TAXMANN'S

PRINCIPLES OF TAXATION LAWS

TAXMANN®'S

Principles of Taxation Laws

Dr. Neha Pathakji
Associate Professor
Director, Centre for Tax Laws
NALSAR University of Law, Hyderabad

Price : ₹ 995

Law stated in this book is as amended by Finance Act, 2023 and updated till April, 2023

Published by :
Taxmann Publications (P.) Ltd.

Sales & Marketing :
59/32, New Rohtak Road, New Delhi-110 005 India
Phone : +91-11-45562222
Website : www.taxmann.com
E-mail : sales@taxmann.com

Regd. Office :
21/35, West Punjabi Bagh, New Delhi-110 026 India

Printed at :
Tan Prints (India) Pvt. Ltd.
44 Km. Mile Stone, National Highway, Rohtak Road
Village Rohad, Distt. Jhajjar (Haryana) India
E-mail : sales@tanprints.com

PREFACE

Tax laws are complex. A large number of law students find taxation laws to be highly intimidating owing to the technicalities. However, it is critical to appreciate that law students are expected to analyse and interpret tax laws rather than harness their computational prowess. A sound foundational and conceptual grounding in Income Tax law calls for balancing the legal and the technical aspects of the statute. Shri B.B. Lal's Income Tax provided this balance of concepts and computations. It is in furtherance of these twin goals of conceptual foundation building and accessible format that the current revision and updation has been carried out. This book is curated for law students. Accessible and student-friendly content remains the cornerstone of this work. The complexities of the Income tax law and provisions have been unbundled for ease of understanding without compromising on the rigour that it requires. Hence, references to computational details have been provided only to the extent they deepen understanding of the legal issue on hand.

This book would not have been complete without the incredible research assistance of my former students and now colleagues Chandini Raj, Piyush Rathi, Rohit Iyengar, and Sughosh Joshi. I am grateful for their valuable input. I am grateful to NALSAR University for all the support and to Taxmann Publications for giving me this opportunity. I shall remain eternally indebted to my mother and sister whose constant support and encouragement keeps me motivated. I am thankful to my students whose close questioning and continuous engagement make it worth all the effort.

NEHA PATHAKJI

CHAPTER-HEADS

PAGE

CONTENTS

PAGE

CHAPTER 3

INTERPRETATION OF TAXING STATUTES

CHAPTER 4

INCOME EXEMPT FROM TAX

CHAPTER 5

RESIDENTIAL STATUS AND SCOPE OF TOTAL INCOME

PAGE

CHAPTER 6

INCOME FROM SALARY

CHAPTER 7

INCOME FROM HOUSE PROPERTY

CHAPTER 8

PROFITS AND GAINS OF BUSINESS OR PROFESSION

PAGE

CHAPTER 13

DEDUCTIONS FROM GROSS TOTAL INCOME

CHAPTER 14

AGRICULTURAL INCOME AND TAX LIABILITY

CHAPTER 15

CHARITABLE TRUSTS AND RELIGIOUS INSTITUTIONS

CHAPTER 16

DIVIDEND

PAGE

CHAPTER 17

DOUBLE TAXATION RELIEF

CHAPTER 18

ASSESSMENT OF INDIVIDUAL

CHAPTER 19

LIABILITY IN SPECIAL CASES

CHAPTER 20

INCOME-TAX AUTHORITIES

CHAPTER 21

PROCEDURE FOR ASSESSMENT

PAGE

CHAPTER 25

DEDUCTION OF TAX AT SOURCE

CHAPTER 26

ADVANCE PAYMENT OF TAX

CHAPTER 27

COLLECTION AND RECOVERY OF TAX

CHAPTER 28

REFUNDS

CHAPTER 29

TAX IMPLICATIONS ON BUSINESS RE-ORGANISATION

PAGE

CHAPTER 30

TAX PLANNING, TAX EVASION, TAX AVOIDANCE

CHAPTER 1

Introduction to the Income-tax Act and Basic Concepts

INTRODUCTION

Taxation serves as a form of fiscal social contract, an agreement amongst rationale people organizing themselves into a society to contribute to the central authority for governance, security, law and order and for providing public goods. Consequently, the power to tax is understood as an inherent power of the sovereign.

While choices about what to tax, how to tax, at what rate to tax, when to tax remains with policies of public finance; the concerns about why to tax, for what purposes to tax is a call that largely remains with the society and its preferred values and norms. Classically three primary tasks are assigned to taxing statutes:

(*a*) ***Augmentation of revenue for financing public goods*** - Taxes ensure that the revenues will be generated by the government to maintain law and order, protect international border by maintaining defense forces, provide physical and social infrastructure for the economy such as roads, bridges, public schools, public hospitals and so on.

(*b*) ***Redistribution of income and wealth*** - It is understood that concentra-tion of wealth and power in the hands of few in the society is not desirable since it leads to inequality, exploitation and denial of opportunity to others, taxes can ensure that the income and wealth is redistributed. Another justification offered for redistributive goals of taxes is that since any income is a fruit of cooperation of several others *i.e.*, the society collectively contributed to enable the generation of that income and therefore needs to have a share in that fruit.

(*c*) ***Regulation*** - Every society identifies certain traits or behaviours that are harmful and therefore ought to be discouraged or encourage certain behaviour by rewarding it. For instance, drinking alcohol, smoking, wasteful spending on luxury goods. Therefore, imposing heavy taxes on alcohol, tobacco, luxury goods are presumed to discourage consumption of such items and thereby regulate behaviour. It is for the same reason that some countries dealing with obesity issues of a large part of its population, impose sugar cess on beverages, eatables that use sugar and its variables. Similarly, when a society wish to encourage saving as a trait, taxing statutes can advance exemptions upon such savings and investments.

Imposing taxes on income often imbibes a combination of two or all three purposes discussed above. India's Income-tax Act, 1961 can be understood to accommodate all three. The revenue generated from levy of income tax is a significant source of public finance. Based on the principle of ability-to-pay, incomes are taxed after providing for deductions for the contingencies that a taxpayer may have encountered, say medical expenditure on a certain illness or for that of a dependent family member that may have affected a taxpayer's ability to pay in that year. Similarly, certain investments are encouraged and thereby savings is rewarded by way of deductions that can be claimed from taxable income.

Having pointed out the justifications for taxes, it is also pertinent to be mindful of certain principles on which taxing statutes are based.

CANONS OF TAXATION

Even as it is conceded that every government will need revenues to fund public expenditure, and by that reason taxes are inevitable, there are some basic principles that must be followed while imposing and collecting taxes. More popularly understood as canons of taxation, these are the attributes or characteristics that makes for a good tax system. The renowned economist Adam Smith in his book An Enquiry into the Nature and Causes of Wealth of Nations published in 1776 had given the following four classic cannons:

(*a*) ***Canon of Equality*** - Since every taxpayer enjoys the protection that government accords and benefits from public expenditure incurred, whether directly or indirectly, the burden of taxation must be distributed equitably among all taxpayers. However, this distribution must be based on the ability to pay. So that those equally situated in their ability to pay, must contribute more or less the same quantum of tax. This essentially requires creating carders of taxpayers who are equal in their ability to pay so that those having greater ability must pay higher taxes as compared to those having lesser ability.

(*b*) ***Canon of Economy*** - Since the assessment, collection and administration of a system involves costs, such costs should be kept as minimum as possible.

(*c*) ***Canon of Certainty*** - The tax which each individual is bound to pay, ought to be certain and not arbitrary. The time of payment, the manner of payment, the quantity to be paid, ought all to be clear and plain to the contributor, and to every other person.

(*d*) ***Canon of Convenience*** - Since taxes imply parting with one's money, every tax ought to be levied at the time, or in the manner, in which it is most likely to be convenient for the contributor to pay it or when he is most likely to have where with all to pay.

INCOME-TAX ACT, 1961

The present law of income tax in India is contained in the Income-tax Act, 1961 and the Income-tax Rules, 1962. It extends to the whole of India and came into force on 1 April 1962 [Sec. 1]. Income-tax Act is enacted by Parliament under Art. 246 read with entry 82 of the Seventh Schedule of the Constitution of India. Thus, Income-tax is levied and collected by the Centre but its proceeds are shared between the Centre and the States (except for any surcharge on income tax) in accordance with the recommendation of the Finance Commission.

In keeping with the aforesaid discussions, Income-tax Act is based on ability-to-pay principles. It fundamentally taxes all revenue receipts and specified capital gains, makes allowance for expenditure that may have been incurred to earn that income and offers deductions for medical contingencies, medical premiums, rewards virtues of charity, savings in certain specified investments and offers tax holidays for certain priority sectors. Similarly, the Income-tax Act embodies various cannons of taxation in its design. Accordingly, incomes of individuals are taxed progressively *i.e.* those who fall in higher tax bracket pay more; provisions of Tax Deducted at Source (TDS) which identifies specific payers to deduct tax at the time of payment and deposit the same with government lead to reducing costs of administration as well as periodic payment of taxes for the taxpayer; option of advance payment of taxes means taxpayers can pay taxes in instalments instead of parting with their money in one go. Overall the Income-tax Act, 1961 discharges the three prime purposes and at the same time aligns itself with the universally accepted principles of taxation.

DOUBLE TAX AVOIDANCE AGREEMENTS

With the advancement of modern means of travel and communication and advent of the Internet age, cross-border trade proliferated and so were instances of double taxation. Since every sovereign has inherent power to tax its residents, individuals and entities having presence in multiple jurisdictions and generating incomes therefrom were subjected to double taxation and multiple taxation. Take for instance an Indian company having its business in Australia would be taxed in India as well as Australia. To avoid such eventuality, countries entered into bilateral agreements known as Double Tax Avoidance Agreement whereby both State Parties agree to either exempt or offer credit for tax paid by such entity in the other country. In present times, DTAAs operate like a stencil over the domestic Income Tax law. The two are to be read so as to offer double taxation relief to a taxpayer.

SCHEME OF INCOME-TAX ACT, 1961

The Income-tax Act, 1961 follows a scheduler scheme of taxing income *i.e.* an item of income is not taxable unless included in a specific schedule. In other words income is only subject to tax if it is listed in a particular schedule (head), and each type of taxable income has its own schedule having separate rate or withholding requirements. As against this, there also exists a global scheme of taxation wherein any item of income is included in taxable income unless specifically excluded. However, countries adopt a mix of scheduler and global scheme.

Section 14 specifies five heads of income and an income has to be brought under one of the five heads to be chargeable under the Income-tax Act, 1961. Sections 15 to 59 lays down the rules for computing income *i.e.* they quantify the total income chargeable to tax. During such quantification, certain permissible deductions are also enumerated. In these terms it is a scheduler scheme. However, there also exists an unwritten principle that all revenue receipts are taxable unless expressly exempted and all capital receipts are exempt unless expressly included which operates on the global scheme.

TABLE 1.1: SCHEME OF INCOME-TAX ACT, 1961

1.	*Income from salaries: [Sec. 15 to Sec. 17]*		
	Income from salary	xxxx	
	Income by way of allowances	xxxx	
	Taxable value of perquisites	xxxx	
	Gross Salary	(xxxx)	
	Less: Deductions under Sec. 16		
	Standard Deduction	xxxx	
	Entertainment allowance	xxxx	
	Professional tax	xxxx	
	Income from salaries		xxxx
2.	*Income from house property: [Sec. 22 to Sec. 27]*		
	Net Annual Value	xxxx	
	Less: Deductions under Sec. 24		
	Income from House Property	(xxxx)	xxxx
3.	*Profits and Gains from business or profession: [Sec. 28 to Sec. 44DB]*		
	Net Profit as per profit and loss account	xxxx	
	Add: Amounts debited to P & L A/c but not allowable as deduction under the Act	xxxx	
	Less: Amounts allowable under the Act but not debited to P & L A/c	xxxx	
	Add: Income not credited to P &L A/c but are taxable under this head under the Act	xxxx	
	Less: Income credited to P & L A/c but are exempt under the Act or taxable under another head under the Act	xxxx	
	Profits and Gains from Business or Profession		xxxx

4.	*Capital gains: [Sec. 45 to Sec. 55A]*		
	Amount of Capital Gains	xxxx	
	Less: Amount exempt under Secs. 54, 54B, 54D, 54EC, 54F, 54G, 54GA	xxxx	
	Income from capital gains		xxxx
5.	*Income from other sources: [Sec. 56 to Sec. 59]*		
	Gross Income	xxxx	
	Less: Deductions under Sec. 57	xxxx	
	Income from other sources		xxxx
	Total (1) + (2) + (3) + (4) + (5)	xxxx	
	Less: Adjustment on account of set-off and carry forward of losses	xxxx	
Gross total Income		xxxx	
Less: Deductions under Secs. 80C to 80U		xxxx	
Net Income (after rounding off to the nearest multiple of ₹ 10) (Sec. 288A)			xxxx

TABLE 1.2: COMPUTATION OF TAX LIABILITY

Tax on Net Income	xxxx
Less: Rebate, if any	xxxx
Tax on Net Income after rebate	xxxx
Add: Surcharge	xxx
Add: Health and education cess	xxx
Less: Pre-paid taxes	xxxx
Tax paid on self assessment	xxxx
Tax deducted or collected at source	xxxx
Tax paid in advance	xxxx
Tax Liability	xxxx

BASIC CONCEPTS

Before exploring the aforesaid five heads of income in the chapters that follow, it is desirable to firstly familiarize with certain foundational concepts and definitions which are central to the scheme of income-tax law.

Assessee [Sec. 2(7)] - An assessee is a person who is liable to pay any tax under the Income-tax Act or in respect of whom any proceeding has been initiated under this Act. It is not necessary that a person is assessed only for his income.

He may be assessed on the income of some other person as well. An assessee, can be thus neatly categorized as follows:

- **Regular Assessee [Sec. 2(7)]** - It is a person by whom any tax or any other sum of money is payable under this Act. Any other sum includes a fine, an interest, a penalty or a surcharge on income tax.
- **Assessee in respect of whom any assessment proceedings have been initiated [Sec. 2(7)(*a*)]** - The "Assessee" includes every person in respect of whom any proceeding under this Act has been initiated, irrespective of whether or not he is liable to pay any tax or any other sum. Such proceedings may be:
  - (*i*) for the assessment of his income or for the income of any other person in respect of which he is assessable; or
  - (*ii*) for the assessment of the loss sustained by him or by such other person; or
  - (*iii*) for the assessment of the loss amount of refund which is due to him or to any other person.

  Therefore, mere initiation of the assessment proceeding against a person makes him an assessee, even if he is not liable to pay any tax or any other sum.
- **Deemed Assessee [Sec. 2(7)(*b*)]** - "Assessee" includes every person who is 'deemed to be an assessee' by law. "Deemed Assessee" is assessed on the income or loss of any other person. For example, the legal representative of the deceased, the guardian of a minor, the agent of a non-resident and the trustee of a trust, etc.
- **Assessee-in-Default [Sec. 2(7)(*c*)]** - "Assessee" includes any person who is deemed to be an assesse-in-default. A person is deemed to be an assesse-in-default if he does not comply with his statutory duty under the Income-tax Act. For example, if any person is required to deduct tax at a source but does not deduct it, or after having deducted fails to pay it to the Central Government, he is deemed to be an assessee-in-default in respect of such tax [Sec. 201(1)].

Person [Sec. 2(*31*)] - The incidence of tax rests on a person and only a person may be an assessee. The definition of 'person' under the Income-tax Act is an inclusive definition and not an exhaustive one. It includes both, a natural person as well as an artificial or a juridical person as follows:

- **Individual [Sec. 2(*31*)(*i*)]** - An individual is a natural person including a minor or a person of unsound mind. However, the income of a minor or a person of unsound mind is assessed in the hands of the legal guardian or manager, acting as a deemed assessee [*Shridhar Udai Nairain* v. *CIT* (1962) 45 ITR 577 (All.)].
- **Hindu Undivided Family [Sec. 2(*31*)(*ii*)]** - The expression "Hindu Undivided Family" is not defined by the Income-tax Act. It is understood in the sense of a joint Hindu family under the personal laws of Hindus.

[*Surjeet Lal Chhabda* v. *CIT* (1975) 101 ITR 776 (SC)]. All those who are governed by the provisions of the "Hindu" code are included in the term Hindu even though their religions may be different. Therefore, Jains and Sikhs are Hindus for the purpose of the Income-tax Law, in absence of any custom or usage to the contrary. [*CWT* v. *Sardar Surjeet Singh* (1982) 138 ITR 136 (Cal.) and *Nathu Sao* v. *CIT* (1934) 2 ITR 463 (Nag.) & *Seth Nathusa Pasusa Ltd*. v. *CIT* 7 ITC 129 (Nag.)].

A joint Hindu family consists of all persons linearly descended from a common ancestor including their wives and unmarried daughters. An amendment in 2005 to the Hindu Succession Act, 1956 recognized the rights of Hindu females to inheritance and coparcenary. Thus, all rights which were available to a Hindu male are now also available to a Hindu female. The eldest female coparcener of an HUF can be its Karta. [*Mrs. Sujata Sharma* v. *Manu Gupta* (2016) 66 taxmann.com 28 (Delhi)]. A single person does not constitute a family which implies plurality of persons [*C. Krishna Prasad* v. *CIT* (1974) 97 ITR 493 (SC)].

- **Company [Sec. 2(*31*)(*iii*) r.w. sec. 2(*17*) & sec. 2(*26*)] -** In brief, a company means an "Indian Company" incorporated under the Companies Act, 1956, or a corporation established by or under a Central, State or Provincial Act, or any corporate incorporated under the laws of a foreign country or any institution, association or body, whether incorporated or not, whether Indian or foreign, declared by the Board to be a company.
- **Firm [Sec. 2(*31*)(*iv*) r.w. sec. 2(*23*)(*i*)] -** "Firm" has the same meaning, assigned to it by the Indian Partnership Act, 1932 and shall include a limited liability partnership as defined in the Limited Liability Partnership Act, 2008.

  According to Sec. 4 of the Indian Partnership Act, 1932, "Partnership" is the relation between persons who have agreed to share the profits of a business carried on by all or any of them acting for all. Persons who have entered into partnership with one another are called individually "partners" and collectively "a firm", and the name under which their business is carried on is called the "firm name".
- **Association of Persons (AoP) [Sec. 2(*31*)(*v*)] -** An "association of persons" is the one in which two or more persons join for a common purpose or common action with a view to produce income, profits or gains. The association need not necessarily be on the basis of a contract; consent and understanding may be presumed [*CIT* v. *N.V. Shanmugam & Co.* (1971) 81 ITR 310 (SC)].
- **Body of Individuals (BoI) [Sec. 2(*31*)(*v*)] -** "Body of Individuals" means a conglomeration of individuals who carry on some activity with the object of earning income. The word "body" would require an association for some common purpose or there must be unity under some common tie or occupation. A mere collection of individuals without a common tie or common aim cannot be assumed to be a "body of individuals".

BoI vs. AoP - A "Body of Individuals" is not identical with an "Association of Persons" though they do have some similarities. An association of persons may consist of non-individuals also, but a body of individuals has to be consisted only of individuals, that is, human beings.

- **Local Authority [Sec. 2(*31*)(*vi*)] -** The term 'local authority' is not defined by the Act. The General Clauses Act, 1897 defines "local authority" shall mean a municipal committee, district board, body of port commissioners or other authority legally entitled to, or entrusted by the government with, the control or Management of a municipal or local fund. The following major tests for treating an authority as a 'local authority' have been carved out from the decision in *Union of India* v. *R.C. Jain* AIR 1981 SC 951 and subsequent decisions:
  - (*i*) The authority must have separate legal existence as corporate body with autonomous status.
  - (*ii*) Must function in a defined area and must ordinarily, wholly or partly, directly or indirectly be elected by the inhabitants of the area.
  - (*iii*) It performs governmental functions such as running a market, providing civic amenities, etc.
  - (*iv*) It must have power to raise funds for the furtherance of its activities and the fulfilment of its projects by levying taxes/fees; this may be in addition to money provided by Government. Control and management of the fund must vest with the authority - *CIT* v. *Agricultural Marketing Produce Committee* [2001] 114 Taxman 484/250 ITR 369 (Delhi).

Merely because the Act which created Corporation regarded it as a local authority and its fund as local fund, assessee could not be considered as local authority for purpose of section 10(20) *[CIT* v. *U.P. Forest Corpn.* [1998] 97 Taxman 259 (SC)].

- **Other Artificial Juridical Person [Sec. 2(*31*)(*vii*)] -** It includes every artificial juridical (legal) person, not falling within any of the preceding sub-clauses. This is a residuary clause. An idol, deity, a university, Guru Granth Sahib and trust, etc., are covered under this clause.

Assessee vs. Person - The concept of a 'person' is much wider as compared to the concept of an 'assessee'. While every assessee is a person, either an individual or an artificial juridical person but every person cannot fall within the ambit of "assessee" unless any proceeding is pending against him under income-tax law.

ASSESSMENT YEAR AND PREVIOUS YEAR

Assessment Year [Sec. 2(9)] - The term "Assessment Year" means the period of 12 months, commencing on the first day of April every year. Thus, the assessment year always begins on 1 April and ends on 31 March every year. This period is nothing but a financial year. The current assessment year is 2023-24, beginning on 1st April, 2023 and ending on 31st March, 2024.

Previous Year [Sec. 3] - Financial year immediately preceding the assessment year is the previous year. Thus, if the assessment year is 2022-23, financial year 2021-22 is the previous year. In simple words, previous year is the year in which income is earned. Income earned in a previous year is charged to tax in the assessment year that immediately follows. [Sec. 4]. For instance, income earned in the previous year 2021-22 is charged to tax in the assessment year 2022-23.

Uniformity in the Previous Year [Sec. 3] - It should be noted that all assessees are required to follow financial year (1st April to 31st March) as the previous year for tax purposes. So that even when an assessee is free to follow an accounting year which is different from the financial year, for the purposes of submitting and filing income tax returns, he is bound to maintain accounts for every financial year.

Previous Year for newly set up business or new source of income [Proviso to Sec. 3]

Where a new source of income comes into existence during any financial year either by way of setting up new business or profession or otherwise, the period of the first previous year begins (*i*) with the date of setting up of the business or profession; or (*ii*) the date on which new source of income comes into existence and ends with the said financial year. Therefore, in such cases the first previous year may be less than 12 months.

Example 1

A new business is set up on 1 November 2019. The first previous year consists of a period of 5 months, beginning on 1 November 2019 and ending on 31 March 2020. In future, the previous year will consist of 12 months, beginning on 1 April and ending on 31 March.

Example 2

A new house property is purchased on 15 October 2019. The first previous year begins on 15 October 2019 and ends on 31 March 2020. Thereafter, the previous year will comprise of 12 months, beginning from 1 April and ending on 31 March.

Example 3

Mr. J is appointed Sales Manager on 1 January 2020. The first previous year consists of a period of 3 months, beginning from 1 January 2020 and ending on 31 March 2020. Thereafter, financial year 1 April to 31 March will be the previous year.

Assessment Year vs. Financial Year vs. Previous Year - Financial year is a period of 12 months, commencing on 1 April and ending on 31 March. Previous year is the financial year during which the income is earned and will be taxed in the assessment year. Assessment year is the financial year immediately following the previous year in which income earned during the previous year is taxed. While a financial year and assessment year are always of 12 months, a previous year may be less than 12 months also, say, in case of a new business or a new source of income.

Exceptions to the Rule of Previous Year - In certain cases, in order to protect the interests of revenue, the income is taxed in the same year in which it is earned. It is an exception to the general rule that income of a previous year is chargeable to tax in the relevant assessment year. The justification for this is the obvious exigency of the situation which calls for prompt recovery of tax before the assessee leaves the country:

(*a*) **Shipping Business of Non-resident [Sec. 172] -** Where a ship, belonging to or chartered by a non-resident, carries passengers, livestock, mail or goods, shipped at a port in India, the ship is allowed to leave the port only when the tax has been paid or satisfactory arrangements have been made for the payment thereof. For this purpose, the Master of the ship is required to furnish the return to the Assessing Officer, disclosing the full amount paid or payable to the owner/charter of the ship or to any other person on his behalf.

For this purposes, Sec. 172 provides a presumptive basis of taxation whereby 7.5% of the amount paid or payable on account of such carriage will be deemed to be the income which will be subjected to regular corporate rates of tax. Regular Scheme of assessment is not comprised in section 44B. The non-resident in question may exercise such an option before the expiry of the assessment year relevant to the previous year in which the date of departure of the ship from the Indian port falls. Where such option is exercised, an assessment is made on the total income of the previous year at the rates applicable in the relevant assessment year. The tax paid in respect of each shipment is then set off against the tax liability determined on assessment. Shortage, if any, is recovered and excess, if any, is refunded to the assessee.

(*b*) **Persons Leaving India [Sec. 174] -** When it appears to the Assessing Officer that an individual may leave India during the current assessment year and has no present intention to return to India, the total income of such individual for the period from the expiry of the previous year in relation to the current assessment year up to the probable date of his departure from India is chargeable to tax in current assessment year itself. For the purpose of making an assessment, the Assessing Officer is required to serve a notice upon such individual requiring him to furnish a return of his total income for each completed previous year and his estimated total income of the broken period from the expiry of the previous year (relevant to that assessment year) up to the probable date of his departure. The return is to be furnished within such time as is prescribed in the notice but not being less than seven days [Sec. 174(4)]. If the assessee does not make a return in response to the notice, a best judgment assessment (under Sec. 144) is to be made by the Assessing Officer. Non-compliance with the notice may also attract penalty (under Sec. 270A/272A) and prosecution (under Sec. 276CC).

Example 4

S, a citizen of South Africa, residing in Bombay for the last 6 years, has submitted returns for the previous year 2018-19 on 31 July, 2019. While assessing him on 15 July, 2020, the Assessing Officer gets an intelligence tip that he will leave India during September 2020 with no intention to come back.

In such case, the Assessing Officer shall make the following three assessments:

(*i*) Income of the previous year 2018-19 will be assessed at the rates, contained in 'Paragraph A of the Part I of the First Schedule to the Finance Act, 2018 for the assessment year 2019-20.

(*ii*) Income for the previous year 2019-20 should be assessed at the rates, contained in 'Paragraph A of the Part I of the First Schedule to the Finance Act, 2019 for the assessment year 2020-21.

(*iii*) Income of the previous year 2020-21, commencing from 1 April, 2020 and upto the date of his departure in the said year, should be assessed at the rates, contained in 'Paragraph A of Part III of the First Schedule to the Finance Act, 2019 for the current assessment year 2021-22.

(*c*) Association of persons or body of individuals or artificial juridical person formed for a particular event or purpose [Sec. 174A] - Where it appears to the Assessing Officer that any AOP, or BOI, or AJP, established for a particular event or purpose is likely to be dissolved in the assessment year, relating to the previous year in which it was formed or immediately thereafter, the total income of such AOP, or BOI, or AJP for the period from the expiry of the previous year for that assessment year up to the date of its dissolution is chargeable to tax in that assessment year. Separate assessments are to be made if the period falls under two different previous years.

Example 5

X, Y, Z & Associates was formed on 1 May, 2019 to complete a construction projects. While assessing its return for the previous year 2019-20, in the assessment year 2020-21, the Assessing Officer reliably learnt that the Association is going to be dissolved during December, 2020, after completing the project. In such case, the Assessing Officer is required to complete the following two assessments during the assessment year 2020-21: (*i*) he has to assess the income of the previous year 2019-20 at the rates applicable to the assessment year 2020-21; and (*ii*) he has also to assess the income of the previous year 2020-21, w.e.f. 1 April, 2020 to 31 December, 2021 at the rates applicable to the current assessment year itself *i.e.* 2020-21; contained in paragraph A of Part III of the First Schedule to the Finance Act, 2019.

(*d*) Person likely to Transfer Property to Avoid Tax [Sec. 175] - If it appears to the Assessing Officer that a person is likely to charge, sell, transfer, dispose of or otherwise going to part with any tax of his asset to avoid payment of any tax liability under this Act, the total income of such person for the period from the expiry of the previous year for that assessment year up to the date when the Assessing Officer commences the proceedings under this section is chargeable to tax in that assessment year. The procedure of assessment is the same as applicable to a person leaving India under Sec. 174.

Example 6

While assessing the income of Mr. Z for the previous year 2019-20 on 15 November, 2020, the Assessing Officer has got a secret information that Mr. Z has concluded a secret deal to dispose of his guest house on 15 January, 2021 to avoid tax liability. Accordingly, the Assessing Officer issued a notice to Mr. Z to submit his return for the period from 1 April, 2020 to 31 January, 2021 by the end of February, 2021. The Assessing Officer is required to make two assessment as below: (*i*) He has to assess the total income of the previous year 2019-20 at the rates applicable for the assessment year 2020-21 contained in Paragraph A of the Part I of the First Schedule to the Finance Act, 2019. (*ii*) Income for the previous year is to be assessed in the current assessment year itself *i.e.* 2020-21 at the rates, contained in Paragraph A of the Part III of the First Schedule to the Finance Act, 2019.

(*e*) Discontinued Business [Sec. 176] - Where any business or profession is discontinued in any assessment year, the Assessing Officer has the discretion either (*i*) to tax the income of the discontinued business in the assessment year in which the business was discontinued or (*ii*) to tax it in the normal assessment year to the previous year in which such business was discontinued.

The term "discontinuance" means complete cessation of business or profession. Discontinuance is different from succession. Discontinuance means disappearance of business altogether while succession implies a change of ownership of business. Where a partnership is dissolved and one partner takes over and continues the business of the partnership, it is a case of succession and not discontinuance [*C.J. Seth* v. *CIT* (1962) 46 ITR 1052 (Mad.)]. There is no discontinuance if customers are merely notified that business would be closed on a certain date but the business continues to be transacted, though it may be simply to complete the outstanding contracts.

In the case of profession, if a professional person gives up his profession or vocation, it amounts to discontinuance. The question whether a professional man discontinued his profession depends on the state of his mind at the time of cessation. Merely because he took to the profession once again later on, it cannot be stated that there was no discontinuance at the time of cesser. For example, a practicing lawyer is appointed a judge. Consequently he stopped practising. It is a case of discontinuance of profession even though he may resign later on and may start his practice again. In these circumstances, the resumption of the practice amounts to starting a new profession, not the continuance of old one which he had discontinued.

Any person discontinuing any business or profession should give to the Assessing Officer notice of such discontinuance within fifteen days thereof

[Sec. 176(3)]. Where any such assessment is to be made, the Assessing Officer may serve on the person whose income is to be assessed or, in the case of a firm, on any person who was a partner of such firm at the time of its discontinuance, or, in the case of a company, on the principal officer thereof, a notice requiring him to furnish the return of the total income within the prescribed time, not being less than seven days [Sec. 176(5)/(7)]. If no return is furnished in response to the notice, a best judgment assessment (under Sec. 144) is to be made by the Assessing Officer.

Any sum received after discontinuance of business [Sec. 176(3A) w.e.f. 1-4-1976] or profession [Sec. 176(4)] is deemed to be the income of the recipient and charged to tax accordingly in the year of receipt, if such sum should have been included in the total income of the person who carried on the business or the profession had such sum been received before such discontinuance. The profession may be discontinued on account of death or retirement or otherwise. This provision is relevant only when the accounts are maintained on cash basis. Under mercantile system of accounting all accrued (outstanding) incomes are taken into accounting. Hence, this provision is not relevant in mercantile system of accounting. Further, this provision constitutes an exception to the rule that business or professional receipts are taxable only if the business or profession is carried on in the year of account.

Example 7

Mr. X discontinues his business on 30 September, 2019. The Assessing Officer may tax the income of the discontinued business at his discretion in the following manner: (*i*) He may tax it during the assessment year 2019-20 at the rates contained in Part III of the First Schedule of that year. Or (*ii*) He may tax it during the assessment year 2020-21 at the rates contained in Part I of the First Schedule of that year.

INCOME [SEC. 2(*24*)]

The concept of income is very important as it is the income which is taxed under the Income-tax Act. The definition of income under this Act is very wide and includes profit and gains, dividends, voluntary contributions, perquisites, allowances, discharge of an obligation, compensation receipts, profits on sale of license, cash assistance received against exports, recovery of loss or expenditure, recovery of bad debts, winnings from lottery, crossword puzzles, races, card games, gambling, betting, etc. A more detailed discussion on the concept of income follows in Chapter 2.

Exempted Incomes [Sec. 10] - These incomes are either fully or partially exempted from income tax and therefore, to the extent of exemption, do not form a part of the total income and hence are not taxable. Exempted incomes are discussed in detail later in the book as a separate chapter.

Deductions from Income - Income-tax Act, 1961 allows certain specific reductions to be made from the income of an assessee while computing the total income. These reductions are termed as deductions. Two types of deductions have been provided under the Act, *i.e.* deductions from the specific heads of income and deductions from gross total income. These have been discussed in detail in the book at appropriate places.

Total Income [Sec. 2(*45*)] - Total income, computed in accordance with residential status under Sec. 5, is arrived at after allowing deductions under Sec. 80C to Sec. 80U from the gross total income. The charge of income tax is on total income of an assessee. Incomes exempted from income tax do not form a part of total income.

Gross Total Income [Sec. 80B(5)] - The aggregate of net taxable income, computed under various heads of income, is termed as "Gross Total Income". This aggregation is not a mathematical process but a legal concept. It is computed after allowing for the deductions specific to various heads of income, set off of losses and allowances or set off of carry forward losses and allowances and clubbing the income of any other person that may be liable to be included in assessee's total income.

SET OFF AND CARRY FORWARD OF LOSSES

Since income tax is only one tax and not as many taxes as there are heads of income, it is only reasonable that there are specific provisions to allow set off of loss from one source of income against profit from another source of income under the same head in the same previous year. Thereafter, any unabsorbed loss is set off against income of other heads in the same previous year and if some portion of the loss still remains unabsorbed, it may be carried forward for set off against income of subsequent previous years. The maximum period for carried forward is limited by the Act. A separate chapter has been devoted later in the book for an exhaustive discussion on set off and carry forward and set off of losses and allowances.

COMPUTATION OF TAX LIABILITY

Income tax is charged in the assessment year on total income of the previous year by applying the prescribed rates of tax. Thereafter the net tax liability is computed by allowing any rebates or relief due to the assessee, adding the surcharge, education cess and giving credit for any tax paid in advance or deducted at source.

Rates of Income Tax - The rates of income tax are prescribed every year by the Finance Act.

Surcharge - Surcharge is a charge, levied on the amount of income tax if total income of an assessee exceeds specified limits. In simple terms, surcharge is a tax on income tax. With abolition of Wealth-tax Act, 1957 in the Finance Act, 2015 additional surcharge was levied on assessees with high net worth.

Health and Education Cess - Health and Education Cess @ 4% is levied on the aggregate amount of income tax and surcharge. Cess is a tax which is earmarked for specific purposes. Proceeds of cess can only be spent for the purposes of which the same are levied. There has been a long standing controversy on the issue whether or not health and education cess can be claimed as an allowable deduction while computing income tax liability. According to the assessees since health and education cess is a tax levied for a specific purpose, it is separate from income tax itself and therefore should be allowed. However, the Revenue Authorities have taken a contrary view and hold that health and education cess is covered within the meaning and scope of tax in Sec. 40(*a*)(*ii*) the same should not be allowed as deduction. The Finance Act, 2022 has put this controversy to rest by inserting *Explanation 3* to Sec. 40(*a*)(*ii*) with retrospective effect from 1st April 2005 that clarifies that the term "tax" shall include and shall be deemed to have always included any surcharge or cess, by whatever name called, on such tax. Accordingly, health and education cess being a part of income tax will not be allowed as deductible expenditure.

Income tax vs. Surcharge vs. Health and Education Cess - Income tax is levied on total income. Surcharge is levied on income tax. Health and Education Cess is charged on the aggregate of income tax and surcharge. It may be noted that under Art. 270 of the Constitution of India unlike revenues collected from the imposition of income tax is a part of the divisible pool to be shared with the State Governments, proceeds collected from surcharge and cess is not shareable and fully remains with the Central Government.

Rebate [Sec. 87] - Rebate is a reduction allowed in the amount of income tax computed in case of certain types of assessee.

Relief from Tax [Sec. 89] - Where an assessee receives arrears of salary or family pension or advance of salary or profits in lieu of salary [Sec. 17(3)] during any previous year and it becomes taxable during the same previous year causing the assessee to be taxed at a higher rate than he would otherwise have been assessed, relief may be allowed under Rule 21A from tax so computed at the higher rate.

Deductions vs. Rebates vs. Relief - While the basic purpose of all the three is to benefit the assessee by reducing the incidence of tax, they differ in their methodology to achieve their common objective and the conditions under which they pass on the relief. While the deductions reduce the amount of income chargeable to tax, rebates and relief reduces the amount of tax computed on the chargeable income.

SETTLEMENT OF TAX LIABILITY

An assessee is required to file his return of income and deposit the tax with the authorities within the prescribed time, failing which the Act provides wide-ranging powers for recovery of tax besides the fines and penalties for late payment.

Advance Tax - Advance tax is payable during any financial year on the estimated total income that would be chargeable to tax in the immediately following assessment provided the tax liability of the assessee is ₹ 10,000, or more. Accordingly, an assessee is required to pay advance tax in four instalments *i.e.*

15th June, 15th September, 15th December and 15th March. This also eases the cash out-flow for the assessee by allowing him to pay in instalments.

Deduction of Tax at Source - Deduction of tax at source is a method of collection of tax whereby it is obligatory for certain persons to deduct tax, surcharge and cess at prescribed rates from certain type of payments and deposit the tax so deducted with the authorities to the credit of the person from whose payment it was deducted. Therefore, it is a tax on income at its very source. It is deducted by the payer and deposited to the government on behalf of the person earning that income. An assessee is entitled to claim credit for any tax deducted at source from his income during the previous year.

Advance Tax *vs.* Deduction of Tax at Source - The primary difference between the two is that while the onus to pay advance tax is on the assessee himself, the responsibility for deducting and paying tax at source lies with the person making the payment. Tax deduction at source is particularly helpful in ensuring tax revenue from individuals and small unregistered entities who otherwise may not disclose these incomes.

Refunds - Where on completion of the assessment, it is determined that the amount of tax paid by the assessee is in excess of what was actually due from him, the excess tax so paid by the assessee is termed as refund. It is paid back to him by the government along with interest, if any.

Administration of Income Tax - Income tax is administered through a hierarchy of officers ranging from Income-tax Officers to Principal Directors General of Income-tax and Central Board of Direct Taxes. Adequate penal provisions have been enacted for non-compliance with the Act. Right of appeal has been provided to an assessee to redress this grievance to appellate authorities, tribunal and courts. These provisions are discussed in detail under separate chapters later in the book.

CHAPTER 2 Concept of Income

INTRODUCTION

The concept of income remains central to the Income-tax Act. A fundamental principle followed for the purposes of Income tax is that all that is income is taxable unless specifically exempted from tax. The definition of the term income, therefore, assumes criticality. The classical approach scopes income narrowly as a periodical monetary return 'coming in' with some sort of regularity, or expected regularity, from definite sources [*CIT* v. *Shaw Wallace & Co.* (1932) 59 IA 206]. However, there has been a departure from the classical approach and the expression income casts a wide net to include every kind of profit and gain, windfall gains, or casual receipts.

INCOME

Income is an expression of a very wide scope and ambit. The statutory definition of the term income comprises in sec. 2(*24*). It is an inclusive definition and not an exhaustive one. While the inclusive definition adds several artificial categories of income, it does not lose the natural connotation of the term 'income.' [*Emil Webber* v. *CIT* (1993) 67 Taxman 532/200 ITR 483 (SC)]. So that even those receipts or benefits which are not specifically defined thereunder can be considered as income in accordance to the natural meaning of income and therefore assessed to tax.

The Income-tax Act has adopted twin phraseology to specify the items that may be assessable to income tax. First, it includes a list of items in the definition of income, and second, it has coined many deeming provisions to bring the notional receipts also within the ambit of the definition of income. The figure below demonstrates the approaches to the definition of Income.

FIGURE 2.1: INCOME

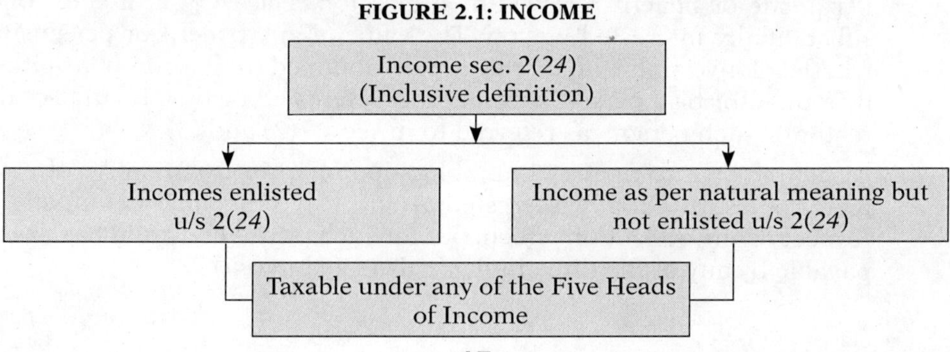

Definition of Income [Sec. 2(*24*)] - The Act has specifically included the following receipts and benefits as income:

(*i*) Profit and gains.

(*ii*) Dividends.

(*iii*) Voluntary contributions received by:

(*a*) a trust or institution, created wholly or partly for charitable or religious purpose or an institution established for such purposes; or

(*b*) scientific research association referred to in Sec. 10(*21*); or

(*c*) sport association referred to in Sec. 10(*23*); or

(*d*) any fund or institution/any trust or institution wholly for public religious/charitable purposes and notified by the Central Government [under Sec. 10(*23C*)(*iv*)/(*v*)]; or

(*e*) any university/educational institution or hospital/other medical institution approved by the prescribed authority under Sec. 10(*23C*(*vi*)/(*via*). From the A.Y. 2007-08 and onwards, voluntary contribution to the aforesaid university, educational institution, hospital or medical institution also includes anonymous donations where such receipts do not exceed ₹ 1 crore. 'Anonymous donation' means any voluntary contribution where its receiver does not maintain a record of the identity and address of the donor [Sec. 115BBC(3)]; or

(*f*) by an electoral trust.

(*iv*) The value of any perquisite or profits in lieu of "salaries".

(*v*) Any special allowance or benefit specifically granted to the assessee to meet his expenses wholly and necessarily and exclusively for the performance of his duties.

(*vi*) City Compensatory Allowance/ Dearness allowance: Any allowance granted to the assessee either to meet his personal expenses at the place where he performs his duties or to compensate him for the increased cost of living.

(*vii*) Perquisite or benefit received by a director, relative of a director or a substantially interested person: The value of any benefit or perquisite, whether convertible into money or not, obtained from a company either by a director or a person substantially interested or by a relative of director or such person as referred to in sec. 17(2) and (3).

(*viii*) Discharge by a company of an obligation of a director, relative of a director or a substantially interested person: Any sum paid by company in respect of any obligation which, but for such payment, would have been payable by any of the three individuals stated in (*vii*).

(*ix*) Benefit or perquisite obtained by a representative assessee: The value of any benefit or perquisite, whether convertible into money or not, obtained by any representative assessee [under Sec. 160(1)(*iii*) or (*iv*)] or beneficiary. Further, any sum paid by the representative assessee in respect of any obligation which, but for such payment, would have been payable by the beneficiary is also an income [Sec. 2(*24*)(*iva*)].

(*x*) Any sum chargeable under sections 28, 41 and 59:

(*a*) Compensation receipts considered as business income under section 28(*ii*) or any amount taxable in the hands of a trade, professional or similar association for specific services performed for its member as its income from business under Section 28(*iii*), and deemed profits which are taxable under Sections 41 and 59 of the Act.

(*b*) Profits on sale of license granted under the Import (Control) Order, 1955, made under the Imports and Exports (Control) Act, 1947.

(*c*) Cash assistance received or receivable by any person against exports under any scheme of the Government of India.

(*d*) Any duty or exercise drawback or custom or excise repaid or repayable as a drawback to any person against exports under the Customs and Central Excise Duties Drawback Rules, 1971.

(*e*) The value of any benefit or perquisite from business or profession, whether convertible into money or not, arising from business or the exercise of a profession [Sec. 28(*iv*)].

(*f*) Any remuneration chargeable under Sec. 28(*v*).

(*g*) Any recovery in respect of loss or expenditure which was allowed to be deducted in any year [Sec. 41(1) or Sec. 59].

(*h*) Excess of sale proceeds of a "scientific research" asset over its amortised value, to the extent of deduction allowed [Sec. 41(3)].

(*i*) Any recovery in respect of a debt which was allowed as a bad debt [Sec. 41(4)].

(*xi*) Capital Gains: Any profits and gains chargeable under Sec. 45.

(*xii*) Insurance Profit: The profits and gains of any business of insurance carried on by a mutual insurance company or by a cooperative society.

(*xiii*) Banking income of a Co-operative Society: The profits and gains of any business of banking (including providing credit facilities) carried on by a cooperative society with its members. It is operative from the AY 2007-08 and subsequent years.

(*xiv*) Winnings from Lottery: Any winnings from lotteries, crossword puzzles, races, card games and other games of any sort or from gambling or betting. The words "other games of any sort" are wide enough to include non-gambling or non-betting activities. Thus, prize won in a car rally is income in its widest sense. Though it is a casual income, it is nevertheless an income [*CIT* v. *Karthikeyan (G.R.)* [1993] 68 Taxman 145/201 ITR 866 (SC)].

"Lottery" includes winnings from prizes awarded to any person by draw of lots or by chance or any other manner, whatsoever, under any scheme or arrangement by whatever name called.

"Card game and other game of any sort" includes any game show, an entertainment programme on television or electronic mode, in which people compete to win prizes or any other similar game [*Explanation*].

(*xv*) Employees' contribution to Provident Fund or Employees State Insurance: Any sum received by the assessee from his employees as contributions to any provident fund or superannuation fund or any fund set up under the provisions of the Employees State Insurance Act, 1948 or any other fund for the welfare of such employees. However, a deduction will be allowed to the assessee to the extent these sums received by him have been duly deposited with the provident fund and ESI.

(*xvi*) Receipts under a keyman insurance policy including the sum allocated by way of bonus is also to be treated as income.

(*xvii*) Non-compete fees received under sec. 28(*va*).

(*xviii*) Monetary gift, exceeding ₹ 50,000 received by an individual or an HUF.

(*xix*) Fair market value of inventory referred to in sec. 28(*via*).

(*xx*) Forfeiture of advance money on account of failure of transfer of a capital asset. It is operative w.e.f. 1-4-2015.

(*xxi*) Any subsidy or grant or cash assistance or duty draw back or waiver or concession or reimbursement by the Government (Central or State) or any other authority or body in cash or kind to the assessee. It does not include any subsidy or grant or reimbursement which is taken into account for determination of the actual cost of the asset [under *Explanation 10* to sec. 43(1)]. It is operative w.e.f. 1-4-2016.

(*xxii*) Sum received by unit holder that represents redemption of units as per sec. 56(2)(*xii*) (w.e.f. 1-4-2024).

(*xxiii*) Any sum received under life insurance policy in which premium exceeds ₹ 5,00,000 as referred to under sec. 56(2)(*xiii*) (w.e.f. 1-4-2024).

DEEMED INCOME [SECS. 23(2), 68 TO 69D]

Income-tax Act has enacted many deeming provisions to bring into tax net notional or fictional incomes which, but for such provisions, would not be assessable as income:

1. Income from self-occupied house [Sec. 23(2)].
2. Unexplained cash credits [Sec. 68].
3. Unrecorded and unexplained investments [Sec. 69, Sec. 69A and Sec. 69B].

4. Unexplained expenditure [Sec. 69C].
5. Amount borrowed or repaid on hundi otherwise by way of an account payee cheque [Sec. 69D].

Income as per its Natural Meaning - As stated earlier, income is a concept of wide scope. It is difficult to confine it to any precise definition. Therefore, what constitutes income has been a subject of frequent litigation with the judiciary often interpreting the natural meaning of income. According to its ordinary and natural meaning, the word income will take in any monetary return "coming in". The following points must be considered while comprehending any receipt or benefit as income for taxation purposes.

Regularity of Income though Important is Not Determinative: The "income" connotes a periodic monetary return coming with some regularity or expected regularity from definite sources. While regularity of income can be a useful indicator as to whether a receipt may be categorised as income, it does not follow that non-regular receipts are not income as even a casual receipt, lump sum receipts, etc., may be taxable income.

Income may be in cash or in kind: Income may be realised in the form of money or money's worth, *i.e.* in cash or in kind. When income is realised in kind, its valuation is made according to the prescribed rules. In the absence of any rule, the market value is generally applied as the basis of valuation. Valuation is an art, not an exact science. Mathematical certainty is neither demanded nor possible. Thus, when a moneylender takes land in satisfaction of his debt, the market value of the land will have to be ascertained. If the market value of the land exceeds the principal sum advanced, the difference between the two sums is treated as interest which is liable to tax.

Income must be real and not fictional: An income is taxed on the basis of receipt or accrual whichever is earlier. When income is received in the hands of an assessee it amounts to receipt of income, when the right to receive the income becomes vested in an assessee, it is an accrual of income. However, for income to be taxed, it should be real income and not fictional. A contingent income is not an income. Until the contingency takes place it cannot be said that income has accrued or arisen to the assessee.

Mere book entry by itself is not Sufficient to Result in Income: Simply because a transaction may or may not have been recognised as income in the accounts books, it does not automatically follow that the same treatment should be followed for the purpose of the Income-tax Act. If income does not result at all, it cannot be assessed to tax, even though in book-keeping, an entry is made about a "hypothetical income", which does not materialise.

Mere relief from expense is not Income: The common parlance wisdom of a 'penny saved is a penny earned' has no holding for the purposes of income tax. A person is chargeable to tax not on what he saves in his pocket but on what goes into his pocket. Therefore, mere relief from expenses cannot be considered as an income. For example, a rebate obtained by a purchaser is not an income [*Harihar Cotton Pressing Factory* v. *CIT* (1960) 39 ITR 594 (Bom.)]. Similarly, the remission of a debt by creditor would not result in the creation of income in the hands of a debtor [*CIT* v. *Hind Construction Ltd*. (1972) 83 ITR 211 (SC)].

Income Tainted with Illegality is also income - The Income-tax law does not make any distinction between legal income and income tainted with illegality. Illegal income is taxable like legal income. To hold otherwise would be to put a premium on dishonesty and fraud. By taxing the illegal income, the State is neither taking part in the crime or condoning it, nor would it become a party to the illegality. The assessee might be prosecuted for the crime and yet be charged on the profits.

Disputed Income is also assessable to tax: Assessment of income cannot be held up because of any dispute in source of the income. The recipient is taxable although there may be a rival claim to the source of income. Where money has been received, a rival claim or a threat of litigation cannot make the income contingent one. On the other hand, a mere claim by a person against another who has actually received the money is not sufficient to make income accrue to the claimant and render him liable for tax.

Case Law : ***Raghuvanshi Mills Ltd.* v. *CIT* (1952) 22 ITR 484 (SC)**

Facts: 'R' had taken a 'Consequential Loss Policy' to insure against loss of profits, agency commission etc. and received ₹ 14 lakh under the said policy after a fire completely destroyed the mill. 'R' argued that the money received was an indemnity for loss of profit, which was a one-off payment contingent upon happening of an eventuality and therefore could not be taxed as income.

Held: The concept of income is very wide and includes "income", "profits" and "gains". The receipt insofar as it represents loss of profits as opposed to loss of capital is income in normal sense of the term. A receipt does not cease to be income just because certain conditions must be fulfilled before it can be claimed. The receipt being inseparably connected with ownership and conduct of business and arose from it, is an income assessable to tax as it has not been specifically exempted.

NEW FORMS OF INCOME: VIRTUAL DIGITAL ASSETS

With advancements in technology, new forms of income and assets have come into existence. Cryptocurrency is among such novel receipt which has gained popularity across the world. Simply understood cryptocurrency is a digital currency that is a kind of tradable digital asset or digital form of money. It exists only in the virtual world and there is no issuing authority or regulatory body that governs crypto and it is built on blockchain technology. While cryptocurrency has not been recognized in India so far, the Cryptocurrency and Regulation of Official Digital Currency Bill, 2021 is to be introduced in Parliament. The Bill aims to facilitate the creation of a framework for the official digital currency to be issued by the Reserve Bank of India and seeks to prohibit private forms of cryptocurrencies with a few exceptions. While the legality or otherwise of cryptocurrency in India is yet to be clarified, the Finance Act, 2022 has imposed a tax on virtual digital assets.

Sec. 2(*47A*) defines the term "virtual digital asset". Accordingly, VDA means any information or code or number or token (not being Indian currency or any foreign currency), generated through cryptographic means or otherwise, by whatever name called, providing a digital representation of value which is exchanged with or without consideration, with the promise or representation of having inherent value, or functions as a store of value or a unit of account and includes its use in any financial transaction or investment, but not limited to, investment schemes and can be transferred, stored or traded electronically. Non-fungible token and any other token of similar nature are included in the definition. Central Government may notify any other virtual digital asset as a virtual digital asset by way of notification in the Official Gazette.

Income from the transfer of any virtual digital asset is taxable @30% under the newly inserted sec. 115BBH and is subject to 1% TDS provisions under Sec. 194S. However, no deduction for expenditure (other than the cost of acquisition) is allowed. Similarly, no set off of any loss shall be allowed to the assessee under any provision of the Act while computing income from the transfer of such asset and such loss shall not be allowed to be carried forward to subsequent assessment years. Gifting of VDA will be covered under Sec. 56(2)(*x*) under the expression property and shall be subject to tax in the hands of the recipient of a gift.

While it is not clear whether VDA is considered as a capital asset or trading asset, Sec.115BBH(3) stipulates that the word "transfer" as defined in Sec. 2(*47*) shall apply to any virtual digital asset, whether capital asset or not.

DOCTRINE OF MUTUALITY

Even as the definition of the term income casts a wide net for tax purposes, it is subject to a fundamental principle that an amount received from oneself cannot be regarded as income. This principle is known as the doctrine of mutuality. Accordingly, a person cannot make a profit from himself. Thus, when a group of persons come together and make contributions to a common fund controlled by this group for a common benefit and they have no dealings with anyone outside the group mutuality principle would apply to them. Any surplus returned to those persons cannot be regarded as income of such persons. For example, clubs, friendly societies, automobile associations have been included as operating upon mutuality. Therefore, even when such persons take the form of being an incorporated entity such as a registered society, association or even a company enjoying a separate and distinct corporate status; they will continue to be governed by the principle of mutuality till they do not have any dealings with the outside world.

However, in order to enjoy this protection of the doctrine of mutuality, the following three essentials must be fulfilled:

(1) *There must be a complete identity of character between contributors and participators of the surplus:* There is nothing *per se* to prevent a company from making a profit from its members but what is required for the appli-

cation of the principle of mutuality is that there should be the complete identity of character between the persons who contribute and the persons who participate in the surplus, that is, the persons must participate in the surplus in the same capacity in which they contributed to it. For example, where a person buys the product of a company of which he is a shareholder, the resultant profit comes back to him in his capacity as a shareholder and not in the capacity as an ordinary buyer. On the other hand, if a person is a member of a club, the resultant benefit to him from using the facilities of the club as a member will also accrue to him in his capacity as a member of the club, thereby resulting in a complete identity of character between the person contributing to the surplus and the person participating in the surplus.

(2) *The incorporation or the manner of incorporation is not relevant so long as the association is for convenience of members, acts as their agents and remains true to its objects:* The fact that an assessee is a corporate entity need not by itself be a bar to the claim for exemption on the basis of the mutuality principle [*CIT* v. *Royal Western India Turf Club Ltd.* (1953) 24 ITR 551 (SC)]. A corporate entity like a company or entities which have limited corporate existence as a registered society or a trust can act as an agent of the members and the principle of mutuality is not defeated in such cases [*JCTO* v. *Young Men's Indian Association* (1970) 26 STC 241 (SC)].

Even if the entity is incorporated as a company but its memorandum and articles of association provided that the funds should be utilised solely for the promotion of its objects and that no portion of the income or property shall be paid or transferred directly or indirectly by way of dividends, bonus to any members or former members, the principle of mutuality may still be applicable [*CIT* v. *Escorts Dealers Development Association Ltd*. [2001] 119 Taxman 849/[2002] 253 ITR 305 (Punj. & Har.)].

(3) *Absolute lack of commerciality:* Insofar as the participators in such clubs or associations continue to trade or provide services among themselves, they remain in a safe harbour. And it does not matter whether they have incorporated themselves as a company or a registered society having a separate corporate existence of its own. Where the trade or activity is mutual, the fact that, as regards certain activities, only certain members of the association take advantage of the facilities which it offers, does not affect the mutuality of the enterprise [*Chelmsford Club* v. *CIT* [2000] 109 Taxman 215/243 ITR 89 (SC)].

Presence of transactions with non-members will not disturb the mutuality of an association vis-à-vis *its members:* The application of the principle of mutuality is not destroyed merely by the presence of transactions with profits derived from non-members. The said principle could still apply to members. The two activities can in appropriate cases be separated. As long as there is complete identity between the contributors and the participators, the principle of mutuality is applicable [*CIT* v. *Madras Race Club* (1976) 105 ITR 433 (Mad.)].

Case Law : ***CIT* v. *Bankipur Club Ltd.* [1997] 92 Taxman 278 (SC)**

Facts: The assessee-clubs were registered under sec. 25 of the erstwhile Companies Act, 1956 as non-profit companies with the main object to afford the usual privileges, advantages, conveniences and accommodation of a club to all members.

Held: Any surplus arising from the sale of drinks, refreshments, etc., or rental amounts by letting out buildings to members, or admission fees, periodical subscriptions and receipts of similar nature from its members would be governed by the principle of mutuality.

Case Law : ***Bangalore Club* v. *CIT* [2013] 29 taxmann.com 29/212 Taxman 566/350 ITR 509 (SC)**

Facts: The assessee-club is an association of person having banks as its corporate members. The Club earned interest from fixed deposits with the member banks which was claimed to be governed by mutuality and therefore taxable.

Held: Till the stage of generation of surplus funds, the setup resembled that of mutuality since the flow of money, to and fro, was maintained within the closed circuit formed by the banks and the club. However, as soon as these funds were placed in fixed deposits with banks, the closed flow of funds between the banks and the club, the privity of mutuality was ruptured as the these funds were exposed to commercial banking operations with member banks using these deposits to advance loans to their clients.

Doctrine of Mutuality is Applicable to All Types of Income Irrespective of the Head under which they are Assessable - Even a Deemed or Notional Income will be Exempt if Mutuality can be Established: The principle of mutuality is applicable to all types of income and cannot be diluted with reference to the head, any head of income, or the nature and character of the income. As long as the conditions of mutuality are satisfied, any income derived by the mutual association will be outside the purview of income tax. For example, even the notional or deemed income by way of the annual value of the property owned by a club or mutual association will not be chargeable to tax [*Chelmsford Club* v. *CIT* [2000] 109 Taxman 215/243 ITR 89 (SC)].

Interest earned through bank deposits - It is interesting to note the consequences when surplus funds contributed by the members are deposited with banks and interest earned thereon to be later on utilised for the purposes of the objectives of the group and its members. Unlike depositing surplus funds in savings account or current account in banks, investment of surplus funds in the form of fixed deposits, securities in banks and financial institutions amounts to a prudent commercial decision motivated by the desire to earn interest and such interest does not fulfil the doctrine of mutuality [*CIT* v. *I.T.I. Employees Death and Superannuation Relief Fund* [1998] 101 Taxman 315/234 ITR 308 (Kar.), *CIT* v. *Common Effluent Treatment Plant (Thane Belapur) Association* [2010] 192 Taxman 238/328 ITR 362 (Bom), *Brigade Plaza Unit Owners Association* v. *ITO* [2021] 129 taxmann.com 51(Kar)].

Exceptions to the Doctrine of Mutuality [*Sec. 2(24)(v)/(vii)*] - Two exceptions have been made in the Act where the surplus of mutual concerns have been made taxable by including them in the definition of income under sec. 2(*24*) under sub-clauses (*v*) and (*vii*):

(*i*) *Trade or Professional Associations:* Income derived by trade, professional or similar association from specific service performed for its members is chargeable to tax as business income [Sec. 28(*iii*)].

(*ii*) *Mutual Insurance Associations:* Profit of insurance business, life or non-life, carried on by a company or a cooperative society computed in accordance with Sec. 44 r.w. First Schedule is liable to tax [Sec. 2(*24*)(*vii*)].

Doctrine of mutuality has not been officially defined by the Income-tax Act, the same is recognised under the Act. Thus, except for the two instances as referred to in Secs. 28(*iii*) and 2(*24*)(*vii*) that makes it expressly chargeble to tax, every other instance involving principle of mutuality has been excluded from the purview of the Act [*Chelmsford Club* v. *CIT* [2000] 109 Taxman 215/243 ITR 89 (SC)].

DIVERSION OF INCOME BY OVERRIDING TITLE

Under the Income-tax Act, every income that accrues or arises in the hands of the assessee is liable to be taxed, irrespective of its subsequent application. However, when on account of a legal obligation, the income is diverted before it reaches the assessee, then such assessee cannot be taxed on such income because the income never reached him/her/it. When diversion of income by overriding title applies, the amount in question cannot be said to be a part of the assessee's income.

For the concept of diversion of income by overriding title to apply, the diversion of income must be effective at the stage when the amount in question leaves the source, on its way to the intended recipient. At that stage, on account of a pre-existing legal obligation, the amount should be diverted to another, who can claim it as of right, based on the pre-existing legal arrangement. The person to whom the amount is diverted should have a legal right that entitles him to claim the amount directly from the source, and without the intervention of the person who would have received the amount but for the said legal arrangement.

Diversion of Income vs. Application of Income - Where owing to an obligation income is diverted before it reaches the assessee, it is not an income in the hands of the assessee and therefore not taxable; but where the income is to be applied to discharge an obligation after such income reaches the assessee, it is merely an application of income and will continue to be taxed in the hands of the assessee.

An income must reach the assessee in order to be available for application. If an income does not reach an assessee, he cannot apply it to discharge an obligation as one cannot apply what does not reach him. It is clarified that the word 'reach' has a wider sense than the word 'receive'. Even if an assessee physically receives the income, but is duty-bound to spend it in a particular manner, then the income cannot be deemed to have reached him.

There is a very thin line between the diversion of income by overriding the title and application of income and drawing a distinction between the two is very important from the point of view of taxation. This fine distinction has not been defined by the Income-tax Act and has therefore been a matter of frequent judicial interventions. Following are various guidelines that distinguish application of income from the diversion of income. However, it is cautioned that these guidelines should not be evaluated in isolation and regard must be paid to the particular circumstances of each individual case.

Mere discharge of an obligation in itself is not sufficient to be categorised as diversion. It is the nature of the obligation which is the decisive factor: There is a difference between an amount that a person is obliged to apply out of his income and an amount that by nature of its obligation cannot be said to be a part of the income of the assessee. [*CIT* v. *Sitaldas Tirathdas* (1961) 41 ITR 367 (SC)].

Voluntary transfer of income is a mere application of the income and therefore will be assessable as income of the transferor: The basic concept has also been given statutory effect by Sec. 60. For example, where the husband assigns the right to receive interest on securities held by him, in favour of his wife, the interest continues to be taxable as the income of the husband. Compulsory deductions from remuneration by the employer are instances of mere application of income and gross salary is chargeable to tax without any allowance for the compulsory deductions.

Case Law : ***Provincial Superior* v. *Union of India* [2021] 129 taxmann.com 154/438 ITR 548 (Kerala)**

Facts: Revenue issued instructions for deduction of tax at source from the payments by way of salary made to nuns, priests being teachers in government aided educational institutions. Writ petitions were filed by different religious congregations and a few nuns and priests individually against such TDS on the grounds that the salary paid to them was diverted income. It was argued that having taken religious vows of poverty, any property that later comes to them becomes the property of the Order to which they belong. So this amounts to diversion of income. That they have undergone civil death under the Canon Law and therefore are not persons for the purposes of Income- tax Act.

Held: The concept of civil death has no application under the Income-tax Act since none of the provision of the Income-tax Act recognize the same. Further Article 25 of the Constitution does not provide any immunity from taxation on basis of religion. The principle of diversion of income by overriding title would not apply to salary received by them.

Mere transfer of income to a trust or benevolent fund in accordance with objects of the assessee without any binding compulsion for such an object is application of income: In order to successfully establish diversion of income by overriding title, one needs to prove that there exists a binding compulsion to transfer directly or indirectly a portion of the income. When an assessee imposes on himself as a part of its internal management, it cannot be a binding obligation. A portion of income that may be credited to a benevolent fund or a trust under objects of incorporation is application of income. [*CIT* v. *Madras Race Cub* (2002) 255 ITR 98/(2003) 126 Taxman 6 (Mad.)].

Case Law : *CIT* v. *Tollygunge Club Ltd.* [1977] 107 ITR 776 (SC)

Facts: 'T', a social and sports club, passed a resolution at general meeting for levying surcharge for local charities on the admission fees it charged on viewers of horse races conducted. The receipts from the surcharge were not credited to the profit and loss account and were carried directly to a separate account styled "charity account".

Held: The surcharge being impressed with an obligation in the nature of trust for being applied to local charities was by this obligation diverted before it reached the hands of the assessee and, at no stage, it became a part of the income of the assessee. If nothing more had been done by the assessee than merely passing a resolution deciding to utilise a part of the admission fee received by it to charitable purposes, no legal obligation would have been created obliging the assessee to utilise this amount for the purpose of charity. Such a resolution would have left it open to the assessee to alter it or to rescind it and it would have been nothing but an expression of the desire or intention of the assessee to apply the amount for charitable purposes. But here a resolution was passed at the general meeting of the assessee for levying the surcharge for local charities and, pursuant to this resolution, the surcharge was paid by the race-goers and received by the assessee for the specific purpose of being applied to local charities.

Case Law : *CIT* v. *Bijli Cotton Mills (P.) Ltd.* [1979] 116 ITR 60 (SC)

Facts: 'B' used to realize a specified amount on account of dharmada (charity) from its customers on sales of yarn and bales of cotton, and credited the amount in a separate account known as dharmada account, and not in its trading account. The money in dharmada account was treated as trust fund and subsequently two trustees were appointed who executed a deed of declaration of trust for the purpose of utilising the monies for altruist religious or charitable purposes.

Held: Right from inception these amounts were received and held by the assessee under an obligation to spend the same for charitable purposes only, with the result that these receipts could not be regarded as forming any income of the assessee. The amount of dharmada was undoubtedly a payment which a customer was required to pay in addition to the price of the goods which he purchases from the assessee but the purchase of the goods by the customer would be the occasion and not the consideration for the dharmada amount taken from the customer.

Diversion of income by creation of a charge on a source of income to discharge an obligation: When a charge is created on a source of income of an assessee in order to discharge a judicial obligation of the assessee, it will result in diversion of the title of income to the person in favour of whom the charge has been created. The assessee will not be in control of the income which will be pledged in favour of the person in favour of whom the charge is created. Such an income cannot reach the assessee and cannot form a part of his income.

Case Law : *Raja Bejoy Singh Dudhuria* v. *CIT* (1933) 1 ITR 135 (PC)

Facts: Under a compromise decree passed under a suit of maintenance, the step-mother of 'R' was to be paid a certain monthly amount and the said amount was declared as a charge upon the properties in the hands of the 'R' by the court.

Held: The amount of maintenance recovered by step-mother was not a case of application of the income of assesse and cannot be taxed in the hands of 'R'.

Case Law : *CIT* v. *Sitaldas Tirathdas* (1961) 41 ITR 367 (SC)

Facts: 'S' was required under a judicial decree to pay a sum of ₹ 25,000 per month to his wife as maintenance expense for her and for their children, and ₹ 2,00,000 as expense for marriage of their daughter. He claimed that these amounts were not a part of his income as they were diverted to his wife as he is under a judicial order.

Held: The assessee remains in control of his income as no overriding charge was created on any of his source of income to discharge the maintenance obligation towards his family. Therefore, the income reaches the assessee as his own, and discharge of the obligation, even if under a judicial decree, is a mere application of income. Therefore, the Assessing Officer is justified in disallowing the deduction claimed by the assessee.

Diversion of income by an agreement to sell an asset along with its income upon transfer of ownership: Ownership of income from an asset during the period between the date of agreement and the actual date of transfer is often a matter of agreement. Where the agreement is silent, such profit-in-law would belong to the seller during the intervening period. But where the agreement provides that the buyer should have the benefit of the same and the transaction finally materialises, it is a case where the seller will not be assessable because of the principle of diversion of income by overriding title in favour of the agreement-holder or purchaser [*Dalmia Cement Ltd.* v. *CIT* (1999) 104 Taxman 97/237 ITR 617 (SC)].

Diversion of income by inheriting an asset with a liability attached to it: Where an assessee inherits an asset along with liability, such a liability would be a charge on the asset with the result that income from such asset would stand diverted by the charge [*Raja Bejoy Singh Dudhuria* v. *CIT* [1933] 1 ITR 135 (PC)]. But where the legal heir receives some assets and some liabilities, while the liability not being a charge on the assets, the inference can well be different. [*CIT* v. *Mathubhai C. Patel* (1999) 238 ITR 403 (SC)].

Case Law : *CIT* v. *Mathubhai C. Patel* (1999) 238 ITR 403 (SC)

Facts: The assessee inherited various assets and liabilities on death of his father and was also required to meet the liability which had accrued out of inherited assets. Amongst the inherited assets were certain shares which were pledged by his father against a bank overdraft taken by the father during his lifetime. The assessee was obliged to pay interest to the bank on the amount outstanding in the overdraft account with the bank. The assessee claimed that the shares were pledged against the overdraft and were therefore intricately linked to it. The income of such shares, to the extent used to settle the interest on overdraft, cannot be considered as his income, as it has been diverted to settle an inherited liability and no real income is earned by him to that extent.

Held: Distinction has to be made between the assets being charged with the obligation to discharge the liability and the income from such assets being charged with the liability. In the instant case, the pledging of the shares was effected by the assessee's father to secure the loan advanced by the bank and it is not a case where the income from the shares had been charged with payment of interest payable on the overdraft. Accordingly, there was no diversion of income by overriding the title and the dividend income of the assessee from shares pledged was assessable to tax.

Transfer of specific income under a pre-existing contractual obligation is diversion of income: Where the assessee has a contract with a third party to contribute its net collections for certain specific days towards certain specified funds, such a contribution will be treated as a diversion of the income. The contract may be oral or written but what is important is that it should be entered before as the income earned in order for it to result in the diversion of income by overriding title [*CIT* v. *Madras Race Club* (1996) 219 ITR 39 (Mad.)]. If such a contract is entered into after earning the income, it will be treated as an application of income [*CIT* v. *Thakar Das Bhargava* (1960) 40 ITR 301 (SC)].

INCOME v. CAPITAL

It is an established law that income is a flow, while capital is a fund. Income can be compared to the fruits of a tree, while the tree being a source is the capital. Income connotes a periodical return in money or moneys coming in with some sort of regularity or expected regularity from a definite source [*CIT* v. *Shaw Wallace & Co. Ltd*. [1932] 6 ITC 178 (Cal.)]. All incomes are liable to income tax unless specifically exempted by the Act and all capital receipts are exempt from income tax unless specifically chargeable. Therefore, the distinction between income and capital receipts is very significant.

Basic Test to Distinguish Income from Capital: The factor which distinguishes an income from a capital receipt is that whatever amount is derived, with the source being intact will be income, while the amount received as compensation for the loss or sterilisation of the source will be capital. In other words, the difference can be drawn by determining whether it is fixed capital or circulating capital. A fixed asset is what the owner turns to profit by keeping it in his own possession; circulating asset is what he makes profit by parting with it and letting it change masters. [*Jon Smith & Son* v. *Moore* (1921) 12 TC 266 (HL)]. What is a capital asset in the hands of one person may be a circulating asset in the hands of the other. For example, say for a consultant, computer is a fixed capital, ownership of which is retained by the consultant but which is nevertheless put to use for his/her work and it enables the consultant to generate profits. But for the dealer in computers, the computer is a circulating capital. Such dealer parts with the ownership of the computer and generates profits by the sale of computer.

Instalments vs. *Lump Sum Receipt of an amount in lump sum or in instalments is not determinative of the character of the receipt as income or capital:* Where capital is repaid in instalments, it retains its character and such instalments received are also treated as capital receipts. On the other hand, if a revenue receipt is received in one lump sum rather than being received every year, it will still retain its character as income. What matters is the true substance of the transaction and not the manner of its receipt. For example, arrears of salary received in one lump sum will still retain the nature of income and cannot be considered to be on capital account merely because they are received in lump sum. Similarly, if consideration for sale of a capital asset is received in instalments, such instalments received will be on capital account and will be settlement of the debt in instalments.

Nomenclature is not decisive: The name which the parties may give to the transaction which is the source of the receipt and the characterization of the receipt by them is of no consequence in determination of the true nature of the receipt.

Motive of the Person Making the Payment is Irrelevant: The nature of the receipt is determined entirely by its character in the hands of the receiver, and the source from which the payment is made has no bearing on its character. When an amount is paid which, so far as the payer is concerned, is paid wholly or partly out of capital, and the receiver receives it as income on his part, the entire receipt is taxable in the hands of the receiver. [*CIT* v. *Kamal Behari Lal Singha* (1971) 82 ITR 460 (SC)].

Treatment of a Receipt under any other Law or as per Accounting Principles is Irrelevant: It is only the character of the receipt under the Income-tax Act which is relevant to determine its nature as income or capital. Manner or treatment under any other law is irrelevant [*Punjab Distilling Industries Ltd.* v. *CIT* (1965) 57 ITR 1 (SC)]. It is the true nature and quality of the receipt and not the head under which it is entered in the account books that would prove decisive. If a receipt is a trading receipt, the fact that it is not shown in the account books of the assessee would not prevent the assessing authority from treating it as an income [*Chowringhee Sales Bureau P. Ltd.* v. *CIT* (1973)/1973 taxmann.com 151/87 ITR 542 (SC)].

Facts and Circumstances of each case to be taken into account: In the determination of the question whether a receipt is capital or income, it is not possible to lay down any single test as infallible or any single criterion as decisive. The question must ultimately depend on the facts of the particular case, and the authorities bearing on the question are valuable only as indicating the matters that have to be taken into account in reaching a decision. Take for example carbon credits. There is an ongoing controversy on whether receipt on sale of carbon credits is a capital or revenue receipt. Several rulings of the Tribunal have held that carbon credits is not an offshoot of business but that of an environmental concern and therefore the same should be taxed as capital receipt and not revenue [*CIT* v. *My Home Power Ltd.* [2014] 46 taxmann.com 314/225 Taxman 8 (AP) (Mag.), *Principal CIT* v. *Lanco Tanjore Power Ltd.* [2021] 131 taxmann.com 31/434 ITR 671 (Mad)]. The matter is currently pending before the Supreme Court of India for determination of this question [*Principal CIT* v. *Lanco Tanjore Power Ltd.* [2021] 133 taxmann.com 93/[2022] 284 Taxman 276 (SC)].

CHAPTER 3 Interpretation of Taxing Statutes

INTRODUCTION

Language is but an imperfect manifestation of human thought and therefore the true intention of the legislature may not always be clear in legislation, thereby leaving ample scope for differences of opinion and ambiguity. Interpretation of statute is a process by which the courts seek to ascertain the meaning of the legislature through the medium of authoritative forms in which it is expressed. Income-tax Act has also been a frequent source of litigation between the taxpayers and the tax administrators. Over the years, judiciary has evolved certain well-established rules to interpret the Act to ascertain the intention of the lawmakers to resolve any ambiguity or difference of opinions. A sound understanding of these rules of interpretation is crucial to understand the Income-tax Act in its true sense and import.

INTERPRETATION v. CONSTRUCTION

Interpretation is an art of finding out the true sense of any form of words, that is, the sense which an author intends to convey and enables others to derive from the same idea which the author wants to convey. Construction, on the other hand, is drawing conclusions about subjects that lie beyond the direct expression of the text from elements known from and given in the text; conclusions which are in the spirit though not within the letter of law. [*Cooley's Constitutional Law*, vol. I, p. 97]. However, the distinction between the two is academic and in practice they are so hard to disentangle that in common usage, interpretation and construction are usually understood as having the same significance and the two expressions are used in the book as synonymous.

The process of interpreting a statutory enactment is not a mechanical task of finding out the dictionary meaning of the words used, as if reading a mathematical formula, but is really an attempt to discover the intent of the legislation from the language used, remembering that language is at best an imperfect instrument for expression of human thought [*Verghese (KP)* v. *ITO* (1981) 7 Taxman 13/131 ITR 597 (SC)]. Rules of interpretation have been evolved to ascertain the intention of the lawmakers. These are not rules of law but only assist the courts to resolve the manifest ambiguity in a provision [*Bhargavy P. Sumathykutty* v. *Janki Sathyabhama* (1996) 217 ITR 129 (Ker.) (FB)]. These rules are not exhaustive and new rules of interpretation may be evolved to meet a new or unique situation [*CIT* v. *Lokmat News Papers (P.) Ltd.* (1995) 80 Taxman

629/216 ITR 199 (Bom.)]. The intention of the legislature is to be gathered from the words used by the statute [*CIT* v. *Sodra Devi* (1957) 32 ITR 615 (SC)].

- **Intention of Legislature should be the true original intention -** In construing an ongoing Act, the interpreter is to presume that the Parliament intended the Act to be applied at any future time in such a way as to give effect to the true original intention. Accordingly, the interpreter is to make allowances for any relevant changes that have occurred, since the passing of Act, in law, social conditions, technology, the meaning of words, and other matters. This means that in its application on any date, the language of the Act, though necessarily embedded in its own time, is nevertheless, to be construed in accordance with the need to treat it as current law [*CIT* v. *Neo Poly Pack (P.) Ltd.* [2000] 112 Taxman 363/245 ITR 492 (Del.)].
- **Object of Legislation v. Legislative Intent -** There is a clear distinction between legislative intention and the purpose or object of the legislation. While the purpose or object of the legislation is to provide a remedy for the malady, the legislative intention relates to the meaning or exposition of the remedy as enacted. [*Shashikant Laxman Kale* v. *Union of India* [1990] 52 Taxman 352/185 ITR 104 (SC)].
- **Equity cannot be taken into account while interpreting legal provisions -** The argument that taxation of such amount would offend the principles of equity and that such tax would create hardships, it was held, would not be a relevant ground in interpretation of tax laws. If there is any hardship or there is any need for reform on grounds of equity, it is for the Government to remove such hardships. [*Karamchari Union* v. *Union of India* [2000] 109 Taxman 1/243 ITR 143 (SC)].

Case Law : ***Karamchari Union* v. *Union of India* [2000] 109 Taxman 1/ 243 ITR 143 (SC)**

Facts: The appellants were employees of Central Government, State Government Central Government undertakings, banks, and general insurance employees receiving various allowances including City Compensatory Allowance, dearness Allowance and House Rent Allowance. They challenged the inclusion of CAA, DA and HRA in their income for the purpose of tax liability contending that such allowances were not incomes but a reimbursement of expenditure and in several cases they were actually expending more than the allowance received. Therefore including these payments as taxable would cause hardship to the honest employees whose source of income is limited and are required to meet extra expenses at the station where they are transferred.

Held: Income-tax is attracted at the point when the income is earned and taxation of income is not dependent upon its destination or the manner of its utilisation. It may be true to the extent that Government or statutory corporations do pay something less than what is required to be reimbursed. However, equity or hardship would hardly be relevant ground for interpretation of tax law. It is for the Government or the statutory bodies to do the needful.

- **Interpretation of Statutes is exclusively the domain of the judiciary -** The task of interpretation of laws is the exclusive domain of the courts [*Grasim* v. *Asstt. CIT* [2000] 245 ITR 677/(2001) 115 Taxman 278 (Bom.) and *Tata Teleservices Limited* v. *CBDT* (2016) 69 taxmann.com 226/240 Taxman 182/286 CTR 465 (Del)]. Since there are several rules governing the construction or interpretation of the statutes, it is for the court to select the most appropriate rule to aid the understanding of a particular provision [*Muddeereswara Mining Industries* v. *CIT* [1993] 204 ITR 550 [1994] 72 Taxman 186 (Kar.)].

Case Law : ***Tata Teleservices Limited* v. *CBDT* [2016] 69 taxmann.com 226/240 Taxman 182 (Delhi)**

Facts: 'T' engaged in the business of providing telecom services, accumulated heavy losses over the years and claimed refund for the tax deducted at source ('TDS') by the payers and deposited with the Government. The refunds were declined citing reasons of pending scrutiny and that in light of relevant section and the Instructions of the CBDT.

Held: While the CBDT has the statutory power under sec. 119 to tone down the rigour of the law for the benefit of the assessee by issuing instructions and circulars to ensure a proper administration of the fiscal statute, this power has certain limitations. The direction or instructions issued by the CBDT should not be "prejudicial to assessees." The task of interpretation of the laws is the exclusive domain of the courts. By the device of issuing an instruction in purported exercise of its power under Section 119 of the Act, the CBDT cannot proceed to interpret or instruct the income tax department to 'prevent' the issue of refund.

FUNDAMENTAL RULES OF JUDICIAL CONSTRUCTION

Rule of Strict and Literal Construction

The cardinal rule to interpret an Act of Parliament is that it must first be constructed in accordance with the intention expressed in the Act itself by way of words used to phrase the legislation. In a taxing statute one has to look at what is clearly said. There is no room for any intendment. There is no equity about a tax. There is no presumption as to a tax. Nothing is to be read in, nothing is to be implied. One can only look fairly on the language used [*Cape Brandy Syndicate* v. *IRC* [1921] 1 KB 64 approved in *CIT* v. *Ajax Products Ltd*. [1965] 55 ITR 741 (SC)].

Therefore, where the words of the legislation are clear, unambiguous and does not lead to any absurdity in law, they should only be given their ordinary grammatical meaning without regards to the wisdom of the legislation or the result. [*Kishor B. Setalvad* v. *CWT* (2002) 256 ITR 637 (2003) 128 Taxman 560 (Guj.); *CWT* v. *Smt.Harmatunnisa Begum* [1989] 176 ITR 98 (SC); *Doshi Accounting Services Pvt. Ltd.* v. *Dy. CIT* [2019] 76 ITR (Trib.) 449 [2020] 113 taxmann.com 521/181 ITD 49 (Ahd.-Trib.)].

Accordingly, where the language of the statute is clear and explicit, effect must be given to each word [*CIT* v. *Swadeshi Cotton Mills Co. Ltd.* [1998] 98 Taxman 388/232 ITR 618 (All); *Doshi Accounting Services Pvt. Ltd.* v. *DCIT* [2019] 76 ITR (Trib.) 449/[2020] 113 taxmann.com 521/181 ITD 49 (Ahd. (Trib.)]. No words should be added or subtracted or altered or modified unless it is plainly necessary to do so in order to prevent a provision from being absurd, unreasonable or unworkable [*Ruchi Soya Industries Limited* v. *Union of India* [2016] 336 ELT

463 (Cal.)]. The courts should not substitute its own notions of justice in place of legislative intent as is apparent from the reading of the statutory provision [*ACIT* v. *Iqbal Jafar* (2014) 51 taxmann.com 189/151 ITD 364 (Luck-Trib.)]. The words of the statute are ultimately to be regarded as decisive when they are unambiguous and the width of its meaning cannot be altered by importing the principles laid down in the cases decided under other statutes in the background of facts which are wholly dissimilar. [*CIT* v. *T. Abdul Wahid and Co.* (2000) 125 Taxman 702/243 ITR 467 (Mad.); *CIT* v. *Khanwaljit Singh* (ITA 602, 607 and 921/2010)].

A taxing statute cannot be construed by making assumptions and presumptions [*Goodyear India Ltd.* v. *State of Haryana* (1990) 1990 taxmann.com 985/(1991) 188 ITR 402 (SC); *CIT* v. *Calcutta Knitwears* (2014) 43 taxmann.com 446/223 Taxman 115 (Mag.) (SC)/6 SCC 444]. Where strict construction does not lead to the intended result, equitable or reasonable construction may be applied in such cases [*Keshavji Ravji and Company* v. *CIT* [1990] 183 ITR 1 (SC)].

Case Law : ***CIT* v. *Swadeshi Cotton Mills Co. Ltd.* [1998] 98 Taxman 388/232 ITR 618 (All.)**

Facts: 'S' engaged in manufacturing textile goods had one main mill and several manufacturing units in different places, claimed a sum to the tune of about ₹ 66,000 as entertainment expense. However, the Assessing Officer considered the overall income of 'S' from all the units and allowed a sum of ₹ 12,000 disallowing the rest. 'S' appealed and contended that the AO should have considered the expenses in respect of each unit separately and therefore the claim of entertainment expense should be considered unit wise.

Held: The cardinal principle of law is that insofar as the language of a provision of a fiscal law is clear and unambiguous, that has to be given full effect without importing into it any foreign word. The relevant section reads 'in case of a company', thereby requiring aggregation at the time of allowing deductions. No doubt units are independent and identifiable nevertheless none of the units of 'S' is an assessee itself or a company. If the contention of 'S' were accepted then the expression "in the case of a company" will have to be read as "in the case of a company and its unit" for which there is no justification.

Case Law : ***ACIT* v. *Iqbal Jafar* [2014] 51 taxmann.com 189/151 ITD 364 (Luck. - Trib.)**

Facts: 'I' earned long term capital gains on sale of land and claimed exemption under sec. 54F having invested double the amount of gain in a residential house situated outside India. The Assessing Officer rejected claims to exemption deeming that the newly invested property should be in India in keeping with the intentions of legislation although the provision itself nowhere use the words 'in India'.

Held: The cardinal rule of interpretation is that the Statute must be construed according to its plain language and neither should anything be added nor should anything be subtracted therefrom unless there are adequate grounds to justify the interference that the Legislature so clearly intended. The meaning of the extent of the statute must be collected from the plain and unambiguous expression used therein, rather than from any notions which may be entertained by the Court as to what is just and expedient. Therefore, the words "in India" cannot be inserted in Sec. 54F and as per plain reading of the section sale proceeds of the capital asset shall be invested in residential house in India or outside India thereby, entitling 'I' to exemption.

Case Law : ***Godrej & Boyce Manufacturing Company Ltd.* v. *Dy. CIT* [2017] 81 taxmann.com 111/247 Taxman 361 (SC)**

Facts: 'G' earned tax free dividend income in respect of shares held in group companies on which the company had paid tax under sec. 115-O. 'G' claimed that since the companies distributing dividend had paid tax thereon, no disallowance could be made in hands of 'G' by invoking provisions of section 14A and expenditure incurred by it should be allowed.

Held: A plain reading of section 14A show that no expenditure should be allowed with respect to such income that is not included in the total income of the assessee. Once the said condition is satisfied, the expenditure incurred in earning the said income cannot be allowed to be deducted. Since income was tax free in the hands of 'G', it was not included in its total income and therefore expenditure incurred cannot be allowed by application of sec. 14A.

GOLDEN RULE

Where the plain and literal interpretation of a statutory provision produces a manifestly absurd and unjust result which could never have been intended by the legislature, the court may modify the language used by the legislature or even do some violence to it, so as to achieve the obvious intention of legislature and produce a rational construction [*Godrej & Boyce Manufacturing Company* v. *Deputy CIT* [2017] 81 taxmann.com 111/247 Taxman 361/394 ITR 449 (SC)].

Thus, where a literal and strict construction defeats the obvious intention of the legislation and produces wholly unreasonable result, the court may follow the rule of reasonable construction [*CIT* v. *J.H. Gotla* [1985] 23 Taxman 14J/156 ITR 323 (SC)]. A correct interpretation would achieve the object of the provision, avoid mischief, advance the cause of justice and make the law workable and enforceable [*Syed Sadiq* v. *CIT* [1999] 239 ITR 263 (SC); *CIT* v. *Chandulal Harjivandas* (1967) 63 ITR 627 (SC); *CIT* v. *Regional Soyabean Products Cooperative Union Ltd.* (1999) 105 Taxman 134/239 ITR 217 (M.P.)]. A construction which renders a provision of an enactment futile, either wholly or partially is not to be adopted [*CIT* v. *Hindustan Bulk Carriers* (2003) 126 Taxman 321/259 ITR 449 (SC); *Manian Transport* v. *Krishna Moorthy* [1991] 191 ITR 1 (Mad.) and *Gopal Engg. Works* v. *C.P. Thanraj* [1995] 211 ITR 303 (Mad.)].

Case Law : ***Principal CIT* v. *IDMC Ltd.* [2017] 246 Taxman 6 (Gujarat)**

Facts: 'I'purchased the plant and machinery but due to certain damage, parts of the machinery were replaced by the supplier at Germany and therefore, the said machinery could be installed only after one year. 'I's claim for additional depreciation under sec.32(1)(*iia*) was rejected by the Assessing Officer stating that the twin condition of acquisition as well as installation for claiming depreciation was not satisfied.

Held: The underlying object and purpose of allowing additional depreciation is to encourage industries like 'I' to set up the new undertaking/ install new plant and machinery. The provisions of sec. 32(1)(*iia*) are required to be interpreted reasonably and purposively as strict and literal reading of sec. 32(1)(*iia*) would lead to an absurd result denying additional depreciation to 'I' though admittedly 'I' had acquired new plant and machinery and, therefore, 'I' was entitled to additional depreciation.

RULE OF BENEFICIAL OR LIBERAL CONSTRUCTION

Where two reasonable constructions of a taxing provision are possible, that construction which is most beneficial or favourable to the assessee should be adopted even if it results in a double advantage to the assessee [*CIT* v. *Vegetable Products Ltd.* [1973] 88 ITR 192 (SC) *Vahid Paper Converters* v. *ITO* [2006] 98 ITD165 (Ahd.-Trib.)]. If a section in a taxing statute is doubtful and of ambiguous meaning, it is not possible out of that ambiguity, to extract a new and added obligation not formerly cast upon the tax-payer. [*CIT* v. *J.V. Kolte* [1999] 235 ITR 239 (Bom.)]. This is based on the premise that the Legislature can always clarify its intention by amending the law with retrospective effect and nullify the decision of the courts [*Krishna Murthy (M.)* v. *CIT* (1985) 23 Taxman 126/ 152 ITR 163 (AP)]. Therefore, if a section in a taxing statute is doubtful and of ambiguous meaning, it must be resolved in favour of the assessee. Similarly, where a case is governed by more than one provisions, it is the prerogative of the assessee to be governed under a provision, which leaves him with a lighter burden.

However, it must be noted that the question of adopting the construction of a fiscal statute beneficial to the assessee arises only if the interpretation of such statute is open to doubt. The theory of beneficial interpretation has no application where the language of the statute is clear and explicit. In such a case, the well-settled principle of interpretation is that the statutory provision should be construed according to the plain natural meaning of its language [*M.H. Daryani* v. *CIT* [1993] 202 ITR 731 (Bom.)].

Case Law : ***Chief Electoral Officer* v. *ITO* [1999] 68 ITD 439 (Chd. - Trib.)**

Facts: The assessee, Chief Electoral Commissioner, Haryana, did not deduct tax at source at the time of making payments to another governmental organisation for preparation and supply of laminated electoral photo identity cards prepared as per specification supplied by the assessee. According to the assessee, the expression 'carrying out any work' as used in sec. 194C read with a specified Circular of the income-tax department did not cover the activity involved in the instant case and it was merely a contract for sale/ supply of goods. Rejecting the assessee's contention, the Assessing Officer held that the activity involved fell within the expression 'carrying out any work' and held the assessee in default in deducting tax at source and levied interest also under section 201(1A).

Held: The expression 'work' has been defined in *Explanation III* to section 194C with effect from 1-7-1995. The said definition is inclusive and the ordinary meaning of the expression 'work' has to be seen. The expression 'carrying out any work' used in Sec. 194C has a wide import and cover 'any work' which could be got carried out through a contractor under a contract including the obtaining of supply of labour under a contract with a contractor for carrying out any work. The Circular excluded contracts where the contractor undertakes to supply any article or thing fabricated according to the specifications given by the Government and the property in such article or thing passes to the Government since the contract will be a contract for sale. Thus, in such a situation, where two interpretations are possible, such interpretation which favours the assessee has to be adopted. Further, the assessee acted *bona fide* in this case on the basis of the said belief and did not deduct tax at source. The tax due on payments in question had been paid by the contractor and no loss of revenue had been caused to the department as the tax due had been paid by one of the parties.

RULE OF HARMONIOUS CONSTRUCTION

When any provision of a taxing statute is interpreted, it must be so constructed that the meaning of such provision must harmonise with the intention of the Legislature behind the provision in particular and the enactment in general *CIT* v. *Chandanben Maganlal* [2002] 120 Taxman 38 (Guj.). Further one provision of the Act cannot be construed in a manner so as to defeat another provision of the Act. Several provisions in the Act must be read together as parts of one larger scheme [*CIT* v. *Dharma Chand* (1993) 70 Taxman 390/204 ITR 787 (Raj.); *Ghisalal* v. *CIT* (2001) 115 Taxman 531/248 ITR 506 (Gau.)]. One provision should be construed with reference to another provision, so as to make a consistent enactment of the whole statute [*CIT* v. *Parekh Bros.* (2002) 120 Taxman 362/253 ITR 43 (Ker.)]. The court always upholds a harmonious construction which reconciles and considers all parts of the Act [*CIT* v. *Hindustan Bulk Carriers* (2003) 126 Taxman 321/ 259 ITR 449 (SC)].

Case Law : ***Sanjeev Lal* v. *CIT* [2014] 46 taxmann.com 300/225 Taxman 239 (SC)**

Facts: 'S' entered into an agreement to sell a house property, received earnest money and purchased a new residential property within one year from date of agreement to sell. Subsequently sale deed could not be executed owing to the pendency of the litigation wherein the validity of the will under which the property had devolved upon was challenged. The execution of sale deed took place only after the final dismissal of the litigation. 'S's claim for exemption from long-term capital gains on the transfer of said property and investment of its proceeds in the new house was rejected on the grounds that the new house was purchased two years before the date of execution of sale deed while under the statutory provisions it should be only before one year.

Held: The provisions of sec. 54 read with sec. 2(*47*), *i.e.* definition of "transfer" give relief to a person who has transferred his one residential house and is purchasing another residential house either before one year of the transfer or even two years after the transfer. The intention of the Legislature is to give him relief on the payment of long term capital gain tax. Although the sale deed could not be executed owing to an interim order of the court restraining 'S' from doing so, considering the definition of "transfer" there was some right in respect of the capital asset in question that had been transferred in favour of the vendee and therefore, some right of 'S' which stood extinguished. Harmonious construction of the provisions which subserve the object and purpose should also be made while construing any of the provisions of the Act and more particularly when one is concerned with exemption from payment of tax. 'S' was allowed exemption.

Case Law : ***CIT* v. *A.K. Ghosh* [2003] 131 Taxman 124/263 ITR 536 (MP)**

Facts: 'A' a Development Officer in the Life Insurance Corporation, claimed deduction for conveyance allowance, additional conveyance allowance and 40 per cent, of the incentive bonus. The AO, after referring to the provision of sec. 10(*14*) and certain guidelines issued by the CBDT wherein it was indicated that the Development Officer was not entitled to get deduction on incentive bonus, disallowed all the claims.

Held: A perusal of sec. 10(*14*) shows that in case of any special allowance or benefit specifically granted to meet the expenses incurred wholly, necessarily and exclusively in the performance of the duties of an office or employment, deductions would be permissible. The emphasis is on the actual expenses incurred by the assessee. Further, The Government of India in notification has specified that the conveyance allowance in performance of duties is to be exempted. Reading the provisions of section 10(*14*) in entirety and appreciating the factual scenario in proper perspective and keeping in view the instructions of the LIC and the Gazette Notification issued by the Government it is clear that the conveyance allowance/additional conveyance allowance received by the Development Officer of the LIC is exempt under section 10(*14*). However, 40% deduction claimed for incentive bonus was not allowed.

- **Words to be Construed in the Context in which they Occur - Words of Analogous Meaning Coupled Together should be Understood in their Cognate Sense -** Every word in a statute should be construed in the context in which it occurs in order to discover its appropriate meaning. A word is known by the company it keeps, *noscitur a sociis*. When two or more words which are susceptible of analogous meaning are coupled together, they should be understood in their cognate sense. [*TEOCO Ltd.* v. *DCIT* ITA No. 1910/Mum/2017].
- **Definition in One Section can Apply to All Sections -** Where there is a definition in an enactment, such definition should have application in respect of the entire enactment and not merely to the section to which the definition is given. [*CIT* v. *G.S. Atwal & Co. (Gua)* (2002) 254 ITR 592/ (2003) 128 Taxman 520 (Cal.)]. A particular word occurring in one section of the Act, having a particular object cannot carry the same meaning when used in different section of the same Act, which is enacted for different object [*DCIT* v. *Datacraft India* (2010) 40 SOT 295 (Mum.-Trib.)(SB)].

  In order to ascertain the legislative intent of any provision of law, regard may be had to the heading of the section as well as the spirit conveyed by the provisions of the entire section. [*CIT* v. *Indian Products Ltd.* [1994] 73 Taxman 245/207 ITR 647 (Cal.) *PCIT* v. *Saumya Construction Pvt. Ltd.* (2017) 81 taxmann.com 292/297 CTR (Guj.) 387].

Case Law : ***Stonecraft Enterprises* v. *CIT* [1999] 103 Taxman 490/237 ITR 131 (SC)**

Facts: 'S' exporting granite claimed deduction available under section 80HHC which was rejected by the revenue authorities stating that 'granite' is a 'mineral' within the meaning of the term found in section 80HHC(2)(*b*)(*ii*) that excluded application of the deduction to 'mineral oil' and 'minerals and 'ores'.

Held: The word 'minerals' in sub-section (2)(*b*) of section 80HHC must be read in the context of 'mineral oil' and 'ores' with which it is associated. These three words taken together are intended to encompass all that may be extracted from the earth. All materials extracted from the earth, granite included, must, therefore, be held to be covered by the provisions of sub-section (2)(*b*) of section 80HHC and the exporter thereof is, therefore, disentitled to the benefit of that section.

EXTERNAL AIDS TO INTERPRETATION

At times, it is not possible to judge the intention of the legislature by analysing mere words and phrases of an enactment as language is at best an imperfect instrument for the expression of human thought. In such cases, we may take clues as the intention of the legislature from a range of relevant sources to arrive at a judicious interpretation of a clause. Such useful aids to construction of taxing statutes are discussed later.

CIRCULARS

The Central Board of Direct Taxes are conferred powers under the Income-tax Act to pass such ciruclars, orders, instructions and directions to the income tax authorities for the proper administration of this Act. Such Circulars or directions, issued by the Central Board of Direct Taxes bind all officers and persons employed in the execution of the Act to the extent they are beneficial to the assessees. If they are prejudicial to the taxpayer, then they cannot prevail over the statute. [*Commissioner of Central Excise* v. *Ratan Melting & Wire Industries* (2008) 17 STT 103 (SC)].

Circulars beneficial to the assessee which tone down the rigour of the law and are issued in exercise of the statutory powers under section 119 are binding on the authorities in the administration of the Act. The benefit of such circulars is admissible to the assessee even though the circulars might have departed from the strict tenor of the statutory provision and mitigated the rigour of the law. This Court, however, clarified that the Board cannot pre-empt a judicial interpretation of the scope and ambit of a provision of the Act. Also a circular cannot impose on the taxpayer a burden higher than what the Act itself imposed. [*Keshavji Ravji & Co.* v. *CIT* [1990] 49 taxman 87/183 ITR 1 (SC)].

Case Law : ***UCO Bank* v. *CIT* [1999] 104 Taxman 547/237 ITR 889 (SC)**

Facts: The assessee bank had advanced loans to various customers and recovery as well as interest of some loans was very doubtful. Such doubtful interests were not brought to the profit and loss account of the assessee-bank and did not form a part of the real income of the bank. CBDT circular was also a general test for deciding what is a doubtful debt in circular dated 9-10-1984 and directed that all ITOs should treat such amounts as not forming part of income of assessee until realised. While the Assessing Officer excluded such interest from the total income of the assessee-bank, the Commissioner concluded that the said amount was includible in the total income.

Held: Under sec.119 a specific power is given to the Board for the purpose of proper and efficient management of the work of assessment and collection of revenue to issue such orders, instructions or directions as the guidelines, principles or procedures to be followed in the work relating to assessment, not being prejudicial to the assessees. As such, the circular would be binding on the department. The relevant circulars of the Board cannot be ignored. So long as such a circular is in force, it would be binding on the departmental authorities in view of the provisions of section 119 to ensure a uniform and proper administration and application of the Act.

- **Board's Circulars Explaining Contemporaneous Law has Greater Sanctity -** The Board's circulars issued at the time of any new law has greater sanctity on the principle of *contemporanea expositio,* as one which explains the intention behind the law at a time contemporaneous with the law itself. But where a circular is issued much later, it cannot be said to be a contemporaneous interpretation with the result it does not have the same degree of authenticity as one issued at the time of the introduction of law. For example, a circular issued in 2005 in respect of a provision made in 1998 cannot command the same respect as otherwise, with the result that the judiciary is free to consider the issue with reference to other criteria and came to a conclusion different from the one enjoined by the circular [*Warren Tea Ltd.* v. *Union of India* [1999] 102 Taxman 501/236 ITR 492 (Cal.)].
- **Circulars, Clarifications and Government Press Releases are Binding Only on the Department - They can Supplement the Law but cannot Run counter to a Statutory Provision -** The power of the Central Board of Direct Taxes to issue instructions to subordinate authorities is limited. Such instructions can be issued only for proper administration of the provisions of the Income-tax Act and not otherwise. It cannot issue any instructions which would be *de hors* the provisions of the said Act [*Shiva Kant Jha* v. *Union of India* (2002) 122 Taxman 952/256 ITR 563 (Delhi); *Azadi Bachao Andolan* v. *Union of India* (2001) 116 Taxman 249/252 ITR 471 (Delhi); *Tata Teleservices Limited* v. *CBDT* (2016) 69 taxmann.com 226/240 Taxman 182/286 CTR (Delhi) 465].

  However, such circulars or directions cannot bind the appellate authority, the tribunal or the court [*ITO* v. *D. Manohar Lal Kothari* (1999) 104 Taxman 139/236 ITR 357 (Mad.); *Commissioner of Central Excise* v. *Ratan Melting & Wire Industries* (2008) 17 STT 103 SC]. The task of interpretation of laws is the exclusive domain of the court [*Grasim Industries Ltd.* v. *ACIT* (2000) 245 ITR 677/(2001) 115 Taxman 278 (Bom.)]. Clarificatory notes or press releases and notifications issued by the Government or the Board have no legal force [*CIT* v. *Anjum M.H. Ghaswala* (2001) 119 Taxman 352/252 ITR 1 (SC); *CIT* v. *A. Raajendra Prasad* (2008) 299 ITR 227 (AP)]. Executive instructions can supplement a statute but they cannot run contrary to the statutory provision or whittle down their effect [*State of MP* v. *GS Dall & Flour Mills* (1991) taxmann.com 887/187 ITR 478 (SC)].

Case Law : ***Union of India* v. *Azadi Bachao Andolan* [2003] 132 Taxman 373/ 263 ITR 706 (SC)**

Facts: With a view to avoid double taxation of income, the Government of India and the Government of Mauritius entered into a double taxation avoidance convention which *inter alia* provided that residents of Mauritius would not be taxable in India on capital gains they make from shares of Indian companies. Allegedly Mauritius became a tax haven and investment was routed through Mauritius by several companies merely having a post box address in Mauritius only to avoid of capital gains tax in India. CBDT had issued Circular No. 789, dated 13-4-2000 whereby a certificate of residence issued by Mauritius authorities was a sufficient evidence for accepting status of residence.

This circular was contested in the courts of law in India stating that the circular curtailed the powers of the Assessing Officer to call in for more evidence and ultra vires the powers vested in Central Board of Direct Taxes.

Held: Under sec. 119 CBDT was entrusted to set things on course by eliminating avoidable wastage of time, talent and energy of the assessing officers discharging the onerous public duty of collection of revenue. The Circular No. 789 does not in any way crib, cabin or confine the powers of the assessing officer with regard to any particular assessment. It merely formulates broad guidelines to be applied in the matter of assessment of assessees covered by the provisions of the DTAC. The circular did not take away or curtail the jurisdiction of the assessing officer to assess the income of the assessee before him.

- **Finance Minister's Speech**

  The speech of the Minister or the mover of the Bill can be taken into consideration to ascertain the legislative intent or the purpose behind the legislation [*Kerala SIDC* v. *CIT of India* [2003] 259 ITR 51 (SC); *DCIT* v. *Datacraft India Ltd.* (2010) 40 SOT 295 (Mum.-Trib.) (SB)].

  However, in absence of ambiguity in a provision, Minister's speech cannot be used as an aid to the interpretation of a provision [*Escorts* v. *UOI* [1991] 189 ITR 81 (Delhi)]. The opinion tendered by the Law Ministry and Minister's reply to a question before Parliament are not binding on the courts [*Builders Associations of India* v. *UOI* (1994) 209 ITR 877 (SC)].

- **Explanatory Memorandum**

  Where the provisions are unambiguous, there is no warrant to refer to external aids of interpretation like notes on clauses of the Finance Bill, and the memorandum explaining its provisions [*CIT* v. *Central Bank of India Ltd.* [1990] 185 ITR 6 (Bom.)]. However, in cases of doubt or difficulties, these may be useful to ascertain the intention of the legislature [*Rangaswami (M)* v. *CWT* (1996) 221 ITR 39 (Mad.); *Shree Shree Ramakrishna Samity* v. *DCIT* (2015) 64 taxmann.com 330/44 ITR(T) 678/ (2016) 156 ITD 646 (Kol. - Trib.)].

Catch Phrases used in Explanatory Memorandum cannot be Relied Upon. Catch phrases of an explanatory memorandum may not give a true indication of the object of the legislation. A catch phrase possibly used as a populist measure to describe some provisions in the explanatory memorandum while introducing the Bill in Parliament can neither be determinative of, nor can it camouflage, the true object of the legislation [*Shashikant Laxman Kale* v. *Union of India* [1990] 52 Taxman 352/185 ITR 104 (SC)].

- **Recommendation of a Commission** - Where an enactment or amendment is the result of the recommendation of a Commission, it is permissible to refer to the relevant report of the Commission [*Mithilesh Kumari* v. *Prem Bihari* [1989] 177 ITR 97 (SC); *R. Dalmia* v. *CIT* (1992) 194 ITR 700 (Delhi)].

- **Provisions of Other Statutes** - Judicially interpreted words and expression, defined in one statute, do not afford a guide to the constitution of the same words or expressions in another statute unless both the statute are *pari materia* (that is, in equal materials) legislation or it is specifically provided in one statute to give the same meaning to the words as defined in another statute [*DCIT* v. *Datacraft India* (2010) 40 SOT 295 (Mum.-Trib.) (SB)]. Resort to a provision of another Act may be permissible in the absence of a definition or the term of a technical nature [*Re Moolamattom* (1999) 106 Taxman 242/238 ITR 630 (Ker.)].

Case Law : *CIT* v. *Shambulal Nathalal & Co.* (1985) 23 Taxman 93/[1984] 145 ITR 329 (Kar.)

Facts: The partnership deed of the assessee-firm did not provide that the firm would continue after the death of any partner. During the relevant accounting year, one partner died and on very next day a new partnership was brought into existence consisting of all three surviving partners of the dissolved firm and two sons of deceased partner. For the relevant assessment year, two returns were filed, one by the dissolved firm and the other by the newly constituted firm. While sec. 187 deals with changes in the constitution of the firm, sec. 188 deals with succession of one firm by another. Sec. 189 deals with dissolution of the firm or the discontinuance of its business. The revenue authorities considered it as a case of 'change in constitution of firm' within the meaning of section 187 justifying a single assessment clubbing both income for periods prior to and after factual dissolution of old firm. The assessee-firm contended that since the firm was dissolved, and it was succeeded by another firm, it would be governed by sec. 188. It also argued that under the Partnership Act the phrase 'change in the constitution of the firm' did not include a case of dissolution and thereby the same phrase used in sec. 187 also could not be held to include dissolution of a firm.

Held: When there is a dissolution of a firm under the law of partnership and a new firm takes over the business of the dissolved firm, it is true that under the general law of partnership the old firm cannot be regarded as being reconstituted. But the legal position of a firm under the income-tax law is different from that under the general law of partnership in several respects. And where the provisions of the Income-tax Act are clear, resort cannot be had to the provisions of another statute like the Indian Partnership Act. Therefore, a firm which is regarded as dissolved under the general law of partnership, can be regarded as being merely reconstituted under the law of income-tax in certain circumstances.

Case Law : *Jaswant Trading Co.* v. *CIT* [1995] 212 ITR 24/(1996) 85 Taxman 639 (Raj.)

Facts: 'J' being a firm, made donations and claimed that the entire amount was allowable as business expenditure since by making such donations there was increase in business turnover. The Assessing Officer rejected 'J's claim for full deduction as business expenditure under sec. 37(1) and allowed only 50% deduction under sec. 80G.

Held: Sec. 37(1) is a general provision and sec. 80G is a specific provision. Sec. 37(1) is a residuary provision for claiming business expenditures and requires that such an expenditure should be laid out or expended wholly and exclusively for the purposes of the business or profession and the burden to prove is on the assessee. Section 80G provides for a deduction in computing the total income of an assessee, on the donation made by the assessee, in specified funds. The deduction allowed is 50% of the donation amount or could even be 100% of the donated sum if so specified.

Applying the *maxim generalia specialibus non-derogant*, if an amount is liable for deduction under section 80G, it cannot be claimed under general provision of section 37(1). If a particular amount of expenditure falls within the category of donation, then the deduction as provided under section 80G alone would be applicable.

◆ *Income-tax Act* v. *Provisions of Double Tax Avoidance Agreements* - In determining the liability of a non-resident company, if there is any Agreement for Avoidance of Double Taxation, the said agreement must prevail over the provisions of the Income-tax Act [unless the statutory provision is more beneficial to the assessee [*UOI* v. *Azadi Bachao Andolan* (2003) 132 Taxman 373/263 ITR 706 (SC); *Danisco India (P.) Ltd.* v. *Union of India* (2018)/90 taxmann.com 295/253 Taxman 500/404 ITR 539 (Delhi)].

Case Law : ***Danisco India (P.) Ltd.* v. *Union of India* [2018] 90 taxmann.com 295/253 Taxman 500/404 ITR 539 (Delhi)**

Facts: 'D' is an Indian assessee, who, in the normal course of its business remits payments to M/s. DuPont Singapore, a non-resident company, located in Singapore. Tax relationship between the two countries is regulated in terms of Indo-Singapore Double Taxation Avoidance Agreement (DTAA). The relevant provisions of DTAA mandates a cap of 10% upon the recovery of amounts, in respect of tax incidence that occurs in the concerned host country. However, 'D' was issued a notice under sec. 206AA (prior to its amendment) resulted in a recovery of an additional 10%, in the event, the non-resident payee, did not possess PAN.

Held: The amendment to sec. 206AA(7) has now rendered the issue rather academic. The amendment is mitigating to a large extent, the rigors of the pre-existing laws. The law, as it existed, went beyond the provisions of DTAA which in most cases mandates a 10% cap on the rate of tax applicable to the state parties. Where reciprocating states mutually agree upon acceptable principles for tax treatment then in such case Double Taxation Avoidance Agreement will acquire primacy. Hence, the provision in sec. 206AA (as it existed) has to be read down to mean that where the deductee *i.e.*, the overseas resident business concern conducts its operation from a territory, whose Government has entered into a Double Taxation Avoidance Agreement with India, the rate of taxation would be as dictated by the provisions of the treaty.

◆ **Dictionary Meaning**

Where a word is not defined in the Act, it may be understood as per its dictionary meaning. However, in case of more than one meaning of a word, it should be interpreted in the context of the provisions of the Act, having regard to the legislative history of the provision and scheme of the Act [*CIT* v. *Venkateswar Hatcheries (P.) Ltd.* (1999) 103 Taxman 503/153 CTR 105 (SC)]. **Dictionary Meaning is Relevant but not Sacrosanct.** Words in the section of a statute are not to be interpreted by having those words in one hand and the dictionary in the other. In spelling out the meaning of the words in a section, one must take into consideration the setting in which those terms are used and the purposes that they are intended to serve [*CGT* v. *N.S. Getti Chettiar* [1971] 82 ITR 599 (SC)]. Therefore, the dictionary meaning of a word or expression used in a statute is relevant but not sacrosanct and the court will not hesitate to depart from the dictionary meaning if the context and the setting in which the word or expression is used so suggests or demands. Courts would also be justified in departing from the literal meaning to be given to an expression if it is satisfied that the literal interpretation is likely to produce a manifestly unjust result which could not have been intended by the Legislature [*Shree Shree Ramakrishna Samity* v. *DCIT* (2015) 64 taxmann.com 330/44 ITR 678/(2016) 156 ITD 646 (Kol. - Trib)].

Case Law : ***CIT* v. *Sri Venkateswara Hatcheries* [1999] 103 Taxman 503/ 237 ITR 174 (SC)**

Facts: 'V', having a poultry farm, were running hatcheries where eggs are hatched on large scale. 'V' claimed to be industrial undertaking engaged in the business of producing article and therefore entitled to development allowance under sec. 43A and deductions under sec. 80HH, sec. 80HHA, sec. 80-I and sec. 80J.

Held: Neither the word 'produce' nor the word 'article' has been defined in the Act. When the word is not so defined in the Act it may be permissible to refer to the dictionary to find out the meaning of that word as it is understood in the common parlance. But where the dictionary gives divergent or more than one meaning of a word the word has to be construed in the context of the provisions of the Act and regard must also be had to the legislative history of the provisions of the Act and the scheme of the Act. Giving such reading it is abundantly clear that those who are engaged in the business of hatcheries are neither industrial undertakings nor engaged in the business of producing articles or things.

- **Meaning of a Word or Expression must be Consistently used Throughout the Act -** It is a cardinal principle in the construction of enactments that, unless the context otherwise requires, the meaning of an expression contained in the Act should prevail throughout the Act. Therefore, whenever a different meaning is sought to be given to that expression occurring at different places in the Act, it is necessary to point out why the context requires different meanings to be given to the same expression occurring at different places in the Act [*CIT* v. *Dredging Corporation of India* (1988) 39 Taxman 301/174 ITR 682 (AP); *Dy. Director of Income Tax* v. *Andhra Pradesh Right to Sight Society* (2012) 24 taxmann.com 1/ 53 SOT 480 (Hyd. - Trib.)].

Case Law : ***Dy. DIT* v. *Andhra Pradesh Right to Sight Society* [2012] 24 taxmann.com 1/53 SOT 480 (Hyd. - Trib.)**

Facts: 'A' is a charitable institution formed with the objective of developing high quality sustainable comprehensive eye care services, aiming towards eradication of blindness. Assessing Officer added ₹ 16 crores being grants and contribution including the ones received by the state government and interest on such grants. AO also withdrew the exemption benefit under sec.11 for the reason that 'A' had applied ₹ 4 crores towards supply of equipments to the government hosptials, that is applied directly or indirectly for the benefit of person (the donor) and so 'A' had fallen foul of sec. 13(3).

Held: The definition of "person" under Section 2(*31*) includes legal authority but not Government itself. It is a cardinal principle in the construction of enactments that, unless the context otherwise requires, the meaning of an expression contained in the Act should prevail throughout the Act. Whenever a different meaning is sought to be given to that expression occurring at different places in the Act, it is necessary to point out why the context requires different meanings to be given to the same expression occurring at different places in the Act. Since State Government cannot be considered as a 'person' under sec. 2(*31*) and the Department has not pointed out any special circumstances as to why a different meaning should be given for the phrase 'person' for the purpose of secs. 11-13 so as to include the State government as a 'person' for these sections only. Hence, the contention of the Revenue that by giving the machines to the Government Hospitals sec.13 has been violated is incorrect.

PRECEDENTS

Though the doctrine of *res judicata* does not apply to income-tax proceedings since each assessment year is independent of the other, but where an issue had been decided consistently in a particular manner for earlier assessment years, for the sake of consistency the same view should continue to prevail for subsequent years unless there is material change in the facts. If there is no single distinguishing feature prompting a different view, the view consistently applied over the past years must prevail [*Raja Bahadur Visheshwara Singh* v. *CIT* [1961] 41 ITR 685 (SC)].

Case Law : ***Raja Bahadur Visheshwara Singh* v. *CIT* [1961] 41 ITR 685 (SC)**

Facts: From 1929, the assessed invested his cash surplus in shares and securities and earned certain amount of profits on sale of these but under orders of the revenue authorities, these sums were not assessed to income-tax. Subsequently, in view of magnitude and frequency and ratio of sales to purchases and, holdings total Tribunal held that assessee was to be regarded as a dealer in shares and securities and, therefore, profits from sale transactions were assessable to income-tax which was challenged by the assesse.

Held: There is no such thing as *res judicata* in income-tax matters. Though for the assessment year assessee was held not to be carrying on any trade, it was open to Tribunal to hold that assessee was a dealer in shares and securities for subsequently assessment years.

Precedents can only Serve as Illustrations and not as Deciding Factors in themselves - No judicial ruling can, strictly speaking, be a precedent which could govern the decisions of a later litigation involving a similar question. Past decisions can be used only by way of illustrations of the different viewpoints which have a bearing on the decision of the case in hand [*Saroj Kumar Mazumdar* v. *CIT* [1959] 37 ITR 242 (SC)].

Decision of a High Court are not Binding on High Courts and Tribunals of Another State - Every High Court established under the Constitution for one or more States, is as independent and supreme, as the Supreme Court itself, in its own territorial sphere and is not subordinate to another High Court and is not bound by the Decisions of other High Courts [*Patil Vijaykumar* v. *Union of India* [1985] 20 Taxman 363/151 ITR 48 (Kar.); *The Commissioner GST, Commissionerate* v. *Shree Krishna Paper Mills and Industries Ltd.* CEA No. 36 of 2019 (O&M)].

On the desirability to have uniformity of decisions, there cannot be two opinions. But, that desirability cannot be elevated to an absolute proposition of law to hold that a High Court is bound to follow a decision of another High Court. Any decision rendered by a High Court either on the validity or the construction of an all India enactment will only be binding on that High Court, the courts and the Tribunals functioning in the territorial area over which it exercises jurisdiction and not on other High Courts, and the courts and the Tribunals functioning in the territorial area of that other High Court [*Patil Vijaykumar* v. *Union of India* [1985] 20 Taxman 363/151 ITR 48 (Kar.)].

However, a court must take into consideration the decision of another Bench even though it may not be binding on it [*CIT* v. *Brigadier B.D. Khurana* [1996] 217 ITR 381 (All.)].

The Principal Laid Down by a Supreme Court Ruling is Binding on High Courts but the Observations made by Supreme Court are not Binding - The ratio or principal laid down by the Supreme Court is binding on the High Courts, but each and every word stated by the Court while deciding a case does not become the law of the land. The pronouncement of the court even if cannot be strictly called the ratio decidendi of the judgment, would certainly be binding on the High Court. [*The Peerless General Finance and Investment Co. Ltd.* v. *CIT* [2019] 107 taxmann.com 228/265 Taxman 413 (SC)].

Case Law : ***The Peerless General Finance and Investment* v. *CIT* [2019] 107 taxmann.com 228/265 Taxman 413 (SC)**

Facts: 'P' floated various schemes that required subscribers to deposit certain amounts by way of subscriptions and at the end of the scheme amounts were ultimately repaid with interest. The scheme also contained forfeiture clauses in which case the amount would become income of 'P'. In the first year 'P' offered the subscription as revenue receipts. However, amounts pursuant to the investment scheme by subscribers never got forfeited and thus, 'P' claimed the subscription as capital receipt. Issue arose whether such subscriptions should be considered revenue reciept or capital receipt in the hands of 'P'. In an earlier ruling the Supreme Court though did not directly focus on the question whether subscriptions so received are capital or revenue in nature, the Court had on general principles held that such subscriptions would be capital receipt business aspect of matter. The High Court took a view since the issue before the Supreme Court in earlier ruling had no direct focus on the said question, that decision was read as not having laid down any absolute proposition of law.

Held: Though the Court's focus was not directly on this, yet, a pronouncement by this Court, even if it cannot be strictly called the *ratio decidendi* of the judgment, would certainly be binding on the High Court.

Precedents and Principles Under the Income-tax Act, 1922 - Where the provisions of the Income-tax Act, 1922 are similar in nature and intent to the corresponding provisions of the Income-tax Act, 1961, the principles and precedents which applied to the provisions of the old Act would still remain valid. [*CIT* v. *T. P. Sidhwa (Smt.)* [1981] 6 Taxman 91/[1982] 133 ITR 840 (Bom.)].

INTERPRETATION OF CERTAIN SPECIFIC PROVISIONS

There are certain fiscal provisions which require to be interpreted correctly to understand the legal implications. Some of them are explained later.

Mandatory or Directory Nature of a Provision, May v. Shall

The nature of a provision—mandatory or directory—is decided by taking into consideration the intent of the legislation, phraseology of the provision, consequences which would follow from construing it one way or the other [*CIT* v. *Shiva Electronics* [1994] 75 Taxman 93/209 ITR 673 (Bom.); *Church's Auxiliary for Social Action* v. *Director General of Income Tax* (2010) 325 ITR 362 (Delhi)]. If the object of the enactment is likely to be defeated by holding it as directory, it should be construed as mandatory. [*Church's Auxiliary for Social Action* v. *Director General of Income Tax* (2010) 325 ITR 362 (Delhi)]. If mandatory interpretation of the enactment gives rise to serious inconveniences to innocent persons without advancing its object, it should be construed as directory. In certain cases, having regard to the nature of the provision and intention of the legislature, the word "may" can be interpreted in mandatory sense and used interchangeably with "shall" [*Church's Auxiliary for Social Action* v. *Director General of Income Tax* [(2010) 325 ITR 362 (Delhi)]. For example, where the word "may" is used in the provision, ostensibly implying it to directory, but if any non-compliance with that provision would make the provision itself *null* and *void*, the use of word "may" should be constructed in a mandatory sense as provisions of law cannot be allowed to be frustrated by mere grammatical interpretation.

Case Law : ***Church's Auxiliary for Social Action* v. *Director General of Income Tax* [2010] 325 ITR 362 (Delhi)**

Facts: 'C' is a registered society withan aim of undertake, promote and assist in the upliftment of the poor, needy and to assist emergency relief work for the victims of flood, famine, and other disaster to assist in resettlement and rehabilitation of displaced persons and repatriates. It was also granted registration under sec. 12A. In 2001 'C' received the contributions/donations aggregating to ₹ 25 crore for relief work at earthquake hit state of Gujarat which was spent on the said purposes. However, since 'C' could not render accounts of the income and expenditure to the prescribed authority by the prescribed date, the entire donation was treated as taxable income. The application for condonation of delay was also rejected stating that there is no provision for condition of delay. 'C'challenged the rejection of the application which resulted in making the entire donation exigible to tax.

Held: The use of the word 'shall' in a statute, though generally taken in a mandatory sense, does not necessarily mean that in every case it shall have that effect. On the other hand, it is not always correct to say that when the word 'may' has been used, the statute is only permissible or directory. It is necessary to ascertain the intention. The word 'shall' is not always decisive. Regard must be had to the context, subject-matter and object of the statutory provision in question in determining whether the same is mandatory or directory. The real intention of the Legislature while enacting sub-section (5C) of Section 80G of the Act was to ensure application of donations to specific purpose by specified date and that part of the provision is mandatory. In order to find out that donations are applied for the stipulated purpose, requirement of rendition of accounts is to be introduced. However, if there is some delay in submitting this accounts, the Legislature never intended that such institutions or funds should pay the taxes on the donations received even when necessary applications with the provisions by expending the donations for specified purposes is made. This could not be and cannot be the purpose behind this provision.

Rules are Mandatory

All the authorities functioning under the Act including the Appellate Tribunal are bound by the Rules and it is not permissible to ignore or refuse to apply a Rule on the ground that it is only directory in nature. The rule cannot be construed in such a manner which prevents its application. Irrespective of the hardships, the provisions of the rule should be applied and if its application results in undue hardships, it is for the Board to intervene by suitable modification in the Rule. [*Commissioner of Income Tax* v. *K. S. Sundaram* [1999] 105 Taxman 317/239 ITR 851 (Mad.)]. A "Form" prescribed by the Rules cannot qualify a statutory provision or impose a time limit that the statute does not provide [*CIT* v. *Trustees of Shri Teckchand Chandiram Trust* [1989] 47 Taxman 468/[1990] 184 ITR 537 (Bom.)].

Case Law : ***CIT* v. *K. S. Sundaram* [1999] 105 Taxman 317/239 ITR 851 (Mad.) (affirmed by the Supreme Court)**

Facts: 'K', previously an employee of a limited company now a director of its subsidiary, was allotted a rent-free accommodation which he continued to hold. After becoming the director the subsidiary company reimbursed the rent of 'K's house to the holding company. The ITO determined the perquisite value of this rent-free unfurnished accommodation by applying rule 3(*a*)(*iii*) which stipulates that value shall ordinarily be a sum equal to 10% of salary. The Tribunal however held that rule 3(*a*)(*iii*) was directory and have no application when the accommodation was hired by the employer.

Held: Mere employment of expression 'ordinarily' in main part of rule 3(*iii*) does not show that said rule is directory and where statute provides for a uniform method of valuation of perquisite, statutory method of valuation of perquisite has to be adopted and it is not permissible to ignore or refuse to apply rule 3 on ground that it is only directory in nature and, hence, is not applicable in a case where accommodation itself is taken on lease by employer and provided to employee free of rent.

Time Limits - Whether Mandatory or Directory?

The law prescribes various time limits, but it cannot be said that all such limits are mandatory. While time limits for filing return or filing appeals have been considered mandatory, subject, of course, to the delay being condoned for sufficient cause as provided in the statute, it cannot be said that every other time limit is similarly mandatory. The consensus in such cases is that where the time limit is concerned with mere procedure, it should ordinarily be taken to be directory to subserve the purpose for which it is intended and not to be treated as a substantive requirement, which would defeat the very purpose of the relief. Distinction should be made between the provisions of the statute, which are substantive in character and those which are merely procedural and technical, consistent with the specific objective of the policy behind the time limit. [*Mangalore Chemicals and Fertilizers Ltd.* v. *Dy. CCT* [1992] Suppl. (1) SCC 21(SC)/[1992] 1992 taxmann.com 24 (SC)].

Construction of Charging Provision and Machinery Provisions

A charging provision has to be construed strictly [*CIT* v. *Calcutta Knitwears* (2014) 43 taxmann.com 446/223 Taxman 115 (Mag.) (SC)/6 SCC 444]. No person can be taxed under a charging section unless there are clear words to bring him within its ambit. No one can be taxed by implication [*CIT* v. *Punjab Financial Corporation* (2002) 121 Taxman 656/254 ITR 6 (Punj. & Har.)]. In interpreting a charging provision, construction that leads to double taxation, should be avoided unless it is expressly provided by the statute or it is implied therein [*CIT* v. *Keshavlal Lallubhai Patel* [1965] 55 ITR 637 (SC)]. Computation provisions may help to determine the scope of the charging section. [*CIT* v. *Calcutta Knitwears* (2014) 43 taxmann.com 446/223 Taxman 115 (Mag.) (SC)/6 SCC 444] The two together constitute an integral code.

A machinery provision cannot qualify the charging section so as to make the latter otiose [*Standard Triumph Motor Co. Ltd.* v. *CIT* [1993] 67 Taxman 160/201 ITR 391 (SC)]. Machinery provision should be construed in a manner that makes the machinery workable, effectuate the levy of tax and advance the object of the provision [*Tity Thomas* v. *TRO* [1994] 72 Taxman 254/207 ITR 1072 (Ker.); *CIT* v. *M.S.P. Exports (P.) Ltd.* (1992) 196 ITR 762/(1993) 67 Taxman 120 (Ker.); *CIT* v. *Calcutta Knitwears* (2014) 43 taxmann.com 446/223 Taxman 115 (Mag.) (SC)/6 SCC 444]. In interpreting such provisions, the benefit of the language should go to the assessee rather than to the revenue [*Kodiayal Foods & Fabs (P.) Ltd.* v. *CIT* [1992] 61 Taxman 99/193 ITR 411 (Ker.)].

Machinery provisions should be construed in a manner that the charge of tax is not defeated [*Kerala State Industrial Development Corpn. Ltd.* v. *CIT* [2000] 111 Taxman 1/246 ITR 330 (Ker.)]. However, the rule of strict interpretation is not applicable while interpreting machinery provisions [*CIT* v. *Punjab Financial Corporation* (2002) 121 Taxmann 656/254 ITR 6 (Punj. & Har.); *CIT* v. *Calcutta Knitwears* (2014) 43 taxmann.com 446/223 Taxman 115 (SC) (Mag.)/6 SCC 444], but a construction that disables the taxing machinery and lets the assessee get away with not paying the due amount of tax should not be adopted [*Jorawar Singh Baid* v. *Asstt. CIT* (1992) 198 ITR 47 (Cal.)].

Case Law : ***Gursahai Saigal* v. *CIT* [1963] 48 ITR 1 (SC)**

Facts: 'G' was charged with interest under as he did not make an estimate of advance-tax and did not pay tax. Under the relevant provision, interest was to be calculated from January 1 on the short-fall between the amount paid and eighty per cent of the tax that was found payable on the regular assessment. 'G' contended that in his case the question of charging interest on short payment of tax did not arise since there was no calculable shortfall in the first place. Since he never paid any tax, the shortfall between eighty per cent of the tax payable on regular assessment and the amount paid did not arise. Therefore he had been wrongly charged with interest.

Held: The relevant provision clearly intended to charge interest on non-payment of advance tax. But the interest has to be calculated in a certain manner. This provision only lays down the machinery for assessing the amount of interest for which liability was clearly created. The proper way to deal with such a provision is to give it an interpretation which makes the machinery workable. In a scenario where no tax is paid, and therefore there is no shortfall, the amount of such shortfall will be the entire eighty per cent.

Construction of a Legal Fiction

A legal fiction is often created by the Income-tax Act by enacting deeming provisions to assume the existence of certain facts which does not really exist. Although, a legal fiction is normally created by way of deeming provisions, such fiction may also be created without the use of word "deemed". A deeming provision is enacted to enlarge the meaning of a particular word and intended to include matters which otherwise may or may not fall within its ambit. [*Government of Andhra Pradesh* v. *Corporation Bank* (2007) 9 SCC 55/(2008) 2008 taxmann.com 1105 (SC)] For example, Section 9 extends the scope of accrual of income and receipt of income. Therefore, the deeming provisions should be construed strictly [*CIT* v. *Khimji Nenshi* (1991) 59 Taxman 278/(1992) 194 ITR 192 (Bom.); *CIT* v. *National Travel Services* [2011] 14 taxmann.com 14/202 Taxman 327/(2012) 249 CTR 540 (Delhi)].

In interpreting a legal fiction a court is to first ascertain the purpose for which the fiction was created and then assume all the facts which are incidental to or corollaries to the fiction but the fiction cannot be extended beyond the purpose for which it was created and its scope cannot be extended by importing another fiction. [*CIT Bombay City II* v. *Shakuntla* AIR 1966 SC 719] [*CIT(Central) Calcutta* v. *Moon Mills Ltd.* AIR 1966 SC 870]. A court has to give full effect to a legal fiction by taking it to its logical conclusion by imagining an assumed situation or fact as real unless the resultant interpretation would lead to absurd results [*CIT* v. *Saroop Krishan* (1985) 21 Taxman 404/153 ITR 1 (P&H)].

A legal fiction is created for some definite purpose and cannot be extended beyond that legitimate field. [*Bengal Immunity Co. Ltd.* v. *State of Bihar* AIR 1955 SC 661]. A legal fiction has to be carried to its logical conclusion, but only within the parameters of the purpose for which the fiction is created. As far as possible, the legal fiction should not be given a meaning so as to cause injustice. [*CIT* v. *Hindustan Petroleum Corporation Ltd.* (1990) 53 Taxman 512/(1991) 187 ITR 1 (Bom.)].

Case Law : ***Addl. ITO* v. *E. Alfred* [1962] 44 ITR 442 (SC)**

Facts: 'E' died intestate and the son of 'E' was assessed to tax for income of 'E' as his legal representative. Subsequent to the assessement a demand notice was issued and later a penalty was imposed on the son which was challenged by the son. High Court quashed the order imposing penalty on ground that the legal representative is not an assessee 'other person'.

Held: The original assessee being dead before the notice, either general or special, issued (*sic*) to him, he could not be treated as an assessee. The process of the Act is, by the fiction, made available against a different person like a legal representative, who was fictionally deemed to be an assessee, for purposes of assessment. It is in this sense that the legal representative becomes an assessee by the fiction, and it is this fiction, which has to be fully worked out. The words 'other person' cannot apply to a legal representative, if he is an 'assessee' by fiction, and the fiction has to be worked out to its logical conclusion. If he falls within the word 'assessee', he does not fall within the words 'other person. The penalty could be imposed on the respondent as an assessee.

Construction of Penal Provisions

The rule of strict interpretation should be applied to provisions which are penal [*Pr. CIT* v. *Shree Sai Developers* (2020) 314 CTR 641 (Guj.)] or quasipenal in nature [*Govind* v. *Dy. CIT* [2000] 246 ITR 787/[2001] 114 Taxman 693 (MP)]. There is no retrospective operation in penal law unless the statute takes it within its fold [*Smt. Thangalakshmi* v. *ITO* [1994] 205 ITR 176 (Mad.)]. For the penal provision to apply, the presumption is that the assessee had the *mens rea* (guilty mind) unless the statute specifically provides for the absence of the same. If there is any ambiguity in a penal provision, the assessee is entitled to the benefit of doubt [*CIT* v. *Gemini Pictures Circuits (P.) Ltd.* [1991] 54 Taxman 3/188 ITR 101 (Mad.)].

Case Law : ***Jarnail Singh* v. *ITO* [1989] 47 Taxman 422/179 ITR 426 (P&H)**

Facts: 'J' filed his returns for assessment years in question but had not maintained any books of account and income was disclosed on an estimate basis in *bona fide* manner. Subsequently, it was found in a department search on 'J's son's premises that it was the son who was the real owner of various business concerns which were being run by his relations including 'J'. The revenue authorities persuaded 'J' and other group of relatives to file revised and were assured that no penalties, interest or prosecution would be initiated against them. Although no concealed assets or income had come to light in the hands of the 'J' in the revised returns, complaints were filed by the ITO and prosecution proceedings were initiated against 'J'.

Held: To bring an act under the provisions of section 276C, the action of the person concerned has to be a wilful attempt to evade any tax, penalty or interest chargeable or imposable under the Act and this word 'wilful' imparts the concept of *mens rea* and if *mens rea* is absent no offence under this section can be made out. In the instant case, the earlier returns filed by 'J' could not be said to be false. 'J' filed the new returns only because of the settlement talks going on with the department. In any case, the new returns were to be considered as protective returns and therefore the prosecutions initiated under section 276C were not valid and were to be quashed.

Construction of Limitation Provisions

The law of limitation is intended to give certainty and finality to legal proceedings and to avoid exposure to risk of litigation to litigant for indefinite period on future unforeseen events. In a fiscal statute provisions regulating period of limitation must receive strict construction. Proceedings, which have attained finality under existing law due to bar of limitation, cannot be held to be open for revival. Unless such provision is amended and the amended provision is clearly given retrospective operation so as to allow upsetting of proceedings, which had already been concluded and attained finality, the proceedings cannot be reopened. [*K.M. Sharma* v. *ITO* (2002) 122 Taxman 426/254 ITR 772 (SC)]. A time-barred proceeding has to be dismissed [*Brahm Datt* v. *Asstt. CIT* (2018) 100 taxmann.com 324/(2019) 260 Taxman 380/306 CTR 114 (Del.)]. If limitation period is extended during the pendency of proceedings, such extended period should be applied to the pending proceedings [*Madhu Jayanti (P.) Ltd.* v. *CIT* (1992) 65 Taxman 485/193 ITR 159 (Cal.)].

Case Law : ***Brahm Datt* v. *Astt. CIT* [2018] 100 taxmann.com 324/[2019] 260 Taxman 380/(2019) 306 CTR 114 (Del)**

Facts: 'B' was a senior citizen non-resident/not ordinarily resident in India, derived income primarily from salary and professional receipts by working and residing in foreign countries. A search and seizure operation was carried out and during the search he clarified that he did not maintain any account with foreign bank in his personal capacity, but had contributed certain amount at the time of settling of an offshore Trust from his income earned from sources outside India. The revenue authorities initiated reassessment proceedings for AY 1998-99 after 8 years on the suspicion that the income of 'B' had escaped assessment. 'B' contended that such re-opening is time barred after six years under sec. 149. The AO relied on the amendment to sec.149(1)(*c*) introduced by the Finance Act, 2012 w.e.f. 1-7-2012 to hold that the proceedings were initiated within the extended period of 16 years from the end of the relevant assessment year

Held: Reassessment for 1998-99 could not be reopened beyond six years in terms of provisions of sec. 149 of the Act as applicable at the relevant time. 'B's return for assessment year 1998-99 became barred by limitation on 31.03.2005. Such assessement could not be revived beyond the period of limitation by taking recourse to the subsequent amendment made in sec. 149. The provision regulating period of limitation ought to receive strict construction. Proceedings, which have attained finality under existing law due to bar of limitation cannot be held to be open for revival unless the amended provision is clearly given retrospective operation. Statutes other than those which are merely declaratory or which relate only to matters of procedure or of evidence are *prima facie* prospectively and retrospective operation should not be given to a statute so as to take away or impair an existing right or create a new obligation or impose a new liability. The reassessment notice and all consequent proceedings were quashed and set aside.

Construction of Deduction, Exemption and Relief Provisions

A provision for deduction, exemption and relief should be interpreted liberally, reasonably and in favour of the assessee [*CIT* v. *South Arcot & Mahindra Ltd.* [1989] 176 ITR 117 (SC); *CIT* v. *Laxmi Metal Industries* [1998] 100 Taxman 619/[1999] 236 ITR 130 (All.)]. It should be construed so as to effectuate the object of the legislature and not to defect it [*CIT* v. *Mahindra & Mahindra Ltd.* [1983] 15 Taxman 1/144 ITR 225 (SC)]. Full effect should be given to the language used in the provision. A rigid or restricted interpretation should be avoided.

While an exemption, deduction and relief provision should be liberally construed, this does not mean that such liberal construction should be made even by doing violence to the plain meaning of such exemption provision. Liberal construction will be made wherever it is possible to be made without impairing the legislative requirement and the spirit of the provision. [*Petron Engineering Construction (P.) Ltd.* v. *Central Board of Direct Taxes* [1988] 41 Taxman 294/[1989] 175 ITR 523 (SC)].

Exemption notification has to be interpreted strictly. The burden of proving its applicability is on the assessee; and in case of any ambiguity, the benefit thereof cannot be claimed by the subject/assessee, rather it would be interpreted in favour of the revenue [*Commissioner of Customs (Import), Mumbai* v. *Dilip Kumar and Company* (2018) 95 taxmann.com 327/69 GST 239/361 ELT 577 (SC)]. The scope and ambit of the exemption provision cannot be expanded or widened at the stage of finding out eligibility and it remains subject to strict interpretation. But once eligibility is decided in favour of the claimant, it could be construed liberally in regard to other requirements, which may be formal or directory in nature. [*UOI* v. *Wood Papers Ltd.* [1991] 1991 taxmann.com 77/[1990] 47 ELT 500 (SC)].

Case Law : ***Ramnath & Co.* v. *CIT* [2020] 116 taxmann.com 885/272 Taxman 275 (SC)**

Facts: 'R', engaged in providing services to certain foreign buyers of frozen seafood, had received service charges from such foreign buyers in foreign exchange and claimed deduction under sec. 80-O. Relying on sec. 80-O *Explanation* (*iii*), the AO rejected the claimon the grounds that services provided by 'R' are services rendered in India and cannot be construed as services rendered from India.

Held: Merely having a contract with a foreign enterprise and earning foreign exchange does not *ipso facto* lead to application of sec. 80-O. Services of 'R' were nothing but of an agent, who was procuring merchandise for its foreign principals and such services as agent were rendered in India, income received by 'R' in foreign exchange did not qualify for deduction.

Construction of Non-obstante Clauses

A non-obstante clause is one which makes an exception from the general provisions relating to such statute. Such clauses are usually worded as "notwithstanding anything to the contrary contained in.........". The effect of the non-obstante clause is that in spite of the provision or Act mentioned therein, the enactment following it will have full operation or that the provisions embraced in the non-obstante clause will not be an impediment for the operation of the enactment [*CIT* v. *ONGC* [2002] 124 Taxman 292/255 ITR 413 (Raj.)]. Its scope has to be ascertained by reading it in the context of the provisions and consistent with the scheme of the enactment [*Bharat Hari Singhania* v. *CWT* [1994] 73 Taxman 3/207 ITR 1 (SC)].

Construction of "Means" and "Includes" Clauses

There are two forms of interpretation clauses. In one, when the word 'defined' is declared to "mean" something, the definition is explanatory and *prima facie* restrictive. In the other, where the word 'defined' is to "include" something, the definition is extensive and the extended meaning of a term does not take away its ordinary meaning [*Patil Vijay Kumar* v. *Union of India* [1985] 151 ITR 48 (Ker.)/*CIT* v. *Anchal Hotels (P.) Ltd.* [2016] 70 taxmann.com330/241 Taxman 108 (Uttrakhand)].

The word "include" is very generally used in interpretation clauses in order to enlarge the meaning of the words or phrases occurring in the body of the statute; and when it is so used these words or phrases must be construed as comprehending, not only such things as they signify according to their natural import, but also those things which the interpretation clause declares that they shall include. But the word "include" is also susceptible of another construction which may become imperative if the context of the Act is sufficient to show that it was not merely employed for the purpose of adding to the natural significance of the words or expressions defined. It may be equivalent to "mean and include", and in that case it may afford an exhaustive explanation of the meaning which, for the purposes of the Act, must invariably be attached to, these words or expressions [*Dilworth* v. *Commissioner for Land & Income Tax* [1899] AC 99 (PC); *CIT* v. *Aanchal Hotels (P.) Ltd.* [2016] 70 taxmann.com 330/241 Taxman 108 (Uttarakhand)].

The inclusive definition is therefore, comprehensive of not only such things as they signify according to their nature and import but also those things which the interpretation clause declares that they shall specifically include *Patil Vijay Kumar* v. *Union of India* [1985] 151 ITR 48 (Ker.)]. It is a well-settled rule of interpretation of inclusive definitions that it is not controlled or confined to the words or expressions which are included in the definition [*CIT* v. *H. D. Dennis* [1981] 7 Taxman 231/[1982] 135 ITR 1 (Bom.)].

Case Law : ***CIT* v. *Aanchal Hotels (P.) Ltd.* [2016] 70 taxmann.com 330 241 Taxman 108 (Uttarakhand)**

Facts: The assessees had set up hotels in Uttarakhand. They claimed deduction from income of hotel under sec. 80IC on the basis of entry 15 of 14th Schedule of the Act, which stated - 'Ecotourism including hotels'. The Assessing Officer disallowed deduction on ground that mere setting up the hotel was not sufficient to claim benefit of deduction but the hotel should also partake of ecotourism.

Held: Government of India issued the Office Memorandum in the year 2002 contemplated benefits for Thrust Industries, which included ecotourism hotels, located in the States of Himachal Pradesh and Uttarakhand. Ordinarily, the use of the word 'include' would mean an extension of the meaning. However, it may also be a case where the use of the word 'include', will have the effect of the word giving an exhaustive meaning. Ecotourism cannot be the same as tourism. Only hotels, which were set up as Ecotourism units or having set up as Ecotourism or units, were expanded as such, would be entitled to the benefit of section 80-IC. The soul of the provision is Ecotourism. Mere procurement of a No Objection from the Pollution Control Board cannot be determinative of a question, whether the hotel fulfils the requirement under section 80-IC.

Construction of a "Proviso"

"Proviso" does not control substantive enactment and cannot set at naught the real object of the main enactment. It functions as an exception to the main provision and deals with a case which otherwise would fall within the general language of the main enactment and its effect is confined to that case [*Gian Chand Ashok Kumar & Co.* v. *UoI* [1991] 56 Taxman 282/187 ITR 188 (H.P.)].

Mavilayi Service Co-operative Bank Ltd. v. *CIT* [2021] 123 taxmann.com 161/279 Taxman 75 (SC)]

However, a "proviso" may also be read as an independent substantive enactment where the context warrants such a construction [*CIT* v. *P. Krishna Warriar* [1964] 53 ITR 176 (SC); *CIT* v. *P. Krishna Warier* (1970) 75 ITR 154 SC]. It must be construed harmoniously with the main enactment [*T.T. (P.) Ltd.* v. *ITO* [1980] 121 ITR 551 (Kar.)].

Case Law : ***Mavilayi Service Cooperative Bank Ltd.* v. *CIT* [2021] 123 taxmann.com 161/279 Taxman 75 (SC)**

Facts: 'M', being a co-operative society registered as 'primary agricultural credit societies' claimed deduction under sec. 80P which was denied on the grounds that agricultural credits given by 'M' to members were very negligible as compared to credits for purposes other than agriculture. Sec. 80P(4) was introduced so as to exclude co-operative banks from taking the benefit of deduction under sec. 80P(1) and (2) where such banks, like any other commercial bank, are lending amounts to members of the general public.

Held: Sec. 80P is a benevolent provision which is enacted by Parliament in order to encourage and promote growth of cooperative sector in the economic life of the country. Therefore, such a provision has to be read liberally, reasonably and in favour of 'M'. The limited object of sec. 80P(4) is to exclude co-operative banks that function at par with other commercial banks *i.e.* which lend money to members of the public. Once sec. 80P(4) is out of harm's way, the Primary agricultural credit societies are entitled to the benefit of the deduction contained in sec. 80P, notwithstanding that they may also be giving loans to their members which are not related to agriculture. Sec. 80P(4) has to be read as a proviso, the proper function of a which is to qualify the generality of the main enactment by providing an exception and taking out as it were, from the main enactment, a portion which, but for the proviso would fall within the main enactment. A proviso must, therefore, be considered in relation to the principal matter to which it stands as a proviso. A proviso should not be read as if providing something by way of addition to the main provision which is foreign to the main provision itself.

Construction of Explanations

An "Explanation" is intended to explain the meaning of certain phrases and expressions contained in a statutory provision. Sometimes, depending upon its language, it is inserted to take away something from the content of a provision. An Explanation to a statutory provision has to be read with the main provision to which it is added as an Explanation. An Explanation appended to a section or a sub-section becomes an integral part of it and has no independent existence apart from it [*CIT* v. *Reunion Engineering Co. (P.) Ltd.* [1993] 203 ITR 274/70 Taxman 546 (Bom.)]

Insertion of an Explanation cannot be treated as an amendment but only intended to clear any mental cobwebs surrounding the meaning of a statutory provision. It is more a legislative exposition or clarification of an existing law than a change in it [*ITO* v. *D. Manoharlal Kothari* (1999) 104 Taxman 139/236 ITR 357 (Mad.)]. An *Explanation* is not a substantive provision but is inserted to clear up any ambiguity in the Section [*CIT* v. *Mohan Meakin Breweries Ltd.*

[1992] 60 Taxman 529/[1991] 192 ITR 134 (HP); *Sedco Forex International Drill Inc* v. *CIT* AIR 2006 SC 428]. It should be read to harmonise it with the Section because it is an integral part of the Section and has no independent existence apart from the Section [*CIT* v. *Reunion Engg. (P.) Ltd.* (1993) 70 Taxman 546/ 203 ITR 274 (Bom.)].

- **Explanations are Normally Retrospective in Operation unless Expressly made Prospective** - An *Explanation* is normally intended to remove an ambiguity and make the intention of the Parliament clear, therefore becomes a part and parcel of the provision from the original date of the provision [*Bengal Immunity Co. Ltd*. v. *State of Bihar* (1955) 6 STC 446 (SC), *Sedco Forex International Drill Inc* v. *CIT* [AIR 2006 SC 428]]. Therefore, an *Explanation* can have an effect even for a period prior to its insertion even though it may not have been expressly made retrospective in its operations [*CIT* v. *Doraiswamy Chetty* [1990] 52 Taxman 346/ 183 ITR 559 (SC) *Sedco Forex International Drill Inc* v. *CIT* AIR 2006 SC 428]. When a provision is enacted for the express purpose of explaining or clearing up issues as to the meaning of a previous enactment, such *Explanation* should normally govern earlier Acts also. An *Explanation* is *prima facie* confined to the subject matter of the prior enactment and governs the same and the presumption is that such an explanatory provision is retrospective. An *Explanation* which though posed as clarificatory but has the effect of expanding the scope of the section it seeks to clarify and resultantly introduces new principle upon which liability arises, then such amendment even though is posed to be as clarificatory would not be given retrospective effect. [*DIT* v. *New Skies Satellite BV* [2016] 68 taxmann.com 8/238 Taxman 577/382 ITR 114 (Delhi)]

Case Law : *Sedco Forex International Drill Inc* v. *CIT* AIR 2006 SC 428

Facts: 'S', non-resident company, entered into a contract with a company resident in India for offshore drilling project within the territorial waters of India. 'S' also entered into agreements with its employees who were residents of UK that included a period of field break during which they were required to undergo training not necessarily in India for upgrading their skills and technique. The Assessing Officer sought to tax salary of employees even during field break by relying on the *Explanation* to sec. 9(1)(*ii*) that was which was added by way of amendment in 1999 w.e.f. 1.04.2000 to include off-period salary in India. By that reason, the explanation was purportedly sought to be applied retrospectively in case of 'S' which was challenged by 'S'.

Held: An *Explanation* to a statutory provision may fulfil the purpose of clearing an ambiguity in the main provision or an Explanation can add to and widen the scope of the main section. If it is in its nature clarificatory then the Explanation must be read into the main provision with effect from the time that the main provision came into force but if it changes the law it is not presumed to be retrospective irrespective of the fact that the phrase used are 'it is declared' or 'for the removal of doubts'. The *Explanation* to sec. 9(1)(*ii*) is prospective in nature given the legislative history of the amendment and the fact that there was no ambiguity in the section.

Construction of Operative Dates of Provisions

All provisions are considered to be prospective except when made retrospective by express words or by necessary intendment. In case of ambiguity, the provisions should be construed as being prospective. [*CIT* v. *Ayodhyakumari (Mrs.)* [1985] 154 ITR 604 (Raj.); *CIT* v. *Vinay Mishra* [2020] 121 taxmann.com 243/[2021] 276 Taxman 68 (Kar.)]:

- **Retrospectivity is not to be inferred but must be stated explicitly -** Retrospective operation of a provision is not to be lightly inferred unless it is specifically stated to be retrospective in its operation. [*Brahm Datt* v. *ACIT* (2019) 306 CTR (Delhi) 114].

  Exception - An Explanation is ordinarily clarificatory in nature and has retrospective operation unless it is made to operate prospectively. For details, please refer to the earlier discussion on interpretation of Explanations in this chapter.

- **Vested Right does not get Divested by Subsequent Change of Law unless the Change is Expressly Retrospective -** Once a right is vested in the assessee, it does not get divested by a mere change in the provisions of law. For example, where an assessee is entitled to a deduction, which if not absorbed in the year of claim, can be carried forward and the deduction is meanwhile deleted from the statute before it could be absorbed, the deduction which had already been vested with the assessee will continue to be available to the assessee notwithstanding the intervening deletion of the statutory provision for deduction itself. The law is well settled that unless there is a clear provision in law nullifying the deduction already allowed, it cannot be treated as unavailable. [*Govinddas* v. *ITO* [1976] 103 ITR 123 (SC); *CIT* v. *Vinay Mishra* [2020] 121 taxmann.com 243/[2021] 276 Taxman 68 (Kar.)].

Case Law : ***CIT* v. *Vinay Mishra* [2020] 121 taxmann.com 243/[2021] 276 Taxman 68 (Kar.)**

Facts: 'V' , a Director of a company, derived income from salary, business, capital gains and other sources. The Assessing officer denied the deduction claimed under sec. 54F(1) on capital gains stating that investment was made in a property outside India.

Held: Since the requirement of investment in a residential house in India for claiming exemption under sec. 54F(1) was incorporated with effect from 1-4-2015 and not prior to that period, 'V's investment which was made prior to 1-4-2015, he would be entitled to claim exemption under section 54F.

The Doctrine of Promissory Estoppel

The State cannot lightly wriggle out of an assurance by citing statutory provisions of public interest, if the assurance was made by proper persons under authority. Statutory provisions do not rule out discretion, which should be deemed to have been exercised when an assurance is given and public interest cannot be understood as requiring penalty in every case.

For example, where an assessee established a factory on the promise of the Government to give exemption from tax, but was not given the same on the ground that the tax law did not provide for such exemption, the assessee was found to be eligible for the same under the powers available to the Government to grant such exemption under the law, as in a case where the promise is made by a person competent to make such promise. It is true that public interest may override the obligations of the promisor, but then something must be shown to have transpired, since the making of the promise to indicate that public interest would be prejudiced, if the promise is required to be kept. [*Motilal Padampat Sugar Mills Co. Ltd.* v. *State of U.P.* [1979] 118 ITR 326/1979 taxmann.com 210 (SC); *Manuelsons Hotels Private Limited* v. *State of Kerala* AIR 2016 SC 2322]. Where such a justification is sought to be made for the breach, it is for the court to balance the public interest as against the damage done to the promisee by breach of the assurance in the nature of a promise. The promisor cannot be the judge of its own liability to repudiate the promise *ex parte* with impunity [*Motilal Padampat Sugar Mills Co. Ltd.* v. *State of U.P.* [1979] 118 ITR 326 /1979 taxmann.com 210 (SC); *Manuelsons Hotels Private Limited* v. *State of Kerala* AIR 2016 SC 2322].

Case Law : ***Prashanti Medical Services & Research Foundation* v. *Union of India* [2019] 107 taxmann.com 382/265 Taxman 504 (SC)**

Facts: 'P' a charitable trust was granted an approval under sec. 35AC for its hospital projects and accordingly donations received by it were entitled to deduction under sec. 35AC in hands of donors from the total income of such donors. However, due to insertion of sub-section (7) to sec. 35AC with effect from 1-4-2017, the benefit of deduction to donors was discontinued. 'P' challenged the constitutional validity of sec. 35AC(7) inter alia on ground the deduction could not be withdrawn for projects already approved.

Held: A plea of promissory estoppel is not available to an 'P'against exercise of legislative power and nor any vested right accrues to 'P' in matter of grant of any tax concession to him. Further 'P's contention that it would have received much higher donation if the benefit of deduction was available to the donors is not acceptable and the constitutional validity of especially a taxing provision cannot be struck down on a plea based on equity or/and hardship.

Doctrine of Supervening Illegality

Distinction has to be made between invalidity in law and irregularity in law. While invalidity is a nullity in law, irregularity is capable of being cured. For example, if an assessment is bad in law *ab initio*, it can only be annulled, but if it is validly initiated and an invalidity creeps in during the assessment proceedings, the order will be required to be set aside but a fresh assessment after removal of irregularity will be permissible. [*Guduthur Bros.* v. *ITO* [1960] 40 ITR 298 (SC)]. Irregularity is capable of being waived and such waiver is inferable by conduct of the parties. It is only an illegality which is not capable of being waived. [*CIT* v. *N. Krishnan* [1999] 235 ITR 386 (Ker.)].

Case Law : ***Guduthur Bros* v. *ITO* [1960] 40 ITR 298 (SC)**

Facts: 'G' failed to file the return within the prescribed time and the ITO issued a show cause notice for imposing penalty. Despite 'G' filing reply, the ITO proceeded to levy penalty without affording hearing to 'G' as required under the statute. On appeal, the Assistant Commissioner set aside the order of ITO and directed refund of the penalty in view of an illegality which had occurred during the course of the assessment proceedings. The ITO then issued a further notice calling 'G' to appear so that they might get opportunity of being heard.

Held: The original show cause notice issued to 'G' did not cease to be operative, because the Appellate Assistant Commissioner pointed out an illegality which vitiated the proceeding after it was lawfully initiated. That notice having remained still to be disposed of, and the ITO was well within his jurisdiction to continue the proceedings from the stage at which the illegality had occurred.

Burden of Proof

Although the onus to prove that the sum in question was chargeable to income tax was on the Department, facts within the special knowledge of the assessee had to be placed and proved by him [*CIT* v. *Bipin Kumar Worah* [1974] 97 ITR 62 (Pat.)].

The onus is on the Revenue to satisfy the court that the case falls strictly within the provisions of the law. If the case is not covered within the four corners of the provisions of the taxing statute, no tax can be imposed by inference or by analogy or by trying to probe into the intentions of the Legislature and by considering what was the substance of the matter. If a Section in a taxing statute is doubtful and of ambiguous meaning, it is not possible out of that ambiguity to extract a new and added obligation not formerly cast upon the tax-payer. [*CIT* v. *J. V. Kolte* [1999] 235 ITR 239 (Bom.)].

However, where an assessee is claiming a benefit or deduction under the Income-tax Act, the burden of proving his claim to such benefit rests with the assessee only.

Retrospectivity in Taxation

The Constitution of India does not prohibit retrospective application laws and the legislative power to pass laws and amendments with retrospective effect. While it is often argued that retrospective amendments tend to make laws unpredictable and arbitrary, it is conceded that the legislation should have the power to correct a flaw in the drafting or inadvertent mistakes in the statute. The Constitution, however does prohibit making any act or omission an offence retrospectively or increasing punishment for an offence retrospectively. Thus creating a back-dated liability is not permissible and thereby retrospective amendments that create a tax liability on an assessee where none existed when the assessee entered into that transaction should not be encouraged. And yet retrospective amendments remain a common feature of tax laws.

The Supreme Court in *Chhotabhai Jethabhai Patel* v. *Union of India* 1962 Supp 2 SCR 1 upheld a retrospective amendment to the Central Excises and Salt

Act, 1944 which imposed excise duty on manufactured tobacco from the date of the introduction of the Bill and not from the date it came into force on the grounds that amendments sought to address the existing flaws which defeated the purpose of the legislation. Retrospective amendments in tax laws have been permissible when these sought to cure the inadvertent defects in the drafting of law that resulted into unintended consequences frustrating the very purpose of the law or amendments which are declaratory or clarificatory in nature. A declaratory amendment merely declares the law as it is and does not have the effect of abrogating a vested right in an assessee. Similarly clarificatory amendments that usually commence with the wordings 'For the removal of doubts it is clarified that....' merely explains or clarifies the legal position as it is which existed even prior to such clarification [*CIT* v. *Vatika Township (P.) Ltd.* (2014) 49 taxmann.com 249/227 Taxman 121/367 ITR 466 (SC)] has laid down the following general principles governing retrospective operation of legislations:

(*a*) unless a contrary intention appears, a legislation is presumed not to be intended to have a retrospective operation

(*b*) legislations which modified accrued rights or which impose obligations or impose new duties or attach a new disability have to be treated as prospective unless the legislative intent is clearly to give the enactment a retrospective effect; unless the legislation is for purpose of supplying an obvious omission in a former legislation or to explain a former legislation

(*c*) if a legislation confers a benefit on some persons but without inflicting a corresponding detriment on some other person or on the public generally, and where to confer such benefit appears to have been the legislators object, then the presumption would be that such a legislation, giving it a purposive construction, would warrant it to be given a retrospective effect

However, tax statute is replete with instances of retrospective amendments so as to nullify the effect of a decision of the Court. In the recent years there has been a spate of retrospective amendments, the one that earned a great amount of disrepute to India is the retrospective amendments made to the Income-tax Act after the Supreme Court ruled in favour of the assessee in *Vodafone International Holdings BV* v. *Union of India* (2012) 17 taxmann.com 202/204 Taxman 408/341 ITR 1 (SC).

The Vodafone tax matter slated to be the biggest corporate tax case in the country involved determination of a dispute whether a share purchase agreement of a non-resident company entered into between two non-resident companies is liable for capital gains tax in India just because the non-resident company whose shares is the subject matter of the agreement had its underlying assets in the Indian telecom joint venture. Simply put, Hutchison Whampoa, a Hong Kong based Company entered into a share purchase agreement with Vodafone International Holdings BV, a Netherlands company. Under the agreement the shares of a company based in Cayman Island controlled by Hutch were sold to Vodafone and since this Cayman Island company held majority stakes in

Hutchison Essar, an Indian telecom joint venture based in India; Vodafone took control over the Indian JV along with its control over the Cayman Island company. The Revenue authorities in India raised a tax demand of a whooping ₹ 22,000 crores including penalties and interest on this transaction claiming a source based jurisdiction over this transaction claiming the essence of the transaction was the control over Indian telecom JV. The Revenue also touted that this sharepurchase agreement of a Cayman Island company was a tax avoidance arrangement whose legal effect must be nullified. The Supreme Court however did not find merit in this argument and ruling in favour of the assessee went on to hold that the existing Income-tax provision did not capture such indirect transfers of capital asset situated in India and so no tax liability arose in India.

The Finance Act, 2012 introduced a range of retrospective amendments to the definition of the term transfer, capital asset as well as Section 9 that deals with incomes deemed to accrue or arise in India and thereafter the Revenue authorities sought to proceed with the tax demand on Vodafone. Pursuant to these tax demands, Vodafone and Cairn invoked arbitration under the Bilateral Investment Treaty. The Arbitration Tribunal ruled in favour of the assessees.

In order to create a positive environment for investment in the country and ensure tax certaints, the Parliament passed the Taxation Laws (Amendment) Act, 2021 amending the Income-tax Act. Accordingly, no tax demand shall be raised for any indirect transfer of Indian assets if the transaction was under taken before 28th May, 2012.

CHAPTER 4 Income Exempt from Tax

INTRODUCTION

While legislating on a matter within its competence if Parliament can grant an exemption, it is also competent for it to withdraw that exemption in exercise of the self-same power [*Madurai District Central Co-operative Bank Ltd.* v. *Third ITO* [1975] 101 ITR 24 (SC)]. Income-tax Act provides a scheme of exemptions, deductions and tax rebates (Fig. 4.1).

FIGURE 4.1: SCHEME OF EXEMPTIONS AND TAX BENEFITS

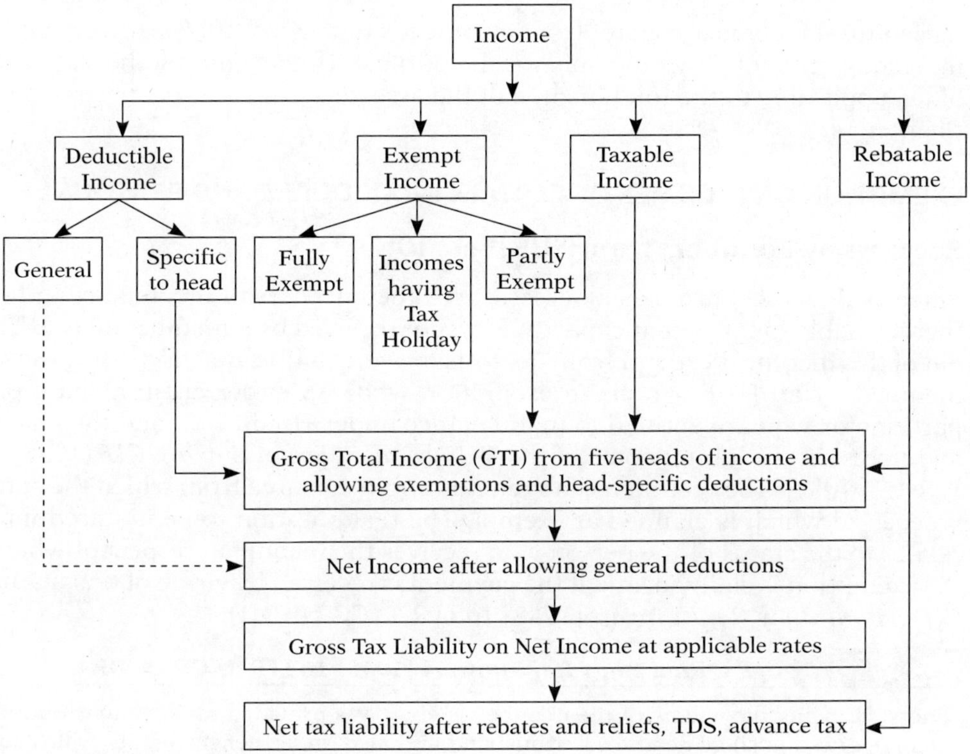

Income

Deductible Income

Exempt Income

Taxable Income

Rebatable Income

General

Specific to head

Fully Exempt

Incomes having Tax Holiday

Partly Exempt

Gross Total Income (GTI) from five heads of income and allowing exemptions and head-specific deductions

Net Income after allowing general deductions

Gross Tax Liability on Net Income at applicable rates

Net tax liability after rebates and reliefs, TDS, advance tax

Incomes fully exempt from income tax do not form part of the total income at all. Incomes partially exempt from tax are to be included in the total income only to the extent to which they are in excess of the quantum of exemption available.

Incomes for which deductions have been specified by the Act are also liable to be included in the gross total income, but a deduction is allowed to the extent of the quantum specified.

Similarly, incomes which are entitled to rebate or relief from tax are basically included in the total income only for the purpose of determining the gross tax liability and a rebate from the gross tax liability is then allowed in the manner specified. Rebatable incomes are, therefore, included in the total income only for determining the slab rate of tax applicable to the assessee. This chapter is devoted to incomes exempt from tax while the deductions from gross total income and rebate from tax liability have been discussed separately in latter chapters.

Burden of Proof for Claiming the Exemption Rests with the Assessee - Where the assessee wishes to claim any exemption under the Act, the burden of proving that the income is exempt from tax rests solely with him. Consider the following exemptions:

EXEMPTION ON AGRICULTURAL INCOME

Agricultural income is exempt from income tax under sec. 10(*1*). However, it is included in the total income only for the purpose of determining the slab rate of tax applicable to the total income of the assessee. This is to be discussed in Chapter 14.

EXEMPTION ON INCOMES OF CERTAIN INDIVIDUALS AND PERSONS

Receipts by Members from HUF [Sec. 10(2)]

Since HUF is recognized as an assessee for the purposes of income tax and is thereby liable to tax in that capacity, any sum received by a member of an HUF out of this income is exempt from tax so as to avoid double taxation. Only those members of an HUF can claim exemption who can either claim a share on partition or who are entitled to maintenance under Hindu Law and thus have an interest in the joint income of the HUF [*Kadar Narian Singh* v. *CIT* (1938) 6 ITR 157 (All.)]. The section has no reference to the source from which the sum is received which is claimed as exempt. The real question to be inquired into relates to the status of the person who receives the income in respect of which the exemption is claimed, and if the payment is received by virtue of that status *CIT* v. *Rani Bijay Raj Kunwari* [1948] 16 ITR 1 (CC-OUDH).

Case Law : ***CIT* v. *Rani Bijay Raj Kunwari* [1948] 16 ITR 1 (CC-OUDH).**

Facts: 'R' being the widow of the member of HUF was provided maintenance out of income of estate since death of her husband and also under her husband's will. The revenue authorities considered that the maintenance allowances were received by her not as member of HUF but under provisions of her husband's will.

Held: The existence of a right to claim maintenance as a member of an Hindu Undivided Family is not necessarily inconsistent with existence of an additional ground of claim based upon a will. Though husband's will fixed amount to be paid to assessee and made it a charge upon estate, it did not alter legal character of the sums paid as a member of an Hindu Undivided Family and was exempt.

Share of Profits from Partnership Firm [Sec. 10(*2A*)]

Since the Income-tax Act recognizes the partnership firm as a separate legal entity profits of which are liable to tax, share in such profits in the hands of partners is exempt. This is for the purposes of avoiding double taxation. Profits includes negative profits. And thereby, losses from a firm cannot be set off by partners against their personal income. The share of loss from a source, the income of which is exempt from tax, cannot be set off against any taxable income from any other source [*CIT* v. *Lallubhai Garothandas Mehta Charitable Trust* (1994) 207 ITR 104/[1995] 78 Taxman 88 (Guj.)].

Case Law : ***Radha Krishna Jalan* v. *CIT* [2007] 165 Taxman 538 (Gauhati)**

Facts: 'J' and two others were partners in a firm. Later 'J' constituted a sub-partnership firm with four others (the assessee) who would supplement the funds required to be invested by 'J' in the business of parent firm. Treating itself as a partner in the parent firm, the assessee-firm claimed exemption from share in profits it derived from the parent firm.

Held: A sub-partnership, which is in receipt of share of profit of a partner in main partnership, has to be deemed to be a partner in main partnership for limited purpose of section 10(2A) and will be entitled to exemption under section 10(2A).

Exemptions to Ex-rulers of Indian States [Sec. 10(*19A*)]

The annual value of any one palace in the occupation of the ex-ruler of Indian State is exempt, provided such annual value was exempt from tax before commencement of the Constitution (Twenty-sixth Amendment) Act, 1971 [Sec. 19A]. It is clarified that the exemption does not extend to capital gains realized on the sale of land forming part of the Official Residence of the ex-ruler [*Smt. Maharani Ushadevi* v. *CIT* (1981) 131 ITR 445/[1982] 8 Taxman 91 (MP)].

Case Law : ***Maharao Bhim Singh of Kota* v. *CIT* [2016] 76 taxmann.com 274/ [2017] 244 Taxman 139 (SC)**

Facts: 'M' was the ex-ruler of the princely state and occupied a palace for his residence. A part of the property was requisitioned by the Defence Ministry and question arose whether the rental income received by 'M' from the requisitioned property by way of rent was taxable in his hands.

Held: As long as an assessee continues to remain in occupation of his official residential palace for his own use, he would be entitled to claim exemption under section 10(19A) for entire palace notwithstanding fact that a part of his official residence has been let out.

Income of a Member of Scheduled Tribe [Sec. 10(26)]

The following incomes of a member of a Scheduled Tribe as defined by Article 366 (25) of the Constitution and residing in the specified areas is exempt from tax:

(*i*) income from any source in the areas, States or Union Territories specified; or

(*ii*) income by way of dividend or interest on securities.

Specified areas: Areas specified in Part I or Part II of Table appended to Paragraph 20 of the Sixth Schedule to the Constitution or in the States of Arunachal Pradesh, Manipur, Mizoram, Nagaland, Tripura and Ladakh region of Jammu and Kashmir.

Income of a Sikkimese Individual [Sec. 10(*26AAA*)]

Under sec. 10(*26AAA*) the following incomes of a Sikkimese individual was exempt:

(*a*) Income accruing or arising from any source in the State of Sikkim; or

(*b*) Income by way of dividend or interest on securities.

However, such exemption was not available to a Sikkimese woman if, on or after 01-04-2008, she married an individual who was not a Sikkimese. Following the Supreme Court decision in *Association of Old Settlers of Sikkim* v. *Union of India* [2023] 146 taxmann.com 271/292 Taxman 73 (SC), the Finance Act, 2023 has omitted the proviso that denied exemption to Sikkimese women marrying non-Sikkimese. The newly replaced sec. 10(*26AAA*) extends the exemption to

(*i*) an individual, whose name is recorded in the register maintained under the Sikkim Subjects Regulation, 1961 read with the Sikkim Subject Rules, 1961, immediately before the 26th day of April, 1975; or

(*ii*) an individual, whose name is included in the Register of Sikkim Subjects by virtue of the Government of India Order No. 26030/36/90-I.C.I. dated the 7th August, 1990 and Order of even number dated the 8th April, 1991; or

(*iii*) any other individual, whose name does not appear in the Register of Sikkim Subjects, but it is established beyond doubt that the name of such individual's father or husband or paternal grandfather or brother from the same father has been recorded in that register; or

(*iv*) any other individual, whose name does not appear in the Register of Sikkim Subjects but it is established that such individual was domiciled in Sikkim on or before the 26th day of April, 1975; or

(*v*) any other individual, who was not domiciled in Sikkim on or before the 26th day of April, 1975, but it is established beyond doubt that such individual's father or husband or paternal grandfather or brother from the same father was domiciled in Sikkim on or before the 26th day of April, 1975;

EXEMPTION TO NON-RESIDENT ASSESSEES

Interest on Notified Securities or Premium on their redemption, Accruing to Non-residents [Sec. 10(*4*)]

Any income accruing to a Non-Resident from interest on such securities and bonds, notified by the Central Government prior to 1 June 2002, is exempt.

Any income to a 'Non-Resident' by way of premium on the redemption of aforesaid bonds is also exempt.

Any interest on moneys standing to the credit of an individual, resident outside India, under Non-resident (External) Account in any bank in India in accordance with Foreign Exchange Management Act, 1999 is exempt. Such account can be maintained only by individual, resident outside India [under sec. 2(*q*) of the Foreign Exchange Regulation Act, 1973] or permitted by Reserve Bank of India.

Income of a non-resident resulting from the transfer of non-deliverable forward contracts entered with an offshore banking unit of an IFSC [Sec. 10(*4E*)]

Any income accrued or arisen to, or received by a non-resident as a result of transfer of non-deliverable forward contracts or offshore derivative instruments or over-the-counter derivatives entered into with an offshore banking unit of an International Financial Services Centre as referred to in sec. 80LA(1A) which fulfils such conditions as may be prescribed is exempt.

Royalty or Interest income on leasing of an aircraft or ship to a unit located in an International Financial Services Centre (IFSC) [Sec.10(*4F*)]

The Finance Act, 2021 inserted sec. 10(*4F*) to provide exemption in respect of income of a non-resident by way of royalty or interest income on account of leasing of an aircraft or ship to a unit located in an International Financial Services Centre (IFSC) as referred to in sec. 80LA(1A) if the unit has commenced its operations on or before the 31st day of March, 2024.

For the purposes of this clause, "aircraft" means an aircraft or a helicopter, or an engine of an aircraft or a helicopter, or any part thereof.

Income received by a non-resident from portfolio of securities or financial products or funds [Sec.10(*4G*)]

The Finance Act, 2022 inserted a new exemption. Any income received by a non-resident from portfolio of securities or financial products or funds, managed or administered by any portfolio manager on behalf of such non-resident, in an account maintained with an Offshore Banking Unit in any International Financial Services Centre referred to in sec. 80LA(1A) to the extent such income accrues or arises outside India and is not deemed to accrue or arise in India.

The Finance Act, 2023 has further extended the scope of this exemption to any income received by a non-resident from the specified activity carried out by the specified person as may be notified by the Central Government.

Exemption to non-residents or IFSC units on the transfer of shares of a domestic company engaged in aircraft leasing business in IFSC [Sec. 10(*4H*)]

The Finance Act, 2023 has inserted a new clause (*4H*) in section 10 with effect from the assessment year 2024-25. This clause provides an exemption to income earned by a non-resident or Unit of an IFSC as referred to in section 80LA(1A). The exemption shall be allowed subject to the following conditions:

(*a*) Non-resident or Unit of an IFSC must be engaged primarily in the business of leasing of an aircraft;

(*b*) Income should be in the nature of capital gains arising from the transfer of equity shares of a domestic company;

(*c*) Domestic company must be a Unit of an IFSC as referred to in section 80LA(1A);

(*d*) Domestic company must be engaged primarily in the business of leasing of an aircraft;

(*e*) Domestic company must commence its operations on or before 31-3-2026;

(*f*) Equity shares of the domestic company must be transferred within 10 years of commencing of its operations. However, if the domestic company commenced its operations before 1-4-2024, the 10-year time limit shall be counted from 1-4-2024.

For the above purposes "aircraft" means an aircraft, helicopter, an engine or part of an aircraft or a helicopter.

Exemption on capital gains to non-resident investors or specified fund upon transfer or relocation of original asset located outside India to a resultant fund in IFSC [Sec. 10(*23FF*)]

In order to encourage transfer due to relocation of capital asset by the original fund located outside India to a resultant fund in IFSC, the Finance Act, 2021 has introduced sec. 10(*23FF*). Accordingly, any income of the nature of capital gains, arising or received by a non-resident or a specified fund, which is on account of transfer of share of a company resident in India, by the resultant fund or a specified fund to the extent attributable to units held by non-resident (not being a permanent establishment of a non-resident in India) in such manner as may be prescribed, and such shares were transferred from the original fund, or from its wholly owned special purpose vehicle, to the resultant fund in relocation, and where capital gains on such shares were not chargeable to tax if that relocation had not taken place.

Interest Payable by any Scheduled Bank in India to any Foreign Bank, Performing Central Banking Functions Outside India [Sec. 10(*15*)(*iiia*)]

Interest payable on the deposits made by any such foreign bank with any scheduled bank in India with the approval of the Reserve Bank of India, is exempt [Sec. 10(*15*)(*iiia*)].

Interest on Bonds and Debentures of a Public Sector Company [Sec. 10(*15*)(*iv*)(*h*)]

Interest on such bonds or debentures of a Public Sector company as are notified by the Government is exempt. The name of the holder of the bonds or debentures must appear on the register of the company to enable him to seek exemption.

Interest on Securities and Deposits for Benefit of Bhopal Gas Victims [Sec. 10(*15*)(*v*)]

Interest on securities held by the Welfare Commissioner for Bhopal Gas Victims in Reserve Bank's SGL Account No. SL/DH048 or interest on deposits for the benefit of the victims of the Bhopal gas leak disaster held in such account with the Reserve Bank of India or with a public sector bank, as the Central Government may notify, is exempt.

Interest on Gold Deposit Bonds [Sec. 10(*15*)(*vi*)]

Any interest on Gold Deposit Bond Scheme, 1999 is exempt from tax [Sec. 10(*15*)(*vi*)].

Interest on Notified Bonds of a Local Authority [Sec. 10(*15*)(*vii*)]

Interest on bonds of a local authority, notified by the Central Government is exempt from tax. From the Assessment Year 2008-09 and onward, interest on bonds, issued by a State Pooled Finance Entity is also exempt. "State Pooled Finance Entity" means such entity which is set up in accordance with the guidelines for the Pooled Finance Development Scheme notified by the Central Government in the Ministry of Urban Development.

Interest on Deposits made by NRI or NOR after 31 March 2005 in an Offshore Banking Unit [Sec. 10(*15*)(*viii*) r.w. Special Economic Zones Act]

Any income by way of interest received by a non-resident or a person who is 'not ordinarily resident', in India as a deposit made on or after 1 April 2005, in an Offshore Banking Unit (*i.e.* a branch of a bank located in Special Economic Zone and which has obtained permission under Sec. 23(1)(*a*) of the Banking Regulation Act, 1949.

Interest, dividend or long term capital gains from a debt or equity investment made in India by Specified persons [Sec. 10(*23FE*)] (w.e.f. 1.4.2021)

Any income of certain specified person being:

(*a*) a wholly owned subsidiary of the Abu Dhabi Investment Authority.

(*b*) a sovereign wealth fund.

(*c*) a foreign pension fund.

When such income is in the nature of dividend, interest or any sum received by unit holder upon redemption of units under sec. 56(2)(*xii*) or long-term capital gains arising from an investment made by it in India, whether in the form of debt or share capital or unit, if the investment will be exempt, if the investment is made in:

(*i*) Business trust specified in sec. 2(*13A*)(*i*)

(*ii*) A company or enterprise or an entity carrying on the business of any infrastructure facility defined in the *Explanation* to sec. 80-IA(4)(*i*) or other notified by the Central Government.

(*iii*) Category I or II Alternative Investment Fund regulated by SEBI (Alternative Investment Fund) Regulations, 2012 having 50% investment in one or more of the entities carrying on business of developing and/or operating and maintaining any specified infrastructure facility as defined in the *Explanation* to Section 80-IA(4)(*i*).

Such investment must be made on or after the 1st day of April, 2020 but on or before the 31st day of March, 2024 and must be held for at least three years.

Thus, exemption under this section could be availed only if the investment was made in Category I or II AIF having 100% investment in the Infrastructure companies. The Finance Act, 2021 has inserted two additional areas where investment made by specified persons above shall be eligible for exemption.

(*iv*) A domestic holding company registered on or after 1-4-2021 having a minimum 75% investments in one or more infrastructure companies.

(*v*) A non-banking finance company registered as an Infrastructure Finance Company or Infrastructure Debt Fund having minimum 90% lending to one or more infrastructure entities.

EXEMPTION TO CERTAIN REGULATORY BODIES, AUTHORITIES AND INSTITUTIONS

Certain Incomes of Local Authorities [Sec. 10(*20*)]

Income of a local authority from the following sources is exempt:

(*i*) Income from house property;

(*ii*) Capital gains;

(*iii*) Income from other sources;

(*iv*) Income from a trade or business which accrues or arises from the supply of a commodity or service within its own jurisdictional area. Income from the supply of electricity or water whether within its own jurisdiction or outside its own jurisdictional area is exempt.

The expression local authority means:

(*i*) Panchayat [as defined by Article 243(*d*) of the Constitution].

(*ii*) Municipality [as defined by Article 243P(*e*) of the Constitution].

(*iii*) Municipal Committee and District Board legally entitled to or entrusted by the Government with the control or management of a Municipal or local fund.

(*iv*) Cantonment Board [Sec. 3 of the Cantonments Act, 1924].

Case Law : ***Calcutta State Transport Corporation* v. *CIT* [1996] 85 Taxman 402 (SC)**

Facts: The assessee was a Road Transport Corporation constituted to render road transport services in the State. The Road Transport Corporations Act which set out the general duties and powers of the assessee established clearly that the assessee was meant mainly and only for the purpose of providing an efficient, adequate, economical and properly coordinated system of road transport services in the State or a part of it. It had no element of popular representation in its constitution.

Held: Merely because it had a fund or merely because it was constituted to provide public service and to employ persons in that connection, it could not be said that its functions were similar to those of local authority.

Income of Research Association [Sec. 10(*21*)]

Any income of research association approved for the purposes of (*i*) scientific research and (*ii*) research in social science or statistical research may be exempt subject to certain conditions.

Any Income of Notified News Agency Set up in India [Sec. 10(*22B*)]

Any income of news agency set up in India solely for collection and distribution of news may be exempt, provided certain conditions are satisfied. The Finance Act, 2023 provides that this exemption shall not be available on or after 1.4.2024.

Income of Professional Association [Sec. 10(*23A*)]

Any income of professional association or institution, established in India, is exempt provided the certain conditions are fulfilled:

Income of Khadi and Village Industries Board [Sec. 10(*23BB*)]

Any income of the *Khadi* and Village Industries Boards set up under State or Provincial Act is exempt from income tax.

Income of Statutory Bodies or Authorities Administering Public Religious or Charitable Trust or Endowments [Sec. 10(*23BBA*)]

Any income of statutory bodies or authorities which are established, constituted or appointed under any law (Central, State or Provincial) for the administration of public religious or charitable trusts or endowments (including *muths*, temples, gurdwaras, wakfs, churches, synagogues, agiaries or other places of public religious worship) or societies for religious or charitable purposes, registered as such under the Societies Registration Act, 1860 or any other law for the time being in force, is exempt from tax.

It may be noted that the exemption does not apply to the income of the trust, endowment, etc. (which is exempt under Secs. 11 and 12).

Income of Trade Unions [Sec. 10(*24*)]

Any income chargeable under the heads "income from house property", and "income from other sources" of a trade union registered under Indian Trade Union Act, 1926, and formed primarily for the purposes of regulating the relations between workmen and employers or between workmen and workmen is exempt from tax.

Association of registered unions also covered: The exemptions also extend to an association of registered unions.

Income of Agricultural Produce Market Committee [Sec. 10(*26AAB*)]

Any income of "an agricultural produce market committee or board" for regulating the marketing of agricultural produce is exempt from tax.

Income of a Corporation/Body/Institution Formed for the Benefit of Scheduled Castes or Scheduled Tribes or Backward Classes [Sec. 10(*26B*)]

Where any corporation which is established by a Central or State or Provincial Act, or any other body, institution or association which is wholly financed by the Government, is formed for promoting the interest of the members of the Scheduled Castes or the Scheduled Tribes or backward classes or of any two or all of them, its entire income is exempt from tax.

Scheduled Caste or Scheduled Tribes will have the same meaning respectively assigned to them in Clause 24 and Clause 25 of Article 366 of the Constitution of India.

"Backward classes" means such classes of citizens other than the Scheduled Castes or the Scheduled Tribes, as may be notified by the Central Government or any State Government from time to time.

Income of a Corporation, Promoting the Interest of a Minority Community [Sec. 10(*26BB*)]

Any income of a corporation established by the Central Government or any State Government for promoting the interest of the members of a minority community is exempt.

Meaning of Minority Community: "Minority Community" means such community as may be notified by the Central Government.

Income of a Corporation Established for Welfare of Ex-servicemen [Sec. 10(*26BBB*)]

Any income of a corporation established by a Central, State or a Provincial Act for welfare and economic upliftment of ex-servicemen is exempt from tax from AY 2004-05 onwards.

Ex-servicemen - Means an Indian citizen who has served in any rank, whether as combatant or as non-combatant, in the armed forces of the Union or armed forces of the Indian States before the commencement of the Constitution for a continuous period of not less than 6 months after attestation and has been released otherwise than by way of dismissal or discharge on account of misconduct or inefficiency.

In case of a deceased or incapacitated servicemen - The term also includes his wife, children, father, mother, minor brother, widowed daughter and widowed sister wholly dependent on such servicemen.

Armed forces for this purpose exclude - The Assam Rifles, Defence Security Corps, General Reserve Engineering Force, Lok Sahayak Sena, Jammu and Kashmir Militia and Territorial Army.

Income of a Cooperative Society formed for the Scheduled Castes or Scheduled Tribes [Sec. 10(*27*)]

Any income of a cooperative society formed for promoting the interests of the members of either Scheduled Castes or Scheduled Tribes is exempt. However, the membership of the said society should consist of only other co-operative societies formed for similar purposes and the finances of the society should be provided by the Government and such other societies.

Income Accruing to Certain Boards or Authorities [Sec. 10(*29A*)]

Any income accruing or arising to certain specified Boards or Authorities is exempt. The exemption applies either from the previous year relevant to the specified assessment year or from the previous year in which the Board is constituted, whichever is later. The following Boards are exempt under this section:

Income of Coffee Board/Rubber Board/Tea Board

Income of Tobacco Board

Income of Marine Products Export Development Authority

Income of Agricultural and Processed Food Products Export Development Authority

Spices Board

Coir Board

Exemption to development authorities etc. (Sec. 10(*46*), 10(*46A*) newly inserted by the Finance Act, 2023)

Under sec. 10(*46*) exemption is granted to any specified income arising to a body or authority or Board or Trust or Commission, or a class thereof which—

(*a*) has been established or constituted by or under a Central, State or Provincial Act, or constituted by the Central Government or a State Government, with the object of regulating or administering any activity for the benefit of the general public;

(*b*) is not engaged in any commercial activity; and

(*c*) is notified by the Central Government in the Official Gazette for the purposes of this clause.

However, the restriction on undertaking commercial activities by such Board/ Authority was subject to litigations. The Supreme Court in the case of *Asstt. CIT* v. *Ahmedabad Urban Development Authority* [2022] 143 taxmann.com 278/[2023] 291 Taxman 11 (SC) held that the expression 'commercial' in sec. 10(*46*)(*b*) will require a consideration whether it is at cost with a nominal mark-up or significantly higher, to determine if it falls within the mischief of "commercial activity". However, it was also held that in case of statutory authorities, boards etc. established by the State government or Central governments for achieving essentially public services, such amounts will fall outside the mischief of being business or commercial receipts.

The Finance Act, 2023 has newly inserted sec. 10(*46A*) w.e.f. 1-4-2024 to expressly provide an exemption to any income arising to a body or authority or Board or Trust or Commission, not being a company, which—

(*a*) has been established or constituted by or under a Central Act or State Act with one or more of the following purposes, namely:—

(*i*) dealing with and satisfying the need for housing accommodation;

(*ii*) planning, development or improvement of cities, towns and villages;

(*iii*) regulating, or regulating and developing, any activity for the benefit of the general public; or

(*iv*) regulating any matter, for the benefit of the general public, arising out of the object for which it has been created; and

(*b*) is notified by the Central Government in the Official Gazette for the purposes of this clause.

EXEMPTION TO INCOMES OF CERTAIN FUNDS

Income of Specified Funds [Sec. 10(*4D*)]

The following income accrued or arisen to, or received by a specified fund will be exempt to tax:

(*a*) income from transfer of capital asset being a bond or Global Depository Receipt, derivative or other notified securities referred to in Sec. 47(*viiab*), on a recognised stock exchange located in any International Financial Services Centre and where the consideration for such transaction is paid or payable in convertible foreign exchange; or

(*b*) income from transfer of securities (other than shares in a company resident in India);

(*c*) income from securities issued by a non-resident (not being a permanent establishment of a non-resident in India) and where such income otherwise does not accrue or arise in India;

(*d*) income from a securitization trust which is chargeable under the head 'Profits and gains from business or profession';

Exemption shall be limited to the income attributable to units held by a non-resident, not being the permanent establishment of a non-resident in India.

Specified fund for the purposes of this section means:

(1) a fund established or incorporated in India in the form of a trust or a company or a limited liability partnership or a body corporate:

(*a*) which has been granted a certificate of registration as a Category III Alternative Investment Fund and is regulated under the Securities and Exchange Board of India (Alternative Investment Fund) Regulations, 2012.

(*b*) which is located in any International Financial Services Centre.

(*c*) of which all the units are held by non-residents other than unit held by a sponsor or manage:

Provided that the condition specified in this item shall not apply where any unit holder or holders, being non-resident during the previous year when such unit or units were issused, becomes resident or deemed resident under Sec. 6(1) or (1A) in any previous year subsequent to that year, if the aggregate value and number of the units held by such resident unit holder or holders do not exceed five per cent of the total units issued and fulfil such other conditions as may be prescribed. (inserted by the Finance Act, 2022 w.e.f. 1.4.2023)

(2) investment division of offshore banking unit which has been:

(*a*) granted a certificate of registration as a Category-III AIF and is regulated under the SEBI (AIF) Regulations, 2012, made under the SEBI Act, 1992 or which has commenced its operations on or before 31-3-2024; and

(*b*) fulfils such conditions including maintenance of separate accounts for its investment division, as may be prescribed.

Income of Regimental Funds, Non-public Funds, set up by Armed Forces [Sec. 10(*23AA*)]

Any income received by any person on behalf of any Regimental Fund or Non-public Fund established by the armed forces of the Union for the welfare of the past and present members of such forces or their dependants is exempt from income tax.

Any Income from Employees Welfare Fund [Sec. 10(*23AAA*)]

Any income received by any person on behalf of a fund for the welfare of employees or their dependants is exempt, provided the certain conditions are satisfied.

Any Income of a Fund set up by LIC under a pension scheme [Sec. 10(*23AAB*)]

Where any fund is set up by LIC on or after 1 August 1996 under a pension scheme to provide pension to the subscriber/widow of the subscriber and such fund is approved by the Controller of Insurance, any income of such fund, by whatever name called, is exempt from tax.

From the assessment year 2002-03, and subsequent years, exemption has also been extended to any income of a fund set up by any other insurer under a pension scheme and which is approved by the Insurance Regulatory and Development Authority established under Sec. 3(1) of the Insurance Regulatory and Development Authority Act, 1999.

Income of Public Charitable Trust or other Institutions from the Business of Khadi or Products of Village Industries [Sec. 10(*23B*)]

Any income from the business of production, sale or marketing of *khadi* or products of village industries to a public charitable trust or an institution registered under Societies Registration Act, 1860, or under any law corresponding to that Act may be exempt if certain conditions are fulfilled.

Income of Specified Funds of National Importance [Sec. 10(*23C*)]

Exemption provisions in respect of certain funds and institutions have been classified as under:

Unconditional Exemption for Certain Funds

Any income received by any person on behalf of the following funds or institutions is exempt. The exemption is unconditional:

(*i*) The Prime Minister's National Relief Fund or the Prime Minister's Citizen Assistance and Relief in Emergency Situations Fund (PM CARES FUND) [Sec. 10(*23C*)(*i*)]; or

(*ii*) The Prime Minister's Fund (Promotion of Folk Art) [Sec. 10(*23C*)(*ii*)]; or

(*iii*) The Prime Minister's Aid to Students Fund [Sec. 10(*23C*)(*iii*)]; or

(*iv*) National Foundation for Communal Harmony [Sec. 10(*23C*)(*iiia*)];

(*v*) The Swachh Bharat Kosh, set up by the Central Government, w.e.f. 1-4-2015 [Sec. 10(*23C*)(*iiiaa*)]; or

(*vi*) The clean Ganga Fund, set up by the Central Government, w.e.f. 1-4-2015 [Sec. 10(*23C*)(*iiiaaa*)].

Income of mutual fund [Sec. 10(*23D*)]

Any income of a mutual fund, either registered under the Securities and Exchange Board of India Act, 1992 or set up by a public sector bank or a public financial institution, authorised by Reserve Bank of India, is exempt.

Any Income of a Venture Capital Company or Venture Capital Fund [Sec. 10(*23FB*)]

Any income of a 'venture capital company' or 'venture capital fund' from investment in a 'venture capital undertaking' is exempt from tax. It is operative from the assessment year 2007-08 and subsequent years. From the assessment year 2016-17 and onward, no exemption applies in respect of any income of a venture capital company or venture capital fund, being an investment fund [under clause (*a*) of *Explanation 1* to sec. 115UB] on or after 1 April, 2016.

Income of Investment Fund [Sec. 10(*23FBA*]

Any income of an 'investment fund' in exempt from tax. However, no-exemption applies for such income if it is not chargeable under the head "Profits and gains of business or profession".

"Investment fund" means any fund established/incorporated in India in the form of a trust/a company/a limited liability partnership/ a body corporate; and which has been granted a certificate of registration as category I or category II

Alternative Investment fund; and it is regulated under the Securities and Exchange Board of India (Alternative Investment Fund) Regulations, 2012, made under the Securities and Exchange Board of India Act, 1992.

Income of a unit holder of an investment funds [Sec. 10(*23FBB*)]

Any income accruing or arising to, or received by, a 'unit holder' of an investment fund, being that proportion of income which is chargeable under the head "Profits and gains of business or Profession", is exempt from tax.

Interest received by a Business Trust [Sec. 10(*23FC*)]

Any interest received or receivable by a business trust from a 'special purpose vehicle ' is exempt from tax.

"Special Purpose Vehicle" means an 'Indian company' in which business trust holds controlling interest and any specific percentage of share holding or interest, required by the Regulations under which such trust is granted registration.

Exemption is operative from the assessment year 2015-16 and subsequent years.

Any income of a real estate investment trust [Sec. 10(*23FCA*)]

Any income of a business trust, being a 'real estate investment trust', from (*i*) renting or letting or (*ii*) leasing or letting any 'real estate asset', owned directly or indirectly by it, is exempt from tax from the assessment year 2016-17 and onward.

Any distributed income, received by a unit holder from the business trust [Sec. 10(*23FD*)]

Any distributed income, received by a unit holder from the business trust is exempt provided it is not covered under sec. 10(*23FC*) w.e.f. 2015-16 or sec. 10(*23FCA*) w.e.f. 2016-17, explained as above.

Any income accruing or arising to, or received by, a unit holder from a specified fund or on transfer of units in a specified fund [Sec. 10(*23FCB*)]

Any income accruing or arising to, or received by, a unit holder from a specified fund or on transfer of units in a specified fund.

Income of Certain Provident Funds [Sec. 10(*25*)]

The following incomes are exempt:

(*i*) Interest on securities, held by a Statutory Provident Fund and any capital gain arising from the sale, exchange or transfer of such securities.

(*ii*) Any income received by the trustees on behalf of a recognised provident fund.

(*iii*) Any income received by the trustees on behalf of an approved superannuation fund.

(*iv*) Any income received by the trustees on behalf of an approved gratuity fund.

(*v*). Any income received by the:

(*a*) Board of Trustees constituted under the Coal Mines Provident Funds and Miscellaneous Provisions Act, 1948 on behalf of the deposit linked insurance fund established under Sec. 3G of that Act; or

(*b*) Board of Trustees constituted under the Employees' Provident Fund and Miscellaneous Provisions Act, 1952 on behalf of the deposit linked insurance fund established under Sec. 6C of that Act.

Income of the Employees' State Insurance Fund [Sec. 10(*25A*)]

Any income of the Employees' State Fund, set up under the provisions of the Employees State Insurance Act, 1948, is exempt.

Income of an infrastructure debt fund [Sec. 10*(47)*]

Any income of an infrastructure debt fund, set up in accordance the guidelines, prescribed by the Central Government, is exempt. The 'Infrastructure Debt fund' may be set up by a 'Non-Banking financial company' in accordance with conditions prescribed by the Reserve Bank of India (under Rule 2F). Its funds can be invested only in the Public Private partnership Infrastructure Projects.

EXEMPTION TO INDUSTRIAL UNITS

Newly Established units in Special Economic Zone [Sec. 10AA]

An 'entrepreneur' is allowed to claim deduction in respect of export profits from his unit which begins to manufacture or producer articles or things or provide any service during the previous year, relevant to the assessment year, commencing on or after 1 April, 2006 but before 1st April 2021. This section also applies to a unit, if proceeds from sale of goods or provision of service is brought as convertible Foreign Exchange [Sec. 10AA(4A)].

'Entrepreneur' means a person who has been granted a letter of approval by the Development commission [under sec. 15(*a*) of Special Economic Zones Act, 2005.] However no such deduction shall be allowed to an assessee who does not furnish a return of income on or before the due date specified under sec. 139(1).

Conditions for claiming the deduction [Sec. 10AA(*ii*)]

The deduction is allowed subject to the following conditions:

(*i*) *Operational period:*

The undertaking should begin to manufacture or produce articles or things or to provide services during the previous year, relevant to the assessment year, commencing on or after 1st April, 2006 in any 'Special Economic Zone'.

(*ii*) *Undertaking to be new:*

It should not be formed by splitting up or Reconstruction of an existing undertaking. However, this condition does not apply where the undertaking is discontinued due to extensive damage or destruction of its building, machinery on account of natural disasters and it is re-established within 3 years.

(*iii*) *Plant and Machinery to be new:*

The undertaking should not be formed by transfering machinery or Plant, previously used for any purpose.

(*iv*) *Inter-Transfer of Goods to be at market value [Explanation to sec. 10AA(4) r.w. Sec. 80-IA(a)]*:

Any inter-transfer of goods from such undertaking or unit to another business of the assessee or *vice versa* should be made at the market value of such goods on the date of its transfer.

Market value for this purpose means the price which the said goods may fetch in the open market.

(*v*) *Adjustment of Profits [Sec.10AA(a) r.w. sec. 80-IA(10)]*:

Where more than ordinary export profits may be expected to arise from the eligible business owing to the close connection between the assessee, carrying on the eligible business and any other person, the Assessing Officer may allow the deduction on the basis of such profits as may be reasonably expected to arise from eligible business.

(*vi*) *Deduction for Export Profits:*

Only profits from sale of goods out of India and requiring custom clearance are eligible for the purpose of availing the benefit under the said provisions.

Profit derived from onsite development of computer software (including services for development of computer software) outside India is also deemed to be export profits [*Explanation 2* to sec. 10AA].

Indirect profits from export business cannot be regarded as export profits. For example, interest received from bank deposits for opening a letter of credit cannot be regarded as export profits [*CIT* v. *Menon Impex (P.) Ltd*. [2003] 128 Taxman 11/259 ITR 403 (Madras)].

(*vii*) *Effect of amalgamation or demerger [Sec. 10AA(5)] :*

Where any unit, entitled to 'Tax Holiday Benefit' is transferred under a scheme of amalgamation or demerger, before the expiry of tax holiday period, the amalgamating or demerged unit of the company, is entitled to claim the benefit of deduction for the unexpired period.

(*viii*) *Tax Exemption under this section prohibits deduction under 'Specified Business' [Sec. 10AA(10) r.w. sec. 35AD(8)]:*

Where deduction is allowed in respect of newly established unit in Special Economic Zone [under Sec. 10AA(1)], no deduction is allowed in respect of profits of specified business under sec. 35AD(8)(*c*) for the same year or any other assessment year.

Case Law : ***Principal CIT* v. *Jewels Magnum* [2020] 120 taxmann.com 316/275 Taxman 134 (Madras)**

Facts: 'J' engaged in business of manufacturing gold jewellery claimed deduction under section 10AA on basis of approval granted to it by Development Commissioner, Special Economic Zone (SEZ) for manufacturing gold bangles and gold pendants. The Assessing Officer disallowed 'J' claim on ground that it had violated approval granted by Special Economic Zone by manufacturing medallions and exporting same instead of manufacturing gold bangles and pendents.

Held: Since a medallion is also classifiable as a pendant, 'J' had not violated terms and conditions of letter of approval by SEZ and was eligible for benefits of exemption under section 10AA.

EXEMPTION TO INCOME OF EDUCATIONAL INSTITUTIONS AND HOSPITALS [SEC. 10(*23C*)]

Where

- any university or other educational institutions exists solely for educational purposes and not for purposes of profit; or
- any hospital or other institution to receive and treat persons suffering from illness or mental defectiveness or requiring medical attention or rehabilitation during their covalence or otherwise exists solely for philanthropic purposes and not for the purposes of profit.

such institutions are eligible for exemption under sec. 10(*23C*). However, the eligibility for exemption is evaluated each year, to find out whether the institution existed during the relevant year solely for such purposes as referred above and not for the purposes of profit [*Aditanar Educational Institution* v. *Addl. CIT* [1997] 90 Taxman 528 (SC)].

Educational Institutions

Solely for the purposes of education **-** While there is no definition of the term 'education', it would surely encompass systematic dissemination of knowledge and training in specialised subjects. It is not necessary to nail down the concept of education to a particular formula or to flow it only through a defined channel. [*Gujarat State Co-Operative Union* v. *CIT* [1992] 195 ITR 279 (Guj.)]. The purpose for which and the object with which the institution is established and the source from which the income is earned are relevant considerations to determine whether the income earned by the assessee is exempted from tax under the provision [*Oxford University Press* v. *CIT* [2001] 115 Taxman 69 (SC)].

In a recent ruling, *New Noble Educational Society* v. *Chief CIT* [2022] 143 taxmann.com 276/[2023] 290 Taxman 206 (SC), the Supreme Court held that the term 'solely' means that such trust, university or other institution should necessarily have all its objects aimed at imparting or facilitating education only. It may be possible that profits may be 'incidentally' generated or earned by the charitable institution the same will continue to be exempt insofar as the objectives of the institution is only providing education. The reference to 'business' and 'profits' in the seventh proviso to sec. 10(*23C*) and sec. 11(4A) merely means that the profits of business which is 'incidental' to educational activity. For example profits relating to education such as sale of text books, providing school bus facilities, hostel facilities, etc.

Foreign University is also eligible for exemption - The basic requirement of the section is the existence of "educational purpose" which, in other words, means the imparting of education which has to be in India. A university established in a foreign country is not excluded from the ambit of exemption in case it is imparting education in India or has some educational activity in India. Where the assessee, though part of a foreign university, was merely running a printing press in India for printing of educational books and their sale, and there was no finding that the assessee was imparting any education or had any educational activity in India, the assessee is not entitled to claim exemption. Any other interpretation would be absurd and manifestly unjust. The absence of the word "India" in this provision is inconsequential. It has to be read into section 10(*22*) - *Oxford University Press* v. *CIT* [2001] 115 Taxman 69 (SC).

Case Law : ***Assam State Text Book Production & Publication Corporation Ltd.* v. *CIT* [2009] 185 Taxman 58/319 ITR 317 (SC)**

Facts: 'A' being a Government company controlled by the State of Assam, was established with the aim to do research, printing and publishing of text books for school students as per norms prescribed and approved by Education Department, State of Assam and thereby implementing the State's policy on education. Exemption was denied on the grounds that it was not an educational institution.

Held: Exemption could not be denied without considering the historical background in which the corporation came to be constituted, source of funding, shareholding pattern and the relevant circulars and notifications of the Income-tax Department.

Hospitals

When dominant purpose of running the hospital is philanthropic, merely because the assessee is running the hospital on commercial lines will not disentitle the assessee from claiming exemption [*CIT* v. *Pulikkal Medical Foundation (P.) Ltd.* [1994] 73 Taxman 402 (Ker.)]. Thus, philanthropy is not restricted understanding of giving free treatment only to extremely poor, but also an extended meaning of giving treatment at a concessional rate to those who though not extremely poor cannot afford to pay full and normal charges - *Breach Candy Hospital Trust* v. *Chief CIT* [2010] 192 Taxman 98 (Bom.)

Case Law : ***CIT* v. *Apeejay Medical Research & Welfare Association (P.) Ltd.* (SLP against the High Court admitted by the Supreme Court in [2018] 99 taxmann.com 303/259 Taxman 318 (SC)**

Facts: 'A', being a private company, had raised welfare fund of certain amount from three of its group companies having health unit at their respective tea gardens. The existing health units were renovated and some other health units and a hospital was constructed within the area of the said tea gardens of the donor companies. 'A' had deposited the said amount and earned interest income thereon which it claimed to be a surplus after expenditure, exempt from tax.

Held: Since 'A' itself did not run any hospital but merely reimbursed expenses incurred by donor companies on providing medical facilities to their (donor's) employees, 'A's claim for exemption under section 10(*22A*)(which is now omitted) in respect of interest income could not be allowed.

Depending upon the mode of financing these institutions, the exemption may be available without making any application for exemption or upon such application.

Government Financed Educational Institutions and Hospitals [Sec. 10(*23C*) (*iiiab*), (*iiiac*)] - Where the educational institution or hospital is wholly or substantially financed by the Government any income of such institution is fully exempt from tax. The vagueness attributable to the meaning of the words 'substantially financed' was removed by introducing an Explanation to this section by the Finance Act, 2014 that clarifies that if more than 50% of grants is by the Government, it is considered substantially financed by the Government.

Since prior to 2014, the method of arriving at substantially financed could be different and it could be qua the total expenditure incurred by the institution or qua the total receipts received by the Institution, a retrospective reading of the *Explanation* would lead to difficulties; in a matter before it, the Bombay High Court proceeded on the basis that the same was not retrospective [*DIT* v. *Tata Institute of Social Science* (2019) 105 taxmann.com 128/263 Taxman 387/413 ITR 305 (Bom.)].

The words 'wholly or substantially financed by Government' cannot be confined only to annual grants as apart from providing annual grant, if Government grants land, invests money in building and infrastructure and also runs educational institutions all these factors have to be taken into consideration to decide whether institution is wholly or substantially financed by Government in order to become eligible to claim exemption [*CIT* v. *Indian Institute of Management* [2014] 49 taxmann.com 136/226 Taxman 301/(2015) 370 ITR 81 (Kar.)]. However, the funds received from Government must be direct grants/contributions from governmental source and not fees collected from students under Statute [*Visvesvaraya Technological University* v. *ACIT* [2016] 73 taxmann.com 286/242 Taxman 247 (SC)].

Private Educational Institutions and Hospitals with annual receipts of ₹ 5 crore or less [Sec. 10(*23C*)(*iiiad*), (*iiiae*)] - Where educational institution and hospital is not financed wholly or substantially by the Government and its annual receipts do not exceed ₹ 5 crore, any income of such institution shall be fully exempt. (The threshold has been raised from ₹ 1 crore to ₹ 5 crore by the Finance Act, 2021). However, from the assessment year 2007-08 and onward, exemption does not apply for anonymous donations in respect of which the donee does not maintain a record of the identity of the donor, indicating his name, address and such other particulars as may be prescribed. [Sec. 10(*23C*) (*iiiad*) r.w. sec. 115BBC].

Such institution is required to furnish the return of income if its total income without giving effect to the provisions of Sec. 10, exceed the maximum limit not chargeable to tax. It is clarified that anonymous donations on which tax is payable under Sec. 115BBC should also be included in the total income [Sec. 139(4C)(*e*)].

It must be noted that there is nothing to indicate that section 10(*23C*)(*iiiad*) requires the educational institutions referred to therein to impart education in any particular subject or in any manner whatsoever. So much so, the term 'education' should enjoy a wide connotation covering all kinds of coaching and training carried on in a systematic manner leading to personality development of an individual [*CIT* v. *St. Mary's Malankara Seminary* [2012] 19 taxmann.com 175/206 Taxman 429 (Ker.)].

Case Law : ***ICAI Accounting Research Foundation* v. *DGIT* [2009] 183 Taxman 462 (Delhi)**

Facts: 'I' a foundation set up by Institute of Chartered Accountants of India (ICAI) with main objective for imparting, and promoting knowledge, learning and education in various fields related to the profession of accountancy. 'I's application for exemption under sec. 10(*23C*)(*iv*) was rejected that it was not for charitable purposes having taken research projects amounting to professionals services.

Held: Merely because 'I' undertook research projects at instance of Government/local bodies and received remuneration for such projects, it cannot be said that essential character of 'I' have been converted into one which carried on commerce or business activity or rendered any service in relation to trade, commerce or business, so as to reject its claim for exemption. Exemption was allowed.

Any other Fund, Institution, Trust, and any other Educational Institution, and Hospital [Sec. 10(*23C*)(*iv*)/(*v*)/(*vi*)/(*via*)/(*iiiae*)]

Any income (other than anonymous donations) of any (*i*) other fund, (*ii*) institution, (*iii*) trust, (*iv*) private educational institution and hospital receiving an annual receipt of more than ₹ 5 crore may be exempt, provided it makes an application for the exemption or having obtained an exemption for the continuation of the same and complies with the following conditions:

Application of income [Third Proviso to sec. 10(23C)]:

(*a*) Income of the fund, institution, trust, university, educational institution or hospital should be applied wholly and exclusively to the objects for which it is established.

(*b*) At least 85% of the total income must be applied solely for the objects for which such institution was established. Voluntary contribution made by the applicant with a specific direction that such contribution shall form part of the corpus any other trust registered under sec. 12AA or any other institution claiming exemption under sec. 10(*23C*) will not be considered as application of income with this meaning [Proviso XII].

(*c*) The applicant may accumulate its income for the objects for which it is established and where more than 15% of its income is accumulated, the period of accumulation should not exceed 5 years. In other words the applicant is allowed to retain up to 15% of total income without any conditions.

(*d*) The applicant must deposit or invest its funds in any forms or modes specified in Sec. 11(5) is discussed in **Chapter 15.**

It must be noted that the aforesaid income shall not include income in the form of voluntary contributions made with a specific direction that they shall form part of the corpus of the applicant. [*Explanation* to the Proviso III]

Application to be considered on payment basis **-** Since existing provision was silent on whether the application of income could be allowed to such trusts on accrual basis following the mercantile system of accounting or on payment basis following the cash system, the Finance Act, 2022 offers some clarity. According to the newly inserted *Explanation 3* to Sec.10(*23C*) application of income by any trust or institution will be on 'payment basis'. In other words, irrespective of the accounting method employed by the trust, any sum payable by any trust or institution shall be considered as application of income only when such sum is actually paid by it.

Exemption for Income from Business Incidental to Attainment of Main Objective. Exemption may apply to the business income of the trust, institution, fund, educational institution or hospital, provided the business is incidental to the attainment of its objective and separate books of accounts are maintained in respect of such business.

No exemption for Anonymous donations: Anonymous donations are liable to be included in the total income and are taxable @ 30% under Sec. 115BBC. "Anonymous donations" means any voluntary contribution where the donee does not maintain the record of the identity of the donor, *i.e.* name, address and such other particulars as may be prescribed.

Voluntary donations received for renovation or repair of temple, mosque etc. - By virtue of newly inserted *Explanation 1A* to Sec. 10(*23C*) through the Finance Act, 2022 an option is provided to the trust covered under sec. 10(*23C*)(*v*) to treat voluntary contribution received for renovation or repair of temple, mosque etc. as a part of corpus. Accordingly, where the property held under a trust or institution includes any temple, mosque, gurdwara, church or other place notified under Sec. 80G(2)(*b*), any sum received by such trust or institution as voluntary contribution for the purpose of renovation or repair of such temple, mosque, gurdwara, church or other place, may, at its option, be treated by such trust or institution as forming part of the corpus of the trust or the institution, subject to the condition that the trust or the institution,—

(*a*) applies such corpus only for the purpose for which the voluntary contribution was made;
(*b*) does not apply such corpus for making contribution or donation to any person;
(*c*) maintains such corpus as separately identifiable; and
(*d*) invests or deposits such corpus in the forms and modes specified under Sec. 11(5).

Where any of these conditions are breached, such voluntary contribution shall be treated as income of the trust/institution in that year. [*Explanation 1B* to Sec. 10(*23C*)] (newly inserted by the Finance Act, 2022).

Compulsory Audit of Accounts [*Tenth Proviso to Sec. 10(23C)*]: Where total income, without giving effect to exemption under Sec. 10, exceeds the maximum exemption limit not chargeable to tax, it is obligatory to get accounts audited by a chartered accountant and audit report should be filed along with the return of income in Form No. 10BB under Rule 16CC.

Filing Return of Income: It is mandatory to furnish the return of income under Sec. 139(4C) if total income without giving effect to exemption under Sec. 10, exceeds the maximum limit not chargeable to tax. It is operative from the assessment year 2006-07 and onward.

New Regime of Registration [First and Second Provisos to Sec. 10(23C)]:

Every such institution that sought to avail exemption for its income under secs.10(*23C*), 11, 12 and 80G deduction were required to register itself under the prescribed procedure. A new registration regime has been put in place by the Finance Act, 2020. The process of registration under the new regime will be completely electronic and a unique registration number (URN) shall be issued to all new and existing charity institutions. All existing institutions being (*i*) fund or (*ii*) trust or (*iii*) institution or (*iv*) university or other educational institution or hospital or other medical institution that have been granted exemption including the one under this Section are required to file fresh applications in the prescribed form and manner to the Principal Commissioner or Commissioner within specified time. There is no perpetual approval and it will be give for only 5 years, after which such fund or trust or institution or university or other educational institution or hospital or other medical institution have to seek reapproval of exemption. Upon receipt of application, the Principal Commissioner may call for such documents and conduct such inquiries to satisfy about (*i*) object of trust (*ii*) genuineness of activities and (*iii*) compliance with requirement of any other law and thereafter pass the orders either approving or rejecting the exemption application.

Rationalisation of exemption regimes

There exists two prevailing exemption regimes for trusts and institutions: (*a*) exemption available for funds, trusts, educational institutions etc. under sec. 10(*23C*) and (*b*) exemption available under sec. 11 to charitable trusts and religious institutions registered under sec.12AB.

In a move to rationalize and provide consistency between the two prevailing regimes, the Finance Act, 2022 has inserted a series of newly inserted *Explanations* that ensures that the two are in alignment and grant similar benefit.

Accordingly, the following changes are made with respect to Fund, Institution, Trust, and any other Educational Institution, and Hospital under sec. 10(*23C*) (*iv*), (*v*), (*vi*), (*via*).

Accumulation Provisions

Under the existing provisions of the Act, a trust or institution is required to apply 85% of its income during any previous year. However, if it is not able to apply 85% of its income during the previous year, it is allowed to accumulate such income for a period not exceeding 5 years. Now, whereas under sec.11(2) such accumulation was granted exemption subject to certain conditions, being a statement to be filed before Assessing Officer stating the purpose of accumulation and investing the money in accordance with sec.11(5); no such condition was stipulated under sec.10(*23C*).

By virtue of newly inserted *Explanation 3* to sec. 10(*23C*) the Finance Act, 2022 extends similar conditions for accumulated income for trusts and institutions covered under sec.10(*23C*). Further under *Explanation 5* to sec.10(*23C*) where the trust could not apply its accumulated income for the reasons beyond its control the same was deemed to be applied to the purposes of the trust upon application to the Assessing Officer and such AO has allowed to apply such income for such other purpose in India as is specified in the application which is in conformity with the objects for which that trust was set up.

Year of Chargeability of accumulated income remaining unutilised or due to non-compliance

There existed an inconsistency in terms of year chargeability of accumulated income remaining untilised or due to non-compliance of conditions. Sec. 11(3) provided specific year of chargeability in case of different types of violation, which *inter alia* comprised a provision that if the accumulated income is not applied within 5 years, it shall be taxed in the sixth year. There were no such specific provisions under sec.10 (*23C*) and therefore, if the accumulated income is not applied within 5 years, the same was taxed in the fifth year itself.

The Finance Act, 2022 has introduced *Explanation 4* whereby a similar provision to sec.10(*23C*) whereby leveled the year of chargeability for such non-compliance, non-utilization of accumulated income. This is as follows:

it is applied to purposes other than religious or charitable	deemed to be the income of the previous year in which it is so applied in
it ceases to be accumulated or set apart for application to religious or charitable purposes	deemed to be the income of the previous year in which ceases to be so accumulated or set apart
it ceases to remain invested in statutory form of investment specified under Sec. 11(5)	deemed to be the income of the previous year in which ceases to remain so invested or deposited

it is not utilised for the purpose for which it is so accumulated or set apart within the allowed period of 5 years or in the year immediately following the expiry thereof	deemed to be the income of the previous year being the last previous year of the period for which the income is accumulated or set apart
it is credited or paid to any other trust or institution registered under sec. 12AA or sec.12AB	deemed to be the income of the previous year in which credited or paid
it is credited or paid to any other fund, institution, trust, hospital, university or other educational institution, or hospital or any other medical institution referred under clauses (*iv*), (*v*), (*vi*) and (*via*) of Sec. 10(*23C*)	deemed to be the income of the previous year in which credited or paid

Maintaining Books of Account [Tenth Proviso to Sec.10(*23C*)]

Under the existing scheme of things, there are no specific books of account that the trust is required to maintain. By virtue of the newly inserted tenth proviso to sec. 10(*23C*), where the total income of the trust/institution exceeds the basic exemption limit, it is required to mandates maintaining books of account that may be prescribed and get its books of account audited.

Cancellation of Registration

The Finance Act, 2022 substitutes the existing fifteen proviso with a new one which stipulates cancellation of registration. Accordingly, where having granted registration of a trust or an institution, the Principal Commissioner or Commissioner:

(*a*) has noticed occurrence of one or more specified violations during any previous year; or

(*b*) has received a reference from the Assessing Officer under Sec. 143(3); or

(*c*) such case has been selected in accordance with the risk management strategy, formulated by the Board from time to time

the such Principal Commissioner or Commissioner shall pass an order in writing cancelling the registration of such trust or institution after calling for such documents and information or making such inquiry and affording a reasonable opportunity of being heard.

Specified Violation in this regard comprise in:

(*i*) application of income of trust for objects other than for the objects of the trust or institution.

(*ii*) application of income of trust for private religious purposes, which does not enure for the benefit of the public.

(*iii*) having a business which is not incidental to the attainment of its objectives.

(*iv*) failure to maintain separate books of account in respect of the business which is incidental to the attainment of its objectives.

(*v*) the trust or institution established for charitable purpose created or established after the commencement of this Act, has applied any part of its income for the benefit of any particular religious community or caste

(*vi*) any activity being carried out by the trust or institution: is not genuine; or is not being carried out in accordance with all or any of the conditions subject to which it was registered. [*Explanation 2* to fifteenth proviso to sec. 10(*23C*)].

(*vii*) where application furnished for registration on the e-portal is incomplete or the information is false or incorrect (inserted by the Finance Act, 2023).

Computation of income of a trust in case of certain non-compliances (newly inserted by the Finance Act, 2022)

Under the existing scheme, there is no explicit provision that determines computation of taxable income due to non-compliances. The Finance Act, 2022 newly inserted new proviso after nineteenth proviso that stipulates computation such income after allowing deductions for revenue expenditure in India to the following conditions:

- Expenditure should not be a donation or contribution to any person.
- Expenditure incurred without withholding appropriate tax or expenditure incurred in cash beyond the prescribed threshold shall not be allowed.
- Expenditure incurred from the corpus or any loan or borrowing shall not be allowed.
- Depreciation on an asset, the cost of which is claimed as application of income in any year, shall not be allowed.

Further no deduction in respect of any expenditure or allowance or set off of any loss shall be allowed to the assessee under any other provision of this Act.

Tax rates applicable on specified incomes [Sec. 115BBI] (newly inserted by the Finance Act, 2022)

Specified Incomes of trust or institutions, that is, income accumulated or set apart in excess of fifteen per cent would be taxable at a flat rate of 30 per cent without reduction of any expenditure or allowances or set off of losses. Other incomes (if any) of the trust/institution will be taxable per the currently applicable provisions.

Exit Tax on trusts, institutions when it cease to exist or converts into a non-charitable entity

There is an exit tax imposed on charitable trusts and religious institutions registered under sec.12AA or sec. 12AB when they voluntarily wind up its activities and dissolve or may also merge with any other non-charitable institution, or to may convert into a non-charitable organization. However, trusts and institutions under sec. 10(*23C*) were not subjected to such tax. The Finance Act, 2022 extended the provisions of Chapter XII-EB and sections 115TD, 115TE and 115TF to the educational institutions, hospitals etc. covered under sec. 10(*23C*) as well. (For details see **Chapter 15**).

EXEMPTION TO POLITICAL PARTIES

Income of Political Party [Sec. 13A]

Any income of a political party which is chargeable under the head "income from house property" or "income from other sources", or capital gains or any income by way of voluntary contribution, other than electoral bonds, received by it from any person, is exempt from tax.

Condition for Exemption

The exemption may be claimed subject to the fulfilment of the following conditions:

(*a*) such political party keeps and maintains such books of account and other documents as would enable the Assessing Officer to properly deduce its income therefrom.

(*b*) if the accounts of the political party are duly audited by the chartered accountant and it maintains a record of each voluntary contribution exceeding ₹ 20,000 along with name and address of the contributor.

(*c*) no donation exceeding ₹ 2000 is received by such political party otherwise than by an account payee cheque drawn on a bank or an account payee bank draft or use of electronic clearing system through a bank account or through such other electronic mode as may be prescribed or through electoral bond.

In order to avail exemption, such political party must furnish a return of income for the previous year in accordance with the provisions of sec. 139 on or before the due date under that section. However, no exemption can be availed if the treasurer of such political party or any other person authorised in this behalf fails to submit a report under 29C(3) of the Representation of the People Act, 1951 for a financial year.

Meaning of Political Party

"Political party" means an association or body of individual citizens of India which is registered or deemed to be registered with the Election Commission of India as political party [under Election Symbols (Reservations and Allotment) Order, 1968].

OTHER EXEMPTIONS

Awards and Rewards [Sec. 10(*17A*)]

(*a*) Any payment made, whether in cash or in kind, in pursuance of awards instituted in the public interest by the Central Government or any State Government or instituted by any other body and approved by the Central Government is exempt.

(*b*) Any payment made, whether in cash or in kind, as a reward by the Central Government or any State Government for such purposes as may be approved by the Central Government in this behalf in the public interest is exempt.

Case Law : ***CIT* v. *J.C. Malhotra* [1998] 230 ITR 361 (Delhi)**

Facts: 'J' an ITO received a reward from Central Government in connection with Voluntary Disclosure Scheme.

Held: Since there was no separate approval by Central Government for exemption had not been given, such reward would not be exempt.

Payment under Bhopal Gas Leak Disaster [Sec. 10(*10BB*)]

Where any payment is made to a person under the Bhopal Gas Leak Disaster (Processing of Claims) Act, 1985, and any scheme framed thereunder, it is fully exempt from income-tax. However, no exemption applies in respect of compensation, received by an assessee in respect of an expenditure incurred and already allowed as deduction, in computing taxable income.

Compensation Received on Account of Disaster [Sec. 10(*10BC*)]

Any amount of compensation received or receivable by an individual or his legal heir on account of any disaster from the Central Government or State Government or a local authority is not to be included in total income. The exemption is not available in respect of the amount received or receivable to the extent such individual or his legal heir has been allowed a deduction under this Act on account of any loss or damage caused by such disaster. It is operative from the assessment year 2005-06, introduced by the Finance Act, 2007.

"Disaster" means a catastrophe, mishap, calamity or grave occurance in any area, arising from natural or man-made causes, or by accident or negligence which results in substantial loss of life or human suffering or damage to, and destruction of property, or damage to, or degradation of, environment, and is of such nature or magnitude as to be beyond the coping capacity of the community of the affected area [Sec. 2(*d*) of the Disaster Management Act, 2005].

Proceeds of ULIP and Bonus on such Policy [Sec. 10(*10D*)]

Any sum received under unit-linked life insurance policy and any sum allocated by way of bonus on such policy is exempt subject to the following:

(*a*) Where an individual or a Hindu undivided family has paid any amount to Life Insurance Corporation or any other insurer for maintenance of a dependant with disability but such person predeceases the insured person, no-exemption is allowed for any amount paid by the LIC or any other insurer to the depositor; or

(*b*) No exemption applies for any sum received under Keyman Insurance policy, taken by a person on the life of his employee; or

(*c*) No-exemption applies for any sum received under an insurance policy issued on or after 1 April, 2003 but before 31 March, 2012 in respect of which premium payable for any year during the term of policy exceeds 20% of the actual sum assured, However, the exemption is available if any sum is received on the death of a person; or

(*d*) No-exemption applies for any sum received under an insurance policy, issued on or after, 1 April, 2012 in respect of which premium payable during the term of policy exceeds 10% the Capital sum assured. However, the exemption is allowed if any sum is received on the death of a person.

However, the maximum limit of 10% of the capital sum assured has been relaxed from 10% to 15% if the policy is issued on or after 1 April, 2013 on the life of any person, who is -

(*i*) a person with disability or a person with severe disability (under sec. 80U), or

(*ii*) suffering from desease or ailment specified in the rules under sec. 80DDB.

The Finance Act, 2021 inserts two new provisos to sec.10(*10D*). According to the Fourth Proviso no exemption shall be available under Sec. 10(*10D*) in respect of ULIPs issued on or after 1-2-2021, if the amount of premium payable for any of the previous year during the term of the policy exceeds ₹ 2,50,000. Further, as per the Fifth Proviso if the premium is payable by a person for more than one ULIPs, the exemption shall be available only for those policies whose aggregate premium does not exceed ₹ 2,50,000, for any of the previous years during the term of any of the policy. Under the Finance Act, 2023 net proceeds received from non-ULIP policies issued on or after 1-4-2023 where premium payable exceeds ₹ 5,00,000 will be taxable as income from other sources. However, amount received on death of person will be exempt.

The income arising from such high-premium ULIPs is proposed to be taxed under sec. 112A. The definition of 'equity-oriented fund' in that section has been amended to cover such high premium ULIPs. Thus, the equity-oriented fund will include ULIPs if such fund invests minimum 90% (in case of investments in other units listed on a recognised stock exchange) or 65% (in any other case) in equity shares of a domestic company.

Payment from Sukanya Samriddhi Account Rules, 2014 [Sec. 10(*11A*)]

To promote the welfare of girl-child, 'Sukanya Samriddhi Account Scheme' has been introduced from the assessment year 2015-16 and subsequent years. The said scheme allows the following tax benefits:

(*i*) investment made in the scheme is eligible for deduction under sec. 80C;

(*ii*) interest accruing on deposits in such account is exempt from tax;

(*iii*) withdrawal from the said account in accordance with the prescribed rules also enjoy exemption from tax.

The scheme is operative from the assessment year 2015-16 and subsequent years.

Educational Scholarship [Sec. 10(*16*)]

Scholarships received by an assessee to meet the cost of his education are exempt from tax.

Actual expense on education is immaterial for the quantum of exemption so long as the purpose of the scholarship is to meet the cost of education. Since the purpose of the payment is to meet the cost of education, the question whether the quantum of payment is adequate or inadequate, or, is or is not in excess of the requirements are all beside the point. It is enough if the whole object of the payment is to meet the cost of education of a person and no further enquiry is called for in order to exclude the amount from the taxable income under Sec. 10(*16*). If the payment is only for the cost of education, the fact that the recipient does not spend the whole of the amount or saves something out of it or utilises it for other purposes would not detract from the character of the payment being one for scholarship. [*CIT* v. *V.K. Balachandran* [1984] 147 ITR 4/ [1985] 23 Taxman 29 (Mad.)]. So that even if scholarship amounts to income in the hands of the recipient, it will remain exempt [*Dr. V. Mahadev* v. *CIT* [1990] 51 Taxman 411 (Mad.)].

Scholarships paid by an employer voluntarily and at its sole discretion to the children of its employees is not a taxable perquisite. Any scholarship paid by an employer directly to the children of its employees, voluntarily, at its sole discretion and without any reference in the terms of employment to scholarship scheme is not assessable as perquisites in hands of the employee u/s 17(2)(*iii*). No right to receive any scholarship is created in favour of any employee as such payment by the employer is entirely gratuitous and at its sole discretion. Moreover, payment of the scholarship amount is received not by the employee but by the children concerned or deposited in the special account referred to in the scheme of scholarship. Even if the amounts were taken as having been paid to the assessee, they will be amounts of scholarship and hence not liable to be included in the computation of the total income of the assessee under the provisions of Sec. 10(*16*). [*CIT* v. *M.N. Nadkarni* [1986] 25 Taxman 9/161 ITR 544 (Bom.)].

Recipient of Scholarship may be a Citizen of India or a Foreign National. If the scholarship is given to meet the cost of education, it does not matter whether the recipient is of Indian origin or is of a foreign origin [*CIT* v. *V. K. Balachandran* [1984] 147 ITR 4/[1985] 23 Taxman 29 (Mad.)].

Any Income from Notified Sporting International Event, held in India [Sec. 10(39)]

Any specified income arising to the person, notified by the Central Government, from any international sporting event, held in India, is exempt subject to the following conditions:

(*i*) such sport event is approved by the international body regulating the international sport relating to such event;

(*ii*) such sport event has participation by more than two countries; and

(*iii*) such sport event is notified by the Central Government.

Any income Financing and Infrastructure Development Institution [Sec. 10(*48D*)] (w.e.f. 1-4-2021)

The Finance Act, 2021 introduced this new sub-section. Any income accruing or arising to an institution established for financing the infrastructure and development, set up under an Act of Parliament and notified by the Central Government for the purposes of this clause, shall be exempt for a period of 10 consecutive assessment years beginning from the assessment year relevant to the previous year in which such institution is set up.

Any Income of a Developmental Financing Institution [Sec. 10(*48E*)] (w.e.f. 1.4.2021)

The Finance Act, 2021 introduced this new sub-section. Any income accruing or arising to a developmental financing institution, licensed by the Reserve Bank of India under an Central Government for the purposes of this clause, shall be exempt for a period of 5 consecutive assessment years beginning from the assessment year relevant to the previous year in which the developmental financing institution is set up.

However the Central Government may, by issuing notification under this clause, extend the period of exemption under this clause for a further period, not exceeding 5 more consecutive assessment years, subject to fulfilment of such conditions as may be specified in the said notification.

Any income which is subject to Equalization levy [Sec. 10(*50*)]

Any income arising from any specified service provided on or after the date on which the provisions of Chapter VIII of the Finance Act, 2016 comes into force or arising from any e-commerce supply or services made or provided or facilitated on or after the 1st day of April, 2021 and chargeable to equalisation levy under that Chapter shall be exempt.

No deduction on expenditure incurred in relation to exempt income [Sec. 14A]

Sec. 14 specifies five heads of income which are chargeable to income-tax. Secs. 15 to 59 lays down the rules for computing income *i.e.* they quantify the total income chargeable to tax. During such quantification, certain permissible expenditures that have been incurred for earning the income are allowed to be deducted. Now there are incomes that are exempt from tax and therefore not chargeable to tax. When an assessee had clearly identifiable and divisible businesses, those which earned taxable income and those that were exempt; expenditure was allowed to be deducted for the former and not allowed for the later.

Difficulty arose when an assessee had a composite and indivisible business which had elements of both taxable and non-taxable income, and then claimed the entire expenditure in respect of said business as deductible. In order to address this situation sec. 14A, based on the principle of apportionment, was introduced by the Finance Act, 2001 with a retrospective effect from April 1, 1962. So that now, expenditure could be apportioned between taxable and non-taxable income and deductions made accordingly.

Section 14A stipulates that no deduction is allowed for any expenditure, incurred by the assessee for any income which does not form part of total income. In other words deductions for only those expenditures will be allowed that pertain to income which is brought under one of the above heads and is chargeable to tax and not when the income is exempt. If the income is exempt, expenditure incurred with respect to the same shall not be allowed.

If the Assessing Officer is not satisfied about the claim of the assessee in respect of such expenditure, he is empowered to determine such expenditure in accordance with such method as may be prescribed in Rule 8D [Sec. 14(2)].

The Assessing Officer is also empowered to examine the claim of the assessee that he has not incurred any expenditure relating to income which does not form part of total income [Sec. 14(3)].

The mandate of sec.14A is clearly to curb the practice of claiming deductions of expenses incurred in relation to exempt income against taxable income [*CIT* v. *Walfort Share & Stock Brokers (P.) Ltd*. [2010] 192 Taxman 211 (SC)]. The application of this section is, however, far more complicated than what appears. Take for instance, when an assessee holds shares as stock-in-trade with a purpose to trade in shares and earn profits and not as investment for earning interest or dividend. In such instances, entire expenditure including administrative costs or interest payouts, if the shares were bought with borrowed capital will be claimed by assessee as allowable expenditure. It must be noted that earning dividend income which was exempt is merely incidental while profits are offered to tax. When shares held as stock-in-trade, profits of which are chargeable to tax as business income, incidentally yields dividends that are exempt from tax, sec.14A gets triggered. Accordingly, expenditure incurred in acquiring those shares will have to be apportioned and disallowed [*Maxopp Investment Ltd*. v. *CIT* [2018] 91 taxmann.com 154/254 Taxman 325 (SC)].

Case Law : ***Maxopp Investment Ltd.* v. *CIT* [2018] 91 taxmann.com 154/254 Taxman 325 (SC)**

Facts: 'M' engaged in the business of finance, investment and trade in shares and securities held shares/securities in two portfolios as investment and as trading assets. It claimed that the shares held as trading assets were for the purpose of acquiring and retaining control over investee group companies. These shared yielded dividend income.

Held: Sec. 14A applies irrespective of whether shares are held to gain control or as stock-in-trade. At the time of investing into those shares 'M' knows that it may generate dividend income as well. Expenditure attributable to exempt dividend income will have to be apportioned and be disallowed under sec. 14A.

Case Law : ***Godrej & Boyce Manufacturing Company Ltd. v. Dy. CIT*** **[2017] 81 taxmann.com 111/247 Taxman 361 (SC)**

Facts: 'G' earned tax free dividend income in respect of shares held in group companies on which the company had paid tax under sec. 115-O. 'G' claimed that since the companies distributing dividend had paid tax thereon, no disallowance could be made in hands of 'G' by invoking provisions of section 14A and expenditure incurred by it should be allowed.

Held: The object behind the introduction of section 14A by the Finance Act of 2001 is clear and unambiguous. The legislature intended to check the claim of allowance of expenditure incurred towards earning exempted income in a situation where an assessee has both exempted and non-exempted income or includible or non-includible income. A plain reading of section 14A would go to show that the income must not be includible in the total income of 'G'. Once the said condition is satisfied, the expenditure incurred in earning the said income cannot be allowed. Deduction cannot be permissible on the ground that the tax on the dividend received by 'G' has been paid by the dividend paying company.

There has been a prevailing confusion whether disallowance under Sec. 14A can be made even in those cases where no exempt income has been earned by an assessee. In its Circular No. 5/2014 dated 11.02.2014, CBDT clarified such disallowance of expenditure to be made even where taxpayer in a particular year has no corresponding exempt income. However, the judicial decisions has been taking a different stance.

The Finance Act, 2022 has amended sec. 14A. Accordingly, a non-obstante clause has been inserted to sec. 14A providing an overriding effect to Sec. 14A over any other provision of the Act. Further, by virtue of an explanation newly inserted to sec. 14A, it has been clarified that disallow of expenditure incurred during the year shall be made even when corresponding exempt income has not been received or not accrued to the assessee in such year.

CHAPTER 5 Residential Status and Scope of Total Income

INTRODUCTION

Taxing statutes extend to assessees' either on the basis of their residence in a tax jurisdiction or on the basis of source of income in the tax jurisdiction. It may be noted that residence for the purposes of tax is not to be confused with nationality or citizenship. While residence-based taxation applies to the assessees' depending upon their physical presence or control over their affairs in a jurisdiction, source-based taxation applies when assessees' earn incomes having economic allegiance with that jurisdiction.

If pure residence-based taxation was to apply, host states would stand to lose tax revenues despite facilitating income generations by providing requisite infrastructure, law and order, stability and consuming markets. Even home states would not fare well with assessee stationing themselves in tax havens. Similarly, pure source-based taxation would also necessarily lead to problems especially when in order attract investment, states would compete amongst themselves by reducing tax rates leading to a race to the bottom.

Since pure residence-based or pure source-based taxation may not be a conducive to tax system, nation states apply both residence-based and source-based approach to taxation. Income-tax Act also adopts a combination of both residence and source based taxation by virtue of sec. 6 and sec. 9.

DETERMINATION OF RESIDENTIAL STATUS

Residential status of an assessee refers to his presence in India during the previous year in accordance with the provisions of sec. 6 of the Income-tax Act. For natural persons it is determined based on physical stay in India for a specified period and for non-natural persons such as a company, a firm etc. residence is determined by virtue of the control and management of its affairs, being exercised in India.

Residential status of an assessee assumes significance for the reason that the incidence of tax and tax liability is highest on a 'resident' and lowest for a non-resident. An assessee who is resident in India is liable to tax in India on his global income *i.e.* irrespective of the fact that the assessee has earned income in other country, he will be liable to tax in India. In respect of non-resident assessee it is only that income the source of which is India will be liable to tax.

The following general rules must be kept in mind while determining the residential status of an assessee:

(1) *Residential Status is Determined Separately for Each Previous Year*: Residential status may differ from year to year. In one year the assessee may be 'resident' while in another year he may be 'non-resident'.

(2) *Residential Status is Always Determined for the Previous Year*: Residential status of an assessee in the assessment year is immaterial for tax purposes.

(3) *Different Residential Status for Different Sources of Income Not Permissible [Sec. 6(5)]*: If a person is resident in India in a previous year in respect of any source of income, he is deemed to be resident in India in respect of each of his other sources of income as well.

(4) *Burden of Proving the Residential Status lies with the Assessee*: The burden of proof usually lies with the claimant of a benefit or an advantage under the Act. Therefore, where an assessee wishes to reduce the incidence of taxation on him by claiming to be a 'non-resident' or 'not-ordinarily resident', the burden of proving his claim will rest on him and he must place all relevant facts, evidence and material before the income-tax authorities to substantiate his claim [*V. Vr. N. M. Subbayya Chettiar* v. *CIT* [1951] 19 ITR 168 (SC)].

An individual may be a resident (R) or a non-resident (NR) in India. If he is a resident, he further may be a 'resident and ordinarily resident' (ROR) or 'resident but not ordinarily resident' (RNOR). So in case of an individual, he may be a

(*i*) ROR

(*ii*) RNOR or

(*iii*) NR

It may be noted that the statutory provisions refers only firstly to R and second to RNOR. No explicit mention is made about NR and ROR category. The same is constructed upon application of the bare provisions.

Determining residential status of an individual is a two-step procedure as follows:

Step 1: Basic Conditions to determine if an individual is "Resident" in India [Sec. 6(1)]

(*a*) Stay in India for a period or periods of 182 days or more during the previous year; or

(*b*) *i.* Stay in India for a period or periods of 60 days or more during the previous year; and

ii. Stay in India for a period or periods of 365 days or more out of 4 years immediately preceding the previous year.

If none of the basic condition (*a*) or (*b*) are fulfilled such individual is non-resident in India during that previous year. No further inquiry is to be made.

If both or one of the basic condition (*a*) or (*b*) are fulfilled such individual is resident in India during that previous year. Thereafter the Step 2 must be followed to find out whether such resident is R but NOR or is R&OR.

Exceptions:

In case an individual falls within any of the following exceptions, basic condition (*b*)(*i*) comprising the threshold of 60 days stay in a given previous year is replaced with 182 days. In other words, while for every other individuals both basic conditions (*a*) and (*b*) above need to be applied, for individuals within the exception only condition (*a*) applies. If their stay do not exceed 182 days, they become non-resident in India. The exceptions are as follows:

(*i*) An Indian citizen leaving India in any previous year as a member of the crew of Indian Ship. Where such individual is a member of the crew of a foreign bound ship leaving India, the period of stay in India for an eligible voyage shall exclude the period as specified in rule 126.

(*ii*) An Indian citizen leaving India in any previous year for the purposes of employment outside India. Since the provision clearly mentions for the 'purposes of employment' this exception does not apply if the individual leave India for any other purposes say for study or medical treatment.

(*iii*) An Indian citizen who, being outside India, comes on a visit to India in any previous year.

(*iv*) An individual being a person of Indian origin comes on a visit to India in any previous year. An individual is deemed to be of Indian origin if he or either of his parents or any of his grandparents were born in undivided India [*Explanation* to Sec. 115C(*e*)].

These exceptions that expands 60 days requirement to 182 days provides relaxation to these individuals allowing them to visit India for longer duration without becoming resident of India.

It was long experienced that period of 182 days specified in respect of an Indian citizen or person of Indian origin visiting India during the year was being mis-used. So that individuals who were otherwise actively carrying out substantial economic activities from India, managed their period of stay in India below 182 days so as to remain a non-resident in perpetuity and thereby were escaping tax on their global income in India. In order to address these concerns, the Finance Act, 2020 introduced an amendment to the relevant explanations to sec. 6 whereby a citizen of India or a person of Indian origin, being outside India, comes on a visit to India shall be considered as RNOR if he fulfils the following conditions cumulatively:

(*i*) total income other than the foreign income of more than ₹ 15 Lakhs and;

(*ii*) Stay in India for a period of 120 days or more but less than 182 days in the previous year and;

(*iii*) Stay in India for a period of 365 days or more in 4 years preceding the previous year.

By virtue of this amendment, such individuals who were previously non-residents in India will now acquire a status of RNOR and consequently the incidence of tax will increase.

Step 2: Additional Conditions to determine if a Resident is RNOR [Sec. 6(6)]

(*i*) He has been a non-resident in India in 9 out of 10 years; or

(*ii*) He has been in India for 729 days or less out of 7 years.

If both or one of the additional condition (*i*) or (*ii*) are fulfilled, such individual is a resident but not ordinarily resident in India.

If none of the additional condition (*i*) or (*ii*) are fulfilled, such individual is not a RNOR. In other words he is a resident and ordinarily resident in India.

Deemed to be Resident [Sec. 6(1A)]

Certain high net worth individuals were emerging as stateless persons by strategically arranging their stay in different countries and avoiding tax residence in no state. Further with advancements in technology and information age, individuals are no longer constrained by conventional office and can work anytime from anywhere. This has given rise to what is popularly known as 'digital nomads'. Since such individuals are constantly on the move, it may not possible to designate a particular country of residence for tax purposes.

To address this situation, the Finance Act, 2020 introduced sub-section (1A) to sec. 6. Accordingly, an individual, being a citizen of India, having total income, other than the income from foreign sources, exceeding ₹ 15,00,000 during the previous year shall be deemed to be resident in India in that previous year, if he is not liable to tax in any other country or territory by reason of his domicile or residence or any other criteria of similar nature. Such a citizen of India who is deemed to be resident in India will be resident but not ordinarily resident in India [Sec. 6(6)(*d*)].

The Place of Stay or the Purpose of Stay is Immaterial - It is not essential that an assessee should stay at the same place during this period [*Kinlock* v. *I. R. C.* 14 TC 736]. He may go from place to place or from house to house or from hotel to hotel. Similarly, the purpose of the visit is of no relevance. It may be that he comes on business or to visit his relatives or to obtain medical advice or he simply visits India for pleasure.

Stay in India Need not be Continuous - The stay of 182 days or more may not be continuous. It is sufficient if it is for a minimum period of 182 days in aggregate. The calculation of the 182 days in respect of broken days should be made on an hourly basis. A total of 24 hours of stay spread over two or more days is to be counted as equivalent to the stay of one day. In counting the period of stay in India, the days of entry and exit, both should be taken into account. In absence of the details of hourly stay of the assessee, the entry and exit days are taken as full days in counting. [Ref. AAR in Petition No. 7 of 1995, *In re* (1997) 90 Taxman 62/223 ITR 462 (AAR – New Delhi), the Authority for Advance Ruling].

The Visit to India during the Four Preceding Years might be Regular or Irregular - Regularity of visits to India is not essential. The individual may come to India every year for a definite duration so that his minimum stay is 365 days in the preceding 4 years or he might have stayed in India for a full year in the first year and there being a complete gap in the remaining three years.

Case Law : ***CIT* v. *Suresh Nanda* [2015] 57 taxmann.com 448/233 Taxman 4/375 ITR 172 (Delhi)**

Facts: 'S' s passport was impounded by CBI on the suspicion of alleged brokering role in contravention of defense purchase policy. It was only subsequent to the appeals in the Higher Courts that his passport was ordered to be released but in the meantime his stay in India had exceeded 182 days.

Held: 'S' had become unwilling resident on Indian soil without his consent and against his will, the period of his involuntary stay in India was to be excluded for determining his residential status under section 6.

Involuntary stay in India due to Corona Virus Outbreak Circular No. 11 of 2020 dated 8.5.2020 and Circular No. 2 of 2021 dated 3.3.2021

There were number of individuals who had come on a visit to India during the previous year 2019-20 for a particular duration and intended to leave India before the end of the previous year for maintaining their status as non-resident or not ordinary resident in India. However, due to declaration of the lockdown and suspension of international flights owing to outbreak of Novel Corona Virus (COVID-19), they are required to prolong their stay in India and chances were that they exceeded their stay in India.

In order to avoid genuine hardship in such cases, the Central Board of Direct Taxes issued Circular No. 11 of 2020 dated 8.5.2020 by virtue of which for determining the residential status under section 6 of the Act during the previous year 2019-20 in respect of an individual who has come to India on a visit before 22nd March, 2020 and

- has been unable to leave India on or before 31st March, 2020, his period of stay in India from 22nd March, 2020 to 31st March, 2020 shall not be taken into account;
- has been quarantined in India on account of Novel Corona Virus (COVID-19) on or after 1st March, 2020 and has departed on an evacuation flight on or before 31st March, 2020 or has been unable to leave India on or before 31st March, 2020, his period of stay from the beginning of his quarantine to his date of departure or 31st March, 2020, as the case may be, shall not be taken into account;
- has departed on an evacuation flight on or before 31st March, 2020, his period of stay in India from 22nd March, 2020 to his date of departure shall not be taken into account.

Since apprehensions were raised by assessees who were exceeding their stay in India even after the relief offered above and consequently losing their non-residential or not ordinarily resident status, CBDT issued Circular 2 of 2021 dated 3.3.2021 that clarifies that most countries have 182 days or more stay for determining residency, when relaxations are provided with respect to 182 days, it may result in double non-residency, that is, a situation where the assessee is not a resident in any state. In any case, be it double residency or double non-residency, the tie breaker rule of a Double Tax Avoidance Agreement that provides for criteria other than minimum number of days of physical stay may be invoked to determine the residential status of the assessee. So that under a DTAA where an individual is a resident of both Contracting States, he shall be deemed to be the resident of the State in which:

(*a*) he has a permanent home available to him;

(*b*) if he has a permanent home available to him in both States, he shall be deemed to be a resident of the State with which his personal and economic relations are closer (centre of vital interests);

(*c*) if the State in which he has his centre of vital interests cannot be determined, or if he does not have a permanent home available to him in either State, he shall be deemed to be a resident of the State in which he has an habitual abode;

(*d*) if he has an habitual abode in both States or in neither of them, he shall be deemed to be a resident of the State of which he is a national;

(*e*) if he is a national of both States or of neither of them, the competent authorities of the Contracting States shall settle the question by mutual agreement.

Residential Status of a Hindu Undivided Family [Sec. 6(2)], Firm [Sec. 6(2)], AOP [Sec. 6(2)] and Other Persons [Sec. 6(4)]

Residential status of HUF, Firm, AOP and every other artificial juridical person is determined on the basis of the place where the control and management of its affairs is situated.

Step 1: Place of control and management of its affairs

- If the control and management of its affairs is wholly situated outside India, the assessee is a non-resident.
- If the control and management of its affairs is partly situated in India and partly outside India, the assessee is a resident.

Except for HUF (which requires a two-step procedure of determination), all others just applies a single step process.

Step 2 (applicable only to HUF): Additional Conditions to determine if a Resident is RNOR [Sec. 6(6)(b)]

(*i*) The Karta has been a non-resident in India in 9 out of 10 years; or

(*ii*) The Karta has been in India for 729 days or less out of 7 years.

If both or one of the additional condition (*i*) or (*ii*) are fulfilled, such HUF is a resident but not ordinarily resident in India.

If none of the additional condition (*i*) or (*ii*) are fulfilled, such HUF is not a RNOR. In other words he is a resident and ordinarily resident in India.

Control and Management

The term "control and management" has not been defined by the Act and therefore has to be understood in accordance with its generally accepted meaning. The Supreme Court in the case of *CIT* v. *Nandlal Gandalal* [1960] 40 ITR 1 (SC) described the term "control and management" as:

> *"Control and management signifies the controlling and directive power, the head and brain and it is normally situated at a place from where such power is exercised with some degree of permanence. As a general rule, the control and management of a business remains in the hand of a person or a group of persons, and the question to be asked is wherefrom the person or group of persons controls or directs the business."*

The Words "Its Affairs" Means Such Affairs as are Capable of being Managed by the Assessee - Where, for instance, coparcener of the Hindu Individual Family enters into partnership with strangers, the Hindu Undivided Family exercises no controlling power of management over the partnership firm. Partnership will lie between the coparcener in his individual capacity and other partners of the firm. It does not lie between HUF and other partners of the firm. Therefore, the partnership firm cannot be an "affair" of the Hindu Undivided Family as such. [*CIT* v. *Nandlal Gandalal* [1960] 40 ITR 1 (SC)].

Case Law : ***CIT* v. *Nandlal Gandlal* [1960] 40 ITR 1 (SC)**

Facts : G & Sons (HUF) carried on cloth business in London. N, a coparcener, came to Mumbai and started a cloth business in partnership with other persons. The capital supplied by N to this firm came from the family. Subsequently, another coparcener G joined the firm as partner. Later, another business was started at Banaras with the same partners and one outsider as partner. A third coparcener of the family also joined this firm. The Assessing Officer made an assessment on G & Sons (HUF) as resident in India.

Held: Partnership is governed by the provisions of the Indian Partnership Act. In this case, partnership is between the coparcener individually and his other partners and therefore, it is not an affair of the HUF. On the death of the coparcener the surviving members of the family cannot claim to continue as partners with others or institute a suit for dissolution of partnership; nor can the stranger partners sue the surviving members as partners for the coparcener's share of the loss. The control and management is in the hands of the individual coparcener who is the partner, and not in the family. The Hindu undivided family is therefore non-resident in India.

Control and Management is exercised by the Principal Decision-makers

The control and management of an entity is exercised not by ordinary employees but by the highest decision-making body in the decision-making hierarchy of the assessee as shown in the Table 5.1.

TABLE 5.1: PRESUMPTIVELY THE CONTROLLERS OF NON-NATURAL PERSONS

Assessee	Control and management vested with
HUF	*Karta*
Firm	Partners
AOP	Principal officer
Any other person	Principal officer or as per facts of the case

Legality of the Power, Exercised by the Principal Decision-makers, is not Relevant - Control and management means *de facto* control and management and not *de jure* control and management. Therefore, the legality of the power exercised by the principal decision-makers is not relevant from the point of view of establishing where control and management is situated. The fact, that the persons who actually manage the affairs have no power in law to do so legally, is not material in this context. It is not what powers the principal decision-makers have, but it is what they actually do and where they do is of importance in determining the question of the place where the control is exercised. [*CIT* v. *Chitra Palayakat Co*. [1983] 15 Taxman 197/[1985] 156 ITR 730 (Mad.)].

Place of Control and Management of the business - Control and management is situated at the place where decisions are taken about vital policies of business, such as extension or contraction of business, raising of finance and their appropriations for specific purposes, the appointment and removal of staff, etc.

If principal decision maker lives outside India, it does not mean that business decisions are also taken outside India - For example, the partner of a firm may live outside India but if he comes to India to take even a single decision concerning the affairs of the firm, control and management of the firm cannot be situated wholly outside India. Similarly, mere fact that a Hindu Undivided Family owns a house in India where some of the members of the HUF live, it does not constitute that place as the seat of control and management of the affairs of the family unless policy decisions are also taken there.

If the Principal Decision-makers of the Assessee are Always Outside India at the Time of Taking the Decisions, Control and Management will be Situated "Wholly Outside India" - On the other hand, if the principal decision-makers of the assessee take even a single decision in India, the assessee will be considered a resident as "part of its control and management" will be situated in India.

Thus, if the partners of an Indian firm always meet to decide the affairs of the firm outside India, the control and management of the firm will be wholly situated outside India. By contrast, if regular accounts and reports of the foreign partnership business are forwarded to the partner in India from time to time by their agents or employees, instructions are sought from the partner regarding the conduct of the foreign business and such instructions are duly sent, these are substantial indications of the control and management situated in India.

However, if the foreign business is carried on from abroad by some partners or by agents with plenary powers of management, the mere fact that the copies of accounts of the foreign business are sent to another partner resident in India, does not amount to control from India.

Onus of Proving that Control and Management was Wholly Situated Outside India is on the Assessee - It is the duty of the assessee to prove that all the decisions regarding the affairs of business were taken outside India. In absence of any such proof, the control and management will by default be in India.

Case Law : ***V. V. R. N. M. Subbayya Chettiar* v. *CIT* [1951] 19 ITR 168 (SC)**

Facts: N & Sons is an HUF. The karta, Mr N is domiciled in Colombo with the family. During the previous year, N had visited India on seven occasions with the total stay period of 101 days to attend to personal legal matters. The Assessing Officer assessed N & Sons (HUF) as resident on grounds that due to the presence of karta in India for 101 days, the HUF was no longer wholly managed from outside India during the previous year. N filed an appeal on grounds that his presence in India was for personal litigation and not for HUF business.

Held: Mere presence of karta in India for part of the year in itself is not sufficient to shift the control and management partly to India. However, the onus of proving that the control and management of affairs lies wholly outside India is on the assessee. In absence of such proof, an HUF will be considered resident by default. Since the HUF was not able to prove that karta did not take any decisions for the HUF while attending to his personal work in India, the HUF will be considered resident by default on grounds of onus of proof.

Case Law : ***CIT* v. *Chitra Palayakat Co.* [1983] 15 Taxman 197/[1985] 156 ITR 730 (Mad.)**

Facts: S was the managing partner of a firm in Burma. The firm was assessed in India as a non-resident. The other partners of the firm, K and T were based in India. S was also a partner in a firm in Chennai from which the Burma firm made most of its purchases. S was in India for 315 days during the PY to arrange the marriage of his daughter. However, before coming to India, he appointed T as his power of attorney agent to look after the affairs of the firm. T then went to Burma to look after affairs of the firm. The AO changed the status of the firm to resident on grounds that the presence of the managing partner in India had shifted a part of the control and management of the firm in India.

Held: Since the managing partner had delegated his powers in favour of its another partner before coming to India for personal reasons and his power of attorney exercised such powers outside India on his behalf, his mere residence in India will not shift the control and management of the Firm to India.

Residential Status of a Company [Sec. 6(3)]

The residential status of a company is determined on the basis of either of the following:

(*a*) Place of incorporation; or

(*b*) Place of effective management.

When the place of incorporation of a company is India *i.e.* under the laws of India, it is an Indian company. An Indian company is always resident in India. In some instances, a company despite being incorporated outside India, under the laws of some other country, can still be a resident company in India for tax purposes if the place of effective management of such company is India. It must be noted that place of effective management is a recent amendment to the statute book and prior to 1.4.2017 the control and management of the affairs test was applicable.

Meaning of "Place of Effective Management" (POEM) - According to the *Explanation* to sec. 6(3) place of effective management means a place where key management and commercial decisions that are necessary for the conduct of the business of an entity as a whole are, in substance, made. An entity may have more than one place of management, but it can have only one place of effective management at any point of time. Since "residence" is to be determined for each year, POEM will also be required to be determined on year to year basis.

In order to facilitate the determination of POEM, the Central Board of Direct Taxes has released Circular No. 06 of 2017 dated 24th January, 2017 that offers the working details in this respect. Accordingly, companies are bifurcated into those engaged in active business outside India (ABOI) and others. The figure below will facilitate better understanding:

FIGURE 5.1: OVERVIEW OF POEM

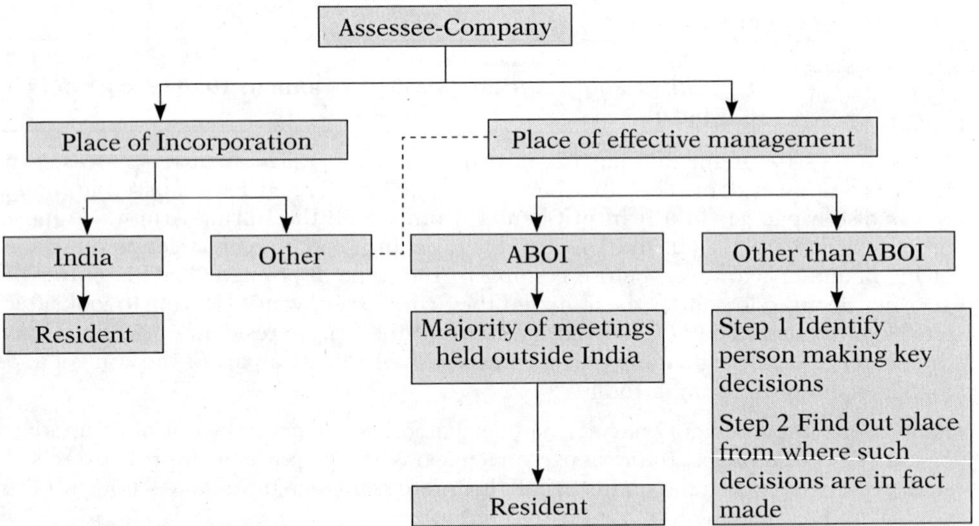

Company engaged in Active Business Outside India (ABOI) - The place of effective management in case of a company engaged in active business outside India shall be presumed to be outside India if the majority meetings of the board of directors of the company are held outside India. However, if on the basis of facts and circumstances it is established that the Board of Directors of the company are standing aside and not exercising their powers of management and such powers are being exercised by either the holding company or any other person(s) resident in India, then the place of effective management shall be considered to be in India.

A company shall be said to be engaged in "active business outside India" if the passive income is not more than 50% of its total income; and

(*i*) less than 50% of its total assets are situated in India; and

(*ii*) less than 50% of total number of employees are situated in India or are resident in India; and

(*iii*) the payroll expenses incurred on such employees is less than 50% of its total payroll expenditure.

For this purposes the average of the data of the previous year and two years prior to that shall be taken into account.

Mere formal holding of board meetings at a place would by itself not be conclusive for determination of POEM being located at that place. If a board has *de facto* delegated the authority to make the key management and commercial decisions for the company to the senior management or any other person the company's place of effective management will ordinarily be the place where these senior managers or the other person make those decisions.

Companies other than those that are engaged in active business outside India the determination of POEM would be a two stage process, namely:- First stage would be identification or ascertaining the person or persons who actually make the key management and commercial decision for conduct of the company's business as a whole. Second stage would be determination of place where these decisions are in fact being made.

With the use of modern technology it is no longer necessary for the persons taking decision to be physically present at a particular location. In such cases the place where the directors or the persons taking the decisions or majority of them usually reside may also be a relevant factor to determine the place of effective management.

SCOPE OF TOTAL INCOME [SEC. 5]

As stated earlier, the incidence of income-tax liability in India is based on the concept of residence. An assessee resident in India is taxable on its global income while a non-resident is taxable only on those incomes which has nexus in India. Therefore, the scope of total income varies according to the residential status of an assessee. The incidence of tax is highest on ordinarily resident, a little lower on not ordinarily resident and lowest on non-resident assessee. The scope of total income with reference to the residential status of an assessee is tabulated below for sake of easy reference.

TABLE 5.2: SCOPE OF TOTAL INCOME

	Particulars of income (During the relevant previous year)	**Residential status and tax liability**		
		ROR	**RNOR**	**NR**
1.	Income received in India	Taxable	Taxable	Taxable
2.	Income deemed to be received in India	Taxable	Taxable	Taxable
3.	Income which accrues or arises in India	Taxable	Taxable	Taxable
4.	Income which is deemed to accrue or arise in India	Taxable	Taxable	Taxable
5.	Income which accrues or arises outside India			
	(*a*) Income which accrues or arises outside India from a business controlled in India or a profession set up in India. [Proviso to Sec. 5(1)]	Taxable	Taxable	Non-Taxable
	(*b*) Income accruing or arising outside India other than in 5(1) above.	Taxable	Non-Taxable	Non-Taxable

Meaning of "Profession Set Up in India"- Profession set up in India would imply that it was started in India and later on extended to foreign countries. The expression "controlled in India" would imply that the head and brain who directs the business activities is situated in India.

Scope of Total Income to be Determined Subject to the Provisions of the Act - The total income is to be computed subject to the provisions of this Act. An income may be taxable according to the provisions of sec. 5, but if it has been exempted under any other provision of this Act, such income is to be excluded from the scope of total income. Similarly, if any other section of the Act contains the provision which is contrary to the provisions of Sec. 5, the provisions of sec. 5 do not apply to that extent in computing the total income of the assessee.

Income may be Derived from Any Source - The source of income is irrelevant for determining the chargeability under this section. If the conditions regarding accruing, arising or receipt as given above are satisfied, the income, irrespective of its source, is liable to be included in the total income.

With respect to non-residents, sec. 5(2)(*b*) stipulates that subject to the other provisions of the Act, the total income of any previous year of a person who is a non-resident includes income from whatever source derived which accrues or arises or is deemed to have accrued or arisen in India during such year. It is, therefore, evident that even if there is no known or disclosed source of income, the income would still be deemed to have accrued to a non-resident of India from undisclosed sources if it is actually found in the hands of his representative assessee [*Hazoor Singh* v. *CIT* [1986] 25 Taxman 211/160 ITR 746 (Punj. & Har.)].

Case Law : ***Hazoor Singh* v. *CIT* (1986) 25 Taxman 211/160 ITR 746 (P&H)**

Facts: H purchased agricultural land in the name of a non-resident for ₹ 96,000 by raising loans from friends and family. The sale was pre-empted and ₹ 96,000 was received back. The Income-tax Officer discovered that the loans were actually income of the non-resident from undisclosed sources and he therefore assessed non-resident on ₹ 96,000 as income deemed to accrue or arise in India. Assessee contended that if the very source of income was undisclosed, it could not be said to accrue or arise in India.

Held: The provisions of Sec. 5(2)(*b*) lay down that the total income of a non-resident includes income from whatever source derived which accrues or arises or is deemed to have accrued or arisen in India during such year. It is, therefore, evident that even if there is no known or disclosed source of income, the income would still be deemed to have accrued to a non-resident of India from undisclosed sources if it is actually found in his hands. Sections 9(1) and 163 are comprehensive enough to include all heads of income mentioned in section. [*Hazoora Singh* v. *CIT* [1986] 25 Taxman 211/160 ITR 746 (Punj. & Har.)].

Income Received in India [Sec. 5]

Receipt of income refers to the occasion when the assessee or its agent gets the actual or constructive control over the income, either in cash or in kind. What is relevant for the purpose of the Act is not just any receipt but receipt of income. Receipt by itself is not sufficient to attract tax until it falls within the ambit of income. For example, discounting of invoices by a bank is a mere advance to a client and not a payment against price of goods and, therefore, it is not a receipt of income [*CIT* v. *Mysore Chromite Ltd.* [1955] 27 ITR 128 (SC)]. Receipt of income has not been defined by the Act and therefore, has to be understood in its general parlance and in accordance with the facts and circumstances of each case.

Following points are essential with respect to bringing such income to tax:

Receipt Means the First Receipt either by the Assessee or his Agent: The receipt of income contemplates the first occasion when the assessee gets the income under his control [*Keshav Mills Ltd.* v. *CIT* [1953] 23 ITR 230 (SC)]. If the assessee has got the income under his control outside India and such income is remitted to India, it cannot be treated as receipt of income in India.

There is No Concept of a Transitional Receipt: Once an income is received in India, it cannot be argued that it was merely a transitional receipt as an intermediary arrangement and will be remitted outside India in due course as per contract. Once an income is received in India and such receipt is the first receipt, the subsequent destination of the receipt is immaterial. [*CIT* v. *Badische Anilin & Soda Fabrik A. G.* [1983] 12 Taxman 107/[1984] 146 ITR 393 (Bom.)]. Even if an amount is credited temporarily in a suspense account pending a final outcome, it will be considered as a receipt within the meaning of Sec. 5(2)(*a*) [*Indulal Kanji Parekh* v. *CIT* [1986] 29 Taxman 399/[1987] 163 ITR 102 (Guj.)].

Receipt of Income by an Agent on Behalf of the Assessee is a Valid Receipt: Receipt by a person who is authorised to collect and give a valid discharge is considered as received by the assessee [*Turner Morrison and Co. Ltd.* v. *CIT* [1953] 23 ITR 152 (SC)]. Such agency may be Express or Implied. It is not necessary that an agent, acting on behalf of the assessee, must act under written authority. For example, where assessee requests a creditor to deliver cheque by post, post office will act as agent of the assessee and income will be considered received by the assessee as soon as it is delivered to the post office [*CIT* v. *Ogale Glass Works Ltd.* [1954] 25 ITR 529 (SC)].

Modes of Receipt of Income - May be in Cash or in Kind: Income may be received in cash as well as in kind [*Raja Mohan Raja Bahadur* v. *CIT* [1967] 66 ITR 378 (SC)]. Receipt of government bonds in lieu of interest or allotment of shares to the underwriters in lieu of underwriting commission are the examples of receipt of income in kind. It is essential that what is received in kind should be the equivalent of cash or, in other words, should be of money's worth. For example, where an income is received in form of a promissory note or an IOU, it is mere replacement of one liability with other and is not a receipt in money's worth. [*CIT* v. *(Maharajadhiraja) Kameshwar Singh* [1933] 1 ITR 94 (PC)]. However, receipt by way of negotiable instruments which can be transferred and realized in money's worth will be a valid receipt. It is well settled that where income is received in money's worth, its value should be determined with reference to the market value, prevailing at the time of receipt of the money's worth [*CIT* v. *Central India Industries Ltd.* [1971] 82 ITR 555 (SC)].

Income Received in Kind must be Valued Even if it is Not Immediately Realisable: The fact that the worth of a receipt cannot be realised in terms of money at once, it is not a sufficient reason for ignoring it for the purpose of income-tax. Difficulty in realising the money's worth of such a receipt may reduce its present value, but it still retains the character of a valid receipt of income. [*Gold Coast Selection Trust Ltd.* v. *Humphrey (H. M. Inspector of Taxes)* [1949] 17 ITR (EC) 19 (HL)].

Receipt by Book Entry under Express or Implied Instructions of Payee is a Valid Receipt: Payee is free to choose the mode of receipt. Therefore, when a person, entitled to receive income, instructs the payer, for whatever reasons, to keep the money in his name as a credit entry, such credit is held in nature of a deposit and not as a trading liability. [*Raghava Reddi* v. *CIT* [1962] 44 ITR 720 (SC)]. Such instructions to accept payment by means of a book credit may even be implied by the practice, normally followed by the parties. [*Standard Triumph Motor Co. Ltd.* v. *CIT* [1993] 67 Taxman 160/201 ITR 391 (SC)]. However, mere credit entry in the books of account of the payer without any express or implied instructions of the payee to accept payment by way of such credit cannot be considered as amount, received by the payee. [*CIT* v. *Toshoku Ltd.* [1980] 125 ITR 525 (SC)].

Date of Receipt of Income: Date of receipt of income is the date when either the assessee or his agent first came in possession of the income. Date of receipt of income is significant to determine in which previous year the income will be liable to tax. However, this is significant only in case of cash system of accounting. Under mercantile system of accounting, the time of accrual of income is significant and not the time of its receipt.

Date of Receipt of Income is Relevant, Not the Date of Realisation: Where income is received by way of a negotiable instrument or in money's worth, the date of actual realisation of the negotiable instrument or the date of actual conversion of money's worth in money is not relevant. Only the date when income was first received is relevant [*CIT* v. *Ogale Glass Works Ltd.* [1954] 25 ITR 529 (SC)]. For example, if a cheque is received on 25.03.2014, but is realised by way of clearing only on 05.04.2014, income will be considered received on 25.03.2014 and not on 05.04.2014.

Place of Receipt of Income in India or Outside India: Place of receipt of income is the territorial place where it is received either by the assessee or his agent. The place of final subsequent remittance to the assessee or its accounting office is immaterial. For example, where an income is received in India by an agent of a non-resident assessee, it will be considered as received in India. Subsequent remittance by the agent to his non-resident principal will not be relevant [*Turner Morrison and Co. Ltd.* v. *CIT* [1953] 23 ITR 152 (SC)].

Burden of Proving, the Chargeability of Income Received by the Assessee is on the Revenue: The onus is on the income-tax department to prove that the assessee has received an income which is assessable under the Act. [*CIT* v. *Bikaner Trading Co. Ltd.* [1970] 78 ITR 12 (SC)].

Income Deemed to be Received in India [Sec. 5]

The expression "deemed to be received in India" means that although the income is not actually received by the assessee or may have been received by him outside India, but it is nonetheless considered to have been received by him in India under the provisions of this Act. Therefore, the deeming provisions for receipt of income affect the place of receipt of income. Such incomes as are deemed to be received in India are explained in the following sub-sections:

Specified Portion of Annual Accretion to the Credit Balance of Employee under a Recognised Provident Fund [Sec. 7(*i*) r. w. Rule 6 of Part A of Fourth Schedule]

Where an employee is a member of a recognised provident fund scheme, the annual accretions during the previous year to his account under the provident fund scheme consisting of:

- employer's contribution in excess of 12% of salary;
- interest credited on the balance to the credit of the employee in excess of 9.5%, is deemed to have been received by the employee in that previous year and is chargeable to tax as income of that previous year. Employer's contribution and interest on the credit balance not exceeding the above specified limits is exempt from tax.

Balance from Unrecognised Provident Fund Transferred to a Newly Recognised Provident Fund [Sec. 7(*ii*) r. w. Rule 11(4) of Part A of Fourth Schedule]

When the employee is a member of unrecognised provident fund which is accorded recognition by the Commissioner of Income Tax for the first time, the balance standing to the credit of the employee under unrecognised fund prior to the date of recognition may be, at the option of the employee, transferred to his credit under the newly recognised provident fund. The balance so transferred is termed as "transferred balance".

The amount so transferred is treated as if it was contributed under recognised provident fund retrospectively from the date of institution of unrecognised provident fund. Thus, aggregate sums out of the balance so transferred, representing:

- employer's contribution in excess of specified rate for the respective years of contribution;
- interest credited on the balance to the credit of the employee in excess of specified rate for the respective year of credit; is deemed to have been received by the employee in that previous year and is chargeable to tax as income of that previous year. Any balance not transferred to the recognised provident fund is taxed in the year of its actual receipt by the assessee.

Government contribution to the Credit of an Employee under a Notified Pension Scheme [Sec. 7(*iii*)]

Where the Central Government or any other employer has made any contribution under a notified pension scheme (under sec. 80CCD) to the credit of an employee, joining service on or after 1 January 2004, such contribution is deemed to have received by him as his income. It is operative w.e.f. 1 April 2004.

Income which Accrues or Arises in India [Sec. 5]

The expression 'accrue' means to augment or increase and 'arise' means to come into existence for the first time. The terms accrue or arise are used in contradistinction to the word received. Income is said to "accrue" when an enforceable right to receive it becomes vested in the assessee. A mere claim to income without an enforceable right thereto cannot be regarded as an accrual of income. Quantification of receipt of income is not necessary for accrual and may follow latter in due course. The right to receive the income depends neither upon the method of accounting employed by the assessee, nor upon the view the assessee may take of his rights or liabilities, but upon commercial reality [*E. D. Sassoon & Company Ltd.* v. *CIT* [1954] 26 ITR 27 (SC)], [*CIT* v. *Ashokbhai Chimanbhai* [1965] 56 ITR 42 (SC)].

Income Accruing vs. Income Arising: The words "accrue or arise" differ only as to the point of time of recognition of income in the books of account. The distinction arises in income tax because under sec. 145 the income from "business-profession" and "other sources" are to be computed in accordance with the method of accounting regularly employed by the assessee. Therefore, an income "accrues" when the assessee becomes vested with the right to receive it but it may "arise" only when the method of accounting recognises it as an income.

For instance, under cash system of accounting an income may accrue in one previous year but it may arise in accounts in the next previous year if it is received by the assessee in that year. On the other hand, under mercantile system of accounting, income will accrue and arise at the same time and will be synonymous to each other.

Income Received vs. *Income "Accruing or Arising"*: The words "accrue" or "arise" are used to contradistinguish the word received. Income is said to be received when it reaches the assessee. It is said to accrue or arise when the right to receive the income becomes vested in the assessee.

Income can be Charged to Tax Either on Receipt Basis or on Accrual Basis [sec. 5, Explanation 2*]*: If an income is taxed on accrual or deemed accrual basis, it cannot be taxed again either in the same year or in a different year on receipt basis. It avoids double taxation on the same income first on accrual or deemed accrual basis and secondly on receipt basis.

Determining Accrual of Income - Guiding Principles

There is no defined criteria to evaluate whether an income has accrued to an assessee or not. Therefore, the question of accrual of income has to be answered after a careful evaluation of all facts and circumstances relevant to each case including, but not limited to, the conduct of the parties. However, certain valuable guiding principles are discussed in the following sub-sections:

Hypothetical Income cannot Accrue-Income Accruing or Arising to an Assessee must be Real Income: Income tax is a levy on income. Though the Income-tax Act takes into account the two points of time at which the liability to tax is attracted, *viz.,* the accrual of the income or its receipt; but the substance of the matter is the income. If income does not result at all, there cannot be a tax on hypothetical income [*Godhra Electricity Co. Ltd.* v. *CIT* [1997] 91 Taxman 351/225 ITR 746 (SC)].

Mere Book Appreciation in the Value of Stock in Trade v. *Gain in Value of Stock of Foreign Currency Balances Resulting from Devaluation of Rupee*: Where stock-in-trade remains unused or unsold, mere book appreciation in the value thereof cannot be brought to tax. However, where such surplus on devaluation results to a bank and is credited to "Provision for contingencies account", the assessee itself could be said to have clearly treated such surplus as its business income. Second, the stock-in-trade in terms of foreign currency was sold and used by the assessee in its normal banking business. What is important is that the profit on account of the difference in exchange rate should have arisen in the course of trading operations of the bank. The bank acquired and sold the foreign exchange assets in the course of its normal banking business and, therefore, the profit arising out of the fluctuation in exchange rates, however large and however unexpected any particular fluctuation may be, arose in the course of and incidental to such business of the bank [*State Bank of Travancore* v. *CIT* [1986] 24 Taxman 337/158 ITR 102 (SC)].

Subsequent Waiver or Surrender or Non-receipt of Income or a Probability of its Non-recovery is of No Consequence: Once an income has accrued, the fact that it may subsequently be surrendered, waived, or is not received at all cannot nullify its accrual. Similarly, mere probability of non-receipt of income, howsoever high, is not sufficient to negate its accrual. The income in such cases will still accrue and be assessed to tax and the assessee can at best take recourse to any relief for its non-recovery (if available) under provisions of the Act. For example, in case of non-recovery of business income, assessee may claim it as an expense in form of bad debt under sec. 36(*vii*) but where salary is not realised, no such benefit can be claimed in absence of any provision to this effect.

Income Accrues when an enforceable right to receive it vests with the assessee - Unless an assessee can enforce his claim to receive income, it cannot accrue to him. A mere claim to receive an amount in itself is not income unless an assessee also has an enforceable right to it. The following will clarify the concept further.

Salary Accrues on a Month to Month Basis: The right to receive salary normally vests with an employee only at the end of the month. Where salary is paid to an employee as a percentage of profits of the company, such profits will have the character of salary and will accrue not at the end of the year when the accounts are finalised but on a month to month basis. It is only the quantification of such salary which may have to wait till the net profits crystallise at the end of the accounting year but the income by way of salary will accrue on monthly basis and not when profits are finally determined. [*CIT* v. *(Smt.) Meenaben Vadilal Parekh* [1991] 187 ITR 158 (Bom.)].

Place of Accrual of Income

Place of accrual of income under the Act can either be within India or outside India. Place of accrual of income is very significant for a "non-resident" and "not-ordinarily resident" from point of view of its taxability under the Act. Since a resident assessee is taxed on total world income, place of accrual of income is immaterial.

Determining the Place of Accrual - In the absence of any firm indication in the Act as to how the place of accrual of income is to be determined, it should be determined according to the general principles of law and in the light of the particular facts. It is nearly impossible to lay down any general test to determine the place of accrual of income. In some cases it may be the place of the formation of the contract, but other matters, *e.g.* the place where the contract is carried out or acts are done under the contract may be decisive in certain circumstances. The question should be decided on the facts of each case.

Place of Accrual of Income in Case of Sale of Goods: When the business consists of buying and selling of goods, profits accrue, as a general rule, at a place where the contract of sale is made (a contract of sale is made at a place where the offer is accepted) or where sales are effected. But the question depends very much upon the facts and circumstances of each particular case.

Place of Accrual of Income in Foreign Trade: In foreign trade, when documents of title deeds are unconditionally given to the buyer or his agent by the seller, the property in goods passes at the seller's place, so the profit also arises at seller's place. For example, if the seller takes the bill of lading in the name of buyer and tenders the same along with other papers to the buyer's agent, the transaction is complete and the seller earns his profits in his own country. If, however, the seller retains his control over the goods by taking the bill of lading in his own name and under the terms of the contract the documents of title deeds are to be given to the buyer or his agent at destination against payment, the property in goods passes at the buyer's place where full payment is made. The profits arise at the buyer's place in such case.

Place of Accrual of Salary: Salary accrues at the place where services are rendered by him.

The Profits of a Company Accrue at a Place where Actual Business of the Company is Done: The place of control and management of the company is irrelevant in this connection.

Manufacturing Profits Arise at the Place where Goods are Manufactured: Where an assessee sells goods of his own manufacturing and place of manufacturing and sales are different, the manufacturing profits arise at a place where goods are manufactured, and not at the place where goods are sold. Therefore, the profits embedded in such a sale must be apportioned and a part should be considered as accruing at the place where the goods are manufactured and a part at the place where they are sold. It is particularly important where one place lies in India and the other is outside India.

Case Law : ***Performing Right Society Ltd.* v. *CIT* [1977] 106 ITR 11 (SC)**

Facts: 'S', a non-resident company, was an association of composers, authors and publishers of copyright musical works, had granted permission to All India Radio to broadcast its musical work. The agreement was signed in England and royalty payments received there.

Held: The income of 'S' accrued in India and no question arose whether it should be 'deemed' to accrue or arise in India. Whether a certain income accrued or arose in India within the meaning of section 5(2) is a question of fact which should be looked at and decided in the light of commonsense and plain thinking.

Income Deemed to Accrue or Arise in India [Sec. 5 r.w. sec. 9]

Sec. 9 of the Income-tax Act embodies the source-based taxation and creates a deeming fiction whereby incomes having their nexus with India are deemed to accrue or arise in India irrespective of their actual place of accrual. Such income is taxable in India irrespective of the residential status of an assessee.

The deeming provision is significant for "Non-residents" and "Not Ordinarily Residents" - Assessees who are resident in India are anyways taxable on their global income. And it hardly matters to them whether income is deemed to accrue or arise in India or not. It is the non-residents and not ordinarily residents for whom the provision is of consequence since their tax liability is limited to Indian incomes. Therefore in case of such assessees' when the income they earn have a live linkage with India, such incomes are taxable in their hands.

FIGURE 5.2: INCOME DEEMED TO ACCRUE OR ARISE IN INDIA [SEC. 9]

Deemed income [sec. 9]

- Through or from any business connection in India
- Through or from any property in India
- Through or from any asset or source of income in India
- Through the transfer of a capital asset situate in India
- Salary earned in India
- Salary paid by govt. to employees outside India
- Dividend Paid by Indian company
- Royalty Income
- Interest Income
- Fees for Technical services
- Cash gifts exceeding ₹ 50,000

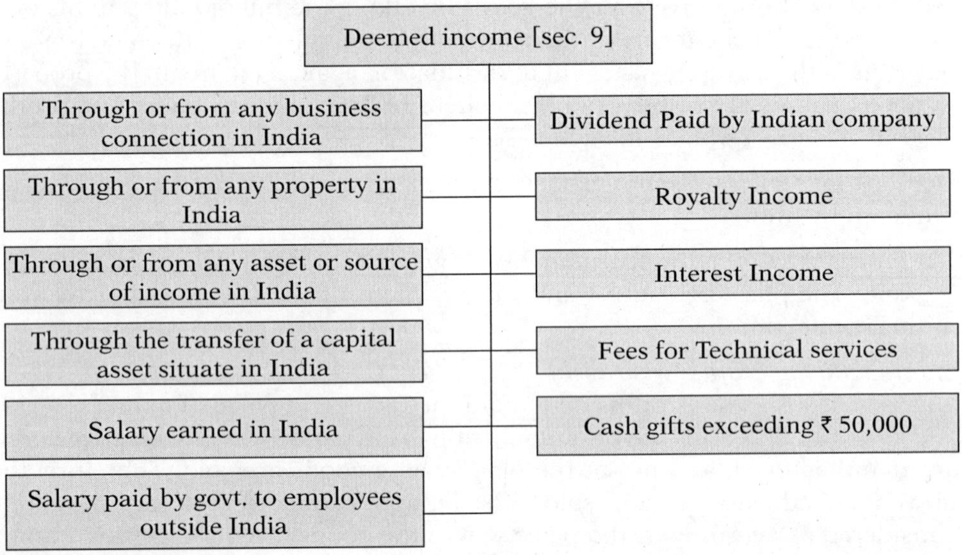

Deemed incomes:

Incomes which are deemed to accrue or arise in India have been enlisted under sec. 9 as under:

(*i*) Income through or from Business Connection in India is deemed to accrue or arise in India [Sec. 9(1)(*i*)]

Income accruing or arising, directly or indirectly, through or from any business connection in India, is deemed to accrue or arise in India. The term business connection does not have an exhaustive definition and is a term of wide import. It is only from the AY 2004-05 by way of an inclusive explanation that certain activities were expressly clarified to be forming business connection. Therefore, what constitutes business connection continues to be constructed as per the judicial decisions. Some of the essentials of business connections are as follows:

Real and Intimate connection - The expression "business connection" postulates a real and intimate relation between the trading activity carried on outside India and the trading activity within India, the relation between the two contributing to the earning of income by the non-resident in his trading activity. [*CIT* v. *R.D. Aggarwal & Co.* [1965] 56 ITR 20(SC)]. It basically involves a relation between the business of the non-resident assessee and some activity in India which contributes directly or indirectly to the earning of profits and gains by the assessee from his business [*CIT* v. *R.D. Aggarwal & Co.* [1965] 56 ITR 20 (SC)].

"Business" Includes Professions and Vocations - The expression "business" u/s 9(1) is much wider than trade or manufacture and includes within its scope professions, vocations and callings for a fairly long time. It is a word of wide import and it means an activity carried on continuously and systematically by a person by the application of his labour and skill with a view to earning an income. [*Barendra Prosad Ray* v. *Income-tax Officer* [1981] 129 ITR 295/6 Taxman 19 (SC)].

Business Connection Predicates an Element of Continuity - A stray or isolated transaction is normally not to be regarded as a business connection. Business connection presupposes an element of continuity between the business of the non-resident and the activity in India. [*CIT* v. *R. D. Aggarwal & Co.* [1965] 56 ITR 20 (SC)]. A one off transaction between two parties may not qualify as a business connection.

The Volume of Business and not the Time Factor is the Test of Continuity - If a large number of orders are given from time to time within a short period and then executed, it is sufficient to constitute a business connection. Whether there is continuity about the connection or whether the agent has entered into stray and casual transaction is a question of fact which depends upon the circumstances of each case [*Anglo-French Textile Co. Ltd.* v. *CIT* [1953] 23 ITR 101 (SC)].

Only So Much of the Income as is Attributable to the Operations Carried Out in India is Deemed to Accrue or Arise in India [Sec. 9(1) Explanation 3] - When all the operations of the non-resident are not carried out in India, only so much of the profits that is attributable to India will be deemed to accrue or arise in India. [See *CIT* v. *R. D. Aggarwal and Co.* [1965] 56 ITR 20 (SC) and *Carborandum Co.* v. *CIT* [1977] 108 ITR 335 (SC)].

FIGURE 5.3: OVERVIEW OF BUSINESS CONNECTION [SEC. 9(1)]

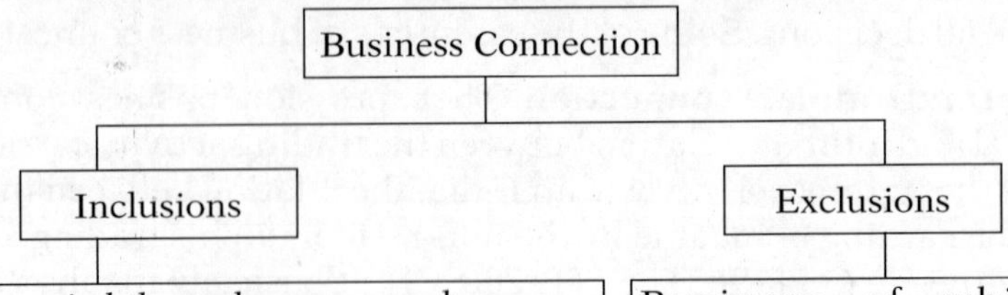

Inclusions

Business activities carried through a person who:

- Has authority to conclude contracts and habitually exercise the same in India
- Has no authority but played major role in concluding contracts
- Maintains stock and regularly delivers therefrom
- Secures orders

Business activities carried through dependent agents *i.e.* the ones who works mainly or wholly on behalf of a non-resident

Non-resident having Significant Economic Presence in India:

- transaction in respect of any goods, services or property including downloading data or software
- systematic and continuous soliciting of business activities
- engaging in interaction with such number of users in India

Operations carried out in India including activities from:

- advertisement targeting Indian customers or customers accessing advertisement through internet protocol address located in India
- sale of data collected from a person who resides in India or from a person who uses internet protocol address located in India
- sale of goods or services using data collected from a person who resides in India or from a person who uses internet protocol address located in India

Exclusions

Business of which operations are confined to purchase of goods in India for export

Individual/firm/company whose operations are confined to the shooting of cinematographic film in India

Non-resident running a news agency or publishing newspapers, etc., whose activities are confined to collection of news and views in India for transmission out of India

Business activities carried through independent agent

Activity of foreign company engaged in the business of diamonds mining confined to display of uncut, unassorted diamonds in notified area

Fund Management Activity by eligible investment fund [Sec. 9A]

Note: The Finance Act, 2021 has inserted a new provision sec. 9B with respect to transfer of a capital asset or stock-in-trade to a partner at the time of dissolution or reconstitution of the firm. For details please see the Chapter 9.

Inclusions to Business Connection [*Explanation 2* to sec. 9(1)] - By virtue introduction to an *Explanation 2* to sec. 9, it has been clarified that certain activities are included as business connection. Accordingly, in the following instances, a non-resident will be having a business connection in India:

(*a*) Business activity carried out through a person who has an authority to conclude contracts on behalf of the non-resident and habitually exercise such authority. [*Explanation 2(a)* to Sec. 9(1)]. Simply having the authority to conclude contracts on behalf of the non-resident is in itself not enough. The person having such authority must also be exercising it habitually in order to constitute his actions as business connection.

It was found that often such persons played a key role in the negotiation of contracts, say for instance the quality of goods, prices, discounts, and other such functions which led to the conclusion of contract but itself did not have any authority to conclude the contract. After all the terms were settled, the non-resident would routinely conclude the contract and circumvent this provision. To curb such practices, the Finance Act, 2018 w.e.f. 1.4.2019 stipulates that business connection will be created even when such person plays a principle role leading to conclusion of contract.

(*b*) Business activities through a person who habitually maintains stock of goods on behalf of the non-resident from which he regularly delivers goods and merchandise on behalf of the non-resident without having any authority [*Explanation 2(b)* to Sec. 9(1)]. Mere maintaining of stock of goods or merchandise on behalf of the non-resident in itself is not enough to constitute business connection. Certain degree of continuity is required both in maintaining the said stock and also its delivery on behalf of the non-resident, provided the person does not act under authority.

(*c*) Business activities through a person who habitually secures orders mainly or wholly for the non-resident or/and other non-resident entities controlling, controlled by or under the same control of the same non-resident person [*Explanation 2(c)* to Sec. 9(1)]. Again, certain degree of continuity is required in securing orders in India on behalf of the non-resident. Securing a few isolated orders on behalf of a non-resident in India may not in itself be enough.

(*d*) Business activities carried on through dependent agents *i.e.* the one who works mainly or wholly on behalf of non-resident. An agent who has economic dependence on the non-resident for its survival in the business will be a dependent agent and a business connection will be established through such dependent agent.

Exclusions from Business Connection [Proviso to *Explanation 1* to sec. 9(1) and sec. 9A w.e.f. 1.4.2016] - The following activities are excluded from business connection:

(*a*) Business activities that are confined to the purchase of goods in India for the purpose of export.

(*b*) Activities of collection of news and views in India for transmission out of India by a news agency or a business that publishes newspapers, magazines or journals.

(*c*) Activities confined to the shooting of any cinematograph film in India.

(*d*) Business activities carried through an Independent agent- Where a non-resident carries on business activities through independent agents, no business connection will be created through such an agent.

(*e*) Activities confined to the display of uncut and unassorted diamond in any special zone notified by the Central Government by a foreign company engaged in the business of mining of diamonds.

(*f*) Fund management activity of an 'eligible investment fund', carried out through an 'eligible fund manager', acting on behalf of such fund.

Apportionment of Deemed Profits [Sec. 9(1)(*i*), *Explanation 1(a)*]

In case of business income, it may be that some business operation may be carried out in India and some outside India. For instance, the goods may be purchased or manufactured in India but may be sold outside India. In such circumstances, it is not just and proper to tax the entire income in India, nor to let the entire income go out of the Indian tax net. Therefore, the Explanation provides that in such cases only such part of the business income as is reasonably attributable to the operations carried out in India, is deemed to accrue or arise in India.

When all operations of business are not carried out in India and only that income attributable to the operations carried out in India; such attributions shall include income:

(*i*) from such advertisement which targets a customer who resides in India or a customer who accesses the advertisement through internet protocol address located in India; or

(*ii*) sale of data collected from a person who resides in India or from a person who uses internet protocol address located in India; or

(*iii*) sale of goods or services using data collected from a person who resides in India or from a person who uses internet protocol address located in India. [*Explanation 3* to sec. 9(1)(*i*) w.e.f. 1.4.2021].

Case Law : ***Volkswagen Finance (P.) Ltd.* v. *ITO (International Taxation)* (2020) 115 taxmann.com 386/184 ITD 872/79 ITR (T) 447 (Mumbai-Tribunal)**

Facts: The assessee being an Indian company made payment to a celebrity for making an appearance at a product launch event in Dubai (UAE). A contigent of 150 persons from India were flown down to Dubai. The event was meant for below the line publicity in India, targeting Indian customers and benefits to be derived in India. Assessee was held liable for failing to withhold tax on the payment.

Held: Since there exists relationship between event in Dubai and business of the assessee in India, income accrues or arises to a non-resident celebrity outside India by means of, in consequence of, or by reason of, any business connection in India, it will be taxable in India under sec. 5(2) read with sec. 9(1)(*i*).

Case law : ***Barendra Prosad Ray* v. *ITO* (1981) 6 Taxman 19/129 ITR 295 (SC)**

Facts: A of Calcutta acted as the solicitor of a German corporation in certain patent suits. On instructions by German corporation he retained B, a U.K. barrister as a co-solicitor. B argued the case in India together with A for 13 days and left India without making any arrangement regarding payment of Indian income tax on the fees earned by him for arguing the case of the German corporation. The ITO treated A as the agent of B on grounds of business connection and proceeded to tax B's income through his agent A.

Held: Fees earned by B is deemed to accrue or arise in India. There was business connection between A and B which was real and intimate and not a casual one and B earned the fees for arguing the case in India only through that connection. The expression "business" does not necessarily mean trade or manufacture only but includes within its scope professions and vocations also.

Business Connection and Permanent Establishment

It may happen that profits of the non-resident that are subjected to tax in India upon application of business connection being a host country are also chargeable to tax in the hands of the non-resident in its home country. This gives rise to the issue of double taxation. Therefore countries enter into Double Tax Avoidance Agreement (DTAAs) that is a bilateral agreement to offer a relief to such assessee who otherwise would be required to pay taxes in both the countries. By virtue of the DTAA, home state and host state reach a compromise as to who gets to tax what income of the assessee in question and to what extent. Accordingly, business profits of any assessee are taxed by the home state unless such assessee has a Permanent Establishment (PE) in the host country. Thus, the purpose of permanent establishment is to enable the host country to tax the business profits attributable to its jurisdiction. Simply understood, Permanent Establishment postulate the existence of a substantial element of an enduring or permanent nature of a foreign enterprise in another country, which can be attributed to a fixed place of business in that country. It should be of such a nature that it would amount to a virtual projection of the foreign enterprise of one country into the soil of another country [*CIT* v. *Visakhapatnam Port Trust* [1983] 15 Taxman 72/144 ITR 146 (AP)].

Article 5 of the DTAAs provide various forms of PE

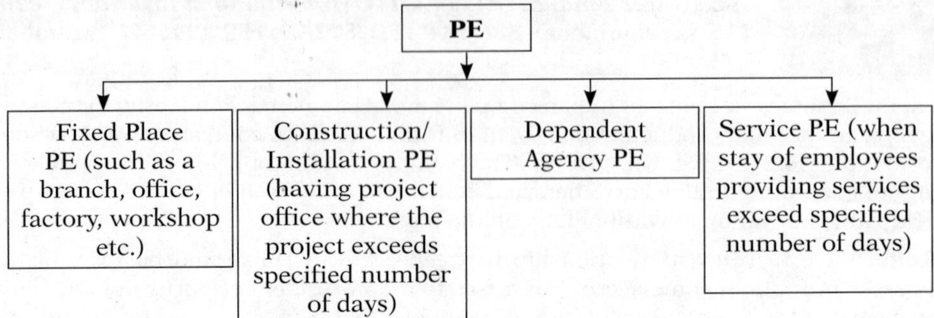

It may be noted that there are lot of similarities in determining activities constituting business connection and forms of PE. However the two concepts serve very different purpose and should not be used interchangeably. Business connection is used for the purposes of domestic law in determining source-based taxation. Permanent Establishment is a concept of international taxation that allows host country to tax a non-resident present in its jurisdiction under any of the given forms. So that even when an activity of a non-resident assessee resulting into profits amounts to business connection in Income-tax Act, in absence of PE such profits of the non-resident cannot be taxed by the host country owing to the commitment made to the home country. Similarly, merely having a PE in a host country without such activity falling within the scope of business connection cannot result into tax liability for the non-resident.

Case Law : ***Dy. DIT* v. *Western Union Financial Services* (2016) 156 ITD 882 (Delhi - Tribunal)**

Facts: 'W' being a company incorporated in the USA was engaged in the business of money transfers world wide. It had appointed Banks, Post Offices, Tour Operators as its agents in India for which they were paid commission. The money transfer transaction involved a remitter in the USA who would deposit the money there, and the computer system of 'W' with exclusive software generates a unique number which is given to the remitter. The remitter passes on this number to the remittee in India who then approaches the agents of 'W' in India along with proof of its identity. The agent's computer is installed with 'W's software who cross verifies this number and makes payment of money to the remittee. The Revenue authorities in India claimed that profits of 'W' which are attributable to transfers in India are taxable in India being business connection in India.

Held: Since the transaction initiated in the USA would not complete without the remittance procedure in India, there was a business connection. However, 'W' did not have a permanent establishment in India as the Post Offices, Banks etc. independent agents and not forming any branch of 'W' or dependent agent of 'W' or installation PE for 'W' and therefore profits of 'W' attributable to India cannot be taxed in India.

Business Connection in the digital age

With the rise of the internet age, businesses could capture the markets in different countries without having physical presence or through aforementioned persons such as agents. The merchandise of business also became more sophisticated in that these could now acquire a relatively intangible form. Say for instance, instead of selling a magazine, a company could allow its customers located in any country to download an article from its website for a subscription amount. Or say, downloading a song/movie from an application instead of selling a CD/ video cassette. Such virtual transactions without the seller obligated to open a shop or appoint an agent in the host country.

The existing framework of domestic law as well as international taxation in the form of the Double Taxation Avoidance Agreement was based on the physical presence test to tax non-resident entities by way office or appointment of agent, or employees and so on was inadequate to respond to the new model of doing business in the virtual world without entering into the political boundaries of tax jurisdictions posed new challenges. So that while the Internet age and globalization increased cross-border trade, it also brought challenges to the tax regime. G20 Finance Ministers called upon the Organisation of Economic Co-operation and Development (OECD) to chalk identify the gaps and loopholes in the existing framework and come up with an action plan to address the Base Erosion and Profit Shifting practices that were causing leakages in the tax revenues of countries around the world. And so emerged OECD/G20 BEPS Project, setting out 15 Actions Plans to equip governments with domestic and international rules and instruments to address tax avoidance, ensuring that profits are taxed where economic activities generating the profits are performed and where value is created. Action Plan 1 referred to the challenges of digitalization and the ways of addressing the same. While it discussed several possible methods of taxing digital economies no particular method was recommended.

India's response to the growing escapement of tax revenues owing to the inadequacy of existing laws came into gradual phases:

(*a*) The Finance Act, 2016 introduced Equalisation Levy which was further expanded in the Finance Act, 2020.

(*b*) The Finance Act, 2018 introduced Significant Economic Presence (SEP).

(*c*) The Finance Act, 2020 introduced TDS provisions on domestic e-commerce participants. These are discussed below:

(*a*) Equalisation Levy

The Finance Act, 2016 Chapter VIII introduced Equalisation Levy. It is a levy at the rate of 6% applicable on the gross amount of:

(*i*) certain "specified services" being online advertisement and any provision for digital advertising space or any other facility or service for the purpose of online advertisement.

(*ii*) when consideration is received by non-residents for providing online advertisement services to residents or non-residents

(*iii*) such non-resident service provider does not have a Permanent Establishment in India.

(*iv*) the transaction is more than ₹ 1 lakh and it is business to business (B2B) transaction.

The scope of this levy was further expanded in the Finance Act, 2020, popularly known as Equalisation Levy 2.0. Accordingly a 2% equalisation levy was imposed on any e-commerce operator, being a non-resident who owns, operates or manages digital or electronic facility or platform for online sale of goods or online provision of services or both. The following activities of an e-commerce operator attracted this levy:

(*i*) online sale of goods owned by the e-commerce operator or

(*ii*) online provision of services provided by the e-commerce operator

(*iii*) online sale of goods or provisions of services facilitated by the e-commerce operator or

(*iv*) a combination of these

The aforementioned supply or services were performed for:

(*i*) Any person resident in India, irrespective of the IP address used by him while ordering such goods or services;

(*ii*) Any person who buys goods or services (or both) using an internet protocol (IP) address located in India;

(*iii*) Any non-resident in respect of offshore purchases of advertisements which targets Indian customers; or

(*iv*) Any non-resident to whom data is sold which is collected from an Indian resident or from a person who uses an IP address located in India.

Exception to the 2% Equalisation Levy

- where the e-commerce operator has a permanent establishment in India and such e-commerce supply or services is effectively connected with such permanent establishment;
- where the Equalisation levy is leviable on online advertisement and related activities; or
- gross receipts of the e-commerce operator from the e-commerce supply or services made or provided or facilitated is less than ₹ 2 crores;
- This threshold limit of ₹ 2 crores is not buyer specific but includes total turnover of the e-commerce operator from all the specified buyers during the previous year.

Residents in India are taxable in India on their global income and non-residents having a PE in India are taxable to the extend income is attributable to such PE. Imposing Equalisation Levy which essentially targets incomes going untaxed despite having economic nexus with India, on such persons was not required. The Finance Act, 2021 therefore excludes these by providing a definition of consideration. Sec. 165A rephrased the inclusive definition of consideration and thereby excludes such consideration from the ambit of Equalisation Levy. Accordingly, when consideration is received in respect of goods owned or provision of services provided by a resident in India or a non-resident having PE in India, such consideration is excluded from the application of Equalisation Levy.

It must be noted that Equalisation Levy is part of the Finance Act, 2016 and not that of the Income-tax Act, 1961. Consequently, no relief can be obtained by such non-residents imposed with Equalisation Levy under the Double Tax Avoidance Agreements because DTAAs only offer relief to tax paid under Income-tax laws and Equalisation Levy falls outside the scope of the Income-tax Act.

(*b*) Significant Economic Presence

The Finance Act, 2019 introduced *Explanation 2A* to sec. 9(1)(*i*) stipulating that significant economic presence (SEP) of a non-resident in India shall constitute "business connection" in India. SEP for this purposes mean:

(*i*) transactions with respect to any goods, services or property carried out by a non-resident with any person in India including provision of download of data or software in India will be constituting business connection of such non-resident in India and be liable to tax in India when payments thereof exceeds the prescribed limits; or

(*ii*) systematic and continuous soliciting of business activities or engaging in interaction with certain minimum prescribed number of users in India will also amount to business connection.

Such transactions or activities shall constitute significant economic presence in India, whether or not

(*i*) the agreement for such transactions or activities is entered in India; or

(*ii*) the non-resident has a residence or place of business in India; or

(*iii*) the non-resident renders services in India.

However, only so much of income as is attributable to the transactions or activities referred to in shall be deemed to accrue or arise in India.

Through a notification dated 3rd May 2021, the threshold for revenue-linked SEP and user-linked SEP has been prescribed. Accordingly, as per the Income-tax Rules, 1962 Rule 11UD, ₹ 2 crores in case (*i*) and 3 lakh users in case (*ii*) above.

It must be noted that since SEP related explanation is a part of domestic law provision, it will have no impact on the international transactions and tax liabilities of non-resident assessees unless the requirement of Permanent Establishment under the DTAAs are also revisited and reframed.

(*c*) TDS on e-commerce operators under Sec. 194-O (effective from 1.10.2020)

The Finance Act, 2020 introduced a tax deducted at source provision under Sec. 194-O whereby sale of goods or provision of services of an e-commerce participant is facilitated by an e-commerce operator through its digital or electronic facility or platform (by whatever name called), such e-commerce operator is required to deduct tax at the rate of 1% of the gross amount of such sale or service or both, at the time of credit of amount of sale or services or both to the account of an e-commerce participant or at the time of payment thereof to such e-commerce participant by any mode, whichever is earlier.

For this purposes,

(*i*) electronic commerce means the supply of goods or services or both, including digital products, over digital or electronic network.

(*ii*) e-commerce operator means a person who owns, operates or manages digital or electronic facility or platform for electronic commerce.

(*iii*) e-commerce participant means a person resident in India selling goods or providing services or both, including digital products, through digital or electronic facility or platform for electronic commerce.

(*iv*) services includes "fees for technical services" and fees for "professional services", as defined in the *Explanation* to Sec. 194. **[*Explanation* to Sec.194-O].**

However, no deduction for TDS is required when the gross amount of sale or services or both of an e-commerce participant, being an individual or Hindu undivided family through e-commerce operator does not exceed ₹ 5 lakh and such e-commerce participant has furnished his Permanent Account Number or Aadhaar number to the e-commerce operator **[Sec.194-O(2)]**.

The following points of difference must be noted:

Particulars	Equalisation Levy	Significant Economic Presence (SEP)	TDS under Sec. 194-O
Statute	Applicable under the Finance Act, 2016	Applicable under the Income-tax Act, 1961	Applicable under the Income-tax Act, 1961
Objective	To neutralise tax on those earning incomes from advertising services and bring within the tax ambit such transactions of a Non-Resident (NR) whose source of income was in India but did not have a base in India	To bring within the ambit of domestic laws such incomes of non-residents having economic nexus with India but where the non-resident did not have physical presence in India	To operate on canon of administrative convenience and ensure that persons earning income does not escape without paying taxes and filing Income Tax Return (ITR)
Type of payment	Payment made by a resident or non-resident for advertising services/ spaces to ◆ a NR not having a PE in India ◆ E-Commerce Supply or service to a resident, NR using Indian IP, data etc.	Payments made by a resident or non-resident to **a non-resident** for transactions with respect to any goods, services or property above prescribed limits or for soliciting of business activities or engaging in	Payment made by E-Commerce operator (**Resident or NR**) to **Resident** E-Commerce Participant

Particulars	Equalisation Levy	Significant Economic Presence (SEP)	TDS under Sec. 194-O
	to NR Ecommerce Operator	interaction with certain minimum prescribed number of users	
Rates	6% on advertisement 2% e-commerce supply	Regular tax rate slab	1% of gross amount of sale or service or both

After the scope of Equalisation Levy was expanded in the Finance Act, 2020 to include an online provision of services provided by the e-commerce operator where such e-commerce operator was defined as a non-resident who owns, operates or manages digital or electronic facility or platform, questions arose if imposition of Equalisation Levy is in addition to the Income-tax Act or are they mutually exclusive. This confusion was also strengthened by the exemption provided under Sec. 10 (*50*) according to income which had suffered equalization levy was exempt from the levy of income-tax.

For instance, when a non-resident provides technical services which is utilised in India through its online platform, the income would be chargeable to tax @10% in India as per Sec. 9(1)(*vii*) of the Income-tax Act. With broadened scope of the Equalisation Levy, the same service may now also attract 2% Equalisation levy as per the new provisions as it includes the services provided online to a resident by a non-resident who owns, operates and manages a digital or electronic facility.

This anomaly is now removed with the Finance Act, 2021 by introducing an *Explanation* to Sec. 163 of the Finance Act, 2016, clarifying that consideration received for specified services and that for e-commerce supply or services shall exclude such consideration which is taxable as royalty or fees for technical services in India under the Income-tax Act read with the DTAA.

(*i*) Income through or from a property in India is deemed to accrue or arise in India [Sec. 9(1)(*i*)]

The term property includes any property, movable or immovable, but which must be tangible. For instance, ABC Ltd. a non-resident company owning a building situated in India is leased to XYZ Ltd. another non-resident company. The lease agreement is entered outside India and the lease charges are directly deposited in the bank account of ABC Ltd. abroad. It is an income deemed to accrue or arise in India as the tangible property is situated in India.

(*ii*) Income through or from any Asset or Source in India is deemed to accrue or arise in India [Sec. 9(1)(*i*)]

The term "asset" includes all intangible rights as opposed to "property" which covers only tangible properties. "The source" means not a legal concept but which a practical man would regard as a real source of income.

Case Law : ***PILCOM* v. *CIT* [2020] 116 taxmann.com 394/271 Taxman 200 (SC)**

Facts: 'P', a joint committee, was formed by the Cricket Control Boards India, Pakistan and Sri Lanka for the purpose of conducting the World Cup Cricket tournament for the year 1996 in these three countries. 'P' opened bank accounts in London in which the receipt from sponsorship, T.V. rights etc. were deposited and expenses were met. The surplus amount remaining in the said Bank account was decided to be divided among the Cricket Boards.

Held: Payments made to non-resident sports in relation to matches played in India was income accruing or arising or deemed to accruing or arising in India and 'P' was liable to deduct tax at source.

(*iii*) Income through the Transfer of a Capital Asset Situated in India is deemed to accrue or arise in India [Sec. 9(1)(*i*)]

Any capital gain from the transfer of the capital asset, situated in India, is deemed to accrue or arise in India. For instance, when ABC Ltd. a non-resident company owning a house property situated in India transfers the same to XYZ Ltd. another non-resident company; even if the agreement to sell is entered outside India and payment is received in foreign currency directly deposited in the bank account of ABC Ltd. abroad, capital gains from such transaction will attract tax in India.

The Vodafone controversy had a lasting impact on this provision and was followed by a series of explanations that were later introduced here. The matter involved a question whether transfer of shares of a non-resident company between two non-resident companies attracts capital gains tax in India. The existing provision required that the capital asset should be situated in India for the income to be deemed to accrue or arise in India. So that when Vodafone International and Hutchinson International, both being non-resident companies entered into a share purchase agreement of another non-resident company based in Cayman Island, the same could not be brought to tax being a transfer of shares *i.e.* capital asset situated outside India. The Revenue Department however contended that since the Cayman Island based company was having a controlling interest in an Indian Telecom joint venture the said company derived its value from India and so the income upon its transfer was taxable in Indian. This contention was further layered with a charge of the arrangement being a tax avoidance scheme which ought to be disallowed. In a comprehensive judgment in 2012, the Supreme Court of India ruled in favour of the assessee-company to hold that when capital asset was situated outside India there was nothing in the existing provision of sec. 9(1)(*i*) to capture such indirect transfers referred to by the Revenue Department. A series of explanations with retrospective effect followed this ruling.

Shares or interest of non-resident entity deemed to be situated in India [*Explanation 5* to sec. 9(1)(*i*)] - Where any asset or capital asset being shares or interest in a non-resident company or entity, directly or indirectly derives its value substantially from the assets located in India, such asset or capital asset is deemed to be situated in India.

For this purposes, the shares or interest will be deemed to derive its value substantially from the assets, tangible or intangible, located in India; if the value of such assets exceeds ₹ 10 crores and represents at least 50% of the value of all the assets, owned by the company or entity. The value of an asset is taken at the fair market value on the specified date without reduction of liability in respect of such asset, if any. [*Explanation 6* w.e.f. 1.4.2016].

However, category-I FPIs under SEBI (FPI) Regulations 2019 is exempt from application of indirect transfer Provisions (third Proviso to *Explanation 5*). Further, no tax demand shall be raised for any indirect transfer if such transaction was undertaken before 28th May 2012. In case tax is already paid such assessee shall be entitled to a refund without interest thereon. (Fourth, fifth and sixth Provisos to *Explanation 5*).

When income from transfer of shares or interest deriving its value substantially from assets in India is not deemed to accrue or arise in India [*Explanation* 7 w.e.f. 1-4-2016]

(*a*) (*i*) If such company/entity directly owns the assets situated in India and the transferor (Whether individually or along with associated enterprises) neither holds the right of management or control of such company or entity nor holds voting power or share capital or interest, exceeding 5% of total voting power or total share capital or total interest of such company or entity at any time within 12 months, preceding the date of transfer; or

(*ii*) If such company or entity indirectly owns the assets situated in India and the transferor (Whether individually or along with associated enterprises) at any time within 12 months preceding the date of transfer complied with the following conditions:

(1) neither he holds the right of management or control in relation to such company or entity,

(2) nor he holds any right in, or in relation to, such company or entity which would entitle him to the right of management or control in the company or entity that directly owns the assets situated in India,

(3) nor he holds such percentage of voting power or share capital or interest in such company or entity which results in holding (either individually or along with associated enterprises) a voting power or share capital or interest exceeding 5% of the total voting power or share capital or interest exceeding 5% of the total voting power or total share capital or interest, as the case may be, of the company or entity that directly owns the assets, situated in India.

(*b*) Where all the assets owned, directly or indirectly, by a company or an entity, referred to in the Explanation 5, are not located in India, the proportionate income from the transfer of a share of such company or interest therein to the non-resident transferor is deemed to accrue or arise to him in India in such proportion as may be reasonably attributable to assets located in India. Such income is determined in such manner as may be prescribed.

(*iv*) Salary Income if earned in India [Sec. 9(1)(*ii*)]

Income which falls under the head of "salary" is deemed to accrue or arise in India if it is earned in India. Salary income is treated as earned in India if it is payable for

(*i*) services rendered in India; or

(*ii*) rest period or leave period which is preceded or succeeded by services rendered in India and forms part of service contract of employment.

Pension Accrues or Arises at a Place where the Services were Rendered [Sec. 9(2)]

Pension is earned by reason of services rendered in past years. Hence, it accrues or arises at a place where the services were rendered. Therefore, the pension is chargeable to tax if the pensioner had worked in India. An exception is, however, enacted in respect of (*i*) civil servants appointed by the Secretary of State or the Secretary in Council before 15 August 1947, and (*ii*) Judges of the High Court and the Federal Court appointed before 15 August 1947 and continuing to serve as civil servants or as Judges after the promulgation of the Constitution. If these persons, on retirement, reside permanently outside India and receive their pensions outside India, such pensions are not deemed to accrue or arise in India.

Case Law : ***CIT* v. *A. P. Kalyanakrishnan* [1992] 195 ITR 534 (Mad.)**

Facts : K, a resident but not ordinarily resident in India, was a pensioner of the Malaysian Government. The pension was paid by Malaysian Government through the Accountant-General, Chennai. The assessee claimed that this pension was not taxable in India as the pension had been received in Malaysia but the Assessing Officer taxed the pension u/s 5(1)(*c*) of the Act.

Held: Receipt means the first occasion when the assessee gets the money under his control. The pension accrues to the assessee outside India and was first received in Malaysia and its remittance to the place where the assessee was living was a matter of convenience and that would not constitute receipt of income in India. Therefore, having regard to provisions of Sec. 5(1)(*a*), the pension remitted to the assessee was not assessable in India.

(*v*) Salary payable by the Government to an Indian citizen abroad is deemed to accrue or arise in India [Sec. 9(1)(*iii*)]

In case of government servants who are citizens of India any income chargeable under the head "Salaries" is deemed to accrue or arise in India even though the services are rendered by them outside India. It is applicable to government employees who are citizens of India and who are posted abroad. They render the services outside India and they may also be paid outside India. Even then they are chargeable to tax for the income falling under the head "Salaries" because their income is deemed to accrue or arise in India by this provision.

(*vi*) Dividends Paid by an Indian Company outside India are Deemed to Accrue or Arise in India [Sec. 9(1)(*iv*)]

Any dividend paid by an Indian company outside India is deemed to accrue or arise in India. Thus, if any dividend is paid to non-residents or not ordinarily resident shareholders outside India by an Indian company, it is liable to be taxed in India by force of this provision.

A dividend paid by a non-Indian company outside India is not deemed to accrue or arise in India. Thus, the dividend paid by a non-Indian company, operating in India, to non-resident or not ordinarily resident shareholders outside India is exempt from tax. The reason of this exemption lies in the fact that a non-Indian company, operating in India, is taxed at a higher rate. Thus, the loss involved in the exemption of dividend is compensated by a higher rate of taxation.

Case Law : ***Pfizer Corporation* v. *CIT* [2003] 129 Taxman 459/259 ITR 391 (Bom.)**

Facts: P, a non-resident company, was a shareholder in its Indian subsidiary, a company registered under the Indian Companies Act. The Indian company declared final dividend amounting to ₹ 50.40 lakh out of which ₹ 25.20 lakh was remitted two years later when the statutory approval from RBI for remitting foreign exchange was received. The department proceeded to tax the amount of dividend received in the assessment year relevant to the previous year in which it was declared on grounds that dividend income accrued to the assessee during the assessment year in which the dividend was declared even though it was received in latter years.

Held: Indian company's obligation to pay dividend to the assessee arose only on obtaining statutory approval of the RBI. In the present case, the debt did not arise in the year in which the dividend was declared. The assessee's right to receive the dividend accrued only in the year the RBI granted approval.

Income by way of Interest [Sec. 9(1)(*v*)]

This is explained with the help of the following Table 5.3.

TABLE 5.3: INCOME BY WAY OF INTEREST

Interest payable by:	Income by way of interest when deemed to accrue or arise in India
Government	Always It is immaterial whether the interest is paid on debt incurred or on moneys borrowed to be utilized in India or outside India
Resident person	Always, except where the interest is payable in respect of any debt incurred, or moneys borrowed and used for business or profession outside India or for earning any income from any source outside India, it is not deemed to accrue or arise in India.
Non-resident person	Only when the interest is payable in respect of a debt incurred, or moneys borrowed and used, for the purpose of business or profession carried on by such person in India.

Interest payable by the permanent establishment of a Non-Resident in India to the Head office outside India [Sec. 9(1)(*v*)(*c*)] w.e.f. 1-4-2016:

If permanent establishment of a 'Non-resident' engaged in banking business, pays any interest in India to the head office or any permanent establishment or any part of such non-resident outside India, it is deemed to accrue or arise in India. In addition to any income, attributable to the permanent establishment in India, it is also chargeable to tax on such income. Permanent establishment is deemed to be a person, separate and independent of the 'Non-Resident person' of which it is a permanent establishment. The provisions of this Act relating to computation of total income, determination of tax and collection and recovery equally apply accordingly. It is operative from the assessment year 2016-2017 and subsequently.

Income by way of Royalty [Sec. 9(1)(*vi*)]

The extent to which an income by way of royalty is deemed to accrue or arise in India is explained with the help of the Table 5.4.

TABLE 5.4: INCOME BY WAY OF ROYALTY

Interest payable by:	Income by way of interest when deemed to accrue or arise in India
Government	Always taxable
Resident person	Always taxable, except where the royalty is payable in respect of any right, property or information used or services carried on by such person outside India or for making or earning any income from any source outside India, it is not deemed to accrue or arise in India.
Non-resident person	Only taxable when royalty is in respect of any right, property or information used or services utilised for business or profession carried on by such persons in India or for making or earning any income from any source in India, is deemed to accrue or arise in India.

Meaning of Royalty - Ordinarily royalty connotes a periodic payment by one person to another for the use of certain exclusive rights belonging to such another person with respect to say a patent, specialized knowledge or rights in respect of publications. The person granting such right to use may have itself obtained an exclusive right under the requisite law. For example, a person may have obtained an exclusive right over an invention under the Patent Laws. In respect of books and publications, the exclusive right of the author is protected and sanctioned by the laws of copyright. Similarly, it is possible for a person carrying out operations of manufacture and production of a particular produce to acquire specialised knowledge in respect of such manufacture and production which is not generally available. A person having such specialised knowledge can claim exclusive right to the same as long as he chooses not to make such specialised knowledge public.

For the purposes of this clause, "royalty" means consideration for:

(*i*) the transfer of all or any rights in respect of; imparting of any information concerning the working of or the use of; the use of a patent, invention model, design, secret formula or trademarks or similar property;

(*ii*) the imparting of any information concerning technical, industrial, commercial, or scientific knowledge, experience or skill;

(*iii*) the use or right to use, any industrial, commercial or scientific equipment but excluding the amount for the use of ships, aircraft, vehicles, drilling units, scientific apparatus and equipment used in connection with business of exploration of mineral oils, etc.;

(*iv*) the transfer of all or any rights including the granting of a licence in respect of any copyright, literary, artistic or scientific work including films or video tapes for use in connection with television or tapes for use in connection with radio broadcasting, but not including consideration for sale, distribution or exhibition of cinematographic films; or

(*v*) Rendering of any services in connection with any of the above.

Exclusions of certain royalties - The following royalty payments subject to the fulfilment of specified conditions are excluded and therefore not taxable in India:

(1) Royalty payable under an agreement approved by the Central Government:

  (*a*) if the agreement is made before 1 April, 1976.

  (*b*) for the transfer outside India of, or the imparting of information outside India.

  (*c*) in respect of, any data, documentation, drawing or specification relating to any patent, invention, model, design, secret formula or process or trade mark or similar property; and

  (*d*) the royalty payable is a lump sum consideration.

  For this purpose, an agreement made on or after 1 April 1976 will be deemed to have been made before that date:

  - in case of a foreign company, if the agreement is in accordance with proposals approved by the Central Government before 1 April 1976 and the foreign company makes a declaration in writing to the Assessing Officer within specified time that the agreement may be regarded as an agreement made before 1 April 1976.
  - in case of any other assessee if the agreement is in accordance with proposals approved by the Central Government before 1 April 1976.

(2) Royalty payable in respect of computer software, if:

  (*a*) lump sum payment is made by a resident;

  (*b*) for transfer of all or any rights relating to computer software supplied along with a computer or computer-based equipment;

(*c*) by a non-resident manufacturer;

(*d*) under any scheme approved under the Policy on Computer Software Export, Software Development and Training, 1986 of the Government of India.

Royalty payment is distinct from outright sale - Where the payment is in consideration of transfer of the full ownership of property, such payment is not in consideration 'for the use of, or the right to use' that property and therefore does not qualify to be a royalty. In other words, if ownership rights have been alienated, it is no longer for use of rights. Such payment will be taxed as business profits or capital gains.

Case Law : ***CIT* v. *Davy Ashmore India Ltd.* [1991] 190 ITR 626 (Cal.)**

Facts: D, an Indian company, placed an order with a UK company for supply of concept designs and drawings for the manufacture of terminal equipment for which a lump sum payment was made. The Income-tax Officer took the view that the payments made to the non-resident UK company were in the nature of royalty.

Held: Since the non-resident company was not retaining the property in the designs and drawings, the consideration paid for transfer of designs and drawings amounts to an outright sale and not royalty.

Royalty payment for contracts of know-how should not be confused with service contract - Under a contract of imparting know-how, one party agrees to impart knowledge or experience (that remains unrevealed to the public) to the other party to be used on his own account. A contract of service is where one party undertakes to use his customary skills to execute the work himself for the other party. For example after sale service.

Right to use computer software: Transfer of Copyright or Copyrighted Article Controversy

Generally speaking computer software is a set of instructions expressed in words, codes or any other form that makes a computer perform a particular task. Computer software can be customized according to a client's requirements. For example, a software developed exclusively for a university to maintain record of its students, their marks, attendance, professor's service record and so on. A software may be standardized so that it can be readily used by any buyer. For example, an anti-virus software which can be bought and used by anyone. Software can be transferred as an integral part of computer hardware or in an independent form like on a CD. For the purposes of section 9(1)(*vi*) the expression "computer software" means any computer programme recorded on any disc, tape, perforated media or other information storage device and includes any such programme or any customized electronic data.

Payments with respect to the grant of a non-exclusive, restricted license to use software have posed difficulties in terms of its characterization *i.e.* whether it is a royalty payment for the use of copyright or is it a payment for a copyrighted article which is business profit. The Courts have been divided on their opinion.

A Special Bench of Delhi Tribunal in *Motorola Inc.* v. *Dy. CIT* [2005] 147 Taxman 39/95 ITD 269 (Delhi)(Trib.)(SB) was called upon to decide whether payments received by Motorola on the sale of GSM equipment comprising of hardware and licensing of application of software to Indian cellular operators amounts to royalty or business income. The Special Bench observed that the cellular operators had a very limited right to use the software and could not exploit the computer software commercially which was the very essence of a copyright within the provisions of the Copyright Act, 1957. It therefore held that the payment by the cellular operator was not for any copyright in the software but was only for the software as such as a copyrighted article. This ruling of the Special Bench has been followed by the Delhi High Court in several other cases. [*DIT* v. *Infrasoft Ltd.* [2013] 39 taxmann.com 88/[2014] 220 Taxman 273/264 CTR (Delhi) *Principal CIT* v. *M. Tech India (P.) Ltd.* [2016] 67 taxmann.com 245/238 Taxman 178/381 ITR 31 (Delhi)].

The Karnataka High Court on the other hand in *CIT* v. *Samsung Electronics Co. Ltd.* [2009] 185 Taxman 313/[2010] 320 ITR 209 (Kar.) and later in *CIT* v. *Synopsis International Old Ltd.* [2012] 28 taxmann.com 162/[2013] 212 Taxman 454 (Kar.), has consistently held that the meaning assigned to the word 'copyright' under sec. 14 of the Copyright Act cannot be transplanted to the understanding the meaning of the word 'royalty' used in the Income-tax Act as defined in *Explanation 2* to section 9(1). Within the meaning of royalty in Income-tax Act, the inquiry that needs to be made is whether the consideration paid to the owner is for transfer of any right in respect of a copyright. The words "in respect of" denotes the intention of the Parliament to give a broader meaning. So that even if a copyrighted article is transferred, it may not be a right in the copyright which is transferred, but it is a right in respect of a copyright contained in the copyrighted article which is transferred which amounts to royalty income.

The controversy has been finally been settled with the recent decision of the Supreme Court in *Engineering Analysis Centre of Excellence (P.) Ltd.* v. *CIT* [2021] 125 taxmann.com 42/281 Taxman 19 (SC). Herein again, the assessee Engineering Analysis Centre of Excellence Pvt. Ltd, a resident of India, was an end-user of shrink-wrapped computer software which it was directly importing from the USA. The revenue authorities considered the assessee being in default under Sec. 201 for failing to deduct tax on the royalty income paid to a non-resident. The Supreme Court held that the assessee being a distributor was only granted a non-exclusive, non-transferable license to resell computer software under an End-User License Agreement which expressly stipulated that no copyright in the computer program is transferred either to the distributor or to the ultimate end-user. The EULAs cannot be understood as the one referred in Sec. 30 of the Copyright Act which requires granting of an interest in any of the rights mentioned in sections 14(*a*) and 14(*b*) of the Copyright Act for it to be license.

The Supreme Court endorsed the view taken in *Tata Consultancy Services* v. *State of A.P.* [2004] 141 Taxman 132 (SC)/2005 (1) SCC 308 which was a matter concerned with the imposition of indirect tax on a software embedded on a hardware, and the Supreme Court there had held that a licensed software supplied by a foreign, non-resident supplier to the distributor in India and resold to the resident end-user, or directly supplied to the resident end-user, is the sale of a physical object which contains an embedded computer program, and is, therefore, a sale of goods. Further the Supreme Court likened the sale of licensed software under EULA with the sale of copyrighted book. Just like an English publisher sells 2000 copies of a particular book to an Indian distributor, who resells the same at a profit, no copyright in the aforesaid book is transferred to the Indian distributor, either by way of license or otherwise, since the Indian distributor only makes a profit on the sale of each book similar is the situation of a distributor of a software under EULA. Therefore, distributor was not an assessee-in-default since no tax was required to be deducted on import of software under EULA.

Payments for Satellite Television Broadcasting services

Characterisation of payments received by satellite broadcasting service providers has also been under a cloud and prompted a few amendments. *Asia Satellite Telecommunications Co. Ltd.* v. *DIT* [2011] 9 taxmann.com 168/197 Taxman 263/332 ITR 340 (Delhi) is a leading authority in this matter. The assessee-company, incorporated in Hong Kong, carried on business of private satellite communications and broadcasting facilities. The assessee leased transponder capacity on its satellites to TV channels and other companies for downlinking programme to various countries including India for which it received payments. Neither the assessee's satellite was positioned over Indian airspace nor its clients had relay stations situated in India. The revenue department contended that the assessee allowed its clients to use a secret process of uplinking and downlinking signals which had its footprint in India and therefore payments received were royalty within *Explanation 2* to section 9(1)(*vi*) income chargeable to tax in India.

The Delhi High Court held that there was no use of 'process' by the TV channels and no such purported use had taken place in India. The assessee as well as its customers was situated outside India and the agreements were executed abroad. Merely because footprint area included India and ultimate consumers/viewers were watching programmes in India, it would not mean that assessee was carrying out its business operations in India.

Following this ruling, the Finance Act, 2012 inserted a clarificatory *Explanation 6* to sec. 9(1)(*vi*) that the expression "process" includes and shall be deemed to have always included transmission by satellite (including uplinking, amplification, conversion for down-linking of any signal), cable, optic fibre or by any other similar technology, whether or not such process is secret.

The Delhi High Court was once again dealing with a similar controversy in *DIT* v. *New Skies Satellite BV* [2016] 68 taxmann.com 8/238 Taxman 577/382 ITR 114 (Delhi). Revenue contended that since the amendment in 2012 has provided an explanation, the ruling in Asia Satellite is no longer applicable and therefore even if the process was not secret, it still falls within the definition of the term royalty to attract sec. 9(1)(*vi*). The Delhi High Court held that since the definition of the term royalty in the DTAA applicable in this matter required the process to be secret, a unilateral and subsequent change in the domestic law definition to the term royalty cannot be applied to hold the assessee taxable in India. Such an amendment to the definition must be jointly made by the parties to the DTAA. The issue is pending before the Supreme Court.

Income by way of Fees for Technical Services [Sec. 9(1)(*vii*)]

The extent to which an income by way of fees for technical services is deemed to accrue or arise in India is explained with the help of the Table 5.5.

TABLE 5.5: INCOME BY WAY OF FEES FOR TECHNICAL SERVICES

Interest payable by:	Income by way of FTS when deemed to accrue or arise in India
Government	Always Taxable
Resident person	Always Taxable, except where the fees for technical services is payable in respect of services utilised in a business or profession carried on by such person outside India or for making or earning any income outside India, it is not deemed to accrue or arise in India.
Non-resident person	Only taxable when the fees for technical services is payable in respect of services utilised in a business or profession carried on by such person in India or for making or earning any income in India, it is deemed to accrue or arise in India.

Exception - Any income by way of fees for technical services payable in pursuance of an agreement made before 1 April 1976 and approved by the Central Government, is not deemed to accrue or arise in India.

For this purpose, an agreement made on or after 1 April 1976 will be deemed to have been made before that date: if the agreement is in accordance with proposals approved by the Central Government before 1.

Meaning of "Fees for Technical Services" - "Fees for technical services" means any consideration (including provision of lump sum consideration) for the rendering of any managerial, technical or consultancy services (including services of any technical or other personnel).

Fees for technical services does not include consideration for any construction, assembly, mining, or like project undertaken by the recipient or consideration which would be income of the recipient chargeable under the head 'salaries'.

Meaning of Managerial, Technical and Consultancy services

Management includes the act of managing by direction, or regulation or administration or control or superintendence of the business [*R. Dalmia* v. *CIT* [1977] 106 ITR 895 (SC)]. The term "Consultant" has been defined as "a person" who gives professional advice or services in a specialized field. Therefore, the service of consultancy necessarily entails human intervention. Since the words "technical services" comes in between the words "managerial and consultancy services" "technical services" would obviously involve services rendered by human efforts.

In general parlance anything that is 'technical' concerns itself with applied and industrial science and quite often provisioning of service. But merely because the activity involves installation of sophisticated equipment and operates through such equipment, it does not result into incomes form such activities being fees for technical services. In other words, when services offered upon intense use of technology and inputs of technical knowledge and experience will not necessarily make it a FTS.

Further, provisioning of technical services denotes catering to the specific needs of the user. It is this feature that distinguishes a service provided from a facility offered. While provisioning service is special and exclusive to the seeker of the service, facility offered, even if termed as a service, is available to all. [*CIT* v. *Kotak Securities Ltd.* [2016] 67 taxmann.com 356/239 Taxman 139/383 ITR 1 (SC)]. When payment is collected, by whatever nomenclature, for the use of standardized facility involving use of technology does not amount to FTS.

Technical Services includes Financial Services also Advice given to procure loan to strengthen finances would be as much a technical or consultancy service, as it would be with regard to management, generation of power or plant and machinery. A business cannot be divided into water-tight compartments, like finance, production, plant and machinery, management, etc., to hold that fees for technical services will relate only to production or plant and machinery but not to technical services related to finance of the project. For example, if a resident assessee hires the services of a non-resident financial consultant for advice in raising financing for its power project in India, fee paid to such non-resident consultant will fall within the ambit of technical fee which is deemed to accrue or arise in India and assessable to tax in India [*G. V. K. Industries Ltd.* v. *Income-tax Officer* [1997] 228 ITR 564/[1998] 96 Taxman 179 (AP)].

Meaning of FTS in DTAA and the 'Make Available' clause Some DTAAs (such as Canada, Finland, Netherlands, UK and US) restrict the scope of the term "FTS" to only technical and consultancy services (*i.e.,* managerial services are not included within the fold of the definition) and with a 'make available' clause. Accordingly, technology is considered to be 'made available' when the person acquiring the service is enabled to apply the technology. The technical knowledge or skills of the provider should be imparted to and absorbed by the receiver so that the receiver can deploy similar technology or techniques in the future without depending upon the provider.

Case Law : ***CIT* v. *Kotak Securities Ltd.* [2016] 67 taxmann.com 356/239 Taxman 139/383 ITR 1 (SC)**

Facts: K, along with other members of Bombay Stock Exchange, availed fully automated facilities of a faceless screen based transaction by Bombay Stock Exchange for a payment of fees. Issue arose whether K should have withheld tax on the payment to BSE since it was a payment towards FTS.

Held: Only payment for services which are specialized, exclusive and according to individual requirements of user or consumer who may approach service provider for such services would come within ambit of 'fees for technical services' in terms of *Explanation 2* to section 9(1)(*vii*) so as to attract TDS under section 194J.

Clarification about Source Rule in respect of Royalty, Interest and Fees for Technical Services [Sec. 9(1)(*v*)/(*vi*)/(*vii*)] [*Explanation 2* to Sec. 9(2)] - The Supreme Court in *Ishikawajama–Harima Heavy Industries Ltd.* v. *Director IT* [2007] 158 Taxman 259/288 ITR 408 (SC) has held that there must be sufficient territorial nexus between deemed income and territory of India. The deeming fiction cannot bring to tax any income of a non-resident received outside India from Indian concerns for services rendered outside India. Fees for technical services can be taxed under deeming fiction if the services have not only been utilised in a business in India, but also have to be rendered in India.

The Explanation introduced by the Finance Act, 2007 retrospectively provides that any income deemed to accrue or arise in India under Sec. 9(1)(*v*), (*vi*) and (*vii*) is to be included in the total income of a non-resident regardless of the fact whether the non-resident has a residence or place of business or business connection in India. In such cases, it is not necessary to establish the territorial nexus between the income deemed to accrue or arise to the non-resident under the said clauses and the territory of India.

Mere Entry in Balance Sheet of a Foreign Income does not in itself Amount to Receipt in India [*Explanation 1* to Sec. 5] - Income accruing or arising outside India is not deemed to be received in India because of the fact that it is taken into account in a balance sheet prepared in India. Thus, where the profits of a foreign branch, not received in India, are incorporated in the account books of Head Office in India, the incorporation of entries in the books of account do not amount to receipt of such profits in India. If such foreign profits (not received in India) are taken not only in account books but are also taken in determining the amount to be paid as dividend, it does not amount to receipt of foreign profits in India. Similarly, the fact that the foreign profits are distributed among the partners in a firm's account in India does not by itself amount to receipt of the profit in India.

Gift to non-residents and not ordinarily residents [Sec. 9(1)(*viii*)]

It was observed that gifts were being made by persons resident in India to non-residents who were claiming the same as non-taxable. Therefore, as an anti-abuse provision, the Finance Act, 2019 extended the deeming fiction of section 9 to such gifts received by non-residents. Accordingly, any sum of money exceeding ₹ 50,000 received by a non-resident without consideration from a person resident in India, on or after the 5th day of July, 2019 was deemed to accrue or arise in India to such non-resident. This provision does not apply to a non-resident who is a company or a foreign company. The Finance Act, 2023 has further extended this fiction to not ordinarily residents as well w.e.f. 1.4.2024 (AY 2024-25 and subsequent years).

CHAPTER 6 Income from Salary

INTRODUCTION

Income-tax is charged on the total income which is computed source wise under different heads. "Salaries" is the first head of income. Any income arising in the hands of a recipient by virtue of a contract of employment is characterized as income from salary. It comprehends every payment, due to or received by an employee from the employer on account of services, rendered to him. Even non-monetary benefits and perquisites provided by an employer to employee are valued in terms of money and taxed accordingly in the hands of employee.

Any income from salary is taxed either on due basis or receipt basis, whichever is earlier. Even arrears of salary, if not taxed earlier on due basis, are taxed during the previous year in which they are received by the assessee. Similarly, where salary is received in advance, it is taxed during the previous year in which it is received and the year of its accrual plays no role in its taxability.

This head of income comprise of three sections that provides a framework of income from salary. The basis of charge is explained under sec. 15. An inclusive definition of salary is contained in sec. 17 that addresses definition of (*a*) salary (*b*) perquisite and (*c*) profits in lieu of salary. Permissible deductions are provided under sec. 16.

TABLE 6.1: COMPUTATION OF SALARY INCOME

Particulars	Amount (in ₹)	Amount (in ₹)
- Salary	XXXXXXX	
- Income by way of allowances	XXXXXXX	
- Taxable value of perquisites	XXXXXXX	
GROSS SALARY	XXXXXXX	
Less: Deductions -Standard Deduction		
-Entertainment Tax	XXXX	
-Professional Tax	2,500	
NET SALARY		XXXXXX

EXISTENCE OF EMPLOYER-EMPLOYEE RELATIONSHIP

The primary requirement for application of this head of income is the existence of a relationship of employer-employee between the payer and payee. An employer may be a present, past or future employer or multiple employer in the same previous year. Employer may be any entity, *e.g.*, a local authority, or a company, or any other public body or association, or Central or State Government, or Foreign Government or any other private employer like a firm, HUF, AOP, company or even an individual. Remuneration may be paid by such employer or 'on behalf of the employer'. Insofar as the reward is on account of employment, income will be chargeable to tax as salary income.

When payments are received from persons other than employer such incomes are chargeable either under the head "Profits and Gains of Business or Profession" or "Income from other sources". For example, examinership fee to a lecturer is assessable under the head "Income from other sources".

Determinants of Employer-Employee Relationship

Control and Supervision Test

Classically control and supervision was considered to be an indicator of the nature of relationship between the parties. Therefore, the degree of authority exercised over the person offered a general yardstick to determine whether the relationship is that an employer-employee or a principal-agent. The greater the amount of direct control over the person employed, the stronger the conclusion of his being an employee. And the greater the degree of independence, the greater the possibility of the services rendered being in the nature of principal and agent. [*Ram Prasad* v. *CIT* (1972) 86 ITR 122 (SC)]

A distinction was drawn between a contract of services and a contract for service. While a contract of services leads to employment, a contract for services results into agency or independent contract. In a contract for service the principal can require what is to be done by the agent, under a contract of service employer can dictate not only what is required to be done but also how it shall be done. Thus, an employer wields direct control and supervision on the employee who is bound to conform to all reasonable orders given to him in the course of his work. An agent is not subject to the direct control and supervision of the principal, though he is bound to be diligent and to further the interest of the principal in a lawful manner. An independent contractor, on the other hand, is entirely independent of any control or interference, and merely undertakes to produce a specified resulted employing his own means to produce that result.

Determination of employer-employee relationship is difficult when the position holder could operate in dual capacity, say for instance a managing director of a company who often discharges his functions in several capacities. He may be a director or an employee or a trustee or an agent of a company. Therefore, in order to prove that a director is an employee it should be established on record as fact and not merely as a paper work. [*CIT* v. *Smt. Shanti Devi* [1992] 64 Taxman 251/[1993] 199 ITR 800 (Orissa)].

In addition to the extent of control and supervision, other factors such as the appointing authority, pay master; power of termination dismiss, tenure of services, nature of job/establishment, exclusivity etc. were also considered before arriving at a conclusion of employer-employee relationship. [*CIT* v. *Ivy Health Life Sciences (P.) Ltd.* [2015] 63 taxmann.com 362/[2016] 236 Taxman 292/380 ITR 242 (Punj. & Har.)]

Case Law : *CIT* v. *B.P. Dalmia* [1993] 71 Taxman 52/[1996] 218 ITR 709 (Cal.)]

Facts: The assesse, being a director of a company, characterized the remuneration received under the head 'Salary' and claimed standard deduction under sec. 16(*i*). The Assessing Officer recharacterised the same as 'Income from Other Sources' on the grounds that since the assessee enjoyed wide power and control over the affairs of company unlike any other employee, he was not an employee.

Held: Upon reference to clauses of Articles of Association of company, it is clear that managing director shall act and discharge all duties and powers subject to direct control and supervision of Board of Directors and that there existed employer-employee relationship.

Hire and Fire Test

Apart from control and supervision, if under the terms of contract, a payer is vested with the right to terminate services, it is indicative of the nature of relationship being an employment. For example, the nature of a director's employment may be determined by the articles of association of a company and/or the agreement, if any, under which a contractual relationship between the director and the company has been brought about. So that when under the terms of agreement of appointment, such managing director could be removed for not discharging the work diligently or if he is found not to be acting in the interest of the company, it would amount to a contract of employment. [*Ram Prashad* v. *CIT* (1972) 86 ITR 122 (SC)]

However, even an agent can be lawfully be terminated before the expiry of the term for fraud, dishonesty, gross negligence, wilful default, misfeasance and the like causes even in the absence of a specific term to that effect in the contract. Therefore, though the power or right to terminate an appointment is a relevant consideration, it does not necessarily lead to an irresistible conclusion that every contract is a contract for and not of service.

Case Law : *Ram Prashad* v. *CIT* (1972) 86 ITR 122 (SC)

Facts: The assessee-director claimed that the commission income, being in the nature of salary income, given up by him could not be included in his total income since the income did not 'accrue'. It was disputed whether the nature of commission was salary income or business income.

Held: The Supreme Court referred to article of association and terms of appointment of the directors. It was observed that the Managing Director exercised powers within the terms and limitations prescribed under articles of association and subject to control and supervision of the Board of Directors. Further, under the terms of agreement, he could be removed for not discharging the work diligently or if he is found not to be acting in the interest of the company. It was therefore held to be a contract of employment.

Case Law : ***Satya Paul* v. *CIT* (1979) 116 ITR 335 (Cal.)**

Facts: The assessee was a managing director of company 'S' for life and of company 'A' for 20 years. There was no separate contract between the assessee and the companies regarding his appointment as the managing director. The articles of association of these companies did not provide for dismissal of the assessee from the office of the managing director.

Held: Calcutta High Court held that (a) Assessee's relationship with company 'S'- since assessee was empowered under the articles to appoint and remove any person as additional director and no employee of any company can appoint a director let alone dismiss him, assessee was not an employee of the company. This was so even where assessee was subject to the supervisory control by company 'S' and its directors and his appointment could be terminated. (b) Assessee's relationship with company 'A' – since the assessee was required to manage the business of the company in accordance with the resolutions of the board of directors and company and its directors exercised a supervisory control over assessee, and by virtue of an overriding article, company had a specific right to remove any director 'before expiration of his period of office by an extraordinary resolution' and if he were so removed, he would automatically be dismissed from office of managing director, assessee, could be said to be an employee of company 'A'.

Exclusivity and/or Non-compete Clause in the agreement are relevant but not determinative

Ordinarily, a contract of service comprises a clause of exclusivity in the sense that an employee is not allowed to take another employment during the continuation of services under that contract. However, merely because the assessee exclusively renders services to one particular entity and receives remuneration from that entity alone cannot be construed as a contract of employment. Further inclusion of non-compete clause in the agreement shall not invalidate the nature of profession. In other words, even if a contract stipulates a non-compete clause, it will continue to remain contract for service.

Case Law : ***Laxminarayan Ram Gopal & Son* v. *The Government of Hyderabad* 1954 AIR 364 (SC)**

Facts: L was appointed by M to be acting as managing agents on behalf of M for a remuneration. Subject to the control and supervision of the Directors, L could enter into contracts, recruite or dismiss staff, purchase and sell properties and continue as managing agents for a period of 30 years. L contended that since they served M exclusively and no other person as managing agents, the remuneration received from M was in the nature of salary and so cannot be taxed as business profits.

Held: It was held that a company incorporated with an object of serving as a managing agent of other companies, operated as managing agents of one company alone and no other, was not a persuasive factor to hold the relationship as that of employment. Thus, remuneration received will be profit from business and not salary.

Case Law : ***CIT* v. *Manipal Health Systems (P.) Ltd.* (2015) 57 taxmann.com 255/231 Taxman 518/375 ITR 509 (Kar.)**

Facts: The assessee-company running a hospital, imposed a condition restricting private practice by visiting doctors so as to make use of the expertise, skill of a doctor exclusively and discourage doctors from transferring patients to their own clinics or any other hospital.

Held: Non-compete clause or restriction will not alter the nature of professional service rendered by the doctors.

Case Law : ***Income-tax Officer* v. *Entertainment Network (I) Ltd.* (2017) 88 taxmann.com 843/185 TTJ 178 (Mumbai-Trib.)**

Facts: FM Radio broadcasting company characterized payments to Radio Jockeys (RJs) as consideration towards professional/consultancy services. As per the Assessing Officer this was salary income.

Held: RJ's were not entitled to various employment benefits such as provident fund, gratuity etc and were free to take assignments from any other company (except with any other Radio broadcasting company). There was nothing in the specific clauses in the agreement or its overall reading that indicated an employer-employee relationship.

Employment incidental to profession does not create employments

Sometimes during the course of practice, a professional may be necessitated to get himself or herself engaged to a particular master temporarily. However, such temporary association will not entail an employment relationship since the professional does not intend to give up his profession. The position is different when a professional permanently accepts an employment and exchanges his profession for service. The remuneration in that case is chargeable to tax under the head "Salaries".

Case Law : ***CIT* v. *Mrs. Durga Khote* (1952) 21 ITR 22 (Bom.)**

Facts: D a film actress entered into a contract with film Production Company for the purposes of acting in different films at fixed remuneration.

Held: D's employment was temporary and incidental to her profession. Since she had no intention to permanently engage herself with any company and was completely free to lend her services to any other company she desired after the contract, there was no employer-employee relationship.

It is an inquiry into Substance over Form

Usually an employee receives fixed remuneration, presents himself for work during the predetermined work hours and is entitled to a number of benefits such as pension, gratuity, leave salary, allowances etc. However, absence of the same may not lead to a conclusive proof that the contract is a contract for service, if the totality of contract indicates otherwise. The real nature of the agreement cannot be camouflaged by clever use of phraseology. The nature of the contract can be deciphered from the intention of the parties as expressed in the terms of contract.

Case Law : ***Hosmat Hospital P. Ltd.* v. *Asstt. CIT* (2016) 73 taxmann.com 147/ 160 ITD 513 (Bangalore-Trib.)**

Facts: The terms of contract entered by the hospital with consultant doctors provided for fixed remuneration, irrespective of number of patients attended by the consultant doctors, fixed timings, a tenure of five years, non-compete clause, and service were to be performed under the direct control and superintendence of the hospital.

Held: It is not the form but the substance of the transaction that matters. The nomenclature used may not be decisive or conclusive to determine the nature of transaction. The intention of the parties is to be ascertained with reference to terms of conditions contained in the agreement.

Case Law : ***Red Chillies Entertainment (P) Ltd.* v. *DCIT* [ITA No. 5271/Mum./2013] order dated 31.5.2016**

Facts : R being a film production company had entered into a service contract agreement with certain personnel and the compensation paid was termed as 'retainership fee'. Upon a perusal of the agreement it was revealed that the staff was required to perform all the duties as may be assigned from time to time, could avail leaves of around 30 days in a year, received fixed remuneration. They were provided company's car and mobile phone.

Held: Although payment of provident fund, gratuity, bonus etc is one of the indicators of existence of employer-employee relationship but it is not a conclusive or the only ingredient of employment. Here exists an employer-employee relationship.

There is no strait jacket formula prescribed under any statute or by any pronouncement on the basis of which it could be said that in a given eventuality, it would be characterized as employer-employee relationship. Such relationship depends upon several factors taken together.

REMUNERATION RECEIVED BY CONSTITUTIONAL FUNCTIONARIES

Members of Parliament and Members of Legislative Assembly - MPs and MLAs are elected by the public and upon such election acquire constitutional position to discharge constitutional functions. MPs and MLAs are not government employees. Government does not exercise any control on the member of the legislature, rather it is the legislature which exercises control over the Government. Therefore remuneration received by MPs and MLAs is not chargeable to income tax under the heads, "salaries" but as income from "other sources" under Sec. 56. [*CIT* v. *Shiv Charan Mathur* (2008) 306 ITR 126 (Raj.)]

Chief Minister of State - By virtue of Article 164(1) of the Constitution of India the Chief Minister is to be appointed by the Governor and he holds office during his pleasure. Article 164(5) of the Constitution provides for salaries and allowances of the Ministers to be determined by the Legislature of the State and until it is so determined, as specified in the Second Schedule to the Constitution. Therefore pay and allowances received by a Chief Minister will be chargeable to tax as salary and not as income from other sources. [*Lalu Prasad* v. *CIT* (2009) 2009 taxmann.com 1035/316 ITR 186 (Patna)]

Judges of High Court or Supreme Court - The relationship between the Government and High Court Judges is not of master and servant. A Judge of the High Court occupies a unique position under the Constitution and is able to function independently and impartially because he is not a Government servant and does not take orders from any one. And therefore the relationship between the Government and High Court Judges is not of master and servant. [*Union of India* v. *Pratibha Bonnerjea JT* 1995 (8) SC 357]. Therefore, High Court and the Supreme Court has no employer. However, Articles 125 and 221 of the Constitution deal with the 'salaries' of Supreme Court and High Court Judges respectively and expressly state that what the Judges receive are 'salaries'. Therefore remuneration received by judges is taxable as income from salary. [*Justice Deoki Nandan Agrawala* v. *Union of India* (1999) 237 ITR 872 (SC)].

Advocate-General - An Advocate-General is essentially a professional person and remuneration paid to him by State is only a retainer fee for services rendered as a professional advocate. An Advocate-General cannot be assumed to have exchanged his profession for service and continues to be a professional person. Therefore, such remuneration is to be assessed as professional income under head Profits and gains of business or profession and not under head Salary. [*CIT* v. *Govindaswaminathan* (1998) 101 Taxman 1/233 ITR 264 (Madras)]

- **Remuneration received by Partner of a Firm**

  Any salary, bonus, commission, etc., to a partner from firm is not treated as salary income [*Explanation 2* to Sec. 15]. It is treated as business income under sec. 28(*v*). A firm is not a legal person and has no legal existence apart from its partners. Though under income-tax law, it is a unit of assessment by virtue of special provisions, it cannot be considered that the firm is the employer of its partner. Salary received by partner is not received from an employer and it constitutes business income. The partners in a firm work for themselves and not for any employer. They are their own masters. Thus, the salary drawn by the partners is only a different name for their share in profits. The doubt, if any, was set at rest by the incorporation of Sec. 28(*v*), wherein it is provided that "any interest, salary, bonus, commission or remuneration, by whatever name called, due to, or received by, a partner of a firm from such firm" is "chargeable to income tax" under the head "Profits and gains of business or profession." [*CIT* v. *Ghansham Dass* [2002] 121 Taxman 355/254 ITR 355 (Punjab & Haryana)].

BASIS OF CHARGE

Sec. 15 is the charging provision for income under the head salary. It points out the time at which tax liability is attracted for salary income. Accordingly to sec. 15 salary is chargeable to tax on receipt or due basis, whichever is earlier. Sec. 15 comprise of three possible timing for taxation:

(*a*) **When salary is due, whether paid or not [Sec.15(1)(a)]** - For example, A's salary is due on the last day of every month. He is yet to be paid salary for the month of March 2019 which was paid to him on 10th April 2019. It will be taxed on due basis for A in the previous year 2018-19. When salary is 'due' it entails an obligation on the part of the employer to pay that amount and a right of the employee to claim the same. It does not cover contingent payment since the employee has no right till the contingency occurs. [*ITO* v. *D.S. Seth* (1987) 35 Taxman 27 (Bombay) (Mag.)] If the employer has denied the employee's claim to salary and the matter is referred to an arbitrator but there is no award or decree passed in employee's favour, it cannot be said that the salary is due. [*X* v. *ITO* (1985) 20 Taxman 7 (Bombay - Trib.)].

(*b*) **When salary is paid or allowed, whether due or not [(Sec.15(1)(b)] -** For example, B received salary of April 2019 and May 2019 in March 2019. This will be taxable for B for the previous year 2018-19. The expression 'allowed', it is said, is of a wider connotation and any credit made in the employer's account is covered thereby. [*CIT* v. *L.W. Russel* (1964) 53 ITR 91 (SC)].

(*c*) **When any arrears of salary paid or allowed, if not earlier charged to income tax in any previous year [Sec.15(1)(c)] -** For example, when arrears of salary are paid on account of revision of pay scales with retrospective effect, such arrears are taxed on receipt basis. Therefore in accordance with *Explanation 1* to sec. 15(1) where any salary paid in advance is included in the total income of any person for any previous year it shall not be included again in the total income of the person when the salary becomes due.

It is immaterial that the arrears relate to a year in which they were not chargeable to tax. Sec. 15(*c*) applies to arrears of salary provided such arrears had not been charged to income tax for any earlier previous year. The words used in clause (*c*) are "if not charged to income tax" and are wide enough to cover cases where the charge could or could not have been imposed.

Case Law: ***CIT* v. *Sardar Arjun Singh Ahluwalia* (1999) 107 Taxman 246/240 ITR 693 (SC)**

Facts: The contract of employment of S was terminated and he was not given his dues during the relevant previous year. Subsequently, after a prolonged litigation and upon a decree by the Court, the salary which was due was received.

Held: Since the said amount was not charged to income-tax for any previous year it falls within sec. 15(*c*) and can be brought to tax in the year of receipt as arrears in salary.

Vested Right to Receive Salary - In order to bring an income under sec. 15 there should be a vested right in an employee to claim any salary from an employer or former employer, whether due or not if paid; or paid or allowed, though not due. In absence of such right, income cannot be taxed under sec.15.

Case Law : ***ITC Hotels* v. *CIT* (2016) 68 taxmann.com 323/239 Taxman 372/384 ITR 14 (SC)**

Facts: Tips were paid to waiters in a hotel on purely voluntary basis by customers for services rendered to them. 'I', being an employer merely collected tips from customers in a fiduciary capacity as a trustee to be subsequently disbursed to employees. However such payment has no reference to the contract of employment at all.

Held: Since there was no such vested right to receive tip because customers may or may not tip the waiter, sec. 15(*b*) of the Income-tax Act, 1961 cannot be attracted and the employer cannot be considered to be an assessee-in-default for failing to deduct tax at source.

Waiver or Forfeiture or Donation of Salary accrued is chargeable to tax

Sometimes an employee may waive his salary either in full or in part or his salary may get forfeited. In such cases, where income has accrued but is subsequently given up, it remains the income of the recipient. [*CIT* v. *Shoorji Vallabhdas and Co.* [1962] 46 ITR 144 (SC)].

The voluntary forgoing by the employee of the salary due to him is normally a mere application of income and the salary is nonetheless taxable. Unless the assessee forgoes his right to salary before the income accrues, it has to be brought to charge. [*CIT* v. *Bawa Singh Chauhan* [1984] 16 Taxman 180/150 ITR 8 (Del.)]. For example, when a Managing Director of a company waives his salary for past few months due to poor financial state of the company, he will still be assessable on the salary waived by him. [*CIT* v. *Rajaratnam (V.R.)* [1979] 119 ITR 89 (Mad.)]. On the other hand, when the board of directors by a resolution decided not to pay any remuneration to the Managing Director on account of continuous loss to the company in its business operations, the Managing Director cannot be assessed on such salary even if there is a provision in accounts for his salary because such salary has not accrued to him at all. [*Trailokyanath Mohanty* v. *CIT* [1977] 110 ITR 254 (Ori.)].

However, an exception is made when a person has surrendered salary under Voluntary Surrender of Salaries (Exemption from Taxation) Act, 1961. By virtue of sec. 2 of the said Act, no income-tax or supper-tax shall be payable by any person (*a*) where his salary paid out of the Consolidated Fund of India or of the Consolidated Fund of a State which he has volunteered to forego in public interest by a written declaration (*b*) in any other case, which has been in the public interest, surrendered in favour of, and paid to. A person may surrender a portion of his salary or allowances in relation to salary for any period after 31st March, 1961. The amount so surrendered shall not be included in his total income. Such surrendered salary is treated as if it was never due to the employee. Surrender of salary should not be confused with donation of salary.

Diversion of salary income by overriding title is not chargeable to tax

Doctrine of diversion of income by overriding title postulates that certain income is received by a person (say 'A'), and that a part of that income is diverted to another person (say 'B') by reason of such person's possessing anterior, overriding superior title to the said part of income. For the doctrine of diversion of overriding title to apply, the diversion of income must be effective at the stage when the amount in question leaves the source, on its way to the intended recipient. It is at that stage that the amount gets diverted to another, who claims it as of right based on the pre-existing legal arrangement. [*Fr. Sunny Jose* v. *Union of India* (2015) 60 taxmann.com 386/233 Taxman 454/276 CTR 512 (Kerala)]

It is crucial to differentiate application of income with diversion of income by overriding titles. "When income has reached the assessee which is then applied to discharge certain obligation of the assessee it is application of income, when income is diverted before it reaches assessee it is diversion of income by overriding title." [*CIT* v. *Sitaldas Tirathdas* (1961) 41 ITR 367 (SC)].

Case Law : ***Fr. Sunny Jose* v. *Union of India* (2015) 60 taxmann.com 386/233 Taxman 454/276 CTR 512 (Kerala)**

Facts: The issue arose with respect to members of religious congregations who were employed as teachers in various aided educational institutions in State and paid salary for the teaching services rendered by them. Upon demands being made to deduct tax at source from such payments, the members contended that according to Canon Law, a member of the religious congregation cannot own any property and whatever he/she receives is a receipt on behalf of the religious congregation of which he/she is a member. It was argued that the principle of diversion of income by overriding title applied in this case since the income never reached the member.

Held: Since payments had accrued to members of religious congregations as their income, subsequent diversion of that income to religious congregations concerned was only a case of application of that income. Salary income was therefore liable to TDS provision.

Case Law : ***Union of India* v. *Society of Mary Immaculate (Tamil Nadu), Madras* (2019) 103 taxmann.com 333/262 Taxman 496 (Madras)**

Facts: Nuns, Sisters, Priests or Fathers who also render their services as teachers in schools receiving Grant-in-aid from the State Government claimed that they could not be taxed in respect of the salary received from the State Government. It was argued that they are bound by the Canon Law for their vows of poverty to the Christ and they have suffered a civil death and renounced the world. The salary directly transferred to the individual Bank Account of the Teachers under ECS Scheme belongs to the Institution, Church or the Religion and therefore, they cannot be subjected to the deduction of tax at source as stipulated in Sec. 192 of the Income-tax Act, 1961.

Held: TDS provision of sec. 192 has nothing to do with the religious character of teachers who are paid such salary by the State government. Salary is paid under contract of employment with which Educational Institution or Church or Diocese is not even a privy to such contract of employment qua the State Government. As a payer of salary income, State Government is not bound by any religious tenets or provisions of Canon Law. It has nothing to do with Religious freedom as guaranteed under Articles 25 and 26 of Constitution of India. Salary is therefore subject to deduction of tax at source.

PLACE OF ACCRUAL OF SALARY

Salary earned in India

Sec. 9(1)(*ii*) of the Income-tax Act, 1961 is a deeming provision that creates an artificial place of accrual of salary. It stipulates that the income chargeable under the head 'Salaries' is deemed to accrue in India if it is earned in India.

Services rendered in India

Explanation (*a*) to sec. 9(1)(*ii*) elaborates that if services under the contract of employment are rendered in India it will be considered as income earned in India. The effect of the *Explanation* is that it is no longer open to an assessee to say that though he rendered services in India, since the contract of employment was entered into outside India, the salary could not be said to have accrued or arisen in India.

Case Law : ***CIT* v. *Morgenstern Werner* (2003) 132 Taxman 214/259 ITR 486 (SC)**

Facts: M, a German technician, was appointed on deputation in India by his employer company K based in Germany. He continued to receive salary in Germany from K but received daily allowance from B, an Indian company for whose work K had deputed him in India. Issue emerged whether his salary was chargeable to tax in India.

Held: Since M was not ordinarily resident in India proviso to sec. 5(1)(*c*) was applicable. Salary received by him in Germany was not taxable in India and the same could not be included in the total income to be assessed in India. Further the daily allowance was received from B on account of absence from normal place of duty, this amount was also not taxable being exempt under sec. 10(*14*)(*i*) of the Income-tax Act, 1961.

Case Law : ***CIT* v. *Eli Lilly & Co. (India) (P.) Ltd.* (2009) 178 Taxman 505/312 ITR 225 (SC)**

Facts: E, an Indian company had entered into a joint venture with EN, a foreign company who had seconded four expatriates to the joint venture in India. The four expatriates continued to remain on the rolls of EN, the foreign partner and received home salary outside India. No tax was deducted in respect of the said home salary paid by the foreign company. Issue arose whether the same was deductible for tax purposes in India.

Held: When the home salary/special allowance was paid by EN but the same was only for rendition of services to E, such payment would be deemed to accrue or arise in India as salary earned in India in terms of sec. 9(1)(*ii*).

Salary not taxable in India for services rendered outside India

If services are rendered outside India, such income would not be taxable in India. Salary received by a non-resident/ not ordinarily resident marine engineer for services rendered by him on a foreign going Indian ship which mainly remained away from the Indian coast during the relevant previous year will not be taxable in India. *CIT* v. *Avtar Singh Wadhwan* [2001] 115 Taxman 536/247 ITR 260 (Bom.) Also see *Smt. Sumana Bandyopadhyay* v. *Deputy Director of Income Tax (International Taxation)* [2017] 88 taxmann.com 847/396 ITR 406 (Calcutta), *Director of Income-tax (International Taxation)* v. *Prahlad Vijendra Rao* [2011] 10 taxmann.com 238/198 Taxman 551/239 CTR 107 (Karnataka). According to the clarification issued by Ministry of Finance vide Circular No.13 of 2017, dated 11-4-2017 salary accrued to a non-resident seafarer for services rendered outside India on a foreign ship shall not be included in the total income merely because the said salary has been credited in the NRE (Non-Resident External) account maintained with an Indian bank by the seafarer.

Salary granted during rest period or leave period - As per *Explanation* (*b*) to sec. 9(1)(*ii*) even the rest period or leave period, which is preceded or succeeded by services rendered in India and forms part of the service contract of employment will be deemed to accrue or arise in India. The expression rest period or leave period has been given an extended reading to include payments as a part of stand-by arrangement or retainership fee.

Case Law : ***Reading & Bates Drilling Co.* v. *CIT* (2005) 147 Taxman 499/277 ITR 253 (Uttaranchal)**

Facts: R, a non-resident company, executed off-shore drilling contracts in India and employed technicians to work on the same. Contract for employment provided for on-periods and off-periods and during off-period the technicians so employed had to go back to country of their residence. It was claimed that salary paid for off-period was not taxable in India.

Held: Since both on-period and off-period were forming an integral part of the contract, it was not possible to give separate tax treatments to the periods. Salary earned during the off-period also had nexus with the services rendered in India and therefore the payment received was for his services in India chargeable to tax.

Case Law : ***CIT* v. *Anant Jain* (2012) 21 taxmann.com 19/207 Taxman 117 (Delhi)**

Facts: In this case the upon termination of employment with E, a non-resident company, A received certain amount as severance and vacation encashment for his services. A contended that this amount had accrued outside India for employment rendered outside India and was received outside India and therefore not liable to tax in India.

Held: Since A was 'not ordinarily resident' in India in the year of receipt of the said amount, this amount was not taxable in India as there was no nexus between the severance/vacation/retirement and the payment made by the erstwhile employer.

Salary Payable by Government of India

By virtue of sec. 9(1)(*iii*) income chargeable under the head "Salaries" payable by the Government of India to a citizen of India for service outside India is deemed to accrue or arise in India in the hands of the assessee and will be therefore chargeable to tax in India. In the case of government servants who are citizens of India, any income chargeable under the head "Salaries" is deemed to accrue or arise in India even though they render the services outside India. It is applicable to government employees who are citizens of India and who are posted abroad. They render the services outside India and they may also be paid outside India. Even then they are chargeable to tax for the income falling under the head "Salaries" because their income is deemed to accrue or arise in India by force of this provision.

SCOPE AND DEFINITION OF SALARY

General

Salary, according to the Shorter Oxford English Dictionary, means "to recompense, reward; to pay for something done". In Jowitt's Dictionary of English Law, salary is explained as "a recompense or consideration generally periodically made to a person for his service in another person's business; also wages, stipend, or annual allowance". In Stroud's Judicial Dictionary (4th edition), the expression salary is explained as "where the engagement is for a period, permanent or substantially permanent in character, and is for other than manual or relatively unskilled labour, the remuneration is generally called 'salary'. [*Krishna Murthy (M.)* v. *CIT* [1985] 23 Taxman 126/152 ITR 163 (AP)]. A contract of employment necessarily involves the rendering of services by the employee to the employer and the use of his skill, energy and time for the benefit of the business in which he is employed. An employer is at liberty to remunerate the employee for those services in accordance with the different measures of his choice. Such remuneration is a compensation for employment. [*CIT* v. *T. Abdul Wahid & Co.* (2000) 125 Taxman 702/243 ITR 467 (Madras)]

Sec. 17 of the Income-tax Act, 1961 provides an inclusive definition of the term salary. Accordingly, 'salary' in sec. 17 provides that apart from actual salary received by the employee, it also includes wages, annuity, pension, gratuity, commission, perquisites or profits in lieu of salary or profits in addition to salary. It is couched in wide terms to take into account the remuneration paid to the employee, whether its nomenclature is salary or not. Nomenclature of such remuneration does not make a difference if there exist an employment. For instance, incentive bonus paid to an employee is a salary. [*CIT* v. *T.K. Ginarajan* (2013) 36 taxmann.com 583/217 Taxman 323/356 ITR 618 (SC)]

The various components of the definition of salary are broadly divided as (*a*) salary (*b*) perquisites (*c*) profits in lieu of salary as further discussed. The definitions of salary, perquisite and profits in lieu of salary is only for the purpose of chargeability under section 15 and deductions under the head "salary" under section 16 and cannot be used for any other purpose. The opening words of Sec. 17 clearly states that "for the purpose of secs. 15 and 16, salary includes...". Therefore, the definitions contained in Sec. 17 are only for the purposes of chargeability under sec. 15 and deductions under sec. 16 and not for any other Sections of the Act [*Y.S.C. Babu* v. *Chairman and Managing Director, Syndicate Bank* (2002) 120 Taxman 88/253 ITR 1 (AP)].

Salary [Sec. 17(1)]

According to sec. 17(1), salary includes

(*i*) **Wages [Sec. 17(1)(*i*)]** - Conceptually, there is no difference between salary and wages both being a recompense for work done or services rendered, though ordinarily the former expression is used in connection with services of non-manual type while the latter was used in connection with manual services. [*Gestetner Duplicators Pvt. Ltd.* v. *CIT* (1979) 1 Taxman 1/117 ITR 1 (SC)]

(*ii*) **Annuity or pension [Sec. 17(1)(*ii*)]** - Pension is a periodic payment, made by the employer to the employee after his retirement. Annuities are annual grants and when paid by employer, these are taxable as salary. Annuity or pensions, paid by the employer, whether paid voluntarily or under contractual obligation, are chargeable under the head, "salaries". Annuities, paid by a person other than the employer, are taxable as "income from other sources".

(*iii*) **Gratuity [Sec. 17(1)(*iii*)]** - Gratuity is paid to an employee for long and meritorious service, rendered by him to the employer. It is not paid to an employee gratuitously or merely as a matter of boon. The object of providing gratuity is to provide a retiring benefit to workmen who have rendered long and unblemished service to the employer, and thereby contributed to the prosperity of the employer. Any gratuity paid by an employer to the employee is taxable as salary.

(*iv*) **Fees, commissions, perquisites or profits in lieu of or in addition to salary or wages [Sec. 17(1)(*iv*)]** - When under the terms of the contract of employment, remuneration in the form of commission is determined at a fixed percentage of turnover achieved by the employee, then such commission will be characterized as salary. Any commission paid or allowed to an employee, which is not based on the turnover achieved by him, is still chargeable u/s 17(*iv*) as commission but does not partake the character of basic salary u/s 17(1)(*i*).

(*v*) **advance of salary [Sec. 17(1)(*v*)]** - If an employee takes an advance of salary, it is taxable on receipt basis

(*vi*) **leave salary [Sec. 17(1)(*va*)]** - Leaves accumulated and later encashed are taxable.

(*vii*) **Annual accretion to the balance of Recognized Provident Fund [Sec. 17(1)(*vi*)]:** When the employee is a member of a Recognised Provident Fund, the amount contributed by the employer in this fund in excess of 12 per cent of the salary of the employee is to be included in the salary income. If interest is credited on or after 1 April 2001 on the accumulated balance standing to the credit under Recognised Provident Fund and the rate of interest does not exceed 9.5%, the amount of interest so credited is fully exempt. If the rate of interest exceeds 9.5%, the amount of interest credited on the accumulated balance at a rate in excess of 9.5% is liable to be included in salary income

(*viii*) **Transferred balance in Recognized Provident Fund [Sec. 17(1)(*vii*)]** - When an unrecognised provident fund is recognised for the first time, the balance in the unrecognised provident fund is known as "Transferred balance". The employer's share (contribution in unrecognised provident fund and interest on employer's share) is included in the salary income for income-tax purposes at the time of such transfer

(*ix*) Contribution by Central Government or any other employer to Employees Pension Account as referred in sec. 80CCD. **[Sec. 17(1)(*viii*)]**

(*x*) Contribution by the Central Government to Agniveer Corpus Fund account of an individual enrolled in the Agnipath Scheme referred to sec. 80CCH **[Sec. 17(1)(*ix*)]**

Perquisites [Sec. 17(2)]

In common parlance the word 'perquisite' is defined as any perk or benefit attached to a position. These are usually non-cash benefits given by an employer to an employee in addition to entitled salary or remuneration. Sec. 17(2) provides an inclusive definition of the term perquisites. Perquisites include all benefits and amenities provided by the employer to the employee in addition to salary and wages either in cash or in kind which are convertible into money. These benefits or amenities may be provided either voluntarily or under service contract. For income-tax purposes, the perquisites are of three types:

(*i*) Taxable Perquisites

(*a*) the value of rent-free accommodation provided to the assessee by his employer

(*b*) the value of any concession in the matter of rent respecting any accommodation provided to the assessee by his employer

(*c*) any sum paid by the employer in respect of any obligation which, but for such payment, would have been payable by the assessee

(*d*) Sum paid by the employer (directly or indirectly) for effecting an assurance on the life of the employee or for providing an annuity. If the amount is paid to a recognised provident fund or an approved superannuation fund, or to a deposit linked insurance fund established under the Coal Mines Provident Fund Act or Employees' Provident Fund Act, the sum so paid is not to be included in the salary income

(*e*) the value of any specified security or sweat equity shares allotted or transferred, directly or indirectly, by the employer, or former employer, free of cost or at concessional rate to the assessee

(*f*) the amount of any contribution to an approved superannuation fund by the employer in respect of the assessee, to the extent it exceeds one lakh and fifty thousand rupees (applicable before 1.4.2021)(replaced with a two new clauses as described in (*g*) and (*h*))

(*g*) the amount of contribution in excess of ₹ 7,50,000 by the employer in recognized provident fund, National Pension Scheme and approved superannuation fund taken together (applicable w.e.f. 1.4.2021)

(*h*) any interest, dividend or any other amount of similar nature on the excess contribution refered to in (*g*) above.

(*i*) the value of any other fringe benefit or amenity as may be prescribed

(*ii*) Perquisites taxable under specified cases

The value of certain benefit or amenity granted or provided free of cost or at a concessional rate in any of the following cases only shall be included in the salary income:

(*a*) by a company to an employee who is director thereof [It is immaterial whether the director is full time or part time director];

(*b*) by a company concern to an employee, being a person who has a substantial interest in the company concern, *i.e.*, employee is the beneficial owner of at least 20 per cent of the equity shares of that company or is entitled to at least 20 per cent share is profit of the concern;

(*c*) an employee whose income chargeable under head salaries (exclusive of the value of all benefits or amenities not provided by way of monetary payments) excess ₹ 50,000, is a specified employed.

Sec. 17 of the Act applies to the cases only where the perquisite is provided to the employees but not to the members of their families.

Case Law : ***ACIT* v. *P.R. Parthasarathy* (1979) 118 ITR 869 (AP)**

Facts: P an officer of an Indian company was invited by the company's London office to visit London and Canada. The company insisted that the wife of the assessee accompanied him on his business tour to London and Canada and the company incurred expenses for both the assessee and his wife.

Held: Foreign tour of wife of assessee at cost of company could not be brought within ambit of definition of 'perquisite' under sec. 17. It was the company that desired that the assessee's wife should also join him in the tour for the reason stated by it in its letter to the assessee. Therefore, it cannot be taxed as perquisite.

Case Law : ***Mrs. Sugra Sulaiman* v. *CIT* (1990) 44 Taxman 1/181 ITR 444 (Madras)**

Facts: The employer company of S incurred expenditure on a foreign tour of S when she accompanied her husband who was the managing director of the same company.

Held: The foreign tour should be considered to be a personal one, an obligation that had been met by the company in which the assessee was an employee. The amount paid by the company in discharge of the obligation of the assessee was regarded as perquisite falling under sec. 17(2)(*iv*).

(*iii*) Tax-free perquisites

The value of the following perquisites is not to be included in the salary income of an employee:

(*a*) The value of any medical facility provided to an employee or his family member in any hospitals, clinics, etc. maintained by the employer.

(*b*) Reimbursement of expenditure actually incurred by the employee on medical treatment for self or for his family members in any hospitals, dispensaries etc. maintained by the Government or local authority or in a hospital approved under the Central Health Scheme or any similar scheme of the state Government or in a hospital, approved by the chief commissioner having regard to the prescribed guidelines for the purposes of medical treatment of the prescribed diseases or ailments. The Finance Act, 2022 extends such reimbursements in respect of any illness relating to COVID-19 subject to such conditions as the Central Government may notify.

(*c*) Group medical insurance obtained by the employer for his employees (including family members of the employees) or all medical insurance payments made directly or reimbursement of insurance premium to such employees who take such insurance.

(*d*) Any expenditure incurred or paid by the employer on the medical treatment of the employee or any family member of the employee outside India, the travel and stay abroad of such employee or any family member of such employee or any travel or stay abroad of one attendant who accompanies the patient in connection with such treatment will not be included in perquisites of the employee.

However, the travel expenditure shall be excluded from the perquisites only when the employee's gross total income as computed before including the said expenditure does not exceed two lakh rupees and further to such conditions and limits as the Board may prescribe having regard to guidelines, if any, issued by the Reserve Bank of India.

Profits in lieu of salary [Sec. 17(3)]

(*i*) **Compensation received from employer** - By virtue of sec. 17(3)(*i*) any due to an assessee-employee as a right under any statute, award or contract of employment or received by him from his employer or former employer irrespective of his entitlement to receive the same, is now included within the meaning of the expression 'profits in lieu of salary'.

(*ii*) **Compensation for termination of employment** - Any compensation received by an employee from his employer in connection with termination of his employment is taxable as profits in lieu of salary. Termination of service can take place either by resignation or by dismissal or by compulsory retirement or on attaining superannuation or by voluntary retirement. Even a notice pay received by an employee is taxable as compensation for termination of employment.

(*iii*) **Compensation for modification of terms and conditions of service** - Though the relationship of employer and employee may continue, the terms and conditions of service may be rearranged or modified. For example, under the modified terms and conditions, the employee may be paid a lump sum in consideration of a cut in his future remuneration. The lump sum so received by way of compensation is taxable as profits in lieu of salary.

(*iv*) **Surrender Value of Keyman Insurance Policy** - Keyman insurance policy is taken by an employer on the life of a keyman employee, *i.e.* an employee whose services contribute substantially to the success of the business. The object of keyman insurance is to indemnify the employer from the loss of earnings resulting from the death of a valuable employee. The amount of keyman insurance can be estimated as the monetary value of the likely setback to the profits of the concern due to the death of keyman. The amount of policy is paid either on the maturity of the policy or death of the keyman, whichever is earlier.

Where an employer assigns a keyman insurance policy to such employee at the time of his retirement as a reward for his services, the surrender value of such policy at the time of retirement is taxable in the hands of such employee as profits in lieu of salary. No exemption is available in this respect.

(*v*) **Payments from Unrecognised Provident Fund** - If any payment from an unrecognised provident fund becomes due and payable to an employee, such receipts to the extent of employer's contribution and interest thereon are liable to be taxed as profits in lieu of salary. Employee's contribution is not charged to tax as it is already taxed in the respective years of contributions as a part of his gross salary. Interest on the employee's contribution from unrecognised provident fund is chargeable to tax as income from "other sources" and not as profits in lieu of salary.

(*vi*) **Any other payment, due or received, from an employer before joining employment or after cessation of employment -** Any other payment from the employer or former employer is taxable as profits in lieu. The clause *"any payment received by an assessee from an employer or a former employer"* used in Sec. 17(3)(*ii*) is wide enough to catch all the payments of the nature paid to the assessee by his employer or former employer to a person for something done as an employee. [*V.R.Granthi* v. *CIT* (1995) 82 Taxman 37/216 ITR 48 (Andhra Pradesh)]

However, payments made to an employee which are not related to any service rendered but on account of personal considerations cannot be charged as profits in lieu of salary. For instance, payment made by the employer to compensate the employee for loss of movable assets, suffered by the employee, cannot be taxed as profit in lieu of salary, as such payment has no relation to the services rendered but is merely to compensate him for a personal loss. Payments made on personal grounds where there is no element of remuneration for services do not fall within the ambit of profits in lieu of salary under sec. 17(3)(*ii*) and are not taxable in their hands. [*Lachhman Dass* v. *CIT* (1980) 3 Taxman 560/124 ITR 706 (Delhi)]. If money accrues to a person by virtue of his office or employment, it does not matter whether it was voluntary or it was compulsory on the part of the person who paid it. Such amount is taxable. [*Herbert (Rev. G. N.)* v. *J. A. McQuade* (1902) 2 KB 631] If the payment is made by an employer as personal gift for appreciation of qualities of employee or for reasons unconnected with employment cannot be considered as profits in lieu of salary. [*Reed* v. *Seymour* (1927) 11 TC 625]

Payment of *ex gratia* amount by employer has posed vexed questions of tax implications. *Ex gratia* is an amount paid by an employer to an employee voluntarily without any obligation. Taxability of such amount in the hands of the employee depends on its nexus with the service rendered by the employee. Where it can be demonstrated that such payment is in fact in connection with services rendered, it is liable to be taxed as profits in lieu of salary. However, to determine the nexus with service, each case should be evaluated carefully on its own merits. It is, however, clarified by Circular No. 573 dated 21-11-1990 that a lump sum payment made gratuitously or by way of compensation or otherwise to the widow or other legal heirs of an employee, who dies while still in active service, is not taxable.

It must be noted that while bringing within its ambit any amount due to or received by an employee 'from any person', sec. 17(3)(*iii*) contemplates two situations - (*a*) when such payment is before his joining any employment with that person or (*b*) after cessation of his employment with that person. Both situations presupposes the existence of an employment. Therefore when an amount was received by a prospective employee 'as compensation for denial of employment', such amount was not in the nature of profits in lieu of salary. It is a capital receipt that could not be taxed as income under any other head. [*CIT* v. *Smt. Rani Shankar Mishra* [2009] 178 Taxman 324/[2010] 320 ITR 542 (Delhi), *CIT* v. *Pritam Das Narang* [2016] 61 taxmann.com 332/235 Taxman 358/[2016] 381 ITR 416 (Delhi)]

Case Law: *Mahesh Anantrai Pattani* v. *CIT* (1961) 41 ITR 481 (SC)

Facts: A Maharaja voluntarily gave an ex-gratia to his long-serving Dewan on termination of his employment with a letter that the amount was a gift as a token of his affection for the assessee and his family.

Held: The *ex gratia* should be considered as a personal gift and therefore not taxable as salary in lieu of profits.

Case Law : *V.R. Granthi* v. *CIT* (1995) 82 Taxman 37/216 ITR 48 (AP)

Facts: G who resigned the job owing to ill-health was paid an amount of four months' salary as *ex gratia* stating that the said amount was as a token of his long and meritorious service to the company.

Held: The amount was paid to G not as personal gift or testimony but for his past services as an employee. The payment should be considered taxed as profit in lieu of salary.

Case Law : *J.K. Helene Curtis Ltd.* v. *CIT* (1999) 103 Taxman 162/236 ITR 403 (Bom.)

Facts: The executive director of the company was paid a certain amount as a special bonus for the exceptional services rendered by him.

Held: The payment was liable to tax as profit in lieu of salary.

Allowances

An allowance is a sum of money, allowed or granted, by an employer to an employee for a particular purpose. While there is no defined list of such allowances, few of the popular instances of allowances that can be cited are: Dearness allowance (DA) or dearness pay, city compensatory allowance (CCA), house rent allowance (HRA), project allowance, medical allowance, refreshment, lunch or tiffin allowance, proctor allowance, warden allowance, non-practicing allowance, telephone allowance, leave travel allowance, rural area allowance, entertainment allowance, family allowance.

Thus, when employees union of B challenged taxability of dearness allowance on the basis that since dearness allowance is paid only to offset erosion in wages it is not income, it was held that dearness allowance paid to offset the rise in prices is still income and cannot be excluded from the ambit of salary. There is no exemption in regard to dearness allowance. On a joint reading of secs. 2(24), 14, 15 and 17 of the Act makes it clear that dearness allowance is part of salary and is liable to be taxed. "Any allowance granted to the assessee either to meet his personal expenses at the place where the duties of his office or employment of profit are ordinarily performed by him or at a place where he ordinarily resides or to compensate him for the increased cost of living". [*Brooke Bond Employees Union* v. *Union of India* (1989) 46 Taxman 203/179 ITR 533 (Patna)]

All Allowances are Taxable Unless Specially Exempt

Sec. 2(24) of the Act which gives a wide and inclusive definition to the word "income" which includes in its scope, *inter alia,* under sec. 2(*24*)(*iiia*), (*iiib*), all allowances or benefits specifically granted to the assessee to meet expenses wholly, necessarily and exclusively for the purpose of the duties of an office or expenses at a place where duties of his office are ordinarily performed. Besides, the word "salary" is also given an exhaustive meaning. Therefore, all allowances, even allowances such as city compensatory allowance, house rent allowance or other such allowances given for reimbursing the expenditure incurred by the employees are also taxable as salaries. Income tax is attracted at the point when the income is earned and taxability of income is not dependent upon its destination or the manner of its utilisation.

In the landmark ruling of *Karamchari Union* v. *Union of India* (2000) 109 Taxman 1/243 ITR 143 (SC) various employees of the Central Government, State Government, banks and general insurance contended that the amount of CCA, DA, HRA paid by employers was merely reimbursing extra cost incurred by employees and in some cases, such allowances fell short of the actual costs incurred by employees. Therefore these payments cannot be treated as 'profits' in the hands of the assessees. Further, taxing these payments caused hardship to honest employees having limited source of income and required to meet extra expenses at the station when transferred. Supreme Court held that in view of the inclusive meaning of 'profits in lieu of salary', 'salary' and 'income' DA, CCA and HRA will be taxable income. Equity or hardship would hardly be relevant ground for interpretation of tax law.

Exemption on Allowances

Exemption on special allowances granted for performance of official duty

Under sec. 10(*14*)(*i*) of the Income-tax Act, 1961 read with rule 2BB(1) of the Income-tax Rules, 1962 any special allowance or benefit which is granted to perform official duties of employment will be exempt from tax to the extent of expenses incurred. However, such allowances

(*a*) should not be a perquisite and

(*b*) must have been specifically granted to meet expenses wholly, necessarily and exclusively incurred in the performance of the duties of an office or employment of profit.

For instance, travel allowance, tour allowance, daily allowance, conveyance allowance, research allowance, helper allowance, uniform allowance are exempt from tax on the basis of actual expenditure incurred or the amount of allowance, whichever is less.

Conveyance Allowance - It must be noted that mere use of the phrase 'conveyance allowance' by itself would not mean that it is to be exempted from tax. In order to avail exemption under sec. 10(*14*)(*i*) it is absolutely essential that the allowance is paid for expenses incurred for performance of duties. If such conveyance allowance is paid all employees whether on duty or not irrespective of his place of residence and the place of his work and also irrespective of whether he is posted in any of the offices, it cannot qualify for exemption. [Life *Insurance Corporation Class-I Officers (Bombay) Association* v. *Life Insurance Corporation of India* [1998] 229 ITR 510 (Bombay)]

Living Allowance/Daily Allowance

When assessee are required to stay away from their homes the daily allowance given to them is relatable to the extra expenditure incurred by them on food etc., which is wholly, necessarily and exclusively for the purpose of duties and as such the allowance is in the nature of reimbursement which would qualify for exemption. [*CIT* v. *Goslino Mario* (2000) 241 ITR 312 (SC). *Also see CIT* v. *Morgenstern Werner* (2003) 132 Taxman 214/259 ITR 486 (SC)].

Uniform Allowance - When an employer grants allowance to its employees to meet the expenditure incurred on the purchase or maintenance of uniform during performance of duties of office, it will squarely fall within the purview of sec. 10(*14*)(*i*). In an interesting case before Gujarat High Court, the employer company had prescribed a uniform to its employees which was later withdrawn but uniform allowance was continued to be paid. The employer suggested that dress code at the work place would qualify as uniform, and expenditure towards the same qualifies for exemption. Dispute arose if the allowance qualified for uniform allowance. High Court observed that there is a distinction between a dress code and a uniform. In common parlance 'dress code' is often referred to as the minimum standard of dressing depending on the place or occasion and can carry a wide range of choices at the command of the person concerned. Uniform on the other hand necessarily include precise instructions as to the dress, design, and colours to attain uniformity in dressing at a work place or at the place of study. It was therefore held that when the employer had not prescribed any uniform, payment made to employees in name of uniform allowance cannot be exempted under sec. 10(*14*)(*i*). [*Oil & Natural Gas Corporation Ltd.* v. *Asstt. CIT* (2016) 73 taxmann.com 273/243 Taxman 105/289 CTR 403 (Gujarat)

Exemption on allowances granted to meet personal expenditure

Under sec. 10(*14*)(*ii*) read with rule 2BB(2) of the Income-tax Rules, 1962 any allowance granted to the employee to meet personal expenses or that are special compensatory allowances will be exempt to the extent of amount received or the limits specified whichever is less. For instance, any special compensatory allowance such as tribal area allowance, high altitude allowance, border area allowance etc. will be exempt according to the limits prescribed. Similarly, any such allowance granted to meet his personal expenses such as children education allowance, children hostel allowance, transport allowance will be exempt as per limits prescribed in rule 2BB(2).

Exemption on House Rent Allowance - By virtue of sec. 10(13A) of the Income-tax Act, 1961 any special allowance granted to an assessee by his employer to meet expenditure actually incurred on payment of rent in respect of residential accommodation occupied by the assessee shall be exempt to the extent prescribed under Income-tax Rules, 1962 rules 2 and 26A. Such an exemption takes into consideration the area or place in which such accommodation is situated and other relevant considerations. However, no exemption can be availed if the residential accommodation occupied by the assessee is owned by him or the assessee has not actually incurred expenditure on payment of rent. In order to avail this exemption it is essential that the assessee furnish evidence of the actual rent paid. A few interesting case laws in this regard will be helpful.

Case Law : ***Mrs. Meena Vaswani* v. *ACIT* (2017) 80 taxmann.com 2/164 ITD 120 (Mumbai - Trib.)**

Facts: M had a self-occupied property jointly held with her husband. M claimed that she lived with her mother in her house for care giving purposes and that she had been paying a rent her mother and therefore sought to avail exemption under sec. 10(13A) for the HRA paid by her employer. The Tribunal considered that receipts were duly produced, however, the mother of M had not filed any tax returns and there was no evidence as leave and license agreement, letter to society intimating about her tenancy etc.

Held: The whole arrangement of rent payment by assessee to her mother was a sham transaction which was undertaken with sole intention to claim exemption of HRA under sec. 10(13A) and M's cannot be allowed exemption.

Case Law : ***Bajrang Prasad Ramdharani* v. *ACIT* (2013) 37 taxmann.com 186/60 SOT 66 (Ahmedabad - Trib.)(URO)**

Facts: B was paying rent to his wife through bank transfer entry for living in the house owned by the assessee's wife.

Held: A verification of the entries showed transfer on the given dates and the twin requirements of the provision, *i.e.*, occupation of the house and the payment of rent were fulfilled.

HRA paid to the High Court and Supreme Court Judges

Sec. 10(13A) of the Income-tax Act, 1961, read with secs. 22A and 22D of the High Court Judges (Conditions of Service) Act, 1954 stipulates that house rent allowance paid to a judge of a High Court will be exempt from income tax. However, the definition of the term 'judge' under the High Court Judges (Conditions of Service) Act, 1954 means only a sitting High Court Judge. Retired Judges of High Court or Supreme Court appointed by the Central Government or State Government for any purpose or to any post would be under the Government of India or the concerned State Government, as the case may be, and not a constitutional post of Chief Justice or Judges of a High Court so as to attract the provisions of sec. 22D of the High Court Judges (Conditions of Service) Act. Therefore cannot claim exemption. [*Justice Challa Kondaiah* v. *CIT* (2001) 119 Taxman 511/252 ITR 854 (Andhra Pradesh]

Exemption on leave travel concession (LTC)/leave fare concession (LFC)

Sec. 10(5) of the Income-tax Act, 1961 read with rule 2B of the Income-tax Rules, 1962 stipulates that the value of any travel concession or assistance received by or due to an assessee from his employer or former employer, as the case may be, for himself and his family, in connection with his proceeding (*i*) on leave to any place in India, or (*ii*) to any place in India after the retirement from service, or (*iii*) to any place in India after the termination of his service. It must be noted that the exemption is available only for travel to any place in India.

The exemption is admissible in respect of actual expenditure incurred for journeys performed, not only by the assessee but also by his family. Here, family includes the spouse and children of the individual and the parents or brothers or sisters wholly or mainly dependent on the individual. However, no exemption is allowed for undertaking overseas travel. [*Om Parkash Gupta* v. *ITO* (2013) 33 taxmann.com 169/58 SOT 304 (Chandigarh - Trib.)]

Exemption to allowances payable to outside India - As per sec. 10(7) any allowances or perquisites paid or allowed as such outside India by the Government to a citizen of India for rendering service outside India are exempt from tax.

Exemption to allowances of MPs/MLAs - By virtue of sec. 10(17) daily allowance and constituency allowance received by Members of Parliament or Members of Legislative Assembly will be exempt from tax.

Exemption to allowances of Chairperson of Union Public Service Commission (UPSC) - Under sec. 10(45) all such allowances or perquisites as notified by the Central Government in the Official Gazette will be exempt in the hands of the Chairman or a retired Chairman or any other member or retired member of the Union Public Service Commission.

DEDUCTIONS UNDER SALARY

Standard Deduction - The Finance Act, 2018 has reinserted standard deduction for the salaried class. It was withdrawn by the Finance Act, 2005. By virtue of sec. 16(*ia*) a standard deduction of ₹ 50,000 will be available under the head salary with effect from 1st April 2019. Standard deduction proceeds on the assumption that an employee would be required to incur certain expenditure in order to earn his salary and consequently, irrespective of the actual amount of such expenditure, a flat deduction is available. Such deduction can be claimed by an assessee whether he is in actual employment or a pensioner. [*CIT* v. *K.R. Patel* [1994] 205 ITR 405/77 Taxman 515 (Gujarat); *CIT* v. *Brigadier B.D. Khurana* [1996] 217 ITR 381 (Allahabad)] According to the response of Central Board of Direct Taxes on FAQs pertaining to salary, since family pension is taxable under the head income from other sources, standard deduction is not applicable in case of Family Pension.

When the assessee receives salary from more than one employer, standard deduction should be computed with reference to aggregate salary due to him and such deduction shall in no case exceed monetary ceiling specified therein. [*CIT* v. *N.Gopalsamy* (2001) 118 Taxman 152 (Madras)]. Since a partner receiving salary from the firm is not characterized as income from salary. Consequently, assessee-partner cannot claim standard deduction. [*CIT* v. *Pramod Kumar Jain* (1995) 80 Taxman 333/216 ITR 598 (Rajasthan)]

Entertainment Allowance - Under sec. 16(*ii*) entertainment allowance granted to a government employee is eligible for the following deduction:

(*a*) a sum equal to one-fifth of his salary (excluding any allowance, benefit or other perquisite) or

(*b*) ₹ 5000/-,

whichever is less. It is evident from the wordings of the sec. that such deduction is not available for non-government employee.

Professional Tax- Article 276 of the Constitution of India empowers State Legislature to impose taxes in respect of professions, trades, callings or employment which shall not exceed ₹ 2500/- per annum. When an employee has paid such a professional tax, the same will be available as a deduction under sec. 16(*iii*).

EXEMPTION FROM SALARY INCOME FOR CERTAIN INDIVIDUALS

Exemption to Remuneration of Diplomats etc. [Sec. 10(6)(*ii*)] - Remuneration received by a Diplomat as an official, by whatever name called, of an embassy, high commission, legation, commission, consulate or the trade representation of a foreign State, or as a member of the staff of any of these officials, for service in such capacity. However, the remuneration received by him as a trade commissioner or other official representative in India of the Government of a foreign State (not holding office as such in an honorary capacity), or as a member of the staff of any of those officials, shall be exempt only if the remuneration of the corresponding officials or, as the case may be, members of the staff, if any, of the Government of India, resident for similar purposes in the country concerned enjoys a similar exemption in that country that such members of the staff are subjects of the country represented and are not engaged in any business or profession or employment in India otherwise than as members of such staff.

Exemption to Remuneration of an Employee of a Foreign Enterprise [Sec. 10(6)(*vi*)]

The remuneration received by him as an employee of a foreign enterprise for services rendered by him during his stay in India may be exempt from tax provided the following conditions are fulfilled:

Conditions:

(*a*) The foreign enterprise is not engaged in any trade or business in India;

(*b*) His stay in India does not exceed in aggregate a period of 90 days in such previous year; and

(*c*) Such remuneration is not liable to be deducted from the income of the employer, chargeable under this Act.

Remuneration to employees of a business concern is an allowable deduction while computing the taxable profits of business. But an exception has been made in this case. The employer cannot deduct the remuneration paid to the employees of a foreign enterprise. Consequently, the taxable profits will go up, and thus the employer is indirectly taxed on such remuneration.

Exemption to Salary of Non-resident Foreign Crew of a Foreign Ship [Sec. 10(6)(*viii*)]

Any income chargeable under the head "Salaries" received by or due to an individual, who is not a citizen of India and also non-resident in India, as remuneration for services rendered in connection with his employment on a foreign ship is exempt, provided his total stay in India does not exceed in the aggregate 90 days in the previous year.

Remuneration of a Foreign Government Employee in Connection with his Training in India at Specified Undertakings [Sec. 10(6)(*xi*)]

Remuneration received by a non-Indian citizen employee of a foreign State during his stay in India in connection with his training is exempt.

Establishments for Training - The training may be imparted in any establishment or office of, or in any undertaking owned by:

(*a*) the government; or

(*b*) any company in which the entire paid-up share capital is held by the Central Government or any State Government or Governments, partly by the Central Government and partly by one or more State Government; or

(*c*) any company which is the subsidiary of a company referred to in item (*b*); or

(*d*) any corporation established by or under a Central, State or Provincial Act; or

(*e*) any society registered under the Societies Registration Act 1860, or under any other corresponding law for the time being in force and wholly financed by the Central Government or any State Government or State Governments, or partly by the Central Government and partly by one or more State Government.

Exemption to salary income of a member of Scheduled Tribe [Sec. 10(*26*)] - Income of a member of a Scheduled Tribe as per article 366(25) of the Constitution is exempt from tax, if following conditions are satisfied:

- Such member resides in any area in the State of Nagaland, Manipur, Tripura, Arunachal Pradesh, Mizoram or district of North Cachar Hills, The Karbi Anglong District, The Bodoland Territorial Areas District, Khasi Hills, Jaintia Hills and Garo Hills or in the Ladakh region of the State of Jammu and Kashmir.
- Such exemption is available in respect of income which accrues/arises from any source in such areas or income by way of dividends/interest on securities arises from any area.

Thus, three conditions which are essential to be entitled to exemption under this sec.: (*i*) The person claiming exemption should be a member of a Scheduled Tribe as defined in Article 366(25) of the Constitution; (*ii*) he should be residing in the specified areas and (*iii*) the income in respect of which exemption is claimed must be an income which accrues or which arises to him (*a*) from any source in the specified area or (*b*) by way of dividend or interest. Benefit of sec. 10(26) is available to all members of the Scheduled Tribes declared as such under article 342 as long as they are residing in the areas specified. Thus, it can be gathered that persons earing income while residing in specified areas and belong to the Scheduled Tribes are entitled to the benefit of exemption from payment of income tax.

The constitutional validity of this exemption section was challenged in *ITO* v. *N. Takin Roy Rymbai* [1976] 103 ITR 82 (SC). Here the assessee was a member of Scheduled Tribe in the State of Meghalaya and posted at Shillong as Secretary to the Government of Assam. The Assam Secretariat building and office, which constitute his place of work was outside area specified for the purposes of this sec. and therefore his salary income was assessed and charged to tax. The assessee claimed that sec. 10(26) was invalid and *ultra vires* Article 14 of the Constitution. Reversing the decision of the High Court, Supreme Court upheld the constitutional validity of this sec. Whilst Supreme Court conceded that taxation law cannot claim immunity from the equality clause in Article 14 of the Constitution, in view of the intrinsic complexity of fiscal adjustments of diverse elements, the State have a wide discretion in the matter of classification for taxation purposes. Given legislative competence, the legislature has ample freedom to select and classify persons, districts, goods, properties incomes and objects which it would tax. So long as the classification made within this wide and flexible range by a taxing statute does not transgress the fundamental principles underlying the doctrine of equality, it is not vulnerable on the ground of discrimination merely because it taxes or exempts from tax some incomes or objects and not others. Nor the mere fact that a tax falls more heavily on some in the same category, is by itself a ground to render the law invalid. Sec. 10(26) was based on a intelligible differentia- the object of this differentiation between income accruing or received from a source in the specified areas and the income accruing or received from a source outside such areas to benefit not only the members of the Scheduled Tribes residing in the specified areas but also to benefit economically such areas.

This intelligible differentia when read in combination with Article 46 of the Constitution which provides a directive principle for state policy for the promotion of educational and economic interest of the weaker secs of the people, particularly the Scheduled Castes and Scheduled Tribes lent constitutional validity to this sec.

However, the scope and ambit of the word 'residing' has to be given its natural meaning that a person has an abode and is living in a particular area for his work and livelihood for a reasonably long length of time. A member of a Scheduled Tribe would be entitled to the benefit of sec. 10(26) only when he is posted in the specified areas. Once he is posted outside the specified areas then he ceases to reside in the specified area and the income does not accrue to him in the specified area. [*Chandra Mohan Sinku* v. *UOI* [2015] 55 taxmann.com 383/230 Taxman 383/372 ITR 627 (Tripura) (FB)].

Case Law : ***Pradip Kr. Taye* v. *Union of India* (2010) 189 Taxman 483/320 ITR 29 (Gauhati) (FB)**

Facts: Assessees who originally belonged to the State of Assam and recognized as Scheduled Tribe (ST), were employed by N, a Government Company on vacancies reserved for the scheduled tribes. Assessees were deputed to work at different places in the State of Arunachal Pradesh which is an area specified in the Sixth Schedule to the Constitution. The issue was whether they would continue to be entitled to the exemption since they had migrated from their place of origin to another place.

Held: The expression "residing in any area specified" occurring under sec. 10(26) cannot be given a narrow and restricted meaning to imply that upon migration from their place of origin to another areas specified, members of scheduled tribe would be disqualified for availing benefits of sec. 10(26).

Remuneration of an employee working under the Co-operative Technical Assistance Programme [Sec. 10(8)] - In the case of an individual who is assigned duties in India in connection with co-operative technical assistance programmes and projects in accordance with an agreement entered into by the Central Government with the Government of a foreign State, the terms of which provide for the exemption from tax, (*a*) the remuneration received by the individual directly or indirectly from the Government of that foreign State for such duties and (*b*) any other income of such individual which accrues or arises outside India (but is not deemed to accrue or arise in India) and in respect of which such individual is required to pay any income-tax or social security tax to the Government of that foreign State, would be exempt from income-tax.

By virtue of the Finance Act, 2022 this exemption has been withdrawn from the assessment year 2023-24.

The expression 'remuneration' in this sec. is a word interpreted to have wider meaning than 'Salary'. It includes salary and other kinds of wages which may be paid a quid pro quo for the services rendered. This exemption will apply to all such employees of the foreign state who are so assigned duties. It does not to restricted to the citizens of that foreign state but covered Indian nationals also who are so assigned duties. **[*CIT* v. *Prem Bhandhu Gupta* [1985] 21 Taxman 228/156 ITR 737 (Delhi)]**.

Case Law : ***Dr. Jyoti Vajpayee* v. *CIT* (2017) 77 taxmann.com 276/392 ITR 518 (Allahabad)**

Facts: 'J', being a member of the U.P. Provincial Medical Services Cadre in the State of U.P., was offered an appointment to work in a collaborative family planning programme entered into between the Government of India and USA. Issue was whether 'J' was entitled to exemption under sec.10(8).

Held: As per the job description offering appointment 'J' was required to perform duties relating to the said project in India. Even if it was not the State government of U.P., the original employer, that had assigned such duties to 'J'.

Remuneration received by an employee of a consultant referred to in Sec. 10(8A) as well income of family member of such employee [Sec. 10(8B)] - Sec. 10(8B) grants exemption to an individual who is assigned to duties in India in connection with any technical assistance programme or project in accordance with an agreement entered into by the Central Government and the international organisation (hereinafter referred to as the agency) from:

(*a*) the remuneration received by him directly or indirectly, for such duties from any consultant referred to in sec. 10(8A)

(*b*) any other income of such individual which accrues or arises outside India, and is not deemed to accrue or arise in India, in respect of which such individual is required to pay any income tax or social security tax to the country of his origin, provided:

(*i*) the individual is an employee of the consultant as defined in Sec. 10(8A) and is either not a citizen of India or, being a citizen of India is not ordinarily resident in India, and

(*ii*) the contract of service of such individual is approved by the prescribed authority before the commencement of his service.

Under Sec.10(9) income of any member of the family of any such employee who accompanied him to India that accrues or arises outside India, and is not deemed to accrue or arise in India was also exempt from tax in India. However it was required that such family member was required to pay any income tax or social security tax with respect to such income to the Government of that foreign State or its country of origin.

By virtue of the Finance Act, 2022, this exemption under sec. 10(8B) and (9) is withdrawn and the same shall not be available from the assessment year 2023-24.

Exemption to employee when his tax liability is borne by employer [Sec. 10(10CC)] – By virtue of sec. 17(2)(*iv*) any sum paid by the employer in respect of any obligation which, but for such payment, would have been payable by the assessee will be treated as perquisite in the hands of the employee chargeable to tax under the head salary. Sec. 10(10CC) was introduced by the Finance Act, 2002 with effect from 1-4-2003 that exempted tax paid by employer on behalf of employee with respect to non-monetary perquisites granted to employee. Take for instance *RBF Rigs Corpn., LIC* v. *ACIT* (2007) 18 SOT 466/109 ITD 141 (Delhi-Trib.) (SB). As per the terms of employment, expatriate secondment employees were to be paid salary 'net of taxes' and taxes were to be borne by the employer company. The Special Bench held that tax paid by the employer on behalf of the employee is discharge of an obligation of the employee which but for such payment would have been payable by the employee himself. It is a perquisite fully covered by sec. 17(2)(*iv*). However, it is not money which is paid to the employee when taxes are paid on his behalf. Even if such discharge may be a monetary gain or monetary benefits to the employee it is not a monetary payment to the employee. Therefore, tax paid by employer on salaries/ remuneration of employees would constitute non-monetary benefits and, as such, same would be exempted under sec. 10(*10CC*). Also see *Yoshio Kubo* v. *CIT* [2013] 36 taxmann.com 1/218 Taxman 164/357 ITR 452 (Delhi) and *DIT (Inter-*

national Taxation) v. *Sedco Forex International Drilling Inc* [2012] 25 taxmann.com 238/210 Taxman 25/252 CTR 448 (Uttaranchal)

EXEMPTION ON TERMINATION/RETIREMENT BENEFITS

Death-cum-retirement Gratuity [Sec. 10(10)]

Fully Exempt [Sec. 10(10)(*i*)] - The amount of any death-cum-retirement gratuity received under the following will be fully exempt from tax:

(*i*) the revised pension rules of the Central Government; or

(*ii*) the Central Civil Services (Pension) Rules, 1972; or

(*iii*) any similar scheme applicable to (*a*), the members of civil services of the Union, or (*b*) holders of posts connected with defence or of civil posts under the Union, or (*c*) the member of All India Services, or (*d*) the members of civil services of a State, or (*e*) holders of civil posts under a State, or (*f*) employees of a local authority, or (*g*) Pension Code or Regulations applicable to the members of the defence services

Where employees are covered by Payment of Gratuity Act, 1972- Any gratuity received under the Payment of Gratuity Act, 1972 will be exempt from tax to the extent it does not exceed an amount calculated in accordance with the provisions of sec. 4(2) and (3) of the Payment of Gratuity Act, 1972.

Where the employees are not covered under the Payment of Gratuity Act, 1972 - Any gratuity not covered under the Payment of Gratuity Act, 1972 received by an employee on his retirement or on his becoming incapacitated prior to such retirement or on termination of his employment, or any gratuity received by his widow, children or dependents on his death, will be exempt as follows:

(*a*) exceed 1/2 month's salary for each year of completed service, calculated on the basis of the average salary for the ten months immediately preceding the month in which any such event occurs, or

(*b*) ₹ 10 lakhs or

(*c*) gratuity actually received

In case where the assessee receive gratuity from more than one employer in the same previous year, the aggregate amount exempt from income-tax under shall not exceed ₹ 10 lakhs. When a benefit of such exemption was availed in any earlier previous year, the limit of exemption will have to be adjusted taking into account such exemption already availed.

Where any such gratuity or gratuities was or were received in any one or more earlier previous years also and the whole or any part of the amount of such gratuity or gratuities was not included in the total income of the assessee of such previous year or years, the amount exempt from income-tax under this clause shall not exceed the limit so specified as reduced by the amount or, as the case may be, the aggregate amount not included in the total income of any such previous year or years.

Pension

Exemption to commuted pension of government employees [Sec. 10(10A)(*i*)] - The commuted value of full pension, received by an employees of the following is fully exempt:

(*i*) Civil Pension (Commutation) Rules of the Central Government

(*ii*) members of the civil services of the Union

(*iii*) holders of the posts, connected with defense

(*iv*) holders of civil posts under the Union

(*v*) members of all India services

(*vi*) members of defense services

(*vii*) members of civil services of a State

(*viii*) holder of civil post under a State

(*ix*) employees of a local authority

(*x*) employees of a Corporation established by a Central, State or Provincial Act

Pension received by erstwhile employee of United Nations Organization is exempt from tax. [*CIT* v. *Dr. P.L. Narula* [1984] 17 Taxman 223/150 ITR 21 (Delhi), *CIT* v. *Dr. P.M. Kaul* [2001] 119 Taxman 139/249 ITR 667 (Delhi)]

Exemption to commuted pension by non-government employee [Sec. 10(10A)(*ii*)] - Where any other employee gets pension commuted, the quantum of exemption depends whether the employee received gratuity or did not get gratuity at the time of retirement:

(*i*) where the employee receives any gratuity, the commuted value of one-third of the pension which he is normally entitled to receive;

(*ii*) where the employee does not receive any gratuity, the commuted value of one-half of such pension.

Exemption to commuted pension from a fund set up by LIC or any other insurer [Sec. 10(10A)(*iii*)] - When any payment is received in commutation of pension from a fund, set up by LIC or any other insurer, approved by Insurance Regulatory Authority [under Sec. 23AAB], it is fully exempt. Commutation of pension received from such fund is not income from "salaries" because it is not a payment from the employer to the employee. It is income from other sources. However, it has been exempted under Sec. 10(10A)(*iii*).

Fund Established for Welfare of Employees [Sec. 10(23AAA)] - It provides for exemption from tax on any income received by any person on behalf of a fund, established for such purposes as may be notified by the Board, for the welfare of employees or their dependents and of which fund such employees are members. The exemption will be available only if the fund applies its income, or accumulates it for application, wholly and exclusively, to the objects for which it is established. The aforesaid fund shall invest its funds and contributions made by the employees and other sums received by it in any one or more of the forms or modes specified in Sec. 11(5). The said fund is to be approved by the Principal Commissioner or Commissioner in accordance with the rules made in this behalf and such approval shall have effect for such assessment year or years not exceeding three assessment years as may be specified in the order of approval.

Pension to individuals awarded gallantry award - Under sec. 10(18) any income by way of pension received by an individual or family pension received by any member of the family of such individual shall be exempt if such individual has been in the service of Central/State Government and has been awarded Param Vir Chakra or Maha Vir Chakra or Vir Chakra or such other gallantry award as may be notified.

Family Pension of member of armed forces - Under sec. 10(19) read with rule 2BBA stipulates that family pension received by the widow or children or nominated heirs of a member of the armed forces (including para-military forces) of the Union, where the death of such member has occurred in the course of operational duties will be exempt.

National Pension System

National Pension System (NPS) is a pension cum investment scheme launched by Government of India to provide old age security to citizens of India. It facilitates long term savings and effective planning of retirement through market-based return. The Central Government had introduced the National Pension System (NPS) with effect from January 1, 2004 (except for armed forces). All the employees of Central Autonomous Bodies (CABs) who have joined on or after 1.1.2004 are mandatorily covered under NPS. Subsequent to Central Government, various State Governments adopted this architecture and implemented NPS with effect from different dates. A State Autonomous Body (SAB) can also adopt NPS if the concerned State Government/UT have adopted the NPS architecture and initiated implementation of the same. Employee contributes towards pension from monthly salary along with matching contribution from the employer.

For the private sector employees NPS Corporate Sector Model exists which is the customized version of NPS to suit various organizations and their employees to adopt NPS as an organized entity within purview of their employer-employee relationship. From 1st May, 2009 any individual not being covered by the government sector or corporate sector can join NPS under the All Citizens of India sector. Any individual citizen of India (both resident and Non-resident) in the age group of 18-65 years can join NPS. NPS offers two types of accounts a) Tier 1 account is non-withdrawable till the person reaches the age of 60. Partial withdrawal before that is allowed in specific cases b) Tier II account is operates like a savings account and subscribers are free to withdraw the money as and whenever they require.

The Scheme is regulated by Pension Fund Regulatory and Development Authority (PFRDA). National Pension System Trust (NPST) established by PFRDA is the registered owner of all assets under NPS. A subscriber contributes periodically and regularly towards NPS during the working life to create the corpus for retirement. On retirement (attaining 60 years) or pre-mature exit from the scheme (before attaining 60 years), the corpus is made available to the subscriber with the mandate that portion of 40% and 80% respectively of the corpus must be invested in to an annuity to provide a monthly pension post retirement or exit from the scheme. Amount invested in purchase of Annuity, is fully exempt from tax. However, annuity income that you receive in the subsequent years will be subject to income tax. There is a lock-in period of 10 years, *i.e.* subscriber cannot exit NPS before completion of 10 years. A subscriber also has an option to continue to contribute to NPS upto 70 years of age and avail benefits of the contribution.

Deduction on employee's contribution to NPS under sec. 80CCD - Employee's contribution to NPS up to 10 per cent of salary (basic + dearness allowance) can be claimed as a deduction under sec. 80CCD(1), subject to a limit of ₹ 1.5 Lakh under sec. 80C. An additional investment up to ₹ 50,000 is also deductible from taxable income under Sec. 80CCD(1B). This is over and above the deduction of ₹ 1.5 lakh available under sec. 80C of Income-tax Act, 1961.

In case of private sector employees, employees' contribution to NPS up to 20 per cent of the gross total income can be claimed as deduction under sec. 80CCD(1).

Employer's Contribution to the Account of an Employee under a Pension Scheme

Employer's contribution to the NPS account of the employee is first included as salary income of the employee by virtue of sec. 17(1)(*viii*) and subsequently a deduction under sec. 80CCD(2) is allowed to the employee as follows:

(*a*) in case of Central Government employer, whole of the amount contributed by the Central Government

(*b*) in case of any other employer, actual contribution or 10% of the salary whichever is less.

Exemption on closure or opting out from NPS [sec.10(12A)] By virtue of sec. 10(12A), 60% of the payment received from NPS to an employee on closure of his account or on his opting out of the pension scheme will be exempt from tax.

Exemption on partial withdrawal from NPS [sec.10(12B)] A withdrawal up to 25% of contribution from NPS tier I account for the purposes specified under the Pension Fund Regulatory and Development Authority Act, 2013 will be exempt from tax.

Reinvestment of the amount received under this section [Sec. 80CCD(5)] Where an assessee has received any amount under this section in any previous year but he has reinvested the said amount for purchasing an annuity plan in the same previous year, it is deemed as if he has received no such amount to avoid its taxability. It is operative w.e.f. 1-4-2009.

Payment received out of an approved Superannuation Fund [Sec. 10(13)]

Any payment from an approved superannuation fund made—

(*i*) on the death of a beneficiary; or

(*ii*) to an employee in lieu of or in commutation of an annuity on his retirement at or after a specified age or on his becoming incapacitated prior to such retirement; or

(*iii*) by way of refund of contributions on the death of a beneficiary; or

(*iv*) by way of refund of contributions to an employee on his leaving the service in connection with which the fund is established otherwise than by retirement at or after a specified age or on his becoming incapacitated prior to such retirement, to the extent to which such payment does not exceed the contributions made prior to 1.4.1962 and any interest thereon; or

(*v*) by way of transfer to the account of the employee under a pension scheme referred to in sec. 80CCD and notified by the Central Government.

Provident Fund

Provident Fund remains an immensely popular social security provision for the retirement age that is created by contributions of the employee and the employer during the employment and interest thereon.

Statutory Provident Fund [Sec. 10(11)]

Provident funds set up under the Provident Funds Act, 1925 are called Statutory Provident Funds. Provident funds of the Central Government, state government, Railways, Reserve Bank of India, State Bank of India, educational institutions such universities maintain Statutory Provident Funds.

Under sec. 10(11) in case of Statutory Provident Fund, the entire amount of employer's contribution without any limit or restriction whatsoever and the interest thereon received by the employee shall not be includible in the total income of the employee both at the time when the contribution is made and at the time when the money is received by or on behalf of the employee on his retirement, death or otherwise.

Recognized Provident Fund [Sec.10(12)]

Provident Funds established under a scheme framed under the Employees Provident Funds Act, 1952 are known as Recognized Provident Funds. Also all Provident Funds recognized by the Commissioner of Income-tax under Rule 3 of Part 'A' of the Fourth Schedule to the Income-tax Act, 1961 will be considered as Recognized Provident Fund. If such recognition is subsequently withdrawn by the Commissioner, the Fund ceases to be a Recognized Provident Fund. The Provident Funds of various Public Sector Undertakings, Semi-Government bodies and other institutions and organizations including companies which are recognized by the Commissioner for income-tax purposes, would be treated as Recognized Provident Funds.

As per sec. 10(12) in the case of a Recognized Provident Fund, the employer's contribution to the Provident Fund is not treated as the employee's income so long as the contribution by the employer does not exceed 12% of the salary of the employee. But if the contribution of the employer exceeds 12% of the employee's salary, the excess of the contribution over 12% of the salary of the employee is to be treated as part of the taxable income from salaries in the hands of the employee in respect of the financial year in which the contributions were made by the employer. The fact that the employee concerned does not receive the money in hand nor is he entitled to get the money immediately does not in any way affect the taxability of the excess over 12% of the employee's salary. The employee's own contribution qualifies for deduction under Sec. 80C of the Income-tax Act.

[Salary for this purpose, includes basic salary; dearness allowance/pay (if the terms of employment so provide) and commission (if based on a fixed percentage of turnover achieved by the employee)]. As regards interest on the contributions to the Provident Fund, only an amount exceeding a sum calculated at 12% per annum on the balance standing to the credit of the employee would be treated as part of the taxable income of the employee. In other words, so long as the amount of interest does not exceed this limit, the interest does not become chargeable to tax in the hands of the employee.

Unrecognized Provident Fund

The Provident Fund which is neither Statutory nor Recognized by the Commissioner of Income-tax nor Public Provident Fund, would be an Unrecognized Provident Fund for income-tax purposes.

In the case of an Unrecognized Provident Fund, the employee's own contribution to the Fund would not be allowed as a deduction. The employer's contribution and the interest thereon would, however, be exempt from tax as and when the contributions are being made. But when the money in lump sum is received back by the employee, that part of the amount attributable to the employer's contribution would be taxable as income from salaries and the interest on the employer's contribution would also be taxable as salary income in the hands of the employee. The employee's own contributions when received back would not be taxable because they do not contain an element of income. However, the interest thereon would be chargeable to tax as income from other sources and not as income from salaries.

Public Provident Fund

Public Provident Fund is a popular long term saving and investment option aimed at mobilizing personal savings of individuals and at the same time offering retirement plan. It was introduced by the Central Government in 1968. Any member of public whether salaried or self-employed can open a PPF account in any branch of Post Office or a nationalized bank (Better to avoid naming Banks). Even private banks have been authorized to provide PPF account. An individual can deposit a minimum of ₹ 500 and a maximum of ₹ 1.5 lakh in a PPF account. It has a lock-in period of 15 years. However, a partial withdrawal of up to 50% of the total deposit can be made before completion of 15 years but after completion of 6 years. However, such withdrawal will be treated as a loan to be repaid into the account. Contribution to the PPF account during the financial year is deductible under sec. 80C of the Income-tax Act, 1961. Further, the accumulated amount and interest is also be exempt from tax at the time of withdrawal of completion of 15 years.

TABLE 6.2: TAX IMPLICATIONS OF CONTRIBUTIONS TO PROVIDENT FUND

	SPF	RPF	UPF	PPF
Employee's contribution to the fund	Exempt	Exempt to the extent of 12% of salary. Excess contribution above 12% is taxable	Exempt	NOT APPLICABLE since employer does not contribute at all
Employer's contribution to the fund	Available as deduction under sec. 80C	Available as deduction under sec. 80C	No Deduction available	Available as deduction under sec. 80C
Interest credited to the fund	Exempt	Exempt up to the rate of interest notified. Any excess interest taxable	Exempt	Exempt from tax
Payment of corpus upon retirement or termination of services	Exempt from tax	Exempt if- employee rendered 5 years of service or resignation before 5 years of service for joining another employer, termination of service due to ill-health, discontinuance of employer's business etc., transfer of balance to NPS in 80CCD	Employer's contribution and interest thereon- taxable as salary Employee's contribution-Exempt Interest on employee's contribution-taxable as income from other sources	Exempt from tax

The Changing Exemption scenario

The major benefit for salaried income individuals was that they received income which was an Exempt-Exempt-Exempt category, that is, the contribution, interest and withdrawal at the time of retirement was all exempt. The Finance Act, 2020 however introduced a threshold for the employer's contribution beyond which the excess amount and interest thereon was chargeable to tax as a perquisite. Accordingly if employer's contribution to the Recognised Provident Fund, National Pension Scheme and approved superannuation fund exceeds ₹ 7,50,000 such contribution over ₹ 7,50,000 and interest thereon is chargeable to tax as perquisite sec. 17(2)(*vii*)/(*viia*).

Further, by virtue of amendment introduced by the Finance Act, 2021 no exemption will be allowed on the interest accredited in the recognized and statutory provident fund to the extent it relates to the contribution made by the employees over ₹ 2,50,000 in a previous year. This amendment is applicable from the assessment year 2022-23. For the said purposes, Sec. 10(11) and (12) have been amended to that extent. A second proviso inserted to Sec. 10(11), (12) stipulates that where an employee is contributing to the fund but there is no contribution to such fund by the employer, then the interest income accrued during the previous year shall be taxable to the extent it relates to the contribution made by the employee to that fund in excess of ₹ 5,00,000 in a financial year.

Payment for Voluntary Retirement [Sec. 10(10C)]

According to sec. 10 (10C) an amount received or receivable by the employee on his voluntary retirement or termination of his service will be exempt from tax to the extent of the actual amount or ₹ 5 lakhs whichever is less. The employees of following will be eligible for such exemption:

(*a*) public sector company or

(*b*) any other company or

(*c*) an authority established under Central, State or Provincial Act or

(*d*) a local authority or

(*e*) a cooperative society or

(*f*) a University established under the State Government or Central Government or Provincial Act or University Grants Commission Act or

(*g*) Indian Institute of Management or

(*h*) any State Government or

(*i*) Central Government or

(*j*) the Institution having importance throughout India or a

(*k*) recognised management institute, on his voluntary retirement or termination of his service, in accordance with any scheme or schemes of voluntary retirement or in the case of a public sector company, a scheme of voluntary separation.

Certain essential conditions of voluntary retirement scheme are stipulated by Rule 2BA. Accordingly, the scheme of voluntary retirement/separation must have been drawn to result in overall reduction in the existing strength of the employees. It applies to an employee. All employees (by whatever name called), including workers and executives who has completed ten years of service or completed 40 years of age. However, this condition of age and years of service is not applicable in case of amount received by an employee of a public sector company under scheme of voluntary separation framed by the said company. Further, directors of the company/cooperative society are not covered under voluntary retirement scheme. It is necessary that the vacancy caused by voluntary retirement/separation is not to be filled up, nor, the retiring employee is to be employed in another company or concern belonging to the same management. This exemption is available only once in the life time of an assessee.

Retrenchment Compensation [Sec. 10(10B)]

Any compensation received by a workman under the Industrial Disputes Act, 1947 or under any other Act or rules, orders or notifications issued thereunder or under any standing orders or under any award, contract of service or otherwise, at the time of his retrenchment. The amount is exempt under this clause to the extent of least of the following limits:

(*i*) Actual amount received

(*ii*) Amount specified by Central Government *i.e.* ₹ 5,00,000.

(*iii*) An amount calculated in accordance with the provisions of clause (*b*) of Sec. 25F of the Industrial Disputes Act, 1947 *i.e.* 15 day's average pay for every completed years of services or part thereof in excess of 6 months.

Compensation referred to in this sec. is the compensation received by a workman at the time of the closing down of the undertaking in which he is employed. This exemption provision will not apply where any compensation is received by a workman under any scheme approved by the Central Government having regard to the need for extending special protection to the workmen in the undertaking to which such scheme applies.

Leave Salary [Sec. 10(10A)]

According to the terms of employment and service rules, an employee may be entitled to certain number of earned leaves. Such leaves may be availed by the employee during his working life or depending upon the service rules when leaves are not availed they may lapse or accumulate. Accumulated leaves may be encashed at the time of retirement or during the continuation of service. Section 10(10AA) does not qualify retirement from service on attaining a particular age, or on some other reasons. The retirement may be of various kinds. It may be on superannuation or it may be voluntary. If there is any voluntary retirement from service upon resignation provisions of sec. 10(10AA) would apply. [*CIT* v. *R.J. Shahney* [1986] 159 ITR 160 (Madras)] Leave encashment received during the continuance of service period is not eligible for exemption. *CIT* v. *Ram Rattan Lal Verma* [2005] 145 Taxman 256 (Allahabad). Also see *CIT* v. *Vijai Pal Singh* [2005] 144 Taxman 504/273 ITR 126 (Allahabad).

According to sec. 10(*10A*)(*i*) any payment received by an employee of the Central Government or a State Government as leave salary at the time of retirement or superannuation or otherwise is exempt from tax.

Sec. 10(*10A*)(*ii*) stipulates tax implications of leave salary for non-government employees including employees of local authority or statutory corporation. Accordingly least of the following will be exempt:

(*i*) Cash equivalent of the leave salary in respect of the period of earned leave standing to the credit of employee at the time of retirement/ superannuation (maximum earned leave entitlement being: 30 days for every year of actual service rendered for the employer from whose service he has retired); or

(*ii*) 10 month's "average salary", *i.e.* salary drawn during the period of 10 months immediately preceding the retirement/superannuation

(*iii*) The amount specified by the Government

(*iv*) Amount of leave encashment actually received

Sec. 10(*12C*) Exemption to payment under Agnipath Scheme (newly inserted by the Finance Act, 2023)

The Ministry of Defence has introduced the Agnipath Scheme, 2022 for enrolment of Agniveers in Indian Armed Forces. It has come into force on 1st November, 2022. Pursuant to the same, a non-lapsable dedicated Agniveer Corpus Fund in the interest-bearing section of the Public Account head has been created. The Agniveer Corpus Fund is a Fund in which consolidated contributions of all the Agniveers and matching contributions of the Government along with interest on these contributions would be held in their respective accounts. On completion of the engagement period of four years, Agniveers will be paid one time 'Seva Nidhi' package, which shall comprise of their contribution including interest thereon and matching contribution from the Government equal to the accumulated amount of their contribution including interest. Payment received by Agniveer or his nominee, from the Agniveer Corpus Fund will be exempt from tax under the newly inserted sec.10(*12C*). Further, any contribution made by Agniveer or the Central Government to his Agniveer Corpus Fund account will be available as a deduction from the total income of Agniveer under sec. 80CCH.

Interest Payable on Retirement Deposits of a Government Employee [Sec. 10(15)(*iv*)(*i*)]

Interest payable by the Government on deposits made by an employee out of money due to him on his retirement, whether on superannuation or otherwise, is exempt. The employee may be of Central Government, State Government or public sector employee. [Sec. 10(*15*)(*iv*)(*i*)].

Scholarship granted to meet education cost of children of employee is exempt [Sec. 10(16)]

Scholarships paid by an employer voluntarily and at its sole discretion to the children of its employees is not a taxable perquisite. Any scholarship paid by an employer directly to the children of its employees, voluntarily, at its sole discretion and without any reference in the terms of employment to scholarship scheme is not assessable as perquisites in hands of the employee u/s 17(2) (*iii*). No right to receive any scholarship is created in favour of any employee as such payment by the employer is entirely gratuitous and at its sole discretion. Moreover, payment of the scholarship amount is received not by the employee but by the children concerned or deposited in the special account referred to in the scheme of scholarship. Even if the amounts were taken as having been paid to the assessee, they will be amounts of scholarship and hence not liable to be included in the computation of the total income of the assessee under the provisions of Sec. 10(16). [*CIT* v. *M.N. Nadkarni* [1986] 25 Taxman 9/161 ITR 544 (Bom.)].

Allowances or perquisites paid to Chairman or Retired Chairman or Members or Retired Members of the Union Public Service Commission [Sec. 10(45)]

Any notified allowance or perquisite, paid by the Central Goverment to the chairman, retired chairman, members or retired member of Union Public Service Commission is exempt from tax.

RELIEF UNDER SEC. 89

Relief in respect of arrears of salary [Sec. 89 read with Rule 21A(2)] - When the assessee is assessed on the salary of more than 12 months for any previous year on account of receipt basis, he is entitled to seek relief about income tax under sec. 89 read with rule 21A. For instance, when assessee receives arrears of salary or advance salary, he will be taxed on receipt basis. He can claim relief under this sec. The relief is applicable even in case of leave salary encashed before retirement. [*CIT* v. *S.N. Chadha* [2001] 118 Taxman 520/249 ITR 31 (Delhi)]

Relief in respect of gratuity [Sec. 89 read with rule 21A(3)] - Such relief is available subject to the following conditions:

(*a*) Gratuity is received in respect of past services for a minimum period of 5 years

(*b*) Gratuity is received by the assessee from his employer in the same year in which it becomes due. Thus, any gratuity received in advance or in arrears is not be eligible for relief.

Relief is Available only for the Taxable Portion of Gratuity. Where a portion of the gratuity is exempt under sec. 10(10), no relief is admissible for such exempted portion of the gratuity. Only the portion of gratuity which is in excess of the amount of exemption under sec. 10(10) and is included in gross salary income is eligible for relief. Where the whole of the gratuity is exempt, no relief is admissible.

Relief in respect of Compensation for Termination of Employment [Sec. 89 read with rule 21A(4)]

Where an assessee received any compensation from his employer or former employer at or in connection with the termination of his employment, relief from any additional tax burden is provided only if the following conditions are satisfied:

(*a*) The compensation is received after rendering a continuous service of not less than 3 years to the employer or the former employer, as the case may be. For example, where an employee gets terminated after 2 continuous years of service and receives compensation from his employer, no relief is admissible to him; and (*b*) The unexpired portion of his term of employment is also not less than 3 years.

Ex gratia compensation, received by an assessee consequent on the termination of his services, is entitled to the relief under Sec. 89 of the Act. It is immaterial if such termination is on account of resignation, dismissal, compulsory retirement or on attaining superannuation. However, if the *ex gratia* amount is not received by the assessee on account of services rendered, it cannot be construed as an income, assessable under Income-tax Act, being received on account of personal considerations. [*CIT* v. *J. Visalakshi* [1994] 74 Taxman 532/206 ITR 531 (Madras)]

No Relief under sec. 89 for voluntary retirement if exemption sought under sec. 10(10C) - Relief under this sec. and exemption on payments received upon voluntary retirement are mutually exclusive in nature. *i.e* the assessee shall not be eligible for relief under this sec. in case he has claimed exemption under sec. 10(10C). On the other hand, if he claims relief under sec. 89, he cannot claim exemption under sec. 10(10C).

Relief in case of Commutation of Pension [Sec. 89 read with rule 21A(5)]

Where an assessee received commuted value of the pension in any previous year, he shall be eligible for relief under sec. 89.

Relief in respect of other payments [Sec. 89 read with rule 21A(6)]

Relief in respect of any other payment (*i.e.,* other than those covered above) will be granted by the Central Board of Direct Taxes, after examining the circumstances of each individual case.

Relief in respect of income from retirement benefit account maintained in a notified country [Sec. 89A]

The Finance Act, 2021 newly inserted Sec. 89A which offers relief to a person resident in India who opened a specified account in a notified country while being non-resident in India and resident in that country. Accordingly, where such specified person maintained an account in a notified country in respect of his retirement benefits and the income from such account is not taxable on accrual basis but is taxed by such country at the time of withdrawal or redemption; such income shall be taxed in India in such manner and in such year as may be prescribed.

RELIEF FOR EMPLOYEES OF FOREIGN ENTITITES

Bilateral Relief to employees of foreign enterprise, foreign ship, foreign government under DTAAs

With globalization and liberalization of economies across the world, there has been an unprecedented growth in cross-border trade and commerce with multinational collaborations and exchange of ideas and resources. As in the past, so even now, employees are deputed to execute work contracted by their employers in other countries or the nature of their job requires them to go globe-trotting for the purposes of employer's business. Countries have entered into bilateral agreements with each other so as to avoid double taxation of income including salary. Such DTAAs are reciprocative in nature and both Contracting Parties (States) agree to provide bilateral relief to the residents of the other.

Accordingly, Article on Dependent Personal Service (DPS) provide for avoidance of double taxation with respect to salary income of employees. As per this Article, salaries, wages and other similar remuneration derived by an individual who is a resident of one of the Contracting States in respect of an employment shall be taxable only in that State unless the employment is exercised in the other Contracting State. If the employment is so exercised, such remuneration as is derived from that exercise may be taxed in that other State. For example, salary income of an individual being a resident in India will be taxable only in India unless, salary is earned in say Australia. In such scenario it is the Australia that will tax the salary income. Thus, the country of source will tax the income.

Further, source country can tax such an individual only if the physical presence of such individual in the source state exceed a certain number of days as specified in the DTAA, the remuneration is paid by, or on behalf of, an employer who is a resident of the source State and the remuneration is deductible in determining taxable profits of a permanent establishment or a fixed base which the employer has in that other State.

With reference to taxability of remuneration derived by an employment exercised aboard a ship or aircraft operated in international traffic by an enterprise, such remuneration will be taxed by the state of residence of such enterprise. Insofar as individuals performing employment services for the government of a contracting state, DTAAs provide that these are taxable only by that state. Diplomats and consular officials who work in a foreign country as members of their government's diplomatic missions are exempt from tax under special agreements or under the rules of international law.

Salary received by a professor/teacher

DTAAs with several countries include an Article for providing double tax relief to remuneration of professors and teachers visiting foreign countries for research or teaching. Accordingly, where a professor or teacher who is a resident of one of the Contracting States visits the other Contracting State for a period not exceeding two years for the purpose of teaching or carrying out advanced study or research at a University, college, school or other educational institution, any remuneration that person receives for such teaching, advanced study or research shall be exempt in the host country to the extent to which such remuneration is or will be upon application of this article, subject to tax in the home country. This Article shall not apply to remuneration which a professor or teacher receives for conducting research if the research is undertaken primarily for the private benefit of a specific person or persons.

Unilateral Reliefs to employees of foreign enterprise, foreign ship, foreign government under Income-tax Act, 1961

Sec. 10 of the Income-tax Act, 1961 comprise of exemption provisions *i.e* those incomes that are not included in the total income of the assessee. This sec. includes relief provided to employees of foreign entities etc. and is basically a unilateral relief offered by India. In other words, even if there is no DTAA between India and the home country of such assessee, exemption will nevertheless will be available.

Remuneration received by foreign individual [Sec. 10(6)(vi)] - The remuneration received by a foreign individual in his capacity as an employee of a foreign enterprise for the services rendered by him during his stay in India would be exempt if the following conditions are fulfilled:

(*a*) The foreign enterprise is not engaged in any trade or business in India.

(*b*) The total period of stay of the individual in India during the previous year does not exceed 90 days.

(*c*) Such remuneration is not liable to be deducted from the income of the employer chargeable to tax in India under the Income-tax Act.

Non-resident employee on a foreign ship [Sec. 10(6)(*viii*)] - Income chargeable under the head 'Salaries' received by or due to any non-resident individual as remuneration for the services rendered by him in connection with his employment on foreign ship is exempt from tax where the total period of his stay in India does not exceed a period of 90 days during the previous year.

Remuneration of employee of foreign Government during his training in India [Sec. 10(6)(*xi*)]

The remuneration received by an individual being a foreign citizen as an employee of the government of a foreign State during his stay in India in connection with his training in any establishment or office of, or in any undertaking owned by:

(*a*) The government; or

(*b*) Any company in which the entire paid-up capital is held by the Central Government, or any State Government or Governments; or partly by the Central Government and partly by one or more State Governments; or

(*c*) Any company which is a subsidiary of a company referred to in (*b*); or

(*d*) Any corporation established by or under a Central, State or Provincial Act; or

(*e*) Any society registered under the Societies Registration Act, 1860, or under any other corresponding law for the time being in force and wholly financed by the Central Government, or any State Government or partly by the Central Government and partly by one or more State Governments.

CHAPTER 7 INCOME FROM HOUSE PROPERTY

INTRODUCTION

This head of income brings to tax the inherent capacity of a house property to generate income. Accordingly, under sec. 22 annual value of a house property consisting of any buildings or lands appurtenant thereto, of which the assessee is the owner is chargeable to tax under this head of income. It must be noted at the very outset that annual value is not to be confused with rent of the house.

House property in common parlance means means 'abode', a dwelling place or building for human habitation. A building for human habitation ordinarily requires to have minimum facilities of washroom, kitchen, electricity, sewerage etc. [*Ashok Syal* v. *CIT* [2012] 24 taxmann.com 274/209 Taxman 376 (Punj. & Har.)]. The expression "land appurtenant thereto" refers to "land usually enjoyed or occupied with building".

This head of income does not concern itself with the purpose for which the house property is used. Thereby, the scope of the expression "house property" is much wider than mere residential house and includes within its ambit even factories, shops, offices, etc. However, such property or any portion thereof which is occupied by the assessee for the purposes of his business or profession, the profits of which are chargeable to tax, is excluded from this head.

CONDITIONS FOR APPLICATION OF THE HEAD INCOME FROM HOUSE PROPERTY

Under sec. 22 annual value of a house property consisting of any buildings or lands appurtenant thereto, of which the assessee is the owner is chargeable to tax. Thus, in order to bring an income to tax under this head, the following conditions must be fulfilled:

1. The property should consist of buildings or lands appurtenant thereto.
2. The assessee should be the owner.
3. The property should not be used by the owner for the purpose of any business carried on by him the profits of which are chargeable to income tax.

(1) Property consisting of any Buildings or Lands Appurtenant thereto

The expression "house property" under this headrefers to a) any buildings or b) lands appurtenant thereto. The first part (*a*) "any building" may include residential houses, bungalows, buildings let out for office use or for storage or warehousing or for use as factory or shops, dance halls, music halls, lecture halls, theatre halls and other public auditoriums. Thus, irrespective of the purpose for which such building is put to use by the assessee-owner such a property will be assessable to tax under this head.

Rent from Vacant Plot not Chargeable under this Head Any rent received from a vacant plot of land is assessable under the head "income from other sources" and not under this head. This head of charge does not include income from vacant lands, though they may be building sites [*Chowdhry Sharafat Hussain* v. *CIT* (1956) 29 ITR 514 (Pat.)]. Annual value of stalls, permanently affixed to the ground is taxable as income from house property [*CIT* v. *Kanaiyalal Nimani* (1979) 120 ITR 892 (Cal.)].

Income from Temporary Hut not Chargeable under this Head If the vacant plot is used for erecting temporary huts or for storing materials, any income from such a plot is assessable under other source.

The second part (*b*) comprise of lands appurtenant thereto. The concept of appurtenance 'thereto' is to be understood in the context of a house and that the land is necessary or connected with the enjoyment of the house. Thus touchstone of "appurtenance" is the dependence of the building. What is integral is not necessarily appurtenant. A position of subordination, something incidental or ancillary or dependent is implied in appurtenance [*M. Ramalakshmi Reddi* v. *CIT* [1998] 100 Taxman 509/232 ITR 281 (Mad.)]. For example, a hundred acres may be spread out in front of a club house for various games like golf. But all these abundant acres are unnecessary nor incidental to the enjoyment of the house in any reasonable manner. The determination whether the land is to be treated as appurtenant or not depends upon the extent and nature of the land and its situation *vis-á-vis* the building thereon [*Maharaj Singh* v. *State of U.P.* AIR 1976 SC 2602]. The appurtenant lands in respect of a residential building may be in the form of a compound and playground, courtyard and backyard, kitchen-garden, cattle-shed, motor garage, etc., forming part of the building. In respect of a non-residential building, the appurtenant lands may be in the form of car parking space, connecting roads between different departments of the factory area, drying grounds, playgrounds, etc., forming part of the building. Only lands appurtenant to buildings come under property. Income from other lands, that is, not appurtenant to buildings and not occupied and enjoyed with them is income from "other sources." For example, say when the owner exploits soil of his land appurtenant to a building for brick making for commercial purposes, such land will no longer remain appurtenant thereto so as to qualify under this head and any gains therefrom will be 'income from other sources'.

Case Law : ***CIT* v. *Kanaiyalal Nimani* (1979) 120 ITR 892 (Cal.)**

Facts: 'K' had taken a premise with a building thereon on a lease and created many stalls in the premise and set up a market therein and claimed income from these stalls to be income from house property.

Held: The stalls were permanently affixed to the ground and the stallholders were using them for selling and storing their merchandise. These stalls not erected temporarily, nor were they capable of being shifted from place to another. The stalls were "buildings" within the meaning of the head house property.

Case Law : ***M. Ramalakshmi Reddi* v. *CIT* [1998] 100 Taxman 509/232 ITR 281 (Mad.)**

Facts: 'R' had allowed two parties to draw water from a well on her house property for a consideration.

Held: Merely because some water was also used by 'R' for her house hold requirements, portion of land in which well was situated could not be said to be appurtenant to her dwelling house. When potable water-spring had been struck, which became a perennial source of potable water which could be independently and commercially exploited easily in order to make considerable gain to the owner thereof such portion of land had become such a valuable assets. It could not continue to remain as an appurtenant landeven assuming that such portion of the land was originally appurtenant land. 'R' cannot claim it as income from house property.

(2) Ownership of the Property

In order to assess the house property under this head, it is critical that the assessee is the a) owner or b) deemed owner of such property during the relevant previous year. Generally, an owner means a person who has got valid title legally conveyed to him after complying with the requirements of law such as the Transfer of Property Act, Registration Act, etc. However, for the purposes of this head 'ownership' is not merely a word of technical legal meaning but it is to be interpreted in its broadest possible meaning. It consists of a bundle of rights. For the purposes of this head, 'owner' is a person who is entitled to receive income from the property in his own right [*R.B. Jodha Mal Kuthiala* v. *CIT* [1971] 82 ITR 570 (SC)]. Thus, it is not only the registered owner of the property who is assessable under this head. The expression owner extends to a legal owner, beneficial owner or deemed owner [*P. Joseph Swaminathan* v. *CIT* [1984] 145 ITR 198/[1985] 22 Taxman 153 (Mad.)].

(*a*) Owner [Sec. 22]

For the purposes of this provision ownership is not necessarily confined to a registered owner alone. Having regard to the object of the Act, namely, to tax the income, owner is a person who is entitled to receive income from the property in his own right [*CIT* v. *Podar Cement (P.) Ltd.* (1997) 92 Taxman 541/226 ITR 625 (SC)]. Broadly, "ownership" rests in one who has dominion over the property. Thus, if, in a given case, it is found as a fact that the assessee is in occupation of the building as owner to all intents and purposes, he is to be considered the owner under sec. 22 even if the sale deed is not yet registered in his favour [*Smt. Kala Rani* v. *CIT* (1981) 6 Taxman 226/130 ITR 321 (Punj. & Har.)]. Even where the assessee has come into the possession of property under an invalid deed of transfer, such person will still be taxed as owner of the property [*Nawab Mir Barkat Ali Khan Bahadur* v. *CIT* (1988) 36 Taxman 317/171

ITR 541 (AP)]. Under Muslim Personal Law, oral gift of house is a valid transfer and does not require compulsory registration. Therefore, income from house property in case of such transfer is assessable in hands of the donor [*CIT* v. *Begum Noor Banu Alladin* [1985] 20 Taxman 44/[1987] 163 ITR 389 (AP)].

However, mere interest of a person in the property is not enough to constitute ownership. [*Madgul Udyog* v. *CIT* [1990] 184 ITR 484/[1991] 54 Taxman 34 (Cal.)]. For example, where a house is inherited by an assessee but under the peculiar terms of the will, the house so inherited can neither be occupied by her for her residence nor could be let out or sold by her, the assessee cannot be termed as owner of the inherited property [*M.P. Gnanambal Ammal* v. *CIT* (1985) 152 ITR 659 (Mad.)].

Ownership need not extend to both, the land on which the building stands, as well as the building: It is not essential that a person who owns a building should be owner of the land upon which it stands for assessing income under this head. Thus, if the terms of the lease-deed show that the ownership of the superstructures is vested in the lessee while the ownership of the site remains in the lessor, the lessee can be assessed in respect of the income from the superstructures under Sec. 22 as income from property [*Shri Ganesh Properties Ltd.* v. *CIT* (1962) 44 ITR 606 (Cal.)].

Income from sub-letting is not assessable to tax under this head: Ownership of the assessee over the house property is an essential requisite to invoke this head of income. Where a tenant sublets house property, such income from sub-letting is taxable as income from "other sources" and not under this head since the tenant is not the owner of the property.

Legatees and not the Executor is owner of property of the deceased: Where a will gives life interest in house property to specific legatee, such legatee is the owner of the property. Annual value of property is assessable in the hands of legatee and not in the hands of executor [*Estate of Ambalal Sarabhai* v. *CIT* [2000] 245 ITR 445/[2001] 114 Taxman 162 (Guj.)].

Ownership of mortgaged property remains with the mortgagor: Mortgagor remains the owner of the property mortgaged by him. Even if under the mortgage there is an absolute transfer in favour of the mortgagee, yet the mortgagor still retains the legal estate in himself. There is no equitable estate recognised in the Transfer of Property Act and what remains to the mortgagor must be regarded as legal estate [*Raja P. C. Lall Choudhary* v. *CIT* (1948) 16 ITR 123 (Pat.)].

Official Receiver cannot be the owner of the property: "Owner" in Sec. 22 of the Act means the owner of the property itself and not the owner of the annual value. A receiver appointed by court merely manages the property under orders of the court and the property in his hands is in *custodialegis* for the person who can make a title to it. The receiver cannot therefore be assessed as owner of the property under Sec. 22. His position is different from that of a trustee or official assignee [*Raja P. C. Lall Choudhary* v. *CIT* (1948) 16 ITR 123 (Pat.)].

Ownership in case of Insolvency may vest with the Official Assignee: If any person is adjudicated insolvent, his house property vests in the official assignee who is assessable as owner [*Re. Official Assignee for Bengal* (1937) 5 ITR 233 (Cal.)].

Property Owned by Firm: Where the house property is owned by a partnership firm, it is assessable in the hands of the firm as owner and not the partners as co-owners u/s 26. [*Sarvamangala Properties Ltd.* v. *CIT* (1973) 90 ITR 267 (Cal.)].

Benami Properties: There is nothing that compels to accept the registered owner as real owner for the purposes of tax assessment under this head, and the Revenue authorities can establish otherwise. However, the burden of proving that a transaction is benami and the owner is not the real owner always rests on the person asserting it to be so. This burden has to be strictly discharged by adducing legal evidence of a definite character which would either directly prove the fact of benami or establish circumstances unerringly and reasonably raising an inference of that fact. [*P. Joseph Swaminathan* v. *CIT* (1984) 145 ITR 198/[1985] 22 Taxman 153 (Mad.)].

Disputed ownership: The assessment proceeding cannot be held up on account of dispute relating to title of the property either in or outside the Court [*Keshardeo Chamria* v. *CIT* (1939) 7 ITR 394 (PC)]. The decision as to who is the owner rests with the Assessing Officer. The person who is in receipt of income is assessed to tax. If, however, the decision of the Court goes against the interim decision of the tax authorities, the back years assessments are to be rectified according the verdict of the Court.

Co-ownership [Sec. 26]: When a house property is owned by two or more persons as co-owners and their respective shares are definite and ascertainable, sec. 26 is applicable. The share of each co-owner in the income from the property is computed separately in accordance with the provisions relating to income from house property (Sec. 22 to Sec. 25) and included in their total income. Such house property cannot be assessed as an association of persons.

Dayabhaga HUF assessable as co-owners under sec. 26 in respect of income from property: The income from house property possessed jointly by the members of the Hindu Undivided Family should be assessed to tax not in the hands of the family but in the hands of the individual members by applying the provisions of Sec. 26 of the Income-tax Act, 1961. [*CIT* v. *Balai Chandra Paul* [1976] 105 ITR 666 (Cal.)]. The essence of a coparcenary under the Dayabhaga Law is unity of possession and not unity of ownership. Every coparcener takes a defined share in the property, and he is the owner of that share. Such share is defined immediately and even before partition any coparcener can say that he is entitled to a particular share. So long as there is unity of possession, no coparcener can say that particular share of the property belongs to him; that he can say only after a partition. Partition, according to the Dayabhaga Law, consists in splitting up joint possession and assigning specific portions of the property to the several coparceners. Thus, the heirs of a Dayabhaga Hindu have defined shares in the properties belonging to them jointly and they are in joint possession. Therefore, the income from house properties which are in the joint-possession of the coparceners of a HUF governed by the Dayabhaga school of Hindu law should be assessed separately in their individual hands in proportion to their shares in the family properties under Sec. 26 of the Act. [*CIT* v. *Prafulla Kumar Panja* [1993] 200 ITR 706 (Cal.)].

(*b*) Deemed Owner [Sec. 27]

A "deemed owner" is also assessable on the annual value of the property. A person is deemed to be owner of house property in the following cases:

(*i*) *Transfer of house property to spouse or minor child without adequate consideration [Sec. 27(i)]*: If an individual transfers any house property to his or her spouse or to a minor child (excluding married minor daughter) without adequate consideration, such individual is deemed to be the owner of the house property. However, where such transfer is to his/her spouse under an agreement to live apart or a married minor daughter, this provision is not applicable. In the two cases, the transferee is the owner of such property.

(*ii*) *Holder of impartiable estate [Sec. 27(ii)]*: An impartiable estate is owned by the Hindu Undivided Family. But under income-tax law, the holder of such estate is deemed to be the owner of all the properties comprised in such estate. The holder of such estate is generally the senior-most member of the family. Therefore, he is assessable on the annual value of the property comprised in such estate.

(*iii*) *Member of cooperative society/company/an association of persons [Sec. 27(iii)]*: A member of a cooperative society/company/an association of persons, to whom a building or part thereof is allotted or leased under a house building scheme of the society/company/association of persons, is deemed to be the owner of that building or part thereof.

(*iv*) *Transferee in possession of building in part performance of a contract referred to under sec. 53A of Transfer of Property Act [Sec. 27(iiia)]*: Where an immovable property is transferred under a written agreement for consideration and the possession is given to the buyer, the buyer is deemed to be the owner of the property for the purpose of the Income-tax Act even though the seller remains the legal owner till the time the registration is executed in favour of the buyer. For example, A contracts in writing on 15 February 2015 to sell his property for ₹ 80,000 to B. A has handed over the possession to B who has paid the consideration to A. No conveyance has been executed till 31 March 2015. B is deemed to be the owner of the property.

(*v*) *A person acquiring right in respect of building [Sec. 27(iiib)]*: When any person acquires any land or building or part thereof or any interest therein by way of sale, exchange or lease for a term of not less than 12 years, and he is allowed to use or retain possession thereof (under part performance of the contract under sec. 53A of the Transfer of Property Act), he is deemed to be the owner of such property.

(*c*) Property must not be used by the owner for his business or profession, profits of which are chargeable to tax

In order to be taxable under the head "Income from house property", an assessee should not occupy the property owned by him for the purposes of carrying on any business or profession, the profits of which are chargeable to tax. Thus, the charging section of the head house property excludes such property that is used by the owner for the purposes of his business or profession, profits of which are chargeable to tax under head profits and gains from business or profession. For example, where a house property owned by an HUF is even partly used for its business by a firm in which the HUF is a partner, the notional income of that part of the property used by the firm for its business cannot be assessed in the hands of the HUF [*CIT* v. *H.S. Singhal and Sons* [2001] 118 Taxman 894/[2002] 253 ITR 653 (Del.)].

The principle is that if the owner of a property carries on business with a property owned by him, the income from that property must be assessed as only "income from business" [*CIT* v. *New India Maritime Agencies P. Ltd.* [1994] 207 ITR 392 (Mad.)]. If the letting of property is only incidental and subservient to the main business of the assessee, the rental income from such letting is not taxable under this head but under the head "business or profession". For instance, income derived by the company by letting out its property to its employees is incidental to the business carried on by it and has to be considered as income from business [*CIT* v. *M.A. Sathar (P.) Ltd.* [1997] 226 ITR 910 (Mad.)].

The criterion is chargeability and not the actual charge, that is the business may not make profits in a particular year or may make profits but may not be taxable on account of total income falling below taxable limit. Thus, the annual value of the buildings or lands appurtenant thereto owned and occupied by the assessee to carry on any business or profession is not assessable under this head provided the profits of the business or profession are chargeable, though not actually taxed for any reason. If the profits of business or profession are not chargeable to tax, that is, being exempt from tax, the annual value of the property is assessable under income from house property.

The same holds true when a business asset is put to use in times of a slowdown. However, it must be noted that there is a marked distinction between "lull in business" and "going out of business". A temporary discontinuance of business may, in certain circumstances, give rise to an inference that a business is going through a lean period of transition and it could be revived if proper circumstances arise. But where an assessee decides to dispose of its property, the plant and machinery are dismantled and taken away from the factory premises, there is not even the slightest chance of the assessee restarting production, and there is no finance available, and even the licences ceased to be effective, it cannot be held that there was a lull in business which was of a temporary nature [*Hindustan Chemical Works Ltd.* v. *CIT* [1979] 1 Taxman 420/[1980] 124 ITR 561 (Bom.)]. Where in order to curtail the losses, the assessee reduces its production and leases the surplus portion of the factory premises on rent, such rental income is assessable as income from business [*CIT* v. *Anand Rubber and Plastics (P.) Ltd.* [1989] 44 Taxman 482/178 ITR 301 (P&H)].

Building Owned by a Partner but Occupied by the Firm - The chargeability of annual value of a building owned by a partner of the firm and occupied by the firm free of rent for its business or profession, the profits of which are chargeable to tax, is judicially controversial. One view is that the partner owning such building is not assessable on its annual value under this head. The business carried on by the firm is regarded as being carried on by all the partners. The user and occupations by the firms of the property belonging to the partner has to be regarded as occupation of the property by the partner for the purposes of business or profession carried on by him [*CIT* v. *K. M. Jagannathan* (1989) 44 Taxman 224/180 ITR 191 (Mad.)]. Hence, partner owning such property is not assessable on its annual value provided the profits of business are chargeable to tax. The other view is that where a house property owned by a partner of firm is used for the firm's business, such partner is assessable on its annual value as he has not occupied it for his own occupation in the capacity as owner [*CIT* v. *K. N. Guruswamy* (1984) 146 ITR 34/17 Taxman 87 (Kar.)]. When a firm carries on business, it is business carried on by the partners of that firm. Every partner is the agent of the other in carrying out that business. Consequently, when a partnership carries on business, each partner thereof must be said to be carrying on that business. Income from house property owned by an assessee and used in business carried on by the partnership firm in which the assessee is a partner would qualify for the exemption provided in Sec. 22 of the Income-tax Act, 1961 [*CIT* v. *Rabindranath Dhol* [1995] 211 ITR 799/79 Taxman 170 (Ori.)]. The Karta of a Hindu Undivided Family can be a partner in a firm either in his individual capacity or in his capacity as Karta representing the Hindu Undivided Family. He occupies a dual position. Qua the partnership, he functions in his personal capacity; qua the third party, in his representative capacity. Where property belonging to a Hindu Undivided Family is occupied by a firm, for purposes of business, the mere fact that the assessee—Hindu Undivided Family as such is not a partner in the firm, but only the Karta who represents the assessee as partner, does not disentitle the assessee to the benefit under Sec. 22 of the Income-tax Act, 1961, where the Hindu Undivided Family in effect occupies for the purpose of its business the portion of the premises in question [*CIT* v. *Champalal Jeevraj* [1995] 215 ITR 289/[1996] 84 Taxman 473 (Mad.)].

Case Laws : ***Maharashtra Fertilizers and Chemicals* v. *CIT* [1984] 150 ITR 317 (Bom.)**

Facts: The assessee–firm being into the business of manufacturing and sale of manure, constructed a godown for its use in business. However, instead of using the godown for its own business, the assessee gave the same on rent to another firm. The Assessing Officer held that the income from rent had to be assessed as income from other sources.

Held: Since the assessee never actually used the godown for its own business purposes, it is not a business asset and income derived from letting out of the godown had to be assessed under the head "income from house property".

Case Law : ***CIT* v. *National Newsprint and Paper Mills Ltd.* [1978] 114 ITR 388 (MP)**

Facts: The assessee, a public sector undertaking, engaged in the business of manufacture and sale of newsprint, with a huge industrial complex. The said complex comprised residential quarters for its employees and also rented buildings to banks, post office, police station etc. so as to facilitate efficient carrying on of its business. The Assessing Officer treated the income from letting as income from property whereas the assessee contended that it should be assessed as business income being incidental to the business carried by it.

Held: The dominant purpose of letting out was to enable the assessee to carry on its business more efficiently and smoothly and the activity of letting had a definite nexus with the business that the assessee was carrying on. Therefore, the rent received from letting out of the accommodations to employees as well as other agencies being incidental to the assessee's business is taxable as income from business and not as house property.

BASIS OF CHARGE [SEC. 22]

The basis of charge under this head is the annual value of the property, consisting of any building or land appurtenant thereto, owned by the assessee excluding such property or portion thereof occupied by him to carry on any business or profession, the profits of which are chargeable to income tax.

It must be noted that the basis of charge is not on rent received from the building or land appurtenant thereto but on the annual value of the building or land appurtenant thereto. Annual value is a notional figure arrived at after an objective consideration of various factors such as municipal valuation, fair rent of the property in a similar location, standard rent under Rent Control Act, actual rent received or receivable, unrealised rent, the period for which the property was vacant and facts and circumstances of a particular case.

The owner of a house property may keep the property vacant or locked, he is assessable on the annual value of such property [*CIT* v. *DLF Housing Construction (P.) Ltd.* (1981) 129 ITR 773 (Del.)].

Income from Property of Mutual Concern is not Assessable on Grounds of Mutuality - No person can trade with himself and make an assessable profit [*Sir Kikabhai Premchand* v. *CIT* [1953] 24 ITR 506 (SC)]. So long there is a complete identity between the contributors and the participators, the principle of mutuality is applicable [*CIT* v. *Madras Race Club* (1976) 105 ITR 433 (Mad.)]. Income of a club from letting out its room solely to its members, is not chargeable to tax on principle of mutuality [*CIT* v. *Cawnpore Club Ltd.* [1983] 14 Taxman 211/ [1984] 146 ITR 181 (All.)]. It was not only the surplus from the activities of the business of the club that was excluded from the levy of income tax, even the annual value of the club house, as contemplated in Sec. 22 of the Act, would be outside the purview of the levy of income tax [*Chelmsford Club* v. *CIT* [2000] 243 ITR 89/109 Taxman 215 (SC)]. For a detailed discussion on the concept of mutuality, please refer to Chapter 2.

TABLE 7.1: COMPUTATION OF INCOME FROM HOUSE PROPERTY

Particulars	**Amount (in ₹)**
Gross Annual Value	xxxxx
Less: Municipal Taxes	xxxxx
Net Annual Value	xxxxx
Less: Deductions under sec. 24	
Standard Deduction	xxx
Interest on borrowed capital	xxxx
Income from House Property	xxxxx

Determining Annual Value of a Property (Sec. 23) - Since this head taxes the inherent capacity of the property to generate income, and such property is assessable to tax even when it is kept locked or vacant by the owner, sec. 23 contemplates different situations for which annual value needs to be determined:

(*a*) when property is deemed to be let out

(*b*) when property is actually let out

(*c*) when property is actually let out and subsequently remains vacant

(*d*) when property self-occupied for the purposes of residence

In instance (*a*), the property has not been actually let out. By virtue of a legal fiction it is deemed as if the property is let out and generating income which is now assessable to tax. In such a scenario, annual value will be a notional sum that a hypothetical tenant would have paid for the property. In (*b*) the owner of the property has actually let out the property and therefore one will be receiving actual rent which may be determined as annual value. Situation (*c*) contemplates a possibility where the property was let out and subsequently falls vacant. In such case annual value will have to be adjusted in accordance with vacancy period. Annual value for each of these three is determined as follows:

(*a*) Property Deemed to be let out [Sec. 23(1)(a)] - The annual value of such is the sum for which the property might reasonably be expected to be let out from year to year. Thus, 'reasonably expected' rent is only a fictitious sum that a hypothetical tenant would have paid for the property. The Income-tax Act does not specify any particular method to determine reasonably expected rent and therefore the question of what would be reasonable depends on the facts and circumstances of a given situation. Ordinarily, "a bargain between a willing lessor and a willing lessee uninfluenced by any extraneous circumstances may afford a guiding test of reasonableness" and in normal circumstances, the actual rent payable by a tenant to the landlord would afford reliable evidence of what the landlord may reasonably expect to get from the hypothetical tenant, unless the rent is inflated or depressed by reason of extraneous considerations such as relationship, expectation of some other benefit, etc. [*Dr. Balbir Singh* v. *MCD* (1985) 20 Taxman 56/152 ITR 388 (SC)].

However, as a general yardstick following considerations are taken into account in determining reasonably expected rent

(*i*) *Municipal valuation*: Municipal valuation is an important guiding factor in arriving at the notional income of a house property. A local authority makes a periodic survey of rental valuations of all buildings within its area for determining municipal taxes payable by a houseowner. The surveyor determines the gross rent.

(*ii*) *Fair rent*: Rent payable for similar and similarly situated property may also be taken into consideration in determining notional income of the house property.

(*iii*) *Standard rent*: In a State in which the Rent Control Act is in operation, the landlord cannot reasonably expect to receive anything more than the standard rent fixed or determinable under the Rent Control Act. Therefore, the standard rent fixed or determinable under the Rent Control Act would be the basis for fixing annual value of the house. [*Mrs. Shiela Kaushish* v. *CIT* (1981) 7 Taxman 1/131 ITR 435 (SC)].

Thus, annual value will be reasonably Expected Rent which is higher of Municipal valuation or fair rent. Notional rent so determined cannot exceed standard rent under the Rent Control Act (wherever in operation).

This is because reasonably expected rent applies to situations where by virtue of a legal fiction, it is assumed as if the property is let out and is generating an income. Such notional amount cannot therefore exceed the amount that the owner can lawfully recover from a tenant [*Dr. Balbir Singh* v. *MCD* (1985) 20 Taxman 56/152 ITR 388 (SC)]. The expected rent can be less than the standard rent having regard to various attendant circumstances and considerations [*Dr. Balbir Singh* v. *MCD* (1985) 20 Taxman 56/152 ITR 388 (SC)]. For example, if the building is not in a proper state of repair or is so situated that it has certain disadvantages from the point of view of easy accessibility or means of transport or any other similar cause, the actual rent which the owner may reasonably expect to receive from a hypothetical tenant may be less than the standard rent determinable on the principles laid down in the Rent Act. It is also possible that in the case of a building recently constructed, the standard rent determinable according to the principles laid down in the Rent Act may be very high having regard to the fantastic inflation in the value of land and the abnormal rise in the cost of construction in the last few years, but it may not be, and perhaps in many cases would not be, possible for the owner to obtain such high rent from a hypothetical tenant. It is equally possible that the building constructed by the owner may be so large as a single unit that it may be difficult for the owner to find a tenant who will be prepared to pay the huge amount of rent which the standard rent is bound to be if determined on the principles laid down in the Rent Act and having regard to the extreme smallness of the number of possible tenants of such a building, the rent which the owner may reasonably expect to receive from a hypothetical tenant may be very much less than the standard rent.

(*b*) Property Actually let out [Sec. 23(1)(*b*)] - Where the property is let out, actual rent is received or receivable from a tenant in occupation of the property. In such instance, actual rent is an important criterion in fixing annual value but it is not the sole criterion. Chances are that actual rent is not genuine or has been deflated due to emergency, relationship, fraud or such other considerations. [*Corporation of Calcutta* v. *Padma Debi* AIR 1962 SC 151].

To address such a possibility, the provision stipulates that actual rent will be taken as annual value if it exceeds reasonably expected rent. Meaning thereby, that if actual rent is less than reasonably expected rent, it is reasonably expected rent which will be taken as annual value.Where actual rent is a genuine figure, no adjustment is required.

Notional interest on interest free advances not to be considered in arriving at actual rent: Where the lessee deposits interest-free deposits for the due performance of the lease, notional interest cannot be added to the rent to arrive at de facto rent [*CIT* v. *J. K. Investors (Bombay) Ltd.* (2000) 112 Taxman 107/(2001) 248 ITR 723 (Bom.)].

Obligations borne by tenant are not included to arrive at actual rent: Where the tenant is statutorily required to bear municipal taxes for the portion occupied by him, amount of such taxes paid by the tenant cannot be added to actual rent to find out de facto rent. Tenant share of municipal taxes, collected in excess by landlord but not paid to municipality, not to be added while fixing de facto rent: Where the tenant's share of municipal taxes is collected in excess by the landlord and the same is not paid to the municipality, the unpaid amount of such taxes cannot be added to actual rent to ascertain de facto rent. To the extent such amount has not been paid to the municipality, the same has to be refunded to the tenant from whom it was collected. Such amount does not acquire the character of income [*CIT* v. *Gillanders Arbuthnot and Co. Ltd.* (1983) 13 Taxman 189/142 ITR 598 (Cal.)].

Charges for services which a landlord is not obliged to render cannot be a part of Annual Value: Where a landlord receives a payment distinct from the rent as service charges for certain services, which he is not obliged to render as landlord, such service charges cannot be treated as part of the rental receipt, but only as income from other sources [*Tarapore and Co.* v. *CIT* (2002) 125 Taxman 446/(2003) 259 ITR 389 (Mad.)]. Such service charges cannot be treated as part of annual value.

Mere claim by a landlord for enhancement of rent cannot be said to be an Amount "Receivable" within the Meaning of Sec. 23(1) of the Act: A mere claim or a demand by itself does not come within the purview of the word "income received or receivable". Although the system of accounting adopted by the assessee may be a relevant factor, even in the mercantile system of account only such amounts can be assessed which the assessee had a right to receive or which had accrued. A mere claim or a mere demand without anything else is not income within the meaning of Sec. 5 of the Income-tax Act. It must be borne in mind that a claim may fructify only after a lapse of many years because of pendency thereof in a court of law and/or prolonged negotiation between the parties. A tenant is not bound to pay rent at an enhanced amount only because the landlord claims the same.

Case Law : ***CIT* v. *Parbutty Churn Law* (1965) 57 ITR 609 (Cal.)**

Facts: The lease deed provided that the tenants shall undertake the costs of petty repairs while those requiring structural changes will be borne by the landlord. Assessing Officer sought to add the cost of repairs by the tenant to the actual rent.

Held: Where tenant bears the repair cost but pays the market rent, it is no ground to hold that annual value must be fixed at a higher figure than the actual rent

(*c*) Property falling vacant subsequent to let out [Sec. 23(1)(*c*)]

There are possibilities that a property which was actually let out subsequently falls vacant either during a part or the whole of the previous year. Say for instance, a property was let out under a tenancy agreement of three years starting from 2018-19. On 1st June 2020 the tenant vacates the place owing to change in job to the other city. The owner could find another tenant only in October 2020 and there onwards. For the previous year 2020-21, the vacancy period subsists through four months.

In such situation, actual rent after deducting the vacancy period will be taken as annual value even if such actual rent is less than expected rent.

Unrealised rent to be excluded

Annual value of property covered by (*b*) and (*c*) above will exclude unrealized rent *i.e.* the amount of rent payable but not paid by the tenant. This exclusion is subject to the fulfilment of the following conditions (under Rule 4) [*Explanation* to Sec. 23(1) r.w. Rule 4]

- The tenancy is *bona fide*.
- The defaulting tenant has vacated, or steps have been taken to compel him to vacate the property.
- The defaulting tenant is not in occupation of any other property of the assessee.
- The assessee has taken all reasonable steps to institute legal proceedings for the recovery of the unpaid rent or satisfies the Assessing Officer that legal proceedings would be useless.

(*d*) Property is self-occupied for residence [Sec. 23(2), (3) & (4)]

When a house property is self-occupied by the assessee-owner, it's annual value is taken as nil in the following two instances:

(*i*) **self-occupied for residence** the house is in occupation of the owner for the purpose of his own residence; or

(*ii*) **could not be occupied owing to business or employment** the house could not be actually occupied for the purpose of his own residence owing to the fact that his employment, business or profession is carried on at a place other than the place of the house owned by him.

Such a benefit of nil annual value can be availed in respect of any two such houses at the option of the assessee provided that the house or any part thereof is not let out or no other benefit is derived thereof.

Benefit for self-occupied house available only to an Individual and HUF: The expression "occupation by the owner for the purposes of his own residence" refers only to a human owner and not a fictional entity. A firm or a company cannot physically reside and so cannot claim the benefit of the provision. For example, it is difficult to contemplate residence by some of the partners or even all of them as self-residence by the owner-firm. In the context of Sec. 23(2), the dichotomy between the firm and its partners, who are independent assessable entities for the purposes of the Act, should be given effect to. The nature of the relief under Sec. 23(2) is such that it is not available in the case of a firm just as it is not available in the case of a company [*CIT* v. *Dewan Chand Dholan Das* (1982) 9 Taxman 172/(1981) 132 ITR 790 (Delhi)].

Nexus between Vacancy and Employment/Business is Must: Some nexus between the fact of residing in a building not belonging to him and his employment, business or profession must be shown before the relief can be claimed for keeping his house vacant. For example, where the assessee owns a residential house at the place of business but lives in the same town in a house owned by his father for the sake of personal convenience and it cannot be proved that by living in his own house, he cannot look after his business, no relief can be allowed to him for keeping his house vacant. [*Shikharchand Jain* v. *CIT* (1982) 11 Taxman 124/(1983) 140 ITR 552 (MP)]. On the other hand, where an official or a dignitary has to reside in official residence as a obligation of office and, therefore, his own residential house at the place of employment is kept vacant for self-occupancy, the benefit of Sec. 23(3) would apply [*CIT/Wealth-tax* v. *Justice Avadh Behari Rohtagi* (1985) 21 Taxman 409/(1986) 157 ITR 441 (Delhi)], provided the house property is not let out and no other benefit is derived therefrom by the owner.

Case Law : *D.R. Sunder Raj* v. *CIT* (1979) 2 Taxman 458/(1980) 123 ITR 471 (AP)

Facts: The assessee let out his house to his employer-company which, in turn, allotted the same to him as rent-free quarter. The assessee claimed that the income from the house property should be taken as nil under sec. 23(2), being self-occupied by him.

Held: The object of Sec. 23(2) is to provide relief to the owner when he, in his capacity as owner, occupies the same for his own residence. The beneficial determination of annual value cannot be accorded in any other capacity. Since the assessee occupied his own house in his capacity as sub-tenant of the employer-company and that of an owner, he is not entitled to the benefit permissible under section 23 (2).

Case Law : *Smt. Jashvidaben C. Mehta* v. *CIT* [1988] 37 Taxman 249/172 ITR 680 (Guj.)

Facts: The assessee had one property which was occupied by her cousin free of rent. The assessee claimed the benefit under sec. 23(2) whereby annual value would be nil.

Held: On a plain reading of the sec. 23(2) the property in question must be in the occupation of the owner for her own residence to avail of the benefit of the said provision. If the house is in occupation of a relative, benefit cannot be granted.

TABLE 7.2: SUMMARIZING DETERMINATION OF ANNUAL VALUE

<table>
<tr><td rowspan="2">(a) Deemed to be let out</td><td colspan="2">(b) Actually let out</td><td>(c) Let out and subsequently vacant</td><td colspan="2">(d) Self-occupied for residence</td></tr>
<tr><td>When Actual rent exceed Expected Rent</td><td>When Actual Rent is less than Expected Rent</td><td>When Actual Rent is less than Expected Rent due to vacancy</td><td>Any two houses at the option of the assessee</td><td>Houses in addition to two [could be (a), (b), (c)]</td></tr>
<tr><td>Expected Rent [Higher of Municipal valuation or Fair rent, (can be less than Standard Rent but cannot be more than Standard Rent)]</td><td>Actual Rent</td><td>Expected Rent</td><td>Actual Rent</td><td>NIL</td><td>As the case may be</td></tr>
<tr><td>--</td><td colspan="2">Deduct unrealized rent, if any</td><td>Deduct unrealized rent, if any</td><td colspan="2">--</td></tr>
<tr><td></td><td colspan="2"></td><td></td><td colspan="2"></td></tr>
</table>

(*e*) Others

(*i*) Annual value where a house is jointly occupied by the tenant and owner - Where a house or its unit is jointly occupied by the owner and the tenant, the annual value of such house/unit is to be determined in accordance with the proportion of holding of the owner as well as the tenant. So that annual value of the portion self-occupied by the owner for the purposes of his residence will be nil while that of the tenant will be determined in accordance with the provisions discussed above.

(ii) **Annual value in case of co-ownership of the property [Sec. 26] -** When the property has two or more co-owners, the benefit of nil annual value for self-occupancy is computed as if each co-owner is individually entitled to relief [*CIT* v. *Bijoy Kumar Almal* (1995) 80 Taxman 76/215 ITR 22 (SC)]. Section 26 contemplates assessment of income from jointly-owned property in the hands of co-owners in separate compartments in accordance with their shares which are required to be ascertained. When the computation of this income is required to be made separately, then, the benefit contemplated under the Act cannot be excluded. The co-owners were not joint-owners, but owners in common for which Sec. 26 had provided a special method of computation of income and if that method was logically applied then to the share of each co-owner, all the benefits and deductions as are available to a full owner would have to be given also to a co-owner (but obviously restricted to his share) [*CIT* v. *Nauser K. Kanga* [1979] 2 Taxman 147/120 ITR 404 (Bom.)]. The provisions of Sec. 26 are mandatory and positively prohibits assessment in the status of an association of persons and directs that the share of each individual in the income from the property is to be included in his individual total income. The provisions leave no choice or option in the hands of the Assessing Officer [*Gora Chand Sen* v. *CIT* [1985] 23 Taxman 410/154 ITR 435 (Cal.)].

(iii) **Annual value when property is a stock-in-trade of a builder [Sec. 23(5)] -** In accordance with this head of income, even when property remains locked, a notional income is chargeable in the hands of the owner. It is also irrelevant that the owner is in the business of selling house property. This created difficulties for assessee-builders and developers who owned house properties as stock-in-trade for the purposes of sale to ultimate buyers. Because ordinarily it takes some time in finalizing the sale of property with the buyer and the moment construction of the house property is complete, this head of income becomes applicable. So to provide a relief to this set of assessees, the Finance Act, 2017 (w.e.f. 1.4.2018) inserted a new sub-section (5) whereby a safe harbour of two years was created for a property held as stock-in-trade. Accordingly, where a property consisting of any building or land appurtenant thereto is held as stock-in-trade which is not let, will be given the benefit of nil annual value for a period of up to two years from the end of the financial year in which the certificate of completion

of construction of the property is obtained from the competent authority.

(*iv*) **Annual Value of a Foreign Property -** A "resident" assessee is taxed on his total world income. Therefore, if such assessee owns a house property in a foreign country, income from such property is also to be included in the total income. In computing annual value of such a house property municipal taxes levied by a local authority of that country and which have been paid, are to be deducted in computing the annual value [*CIT* v. *R. Venugopala Reddiar* (1965) 58 ITR 439 (Mad.)].

(*v*) **Annual Value when a furnished house is let outand the letting is separable -** If a furnished house property is let out, the annual value of such house should be estimated exclusive of the rent of the furniture. The rent attributable to furniture is to be taxed separately either under the head "business" or under the head "other sources". Similar is the position about monies charged in respect of other services provided by the landlord. When the letting is inseparable, income therefrom is taxed either under the head 'Profits and Gains from Business or Profession' or 'Income from Other sources'. (Discussed further in this chapter)

MUNICIPAL TAXES

Municipal Taxes paid by Owner - The deduction for municipal taxes is on payment basis. Thereby, full value municipal taxes, paid by the owner, is deductible. So that where arrears of municipal taxes of earlier years are paid during the previous year, deduction should be allowed to the assessee provided such taxes were not allowed as deduction on due basis during the earlier years [*CIT* v. *Parachuri Siva Lakshmi* [1998] 229 ITR 697 (AP)].

However, no deduction is allowed when municipal taxes are to be borne and paid by the tenant and not the owner.

Municipal taxes include service taxes levied by a local authority in respect of the property [Sec. 27(*vi*)] e.g. water tax, scavenging tax or halalkore tax, fire tax, education cess, etc. Municipal taxes do not include any tax levied by the State Government. For example, state education cess and urban land tax levied by a State Government are not deductible under municipal taxes.

No roll back of deduction upon refund of Municipal Taxes - Unlike sec. 41 that treats the recovery of any amount as business income when such amount was allowed as deduction in earlier year, there is no provision in this head that rolls back deduction on municipal taxes. Thus in absence of similar provision under the head "house property" refund of municipal taxes cannot be treated as income from house property [*CIT* v. *India Automobiles (1960) Ltd.* (2001) 119 Taxman 965/251 ITR 117 (Cal.)]

No Deduction for Municipal Taxes allowed for a Self-occupied House or a House kept Vacant for Self-occupancy - There is no provision in Sec. 23 of the

Income-tax Act, 1961, whereby for the purposes of computing the annual letting value of the self-occupied house property, local or municipal taxes paid by the owner can be deducted. [*CIT* v. *Arvind Narottam Lalbhai Dalpatbhai Vada* [1976] 105 ITR 378 (Guj.) and *Addl. CIT* v. *M.B. Rajeswari* [1977] 110 ITR 443 (Mad.); dissented from [*CIT* v. *I. Chatterji* [1986] 24 Taxman 251/161 ITR 535 (Bom.)].

Deduction in Computing Income from House Property [Sec. 24]

The following deductions are allowed in computing the income from house property:

Statutory Deduction @ 30% of Net Annual Value [Sec. 24(*a*)]

Where a house property is let out or deemed to be let out, statutory deduction @ 30% of Net Annual Value is allowed in computing its income. This deduction is not to be allowed in respect of a house, occupied by the owner for his own residence or kept vacant for self-occupancy, fulfilling the conditions of Sec. 23(2)(*a*) and Section 23(2)(b).

Interest on Borrowed Capital [Sec. 24(*b*)] - Where the property has been acquired, constructed, repaired, renewed or reconstructed with borrowed capital, interest on such borrowed capital is allowed as deduction in the following manner:

(*a*) *House occupied by owner:*

Where, the property is in occupation of the owner for the purpose of his own residence; orit cannot be occupied by the owner by reason of the fact that owing to his employment, business or profession being carried on at other place, he has to reside at that other place in a building not belonging to him; deduction of interest is available as follows:

(*i*) **Where capital is borrowed before 1 April, 1999 -** When capital is borrowed for acquiring, construction, repairs, reconstruction or renewal of the property, interest thereon is allowed as deduction subject to a maximum limit of ₹ 30,000.

(*ii*) **Where capital is borrowed on or after 1 April, 1999 for acquisition or construction -** When capital is borrowed on or after 1 April, 1999 for the purposes of acquisition or construction of house property, interest thereon is allowed as deduction to a maximum limit of ₹ 2,00,000 subject to the following conditions:

- such acquisition or construction is completed within five years from the end of the financial year in which the capital was borrowed.
- Certificate of Interest to be Furnished by the Assessee: The deduction of such interest is allowed provided the assessee furnishing a certificate from the person to whom any interest is payable on the capital borrowed. The certificate should specify the amount of interest payable by the assessee for the purpose of such acquisition or construction of the property or conversion of the whole or any part of the capital borrowed which remains to be repaid as a new loan.

(*iii*) **Where capital is borrowed on or after 1 April, 1999 for repairs, renewals or reconstruction of property:** When capital is borrowed for repairs, reconstruction or renewal of the property, interest thereon is allowed as deduction subject to a maximum limit of ₹ 30,000.

For this purpose, "new loan" means the whole or any part of the loan taken by the assessee subsequent to capital borrowed, for the purpose of repayment of such capital [Third Proviso to Sec. 24(b)]. It is operatire from the AY 2003-2004 and subsequent years.

(*b*) *House let out:* The amount of any interest payable on capital borrowed for acquiring, construction, repairs, reconstruction or renewal of the property is allowed as deduction from annual value without any limit even if it exceeds annual value [*CIT* v. *Justice P.C. Jain* (1989) 46 Taxman 337/179 ITR 572 (P&H)].

(*c*) *House partly let out and partly self-occupied:* Where the deduction of interest on a loan is claimed in respect of house property, which is occupied by the owner for the purposes of his residence and let out a part thereof, interest on loan is fully allowed.

(*d*) *House deemed to be let out:* Where loan is taken to acquire a house occupied by the owner but treated as deemed let out, interest on such loan is fully deducted.

TABLE 7.3: OVERVIEW OF DEDUCTION OF INTEREST ON BORROWED CAPITAL

Deemed to be let out	Actually let out	Self-Occupied			Partly let out and partly self-occupied
		Loan borrowed before 1.4.1999	Loan borrowed on or after 1.4.1999		
		Acquiring, construction, reconstruction, repairs, renewals	Acquiring or Construction (subject to fulfilment of conditions)	Repairs, renewals, reconstruction	
Any amount of interest	Any amount of interest	Restricted to ₹ 30,000	Restricted to ₹ 2,00,000	Restricted to ₹ 30,000	Any amount of interest

Interest for Pre-acquisition Period to be Allowed in 5 Annual Instalments [Explanation 1 to Sec. 24] - Where loan is taken to acquire a house property but the property is not acquired, either by way of purchase or construction, in the year in which loan is taken but it is acquired in a subsequent year, interest for pre-acquisition period or pre-construction period, as the case may be, is allowed to be deducted in five annual instalments, commencing from the previous year in which the property is acquired.

For instance, an assessee borrowed loan of ₹ 30 lacs on 1st June 2019 and commences construction of a house property which is completed in 1st June 2020. The entire amount of loan was repaid in June 2021. That essentially means that for the purposes of income-tax, the house property comes into existence only in June 2020 *i.e* for the previous year 2020-21. But interest would have been paid right from June 2019 till June 2022. Now the interest that was paid before the house property came into existence *i.e.* between June 2019 to June 2020 ought to be allowed as deduction to the assessee.

For this purposes, pre-construction period begins from the date of borrowing *i.e.* 1st June 2019 in our example and it goes (*i*) either up to 31 March, immediately preceding the previous year in which the property is acquired/constructed *i.e.* 31st March, 2020 (*ii*) or the date of repayment of loan *i.e.* 1st June 2021, whichever is earlier. Pre-construction period is 1st June 2019 to 31st March, 2020. All the interest paid during this time will be divided in five equal instalments and allowed as deduction beginning from the previous year in which the house property come into existence. Thereby the interest deductible will include current year's interest as well as interest of pre-construction period. The usual limits of deductions will apply, as the case may be.

FIGURE 7.1: PRE-CONSTRUCTION PERIOD

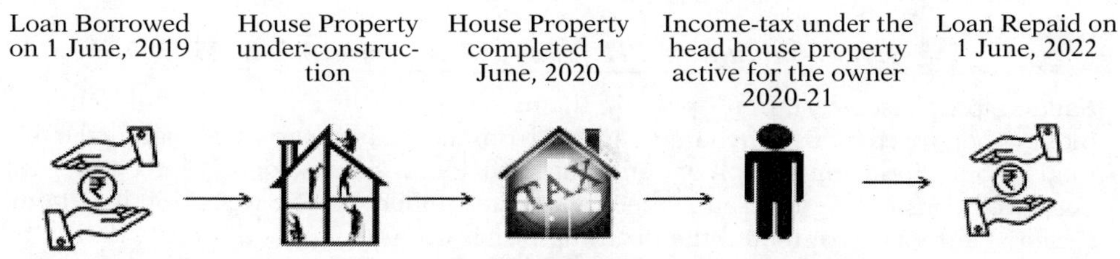

Pre-Construction period

From: Date of borrowing *i.e.* 1 June, 2019

To : 31 March immediately preceding the previous year in which property is constructed *i.e.* 31 March, 2020 or Date of repayment of loan *i.e.* 1 June 2022 whichever is earlier *i.e.* 1 June, 2019 to 31 March, 2020

Deduction on interest allowed on Due Basis: The deduction for interest is allowed on due basis, *i.e.* whether interest is paid or not. Even if the assessee follows cash system of accounting, interest is allowed to be deducted on due basis. Once the nexus between the borrowed capital and the acquisition, construction, etc., of property is established and proved, the claim for deduction of interest on borrowing cannot be resisted. sec. 24(*b*) permits deduction of the interest "payable" on borrowed capital utilised for the construction, etc., of property. The deduction has not been made dependent on the actual payment of the amount claimed as deduction [*CIT* v. *Devendra Brothers and Co.* [1993] 200 ITR 146 (All.)].

Interest on Loan Taken to Repay the Original Borrowing is also Eligible: Where a fresh loan has been raised to repay the original loan taken for the aforesaid purpose, the interest payable in respect of the second loan is also admissible as deduction [Circular No. 28, dated 20.08.1969].

Interest paid on outstanding purchase price allowed: Where buyer of property agrees to pay interest to the seller on unpaid purchase price, unpaid purchase consideration is treated as capital borrowed for acquiring the property. The buyer may claim deduction in respect to such interest [*CIT* v. *R.P. Goenka and J.P. Goenka* (1998) 99 Taxman 13/233 ITR 123 (Cal.)].

Interest on House Building: Advance Interest on house building advance taken by Government employees under House Building Advance Rule 6, is allowed to be deducted on accrual basis.

Property Mortgaged for Raising the Loan need not be the Same Property for which the Loan is Raised: Where loan is taken to acquire a property by mortgaging some other property, interest on such loan is to be deducted from annual value of the property acquired. Take an example. Loan is taken by mortgaging property J to acquire property M. Interest is deductible from the annual value of property M. However, where the property, acquired with loan money, is sold prior to redemption of the loan, interest on outstanding loan money cannot be deducted from the income of other property.

Interest on Arrears of Interest not Deductible: If interest is paid on the arrears of interest, no deduction is be allowed for such interest.

Expenses in Connection with Loan are not Deductible: No deduction is allowed for any brokerage or commission or any other expense incurred in raising the loan.

Case Law : ***S.M.A. Siddique* v. *CIT* [1984] 17 Taxman 14/148 ITR 307 (Mad.)**

Facts: S purchased certain property in the name of his wife and minor children with moneys borrowed in his own name. Income from the said property was included in his total income upon application of clubbing provision. S claimed deduction on interest borrowed considering himself as deemed owner under sec. 27. Rejecting his claim, Revenue authority contented the deeming provision introduces a limited fiction by virtue of which S was deemed as owner of the house in name of his wife and cannot be extended so as to deem even the borrowing by S.

Held: The fiction in section 27(1) which makes the transferor continue to be the owner of the transferred assets itself, comprehends the conception that the borrowing by the assessee must be so regarded and given effect to that the computation of the income from the transferred property is to be arrived at precisely in the same manner and to the same extent as it would be if the assessee had not transferred the property at all to his wife or minor children. S was entitled to deduction.

Interest Payable Outside India to be Deducted Subject to Deduction of Tax at Source [Sec. 25] - If interest is payable outside India, and it is chargeable to tax in India, it cannot be deducted unless the tax on it has been paid or deducted at source. However, the condition of payment of tax or deduction of tax at source does not apply if such interest is paid on a loan issued for public subscription before 1 April 1938 or there is a person in India who may be treated an agent (under sec. 163) of the recipient of such interest. In such a case, the interest is deductible even if no tax on it has been paid or deducted at source

Recovery of arrears of rent and unrealised rent in subsequent years [Sec. 25A] - When the assessee-owner receives arrears of rent or unrealised rent subsequently from a tenant, such receipts shall be deemed to be the income from house property in respect of the financial year in which it is received. It is to be classified under this head "Income from house property" even when the assessee may not continue to remain the owner of that property.

Further, a deduction of thirty per cent of this amount shall be available to the assessee.

GENERAL DEDUCTION

Deduction for the repayment of the principal amount [Sec. 80C(2)(*xviii*)]

While interest on capital borrowed for the purchase or construction of a house property is deductible under sec. 24, principal amount of the loan for the purchase or construction of such property repaid by the assessee is also eligible for deduction as a general deduction under sec. 80C. The upper limit of such deduction is ₹ 1,50,000 (which is an aggregation with other investments under secs. 80C, 80CCC and 80CCD. For details see Chapter 13 deductions from Gross Total Income.

Following payments are eligible for this deduction:

(*a*) Any payment by way of instalment or part payment of the amount due under self-financing or other schemes of any development authority, housing boards, etc., engaged in the construction and sale of house property on ownership basis; or

(*b*) Any payment by way of instalment or part payment of the amount due to any company or cooperative society of which the assessee is shareholder or member towards the cost of the house allotted to him; or

(*c*) Repayment of the loan borrowed by the assessee from (*i*) the Central Government or any State Government; or (*ii*) any bank including a co-operative bank; or (*iii*) the Life Insurance Corporation; or (*iv*) National Housing Bank; or (*v*) any public company, formed and registered in India with the main object of carrying on the business of providing long-term finance for the construction or purchase of houses in India for residential purposes and which is entitled to claim deduction in respect of special reserve [under Sec. 36(1)(*viii*)]; or (*vi*) any company in which public are substantially interested or any cooperative society where such company or society is engaged in the business of financing the construction of houses; or (*vii*) the assessee's employer where such employer is an authority or a board or a corporation or any other body established or constituted under a Central or State Act; or (*viii*) the assessee's employer where such employer is an authority or a board or a corporation or any other body established or constituted under a Central or State Act; or (*ix*) the employer of the assessee, where such employer is public company; or (*x*) public sector company, or university or its affiliated college, or a local authority.

(*d*) Any payment of stamp duty, registration fee and other expenses for the purpose of the transfer of such house property to the assessee.

Some payments are not eligible for deduction as they are not treated towards the cost of the house. Such payments are as follows:

(*i*) admission fee, cost of share/initial deposit which a shareholder of a company or member of a cooperative society has to pay for becoming shareholder or member; or

(*ii*) the cost of land, except where the consideration for the purchase of the house property is composite amount and the cost of the land alone cannot be separately ascertained; or

(*iii*) the cost of any addition, alteration, renovation, repair of the house, incurred either after the issue of completion certificate or after the house has been occupied by the assessee or any person on his behalf or after the house has been let out; or

(*iv*) any expenditure in respect of which deduction is allowable while computing the income from house property (under Sec. 24).

Where the rebate has been allowed to an assessee in any previous year in respect of any sum covered under clause (*a*) or (*b*), (*c*) or (*d*) aforesaid and subsequently such sum is refunded or received back by the assessee in any previous year, there are two-fold tax-effects of such refund.

(*i*) No rebate is admissible in respect of any sum paid in the relevant previous year (in which refund is received); and

(*ii*) The aggregate amount of the rebate allowed in the previous year(s) preceding the relevant previous year is deemed to be tax due from the assessee in the relevant previous year.

Roll back of deduction if property transferred within five years: There is a lock-in-period to avail deduction under sec. 80C whereby the assessee cannot transfer the property for a period of five years. If the assessee transfers the house property so acquired before the expiry of five years from the end of the financial year in which possession of such property is obtained by him receives back, whether by way of refund or otherwise, any sum covered under aforesaid clauses—(*a*), (*b*), (*c*) and (*d*) no deduction is allowed to the assessee in respect of any sum so paid in such previous year and the aggregate amount of the deduction of income so allowed in respect of the previous year or years preceding such previous year, is deemed to be the income of the assessee of such previous year and is liable to tax in the assessment year relevant to such previous year [Sec. 80C(3)].

The scope of the term "transfer" in relation to immovable property has been given extended meaning. It includes transfer of such property by way of sale or exchange or lease for a term not less than 12 years.

It also includes allowing possession of such property to be taken or retained in part performance of a contract under Sec. 53A of the Transfer of Property Act, 1982 [Sec. 269(4A)(*f*)].

Additional deduction for interest [Sec. 80EE]

From the assessment year 2017-18 and onwards, an individual assessee, being the first time home buyer, can avail an additional deduction of upto ₹ 50,000 on the interest payable on loan provided the following conditions are fulfilled:

(*i*) The loan is borrowed from a bank or a housing finance company between 1.4.2016 and 31.3.2017.

(*ii*) the amount of loan sanctioned is not more than ₹ 35 lac

(*iii*) the value of residential house property does not exceed ₹ 50 lac

(*iv*) the assessee does not own any residential house property on the date of sanction of loan.

It must be noted that this additional deduction is only for individual assessees and not any other category such as HUF or company or others.

Additional Deduction for interest who is ineligible under sec. 80EE [Sec. 80EEA]

An individual assesse who is a first time home buyer but is ineligible under sec. 80EE can avail an additional deduction on interest payable on loan taken by him for the purposes of acquisition of residential house property upto ₹ 1,50,000 provided he fulfils the following conditions:

(*i*) the loan has been sanctioned by any bank or housing finance company between 1.4.2019 and 31.3.2021.

(*ii*) the stamp duty value of residential house property does not exceed ₹45 lac.

(*iii*) the assessee does not own any residential house property on the date of sanction of loan.

Characterisation of Income derived from a Building: Property Income *v.* Business Income *v.* Income from Other Sources

Ownership of property and leasing it out may be done as a part of business or it may be done as a landowner. It is therefore capable of being characterized under either of the three possible heads- house property income, business income and income from other sources. Merely because income is earned from an immoveable property does not mean that it is income from house property. For example, letting out of building for marriages and other functions along with chairs, mike, etc., for limited periods is assessable as business income. This activity can be described as a business carried on by the assessee with the intention of earning income (profits) from the building. The income earned thereby is assessed as business income and not as income from house property [*CIT* v. *Halai Nemon Association* [2000] 111 Taxman 326/243 ITR 439 (Mad.)]. Therefore, income received on account of letting of a building need not always be treated as income from house property.

To ascertain whether an income received by an assessee from leasing or letting out of assets would fall under the head "profits and gains of business or profession" or under the head "income from house property" no precise test can be laid down. This decision is a mixed question of law and facts. One must see not the form which it gave to the transaction but to the substance of the matter. Whether it is the one or the other must necessarily depend upon the object with which the act is done. It is essential to find out the user of the property and the character in which that property is used. Let us have a look at a fundamental approach towards income from house property.

House Owning and Bare Letting carried on as business - Income from House Property - House owning, howsoever profitable, is not a trade or business within the meaning of Income-tax Act. Even if it is the business of the assessee is to let out houses, the rental income cannot be taxed as business income under Sec. 28. The annual value of house properties of which the assessee is the owner and which are not used for the purposes of his business or profession, the profits of which are chargeable to tax, is assessable under this head even if the house properties constitutes stock-in-trade of the assessee. Thus, where a company is incorporated with the object of promoting and developing markets, the rental income in respect of market shops and stalls owned by it, is assessable under the head "house property". The character of the income would not be altered merely because it is company incorporated with the object of letting out properties. [*East India Housing & Land Development Trust Ltd.* v. *CIT* (1961) 42 ITR 49 (SC)].

The source of Indian jurisprudence in this respect is the English case law on the matter in *Fry* v. *Salisbury House Estates Co. Ltd.* [1930] AC 432. There a company, being formed to acquire, manage and deal with buildings, let out unfurnished offices to the tenants and also provided staff to operate the lifts and to act as porters and watch and protect the building; in addition to certain services such as heating and cleaning to the tenants at an additional charge. The House of Lords while deciding on the issue pertaining to classification of income, held that the profits arose by ownership of land and is property income and not trade receipts. Thus, when subject matter of letting is simple income derived therefrom is income from house property, irrespective of the fact whether it is an individual or a company. When it is found that main intention is for simply letting out of property or any portion thereof, resultant income must be assessed as income from house property.

Case Law : ***Keyaram Hotels (P.) Ltd. v. Dy. CIT* [2014] 52 taxmann. com 469/ [2015] 228 Taxman 354 (Madras)**

Facts: The assessee company derived rental income from letting out a commercial complex and declared income under the head 'business' claiming all expenses and deductions allowable while computing the income under the head 'business'. The expenses were disallowed by the revenue authorities claiming that it was rental income.

Held: Even if the assessee's business letting, income on letting out of the property was to be assessed as "income from house property".

Letting of Building along with services and other amenities - In certain instances, apart from letting out the building, assessee-owner provides amenities such as lift, air-conditioning, security, cleaning etc. or for furniture and other gadgets. Such arrangements often take the form of a composite rent *i.e.* the rent for building includes the consideration for amenities or a separate charge *i.e* where the rental amount and that towards amenities are individually assigned. When the amounts are separable, that towards amenities is taxable as business profits or income from other sources and the one attributable to rent is taxable as property income. [*CIT* v. *Model Manufacturing Co. P. Ltd.* (1985) 21 Taxman 338/(1986) 159 ITR 270 (Cal.)].

In such instances, income that should be attributed to the property as such alone should be assessed under Sec. 22 of the Income-tax Act, 1961. The composite rent received by the assessee from its tenants should be split and the amounts attributable to the property only should be assessed under the head "income from property", while the amount attributable to amenities provided/services rendered by the assessee to the tenants should be assessed under the head "other sources" [*CIT* v. *Shkankaranarayana Hotels (P.) Ltd.* [1993] 67 Taxman 520/201 ITR 138 (Kar.)].

Case Law : ***CIT* v. *Mysore Intercontinental Hotels (P.) Ltd.* [2011] 9 taxmann. com 109/198 Taxman 514 (Kar)**

Facts: The assessee rented out premises fitted with some fittings to make it suitable for a tenant to use it as an office premises for carrying on software business activities. Revenue authorities split the composite rent as 90% towards house property income and 10% as Income from other sources.

Held: The question about what percentage of composite rent ought to be attributed to property income and business income or income from other sources is a question of fact. Having regard to the terms and conditions indicated in the agreement between the parties and for the facilities provided 40 per cent of the amount was to be apportionedas business income.

Complexity of the subject let out- Business Profits

When composite rent is charged from the tenants, and services rendered by assessee to its tenants are the result of its activities a) carried on continuously b) in an organized manner, c) with a set purpose and with a view to earn profits, those activities are business activities and income arising therefrom is chargeable to tax as business profits [*Karnani Properties Ltd.* v. *CIT* (1971) 82 ITR 547 (SC)].

So that while income from bare letting out is classified as house property income and is taxed accordingly, when the subject hired out is a complex one and the income obtained is not so much because of the bare letting of the tenement but because of the facilities and services rendered, it is a business income. [*CIT* v. *National Storage P. Ltd.* (1967) 66 ITR 596 (SC)]

Case Law : ***Raj Dadarkar & Associates* v. *Asstt. CIT* [2017] 81 taxmann. com 193/248 Taxman 1/394 ITR 592 (SC)**

Facts: The assessee obtained a market premise on lease, made substantive structural changes to the same and constructed shops and stalls on it which were given on rent.

Held: Since assessee was not engaged in systematic or organized activity of providing service to occupiers of shops/stalls, income from sub-licensing was to be taxed as income from house property and not as business income.

Case Law : ***Manohar Singh* v. *CIT* (1965) 58 ITR 592 (Pun. & Har.)**

Facts: The assessee purchased a piece of land and a constructed a house consisting of 13 well-furnished rooms and gave the suits on rent for a period extending to a day to months together with facilities of lunches, dinners, bed sheets, blankets, bath towels, face towels, etc.

Held: Rental income is derived not merely for letting of tenements but because of facilities and services rendered by the assessee. Rental income is chargeable as business income.

Case Law : ***CIT* v. *Veerabhadra Industries* [1999] 106 Taxman 370/240 ITR 5 (AP)**

Facts: The assessee-firm, after constructing godowns, let out the same on rent. It showed rental income as business income which was not acceptable to the revenue authorities.

Held: A single act of constructing a godown and letting it out cannot be treated as a business. The expression 'business' contemplates continuous activity from year to year. Unless the assessee is continuing the activity of constructing godowns and letting them out from year to year. Therefore, the income from a simple letting out of the godown could not be treated as business income for the purpose of the Income-tax.

No precise test can be laid down: Determination of income from buildings as house property income or business income is a knotty issue and the courts have time and again conceded that there is no precise test to ascertain whether the income is one or the other. It is a mixed question of law and fact and has to be determined from the point of view of a businessman in that business on the facts and in the circumstances of each case, including true interpretation of the agreement under which the assets are let out [*Universal Plast Ltd.* v. *CIT* (1999) 103 Taxman 493/237 ITR 454 (SC)].

Intention of the assessee as a determinant - In deciding whether income from letting out an asset is business income or income from property what has to be seen is whether the main intention of the assessee is to let out the property or any portion thereof, is for the purpose of enjoying the rent or if the primary object is to exploit the immovable property commercially [*CIT* v. *Shambhu Investment Pvt. Ltd.* [2001] 116 Taxman 795/249 ITR 47 (Cal.)]. In general parlance, when property is exploited commercially, the owner usually ends up incurring considerable expenditure which is ordinarily not incurred by a landlord who turns his house property to profitable account. This gives an indication that the property is being exploited for business and not as ownership rights. The distinction between the two is a narrow one and has to depend on certain facts peculiar to each case [*CIT.* v. *New India Industries Ltd.* [1993] 201 ITR 208 (Guj.)].

Where the object of an assessee is to acquire and possess properties and there is no indication that he intended to sell those properties or even turn them to account by way of leasing them as part of its business activities, the income from such properties is assessable as income from property and cannot be attributable to business [*Anaikar Trades and Estates (P.) Ltd. (No. 1)* v. *CIT* [1990] 51 Taxman 350/186 ITR 175 (Mad.)]. If the dominant object of leasing out is incidental to and for the purposes of the assessee's business, the income would be business income. What was to be discovered is whether the property is subservient to the main business of the assessee [*CIT* v. *New India Industries Ltd.* [1993] 201 ITR 208 (Guj.)].

Inseparable Letting of Building along with Machinery, Plant or Furniture - Assessed as Income from Other Sources and not as Income from Property - Sec. 56(2)(*iii*) of the Act specifically provides that where an assessee lets on hire machinery, plant or furniture belonging to him and also buildings and the letting of buildings is inseparable from letting of the said machinery, plant or furniture, the income from such letting, is not chargeable as business income but is assessed as income from other sources. The inseparability referred is one that arises from the intention of the parties and not necessarily by the physical inseparability by its very nature. It does not matter if the building or plant, machinery of furniture are let out under the same lease or separate lease as long as the intention is that they should be enjoyed together [*Sultan Brothers Pvt. Ltd.* v. *CIT* (1964) 51 ITR 353 (SC)]. For example, where an assessee leases a building along with furniture and fixtures for use by the lessee as a hotel, the rental income is assessed under other sources even if the rent for building and furniture and fixtures is specified separately in the lease agreement [*Sultan Brothers Pvt. Ltd.* v. *CIT* (1964) 51 ITR 353 (SC)]. Similarly, an assessee constructs a factory shed but is not able to start business due to some delays and lets the factory out on rent. The factory has electric installations and electrical equipment installed therein as an integral part and could not be used otherwise than with the factory. Income from renting the factory is assessed as income from other sources [*CIT* v. *Ajmera Industries Private Ltd.* (1976) 103 ITR 245 (Cal.)].

Exemptions to certain house properties - The income derived from the following are exempt:

(*i*) Income from farm house [Sec. 2(*1A*)(*c*)].

(*ii*) Annual value of any one place of an ex-Ruler [Sec. 10(*19A*)].

(*iii*) Income from house property of a local authority [Sec. 10(*20*)].

(*iv*) Income from house property of an approved scientific research association [Sec. 10(*21*)].

(*v*) Income from house property of an educational institution and hospital [Sec. 10(*23C*)].

(*vi*) Income from house property of a registered trade union [Sec. 10(*24*)].

(*vii*) Property held for charitable purposes. Income from property held for charitable or religious (public) purposes is exempt (under Sec. 11).

(*viii*) Property used for own business or profession, profits of which are chargeable to tax.

(*ix*) Self-occupied building or building, remaining vacant for self-occupation only.

Deduction to house property income of a Co-operative Society

Income derived by a cooperative society from a house property given below is includible in its total income and later on a deduction is allowed from the gross total income:

(i) *Letting of godowns [Sec. 80P(2)(e)]*: Whole of the income derived by a cooperative society from the letting of godowns or warehouses for storage, processing or facilitating the marketing of commodities is deductible in computing its total income.

(ii) *Income from any other property [Sec. 80P(2)(f)]*: If the gross total income of a cooperative society, not being a housing society or an urban consumers' cooperative society or a society carrying on a transport business, does not exceed ₹ 20,000; any income from house property is deductible in computing its total income.

CHAPTER 8

Profits and Gains of Business or Profession

INTRODUCTION

Revenue receipts of businesses and professions are brought to tax under the head 'Profits and Gains of Business or Profession.' The expression profits and gains should be understood to include negative incomes as well. So that while profits and gains represent "plus income", losses represents "minus income". Both positive and negative profits are of revenue character and therefore both must be taken into account in computing taxable income under this head [*CIT* v. *Harprasad & Co. Pvt. Ltd.* (1975) 99 ITR 118 (SC)].

Since this head computes revenue receipts, as a matter of principle, capital outlays are not allowed while arriving at profit figures for this head. However, some exceptions have been made in this regard in the relevant provisions. Profits and gains of business or profession are required to be computed in accordance with the method of accounting regularly followed by the assessee [Sec. 145].

Sec. 28 is the charging provision that essentially entails incomes that are chargeable to tax as profits under this head. In addition to what is recognized as profit under sec. 28, there are certain incomes that are deemed to be profits for the purposes of this head. Sec. 41 and secs. 68 to 69D comprise of incomes that are deemed to be profits and taxable for the assessee. Sec. 29 permits deductions and allowances comprised in secs. 30 to 37 to be availed by the assessee while computing profits and gains under this head. Secs. 40, 40A and 43B list out expenses that are not allowed as deductible from profits.

COMPUTATION OF TAXABLE PROFITS

Taxable profits of business or profession are computed in accordance with the method of accounting regularly followed by an assessee (Sec. 145). There are two systems of book keeping - Cash system and Mercantile system.

Cash System of Book Keeping - According to the cash basis of accounting, a record is kept of actual receipts and actual payments, entries are made only when money is actually collected or disbursed. If the profits of a business or profession are accounted in this way, the tax is payable on the difference between the receipts and the disbursements for the period in question. Under this method, deduction for expenditure is allowed only in the year of disbursement, irrespective of the question when the liability to pay the same arose [*Re B.M. Kamdar* (1946)14 ITR 10 (Bom.) *CIT* v. *E.A.E.T. Sundararaj* (1975) 99 ITR 226 (Madras)]. Income is taxable on receipt basis irrespective of the timings of its accrual.

Mercantile System of Book Keeping - Under this system, the net profit or loss is calculated after taking into account all the income and the expenditure relating to the period whether such income has been actually received or not and whether such expenditure has been actually paid or not. Thus, the profit computed under the system is the profit actually earned, though not necessarily realised in cash, or the loss computed under this system is the loss actually sustained, though not necessarily paid in cash. If the accounts are kept on mercantile basis, the income is taxable when it accrues or is earned, irrespective of receipt, the charge being on the net "book profits".

A mere claim against the assessee is not sufficient to justify a deduction—a liability to pay must definitely arise [*CIT* v. *Swadeshi Cotton & Flour Mills (P.) Ltd.* (1964) 53 ITR 134 (SC)]. If an assessee has been taxed on "book-profits", which have accrued but not received, he cannot be taxed on the same sum of money when they are actually received in a later year of assessment [*Explanation* 2 to Sec. 5].

COMPUTATION OF TAXABLE PROFITS IN CASE OF CASH SYSTEM OF BOOK-KEEPING

Those who follow cash system of accounting prepare "receipts and payments account", whereas the assessee following mercantile system of accounting, prepare the "profit and loss account". In order to compute taxable profits, the "receipts and payment accounts" or, as the case may be, the "profit and loss account" has to be adjusted in the light of the income-tax provisions, as demonstrated below.

TABLE 8.1: COMPUTATION OF PROFITS AND GAINS FROM BUSINESS OR PROFESSION

Particulars	Amt. (in ₹)	Amt. (in ₹)
Net Profits as per profit and loss account		xxxx
Add:		
(*a*) Amounts debited to P & L A/c but not allowable as deduction under the Income-tax Act	xxx	
(*b*) Income not credited to P & L A/c but are taxable under this head under the Income-tax Act	xxx	
		xxx
Less:		
(*a*) Amounts allowable under the Act but not debited to P & L A/c	xxx	
(*b*) Income credited to P & L A/c but are exempt under the Act or taxable under another head under the Act	xxx	
		xxx
Profits and Gains from Business or Profession		xxxx

MEANING OF BUSINESS [SEC. 2(*13*)]

According to the definition in sec. 2(*13*) business includes any trade, commerce, or manufacture or any adventure or concern in the nature of trade or commerce or manufacture. Ordinarily, the term business is used in the sense of an occupation or profession, which occupies time, attention and labour of a person, normally with the object of making a profit [*State of Andhra Pradesh* v. *H. Abdul Bakshi and Bros.* (1964) 15 STC 644 (SC)]. "Business" being an inclusive definition and not an exhaustive one is therefore capable of having an expansive understanding [*Dr. Vadamalayan P* v. *CIT* (1969) 74 ITR 94 (Mad.)]. Nevertheless, in judicial interpretation of the term 'business' has often identified the following key essentials:

Systematic and Organised Activity: Business means some real, substantial and systematic or organised course of activity or conduct with a set purpose Business means an activity carried on continuously and systematically by a person by the application of his labour and skill with a view to earning an income [*Barendra Prosod Ray* v. *ITD* (1981) 6 Taxman 19/129 ITR 295 (SC)].

Profits motive not essential: Though the element of profit is generally present in "business" but the motive of making profit or actual earning of profit is not an essential ingredient of business. For instance, mutual concerns and societies carry on business though not with a profit motive.

Business includes trade, commerce: Trade implies buying goods and selling them to make profit. If such transactions are done on a large scale, it is called commerce. Nobody can define the volume of business, which would convert a trade into commerce. But everybody understands the distinction between the two with sufficient vagueness [*Sri Gajalakshmi Ginning Factory Ltd.* v. *CIT* (1952) 22 ITR 502 (Mad.)].

"Business" is not merely confined to purchase and sale of articles or goods. It may consist of rendering services to others, *i.e.* communication service (*i.e.* telephone, telegraph, etc.) or transport (*i.e.* railways, bus, and aeroplane, etc.). There is no antithesis between service and business.

Business includes manufacture: The Finance Act, 2009 inserted the definition of the term manufacture. Accordingly under sec. 29BA manufacture with its grammatical variations, means a change in a non-living physical object or article or thing (*a*) resulting in transformation of the object or article or thing into a new and distinct object or article or thing having a different name, character and use or (*b*) bringing into existence of a new and distinct object or article or thing with a different chemical composition or integral structure. "Manufacture" implies a change but every change is not "manufacture".

It is only when the change, or a series of changes take the commodity to the point where commercially it can no longer be regarded as the original commodity but instead it is recognised as a new and distinct article, having its own name, identity character and end use [*CIT* v. *Oceanic Products Exporting Co.* (1996) 85 Taxman 554/219 ITR 293 (Ker.); *Assistant CIT* v. *Soni Photo Films P. Ltd.* (2000) 245 ITR (AT) 11 (Del.) (AT)].

Business includes any adventure or concern in the nature of trade or commerce - The word "business" in its commercial sense implies an element of continuity. But the income-tax law the wide definition of business does not require that there should be a series of transactions to constitute business. Even a single and isolated transaction may fall within the definition of business as being an adventure in the nature of trade, provided the transaction bears clear indication of trade. A transaction can be termed as an adventure in the nature of trade, commerce or manufacture if some elements of trade or business are present therein and not necessarily all elements be present. A single plunge may be enough, provided it is clearly demonstrated that the plunge is made in the water of trade.

It is a mixed question of facts and law whether a transaction constituted an adventure in the nature of trade, commerce, or manufacture. No hard and fast rule can be laid down in this respect. Each case has to be examined in the light of available facts. However, some guidance may be sought from the following broad principles, which are based on judicial pronouncements:

(*i*) *Intention to resell:* When the purchase is made solely with an intention to resell at a profit and purchaser has no intention of holding the property for himself, the transaction is an adventure in the nature of trade. Where the purchase of any article is made without an intention to sell at a profit, a resale under changed circumstances is only a realisation of capital investment and does not stamp the transaction with a business character.

(*ii*) *Transaction relating to business:* If a transaction is related to the business which is normally carried on by an assessee, though not directly part of it, it may be inferred that the transaction is an adventure in the nature of trade. For example, Mr. X is a cotton merchant. During a crisis in the cotton market, he is appointed under the power of attorney to wind up the affairs of a cotton firm and to dispose of the cotton bales and distribute the sale proceeds. The commission that he receives is taxable as business profits.

(*iii*) *The quantity of the commodity purchased:* Where the transaction is unrelated to business, which is normally carried on by an assessee, the quantity purchased and sold may throw some light on the nature of the transaction. If the quantity purchased is quite large which cannot be consumed by an assessee and his family in a reasonable time, and it does not give him any pride or possession, such transaction may be inferred as an adventure in the nature of trade.

(*iv*) *Where the purchased property undergoes alteration and then sold:* Where a commodity is purchased, altered, repaired or converted into a different property and then sold, it may be readily inferred that the transaction is an adventure in the nature of trade.

(*v*) *Concern in the nature of a trade:* A concern in the nature of trade, commerce, or manufacture also falls within the definition of "business". A concern in the nature of trade implies that it has an adequate degree of business organisation for the purpose of carrying on an undertaking. The size of organisation must necessarily depend upon the character of the concern itself.

Case Law: ***Raja J. Rameshwar Rao* v. *CIT* (1961) 42 ITR 179 (SC)**

Facts: 'R' acquired some land with a view to develop it and further goes further and divides the land into plots and sells the land not as a single unit, but in parcels.

Held: Even a single venture may be regarded as in the nature of trade or business. When a person acquires land with a view to selling it later after developing it, he is carrying on an activity resulting in profit, and the activity can only be described as a business venture.

Case Law: ***G. Venkataswami Naidu & Co.* v. *CIT* (1959) 35 ITR 594 (SC)**

Facts: 'V' a firm into the business of managing agency, purchased four different plots of lands over a period of two years. Such lands were adjacent to the mills it was managing. 'V' never used the lands either for cultivation or building on it but with an intention to sell it for profit to the mills.

Held: Instances of realization of investments by purchase and profitable resale are clearly outside the domain of adventures in the nature of trade. But when purchase had been made solely and exclusively with the intention to reselling it at a profit and the purchaser has no intention of holding the property for himself or otherwise enjoying or using it; it would raise a strong presumption that the transaction is an adventure in the nature of trade. 'V' purchased four plots with the sole intention of selling them to the mills at a profit and this intention raised a strong presumption that it was an adventure in the nature of trade.

Case Law: ***CIT* v. *Moti Chand Khajanchi* [1987] 34 Taxman 498/[1988] 171 ITR 280 (Rajasthan)**

Facts: 'M' derived income from interest, dividends and shares from three partnership firms, besides income from property. 'M' had a hobby of collection of paintings and sold some of them to National Museum, New Delhi in national interest. 'M' claimed that receipt from the sale of paintings was not liable to tax as it was neither a business profit nor a capital gain.

Held: Since receipts from the sale of paintings were of a casual and non-recurring nature, it was not an adventure in the nature of trade or commerce.

MEANING OF PROFESSION [SEC. 2(*36*)]

A "profession" is an occupation requiring either purely an intellectual skill or manual skill, controlled by the intellectual skill of the operator. Examples of profession are medicine, law, engineering, auditing, painting, etc.

All professions are business, but all business are not professions. Only those businesses are professions the profits of which are dependent mainly upon the personal qualifications and in which no capital expenditure is required or only capital expenditure of a comparatively small amount is required. Politics is a profession or vocation [*CIT* v. *PVG Raju* (1975) 101 ITR 465 (SC)].

Profession includes Vocation [Sec. 2(*36*)] - A vocation, as normally understood, is a calling in which a person passes his life. It may even be stated to a way of living or a sphere of activity for which one has a special fitness, though it is not necessary that the activity should be indulged in for the purposes of livelihood [*K. Ramaswami Gounder* v. *CIT* (1984) 19 Taxman 5/(1987) 163 ITR 94 (Mad.)]. Social work and preaching religion may amount to vocation. Teaching is a vocation if not a profession, a teaching of vedant, even as a matter of religion, amounts to carrying on a vocation [*P. Krishna Menon* v. *CIT* (1959) 35 ITR 48 (SC)].

Distinction between Business, Profession is of no Importance - Distinction between business, profession and vocation is of no importance in the computation of taxable income. What does not amount to "profession" may amount to "business", and what does not amount to "business" may amount to vocation. The Act treats them on an equal footing and the charging provisions for computing taxable income are the same for all of them.

BASIS OF CHARGE [SEC. 28]

The following receipts/incomes are chargeable to income tax under the head "profits and gain of business or profession":

Profits and Gains of any business or profession carried on by the assessee at any time during the Previous Year [Sec. 28(*i*)]

The charge under the head is on profits and gains and not on the gross receipts or sale proceeds of the business or profession. The following points may be noted in this context:

Profits of each business be computed separately: If one and the same business is carried on at a number of places, there is only one business. Net profits of the business have to be ascertained by aggregating the profits earned in all the branches and reducing them from all the allowable expenses. If more than one business is carried on by the assessee, profits of each business must be computed separately.

Capital Receipts not Chargeable: Capital receipts are outside the purview of this clause unless specifically required to be included by the statutes. Take an example. The supplier of bottles received compensation from an American company for destroying empty bottles of Coca-cola and Fanta as the Government refused permission for bottling agreement. The A.O. did not tax the amount of compensation. The CIT revised the Order under Sec. 263 and taxed it. Held, the empty bottle being a capital asset, the compensation received for their distruction was a capital receipt [*CIT* v. *Soft Beverages P. Ltd.* (2001) 118 Taxman 846/249 ITR 552 (Mad.)].

Chargeability of Revenue Receipts: In order to be chargeable, the receipts must be of revenue nature either by way of sales or consultancy fees or in some other form. Receipts should be a part of consideration for goods or services. It should not be a capital receipt or a returnable deposit.

Receipt may be in cash or kind: Receipts may be in money or money's worth, in cash or in kind. When a company sells its trading asset for fully paid shares in another company, the profit of the transaction is assessable although no cash passes [*British South Africa Co.* v. *CIT* (1946) 14 ITR 17 (PC)] (SUPP).

Voluntary Payments - All revenue receipts arising from business or the exercise of profession or vocation are chargeable under this section. Voluntary payments by persons who are under no obligations to pay anything at all would be income receipts in the hands of the receiver if those are received in the course of business or in the exercise of profession. Thus, an amount paid to the lawyer by a person who was not a client who had benefited by his professional services to another [*Susil C. Sen*, In re (1941) 9 ITR 261 (Calcutta)] or a voluntary payment made to an actress by a producer of film who had engaged her services [*C. Lakshmi Rajyam* v. *CIT* (1960) 40 ITR 340 (Madras)] are taxable under this clause.

Illegal Business: The income-tax law is not concerned with the legality or illegality of the business. The illegality of a business, profession or vocation does not exempt its profits from being taxed. Profits from carrying on the business of smuggling are thus taxable. Likewise, profits from illicit trafficking in drugs or illicit trafficking in liquor, contrary to prohibition laws, are chargeable to tax. Similarly, a man who lives by regularly receiving and reselling stolen goods is liable to be taxed on such profits.

The loss in illegal business can also be set off against the profits of such business. Thus, where an assessee carries on the business of dealing in smuggled gold and the gold is confiscated by the custom authorities, the loss due to confiscation of gold can be set off against the income in respect of such gold business [*CIT* v. *Piara Singh* [1980] 3 Taxman 67/124 ITR 40 (SC). Also see C. *Krishanalal Jain* v. *CIT* (1986) 26 Taxman 452/(1987) 163 ITR 747 (Kar.)].

Ownership of Business not essential for Chargeability: A person carrying on the business profession is assessable on business profits. Normally, this right is vested with the owner of business and so he would be assessable on business profits.

However, in a few cases, the right to carry on the business may not vest with its owner even though the profits may accrue to him. In such cases, the Revenue would charge the person who is vested with the right to carry on the business. Thus, promoters are assessable on pre-incorporation profits and not the company even though it might have ratified all pre-incorporation deals and accepted pre-incorporation profits [*CIT* v. *City Mills Distributors (P.) Ltd.* (1996) 85 Taxman 352/219 ITR 1 (SC)].

Where a guardian of a minor has the right to carry on business, he is to be assessed on such profits. Similarly, where the court takes away the right of the owner to carry on his business and appoints somebody else to carry on the business, the person appointed by the court is assessable on business profits. The owner is not assessable as he is not carrying on the business [*Saifudin Alimohamed* v. *CIT* (1954) 25 ITR 237 (Bom.)].

Business to have been carried on during the previous year: For chargeability of business profits, it is necessary that the business should have been carried on by the assessee at any time during the previous year. It is not necessary that business should have been carried on throughout the previous year [*CIT* v. *Express Newspapers* (1964) 53 ITR 250 (SC)].

Receipt after Discontinuance of Business, following Cash System of Accounting [Sec. 176(3A)/(4)]: In a business–profession, following cash system of accounting, profits and gains received after its discontinuance could not have been taxed as income from business or profession because no business–profession exists during the year of receipts.

Section 176(3A) and (4) plug this loop-hole. It provides that receipts from a discontinued business profession, following cash system of accounting, would still be taxable as the income from business–profession even though no source of income exists during the year of receipts.

The exception has no relevance to a business or profession, following mercantile system of accounting where profits might have accrued and charged to tax during the continuance of business or profession.

Receipts prior to setting up business: A business must be carried on before there can be any profits and gains. Any receipt, received before the business is carried on, is not a business receipt and if any expenditure is incurred before the business has started, it is also not a business expense. Where the assessee received grants-in-aid before it started business, it could not be treated a business receipt [*CIT* v. *State Trading Corporation of India Ltd.* (1973) 92 ITR 294 (Delhi)].

Case Law: ***CIT* v. *T.V. Sundaram Iyengar & Sons Ltd.* [1996] 88 Taxman 429/222 ITR 344 (SC)**

Facts: 'S' received certain deposits from customers in course of its business which were originally treated as capital receipt but subsequently written back in profit and loss because since these remained unclaimed had become time barred. Assessing Officer treated such amount as its trading receipt.

Held: Although the amounts received originally was not of revenue in nature and therefore were not taxable in the year of receipt, the amount changed its character when the amount became the assessee's own money because of limitation or by any other statutory or contractual right and treated as trade surplus.

Compensation for loss of office [Sec. 28(*ii*)]

Any compensation or other payment due to (under the mercantile system of accounting) or received (under cash system of accounting) by any person for the loss of office in the specified cases is chargeable to tax as business income. Such specified cases are given below:

(*a*) Compensation due to or received by any person who is managing the affairs of an Indian company wholly or substantially for the termination of his management or for the modification of the terms and conditions relating thereto.

(*b*) Compensation due to on received by any person who is managing the affairs of any other company in India at the termination of his office or modification of the terms and conditions relating thereto.

(*c*) Compensation due to or received by any person who is holding an agency in India for any part of the activities relating to the business of any other person for the termination of the agency or the modification of the terms and conditions relating thereto.

(*d*) Compensation due to or received by any person for vesting of the management of any property or business in the government or in any corporation owned or controlled by the government.

(*e*) Compensation due to or received by any person at or in connection with the termination or the modification of the terms and conditions, of any contract relating to his business (inserted w.e.f. 1.4.2019).

Income of trade or Professional Association from specific service [Sec. 28(*iii*)]

This clause makes an exception to the general rule that income of mutual associations is exempt from tax. Income derived by trade, professional or similar association from specific services performed for its members is chargeable to tax as "profits and gains of business or profession".

Specific services mean "conferring particular benefits" which may be available only on payment of the specific fee charged for such benefits. Income derived from general services, performed for its members continues to be exempt from tax. For example, where Miners' Association allows higher quota of coal to a member on payment of royalty, such royalty is taxable under this clause. Similarly, where chamber of commerce intervenes to settle the dispute between members on payment of arbitration fees, such fees is taxable under this clause.

Income derived from specific services performed for non-members is chargeable to tax either under the "other sources" or under clause (*i*) of sec. 28 but not under this clause. The applicability of this clause is restricted only to the members.

Social clubs fall outside the preview of this provision. Therefore, surplus accruing to a social club even from specific services to its members would be governed by the general principle of mutuality and hence not assessable [*CIT* v. *Delhi Race Club (1940) Ltd.* [1970] 75 ITR 111 (Delhi)].

Profit on sale of licence [Sec. 28(*iiia*)]

Profit on sale of a licence granted under the Imports (Control) Order, 1955, is chargeable as business profit. Thus, sale proceeds of import entitlements is to be statutorily taxed as business income.

Cash assistance against exports [Sec. 28(*iiib*)]

Cash assistance (by whatever name called) received or receivable by any person against exports under any scheme of Government of India is taxable as business income. Thus, where an exporter gets cash compensatory support (CSS) from the government or receives any other subsidy, it is taxable as business income.

Repayment of any duty of custom or excise [Sec. 28(*iiic*)]

Repayment of any duty of custom or excise as drawback to any person against the exports under the Customs and Central Excise Duties Drawback Rules, 1971 is chargeable to tax as business income.

Profit on the transfer of Duty Entitlement Pass Book Scheme (DEPS) [Sec. 28(*iiid*)]

Any profit on the transfer of the DEPS, being Duty Remission Scheme, under the export and import policy formulated and announced under sec. 5 of the Foreign Trade (Development and Regulation) Act, 1992 is chargeable to tax as business income.

Profit on the transfer of Duty Free Replenishment Certificate (DFRC) [Sec. 28(*iiie*)]

Any profit on the transfer of the DFRC, being Duty Remission Scheme, under the export and import policy formulated and announced under sec. 5 of the Foreign Trade (Development and Regulation) Act, 1992 is chargeable to tax as business income.

Value of Benefits or Perquisite [Sec. 28(*iv*)]

The value of any benefit or perquisite, whether convertible into money or not, or cash or in kind or partly in cash and partly in kind, arising from the exercise of business or a profession, is chargeable to tax as "profits and gains of business or profession". For instance, in addition to payment of medical fees, a patient also gives gift to a doctor who has cured him from chronic disease. The market value of such gift is also assessable as income from profession. A gift is taxable as business income if it has been received in the course of the business. Similarly, where a partner uses the residential premises, car, telephone belonging to the firm, the value of perquisites is taxable in his hands as business income [*V. P. Warrier* v. *CIT* (1990) 49 Taxman 314/181 ITR 303 (MP)] Award received by a professional sportsman is in the nature of a benefit in the exercise of his profession, and therefore, it is taxable.

Thus, the benefit or perquisite under the provision is other than in shape of money. If it is money, it does not fall in this provision. All revenue receipts arising from business profession or vocation are chargeable even if they are of non-recurring nature. Benefits assessable under this clause would not qualify for exemption under sec. 10(*2A*).

Case Law: ***Commissioner* v. *Mahindra and Mahindra Ltd.* [2018] 93 taxmann.com 32/255 Taxman 305 (SC)**

Facts: 'M' entered into an agreement with 'K' for the purchase of tools and other equipments for which 'K' agreed to provide a loan. Subsequently, 'K' was taken over by another company 'A' which waived the loan of 'M'. Issue was whether waiver of loan by 'A' was a perquisite for 'M'.

Held: The very first condition for application of this provision is that any benefit or perquisite arising from the business shall be in the form of benefit or perquisite other than in the shape of money. Since waiver amount represented cash/money, provisions of section 28(*iv*) were inapplicable.

Case Law: ***Ms. Priyanka Chopra* v. *Dy. CIT* [2018] 89 taxmann.com 286/169 ITD 1 (Mum. - Trib.)**

Facts: 'P', a film actress had done promotional activity on being brand ambassador of a campaign and received a car as a gift which was added as perquisites. 'P' contended that the gift of car was not a part of her fee/remuneration for the campaign.

Held: The car received by 'P' is a part and parcel of the agreement for the professional services rendered by her and is rightly added as perquisite.

Case Law : ***ACIT* v. *Shahrukh Khan* [2017] 84 taxmann.com 209/189 TTJ 547 (Mumbai)**

Facts: 'S', being a film actor by profession, received a gift of Villa from 'N' a Dubai based company. The Revenue authorities contended that the villa was a professional receipt in lieu of 'S' having attended the annual day celebration of the said company. 'S' claimed that the villa was a unilateral act of gift by his friend who happened to be the Executive Director of 'N' company on account of natural love and affection.

Held: No addition could be made merely on the basis of mere suspicion, conjectures or surmises. The gift was offered to 'S' in the year 2004, whereas, the Annual Day took place in the year 2007 and, therefore, 'S' was under no obligation to attend the same and undertake any sort of brand endorsements for donor company. It is not a professional receipt under sec. 28(*iv*).

Remuneration due to or received by a partner from the firm [Sec. 28(*v*)]

Any interest, salary, bonus, commission or remuneration due to or received by a partner from the firm is taxable as his business income, provided such payments were deducted while computing taxable profits of the firm. For example, R is a partner in a firm. He receives a sum of ₹ 50,000 as salary, interest, bonus and commission. While computing taxable profits of the firm, a sum of ₹ 20,000 was disallowed on account of these payments. R is assessable on a sum of ₹ 30,000 as his business income.

Non-compete fees and fees for exclusivity rights [Sec. 28(*va*)]

Any sum received or receivable under agreement for not carrying out any activity in relation to any business (but not profession) is chargeable to tax as business income.

Similarly, any sum received or receivable under an agreement for not sharing any know-how, patent, copyright, trademark, licence, franchise or any other business or commercial rights of similar nature or information or technique likely to assist in the manufacture processing of goods or provision for services is taxable as business income.

Payment for non-compete fees and fees for exclusivity rights may be paid in cash or kind.

However, any sum received or receivable for not carrying out any activity is not treated as business income in the following two cases:

(*i*) any sum, received or receivable in cash or kind, on account of transfer of the right to manufacture, produce or process any article or thing or right to carry on any business which is chargeable under the head "capital gains".

(*ii*) any sum received as compensation from the multilateral fund of the Montreal Protocol on Substances that deplete the Ozone layer under the United Nations Environment Programme in accordance with the terms of agreement entered into with the Government of India.

"Agreement" includes any arrangement, understanding or action in concert. It may be formal or in writing. It may not be intended to be enforceable by legal proceedings.

"Service" means service of any description, which is made available to potential users. It includes the provision of services in connection with business of any industrial or commercial nature, such as accounting, banking, communication, conveying of news of information, advertising, entertainment, amusement, education, financing, insurance, chit funds, real estate, construction, transport, storage, processing, supply of electrical or other energy boarding and lodging.

It must be noted that payment received as non-competition fee under a negative covenant was not taxable before 1-4-2003 as it was a capital receipt. It is only after 1-4-2003 by virtue of Finance Act, 2002 that non-competition fees under a negative covenant is taxable under sec. 28(*va*).

Case Law : ***Shiv Raj Gupta* v. *CIT* [2020] 117 taxmann.com 871/272 Taxman 391 (SC)**

Facts: 'S' and his family, being controlling shareholders of company C, sold their shares to company SWC. 'S' received a consideration towards non-competition fee from SWC. The revenue authorities contended that true nature of the transaction was that of payment received as compensation for terminating management of 'S' in company C. Non-compete fee was a colourable device to avoid payment of tax.

Held: There was no colourable device involved in having two separate agreements for two entirely separate and distinct purposes. Since non-competition fee under a negative covenant was always treated as a capital receipt till assessment year 2003-04 and 'S' had entered the agreement within during this time, amounts received by him were such capital receipts that not were not chargeable to tax.

Receipt under a keyman insurance policy [Sec. 28(*vi*)]

Any sum received under a keyman insurance policy including the sum allocated by way of bonus is also treated as business income.

Keyman insurance policy is taken by a business concern on the life of an employee (keyman) whose services contribute substantially to the success of the business. The object of the keyman insurance is to indemnify a business concern from the loss of earnings resulting from the death of a valuable employee. The amount of keyman insurance can be estimated as the monetary value of the likely setback to profits of the concern due to the death of the keyman. Any sum received by a business house on such policies including bonus is taxed as business income. The exemption under sec. 10(*10D*) is not available in respect of such policy.

FMV of inventory converted into capital asset [Sec. 28(*via*)]

The Finance Act, 2019 inserted a new category to be charged as profits under this head. The fair market value of inventory on the date on which it is converted into, or treated as, a capital asset will be brought to tax as profits.

Any sum received on demolition of capital asset [Sec. 28(*vii*)]

Any sum, received or receivable, in cash or kind, on account of demolition, destruction, dismissal or transfer of any capital asset, (other than land or goodwill or financial instrument) is taxable as business income provided the whole of the expenditure on such capital asset has been allowed as deduction (under sec. 35AD).

Speculative profits [*Explanation 2* to Sec. 28]

Where speculative transactions, carried on by an assessee, constitute business, the speculation business is deemed to be distinct and separate from any other business (under *Explanation 2* of Sec. 28).

Speculative Transaction Defined [Sec. 43(5)]

"Speculative transaction" means a transaction in which a contract for the purchase or sale of any commodity including stock and shares is periodically or ultimately settled otherwise than the actual delivery or transfer of the commodity or scrips [sec. 43(5)]. For example, N agrees to supply 10 cotton bales to M @ ₹ 5,000 per cotton bale after one month. On the date of delivery market price has fallen from ₹ 5,000 to ₹ 4,200 per bale. Both the parties agree to settle the contract by realising difference of prices. Thus, N gains ₹ 8,000 and M loses ₹ 8,000. It is speculation profit/speculation loss.

The term "commodity" signifies a thing, produce, merchandise or goods. Therefore, contracts in real property, and, houses do not fall within the scope of "speculative transaction". A renunciation letter in relation to right of allotment of shares is neither a share nor a commodity [*CIT* v. *Nirmal Trading Company* (1971) 82 ITR 782 (Cal.)]. Units of the Unit Trust of India are held not to be shares for the purposes of this sole-section [*CIT* v. *Appollo Tyres Ltd.* [1998] 101 Taxman 167/[1999] 237 ITR 706 (Ker.) *affirmed by SC in Appollo Tyres Ltd.* v. *CIT*

[2002] 122 Taxman 562/255 ITR 273 (SC)]. Thus, a contract for sale or purchase of units of UTI, settled without delivery, is not a speculative transaction.

The term "actual delivery" should not be understood as physical delivery, but it should be understood as per of the custom of the trade. Thus, where obtaining delivery order, without taking physical delivery of goods, is treated as actual delivery as per custom of the trade, any profit or loss on the sale of goods on the basis of delivery order cannot be treated as speculative profit or loss [*Raghunath Prasad Poddar* v. *CIT* [1973] 90 ITR 140 (SC)].

Under Sales of Goods Act, the concept of delivery entails that it can be made either by physical delivery of the commodity directly to the purchaser or to the carrier for him or by transferring the documents of title to the commodity. An ordinary contract for sale of goods should not be held to be speculative merely because the actual delivery could not be effected because of the supervening circumstances [*CIT* v. *Panachand Khemchand* [1994] 210 ITR 1053 (Guj.)].

At the outset of the contract the parties might have decided to settle the contract by taking actual delivery but if ultimately the contract is settled by accepting the difference in prices it becomes a speculative transaction.

Isolated speculative transaction not to constitute speculation business: *Explanation 2* refers to "speculative transactions". A single speculation transaction would not amount to a speculation business. Accordingly, an isolated speculative transaction would not constitute a speculation business.

Breach of contract settled without delivery not to be treated speculative transaction: A transaction is considered to be speculative if it is settled otherwise than by the actual delivery or transfer of the commodity or scrips but it does not follow that all contracts which are settled or adjusted without delivery are speculative. There may be a number of cases where there may not be any delivery for various reasons, that is, the party has become insolvent or the business of the party has been banned or one party is unable to give the delivery or the other party is unable to take the delivery. Where the obligation to supply or take the delivery comes to an end through impossibility or by operation of law, any compensation paid for breach of contract cannot be treated a speculative loss. It must be noted that sec. 43(5) speaks of a settlement of contract and, consequently, where there is a breach of the contract resulting in a dispute between the parties and culminating in award of damages as compensation by an arbitration award, the transaction cannot be treated as a 'speculative transaction' within the meaning of section 43(5) [*CIT* v. *Shanti Lal (P) Ltd.* (1983) 14 Taxman 1/144 ITR 57 (SC)].

Non-recovery of loss suffered by a broker in speculative transactions: Where a broker/commission agent carries out speculative transactions on behalf of his clients and the loss suffered in such speculative transactions cannot be recovered from the clients, such loss is not a speculative loss. It is a normal business loss from the commission business. Such loss can be set off against business profits.

If the speculation business is done by the commission agent on his behalf, such loss is a speculative loss, It cannot be set off against the profits of commission business [*CIT* v. *Pangal Vittal Nayak and Company (P.) Ltd.* (1969) 74 ITR 754 (SC)].

Case Law : ***CIT* v. *Pangal Vittal Nayak and Co. (P.) Ltd.* (1969) 74 ITR 754 (SC)**

Facts: 'P' a company was a member of an association for speculation in coconut oil. 'P' speculated for its own business and also entered into forward contracts on behalf of its clients and received commission in respect of such transactions, irrespective of whether the clients made profits or suffered losses. 'P' claimed to set off losses from its speculation business against this commission income since it claimed that commission was also a part of its speculation business.

Held: The receipts of commission business was entirely of a different character from the profits and losses of the speculative transactions. There was thus no element of speculation in the commission income received by 'P' and the commission was earned and received by him independently of the profit or loss sustained by the his clients in the transaction. Accordingly, 'P' was not entitled to get the commission receipts assessed under the head "speculation business" and therefore cannot set off speculation loss against said income.

Hedging transactions not to be treated speculative transactions: Hedging transactions are not deemed to be speculative transactions. Such transactions are entered into by manufacturers and merchants in the course of business to guard against loss through future price fluctuations. A hedging loss is treated as business loss and is allowed to be set off against business profits. Likewise, hedging profit is treated as business profits.

Scope of Hedging Transactions: Hedging transactions include the following:

(*a*) a contract in respect of raw material or merchandise entered into by a person in the course of his manufacturing or merchanting business to guard against loss through future price fluctuations in respect of his contracts for actual delivery of goods manufactured by him or merchandize sold by him; or

(*b*) a contract in respect of stocks and shares entered into by a dealer or investor therein to guard against loss in his holdings of stocks and shares through price fluctuations; or

(*c*) a contract entered into by a member of a forward market or a stock exchange in the course of any transaction in the nature of jobbing or arbitrage to guard against the loss which may arise in the ordinary course of his business as such member.

(*d*) An eligible transaction carried out in respect of trading in derivatives (referred to in Sec. 2(*ac*) of the Securities Contracts (Regulation) Act, 1956), in a recognised stock exchange is not deemed to be a speculative transactions.

"*Eligible transaction*" means any transaction—

(*i*) carried out electronically on screen board-based system through a stock broker or sub-broker or such other intermediary registered under sec. 12 of the Securities and Exchange Board of India

Act in accordance with the provision of the Securities Contracts (Regulation) Act, 1956 or the Securities and Exchange Board of India Act, 1952 or the Depositories Act, 1996; and

(*ii*) which is supported by a time-stamped contract note issued by such broker or sub-broker or such other intermediary to every client indicating in the contract note the unique client identity number allotted under any Act referred to sub-clause (*A*) and permanent account number under this Act.

RECEIPT FROM HOUSE PROPERTY USED FOR BUSINESS OR PROFESSION [SEC. 22]

Where a house property owned by the assessee and used for his business or profession, the profits of which are chargeable to tax, the annual value of such property is not assessable under the head "house property". Income from such property is taxed as business income.

COMPUTATION OF PROFITS AND GAINS [SEC. 29]

For the purposes of this head, the computation of profits should be in accordance with the provisions contained in secs. 30 to 43D (Sec. 29). The list of allowances enumerated in secs. 30 to 43D is not exhaustive. An item of expenditure or loss which is incidental to business or profession may be allowed under this section on the basis of ordinary commercial principles even though there may be no express provision under these sections [*G.G. Dandekar Machine Works Ltd.* v. *CIT* (1993) 202 ITR 161 (Bom.)].

Enquiry to be held about justification for deduction - In order to determine whether a particular item (not covered by Secs. 30 to 37) may or may not be deducted from profits under this section, one should first ascertain whether its deduction is expressly prohibited under any of the sections, and if not, whether it is of such nature that its deduction may be allowed on ordinary commercial principle in computing taxable profits. If the answer is in the affirmative, the deduction may be allowed.

Allowance for Business Losses - Business losses, though fall outside the purview of secs. 30 to 43D, may be allowed under this section on the basis of ordinary commercial principles provided following conditions are satisfied:

(*i*) Losses are not of capital nature [*Mandani Development Corpn. (P.) Ltd.* v. *CIT* (1986)161 ITR 165 (SC)].

(*ii*) They are not merely connected with the trade but are incidental to the trade itself [*CIT* v. *Textool Co. Ltd.* (1982) 10 Taxman 293/135 ITR 200 (Mad.)]

(*iii*) There is no provision, direct or indirect, against such deduction. These principles were affirmed by Supreme court in [*Badridas Daga* v. *CIT* (1958) 34 ITR 10 (SC) and *CIT* v. *Nainital Bank Ltd.* (1965) 55 ITR 707 (SC)].

If there is a direct and proximate nexus between the business operation and the loss, such loss is deductible because without business operation and without doing all that is incidental to it, no profit can be earned. It is in this scene that such a loss is considered as trading loss from commercial standard and becomes deductible from the total income [*Ramchandar Shivnarain* v. *CIT* (1978)111 ITR 263 (SC)].

Burden of Proof - Where an assessee seeks to deduct from his business profits certain items under this Section, the onus of proving that such deductions are permissible, falls on him [*CIT* v. *Calcutta Agency Ltd.* (1951) 19 ITR 191 (SC)].

Some of the usually occurring type of trading losses, covered under this section, are described below:

(*i*) *Loss of stock-in-trade:* A loss of stock-in-trade occasioned by enemy action or by ravages of white ants or by fire or by negligence or fraud of employees or by natural causes or loss of stock-in-trade in transit is deductible as a trading loss. If the assessee, for reasons beyond his control, cannot prove the exact amount of stock-in-trade destroyed, the loss may be estimated from such materials as are available.

Any compensation received in lieu of loss of stock-in-trade is a trading receipt [*CIT* v. *S.N.A.S.A. Annamalai Chettiar* (1972) 86 ITR 607 (SC)]. For example, an assessee mortgaged his stock-in-trade to secure loan. The stock-in-trade was damaged in the custody of bank. The assessee was awarded compensation by the bank for the damage caused to the stock-in-trade. The compensation is taxable as the income of the previous year in which it is received [*Ramesh Narain Saxena* v. *CIT* (1996) 220 ITR 19 (SC)].

(*ii*) *Loss through embezzlement by employee or agent:* An amount embezzled by the assessee's employee or agent is deductible in computing business profits. Loss caused by embezzlement is allowable as a deduction not necessarily in the year, in which the embezzlement takes place, but when there is no reasonable chance of obtaining restitution and the amount is found to be irrecoverable [*Associated Banking Corporation of India Ltd.* v. *CIT* (1965) 56 ITR 1 (SC)].

(*iii*) *Loss on account of non-recovery of advance, made during the course of business:* Where the assessee makes an advance during the course of the business and such advance is not recovered, the loss arising on account of non-recovery of such advance is allowable as a trading loss.

(*iv*) *Loss by robbery or theft:* If the loss of cash by theft or robbery is incidental to the operations of the business such loss is deductible in computing taxable profits of business or profession. For instance, when an employee who is entrusted with funds for purpose of distribution amongst sugar cane growers in accordance with statutory rules, is robbed of them on the way, the loss is deductible [*Motipur Sugar Factory Ltd.* v. *CIT* (1955)

28 ITR 128 (Pat.)]. If stolen moneys which are allowed as a deduction in any year are subsequently recovered, such receipts are taxable as the income of the previous year in which stolen moneys are received [Sec. 41(1)]. Similarly, when an assessee or his employee carrying cash to bank is robbed on the way such loss is an allowable deduction.

Likewise, the loss of cash in the robbery committed at night in the bank premises is an allowable deduction as a bank is under statutory obligation to maintain a certain amount of cash at the close of the business everyday [*CIT* v. *Nainital Bank Ltd.* (1965) 55 ITR 707 (SC)]. Similarly, keeping cash is found inevitable to carry on business operations on the next day, loss of cash due to theft or burglary in factory premises during or after working hours is deductible [*CIT* v. *Serya Sugar Mills (P.) Ltd.* (1968) 70 ITR 109 (All.)]. Also, see [*Ramachandar Shivanarayan* v. *CIT* (1978) 111 ITR 263 (SC)].

ALLOWABLE DEDUCTIONS [SECS. 30 TO 35]

EXPENSES IN RESPECT OF BUSINESS PREMISES [SEC. 30]

Deduction in respect of expenses incurred for premises, used for business, is allowed in accordance with the following provisions:

(*i*) Rent - Deduction of rent is governed by the following provisions:

(*a*) *Business premises hired by the assessee:* Where premises are taken on rent by an assessee, rent paid for the premises is an allowable deduction if the premises are used for business. The word "paid" means actually paid or incurred according to the method of accounting adopted by an assessee [Sec. 43(2)]. Where the assessee maintains the accounts on mercantile basis, "paid" signifies the accounting year in which the liability to pay the rent first accrued. In other words, the rent payable for a previous year is allowable on due basis even when not actually paid.

(*b*) *Rent of guest house:* The rent paid for a guest house, used for the purposes of business is fully allowable under this section.

(*c*) *Chargeability of rent in the hands of receiver not a condition for deduction:* Rent payable for the business premises is deductible even though the recipient of the rent may not be assessable on such rent.

(*d*) *Sub-letting of business premises* vs. *deduction of rent:* Where a part of the business premises are sub-let, the rent from sub-letting would be set off against the amount of rent payable. Thus, net rent payable would be deducted.

(*e*) *Premium paid for lease of business premises:* Premium (*salami* or *pugri*) paid for obtaining lease or for a renewal of lease cannot be equated with rent. Such premium is a capital expense and cannot be deducted.

(*f*) *Payment of rent arrears of the previous tenant:* If a tax-payer takes business premises on lease for carrying on a business and agrees to pay arrears of rent of the previous occupier, whether voluntarily or under legal obligation, such arrears or rent cannot be deducted under this section because it is not the rent payable for the period during which the premises are used for the purposes of the business [*CIT* v. *Maharajadhiraj Kameshwar Singh* (1933) 1 ITR 94 (PC)].

(*g*) *Rent paid for unexpired lease period in respect of premises not used for business:* If the business premises have been taken on a long-term lease which is still subsisting but the business ceases to be carried on in those premises and it is carried on elsewhere, the rent paid for the premises under the old lease cannot be deducted under this clause. It can be claimed under "general deductions" (under sec. 37) if it can be proved that the liability could not be terminated when the business came to an end [*Pohoomal Bros.* v. *CIT* (1958) 34 ITR 64 (Bom.)].

(*h*) *Rent of the business premises, partly occupied by the assessee/employee:* Where part of the business premises taken on rent are used by an assessee as his dwelling house, a proportionate deduction on account of rent in respect of the portion so occupied is to be disallowed (Sec. 38). But if such premises are occupied by the employees of the business, the rent of the premises so occupied is an allowable deduction under this clause or in any case under "general deduction" (under sec. 37).

(*i*) *Notional rent of the premises owned by the assessee not to be deducted:* If business premises are owned by a taxpayer, no deduction is allowed on account of notional rent. In such event, the annual value of business premises is not assessable under sec. 22.

***(ii)* Repairs** - Expenditure on repairs is incurred to preserve and maintain an existing asset. The objective of repairs is neither to bring a new asset into existence nor to obtain any fresh advantage. Repairs restore what has been lost by way of wear and tear [*New Shorrock Spinning & Manufacturing Company Ltd.* v. *CIT* (1956) 30 ITR 338 (Bom.)].

Following points may be noted in this connection:

(*a*) *Repairs borne by tenant:* If the business premises are taken on rent by a taxpayer and he has also undertaken to bear the cost of repairs (by the terms of tenancy) of such premises, he is entitled to an allowance of the cost repairs.

Even if he has not undertaken to bear the cost of repairs, but for reasons of commercial expediency he effects repairs to the premises let out to him, the expenditure though not allowable under this clause, may be allowed under "general deductions" [under sec. 37(1)] as incurred wholly and exclusively for the purposes of the business [*CIT* v. *Goyal Oil Mills* (1970) 78 ITR 414 (Punj. & Har.)].

Cost of repairs borne by the tenant should not include any expenditure in the nature of capital expenditure.

(*b*) *Repairs borne by the owner:* If the assessee occupies the business premises other than as a tenant, that is as owner or mortgagee in possession, deduction is allowed subject to the following conditions:

1. *Repairs should be current repairs:* Expenditure on current repairs is allowed to be deducted provided it is not of capital nature. Nature of the expenditure, capital or revenue, is not a question of law. It is a question of facts.

   The expression "current repairs" connotes repairs which are attended to when the need for them arises from the businessman's point of view and which are not allowed to fall into arrears to be accumulated. Current repair does not mean petty repairs but it means belonging to the present time [*Mahalakshmi Textiles Mills Ltd.* v. *CIT* (1967) 66 ITR 710 (Mad.)]. The "current repairs" are necessary repairs, which are needed for the maintenance of an asset [*Humayun Properties Ltd.* v. *CIT* (1962) 44 ITR 73 (Cal.)]. Thus, replacement of worn out cement sheets by new cement sheets or repairs of walls which had collapsed due to heavy rains are examples of current repairs.

   Thus, expenditure incurred for substituting worn out door by fire-proof doors as per factory rules and expenditure incurred for renewal of the roof of the backing house, to get more light into the factory, is allowable as expenditure on current repair [*Addl. CIT* v. *India United Mills Ltd.* (1983) [1982] 8 Taxman 182/141 ITR 399 (Bom.)].

2. *Capital expenditure on current repair not to be allowed [Explanation to sec. 30].* The amount paid on account of current repairs does not include any expenditure in capital nature. Thus, expenditure incurred on modernizing the cinema house by replacing old wooden chairs with new cushioned chairs and constructing office, side rooms, bathrooms that brings enduring benefit is capital expenditure and cannot be allowed [*Silver Screen Enterprises Ltd.* v. *CIT* (1972) 85 ITR 578 (Punjab and Haryana)].

3. *Repairs of business premises, partly occupied by the assessee:* When part of the business premises is used as a dwelling house by the assessee, a proportionate repair allowance in respect of such premises (occupied as dwelling house) is disallowed [Sec. 38].

4. *Accumulated repairs not allowed under this clause:* The expression "current repairs" denotes repairs which are attended to when the

need for them arises from the businessman's point of view and which are not allowed to fall into arrears or to be accumulated [*Modi Spinning & Weaving Mills Co. Ltd.* v. *CIT* (1993) 200 ITR 544 (Delhi)]. Accumulated repairs done in one year are not allowable under this clause but they may be allowed under Sec. 37(1) [*CIT* v. *Kalyanji Mavji & Co.* (1980) 122 ITR 49 (SC)].

(*iii*) Land revenue, local rates, or municipal taxes - Deduction for land revenue or local rates or municipal taxes paid in respect of premises used for the purposes of business is allowed subject to the following conditions:

1. *Deduction is allowed when such taxes are paid [sec. 30 r.w. sec. 43B]:* Deduction is allowed provided such taxes have been actually paid. Even if an assessee follows mercantile system, deduction is allowed on payment basis. When such taxes are paid on or before the due date fixed for furnishing the return of income for the relevant previous year, deduction is allowed during the same previous year in which the liability to pay has accrued. If the date of payment falls after the said date, deduction in respect of such taxes is allowed in the previous year in which the date of payment falls.
2. *Business premises partly occupied by the assessee for personal use: Proportionate taxes for personal use not to be allowed:* If a part of the premises are occupied by the assessee for his dwelling purposes, proportionate taxes in respect of premises for personal use cannot be allowed.
3. *One-time local tax paid on newly constructed building held not allowable:* One-time payment of local tax in respect of newly constructed building has been held not allowable under this clause as it is not paid in the capacity as trader. Deduction is also denied under sec. 37(1) as it is a capital expenditure [*Michael Joseph & Co.* v. *CIT* [1996] 89 Taxman 521/[1997] 225 ITR 786].

(*iv*) Insurance premium - The amount of any premium paid in respect of insurance against risk of damage or destruction of the business premises is an allowable deduction.

Proportionate premium in respect of premises used by the assessee, disallowed: If any part of the premises is used as dwelling house by the assessee, a proportionate deduction on account of insurance premium in respect of such premises is disallowed (sec. 38).

REPAIRS AND INSURANCE OF MACHINERY, PLANT AND FURNITURE [SEC. 31]

Any expenditure incurred on repairs and insurance in respect of machinery, plant and furniture, used for the purposes of business profession, is deducted in accordance with the following provisions:

(*i*) **Use of assets for the purposes of business or profession -** Deduction of repairs and insurance in respect of machinery, plant and furniture is allowed, provided the assets are used for the purposes of business or profession:

(*a*) *Use may be active use or passive use:* The word "use" should be understood in a wider sense so as to include passive as well as active use. [*Whittle Anderson Ltd.* v. *CIT* (1971) 79 ITR 613 (Bom.)]. When machinery is kept ready for the use at any moment, it can be said to be used for the purpose of the business even if it has not actually worked. Sometimes, the manufacturing concerns have to keep in readiness stand-by plants to provide against breakdowns or other unforeseen circumstances. Such plants also qualify for full repair allowance though they have not been actively used in business during the previous year. Examples are (*i*) additional boilers in all factories driven by steam power, and (*ii*) stand-by generators of an electricity supply company.

(*b*) *Degree of use is immaterial:* It is not necessary that the machinery, plant or furniture should be used throughout the accounting year. Even if they have worked only for part of the year, the assessee should be granted the full allowance permissible under this section, and not merely an amount proportionate to the period of user [*Western States Trading Co. (P.) Ltd.* v. *CIT* (1971) 80 ITR 21 (SC)].

(*c*) *Proportionate expenditure in respect of assets used by the assessee for personal purposes not allowed (sec. 38):* Where a machinery or plant is not exclusively used for business or profession, proportionate repair for non-business use is disallowed (sec. 38).

(*d*) *Inclusive definition of Plant [Sec. 43(3)]:* The term "plant" include ships, vehicles, books, scientific apparatus and surgical equipment used for the purposes of the business or profession [Sec. 43(3)].

It does not include tea bushes or livestock or buildings or furniture and fittings.

(*ii*) **Repair should be current repairs -** Payments on account of "current repairs" must be understood in contradiction to payments for "addition" or "improvement". The simple test that must be instantly borne in mind is that as a result of the expenditure which is claimed as an expenditure for repairs what is really being done is to preserve and maintain an already existing asset. The objective of expenditure should not be to bring a new asset into existence [*CIT* v. *Chowgule & Co. (P.) Ltd.* (1995) 81 Taxman 384/214 ITR 523 (Bom.)].

(*iii*) **Capital expenditure on current repairs not allowed [*Explanation* to Sec. 31] -** Amount laid on current years should not include any expenditure, which is of capital nature. It is operative from the assessment year 2004-2005 and onwards.

Expenditure on current repairs should be of revenue nature. The replacement cost of the asset, at time, be used as an indication of the true character of the expenditure. If expenditure on repairs, added to the written down value or disposal value exceeds the replacement cost of the asset, the presumption is possible that it is not a revenue expenditure but an expenditure of capital nature. Such presumption, of course, on facts of a case may be rebuttable.

Ordinarily, substitution in the machine of new parts for old parts is in the nature of current repairs or revenue expenditure [*CIT* v. *Mahalakshmi Textile Mills Ltd*. [1967] 66 ITR 710 (SC)]. However, if the cost of substitution of new parts substantially change the identity of the machine or effect a substantial improvement, it would be capital expenditure and would not be allowed as the cost of current repair [*Ratan Singh* v. *CIT* [1926] 2 ITC 294, *Dy. CIT* v. *S.T.N. Textiles Ltd.* [2002] 257 ITR 161/[2003] 131 Taxman 73 (Ker.)].

Where the productive unit, set up by the assessee, remains the same but a part of it which has become unsuitable for its use is replaced by something which makes it possible for the existing set up to function effectively, the cost incurred on such replacement would be revenue.

(*iv*) **Accumulated repairs not to be allowed** - Cost of arrears of repairs done in one year cannot be allowed under current repairs. Accumulated repair may be allowed under sec. 37(1) if incurred wholly and exclusively for the purposes of business, provided these are not of capital nature.

(*v*) **Insurance premium against damage or destruction** - The amount of insurance premium paid against the risk of damage or destruction of machinery, plant or furniture is allowed to be deducted in computing taxable profits.

The word "paid" means actually paid or incurred according to the method of accounting followed by the assessee in computing taxable profits [sec. 43(2)]. Thus, the deduction under mercantile system may be allowed on accrual of the liability to pay.

DEPRECIATION [SEC. 32]

The term "depreciation" has not been defined in the Income-tax Act. Therefore, it has to be understood in its usual commercial sense. Depreciation means "a decrease in the value of property through wear and tear, or obsolescence". Depreciation is the inherent decline in the value of an asset from any cause whatsoever. In computing taxable profits of a business or profession, the income-tax law permits the deduction of depreciation so that the business is provided for a cost of replacement over a period of time. This deduction is subject to certain conditions.

ASSET ELIGIBLE FOR DEPRECIATION [SEC. 32(1)]

Depreciation is allowed in respect of the following assets:

(*a*) *Tangible assets:* Depreciation is allowed on tangible assets, being building, plant, machinery and furniture. Thus, no depreciation is allowed on land.

(*b*) *Intangible assets:* From the assessment year 1999-2000 and subsequent years, depreciation is also allowed on intangible assets, being know-how, patents, copyrights, trademarks, licenses, franchises or any other business or commercial rights of similar nature.

(A) Tangible Assets

(*i*) *Building:* "Building" is that which is built; specifically a faleric or edifice, framed or constructed, designed to stand more or less permanently and covering a space of land, for use as a dwelling, store-house, factory, shelter for beasts or some other useful purpose.

The term "building" means the superstructure only and does not include site. The land neither requires insurance against destruction, nor any repairs, nor does it depreciate in value by use. So, the depreciation is provided only in respect of building and not lands [*CIT* v. *Alps Theatre* (1967) 65 ITR 377 (SC)].

Scope of Building: "Buildings" include roads, bridges, culverts, wells and tube-wells. The buildings may be factory buildings or non-factory buildings, that is, building used for office, storage, employees' quarters or welfare of employees, *e.g.*, workers' canteen or sports pavilion, etc. Building include a part of a building.

Building constructed on leasehold land is eligible for depreciation even if the building may be handed over to the lessor after the expiry of lease. It is not necessary that building should have a roof for claiming depreciation. A large stadium or an open swimming pool would be a building as it is a permanent structure and designed for a useful purpose. It would qualify for depreciation.

(*ii*) *Machinery:* The word "machinery" has not been defined in the Act. "Machinery" is a contrivance whereby several things are put together to work in such a way that force may be applied at most convenient point in a most convenient way to get a particular work or an item of work done to produce a specific article or manufactured goods [*D.B. Bhandari* v. *State of Mysore* (1967) 20 STC 25 (Mys.)].

(*iii*) *Plant:* The term "plant" includes ships, vehicles, books, scientific apparatus and surgical equipment used for the purposes of the business or profession [sec. 43(3)] but does not include "tea bushes" and livestock.

The definition of the word "plant" is inclusive and not exhaustive and hence it has to be given a wider meaning. The word "plant" therefore, includes whatever apparatus or instrument, any article or object, fixed or movable, used by a businessman in carrying on his business and it is not confined to an apparatus used by mechanical operator.

(*iv*) *Furniture:* There is no definition of the word "furniture" in the Act. All articles of convenience or decoration, used for the purpose of furnishing a dwelling place or a place of business or an office, are articles of furniture.

(B) Intangible Assets - From the assessment year 1999-2000 depreciation is also allowed on "intangible assets", being know-how patents, copyrights, trademarks, licences, franchises or any other business or commercial rights of similar nature.

Intangible Assets not owned by the assessee - Any payment for use of intangible rights, not owned by the assessee, would not be covered under the scheme of depreciation. Such payment would be allowed as revenue expenditure under sec. 37(1). For example, if a lump sum payment is made for use of "trademark" for a period of three years, no depreciation can be allowed because the trademark is not owned by the assessee. Lump sum payment for the use of trademark would be allowed as revenue expenditure under sec. 37(1).

Assets not entitled to Depreciation

It may be noted that 'goodwill' as one of the forms of intangible assets is not included in this list of intangible asset for the purposes of depreciation. Further the block of assets under sec. 2(*11*) also does not include goodwill. However, the Supreme Court in *CIT* v. *Smifs Securities Ltd.* [2012] 24 taxmann.com 222/210 Taxman 428 (SC) held that goodwill which was acquired in a scheme of amalgamation will be a capital right which would fall under the expression 'any other business or commercial right of a similar nature' and hence eligible for depreciation while computing business income. In a recent decision, the Supreme Court in the case of *Principal CIT* v. *Zydus Wellness Ltd.* [2020] 113 taxmann.com 154/269 Taxman 57 (SC) dismissed the Special Leave Petition (SLP) against the order wherein the High Court had upheld Tribunal's ruling allowing assessee's claim for depreciation on goodwill.

Thus, while Supreme Court has time and again held that goodwill of a business or profession is a depreciable asset under sec. 32, the actual calculation of depreciation of goodwill poses difficulties when other relevant provisions for its computation are applied. For instance in business reorganization through amalgamation depreciation on goodwill cannot be computed since its actual cost being zero, the written down value of that assets in the hands of amalgamating company also being zero.

The Finance Act, 2021 has set to rest the controversy whether or not goodwill is eligible for depreciation by expressly excluding goodwill from the very definition of the block of asset. Thus, the definition of **'block of asset' under sec. 2(*11*) expressly excludes 'goodwill of a business or profession'.** Further, an amendment has been made to *Explanation 3(b)* to sec. 32(1) which defines the expression 'assets'. The said explanation now clearly stipulates that 'goodwill of a business or profession' shall not be treated as an 'intangible asset' for sec. 32(1).

Further where goodwill is forming a part of the block of asset and depreciation has been claimed on it, the Central Board of Direct Taxes shall be prescribing a method to determine the written down value in such case. [Sec. 50(2)].

Conditions for the Allowability of Depreciation

Depreciation is an admissible deduction subject to the following conditions:

(1) Assets must be owned by the assessee whether wholly or partly [Sec. 32(1)]

Depreciation is allowed on the asset which is owned by the assessee, whether wholly or partly.

Meaning of the Term "Owned" - An asset is owned by an assessee if he is the legal owner of it. However, the term "owned" as occurring in sec. 32(1) must be assigned a wider meaning. Anyone in possession of the property in his own title exercising such dominion over the property as would enable other being excluded there from and having right to use and occupy the property and/or to enjoy its usufruct in his own right would be the owner of the building though a formal deed of title may not have been executed and registered as contemplated by the Transfer of the Property Act, 1882, Registration Act. Thus, where an assessee has taken possession of the building by making part payment, to the exclusion of others, he is deemed to be the owner of the building for the purposes of claiming of depreciation even though no conveyance deed has been executed in his favour [*Mysore Minerals Ltd.* v. *CIT* (1999) 106 Taxman 166 (SC)].

Capital Expenditure on a building not owned by the assessee entitled to depreciation - Where the business is carried on in a building not owned by the assessee but in respect of which he holds a lease or other right of occupancy and he incurs any capital expenditure on the construction of any structure he is deemed to be its owner. He is entitled to claim depreciation on such structure/renovation/extension/improvement, etc. [*Explanation 1* to Sec. 32].

Firm entitled to claim depreciation on a building contributed by a partner as his capital - Where partners have brought assets as their capital contribution, the firm is entitled to depreciation because all properties and rights which the partners have brought in the common stock as their contribution to the common business are treated as parts of the partnership property. Thus, where a partner brings building as capital contribution in the firms, the firm is entitled to depreciation on building even though the partnership deed may provide that building would go back to the partner on dissolution of the firm [*CIT* v. *Amber Corporation* (1994) 74 Taxman 302/207 ITR 435 (Raj.)].

Depreciation on assets acquired under hire purchase - The allowability of depreciation in respect of assets acquired under hire-purchase system is guided by the Board circular which allows depreciation in such cases on the initial value of the asset, that is, the amount for which the hired asset would have been sold for cash at the date of agreement. Where the asset is purchased under instalment selling, depreciation is allowed on the entire purchase price [Circular No. 9 dated 23-3-1943 and Instruction No.1097 dated 19 September 1977].

Depreciation in a leasing business - In a leasing business the lessor is entitled to claim the depreciation. Lessee cannot claim the depreciation.

(2) The asset should be used in business [Sec. 32(1)]

The depreciation is allowed where the depreciable asset is owned by the assessee and used for the purpose of his business or profession in the accounting year.

Nature of Use: Active or Passive - The user may be active or passive, that is, the depreciable asset is kept ready for use in business or profession though it may not have actually been used in the accounting year. For instance, the manufacturing concerns have to keep in readiness additional generators to be driven by steam power to provide against unforeseen contingencies or breakdowns. Depreciation on such assets is also allowed. Similarly, where a building is purchased for shifting the factory in a particular previous year but actual shifting is done in the subsequent year, depreciation would be allowed for the year of purchase [*CIT* v. *O.P. Khanna & Sons* (1982) 10 Taxman 243 (Punj. & Har.)].

Assets used by employees entitled to depreciation - Residential quarters occupied by the employees whose residence is subservient to and necessary for business are eligible to depreciation if such quarters are owned by the assessee. Occupancy of such quarters by the employees of business is considered business use of the property. Similarly, fans, air-conditioners, refrigerators, furniture, etc., owned by the assessee and provided to the employees at their quarters are eligible to depreciation.

Assets partly used for business and partly for other purposes - If the depreciable asset, being building, machinery, plant and furniture is used partly for business or profession and partly for private purposes only such proportionate depreciation for the business use as is reasonable in the opinion of the Assessing Officer is allowed [Sec. 38(2)]. Sec. 38(2) does not cover intangible assets. Thus, if intangible assets are used partly for business purposes and partly for other purposes, no disallowance can be made.

Depreciation on Assets acquired during the year and put to use during the year for less than 180 days: Depreciation to be Allowed 50% of the Normal Rate [Second Proviso to Sec. 32(1)(*ii*)] - Where an asset falling within a block of assets is acquired by the assessee during the previous year and is used for the purposes of business or profession for less than 180 days in that previous year, depreciation is allowed @ 50% of the prescribed rate [Second Proviso to sec. 32(1)(*ii*)].

Following points may also be noted in this connection:

Applicability of the Second Proviso: It applies only during the year of purchase. It has no application in subsequent years. Thus, where an asset is acquired during the year at a time when it can be used only for less than 180 days, but the asset is put to use in a subsequent year, the 'Second Proviso' has no application.

Passive user also to be taken into account: Use may be actual use or passive use. Thus, the asset is kept ready for being used for 180 days or more but actually used for less than 180 days, depreciation is allowed at the normal rates.

BLOCK OF ASSETS [SEC. 2(*11*)]

"Block of assets" means a group of assets, falling within a class of assets, comprising tangible or intangible assets, in respect of which the same percentage of depreciation is prescribed.

Tangible assets include building, machinery, land or furniture.

Intangible assets include know-how, patents, copyright, trademarks, licences, franchises or any other business or commercial rights of similar nature.

Formation of Block Assets - Assets falling within the same class and having same rate of depreciation are grouped under one block. For example, factory building and furniture bear a rate of 10%. However, they cannot be grouped under one block because their class/nature is different.

Similarly, know-how and trademarks are intangible assets and bear rate of 25%. However, they cannot be put under one block because know-how and trademarks belong to a different class.

BASIS OF DEPRECIATION [SEC. 32 (1)(*i*)/(*ii*)]

Where the Assessee is Electricity Undertaking - An undertaking, engaged in generation or generation and distribution of power, is entitled to claim depreciation under any of the following two methods:

(*i*) Either on written-down value under Block System; or

(*ii*) On cost price under straight line method.

The electricity undertaking is required to exercise its option in the first assessment year at the time of furnishing the return of income under sec. 139(1). The option once exercised is final for subsequent years.

Where the assessee is other than electricity undertaking - Any other assessee can claim depreciation only on written down value under Block System.

Claim of Depreciation Obligatory - The Assessing Officer has to allow depreciation even if it is not claimed by the assessee. Thus, the claim of depreciation is now obligatory. It is operative from the assessment year 2002-2003 and subsequent years.

Allowability of Depreciation - Depreciation is allowed to an assessee if it is established that business has been set up even though commercial production has not started [*Chakradhari Wheels (P) Ltd.* v. *ITO* (2006) 154 Taxman 77 (Delhi - Trib.) (Mag.)]

WRITTEN DOWN VALUE (WDV) UNDER BLOCK SYSTEM [SEC. 43(6)(*c*)(*i*)(A)/(B)/(C)]

An assessee is allowed depreciation at the prescribed rate as per Rule 5 on the aggregate written down value of the block of assets at the end of the previous year. The mode of computing written-down value is given below:

Particulars	₹	₹
WDV of the block of assets at the beginning of the previous year:		xxx
Add: Actual cost of any asset acquired during the previous year under that block		xxx
Aggregate value of assets falling under the block		xxx
Less: (*i*) Money payable in respect of any asset, sold, destroyed discarded, or demolished during the previous year	xxx	
(*ii*) WDV of the assets, transferred under "slump sale" falling under that block	xxx	
	xxx	(-) xxx
WDV at the end of the previous year; but it cannot be negative figure:		xxx

WDV to be taken Nil - Scheme of Depreciation is Closed:

1. *Entire block of assets ceases to exist:* Where entire block of assets ceases to exist, scheme of depreciation comes to an end. The scheme of capital gain/loss is operative in such case under sec. 50.
2. *Money payable of partial sale exceeding opening WDV + additions made during the year:* Where money payable in respect of asset sold, destroyed, discarded or demolished during the year exceeds the opening WDV plus cost of assets acquired during the year under that block, scheme of depreciation comes to an end. Such case is covered under the scheme of capital gain under sec. 50.

DETERMINING ACTUAL COST [SEC. 43(1)]

"Actual cost" means, the actual cost of the assets to the assessee reduced by that portion of the cost of the assets to the assessee which is met directly or indirectly by any other person or authority [Sec. 43(1)].

The expression "actual cost" has to be understood in the commercial sense as per normal rules of accountancy prevailing in the commercial/industrial world

[*Challapalli Sugars Ltd.* v. *CIT* (1975) 98 ITR 167 (SC)]. Thus, it would include within its ambit:

(*i*) Purchase price of an asset.

(*ii*) Expense incurred for the acquisition of the asset, *e.g.* interest on loan taken for purchasing an asset; commission paid to the bank for giving guarantee to the supplier of the asset, travelling expenses of the staff deputed to purchase the machinery in India or outside India, legal expenses relating to purchase of the asset, etc., payment of additional premium or commercialisation charges for permitting increase in the floor area of building [*CIT* v. *Hindustan Times Ltd.* (1988) 169 ITR 1/[1987] 34 Taxman 48 (Delhi)].

(*iii*) Expenses incurred to bring the asset to the site of installation, e.g. cost of freight, import duty, insurance in transit, dock charges, demurrage, etc.

(*iv*) Expenses incurred for installation and putting the plant and machinery in the working condition, e.g. staff training expense relating to installation but not relating to maintenance [*Sunil Synchem Ltd.* v. *CIT* [1986] 24 Taxman 399/(1987) 163 ITR 467 (Raj.)], expenses incurred for insurance, power, fuel and trial run cost before the commencement of the production, *mahurat* expenses on the foundation laying ceremony of the building. [*Challapalli Sugars Ltd.* v. *CIT* (1975) 98 ITR 167 (SC)].

NOTIONAL COST [*EXPLANATION* TO SEC. 43(1)]

In certain cases, the concept of "actual cost" has been substituted by "notional cost". The concept has been introduced to avoid double deduction or to prevent avoidance of tax. Various *Explanations* to sec. 43(1) deal with different situation and substitute "actual cost" by "notional cost". Such costs are explained below:

(*i*) **Cost of the asset introduced in business after being used for scientific research [*Explanation 1*]** - Where an asset is used in the business after it ceases to be used for scientific research related to the business, and a deduction has to be made for the purposes of depreciation in respect of that asset, the actual cost of such asset to the assessee is taken to be the actual cost to the assessee as reduced by the amount of any deduction for capital expenditure on scientific research in respect of that asset.

(*ii*) **Cost of the asset used as inventory [*Explanation 1A* to sec. 43(1)]-** Where a capital asset referred to in clause (via) of section 28 is used for the purposes of business or profession, the actual cost of such asset to the assessee shall be the fair market value which has been taken into account for the purposes of the said clause.

(*iii*) **Cost of the asset acquired under gift [*Explanation 2* to Sec. 43(1)] -** Where an asset is acquired by the assessee by way of gift or inheritance, the actual cost of the asset to the assessee is taken at the actual cost to the previous owner, as reduced by (*a*) the amount of depreciation actually allowed in respect of any previous year relevant to the assessment year commencing before 1 April 1988; and

(*b*) the amount of depreciation that would have been allowable to the assessee for any assessment year commencing on or after 1 April 1988, as if the asset was the only asset in the relevant block of asset.

It is operative from the assessment year 1988-1989 and subsequent years.

(*iv*) **Cost of the second-hand asset [*Explanation 3* to Sec. 43(1)] -** Where before the date of acquisition by the assessee, the assets were at any time were used by any other person for the purposes of his business or profession and the Assessing Officer is satisfied that the main purpose of the transfer of such assets, directly or indirectly to the assessee, was the reduction of income tax liability by claiming depreciation with reference to an enhanced cost, the actual cost of such asset to the assessee is taken at such amount as the Assessing Officer with the previous approval of the Joint Commissioner, may determine, having regard to all the circumstances of the case. The *Explanation* cannot be invoked in *bona fide* cases where the purpose is not to reduce tax liability. For example, firm assets were revalued on the death of a partner with the help of three leading members of the locality to settle their dispute. Some assets were taken over by the partners at revalued figure. The ITO allowed depreciation on written-down value by invoking *Explanation 3* to Sec. 43(1). Held, the *Explanation 3* is not applicable to the instant case as the object of revaluation was not to avoid any tax liability but to settle the dispute [*CIT* v. *Sekar Offset Press* (1995) 83 Taxman 436/214 ITR 516 (Mad.)].

(*v*) **Cost of the asset reacquired by the assessee [*Explanation 4* to Sec. 43(1)] -** Where any asset which had once belonged to the assessee and had been used by him for the purpose of his business or profession and thereafter ceased to be his property because of transfer or otherwise, is reacquired by him, the actual cost of such asset to the assessee is taken to be:

(*i*) the actual cost to him when he first acquired the asset as reduced by (*a*) the amount of depreciation actually allowed to him in respect of any previous year relevant to the assessment year commencing before 1 April 1988, and (*b*) the amount of depreciation that would have been allowable for any assessment year commencing on or after 1 April 1988, as if the asset was the only asset in the relevant block of assets (till the date of its original transfer), or

(*ii*) the actual price for which the asset is reacquired by him.

Whichever is less, is taken as the cost of such asset

(*vi*) **Cost of the asset acquired under SLB [*Explanation 4A* to Sec. 43(1)] -** Where any person who has claimed depreciation in respect of assets, used by him for his business or profession, transfers such assets to any other person but subsequently reacquires them on lease, hire or otherwise from such other person, notwithstanding anything contained in *Explanation 3* (as explained above), the cost of acquisition of such assets is the written down value of the said assets at the time of transfer of such assets to the transferee. The practice of sale and lease back transactions has been used as a tax avoidance device to reduce tax liabilities. The assets having nil or nearly nil written-down value are being sold at higher prices, especially where rate of depreciation is 100% to enable the buyer to claim the depreciation at the sale price. *Explanation 4A* puts an end to this practice. Thus, *Explanation 4A* applies where transfer is at higher value to claim more depreciation.

(vii) **Cost of building, previously owned by the assessee, introduced in business [*Explanation 5* to Sec. 43(1)]** - When a building, which was previously the property of the assessee, is brought into use for the purpose of the business or profession after 28 February 1946, the actual cost of such building to the assessee is taken to be the actual cost of the building to the assessee, as reduced by the amount of depreciation calculated at the rate in force on that day that would have been allowable had the building been used for the aforesaid purposes since the date of its acquisition by the assessee.

(viii) **Cost of the assets transferred by holding company to its subsidiary or *vice versa* [*Explanation 6* to Sec. 43(1)]** - Where the holding company transfers any capital asset (on which no depreciation has been claimed) to its Indian subsidiary whose 100% share capital is held by the holding company, or subsidiary company transfers any capital asset to its Indian holding company which holds 100% share capital of its subsidiary company, the actual cost of the capital asset transferred to the transferee company is taken to be the same as it would have been if the transferor company had continued to hold the capital asset for the purposes of its business [*Explanation 6* to Sec. 43(1)].

Where the holding company transfers any block of assets to its Indian subsidiary whose 100% share capital is held by the holding company or the subsidiary company transfers any block of assets to its Indian holding company which holds 100% share capital of the subsidiary company, the actual cost of the block of assets to the transferee company is the written-down value of the block of assets to the transferor company for immediately preceding previous year as reduced by the amount of depreciation actually allowed in relation to the said previous year [*Explanation 2(a)* r.w. Sec. 43(6)(*c*)].

For the purposes of computing written-down value, unabsorbed depreciation is deemed to be depreciation "actually allowed".

(ix) **Cost of asset acquired in a scheme of amalgamation [*Explanation 7* to Sec. 43(1)]** - Where an amalgamating company transfers any capital asset (on which depreciation has not been claimed) to the amalgamated

company and the amalgamated company is an Indian company the actual cost of the asset transferred to the amalgamated Indian company is taken to be the same as it would have been if the amalgamating company had continued to hold the capital asset for the purposes of its own business [*Explanation* 7 to Sec. 43(1)].

Where an amalgamating company transfers any block of assets to amalgamated company and the amalgamated company is an Indian company, the actual cost of the block of asset to the amalgamated company is written-down value of the block of assets as applicable to the amalgamating company for the immediately preceding previous year as reduced by the amount of depreciation actually allowed in relation to the said preceding previous year [*Explanation 2(b)* to Sec. 43(6)].

Unabsorbed depreciation is deemed to have been actually allowed [*Explanation 4* to Sec. 43(6)].

(*x*) **Cost of assets acquired in a scheme of demerger [*Explanation 7A* to Sec. 43(1)] -** Where a demerged company transfers any capital asset to a resulting company and the resulting company is an Indian company, the actual cost of the transferred capital asset to the resulting company is taken to be the same as it would have been if the demerged company had continued to hold the capital asset for the purposes of its own business. It is operative from the assessment year 2000–2001 and onward [*Explanation 7A* to Sec. 43(1)]. However, such actual cost should not exceed the written-down value of such capital asset in the hands of demerged company [Proviso to *Explanation 7A*].

(*xi*) **Capitalisation of interest for determining cost of acquisition [*Explanation 8* to Sec. 43(1)] -** Where any amount is paid or is payable as interest in connection with the acquisition of an asset, so much of such amount as is relatable to any period after such asset is first put to use cannot be included in the actual cost of such asset.

(*xii*) **Adjustment to Modvat Credit [*Explanation 9* to Sec. 43(1)] -** Where any excise duty/custom duty is included in the cost of an asset, any modvat credit allowed in respect of such duty should be excluded in determining the cost of such asset. It is operative from 1 March 1994.

(*xiii*) **Exclusion of subsidy from cost [*Explanation 10* to Sec. 43(1)] -** Where an assessee acquires any asset and its cost is met, directly or indirectly, by the government or any other authority (established under law) by way of subsidy, grant or reimbursement, the cost of such asset is reduced by the amount of such subsidy, grant or reimbursement.

Where such subsidy, grant or reimbursement is not directly relatable to the asset acquired, a proportionate amount of total subsidy/grant/reimbursement in proportion as such asset bears to all the assets, is excluded from the cost of the asset (proviso to *Explanation 10*). Thus, where an incentive subsidy is not directly relatable to the asset acquired, the total subsidy has to be apportioned over various assets to reduce their cost for the purposes of depreciation. *Explanation 10* is operative from the assessment year 1999-2000 and subsequent years.

(*xiv*) **Cost of the asset acquired by a non-resident outside India [*Explanation 11* to Sec. 43(1)]** - Where a non-resident has acquired an asset outside India and such asset is brought into India by him to be used for the purposes of his business or profession, the actual cost of such asset is taken at its written-down value which is to be computed as below:

Actual cost of such asset	xxx
Less: Depreciation of the rate in force in India since the date of its acquisition	(–) xxx
Written-down value to be taken as the actual cost	xxx

(*xv*) **Cost of acquisition of assets, acquired under scheme of corporatisation [*Explanation 12* to Sec. 43(1)]** - Where any capital asset is acquired by the assessee under a scheme of corporatisation of a recognised stock exchange in India, the actual cost of the asset is deemed to be the amount which would have been regarded as actual cost had there been no such corporatisation. The provision applies where scheme of corporatisation is approved by the Securities and Exchange Board of India.

(*xvi*) **Cost of acquisition of block of assets transferred by a private company to a limited liability partnership [*Explanation 2C* of Sec. 43(6)]** - Where any block of assets is transferred by a private company or unlisted company to a limited liability partnership, the actual cost of the block of assets in the case of limited liability partnership is taken at the written down value of the block of assets in the said company on the date of conversion of the company into limited liability partnership. It is operative w.e.f. 1-4-2011 [(*Explanation 2C* to Sec. 43(6)].

COMPUTATION OF DEPRECIATION UNDER BLOCK SYSTEM [SEC. 32]

A "Block of assets" includes all assets having the same rate of depreciation eventhough these may belong to different units of an undertaking. Computation of depreciation differs according to the rate of depreciation and degree of the use of an asset.

(A) Computation of depreciation where block of assets do not include any asset acquired during the year and put to use for less than 180 days:

Depreciation is computed as under:

WDV of the block of assets at the end of the previous year × Prescribed rate of depreciation.

Scheme of depreciation applies if there is positive written-down value at the end of the previous year.

(B) Computation of depreciation, where block of assets includes assets acquired during the year and put to use for less than 180 days during the year [Second proviso to Sec. 32(1)(*ii*)].

For calculating normal depreciation, it has to be ascertained whether or not WDV at the end of the year exceeds the cost of asset, acquired during the year and put to use for less than 180 days during that year, or WDV at the end of the year is equal to or less than the cost of such assets?

(a) *Where WDV of the block of assets at the end of the year exceeds the cost of the asset acquired during the previous year and put to use for less than 180 days in that year:*

   (*i*) WDV of the block of assests, equal to the cost of such asset used for less than days 180 × Rate of depreciation ×

   (*ii*) Balance of WDV of the block of assets × Rate of depreciation.

(b) *Where WDV of the block of asset at the end of the accounting year is equal to or less than the cost of asset, acquired and put to use for less than 180 days during the previous year.*

It is presumed that the entire WDV relates to the cost of such assets as were used for less than 180 days. Accordingly, depreciation is calculated as below:

WDV of the block of assets × Rate of depreciation × 50%.

ALLOWANCE OF BALANCE 50% ADDITIONAL DEPRECIATION [THIRD PROVISO TO SEC. 32(1)(*ii*)]

Where an asset, referred to in Sec. 32(1)(*iia*) (*i.e.* eligible for additional depreciation @ 20%) is put to use for the purposes of business for a period of less than 180 days during that previous year, and deduction was restricted to 50% the prescribed rate, the balance deduction of 50% is allowed in the immediately succeeding previous year in respect of such asset.

Electricity Undertaking Claiming Depreciation under Straight Line Method

From the assessment year 1998–1999 and subsequent years, power generation/ distribution units may claim depreciation either (*i*) under straight line method or (*ii*) written-down value method under block system. Such option may be exercised at any time, fixed for furnishing return of income under Sec. 139(1). The option is exercised in the first assessment year and it holds good for subsequent years [Rule 5(1A)].

When depreciation is claimed under straight line method, the total depreciation allowable during the working life of the asset cannot exceed the cost of acquisition of the asset. However, where an asset is sold during the currency of its working life, the provisions of terminal depreciation or balancing charge may be operative to allow final deficiency or to tax the surplus. The scheme of terminal depreciation or balancing charge is discussed/illustrated as below:

Terminal depreciation on tangible assets [Sec. 32(1)(iii) r.w. Sec. 32(1)(i)]. Where any tangible assets (*i.e.* building, machinery, plant or furniture) of electricity undertaking is sold, discarded, demolished or destroyed in the previous year, and the money payable plus scrap value of the asset, if any, falls short of its written-down value, such deficiency is deducted by way of terminal depreciation.

Intangible assets of electricity undertaking are not covered under the scheme of terminal depreciation. Any loss on their sale is allowed as capital loss under Sec. 50A.

Provisions of terminal deficiency do not apply when any tangible asset is sold in the previous year in which it was first brought to use. In that event, the deficiency is allowed as short-term capital loss.

Balancing charge [Sec. 41(2)] - Where any tangible assets (*i.e.* building, plant, machinery or furniture) of electricity undertaking, used for its business, is sold, discarded, demolished or destroyed in the previous year and the money payable together with scrap value, if any, exceeds its written-down value such excess to the extent of depreciation allowed is taxable as balancing charge. If such excess is more than depreciation allowed, such excess is taxable as capital gain.

The word "money" used in Sec. 41(2) has to be interpreted only as actual money or cash and not as any other thing or benefit which could be evaluated in terms of money. Thus, where insurance company restores the destroyed assets to the insured assessee, the excess of market value of replaced assets over the written-down value of the destroyed asset cannot be taxed as balancing charge [*CIT* v. *Kasturi and Sons Ltd.* (1999) 103 Taxman 342/237 ITR 24 (SC)].

The scheme does not apply where tangible asset is sold in the previous year in which it was first brought to use. The surplus is taxable in that event as capital gain.

For the applicability of balancing charge, it is not necessary that the business in which tangible asset was used, should be in existence [*Explanation* to Sec. 41(2)].

Provisions of balancing charge do not apply to intangible assets. Any profit on the sale of intangible assets is taxable under the scheme of capital gain.

SET-OFF OF CURRENT YEAR DEPRECIATION

Current year depreciation is set-off in the following manner:

(*i*) *Depreciation to be set-off to the extent of profits*: Depreciation is allowed to be set-off to the extent of the profits and gains of the business profession. Where profits are not sufficient to absorb the full amount of depreciation, the balance amount of depreciation becomes unabsorbed depreciation.

(*ii*) *Unabsorbed depreciation of one business to be set-off against the profits of another business*: The unabsorbed amount of current year depreciation of one business can be set-off against the profits and gains of any other business profession, carried on by the assessee and assessable for that assessment year. For example, unabsorbed depreciation of "timber business" may be set-off against the assessable profits of "sugar business".

Similarly, unabsorbed depreciation of speculative business may be set-off against the profits of any other business even though the speculative loss cannot be set-off against business-profits.

(*iii*) *Unabsorbed depreciation to be set-off against the income of any other head:* If current year depreciation cannot be fully set-off against the profits of any other business, it can be set-off against the income of any other head, for example, salary, house property, capital gains, etc., but not against winnings, covered under Sec. 115BB. Finally, if current year depreciation can neither be set-off under the head business–profession, nor against the income of any other head, it is treated as finally unabsorbed depreciation of that year.

(*iv*) *Business loss and unabsorbed depreciation*: If there is business loss, prior to setting-off current year depreciation, the whole depreciation remains unabsorbed. Under inter-head adjustment, current year business loss has got a priority over current year unabsorbed depreciation.

(*v*) *Carry forward of unabsorbed depreciation*: Unabsorbed depreciation is carried forward for future set-off, without any time-limit.

CARRY FORWARD AND SET-OFF OF UNABSORBED DEPRECIATION [SEC. 32(2)]

Unabsorbed depreciation to be carried forward without any time-limit: If current year depreciation cannot be set off in accordance with the prescribed procedure, the unabsorbed amount is carried forward without any time-limit. Business loss has got priority over unabsorbed depreciation in the matter of set off.

Right of carry forward and continuity of business: For the purposes of carry forward of unabsorbed depreciation, it is not necessary that the business in which it remained unabsorbed should be continued. It is operative from the assessment year 2001-2002 and onward.

Mode of set-off:

(*i*) *Where no business loss is being carried forward*: Unabsorbed depreciation is added to current year depreciation. It is set-off first against business profits and then against the income from any other head. Where there is no current year depreciation, unabsorbed depreciation is treated as current year depreciation. It is set-off first against business profits and then against the income from any other head.

(*ii*) *Where unabsorbed business loss/speculation loss and unabsorbed depreciation, both are being carried forward*: Unabsorbed business loss [Sec. 72(2)] and unabsorbed speculation loss [Sec.73(2)] have got priority over unabsorbed depreciation in the matter of set-off. Thereafter, unabsorbed depreciation whether from business activity or speculative activity, is set-off against business profits including speculation profits, if any.

Balance of the unabsorbed depreciation can be set-off against the income of any other head, for example, income from salaries, income from house property, capital gain, and income from other sources (excluding winnings), etc. If it still remains unabsorbed, it may be carried forward without any time-limit and can be set-off in the same manner as outlined above. It is operative from the assessment year 2002-2003 and subsequent years.

Meaning of Business Profits for the Purposes of Carry Forward and Set-off - For the purposes of setting-off carried forward business loss or carried forward unabsorbed depreciation, business profits includes any income which is essentially from business activity though it has been classified for the purposes of computation of income under any other head [*CIT* v. *Chugandas & Co.* (1965) 55 ITR 17 (SC)]. The following incomes are treated as business income for the purposes of set-off:

(*a*) Interest on securities or dividends on shares, held as stock-in-trade.

However, dividend declared, distributed or paid by a domestic company on or after 1 April 2003 is exempt in the hands of the shareholder under Sec. 10(*34*). Therefore, exempted dividends under Sec. 10(*35*) do not form part of business profits.

(*b*) Rent earned by exploitation of business assets [*CIT* v. *Smt. Indermani Jatia* (1970) 77 ITR 133 (All.)].

(*c*) Interest on investment of surplus business funds in short-term bank deposits [*Sham Progetti S.P.A.* v. *Addl. CIT* (1981) 132 ITR 70/(1982) 10 Taxman 86 (Del.)].

(*d*) Balancing charge to the extent of depreciation allowed would be business profits.

(*e*) Surplus of speculation profits.

(*f*) Withdrawal from special reserve would be business profits [Sec. 36(1)(*viii*)].

INVESTMENT IN NEW PLANT AND MACHINERY IN NOTIFIED BACKWARD AREAS IN CERTAIN STATES [SEC. 32AD W.E.F. 1-4-2016]

If any assessee sets up an undertaking or enterprise to manufacture or produce any article or thing on or after 1 April, 2015 but before 1 April, 2020 in any backward area notified by the Central Government in the (*i*) State of Andhra or (*ii*) State of Bihar, or (*iii*) State of Telangana or (*iv*) State of West Bengal and acquires new plant and machinery other the ship or aircraft, after 31 March, 2015 but before 1 April, 2020 in the said backward area, it is allowed prescribed deduction, subject to the specified conditions:

Conditions to allow the deduction [Sec. 32AD(2)(4)]:

(*i*) New machinery or plant, acquired and installed, should not be transferred within 5 years from the date of its installation, failing which the deduction allowed is deemed to be business profits of the previous year in which it is sold or transferred.

In addition, the defaulter company is also be liable to be taxed in respect of capital gain, if any.

However, the restriction does not apply if such machinery or plant is transferred under the scheme of amalgamation or demerger or reorganisation to a company [under Sec. 47(*iii*) or 47(*xiv*)] or limited liability partnership [Sec. 47(*xiiib*)] before the expiry of 5 years. In that case, the transferee company partnership is bound to comply with this condition for the unexpired period of 5 years to avoid their tax liability for the business profits and capital gains, if any [Sec. 32AD(3)].

(*ii*) New plant or machinery, entitled for deduction, should not include:

(*a*) any plant or machinery which is used before its installation by any person either in India by any other person;

(*b*) any plant or machinery, installed in any office premises or any residential accommodation, including accommodation in the nature of guest house;

(*c*) any office appliance including computer software;

(*d*) any vehicle; or

(*e*) any plant or machinery, the whole cost of which is deducted (Whether by way of depreciation, or otherwise) in computing the income, chargeable to tax under the head "profits and gains of business" or profession of any previous year [Sec. 32AC(4)].

Amount of deduction [Sec. 32AD(1)]

The assessee is allowed a deduction @ 15% of the actual cost of such new asset for the assessment year relevant to the previous year in which such new plant and machinery is installed.

TEA DEVELOPMENT ACCOUNT, COFFEE DEVELOPMENT ACCOUNT AND RUBBER DEVELOPMENT ACCOUNT [SEC. 33AB]

The deduction under the Tea Development Account is operative from the assessment year 1991-1992 and subsequent years. From the assessment year 2004-2005 and onward, deduction is also allowed for Coffee Development Account and Rubber Development Account.

Conditions for claiming the deduction [Sec. 33AB(1)/(2)/(3)/(8)]

The deduction is allowed if the following conditions are satisfied first:

(*i*) *Business of growing and manufacturing tea or coffee or rubber*: The assessee should be engaged in the business of growing and manufacturing tea or coffee or rubber in India. The provision requires both growing as well as manufacturing. So that if the assessee is engaged in the business of growing tea-leaves but is not engaged in processing/manufacturing the tea-leaves into tea, fit for human consumption, the section does not apply. Similarly, where the assessee is not engaged in growing tea-leaves but is engaged in processing them, the section has no application.

(*ii*) *Deposit in a special account with NABARD or deposit in Tea Deposit Account*: The assessee should make a deposit of any amount in a special account with National Bank for Agriculture and Rural Development (NABARD) under a scheme approved by the Tea Board or Coffee Board or the Rubber Board or deposit any amount in Deposit Account under any scheme framed by the Tea Board or the Coffee Board or the Rubber Board and approved by the Central Government. The deposit may be of any amount. It may be in any one account or both.

(*iii*) *Time to make the deposit*: The deposit may be made:

(*a*) within 6 months from the end of the previous year, or

(*b*) before the due date of furnishing the return of income, whichever is earlier.

(*iv*) *Audit accounts*: The accounts of the business of the assessee should be audited by a Chartered Accountant. The report of such audit should be furnished along with the return of income. The condition may not apply where accounts are required to be audited under any other law and the assessee gets them so audited and furnishes a report of such audit [sec. 33AB(2)].

Quantum of Deduction [Sec. 33AB(1)] - The quantum of deduction is computed as below:

(*i*) the amount of deposit or aggregate amounts of deposit as per the scheme.

(*ii*) 40% of the profits of such business, computed under the head "business or profession" before making any deduction under this section,

Whichever is less, is deducted in computing taxable profits of business. Such deduction is allowed before setting off the carried forward business loss (under sec. 72).

Computation of business profits for the purposes of deduction: Where separate accounts are maintained for the business of growing and manufacturing tea, coffee or rubber, profits is computed in accordance with provisions contained in secs. 28 to 44D.

Where separate accounts are not maintained, business profits may be computed proportionately *i.e.* in the ratio, the turnover from such business bear to the total turnover of the business:

Application of Rules 7A, 7B and 8: After computing profits from business–profession, taxable profits should be computed in accordance with relevant

Rules 7A (Rubber), Rule 7B (Coffee) and Rule 8 (Tea), as the case may be **[See Chapter 14 (Agriculture Income and Tax Liability)]**.

Withdrawal of the Deposit [Sec. 33AB(3)] - The amount standing to the credit of the assessee in the special account or deposit account is allowed to be withdrawn for the purposes specified in the scheme or as the case may be in the deposit scheme. However, withdrawal of the deposit is also allowed in the circumstances specified below:

(*a*) closure of the business;

(*b*) death of an assessee;

(*c*) partition of a Hindu Undivided Family;

(*d*) dissolution of the firm;

(*e*) liquidation of the company.

Chargeability of the Deposit - The deposit made under the scheme is treated as business income in the following cases:

(*i*) *Withdrawal of the deposit on closure of the business or dissolution of the firm [Sec. 33AB(5)]*: Where the deposit is withdrawn on the closure of the business or dissolution of the firm, whole of the amount so withdrawn is chargeable to tax as business income of that previous year. Since, it is income partly from business and partly from agriculture, taxable profits be computed in accordance with Rule 7A, Rule 7B or Rule 8, as the case may be.

(*ii*) *Bar on utilisation of deposit for the purchase of certain machinery and plant [Sec. 33AB(4)]*: The assessee should not utilise the amount of deposit, released or withdrawn for the purchase of machinery or plant to be utilised for the following purposes:

(*a*) any machinery or plant to be installed in any office premises or residential accommodation, including any accommodation in the nature of guest house;

(*b*) any office appliances (not being computers);

(*c*) any machinery or plant, the whole of the actual cost of which is allowed as a deduction (whether by way of depreciation or otherwise) in computing the income chargeable under the head "business or profession";

(*d*) any new machinery or plant to be installed in an industrial undertaking for the purposes of business of construction, manufacture or production of any article or thing specified in the Eleventh Schedule.

The deposit utilised for the purchase of prohibited machinery and plant is deemed to be profits and gains of business or profession and accordingly it is chargeable to income tax as the income of that previous year.

(*iii*) *Unutilised amount of deposit [Sec. 33AB(7)]*: Where the amount of deposit is released by the Bank, or it is withdrawn by the assessee from Tea Deposit Account, it should be utilised in accordance with the relevant scheme in the said previous year. If it is not so utilised, the unutilised amount is deemed to be business income of that previous year. However, the provision does not apply to a case where the deposit is released by the Bank, (*a*) on the death of the assessee, or (*b*) on the partition of a Hindu Undivided Family, or (*c*) on the liquidation of a company.

Taxable deemed business profits in the above cases are computed in accordance with the relevant Rules, that is Rule 7, Rule 7A, or Rule 8, as the case may be [*refer to* **Chapter 14 (Agricultural Income and Tax Liability)**].

(*iv*) *Sale of assets within lock-in-period (proportionate deduction deemed to be business profits) [Sec. 33AB(8)]:* Where any asset, acquired under the relevant scheme, is sold or otherwise transferred within 8 years from the end of the previous year in which it was acquired, the proportionate amount of deduction, relatable to the cost of such asset is deemed to be business income of that previous year.

Exceptions: However, the provision does not apply in the following cases:

(*i*) where the asset is sold or otherwise transferred to the government, a local authority, a statutory corporation (established under a Central, State or Provincial Act), or a government company as defined under Sec. 617 of the Companies Act; or

(*ii*) where a firm is succeeded in business by a company and any asset acquired by the firm under the relevant scheme is sold or otherwise transferred to the company under the scheme of succession, the deeming provision does not apply to the firm. The firm gets the tax benefit under this provision, provided the following conditions are satisfied:

(*a*) all the properties of the firm relating to the business or profession, immediately before the succession become the property of the company;

(*b*) all the liabilities of the firm relating to the business or profession, immediately before the succession become the liabilities of the company; and

(*c*) all the shareholders of the company were partners of the firm immediately before the succession.

The tax incentive has been allowed to the firm subject to the condition that the successor-company complies with all the conditions of the scheme. Thus, the successor-company is required to apply the deposit in accordance with the scheme. The successor-company should not transfer such assets within unexpired period of 8 years.

SITE RESTORATION FUND [SEC. 33ABA]

The deduction under Site Restoration Fund is operative from the assessment year 1999–2000 and subsequent year. The scheme of deduction is explained as below:

Conditions for the claiming the deduction [Sec. 33ABA(1)/(2)]

The deduction is allowed if the following conditions are satisfied:

(*i*) *Business should be of prospecting, or extraction, or production of petroleum or natural gas:* The assessee should be engaged in the business of prospecting or extracting or production of petroleum or natural gas or both in India under an agreement with the Central Government.

(*ii*) *Deposit in a special account/or the Site Restoration Account:* The assessee should make a deposit:

(*a*) in the special account with the State Bank of India under a scheme approved by the Ministry of Petroleum and Natural Gas, Government of India; or

(*b*) in the Site Restoration Account under a scheme framed by the Ministry of Petroleum and Natural Gas, Government of India.

Interest credited to the special account or Site Restoration Account is also treated deposit for the purposes of deduction under this Section [Fourth Proviso to Sec. 33AB(1)].

(*iii*) *Time to make the deposit:* The deposit should be made at any time before the end of the previous year. Thus, any deposit made after the end of the previous year does not qualify for deduction.

(*iv*) *Audit of accounts:* The accounts of the business of the assessee should be audited by a Chartered Accountant. The report of such audit should be furnished along with the return of income. The condition does not apply where accounts are required to be audited under any other law and the assessee gets them so audited and furnishes a report of such audit in Form No. 3AD under Rule 5AD [Sec. 33ABA(2)].

Quantum of Deduction [Sec. 33ABA(1)] - The amount of deduction is computed as below:

(*i*) the amount of deposit or aggregate amount of deposits including interest in special account or Site Restoration Account under the scheme; or

(*ii*) 20% of the profits of such business, as computed under the head "Business or Profession" before making any deduction under this section.

Whichever is less, is to be deducted. Such deduction is allowed before setting-off the carried forward business loss (under Sec. 72).

Double deduction not allowed - Where deduction has been allowed under this Section to a firm, an association of persons or body of individuals, no deduction is to be allowed in computing the income of the partner or member of such association or of persons/body of individuals [First Proviso to Sec. 33ABA(1)].

Where the deduction has been allowed under this Section in respect of such deposit in any previous year, no deduction is to be allowed in respect of such amount in any other previous year [Second Proviso to Sec. 33ABA(1)].

Where the amount of deposit is utilised for the purpose of business in accordance with the scheme, no deduction is allowed for such expenditure. This is to prevent the benefit of double deduction [Sec. 33ABA(6)].

No Dedution for Utilisation of Deposit

The amount of deposit may be withdrawn from "Special Account" or "Site Restoration Fund" for the purposes specified in the relevant scheme [Sec. 33ABA(3)]. It should be utilised for the said purpose. Where deposit is utilised for the purposes of any expenditure in connection with such business in accordance with the scheme or the deposit scheme, no deduction is allowed for such expenditure in computing business profits [Sec. 33ABA(6)].

Similarly, no deduction is permissible under Sec. 33ABA(1) in respect of any amount utilised for the purchase of machinery or plant for the following purposes:

(*a*) any machinery or plant to be installed in any office premises or residential accommodation including a guest house;

(*b*) any office appliances (not being computers);

(*c*) any machinery or plant, the whole cost of which is allowed is deduction (whether by way of depreciation or otherwise) in computing taxable profits of business or profession of any previous year;

(*d*) any machinery or plant to be installed in an industrial undertaking for the purpose of business of construction, manufacture or production of any article or thing specified in Eleventh Schedule to Income-tax Act [Sec. 33ABA(4)].

Chargeability of the deposit as profits and gains of business or profession - The deposit made under the scheme may be treated as business income in the following cases:

(*i*) *Withdrawal of the deposit on the closure of the business [Sec. 33ABA(5)]:* The amount of the deposit may be withdrawn for the purposes specified in the scheme [Sec. 33ABA(3)].

Where any amount standing to the credit of the assessee in the special account or Site Restoration Account is withdrawn on the closure of the account during any previous year, the amount so withdrawn reduced by the amount, if any, payable to the Central Government by way of profit or production share as provided in the agreement, referred to in Sec. 42, is deemed to be business income of that year. Accordingly, it is chargeable to tax as business income. If the business is no longer in existence in such previous year, it is presumed as if the business is in existence.

(*ii*) *Unutilised amount of deposit [Sec. 33ABA(7)]:* Where the amount is released from the "Special Account" by the State Bank or where the amount is withdrawn from "Site Restoration Account" during any previous year, such amount including accrued interest should be utilised in accordance with the scheme. If it is not so utilised, the unutilised amount is deemed to be business income of that previous year.

Sale of assets within lock-in-period: Deduction allowed is deemed to be business profits [Sec. 33ABA(8)] - Any asset acquired under the scheme should not be transferred within next 8 years from the end of the previous year in which it was acquired. [Sec. 33ABA(8)].

Where any asset acquired under the relevant scheme is sold or otherwise transferred within 8 years from the end of the previous year in which it was acquired, the proportionate amount of deduction, relatable to the cost of such asset, is deemed to be business income of that previous year.

However, the provision does not apply in the following cases:

(*i*) Where the asset is sold or otherwise transferred to the government, a local authority, a corporation established under a Central or State or Provincial Act or a Government Company; or

(*ii*) Where a firm is succeeded in business by a company and any asset acquired by the firm under the relevant scheme is sold or otherwise transferred to the company under the scheme of succession, the deeming provision does not apply to the firm. The firm gets the tax benefit under this provision, provided the following conditions are satisfied:

   (*a*) all the properties of the firm relating to the business or profession immediately before the succession become the property of the company;

   (*b*) all the liabilities of the firm relating to the business or profession immediately before the succession become the liabilities of the company; and

   (*c*) all the shareholders of the company were partners of the firm immediately before the succession.

Tax concession to the predecessor firm also requires the successor–company to comply with all the conditions of the scheme. Thus, the successor-company is required to apply the deposit in accordance with the scheme. The successor-company should not transfer such assets within unexpired period of 8 years.

EXPENDITURE ON SCIENTIFIC RESEARCH [SEC. 35]

Under Sec. 43(4) Scientific research means any activity for the extension of knowledge in the fields of natural or applied science including agriculture, animal husbandry or fisheries. The research is said to be related to business if it leads to an extension of the business or if it is research of a medical nature which helps in the welfare of the business employees.

The following deductions are allowed in respect of any expenditure incurred for scientific research:

Deduction for Contributions to Outsiders

Section	Contributions made to	Deduction allowed	Particulars
35(1)(*ii*)	Contribution to approved scientific research association with an objective of undertaking scientific research or an approved institution a university, college or other institution	150% of the amount paid till AY 2020-21 100% of the amount paid till AY 2021-22	Such research association or institution must be (*a*) approved by the prescribed authority and (*b*) fulfil all the prescribed rules and regulations. The research programme may be related to business or not related to business. If any question arises whether any activity constitutes scientific research or an asset is or was used for scientific research, the decision of the Central Government is final.
35(1)(*iii*)	Contribution to a company	100% of the amount paid	The donee-company must be: (*i*) it is registered in India; (*ii*) its main object is scientific research and development; and, (*iii*) it is approved by the prescribed authority in the prescribed manner
35(1)(*iii*)	Contribution for research in social science or statistical research or to a university, college or other institution to be used for research in social science or statistical research	100% of the amount paid	Such research association or institution must be (*a*) approved by the prescribed authority and (*b*) fulfil all the prescribed rules and regulations.
35(2AA)	Contribution to National Laboratory a University or an Indian Institute of Technology or a specified person	150% of the amount paid till AY 2020-21 100% of the amount paid till AY 2021-22	Sum is paid with a specific direction that it shall be used for scientific research undertaken under a programme approved in this behalf by the prescribed authority.

No deduction to the donor without statements and certificates issued by the done [Sec. 35(1A) w.e.f. 2021] - The Finance Act, 2021 introduced a new provision by virtue of sub-section (1A) according to which the donor shall not be entitled to deduction under the respective under this section unless such research association, university etc. or company—

(*i*) prepares such statement for such period as may be prescribed and deliver or cause to be delivered to the said prescribed income-tax authority or the person authorised by such authority such statement in such form, verified in such manner, setting forth such particulars and within such time, as may be prescribed. The done may also deliver to the prescribed authority a correction statement for rectification of any mistake or to add, delete or update the information furnished in the statement delivered in such form and verified in such manner as may be prescribed;

(*ii*) furnishes to the donor, a certificate specifying the amount of donation in such manner, containing such particulars and within such time from the date of receipt of sum, as may be prescribed.

Withdrawal of the approval subsequent to donation, not to affect the donor [*Explanation* to Sec. 35(1), and Sec. 35(2AA)] - Where subsequent to the donation to any such institution, its approval is withdrawn, the deduction to the donor cannot be denied on this ground.

PROCEDURE FOR GRANTING APPROVALS

Prior to 1-4-2020 - The research association, university, college or other institution referred to above shall make an application in the prescribed form and manner to the Central Government for the purpose of grant of approval, or continuance thereof [First Proviso to Sec. 35(1)].

Before granting approval to the research association or the institution referred above, the Central Government may call for such documents (including audited annual accounts) or information from the research association, university, college or other institution as it thinks necessary in order to satisfy itself about the genuineness of the activities of the research association, university, college or other institution and that Government may also make such inquiries as it may deem necessary in this behalf [Second Proviso to Sec. 35(1)].

Such approval notification shall remain in force for maximum three assessment years (including an assessment year or years commencing before the date on which such notification is issued) [Third Proviso to Sec. 35(1)].

Such an application shall be disposed of either accepting or rejecting the same within 12 months from the end of the month of receipt of such application [Fourth Proviso to Sec. 35(1)].

Post 1-4-2020 - With effect from 1-4-2020 every such approval notification in respect of the research association, university etc. or in respect of the company issued on or before 1-4-2020 shall be deemed to have been withdrawn unless such research association, university etc. or the company makes an intimation to the prescribed income-tax authority in prescribed form and prescribed manner within three months from the date on which this proviso has come into force. Such approval notification shall be valid for a period of five consecutive assessment years beginning with the assessment year commencing on or after the 1st day of April, 2022 [Fifth Proviso to Sec. 35(1)].

Any approval notification issued by the Central Government in respect of the research association, university etc. or in respect of the company after 1-4-2020 shall, at any one time, have effect for such assessment year or years, not exceeding five assessment years as may be specified in the notification.

Expenditure on In-house Scientific Research

Section	Contributions made to	Deduction allowed	Particulars
35(1)(*i*)	Revenue expenditure on in-house research relating to business	100% deductible to the extent the profits in the previous year in which such expenditure is incurred	Any expenditure of revenue nature, incurred on scientific research, related to business
Explanation to 35(1)(*i*)	Expenditure on in-house research, incurred before the commencement of the business	100% deductible to the extent the profits in the previous year in which such expenditure is incurred	◆ expenditure is incurred before the commencement of the business either by way of salary of the research staff or for purchasing raw material for scientific research, ◆ such expenditure incurred within 3 years prior to the commencement of the business ◆ deduction is allowed only for such expenditure as is certified by the prescribed authority
35(1)(*iv*) r.w. 35(2)(*ia*)(*iv*) and r.w. 35(4)	Capital expenditure on in-house scientific research, relating to business (excluding the capital expenditure incurred after 29 February 1984 on the acquisition of any land)	100% deductible to the extent the profits in the previous year in which such expenditure is incurred	Any capital expenditure, incurred on scientific research
35(4)	Carry forward of unabsorbed capital expenditure on in-house scientific research	-	Unabsorbed amount can be carried forward and may be set-off against the income of any other head. If it still remains unabsorbed, it can be carried forward without any time-limit. Carried forward business loss or speculation loss has got priority over unabsorbed capital expenditure on scientific research

Section	Contributions made to	Deduction allowed	Particulars
35(5)	Unabsorbed capital expenditure on in-house scientific research in a scheme of amalgamation	-	Amalgamated company can claim carry forward and set off of unabsorbed capital expenditure provided it is an Indian company

EXPENDITURE ON IN-HOUSE SCIENTIFIC RESEARCH INCURRED BY A COMPANY–ASSESSEE [SEC. 35(2AB)]

Section	Contributions made to	Deduction allowed	Particulars
35(2AB)	Company is engaged in the business of bio-technology or any business of manufacture or production of any article or thing; other than an article specified in Eleventh Schedule	150% of the expenditure till AY 2020-21 100% of the expenditure till AY 2021-22	Any expenditure on in-house scientific research and development but other than any expenditure on any land or building

Meaning of expenditure on scientific research - Expenditure on scientific research in relation to drugs and pharmaceuticals, shall include expenditure incurred on clinical drug trial, obtaining approval from any regulatory authority under any Central, State or Provincial Act and filing an application for a patent under the Patents Act, 1970.

Expenditure for obtaining right to use spectrum for telecommunication services [Sec. 35ABA] - The Finance Act, 2016 w.e.f. 1-4-2017 introduced this provision that allows deduction in respect of expenditure for acquiring spectrum rights for telecommunication services:

(*a*) *Payment of spectrum fee made before the commencement of the business:* Deduction is allowed from the previous year in which business is commenced.

(*b*) *Payment of spectrum fee made on or after the commencement of business:* Deduction is allowed from the previous year in which spectrum fee is actually paid.

The other provisions with respect to sale of spectrum rights are same as that of sec. 35ABB that deals with expenditure incurred for obtaining licence to operate telecommunication services.

EXPENDITURE FOR OBTAINING LICENCE TO OPERATE TELECOMMUNICATION SERVICES [SEC. 35ABB]

From the assessment year 1996-1997 and subsequent years, every assessee is entitled to claim the deduction in respect of capital expenditure incurred to acquire a license for operating telecommunication services, in accordance with the following provisions:

(*a*) *Payment of licence fee made before the commencement of the business:* Deduction is allowed from the previous year in which business is commenced. The amount of instalment to be allowed is determined as follows:

Licence fee actually paid ÷ Working life of the licence, remaining in force after commencement of the business

(*b*) *Payment of licence fee made on or after the commencement of business:* Deduction is allowed from the previous year in which licence fee is actually paid. The amount of instalment to be deducted is determined as below:

Licence fee actually paid ÷ Working life of the licence, remaining in force after commencement of the business

Sale of the Licence: The assessee may opt to transfer the licence before the expiry of its full terms. He may choose to transfer it fully or in part. In such cases, no regular deduction is allowed in the year of sale. Instead, if there is any deficiency, it is fully allowed as deduction in that year. However, any surplus to the extent of deduction already allowed is taxable profit of business and further excess, if any, is taxable as capital gain, short-term or long-term, depending on the period of holding. In the year of sale, business may or may not be in existence. If the licence transferred is a long-term capital asset, the assessee is entitled to claim deduction for indexed cost of acquisition in computing long-term capital gain.

Deficiency, or surplus is determined as under:	₹
Add: (*i*) Sale price of the licence	xxx
(*ii*) Deduction allowed	xxx
	xxx
Less: Cost of acquisition of the licence	xxx
Deficiency or surplus	(–)xxx

Partial sale of the licence: Where the licence to operate telecommunication services is transferred in part, regular deduction is not be allowed in such case. If there is a deficiency, it is amortised over the unexpired operational period of licence remaining in-force. Unexpired operational period of licence is taken on the first day of the previous year in which licence is transferred. For example, if the Telecom Licence, obtained on 1 April 2012 for 10 years, is transferred on 1 October 2014, unexpired operational period is 8 years as on 1-04-2014 and not 7.5 years as on the date of actual transfer, 1-10-2014. Surplus if any, to the extent of deduction allowed is taxable as deemed business profit. If there is further excess, it is taxable as capital gain, short-term or long-term.

Amortisation in a scheme of amalgamation or demerger [Sec. 35ABB(6)/(7)]: Where an amalgamating company or a demerged company transfers the telecom licence in a scheme of amalgamation or demerger to Indian amalgamated company or Indian resulting company, the provisions of amortisation of deficiency or deemed profit or capital gains, as the case may be, apply to Indian amalgamated company or Indian resulting company in the same manner as they would have applied to the amalgamating company or demerged company.

Scheme of depreciation not to apply [Sec. 35ABB(8)]- Amortisation of telecom/ licence fee under this section debars an assessee to make a claim for depreciation in respect of such fees.

DEDUCTION IN RESPECT OF EXPENDITURE, ON SPECIFIED BUSINESS [SEC. 35AD]

An assessee is allowed deduction in respect of capital expenditure, relating to 'specified business', incurred either during the previous year in which business is commenced or prior thereto, subject to the prescribed conditions [Sec. 35AD(1)].

Any expenditure of capital nature does not include any expenditure incurred on the acquisition of any land or goodwill or financial instrument [Sec. 35A(8)(*f*)].

'Specified Business' [under sec. 35(8)(*c*)] includes the following, namely:—

(*i*) Cold chain facility;

(*ii*) Warehousing facility for storage of agriculture produce;

(*iii*) Pipeline network for distribution of natural gas or patrolium oil;

(*iv*) Hotel of two star or above category;

(*v*) Hospital of atleast 100 beds;

(*vi*) Building and developing housing project for slum redevelopment;

(*vii*) Building and developing affordable housing project;

(*viii*) Production of fertilizer;

(*ix*) Setting up and operating an inland container depot/container freight system;

(*x*) Bee-keeping and production of honey/beeswax;

(*xi*) Warehousing facility for storage of sugar;

(*xii*) Laying and operating a slurry pipeline for the transportation of iron ore; and

(*xiii*) Setting up and operating a semi-conductor wafer fabrication manufacturing unit notified by the Board.

Conditions for deduction [Sec. 35AD(2)] - The prescribed deduction, relating to 'specified business', is allowed if the following conditions are satisfied:

(*a*) it is not set up by splitting up, or the reconstruction of a business already in existence;

(*b*) machinery or plant, previously used for any purpose, should not be transferred to the 'specified business';

Exception:

Machinery or plant cannot be treated as previously used in the following cases:

(*i*) it was not used in India prior to its installation by the assessee;

(*ii*) it is imported into India from any country outside India;

(*iii*) no depreciation has been allowed in respect of such plant and machinery in computing total income of any person for any period prior to its installation by the assessee;

(*iv*) if the total value of machinery or plant previously used for any purposes does not exceed 20% of the total value of machinery or plant used in such business, this condition is deemed to have be complied with.

(*c*) Where the business relates to laying and operating natural gas or crude or petroleum oil pipeline net work for distribution, it is further required to fulfil the following conditions:

1. Ownership: It is owned by a company, formed and registered in India under the Companies Act, 1956 or by a consortium of such companies, or by an authority or a board or a corporation, established or constituted under any Central State Act;
2. Approval: It has been approved by the Petrolium and Natural Gas Regulatory Board;
3. Pipeline capacity: The prescribed capacity of its pipelines is available for use on common carrier basis by any person, other than the assessee or an associated person;
4. Any other condition: It fulfils any other condition as may be prescribed.

Double deduction not allowed [Sec. 35AD(3) & (4)] - Where the assessee has claimed deduction in respect of 'specified business' for any assessment year, no deduction is allowed neither 'in respect of newly established units' in 'Special Economic Zone' (under Sec. 10AA) nor in respect of any income, allowed in computing total income [Sec. 35AD(3)].

Similarly no deduction is allowed in respect of capital expenditure, allowed under Sec. 35AD(1), in any other section in any previous year or under this section in any other previous year.

Schedule of commencement of the prescribed business activities:

Sl. No.	Specified Facility	Date of Commencement
1.	Cold storage facility	on or after 1 April, 2009
2.	Storage of agricultural produce	on or after 1 April, 2009
3.	Laying and operating cross country natural gas	on or after 1 April, 2007
4.	Building/operating 2 star hotel	on or after 1 April, 2010
5.	Hospital of 100 beds	on or after 1 April, 2010

Sl. No.	Specified Facility	Date of Commencement
6.	Housing project	on or after 1 April, 2010
7.	Housing project	on or after 1 April, 2011
8.	Production of fertilizer in India	on or after 1 April, 2011
9.	Setting & operating an inland container depot/a container freight station	on or after 1 April, 2012
10.	Bee keeping, production of honey & beeswax	on or after 1 April, 2012
11.	Setting up & operating a warehouse facility for storage of sugar	on or after 1 April, 2012
12.	Laying & operating a slurry pipeline for transportation of iron ore	on or after 1 April, 2014
13.	Setting up & operating a second conductor wafer fabrication manufacturing	on or after 1 April, 2014
14.	Laying & operating slurry pipeline for transportation of iron ore	on or after 1 April, 2015
15.	Setting up & operating a semi-conductor wafer fabrication manufacturing unit	on or after 1 April, 2015

Life-span of usable asset [Sec. 35AD(7A)] - Any assets, in respect of which the deduction has been claimed and allowed, should be used only for the specified business for a period of 8 years, commencing from the previous year in which the asset is acquired or construed. It is operative from the assessment year 2015-2016 and subsequent years.

Consequences of using the asset for non-specified purposes [Sec. 35AD(7B), (7C)] - Any asset acquired for 'specified business' and in respect of which a deduction has been claimed and allowed under sec. 35AD, it should be used only for the specified purpose during its prescribed life-term [under sec. 35AD(7A)]

If such asset is used for any other purpose in one or more previous year, the total amount of deduction so claimed and allowed during this period, reduced by the amount of depreciation allowable, is deemed to be business income [under sec. 28(*vii*)].

However, this provision does not apply to a company which has become sick during its allowable life-term of eight year [under sec. 35AD(7A)].

PAYMENT TO ASSOCIATIONS AND INSTITUTIONS FOR CARRYING OUT RURAL DEVELOPMENT PROGRAMME [SEC. 35CCA]

Every assessee is entitled to claim deduction in respect of expenditure for carrying out rural development programme, subject to the following conditions:

(A) *Contributions for rural development programme*: Payment should be made by an assessee for rural development programme which was approved before 1 March 1983.

Scope of rural development programme: Rural development programme should relate to the following:

(*a*) construction of any building or structure to be used as dispensary, school, training or welfare centre, or workshop or any other purpose; or

(*b*) laying of any road; or

(*c*) boring a well/tube well; or

(*d*) installation of any machinery or plant.

Approval of the association or institution: The association or institution-undertaking the programme of rural development, should be approved by the prescribed authority.

Approval and commencement of the programme: Rural Development Programme has been approved before 1 March 1983 by the prescribed authority, and it should commence before 1 March 1983.

Assessee to Furnish a Certificate from Association or Institution- The assessee is required to furnish a certificate from the association or institution to the above effect. The association or institution cannot issue such certificate unless it has obtained authorisation in writing from the prescribed authority to issue such a certificate.

Prescribed authority [Rule 6AAA] - It consists of the following:

(*i*) The Chief Commissioner or Commissioner of Income Tax who exercises jurisdiction over the State/Union Territory in which programme of rural development is to be carried out—Chairman.

(*ii*) An officer not below the Secretary to the Government of the State/ Union Territory in which the programme of rural development is to be carried out—member.

Subsequent Withdrawal of Approval not to Affect the Deduction Allowed [*Explanation to Section 35CCA*] - The deduction allowed to the donor cannot be withdrawn merely on the ground that subsequent to the payment of such sum by the donor, the approval granted to the programme of rural development or to the association or institution has been withdrawn. It is operative from the assessment year 2006-2007 and onward.

(B) *Contributions for training persons in rural development programme* - Any payment to association or institution for training persons in rural development programme is allowed to be deducted subject to the following conditions:

(*i*) *Object of the association or institution:* The payment should be made to an association or institution, which has the object to train persons for implementing programme of rural development.

(*ii*) *Approval of the association or institution:* The association or institution has been approved by the prescribed authority before

1 March 1983. Once the approval is granted to the institution, donor cannot be disallowed deduction on the ground that either the institution is not traceable after a notice was issued to it or that the institution was not carrying out the rural development work [*CIT* v. *Chotatingrai Tea* [2003] 126 Taxman 399/(2002) 258 ITR 529 (SC)]. The withdrawal of the approval, granted to an association or institution, can only be prospective and not retrospection [*CIT* v. *Bachraj Dugar* (1998) 232 ITR 290 (Gauhati)].

From the assessment year 2006-2007 and onward, statutory amendment has been introduced to this effect by the *Explanation* to sec. 35CCA(2A).

(*iii*) *Commencement of the training:* The training of persons for implementing any programme of rural development has been started by the association or institution before 1 March 1983.

(*iv*) *Furnishing a certificate:* The assessee should furnish a certificate from the association or institution to the above effect. The association or institution cannot issue such certificate unless it has obtained authorisation in writing from the prescribed authority to issue such a certificate.

(C) *Payment to National Fund for Rural Development:* Any sum paid to a rural fund, set up, and notified by the Central Government in this behalf, is allowed to be deducted. The Central Government has notified the National Fund for Rural Development in this behalf.

(D) *Payment to National Urban Poverty Eradication Fund:* Any sum paid to National Urban Poverty Eradication Fund is allowed to be deducted. It is operative from the assessment year 1996–1997 and subsequent years.

Double deduction not allowed [sec. 35CCA(3)]: Where any deduction has been claimed and allowed in respect of any sum paid to an approved association or institution to carry out the approved rural development programme or to train persons for implementing rural development programme, no deduction is allowed for such amount under Sec. 80G or any other provisions of this Act for same year or any other assessment year.

EXPENDITURE ON, AGRICULTURAL EXTENSION PROJECT [SEC. 35CCC]

Where an assessee has incurred any expenditure, on agricultural extension project, notified by the Board in accordance with the prescribed guidelines (under Income-tax Rules 6AAD and 6AAE), a deduction of 150% (100% from the assessment year 2021-22 and subsequent years) of such expenditure is allowed to be deducted [sec. 35CCC(1)].

Double deduction not allowed [Sec. 35CCC(2)] - Where any deduction is claimed and allowed for any assessment year, in respect of the aforesaid expenditure, no deduction is allowed in respect of such expenditure under any other provisions of this Act either for the same or any other assessment year. It is operative from the assessment year 2013-2014 and subsequent years.

EXPENDITURE ON SKILL DEVELOPMENT PROJECT [SEC. 35CCD]

Where a company incurs any expenditure on any 'skill-development project', notified by the Board in accordance with the prescribed guidelines [under Rules 6AAF to 6AAH], a deduction of 150% (100% from the assessment year 2021-22 and subsequent years) of such expenditure is allowed to be deducted [Sec. 35CCD(1)].

However, no deduction is allowed on any expenditure incurred on the cost of land or building.

Double deduction not allowed [Sec. 35CCD(2)] - Where any deduction is claimed and allowed for any assessment year in respect of the aforesaid expenditure, no deduction is allowed in respect of such expenditure under any other provisions of this Act either for the same or any other assessment year. It is operative from the assessment year 2013-14 and subsequent years.

AMORTISATION OF CERTAIN PRELIMINARY EXPENSES [SEC. 35D]

A special provision has been enacted to allow certain preliminary expenses which otherwise could not have been allowed on the ground of being an expenditure of capital nature. The provision has been enacted to allow such expenses subject to certain conditions. The deduction is allowed either to (*i*) an Indian company or (*ii*) any assessee who is 'resident' in India (under Sec. 6). Thus, a 'non-resident' or 'non-company' assessee cannot claim this deduction.

Timing of Incurring Expenditure - Expenditure should be incurred after 31 March 1970. It may be incurred before the commencement of the business or after the commencement of the business. There is no time-limit to incur the expenditure either before the commencement or after the commencement of the business.

Expenditure incurred before the commencement of the business or after the commencement of the business may be incurred on trading ventures or industrial ventures.

Mode of Incurring the Expenditure - Expenditure may be incurred by the assessee himself or through consultancy concerns as may be approved by the Board in this behalf. Foreign concerns are not approved by the Board in areas where Indian expertise is available. As a measure of tax planning, this function may not be assigned to a foreign collaborator, if Indian expertise is available.

Expenditure Qualifying for Deduction - Expenditure should be related to the following items:

(*a*) *In case of any assessee*:

(*i*) preparation of the feasibility report;

(*ii*) preparation of project report;

(*iii*) conducting a market survey or any other survey necessary for the business of the assessee;

(*iv*) engineering services relating to the business of the assessee;

(*v*) legal charges for drafting any agreement between the assessee and any other person for any purpose relating to the setting up or for conduct of the business of the assessee.

The word "survey" would include attracting customers to a particular spot, demonstrating to them the utility and value of the assessee's products and studying therefrom the business possibilities or determining the action necessary to extend the business [*Madras Fertilizers Ltd.* v. *CIT* (1994) 209 ITR 177 (Mad.)].

(*b*) *In case of company assessee only:* In addition to the aforesaid items, a company assessee may also incur an expenditure on one or more of the following items:

(*i*) legal charges for drafting the memorandum and articles of association of the company;

(*ii*) printing of the memorandum and articles of association;

(*iii*) registration fees of the company payable under the Companies Act, 1956 now Companies Act, 2013. Fees paid for increase of the share capital is not fees for registration of the company. Hence, it is not amortisable under this provision [*CIT* v. *Hindustan Insecticides Ltd.* [2001] 116 Taxman 406/250 ITR 338 (Del.)].

(*iv*) expenses in connection with issue of shares for public subscription or issue of debentures. Such expenses include underwriting commission, brokerage and charges for drafting, typing, printing and advertisement for the prospectus, expenses incurred in connection with refund of the amount over-subscribed.

The expression in connection with the issue of public subscription would include the stamp duty payable by the assessee on the issue of debenture issue. Hence, stamp duty paid qualifies for deduction [*CIT* v. *Mahindra Ugine & Steel Co. Ltd.* [2001] 120 Taxman 250/250 ITR 84 (Bom.)].

(*v*) such other items of expenditure (not being an expenditure which is deductible under any other provision of the Act) as may be prescribed.

Double Deduction not allowed - Where any expenditure, covered under sec. 35D, is also deductible under any other provisions of the Act, the deduction may be claimed under either of the sections, beneficial to assessee. For example, expenses on engineering services on the installation of plant and machinery may also be capitalised. Accordingly, the assessee may claim depreciation and accumulate the cost much faster, depending on the rate of depreciation. There is no ceiling under sec. 32 as it exists under sec. 35D.

Where a deduction is claimed and allowed for any assessment in respect of the qualifying expenditure (under sec. 35D) no deduction is allowed in respect of such expenditure under any other provisions of this Act for the same year or any other assessment year [sec. 35D(6)].

Audit of Accounts [Sec. 35D(4)] - The accounts of the assessee are required to be audited by a Chartered Accountant. Since the accounts of a company assessee and cooperative society are already required to be audited under the relevant law no separate audit is required for this purpose. The report of the audit should be furnished along with the return of income. It should be in the prescribed form and duly signed and certified by the chartered accountant.

Qualifying Amount for Deduction - The deduction is not allowed for actual expenditure. It is allowed for the qualifying amount, which is computed as below.

Non-company assessee	Indian company
(*i*) Actual expenditure incurred on specified items as above, on specified items as above;	(*i*) Actual expenditure incurred
or	or
(*ii*) 5% of the cost of project, cost of whichever is less, is the qualifying amount for deduction	(*ii*) At the option of the assessee, either 5% of the project or 5% of capital employed. Whichever is less, is the qualifying amount for deduction

Cost of the project before the commencement of the business: "Cost of the project" means actual cost of fixed assets, which are shown in the books of the assessee as on the last day of the previous year in which the business of the assessee commences.

Fixed assets include: land buildings, leaseholds, plant, machinery, furniture, fittings and railway siding including expenditure on development of lands and buildings.

Cost of project after the commencement of the business:

(*a*) *Expansion of industrial undertaking:* Cost of project means cost of fixed assets, as are shown in the balance sheet on the last day of the previous year in which the extension is completed and as are acquired in connection with such extension.

"Fixed Assets" include: land buildings, leaseholds, plant, machinery, furniture, fittings and railway siding including expenditure on development of lands and buildings.

(*b*) *Setting up a new undertaking:* "Cost of project" means cost of fixed assets as are shown in the balance sheet on the last day of the previous year in which the new undertaking commences production and as are acquired in connection with setting up of such undertaking.

"Fixed assets" include: land buildings, leaseholds, plant, machinery, furniture, fittings and railway siding including expenditure on development of lands and buildings.

Capital Employed in case of Company Assessee before the Commencement of the Business - "Capital employed" is the aggregate of (*i*) issued share capital (*ii*) debentures and (*iii*) long-term borrowings, as on the last day of the previous year in which the company commences business.

Capital Employed in case of Company Assessee after the Commencement of the Business:

(*a*) *Expansion of undertaking:* "Capital employed" is the aggregate of (*i*) issued share capital (*ii*) debentures and (*iii*) long-term borrowing, as are on the last day of the previous year in which the extension of the undertaking is completed and which have been issued or obtained in connection with extension of the undertaking.

(*b*) *Setting up new industrial undertaking:* "Capital employed" is the aggregate of (*i*) issued capital (*ii*) debentures and (*iii*) long-term borrowings, as on the last day of the previous year in which new undertaking commences production or operation and which have been issued or obtained in connection with setting up of new undertaking.

"Long-term borrowing" means

(*i*) any moneys borrowed by the company from the government or the Industrial Finance Corporation of India or the Industrial Credit and Investment Corporation India or any other financial institution which is eligible to claim deduction under Sec. 36(1)(*viii*) or any banking institution; or

(*ii*) any moneys borrowed or debt incurred by it in a foreign country for the purchase of capital plant and machinery outside India, where the term of borrowing or debt incurred provide for its repayment during the period of the not less than 7 years.

Mode of the Deduction [Sec. 35D(1)] - Deduction of qualifying amount is allowed in five equal annual instalments beginning with the previous year in which the business is commenced or, as the case may be, the previous year in which extension of the undertaking is completed or the new undertaking commences production. It is operative from the assessment year 1999-2000.

Deduction in Respect of Unamortised Amount in a Scheme of Amalgamation or Demerger [Sec. 35D(5A)] - Where the undertaking of an Indian Company is transferred before the expiry of 5 years in a scheme of amalgamation or demerger to another Indian amalgamated company or to another resulting company, no deduction is allowed to the amalgamating company or demerged company for the previous year in which amalgamation or demerger takes place. Instead, the amalgamated Indian company or resulting company is entitled to claim the deduction for the unexpired period of 5 years.

Double deduction not allowed [Sec. 35D(6)] - Where deduction has been allowed in respect of 'preliminary expenses' [sec. 35D(2)], no deduction is allowed for such expenses under any other provision of this Act for the same or any other assessment year.

AMORTISATION OF EXPENDITURE IN CASE OF AMALGAMATION OR DEMERGER [SEC. 35DD]

Where an Indian company incurs any expenditure wholly and exclusively for the amalgamation or demerger of an undertaking it may claim deduction of such expenditure in five annual instalment for each of the 5 successive previous years, beginning with the previous year in which the amalgamation or demerger takes place [sec. 35DD(1)].

No deduction is allowed for such expenditure under any other provision of the Act. [Sec. 35DD(2)]. It is operative on or after 1 April, 1999.

AMORTISATION OF EXPENDITURE INCURRED UNDER VOLUNTARY RETIREMENT SCHEME [SEC. 35DDA]

Where an assessee-employer pays any sum to an employee in accordance with any scheme of voluntary retirement, such amount is allowed to be deducted in five equal yearly instalments in computing taxable profits and gains of the business [Sec. 35DDA(1)].

Where an undertaking of an Indian company, entitled to the aforesaid deduction, is transferred to another Indian company in a scheme of amalgamation before the expiry of 5 years, the successor Indian company is entitled to claim the remaining instalments during unexpired period of 5 years [Sec. 35DDA(2)].

Where undertaking of an Indian company, entitled to the aforesaid deduction [under sec. 35DDA(1)] is transferred to another company in a scheme of demerger before the expiry of 5 years, the resulting company is entitled to claim the balance deductions over the remaining period of 5 years as if the demerger had not taken place [Sec. 35DDA(3)].

Where a firm or proprietary concern is succeeded by a company under scheme of business reorganisation and the conditions of sec. 47(*xiv*), have been fulfilled, the successor company is entitled to claim the balance amount of deduction during the unexpired period of 5 years [Sec. 35DDA(4)].

Where a private company or unlisted public company in succeeded in a scheme of business reorganisation by a limited liability partnership and the conditions of sec. 47(*xiv*) have been fulfilled, the successor limited liability partnership in entitled to claim the balance amount of deduction during the unexpired period of 5 years [sec. 35DDA(4A)]. It is operative from the assessment year 2011-12 and subsequent years.

In the case of any succession as above, no deduction is allowed to the successor in the previous year in which amalgamation, demerger or succession takes place [Sec. 35DDA(5)]

To avoid double deduction, it has been specified that no deduction is allowed about the aforesaid amount (under sec. 35DDA) under any other provision of the Act [Sec. 35DDA(6)].

EXPENDITURE ON PROSPECTING, ETC., FOR CERTAIN MINERALS [SEC. 35E]

Where an Indian company or a person resident in India incurs expenditure (*i*) in prospecting or extraction or production of any mineral or group of associated minerals, specified in Part A or part B of Seventh Schedule or (*ii*) on development of a mine or other natural deposit of any such mineral or group of associated mineral after 31 March, 1970, such assessee is entitled to claim the prescribed deduction in computing to its income.

"Prospecting" means any operation undertaken for the purpose of exploring, locating or proving deposits of any mineral and includes any such operation which proves to be infructuous or abortive [Sec. 35E(5)(1)(*a*)]

Expenditure to be incurred on specified items [Sec. 35E(2)] - Expenditure should be incurred after 31 March 1970 on specified items at any time during the year of commercial production and in any one or more of the 4 years, immediately preceding that year.

The specified items include expenditure:

(*a*) for the purposes of exploring, locating or proving deposits of any minerals (as specified in Part A of the Seventh Schedule) or group of associated minerals (as specified in Part B of the Seventh Schedule); or

(*b*) for the development of a mine or other natural deposits of any such mineral or group of associated minerals.

The expenditure eligible for deduction does not include the following [Sec. 35E]:

(*i*) any expenditure on the acquisition of the site of the source of any mineral or group of associated minerals aforesaid or of any rights in or over such site;

(*ii*) any expenditure on the acquisition of the deposits of such mineral or group of associated minerals or of any rights in or over such deposits;

(*iii*) any expenditure of a capital nature in respect of any building, machinery, plant or furniture for which deduction by way of depreciation is admissible; and

(*iv*) any expenditure, though eligible for deduction, met directly or indirectly by any other person or authority [Sec. 35E(2)].

Further, the qualifying amount of expenditure is to be reduced by any sale, salvage, compensation or insurance moneys realised by the assessee in respect of any property or rights brought into existence as a result of such expenditure [Proviso to Sec. 35E(2)].

Audit of accounts [Sec. 35E(6)] - Where the assessee is a person, other than company or a cooperative society, no deduction in admissible unless the accounts of the assessee for the year or years in which the expenditure is incurred has been audited by a Chartered Accountant and the Report of such audit is furnished along with the return of income for the first year in which the deduction is claimed.

Mode of deduction [Sec. 35E(4)] - The deduction is allowed with reference to the qualifying expenditure in 10 equal annual instalments, beginning with the year of commercial production.

Deduction to be allowed against profits of newly developed mineral including profits of such mineral already developed - Such deduction is allowed only against the profits arising from the commercial exploitation of the mineral in respect of which the qualifying expenditure was incurred, including the profits derived from commercial production of the same mineral already established by the assessee. If such profits during any year fall short of the annual amount of one-tenth deduction, the amount of shortfall is carried forward and added to the succeeding year's deductible amount and the total sum is allowed as a deduction from similar profits, and so on, up to a period of 10 years reckoned from the initial year of commercial production.

Prohibition of double deduction [Sec. 35E(8)] - Where a deduction is claimed and allowed for any assessment year in respect of the qualifying expenditure [under sec. 35E] no deduction in respect of that expenditure can be allowed under any other provisions of this Act for the same year or any other assessment year.

Unamortised amount in a scheme of amalgamation or demerger [Sec. 35E(7), (7A)] - Where undertaking of an Indian company which is entitled to the deduction [under sec. 35E] is transferred, before the expiry of 10 years to another Indian company in a scheme of amalgamation or demerger, no deduction is allowed to the amalgamating company or the demerged company for the previous year in which the amalgamation or demerger took place. Instead, the amalgamated Indian company or resulting company is entitled to the deduction (under sec. 35E) in respect of qualifying expenditure, remaining unabsorbed, over the unexpired period of 10 years reckoned from the initial year of commercial production.

OTHER DEDUCTIONS [SEC. 36]

Insurance Premium [Sec. 36(1)]

Insurance Premium paid against risk to stocks [Sec. 36(1)(*i*)] - The amount of insurance premium paid against risk of damage or destruction of stocks, used for the purposes of the business or profession, is fully deductible in computing the taxable profits of a business or profession. The expression 'stocks or stores' has not been defined and must, therefore, be given its ordinary meaning. The word 'damage' would mean injury or harm that impairs the value of any property. Destruction of property would take place where the injury caused thereto is beyond repair or reduces the utility of the property to nil or results in complete ruination of the property. [*CIT* v. *Khodidas Motiram Panchal* (1986) 27 Taxman 208/161 ITR 99 (Guj.)]

Insurance Premium Paid by the Federal Milk Society [Sec. 36(1)(*ia*)]- Insurance premium paid by federal milk cooperative society on the life of cattle, owned by a member of primary milk cooperative society, affiliated to it, is deductible in computing the taxable profits of the federal milk cooperative society. The provision is operative from the assessment year 1980-1981 and onward.

Premium under Health Insurance Scheme paid by Cheque [Sec. 36(1)(*ib*)] - The amount of any premium paid by any mode other than cash (w.e.f. AY 2008-2009 and onward) by the assessee–employer to effect or to keep in force an insurance on the health of his employees under a scheme framed by the General Insurance Corporation of India and approved by the Central Government, or under a scheme framed by any other insurer and approved by the Insurance Regulatory and Development Authority, established under Sec. 3(1) of the Insurance Regulatory and Development Authority Act, 1999, is also deducted in computing taxable profits of business or profession.

Case Law : ***CIT* v. *Khodidas Motiram Panchal* (1986) 27 Taxman 208/161 ITR 99 (Guj.)**

Facts: 'K' being a firm took life insurance policy for its partners with an underlying object to ensure the availability of liquid cash (capital) for payment to the legal representatives of in the event of the death of a partner so as to enable the surviving partners to continue the business of the firm without interruption.

Held: Insurance policies in question did not cover any risk of damage or destruction of stocks used for the purposes of business within the meaning of sec. 36(1)(*i*). The amount paid by way of insurance premia was for securing this liquid cash, capital asset, the expenditure incurred therefor could only be said to be in the nature of capital expenditure. Therefore, the insurance premia was not deductible under section 37(1) either.

Bonus or Commission to Employees [Sec. 36(1)(*ii*) r.w. sec. 43B]

Bonus or commission paid to an employee for services rendered is deducted subject to the following two conditions:

(*i*) *Such sum would not have been payable as a profit or dividend if not paid as bonus or commission:* The provision has been designed to check *inter alia* private companies, from avoiding tax by distributing their profits to their members (showing them to be their employees) by way of bonus and not by way of dividend. But if such shareholders are actually the employees of the company and are given bonus based on their salary, deduction for the amount so paid cannot be refused [*Loyal Motor Service Co. Ltd.* v. *CIT* (1946) 14 ITR 674 (Bom.)].

(*ii*) *Such sum has been actually paid on or before the due date of furnishing return of income for the relevant previous year [sec. 43B]:* Even if an assessee follows mercantile system of accounting, deduction of bonus or commission is allowed on actual payment.

Sec. 36(1)(*ii*) does not postulate that there should be any extra services rendered by an employee before payment of commission to him can be justified as an allowable expenditure. It is not necessary that the commission should be paid under a contractual obligation. It may be purely voluntary. [*Shahzada Nand & Sons* v. *CIT* [1977] 108 ITR 358 (SC)].

For claiming the deduction of bonus or commission during the previous year in which the liability to pay has accrued, bonus or commission should be paid either during the previous year itself or as an extended facility under sec. 43B, it can be paid on or before the due date fixed for furnishing return of income for that previous year. In such cases, deduction is allowed during the previous year in which liability to pay accrues.

If bonus or commission is paid after the due date fixed for furnishing the return of income for the relevant previous year, the deduction is allowed in the previous year in which bonus or commission is actually paid.

Proof of payment - For claiming the deduction, the assessee is required to furnish the proof of payment along with the return of income.

Interest on Borrowed Capital [Sec. 36(1)(*iii*) r.w. sec. 40(*b*), sec. 40(*ba*) and sec. 43B]

Interest on borrowed capital is deducted in computing taxable profits of business or profession in accordance with the following provisions:

(*i*) *There should be a borrowing:* Borrowing implies a creditor and a debtor. No one can borrow from himself. Thus, interest on own capital cannot be allowed as deduction.

A mere purchase of a capital asset on a long-term credit with a stipulation for payment of interest on the unpaid balance of the price does not amount to the borrowing of capital within the meaning of this clause. Such a transaction is not a loan transaction but one of purchase [*Bombay Steam Navigation Co. [1953] (P.) Ltd*. v. *CIT* (1965) 56 ITR 52 (SC)]. Interest payable on such credit purchases is not deductible under this clause but may be deducted under general deductions [Sec. 37(1)].

Similarly, interest paid to the directors on the amount of their undistributed salaries is not deductible under this clause as there is no borrowing [*CIT* v. *Saraswati Chemicals and Allied Industries (P.) Ltd*. (2001) 114 Taxman 564/249 ITR 235 (Del.)].

Share capital of a company is not capital borrowed. Therefore, guaranteed interest paid by a company to its shareholders on the capital contributed by them is not deductible under this clause [*Kirloskar Electric Co. Ltd*. v. *CIT* (1997) 228 ITR 674 (Karnataka)].

(*ii*) *Borrowing should be for the purposes of business:* Interest on borrowed capital is allowed provided the borrowing is for the purposes of business. The expression 'for the purpose of business' occurring under the provision of section 36(1)(*iii*) is wider in scope than the expression 'for the purpose of earning income, profits or gains [*Madhav Prasad Jatia* v. *CIT* AIR 1979 SC 1291]. The decisions relating to section 37 will also be applicable to section 36(1)(*iii*) because in section 37 also the expression used is 'for the purpose of business'.

Thus, in order to claim a deduction, it is enough to show that the money is expended not out of necessity but even at times voluntarily on grounds of commercial expediency and in order to indirectly facilitate the carrying on of the business [*Atherton* v. *British Insulated & Helsby Cables Ltd*. [1925] 10 TC 155]. The expression 'commercial expediency' is an expression of wide import and includes such expenditure as a prudent businessman incurs for the purpose of business. The expenditure may not have been incurred under any legal obligation, yet it is allowable as a business expenditure if it was incurred on grounds of commercial expediency [*S.A. Builders Ltd*. v. *CIT* [2007]/58 Taxman 74/288 ITR 1 (SC)].

If borrowed money is used for acquiring controlling interest in other companies and the same is in the assessee's business interest, interest on such borrowing is deductible [*CIT* v. *Rajeeva Lochan Kanoria* (1995) 80 Taxman 572/[1994] 208 ITR 616 (Calcutta)].

The expression "for the purposes of the business" is much wider than "for the purposes of earning the profit". It may include (*i*) day-to-day running of the business; (*ii*) rationalisation of its administration and modernisation of its machinery; (*iii*) measures for the preservation of business and for the protection of its assets and property from expropriation, coercive process or assertion of hostile title; (*iv*) payment of statutory dues and taxes imposed as precondition to commencement or for carrying on of a business; and (*v*) things and many other acts incidental to the carrying on a business [*CIT* v. *Malayalam Plantations Ltd*. (1964) 53 ITR 140 (SC)].

The borrowing for the purposes of the business may be to acquire stock-in-trade, or to pay-off a trading debt. Thus, interest on money borrowed to purchase material or to pay salaries or to pay retrenchment compensation is deductible.

The interest paid on moneys borrowed, utilised for payment of dividends to the shareholders of the company, is deductible as the payment of dividend is part of the business of a company [*CIT* v. *Shree Changdeo Sugar Mills Ltd*. (1983) 143 ITR 449 (Bom.)].

Interest paid on delayed payment of loan taken to pay purchase tax or sales tax to the government is also deductible.

But interest on loan taken to pay advance tax/income tax is not deductible, as income tax is the personal liability of the assessee.

Chargeability of business profit is a condition for deduction: The borrowing must be for the purposes of business or profession whose profits are liable to tax. If money is borrowed for a business, the income of which is not taxable at all, no deduction can be allowed in respect of the interest on such borrowing [*M.S.P. Raja* v. *CIT* (1976) 105 ITR 295 (Mad.)].

Where an indivisible business is carried on by an assessee, the profits of which are partly exempt and partly taxable, the interest on loan is fully deductible even if part of the borrowing has been used to earn non-taxable income. For example, cultivation of sugar cane and manufacturing of sugar is one single indivisible business. The market value of the sugar cane grown is treated as agriculture income (under Rule 7) which is exempt. But the interest paid on money borrowed and used for cultivation of sugar cane is to be allowed as deduction [*Addl. CIT* v. *Chellappalli Sugars Ltd*. (1979) 116 ITR 255 (AP)].

(*iii*) *Reasonability of expenditure or rate of interest is no ground for disallowance:* Once it is established that there is nexus between expenditure and purpose of business revenue cannot justifiably claim to put itself in arm-chair of businessman or in position of Board of Directors and assume role to decide how much is reasonable expenditure having regard to circumstances of case [*Hero Cycles (P.) Ltd.* v. *CIT* [2015] 63 taxmann.com 308/[2016] 236 Taxman 447 (SC)]. Where the borrowing is for genuine business purposes, the department cannot disallow any part of the interest on the ground that the rate of interest is unreasonably high [*East India Industries Madras Ltd*. v. *CIT* (1957) 31 ITR 803 (Madras), *Birla Gwalior Private Ltd*. v. *CIT* (1962) 44 ITR 847 (Madhya Pradesh)] or on the ground that the assessee had enough funds and need not to have recourse to borrowing [*Amnabai Hajee Issa* v. *CIT* (1962) 51 ITR 385 (Madras)] or that he charged a lower rate of interest on the money lent [*CIT* v. *Pudukottai Company (P.) Ltd* (1972) 84 ITR 788 (Madras)].

(*iv*) *Interest "paid", meaning thereof:* Interest "paid" on the borrowed money for the purposes of business is allowed. The word "paid" should be interpreted according to the system of accounting [Sec. 43]. Therefore, where assessee follows mercantile system of accounting, interest is allowed on accrual basis.

In cash system of accounting, interest is allowed on actual payment basis.

(*v*) *Interest is allowed on actual payment basis in case of borrowings from certain institutions [Sec. 43B]:* Any interest payable on any loan or borrowing from any (*a*) public financial institution, or (*b*) a State financial corporation or (*c*) a State industrial investment corporation and (*d*) any interest payable on term loan from a scheduled bank is deducted on actual payment irrespective of system of accounting followed by the assessee.

"Scheduled Bank" also includes a cooperative bank. It is operative from the assessment year 2001-2002 and onwards.

Interest paid on or before due date of furnishing return: Where interest in the above cases is paid on or before the due date fixed for furnishing return of income for the previous year in which the liability to pay interest has accrued, deduction is allowed in that very year.

If interest is paid after the said date, deduction is allowed in the previous year in which the date of payment falls.

(*vi*) *Interest paid on money borrowed to acquire capital asset not be allowed [Proviso to Sec. 36(1)(iii)]:* Where any capital is borrowed for acquisition of an asset, interest paid on such capital for the period from the date of borrowing to the date on which such asset is first put to use, is not be deducted Accordingly, the assessee should capitalise such interest and claim depreciation.

(*vii*) *Deduction of interest subject to TDS and its payment within the prescribed period [Sec. 40(a)(i)/(ia)]:* Where any interest on borrowed moneys is payable outside India to any person (*i.e.* resident or non-resident) or where it is payable in India either to a non-resident, not being a company, or to a foreign company, or where interest is payable to a resident (in India) [sec. 40(*ia*)], and tax is required to be deducted at source on the amount of interest, such interest is allowed to be deducted, provided tax has been deducted at source in accordance with the provisions applicable to TDS and tax deducted at source has been paid within the prescribed time-limit under Sec. 200(1).

Thus, where such tax has not been deducted or, after deduction, has not been paid during the previous year, or in subsequent year before the expiry of the time prescribed under Sec. 200(1), no deduction is allowed for such interest during the previous year in which it is allowable.

Where tax has not been deducted from interested payable during the previous year but tax has been deducted in any subsequent year or has been deducted in previous year (in which such interest is allowable) but paid in any subsequent year after the expiry of the time prescribed under Sec. 200(1), such interest is allowed as a deduction in computing the income of the previous year in which such tax has been paid.

(*viii*) *Interest paid by a firm to a partner [Sec. 40(b)]:* Any payment of interest paid by a firm, to a partner is allowed to be deducted provided rate of interest does not exceed 12% p.a. and it is authorised by the partnership deed.

(*ix*) *Interest paid by an AOP or BOI to a member [Sec. 40(ba)]:* No deduction is allowed in respect of any interest paid by an association of person or body of individual to its member.

(*x*) *Expenses in connection with borrowing:* Interest on borrowing is covered under sec. 36(1)(*iii*) but expenses in connection with borrowing, *e.g.* brokerage, commission, legal expenses, stamp duty, etc., are not covered under sec. 36(1)(*iii*). Such expenses may be claimed as deduction under Sec. 37(1).

Case Law : ***Hansa Estates (P.) Ltd.* v. *ACIT* [2020] 118 taxmann.com 244 (Madras)**

Facts: 'H' claimed to have given interest free loan to its holding company for acquiring a land on its behalf in a joint development agreement. It was noted that the holding company had borrowed loans from banks and thus there was no need for holding company to take advance from assessee for purpose of purchase of land.

Held: When the assessee failes to prove that interest-free loan to sister concern was given for commercial purpose, deduction cannot be allowed.

Discount on Zero Coupon Bond [Sec. 36(1)(*iiia*)]

Discount on Zero Coupon Bond issued by Infrastructure Capital Company (ICC) or infrastructure Capital Fund (ICF) or public sector company schedule bank is allowed on *pro rata* basis, having regard to the period of life of such bond, calculated in the manner as may be prescribed.

"Discount" means the difference between the amount received or receivable and the amount payable on maturity or redemption by such company or fund.

"Period of life of the bond" means the period commencing from the date of issue of the bond and ending on the maturity or redemption of the bond.

"ICC" means such company which makes investments by way of acquiring shares or providing long-term finance to any enterprises or undertaking wholly engaged in the business referred to in Sec. 80-IA(4) or Sec. 80-IAB(1), or an undertaking developing and building a housing project referred to in Sec. 80-IB(10), or a project for constructing hotel of not less than three-star category as classified by the Central Government or a project for constructing a hospital with at least 100 beds for patients [Sec. 2(*26A*)].

"ICF" means such fund operating under a trust deed registered under the provisions of the Registration Act, 1908 established to raise moneys by the trustees for investment by way of acquiring shares or providing long-term finance to any enterprise or undertaking wholly engaged in the business referred to in Sec. 80-IA(4) or Sec. 80-IAB(1), or an undertaking developing and building a housing project referred to in Sec. 80-IB(10), or a project for constructing a housing project referred to in Sec. 80-IB(10), or a project for constructing a hotel of not less than three-star category as classified by the Central Government or a project for constructing a hospital with at least one-hundred beds for patients [Sec. 2(*26B*)].

Employer's Contribution to Provident Fund [Sec. 36(1)(*iv*), (*iva*), (*v*) and r.w. sec. 43B and sec. 40(*a*)(*iv*)]

Employer's contributions to the following funds is allowed:

(*i*) contribution towards a recognised provident fund or an approved superannuation fund, subject to such limits as may be prescribed (*ii*) contribution towards a pension scheme of the Central Government, to the extent it does not exceed ten per cent of the salary of the employee in the previous year

(*iii*) any sum by way of contribution to an approved gratuity fund created for the exclusive benefit of employees under an irrevocable trust

Employer's contribution to unrecognised provident fund are allowed as and when the amount standing to the credit of an employee in the fund is actually paid to him (on leaving the service) under general deductions [*CIT* v. *Bombay Burma (Rangoon)* [1933] Trading Corpn.1 ITR 152; *Allahabad Bank* v. *CIT* [1953] 24 ITR 519 (SC)].

Year of the allowability [Sec. 43B] - Irrespective of the method of accounting followed by the employer, deduction for employer's contribution is allowed during the previous year in which it is actually paid. However, where such contribution is paid on or before the due date fixed for furnishing return of income for the previous year in which liability to pay has accrued, deduction is allowed in that very year in which such liability accrues.

Effective arrangement to ensure deduction of tax at source [sec. 40(a)(iv)]- Employer's contribution to a provident fund or other fund established for the welfare of the employees cannot be deducted unless the employer has made effective arrangements to ensure that tax will be deducted at source from any payment made from the fund which is chargeable under the head "salaries".

Employees' Contribution to the Fund [Sec. 36(1)(va) r.w. Sec. 2(*24*)(*x*)]

Employees' contribution to a provident fund is allowed subject to the following provisions:

(*i*) *Employee's contribution to be treated as income of the employer [Sec. 2(24)(x)]:* Any sum received by the employer from the employees as their contribution to a provident fund (*i.e.* recognised provident fund, approved superannuation fund or approved gratuity fund) is treated as business income of the employer. Thus, it should be credited to the profit and loss account of the business.

(*ii*) *Deduction to be allowed on actual payment to be made on due date, under service agreement or provident fund rules:* Employee's contribution should be paid to the credit of their account on the due date as provided either under agreement or provident fund rules.

If the payment is made on due date by cheque but cheque is encashed after the due date, the deduction is allowable.

(*iii*) *Employees' contribution to unrecognised fund:* Deduction is allowed under Sec. 37(1) only during the year when such contribution is actually paid to an employee, that is on his leaving the service.

Loss on Animals [Sec. 36(1)(*vi*)]

Deduction is allowed in respect of animals, which have been used for the purposes of the business but other than stock-in-trade of the business. Thus, where an assessee deals in the sale and purchase of animals, any loss on their sale is not covered under this clause.

Deduction is allowed in the previous year in which the animal had died or become permanently useless for the business. When an animal is found useful and healthy, any loss on the sale of such animals is not allowed. The quantum of deduction is the difference between the actual cost of the animals and the amount, if any, realised in respect of the carcasses or animals.

Case Law : ***Union Drug Co. Ltd.* v. *CIT* [1974] 93 ITR 91 (Cal.)**

Facts: 'U', being into the business of manufacturing medicines, drugs and chemicals, suffered loss for number of years in manufacture of serum and permanently discontinued manufacture of serum. Animals which were kept by for manufacture of serum became useless and were sold at a loss.

Held: the loss suffered by 'U' was one which came within the terms of the requirements of this section and therefore allowed.

Case Law : ***K.S. Venkatasubba Reddiar* v. *CIT* (1980) 125 ITR 750 (Mad.)**

Facts: 'V' was engaged in the business of horse-racing and the horse is sold at a loss due to cancellation of licence by race club authorities.

Held: The horse had become permanently useless for participating in business of races and, therefore, loss incurred by 'V' on sale of such horse was deductible under section 36(1)(*vi*).

Bad Debt [Sec. 36(1)(*vii*) & Sec. 36(2)]

Deduction of bad debt is allowed in accordance with the following provisions:

Conditions for the allowance:

(*i*) *Relationship of the debtor and creditor:* A bad debt presupposes the existence of a debt and, therefore, a relationship of debtor and creditor is essential. Unless there was an admitted debt and it became irrecoverable, it cannot be written off as bad debt.

(*ii*) *Bad debt written-off in accounts:* A claim for bad debt is allowed in the year in which such bad debt is actually written-off by the assessee in the accounts as irrecoverable. No deduction is allowed for bad debts on the basis of provision for bad and doubtful debts [*Explanation* to Sec. 36(1)(*vii*)].

(*iii*) *Debt is taken into account in income computation or represents money lent in the business of banking or money lending [36(2)(i)]:* Claim of bad debt may be considered in two cases:

(*a*) *Bad debt under mercantile system:* The amount of debt must have been taken into account in computing the income of the assessee of that previous year or an earlier previous year.

When accounts are kept on the basis of mercantile system of accounting, the tax is charged on profits, which may not have been realised by the assessee. If the debts of business or profession become irrecoverable, a deduction for such bad debts becomes necessary in order to arrive at the true profits and gains. Thus, no claim of bad debt can arise where accounts are kept on cash basis because a receipt goes to swell the profits only when it is actually realised. Thus, no tax is paid on due basis. Hence, no claim for bad debt can arise in such a case.

Thus, deduction of bad debt is allowed under mercantile system if it was taken into account in the computation of income. If a debt becomes irrecoverable on the basis of income computation and Disclosure Standards (ICDS), notified under Sec. 145(2), but it was not taken into account, no deduction is allowed [under sec. 36(1)(*vii*).]

From the assessment year 2016-2017 and subsequent years, if a debt becomes irrecoverable on the basis of 'Disclosure Standards' (ICDS) without recording it in the books of account, it is allowed to be deducted in the previous year in which it becomes irrecoverable.

(*b*) *Bad debt in the business of banking or money-lending:* In case of banking or money-lending business, the assessee is entitled to deduction in respect of irrecoverable loans advanced in the ordinary course of business, irrespective of the method of accounting employed. The reason is that money is the stock-in-trade or the circulating capital of a banker or money-lender.

In the business of money-lending, each and every lending may not be in the ordinary course of business. For example, where a money-lender invests his capital or accumulated profits in government securities and debentures and suffers a loss on the investment such a loss is capital loss and cannot be deducted as bad debt against the profits and gains of money-lending business.

Final adjustment of bad debt [Sec. 36(2)(ii)]: The deduction of bad debt under mercantile systems is initially claimed on estimate basis and adjustments are made in the light of final recovery of such debts in the following manner:

		₹
Adjustment in the year of final recovery:		
Add:	(*i*) Final amount of recovery	×××
	(*ii*) Amount of bad debt allowed	×××
		×××
Less: Total debtors		(–) ×××
Deficiency/surplus		×××

If there is deficiency, it is further allowed as bad debts.

If there is surplus, it is taxable business profit [under Sec. 41(4)].

No allowance for bad debt of a discontinued business: No deduction is allowed for a bad debt of a business, which has been discontinued before the commencement of the accounting year. Such a bad debt cannot be deducted from the profits of a separate existing business. An assessee can claim the deduction for a bad debt of a business, which is carried on by the assessee in the accounting year.

Successor entitled to write off predecessor's bad debts: The right to claim a debt as bad is attached to the business and not to particular assessee. If there is continuity of business without any break, the successor, is entitled to claim the debts of the predecessor as bad. For example, on dissolution of partnership, a firm is taken over by one of its partners. The succeeding partner may claim the debts of the firm as bad if they are not recovered subsequently. Similarly, a partnership firm is converted into a private company where all the partners have become shareholders, the succeeding company may claim the deduction in respect of debts of the firm as bad if they are not recovered. Likewise, a company may also claim deduction in respect of bad debt relating to a business taken over from a sick company [*CIT* v. *Veerabhadra Rao* (1985) 22 Taxman 45/155 ITR 152 (SC)].

Case Law : ***CIT* v. *Millennia Developers (P.) Ltd.* [2018] 100 taxmann.com 369/ [2019] 260 Taxman 142 (Karnataka) (SLP filed against the High Court dismissed by the Supreme Court in *CIT* v. *Millennia Developers (P.) Ltd.* [2019] 109 taxmann.com 94/266 Taxman 186 (SC))**

Facts: 'M', being a private company with two directors and their other family members who were also shareholders; transferred certain properties to the relatives of the shareholders as a part of family arrangement and partition recognized under sec.171. However, 'M' waived off its right to receive sale consideration of these properties as an amount settled among the HUF and this amount was written off as bad debts. The said waiver was to avoid deadlock in management of company on account of any disputes arising between family members who were also shareholders of 'M'. Issue arose if such waived off amount could be treated as bad debts under sec. 36(1)(*vii*).

Held: Since an order of partition was passed under section 171 and amount was duly written off in books of account, 'M's claim for deduction of said amount as bad debts was allowed.

Expenditure incurred by a Company to Promote Family Planning among its Employees [Sec. 36(1)(*ix*)]

Where a company assessee incurs *bona fide* expenditure to promote family planning among its employees, deduction in respect of such expenditure is allowed in accordance with the following provisions:

(*i*) *Revenue expenditure:* Full deduction is allowed in respect of revenue expenditure incurred on family planning. If profits are not sufficient to absorb the amount of deduction, it may turn into business loss and be treated accordingly.

(*ii*) *Capital expenditure:* Deduction in respect of capital expenditure on family planning is allowed in five equal annual installments, commencing from the previous year in which such expenditure is incurred. Deduction is allowed to the extent of business profits. The unabsorbed amount is treated like unabsorbed depreciation as per provisions of Sec. 32(2).

Unclaimed deduction in case of amalgamation - If a company amalgamates with an Indian company before the expiry of 5 years, Indian amalgamated company is allowed to claim deduction for the unexpired period.

Scheme of depreciation not applicable - Where any capital asset is required for the purposes of family planning, no depreciation is allowed in respect of such asset. The provision prevents double deduction.

Securities Transaction Tax [Sec. 36(1)(*xv*)]

"Securities transaction tax" paid by the assessee in respect of taxable securities transactions entered into in the course of his business during the previous year is allowed to be deducted, provided income arising from such taxable securities transactions is included in the income, computed under the head "Profits and gains of business or profession".

'Securities transaction tax' provides for a levy of a tax on taxable securities transaction entered in a recognised stock exchange in India payable by the purchaser.

Commodities Transaction Tax [Sec. 36(1)(*xvi*)]

"Commodities transaction tax" paid by the assessee in respect of taxable commodities transactions entered into the course of his business during the previous year, provided such income, arising from such taxable commodities transactions is included in the total income, computed under the head, 'Profits and gains of business or professions'.

"Commodities transaction tax" provides for a levy of a tax on 'taxable commodities transactions' which means a transaction of purchase or a sale of option in goods, or option in commodity derivative, or any other commodity derivative, traded in recognised associations. It is payable by the purchaser or seller, as the case may be.

Marked to Market Loss [Sec. 37(1)(*xviii*)]

This provision has been inserted from the assessment year 2017-18. Marked-to-market loss means that the asset value is adjusted to reflect its market price by recognizing the decrease in value. The decrease in value represents loss for the purpose of computing total income of the assessee. Accordingly deduction in respect of any marked to market loss (or other expected loss) shall be allowed. However, the loss must be computed in accordance with notified Income Computation and Disclosure Standards.

GENERAL DEDUCTION

Section 37(1) allows residuary business expenditure which is not covered under Secs. 30 to 36, laid out or expended, wholly and exclusively for the purposes of business or profession but no deduction is allowed for any expenditure which is of capital nature or personal expenses. However, no deduction or allowance shall be made for any expenditure incurred for any purpose which is an offence or which is prohibited by law [*Explanation 1* to sec. 37(1)]. Thus the following essential elements emerge out of the provision:

(*i*) It should be an expenditure

(*ii*) Such expenditure is not covered under secs. 30 to 36

(*iii*) It is not capital in nature

(*iv*) It is not personal expenses

(*v*) Expenditure is incurred wholly and exclusively for the purposes of business

(*vi*) Expenditure is not for any offence

Further, any expenditure incurred on the activities relating to corporate social responsibility referred to in sec. 135 of the Companies Act, 2013 shall also be not allowed as deduction [*Explanation 2* to sec. 37(1)]. No allowance shall be made in respect of expenditure incurred by an assessee on advertisement in any souvenir, brochure, tract, pamphlet or the like published by a political party.

(*i*) Outlay should be an expenditure - Sec. 37(1) allows deduction for an expenditure which denotes "spending" or "paying out" or "paying away". The fact that an assessee has set apart a particular amount to meet a possible liability in the future by itself cannot make it an expenditure. It has not gone out irretrievably. If the setting apart of the amount is only to meet a contingency which may arise or may not arise, the assessee cannot be held to have incurred any expenditure. [*Mysore Lamp Works Ltd.* v. *CIT* (1990) 52 Taxman 260/185 ITR 96 (Kar.)].

An expenditure should be distinguished from contingent liability which cannot be deducted even under mercantile system [*Indian Molasses Co. (P.) Ltd.* v. *CIT* [1959] 37 ITR 66 (SC)]. Thus, a claim made by a third party against the assessee but not admitted by the assessee or an unascertained liability to pay damages at a future date [*M.S.P. Senthikumara Nadar and Sons* v. *CIT* [1957] 32 ITR 138 (Mad.)] or registration charges for a property not yet lodged for registration [*CIT* v. *Vishal Builders (P.) Ltd.* [2002] 123 Taxman 11/254 ITR 55 (Delhi) *CIT* v. *Pragati Construction Co.* [2002] 123 Taxman 77/256 ITR 593 (Delhi)] cannot be allowed. Similarly, a liability claimed on the basis of show-cause notice when no demand notice is issued, is not allowable as it is a contingent liability [*Indian Smelting & Refining Co. Ltd.* v. *CIT* [2001] 116 Taxman 606/248 ITR 4 (SC)].

On the other hand where a company issues debentures on a discount, it incurs a liability to pay larger amount than what it has borrowed. The liability to pay the discount amount over and above the amount received for the debenture is a liability which has been incurred by the company for the purposes of business in order to generate funds for its activities. This would, therefore, be an "expenditure". Proportionate discount may be deducted over the period of redemption of debentures [*Madras Industrial Investment Corporation Ltd.* v. *CIT* (1997) 91 Taxman 340/225 ITR 802 (SC)].

The expression "laid out or expended" should be interpreted according to the system of accounting followed by the assessee. Thus, where the assessee follows cash system of accounting, deduction should be allowed on actual payment basis. In case of mercantile system of accounting, the deduction is allowed on accrual basis. However, a definite obligation to pay must arise during the year. The mercantile system can never be stretched to embrace all sort of provisions, notional or contingent, which the assessee considers that he might ultimately be called upon to pay. Provision for contingent or unaccrued liability is not allowable deduction [*New Victoria Mills Co. Ltd.* (1966) 81 ITR 305 (All.)].

Expenditure* v. *Loss - An expenditure should be distinguished from loss. An expenditure is voluntarily incurred, while a business loss is accidental and involuntary. An expenditure is a planned one but a loss is something different which is not sustained by calculation and intention. Thus, losses cannot be claimed as deduction under Sec. 37(1) but can be claimed as deduction under Sec. 29 if found incidental to trade like loss by robbery or theft [*Motipur Sugar Factory Ltd.* v. *CIT* (1955) 28 ITR 128 (Pat.)], loss through non-recovery of advance given to suppliers of raw material or loss of stock-in-trade by fire, etc.

Whether Profit Foregone could be an "Expenditure"- Where the assessee forbears from making profit out of commercial considerations, such forbearance of profit could be well-treated an expenditure. Thus, where the managing agents of a company give up the whole or a part of the managing agency commission which has accrued to them and is, therefore, assessable as income under mercantile system, and the commission is found to be remitted for purely business consideration or on grounds of commercial expediency, the amount not so received be allowable as expenditure wholly and exclusively for the purposes of business [*CIT* v. *Chandulal Keshavlal & Co.* (1960) 38 ITR 601 (SC)] followed in [*CIT* v. *Birla Gwalior (P.) Ltd.* (1973) 89 ITR 266 (SC)].

Similarly, if a bank decides, in the interest of its business, not to recover loan from customers whose ornaments, pledged with the bank, had been lost by dacoity, the amount of unrecovered loan would constitute an expenditure [*CIT* v. *Punjab Agro Industries Corpn. Ltd.* (2001) 119 Taxman 860/(2002)253 ITR 788 (Punj. & Har.)].

Expenditure incurred in relation to exempted income, not deductible - Where an assessee is carrying a business in various ventures and some of them yield taxable income and the others do not, a proportionate expenditure relating to exempted income is not to be allowed (Sec. 14A). However, in case of an indivisible business, producing taxable and exempted income, whole of the expenditure is allowed to be deducted. Thus, where loan is taken for cultivation of sugarcane and manufacture of sugar, the interest on such loan is fully allowed to be deducted and cultivation of sugarcane and manufacture of sugar is one indivisible business.

Expenditure to be incurred in connection with Assessee's Own Business - Expenditure is allowed to be deducted if it is incurred in connection with the assessee's own business. A parent company cannot be allowed a deduction in respect of a loss or expenditure incurred by or for the purposes of its subsidiary [*CIT* v. *United Breweries* (1973) 89 ITR 17 (Mysore)].

If the expenses are primarily incurred for the purpose of the assessee's business, an allowance should be made even if the expenditure is also for the benefit of a third party. Thus, where the assessee's own business included furnishing guarantees to debts owed by its subsidiary companies, the payment made to clear the overdrafts of the subsidiary which went into liquidation was held to be an allowable loss [*CIT* v. *Amalgamation (P.) Ltd*. (1997) 92 Taxman 132/226 ITR 188 (SC)].

Expenditure be incurred in connection with the business, carried on by the assessee during the Accounting Year

Expenditure should be incurred for the purpose of own business which is carried on by the assessee in the accounting year. Expenditure cannot be allowed if the business was discontinued before the commencement of the accounting year. This section does not apply to the businesses so discontinued. Thus, travelling and litigation expenses incurred for realising the sale consideration for the factories left in Pakistan have been held not be deductible, as not being pertaining to any business "carried on" by the assessee during the accounting year but pertaining to realisation of sale consideration of fixed assets of a discontinued business [*Dalmia Dairy Industries Ltd.* v. *CIT* (1999) 107 Taxman 544/(2000) 241 ITR 9].

Mere realisation of assets by the liquidator during the course of winding up of the company does not amount to "carrying on" the business and therefore, expenses such as salaries, legal fees, liquidation, expenses, etc., cannot be deducted from the interest income earned during that period [*Vijya Laxmi Sugar Mills Ltd.* v. *CIT* (1991) 59 Taxman 22/191 ITR 641 (SC)].

The expenses of a discontinued business are not allowed to be set-off against the profits of a separate existing business. However, where receipt from a discontinued business or profession is taxed under Sec. 176(3A) or (4) as the income of a year subsequent to the year of discontinuance, expenditure incurred to earn that income is allowed.

Superseding Provisions - Expenditure which is otherwise deductible under Sec. 37(1) may still be disallowed because of superseding provisions contained in some other sections, e.g. Secs. 40, 40A, 43B.

(*ii*) Expenditure should not be covered by Secs. 30 to 36

Section 37(1) and Secs. 30 to 36 are mutually exclusive. Where an expenditure is covered for deduction under a particular section, falling under Sec. 30 to Sec.

36, but no deduction is allowed under that Section because of non-compliance of its conditions, such expenditure cannot be deducted under Sec. 37(1). For instance, Sec. 30 allows certain expenses in respect of business premises, *e.g.* rent, current repairs, insurance and municipal taxes. However, brokerage paid in respect of business premises or registration expenses of the tenancy agreement or advertisement inserted in a newspaper for suitable location of business premises are not covered under Sec. 30. Such expenses may be allowed under Sec. 37(1).

Likewise, Sec. 31 allows current repairs in respect of plant, machinery and furniture. Accumulated repairs are not covered under Sec. 30. Such repairs could be allowed under Sec. 37(1) on account of business expediency.

Similarly, repair, insurance and taxes in respect of premises used for business are allowed under Sec. 30. However, if premises are held for business use but are not actually used for business repair, insurance and taxes in respect of such premises may be allowed under Sec. 37(1).

(iii) No Deduction for Personal Expenses of the Assessee

Personal expenses of the assessee are not deductible, even though such expenses may be necessitated by the business or professional activities. Thus, where an assessee contracted an illness as a result of his professional activities and incurred medical expenses, deduction of such expenses was not allowed as they were personal expenses and could not be said to have been incurred for the purposes of the profession [*Norman* v. *Golder* (*Inspector of Taxes*) 26 TC 293 (CA)/(1945)13 ITR Suppl. 21]. Thus, insurance premium paid on the life of the assessee, expenses of the premises occupied by the proprietor of the business, holidaying or club expenses of the assessee or drawings and personal conveyance expenses of the assessee are not to be allowed.

(iv) Capital Expenditure not Allowed

No deduction is allowed for an expenditure which is in the nature of capital nature. Thus, the expenditure, eligible for deduction, must be of revenue nature.

Capital expenditure* v. *revenue expenditure - The expression "capital expenditure" is not defined. The distinction between capital and revenue expenditure is a commercial distinction and must be answered in accordance with sound accounting principles, taking into accounts the facts of the case. The following tests are generally applied to distinguish between capital and revenue expenditure but none of the test is conclusive or of universal application.

(*i*) *Test of "enduring benefit"*: "Capital" connotes permanency. Capital expenditure is, therefore, closely akin to the concept of securing something which is intended to be of lasting value. Therefore, an expenditure which brings into existence an asset or advantage of enduring nature must be properly regarded on capital account in absence of special circumstances, leading to an opposite conclusion [*CIT* v. *Finlay Mills Ltd.* (1951) 20 ITR 475 (SC)]. For example, shifting expenses of a sugar mill to an area which was not flood-prone and supply of good quality sugarcane was available in abundance, were held to be of capital nature. The expenditure was not incurred in earning the profit but it was incurred for improving the profit earning capacity of the concern and so it brought and advantage of enduring nature [*Sitalpur Sugar Works Ltd*. v. *CIT* (1963) 49 ITR 160 (SC)].

The basic test of enduring benefit is not the time-limit of a fixed period—*i.e.* 5 years or 15 years. The only point to be considered is whether the threat, which is perceived at the time of agreement/incurring the expenditure would cease to exist thereafter or it would recur again. If the threat has the potential of reoccuring after the agreed period, the benefit cannot be said to be of enduring nature [*Smartchem Technologies Ltd*. v. *ITO* (2006) 150 Taxman 63 (Ahd.-Trib.)(Mag.)].

The expenditure on a scheme which increases the value of a capital asset is capital expenditure [*Union Cold Storage* v. *Ellerker* 22 TC 547]. Thus, betterment charges paid to municipal corporation under Town Planning Act is capital expenditure as the value of land will appreciate due to planned development undertaken by the Corporation [*Arvind Mills Ltd*. v. *CIT* (1992) 63 Taxman 493/197 ITR 422 (SC)].

The advantage need not be of a positive character- It may even consist in getting rid of an item of fixed capital that is of onerous character. Thus, a payment made by the assessee to free himself from an onerous lease is capital expenditure [*Malleti* v. *Stavelly* 13 TC 772].

It is the object which counts and not the result- If an expenditure is incurred "with a view" to bringing an asset or an advantage of enduring nature into existence, the expenditure is on capital account though the intended asset or advantage may not have been acquired. Thus, a sum spent in trying to procure an agency or a licence is capital expenditure though the intended agency or licence ultimately may not be secured. Similarly, an expenditure incurred on an unsuccessful attempt to bore a well may be on capital account [*CIT* v. *Bazpur Operative Sugar Factory Ltd*. (1982) 10 Taxman 246 (1983)142 ITR 1 (All.); *Fancy Corpn. Ltd*. v. *CIT* (1986) 24 Taxman 155/162 ITR 827 (Bom.); *Shree Digvijay Woollen Mills Ltd*. v. *CIT* [1993] 204 ITR 398/[1994] 77 Taxman 30 (Guj.)].

Expenditure on acquisition of an asset is capital expenditure but expenditure on its maintenance or replacement of its worn out parts is of revenue nature. Thus, replacement of an old diesel motor engine by the new diesel engine is revenue expenditure. Replacement of a petrol engine by diesel engine because of steep rise in petrol cost is also on revenue account, as it reduces operational cost and thereby augments business profits. By incurring such expenditure no new asset was brought into existence [*CIT* v. *Mohd. Ishaque Mohd. Gulam* (1995) 78 Taxman 323/(1994) 210 ITR 817 (MP); *CIT* v. *Polyolefine Industries Ltd*. (1987) 35 Taxman 76/(1988) 169 ITR 538 (Bom.)].

(*ii*) *Expenditure on assets, belonging to thirty party:* An expenditure incurred by an assessee on a capital asset is to be taken on capital account if the asset belongs to the assessee. However, such expenditure may be deductible as revenue expenditure if the asset belongs to a third party. Thus, the contribution made by a sugar mill towards boring of wells and construction of godown on the land belonging to cane growers, were held deductible as revenue expenditure as those were not properties of the assessee but of the cane growers [*R.B. Narain Singh Sugar Mills (P.) Ltd.* v. *CIT* (1980) 4 Taxman 519/(1981) 129 ITR 698 (Delhi)].

Demolition expenses of an old building and construction expenses of a new building on a land, taken on a long-term lease of 35 years by the assessee on extremely low rent, was held to be of revenue nature since the building, though constructed by the assessee, belonged to the lessor and the assessee did not acquire any capital asset [*CIT* v. *Madras Auto Service (P.) Ltd*. (1998) 99 Taxman 575/233 ITR 468 (SC)].

(*iii*) *Expenditure relating to fixed capital* v. *circulating capital:* An expenditure relating to fixed capital or capital assets is on capital account whereas an expenditure relating to circulating capital or stock-in-trade is revenue expenditure. "Fixed Capital" is what the owner turns to profit by keeping it in his own possession. Circulating capital is what the owner parts with for making profit [*John Smith* v. *Moore* 12 TC 266, 282 (HL)].

(*v*) Expenditure to be laid Out or expended, wholly and exclusively, for the purposes of the business

Where an expenditure has qualified all the preceding tests, it should also stand to scrutiny that it should be laid out or expended (*a*) wholly and exclusively (*b*) for the purposes of the business.

(*a*) Wholly and Exclusively - The word "wholly" refers to the quantum of the expenditure and the word "exclusively" refers to the motive, object and purpose of the expenditure and gives justification to the taxing authority to examine whether the expenditure was exclusively incurred for the purposes of the business and disallow an expenditure not incurred for the purposes of the business.

Once the expenditure is incurred on account of commercial expediency, wholly and exclusively for the purposes of business, the taxing authority cannot invoke the test of reasonableness to disallow a part of the expenditure as being unreasonable. The test of reasonableness has to be judged from the point of view of businessman and not of revenue. The Department cannot justifiably claim to put itself in the armchair of a businessman or in the position of board of directors and assume the said role to decide how much expenditure is reasonable having regard to the circumstances of the case [*CIT* v. *Dalmia Cement (P.) Ltd.* (2002) 121 Taxman 706/254 ITR 377]. For example, while fixing the remuneration of the employee, the employer may take into account the extent of the business, the nature of the duties to be performed and the special attitude of the employee, future prospects of extension of business and a host of other related circumstances. The rule that increased remuneration can only be justified if there be corresponding increase in the profits of the employer is erroneous [*CIT* v. *Walchand & Co. (P) Ltd*. (1967) 65 ITR 381 (SC)].

(*b*) **"For the Purposes of the Business"-** The phrase "for the purposes of the business" has a wider purport. It is to be assigned a meaning according to the circumstances of each case. It cannot be assigned a limited meaning. The expression "for the purposes of the business" is wider in scope than the expression "for the purpose of earning profit", its range is wide.

Whether the expenditure has been incurred for the purposes of the business or not is a question of facts. The following tests are generally useful in determining whether the expenditure is laid out or expanded wholly and exclusively for the purposes of business.

Expenditure to be incurred as a trader: One of the tests to be applied to determine the business purpose is whether the expenditure has been incurred by the assessee in his character as a trader or in a different capacity, *e.g.*, as a house-owner or as a man of religion or as a custodian of the society, etc. Thus, where an assessee pays donation for the worship of his deity as a man of religion, donations are not allowed. The purpose of the business is to earn profits and not to distribute profits by way of donations and charities. Similarly, breach of law is no function of a trader. Whatever he does, he has to do it within the four corners of the law. Therefore, fine and penalties be imposed on him for the breach of law are not allowed.

Where as a house-owner or house-holder, he makes gifts on the birthdays of his children or the wedding anniversary of his wife, and debit them to business accounts, no deduction can be allowed for such gifts. However, where as a trader he makes gifts to business customers, such gifts may be allowed.

Expenditure to be linked with some benefits: The assessee should incur the expenditure with a view to get some benefit—direct or indirect, immediate or deferred. The correct approach is to see whether the expenditure is being incurred on account of commercial expediency for the ultimate benefit of the business. [*J.R. Patel & Sons (P.) Ltd*. v. *CIT* (1968) 69 ITR 782 (Guj.)]. Deduction for such expenditure is allowed if the answer is in the affirmative.

Thus, where expenditure is incurred in providing educational scholarship to the poor children of the weaker sections of the society, it is not allowed even though it may be a noble cause for the nation building. However, where educational scholarships are provided to the poor meritorious children of business employees, such expenditure may be deducted as it would make the employees happy and would promote industrial peace, so vital for the business prosperity.

Expenditure benefitting a third party: Where an expenditure is incurred for protecting business interests, deduction may be allowed for such expenditure even though a third party, other than the assessee, is also benefited by such expenditure. Take an example, on the request of the board of directors of the managed company, an assessee–firm gave up a substantial part of its commission–income considering the bad financial position of the managed company. The surrender of the commission was held an allowable expenditure as it would make the company financially strong and will provide an opportunity to the assessee-firm to earn more commission in future [*CIT* v. *Chandulal Keshavlal & Co*. (1960) 38 ITR 601 (SC)].

Expenditure promoting business interests: Where an expenditure is incurred on account of business necessity for promoting business interests, such expenditure is treated as having been incurred for the purposes of the business. The term business interest is a commercial term and be viewed and analysed in larger perspective. Foreign travel expenses and hotel charges, etc., for the purposes of the business are allowable. Expenses incurred by an author of a book, to attend a seminar to generate interest in the book, are deductible [*G.S. Ramaswamy* v. *CIT* [2002] 125 Taxman 46 (Mad.)].

There are diverse views with regard to allowability of travelling expenses of the spouse of the assessee or director or partner. If the object of the foreign tour by the assessee's wife was to attend to the assessee's personal comforts, the expenditure would not qualify for deduction but where the object of the foreign tour, undertaken by the assessee's wife was for the purposes of the assessee's business and incidentally she attended to her husband who was a cardiac patient, the expenditure would be allowable [*D.B. Madan* v. *CIT* (2002) 125 Taxman 324/ (2003) 261 ITR 193 (Mad.)].

(*vi*) Expenditure tainted with illegality [Explanation to Sec. 37(1)] - Any expenditure incurred by an assessee for any purpose which is an offence or which is prohibited by law cannot be deemed to have been incurred for the purposes of business or profession. No deduction or allowance will be made in respect of such expenditure.

There had been instances when assessees were claiming deductions on expenditure incurred in offering certain benefits or perquisite to a person such as meeting his expenditure related to travel, hospitality, conference etc. In certain such cases acceptance of such benefit or perquisite by such person was in violation of regulations or guidelines governing the conduct of such person. For instance there had been an ongoing controversy whether pharma companies can claim deduction for expenditures incurred on offering freebies or trips to medical practitioners who were prohibited by the rules of the Indian Medical Council (Professional Conduct, Etiquette and Ethics) Regulations, 2002 from accepting such freebies.

Further, disallowance of expenses that were offences were interpretated by some assesses as confined only those pertaining to domestic law and not those under foreign law.

In order to clarify such anomalies, the Finance Act, 2022 inserts *Explanation 3* to sec. 37. For the removal of doubts, it is hereby clarified that the expression "expenditure incurred by an assessee for any purpose which is an offence or which is prohibited by law" under *Explanation 1*, shall include and shall be deemed to have always included the expenditure incurred by an assessee—

(*i*) for any purpose which is an offence under, or which is prohibited by, any law for the time being in force, in India or outside India; or

(*ii*) to provide any benefit or perquisite, in whatever form, to a person, whether or not carrying on a business or exercising a profession, and acceptance of such benefit or perquisite by such person is in violation of any law or rule or regulation or guideline, as the case may be, for the time being in force, governing the conduct of such person; or

(*iii*) to compound an offence under any law for the time being in force, in India or outside India.

Violation of other statutes to be condemned - In making the assessment under the Income-tax Act, the income-tax authorities are required not to close their eyes to the infraction of other statutes and allow the assessee to reap the benefit of their violation. It would be against 'public policy'. However, there is a difference between an an infraction of law and breach of obligation in buinsess. Further, whenever any statutory impost paid by an assessee by way of damages or penalty or interest is claimed as an allowable expenditure under section 37(1), the assessing authority is required to examine whether under the scheme of the provisions of the relevant statute, the impost is compensatory or penal in nature, irrespective of the nomenclature of the impost. The authority has to allow deduction under section 37(1) wherever such examination reveals the concerned impost to be purely compensatory in nature. Wherever such impost is found to be of a composite nature, that is partly of compensatory nature and partly of penal nature, the authorities are obligated to bifurcate the two components of the impost and give deduction to that component which is compensatory in nature and refuse to give deduction to that component which is penal in nature [*Prakash Cotton Mills (P.) Ltd.* v. *CIT* [1993] 67 Taxman 546/201 ITR 684 (SC)].

Damages or compensation paid by an assessee- Damages or compensation paid by an assessee may be allowed, provided the expenditure is incurred by the assessee as a trader. Thus, compensation payable to a customer for injuries caused by defect in goods sold is an allowable deduction but damages payable by a sugar broker for defaming a rival in the trade are not allowable [*Farrie* v. *Hall* 28 TC 200].

Compensation payable as a result of negligence of the assessee or his employees, in carrying on the business is allowable [*Anamalai Timber Trust Ltd.* v. *CIT* (1963) 47 ITR 814 (Ker.)]. Similarly, damages paid for a breach of warranty [*CIT* v. *Prafulla Kumar Mallick* (1969) 73 ITR 119 (Orissa)], or for failure to perform or delay in performing a trading contract [*Hind Mercantile Corporation Ltd.* v. *CIT* (1963) 49 ITR 23 (Mad.)] or payment made to seek extension of time for performance of a contract [*Central Trading Agency* v. *CIT* (1965) 56 ITR 561 (All.)] are allowable deductions. But liability for damages, occasioned by deliberate and dishonest breaches of contract, is not allowable [*Mask & Co.* v. *CIT* (1943) 11 ITR 454 (Mad.); *Northern India Chemicals Distributors Ltd.* v. *CIT* (2001) 114 Taxman 332/248 ITR 790 (Delhi)].

Expenditure on Corporate Social Responsibility not allowed as deduction [*Explanation 2*]

The Companies Act, 2013 by virtue of sec. 135 makes it mandatory for companies meeting a certain threshold to spend at least 2% of its profits towards Corporate Social Responsibility (CSR). Schedule VII to the Companies Act, 2013 also provides an indicative list of areas on which CSR expenditure can be made. The accompanying rules to CSR stipulate that anything which is done by the company in its ordinary course of business shall not be considered as CSR.

Explanation 2 to sec. 37 disallows expenditure on CSR while computing profits of the company for the purposes of this head of income. Therefore when companies incur expenditure on CSR activities towards it the fulfilment of its statutory obligation under sec. 135 of the Companies Act, 2013, it cannot be claimed as a deduction for the purposes of income tax. However, there is some confusion whether expenditure of companies towards CSR in the form of donations to specific funds that are also covered by general deduction under sec. 80G would continue to avail such deduction under that section.

A recent ruling of the Kolkata Tribunal in *JMS Mining (P.) Ltd.* v. *PCIT* [2021] 130 taxmann.com 118/190 ITD 702 (Kolkata - Trib.) shed some light on this controversy. Here the assessee-company was a mining service provider engaged in the business of management and operation of mines. It claimed deduction under section 80G being donation of sum of certain amount which was given to certain trusts as contribution towards Corporate Social Responsibility (CSR) activities. While the Assessing Officer allowed same, the Principal Commissioner invoked revision jurisdiction under sec. 263 and disallowed the same in view of *Explanation 2*. The Tribunal ruled that the said *Explanation 2* cannot be extended or imported to CSR contributions which is otherwise eligible for deduction under any other provision or Chapter, to say donations made by charitable trust registered under section 80G.

The Bangalore Tribunal in *Sling Media (P.) Ltd* v. *Dy. CIT* [2022] 135 taxmann.com 164/194 ITD 1 (Bangalore - Trib.) also took a similar line while allowing CSR expenditure which were in the form of donation that was allowed to avail deduction under sec. 80G. Thus courts have been taking a view that disallowance for CSR expenditure under *Explanation 2* to sec. 37 must to be restricted only to computing profits chargeable under head 'Profits and Gains from Buisness and Profession'. Such disallowance has no application when it comes to computing total taxable income and deductions that are allowed under sec. 80G.

EXPENSES AND PAYMENTS DISALLOWED AND RESTRICTED FOR DEDUCTIONS [SECS. 40, 40A]

While claiming deductions for expenditures as discussed above, certain expenditures and payments are (*i*) disallowed [Sec. 40] or (*ii*) have a restriction on the amounts that may be claimed for the purposes of deduction [Sec. 40A].

(*i*) Disallowed Expenses and Payments

The following expenditures are not allowed to be deducted for the computation of profits and gains from business or profession:

Expenditures disallowed when the assessee fails to deduct tax [Sec. 40(*a*)(*i*),(*ia*),(*ib*)]

When an assessee having incurred an expenditure of the nature described below, fails to deduct the tax at source on such income, such expenditure even though allowed under the provisions as seen above are disallowed. This can be understood as a measure to seek compliance from the assessees and to put them on alert at the time of making such payments as they would be put at a disadvantage if they fail to deduct the tax by being denied a deduction of such expenditures from their profits. The table below provides a quick overview of the relevant disallowance provisions:

TABLE 8.2: EXPENDITURES DISALLOWED FOR FAILURE TO DEDUCT TAX

Particulars	Conditions for disallowance	Quantum of expenditure disallowed	Expenditure allowed if subsequent compliance	Deemed to be deducted if the payee has paid the tax on such income
Interest, Royalty, Fees for Technical Services or any other sum payable to any Person Outside India or to a Non-resident/Foreign company in India [sec. 40(*a*)(*i*)]	◆ If the tax has not been deducted at source on such income (under Sec. 192 to Sec. 206)	100% of such expenditure is disallowed	If deducted in the subsequent year, expenditure is allowed in the year in which tax is deducted and deposited	where an assessee fails to deduct the tax on any such sum the payee (*i*) has furnished the return of income [under Sec. 139(1)], (*ii*) has included the payment in his return, and (*iii*) has paid tax thereon has filed the return had taken such sum for its computing its income and paid tax declared on such return, it shall be deemed that the assessee
	◆ If tax has been deducted but after its deduction, it has not been paid on or before the due date of furnishing the return of income [under Sec. 139(1)]	100% of such expenditure is disallowed	If deposited after due date or date of IT return, expenditure is allowed in the year in which tax is deposited	

Particulars	Conditions for disallowance	Quantum of expenditure disallowed	Expenditure allowed if subsequent compliance	Deemed to be deducted if the payee has paid the tax on such income
				has deducted and paid the tax on such sum on the date of furnishing of return of income. Where an assessee fails to deduct the tax on any such sum the payee
Any sum payable to a resident [sec. 40(*a*)(*ia*)]	◆ If the tax has not been deducted at source on such income	30% of such expenditure is disallowed	If deducted in the subsequent year, 30% of expenditure which was earlier disallowed is allowed in the year in which tax is deducted and deposited	(*i*) has furnished the return of income [under Sec. 139(1)], (*ii*) has included the payment in his return, and (*iii*) has paid tax thereon has filed the return had taken such some for its computing
	◆ If tax has been deducted but after its deduction, it has not been paid on or before the due date of furnishing the return of income [under Sec. 139(1)]	30% of such expenditure is disallowed	If deposited after due date or date of IT return, 30% of expenditure which was earlier disallowed is allowed in the year in which tax is deposited	its income and paid tax declared on such return, it shall be deemed that the assessee has deducted and paid the tax on such sum on the date of furnishing of return of income.
Payment on which Equalisation Levy is deductible [sec. 40(*a*)(*ib*)]	If the tax has not been deducted at source on such income	100% of such payment is disallowed	If deducted in the subsequent year, expenditure is allowed in the year in which tax is deducted and deposited	Where an assessee fails to deduct the tax on any such sum the payee (*i*) has furnished the return of income [under Sec. 139(1)], (*ii*) has included the payment in his return, and (*iii*) has paid tax thereon has filed the return had

Particulars	Conditions for disallowance	Quantum of expenditure disallowed	Expenditure allowed if subsequent compliance	Deemed to be deducted if the payee has paid the tax on such income
	If tax has been deducted but after its deduction, it has not been paid on or before the due date of furnishing the return of income [under Sec. 139(1)]	100% of such payment is disallowed	If deposited after due date or date of IT return, 30% of expenditure which was earlier disallowed is allowed in the year in which tax is deposited	taken such some for its computing its income and paid tax declared on such return, it shall be deemed that the assessee has deducted and paid the tax on such sum on the date of furnishing of return of income.
Salaries paid outside India, whether to a resident or to a non-resident [sec. 40(*a*)(*iii*)]	if the tax has not been paid thereon nor deducted therefrom	100% of the amount	-	-
Salaries paid outside India to a non-resident [sec. 40(*a*)(*iii*)]	if the tax has not been paid thereon nor deducted therefrom			
Any payment to a provident or other fund established for the benefit of employees of the assessee [sec. 40(*a*)(*iv*)]	when assessee has not made effective arrangement to deduct tax at source			

Disallowance of certain taxes paid [Sec. 40(*a*)(*ic*), (*ii*), (*iia*)]

Any sum paid on account of any rate or tax levied on the profits or gains of any business or profession or assessed at a proportion of, or otherwise on the basis of, any such profits or gains shall not be deducted in computing the income chargeable under the head "Profits and gains of business or profession". The table below lists out such taxes:

TABLE 8.3: TAXES DISALLOWED FOR DEDUCTION

Particulars	Quantum of Expenditure
Fringe Benefit Tax [Sec. 40(*a*)(*ic*)]	100% of the sum paid as tax is disallowed
Income tax on the profits of business or profession [sec. 40(*a*)(*ii*)	100% of the sum paid as tax is disallowed
Foreign taxes eligible for double taxation relief under sec. 90 or 91 (however assessee is eligible for credit) [*Explanations 1* and *2* to sec. 40(*a*)(*ii*)]	100% of the sum paid as tax is disallowed

Particulars	**Quantum of Expenditure**
Wealth Tax [sec. 40(*a*)(*iia*)]	100% of the sum paid as tax is disallowed
Foreign Tax similar to nature of wealth tax or such foreign tax having reference to the value of assets of, or the capital employed in a business or profession [sec. 40(*a*)(*iia*)]	100% of the sum paid as tax is disallowed
Tax Paid by the Employer on the Value of Non-monetary perquisite provided to his Employee [sec. 40(*a*)(*v*)]	100% of the sum paid as tax is disallowed

There had been an ongoing controversy whether education and health cess imposed at the time of income tax liability was an allowable deduction for the purposes of this section. Some assesses claimed that since 'cess' has not been specifically mentioned in the aforesaid provisions of section 40(*a*)(*ii*), cess is an allowable expenditure. The Bombay High Court in the case of *Sesa Goa Limited* v *Jt. CIT* (2020) 117 taxmann.com 96 (Bom.) and the Rajasthan High Court in the case of *Chambal Fertilizers & Chemicals Ltd* v. *Jt. CIT* [2019] 107 taxmann.com 484 (Rajasthan) held that 'education cess' can be claimed as an allowable deduction while computing profits under this head. The Courts had relied on the CBDT Circular No. 91/58/66-ITJ(19) dated 18-5-1967. However a recent ruling of Kolkata Tribunal in Kanoria Chemicals & Industries Ltd. discussed the two High Court judgments as well as other judgments held that the "Cess" is not to be allowed as deduction. While arriving at its ruling, the Tribunal placed relevance on the Supreme Court decision in *CIT* v. *K. Srinivasan* (1972) 83 ITR 346 (SC) which held that surcharge and additional surcharge are part of the income tax. Tracing the history of education and health cess, the Kolkata Tribunal held that though named as a cess it was an additional surcharge and was very much a part of income tax. Therefore the same cannot be allowed as deduction for the purposes of sec. 40(*a*)(*ii*).

This controversy has been set to rest by the Finance Act, 2022 by virtue of an *Explanation 3* that has been inserted to sec. 40(*a*)(*ii*). Accordingly, it has been clarified that the term "tax" shall include and shall be deemed to have always included any surcharge or cess, by whatever name called, on such tax. The Explanation has been inserted with retrospective effect from 1-4-2005.

Disallowance of certain royalty, licence fee, charge, etc. in the case of State Government Undertakings [Section 40(*a*)(*iib*)]

State Government Undertakings are separate legal entities distinct from the State Government and are liable to income-tax. When such undertakings pay dividends to State Government which owns them, dividend attracted dividend distribution tax under sec. 115-O and such dividend payments were not deductible as expense. In order to allegedly neutralize such tax implications, State Governments instead of taking profits from such undertakings in the form of dividends, imposed certain levies exclusively on such undertakings alone in the form of royalty, privilege fee etc. and the undertakings claimed such payments as deductions from their profits.

Dispute arose whether such exclusive levies or charge by the State Government exclusively on its undertakings are deductible or not since this would essentially mean leakage in the revenue collections for the Central government imposing income tax. Thus, the Finance Act, 2013 has amended section 40 by inserting new sub-clause (*iib*) in section 40(*a*) with effect from 1-4-2014. Accordingly, no deduction is allowed from the assessment year 2014-15 and subsequent years in respect of the following:

(*i*) Any amount paid by way of royalty, licence fee, service fee, privilege fee, service charge or any other fee or charge which is levied on a State Government undertaking by the State Government.

(*ii*) Any amount which is appropriated, directly or indirectly from a State Government undertaking by the State Government.

Scope of State Government undertaking [*Explanation* to Sec. 40(*a*)(*iib*)]

A State Government undertaking for this purpose includes—

(*i*) a corporation established by or under any Act of the State Government;

(*ii*) a company in which more than 50% of the paid up equity capital is held by the State Government;

(*iii*) a company in which more than 50% of the paid up equity share capital is held by the entity referred in clause (*i*) or clause (*ii*) as above, whether singly or taken together;

(*iv*) a company or corporation in which the State Government has the right to appoint the majority of the directors or to control the management or policy decisions, directly, or indirectly, including by virtue of its shareholding or management rights or shareholders agreement or voting agreements or in any other manner;

(*v*) an authority or a board or an institution or a body established or constituted by or under any Act of the State Government or owned or controlled by the State Government.

(*ii*) Restricted Expenses

Payments to Relatives and other Specified Persons [Sec. 40A(2)]

Where an assessee incurs any expenditure in respect of which payment has been made or is to be made to any relative of the assessee or other specified persons and such payment is found excessive or unreasonable having regard to the fair market value of the goods, services or facilities for which the payment is made or the legitimate needs of the business or profession of the assessee or the benefit derived or accruing to him therefrom, the Assessing Officer is required to disallow so much of the expenditure as is found by him excessive or unreasonable. The object of this provision is to check evasion of tax through excessive or unreasonable payments to relatives and other specified persons.

Type of assessee	*Prescribed person covered under Sec. 40A(2)*
Where the assessee is an individual	Any relative of the assessee-individual.
Where the assessee is a firm	Partner of the firm and any relative of such partner
Where the assessee is an AOP	Member of the AOP and any relative of such member
Where the assessee is an HUF	Member of HUF and any relative of such member
Where the assessee is a company	Any director of the company or any relative, of such director
Where the assessee is any person	(*a*) An individual having substantial interest in the business of the assessee or any relative of such individual.
	(*b*) A company having substantial interest in the business of the assessee or any director of such company or any relative of such director.
	(*c*) A firm having substantial interest in the business of assessee or any partner of such firm or any relative of such partner
	(*d*) An AOP having substantial interest in the business of the assessee or any member of such AOP or any relative of such member
	(*e*) An HUF having substantial interest in the business of the assessee or any' member of such HUF or any relative of such member
Where a director of a company has substantial interest in the business of any assessee.	Company in which director has substantial interest, or such director or any relative of such director.
Where a partner of the firm has substantial interest in the business of any assessee	Firm in which a partner has got substantial interest in the business of the assessee or any such partner or any relative of such partner
Where a member of AOP has got substantial interest in the business of any assessee.	The AOP in which a member has substantial interest in the business of the assessee or any such member or any relative of such member
Where a member of HUF has got substantial interest in the business	The HUF in which a member has got substantial interest in the business of the assessee or any such member of HUF or any relative of such member

Substantial interest explained- A person is deemed to have substantial interest in the business or profession if such person is the benficial owner of at least 20% equity capital of a company (which carries on business or profession) at any time during the relevant previous year and in any other case if he is entitled to at least 20% of the profits of a concern (which carries on business or profession) at any time during the previous year.

Relative defined - The term "relative" in relation to an individual means the husband, wife, brother or sister or any lineal ascendant or descendant of that individual.

Sec. 40A(2) and Transfer Pricing Regulations - Transfer Pricing Regulations comprised in Chapter X of the Income-tax Act are similar to sec. 40A(2) in that they also have an underlying objective to curb tax avoidance practices but transfer pricing are special rules for anti-avoidance. From the financial year 2012-13, transfer pricing provisions were also made applicable to the specified domestic transactions with related parties. So that between 2012-2016, assessee had to comply with the arms length pricing requirements under transfer pricing provisions as well as that of sec. 40A(2). This led to heavy compliance burden on domestic payers. Therefore, Finance Act, 2017 inserted a proviso that stipulates that no disallowances would be made under this section *i.e.* 40A(2) in respect of specified domestic transactions, if such transactions are at arm's length as defined under section 92F.

Payments exceeding ₹ 10,000 to be disallowed when made otherwise than by Account Payee Cheques or Account Payee Bank Drafts [Sec. 40A(3), (3A)]

Payments for Expenditure [Sec. 40A(3)] - Where the assessee incurs any expenditure which is as such allowed as a deduction but which is paid otherwise than an account payee cheque or an account payee demand draft or use of electronic clearing system through bank account or through such other electronic mode as may be prescribed or; such expenditure will be disallowed.

Expenditure covers any payment deductible in computing gross profit: The word "expenditure" is of wide import and includes expenses which are taken into account while determining the gross profit. It includes the price paid for stock-in-trade or raw material, etc. [*Fakri Automobiles* v. *CIT* (1986) 160 ITR 504/24 Taxman 578 (Raj.)]. The expenditure under Sec. 40A(3) is not confined to expenditure deductible under Sec. 37. It refers to any payment made by the assessee and taken into account in computing the total income under the provisions of the Act [*CIT* v. *Avtar Singh & Sons* (1981) 129 ITR 67 (P&H)/[1981] 5 Taxman 61 (P&H)].

Payment of any liability [Sec. 40A(3A)] - Sec. 40A(3) disallowed only cash payments made in respect of an 'expenditure' and not a ' liability'. Therefore to plug this loophole sec. 40A(3A) was inserted. Accordingly where an allowance has been made in the assessment for any year in respect of any liability incurred by the assessee for any expenditure and subsequently the assessee makes payment thereof, otherwise than by an account payee cheque, the payment so made is deemed to be business, profit, chargeable to tax if the payment or aggregate payment exceeds ₹ 10,000.

Limit applies to individual payment: The word 'sum' in the Act mentions a single sum. If the single sum is below ₹ 10,000, no question about contravention of Sec. 40A(3) arises, irrespective of the style adopted by the assessee for making payment of the sum. Thus, the statutory limit of ₹ 10,000 applies to payment made to a party at a time and not to the aggregate of the payments made to a party in the course of the day as recorded in the cash book [*CIT* v. *Aloo Supply Co.* (1980) 121 ITR 680 (Ori.)]

No disallowance where income is computed on presumptive basis: The disallowance can be made in respect of deductions allowed to the assessee in computing his total income. Thus, where the books of account of the assessee were rejected and the profits were computed by applying a flat rate on gross sales, no addition can be further made to such profits by applying Sec. 40A(3) [*CIT* v. *Banwari Lal Banshidhar* (1998) 229 ITR 229 (All.)].

Exception (Rule 6DD): The disallowance in respect of any payment exceeding ₹ 10,000 made otherwise than account payee cheque or account payee bank draft, does not apply in the following cases where it is made to—

(*a*) *Specified Institutions:* No disallowance operates where the payment is made to the following specified institutions:

(*i*) The Reserve Bank of India or any banking company as defined under Sec. 5(*c*) of the Banking Regulation Act, 1949;

(*ii*) The State Bank of India or any subsidiary bank as defined under Sec. 2 of the State Bank of India (Subsidiary Banks) Act, 1959;

(*iii*) Any cooperative or land mortgage bank;

(*iv*) Any primary agricultural credit society or any primary credit society as defined under Sec. 56 of the Banking Rgulation Act, 1949;

(*v*) The Life Insurance Corporation of India;

(*b*) *Payment in Legal Tender to Government:* Where any payment is required to be made in legal tender to the government, no disallowance operates.

(*c*) *Payment by specified modes:* No disallowance operates where the payment is made by the following specified modes:

(*i*) any letter of credit arrangements through a bank;

(*ii*) a mail or telegraphic transfer through a bank;

(*iii*) a book adjustment from any account in a bank to any other account in that or any other bank;

(*iv*) a bill of exchange made payable on a bank;

(*v*) the use of electronic clearing system through a bank account;

(*vi*) credit card;

(*vii*) a debit card.

(*d*) *Payment by adjustment of a liability for goods supplied or services rendered:* Where the payment is made by way of adjustment against the amount of any liability incurred by the payee for any goods supplied or services rendered by the assessee to such payee, no disallowance operates.

(*e*) *Payment to a cultivator/grower/producer for specified purchases:* No disallowance operates where payment is made to cultivator, grower or producer for the following purchases:

(*i*) agriculture or forest produce; or

(*ii*) the produce of animal husbandry (including hides and skins) or dairy or poultry farming; or,

(*iii*) fish or fish products; or,

(*iv*) the products or horticulture or apiculture (bee-keeping for sale of honey);

Produce of animal husbandry would include livestock, meat, hides and skin. Benefit of Rule 6DD(*f*)(*ii*) is available if the purchase livestock, meat, hides and skin is made from a person who is the producer of these goods. If the purchase of these goods are made from a trader, broker or any other middleman, the benefit of exception is not available.

Any person who buys animals from farmers, slaughters them and then sells raw meat, carcasses to the meat processing factories or the traders/retail outlets may be considered as producer of livestock and meat. Subject to certain conditions.

(*f*) *Payment for the products, manufactured in a cottage industry without the aid of power:* No disallowance operates where the payment is made to a producer for the purchase of the products manufactured or processed without the aid of power in a cottage industry.

(*g*) *Payment at a place, not served by bank:* No disallowance operates where any payment is made in a village or town, to any person who ordinarily resides or is carrying on any business, profession or vocation, in any such village or town which, on the date of such payment, is not served by bank.

(*h*) *Terminal payments to low paid employees:* No disallowance operates where any payment by way of gratuity, retrenchment compensation or similar terminal benefit, is made to an employee of the assessee or the heirs of any such assessee on or in connection with the retrenchment, resignation, discharge or death of such employee, if the income chargeable under the head "salaries" of the employee in respect of the financial year in which such retirement, resignation, discharge or death took place or in the immediately preceding financial year did not exceed ₹ 50,000.

(*i*) *Salary payment after TDS at a place other than normal place of duty or on ship and the employee having no bank account at such place or ship:* Where salary is paid after deducting tax by an employer to an employee, no disallowance operates, provided the following conditions are satisfied:

(*i*) such employee is temporarily posted for a continuous period of 15 days or more in a place other than his normal place of duty or on a ship; and

(*ii*) he does not, maintain any account in any bank at such place or ship (w.e.f. 1-12-1995).

(*j*) *Payment on a bank holiday or strike:* No disallowance operates where the payment was made on a day on which the banks were closed either on account of holiday or strike.

(*k*) *Payment to agent:* No disallowance operates where the payment is made by any person to his agent who is required to make payment in cash for goods or service on behalf of such person.

(*l*) *Payment made by authorised dealer:* Authorised dealers and money changers are required normally to pay cash against purchase of foreign currency or travellers' cheques in the normal course of their business. Hence, no disallowance operates for any cash payments made by them.

"Authorised dealer" or "money changer" means a person authorised as authorised dealer or money changer to deal in foreign currency or foreign exchange "under any law for the time being" in force.

Exception in the case of goods carriage

Where any payment is made for playing, hiring or leasing goods carriages, the ceiling of ₹ 20,000 has been raised to ₹ 35000. It is operative w.e.f. 1st September, 2009. [Sec. 40A(3A) first proviso].

Provisions for Gratuity [Sec. 40A(7)]

No deduction is admissible in respect of any provision made by an assessee for the payment of gratuity to his employees on their retirement or on termination of their employment for any reason.

Exceptions: The restriction does not apply in the following cases:

(*i*) any provision made for the purpose of payment of a sum by way of contribution towards an approved gratuity fund; or

(*ii*) any provision for the purpose of any payment of gratuity that has become payable during the previous year. It may be noted that where such provision for the payment of gratuity has been allowed as deduction in computing the profits of business or profession, no deduction again is allowed when gratuity is actually paid out of such provision.

Contribution to Employees' Welfare Fund [Sec. 40A(9)]

Revenue expenditure actually incurred for the welfare of the employees is deductible in computing taxable profits. But no deduction is allowed in respect of contributions paid to any fund, trust, company, association of persons, body of individuals, societies registered under the Societies Registration Act, or any other institution for any purpose [Sec. 40A(9)]. The restriction does not apply to any contribution paid to a recognised provident fund, employer contribution towards a pension scheme (w.e.f. 1-4-2012) or approved gratuity fund to the extent such contribution is permissible under income-tax law [under Sec. 36(1) (*iv*)/(*v*)] or under any other law for the time being in force.

Certain Deductions to be allowed only on Actual Payment [Sec. 43B]

Profits and gains of business–profession have to be computed in accordance with the system of accounting. However, certain deductions have to be allowed only on actual payment even though the assessee is following mercantile system of accounting.

Such deductions are explained as follows:

(*i*) *Any tax or duty:* Any sum payable by way of tax, duty, or fee, by whatever name called, under any law for the time being in force, is deducted on payment basis.

The term "duty" should be distinguished from "interest". Thus, interest payable for warehousing beyond the statutory period is not a duty. Provisions of Sec. 43B do not apply to it [*Hindustan Motors Ltd.* v. *CIT* [1996] 218 ITR 450 (Cal.)]. Similarly, where interest is payable on outstanding municipal taxes, deduction cannot be denied for such interest on the ground that interest is a part of municipal tax itself and liable to be disallowed under Sec. 43B as municipal tax remain outstanding. The interest payable for arrears of municipal taxes is compensatory in nature. It is not a tax or penalty [*CIT* v. *Orient Beverages Ltd*. [2001] 117 Taxman 106/247 ITR 230 (Cal.)].

The "fees" cannot be equated with levy of audit charges, payable for getting the audit of the accounts done. Thus, deduction cannot be refused for outstanding audit fees payable [*CIT* v. *Shree Warna Sahakari Sakhar Karkhana Ltd*. [2001] 119 Taxman 422/[2002] 253 ITR 226 (Bom.)].

(*ii*) *Contribution to provident fund:* Any sum payable by employer by way of contribution to any provident fund or superannuation fund or gratuity fund or any other fund for the welfare of employees is allowed on payment basis.

(*iii*) *Bonus or commission:* Any sum payable as bonus or commission to an employee [under Sec. 36(1)(*ii*)] is allowed on payment basis.

(*iv*) *Interest on borrowings from certain institutions:* Any interest payable on any loan or borrowing from any public financial institution or a state financial corporation or a state industrial investment corporation is deducted on actual payment.

If interest on any loan or borrowing or advance is converted into a loan or borrowing or advance, the interest so converted is not deemed as actual payment. No deduction is allowed in respect or such interest [*Explanation 3C* to Sec. 43B w.e.f. 1-4-1989].

(*v*) *Interest on borrowings from non-banking financial company:* Any interest on any loan or borrowing from a such class of non-banking financial companies as may be notified by the Central Government or systemically important non-deposit taking non-banking financial company, is deducted on actual payment.

(*vi*) *Interest on loan or advances from a scheduled bank:* Any sum payable as interest on loan or advances from a scheduled bank is deducted on payment basis. Advances would cover cash credit and overdraft facility.

If interest on any loan or borrowing or advance is converted into a loan, or borrowing or advance, the interest so converted is not deemed as actual payment. No deduction is allowed in respect or such interest [*Explanation 3D* to Sec. 43B w.e.f. 1-4-1997].

(*vii*) *Encashment of earned leave:* Any sum payable by an employer in lieu of any leave at the credit of his employee is deducted on actual payment.

Where any deduction has been allowed in respect of any provision of earned leave, standing to the credit of an employee, no deduction is allowed again in the previous year in which such sum is actually paid [*Explanation 3B* to Sec. 43B]. In *Bharat Earth Movers* v. *CIT* [2000] 112 Taxman 61/245 ITR 428 (SC), the Supreme Court allowed the deduction in respect of provisions for encashment of earned on accrual basis. The decision has been superseded from the assessment year 2002–2003. Now the deduction is not allowed on accrual basis but on payment basis.

Year of the allowance - In the aforesaid cases, deduction is allowed in the previous year in which such sum is actually paid. However, if any such sum is not paid during the previous year in which the liability to pay has accrued but it is paid in subsequent year on or before the due date for furnishing return of income relevant to that previous year, deduction for such sum is allowed in the same previous year in which the liability to pay has accrued.

For claiming the deduction, the assessee should furnish the evidence of such payment along with return of income.

DEEMED BUSINESS PROFITS

Although profits chargeable under this head of income are the ones enlisted under sec. 28 and the ones which fall within the natural meaning of profits, certain receipts are considered as deemed profits. The deemed receipts are those that were allowed as deductions and are now treated as profits of business even though the business or profession may not be in existence in the year of recovery/receipts. Such deemed profits are described as below.

Recovery against Deduction [Sec. 41(1)]

Where any deduction has been allowed in the assessment for any year in respect of loss, expenditure or trading liability incurred by the assessee and subsequently during any previous year the assessee has obtained any amount in respect of such loss, or expenditure or some benefit in respect of such trading liability by way of remission or cessation thereof, the amount obtained by him or benefit accruing to him is deemed to be profits and gains of business or profession. It is chargeable to income tax as the income of that previous year in which such amount/remission, is obtained.

Conditions for chargeability: Section 41(1) applies if two conditions are satisfied:

(*i*) the assessee was allowed a deduction in an earlier year; and

(*ii*) there is a recovery against such deduction in a subsequent year or the assessee gets some benefit by way of cessation or remission of liability.

Deduction allowed to predecessor, successor taxable for its refund, if any - Where an assessee who has been allowed any deduction on account of any expenditure or loss or trading liability, is succeeded in his business, the successor is chargeable to tax on any amount received or benefit accruing to him in relation to which deduction or allowance has been made to the predecessor. The identity of the person who got the deduction and who got the benefit in subsequent years need not be the same. Thus, where an amalgamated company recovers any amount in respect of which a deduction has been allowed to the amalgamating company, the amalgamated company is assessable on such recovery. Similarly, if a reconstituted firm gets any benefit in respect of which a deduction has been allowed to the predecessor firm, the successor firm is assessable on the value of such benefit.

Likewise, where there has been a demerger and a deduction has been allowed to the demerged company, any recovery against such deduction is taxable in the hands of the resulting company.

Trading liability written-off unilaterally liable to be taxed: Where an assessee or successor writes off any trading liability by a unilateral act in his accounts, unilateral writing-off of a liability also amount to remission or cessation of the liability. The amount of liability so written-off is deemed to be business profits of the year in which the liability has been written-off. Thus, where a time-barred debt is written off by a debtor unilaterally in his accounts, it is deemed to be business profits [*Explanation 1* to Sec. 41(1)].

Balancing Charge [Sec. 41(2)]

When any depreciation had been allowed on plant, machinery, building etc. and subsequently such plant and machinery was sold, discarded or destroyed, the assessee might get some value either as a result of sale or insurance or from salvage or compensation thereabout. Such receipts were not being left out of taxation. Sec. 41(2) plugs this leakage by deeming such incomes as profit. Accordingly, where any building, machinery plant or furniture owned by the assessee and used for the purpose of business for which depreciation under Section 32(1)(*i*) is claimed, is sold, discarded, demolished or destroyed and the money payable together with scrap value in respect of such assets exceeds the written down value, the excess to the extent of difference between the actual cost and the written down value shall be taxable as business income in the previous year in which the moneys payable become due. Even if in the year the moneys payable becomes due, the business for which these assets were used is no longer in existence, the provisions of this section shall apply as if the business is in existence in that previous year.

Sale of an Asset used for Scientific Research [Sec. 41(3)]

Where an asset representing capital expenditure on scientific research [under Sec. 35(1)(*iv*)/(2)], is sold without having been used for any other purpose and the sale price together with the amount of deductions allowed exceeds the amount of the capital expenditure, such excess or the amount of deductions allowed whichever is less, is chargeable to tax as business income of the previous year in which the sale took place. It is immaterial whether the business is in existence in such year or not.

Where an asset used for scientific research is sold after introducing it in business, Sec. 41(3) does not apply. Thus, tax incidence under two alternatives must be analysed before the option is exercised. An option which minimises the tax incidence should be preferred.

Section 41(3) has not been extended to Sec. 35(2AB). Thus, where a capital asset is used for scientific research as per provisions of Sec. 35(2AB), and such asset is sold without being introduced in business, the deeming provision of Sec. 41(3) is not applicable.

Recovery against Bad Debt [Sec. 41(4)]

Where the deduction had been allowed in respect of a debt or part thereof and subsequently any amount is recovered in respect of such debt and the amount of recovery together with the amount of bad debt allowed as deduction, exceeds the amount of such debt, such excess is chargeable to tax as business income of the previous year in which such recovery is made.

Withdrawal from Special Reserve [Sec. 41(4A)]

Where financial corporation has been allowed deduction under sec. 36(1)(*viii*) for creating and maintaining special reserve, any withdrawal from such reserve is taxable as business income of that year.

Set off of Losses of a Defunct Business against Deemed Profit [Sec. 41(5)]

Where the business or profession referred to in this section is no longer in existence, any loss arising to such business or profession, during the previous year in which it ceased to exist and which could not be set off against any other income of that previous year can be set off against deemed profits being recoupment of loss, balancing charge, recovery of bad debt, withdrawal from special reserve discussed above. Such loss however should not be a loss in speculation business.

SPECIAL PROVISIONS WITH RESPECT TO CERTAIN BUSINESSES

Special Provisions for Deduction for Prospecting/Extracting or Production of Mineral Oils [Sec. 42]

This Section grants certain special deductions which are otherwise inadmissible on the ground of capital expenditure, initial expenditure, or amortisation of a wasting asset under this Act, to an assessee who carries on the business of prospecting, extraction or production of mineral oils, petroleum or natural gas in association with the Central Government or with any person authorised by it. The deductions allowable under this agreement may be in lieu of or addition to the allowances admissible under this Act.

Following provisions have been enacted in this respect [Sec. 42(1)]:

Allowances, specified in the agreement, may be computed and allowed in the manner specified in the agreement. Such allowances may be in relation to the following:

(*a*) Expenditure incurred on survey, prospecting and exploration of mineral oil in any area which has turned out to be infructuous or abortive is deductible if such area is surrendered prior to the beginning of commercial production.

(*b*) Expenditure incurred, whether before or after the beginning of commercial production, by the assessee in respect of drilling or exploration activities or services or in respect of physical assets used in that connection and whereon no depreciation is allowable, is to be deducted in the computation of business income after the beginning of the commercial production by the assessee. If the agreement has been entered into after 31 March 1981, expenditure in respect of physical assets has to be deducted irrespective of the fact whether claim for depreciation in respect of such assets is admissible or not.

(*c*) Any allowance for the depletion of mineral oil in the mining area in respect of the assessment year relevant to the previous year in which commercial production is begun and for such succeeding year or years as may be specified in the agreement.

Such allowances are allowed if the agreement so provides and are to be computed and made in the manner specified in the agreement.

Allowing Deficiency or Taxing Surplus in Cases where such Business is Transferred in Accordance with such Agreement [Sec. 42(2)] - Where the business is of propecting/extraction/production of petroleum and natural gas and such business is transferred, wholly or partly or any interest in such business is transferred in accordance with the agreement with the Central Government, following provisions have been introduced to allow deficiency or to re-tax excess deduction from the assessment year 1999-2000 and onward:

(*a*) *Deficiency to be allowed as deduction:* Where unallowed expenditure exceeds the sale proceeds of the transfer such deficiency is allowed as deduction in the previous year in which such business/interest is transferred.

(*b*) *Excess amount of deduction to be taxed as business income:* Where the sale proceeds of transfer exceed the unallowed expenditure, such excess to the extent of deduction allowed is to be treated as business income of the previous year in which such business/interest is transferred.

Where the business or interest in such business is transferred in a previous year in which such business is no longer in existence, the provisions of this section will apply as if the business is in existence in that previous year.

(*c*) *Denial of deduction:* Where sale proceeds of the transfer of a capital asset are not less than the amount of unallowed expenditure, no deduction is allowed in respect of such expenditure in the previous year in which the business or interest in such business is transferred or in a subsequent year.

Transfer of Business in a Scheme of Amalgamation [Proviso to Sec. 42(2)]- Where such business or interest in such business is transferred in a scheme of amalgamation or demerger and the amalgamated company or resulting company is an India company, the provisions of this Section do not apply to the amalgamating company or demerged company. The amalgamated company or the resulting company will continue to claim the deduction available to the amalgamating company as if no amalgamation or demerger had taken place.

Special Provision for full value of consideration for transfer of assets other than capital assets in certain cases [Sec. 43CA]

In order to check black money generation by resorting to under valuation of immovable property transaction, Sec. 50C was introduced which addressed transfer of a capital asset. Under Sec. 50C when a capital asset, being immovable property, is transferred for a consideration which is less than the stamp duty valuation of such property by authority of a State Government, then such value (stamp duty value) is taken as full value of consideration. However, these provisions did not apply to transfer of immovable property held by the transferor as stock-in-trade. Therefore to plug this loophole, Sec. 43CA was introduced by the Finance Act, 2013, w.e.f. 1-4-2014 to extend a similar provision to immovable property held as stock-in-trade.

Where the consideration received or accruing on account of transfer of an asset (other than a capital asset), being land or building or both, is less than the value adopted or assessed or assessable by any authority of State Government for the purpose of payment of stamp duty, it is such stamp duty valuation which is taken as full consideration. If the date for fixing the value of consideration for the transfer of asset and the date of registration of transfer of such asset are not the same the value of such asset for the purpose of payment of stamp duty is taken on the date of agreement.

The Finance Act, 2021 has inserted a new proviso to Sec. 43CA whereby in case of transfer of an asset which is a residential unit, the full value of consideration shall be taken as 120% of the stamp duty value as referred above, provided the following conditions are fulfilled:

(*a*) the transfer of such residential unit takes place during the period beginning from the 12th day of November, 2020 and ending on the 30th day of June, 2021;

(*b*) such transfer is by way of first time allotment of the residential unit to any person; and

(*c*) the consideration received or accruing as a result of such transfer does not exceed ₹ 2 crore.

An *Explanation* further clarifies that a "residential unit" means an independent housing unit with separate facilities for living, cooking and sanitary requirement, distinctly separated from other residential units within the building, which is directly accessible from an outer door or through an interior door in a shared hallway and not by walking through the living space of another household.

Special Provisions for certain businesses of non-residents Profits of a Non-resident from the Business of Exploration of Mineral Oils [Sec. 44BB]

Where a non-resident is engaged in the business of:

(*a*) providing services or facilities in the prospecting for or extraction or production of mineral oils; or

(*b*) supplying plant and machinery on hire, used or to be used for the said purposes, such an assessee is taxable on a presumptive basis.

Accordingly 10% of the aggregate of the following amounts is deemed to be the profits of such assessee:

(*i*) Amounts paid or payable (whether in or out of India) to the assessee or to any person on his behalf, for providing services or facilities in connection with prospecting for or extraction or production of mineral oils in India or for the supply of plant and machinery on hire used or to be used for the said purposes.

(*ii*) Amounts received or deemed to be received in India by or on behalf of the assessee for providing services or facilities in connection with prospecting for or extraction or production of mineral oils outside India or supply of plant and machinery on hire used or to be used for the said purposes outside India.

"Plant" includes ships, aircrafts, vehicles, drilling units, scientific apparatus and equipment for the purpose of the said business.

"Mineral oil" includes petroleum and natural gas.

Option of Rebuttal in respect of Deemed Income

From the assessment year 2004-2005 and onward, the assessee has the option to claim his income lower than the deemed income, provided he maintains books of account referred in sec. 44AA(2) and gets his accounts audited and furnishes a report of such audit as required under sec. 44AB. Thereafter, the Assessing Officer is required to make a scrutiny assessment and may determine the income or loss under sec. 143(3) and determine the sum payable by or refundable to the assessee.

Case Law : ***Oil & Natural Gas Corporation Ltd.* v. *CIT* [2015] 59 taxmann. com 1/233 Taxman 495 (SC)**

Facts: 'O' had entered into an agreement with a non-resident company by virtue of which the non-resident company had agreed to provide various services in connection with prospecting, extraction or production of mineral oil along with certain ancillary works contemplated there under.

Held: Payments received by non-resident under the said contracts is more appropriately assessable under the provisions of sec. 44BB and not sec. 44D. Sec. 44D contemplates an income of a foreign company with which the government or an Indian concern had an agreement executed before 1-4-1976 or on any date thereafter the computation of income extending to fees for technical service within the meaning of *Explanation 2* to sec. 9(1)(*vii*) which in turn excludes payments made in connection with a mining project.

(*i*) The amount paid or payable (whether in India or outside India) to the assessee or to any person on his behalf, on account of the carriage of passengers, livestock, mail or goods from any place in India.

(*ii*) The amount received or deemed to be received in India by the assessee or any person on his behalf, on account of the carriage of passengers, livestock, mail or goods from any place outside India.

Profits of a Foreign Company from Civil Construction Business in Turnkey Power Projects [Sec. 44BBB]

Where a foreign company is engaged in the business of (*i*) civil construction, or (*ii*) erection of plant, or (*iii*) testing or commissioning of such plant and machinery in connection with a turnkey power project, duly approved by the Central Government, it is assessed on a presumptive basis on the income from such project.

A sum equal to 10% of the amount paid or payable on account of such project is deemed its income. The amount may be paid in India or outside India. It may be paid to the assessee-company or to any other person on its behalf.

OPTION OF REBUTTAL IN RESPECT OF DEEMED INCOME

From the assessment year 2004–05 and onward, the assessee has the option to claim his income lower than the deemed income, provided he maintains books of account referred in sec. 44AA(2) and gets his accounts audited and furnishes a report of such audit as required under sec. 44AB. Thereafter, the Assessing Officer is required to make a scrutiny assessment and may determine the income or loss under sec. 143(3) and determine the sum payable by or refundable to the assessee.

Deduction of Head Office Expenses in the case of Non-residents [Sec. 44C]

It was often experienced that foreign companies operating through branches in India sometimes tried to reduce the incidence of tax in India by inflating their claims in respect of head office expenses CBDT Circular No.202 in July 1976. Therefore sec. 44C was introduced so as to put a curb on such practices by one, defining what constitutes head office expenses and two, specifying a limit to which such expenses could be claimed as deduction.

Accordingly, where a non-resident has a head office abroad and a branch in India, the following head office expenses being the executive and general administration expenditure incurred by the assessee outside India, including expenditure incurred in respect of:

(*i*) rent, rates, taxes, repairs or insurance of any premises outside India used for the purposes of the business or profession;

(*ii*) salary, wages, annuity, pension, fees, bonus, commission, gratuity, perquisites or profit in lieu of or in addition to salary, where paid or allowed to any employee or other person employed in, or managing the affairs of, any office outside India.

(*iii*) travelling by any employee or other person employed in, or managing the affairs of any office outside India; and

(*iv*) such other matters connected with executive and general administration as may be prescribed are deductible.

Where an Indian branch office remits technical fees to the head office of a non-resident outside India for rendering technical services, payment of such fees is fully deductible in computing the taxable income of the branch office in India. Such fees is taxable in the hands of the head office [Circular No. 649 dated 31-3-1993].

The deductions mentioned above are allowed upto the specified limits below:

(*a*) 5% of the adjusted total income; or

(*b*) Actual head office expenditure, attributable to the Indian business;

whichever is less, is the specified limit.

"Adjusted total income" means the total income computed in accordance with the provisions of this Act (that is, income computed under different heads aggregated together as per secs. 70 and 71) but before deducting the following:

(*i*) unabsorbed depreciation [under sec. 32(2)];

(*ii*) any capital expenditure incurred by a company for the purposes of promoting family planning amongst its employees [Sec. 36(1)(*ix*)];

(*iii*) carried forward losses [Sec. 72(1) or 73(2) or 74(1) or 74A(3)];

(*iv*) deductions in computing total income (Secs. 80C to 80U).

Where adjusted total income of the assessee is a loss, the amount under (*a*) is computed at 5% of the average adjusted total income of the assessee.

"Average adjusted total income" is taken on the basis of average for a period of three assessment years immediately preceding the relevant assessment year.

Special Provision for Computing Income by way of Royalties and so on, in case of Non-residents [Sec. 44DA]

Where a non-resident (not being a company) or a foreign company carries on business in India through a permanent establishment situated therein or performs professional services from a fixed place of profession situated therein, any income by way of royalty or fees for technical services received from Government or an Indian concern is computed under the head 'Profit and Gains of Business or Profession' in accordance with sec. 28 to sec. 43D, provided the following conditions are satisfied:

(*i*) Royalty or fees for technical services is received from government or an Indian concern in pursuance of an agreement entered into after 31 March 2003;

(*ii*) The right, property or contract in respect of which royalty or fees are paid, should be effectively connected with such permanent establishment or fixed place of profession.

(*iii*) Provisions of section 44BB do not apply in respect of such income.

Permanent Establishment

It includes a fixed place of business through which the business of the enterprise is wholly or partly carried on.

Disallowance of Certain Expenses

In computing taxable income from royalty or fees for technical services, no deduction is allowed in respect of:

(*i*) Expenditure or allowance which is not wholly and exclusively incurred for the business of such permanent establishment or fixed place of profession in India; or

(*ii*) Amounts, if any, paid by the permanent establishment to its head office or to any of its other offices.

However, actual reimbursement of expenses to the head office or other offices is allowed.

Maintenance of Books of Account

The assessee should keep and maintain books of account and other documents in accordance with provisions contained in sec. 44AA and get his accounts audited by a Chartered Accountant and furnish the report of such audit in prescribed form and verified by such accountant.

PRESUMPTIVE BASIS OF TAX

Income-tax Act has enacted certain provisions which supersede the normal produce of computation of profits under Secs. 28 to 44D. In certain cases, taxable, profits have to be computed on presumptive basis, that is, instead of computing the profits of such businesses by the regular method of allowable expenditures, disallowable expenditure, additions to profits etc., a certain percentage of profit is presumed to be earned and thereafter taxed at the specified rate. This is offered to small and medium scale assessees and spare them the elaborate process of book-keeping, computation of profits by simplifying the process for them which would in turn result into better compliance. Such cases are explained as below:

Computation of Profits and Gains of Business on Presumptive Basis [Sec. 44AD]

Income-tax law has specified a summary scheme of presumptive assessment in case of (*i*) an individual or (*ii*) Hindu undivided family, or (*iii*) partnership firm (excluding limited liability partnership) engaged in any business, other than (*i*) the business of plying, hiring or leasing goods carriage and (*ii*) whose total turnover or gross receipts does not exceed ₹ 2 crore during the previous year.

Mode of presumptive computation [Sec. 44AD(1)]: Income-tax law determines the taxable income of such assessee as below:

(*i*) 8% of the total turnover or gross receipts of the assessee during the previous year on account of such business,

Or

(*ii*) A sum higher than the aforesaid sum, claimed to have been earned by the assessee.

Deeming Provisions [Sec. 44AD(2)/(3)]: Deductions allowable in computing business profits (under Secs. 30 to 38) are deemed to have been allowed and no further deduction is admissible.

However, where the assessee is a firm, deduction in respect of salary and interest to partners are admissible [under Sec. 40(*b*) r.w. Sec. 44AD(2)].

Written down value of any asset of an eligible business is deemed to have calculated and allowed [Sec. 44AD(3)].

No payment of advance tax [Sec. 44AD(4)]: Provisions of advance tax do not apply to the profits and gains, computed on presumptive basis.

Maintenance of accounts [Sec. 44AD(5)]: Where the assessee claims his profits are lower than the statutory presumption of 8% of total turnover, and his total income exceeds the exemption limit, he is required to maintain the books of account and other documents [under Sec. 44AA(2)], get them audited and furnish a report of such audit [under Sec. 44AB].

Non-applicability of deeming provisions [Sec. 44AE(6)]: Deeming provisions to compute total income @ 8% of total turnover do not apply in the following cases :

(*a*) **Assessee engaged in profession -** Where any person is engaged in specified profession of (*i*) Law, (*ii*) Medical, (*iii*) Engineering, (*iv*) Architecture, (*v*) Accountancy, (*vi*) Technical consultancy, (*vii*) Interior decoration and (*viii*) Any other profession, notified by the Board; profits cannot be computed on presumptive basis.

(*b*) **Business of commission or brokerage -** Where an assessee is engaged in the business of commission or brokerage, profits cannot be computed on presumptive basis.

(*c*) **Agency business -** Where an assessee is engaged in any agency business taxable profits cannot be computed on presumptive basis.

Computation of Profits and Gains of Profession on Presumptive Basis [Sec. 44ADA]

Since the existing scheme of taxation provided for a simplified presumptive taxation scheme only for businesses and not for professional incomes, it was a felt need to rationalise the presumptive taxation scheme and to reduce the compliance burden of the small tax payers having income from profession as well and thereby facilitate the ease of doing business. The Finance Act, 2016 extended a presumptive basis of taxation to professional as well and introduced sec. 44ADA w.e.f. 1-4-2017.

An assessee being a resident (*i*) an individual (*ii*) Hindu undivided family or (*iii*) partnership firm (excluding Limited Liability partnership firm) who is engaged in a profession referred to sec. 44AA, such as legal, medical, engineering or architectural profession or the profession of accountancy or technical consultancy or interior decoration or any other profession as is notified by the Board in the Official Gazette and whose total gross receipts does not exceed ₹ 50 lakh in a previous year, can avail presumptive basis of tax under this section where the assessee's receipts in cash does not exceed five per cent of total gross receipt, the unit is ₹ 75 lakhs instead of ₹ 50 lakhs.

The Finance Act, 2021 restricts the scope of application of presumptive taxation under this section by excluding HUFs. Thus from the Assessment Year 2021-22, HUF cannot avail the benefit of presumptive taxation under this section.

Mode of presumptive computation [Sec. 44ADA(1)]: Income-tax law determines the taxable income of such assessee as below:

(*i*) a sum equal to 50% of the total gross receipts of the assessee in the previous year on account of such profession or, as the case may be,

(*ii*) a sum higher than the aforesaid sum claimed to have been earned by the assessee.

Deeming Provisions [Sec. 44AAD(2)/(3)]: Deductions allowable in computing business profits (under sections 30 to 38) are deemed to have been allowed and no further deduction is admissible.

Written down value of any asset of an eligible business is deemed to have calculated and allowed.

Maintenance of accounts [Sec. 44AAD(4)]: Where the assessee claims his profits are lower than the statutory presumption of total turnover, and his total income exceeds the exemption limit, he is required to maintain the books of account and other documents [under Sec. 44AA(1)], get them audited and furnish a report of such audit [under Sec. 44AB].

Computation of Profits and Gains of Business of Plying, Hiring or Leasing Goods Carriages [Sec. 44AE]

Where an assessee is engaged in the business of plying, hiring or leasing goods carriages and does not own more than 10 goods carriages at any time during the previous year, the income from such business in the aggregate of the profits and gains from all goods carriages owned by him during the previous year.

Goods carriage defined [Sec. 2(14) of the Motor Vehicles Act, 1988]: The "goods carriage" means any motor vehicle constructed or adopted for use solely for the carriage of goods or any motor vehicle not so constructed or adopted when used for the carriage of goods [Sec. 2(14) of the Motor Vehicles Act, 1988]. "Goods" includes livestock and anything (excluding equipment ordinarily used with the vehicle) carried by a vehicle except living persons but does not include luggage or personal effects carried in a motor car or in a trailer attached to a motor car or the personal luggage of the passengers travelling in the vehicle [Sec. 2(13) of the Motor Vehicles Act, 1988].

Computation of income [Sec. 44AE(2)]: Profits and gains from each goods carriage is computed as below:

(*i*) ₹ 7,500 for every month or part thereof during which the goods carriage is owned by the assessee in the previous year;

or

(*ii*) An amount actually earned from the vehicle;

whichever is higher, it is taxable.

It is operative from the assessment year 2015-16 and subsequent years.

The assessee has the option to declare a higher income in his return from such business. Where he declares his income more than ₹ 7500 per month or part thereof during which the goods carriage is owned by the assessee, such higher amount is deemed to be his income from such business.

The assessee has also the option to declare his income at an amount, lesser than the presumptive amount. In such a case, the assessee should maintain the accounts and get them audited. The Assessing Officer may compute the total income of the assessee by way of scrutiny assessment [Sec. 40AE(7)].

The assessee cannot claim any deduction under Secs. 30 to 38 from the aforesaid deemed profits. All deductions including depreciation is deemed to have already been allowed [Sec. 44AE(3)] and written down value of the assets used for goods carriage is deemed to have been calculated for each relevant assessment year [Sec. 44AE(3)/(4)].

Where any salary, bonus, commission and interest, etc., is paid by a firm to its partners, the firm is entitled to claim the deduction in respect of such remuneration and interest in accordance with the provisions of Sec. 40(*b*) from the estimated profits computed under Sec. 44AE. The Finance Act, 1997 has made it operative retrospectively from the assessment year 1994–1995 and subsequent years.

The provisions of (*i*) aggregation (under Secs. 70-71) and (*ii*) deductions in computing total income (Secs. 80C to 80U), also equally apply to such income.

Maintenance of accounts [Sec. 44AE(5)]: The assessee is neither required to maintain books of account (under Sec. 44AA) nor required to get his accounts audited (under Sec. 44AB) in respect of such business. However, requirements of compulsory maintenance of accounts and compulsory audit of accounts in respect of any other business, not covered under the scheme, equally apply. For calculating the ceiling for the purpose of compulsory maintenance of accounts or compulsory audit of accounts in respect of the business of goods carriage, covered under the scheme, are excluded.

Where the assessee claims that his profits from the business of goods carriage are less than the presumptive rate of ₹ 7,500 p.m., per truck, he is compulsorily required to maintenance the accounts and get them audited [under Sec. 44AA].

COMPULSORY MAINTENANCE OF ACCOUNTS BY CERTAIN PERSONS CARRYING ON PROFESSION OR BUSINESS [SEC. 44AA]

(*a*) *Maintenance of books of account in respect of specified profession [Sec. 44AA(1) r.w. Rule 6F(1)]:* Every person carrying on legal, medical, engineering or architectural profession or the profession of accountancy or technical consultancy or interior decoration or any other profession as is notified by the Board in the Official Gazette shall keep and maintain such books of account and other documents so that Assessing Officer is enabled to compute his total income.

(*b*) *Maintenance of books of account in respect of a business or profession, not specified as above [Sec. 44AA(2)]:* If income of any person from business or profession (excluding such profession as aforesaid) carried on by him exceeds ₹ 1,20,000 or his total sales, turnover or gross receipts, as the case may be, in business or profession exceeds ₹ 10,00,000 in any one of the three years immediately preceding the previous year, he is required to maintain such books of account and other documents as may enable the Assessing Officer to compute his total income in accordance with the provisions of this Act.

For new entrants, that is when such business or profession is newly set up, the aforesaid provisions are applicable if their income or turnover, etc., is likely to exceed ₹ 10,00,000 or gross receipts in profession exceeds ₹ 10,000 during the previous year in which such business or profession is newly set up.

Where such professional is an individual or HUF, maintenance of such accounts is required if the income or turnover, etc., is likely to exceed ₹ 25,00,000 or gross receipts in profession exceeds ₹ 2,50,000.

(*c*) *Maintenance of books of account in a case where presumptive computation applies:* Where in the business of civil construction [under Sec. 44AD(1) or business of goods carriage under Sec. 44AE(2) or business of retail trade under Sec. 44AF(1)], an assessee is taxable on the presumptive profits but he claims the profits from the said business to be lower than the presumptive profits, he is compulsorily required to maintain the accounts and get them audited. Thus, where in the business of civil construction an assessee claims the profits to be lower than 8% of the receipts, or where in the business of goods carriage, an assessee claims the profits to be lower than ₹ 7,500 per month or part thereof the maintenance and audit of accounts has been made compulsory.

COMPULSORY AUDIT OF ACCOUNTS OF CERTAIN PERSONS CARRYING ON BUSINESS OR PROFESSION [SEC. 44AB]

If the total sales/turnover/gross receipts in the business for the previous year or years exceeds ₹ 1 crore and in case of a profession if its gross receipts exceeds ₹ 50 lakhs, it is obligatory for a person carrying on such business or profession to get his accounts audited, before the specified date and furnish the report of such audit in the prescribed form by that date [Sec. 44AB].

The Finance Act, 2020 added a proviso whereby the limit of ₹ 1 crore has been extended to ₹ 5 crore (and after the Finance Act, 2021 - ₹10 crore) in the case of a person whose —

(*a*) aggregate of cash receipts including amount received for sales, turnover or gross receipts during the previous year does not exceed 5% of the said amount; and (*b*) aggregate of cahs payments made including amount incurred for expenditure during the previous year does not exceed 5% the said payment [First Proviso to Sec. 44AB].

The Finance Act, 2021 also inserts a new proviso that for computation of the threshold limit of ₹ 10 crores. Thus according to the Second Proviso to Sec. 44AB the payment or receipt settled through a non-account payee cheque or non-account payee bank draft shall be deemed to be cash payment or cash receipt respectively. Thus, the same shall be included while computing 5% cash transaction limit.

Business Covered under Presumptive Computation Scheme Liable for Compulsory Audit if Profits are Claimed to be Lower than the Statutory Minimum Fixed under the Scheme - Where an assessee engaged in the business of civil construction [Sec. 44AD], or business of plying leasing goods carriage [Sec. 44AE], or business of mineral oil [Sec. 44BB] or business of civil construction in turnkey power projects [Sec. 44BBB], and such assessee claims his profits to be lower than what is presumed under the scheme, he is required to get his accounts compulsorily audited.

Out of pocket expenses - Out of pocket expenses collected by a profession in advance are excluded where the same are credited in a separate client's account and utilised for making payments such as stamp duty, registration fee, travelling, etc., on behalf of the client. If, however, such out of pocket expenses are not specifically collected but are included/collected by way of consolidated fees, the whole amount so collected forms part of the gross receipts. No adjustment should be made in respect of actual expenses paid by the professional person on behalf of his client out of the gross fees so collected.

Carrying on a business as well as a profession - Where any person is engaged in a business as well as a profession, and neither gross receipts from business nor gross receipts from profession exceed the respective prescribed limit in this behalf, he is not required to get his accounts audited even if the aggregate limit of the two exceed ₹ 1 crore.

Time-limit of Audit - A person carrying on business or profession should get his accounts audited before the specified date if his turnover or gross receipts for the previous year or years exceeds or exceed ₹ 1 crore. Such persons are required to furnish a report of such audit by the chartered accountant in the prescribed form by the specified date. The specified date is the due date for furnishing the return of income under Sec. 139(1). [*Explanation* to Sec. 44AB].

Non-applicability of Compulsory Audit-

(*i*) *Certain business, carried on by a non-resident:* The provisions of compulsory audit do not apply to the person who derives income from the shipping business carried on by non-resident (under Sec. 44B), or operation of aircraft by non-resident (under Sec. 44BBA) [First proviso to Sec. 44AB].

(*ii*) *Accounts already audited under any other law:* Where the accounts of a person are required to be audited under any other law, it is sufficient if such person gets his accounts audited under such other law before the specified date and furnish a report of such audit by the chartered accountant in the prescribed form by the said date. Thus, a company assessee or cooperative society may not get its accounts audited again if the accounts have already been audited under the Companies Act or Societies Registration Act [Second Proviso to Sec. 44AB].

UNEXPLAINED RECEIPTS AND INVESTMENTS

There are certain receipts/expenditure/assets, which are deemed to be the income of the assessee in the specified circumstances. In order to curb the generation and proliferation of black money certain provisions have been enacted to treat unexplained (*i*) cash credit, (*ii*) investment, (*iii*) money bullion, and (*iv*) expenditure as the deemed income of the assessee. These provisions are explained as follows:

Cash Credits [Sec. 68]

Where any sum is found credited in the books of an assessee maintained for previous year, and the assessee offers no explanation about the nature and source thereof or the explanation offered by him is not satisfactory, in the opinion of the Assessing Officer, the sum so credited may be charged to income tax as the income of the assessee of that previous year. The opinion of the Assessing Officer for not accepting the explanation offered by the assessees as not satisfactory is required to be based on proper appreciation of material and other attending circumstances available on record [*CIT* v. *P. Mohanakala* [2007]161 Taxman 169/291 ITR 278 (SC)]. Thus, sec. 68 constitutes a charging provision which applies when the assessee's explanation regarding a cash credit is rejected as being unsatisfactory or when the assessee does not render any explanation.

Where any amount is found credited in the books of company by way of share application money, share capital, share premium etc., the explanation of the company cannot be deemed to be satisfactory unless the person, being a resident, offers a satisfactory explanation about the source of such some, found credited.

However, it does not apply if the person in whose name the credit entry stands, is a venture capital fund or venture capital company [under Sec. 10(*23B*)].

Onus on the assessee: The onus of proving the source of a sum of money found to have been received by the assessee is on him. If he disputes liability for tax, it is for him to show either that the receipt was not income or that if it was, it was exempt from taxation under the provisions of the Act. In the absence of such proof, the ITO is entitled to treat it as taxable income [*Kale Khan Mohammad Hanif* v. *CIT* [1963] 50 ITR 1 (SC)]. While the assessee is not expected to explain the "source of the source" but it has to satisfy the other sine qua non, viz., identity and capacity of the creditor to advance money and the genuineness of the transaction [*CIT* v. *Y.M. Singla* [2014] 50 taxmann.com 410/[2015] 228 Taxman 90/[2014] 366 ITR 242 (Punj. & Har.)].

In case credits received by the assessee in the form of loan or borrowing, the judicial decisions have held that only identity and creditworthiness of creditor and genuineness of transactions for explaining the credit in the books of account is sufficient, and the onus does not extend to explaining the source of funds in the hands of the creditor. Therefore, the Finance Act, 2022 inserts a new proviso imposing onus of proof of satisfactorily explaining the source in the hands of the creditor. This new proviso will be effective from the Assessment Year 2023-24. Accordingly, where the sum so credited consists of loan or borrowing or any such amount, by whatever name called, any explanation offered by such assessee shall be deemed to be not satisfactory, unless,—

(*a*) the person in whose name such credit is recorded in the books of such assessee also offers an explanation about the nature and source of such sum so credited; and

(*b*) such explanation in the opinion of the Assessing Officer aforesaid has been found to be satisfactory.

However, it does not apply if the person in whose name the credit entry stands, is a venture capital fund or venture capital company.

Cash credit be found appearing in the books of assessee - For chargeability, cash credit should be found appearing in the books of the assessee himself and not of any other person. The books of account of the firm in which the assessee is a partner, cannot be treated as the books of the assessee for the purposes of this Section. [*Sunder Lal Jain* v. *CIT* [1979] 117 ITR 316 (All.), *Anand Ram* v. *CIT* [1997] 233 ITR 544]. A bank pass book is not a book maintained by the assessee for treating unexplained cash credit as his income [*CIT* v. *Bhaichand N. Gandhi* [1982] 11 Taxman 59/[1983] 141 ITR 67 (Bom.)].

No Deduction of any Head is Available from Cash Credit - Where the assessee fails to explain the source of cash credit satisfactorily, it is deemed to be his income and no source of income, not even other sources, can be assigned to it. Thus, the deductions which are available under any head of the income, are not applicable [*Fakir Mohmed Hazi Hasan* v. *CIT* (2001) 247 ITR 290/(2002) 120 Taxman 11 (Guj.)].

Income-addition on Account of Cash Credit, No Ground for Automatic Imposition of Penalty - Additions to income on the ground of unexplained cash credit do not automatically justify the impastation of a penalty [*National Textiles* v. *CIT* [2001] 114 Taxman 203/249 ITR 125 (Guj.)].

Cash Credit Appearing on the First Day of Previous Year - Cash credit appearing in books on the first day of the accounting year may also be treated income of the assessee in absence of any satisfactory explanation [*CIT* v. *Ashok Timber Industries* (1980)125 ITR 336 (Cal.)].

Case Law : ***E. Ummer Bava* v. *CIT* [2016] 72 taxmann.com 123 (Ker.)**

Facts: 'U' claimed to have received a gift of ₹ 35 lakhs from his brother, a NRI.

Held: since assessee failed to establish creditworthiness of donor and genuineness of transaction, the amount was chargeable to tax under sec. 68.

Unexplained Investments [Sec. 69]

Where an assessee had made investments but failed to record them in books of account, if any, maintained by him for any source of income, the value of such investments is deemed to be his income, provided (*i*) the assessee offers no explanation about the nature and source of investments or (*ii*) the explanation offered by him is not found satisfactory by the Assessing Officer.

Financial year in which the investment is made may be taken as the previous year for this purpose [*Ram Swarup Cold storage and Allied Industries* v. *Asstt. CIT* (1991) 59 Taxman 245/192 ITR 537 (All.)].

Where the assessee gives a credible explanation that is found to be satisfactory, no addition can be made to his income [*CIT* v. *Nitin Kumar* (2001) 118 Taxman 651/248 ITR 478 (Punjab & Haryana)].

Explanation Should Not be Called for Belatedly - The length of time after which an assessee is called upon to explain a transaction is relevant factor while considering the sufficiency of the evidence. After the lapse of a decade, an assessee should not be placed upon the rack and called upon to explain not merely the origin and source of capital contribution but also the origin and source of that source as well [*S. Hastimal* v. *CIT* (1963) 49 ITR 273 (Mad.); *Upasana Hospital and Nursing Home* v. *CIT* [1998] 229 ITR 220 (Ker.)].

Case Law : ***CIT* v. *G. Anandarajan* (1997) 228 ITR 664 (Ker.)**

Facts: 'A' a wholesale dealer in liquor owned two shops with opening balance approx. ₹ 19,000 and sale during the first five days of the year at ₹ 2 lacs when no purchases were made for a year before that year. The ITO inferred that the amount would have to be understood as concealed income and sought explanation.

Held: If books of account reveal sales and in regard thereto there is no material of corresponding nature that assessee could purchase commodity for purpose of offering for sale, situation becomes an invitation for assessee to explain and as to how and from what source he had amount of commodity with regard to its purchase before it is offered for sale and in absence of such explanation, deeming provision of section 69 would come into effect.

Case Law : ***CIT* v. *R. Mallika* [2013] 36 taxmann.com 213 (Madras)/[2013] 219 Taxman 244 (Mad.) [SLP against this order dismissed by the Supreme Court in [2017] 79 taxmann.com 117/246 Taxman 59 (SC)]**

Facts: 'R' had made an investment in a property for a sum of ₹ 22 lakhs and explained that she had funded this investment by a combination of her salary income and cash in hand, loans borrowed from her son-in-law and sale of her jewellery through auction by one 'G'.

Held: There was no material evidence to support this explanation since 'R' did not produce anything apart from Form 16, with 'G' declining any such sale of or auction of jewellery through his concern and no evidence of loan by son-in-law. 'S' had not discharged burden as regards source from which investment had been made and this was investment in property was an unexplained investment and same was rightly added to income of 'R'.

Unexplained Money and other Assets [Sec. 69A]

Where an assessee is found to be the owner of any money bullion, jewellery or other valuable articles but fails to record them in books of account, if any, maintained by him for any source of income, the money and the value of the bullion, jewellery, or other valuable article may be deemed to be his income, provided (*i*) the assessee offers no explanation about the nature and source of their acquisition, (*ii*) the explanation offered by him is not found satisfactory by the Assessing Officer. The expression 'income' as used in section 69A has wide meaning and means anything which comes in or results in gain [*Chuharmal* v. *CIT* (1988) 38 Taxman 190/172 ITR 250 (SC)].

The financial year in which the assessee is found to be their owner is taken as the previous year for assessing such undisclosed income.

Possession of Assets is *Prima Facie* Proof of Ownership - The question whether the assessee is the owner of any money, bullion, jewellery or other valuable article, depends on the facts of each case. Section 110 of the Evidence Act presumes that possession is *prima facie* proof of ownership [*Kantilal Chandulal & Co.* v. *CIT* (1982) 10 Taxman 265/136 ITR 889 (Cal.)].

Date of Possession of Money and other Valuable Articles, Determines the Year of Assessment - The date on which the assessee is found to be the owner of money, bullion, jewellery or other valuable article in search proceedings, determines the year of assessment. The date on which the search finding is concluded or recorded is not relevant.

No deduction with respect to unexplained money - When source of investments, or source of acquisition of money, bullion etc. owned by the assessee are not explained, source of such income is not known. It would therefore not be possible to classify such deemed income under any of the heads mentioned in sec. 14 and consequently none of the deduction corresponding to such heads can be allowed to such unexplained incomes covered under Secs. 69, 69A, 69B and 69C [*Fakir Mohamed Hahi Hasan* v. *CIT* (2001) 247 ITR 290/(2002) 120 Taxman 11 (Guj.)].

Investments and other Valuable Articles not Fully Disclosed in Books of Account [Sec. 69B]

Where the assessee has made investments or is found to the owner of any bullion, jewellery or other valuable article, and the Assessing Officer finds that the amount expended on making such investments, or in acquiring such bullion, jewellery or other valuable article exceeds the amount recorded in the books of account, maintained by the assessee for any source income, such excess amount may be deemed to be the income of the assessee, provided (*i*) the assessee offers no explanation about such excess or (*ii*) the explanation offered by him is not found satisfactory by the Assessing Officer.

The financial year in which the assessee has made investment or is found to be the owner of any bullion jewellery or other valuable article is taken as the previous year for assessing the deemed income.

Accounts Must be Maintained: Where accounts are not maintained, additions made as unexplained investment would not be sustainable under Sec. 69B [*Dr. Prakash Tiwari* v. *CIT* (1983) 14 Taxman 252/(1984) 148 ITR 474 (MP)].

Burden of Proof is on the Revenue: The burden to prove that the real investments exceed the investment shown in the books of account of the assessee is on the department and no addition can be made under Sec. 69B merely on the basis of fair market value.

Case Law : ***CIT* v. *Mantri Share Brokers (P.) Ltd.* [2018] 96 taxmann.com 279 (Raj.) [SLP against the order of the High Court dismissed by the Supreme Court in [2018] 96 taxmann.com 280/257 Taxman 337 (SC)]**

Facts: Though assessee-company never admitted any concealment of income, during the course of survey proceedings in premises, the director of assessee-company admitted an additional income in various concerns in various years by the company. In order to purchase the peace and to honour, the commitment made by the director of the assessee-company, the balance amount had been accepted as the income by the assessee-company but no evidence towards the same was found.

Held: When except for the statement of director of assessee-company offering additional income during survey in his premises, there was no other material either in form of cash, bullion, jewellery or document or in any other form to conclude that statement made was supported by some documentary evidence, said sum could not be added in hands of assessee-company as undisclosed investments

Unexplained Expenditure [Sec. 69C]

Where in any financial year an assessee has incurred any expenditure and he offers no explanation about the source of such expenditure or part thereof or the explanation, if any, offered by him is not satisfactory in the opinion of the Assessing Officer, the amount covered by such expenditure or part thereof as the case may be, may be deemed to be the income of the assessee for such financial year.

Marriage expenses - A noted industrialist had shown an expenditure of ₹ 1.50 lakh on the marriage of his son and daughter in the year 1959–1960 but had not given complete details. Tribunal made an addition of ₹ 1 lakh. Considering the fact that the industrialist had spent ₹ 4 lakh in the year 1941-1945 on the marriage of another son and daughter, the addition was held sustainable [*L.M. Thapar* v. *CIT* (1984) 149 ITR 383 (Cal.)].

Case Law : ***Sunil Balasubramaniam Shankar* v. *ITO* [2019] 107 taxmann.com 55/265 Taxman 7 (Madras)**

Facts: 'S' claimed to have allowed his friend to use his credit cards as an extension of a huge loan to this friend, a fact denied by the friend of having used the credit cards before income tax authorities.

Held: The said amount is taxable in the hands of 'S' as unexplained income/ expenditure.

Amount Borrowed or Repaid on *Hundi* [Sec. 69D]

From the assessment year 1977-1978 and onward, any borrowing on a *hundi* or any repayment of *hundi* loan including interest thereon should be done through an account payee cheque drawn on a bank, failing which the amount borrowed or repaid is deemed to be the income of that person who is borrowing or repaying during that previous year.

The borrowing of *hundi* loan may be from any person and repayment of *hundi* loan may be to any person.

Demand Draft should be Treated a "Cheque"- The omission to refer to an account payee demand draft in Sec. 69D is probably inadvertent. An account payee demand draft should also be treated as an account payee cheque drawn on a bank for the purposes of Sec. 69D [*CIT* v. *Intraven Pharmaceuticals (P.) Ltd*. (1995) 80 Taxman 601 (AP)].

***Hundi* be Distinguished from Cheque -** A *hundi* should be distinguished from cheque. Section 69D applies to a *hundi* loan and not a loan by Cheque. The main characteristics of *hundi* transactions are:

(*i*) A *hundi* loan is normally in oriental language as per mercantile system.

(*ii*) There are three parties in a *hundi*. They are the drawer, the drawee and the payee. The drawer cannot himself be the drawee. If the transaction is bilateral, it is very strong indication to show that it is not a *hundi* transaction.

(*iii*) A *hundi* is payable to a person or order but negotiable without endorsement by the payee. The holder of *hundi* is entitled to sue on its basis without any endorsement in his favour.

(*iv*) In the case of a *hundi*, the owner can claim duplicate or triplicate from the drawer and present the same to the drawee for claiming payment.

Thus, where an assessee borrowed amounts totalling ₹ 2,10,000 from more than one party by account payee cheque but the repayments including interest were made in cash, the Income-tax officer cannot make an addition of ₹ 2,10,000 under Sec. 69D [*CIT* v. *Dexan Pharmaceuticals Pvt. Ltd*. (1995) 82 Taxman 620/214 ITR 576 (AP)].

Document in English not Excluded - Normally, *hundies* are written in the vernacular language, as the traders who used *hundies* in the past, by and large were illiterate in English. However, it does not lead to the conclusion that if a document which is otherwise a *hundi* is written in the English language, such a document cannot be regarded as a *hundi*. It is the content of the document that matters and not the language in which it is written [*CIT* v. *K P Abdullah* (2001) 117 Taxman 530 (Mad.)].

CHOICE OF METHOD OF ACCOUNTING

As discussed at the outset of this chapter, assessees can follow any method of book keeping of their choice, whether cash system or mercantile system. However, the Central Government is empowered to notify from time to time income computation and disclosure standards to be followed by any class of assessees or in respect of any class of income [Sec. 145(2)].

Where an assessee has adopted a regular method of accounting and the same has been accepted by the department, such acceptance does not imply acceptance of the profit figure disclosed by books of account. If the true and correct profits cannot be ascertained therefrom, the Assessing Officer is bound to apply special considerations, depending upon the facts of each case, in order to compute true and correct profits.

Thus, if a contractor maintains separate accounts for each contract, closes them on their completion, the profit of each year may not be deducible from such accounts, because a contract may take several years to be completed and payments thereunder may be received in several years. In such a case, the Assessing Officer may assess the profits of each year by employing a proper method of computing profits, arising under incomplete contracts [*Sukhdeodas Jalan* v. *CIT* (1954) 26 ITR 617 (Patna)].

An assessee may regularly follow a recognised method of accounting, *e.g.* LIFO or "base stock system". The Assessing Officer may reject it if the method does not show correct profits of the year [*Minister of National Revenue* v. *Anaconda American Brass Ltd.* (1956) 30 ITR 84 (PC)].

Rejection of Accounts [Sec. 145(3)]

The Assessing Officer is free to estimate the profits of an assessee according to the best of his judgment in the following cases.

Correctness or Completeness of the Accounts is in Doubt - Where the Assessing Officer is not satisfied about the correctness or completeness of the accounts of the assessee or where the method of accounting [under Sec. 145(1)] has not been regularly followed by the assessee or income has not been computed in accordance with the notified standards, the Assessing Officer may make an assessment to the best of his judgment [under Sec. 144].

The Assessing Officer cannot reject the accounts merely on the ground that they are not balanced. The fact that the yield disclosed by the books of account does not satisfactorily compare with the yield as estimated by the department for the preceding year, is no ground for rejecting the accounts of the assessee as yield may vary from year to year.

Where an assessee furnished no explanation at all as to way the profit at the normal rate was not earned and certain sales were kept out of books, it is open to the Assessing Officer to estimate the gross profit at a rate at which the profit is earned in similar business by rival merchants.

Where the accounts are rejected as incorrect or incomplete or unreliable, the Assessing Officer must give a definite finding to the effect. He may, then, compute profits by applying a flat rate of a percentage on receipts or sales as estimated by him. In adopting the flat rate of profit, the Assessing Officer may take into consideration the rate of profits shown by the assessee in the past years, the average profits made by other traders in the line and other relevant factors. The assessee is entitled to know the basis on which the Assessing Officer has computed the taxable profits and he has a right to rebut the basis as adopted by the Assessing Officer.

Method of Accounting or Accounting Standards, not Followed Regularly - Where an assessee does not follow regular method of accounting or accounting standard, notified by the Central Government, the Assessing Officer may reject the books of account and compute the income according to the best of his judgment [Sec. 145(3)].

CHAPTER 9 Capital Gains

INTRODUCTION

Under the head of capital gains, any profit or gain arising from *"transfer"* of a *"capital asset"* is taxable on accrual basis during the previous year in which such transfer takes place [sec. 45(1)]. Thus, capital gain arises when two conditions are satisfied:

(*i*) there is a capital asset; and

(*ii*) there is a transfer of the said capital asset.

However, each and every transfer of a 'capital asset' does not give rise to capital gain because

(*i*) some transactions either are not treated 'transfers' [under sec. 47] or

(*ii*) excluded from the purview of capital asset [under sec. 2(*14*)] or

(*iii*) enjoy exemption [under sec. 54 to sec. 54GB].

CAPITAL ASSET [SEC. 2(14)]

The first condition to attract capital gains tax is that there should be a capital asset. Sec. 2(*14*) defines the term capital asset. It contains a wide definition of the term capital asset and also specific exclusions from the definition.

Inclusions in Capital Asset

Accordingly, 'Capital asset' means —

(*a*) property of any kind, held by an assessee, whether or not connected with his business or profession;

(*b*) any securities held as a foreign institutional investor which has invested in such securities in accordance with the Regulations made under the Securities and Exchange Board of India Act, 1992.

Property of any kind :

"Property" is a term of the widest import and subject to any limitation or qualification which the context may require, it signifies every possible interest which a person can clearly hold and enjoy [*J.K. Trust* v. *CIT* (1957) 32 ITR 535 (SC)]. In common parlance, "property" has got four attributes, i.e. one can hold it, enjoy it, transfer it and it has got money value. Thus, anything which has got money value is property and so a capital asset. The words 'property of any kind' carries no words of limitation. It includes all kinds of property, movable, tangible or intangible, fixed circulating [Sec. 2(*14*)].

It must be noted that the legislation uses the words 'property of any kind held by an assessee' and not 'owned' by the assessee. The words "held by an assessee" include physical, actual, constructive and also symbolic possession of property of any kind [*CIT* v. *All India Tea & Trading Co. Ltd.* (1979) 117 ITR 525 (Cal.)]. The word "hold" means to possess: as owner, holder or tenant (of property, stock, land, etc.). Thus, a person can be said to be holding the property as an owner, as a lessee, as a mortgagee or on account of part performance of an agreement under Sec. 53A of the Transfer of Property Act. Therefore, in computing the period of holding of an asset, the period for which the asset was held as lessee, or mortgagee or tenant, etc., should also be taken into account [*CIT* v. *Ved Parkash and Sons (HUF)* (1994) 73 Taxman 70/207 ITR 148 (P&H)].

Controlling rights and management rights is a capital asset

The Supreme Court ruling in Vodafone *International Holding* v. *Union of India* had rejected a proposition that controlling interest are capital assets. The Court held that in a share transfer agreement when a party comes into the ownership of shares, it may, in certain situations, result in the assumption of an interest which has the character of a controlling interest in the management of the company whose shares were transferred. However, a controlling interest is an incident of ownership of shares in a company and controlling interest is, therefore, not an identifiable or distinct capital asset independent of the holding of shares.

It was in response to the aforesaid ruling that the Finance Act, 2012 inserted an explanation to the definition of the capital asset under sec. 2(14) with retrospective effect from 1.4.1962 that clarified that "property" includes and shall be deemed to have always included any rights in or in relation to an Indian company, including rights of management or control or any other rights whatsoever. By virtue of this explanation, controlling interest and management rights in themselves have been identified as distinct capital asset.

Case Law : ***CIT* v. *Parle Soft Drinks (Bangalore) (P.) Ltd.* [2018] 97 taxmann.com 136/258 Taxman 61 (SC) (Dismissing the Special Leave Petition against the High Court's Order)**

Facts: Parle group of companies received certain amount as compensation from Coco Cola company for the breach of an agreement whereby Parle company was to set up a bottling plant for Coca Cola but subsequent to a policy decision Coco Cola decided to set up its own plant. Parle claimed the compensation amount as exempt capital gain.

Held: The breach of obligation by Coco Cola deprived the assessee of the potential right to set up a bottling plant, a profit making apparatus, resulting in loss of source of income. The compensation received was capital receipt. However, since there was no transfer or extinguishment of any right, there was no question of capital gains.

Exclusions from Capital Asset :

Following will not be considered as capital asset:

(*i*) **Stock-in-trade, Consumable Stores or Raw Material held for the Purpose of Business or Profession -** Any stock-in-trade, consumable stores or raw material held for the purpose of business or profession have been excluded from the purview of capital asset. Any profit or loss on their sale fall under the head "profits and gains from business or profession". 'Stock-in-trade' does not include "Securities", defined under sec. 2(*h*) of the Securities Contracts (Regulation) Act, 1956.

(*ii*) **"Personal effects" -** Movable property held for personal use of the assessee or any member of his family, dependent on him, is not treated a capital asset. Wearing apparel, furniture, car/scooter, TV, refrigerator, musical instruments, gun, revolver, generator, paintings, etc., are examples of personal effects.

Intimate and Common Use by an Assessee is Essential: The expression "personal effects" means such items of movable property as are necessary adjuncts to an individual's own personality where an intimate connection exists between the effects and the person of the assessee. Such articles must be normally, commonly or ordinarily intended for personal or household use by the assessee and not merely capable of being put to personal or household use. [*H. H. Maharaja Rana Hemant Singh Ji* v. *CIT* (1976) 103 ITR 61 (SC)]. However, it is not necessary in order to qualify as personal effects the same should be used daily. So long as they were meant for personal use, they are considered as personal effects [*Jayantilal A. Shah* v. *K.N. Anantharama Aiyar, CIT* [1985] 23 Taxman 14/156 ITR 448 (Bom.)]. Merely because in view of nature of property it can be used only on ceremonial occasions, it does not follow that property is not held by assessee for personal use [*CIT* v. *H. H. Maharani Usha Devi (H.H.)* [1998] 98 Taxman 309/231 ITR 793 (SC)].

Treatment of Gold and Silver Utensils and Coins: Personal use means that the article should normally, commonly or ordinarily be intended for personal or household use and not merely capable of being intended for personal or household use [*H. H. Maharaj Rana Hemant Singhji* v. *CIT* [1976] 103 ITR 61 (SC)]. Therefore, whether silver utensils are personal effects or not is primarily a question of fact and the answer depends mainly on the nature of use of the articles sold. If an intimate connection between such utensils and their personal use by the assessee can be established on facts of a case, they qualify as personal effects. [*CIT* v. *Benarashilal Kataruka* (1990) 185 ITR 493/(1991) 54 Taxman 300 (Cal.)]. For example, mere fact that certain gold or silver articles are made in the shape of household utensils like cups, saucers, etc., do not in itself qualify them as personal effects if the said articles were kept in a show-case in the drawing room of the assessee as such articles are mere show pieces not intended for personal and intimate use by the assessee. [*G. S. Poddar* v. *CWT* [1965] 57 ITR 207 (Bom.)]. Similarly, gold and silver coins, bars and utensils used for puja of deities as a matter of pride or ornamentation are also not personal effects as it is difficult to characterise such user as personal in nature [*H. H. Maharaja Rana Hemant Singh Ji* v. *CIT* (1976) 103 ITR 61 (SC)].

Revenue must investigate factum of personal use: Irrespective of the claim put forward by the assessee that he is having the articles for personal use, the revenue has to investigate whether the articles are required for the personal use of the assessee as claimed by him or whether the articles are in excess of the requirement of the personal use of the assessee [*R. Ramanathan Chettiar* v. *CIT* [1985] 20 Taxman 52/152 ITR 493 (Mad.)].

What is not a Personal Effect - Personal effects, however, do not include the following:

(*i*) *Jewellery is not a personal effect:* "Jewellery" is excluded from personal effects and as such it is a capital asset and any gain arising on its transfer may be chargeable to tax. Jewellery includes:

(*a*) Ornaments made of gold, silver, platinum or any other precious metal or any alloy containing one or more such precious metals whether or not worked or sewn into any wearing apparel.

(*b*) Precious or semi-precious stones, whether or not set in any furniture, utensil or other article or worked or sewn into any wearing apparel.

(*ii*) archaeological collections;

(*iii*) drawings;

(*iv*) painting;

(*v*) sculptures; and

(*vi*) any work of art.

Case Law : ***CIT* v. *H.H. Maharani Usha Devi* [1998] 98 Taxman 309/231 ITR 793 (SC)**

Facts: 'H' being an the ex-ruler had accepted certain heirloom jewellery as private properties that were used on ceremonial occasions. 'H' sold two items of heirloom jewellery and claimed that the sold items constituted personal effects.

Held: Heirloom jewellery was meant for the personal use of the assessee, though meant for use on ceremonial occasions only and not daily use did not deprive such jewellery of its character as jewellery meant for personal use.

(*iii*) Agricultural land in India [Sec. 2(14)(*iii*)] - Any agricultural land situated in rural are in rural area in India is not a capital asset. Thus, two conditions need to be fulfilled: a) it is an agricultural land b) it is situated in rural area in India. If both these conditions are met, the said land will not be a capital asset for the purposes of this definition and therefore will not be liable to capital gains tax:

(*a*) It is an agricultural land - *Prima facie*, a land could be said to be agricultural if it is either actually used, ordinarily used, or is meant to be used for agricultural purposes. Potential use of the land as agricultural land is wholly immaterial. Entries in the revenue record are good *prima facie* evidence regarding presumption of land as agricultural and unless such presumption is dislodged by the presence of other factors in a specific case, the land should be treated as agricultural [*Chandravati Atmaram Patel (Smt.)* v. *CIT* (1978) 114 ITR 302 (Guj.)].

Agricultural Character of the Land to be Verified on the Date of Sale—Future Potential Factors not Relevant: In order to qualify for exemption, it is not enough that the land was once agricultural land. It must be agricultural land at the time of sale [*Sarifabibi* v. *CIT* [1993] 70 Taxman 301/204 ITR 631 (SC)]. The future intended use of land is immaterial [*Motibhai D. Patel (No. 2)* v. *CIT* [1981] 5 Taxman 147/127 ITR 671 (Guj.)]. Mere fact that after the sale the purchaser will put the land to non-agricultural use, it does not follow that the land has ceased to be agricultural land at the date of sale [*Gordhanbhai Kahandas Dalwadi* v. *CIT* [1981] 127 ITR 664 (Guj.)].

All Relevant Factors to be Considered Cumulatively and not just mere Cultivation of the Land: In a case where the land is not being actually put to any use, the test to be applied is not whether the land is capable for being used for agricultural purpose, but whether, having regard to the various relevant factors, the general nature or character of the land is such that it can be regarded as agricultural land. [*Rasiklal Chimanlal Nagri* v. *CWT* (1965) 56 ITR 608 (Guj.)].

Treatment of things Attached to or Situated on Agricultural Land: The well-known English principle that the thing attached to the land belongs to the land and the character of the thing attached to the land will be the same as the character of the land does not find acceptance in Indian jurisprudence. Therefore, things attached to or situated on an agricultural land does not necessarily acquire the character of being agricultural land themselves [*Clen Leven* v. *CIT* [1973] 91 ITR 391 (Ker.)]. Therefore, treatment of assets like trees, house for agricultural workers, etc., depends on whether such assets are sold together with the agricultural land or as a separate transaction [*Clen Leven Estate Ltd.* v. *CIT* (1973) 91 ITR 391 (Kerala)]. However, where trees are sold along with agricultural land, they constitute part of agricultural land. Trees, until they are cut and removed, form an integral part of such land. When the land is sold with standing trees, the sale is an integral one in respect of the land. It does not involve a separate sale for trees as a distinct asset. The sale consideration cannot be bifurcated to compute capital gain arising on the sale of trees [*CIT* v. *Alamickal Co. Ltd.* (1986) 157 ITR 630 (Ker.)].

(b) It is a land situated in rural area - For an agricultural land to be qualified as one, it is essential that it is situated in rural area. If the land situated in urban area, even if it is used for agricultural purposes, it cannot be an agricultural land for the purposes of exclusion under capital asset and therefore any transfer of such land will attract capital gains tax.

Agricultural land is a capital asset in India in the following cases:

- Agricultural land, situated within the jurisdiction of the municipality or cantonment board, having a population of 10,000 or more, is a capital asset.
- If agricultural land is situated beyond its jurisdiction, it may still be a 'capital asset' keeping in view of (*i*) its distance from the local limits and (*ii*) its population as explained below:

Distance of land from the local limits of municipality/cantonment board	Population of the municipality or cantonment board, figures of which have been published before first day of the previous year
(*i*) up to 2 Kilometers from the local limits of the municipality/cantonment board Population of the municipality/cantonment board	Population of the municipality/cantonment board exceeds 10,000 but does not exceed 1,00,000
(*ii*) up to 6 kilometers from the local limits of the municipality/cantonment board Population of the municipality/cantonment board	Population of the municipality/cantonment board exceeds 1,00,000 but does not exceed 10,00,000
(*iii*) up to 8 kilometers from the local limits of the municipality/cantonment board	Population of the municipality/cantonment board exceeds 10,00,000

Population Ceiling applies to Municipality as a Whole It is the population of the municipality or cantonment board that has to be taken into account as a whole and not the population of the street, ward, village where the agricultural land is situated.

The question whether a land is an agricultural land or not is a question of fact - This is a question of fact. Ordinarily, the fact that the land is entered as agricultural land in the revenue records and is assessed as such under the Land Revenue Code would be a circumstance in favour of conclusion that it is an agricultural land. The said presumption can be destroyed by other circumstances pointed to the contrary conclusion and the onus to dislodge the said presumption is on the revenue. [*CIT* v. *Ashok Kumar Rathi* (2018) 89 taxmann.com 406/404 ITR 173 (Madras)]. However, merely because the land has been categorised in the revenue records as such would not be sufficient to raise a valid claim of exemption.[*CIT* v. *GRK Reddy & Sons (HUF)* [2021] 123 taxmann.com 291/277 Taxman 127 (Madras)].

The Supreme Court in *Smt. Sarifabibi Mohmed Ibrahim* v. *CIT* [1993] 70 Taxman 301 (SC) evolved a set of 13 questions that may be asked to determine if the land is an agricultural land. To mention a few:

(1) Whether the land was classified in the revenue records as agricultural and whether it was subject to the payment of land revenue?

(2) Whether the land was actually or ordinarily used for agricultural purposes at or about the relevant time?

(3) Whether such user of the land was for a long period or whether it was of a temporary character or by way of a stop-gap arrangement?

(4) Whether the land, on the relevant date, had ceased to be put to agricultural use? If so, whether it was put to an alternative use? Whether such cesser and/or alternative user was of a permanent or temporary nature?

(5) Whether the land, though entered in revenue records, had never been actually used for agriculture, that is, it had never been ploughed or tilled? Whether the owner meant or intended to use it for agricultural purposes?

(6) Whether the land was situated in a developed area? Whether its physical characteristics, surrounding situation and use of the lands in the adjoining area were such as would indicate that the land was agricultural?

Further, the fact that a land shown as agricultural land in revenue records had been sold to an industrial unit and had potential to be used for industrial purpose it will not lose the character of being an agricultural land for the assessee-seller [*Pr. CIT* v. *Heenaben Bhadresh Mehta* [2018] 96 taxmann.com 164/257 Taxman 219 (Gujarat)].

Case Law : ***CIT* v. *Gemini Pictures Circuit (P.) Ltd.* [1996] 85 Taxman 594/220 ITR 43 (SC)**

Facts: 'G' purchased a land situated within municipal limit, and constructed two buildings thereon that were used for business purposes and the remaining land was used for raising vegetation. Subsequently 'G' sold the land to various business houses for commercial use and claimed it to be a sale of agricultural land not attracting capital gains tax.

Held: The said land was registered in the Municipal records as an urban land and Urban Land Tax was levied thereon. The mere fact that vegetables were being raised thereon at the time of the sale or for some years prior thereto did not change the nature and character of the land. Obviously, it was only a stopgap activity. It was not a true reflection of the nature and character of the land. It was not 'agricultural land in India' and hence not excluded from the definition of the words 'capital asset'.

(*iv*) **Gold Bonds** - Six-and-a-half per cent Gold Bonds, 1977 or 7% Gold Bonds, 1980 or National Defence Gold Bonds, 1980, issued by the Central Government, are not to be treated as capital assets.

(*v*) **Special Bearer Bonds 1991** - Special Bearer Bonds, 1991, issued by the Central Government have also been excluded from the purview of capital assets.

(*vi*) **Gold Deposit Bonds** - "Gold Deposit Bonds", issued under Gold Deposit Scheme, 1999, have been excluded from the purview of the capital asset. Thus, no capital gain will arise on their redemption.

SHORT-TERM AND LONG-TERM CAPITAL ASSETS

For the purpose of computing capital gain, capital assets have been bifurcated into short-term capital assets or long-term capital assets depending upon the period of holding. This distinction is important as the tax-liability of capital gain also differs according to the type of capital gain, whether (i) it is 'short-terms' [under sec. 111A] or (ii) it is 'long-term' [under sec. 112]. The incidence of tax is higher for short-term capital gains as compared to the long-term capital gains. Except in case of depreciable assets which are always considered to be short-term under sec. 50, the distinction between a long-term and short-term capital asset is based on the period for which it is held by the assessee.

Long-term Capital Asset [Sec. 2(29A)] - "Long-term capital asset" means a capital asset which is not a short-term capital asset.

Short-term Capital Asset [Sec. 2(42A)] - As a general rule, "Short-term capital asset" means a capital asset, held by an assessee for not more than 36 months, immediately preceding the date of its transfer. In other words, if an assessee has held capital asset for more than 36 months, it is a long-term capital asset. However, in the following special cases this period of holding is different:

Asset	Period of Holding
◆ Units of Unit Trust of India ◆ Units of an equity oriented mutual fund ◆ Zero Coupon Bonds ◆ Equity or preference shares in a company (Listed in a recognized stock exchange in India)(if transfer takes place after July 10, 2014)	Period of holding is not more than 12 months (If it is more than 12 months, it is long-term capital asset)
◆ Securities (such as debentures, bonds, derivatives etc.) other than a unit, listed in a recognized stock exchange in India (if transfer takes place after July 10, 2014)	
◆ share of a company (not being a share listed in a recognised stock exchange in India (if transfer takes place on or after April 1, 2016) ◆ an immovable property, being land or building or both (if transfer takes place on or after April 1, 2017)	Period of Holding is not more than 24 months (If it is more than 24 months, it is long-term capital asset)

Determining the Period of Holding [Explanation 1 to Sec. 2(42A)]

Usually, the period of holding of a capital asset is reckoned from the date of its purchase or from the date when an assessee acquired title to it. However, in certain special cases, the period of holding of a capital asset is determined in accordance with the following provisions:

Shares of a Company in Liquidation - Where shares are held in a company which is under liquidation, the period subsequent to the date on which the company goes into liquidation is excluded in computing the period of holding [*Explanation 1(a)* to Sec. 2(*42A*)].

Capital Assets Acquired by way of Operation of Law specified under Sec. 49(1) - Where an assessee acquires a capital asset not by purchase but by way of operation of law as specified under Sec. 49(1), the period of holding is reckoned from the date of holding of the asset by its last previous owner who acquired the asset by way of purchase [*Explanation 1(b)* to Sec. 2(42A)].

Transfer by way of operation of law includes the following:

(*i*) partition of an HUF; or (*ii*) gift or will; or (*iii*) succession, inheritance or devolution; or (*iv*) dissolution of a firm or. Body of Individuals or Association of Persons before 1 April 1987; or (*v*) liquidation of a company; or (*vi*) transfer to a revocable or irrevocable trust; (*vii*) transfer from parent company to 100% Indian subsidiary company; or (*viii*) transfer by 100% subsidiary company to its Indian parent company; or (*ix*) any transfer of capital asset by a banking company to a banking institution in a scheme of amalgamation, or (*x*) any transfer by the predecessor co-operative bank to its successor in a business reorganisation; (*x*) any transfer of shares by a shareholder in the predecessor co-operative bank to successor co-operative bank in a business reorganization; (*xi*) any transfer of capital asset by a firm to a company in a scheme of succession; (*xii*) any transfer of capital asset by a firm to a company as a result of succession; (*xiii*) any transfer by a sole proprietary concern to a company.

In all such cases, the period of holding of the last previous owner who acquired the asset by mode of acquisition other than the ones mentioned above is also be included for the purpose of determining the period of holding by the assessee.

Shares held in an Amalgamated Indian Company which were Allotted in lieu of Shares Held in the Amalgamating Company - Where in a scheme of amalgamation, a shareholder of the amalgamating company transfers his shares to the amalgamated company for consideration of allotment of shares in the amalgamated company, the period of holding of the original shares held in the amalgamating company, is also included in computing the period of holding of the shares in the amalgamated company, provided the amalgamated company is an Indian company [*Explanation 1(c)* to Sec. 2(*42A*)].

Shares or any other Security Subscribed on the Basis of Rights Entitlement - Where a person has acquired any share or security on the basis of his rights entitlement or on the basis of rights renounced in his favour, the period of holding is reckoned from the date of allotment of such share or security [*Explanation 1(d)* to Sec. 2(*42A*)].

Right to Subscribe a Share or any other Security - In case of a capital asset, being the right to subscribe to shares or any other security and which is renounced in favour of any other person, the period of holding is reckoned from the date when such offer was made by the company or institution to the date of renouncement [*Exp. 1(e)* to Sec. 2(*42A*)]. But where debentures are converted into equity shares, which are sold subsequently, the period of holding of the equity shares will be reckoned from the date of allotment of such shares. The period of holding of the debentures should not be taken into account to determine whether the shares are short-term or long-term capital asset [*Mrs A. Ghosh* v. *CIT* (1983)141 ITR 45/13 Taxman 73 (Cal.)].

Shares or any other Securities allotted as a Bonus - Where shares or any other security is allotted without any payment on the basis of holding of any other shares or security, the period of holding is reckoned from the date of allotment of such shares or security [*Explanation 1(f)* to Sec. 2(*42A*)].

Shares of an Indian Company allotted in Consideration of a Demerger - Where an assessee holds shares of an Indian company that were allotted to him in a scheme of demerger in lieu of his shareholding in the demerged company, period of holding is counted from the date of holding of the shares in the demerged company and not from the date of allotment of the shares in the resulting company [*Explanation 1(g)* to Sec. 2(*42A*)].

Trading or Clearing Rights or Equity Shares acquired on Demutualisation or Corporatisation of the Recognised Stock Exchange in India - Period for which the person was a member of the recognised stock exchange in India, immediately prior to such demutualisation or corporatisation, is also to be included to determine the period of holding by the assessee [*Explanation 1(h)* & *(ha)* to Sec. 2(*42A*)].

Specified Security or Sweat Equity Shares - Where such securities or shares are allotted or transferred, directly or indirectly, by the employer free of cost or at concessional rate to his employees (including former employee or employees) the period of holding is reckoned from the date of allotment or transfer of such specified security or sweat equity shares [*Explanation 1(hb)* to Sec. 2(*42A*)].

Unit of business trust [Sec. 2(*42A*)(*hc*)]

Where units of business trust are allotted [under sec. 47 (*xvii*)] on account of transfer of shares, the period for which the shares were held by the assessee is also included in counting the time-limit for which the said units were held.

Units held under consolidation scheme [Sec. 2(*42A*)(*hd*)]

Where unit or units become the property of the assessee in the consolidating scheme of a mutual fund, the period for which the unit or units were held under consolidating scheme is also included:

Share of a company acquired on redemption of Global Depository Receipts [Sec. 2(*42A*)(*he*)]

Where a non-resident acquires share/shares of a company on redemption of Global Depository Receipts, the period of holding is counted from the date on which a request for such redemption was made.

Shares and Securities listed on Stock Exchange - Shares/securities, listed on stock exchange, are sold through brokers. The seller is entitled to consideration on the date of contract though the shares/securities are taken up for the delivery later. Therefore, the date of broker's note is treated as the date of transfer, provided the contract is followed up by delivery. Thus, the period of holding should be counted from the date of broker's note.

In case the trasaction takes place directly between the parties and not through stock exchange, the date of contract of sale as declared by the parties is treated as the date of transfer, provided it is followed by actual delivery of shares and the transfer deeds [Circular No. 704, dated 28.04.1995].

Securities Acquired at Different Points of Time in Several Lots - Where securities are acquired in several lots at different points of time, the First-in–first-out (FIFO) method is adopted to reckon the period of the holding of the security, in cases where the dates of purchase and sale could not be correlated through specific numbers of the scrips. In other words, the assets acquired last is taken to be remaining with the assessee while assets acquired first is treated as sold. [Circular No. 704, dated 28.04.1995].

Allotment of Assets by a Firm to its Partner - Where an asset is allotted by a firm to a partner on retirement/dissolution or otherwise, the period for which the asset was held by the firm, is also be taken into account in computing the period of holding by the partner. The partners in a firm are always the owner of the property, held in the name of the firm [*CIT* v. *Smt. S. Vijayalakshmi* (2002) 122 Taxman 949/(2000) 242 ITR 46 (Mad.)].

Period of Holding in case of any other Capital Asset - Period of holding is determined subject to any rule which the Board may make in this behalf [*Exp.* (*1*)(*ii*) to Sec. 2(*42A*)].

"TRANSFER" OF CAPITAL ASSET [SEC. 2(47)]

The second condition to be fulfilled for attracting tax under this head is that there should be a transfer of a capital asset by the assessee. In its general sense, the expression "transfer of property" connotes the passing of rights, either fully or partly, in a property from one person to another. For the purposes of income tax, the definition of the term "transfer" is comprised under sec. 2(*47*). It is an inclusive definition and does not exhaust other kinds of transfer [*Sunil Siddharthbhai* v. *CIT* (1985) 23 Taxman 14w/156 ITR 509 (SC)]. "Transfer" is, therefore, a word of widest import and includes every means by which the property may be passed from one person to another. Transfer may be permanent or temporary. For example, assignment of leasehold rights to exploit an asset for limited period is a temporary transfer, giving rise to capital gain. The inclusive definition refers to the following modes of transfer:

(*i*) Transfer by way of Sale [Sec. 2(*47*)(*i*)]

Transfer includes sale of a capital asset. The sale may be voluntary or involuntary. For example, sale at the instance of decree holder under court orders also results in transfer of property.

However, the transfer of assets on account of family arrangement offers an interesting set of disputes. Thus, even as it is a settled position that family arrangement is partition and partition does not amount to transfer, no capital gains can be charged (*CIT* v. *R. Nagaraja Rao* [2012] 21 taxmann.com 101/207 Taxman 236 (Kar.); a few interesting case laws have emerged in this area. For instance, the Bombay High Court in *B.A.*

Mohota Textiles Traders (P.) Ltd. v. *DCIT* (2017) 82 taxmann.com 397/248 Taxman 490/397 ITR 616 held that when a family-managed limited company transfers shares to another company and in favour of other family members under the family arrangement through a Court order, capital gains tax would still be attracted. This is because company has a separate legal existence other than its shareholders and therefore company is not a part of family arrangement. However, the Mumbai Tribunal in *Sujan Azad Parikh* v. *DCIT* (2022) 145 taxmann.com 167/[2023] 198 ITD 83 held that when assessee had transferred shares under family arrangement only as per the directions of Company Law Board, no capital gain tax was liable to be paid. This matter pertains to a dispute that arose in the functioning of group of companies headed by different family members. All family members agreed to family arrangement by filing a petition before the Company Law Board. Based on the conditions specified in the order of the Company Law Board, the assessee individual transferred shares of the company to another group company on the buyback terms. Thus, distinguishing from Mohota Textiles, the Mumbai Tribunal held that unlike in Mohota Textile where the transferor was a legal entity, in this matter transferor was an individual and therefore applying Nagaraja Rao ruling no capital gains tax was chargeable.

(*ii*) Transfer by way of Exchange [Sec. 2(*47*)(*i*)]

Transfer includes exchange. When two persons mutually transfer the ownership of one thing for the ownership of another, but none of the things is money, the transaction is called exchange [sec. 118 of the Transfer of Property Act, 1982]. The word "exchange" is not limited to immovable property. It also includes barter of chattels. Thus, conversion of preference shares into ordinary shares is an "exchange". Similarly, where assets are transferred to a company in lieu of allotment of shares, it is a case of an "exchange" and not sale.

Lending of Securities under Securities Lending Scheme of SEBI does not Result in Exchange: The meaning of the word "exchange" necessarily involves exchange of two different assets. Shares are fungible assets, *i.e.* one share of a company is good replacement for another share of the same company. The market does not lay any emphasis on the distinctive numbers. Therefore, when the lender of shares under securities lending scheme of SEBI gets back equivalent number of shares of the company with different distinctive numbers, it is not a case of exchange of assets [Circular No. 751, dated 10-02-1997].

(*iii*) Transfer by way of Relinquishment [Sec. 2(*47*)(*i*)]

A relinquishment takes place when the owner withdraws himself from the property and abandons his right thereto. The property continues to exist after relinquishment [*CIT* v. *Rasiklal Maneklal (HUF)* (1989) 43 Taxman 259/177 ITR 198 (SC)]. For example, relinquished one's right, title and interest in a disputed property in favour of other co-owners for a cash consideration amounts to "transfer" giving rise to capital gain [*CIT* v. *Smt. Vimla Lal* (1983) 13 Taxman 79/143 ITR 16 (All.)].

Relinquishment of Undivided Interest by a Member of HUF prior to Partition is not Transfer: Where a coparcener of an HUF relinquishes his interest in HUF property prior to partition, it does not amount to transfer. A coparcener has indeterminate share in the joint-family property and becomes entitled to a definite share only after partition. In view of this, relinquishment of such right prior to partition does not amount to transfer under Sec. 2(47) for the purpose of computing capital gain under Sec. 45.

(*iv*) Transfer by Extinguishment of a Right in a Capital Asset [Sec. 2(47)(*ii*)]

"Transfer" includes extinguishment of right in any capital asset. The words "extinguishment of rights" covers every possible transaction and situation which results in the destruction, annihilation, extinction, termination, cessation or cancellation of any bundle of rights, either qualitative or quantitative, which the assessee has in the capital asset, comprising either movable or immovable property.

Reduction of Share Capital by a Company amount to Extinguishment: It would constitute transfer within the meaning of Sec. 2(*47*)(*ii*). After reduction of the share capital, though the shares remain but the right of the shareholder to dividends or his right to share in the distribution of the net assets upon liquidation of the company gets extinguished proportionately to the extent of reduction in the capital.

Amount distributed by a company on reduction of its share capital has two components, viz., distribution attributable to accumulated profits and distribution attributable to capital. Therefore, any distribution which is made by a company on a reduction of its share capital which can be correlated with the company's accumulated profits will be dividend in the hands of the assessee by virtue of application of sec. 2(*22*)(*e*).

It is only when the distribution is over and above the accumulated profits of the company (whether capitalised or not), such excess would be considered a capital receipt in the hands of shareholder, giving rise to capital gain. When the capital receipt is in excess of the original cost of acquisition of that interest which stands extinguished, there is a capital gain [*CIT* v. *G. Narasimhan* (1999) 102 Taxman 66 (SC)].

(*v*) Transfer by way of Compulsory Acquisition in Law [Sec. 2(*47*)(*iii*)]

Compulsory acquisition under any law is also treated transfer. To that extent, compulsory acquisition is not voluntary transfer. But as noted earlier, the definition of the term transfer is broad enough to cover both voluntary and involuntary transfers.

(*vi*) Transfer by Conversion of a Capital Asset into Stock-in-Trade [Sec. 2(*47*)(*iv*)]

Where a capital asset is converted by the owner thereof into, or is treated by him as, stock-in-trade of a business carried on by him, such conversion or treatment of the capital asset is also regarded as a transfer of the asset [Sec. 45(2)].

(*vii*) Maturity or Redemption of Zero Coupon Bond [Sec. 2(47)(*iva*)]

Transfer includes redemption of zero coupon bond, issued by any infrastructure capital company or infrastructure capital fund on or after 1 June 2005 and specified by the Central Government. Maturity of such bonds is also treated a transfer.

(*viii*) Transferring Beneficial Possession of Immovable Property [Sec. 2(47)(*v*)/(*vi*)]

Any transaction allowing the possession of any immovable property in part performance of the contract (under Sec. 53A of the Transfer of the Property Act, 1882) is a transfer even though the legal ownership may not have been transferred under the general law of the land. Since sec. 53A of the Transfer of Property Act, 1882 has been embodied in sec. 2(*47*)(*v*), all the essential ingredients of sec. 53A are required to be fulfilled for sec. 2(*47*)(*v*) to apply.

Accordingly, where an assessee enters into an agreement with the builders/developers for developing property, e.g. constructing flats and providing other facilities and confer privileges of ownership under power of attorney without executing conveyance deed, capital gain in such cases is taxable in the year in which such transaction is entered into even if the transfer of immovable property is not effective or complete under general law. Thus, joint development agreements entered into between the parties attracted capital gains tax for the assessee-land owner upon transfer of possession to the developer to develop the property.

However, the provisions of sec. 53A of the Transfer of Property Act and secs. 17 and 49 of the Registration Act, 1908 were amended w.e.f. 24.09.2001 whereby the requirement of registration of agreement was made mandatory. Prior to 2001 when sec. 53A was applicable irrespective of whether the contract between the parties had been registered or not, post 2001 this relaxation was done away with. These amendments had its repercussions on sec. 2(47)(*v*) as well. In absence of registration of joint development agreement, the agreement does not fall under section 53A of Transfer of Property Act, 1882 and, consequently, section 2(*47*)(*v*) does not apply. [*CIT* v. *Balbir Singh Maini* [2017] 86 taxmann.com 94/251 Taxman 202 (SC). Also see [*Pr. CIT* v. *Chuni Lal Bhagat* [2019] 103 taxmann.com 379/262 Taxman 209 (SC)]. Now, even when parties under part performance of contract of the nature referred in sec. 53A allowed possession of the land to the builder, the same was taxable as capital gains if the agreement was not registered.

(*ix*) Any transaction which has the effect of transferring or enabling the enjoyment of any immovable property is also a transfer [Sec. 2(47)(*vi*)].

Such transaction may be by way of becoming a member of, or acquiring shares in a cooperative society, company or other association of persons or it may be by way of agreement or arrangement or in any other manner whatsoever. Oftentimes, flats in apartments or houses in a housing society are held in the name of the registered co-operative housing society formed by individual holders. In such scenario, co-operative housing society is a legal owner and the individual members of the society are deemed owners. When deemed owners transfer the rights to use or enjoy the house by transferring the membership in the name of another person, it will amount to transfer.

By virtue of an amendment in the Finance Act, 2012, an explanation was inserted to the definition of the term "transfer" whereby it is clarified that the term transfer includes and shall be deemed to have always included disposing of or parting with an asset or any interest therein, or creating any interest in any asset in any manner whatsoever, directly or indirectly, absolutely or conditionally, voluntarily or involuntarily, by way of an agreement (whether entered into in India or outside India) or otherwise, notwithstanding that such transfer of rights has been characterised as being effected or dependent upon or flowing from the transfer of a share or shares of a company registered or incorporated outside India.

TRANSACTIONS NOT REGARDED AS TRANSFER [SEC. 47]

Every transfer of a capital asset does not attract the levy of the capital gain tax. The income-tax law has specifically excluded certain types of transfer from the scope and meaning of the word "transfer" in relation to a capital asset. Consequently, no capital gain may arise from such a transfer. The following cases cover such transfer:

Section	*Particulars*
Sec. 46	Distribution of assets in kind by a company to its shareholders upon liquidation.
Sec. 47(*i*)	Distribution of any capital assets in kind by a HUF to its members at the time of total or partial partition.
Sec. 47(*iii*)	Transfer of any capital asset under gift or Will or an irrevocable trust. However if an administrator under a Will sells the capital assets and distributes the sale proceeds amongst the legatees, any capital gain arising on such sale is taxable in the hands of the administrator.
47(*iv*) & (*v*)	Transfer of any capital asset between a parent company and its wholly owned subsidiary company, provided the transferee company is an Indian company.
Sec. 47(*vi*), (*vib*)	Transfer of any a capital asset in the scheme of amalgamation/demerger, if the transferee company is an Indian company
Sec. 47(*via*), (*vic*)	Transfer of any shares of an Indian company by a foreign company to another foreign company, in a scheme of amalgamation/demerger of the two foreign companies subject to certain conditions.
Sec. 47(*viab*), (*vicc*)	Transfer of any shares of a foreign company which derives its value, directly or indirectly, from the shares of an Indian company in a scheme of amalgamation/demerger subject to certain conditions.

Section	*Particulars*
Sec. 47(*viaa*)	Transfer of any capital asset by a banking institution in a scheme of amalgamation, sanctioned and brought into force by the Central Government under Sec. 45(7) of the Banking Act, 1949.
Sec. 47(*vica*)	Transfer of any capital asset by the predecessor co-operative bank to the successor co-operative bank or to the converted banking company in a business reorganisation
Sec. 47(*vicb*)	Transfer of shares by a shareholder in the predecessor co-operative bank in lieu of the shares in successor co-operative bank or to the converted banking company in a scheme of business reorganisation
Sec. 47(*vid*)	Allotment of Shares by the Resulting Company to the Shareholders of the Demerged Company in a Scheme of Demerger
Sec. 47(*vii*)	Allotment of Shares in Amalgamated Company to the Shareholders of Amalgamating Company
Sec. 47(*viia*)	Any transfer of bonds or Global Depository Receipts of an Indian company by a non-resident to another non-resident outside India, provided these were purchased under a scheme approved by Government
Sec. 47(*viiaa*)	Any transfer, made outside India, of a capital asset being rupee denominated bond of an Indian company issued outside India, by a non-resident to another non-resident
Sec. 47(*viiab*)	any transfer of a capital asset bond or Global Depository Receipt under Sec. 115AC(1), rupee denominated bond of an Indian company, derivative or such other securities as may be notified by the Central Government in this behalf made by a non-resident on a recognised stock exchange located in any International Financial Services Centre and where the consideration for such transaction is paid or payable in foreign currency
Sec. 47(*viiac*) (w.e.f. 1.4.2022)	any transfer, in a relocation, of a capital asset by the original fund to the resulting fund
Sec. 47(*viiad*) (w.e.f. 1.4.2022)	any transfer by a shareholder or unit holder or interest holder, in a relocation, of a capital asset being a share or unit or interest held by him in the original fund in consideration for the share or unit or interest in the resultant fund
Sec. 47(*viiae*)	Any transfer of a capital asset by Indian Infrastructure Finance Company Limited to institution established for financing infrastructure and development, set up under an Act of Parliament and notified by the Central Government
Sec. 47(*viiaf*)	any transfer of a capital asset by a public sector company to another notified public sector company, Central Government or State Government, provided such transfer is as per the plan approved by the Central Government
Sec. 47(*viib*)	Transfer of government security where interest is paid outside India, by a non-resident to another non-resident outside India

Section	*Particulars*
Sec. 47(*viic*) w.e.f. 1.4.2024	Any transfer of capital asset being conversion of gold into Electronic Gold Receipt issued by vault manager or conversion of Electronic Gold Receipt into gold.
Sec. 47(*viii*)	Any transfer of agricultural land in India effected before 1 March 1970
Sec. 47(*ix*)	Transfer of any work of art, archaeological, scientific or art collection, book, manuscript, drawing, painting, photograph or print are transfered to the Government or a University or the National Museum, National Art Gallery, National Archives, any other public museum or institution as may be notified by the Central Government
Sec. 47(*x*)	Conversion of any bonds, debentures, debenture-stock or deposit certificate of a company into shares or debentures of that company in any form
Sec. 47(*xa*)	Conversion of Foreign currency exchange bonds (FCEB), issued to non-residents by established Indian companies (under Sec. 115AC) into shares of any company
Sec. 47(*xii*)	Transfer of the land of an industrially sick company subject to certain conditions
Sec. 47(*xiii*), (*xiv*)	Transfer of capital assets or intangible asset on succession of a firm or Sole Proprietory concern by a Company
Sec. 47(*xiiia*)	Transfer of Membership Right of Recognised Stock Exchange in India
Sec. 47(*xiiib*)	Transfer of any capital asset or intangible asset by a private company or unlisted public company to a limited liability partnership or where a shareholder transfers any share/shares on account of conversion of a company into limited liability partnership
Sec. 47(*xiv*)	Transfer of any capital asset or intangible asset by a sole proprietary concern to its successor company
Sec. 47(*xv*)	Transfer in a scheme for lending of any securities
Sec. 47(*xvi*)	Transfer of a Capital Asset under Reverse Mortgage Scheme
Sec. 47(*xvii*)	Transfer of share by an Indian company to a business trust
Sec. 47(*xviii*)	Transfer of unit or units by a unit holder under consolidating scheme of a mutual fund
Sec. 47(*xx*)	Any transfer of capital asset being on interest in joint venture held by a public sector company in exchange of shares of a company incorporated outside India by the Government of a foreign State.

BASIS OF CHARGE

General - Sec.45 is the charging provision for the head capital gains. Accordingly, any profits or gains arising from the transfer of a capital asset effected in the previous year shall be chargeable under the head 'Capital Gains' except when exemptions under secs. 54, 54B, 54D, 54E, 54EA, 54EB, 54F, 54G and 54H applies.

Charge on receipts of insurance claim on account of destruction or damage of a capital asset [Sec. 45(1A)]

Receipt of insurance claim on the destruction or damage of a capital asset gives rise to capital gains even though there may not be any transfer of a capital asset on account of its destruction. It is operative from the assessment year 2000-2001 and subsequent years. Thus, the Supreme Court's decision in *Vania Silk Mills (P.) Ltd.* v. *CIT* [1991] 59 Taxman 3 (SC) has been superseded. The whole scheme of capital gain under Sec. 45(IA) is discussed below:

Insurance Claim to be Received under Specified Cases: Capital gains accrues or arises in specified cases which include flood, typhoon, hurricane, earthquake or convulsion of nature, riot or civil disturbances, accidental fire or explosion, action by enemy or action taken in combating an enemy (whether with or without waging a war). Thus, where insurance compensation is received on account of theft, burglary, dacoity or road accident, etc., it does not give rise to capital gain.

Accrual of Liability on Receipt Basis: Liability to capital gains arises in the previous year in which insurance claim is received on account of damage or destruction of a capital asset. Thus, where insurance claim was accepted in the year 2012-2013 but it is received in the previous year 2014-2015, capital gain is taxable in the previous year 2014-2015, relevant to the assessment year 2015-2016.

Receipt of Claim may be in Cash or Kind: Insurance claim may be received in money or in kind or in both. Where it is received in kind, market value of the property is taken as the full value of consideration for the purposes of computing capital gain. Where it is received partly in money and partly in kind, the aggregate of (*i*) money value and (*ii*) the market value of the property is deemed to be the full of consideration for the purposes of computing capital gain.

Applicability of sec. 45(1A) to Depreciable Assets: Section 45(1A) applies to a depreciable asset only to the extent that receipt of insurance compensation on the destruction of the depreciable asset may also give rise to capital gain even though there may be no transfer in the common parlance. Capital gain, however, is computed in accordance with the provisions of Sec. 50 only.

Charge on conversion of a capital asset into stock-in-trade [Sec. 45(2)] - Where a capital asset is converted by the owner thereof into, or is treated by him as, stock-in-trade of a business carried on by him, the capital gain in such cases is charged to tax in the previous year in which such stock-in-trade is sold or otherwise transferred [Sec. 45(2)].

FMV of the Capital Asset on the Date of Conversion is Deemed to be the Full Value of Consideration: For the purposes of computing capital gain in such cases, the fair market value of the capital asset on the date on which it is converted or treated as stock-in-trade is deemed to be the full value of the consideration received or accruing as a result of the transfer of the capital asset.

Charge on Transfer of Beneficial Interest in Securities by the Depository [Sec. 45(2A)] - Section 45(2A) was inserted by the Depositories Act, 1996 w.e.f.

20.9.1995. The said Act provides dematerialisation of securities to avoid physical movement of scrips in order to ensure faster settlement of trade. In the register of the issuing company, the depository (a company registered with SEBI) appears as the registered owner of the dematerialised securities. In the books of the depository, the real owner of the securities appears as the beneficial owner.

A depository interacts with the investors through participants (agents of depository). For this purpose investors have to enter into an agreement and open an account (which is just like a bank account) with a participant. An investor may hold his dematerialised holdings in more than one account with one or more depositories. All the transactions of sale and purchase of dematerialised securities are through the participants and are entered in the respective accounts. The ownership is transferred through book entries in these statements of accounts.

Capital Gain Accrues to the Beneficial Owner (i.e. the Investor) Where any beneficial interest in securities is transferred by the depository or participant, any profit or gain on such transfer is taxable as the income of beneficial owner of the previous year in which transfer took place. It is not treated as the income of the depository who is registered owner of securities [under Sec. 10(1) of the Depositories Act, 1996]

Cost of Acquisition and Period of Holding is to be Determined according to the FIFO Method FIFO method applies only for dematerialised holdings. Where an investor has more than one account, FIFO method is applied account wise. If in an existing account of dematerialised stock, old physical stock is dematerialised and entered at later date, the basis for determining the movement out of the account under the FIFO method, is the date of entry in the account [Circular No. 712 dated 24.06.1998].

Charge in cases where any person transfers a capital asset to a firm in which he is or he becomes a partner [Sec. 45(3)] - Where any person transfers a capital asset either as capital or otherwise to a firm in which he is or becomes a partner, he is chargeable for any capital gain which may accrue to him on such transfer during the said previous year.

Amount Recorded in the Books of Firm is Treated as Full Value of Consideration Received or Accruing as a Result of Such Transfer. The provision is also applicable to an association of persons or body of individuals but does not apply a company or a cooperative society.

Charge on distribution of capital assets by firm/AOP/BOI to its partners or members on its reconstitution [Sec. 45(4)] - When a firm distributed capital asset or money to its partners upon dissolution of the firm or its reconstitution, such distribution were sought to have certain tax implications. The Supreme Court in *Malabar Fisheries Co.* v. *CIT* [1979] 2 Taxman 409 (SC) held that since under the Indian Partnership Act, 1932, a partnership firm is not a distinct legal entity separate from its partners and the firm as such has no separate rights of its own in the partnership assets; distribution of assets to partners upon its dissolution cannot amount to transfer. Such distribution of capital asset upon dissolution of the firm is nothing but a mutual adjustment of rights between the partners and there is no question of any extinguishment of the firm's rights in the partnership assets amounting to a transfer of assets within the meaning of sec. 2(*47*) so as to attract capital gains tax.

In order to sidestep this position of law, a deeming fiction was created under sec. 45(4) whereby when a firm distributed its capital assets to partners at the time of its dissolution or otherwise, amounted to transfer. Capital gain arising on such distribution was taxable in the previous year in which the said distribution/transfer takes place. Thus, the firm has to pay tax on such capital gain. The provision also applied to an association of persons or body of individuals but it did not apply to a company or co-operative society.

Sec. 45(4) fastens the liability only on the distribution of assets and not on the date of dissolution. The relevant date for ascertaining the year in which the tax is to be levied is the year in which the transfer takes place. That year may or may not be the year in which dissolution takes place.

FMV on the Date of Distribution is Deemed to be Full Value of Consideration: For the purposes of computing capital gains (under sec. 48), the fair market value of the asset on the date of such distribution is deemed to be the full value of the consideration received or accruing as a result of the transfer.

The cost of acquisition of the capital asset to the partner is taken at its agreed value and not the fair market value on the date of distribution: Thus, where a partner takes building at agreed value of ₹ 5,00,000, but its fair market value is ₹ 6,00,000, the cost of acquisition of the building to the partner is the agreed value, *i.e.* ₹ 5,00,000.

Since sec. 45(4) used the expression 'dissolution or otherwise', it was sought to be extended to cases of subsisting partners transferring assets in favour of retiring partners. Retirement *prima facie* is not covered by sec. 45(4). However, the department took the view that the words 'or otherwise' immediately succeeding "dissolution" would cover even retirement. The word "otherwise" used in sec. 45(4) takes into its sweep not only the cases of dissolution but also the cases of subsisting partners of the partnership, transferring assets in favour of a retiring partner. This interpretation created confusion since different courts took different position with respect to the same. So while the Bombay High Court in *CIT* v. *A.N. Naik & Associate* [2004] 136 Taxman 107/265 ITR 346 (Bom.) held that when a firm ceases to have any right in the property which is so transferred, the firm's right to the property stands extinguished and the retiring partners acquires absolute title to the property and sec. 45(4) applies; the Karnataka High Court in *CIT* v. *Dynamic Enterprises* [2013] 40 taxmann.com 318/[2014] 223 Taxman 331 (Kar.)(FB) held that cash representing the value of a retiring partner's share given to such retiring partner by subsisting partners and the partnership and its business continues, the firm's right is not extinguished and does not attract capital gains tax.

Further, when a partnership firm was re-organising its business by reconstitution of the firm whereby some partners were retired and fresh partners were inducted and such re-constitution permitted the firm to carry out business in same name and style; it was not a dissolution of the firm [*Asstt. CIT* v. *G.H. Reddy and Associates* [2020] 119 taxmann.com 395/274 Taxman 283 (SC)] (Dismissing the Special Leave Petition against the High Court's order).

In order to settle the prevailing controversy about the tax implication of transfer of assets by the firm at the time of dissolution, the Finance Act, 2021 has substituted sub-section (4) to sec. 45 with a new sub-section; inserted sec. 48(*iii*) to compute capital gains and inserted sec.9B.

Under the newly substituted sub-section (4), where a partner receives any money or capital asset or both from a firm in connection with the reconstitution of such firm, then any profits or gains arising from receipt of such money by the partner shall be deemed to be the income of the firm and chargeable as capital gains in the hands of such firm in the previous year in which such money or capital asset or both were received by the partner. Such profits or gains are computed as:

Capital Gains = Value of money received + Fair Market value of capital asset received – balance in capital account of the partner

If it is capital loss, instead of gains, it will be taken as 'Zero'.

While computing the balance capital account, the following shall be excluded:

(*a*) Revaluation of asset

(*b*) Self-generated asset such as goodwill

(*c*) Any other self-generated asset

Explanation 2 to sec. 45(4) stipulates that where a capital asseet is received by a partner from a firm in connection with the reconstitution of firm, the provisions of sec. 45(4) shall operate in addition to the provisions of sec. 9B and the taxation under both the provisions shall be worked out independently. Thus, sec. 45(4) provides for the computation of capital gain which arises to a partner on extinguishment or relinquishment of his right in the firm in connection with reconstitution of the firm. Though the income arises to partner but it is deemed as income of the firm. It must be noted that such tax liability is attracted under sec. 45(4) only upon reconstitution and not on dissolution.

Income on receipt of capital asset or stock-in-trade by a partner from a firm [Sec. 9B]

When a partner disassociates from the partnership firm whether by virtue of dissolution of the firm, or retirement or upon reconstitution of the firm and thereby receives capital asset or money in lieu thereof, as such there is no transfer thereof either by the firm or the partner. This is because unlike companies, a partnership firm is not a separate legal entity other than its partners and the firm hold no separate rights of its own in the partnership assets but it is the partners who own jointly in common its assets. Hence, there is no transfer involved. However, by virtue of a legal fiction, sec. 45(4) and the newly inserted sec. 9B identifies two sets of transfers involved upon such dissolution, reconstitution etc. : (*a*) transfer of right in the firm by the partner and (*b*) transfer of property by the firm to the partner. The former transaction is dealt with under sec. 45(4) and the latter in sec. 9B. Under sec. 45(4) even though it is the partner who has extinguished or relinquished its right in the firm upon its reconstitution, the income is deemed as income of the firm and capital gains tax is chargeable in the hands of the firm. Under sec.9B since there is a transfer of property by the firm, it is income in the hands of the firm and therefore chargeable on firm.

Sec. 9B provides that where a partner receives any capital asset or stock-in-trade or both from a firm in connection with the dissolution or reconstitution of such firm, then the firm shall be deemed to have transferred such capital asset or stock-in-trade or both, as the case may be, to the partner in the year in which such capital asset or stock-in-trade or both are received by that partner [Sec. 9B(1)].

Where stock-in-trade is transferred - Any profit and gains arising from deemed transfer of stock-in-trade shall be deemed to be income of the firm of the year in which such stock is received by the partner and, accordingly, it shall be charged to tax under the head "Profit and gains from business or profession" [Sec. 9B(2)].

The fair market value of the stock on the date of its receipt by the partner shall be deemed to be the full value of consideration [Sec. 9B(3)]. In other words, the FMV of stock transferred to the partner shall be recorded as sale by the firm as the same shall form part of the business of the firm under sec. 28.

Where capital asset is transferred - Any profit and gains arising from deemed transfer of capital asset shall be deemed to be income of the firm of the year in which such capital asset is received by the partner. It shall be charged to tax under the head "Capital Gains".

The fair market value of capital asset on the date of its receipt by the partner shall be deemed to be the full value of consideration while computing capital gain arising from deemed transfer of such capital asset by the firm [Sec. 9B(3)].

Since under sec. 9B as well as under sec. 45(4), it is the firm which is chargeable to tax upon capital asset being distributed, it will amount to double taxation of the firm on the same asset. Hence to avoid such consequence, sec. 48(*iii*) has been inserted which allows the amount of capital gain computed under section 45(4) attributable to capital asset being transferred by the firm to be deducted while computing capital gain in the hands of the firm in respect of such capital asset.

Particulars	Amount
Full value of consideration received or accrued (FMV of capital asset)	xxx
Less:	(xxx)
(*a*) Expenditure incurred wholly and exclusively in connection with transfer;	(xxx)
(*b*) Cost of Acquisition/Indexed cost of acquisition;	(xxx)
(*c*) Cost of improvement/Indexed cost of improvement; or	(xxx)

Particulars	Amount
(*d*) Amount chargeable to tax as income of firm under section 45(4) which is attributable to capital asset being transferred by the firm Gross Amount	(xxx)
Less: Exemption under sections 54 to 54GB to the extent of net result of above calculation Short-term/Long-term Capital Gains	(xxx)

It must be noted that the provisions of secs. 9B, 45(4) and 48(*iii*) are applicable to the Association of Persons as well as Bodies of individuals, not being a company or a co-operative society.

Charge on compulsory acquisition of a capital asset by Government [Sec. 45(5)] - Where a capital asset is acquired under any law by the government, or where the consideration for the transfer of a capital asset is to be determined or approved by the government or the Reserve Bank of India, the following points may be noted while computing capital gain:

Liability on Receipt Basis In the matters of compulsory acquisition, while the right to receive compensation comes into being the moment Government takes possession of the property acquired; a corresponding completion of transfer of the property under acquisition does not always follow. Capital gains is therefore chargeable in the previous year referable to the date of award of compensation and not the date of notification for acquisition. [*Raj Pal Singh* v. *CIT* [2020] 118 taxmann.com 508/273 Taxman 375 (SC)]

Thus, capital gain is chargeable to tax in the previous year in which such compensation/consideration or part thereof is first received. However, if any amount of compensation is to be received in pursuance of an interim order of a court, Tribunal or other authority, it is deemed to be income chargeable under the head "capital gains" of the previous year in which the final order of such court, Tribunal or other authority is made. It is operative from the assessment year 2015-16 and subsequent years.

Cost of Acquisition to be deducted in full on first instalment: Where such compensation is received in instalments, the cost of acquisition or cost of improvement is allowed to be deducted in full in the year of first computation on receipt basis. It is not to be apportioned over different instalment.

Realisation Expenses to be deducted in subsequent computation also: If the assessee incurs realisation expenses or legal expenses, etc., in respect of subsequent instalments, the deduction is allowed for such expenses in computing capital gain.

Nature of Capital Gain in Subsequent Computation: In subsequent computation of capital gain, the nature of capital gain is determined with reference to first computation. Thus, if the capital gain under first computation was long-term, it will remain so in subsequent computation also.

Enhancement of Compensation: Where compensation is enhanced or further enhanced by any court, or Tribunal or other authority, capital gain resulting from enhancement of compensation is also taxable on receipt basis. For computing capital gain from such enhancement, cost of acquisition/cost of improvement is taken at nil. Thus, only realisation expenses may be claimed as deduction under Sec. 48(*i*) in computing capital gain from enhancement of compensation.

Receipt of enhanced compensation by any other person: Where due to the death of the original transferor or for any other reason, enhanced compensation is received by any other person, recipient of such compensation is taxable on such capital gain. The provision is also applicable to transfer made prior to 1 April 1988 [*Explanation* to Sec. 45(5)].

Interest on Enhanced Compensation: Where the assessee is following mercantile system of accounting, interest on enhanced compensation should be spread over on accrual basis and be taxed accordingly [*Rama Bai* v. *CIT* (1991) 54 Taxman 496/(1990)181 ITR 400 (SC)].

Reduction in Compensation: Where compensation is reduced subsequently by any Court or Tribunal or other authority, the assessed capital gain of that year is re-computed with reference to reduced compensation, taking it as the full of full consideration.

Charge on development agreement [Sec. 45(5A)]

Where capital gains arises to an assessee, being an individual or a Hindu undivided family, from the transfer of a capital asset, being land or building or both, under a development agreement, the capital gains shall be chargeable in the previous year in which the certificate of completion for the whole or part of the project is issued by the competent authority. For the purposes of computation of such capital gains, full value of consideration will be taken as the stamp duty value on the date of issue of the said certificate as increased by the consideration received in cash or by a cheque or draft or by any other mode.

However, if the assessee has transferd his share in the project on or before the date of issue of the said certificate of completion, and the capital gains shall be deemed to be the income of the previous year in which such transfer takes place.

Capital Gain Arising on Repurchase of Units Issued under Equity Linked Savings Scheme [Sec. 45(6)] - Where an individual or an HUF had purchased units of UTI or Mutual Fund [Sec. 10(*23D*)] under equity linked savings scheme out of his taxable income, and such units are later on repurchased by the issuing authority, capital gain on such repurchase of the units would be the difference between the repurchase price and the capital value of units (i.e. the amount invested in such units).

COMPUTATION OF CAPITAL GAINS [SEC. 48]

The process of computing capital gain depends upon the nature of the capital asset, whether it is short-term capital asset or long-term capital asset.

TABLE 9.1: MODE OF COMPUTATION OF CAPITAL GAIN

Computation of Short-term Capital Gain		Computation of Long-term Capital Gain	
Full value of Consideration	xxxxx	Full value of Consideration	xxxxx
Less:		Less:	
◆ Expenditure Incurred wholly and exclusively in connection with such transfer	xxxx	◆ Expenditure Incurred wholly and exclusively in connection with such transfer	xxxx
◆ Cost of Acquisition	xxx	◆ Indexed Cost of Acquisition	xxx
◆ Cost of Improvement	xxx	◆ Indexed Cost of Improvement	xxx
Gross Amount	xxxx	Gross Amount	xxxx
Less:		Less:	
◆ Exemptions under sec. 54B, 54D, 54G or 54GA	xxx	◆ Exemptions under secs. 54, 54B, 54D, 54EC, 54EE, 54F, 54G, 54GA, 54GB	xxx
Short-term Capital Gain/Loss	xxxx	Long-term Capital Gain/Loss	xxxx

Different elements, relevant to the computation of capital gains are explained as follows.

Full Value of Consideration - The Act has not defined the phrase "full value of consideration" and therefore it has to be understood in commercial sense according to the prevalent usage. Following points may be noted in this connection:

Sale price bargained by the parties is full value of consideration: The expression "full value of considerations" cannot be construed as the market value. It refers to the price bargained for by the parties to the sale. The expression "full value" means the whole price, bargained by the parties without any deduction whatsoever and it cannot refer to the adequacy or inadequacy of the price bargained for [*CIT* v. *George Henderson & Co. Ltd*. (1967) 66 ITR 622 (SC)].

Solatium forms part of full value of consideration: Solatium is an extra payment provided for under the Land Acquisition Act for the compulsory nature of the acquisition. Solatium paid for the transfer of the undertaking is a part of the sale consideration and forms part of the capital gains [*Karvalves Ltd.* v. *CIT* (1992) 197 ITR 95 (Ker.)].

Interest Payable on Unpaid Sale Price not to Form part of Sale Consideration: Where the agreement for sale provides for payment of part of the sale price in instalments along with interest after the sale deed was registered, interest received on unpaid sale price is a revenue receipt and cannot be treated as "profits and gains" arising from the transfer of capital asset [*Mount Stuart Tea Estate and Amar Coffee Plantation* v. *CIT* (1998) 99 Taxman 299/(1999) 239 ITR 489 (Mad.)].

Payment made by vendee to vendor's creditors is a part of consideration: Where an assessee sells a mortgaged property and the vendee pays a part of the consideration to the mortgages and creditors of the assessee, the consideration so paid to mortagees or creditors forms a part of the full value of consideration [*CIT* v. *N. Vajrapani Naidu* (1999) 107 Taxman 277/(2000) 241 ITR 560 (Mad.)].

Market Value of Indexed Bonds Issued by the Government, to be Treated as Full Value of Consideration in Cases of Gift [Fourth proviso to Sec. 48]: Where indexed bonds, issued by the government, are transferred under a gift or an irrevocable trust, the market value on the date of such transfer is deemed to be the full value of consideration received or accruing as a result of transfer.

Special provision for full value of consideration [Sec. 50C] - Since huge amounts black money was being generated especially in the transfer of immovable property by under valuing the property in question, Sec. 50C was introduced to curtail this menace. From the assessment year 2004–2005 and onward, where the consideration received or accruing as a result of the transfer of a capital asset being land or building or both is less than the value adopted or assessed or assessable by the "stamp valuation authority" for the purposes of payment of stamp duty in respect of such transfer, the value so adopted or assessed or assessable is deemed to be the full value of the consideration received or accruing as a result of such transfer.

The expression 'assessable' means the price which the stamp valuation authority would have adopted or assessed if it were referred to such authority for the purposes of the payment of stamp duty.

It must be noted that sec. 50C only addressed the transfer of land or building or both being held as capital asset and not as stock- in-trade. In instances where land or building or both were held as stock-in-trade and transferred in that capacity, the relevant provision is sec. 43CA and any gains on account of such transfer is chargeable under the head 'Profits and Gains from Business or Profession'. (For details please refer Chapter 8).

Reference to Valuation Officer in cases where value adopted by the Stamp Valuation Authority exceeds the Fair Market Value of the property: Where the assessee claims that the value adopted or assessed by the stamp valuation authority exceeds the fair market value of the property (i.e. the price which the capital asset would ordinarily fetch in the open market) on the date of the transfer, and the assessee has not disputed such value in any appeal or revision and no reference has been made before any other authority or Court or High Court, the Assessing Officer is required to refer such case to the Valuation Officer.

Where a case is referred to Valuation Officer, "full value of consideration" is determined as below:

(*a*) value ascertained by the Valuation Officer, or

(*b*) value assessed/adopted by the stamp valuation authority.

Whichever is less, is the full value of consideration.

Fair market value deemed to be full value of consideration in certain cases [Sec. 50D] - Where consideration received for the transfer of capital asset by the assessee is either not ascertainable or cannot be determined for computing capital gain, the fair market value of the said asset on the date of transfer is deemed to be the full value of consideration received or accruing as a result of such transfer.

COST OF ACQUISITION [SEC. 49 AND SEC. 55]

Cost of acquisition of an asset must be understood in its common sense that is, it must represent expenditure incurred in acquiring asset. It is reasonable to include in the actual cost of a capital asset all the expenses which were incurred by the assessee in acquiring it as distinct from the expenditure, which was incurred by him for retaining or maintaining the capital asset.

However, cost of acquisition or cost of improvement for a house property shall not include interest on money borrowed for the construction or purchase of the said house property for which deduction has already been availed under sec. 24B or Chapter VIA (w.e.f. 1-4-2024).

Cost of Acquisition of a Property, which is not a Capital Asset at the Time of its Acquisition but Becomes Capital Asset Subsequently: Where a property becomes a capital asset after the date of its acquisition, cost of acquisition of such property is to be taken with reference to the date of its acquisition and not with reference to the date on which it became a capital asset [*Ranchhodbhai Bhaijibhai Patel* v. *CIT* (1971) 81 ITR 446 (Guj.); *CIT* v. *V. M. Ramiah Reddy* (1986) 158 ITR 611 (Kar.); *CIT* v. *Smt M. Subaida Beevi* (1987) 30 Taxman 50/(1986) 160 ITR 557 (Ker.)].

Purchase Price to be the Cost of Acquisition: Where an assessee has acquired a capital asset by way of purchase, its purchase price is taken to be the cost of acquisition.

Discharge of Mortgage Debt created by the owner himself is not allowed: where the mortgage is created by the assessee himself, then the expenditure incurred by the assessee to repay the mortgage debt cannot be held to be the cost of acquisition or cost of improvement allowable under section 48. The expenditure incurred by the assessee to discharge the mortgage debt created by the previous owner to acquire absolute interest in the property is treated as 'cost of acquisition' and is deductible from the full value of the consideration received by the assessee on transfer of that property. However, where the assessee acquires a property which is unencumbered and himself creates a mortgage on the property, such amount cannot be allowed as deduction. [*V. S. M. R. Jagadishchandran* v. *CIT* (1997) 93 Taxman 389/227 ITR 240 (SC)].

Cost of Acquisition includes Interest on Funds Borrowed Immediately after the Purchase of a Capital Asset to Pay the Vendor and meet the Cost of Stamp Duty: The cost of acquisition includes the cost of the borrowing made by an assessee for the purpose of paying the vendor and obtaining the sale deed. Such borrowing directly relates to the acquisition and it is irrelevant that the borrowing was made after registering the sale deed. The assessee has to first acquire the title before encumbering the same. [*CIT* v. *K Raja Gopala Rao* (2002) 125 Taxman 148/(2001) 252 ITR 459 (Mad.)].

Case Law : *CIT* v. *Attili N. Rao* (2001) 119 Taxman 1030/252 ITR 880 (SC)

Facts: 'A' mortgaged his immovable property to the State Excise Department to provide security for the amounts of 'kist' which were due by him to the State. The State sold the immovable property by public auction to realise its dues, applied the required some towards the same and paid over the balance to 'A'.

Held: Outstanding dues against mortgaged property cannot be deducted from sale price of the property while computing capital gain.

Case Law : *Meccane Industries Ltd.* v. *CIT* (2003) 127 Taxman 460/[2002] 254 ITR 175 (Madras)

Facts: 'M' purchased a piece of land along with a factory and godown buildings and continued agricultural activities in open area. Subsequently, 'M' sold the open land for purpose of house site and claimed that cost of acquisition of the land should be market value of the land on date when it was converted to non-agricultural use from agricultural use.

Held: Cost of acquisition was cost of acquisition of agricultural land and not notional cost as on date lands were put to non-agricultural use.

Capital Gains with respect of self-generated assets - The computation of capital gains is comprised in sec. 48. It must be noted that the computation provision and the charging provision sec. 45 constitute an integrated code for the purpose of ascertaining whether the transfer of the capital asset gives rise to a capital gain for the purposes of the Act. If the computation provisions cannot apply to a given case, then such a case could not be intended by the Legislature to fall within the charging section [*CIT* v. *B.C. Srinivasa Setty* [1981] 5 Taxman 1/128 ITR 294 (SC)].

Such difficulties in meeting with the requirements of computation provision will be encountered particularly in cases were asset is self-generated, that is, no cost was incurred to acquire those assets. These are such assets which did not cost anything to the assessee in terms of money in its creation or acquisition. In absence of such cost of acquisition, the computation provision fails and so does the charging provision because the presumption it raises is that the Legislature never intended to bring such capitals assets within the fold of capital gains tax. For example, asset like goodwill which is a capital asset in general law, but for the original owner, there is no cost of acquisition and hence when such owner sell or transfer goodwill, it would not attract tax on capital gains.

In order to overcome difficulties created by such assets, sec. 55 has been amended from time to time to provide that in case of specified assets, cost of acquisition shall be taken as nil. Thus, assets like goodwill, trade mark, brand name, right to manufacture an article or thing, loom hours, tenancy rights, route permit shall be nil and where it has been purchased, the cost will be taken to be the actual price paid for it.

The Finance Act, 2021 has substituted Sec. 55(2)(*a*). According to the newly substituted clause the cost of acquisition of a capital asset, being goodwill of a business or profession, or a trade mark or brand name associated with a business or profession, or any other intangible asset or right, or right to manufacture, produce or process any article or thing, or right to carry on any business or profession, or tenancy rights, or stage carriage permits, or loom hours or any other rights shall be as follows:

(*a*) in the case of acquisition of such asset by the assessee by purchase from a previous owner, means the amount of the purchase price

(*b*) in the case of acquisition of such asset by partition of HUF, will or gift, succession, liquidation of company etc. specified under Sec. 49(*i*) to (*iv*), and such asset was acquired by the previous owner by purchase, means the amount of the purchase price for such previous owner

(*c*) in any other case nil.

However, for the assessment year commencing on or after 1.4.2022 where depreciation was availed on goodwill being a capital asset, the purchase price in clauses (*a*) and (*b*) above shall be reduced by such depreciation availed.

Case Law : ***CIT* v. *Manoharsinhji P. Jadeja* [2006] 281 ITR 19 (Gujarat)**

Facts: 'M' sold certain property inherited by him on death of his father, which was acquired by his fore fathers by conquest. Issue was whether there was any cost of acquisition.

Held: Since neither cost nor date of acquisition of property were ascertainable, no capital gain could be brought to tax in respect of said property.

COST OF IMPROVEMENT

Section 55(1)(*b*) defines cost of improvement. It provides that where the capital asset became the property of the previous owner or the assessee before 1.4.2001, the cost of any improvement means all expenditure of a capital nature incurred in making any additions or alterations to the capital asset on or after the said date by the previous owner or the assessee. In other cases, it means all capital expenditure in making any additions or alterations by the assessee after it became his property and where the capital asset became the property of the assessee by any of the modes specified in Section 49(1) by the previous owner as the case may be. Where the capital asset is a goodwill or any other intangible asset of a business, or a right to manufacture, produce or process any article or thing or a right carry on any business or profession or any other right, the cost of improvement shall be taken as nil.

Double deduction not allowed: If any part of the expenditure is deductible in computing the income chargeable under the head "Interest on securities", "Income from house property", "Profits and gains of business or profession" or "Income from other sources", such expenditure cannot be included as cost of improvement. This is basically to ensure that double deduction is allowed for the same expenditure.

No Cost of any improvement for goodwill: As per sec. 55(1)(*b*) in relation to a capital asset being goodwill of a business, cost of improvement shall be taken to be nil.

Expenses must have been Actually Incurred: Only those expenses, which have been actually incurred by the assessee in making additions and improvements in the property, ought to be taken into consideration as "cost of improvement" [*Parmanand Bhai Patel* v. *CIT* (1985) 21 Taxman 273/(1984) 149 ITR 80 (MP)].

Improvement must be on the Asset itself and not on the Title to the Asset: Cost of improvement would cover a case where the amount is expended on the asset itself. Improving the owner's title to the asset is different from improving the asset itself. Therefore, compensation paid to a person who disputed the title of the assessee cannot be said to be expenditure by way of any improvement to the asset as such [*CIT* v. *V. Indira* (1980) 3 Taxman 155/(1979) 119 ITR 837 (Mad.)].

Betterment Charges: The expenditure incurred by way of betterment charges paid under town planning scheme for acquiring an enduring benefit are in the nature of capital expenditure and go to improve the cost of land. Hence, they would fall under Sec. 48(*ii*) [*Mathurdas Mangaldas Parekh* v. *CIT* (1980) 4 Taxman 431/126 ITR 669 (Guj.)].

Case Law : ***CIT* v. *Miss Piroja C. Patel* (2002) 122 Taxman 752/(2000) 242 ITR 582 (Bom.)**

Facts: 'P' owned a land which was notified for compulsory acquisition under the Land Acquisition Act, 1894. Hutment dwellers on the land claimed occupancy rights thereon and agreed to vacate upon payment of compensation.

Held: Compensation paid to evict hutment dwellers is allowed as cost of improvement.

Case Law : ***CIT* v. *V. Ramaswamy Mudaliar* (1993) 66 Taxman 469/(1992) 196 ITR 939 (Mad.)**

Facts: 'R' purchased a mare with a view to run it in races but later sent to a stud farm where it gave birth to off-springs. The mare and off-springs were later sold giving rise to capital gains. 'R' claimed expenses incurred on upkeep and maintenance of mare at stud-farm till it gave birth to offsprings as cost of acquisition of off-springs and training fee on mare and offsprings as cost of improvement.

Held : The animals had been subjected to training and such training adds value to the animals amounting to improvement in capital asset sold. Expenditure incurred on training of mare and off-springs amounts to cost of improvement.

Indexed Cost of Acquisition and Improvement [Explanations (*iii*), (*iv*) and (*v*) of Sec. 48]:

"Indexed cost" allows a higher deduction in respect of cost of acquisition to neutralise the effect of inflation. However, it neutralises the effect of inflation only to the extent of 75%. Indexed cost of acquisition is allowed as deduction is computing long-term capital gains.

The terminology for converting 'cost of acquisition' and "cost of improvement" into "Indexed cost" is defined as under:

"Indexed cost of acquisition" means an amount which bears of the cost of acquisition the same proportion as Cost of Inflation Index for the year in which the asset is transferred bears to the Cost Inflation Index for the first year in which the asset was first held by the assessee or for the year beginning on the 1st day of April, 1981 whichever is later [*Explanation iii*].

"Indexed cost of any improvement" means an amount which bears to the cost of improvement the same proportion as cost Inflation Index for the year in which the asset is transferred bears to the cost Inflation Index for the year in which the improvement to the asset took place [*Explanation iv*]

"Cost Inflation Index" in relation to a previous year, means such index as the Central Government may, having regard to seventy-five percent of average rise in the consumer price index for urban non-manual employees for the immediately preceding previous year to such previous year, by notification in the Official Gazette, specify in this behalf [*Explanation v*].

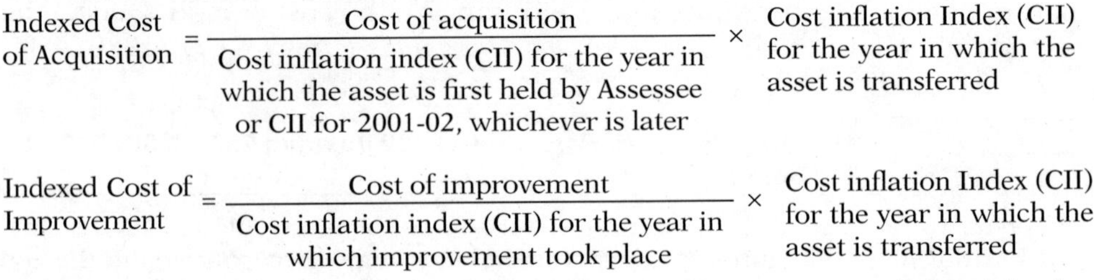

$$\text{Indexed Cost of Acquisition} = \frac{\text{Cost of acquisition}}{\text{Cost inflation index (CII) for the year in which the asset is first held by Assessee or CII for 2001-02, whichever is later}} \times \text{Cost inflation Index (CII) for the year in which the asset is transferred}$$

$$\text{Indexed Cost of Improvement} = \frac{\text{Cost of improvement}}{\text{Cost inflation index (CII) for the year in which improvement took place}} \times \text{Cost inflation Index (CII) for the year in which the asset is transferred}$$

Expenditure Incurred Wholly and Exclusively in Connection with the Transfer - Any expenditure, incurred wholly and exclusively, in connection with transfer of a capital asset is allowed as a deduction in computing capital gain. Thus, the brokerage or commission, stamp duty, registration fee, travelling expenses and legal expenses, etc., incurred in connection with transfer are allowed to be deducted in computing capital gain. The following comments may be noted in this regard:

Payment made to remove any encumbrances on the property are allowed: Amount paid by assessee to clear encumbrances will be treated as a part of cost of acquisition or cost of improvement and be allowed as deduction [*R.M. Arunachalam* v. *CIT* [1997] 93 Taxman 423/227 ITR 222 (SC)]. Where the building is occupied by the tenant and the purchaser insists on vacant possession, payment made to the tenant to secure the vacant possession is also deductible in computing capital gains [*CIT* v. A. *Venkatraman* (1982) 10 Taxman 298/137 ITR 846 (Mad.) and also see *Naozar Chenoy* v. *CIT* (1998) 234 ITR 95 (AP)].

Legal expenses incurred for enhancement of compensation in respect of a capital asset acquired by the Government to be allowed: Legal expenses incurred for getting compensation for compulsory acquisition are deductible, as they are incurred in connection with the transfer. Such legal expenses may be incurred prior to the award or after the award.

Treatment of Embezzlement of Consideration: In order to claim a deduction, an assessee must establish that the embezzlement of consideration took place during the operations of the transaction and was incidental to the operations of the transaction. Whether the loss is incidental to the operations of the transaction is a question of fact. For example, where the loss occurred after the transaction is complete, such loss is not incidental to the transaction but is incurred as owner of the property and hence not deductible [*Mrs. G.Y. Chenoy* v. *CIT* (1999) 102 Taxman 406/(1998) 234 ITR 89 (AP)].

Securities Transaction Tax not to be Deducted [Fifth Proviso to Sec. 48]: No deduction is allowed in respect of any sum paid on account of securities transaction tax from the assessment year 2005-2006 and subsequent years.

ADJUSTMENT OF FORFEITURE OF ADVANCE MONEY [SEC. 51]

Where transfer of any capital asset was subject to infructuous negotiation at any time, any advance or other money received and retained (forfeited) by the assessee in respect of such negotiations is liable to be deducted from the cost of acquisition for which the asset was acquired or from the written-down value or the fair market value, as the case may be. Forfeiture of advance by any other person cannot be adjusted against cost of acquisition. However, where the amount of advance or other money forfeited exceeds the cost of acquisition of the capital asset, such excess cannot be taxed as capital gain because there is no transfer of the capital asset. Such excess is a capital receipt, not chargeable to tax [*Travencore Rubber and Tea Company Ltd.* v. *CIT* (2000) 109 Taxman 250/243 ITR 158 (SC)].

Exception

Where any sum of money, received as an advance or otherwise in the course of negotiations for transfer of a capital asset, has been included in the total income of the assessee for any previous year as income from other sources [under sec. 56(2)(*ix*)], such income cannot be deducted from the cost for which the asset was acquired or the written down value or the fair market value, as the case may be, in computing the cost of acquisition [Proviso to sec. 51]

EXEMPTIONS IN RESPECT OF CAPITAL GAINS

Exemption on capital gains arising from transfer of residential house property [Sec. 54]

Exemption available to	An individual or a HUF
Exemption available when	Long-term residential house property is transferred
Exemption available if	One residential house property is ◆ **purchased** within 1 year before transfer or within 2 years after transfer **OR** ◆ **constructed** in India within 3 years from transfer or ◆ **Bank Deposit** in Capital gain deposit account scheme and amount withdrawn from this deposit for purchase or construction above

Exemption available to the extent of	Investment in new asset or capital gain, whichever is less
Exemption availed is withdrawn	If new asset is transferred within 3 years of its acquisition
Consequences of withdrawal of exemption	The cost of acquisition of the new asset so transferred is reduced by the amount of exemption allowed

The Finance Act, 2019 inserted a proviso to Sec. 54 w.e.f. 1.4.2020 according to which where the amount of the capital gain does not exceed ₹ 2 crore, the assessee may, at his option, purchase or construct two residential houses in India. However, this is only a one-time option available to the assessee. So that where the assessee has exercised this option in any assessment year, he shall not be subsequently entitled to exercise the option for the same or any other assessment year. Where the cost of new asset exceeds ₹ 10 crore, the amount exceeding ₹ 10 crore shall not be taken into account for this exemption. (w.e.f. 1.4.2024)

The following points must be noted:

Purchase of more than one house: The expression "a residential house" would mean "any residential house" and would not refer to a numerical limitation of "one". Whenever the legal intent is to restrict the benefit, it has clearly employed the numerical expression "one" as in the case of Sec. 54F of this Act. An exemption provision be liberally construed. The only requirement is that it should be for the residential use and not for commercial use.

An assessee is at liberty to construct a house in accordance with his own plans and requirements or compulsions. For instance, a person may construct a residential house in such a manner that he may use the ground floor for his own residence and let out the first floor having an independent entry which can be later let out. One may build a house consisting of four bedrooms (all in the same or different floors) in such a manner that an independent residential unit consisting of two or three bedrooms may be carved out with an independent entrance so that it can be let out. The fact that the residential house consists of several independent unit cannot restrict benefit under this section [*CIT* v. *Gita Duggal* [2013] 30 taxmann.com 230/214 Taxman 51 (Delhi) (SLP against High Court order rejected by Supreme Court in *CIT* v. *Gita Duggal* [2014] 52 taxmann.com 246/[2015] 228 Taxman 62 (SC)].

It is not necessary that the sale consideration itself should be used to purchase the house: Sec.54 does not insist that sale consideration obtained by assessee itself should be utilized for purchase of house property. Therefore, advance payment made by assessee for purchase of a residential flat would constitute part of purchase, even when such advance was made prior to date of sale of capital asset [*Ms. Moturi Lakshmi* v. *ITO,* Non-corporate ward (2020) 119 taxmann.com 488/274 Taxman 286/428 ITR 462 (Madras)].

It is not necessary to purchase or construct a whole house: For claiming the exemption, it is not necessary that the assessee should purchase or construct a whole house or it should be a new house. The house purchased may be a new house or an old house or part thereof. Capital gains invested in the construction of first floor on the existing house is also eligible for the exemption [*CIT* v. *P.V. Narasimhan* (1989) 47 Taxman 89/(1990) 181 ITR 101 (Mad.)].

Legal title not necessary: The word "purchase" is not used in the sense of legal transfer but beneficial transfer. The execution of sale deed under the Transfer of Property Act is not a condition precedent to claim exemption. If the assessee has taken possession of the house by investing capital gain within the prescribed time-limit, he can claim the exemption even though the sale deed has not been executed within the permissible time-limit [*CIT* v. *Dr. Laxmichand Narpal Nagda* (1995) 78 Taxman 219/211 ITR 804 (Bom.)].

Allotment of flats under self-financing scheme: The allotment of flats under self-financing scheme of Delhi Development Authority or under similar scheme of co-operative societies or other institutions be treated as cases of construction for the purposes of exemption [Circular No. 471 dated 15.10.1986 and Circular No. 472 dated 16.12.1993].

Date of commencement of construction is not relevant: The date of commencement of the construction of the new house is not material. To get the benefit of exemption, the assessee must complete the construction within the prescribed time-limit from the date of sale of old house [*CIT* v. *J. R. Subramanya Bhat* (1986) 28 Taxman 578/(1987) 165 ITR 571 (Kar.)].

Exemption for capital gain cannot be refused to the assessee simply on the ground that the construction of the new house had begun before the sale of the old house [*CIT* v. *H.K. Kapoor* (1998) 150 CTR 128 (All.)].

Cost of the plot: If the amount of capital gain is appropriated towards the cost of a plot and also towards construction of a residential house thereon, the aggregate cost should be considered for determining the quantum of deduction, provided the acquisition of the plot and also the construction thereon, are completed within the prescribed time-limit [Circular No. 667 dated 18.10.1993].

Special Provision to Extend the Time-limit of Investment of Capital Gains [sec. 54H]. Where the transfer of a residential house is by way of compulsory acquisition and the assessee has not received the amount of compensation on the date of transfer, the period of investment either in the purchase or construction of residential house or deposit in a bank under Capital Gain Scheme Account is counted from the date on which compensation is received.

Case Law : ***CIT* v. *T.N. Arvinda Reddy* (1979) 2 Taxman 541/120 ITR 46 (SC)**

Facts: 'A' the eldest brother in a coparcenary, comprising four brothers, sold his own house and acquired the common house from his three brothers who executed release deeds for a consideration. Question arose if this qualifies as 'purchase' for the purposes of availing exemption under sec. 54.

Held: The word "purchase" should be interpreted in its ordinary meaning, that is, buying for a price or equivalent of price by payment in kind or adjustment towards an old debt or for other monetary consideration.

Case Law : ***CIT* v. *Girish L. Ragha*** **[2016] 69 taxmann.com 95/239 Taxman 449 (Bom.)**

Facts: 'G' invested proceeds of from capital gains in for the purchase of flat by a developer. The construction was completed only after 4 years owing to a dispute with respect to the project and occupancy certificate was obtained only after 4 years.

Held: Since the payment of the total consideration was paid by 'G', merely because the residential premises were not occupied, as the possession was not delivered to 'G' by the developer and the deed of conveyance was not executed within such period would not by itself be a ground to deprive 'G' from availing the deduction under sec. 54.

Exemption on capital gains on transfer of agricultural land [Sec. 54B]

Exemption available to	An individual or a HUF
Exemption available when	Any agricultural land, short-term or long-term is transferred provided that it was used by the individual or his parents or HUF for agricultural purposes for 2 years immediately prior to transfer
Exemption available if	◆ Another agricultural land, may be in rural area or urban area, is acquired within 2 years from the date of transfer or ◆ **Bank Deposit** in Capital gain deposit account scheme and amount withdrawn from this deposit for acquiring the land above
Exemption available to the extent of	Investment in new asset or capital gain, whichever is less
Exemption availed is withdrawn	If new asset is transferred within 3 years of its acquisition
Consequences of withdrawal of exemption	The cost of acquisition of new asset so transferred is reduced by the amount of exemption allowed

Exemption on capital gains on the compulsory acquisition of land or building, forming part of an industrial undertaking [Sec. 54D]

Exemption available to	Any assessee
Exemption available when	Any land or building, short-term or long-term, is compulsorily acquired by the Government provided such land or building was forming part of an industrial undertaking and used for industrial purposes for 2 years prior to its acquisition
Exemption available if	◆ Another land or building is acquired within 3 years from the date of receipt of compensation or ◆ **Bank Deposit** in Capital gain deposit account scheme and amount withdrawn from this deposit for acquiring the land or building above
Exemption available to the extent of	Investment in new asset or capital gain, whichever is less

Exemption availed is withdrawn	If new asset is transferred within 3 years of its acquisition
Consequences of withdrawal of exemption	The cost of acquisition of new asset so transferred is reduced by the amount of exemption allowed

Meaning of industrial undertaking. "Industrial undertaking" must be understood in its popular meaning. An undertaking is one which is maintained by a person for the purpose of carrying on his business. The demonstrative adjective "industrial" qualifying the word "undertaking" shows that the undertaking must be one, which partakes the character of business. Since the word "business" is of wide import, the word "industrial undertaking" should be understood to have been used in a wide sense, taking in its fold any project or business a person may undertake [*CIT* v. *Hemsons Industries* (2001) 118 Taxman 903/251 ITR 693 (AP)].

An industrial undertaking would include setting up the business of running a lodging house [P. *Alikunju* v. *CIT* (1987) 34 Taxman 169/166 ITR 804 (Ker.)].

Exemption for capital gains on transfer of any long-term capital asset [Sec. 54EC]

Exemption available to	Any assessee
Exemption available when	Any long-term capital asset being land or building or both
Exemption available if	Investment is made in Bonds of National Highways Authority of India or Rural Electrification Corporation (REC) or notified bonds provided such investment, wholly or partly, is made within 6 months from date of transfer of asset and the amount of investment in the year of transfer of asset and in subsequent financial year does not exceed ₹ 50 lakhs
Exemption available to the extent of	Investment in new asset or capital gain, whichever is less
Exemption availed is withdrawn	If new asset is transferred within 5 years of its acquisition (3 years if investment is made before 1.4.2018) or converted into money or any loan or advance taken against it within 5 years of its acquisition
Consequences of withdrawal of exemption	Exemption is rolled back and become taxable as long-term capital gains in the year of default

Investment in Long-term Specified Asset, not Eligible for Deduction under Sec. 80C - Where the assessee has claimed exemption for investment in long-term specified asset under Sec. 54EC, he is not entitled to claim deduction for such investment under Sec. 80C. The provision denies/prevents double benefit for the same investment.

Exemption for capital gains on transfer of long-term capital asset [Sec. 54EE]

Exemption available to	An individual or a HUF
Exemption available when	Long-term capital asset
Exemption available if	Invested within 6 months of transfer in long-term capital asset specified assets notified by the Central Government to finance start-ups and such investment does not exceed ₹ 50 lakhs
Exemption available to the extent of	Investment in new asset or capital asset, whichever is less
Exemption availed is with-drawn	New asset is transferred within 3 years from date of acquisition or a loan or advance is taken against the security of such new asset within 3 years of date of acquisition
Consequences of withdraw-al of exemption	Exemption becomes taxable as long-term capital gains

Exemption for capital gains on transfer of a Long-term Capital Asset, other than a Residential House [Sec. 54F]

Exemption available to	An individual or a HUF
Exemption available when	Long-term capital asset other than a residential house property is transferred, provided on the date of transfer the assessee does not own more than one residential house property (other than the new house property below)
Exemption available if	One residential house property is ◆ **purchased** within 1 year before transfer or within 2 years after transfer **OR** ◆ **constructed** in India within 3 years from transfer or ◆ **Bank Deposit** in Capital gain deposit account scheme and amount withdrawn from this deposit for purchase or construction above
Exemption available to the extent of	Investment in new asset ÷ Net Consideration × capital gain. Exemption cannot exceed capital gains.
Exemption availed is with-drawn	If new asset is transferred within 3 years of its acquisition If another residential house property is purchased in India or outside India within 2 years from the date of transfer of original asset If construction of another residential house property in India or outside India is completed within 3 years from the date of transfer of original asset
Consequences of withdraw-al of exemption	Exemption becomes taxable as long-term capital gains

Where the cost of new asset exceeds ₹ 10 crores, the amount exceeding ₹ 10 crores shall not be taken into account for this exemption. (w.e.f. 1.4.2024)

Legal title not necessary: The word "purchase" is not used in the sense of legal transfer but beneficial transfer. The relevant date for the purposes of Sec. 54F is when the assessee paid the full consideration amount for the flat/house and obtained its possession and not the date of registration of the agreement of purchase [*CIT* v. *Smt. Beena K. Jain* (1994) 75 Taxman 145 (Bom.)]

Date of the commencement of construction not relevant: Exemption for capital gain cannot be refused to the assessee simply on the ground that the construction of new house had begun before the transfer of capital asset [*CIT* v. *H.K. Kapoor* (1998) 150 CTR 128 (All.)].

Allotment of flats under self-financing scheme: The allotment of flats under self-financing scheme of Delhi Development Authority or other similar institutions or housing societies be treated as case of construction of the house for the purposes exemption [Circular No. 471 dated 15.10.1986 and Circular No. 672 dated 16-12-1993]

Cost of plot: If the amount of net consideration is appropriated towards the cost of the plot and also towards construction of a residential house thereon, the aggregate of the cost should be considered for determining the quantum of deduction, provided that the acquisition of the plot and also construction thereon, are completed within the prescribed time-limit [Circular No. 667 dated 18-10-1993].

Concurrent Jurisdiction of Sec. 54EC and Sec. 54F. Where the assessee invests net consideration from the transfer of long-term capital asset under Sec.54EC and Sec.54F simultaneously, he is entitled to claim the exemption under both the Sections, provided the required conditions of two sections are satisfied. The scope of the two sections is not mutually exclusive.

Exemption from capital gains on transfer of assets in the course of shifting of industrial undertaking from urban area [Sec. 54G]

Exemption available to	Any taxpayer
Exemption available when	Long-term or short-term capital assets being land, building, plant or machinery is transferred for shifting an industrial undertaking from an urban area to rural area
Exemption available if	Land, building, plant or machinery is acquired to shift the undertaking to a rural area is ◆ **Purchased** within 1 year before transfer or within 3 years after transfer ◆ **Bank Deposit** in Capital gain deposit account scheme and amount withdrawn from this deposit for purchase or construction above
Exemption available to the extent of	Investment in new asset or capital gain whichever is less
Exemption availed is withdrawn	If new asset is transferred within 3 years of its acquisition

Consequences of withdrawal of exemption	The cost of acquisition of new asset so transferred is reduced by the amount of exemption allowed

Exemption for capital gains on transfer of assets in the course of shifting of Industrial Undertaking from Urban Area to any Special Economic Zone [Sec. 54GA]

Exemption available to	Any taxpayer
Exemption available when	Long-term or short-term capital assets being land, building, plant or machinery is transferred for shifting an industrial undertaking from an urban area to any special economic zone
Exemption available if	Land, building, plant or machinery is acquired to shift the undertaking to a special Economic zone is ◆ **Purchased** within 1 year before transfer or within 3 years after transfer ◆ **Bank Deposit** in Capital gain deposit account scheme and amount withdrawn from this deposit for purchase or construction above
Exemption available to the extent of	Investment in new asset or capital gain whichever is less
Exemption availed is withdrawn	If new asset is transferred within 3 years of its acquisition
Consequences of withdrawal of exemption	The cost of acquisition of new asset so transferred is reduced by the amount of exemption allowed

Exemptions for capital gains on transfer of residential property [Sec. 54GB]

Exemption available to	An individual or HUF
Exemption available when	Long-term residential property is transferred during 1.4.2012 and 31.3. 2022
Exemption available if	◆ Equity shares in an eligible company are acquired on or before due date of filing return of income under sec. 139(1) and the eligible company should utilize this amount for the purchase of new asset within 1 year from the date of subscription of equity shares
	◆ **Bank Deposit** in Capital gain deposit account scheme and amount withdrawn from this deposit for purchase or construction above
Exemption available to the extent of	Investment in new asset ÷ Net Consideration × capital gain. Exemption cannot exceed capital gains.
Exemption availed is withdrawn	If equity shares in eligible company are **transferred** within 5 years of its acquisition or the new asset is sold or transferred by the eligible company within 5 years of tis acquisition (where the new asset is a computer or computer software of eligible start up which is transferred in 3 years) **if the deposit account is not utilized fully**

	or partly by the eligible company to purchase new asset within 1 year of subscription
Consequences of withdrawal of exemption	Exemption is rolled back and become taxable as long-term capital gains in the year of default

Eligible company [under Sec. 54GB(6)(b)] is one which fulfils the following conditions:

(*a*) it is incorporated in India up to the due date of furnishing the return of the previous year in which capital arises;

(*b*) it is engaged in the business of any article or thing;

(*c*) it qualifies to be a small or medium enterprises under Micro, Small and Medium Enterprises Act, 2006; and

(*d*) the assessee (seller of the residential house or plot) has more than 50% share capital or 50% of the voting rights.

New machinery or plant does not include—

(*a*) any machinery or plant, used by any other person either within or outside India.

(*b*) any machinery or plant, installed in any office premises or any residential accommodation or guest house;

(*c*) any office appliance including computer or computer software;

(*d*) any vehicle, or

(*e*) any machinery or plant, the whole cost of which is allowed as deduction in computing profits and gains of business or profession.

Common Points for consideration for all exemptions above where an option to deposit the capital gains in the Deposit Scheme is available

Consequences of non-utilisation of bank deposit: Where bank deposit is not utilised in purchasing a residential house within 2 years after the date of transfer or in constructing a residential house within 3 years of the date of transfer, unutilised deposit is deemed to be long-term capital gain of the relevant previous year in which the time-limit of 3 years expires.

Deposit remaining untilised due to the death of the depositor: Where the assessee individual dies without utilising the deposit within the prescribed period, the unutilised amount cannot be treated income of the deceased. This amount is not taxable in the hands of legal heirs also as the untilised deposit does not partake the character of income in their hands. It is only part of the estate, devolving upon them [Circular No. 743 dated 6.5.1996].

Consequences of not Investing Capital Gain on or before the Due Date of Furnishing Return: Where the assessee has not purchased a residential house within one year before the date of the transfer or has not purchased or constructed a residential house on or before the due date of furnishing return of income, or has not deposited the unutilised capital gain before the due date of furnishing return of income under Capital Gain Scheme Account, 1988, capital gain becomes chargeable to tax during that previous year. Accordingly, he has to pay tax.

COMPUTATION OF CAPITAL GAINS IN SPECIFIED CIRCUMSTANCES

Capital Gains on Distribution of Assets by a Company in Liquidation [sec. 46] - Where the assets of a company are distributed to its shareholders on its liquidation, such distribution shall not be regarded as a transfer by the company for the purposes of Section 45. Only where the assets of a company are distributed in specie to its shareholders on its liquidation, it is not regarded as transfer by the company. If, however, the liquidator sells the assets of the company resulting in capital gain, company is chargeable to tax on such capital gain [*Sri Kannan Rice Mills Ltd.* v. *CIT* (1954) 26 ITR 351 (Mad.)].

Tax liability of a Shareholder on Distribution of Assets by a Company in Liquidation [sec. 46(2)]: As such money received by a shareholder from the company upon liquidation would not be taxable since the money received by him represents only satisfaction of the right belonging to such shareholder by virtue of his holding the shares and not by operation of any transaction which amounts transfer such as sale, exchange, relinquishment or other transfer of his shares [*CIT* v. *Madurai Mills Company Ltd.* (1973) 89 ITR 45 (SC)]. Therefore, the distribution of assets to shareholders by a company is deemed to be a transfer under sec. 46(2).

Thus, where a shareholder receives any money or other assets from the company on liquidation of the company, capital gains tax is chargeable in the hands of the shareholder. The portion of distribution attributable to the accumulated profits is chargeable to tax as divided income [under sec. 2(22)]. The balance portion of distribution, if any, is taken as the full value of consideration for ascertaining the capital gains.

Where payment is made in instalments, cost of acquisition to be deducted against first instalment: If the payment by liquidator is made in instalments, the cost of acquisition cannot be deducted at every point of time when there is a receipt from the liquidator. The entire cost of acquisition should be deducted at the time when first instalment is paid. It may result into capital loss. Such loss may be set off/carried forward as per rules in this behalf. When any subsequent instalment is received, it is fully taxable as capital gain [*CIT* v. *Inland Agencies (P.) Ltd.* [1982] 11 Taxman 218/(1983) 143 ITR 186 (Mad.)].

Value of asset received on liquidation to be determined by the Assessing Officer: The value of the assets received by a shareholder on liquidation is determined (for the purpose of capital gains) by the Assessing Officer. The value as determined by the Assessing Officer may be independent from what the liquidator has evaluated. The Assessing Officer is required to value such asset on its market value.

Computation of Capital Gain on Subsequent Transfer of a Capital Asset, Received by a Shareholder on Liquidation: Where a shareholder is assessed to income tax under the head "capital gains" in respect of the asset acquired on the liquidation of a company, the cost of acquisition of the capital assets acquired by him on the liquidation of the company is taken to be its fair market value (as determined by the Assessing Officer on the date of such distribution [Sec. 55(2)(*b*)(*iii*).].

If he has not been assessed to income tax, the cost of acquisition of assets acquired on the liquidation of a company is deemed to be the cost for which the company (under liquidation) acquired it, as increased by the cost of any improvement of the assets incurred or borne by the company or the assessee [Sec. 49(1)(*iii*)(*c*)].

If a shareholder, after receipt of any assets on the liquidation of the company transfers it at a price which is in excess of his cost of acquisition (as aforesaid) he is liable to income tax on such excess, as capital gains.

CAPITAL GAIN ARISING ON BUY BACK OF SHARES [SEC. 46A]

Where a company buys back its shares or securities, the difference between the value of consideration received and cost of acquisition is taxed in its hands of the shareholders as capital gain in the year in which such shares were purchased by the company.

A recent decision of Bangalore Bench of Tribunal held that buyback of shares by subsidiary company from its parent company will be taxable in the hands of the parent company under sec. 46A and the subsidiary company ought to have withheld tax on payment. It was held that exemption under sec. 47(*iv*) was not available since parent company was not holding whole of share capital of subsidiary company along with nominees, transaction of buy back of shares was not covered under section 47(*iv*) [*Acciona Wind Energy (P.) Ltd.* v. *Dy CIT* (2020) 113 taxmann.com 443/180 ITD 792 (Bang-Trib.)].

CAPITAL GAINS IN CASE OF SLUMP SALE [SEC. 50B]

"Slump sale" means the transfer of one or more undertakings as a result of the sale for a lump sum consideration without values being assigned to the individual assets and liabilities in such transfer [Sec. 2(*42C*)]. Any profit and gains, arising from slump sale in the previous year, is chargeable as capital gains arising from the transfer of long-term capital asset and is deemed to be profits of the previous year in which transfer took place. However, where the undertaking is held by the assessee for not more than 36 months prior to the date of its transfer, the capital gain is chargeable to tax as short-term capital gain.

Since the statute uses the term slump 'sale' there existed a controversy whether it should be strictly construed so as to cover only those transactions that meet the classical requirement of sale, that is when transfer is accompanied by monetary, and only monetary consideration; or could slump sale provision also apply when consideration was received in the form of shares and thereby being an exchange. The courts were divided in their opinion on this issue. The Bombay High Court in *CIT* v. *Bharat Bijlee Ltd.*[2014] 46 taxmann.com 257/224 Taxman 282/365 ITR 258 (Bom.) restricted the meaning of slump sale as only transfers that were purely sale in return of monetary consideration, so that when preference shares or bonds were received as consideration, it was an exchange and hence no longer a sale. The Delhi High Court in *SREI Infrastructure Finance Ltd.* v. *Income-tax Settlement Commission* [2012] 20 taxmann.com 476/207 Taxman 74/251 CTR 129 (Delhi) took a view that the expression 'sale' in the term 'slump sale' should not be given a restrictive meaning so as to apply it only to 'sales' in a narrow sense and not to 'transfers' under section 2(*47*) that included exchange.

The Finance Bill, 2021 has put this controversy to rest. Slump sale has been defined as the transfer of one or more undertakings by any means for a lump sum consideration without values being assigned to the individual assets and liabilities in such sales [Sec. 2(*42C*)]. Thus, the broad view taken by the Delhi High Court has been endorsed by the legislature.

Thus, the following conditions should be satisfied to treat a sale as slump sale:

(i) *Transfer of an undertaking:* There should be transfer of an undertaking. For the purposes of this clause an "undertaking" includes any part of an undertaking or a unit or division of an undertaking or a business activity as a whole but does not include individual assets or liabilities or any combination thereof not constituting a business activity [*Explanation I* to Sec. 2(*19AA*)].

(ii) *Transfer should be by way of sale:* It is a voluntary transfer for money consideration. Thus, other forms of transfer, *i.e.* exchange or compulsory acquisition, etc., are not covered by slump sale.

(iii) *Transfer for lump sum consideration:* The transfer of undertaking should be made for a lump sum consideration without assigning values to individual assets and liabilities, If it is possible to identify the price attributable to individual assets separately from the slump price, the transaction would not be regarded as in the nature of slump sale [*CIT* v. *Electric Control Gear Manufacturing Co*. (1997) 93 Taxman 384/227 ITR 278 (SC)].

However, determination of the value of an asset or liability for the sole purpose of payment of stamp duty, registration fees or other similar taxes is not regarded as assignment of values to individual assets or liabilities [Explanation 2 to Sec. 2(*42C*)].

Computation of capital gains:

It is computed as below:	₹
Sale consideration of the undertaking	....
Less : Net worth of the undertaking	(-) ....
Capital gain : Short-term or Long-term on the basis of period of holding	....

Computation of Net worth and Fair Market Value - The Finance Act, 2021 has substituted the existing provision of Sec. 50B(2) as follows: Net worth of the undertaking or the division, as the case may be, shall be deemed to be the cost of acquisition and the cost of improvement for the purposes of Sec. 48 and Sec. 49 and no regard shall be given to the provisions contained in the second proviso to Sec. 48 with respect to indexing cost of acquisition and improvement. Fair market value of the capital assets as on the date of transfer, calculated in the prescribed manner, shall be deemed to be the full value of the consideration received or accruing as a result of the transfer of such capital asset. In the case of capital asset being goodwill of a business or profession, which has not been acquired by the assessee by purchase from a previous owner, nil [*Explanation 2(aa)*].

The assessee is required to attach a certificate of the Chartered accountant along with the return to the effect that net worth has been correctly computed [Sec. 50B(3)].

CAPITAL GAINS IN CASE OF DEPRECIABLE ASSETS [SEC. 50]

The capital gain on the transfer of a depreciable asset is computed in the following manner:

Where the entire Block of Asset does not cease to exist: In case of partial sale of block of assets, if sale consideration exceeds the aggregate of (i) expenditure incurred in connection with transfer + cost of acquisition of block of assets (*i.e* opening written down value + cost of any asset acquired during the year), such excess shall be deemed as short term capital gain.

Where the entire Block of Asset ceases to exist [Sec. 50(2)]: The scheme of depreciation is closed and written down value of the block of assets is taken as nil.

FMV Not Applicable in Respect of Depreciable Assets: The cost of the acquisition depreciable asset is bound to be computed in accordance with sec. 50. Where an assessee has enjoyed depreciation allowance, its cost of acquisition is determined as provided in Sec. 50 which has a reference to written down value only and which has nothing to do with fair market value. Sec. 55(2) is applicable only in respect of sections 48 & 49 of the Act and it has no application to Sec. 50 of the Act (*Common Wealth Trust Ltd.* v. *CIT* (1997) 94 Taxman 137/228 ITR 1 (SC); *CIT* v. *Peirce Leslie & Co. Ltd*. [1998] 99 Taxman 471/(1997) 227 ITR 759 (Mad.)].

From the assessment year 2021-2022, goodwill of a business or profession is not considered as a depreciable asset and there would not be any depreciation on goodwill. However, where goodwill is purchased by an assessee, the purchase price of the goodwill will continue to be considered as cost of acquisition for the purpose of computation of capital gains under sec. 48. If depreciation was obtained by the assessee in relation to such goodwill prior to the assessment year 2021-22, then the purchase price of the goodwill will be reduced by depreciation so obtained. Accordingly Finance Act, 2021 inserted a proviso to sec. 50 with respect to goodwill. A further consequential clarification has been inserted by virtue of an Explanation by the Finance Act, 2022. It is clarified that for the purposes of sec. 50 reduction of the amount of goodwill of a business or profession, from the block of asset in accordance with sec. 43(6)(*c*) item (*ii*) of sub-item (B) shall be deemed to be transfer.

Special Provision for computation of Capital Gains in case of Market Linked securities and Specified Mutual Fund (newly inserted sec. 50AA)

The Finance Act, 2023 newly inserted sec. 50AA for the computation of capital gains arising on transfer or redemption or maturity of Market Linked Debenture or Specified Mutual Funds. Accordingly, irrespective of the period of holding of MLDs or Specified Mutual Fund, the capital gains arising there from shall be deemed to be a short-term capital gain.

For the purposes of this section "specified mutual fund" means a mutual fund where not more than 35% of its total proceeds is invested in the equity shares of domestic companies. "Market Linked Debenture" means a security which has an underlying principal component in the form of a debt security and where the returns are linked to market returns on other underlying securities or indices and include any security classified or regulated as a market linked debenture by the Securities and Exchange Board of India.

REFERENCE TO VALUATION OFFICER BY THE REVENUE IN CERTAIN CASES [SEC. 55A]

With a view to ascertaining the fair market value of a capital asset for computing the capital gains, the Assessing Officer may refer the valuation of the capital asset to a Valuation Officer in the following cases:

(*a*) Where the assessee has got the asset valued by a registered valuer and the Assessing Officer is of the opinion that the value as estimated by the registered valuer is less than the fair market value of the asset.

(*b*) (*i*) Where the Assessing Officer is of the opinion that the fair market value of the asset exceeds the value of the asset as claimed by the assessee by more than 15% of or by more than ₹ 25,000, whichever is less (Rule 111AA).

(*ii*) Where having regard to the nature of the asset and other relevant circumstances, the Assessing Officer considers it necessary to do so. It is open to the Assessing Officer to make a reference to the Valuation Officer in such a case [under Sec. 55A(*b*)(*ii*)].

Assessing Officer is bound to give Due Consideration to All Material Available to him: The powers under Sec. 55A is not arbitrary and has to be exercised by the Assessing Officer on the basis of the materials on record, nature of the asset and other relevant circumstances. For example, where an assessee determines the cost of acquisition of a building constructed by it on the basis of books of account maintained and supported by it, a reference to the District Valuation Officer may arise only in a case where either the Assessing Officer has strong reason to disagree with the accounts of construction produced or where even though such account is kept but the assessee instead relies on the valuation report of the registered valuer. [*CIT* v. *Hotel Joshi* [2000] 108 Taxman 199/(2002) 242 ITR 478 (Raj.)].

Assessment to be quashed when made without considering valuation report after making a reference: Where, after making a reference to the Valuation Officer under Sec. 55A, the ITO completes the assessment even before the receipt of the Valuation Officer's report, the valuation proceedings are liable to be quashed [*Reliance Jute & Industries Ltd.* v. *ITO* (1984) 150 ITR 643 (Cal.)].

Second Reference is Permissible: The ITO is not prohibited from making a second reference when the first reference is found to be not competent [*Daulatram* v. *CIT* (1990) 181 ITR 119 (AP)].

Opportunity of being Heard to be Given: Reference to Valuation Officer cannot be made without giving assessee an opportunity of being heard and without disclosing reasons therefor [*Prem Hotel* v. *ITO* (1997) 93 Taxman 237 (J&K)].

EXEMPTIONS ON CERTAIN CAPITAL GAINS [SEC.10]

◆ **Capital Gains on transfer of bond or Global Depository Receipt, rupee denominated bond of an Indian company etc. by a non-resident [Sec.10(4C)]**

Any income accrued or arisen to, or received by a specified fund as a result of transfer of capital asset referred to in sec. 47(*viiab*) on a recognised stock exchange located in any International Financial Services Centre and where the consideration for such transaction is paid or payable in convertible foreign exchange, to the extent such income accrued or arisen to, or is received in respect of units held by a non-resident.

◆ **Capital Gains on Transfer of a Unit of Unit Scheme, 1964 of UTI [Sec. 10(33)]**

Where a unit of the Unit Scheme, 1964, referred to in the Schedule I of the Unit Trust of India (Transfer of Undertaking and Repeal) Act, 2002 is transferred on or after 1 April 2002, any capital gain, whether short-term or long-term, arising from such unit is exempt from tax.

◆ **Capital Gain arising to an individual or an HUF from compulsory acquisition of agricultural land situated in rural areas [Sec. 10(37)]**

An individual or a Hindu undivided family is entitled to claim exemption in respect of capital gain, which accrues or arise from the compulsory acquisition of agriculture land, subject to the following conditions:

(*i*) **Agricultural land must be situated in rural area as defined in sec. 2(14)(*iii*)** - Agriculture land should be situated in 'Rural Area'. Thus, if agriculture land is situated in 'Urban Area', no exemption is available for any capital gain which accrues or the transfer of such land.

(*ii*) **Such land must be used for agriculture purposes for 2 Years** - HUF or the individual or any of the parent of the individual should have used the land for agricultural purposes for 2 years prior to the date of transfer.

(*iii*) **Transfer is by way of Compulsory Acquisition or Consideration for Transfer is Determined by the Government** - The transfer of land should be by way of compulsory acquisition under any law or the consideration for its transfer should be determined or approved by the Central Government or the Reserve Bank of India. Such "compensation or consideration" also includes compensation or consideration enhanced or further enhanced by any court, Tribunal or authority or (*iii*) a unit of business trust (w.e.f. 01-04-2015).

(*iv*) **Receipt of Compensation or Consideration** - It should be received on or after 1 April 2004.

Interest on compensation would partake of character of compensation and would be eligible for exemption under section 10(37) [*Smt. Lakshmamma* v. *ITO* [2020] 113 taxmann.com 572/182 ITD 408 (Bangalore Trib.)].

◆ **Capital Gain arising to an individual or an HUF from transfer of land or building under Land Pooling Scheme of Andhra Pradesh [sec.10(37A)]**

An individual or a Hindu undivided family is entitled to claim exemption in respect of capital gains, which accrues or arise from transfer of land or building or both where such assessee was the owner of such capital asset as on the 2nd day of June, 2014 and transferred the same under the Land Pooling Scheme covered under the Andhra Pradesh Capital City Land Pooling Scheme (Formulation and Implementation) Rules, 2015 made under the provisions of the Andhra Pradesh Capital Region Development Authority Act, 2014.

◆ **Capital Gain Arising from the Transfer of assets by a Power Generation Undertaking to Notified Indian Company [Sec. 10(41)]**

Where an asset of an undertaking, engaged in the business of generation, transmission or distribution of power, is transferred on or before 31 March 2006 to an Indian company, notified by the Central Government under Sec. 80-IA(4)(*a*)(*v*), any income by way of capital gain from such transfer is exempt from tax.

TAX ON CAPITAL GAINS

Long-term Capital Gains Tax		**Short-term Capital Gains Tax**	
All assesses (sec.112) Where 'individual or 'Hindu undivided family' is 'resident' in India during the previous year and total income after reducing 'long-term capital gain' is below the exemption limit, the amount of long-term capital gain, after reducing it by the amount of such deficiency, is charged @ 20%	20%	Where short-term capital gain arises from the transfer of equity shares or a unit of an equity oriented fund or a unit of business trust and such transaction is chargeable to STT (securities transaction tax) (sec.111) Where total income as reduced by the amount of short-term capital gain, is less than the exemption limit, such	15%

Long-term Capital Gains Tax		Short-term Capital Gains Tax	
		amount is deducted from short-term capital gain for calculating tax thereon Where gross total income includes short-term capital gain, deductions from gross total income are allowed after deducting short-term capital gain' from gross total income. (sec. 111A).	
Where Non-Residents earn long-term capital gain from unlisted securities (sec. 112)	10%		

Long term capital gains on Equity Shares/Units of Equity Oriented Fund/ Units of Business Trust [Sec. 112A]

The Finance Act, 2018 inserted a new Sec. 112A to provide the rate of tax on long term capital gains arising on the transfer of equity shares in a company or unit of Equity oriented fund or units of a business trust. Earlier by virtue of Sec. 10(38) these capital assets being equity shares, units etc were exempt from long term capital gain if securities transaction tax (STT) was paid. However, it was observed that with the equity market becoming buoyant, a large part of the exempted capital gains from listed shares and units accrued in the hands of the corporates and LLPs. This had led to an investment bias whereby more business surpluses were being invested in financial assets instead of in manufacturing. Since the return on investment in equity was already quite attractive even without tax exemption, the exemption was therefore sought to be withdrawn and the long term capital gains on transfer of equity shares, units etc. are now taxed under Sec. 112A. However, transactions undertaken on a recognised stock exchange located in any International Financial Services Centre and where the consideration for such transaction is paid or payable in foreign currency are outside the scope of Sec.112A and continue to enjoy exemption under Sec.10(38).

The following conditions must be fulfilled before applying Sec. 112A:

(*a*) The transfer should be that of listed equity shares, units of a mutual fund and units of a business trust

(*b*) It should be a long-term capital asset

(*c*) STT is paid on listed equity shares both at the time of acquisition and transfer; and at the time of transfer in case of units of equity oriented funds or business trust.

The Finance Act, 2021 has amended the definition of 'equity-oriented fund' [*Explanation (a)*] to cover the high premium ULIPs (Unit Linked Insurance Premiums) if such fund invests minimum 90% (in case of investments in other units listed on a recognised stock exchange) or 65% (in any other case) in equity shares of a domestic company.

Accordingly, where the long term Capital Gain on the transfer of the equity shares, units etc exceeds ₹ 1,00,000, then the amount in excess of ₹ 1,00,000 shall be chargeable to tax at the rate of 10%.For example, if an assessee has a long term capital gain of ₹ 3,00,000 under Sec. 112A, tax @10% is payable on ₹ 2,00,000 (being ₹ 3,00,00 – ₹ 1,00,000).

Further, according to the proviso to Sec. 112A(2) in case of a resident individual or HUF whose total income after reducing the long-term capital gains is below the basic exemption limit, the long-term capital gains under this section stands reduced by such shortfall. For example, assuming 'A' in the above example is a resident individual with total income is ₹ 4,00,000 and the net long-term capital gains as calculated above is ₹ 2,00,000. Here, the balance income after reducing capital gains is ₹ 2,00,000 which is below the basic exemption limit applicable to such individual ₹ 2,50,000. The amount by which the reduced total income falls short of basic exemption limit is ₹ 50,000 (₹ 2,50,000 – ₹ 2,00,000). The 10% tax rate under Sec. 112A will be applied on ₹ 1,50,000 (₹ 2,00,000 – ₹ 50,000) (and not ₹ 2,00,000).

With the insertion of Sec.112A w.e.f. 1.4.2019, a corresponding clause was also inserted in Sec. 55(2) to provide for the determination of cost of acquisition of the assets referred to in this section. Accordingly, where an equity share, units etc. referred in this section is acquired before 1st February 2018, the cost of acquisition of such asset shall be :-

(*a*) Cost of Acquisition of the asset and

(*b*) least of (*i*) fair market value of the asset as on 31st January, 2018 and (*ii*) Full value of consideration received or receivable as a result of the transfer;

whichever is higher [Sec. 55(2)(*ac*)].

CHAPTER 10 Income from Other Sources

INTRODUCTION

Income from other sources is a residuary head of income and sweeps in all such incomes which fall outside the specific heads. The residuary head is resorted to if none of the specific head is applicable. However, if the charge under that head exhausts the taxability of the income, no part of such income can be brought to tax under the residuary head [*Nalinikant Ambalal Mody* v. *S.A.L.Narayana Rao, CIT* (1966) 61 ITR 428 (SC)].

Income under the head "income from other sources" must come from a definite source which would be regarded as a real source of income [*Rhodesia Metals Ltd.* v. *Commrs of Taxes* (1941) GIR 451 (PC); *CIT* v. *Shaw Wallace & Co.* AIR 1932 PC138]. There may be many sources under "other sources"—Income of each source is computed in accordance with the method of accounting regularly followed by the assessee, provided the method is such that the income can be properly deduced therefrom. Thus, in case of an assessee adopts cash system of accounting, his income falling under the head "income from other sources" is to be computed on cash basis and not on accrual basis. However, dividend income is assessable when it is declared or distributed but interim dividend is taxable on receipt basis [Sec. 8].

CHARGING PROVISION

Sec. 56(1) provides that any income which is not chargeable to tax under the four heads of income - Salary, House Property, Profits and Gains from Business or Professions, Capital Gains shall be chargeable under the head Income from Other Sources. Sec. 56(2) specifically provides for those incomes which may be taxable under this head.

INCOMES SPECIFICALLY CHARGEABLE UNDER OTHER SOURCES [SEC. 56(2)]

The following incomes are specifically provided to be taxable under this head:

Dividends [sec. 56(2)(i)] (for detailed discussion on dividend, please refer to Chapter 16 Dividend)

Divided received by shareholders from domestic company: Since domestic companies were liable to pay tax on distribution of dividend on dividends declared by them, such dividend income was exempt in the hands of shareholders u/s

10(34). However, the Finance Act, 2020 has abolished DDT and therefore the liability to pay tax on dividend income is now placed on the door step of the shareholder and tax rate will apply in accordance with the tax slab of their total income be it individual shareholders or corporate shareholders.

Dividend received by shareholders from a foreign company: Dividend Incomes received from foreign companies is taxable as Income from Other sources and chargeable to tax as per the slab rates applicable to the shareholder. Insofar as corporate shareholders are concerned when resident companies receive dividend from other domestic companies, they shall be taxed as per the applicable corporate tax rates. When Indian Holding companies receive dividend income from their Foreign Subsidiary, such dividend is taxable @15% under sec. 115BBD without any allowance for deducting expenditures.

Any Winnings [sec. 56(2)(*ib*)]

This includes winning lotteries, crossword puzzles, races, including horse races, card games and other games of any sort or from gambling or betting of any form or nature whatsoever.

In computing the taxable income from any winning by way of lottery, crossword puzzle, races including horse races, card games and other games of any sort or from gambling or betting, no deduction is allowed in respect of any expenditure incurred in earning such income [Sec. 58(4)]. However, an assessee is entitled to claim deduction for any revenue expenditure incurred in owing and maintaining race horses to run in horse race on which wagering or batting is lawfully allowed [Proviso to Sec. 58(4)].

Income from lottery winning, crossword puzzle and horse race winning is subject to deduction of tax at source. Tax at source is deducted when winning from lottery, crossword puzzle card game or any other game (sec.194B) and in case of winnings from horse race (sec. 194BB) when these exceed ₹ 10,000.

Case Law : ***CIT* v. *G.R. Karthikeyan* (1993) 68 Taxman 145/201 ITR 866 (SC)**

Facts: 'G' participated in a motor rally that was organized to test the endurance driving and reliability of automobile. He won first prize. Chargeability of the prize money was rendered questionable whether the same was winnings from a race or game. Tribunal had held that a rally was neither a race nor a game, therefore prize money could not be charged to tax.

Held: The rally was a contest, if not a race. the concerned receipt being prize money was a casual receipt but nevertheless an income chargeable to tax as income from other sources.

Case Law : ***CIT* v. *A. U. Chandrasekharan* (1998) 229 ITR 406 (Madras)**

Facts: Ten persons entered into a written agreement to jointly purchase lottery tickets and had an oral understanding of dividing the money equally, if any of the tickets won. One such ticket won and the amount which was equally divided within the ten people.

Held: The income is to be treated as 'income from other sources' in the hands of the ten persons as an Association of Persons.

Employee's Contribution to Provident Funds [Sec. 56(2)(*ic*)]

Contributions received by the assessee-employer from his employees of any provident fund or superannuation fund or any fund set up under the provisions of the Employees' State Insurance Act, 1948 or any other fund for the welfare of the employees, are treated as taxable income if such contributions have not been credited to the account of employees under the relevant fund on or before the due date under the relevant law or contract of service. Such income is taxable under other sources if it is not taxable as business income.

Interest on Securities [Sec. 56(2)(*id*)]

This will be discussed later in this chapter. If this type of income is not taxable as business income, then they are taxable under this head.

Meaning of Interest on securities - Interest on securities means—

(*i*) interest on any security of the central government or a state government;

(*ii*) interest on debentures/other securities for money, issued by or on benefit of a local authority or a company or a corporation, established by a central or state or provincial Act [Sec. 2(*28B*)].

Securities may be classified with reference to issuing authority and with reference to mode of payment of interest as below:

"Less tax" security implies that tax is deducted at source and the net amount is paid to the security-holder. In practice, the word "less tax" is generally not used. Security is always presumed to be "less tax" unless specified to be "tax free".

The word "tax free" security implies that no tax has been deducted at source. The security-holder has been paid "gross interest" without deduction of tax at source. Only the government has a right to issue such securities. If any company or any other authority issues tax-free security, it has to pay income tax to the government on the amount of interest paid to the security-holder without deduction of tax at source. Hence, interest from commercial (private) tax-free securities is always to be grossed up.

Basis of Charge - If the assessee follows mercantile system of accounting, interest on securities is taxable on due basis. If he follows cash system of accounting, it is taxable on receipt basis.

Sale of Securities and Chargeability of Interest - Interest on securities does not accrue from day-to-day but it accrues on specific date, *i.e.* yearly, half-yearly or quarterly. Therefore, the interest on securities is chargeable to tax in the hands of one who holds the securities on the due date of interest. This rule remains unaffected by the sale of securities. Where securities are sold before the due date of interest, the price as paid to the seller by the purchaser may include the interest due to the seller up to the date of sale. But for the purposes of taxation the amount of interest is not apportionable on a time basis between the seller and the purchaser. The purchaser is assessable on the whole interest as he holds the securities on the due date of interest.

Income from Letting of Machinery, Plant or Furniture [Sec. 56(2)(*ii*)]

If these assets belong to the assessee, any income from their letting is not chargeable to income tax under the head "profits and gains of business or profession".

Machinery, plant or furniture are commercial assets: Any lease thereof is to be regarded as a business transaction, yielding a business income. Two tests are applied to distinguish a lease from a business transaction. First, if a machinery, plant or furniture is let out when it is no longer a commercial asset (*i.e.* it is now obsolete or old and so not fit for business use), the rental income derived from such letting is chargeable to tax under "other sources". Second, even if it is a commercial asset but the assessee closed down or decided to close down his business, the rental income from machinery, plant or furniture in such a case is regarded as an income from "other sources". If neither of the two characteristics appear in a transaction of lease of machinery, plant or furniture, such transaction is regarded as a business transaction. Any income resulting therefrom is chargeable as a "business income".

If the machinery, plant or furniture do not belong to the assessee, the rental income therefrom is always a business income. So, in a case where the assessee is himself a hirer of the machinery, plant or furniture the income derived by him from sub-letting of machinery, plant or furniture is a business income.

Case Law: ***Express Newspapers (P.) Ltd. v. CIT* [1997] 92 Taxman 496/227 ITR 325 (Madras)**

Facts: 'E' a private limited company, discontinued its activity of publishing newspapers and got them published through its sister concern and received hiring charges for the printing machinery and motor vehicles which according to 'E' ought to be assessed as its business income.

Held: When the income is not earned in the course of business, it cannot be assessed under the head 'Business income'. In order to consider whether an asset is a commercial asset 'E' must do his business by exploiting the said asset. Admittedly the business of publication and printing was discontinued. Therefore, the printing machinery and the motor vehicles could not be considered to be commercial assets. the income derived by letting out the machinery and the motor vehicles as income 'from other sources'.

Income under Inseparable Letting of Plant and Machinery along with Building [Sec. 56(2)(*iii*)]

Income from letting of machinery, plant or furniture belonging to the assessee along with building under an inseparable letting, is chargeable as income from 'other sources' if the same is not chargeable to tax under the head, "profits and gains of business or profession".

Normally, the income from letting of a building is chargeable to tax under the head "income from house property". But where machinery, plant or furniture belonging to the assessee are let along with building and the letting of building is inseparable from the letting of the said machinery, plant or furniture, the rental income from such letting may be chargeable to tax under "other sources", if the same is not chargeable to tax as a business income. The word "inseparable" does not connote that the machinery, plant or furniture should by its very nature be inseparable from the building so that the building has also necessarily to be let along with it, or that it should be fixed to building. The inseparability arises from the intention of the parties—the parties should intend that the subject matters of the lease should be enjoyed together and the letting of the building and of the other assets should be practically on letting.

Inseparability of the plant, machinery etc. and the building: The inseparability referred is one that arises from the intention of the parties and not necessarily by the physical inseparability by its very nature. It does not matter if the building or plant, machinery of furniture are let out under the same lease or separate lease as long as the intention is that they should be enjoyed together [*Sultan Brothers Pvt. Ltd.* v. *CIT* (1964) 51 ITR 353 (SC)]. The Supreme Court in *Sultan Brothers Pvt. Ltd.* v. *CIT* (1964) 51 ITR 353 (SC) gave the following three tests to ascertain if the intention of the parties was to make the two lettings inseparable or not:

(*i*) Was it the intention in making the lease-and it matters not whether there is one lease or two, that is, separate leases in respect of the furniture and the building-that the two should be enjoyed together?

(*ii*) Was it the intention to make the letting of the two practically one letting?

(*iii*) Would one have been let alone and a lease of it accepted without the other?

If the answers to the first two questions are in the affirmative, and the last in the negative then, it has to be held that it was intended that the lettings would be inseparable.

Case Law: ***Jay Metal Industries (P.) Ltd.* v. *CIT* [2017] 84 taxmann.com 11/ 249 Taxman 450 (Delhi)**

Facts: 'J' a company let out the premises comprising of basement, ground floor, first floor and second floor to one party on monthly rent with the amenities like wooden cabins and wooden empanelling, central air conditioning, adequate power back up and treated incomes thereof as 'Income from House Property'. The Assessing Officer characterized the same as 'Income from other sources'.

Held: The preamble clauses of the lease deed make it plain that letting is not merely of the building but a composite letting of both, the building as well as the equipment, furniture etc. and thereby section 56(2)(*iii*) was attracted.

Case Law : ***M. K. Dar* v. *CIT* (1982) 8 Taxman 176 (Allahabad)**

Facts: 'M' and another person purchased a land, constructed and furnished a cinema building and leased it. They entered into two separate lease deeds and received rent for the building and the furnishing and fixtures separately.

Held: There were two leases—one letting out of the fully furnished cinema building and the other relating to the fixtures, furnishing and electrical fittings, etc. It was specifically provided that the hirer would not remove from the fixtures from cinema building which would continue to be used in the same manner and that the hiring of the furniture would be renewed along with that of the lease of the cinema building. It was thus apparent (i) that the two leases were intended to be enjoyed together and the intention was to have a single transaction split into two documents ', and (ii) that the lease of the fixtures and furnishing, etc., would not have been accepted without the lease of the cinema building. Therefore, the income from the cinema building and furniture was inseparable and composite and would be assessable as income from other sources.

Sum received under a Keyman Insurance Policy [Sec. 56(2)(*iv*)]

Any sum received under a "keyman insurance policy" including the sum allocated by way of bonus on such policy is treated as income from "other sources", if the same is not taxable under the head "profits and gains of business or profession" or under the head "salaries".

Forfeiture of advance money [Sec. 56(2)(*ix*)]

Any money that was received as advance for the transfer of capital asset which is later on forfeited and the negotiations does not result in transfer of the asset will be taxable under this head.

Share Premium received by a closely held company [Sec. 56(2)(*viib*)]

Any consideration received by a private company (closely held company) as share premium from any person shall be taxable.

This clause does not apply for consideration for issue of shares received by a venture capital undertaking from a venture capital company or a venture capital fund or a specified fund or by a company from a class or classes of persons so notified by the Central Government. For this purposes, specified fund means a fund established or incorporated in India in the form of a trust or a company or a limited liability partnership or a body corporate which has been granted a certificate of registration as a Category I or a Category II Alternative Investment Fund and is regulated under the Securities and Exchange Board of India (Alternative Investment Fund) Regulations, 2012 made under the Securities and Exchange Board of India Act, 1992 or (w.e.f. 1.4.2023) regulated under the International Financial Services Centres Authority Act, 2019.

Where a company having fulfilled these conditions subsequently fails to comply, share premium will be treated as income of such company in the year of such default and will be deemed that the company has under reported its income and the consequences of misreporting shall follow [Proviso II to sec. 56(2)(*viib*) w.e.f. 1.4.2020].

Any gift of money, immovable property etc received from unrelated persons on or after 1 April 2017 [Sec. 56(2)(*x*)]

The Gift Tax Act, 1958 imposed a gift tax on the donor at a flat rate of 30%. However in October 1998 gift tax was abolished. Later on in the year 2004 it was re-introduced under the head 'Income from other sources' and is taxable in the hands of the recipient at regular tax rates applicable to such recipient. As it stands today, the following form of gifts received by a person from another unrelated person will be its income from other sources:

Money Gift - Where any sum of money, the aggregate value of which exceeds ₹ 50,000, is received without consideration, the whole of the aggregate value of such sum is taxable.

Immovable Property:

(*a*) *Received without consideration:* Where any immovable property with a stamp duty value exceeding ₹ 50,000 is received without consideration, the stamp value of such property is taxable.

(*b*) *Received without adequate consideration:* Where such immovable property is received for a consideration and the stamp duty value of such property exceeds consideration by more than ₹ 50,000 and the amount equal to 20% of the consideration. Where the stamp duty value of immovable property is disputed by the assessee under sec. 50C(2), the Assessing Officer may refer the valuation of such property to a Valuation Officer and such value shall apply for this section.

Any Property Other than immovable property:

(*a*) *Received without consideration:* Where any property other than immovable property is received without consideration and the aggregate fair market value of such property exceeds ₹ 50,000, the entire aggregate fair market value is taxable.

(*b*) *Received without adequate consideration:* Where such property is received for consideration which is less than the aggregate fair market value of the property, by ₹ 50,000, the difference between the two is taxable.

For this purposes property means the following capital asset of the assessee, namely

(*i*) immovable property being land or building or both

(*ii*) shares and securities

(*iii*) jewellery

(*iv*) archaeological collections
(*v*) drawings
(*vi*) paintings
(*vii*) sculptures
(*viii*) any work of art
(*ix*) bullion

The Finance Act, 2022 has further provides that the expression "property" shall include virtual digital asset.

Exception [Proviso to Sec. 56(2)(x)] - Money or property received is not taxable in the following cases:

(*i*) individual from any relative;

(*ii*) on the occasion of the marriage of the individual;

(*iii*) under a Will or by inheritance;

(*iv*) received in contemplation of death of the payer or donor;

(*v*) received from any local authority as defined in the *Explanation* to Sec. 10(20);

(*vi*) received from any fund or foundation or university or other educational institution or hospital or other medical institution or any trust or institution under Sec. 10(23C) (however w.e.f. 1.4.2023 where any sum of money or any property has been received by any person referred to in sec. 13(3) including the founder or author of the trust or the relative of the trust etc., this exception shall not apply [newly inserted Proviso II to sec. 56(2)(*x*) by the Finance Act, 2022]);

(*vii*) from or by any trust or other institution registered under Sec. 12A or 12AA or 12AB (however w.e.f. 1.4.2023 where any sum of money or any property has been received by any person referred to in sec. 13(3) including the founder or author of the trust or the relative of the trust etc., this exception shall not apply [newly inserted Proviso II to sec. 56(2)(*x*) by the Finance Act, 2022]);

(*viii*) by any fund or trust or foundation or university other educational institution or any hospital or any other medical institution referred to in sub-clause (*iv*) or sub-clause (*v*) or sub-clause (*vi*) or sub-clause (*via*) of Sec. 10(*23C*);

(*ix*) by way of transaction not regarded as transfer under Sec. 47(*i*), (*iv*), (*v*), (*vi*), (*via*), (*viaa*), (*vib*), (*vic*), (*vica*), (*vicb*), (*vid*), (*vii*) as well as (*viiac*), (*viiad*), (*viiae*), (*viiaf*) w.e.f. 1.4.2022;

(*x*) from an individual or trust created or established solely for the benefit of relative of the individual;

(*xi*) from such class of persons and subject to such conditions, as may be prescribed.

For this purposes "relative" means,—

(*i*) in case of an individual—

(A) spouse of the individual;

(B) brother or sister of the individual;

(C) brother or sister of the spouse of the individual;

(D) brother or sister of either of the parents of the individual;

(E) any lineal ascendant or descendant of the individual;

(F) any lineal ascendant or descendant of the spouse of the individual;

(G) spouse of the person referred to in items (B) to (F); and

(*ii*) in case of a Hindu undivided family, any member thereof

Gift of money made by a non-relative to a minor: Gift of money made by a relative to a minor cannot be treated income of minor. If such gifts are made by a non-relative to a minor, it is treated income of the minor and it is included in the total income of that parent whose income is greater [Sec. 64(1A)].

Sum of money received on the occasion of the marriage: The phrase 'on the occasion of marriage' does not imply on the date of marriage [*CGT* v. *KBB Subudhi* (1993) 201 ITR 741 (Ori.)]. If the gift was associated with the event of the marriage or if the reason of immediate cause of gift was marriage, it is covered by the expression 'on the occasion of marriage' and exemption would apply [*CGT* v. *Dr. (Mrs.) Neelam Ramaswami* [1986] 24 Taxman 287/(1987) 164 ITR 369 (Mad.)]

Gift maurtiscausa: Such gifts are made by an individual who expects to die shortly because of illness. Such gifts are of movable property only. Title of such gifts pass to the donee only after the death of the donor. Thus, if the donor recovers from illness, the gift becomes void and donee has to return it back to the donor.

Individual as well as an HUF may claim exemption in respect of gifts, received in contemplation of death of the donor.

Sum of money received from charitable entity: The exemption is available to both—an individual and an HUF.

Burden of proof on the donee: The donee may claim exemption if he can prove that it was a *bona fide* gift, entitled to exemption. Therefore, it is advisable for him to obtain written confirmation from the donor along with other details including his PAN, etc. If the donee fails to prove the credentials of the gift, the Assessing Officer is free to invoke the provisions of Sections 68 to 69C and the threshold limit of ₹ 50,000 under Sec. 56(2)(*vi*) would not apply.

The Finance Act, 2022 makes an exception of not taxing the receipt under this provision as income from other sources when the money or any property was received for any illness related to COVID-19. The newly inserted exceptions shall apply with retrospective effect from 1.4.2020. Accordingly, when an individual received money or any property from any person, in respect of any expenditure actually incurred by him on his medical treatment or treatment of any member of his family, for any illness related to COVID-19 subject to such conditions, as the Central Government may, by notification in the Official Gazette, specify in this behalf [clause (*xii*) to Proviso to sec. 56(2)(*x*)]. Further, when upon death of an individual due to illness related to COVID-19, a family member of such deceased person received any sum from the employer of the deceased person or any sum from any person not exceeding ₹ 10 lacs will also form an exception. Such payment should be received within twelve months from the date of death of such person; and subject to such other conditions, as the Central Government may, by notification in the Official Gazette, specify in this behalf [clause (*xii*) to Proviso to sec. 56(2)(*x*)].

Income by way of interest received on compensation or enhanced compensation [Sec. 56(2)(*viii*)]

Interest received on compensation or enhanced compensation as referred to in Section 145B.

Sum received during negotiations for transfer of a capital asset [Sec. 56(2)(*ix*)]

Any sum of money received as an interest or otherwise in the course of negotiations for transfer of a capital asset, if the sum is forfeited during the course of negotiations, or if the negotiations do not result in transfer of such capital asset.

Compensation in connection with termination of employment [Sec. 56(2)(*xi*)]

Any compensation or other payment, due to or received by any person, in connection with the termination of employment or the modification of the terms and conditions relating to employment.

Sum received on redemption of units by business trust [Sec. 56(2)(*xii*)]

Income from Insurance Policies [Sec. 56(2)(*xii*)] - Where premium or aggregate of premium is ₹ 5,00,000 or more and any sum is received under an insurance policy (other than ULIP) issued after 1.4.2023, such sum will be charged as income from other source

Miscellaneous instances of incomes chargeable under this head

Besides the aforesaid incomes, the following incomes are chargeable under this head as they are not covered under any other head:

(1) Director's fees and director's commission for underwriting shares of a new company.

(2) Income derived by sub-letting a house by a tenant.

(3) The salaries of a Member of Parliament.

(4) Examinership fee received by a lecturer from a university.

(5) Unexplained investments in the construction of house property.

(6) Interest on own contribution to an unrecognised provident fund.

(7) Interest on loans, bank deposit or current account, and interest payable under a decree.

(8) Interest received on excess payment of advance tax (u/s 234B) or interest received on delayed refunds (u/ss 243 and 244).

(9) Interest under National Deposit Scheme is taxable (u/s 56) in the year of accrual.

(10) Interest on cumulative deposit scheme of private sector is taxable (u/s 56) on accrual basis annually.

(11) Income from sub-letting any vacant plot of land.

(12) Ground rent.

(13) Insurance commission.

(14) Beneficiary getting income portion from Wakf.

(15) Income from market rights, fisheries, rights of ferry or moorings, grazing rights.

(16) Mining rent and royalties.

(17) Annuity payable under Will.

(18) Income from forest produce.

(19) Interest on foreign government securities.

(20) Family pension, *i.e.* a regular monthly payment by an employer to the heir of a deceased employee.

Case Law: ***Tuticorin Alkali Chemicals & Fertilizers Ltd.* v. *CIT* (1997) 93 Taxman 502 (SC)**

Facts: 'T' had borrowed funds for the purposes of setting up of the factories and during construction and establishment of its factory but before commencement of manufacturing activities, invested the said funds in short-term deposits with banks and earned interest thereon. In its return, it disclosed the interest earned as income from other sources and after setting off same against business loss claimed carry forward of remaining loss. Later on, it filed revised return claiming that interest will have to be capitalised and since the interest income will go to reduce the pre-production expenses, the interest income was not exigible to tax.

Held: Tax is attracted at the point when the income is earned Taxability of income is not dependent upon its destination or the manner of its utilisation. It has to be seen whether at the point of accrual, the amount is of the revenue nature and if so, the amount will have to be taxed. The interest earned by the assessee was clearly its income and unless it could be shown that any provision like section 10 had exempted it from tax, it will be taxable.

Case Law : *CIT* v. *Bokaro Steel Ltd.* (1999) 102 Taxman 94/236 ITR 315 (SC)

Facts: 'B' was a company being set up to produce steel and while the steel plant was yet under-construction, 'B' earned interest on advances to contractor, rent from quarters let out to employees of the contractor, hiring charges for letting plant and machinery to the contractor, royalty income for excavation and use of stones lying on 'B's land for construction work.

Held: Unlike interest earned by investing borrowed capital in short-term deposits which was an independent source of income not connected with the business activities; incomes earned through the utilisation of various assets of the company and the payments received for such utilisation are directly linked with the activity of setting up the capital structure *i.e.* steel plant of the assessee. Such incomes are capital receipts and not income from other sources.

Case law : *CIT* v. *Shree Rama Multi Tech Ltd.* (2018) 92 taxmann.com 363 /255 Taxman 136 (SC)

Facts: 'S' engaged in the manufacture of plastic products, was statutorily required to keep share application money in the separate account till the allotment of shares was completed. 'S' earned interest income on this money and issue arose if it is chargeable as income from other sources.

Held: Since the share application money that is received is deposited in the bank in light of the statutory requirement, the accrued interest is not liable to be taxed and is eligible for deduction against the public issue expenses

ALLOWABLE DEDUCTIONS [SEC. 57]

The following expenditures are allowed to be deducted from various incomes earned under this head:

- **Expenditures for earning dividend income [sec. 57(i) and (iii)]** - Where dividend is assessable to tax as business income, any expenditure, which is neither of capital nature, nor of personal nature, incurred wholly and exclusively for the purposes of earning dividend income is fully deductible. Thus, any reasonable sum paid for collecting the dividend income is fully deductible. Thus, commission paid to bank or remuneration payable to any person for realising the dividend income on behalf of the assessee is deductible. A foreign company is not entitled to this deduction in computing its taxable income from dividend [Sec. 115A(3)].

  Interest on moneys borrowed for purchasing the shares is allowed to be deducted against income from shares. The deduction is allowed even if no income is earned from shares by way of dividend. Section 57(*iii*) does not say that the deduction is permissible only when the income has been earned or profit or gain made. All that it speaks of is that the expenditure must have been laid out solely for the purposes of earning dividend income [*CIT* v. *Rajendra Prasad Moody* (1978) 115 ITR 519 (SC)].

  Interest paid on borrowing utilised by the assessee to purchase the shares in the name of his wife and minor child, is an allowable deduction in computing his taxable income [*Amar Chand Jalan* v. *CIT* (1986) 24 Taxman 468 (Bom.)].

Interest paid on loan treated as dividend under Sec. 2(22)(*e*) is not to be deducted [*Nandlal Kanoria* v. *CIT* (1980) 122 ITR 405 (Cal.)].

Where any interest, chargeable to tax, is payable outside India, no deduction is allowed if tax has not been deducted or paid in accordance with TDS provisions. The restriction does not apply to a loan, issued for public subscription before 1 April 1938. [Sec. 58(1)(*a*)(*ii*)].

Where dividend is taxable under the head other sources, the assessee can claim deduction of only interest expenditure which has been incurred to earn that dividend income to the extent of 20% of total dividend income.

No Deduction is allowed against Exempted Dividends. No deduction is allowed in respect of any interest or any expenditure incurred in relation to income which does not form part of total income [Sec. 14A]. In other words, any expenditure incurred in relation to exempted income cannot be deducted. For details, please refer to Chapter 4 "Incomes Exempt from Tax".

Thus, where a domestic company paid dividend distribution tax under Sec. 115-O on the amount of dividends paid or distributed, such dividend was exempt from tax [Sec. 10(34)]. Hence, no deduction was allowed in respect of any interest or collection charges against such dividends.

- **Expenditures on earning interest on securities [Sec. 57(i) and (iii)] -** Any reasonable sum paid by way of commission or remuneration to a banker or any other person for the purpose of realising such interest on behalf of the assessee.
- **Contributions credited to the Employee's Provident Fund [Sec. 57(*ia*)] -** When employers having received contributions from his employees towards any provident fund or superannuation fund etc. had not credited these to the account of employees under the relevant fund on or before the due date under the relevant law or contract of service, such amounts were treated as income from other sources for the employer. A deduction shall be allowable in accordance with the provisions of sec. 36(1)(*va*), *i.e.*, if the employer has credited the employee's accounts in the respective funds with the amounts of contributions received, the employer shall be allowed credit thereof.
- **Expenditure on income derived from letting [Sec. 57(ii), (iii)] -** The following expenditures are allowed as deduction from income derived from letting out of machinery, plant etc. and also when these are let together with building and two is inseparable:
  - (*i*) Current repairs of building
  - (*ii*) Insurance premium against risk of damage or destruction to premises

(*iii*) Repairs and insurance of machinery, plant or furniture

(*iv*) Depreciation

Where the expenses referred to at (*a*) to (*d*) hereinabove are incurred on property used partly for the business of the assessee, a proportionate deduction shall be allowed.

- **Standard deduction on income in the nature of family pension [Sec. 57(*iia*)]** - When family pension is received *i.e.* a regular monthly amount payable by an employer to the family of the deceased employee, a sum equal to 33-1/3% of the income or ₹ 15,000, whichever is less, is allowable as a deduction.
- **50% deduction on Interest on compensation or enhanced compensation [Sec. 57(iv)]** - When compensation is received for termination of employment, 50% of such compensation or enhanced compensation is allowed as deduction. However, no deduction shall be allowed under any other clause of this section.
- **Other deductions [Sec. 57(iii)]** - Any other expenditure incurred wholly and exclusively for the purpose of earning the income is deductible, provided it satisfies the following conditions :

  (*i*) It must not be in the nature of personal expenditure of the assessee;

  (*ii*) It must not be in the nature of capital expenditure; and

  (*iii*) It must be laid out or expended in the relevant previous year and not in any prior or subsequent year.

  No deduction other than expenditure on interest shall be allowed from the dividend income or income in respect of units of a Mutual Fund specified under sec. 10(*23D*) or units of specified company defined in *Explanation* to sec. 10(*35*). Such deduction shall be restricted to maximum at 20% of dividend income included in the total income [Proviso to sec. 57 w.e.f. 1.4.2021).

AMOUNTS NOT DEDUCTIBLE [SEC. 58]

Following expenses cannot be allowed in the computation of taxable income:

(*i*) Any personal expenses of the assessee

(*ii*) Any interest, chargeable under this Act, which is payable outside India on which tax has not been paid or deducted at source.

(*iii*) Any payment, chargeable under the head "salaries", payable outside India is not to be deducted unless tax has been paid or deducted therefrom in accordance with provisions of TDS.

(*iv*) Any payment which is not deductible in computing taxable profits of business or profession under Sec. 40A is also disallowed.

CHAPTER 11 Income of Other Persons included in Assessee's Total Income

INTRODUCTION

As a general rule an assessee is taxed only in respect of its own income and not that of others. However, in certain specified circumstances, an exception is made to the above rule and the assessee is liable to tax for income of another person. Such clubbing of income of another in the hands of the assessee is resorted to address strategic tax reduction arrangements of the assessee. Accordingly, sec. 60-64 specify conditions under which incomes of another person are clubbedin with the total income of the assessee. It is important to note that the clubbing provisions are not charging provisions, but have been enacted with the intention of preventing tax avoidance, by plugging loopholes which permit taxpayers to divert their income into the hands of others, while still enjoying the benefits of it. [*R.P. Sarathy* v. *Joint Commissioner of Income Tax* (2019) 104 taxmann.com 92/263 Taxman 149/414 ITR 161 (Madras)].

INCOME ARISING TO THE SPOUSE

Remuneration earned by the spouse without the necessary qualifications from a concern where assessee has substantial interest [Sec. 64(1)(*ii*)]

If an individual has got a substantial interest in a concern, any income by way of salary, commission, fee or in any other form of remuneration to the spouse of the said individual from that concern is included in the total income of such individual, provided the earning spouse of the said individual does not possess technical or professional qualification, or if the spouse does possess technical or professional qualification, then the income received was not attributable to said qualification [Sec. 64(1)(*ii*)]. The income to the spouse of the said individual from that concern may arise directly or indirectly and it may be in cash or in kind.

Clubbing provision is applicable if the following conditions are satisfied:

(*i*) *Relationship of spouse at the time of accrual of income:* The relationship of husband and wife must exist at the time of accrual of such income. Thus, income of the spouse derived before marriage cannot be clubbed [*Philip Job Plask Thomas* v. *CIT* (1963) 49 ITR 97 (SC)].

Clubbing provisions will apply if the relationship of husband and wife exists at time of accrual of income during the previous year but it does not exist in the assessment year.

(ii) *Income not attributable to the technical or professional qualification of the earning spouse:* Clubbing provisions are applicable, provided remuneration is not attributable to the technical or professional qualifications, possessed by the earning spouse. Where income is solely attributable to the application of technical or professional qualification, possessed by the earning spouse, clubbing provisions do not apply. Such remuneration is assessable as the personal incomes, of the earning spouse.

However, mere possession of technical or professional qualification will be not sufficient and it must be shown that such technical and professional knowledge and experience was also applied to earn the income. These two conditions are cumulative and not alternative. It is only on satisfaction of the first condition that the second condition would be looked into. The first condition determines the eligibility of the spouse, while the second condition determines which income would be saved from being clubbed with that of the assessee [*Yashwant Chhajta* v. *Dy. CIT* (2013) 29 taxmann.com 393/214 Taxman 280 (Himachal Pradesh)]. Thus, where Mrs. R, a practising lawyer, is engaged by G Ltd., where her husband holds substantial interest therein, fees paid to Mrs. R by G Ltd., is assessable as her income because such income is solely attributable to the application of professional qualification.

(iii) *Liberal construction of the words 'technical' or 'professional':* The words "technical or professional qualification" must receive a liberal construction, as the term has not been defined in the Section or anywhere else in the Act [*CIT* v. *Mrs. R. Jaya Lakshmi* [1998] 101 Taxman 350/[1999] 240 ITR 773 (Mad.)]. Technical or professional qualification does not imply obtaining a certificate, diploma or a degree from a recognised body like a university, or institute. Requisite experience is also a qualification. Thus, where the husband, an experienced salesman, earns commission on sales from a concern, such commission cannot be included in the total income of the wife, holding substantial interest in the concern [*CIT* v. *Madhubala Shrenik Kumar* (1989) 47 Taxman 85/(1990) 181 ITR 180 (MP)].

(iv) *Test of substantial interest:* The spouse of the individual, who earns remuneration from the concern, must hold substantial interest in the concern.

An individual is deemed to have substantial interest in a company if its equity shares carrying not less than 20% of the voting power are, at any time during the previous year, owned beneficially by such individual either alone or with one or more of his/her relatives.

In case of a non-company concern, an individual is deemed to have a substantial interest therein if he/she, either by self or with one or more relatives, is entitled in the aggregate, at any time during the previous year, to not less than 20% of the profits of such concern [*Explanation 2* to Sec. 64(1)(*ii*)].

"Relative" in relation to an individual means the husband, wife, brother, or sister or any lineal ascendant or descendant of that individual [Sec. 2(41)].

The expression "concern" is a word of wide importance and take within its sweep and ambit of all organisations or establishment, engaged in business or profession, whether owned by a company, partnership, or individual or any other entity [*Dr. J.M. Makashi* v. *CIT* [1994] 72 Taxman 98/207 ITR 252 (Mad.)].

(*v*) *Application of clubbing provisions where both spouses have got substantial interest*: Where both husband and wife have substantial interest in the concern and both are in receipt of remuneration from such concern, the remuneration from such concern is included in the total income of the husband or as the case may be, the wife whose total income excluding such remuneration is greater [*Explanation 1* to Sec. 64(1)(*ii*)].

(*vi*) *Clubbing provision mandatory:* If the requisite conditions have been satisfied, the clubbing provision is bound to operate even though tax burden of the assessee is reduced.

Case Law : ***Yashwant Chhajta* v. *Dy. CIT* (2013) 29 taxmann.com 393/214 Taxman 280 (Himachal Pradesh)**

Facts: The assessee was engaged in the business of civil construction, where his wife was employed and was drawing a salary. The wife held a degree in electrical engineering, and the assessee claimed a deduction on the amount of salary that was paid to her, so that the amount would not be clubbed within his total income.

Held: For the proviso to Sec. 64(1)(*ii*) to apply, not only must the spouse hold a technical or professional qualification (which she did in this case), but also that they applied this technical or professional knowledge when deriving the income in question. The Proviso must be strictly construed and therefore, the burden is on the assessee to conclusively prove that the wife was involved in the plans for executing the work or in the administrative decisions. As he failed to do so, the deduction was disallowed, and the income was clubbed with his total income.

Case Law : ***A.D. Kushalappa* v. *Income Tax Officer* (2004) 91 ITD 212 (Bangalore)**

Facts: The assessee and his wife were both partners in a firm. The wife was also receiving certain remuneration from the firm. The issue before the Bangalore ITAT was whether the wife's graduate degree in arts was sufficient technical qualification to run a hardware shop, thereby preventing her income from being clubbed into the total income of her husband.

Held: The Tribunal held that in the case of a working partner in a firm, it is not necessary for the spouse to hold a degree or diploma from a university, but it would be enough to hold an educational qualification which is sufficient to allow her to discharge the duties which earn her the remuneration. Accordingly, her income in the present case was not clubbed with that of her husband's under Sec. 64(1)(*ii*).

Income from an asset transferred by the assessee to the spouse for inadequate consideration [Sec. 64(1)(*iv*)]

Where an individual transfers an asset, directly or indirectly, to his/her spouse for inadequate consideration, income arising from the transferred asset is included in the total income of the transferor [Sec. 64(1)(*iv*)]. For instance, Mr. A gifts bonds and debentures to Mrs. A. Interest income from bonds/debentures is to be included in the total income of Mr. A.

Clubbing provision is applicable if the following conditions are satisfied:

(i) *Relationship of spouse to exist on the date of transfer as well as during the year:* The relationship of husband and wife must exist among the transferor and transferee at the time of transfer as well as at the time of accrual of income during the year [*Vinod Kumar Ratilal* v. *CIT* 100 ITR 564 (Guj.) & *CIT* v. *Ashok Kumar* [1996] 84 Taxman 138/217 ITR 251(All.)]. Thus, transfers made prior to marriage do not fall within the ambit of taxing provision [*Philip John Plasket Thomas* v. *CIT* [1963] 49 ITR 97 (SC)]. The word "wife" or "spouse" does not include a female with whom the assessee has an illicit connection, even for a long period - Executors of the will of T.V. [*Krishna Iyer* v. *CIT* [1960] 38 ITR 144 (Ker.)].Therefore, any income derived by a concubine from an asset transferred to her by her "keeper", cannot be included in the total income of her "keeper". If either of the spouse dies, the clubbing provision does not apply.

(ii) *Transfer of Asset be made for Inadequate Consideration:* The clubbing provision is applicable if the transfer of asset by one spouse to the other spouse is made for inadequate consideration. If the transfer of asset is made for adequate consideration, clubbing provision does not apply. Love and affection do not constitute adequate consideration [*Tulsidas Kilachand* v. *CIT* [1961] 42 ITR 1 (SC)]. As one of the conditions for the application of this provision is that the consideration for the asset be inadequate, it is also necessary that the adequacy of the consideration be such that its value is measurable in either terms of money or money's worth [*Potti Veerayya Sresty* v. *CIT* (1972) 85 ITR 194 (AP)].

Transfer of property by a Hindu father in discharge of his obligation to provide for his daughter's marriage and maintenance may be a transfer for adequate consideration [*CGT* v. *Bandi* [1987] 32 Taxman 88/167 ITR 66 (AP)]. Similarly, transfer of property by a Muslim to his wife in discharge of his liability for deferred dower debt to her is a transfer for adequate consideration [*Ghiasuddin Babu Khan* v. *CIT* [1986] 25 Taxman 252/[1985] 153 ITR 707 (AP)].Where the consideration for the transfer is inadequate, proportionate income to the extent of inadequacy of consideration may be included in the income of the transferor spouse [*H. N. Patwardhan* v. *CIT* (1970) 76 ITR 279 (Bom.)]. Also *see, Dr. N. Kumara Rao* v. *CIT* [1987] 35 Taxman 142/(1988) 169 ITR 128 (AP)]. However, the other view is that entire income is to be clubbed with the income of the transferor-spouse. The Section does not postulate the principle of proportionality, determined by inadequancy of consideration.

Transfer may be a direct transfer, a cross transfer or an indirect transfer: Transfer may be (*i*) direct, (*ii*) a cross transfer, or (*iii*) an indirect transfer including when the original asset is converted into another asset. Thus, assets transferred to a trust for the benefit of settler's spouse is covered by indirect transfer.

"Cross transfer" is also covered by Indirect Transfer: If two or more transfers are inter-connected and are parts of the same transaction in such a way that it can be said that the circuitous method has been adopted as a device to evade implication of the provisions of Sec. 64, the case falls within this Section [*CIT* v. *Keshavji Morarji* (1967) 66 ITR 142 (SC)].

The question of inter-connection between two transfers being parts of the same transaction and being a device to evade the implications of these provisions is a question of fact to be decided in each case by looking at the evidence on record. For example, A gifts ₹ 1,00,000 to the wife of his brother, Mrs. B. B in turn transfers an asset of equal worth to Mrs. A, wife of his brother A. Each of the two transfers (by A and B) may be regarded as an indirect transfer by each to his own wife [*Sital Chaudhry* v. *CIT* (1979) 119 ITR 698 (Cal.)].

Indirect Transfer Covers Conversion of Original Asset into some other Asset: Thus, where securities gifted by A to Mrs. A are converted by Mrs. A into shares of a foreign company, dividend income falls within the clubbing net [*CIT* v. *CM Kothari* (1963) 49 ITR 107 (SC)].

Capital Gains arising to the transferee from the subsequent transfer of the asset are also clubbed: Where an individual transfers an asset directly or indirectly to his spouse without adequate consideration, income from such asset is included in the total income of the transferor [Sec. 64(1)(*iv*)]. Income includes capital gain [Sec. 2(24)]. Hence, capital gain arising on the transfer of such asset is also included in the total income of the transferor.

When the asset is invested by the spouse into a business, the proportionate business income is also clubbed with that of the assessee: Where the assets transferred directly or indirectly by an individual to his spouse without adequate consideration are invested by the transferee-spouse in business, income arising from the business to the transferee-spouse is to be apportioned in proportion of the value of transferred assets to the total investment of the transferee-spouse in the business on the first day of the previous year. The proportionate amount of income relating to the proportionate value of the transferred asset without adequate consideration is includible in the income of the transferor-spouse (*Explanation 3* to Sec. 64).

Assessee cannot claim Adjustment of Advance Tax paid by Transferee on Income from the Transferred Asset: There is no provision under the Income-tax Act to enable the transferor to seek adjustment of the advance tax paid by the transferee on the income from the assets transferred. The transferee should seek a refund of tax in such cash [*Shanti Lal* v. *CIT* (1984)145 ITR 789 (MP)].

Clubbing Provisions are to be read Harmoniously with the other Provisions of the Act: Where an asset is transferred by a non-resident individual to his spouse for inadequate consideration, clubbing provisions remain applicable if income from asset transferred is received or deemed to be received in India or such income is accruing/arising or deemed to accrue or rise in India as per provisions of Sec. 5. If such income does not satisfy the test of Sec. 5, the transferor cannot be assessed on such income under Sec. 64 [*CIT* v. *FY Kambty* (1986) 24 Taxman 29/159 ITR 203 (Bom.)].

Exclusions from the Scope of Clubbing

Pin Money not to be Clubbed Pin-money is an allowance made to a woman by her husband for meeting her personal expenses or for running the household. Such sum and any saving made by the wife out of such sum would be the separate property of wife and cannot be aggregated with the income of the husband [*R. Dalmia* v. *CIT* (1982) 9 Taxman 171/133 ITR 169 (Delhi)].

Income from accretion to the asset not to be clubbed Any income from the accretion of transferred asset is not to be clubbed with the income of transferor. Similarly, if husband gifts certain properties to his wife, the income from such properties is to be included in the income of the husband, but if the wife utilises such income to acquire further property, the income out of such further property is not included in the income of the husband. For example, Mr. J gifted shares of F Ltd., a foreign company, to Mrs. J during PY 2010-2011. F Ltd., issued bonus shares to Mrs. J during the year 2014-2015 and paid dividends of ₹ 40,000 including ₹ 10,000 on bonus shares. Dividends of ₹ 30,000 is assessable in the hands of Mr. J and dividends of ₹ 10,000 is included in the total income of Mrs. J.

Exceptions to the Rule on Clubbing

Transfer of Asset in Connection with an Agreement to Live Apart Where an individual transfers an asset, directly or indirectly, to his/her spouse under an agreement to live apart, income from such asset is assessable in the hands of the transferee spouse.

Transfer of House Property for Inadequate Consideration Where an individual transfers a house property to his/her spouse for inadequate consideration, and the income from house property is chargeable under the head "income from house property", the transferor is deemed to be the owner of the such property [Sec. 27(*i*)]. Thus, the transferor spouse is assessable on the income from such house property.

Case Law : ***Auto Sales Properties* v. *CIT* (2007) 294 ITR 507 (Allahabad)**

Facts: The two assessees let out a building to a firm in which their wives each had a 47% share. The ordinary rent for the building was ₹ 7,515 per month, but the building was leased to their wives' firm at a rent of ₹ 4,000 per month. The revenue department clubbed the income earned by the firm from the building with that of the husbands.

Held: For Sec. 64(1)(*iv*) to apply, there were two conditions to be met: *first* that there was a direct or indirect transfer of the asset to the spouse; and *second*, that the transfer was neither for adequate consideration nor under agreement to live apart. The first condition was met, as the transfer was made to a partnership firm where the wives held a 94% share, effectively making it an indirect transfer of the asset in their favour.

The second condition was also met, as they were given the building at nearly half its ordinary rate, and there was no evidence of any agreement to live apart. Therefore, Sec. 64(1)(*iv*) was applicable in this case.

Case Law : ***ITO* v. *Gulam Abbas Abdullabhai Makati* (1994) 49 TTJ 620 (Ahmedabad - Trib.)**

Facts: The assessee and his brother gifted each other's wives identical sums of cash, which then enabled them to become partners of a firm. The issue was whether the income would be clubbed even though the transfer of the asset had not been made to the spouse of the assessee.

Held: The two gifts were clearly part of the same transaction, and that the arrangement had been entered into with the intention of circumventing the implications of Sec. 64(1)(*iv*). Accordingly, the provisions of the section would apply to the cross gifts, and the assessee's total income would include the income earned by his wife from the partnership.

Case Law : ***Damodar K. Shah* v. *CIT* (2001) 119 Taxman 882/252 ITR 235 (Gujarat)**

Facts: 'D' took a life insurance policy with his wife as the beneficiary and paid the premiums on the policy and his wife received certain amounts, which she then invested and earned interest incomes from it. The revenue authorities clubbed this interest with the income of 'D', which he appealed on the grounds that his obligation to pay the premium was a contractual one, and therefore, it could not be said that the amounts later received by his wife were transferred to her by him for immediate or later benefit.

Held: The Court observed that the initial wording of Sec. 64(1) includes all income arising *directly or indirectly*, and later on in sub-clause (*iv*), this income could arise from a transfer of assets which could be *direct or indirect*. The use of the term 'indirectly' at two separate places meant that the provision was broad enough to be interpreted in light of the objective, *i.e.* to tax the income of the wife in the hands of the husband where the income arises from the transfer of an asset by the husband to the wife. In the present case, the interest on the investments indirectly arose out of the income received by the wife through the cash money which was transferred to her indirectly, having been converted from insurance payments into the final payout. Therefore, the full amount of interest earned by investing the maturity returns of the policy were liable to be clubbed with the income of the assessee.

Case Law : ***Sevantilal Maneklal Sheth* v. *CIT* (1968) 68 ITR 503 (SC)**

Facts: 'S' gifted his wife certain ordinary shares as well as certain preference shares in a company that were subsequently sold by his wife and earned capital gains. This gain was then invested as deposit in a firm where 'S' and his son were partners, where the money earned some interest.

Held: There was no distinction between income arising from the asset transferred and income from the sale of the asset transferred. Accordingly, the capital gains were to be included in 'S's total income.

Case Law : ***Uday Gopal Bhaskarwar* v. *ACIT* (2020) 113 taxmann.com 378/182 ITD 216 (Pune - Trib.)**

Facts: 'U' gifted certain amount to his wife, who then used this sum to start a business of Futures and Options (F&O). This business subsequently incurred losses, for which a set off was sought by 'U'.

Held : Such entire amount of loss incurred in the business by the wife could be clubbed with the income of the 'U'.

Income from an asset transferred to son's wife for inadequate consideration [Sec. 64(1)(*iv*)]

Where an asset is transferred by an individual to son's wife directly or indirectly, on or after 1 June 1973, without adequate consideration, the income from such asset is to be included in the total income of the transferor. Where the assets are invested by the transferee in any business or as a partner in a firm, *Explanation 3* would still apply.

Transfers effected up to 31 May 1973 are unaffected by these provisions. The clubbing applies only to the extent of inadequacy of consideration. Relationship of son's wife must exist at the time of transfer as well as at the time of accrual of income.

Case Law : ***Om Dutt* v. *CIT* (2005) 277 ITR 63 (Punjab and Haryana)**

Facts: The two assessees - A and B - were partners in a firm. C, the daughter-in-law of A, and D, the daughter-in-law of B were then inducted into the partnership. C invested a sum of money which was gifted to her by B, and D invested a sum of money which was gifted to her by A. The issue was then whether the shares of income accruing to C and D could be included within the total income of A and B respectively.

Held: The Court held that the Assessing Officer was justified in clubbing the income of C and D with the total income of A and B, and the cross gifts were merely an attempt to indirectly transfer the assets to their sons' wives and therefore, it was rightly clubbed with the income of the donors.

INCOME ARISING TO A MINOR CHILD [SEC. 64(1A)]

Income arising to a minor child (legal child, including an adopted child or stepchild) is included in the income of the parent who [Sec. 64(1A)]:

- Where the marriage subsists, has a higher income
- Where the marriage no longer subsists, maintains the child

Where marriage of the parents subsists, any income accruing or arising to the minor child is included in the total income of that parent whose income, before inclusion of such income, is greater. Where the income of the minor child is included in the income of one parent, it cannot be included in the total income of the other parent in subsequent years. The Assessing Officer may, however, club the minor's income with that of the other parent if he considers it necessary to do so. For this purpose, he has to give the other parent an opportunity of being heard [*Explanation* to Sec. 64(1A)].

Where marriage of the parents does not subsist, any income accruing or arising to the minor child is included in the total income of that parent who maintains the child. Once any such income is included in the total income of either parent, the same income arising in a subsequent year shall not be switched to the total income of the other parent unless the Assessing Officer has given that parent a sufficient opportunity to be heard [*Explanation* to Sec. 64(1A)].

The term "minor" has not been defined in the Act. A child continues to be minor till he attains the age of 18 years. Where guardian has been appointed by the Court, the child continues to be minor till he attains the age of 21 (Sec. 3 of the Majority Act, 1957). Clubbing applies only in respect of the income of a legitimate child. Adopted child or step child is a legal child. Clubbing provisions do not apply to the income of an illegal child.

Income to be clubbed is computed under each head of income and is clubbed under each head of the income of the parent. Permissible deductions are allowed from the income so clubbed [*Amarchand Jalan* v. *CIT* (1986) 24 Taxman 468/160 ITR 805 (Bom.)].

Rules on Clubbing

Agricultural Income is Excluded

When the income accruing to the minor children is in the nature of agricultural income, the same is not included in the total income of the parent for the purposes of clubbing under Sec. 64(1A). Reading Sec. 2(10) with Sec. 5 and Sec. 10(1), agricultural income does not form a part of the total income of either the minor or the parent [*Smt. Babita P. Kanungo* v. *Dy. CIT* (2005) 96 ITD 91 (Mum. - Trib.)].

Accrual of Income during Minority

Clubbing of income applies where income accrues during the minority and it is enjoyed by the minor during the period of minority. Thus, where income accruing to the minor under certain settlement is required to be accumulate during minority and has to be given to him after he attains majority, the clubbing provision falls to the ground [*CIT* v. *M.R. Doshi* [1996] 85 Taxman 591/ [1995] 211 ITR 1 (SC)].

Where a minor has been admitted for benefits in a partnership firm and he has attained majority during the year but profits under the partnership deed are to be ascertained only at the end of the accounting year, proportionate profits up to the date when he attained majority cannot be clubbed with the income of parent [*Bhogilal Leharchand* v. *CIT* [1955] 28 ITR 919 (Bom.)].

Exceptions to the Rule on Clubbing

Income earned by Manual Work: Any income derived by the minor child from manual work is excluded from clubbing provision. Minor child is assessable on such income through his guardian.

Income earned by Skill: Any income derived by a minor child by application of his skill, talent or specialised knowledge and experience is excluded from clubbing provision. Minor child is assessable on such income through his guardian. Thus, income earned by a minor child from acting in a film or from stage performance is taxable in his hands. Similarly, income derived by a minor child from winning crossword puzzle or card games remain outside the clubbing provision. However, income earned from lottery winnings is covered by clubbing provision.

Minor Child suffering from physical disability: Income of a minor child suffering from physical disability, has been excluded from the clubbing provisions from the assessment year 1995-1996.

Case Law : ***R.P. Sarathy* v. *Jt. CIT* (2019) 104 taxmann.com 92/263 Taxman 149/414 ITR 161 (Madras)**

Facts: The assessee was a minor, whose parents both passed away in a car accident, leaving the assessee with some income from different sources (agricultural income, money-lending and income from a coffee partnership business). The assessee contended that as the clubbing provisions of Sec. 64(1A) could not apply in this case, the income must be left untaxed.

Held: The High Court noted that the clubbing provisions of Sec. 64(1A) would not be attracted in the present case. However, these clubbing provisions are not the charging provision but are merely anti-evasive measures to plug loopholes in taxing the income of minors. Prior to the insertion of Sec. 64(1A), it was not the case that the income of a minor is entirely untaxable. Where neither parent is still alive, Sec. 160(1)(*ii*) would apply, wherein the guardian of a minor is the representative assessee who must discharge the obligations arising from the income in question. Therefore, in the present case, the assessee's income would be taxed in the hands of her guardian, which was her grandfather.

INCOME ARISING FOR THE BENEFIT OF THE SPOUSE OR SON'S WIFE [SEC. 64(1)(*vii*)]

Where the income from an asset transferred for inadequate consideration arises to any other person or association of persons, but is wholly or partly used for the benefit of the assessee's spouse or son's wife (in the latter case, provided the transfer is made after 1 June 1973), the income to that extent is included in the assessee's hands.

All income arising directly or indirectly to any person or association of persons from the assets transferred by the assessee directly or indirectly, without adequate consideration is included in the total income of the transferor only to the extent such income is used by transferee for the immediate or deferred benefit of the transferor's spouse [Sec. 64(1)(*vii*)] (this provision also extended to minor children of the assessee, until the Finance Act of 1992 restricted it solely to the spouse).

Where the beneficiaries under the transfer through the media of the third person or association of persons are, besides the spouse of the transferor, certain strangers too, the clubbing operates only to the extent the income is used for the benefit of spouse of the transferor.

The expression "deferred benefit" refers to a benefit deferred to a year subsequent to the accounting year in which the income is taxable.

All income arising directly or indirectly to any person or association of persons from the assets transferred directly or indirectly by an individual on or after 1 June 1973, without adequate consideration is included in the total income of the transferor only to the extent such income is used by the transferee for the immediate or deferred benefit of transferor son's wife.

Case Law : ***CIT* v. *Behram B. Dubash* (2005) 149 Taxman 615/279 ITR 377 (Bombay)**

Facts: The case arose prior to the 1992 amendment which excluded minors from the scope of the provision. In pursuance to a decree for divorce in suit filed by his wife, the assessee created a trust for the proper maintenance of their minor child. The issue was whether the legal obligation by virtue of the decree was sufficient consideration for the creation of the trust.

Held: The decree for divorce contained directions to the assessee to provide for the maintenance of the child through the creation of a trust. As the trust was created in order to discharge the pre-existing legal obligation of the assessee, it could not be said that it was made for inadequate consideration and therefore, the provisions of Sec. 64(1)(*vii*) would not be attracted.

INCOME ARISING WHOLLY TO OTHER PERSONS

Income from an asset transferred by the assessee without transfer of the asset itself [Sec. 60]

If any person transfers the income from any asset without transferring the asset, such income is included in the total income of the transferor [Sec. 60]. It is immaterial whether the transfer is revocable or irrevocable, and whether it was made before the commencement of this Act (that is, before 1 April 1962) or after the commencement of this Act. For example, a security holder confers on his nephew the right to receive interest on securities, held by him. Such interest is included in the total income of the transferor.

Mode of transfer: Income may be transferred by any mode. It may be transferred by the way of settlement, trust, covenant, agreement or arrangement. The word "arrangement" is not a word of art; it is used here in a business sense. Dealing with a private company of a family character, with the object of carrying into effect a scheme, may amount to an arrangement.

Where the amounts advanced by the assessee to his three children and his wife could not be considered to be genuine loans, the expression arrangement under Sec. 63(*b*) would clearly cover the transaction of this kind [*S.P. Jaiswal* v. *CIT* 224 [1997] 91 Taxman 99/224 ITR 619 (SC)].

Clubbing Provision Applies even where the Transfer is Irrevocable: If there is a transfer of income but no transfer of the asset from which the income arises, the transferor is chargeable under Sec. 60 even though the transfer may be irrevocable during the life-time of the transferee, and the transferor may derive no direct or indirect benefit from the income transferred.

Section 60 applies to "any person" which includes HUF, firm and company. Thus, where an HUF assigns the right to receive rental income from leasing an asset, in favour of a member of an HUF, the income from leased out asset is included in the total income of HUF.

Section 60 has no application where assets, producing income, are transferred along with the income. That may be the field of operation of Secs. 61 to 64 but certainly not of Sec. 60.

Exception: Where Income is Transferred by Overriding Title

Section 60 has no application where the income stood diverted by an overriding title as a matter of fact even before the accrual of income [*Dalmia Cement* v. *CIT* [1999] 104 Taxman 97/237 ITR 617 (SC)]. Where a portion of the income of an assessee by way of commission was transferred without a transfer of the underlying asset, it would be treated as an application of the income by the assessee for a particular purpose and not a diversion of the income by transfer of overriding title [*CIT* v. *Banwari Lal Agarwala* (1987) 32 Taxman 260/167 ITR 321 (Patna)]. However, where the assessee's right to share in the profits of the firm were transferred to a trust, it would amount to a transfer of the underlying asset and accordingly, Sec. 60 would be excluded from applying to such a transfer [*CIT* v. *Jayantilal D. Patel* [(2007) 162 Taxman 385/295 ITR 386 (Gujarat)]

Case Law : ***CIT* v. *Manharlal Girdharlal Doshit* (1998) 100 Taxman 131/231 ITR 89 (Gujarat)**

Facts: 'M' retired from being a partner in a solicitor firm, following which he was entitled to receive certain share of fees with respect to work he had done prior to his retirement which was irrevocably assigned to a trust through a deed of settlement. 'M' then claimed that as he did not retain any right or entitlements towards income from the firm, the provisions of Sec. 60 would not apply.

Held: From the terms of the settlement, it was clear that 'M' had completely given up any right to receive any income from the firm henceforth and it could not be said that there was no transfer of asset under Sec. 60. 'M' had diverted the income producing apparatus, thereby creating an overriding title in favour of the trust. Since he did not retain any asset with himself w.r.t. the firm, Sec. 60 would not apply in this case.

Case Law : ***Dalmia Cement* v. *CIT* (1999) 104 Taxman 97/237 ITR 617 (SC)**

Facts: The assessee was the owner of a factory in Pakistan, which it agreed to sell to 'M' by an agreement on 24 July 1962. The agreement stated that the profits from 30 September 1962 onwards would be for the benefit of 'M' on the completion of the sale. The sale was finally completed on 30 September 1964. The dispute arose as to whether the income from the factory between 1 October 1962 to 30 September 1964 would be taxable in the assessee's hands.

Held: Once the sale agreement was entered into between the parties in 1962, there was no possibility of the assessee being able to retain the income in their own hands since the overriding title had been transferred to 'M'. It was held that Section 60 would not apply to this case and the profits would not be included in the assessee's total income.

Case Law : ***CIT* v. *Banwari Lal Agarwala* (1987) 32 Taxman 260/167 ITR 321 (Patna)**

Facts: The assessee received a commission from a company to which it had leased out certain coal bearing lands and coal mines among other assets. Under the agreement between them, one third of the commission was paid to the assessee, while the remaining two thirds were paid to a private trust with him and certain family members. The ITO assessed the entire commission as part of the total income of the assessee.

Held: On a comprehensive reading of the agreement between the assessee and the company, there was no transfer of the assets from which the income arose (the coal bearing lands and coal mines). Therefore, the provisions of Sec. 60 would apply, and the entire amount would be included within the assessee's total income.

Case Law : ***CIT* v. *Jayantilal D. Patel* (2007) 162 Taxman 385/295 ITR 386 (Gujarat)**

Facts: The Assessee was a partner in a firm with 60% share. He created a trust for benefit of his children and gifted half of his partnership share to the trust. For the subsequent assessment year, the assessee claimed a deduction of 50% of the profits from his share in the firm, by virtue of the transfer made in favor of the trust. The AO contended that this was an application of the income and not a diversion from the source and therefore, Sec. 60 would apply.

Held: The transfer was not just of the income arising out of the assessee's share in the partnership, but of the assessee's right to share the profits of the firm (which would also include liability to contribute to losses). Therefore, it could not be said that there was no transfer of the asset from which the income arose. Since the income producing apparatus stood transferred, Sec. 60 would not apply.

INCOME ARISING TO ANOTHER PERSON FROM A REVOCABLE TRANSFER OF ASSETS [SEC. 61]

All income arising to any person by virtue of a revocable transfer of assets is included in the total income of the transferor [Sec. 61].

Meaning of revocable transfer When a transfer is deemed to be revocable [Sec. 63]:

(*i*) Where it contains any provision for the transfer, directly or indirectly, of the whole or any part of the income or assets to the transferor [Sec. 63(*a*)(*i*)]; or

(*ii*) Where it gives the transferor a right to resume power, directly or indirectly, over the whole or any part of the income or assets [Sec. 63(*a*)(*ii*)].

Scope of Clubbing Applies to the Whole Income If the transfer is revocable, the entire income of the transferred asset is included in the total income of the transferor. This is so even if only part of the income of the transferred asset had been applied for the benefit of the transferor.

Case Law : *Jyotendrasinhji* v. *S.I. Tripathi* (1993) 68 Taxman 59/201 ITR 611 (SC)

Facts: 'V' executed certain deeds of settlement in the U.S, whereby a trust was created with a bank 'M' as the trustee, which was empowered to collect the income from the trust properties and had absolute discretion on how the income would be distributed. Under the settlement agreement, the income could be paid over to the settlor's family only with the consent of the transferor and the trustee both. On V's death, his son, the appellant contended that the income from the settlements could not be included in his total income, as this was not a revocable transfer under sec. 63 given that the transferor did not have the absolute power to revoke the transfer.

Held: The Supreme Court held that sec. 63 neither requires that the transferor's power of revocation be absolute or unconditional, nor that the transferor have the exclusive power to effect a revocation of the transfer.

Case Law : *CIT* v. *Jitendra Nath Mallick* (1963) 50 ITR 313 (Calcutta)

Facts: The assessee owned certain immovable properties, which he settled through a trust deed, for the benefit of himself and his three sons. The revenue department contended that, as the trust deed contained multiple provisions providing for the revocation of the transfer, sec. 16(1)(*c*) [corresponding to the current sec. 61] would apply in this case and all the income from the property would be deemed as the assessee's income and taxed accordingly.

Held: The Calcutta High Court noted that sec. 16(1)(*c*) covered all income arising out of the transferred property which may accrue to *any person*, whether the transferor or some other beneficiary. Therefore, the entire income of the trust would be taxable in the hands of the assessee.

Exceptions to the Rule on Clubbing

The above rules on clubbing do not apply in the following cases:

A. Transferor deriving no benefit from a revocable transfer made for the life-time of beneficiary or transferee [Sec. 62(1)(*i*)]:

   Where an asset is transferred under a revocable transfer, made by way of trust or otherwise, for the life-time of the beneficiary or transferee but the transferor derives no benefit, directly or indirectly, from such transfer, income arising from such transfer is taxable in the hands of beneficiary or transferee. Transferor is not assessable on such income.

   For example, Mr. J settled certain properties on a trust for the benefit of C for his life-time. He appoints B as the trustee. If Mr. J derives no benefit, either direct or indirect, from such transfer, either the trustee, B or the beneficiary, C is assessable on such income. However, if Mr. J derives any benefit, direct or indirect from such transfer, the whole income from the settled properties is to be included in the total income of Mr. J who is assessable on such income.

B. Transfer made before 1 April 1961, not revocable for a period exceeding 6 years and transferor deriving no benefit therefrom [Sec. 62(1)(*ii*)]:

   Where any transfer was made before 1 April 1961 for a period exceeding 6 years and the transferor derives no direct or indirect benefit from such transfer, income arising from such transfer is assessable in the hands of the beneficiary.

However, as and when the power to revoke the transfer arises, any income by virtue of such transfer is included in the total income of the transferor [Sec. 62(2)]. It is not necessary that the transfer should be actually revoked. It is sufficient if the power to revoke has arisen in favour of the transferor.

For example, Mr. T transferred certain securities/properties in 1960 to Mr. N, his nephew for 50 years. N is free to apply the income from the transfer at his discretion. However, T reserved the power to make loans without security, out of the income from the settlement to any person including himself. Here, power to make loans, without security, vested with T, amounted to deriving indirect benefit from such transfer. It is not relevant whether such power is actually exercised or not. Income from transfer is to be included in the total income of T who is assessable on such income.

Case Law : ***CIT* v. *Tamilnadu Urban Development Fund* (2019) 104 taxmann.com 361/263 Taxman 318 (Madras)**

Facts: The assessee was a trust created by the State Government for infrastructure development, which received contributions from HDFC, ICICI and IL&FS. These contributions were revocable after a specified period of three years.

Held: In light of the fact that the contributions were revocable within a period of 3 years, sec. 62(2) would be attracted regardless of whether the contributions were in fact actually recalled by the transferors or not. Therefore, the income that was earned by the trust from the assets in question would be taxable in the hands of the transferors.

INCOME FROM PROPERTY CONVERTED TO THE ASSESSEE'S HUF's PROPERTY [SEC. 64(2)]

Where a member of an HUF has converted his separate property into joint-family property after 31 December 1969, the entire income from the converted property is taxable as income of the converting member. Such income is not taxable as the income of the joint family.

Gift of Property to HUF - From the assessment year 1980-81 and subsequent year, where a member of HUF transfers his separate property directly or indirectly to the Hindu undivided family otherwise than for adequate consideration, the income from such property is included in the total income of such member. In other words, where he makes a gift of his separate property to the HUF, the income from such property is included in the total income of the individual.

Partition of Converted/Gifted Property - If the converted property or gifted property is subsequently partitioned (whether partial or total) among the members of the family, proportionate income derived from the converted property relating the share of the converting member, and the share of his spouse is inclusible in the total income of the converting member. In fact, the share of income to the spouse from the partitioned converted property is deemed to arise from assets transferred indirectly by the converting member and hence the provisions of sec. 64(1)(*iv*) may apply accordingly.

- ***Recovery of Tax [Sec. 65]*** - Where a person is assessed in respect of income of other persons under the provisions of this chapter, the Assessing Officer may recover the tax either from the person assessed or from such other persons to whom the income really belongs. The Assessing Officer may serve notice of demand on such other person for the proportionate amount of tax attributable to such income beneficially held by him. Where any asset is held jointly by more than one person, they are jointly and severely liable to pay the tax which is attributable to the income from the transferred asset so included.

CHAPTER 12

Aggregation of Income, Set-off and Carry Forward of Losses

INTRODUCTION

Income tax is charged on the total income of an assessee. Therefore, in order to arrive at the total income, incomes computed under different heads of income are to be aggregated. During this computation, loss from one source or head of income may be set-off against the income from another source/head. As a matter of rule, first one makes intra-head adjustment. If losses still exist, one next sets off such losses through inter-head adjustment. Any losses that remain unabsorbed are then carried forward in the next assessment year to be then adjusted intra-head. The Income-tax Act does not specify any particular mode of set-off either under intra-head or inter-head adjustment. The assessee is free to adopt a mode of set-off which is most beneficial to him. The mode of set-off opted by the Assessing Officer is not tenable in law. [Circular No. 26 dated 7-7-1955; Also, see: *Seth Jamnadas Daga* v. *CIT* (1961) 41 ITR 630 (SC)]

However, the aggregation of income is not a mathematical exercise. Income-tax Act contains certain provisions which do not allow to set off certain losses, but allow some of them in a particular manner and thus make the aggregation a legal concept. The complete process of aggregation of income, computed under different heads, is discussed in this chapter.

INTRA-HEAD ADJUSTMENT [SEC. 70]

Loss of one source is set-off against the income of another source falling under the same head [Sec. 70]. If there are several sources of income, falling under any head of income, the loss from one source of income may be set-off against the income from another source, falling under the same head of income. Short-term capital loss can be set off against any capital gain, whether short-term or long-term [Sec. 70(2)]. Intra-head set-off has to be allowed in full. Partial set-off is not permissible.

Exceptions this rule - In the following cases, intra-head set off is restricted by pairing it up with a particular source in the same head:

(*i*) *Speculation loss [Sec. 73(1)]:* Speculation loss can be set-off only against speculation profits. It cannot be set-off against business profits though both of them fall under the same head, "profits and gains of business or profession".

(*ii*) *Loss from specified business [Sec. 73A r.w. sec. 35AD]:* Any loss in respect of 'specified business' (under sec. 35AD) can be set off against profits and gains of any other specified business.

(*iii*) *Long-term capital loss [Sec. 70(3)]:* Long-term capital loss can be set-off only against long-term capital gains [Sec. 70(3)]. It cannot be set-off against short-term capital gains though both of them fall under the same head "capital gains".

(*iv*) *Loss from owning and maintaining race horses:* Any loss on account of revenue expenditure, incurred on maintenance of race horses, can be set-off only against the income from the same source maintenance of race horses. Such loss cannot be set-off against any other income falling under the head "income from other sources".

(*v*) *Loss from gambling activity [Sec. 58(4)]:* Any loss from winnings of lottery, crossword puzzle, races including horse races, card games and gambling or betting on any of them cannot be set-off against the income from the same source or any other source, falling under the head "other sources".

(*vi*) *No Loss under "other sources" can be set off against income from gambling activity:* No loss in respect of any income from any source falling under "other sources" can be set-off against the income from winnings from lottery, crossword puzzle, races including horse races, card games and gambling or betting [Sec. 58(4)].

Losses relating to exempted source cannot be set off: Loss from a source, income of which is exempt, cannot be set off against income from taxable source [*CIT* v. *S.S. Thiagarajan* [1981] 129 ITR 115 (Mad.)]. For example, the income of an educational institution is exempt under Sec. 10(*23C*). The deficit of such institution cannot be set-off against the profits of any other business [*CIT* v. *Lallubhai Gordhandas Mehta Charitable Trust* [1995] 78 Taxman 88/(1994) 207 ITR 104 (Guj.)]. Similarly, the loss from "agriculture business" cannot be set-off from the profit of "timber business" because agricultural income is exempt under Sec. 10(1).

However, the loss from a source, the income from which is eligible for 100% deduction under Sec. 80-IA or Sec. 80-IB or Sec. 80JJAA, is fully eligible for set-off from other taxable incomes of the assessee. Income from these sources is not exempt from tax. Loss from illegal business cannot be set off againsts of a legal business, carried on during the previous year [*CIT* v. *Kurji Jinabhai Kotecha* [1977] 107 ITR 101 (SC)].

Intra-head Set-off is Mandatory Loss of one source has to be set-off against the profits of another source subject to the exception prescribed in this respect [*CIT* v. *Milling Trading Co. (P.) Ltd.* [1994] 76 Taxman 389/(1995) 211 ITR 690 (Guj.)].

INTER-HEAD ADJUSTMENT [SEC. 71]

If after applying intra-head set off, the net result is still a loss, such loss under one head of income may be set-off against the income of another head in the same previous year.

Exceptions to rule:

(*i*) Speculation loss cannot be set-off against the income of any other head, *e.g.* salaries, house property, capital gains and other sources [Sec. 73(1)].

(*ii*) Business loss cannot be set-off against the income assessable under the head "salaries".

(*iii*) Capital loss, short-term or long-term, cannot be set-off against the income of any other head [Sec. 71(3)].

(*iv*) Loss from the activity of owning and maintaining race horses cannot be set-off against the income of any other head [Sec. 74A(3)].

(*v*) Loss from House Property can be set off against income of any other head only to an extend of ₹ 2,00,000 [Sec.71(3A)].

(*vi*) Losses from gambling activity, *e.g.* loss from winning of lotteries, cross-word puzzle, card games, betting on race horses, etc. cannot be set-off against the income of any other head [Sec. 58(4)].

Set-off permissible against deemed income, included in the total income of the assessee under clubbing provisions: An assessee is also entitled to claim set-off of any loss either under intra-head or inter-head adjustment in accordance with law against any such income as are included in his total income under clubbing provisions.

Inter-head set-off to be mandatory: Subject to the exception prescribed in this behalf, inter-head adjustment of losses is a mandatory provision of law. An assessee cannot choose to carry forward a loss which is otherwise permissible against available profits.

Current year losses to have priority over carried forward losses: While aggregating the income either under intra-head or under inter-head, current year losses, eligible to be set-off in accordance with law, have got priority in the matter of set-off over carried forward losses.

CARRY FORWARD AND SET-OFF OF LOSSES

Losses, which cannot be set-off first under the same head and thereafter under inter-head adjustment in accordance with law in any previous year are carried forward and set-off in accordance with following provisions.

Loss from House Property [Sec. 71B]

Carry forward [Sec. 71B]: Where any loss from house property cannot be set-off by applying intra-head adjustment (under sec. 70) and thereafter by applying inter-head adjustment (under sec. 71), such loss can be carried forward for 8 assessment years immediately following the year for which the loss was first computed.

Set-off: Carried forward loss from house property is set-off only against the income from house property. It cannot be set-off against the income of any other head of income in subsequent years.

Business Loss [Sec. 72]

Carry forward [Sec. 72(3)]: Where any business loss, other than speculation loss, cannot be set-off by applying intra-head adjustment (under sec. 70), and thereafter by applying inter-head adjustment (under sec. 71) as discussed above, such loss can be carried forward for 8 assessment years immediately following the assessment year for which the loss was first computed. For example, if the business loss relates to the assessment year 2007-08, it can be carried forward for 8 assessment years, that is, upto 2015-16.

Carried forward business loss does not include unabsorbed depreciation [Sec. 32(2)], unabsorbed capital expenditure either on scientific research [Sec. 35(4)] or family planning [Sec. 36(1)(*ix*)].

Following provisions may be noted for the purposes of carry forward:

(*i*) *Carry forward and set-off to be allowed only in respect of taxable sources:* The loss can be carried forward and set-off, provided it arises from a source, profits of which are taxable. For instance, the foreign income of the non-resident is not chargeable to tax. Therefore, the foreign losses cannot be carried forward and set-off against profits of a business or profession carried on by the non-resident in India [Circular No. 22 dated 29 July 1944. Also see: *Indore-Malwa United Mills Ltd.* v. *CIT* (1962) 45 ITR 210 (SC)]. Similarly, the loss from a source the income of which is exempt cannot be carried forward and set-off. Thus, the losses arising from 100% export-oriented units, income of which is exempt under Sec. 10B, cannot be allowed to be carried forward and set-off.

(*ii*) *Business need not be continued to carry forward losses:* From the assessment year 2000-01, it is no longer necessary that the business where such losses were incurred and are now being carried forward should continue. Thus, the loss from a business allowed to be carried forward even if such business is discontinued in the said previous year or thereafter.

(*iii*) *Carry forward permissible to the same assessee:* Even though business may be discontinued and losses carried forward, it must be noted that such carry forward and set-off of loss is allowed to the same assessee who incurred such loss. Where an HUF is disrupted on partition and its members form a partnership firm, such firm cannot carry forward the loss suffered by the HUF before its disruption [*Keshrichand Bhanabhai* v. *CIT* (1951) 20 ITR 201 (Bom.)].

However, there are following exceptions where someone other than the assessee is allowed to carry forward and set off losses:

(*a*) **Loss by Inheritance [Sec. 78(2)] -** Where an individual succeeds in the business of his predecessor by inheritance, the successor is entitled to carry forward the loss incurred by the predecessor. However, the total period of carry forward cannot exceed 8 assessment years immediately succeeding the assessment year for the loss was first computed.

(*b*) **Restriction on set-off of losses in the case of closely held Companies [Sec. 79] -** It was being experienced that as a shrewd measure of tax saving tactics, profit making companies were acquiring loss making companies and claiming set off and carry forward of losses of such companies from the profits made by healthy companies, causing the exchequer revenue losses. Hence, restrictions are placed for claiming the set-off of losses by closely held companies, generally known as private companies.

A closely held company is not allowed to carry forward and set-off of its losses incurred in any prior year against the income of the current previous year, when there has been a substantial change in shareholding in the said company which is more than 49% of such shareholding.

Further, in case of an eligible start-up referred to in sec. 80-IAC, the carry forward and set off of the loss incurred in any prior year shall be allowed against the income of the previous year provided there is no change in the shareholding and such loss has been incurred during the period of ten years beginning from the year in which such company is incorporated.

Following points may be noted in this connection:

(*i*) **Comparison of shareholding at two points of time -** For the purposes of set-off, sec. 79 contemplates comparison of the shareholding pattern at two points of time, that is, on the last day of the previous year in which the loss was incurred and on the last day of the previous year in which the loss is set-off. There is nothing warranting any interpretation that once the set-off is denied in a particular year there should be no further set-off of losses in subsequent year. Applicability of sec. 79 can be considered in each year.

(*ii*) **Registered shareholding *v.* beneficial shareholding -** The provisions speak of beneficial holding and not the registered shareholding. Thus, where shares are held by a trust, any change in the trustees does not affect the right of set-off. Similarly, where shares are held by guardians/wards on behalf of the minors, any change in the guardians/wards, is ignored for the purposes of sec. 79.

(*iii*) **Change of shareholding within the group not a bar on set-off -** The prohibition contained in sec. 79 does not come into play if shares carrying 51% of the voting power continue to be held by the same group which held them on the last day of the previous year in which loss was incurred and on the last day of the previous year in which such loss is set off, even though there is an interchange of shareholding within the group.

(*iv*) **Unabsorbed allowances not affected by the restriction -** The restriction does not apply to the carry forward of unabsorbed depreciation [under sec. 32(2)], unabsorbed capital expenditure on promotion of family planning [Sec. 36(1)(*ix*)] and unabsorbed capital expenditure on scientific research [under sec. 35(4)]. The restriction applies to losses and not unabsorbed allowances. Accordingly, these can be carried forward and set-off, irrespective of change in shareholding.

(*v*) **Non-application of the provision in one year not a bar to consider its application in a subsequent year -** The fact that the Assessing Officer did not invoke this provision in the year in which a change in shareholding took place, is no bar to prevent him from considering the question of its application in a subsequent year to which the unabsorbed loss is carried forward [*CIT* v. *Shri Subhalaxmi Mills Ltd.* (1983) 143 ITR 863 (Guj.)].

(*vi*) **Exception to the rule of change in voting power -** Any change in the shareholding does not affect the right of set-off in the following cases:

(*a*) *Change in shareholding on account of death:* Where a change in the voting power takes place on account of the death of a shareholder, the right of set-off of losses is not affected.

(*b*) *Change in shareholding on account of gift of shares to a relative:* Where a change in the shareholding takes place on account of transfer of shares by way of gift to any relative of the shareholder, making such gift, the closely held company is entitled to claim the set-off of losses.

(*c*) *Change in shareholding of an Indian subsidiary of a foreign company:* Where a change in the said voting power of an Indian company, a subsidiary of a foreign company, takes place in a previous year as a result of amalgamation or demerger of a foreign company, set-off is allowed, provided 51% of shareholders of the amalgamating or demerged foreign company continue to be shareholders of the amalgamated or the resulting foreign company.

(*d*) *Change in shareholding under the IBC:* Where a change in the shareholding takes place in a previous year takes place pursuant to a resolution plan approved under the Insolvency and Bankruptcy Code, 2016 after affording a reasonable opportunity of being heard to the jurisdictional Principal Commissioner or Commissioner, set off is allowed.

(*e*) *Change shareholding owing to the Company Law Tribunal:—*

(*i*) where on an application moved by the Central Government under sec. 241 of the Companies Act, 2013 a company and its subsidiary and the subsidiary of such subsidiary; the Company Law Tribunal has suspended the Board of Directors of such company and has appointed new directors nominated by the Central Government, under sec. 242 of the said Act, set off is allowed; and

(*ii*) where a change in shareholding of such company, and its subsidiary and the subsidiary of such subsidiary, has taken place in a previous year pursuant to a resolution plan approved by the Tribunal under section 242 of the Companies Act, 2013 after affording a reasonable opportunity of being heard to the jurisdictional Principal Commissioner or Commissioner, set off is allowed.

(*f*) to a company to the extent that a change in the shareholding has taken place during the previous year on account of relocation referred to in the *Explanation* to clauses (*viiac*) and (*viiad*) of sec. 47 (w.e.f. 1.4.2022)

(c) Losses of Amalgamating Company/Demerged Company to be carried by Amalgamated Company/Resulting Company [Sec. 72A and Sec. 72AA]: See Chapter 29 "Tax Implications of Business Reorganisation" for details

(*iv*) *Carry forward is allowed if return of loss is furnished withing the prescribed period [Sec. 80]:* The assessee is entitled to carry forward and set-off of the business loss provided the loss return is filed under sec. 139(3) in accordance with the provision of sec. 139(1). If such return is not filed within the prescribed time-limit of sec. 139(1), the right of carry forward and set-off is lost.

(*v*) *Condonation of delay:* The Central Board of Direct Taxes is empowered to condone the delay in furnishing return of loss. Circular No. 8/2001 dated 16-5-2001 contains the necessary provisions in this regard. These provisions are described below:

(*a*) Loss not exceeding ₹ 10,000: Where the delayed loss return does not exceed ₹ 10,000, the Assessing Officer is empowered to condone the delay with the prior permission of the Commissioner of Income Tax.

(*b*) Loss exceeding ₹ 10,000 but not exceeding ₹ 1,00,000: Where the delayed loss return exceeds ₹ 10,000 but does not exceed ₹ 1,00,000 the Assessing Officer may condone the delay with the prior approval of the Chief Commissioner of Income tax or Director-General of Income tax.

(*c*) Loss exceeding ₹ 1,00,000: The power of condonation or rejection lies with the Central Board of Direct Taxes.

(*vi*) *Delay in filing return of loss not to affect the carry forward and setting off the depreciation:* The condition of filing the loss return does not apply to depreciation. Thus, if the loss return is delayed or is not filed, the assessee is entitled to carry forward and set-off unabsorbed depreciation.

(*vii*) *Delay in filing return of loss not to affect intra-head and inter-head adjustment:* The restriction of filing loss return under sec. 139(3) does not apply to intra-head and inter-head adjustments. Thus, if the loss return is delayed, the assessee's right to claim inter-source adjustment under Sec. 70 or inter-head adjustment under sec. 71 is not affected. Take an example. An assessee suffers business loss of ₹ 5,00,000 and earns income from other sources ₹ 2,00,000 during the previous year 2014-15. Loss return of ₹ 3,00,000 is delayed. The assessee's right to carry forward the loss is lost but he cannot be asked to pay tax on ₹ 2,00,000. Inter-head adjustment under sec. 71 has to be allowed.

(*viii*) *Income return, furnished within the time-limit of sec. 139(1), may be revised into a loss return:* Where the assessee files income return within the prescribed time-limit of sec. 139(1), but later on revises such return under sec. 139(5) declaring a loss, the right of carry forward and set-off loss is not lost. A revised return steps into the shoes of the original return. A revised return filed under sec. 139(5) is, in law, a return filed under sec. 139(1) [*Niranjan Lal Ram Chandra* v. *CIT* (1982) 134 ITR 352 (All.)]. Carry forward of loss as per revised return is allowed if the original profit return was filed within the time-limit of sec. 139(1).

Similarly, original loss return, furnished under sec. 139(1) time-limit, can also be revised within the time-limit of sec. 139(5) declaring the loss at higher figure as compared to original return.

Set-off: The carried forward business loss is set-off only against the profits and gains of any business or profession carried on by the assessee and assessable for that assessment year.

Carried forward business loss may be set-off against speculative profits.

Unabsorbed business loss is first set-off against the profit of the same business in which it was incurred. If it is not fully set-off, it may be set-off against the profits of any other business including a newly started business.

Carried forward business loss cannot be set-off against the income under any other head, *e.g.* salary, house property, capital gains, other sources, etc.

Case Law : ***CIT* v. *Cocanada Radhaswami Bank Ltd.* (1965) 57 ITR 306 (SC)**

Facts: 'C' being a private limited company carrying on banking business, derived incomes from banking business and interest from government securities shown under two separate heads of incomes. Subsequently when losses were carried forward and sought to be set off against interest from securities, such set off was disallowed stating that under the relevant provisions losses carried forward from earlier years could be set off only against income from 'profits and gains of the assessee from the same business'.

Held: Though for the purpose of computation of the income, interest on securities is separately classified, income by way of interest from securities does not cease to be part of the income from business if the securities are part of the trading assets. Since the securities which yielded income formed part of 'C"s trading assets, such interest income was part of its income in the business and the loss could be set off against that income from securities. [Also see *Western States Trading Co. (P.) Ltd.* v. *CIT* (1971) 80 ITR 21 (SC).]

Sequence of set-off [Sec. 72(2)]: Where unabsorbed business loss, unabsorbed depreciation, and unabsorbed capital expenditure on scientific research and unabsorbed capital expenditure on family planning incurred by a company are carried forward simultaneously, unabsorbed business loss is set-off first in computing total income. Where profits are insufficient to absorb brought forward losses/allowances and current year depreciation, the same should be deducted in the following order:

1. Current year expenditure on scientific research [Sec. 35(*1*)]
2. Current year depreciation [Sec. 32(*1*)]
3. Carried forward business profession losses [Sec. 72(*1*)]
4. Unabsorbed expenditure on family planning [Sec. 36(*1*)(*ix*)]
5. Unabsorbed depreciation [Sec. 32(*2*)]
6. Unabsorbed capital expenditure on scientific research [Sec. 35(4)].

Loss of industrial undertaking-discontinued but rehabilitated: Losses of discontinued business of an industrial undertaking, subject to certain conditions, is allowed to be carried forward to the assessment year relevant to the previous year in which such business is revived/rehabilitated.

Losses of such business may be set-off against its profits assessable for that year. If profits are insufficient, such loss may be set-off against the profits of any other business, assessable for that year.

Unabsorbed business losses may be carried forward for 7 assessment years immediately succeeding the year of revival/rehablitation.

Conditions:

(*i*) The business of the industrial undertaking, carried on in India, was discontinued due to damage or destruction of its building, machinery, plant or furniture on account of flood, earthquake, riot, fire, war, etc.

(*ii*) The business has been revived/rehabilitated within 3 years from the end of the previous year in which it was discontinued.

Speculation Loss [Sec. 73]

Income-tax law has applied different yard sticks for speculation loss and business loss though both of them fall under the same head of income.

Carry Forward [Sec. 73(4)]

If the whole or part of the speculation loss cannot be set-off against speculation profits of another line, earned in the same year, the unabsorbed loss may be carried forward for future set-off for a maximum period of 4 assessment years immediately succeeding the assessment year for which the loss was first computed [Sec. 73(4)].

Conditions for carry forward: Speculation loss is allowed to be carried forward if other conditions are also satisfied:

(*i*) Return of loss to be submitted within the time-limit of sec. 139(1).

(*ii*) Right of carry forward and set-off is allowed to the same assessee who sustained the loss.

Sale and purchase of shares by companies to be treated speculation business [*Explanation to Sec. 73*]: Where the business of the company consists in the sale and purchase of shares of other companies such company is deemed to be carrying on a speculation business.

If the income is derived by the company partly from the share business and partly from any other source, only proportionate profit to the extent the business consists of purchase and sale of shares is deemed to speculative profit.

Exceptions - However, sale or purchase of shares is not to be treated a speculative business in the case of the following companies:

(*a*) Investment company whose gross total income mainly consist of income chargeable under the heads "income from house property", "capital gains" and "income from other sources";

(*b*) Company whose principal business is the business of banking; and

(*c*) Company whose principal business is the business of granting of loans.

Losses in illegal speculative transaction not entitled to be carried forward and set-off: Losses incurred by an assessee in speculative transactions of banned items under Forward Contracts (Regulation) Act, 1952, can neither be set-off against the profits of the speculative business of the same previous year nor can be carried forward for future set-off [*CIT* v. *Kurji Jinabhai Kotecha* (1977) 107 ITR 101 (SC)].

Law assumes an illegal business to die out of existence with all its losses to the assessee in the year of loss itself. It so because "speculative transaction" has been defined under sec. 43(5) by reference to a "contract" and "contract" means legal and enforceable contract and does not include an illegal agreement, which is unenforceable.

Set-off [Sec. 73(2)]: The carried forward speculation loss may be set-off against profits and gains of any speculation business carried on by the assessee and assessable for that assessment year. It may be noted that the speculative business in which the speculation loss was originally incurred need not be continued by the assessee. In other words, the loss of discontinued speculation business may be carried forward and set-off against the profits of any speculation business carried on by the assessee. Speculative transactions in different commodities are to be treated as one business.

Carried forward speculation loss to have priority over current year business loss in the matter of set off: Since the speculation loss can be set-off only against speculation profits over a period of 4 assessments immediately succeeding the year for which the loss was first computed, it has got priority in the matter of set-off over current year business loss.

Thus, current year surplus of speculation profits may be applied first to set-off carried forward speculation loss and then to adjust current year business loss [Circular No. 23, dated 12-9-1960 and *CIT* v. *New India Investment Corpn. Ltd.* (1994) 205 ITR 618 (Cal.)].

The carried forward speculation loss has got priority over carried forward depreciation, carried forward capital expenditure on scientific research or carried forward capital expenditure on family planning [Sec. 73(3)].

Speculation loss from a solitary speculative transaction not allowed to be set-off: Where speculative transactions carried on by an assessee are of such a nature so as to constitute a business, it is deemed to be "speculation business", which is treated distinct and separate from any other business [*Explanation 2* to Sec. 28]. The plurality of speculative transaction is an essential condition to treat it a separate and distinct business. Hence, any speculation loss arising out of a solitary transaction cannot be carried forward under this Section or under any other provision. It is only when the transactions amount to a 'speculation business', the carry forward of loss is permitted. A solitary transaction may be a speculative transaction but the loss is not a speculative loss [*Addl. CIT* v. *Maggaji Shermal* (1978) 114 ITR 862 (AP)].

Case Law : ***CIT* v. *Pangal Vittal Nayak and Co. (P.) Ltd* (1969) 74 ITR 754 (SC)**

Facts: 'P' a company was a member of an association for speculation in coconut oil. 'P' speculated for its own business and also entered into forward contracts on behalf of its clients and received commission in respect of such transactions, irrespective of whether the clients made profits or suffered losses. 'P' claimed to set off losses from its speculation business against this commission income since it claimed that commission was also a part of its speculation business.

Held: The receipts of commission business was entirely of a different character from the profits and losses of the speculative transactions. There was thus no element of speculation in the commission income received by 'P' and the commission was earned and received by him independently of the profit or loss sustained by the his clients in the transaction. Accordingly, 'P' was not entitled to get the commission receipts assessed under the head "speculation business" and therefore cannot set off speculation loss against said income.

Losses by specified business [Sec. 73A]

Any loss computed in respect of any specified business (explained in Chapter 8 under sec. 35AD) can be set off against profits and gains of any specified business [Sec. 73A(1)/r.w. sec. 35AD]. Where the loss from specified business has not been set off either fully or partially, it may be carried forward for future set off without any time-limit. Such carried forward loss can be set off only against the profits of any other specified business (computed under sec. 35AD) without any time-limit.

Capital Loss [Sec. 74]

From the assessment year 2003-04 and subsequent years, following provisions govern the carry forward and set-off of capital losses:

Carry forward [Sec. 74(2)]: Unabsorbed capital losses, short-term or long-term, can be carried forward for 8 assessment years, immediately succeeding the assessment years, in which the loss was first computed.

Conditions for carry forward:

(*a*) Return of loss should be furnished within the time-limit under Sec. 139(1).

(*b*) Carry forward and set-off is allowed to the same assessee who incurred the loss.

Set-off of short-term capital losses: A short-term capital loss may be set-off against short-term capital gain as well against long term capital gains, assessable for that year.

However, a short-term capital loss cannot be set-off against the income of any other head [Sec. 71(3)].

Set-off of long-term capital loss: A long-term capital loss can be set-off only against long-term capital gains, assessable for that assessment year.

It can neither be set off against short-term gain nor against the income of any other head [Sec. 71(3)].

Case Law : ***CIT* v. *K.P.D. Sigamani* [2020] 120 taxmann.com 255/275 Taxman 4 (SC)**

Facts: Assessees are brothers and founder shareholders of various companies commonly known as KPR Group. In the year 2005-06 they received shares under a scheme of amalgamation between two companies in the group and subsequently sold the shares in 2007-08, thereby earning long-term capital gain. This gain was sought to be set off against short term capital loss which arose on account of forfeiture of call monies paid to a company which was promoted by the assessees and other family members. The Assessing Officer rejected the set off on the grounds that the claim was merely a sham as it was structured only to evade tax arising on sale of shares.

Held: In the absence of claim that the forfeiture of shares to be bogus neither it has been shown to be a fraud or colourable devise. Set off of capital gains on sale of shares allowed against loss on forfeiture of share money.

Loss from the activity of owning and maintaining Race Horses [Sec. 74A]

An assessee being the owner of horses, maintained by him for running in horse races upon which wagering or betting is lawfully made, is entitled to claim the set-off and carry forward of any loss incurred by him in the activity of owning and maintaining race horses. Thus, if an assessee who owns and maintains horses for running in horse races upon which wagering or betting cannot be lawfully made, any loss incurred in the activity of owning and maintaining such horses neither can be claimed to be set-off nor allowed to be carried forward.

Carry forward: Where the income by way of stake money is less than amount of expenditure, not being capital expenditure, expanded wholly and exclusively for the purposes of owning and maintaining race horses, the amount of loss can be set-off against the income from the same source. "Income by way of stake money" means the gross amount of prize received on a race horse or race horses. If such loss cannot be fully set-off, the unabsorbed amount is carried forward for 4 assessment years immediately succeeding the assessment year for which the loss was first determined.

Conditions for carry forward: Following conditions should be satisfied for this purpose:

(*a*) *Activity of the owning and maintaining race horses must be continued:* Carried forward loss is allowed to be set-off provided the activity of owning and maintaining race horses is carried on by the assessee during the previous year relevant for the assessment year in which set-off of such loss is claimed.

However, it is not necessary that such horses should have participated in the race in the relevant assessment year [*CIT* v. *RMS & Sons* (2002) 120 Taxman 237 (Mad.)].

(*b*) *Furnishing the return of loss within the prescribed time-limit:* The assessee has to furnish the return of loss within the time-limit of sec. 139(1).

Failure to file such return [under Sec. 139(1)], within the prescribed time, will disentitle him to claim the right of carry forward and future set-off.

Set-off: The amount of carried forward loss in the activity of owning and maintaining race horses, is set-off only against the income earned from the activity of owning and maintaining race horses, assessable for that assessment year.

No set off of losses consequent to search, requisition and survey [Sec. 79A] (newly inserted by the Finance Act, 2022)

It was noticed that in some cases, assessees claim set off of losses or unabsorbed depreciation against undisclosed income detected during the course of search or survey proceedings. Making such allowance amounts to offering undue advantage to a wrong doer. The Finance Act, 2022 newly inserted sec. 79A that categorically disallows such a set off. The section shall take effect from 1-4-2022.

Accordingly, notwithstanding anything contained in the Act, where consequent to a search initiated under sec. 132 or a requisition made under sec. 132A or a survey conducted under sec. 133A (other than under sec. 133A(2A), the total income of any previous year of an assessee includes any undisclosed income, no set off, against such undisclosed income, of any loss, whether brought forward or otherwise, or unabsorbed depreciation under sec. 32(2) shall be allowed to the assessee.

For the purposes of this section, the expression "undisclosed income" means,—

(*i*) any income of the previous year represented, either wholly or partly, by any money, bullion, jewellery or other valuable article or thing or any entry in the books of account or other documents or transactions found in the course of a search under sec. 132 or a requisition under sec. 132A or a survey under Sec. 133A [other than under sec. 133A(2A)], which has,—

(A) not been recorded on or before the date of search or requisition or survey, as the case may be, in the books of account or other documents maintained in the normal course relating to such previous year; or

(B) not been disclosed to the Principal Chief Commissioner or Chief Commissioner or Principal Commissioner or Commissioner before the date of search or requisition or survey, as the case may be; or

(*ii*) any income of the previous year represented, either wholly or partly, by any entry in respect of an expense recorded in the books of account or other documents maintained in the normal course relating to the previous year which is found to be false and which would not have been found to be so, had the search not been initiated or the survey not been conducted or the requisition not been made.'

CHAPTER 13

Deductions from Gross Total Income

INTRODUCTION

An assessee is taxed on the total income of the previous year in the relevant assessment year. In computing the total income, certain deductions are allowed from the gross total income. Some of them relate to contributions to promote social justice while others are related to incomes in the larger interest to promote economic growth. These are staggered under different provisions, contained under sections 80A to 80U. A few general provisions may be noted in this connection.

General Provisions

In computing total income of an assessee, deductions specified under sections 80C to 80U are allowed from gross total income in accordance with the following provisions [Sec. 80A(1)] :

(1) Deductions cannot result in negative figure [Sec. 80A(2)] - The aggregate of the deductions, allowable under sections 80C to 80U, is limited to amount of gross total income of the assessee and the same cannot exceed such total income so as to result in a negative figure or a loss. Gross total income means the total income computed in accordance with the provisions of this Act, before making any deduction under this Chapter [sec. 80C]. The gross total income of the assessee will excluding long-term capital gain (Sec. 112), short-term capital gain under sec. 111A, winnings from lotteries, races, etc., and certain incomes accruing to a non-resident assessee under sections 115A, 115AB, 115AC, 115ACA, 115AD, 115BBA and 115D.

(2) Deduction to be allowed on the basis of income, included in the gross total income [Sec. 80AB] - Deduction available under any section of the heading *"C.—Deductions in respect of certain incomes"* (*i.e.* sec. 80HH to sec. 80RRB) is allowed on the net income which is included in the gross total income.

Such income implies :

(*i*) computation of income head-wise;

(*ii*) clubbing of income, if any, has been applied;

(*iii*) intra-head and inter-head adjustment has been applied;

(*iv*) brought forward losses or depreciation has been allowed;

(*v*) brought forward expenditure on scientific research, and family planning have been adjusted.

(3) Claim of Deductions to be made by the assessee [Sec. 80A(5)] - The deductions are to be allowed if the assessee claims any of them and establishes the circumstances, warranting such deduction. It would then be the duty of the Assessing Officer to allow any such deduction. If no such deduction is claimed, the assessing authority is not, ordinarily bound to allow any such deduction. The assessee should place all the relevant material before the assessing authority and prove that he is entitled to obtain the concession. The burden is on the assessee to prove that his case falls within the particular provisions, claimed by him. If the claim is not made in computation, but the claim is evident from the notes or annexures which form part and parcel of return of income then it cannot be said that claim for deduction was not made.

(4) Double Deduction not allowed [Sec. 80A(3), (4), (7)]

- Once deductions are availed by an AOP or BOI for computing their total income, such deductions cannot be then claimed by members of such AOP or BOI in computing their income.
- Where deduction has been allowed in respect of (*a*) any income in respect of newly established undertaking in force trade zone (under sec. 10A) or (*b*) newly established units in Special Economic Zone (under sec. 10AA) or (*c*) any income in respect of newly established 100% export oriented undertakings (under sec. 10B) or (*d*) any income in respect of export of certain article or thing (under sec.10BA) or (*e*) any other income under chapter C "in respect of certain incomes" (*i.e.* deduction under sec. 80HH to sec. 80RRB) in any assessment year, deduction in respect of such or income or to the extent of such profits cannot be allowed under any other provision of this Act for such assessment year and cannot exceed the profits and gains of such undertaking or unit or enterprise, as the case may be. **[Sec. 80A(4)]**
- The assessee has the option to claim deduction in respect of specified business either under Sec. 35AD or under this chapter under the heading *"C - Deduction in respect of certain incomes"* **[Sec. 80A(7) r.w. Sec. 35AD]**.

(5) Deduction not to be allowed unless return of income is furnished [Sec. 80AC] - Where any deduction is claimed by an assessee on or after:

(*i*) 1-4-2006 but before 1-4-2018 in respect of (*i*) profits and gains from industrial undertaking or enterprise engaged in infrastructure development (under sec. 80-IA), or (*ii*) profits and gains by an undertaking or enterprise, engaged in development of special Economic Zone (Sec. 80-IAB), or (*iii*) profits and gains from industrial undertakings other than infrastructure development undertakings, (under sec. 80-IB), or (*iv*) undertakings or enterprise in certain special category states (sec. 80-IC), or (*v*) Business of hotels and convention centres in specified area (sec. 80-ID); or (*vi*) undertaking in North-Eastern States [Sec. 80-IE].

(*ii*) 1-4-2018 in respect of deduction admissible under the provision of this chapter under the heading *"C.—Deductions in respect of certain incomes"* (*i.e.* deduction under sec. 80HH to sec. 80RRB)

no such deduction is allowed unless the assessee has furnished the return of income on or before the due date specified under sec. 139(1).

(6) Inter-transfer of goods or services at arms length price [Sec. 80A(6)] - Where inter-transfer of goods or services are made from one department to another department at less than market value, then for the purposes of any deduction under this chapter, the profit of such undertaking or unit or enterprise are bound to be computed as if the transfer had been made at the market value of such goods or services.

Simply put, this provision requires that for the purposes of computing deduction under this chapter, the inter-unit transfer of goods or services between eligible and other units of the assessee should be recognized at market value. As it is when specified domestic transactions cross the threshold of ₹ 20 crores these are subject to provisions of transfer pricing regulation and arms length computed thereunder. If these do not cross the threshold of ₹ 20 crore, the same will continue to be governed by the provisions of this sec. 80A(6) and the market value will be computed on general principles.

DEDUCTION FOR CERTAIN SOCIAL SECURITY INVESTMENTS, MEDICAL PREMIUMS, EDUCATION LOANS ETC. BY INDIVIDUALS AND HUFs

In keeping with ability-to-pay principle discussed in Chapter 1, a range of deductions are offered to assessees being natural persons. Some of these deductions accommodate situations such as medical expenditures in the family or offer relief when such assessee become first time home owners discharging liabilities or have education loans or paying rents. Certain other deductions incentivise savings and investments. The following figure gives an overview of the different kinds of deductions that can be availed by these assessees. Not all of these are available to both individuals and HUFs. A few more such as donations etc. are available to every assessee. The detailed discussion on each deduction follows.

FIGURE 13.1: DEDUCTIONS FOR INDIVIDUALS AND HUFs

Deductions for individuals and HUFs

Contribution towards certain social securities and investments:
- ◆ Approved savings (Sec. 80C)
- ◆ Pension Funds (Sec. 80CCC)
- ◆ National Pensions Scheme (Sec. 80CCD)
- ◆ Agnipath Scheme (Sec. 80CCH)

Medical situations:
- ◆ Mediclaim Premium (Sec. 80D)
- ◆ Medical treatment, maintenance of a dependent with disability (Sec. 80DD)
- ◆ Medical Treatment (Sec. 80DDB)

Interest on Higher Education Loan (Sec. 80E)

Interest on loan taken for residential house property (Secs. 80EE, 80EEA)

Purchase of electronic vehicle (Sec. 80EEB)

Deductions in respect of rents paid (Sec. 80GG)

Interest on Deposits in certain savings accounts (Sec. 80TTA)

Deduction in respect of interest on deposits in case of senior citizens (Sec. 80TTB)

Deduction for individual with disability (Sec. 80U)

Deduction for book authors and patentees (Secs. 80QQB and 80RRB)

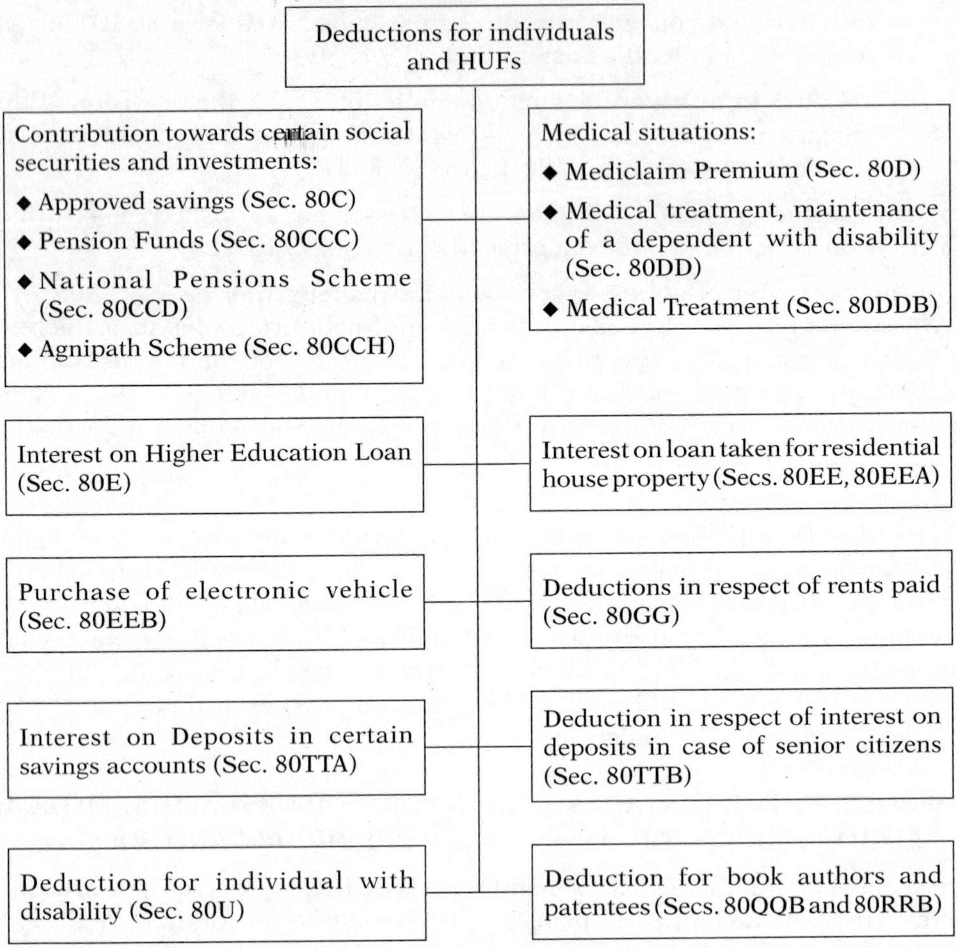

(1) Contributions to approved savings, pension scheme etc.

The following three deductions are amongst those critical deductions that can be availed by individual assessees (except sec. 80C which is available to HUF also) that incentivize savings and social security arrangements made by such assessees:

(*i*) contributions to approved savings [Sec. 80C];

(*ii*) contributions to certain pension funds [Sec. 80CCC]; and

(*iii*) contributions for pension scheme of the Central Government [Sec. 80CCD].

However, a cumulative limit applies to these three deductions which cannot exceed ₹ 1,50,000 [Sec. 80CCE]. In other words maximum deduction that can be availed by the assessee under Secs. 80C, 80CCC and 80CCD taken together is ₹ 1,50,000 and not more. However, the deduction of ₹ 50,000 under sec. 80CCD(1B) is over and above over the ceiling of ₹ 1,50,000.

(*i*) Contributions to approved savings - Life Insurance Premium, Contributions to Provident Fund, etc. [Sec. 80C, w.e.f. AY 2006-07] - The object of this section 80C is to encourage thrift and is required to be interpreted in such a manner as not to nullify that object. It is a normal behaviour of an individual's private life that all incomes are amalgamated and spent. Therefore the Income-tax Act does not require that the investment should be made from the same amount which an assessee had earned by way of income. *CIT* v. *Ramesh Chandra Khandelwal* [2005] 145 Taxman 11/273 ITR 363 (All.). Thus, an assessee is entitled to deduction under section 80C in respect of say, life insurance premium paid or national saving certificates even if purchased out of moneys borrowed [*Kasturi Lal Dewan & Sons* v. *CIT* [2005] 147 Taxman 625 (All.)].

When an individual or a Hindu undivided family makes contributions in the following approved savings, a deduction of maximum ₹ 1,50,000 can be availed as deduction :

1. Insurance Premium [Sec. 80C(2)(*i*)] - Insurance premium may be paid by an individual to effect or to keep in force a policy of insurance on his life or on the life of the spouse or any of his child. The spouse or the child may be dependent or not dependent on the assessee. Premium paid for married daughter also qualifies for rebate. The child may be minor or major, unmarried or married, step-child or adopted child. Thus, where an assessee individual takes a policy on the life of his father/mother/brother/uncle/nephew, etc., premiums paid on such policies cannot be deduction.

An HUF may take the policy on the life of any member, male or female, minor or major.

Maximum ceiling of insurance premium [Sec. 80C(3)/(3A)]

The insurance premium should not exceed the specified limit, given as below :

Year when Policy is issued	Maximum ceiling of insurance premium which may be deducted in computation of total income	
	Insured is person with disability or sever disability or a person suffering from illness referred in sec. 80DDB	Any other person
Where policy is issued on or before 31st March 2012	20% of Capital sum assured	20% of Capital sum assured
Where policy is issued on or after 1st April 2012	10% of Capital sum assured	10% of Capital sum assured
Where policy is issued on or after 1st April 2013	15% of Capital sum assured	10% of Capital sum assured

In calculating the amount of "actual capital sum assured", the value of any premium agreed to be returned or any benefit by way of bonus or otherwise over and above the sum actually assured is not to be taken into account.

Policy not to be discontinued before the expiry of 2 years [Sec. 80C(5)] - Where an assessee has subscribed any single premium policy, it should not be discontinued within 2 years after the date of commencement of insurance. In any other policy, contract of insurance should not be terminated before premiums have been paid for 2 years.

Consequences when policy is discontinued before the expiry of 2 years [Sec. 80C(5)] - Where an assessee terminates the contract of insurance before the expiry of two years of its commencement, no deduction is allowed in respect of the premiums paid in the previous year in which the policy is terminated. Furthermore, deductions allowed in earlier previous year or years is deemed to be the income of the assessee and is liable to tax.

2. Contract for deferred annuity [Sec. 80C(2)(*ii*)] - Any sum may be paid by an individual to effect or keep in force a contract for a deferred annuity on his life or on the life of the spouse or any child of the assessee.

But the contract for the deferred annuity should not contain any provision regarding commutation of annuity. If such contract entitles the assessee to receive a lump sum in commutation of annuity, no deduction is allowed for any sum paid to effect or to keep in force such a contract of deferred annuity.

3. Contribution by a Government employee for deferred annuity [Sec. 80C(1)(*iii*)] - Contribution deducted from the salary of a government employee, in accordance with the conditions of his service for securing him a deferred annuity or making provision for his wife and children, qualify for deduction. However, contribution deducted from salary should not exceed 20% of the salary.

4. Contribution to statutory provident fund [Sec. 80C(2)(*iv*)] - Contribution made by an employee from his salary to statutory provident fund is eligible for deduction.

5. Contribution to the public provident fund [Sec. 80C(2)(*v*)] - Any contribution made by the assessee to the Public Provident Fund, subject to a minimum of ₹ 500 and a maximum of ₹ 70,000 qualifies for deduction. The scheme of Public Provident Fund is operative from 1 July 1968. The membership of the fund is open to every individual and HUF. The deposit may be made by the individual in his own name or in the name of his spouse or in the name of any of his child, minor or major, unmarried or married. An HUF may make the deposit in the name of any member.

6. Contribution to recognised provident fund [Sec. 80C(2)(*vi*)] - Contribution made by an employee from his salary to recognised provident fund is eligible for deduction. An employee is free to contribute any amount.

No deduction is available for employees' contribution under unrecognised provident fund.

7. Contribution to approved superannuation fund [Sec. 80C(2)(*vii*)] - Any contribution made by an employee from his salary to an approved superannuation fund qualifies for deduction.

8. Subscription to notified Government securities and deposit scheme [Sec. 80C(2)(*viii*)] - Subscription to any such security of the Central Government or any such deposit scheme as that government may notify qualify for deduction in computing total income. The Central Government has notified 'Sukanya Samriddhi Account' under this clause w.e.f. 21-1-2015, [Notification No. SO 210(E)]. The deposit may also be made in the name of girl child for whom the depositor in the legal guardian.

9. Subscription to 6-year National Savings Certificate VIII Issue [Sec. 80C(2)(*ix*)] - Subscription to any such savings certificates [defined under Sec. 2(*c*) of the Government Savings Certificates Act, 1959] as the Central Government may specify.

The Central Government has specified National Savings Certificates (VIII Issue) for the assessment year 2006-07 and subsequent years [Notification No. 223/2005 dated 3-11-2005]. Accrued interest for first 5 years also qualify for deduction as it is deemed to have been reinvested.

10. Contribution to ULIP of UTI [Sec. 80C(2)(*x*)] - Contribution to Unit-linked Insurance Plant (ULIP) 1971, specified in the Schedule II of the Unit Trust of India (Transfer of Undertaking and Repeal) Act, 2002, by an individual or an HUF is eligible for deduction.

An individual may contribute either in his own name or in the name of his spouse or in the name of his child, minor or major. An HUF may contribute in the name of any member.

Where the assessee withdraws his participation before the expiry of 5 years no deduction is allowed to him for any contribution paid in such year. Besides, the aggregate amount of deduction of income allowed in previous year or years preceding such previous year, is deemed to be the income of the assessee of such previous year. Accordingly, it is liable to be taxed in the assessment year relevant to such previous year [Sec. 80C(5)].

11. Unit-linked plan of the LIC Mutual Fund [Sec. 80C(2)(*xi*)] - Any contribution for participation in any such unit-linked insurance plan of the LIC mutual fund notified under sec. 10(*23D*), as the Central Government may specify by Notification in the Official Gazette. The individual may contribute in his own name or in the name of his spouse or in the name of his child. An HUF may contribute in the name of any member.

12. Contributions in respect of annuity plans of LIC or any other insurer [Sec. 80C(2)(*xii*)] - Any payment made to effect or to keep in force a contract for such annuity plans of LIC or any other insurer as the Central Government may specify by notification in this behalf. The Central Government has specified New Jeevan Dhara, New Jeevan Dhara I, New Jeevan Akshay, New Jeevan Akshay I, New Jeevan Akshay II plans of LIC and Jeevan Akshay III plans of LIC.

13. Subscription to units of any notified mutual fund or units of UTI [Sec. 80C(2)(*xiii*)] - Subscription to any units of any mutual fund, referred to in Sec. 10(*23D*) or units from administrator or specified company as [referred to under Sec. 2 of the Unit Trust of India (Transfer of Undertaking and Repeal) Act, 2005] under any plan formulated in accordance with such scheme as the Central Government may specify by Notification in this behalf. The Central Government has specified Equity Linked Savings Scheme, 2005 [Notification No. 226/2005, dated 3-11-2005].

14. Contribution to pension fund set up by mutual fund or unit trust [Sec. 80C(2)(*xiv*)] - Contribution by an individual to any pension fund set up (*i*) by any mutual fund, referred to in sec. 10(*23D*), or (*ii*) by the administrator or the specified company [as referred to under sec. 2 of the Unit Trust of India (Transfer of Undertaking and Repeal) Act, 2005] as the Central Government may specify by Notification in this behalf. The Central Government has specified the UTI-Retirement Benefit Pension Fund set up the specified company for the purposes of this clause for the assessment year 2006-07 and subsequent years.

15. Subscription/deposit to any deposit scheme or pension fund set up by National Housing Bank [Sec. 80C(2)(*xv*)] - Any subscription or deposit to any such (*i*) deposit scheme or (*ii*) pension fund, set up by National Housing Bank, as the Central Government may specify by notification qualify for deduction.

Any deposit made in the Home Loan Account Scheme of the National Housing Bank is eligible for deduction under this clause.

16. Deposit with public sector company or housing Board [Sec. 80C(2)(*xvi*)] - Any subscription made to any notified scheme of (*i*) a public sector company which is engaged in providing long-term finance for construction or purchase of houses in India for residential purposes; or (*ii*) any housing board constituted in India to satisfy the need of housing accommodation or to ensure planned development of cities, towns or villages also qualify for deduction.

17. Tuition fees for full-time education in India [Sec. 80C(2)(*xvii*)] - Payment of tuition fees by an individual for any of his two children for full-time education in a school, college, university or any other educational institution in India qualifies for deduction. There is no ceiling for tuition fee. However, deduction is allowed only in respect of two children of the individual.

Tuition fees may be paid at the time of admission or thereafter. Any payment made towards any development fees or donation or payment of similar nature, whether at the time of admission or thereafter does not qualify for deduction.

18. Payment for the construction of residential house [Sec. 80C(2)(*xviii*)] - Any specified payment for the purchase or construction of a residential house, the income from which is chargeable under the head "income from house property" is eligible for deduction.

Specified payments are given below:

(*a*) Any payment by way of instalment or part payment of the amount due under self-financing or other schemes of any development authority, housing boards, etc., engaged in the construction and sale of house property on ownership basis; or

(*b*) Any payment by way of instalment or part payment of the amount due to any company or co-operative society of which the assessee is shareholder or member towards the cost of the house allotted to him; or

(*c*) Repayment of the loan borrowed by the assessee from (*i*) the Central Government or any State Government; or (*ii*) any bank including a co-operative bank; or (*iii*) the Life Insurance Corporation; or (*iv*) National Housing Bank; (*v*) any public company, formed and registered in India with the main object of carrying on the business of providing long-term finance for the construction or purchase of houses in India for residential purposes and which is entitled to claim deduction in respect of special reserve [under Sec. 36(1)(*viii*)]; or (*vi*) any company in which public are substantially interested or any co-operative society where such company or society is engaged in the business of financing the construction of houses; or (*vii*) the assessee's employer where such employer is an authority or a board or a corporation or any other body established or constituted under a Central or State Act; or (*viii*) the assessee's employer where such employer is an authority or a board or a corporation or any other body established or constituted under a Central or State Act; or (*ix*) the employer of the assessee, where such employer is public company; or (*x*) public sector company, or university or its affiliated college, or a local authority.

(*d*) Any payment of stamp duty, registration fee and other expenses for the purpose of the transfer of such house property to the assessee.

Some payments are not eligible for deduction as they are not treated towards the cost of the house. Such payments are as follows:

(*i*) admission fee, cost of share/initial deposit which a shareholder of a company or member of a co-operative society has to pay for becoming shareholder or member; or

(*ii*) the cost of land, except where the consideration for the purchase of the house property is composite amount and the cost of the land alone cannot be separately ascertained; or

(*iii*) the cost of any addition, alteration, renovation, repair of the house, incurred either after the issue of completion certificate or after the house has been occupied by the assessee or any person on his behalf or after the house has been let out; or

(*iv*) any expenditure in respect of which deduction is allowable while computing the income from house property (under Sec. 24).

Where the rebate has been allowed to an assessee in any previous year in respect of any sum covered under clause (*a*), (*b*), (*c*) or (*d*) aforesaid and subsequently such sum is refunded or received back by the assessee in any previous year, there are two-fold tax-effects of such refund:

(*i*) No rebate is admissible in respect of any sum paid in the relevant previous year (in which refund is received); and

(*ii*) The aggregate amount of the rebate allowed in the previous year(s) preceding the relevant previous year is deemed to be tax due from the assessee in the relevant previous year.

Where an assessee transfers the house property so acquired before the expiry of five years from the end of the financial year in which possession of such property is obtained by him receives back, whether by way of refund or otherwise, any sum covered under aforesaid clauses (*a*), (*b*), (*c*) and (*d*) no deduction is allowed to the assessee in respect of any sum so paid in such previous year and the aggregate amount of the deduction of income so allowed in respect of the previous year or years preceding such previous year, is deemed to by the income of the assessee of such previous year and is liable to tax in the assessment year relevant to such previous year [Sec. 80C(3)].

The scope of the term "transfer" in relation to immovable property has been given extended meaning. It includes transfer of such property by way of sale or exchange or lease for a term not less than 12 years.

It also includes allowing possession of such property to be taken or retained in part performance of a contract under sec. 53A of the Transfer of Property Act, 1982 [Sec. 269(4A)(*f*)].

19. Subscription to equity shares or debentures where their proceeds to be wholly utilised for specified facilities [Sec. 80C(2)(*xix*)] - Where the entire proceeds of the shares or debentures, issued by an Indian public company or a public financial institution is to be utilised for the purposes of developing, operating and maintaining infrastructure facility or industrial park or special economic zone or for generating and distributing power or for providing telecommunication services, deduction is admissible for such subscription. The public company or public financial institution (specified under sec. 4A of the Companies Act) is required to obtain the approval of the Board for making such an issue. The application for the approval of the Board should be made in Form No. 59.

The assessee should not transfer such shares or debentures within three years from the date of acquisition. If he transfers them within the lock-in-period of three years, the aggregate amount of the deduction so allowed in respect of such equity shares or debentures in the previous year or years preceding the previous year in which such sale or transfer has taken place is deemed to be the income of the assessee of such previous year and is liable to tax in the assessment year relevant to such previous year. [Sec. 80C(6)].

20. Subscription to units of mutual fund where proceeds to be utilised for providing specified facilities [Sec. 80C(2)(*xx*)] - Subscription to any units of any mutual fund [specified under Sec. 10(*23D*)] qualifies for rebate, provided such units are approved by the board and the entire subscription is utilised for the purposes of infrastructure facilities or for generating/distributing power or for providing telecommunication facilities. The mutual fund should seek the approval of the Board by making an application in Form No. 59A before making such an issue.

21. Bank deposit for a fixed term of not less than 5 years [Sec. 80C(2)(*xxi*)] - An individual or an HUF may deposit with any schedule bank any sum, subject to a maximum of ₹ 1,50,000, for a fixed period of not less than 5 years. The amount of deposit should be in multiples of ₹ 100. The deposit amount cannot be pledged to secure loans. The interest on term deposit is chargeable as per method of accounting followed by the assessee either on receipt basis or accrual basis.

The term deposit may be transferred from one branch to another branch of the same scheduled bank. It cannot be transferred from one scheduled bank to another scheduled bank.

Scheduled bank is defined as SBI, subsidiaries of SBI, nationalised banks and other banks, included in the Second Schedule of the RBI Act, 1934.

The provision is operative from the assessment year 2007-08 and subsequent years.

22. Subscription to National Bank for Agriculture and Rural Development [Sec. 80C(2)(*xxii*)] - From the assessment year 2008-09 and subsequent years, subscription to such bonds, issued by National Bank for Agriculture and Rural Development, and notified by the Central Government also qualify for deduction in computing total income in accordance with the provisions of sec. 80C.

23. Deposit under Senior Citizen Savings Scheme [Sec. 80C(2)(*xxiii*)] - From the assessment year 2008-09 and subsequent years, deposit in an account under Senior Citizen Savings Scheme also qualifies for deduction in accordance with the provisions of Sec. 80C also qualifies for deduction in computing total income.

24. 5-year Time Deposit in Post Office [Sec. 80C(2)(*xxiv*)] - From the assessment year 2008-2009 and subsequent years, 5-year time deposit in an account under Post Office Time Deposit Rules, 1981 also qualifies for deduction in computing total income in accordance with the provisions of Sec. 80C.

Where any amount is withdrawn by the assessee from such account (including accrued interest on deposit) before the expiry of 5 years from the date of its deposit, the amount so withdrawn is deemed to be the income of the assessee of the previous year in which the amount is withdrawn.

However, if amount so received or withdrawn (including accrued interest) has already been taxed in earlier years, such amount cannot be taxed again.

Where the nominee or legal heir of the assessee gets any amount excluding accrued interest on such deposit, refund of such deposit is not taxable. Thus, any accrued interest on the deposit is taxable [Sec. 80C(6A)].

25. Deposit by Central Government Employee [Sec. 80C(2)(*xxv*)] - From the assessment year 2020-21 the amount paid or deposited by a Central Government employee as contribution to specified account of the National Pension Scheme as referred to in sec. 80CCD for a fixed period of three years or more and which is in accordance with the scheme as may be notified by the Central Government in the Official Gazette would also qualify for deduction in computing total income in accordance with the provisions of sec. 80C.

(*ii*) Contribution to Certain Pension Funds [Sec. 80CCC]

This deduction of maximum ₹ 1,50,000 is available only to an individual assessee for contribution to the following pension funds:

(*a*) **Deposit or Payment under Annuity Plan of LIC** - The assessee–individual has paid or deposited any amount to effect or keep in force a contract for any annuity plan of Life Insurance Corporation of India (LIC) or any other insurer (w.e.f. AY 2002-03) for receiving pension from the fund referred to under Sec. 10(*23AAB*).

(*b*) **Payment or Deposit to be made out of Income Chargeable to Tax** - The assessee-individual should make the said deposit/payment out of his taxable income. The amount paid or deposited under the said annuity plan does not include interest or bonus accrued or credited to the assessee's account.

Taxable when pension received/annuity is surrendered [Sec. 80CCC(2)] - Such contribution together with the interest or bonus accrued or credited to the assessee's account is received by the assessee or his nominee as pension, the same is chargeable to tax. Further, any amount refunded to the assessee or his nominee on account of surrender of the annuity plan, before its maturity, whether in whole or in part, the amount of surrender value is taxable as the income of that previous year in which it is received.

Pension Funds Deposit (under Sec. 80CCC) not deductible under sec. 80C [Sec. 80CCC(3)] - Deposit made under pension funds is not eligible for any deduction, allowed for contributions to approved savings under Sec. 80C. The provision prevents double deduction.

(*iii*) Contribution to National Pension Scheme of Central Government [Sec. 80CCD]

The scheme applies to an employee who is employed:

(*i*) by the Central Government or the State Government;

(*ii*) any other employer on or after 1 January 2004. The scheme was further extended to any other individual, w.e.f. 1-4-2009, by Finance (No. 2) Act, 2009.

Deduction on employee's contribution to NPS under sec. 80CCD - Employee's contribution to NPS up to 10 per cent of salary (basic + dearness allowance) can be claimed as a deduction under sec. 80CCD(1), subject to a limit of ₹ 1.5 Lakh under sec. 80C. An additional investment up to ₹ 50,000 is also deductible from taxable income under Sec. 80CCD(1B). This is over and above the deduction of ₹ 1.5 lakh available under sec. 80C of Income-tax Act, 1961.

In case of private sector employees, employees' contribution to NPS up to 20 per cent of the gross total income can be claimed as deduction under sec. 80CCD(1).

Employer's Contribution to the Account of an Employee under a Pension Scheme

Employer's contribution to the NPS account of the employee is first included as salary income of the employee by virtue of sec. 17(1)(*viii*) and subsequently a deduction under sec. 80CCD(2) is allowed to the employee as follows:

(*a*) in case of Central Government employer or State Government employer , whole of the amount contributed by the Central Government or the State Government.

(*b*) in case of any other employer, actual contribution or 10% of the salary whichever is less.

Exemption on closure or opting out from NPS [Sec. 10(*12A*)] - By virtue of sec. 10(*12A*), 60% of the payment received from NPS to an employee on closure of his account or on his opting out of the pension scheme will be exempt from tax.

Exemption on partial withdrawal from NPS [Sec.10(*12B*)] - A withdrawal up to 25% of contribution from NPS tier I account for the purposes specified under the Pension Fund Regulatory and Development Authority Act, 2013 will be exempt from tax.

Assessee Contribution, not Eligible for Deduction under sec. 80C [Sec. 80CCD(4)]

Where any amount, paid or deposited by the assessee, has been deducted in computing his total income under this Section (*i.e.* either under sec. 80CCD(1) or sec. 80CCD(1B), no deduction is allowed with reference to such amount under sec. 80C for any assessment year beginning on or after 1 April 2006. Contributions made by an employee to his pension scheme but not deducted in computing his total income, do not qualify for deduction under Sec. 80C as it contains no provision to this effect. Thus, where an employee contributes more than 10% his salary to pension fund, neither he gets any deduction for such amount under sec. 80CCD nor he gets any deduction under sec. 80C.

Reinvestment of the amount received under this section [Sec. 80CCD(5)]

Where an assessee has received any amount under this section in any previous year but he has re-invested the said amount for purchasing an annuity plan in the same previous year, it is deemed as if he has received no such amount to avoid its taxability.

(2) Deduction in respect of contribution to *Agnipath* Scheme [Sec. 80CCH newly inserted by the Finance Act, 2023]

Where an assessee, being an individual enrolled in the *Agnipath* Scheme and subscribing to the *Agniveer* Corpus Fund on or after the 1st day of November, 2022, has in the previous year paid or deposited any amount in his account in the said Fund, he shall be allowed a deduction in the computation of his total income, of the whole of the amount so paid or deposited. Where the Central Government makes any contribution to the account of an assessee in the *Agniveer* Corpus Fund referred to in sub-section (1), the assessee shall be allowed a deduction in the computation of his total income of the whole of the amount so contributed.

(3) Payment of Medical Insurance Premium [Sec. 80D]

An individual or a Hindu undivided family is entitled to claim the deduction in respect of medical insurance premium according to the following table:

TABLE 13.1: MEDICAL INSURANCE PREMIUM

Particulars	Deduction for Individual		Deduction for HUF
	Self+ Spouse+ Dependent Children	Parents	
◆ Medical Insurance Premium ◆ Contribution to Central Govt. Health Scheme or other notified scheme ◆ Preventive health check-up (capped at ₹ 5,000)	₹ 25,000 (₹ 50,000 if senior citizen)	₹ 25,000 (₹ 50,000 if senior citizen)	₹ 25,000 (₹ 50,000 if senior citizen)
Medical Expenditure on the health of the person who is a senior citizen there is no medical claim insurance	₹ 50,000	₹ 50,000	₹ 50,000
Maximum Deduction under sec. 80D	₹ 50,000	₹ 50,000	₹ 50,000

Payments for mediclaim insurance should meet the following conditions:

- The payment should be made out of income chargeable to tax.
- Payment should be made by any mode other than cash. However, when payment is on account of preventive health check-up, it can be any mode including cash.

Proportionate deduction of insurance premium paid in lump sum [Sec. 80D(4A)] - The Finance Act, 2018 introduced a new provision for claiming a deduction with regards to single premium health insurance policies. Under sec. 80D(4A) where an assessee has made a lump sum premium payment in a single year for keeping in force health insurance for more than one year, deduction can be equal to the appropriate fraction of the amount, under Section 80D. The appropriate fraction is arrived at, by dividing the lump sum premium paid, by the number of years of the policy. However, this would again be subject to the limits of ₹ 25,000 of ₹ 50,000 as the case may be.

(4) Deduction in respect of maintenance including medical treatment of dependant with disability [Sec. 80DD]

An individual or a Hindu undivided family, resident in India, is allowed a deduction of ₹ 75,000 (₹ 1,25,000 if dependant is a person with sever disability) when such assessee:

(*a*) incurs expenditure on medical treatment (including nursing), training and rehabilitation of a dependant who is person with disability, or

(*b*) pays or deposits any amount under a scheme framed by LIC or any other insurer or Administrator (defined under sec. 2 of the Unit Trust of India) and approved by the Board for the benefit of the dependent who is a person with disability. [under Sec. 80DD(1)].

Dependant defined [*Explanation (b)*]

For this purposes dependant in case of an individual means the spouse, children, parents, brothers and sisters of the individual or any of them and in case of a Hindu undivided family, 'dependant' means a member of Hindu undivided family who is wholly or mainly dependant on such individual or Hindu undivided family for his support and maintenance. Such dependant person should not claim any deduction under sec. 80U in computing his total income for the assessment year, relating to that previous year.

The term "disability" shall have the meaning assigned under the Rights of Persons with Disability Act, 2016 or National Trust for Welfare of Persons with Autism, Cerebral Palsy, Mental Retardation and Multiple Disabilities Act, 1999. A "person with severe disability" means a person with eighty per cent or more of one or more disabilities, as referred Rights of Persons with Disability Act, 2016 National Trust for Welfare of Persons with Autism, Cerebral Palsy, Mental Retardation and Multiple Disabilities Act, 1999.

An individual claiming deduction under this section must furnish a copy of the certificate issued by the medical authority in the prescribed form and manner along with the return of income under sec. 139. Where 'medical certificate' specifies the period of disability, no deduction can be allowed after its expiry unless the 'disability certificate' is renewed by the medical authority.

Thus, under the existing provisions, the deduction with respect to deposits in annuity schemes was allowed only if such scheme provided for payment of annuity or lump sum amount for the benefit of a dependant person with disability in the event of the death of the subscriber-assessee. [Sec.80DD(2)] Further, if the dependant person with disability predeceased the subscriber-assessee the amount was deemed to be the income of such subscriber-assessee. [Sec. 80DD(3)].

Such schemes that allowed payments only upon death of the subscriber created hardships for the parents/guardians as well as persons with disabilities especially when amounts were required during the lifetime of the subscriber parent. In the matter of *Ravi Agrawal* v. *UOI* (2019) 101 taxmann.com 70/260 Taxman 352/410 ITR 399 (SC), a Public Interest Litigation (PIL) was filed before the Supreme

Court in the interest of children with disabilities whose parents had subscribed to the scheme of Jeevan Aadhar with Life Corporation of India (LIC) that was devoid of maturity claim. So that despite having paid the entire premium, no amounts could be paid for the benefit of the person disability during the lifetime of the subscriber. When such scheme was read with sec.80DD and the CBDT circular Circular No. CO/CRM/PS/622/23 dated January 24, 2008, no benefit could be paid to the dependent till the proposer/life assured survives. The Supreme Court observed that that there could be harsh cases where persons with disabilities may need payment of annuity or lumpsum during the lifetime of their partents/guadians and that the Legislature may take into consideration all the aspects and provide suitable provision by making necessary amendments in sec. 80DD of the Act.

Therefore, to remove the genuine hardship contained in sec.80DD, the Finance Act, 2022, the deduction allows when such subscriber-assessee attains 60 years or more years and the payment or deposit to such scheme has been discontinued (w.e.f. 1-4-2023). Further, when such annuity or lump sum is received by the dependent being a person with disability during the lifetime of the parent/ guardian, such amount shall not be deemed to be the income of the assessee-subscriber. (Sec. 80DD(3A) inserted by the Finance Act, 2022) [Sec. 80DD(3A)].

(5) Deduction for Medical Treatment [Sec. 80DDB]

Where an assessee individual or HUF, resident in India, incurs expenditure for medical treatment of specified diseases for himself or his dependant person or any member of its family respectively, he is allowed deduction to the extent of actual expenditure or ₹ 40,000 whichever is less. Such deduction is further reduced by any reimbursements received by the assessee from the insurer or employer. When such expenditure is incurred for a senior citizen, the ceiling is ₹ 1,00,000 instead of ₹ 40,000.

For this purposes, in case of individuals, dependent means the spouse, children, parents, brothers, and sisters of the individual or any of them; in case of HUF dependent means a member of the HUF. **Senior citizen** means an individual, resident in India, who is 60 years of age of more at any time during the previous year.

Specified Diseases - Payment for medical treatment should be for specified diseases and ailments which are given as follows:

(*a*) *Neurological diseases:* (*i*) Dementia; (*ii*) Dystonia Musculorum Deformans; (*iii*) Motor neuron disease; (*iv*) Ataxia; (*v*) Chorea; (*vi*) Hemiballismus (*vii*) Aphasia; (*viii*) Parkinson's disease.

Chronic neurological diseases: The above-mentioned diseases are to be treated as chronic and protracted, if the disability has been certified to be 40% and above.

(*b*) *Other diseases:* Cancer;

(*c*) Full blown acquired immuno-deficiency syndrome (AIDS);

(*d*) Chronic renal failure;

(*e*) Hemophilia

(*f*) Thalassaemia.

Certificate from Prescribed Specialist working in a Government Hospital - The assessee must furnish a certificate from a neurologist, an oncologist, a urologist, a hematologist, an immunologist, or such other specialist as may be prescribed. Prior to 1-4-2016, it was mandated that such certificate should be issued by a specialist in government hospitals. However, since this requirement was causing undue hardship the assessees and given a possibility that government hospital may not have specialists in above branches of medicine, the requirement of certificate from government doctor is has been done away with in the Finance Act, 2015 w.e.f. AY 2016-17.

(6) Repayment of interest on loan taken for higher education [Sec. 80E]

Where an assessee being an individual has taken loan from any financial institution or approved charitable institution for pursuing his higher education or for the purpose of higher education of his 'relative', he is allowed to deduct the amount of interest paid on such loan in computing his taxable income.

Period of deduction for interest - The borrower is allowed to deduct the interest on such loan in computing total income (*i*) during the period of 8 assessment years, commencing from the assessment year in which the assessee starts repaying the interest on loan (*ii*) or until the interest is paid in full, whichever period is earlier.

Repayment of Principal amount of loan not allowed as deduction - No deduction is allowed in respect of repayment of loan taken for higher education.

Terms defined:

(*a*) "Higher Education" - Means full-time studies for any graduate or postgraduate course in engineering, medicine, management, or postgraduate courses in applied sciences or pure sciences including mathematics and statistics. Graduate or postgraduate studies in engineering would include studies in architecture [Circular No. 688, dated 23-8-1994].

(*b*) Approved charitable institution - Means an institution established for charitable purposes and notified by the government under sec. 10(*23C*) or an institution referred to in sec. 80G(2)(*a*).

(*c*) Financial institution - Means a banking company to which Banking Regulation Act, 1949 applies or any other financial institution as the Central Government may notify in this behalf.

(*d*) Relative - The term "relative" in relation to an individual means the spouse and the children of that individual or the student for whom the individual is the legal guardian.

"Spouse" means legally wedded spouse. The relationship of spouse must exist at the time when interest is paid on education loan.

"Child" means legal child. Adopted child is a legal child. There is no restriction about the number of children. Thus, interest on loan for higher education may be paid for any number of children.

(7) Repayment of interest on loan taken for residential house:

(*a*) Loan sanctioned between 1st day of April, 2016 and ending on the 31st day of March, 2017 [Sec. 80EE]

Where an assessee being an individual borrows a loan from any financial institution for the purposes of acquisition of residential house property, interest payable on loan up to maximum ₹ 50,000 can be claimed as deduction provided the following conditions are fulfilled:

(*i*) the loan has been sanctioned by the financial institution during the period beginning on the 1st day of April, 2016 and ending on the 31st day of March, 2017;

(*ii*) the amount of loan sanctioned for acquisition of the residential house property does not exceed ₹ 35,00,000;

(*iii*) the value of residential house property does not exceed ₹ 50,00,000;

(*iv*) the assessee does not own any residential house property on the date of sanction of loan.

Where a deduction under this section is allowed for any interest, deduction shall not be allowed in respect of such interest under any other provision of this Act for the same or any other assessment year.

It may be inferred that the deduction under this section is in addition to the amount of ₹ 2,00,000 available under the head, 'income from house property' (Sec. 24(*b*) r.w. second proviso) and further amount of deduction which the assessee may claim under sec. 80C(2)(*xviii*).

(*b*) Loan sanctioned between 1st day of April, 2019 and ending on the 31st day of March, 2020 [Sec. 80EEA]

Where an assessee being an individual not eligible to claim deduction under section 80EE, borrows a loan from any financial institution for the purposes of acquisition of residential house property, interest payable on loan up to maximum ₹ 1,50,000 can be claimed as deduction provided the following conditions are fulfilled:

(*i*) the loan has been sanctioned by the financial institution during the period beginning on the 1st day of April, 2019 and ending on the 31st day of March, 2022;

(*ii*) the stamp duty value of residential house property does not exceed ₹ 45,00,000;

(*iii*) the assessee does not own any residential house property on the date of sanction of loan.

Where a deduction under this section is allowed for any interest, deduction shall not be allowed in respect of such interest under any other provision of this Act for the same or any other assessment year.

(8) Loan taken for purchase of electric vehicle [Sec. 80EEB]

Where an assessee being an individual borrows loan from a financial institution for the purposes of purchasing electric vehicle, interest payable thereon upto maximum ₹ 1,50,000 can be claimed as deduction. Such deduction will be allowed only when the loan has been sanctioned by the financial institution during the period beginning on the 1st day of April, 2019 and ending on the 31st day of March, 2023.

Where a deduction under this section is allowed for any interest referred herein, no deduction shall be allowed in respect of such interest under any other provision of this Act for the same or any other assessment year.

For the purposes of this section Electric vehicle has been defined as a vehicle which is powered exclusively by an electric motor whose traction energy is supplied exclusively by traction battery installed in the vehicle and has such electric regenerative braking system, which during braking provides for the conversion of vehicle kinetic energy into electrical energy. [Sec. 80EEB(5)].

(9) Deduction in case of a Person with Disability [Sec. 80U]

A deduction of ₹ 75,000 is allowed to an assessee being a resident individual is certified by the medical authority to be a person with disability. In case of sever disability this deduction is ₹ 1,25,000. However, an individual claiming deduction under this section must furnish a copy of the certificate issued by the medical authority in the prescribed form and manner along with the return of income under sec. 139. Where 'medical certificate' specifies the period of disability, no deduction can be allowed after its expiry unless the 'disability certificate' is renewed by the medical authority.

The term "disability" shall have the meaning assigned under the Rights of Persons with Disability Act, 2016 or National Trust for Welfare of Persons with Autism, Cerebral Palsy, Mental Retardation and Multiple Disabilities Act, 1999. A 'person with severe disability" means a person with eighty per cent or more of one or more disabilities, as referred Rights of Persons with Disability Act, 2016 National Trust for Welfare of Persons with Autism, Cerebral Palsy, Mental Retardation and Multiple Disabilities Act, 1999.

(10) Interest on deposits in savings account [Sec. 80TTA]

Where gross total income either of an individual or a Hindu undivided family, other than the income referred to in sec. 80TTB (inserted by Finance Act, 2018 w.e.f. 1-4-2019), includes interest on saving account, either held with:

(*i*) bank, or

(*ii*) co-operative society, engaged in banking business (including co-operative land Mortgage Bank or a Co-operative land development bank), or

(*iii*) a post office,

such assessee is allowed a deduction upto ₹ 10,000.

However, such deduction is not allowed when interest is credited on any deposit in saving account held on behalf of a (*i*) firm or (*ii*) an association of persons or (*iii*) body of individuals.

(11) Deduction in respect of interest on deposit (with bank/post-office) in case of senior citizen [Sec. 80TTB]

The Finance Act 2018 inserted this section w.e.f. 1-4-2019 that allows deduction of upto ₹ 50,000 to senior citizens, being resident individuals with age of 60 years and above, earning interest income on deposits with:

(*i*) bank, or

(*ii*) co-operative society, engaged in banking business (including co-operative land Mortgage Bank or a Co-operative land development bank); or

(*iii*) a post office,

However, such deduction is not allowed when interest is credited on any deposit in saving account held on behalf of a (*i*) firm or (*ii*) an association of persons or (*iii*) body of individuals.

(12) Deduction in respect of royalty income, etc., of authors of certain books other than textbooks [Sec. 80QQB]

An assessee being an author who is an individual resident in India is allowed a deduction under this section with respect to income being:

(*i*) any lump sum consideration for assignment of his interest in the copyright of any book of literary, artistic or scientific nature, or

(*ii*) royalty or copyright fees in respect of such book.

The quantum of deduction is (*i*) either of the whole amount or (*ii*) ₹ 3,00,000, whichever is less.

Following points must be noted:

(*i*) Book does not include brochures, commentaries, diaries, guides, journals, magazines, newspapers, pamphlets, text book for schools, tracts and other publications of similar nature, by whatever name called.

(*ii*) The maximum ceiling is not 'per book' but it is 'per assessee'. Thus, if the assessee gets royalty from more than one book, the maximum ceiling of deduction in respect of royalty from all such books during the previous year remains ₹ 3,00,000.

(*iii*) *Rate of royalty should not exceed 15%* - Where the income by way of such royalty or copyright fee is not a lump sum consideration in lieu of all rights of the assessee in the book, so much of the income, before allowing expenses attributable to such income, as is in excess of 15% of the value of the such books sold during the previous year, is to be ignored. In other words, the amount of eligible income, in respect of which deduction is to be allowed, should not exceed 15% of the value of the books sold during the previous year. Any excess over 15% of the value of books sold during the previous year is not to be considered for the purposes of deduction.

(*iv*) ***Remittance not deductible*** - No deduction is allowed in respect of any such income as is earned outside India in convertible foreign exchange but which is not brought into India within 6 months from the end of the previous year or such extended time as may be allowed by the competent authority.

Furnishing of a certificate [Sec. 80QQB(3)(4)] - No deduction is allowed to such assessee unless a certificate in Form No. 10CCD (under Rule 19AC) is furnished along with the return of income.

No deduction is allowed in respect of any income earned from any source outside India unless the assessee furnishes a certificate in Form No. 10H [under Rule 29(1)].

Double Deduction Prohibited [Sec. 80QQB(5)] - Where any deduction has been allowed in for any previous year in respect of royalty or copyright fee under this Section, no deduction in respect of such income is allowed again under any other provision of the Act.

(13) Deduction in respect of Royalty Patents [Sec. 80RRB]

Where a patentee being an individual resident in India receives royalty income in respect of a patent registered on or after 1st April, 2003 under the Patents Act, 1970, such individual is allowed a deduction for such income subject to the following conditions:

(*a*) *Certificate to be furnished:* Assessee should furnish a certificate along with the return of income in prescribed form, duly signed by the prescribed authority and setting forth such particulars as may be prescribed.

A separate certificate need to be furnished in respect of royalty earned from any source outside India.

(*b*) *Royalty earned outside India to be brought into India within the prescribed time-limit:* Royalty earned from any source outside India should be brought into India for or on behalf of the assessee in convertible foreign exchange within 6 months from the end of the previous year or such extended time as may be allowed by the Reserve Bank of India or any other authority as is authorised under any law for the time-being in force for regulating payments and dealing in foreign exchange.

Where only a part of the royalty is brought into India within the prescribed limit, only the part so brought into India will be eligible for deduction.

Quantum of Deduction

The amount of deduction to allowed is as follows:

(*i*) Actual amount of royalty, or

(*ii*) ₹ 3,00,000

Whichever is less.

Royalty received under Compulsory Licence - Where compulsory licence is granted in respect of any patent under the Patents Act, 1970, the amount of royalty allowed as deduction cannot exceed such amount as is settled under the terms of the licence settled by the Controller under the Patents Act.

Deductions for donations, contributions etc.

(14) Donations to Certain Funds, Charitable Institutions [Sec. 80G]

To promote charitable institutions in the larger social interest, income-tax law allows deduction in respect of donations in accordance with the following provisions:

Conditions for claiming the deduction :

(*i*) **Donations must be Paid in Money and not in Money's Worth [*Explanation 5* to Sec. 80G] -** The deduction is allowed if donations are paid in monetary terms only, that is, either by cash or cheque. No deduction is allowed for donation paid in kind. For example, donations made by supplying goods of various kinds such as building, vehicle, shares or any other tangible property does not qualify for deduction u/s 80G even though such donations may be convertible in terms of money. *Explanation 5* to Sec. 80G makes the legislative intent very clear. It allows no deduction in respect of any donation unless it is a sum of money. [*H.H. Sri Rama Verma* v. *CIT* [1991] 187 ITR 308/57 Taxman 149 (SC)].

(*ii*) **Donations must be paid only to specified funds, institutions or trust, etc. -** No deduction is allowed if donations are paid to Funds, Institutions or Trusts not specified u/s 80G.

(*iii*) **Deduction cannot be claimed twice [Sec. 80G(5A)] -** Where a deduction is claimed and allowed u/s 80G, the sum in respect of which deduction is allowed does not qualify for deduction under any other provision either for the same or any other assessment year.

There may be a case where a donation falls within the category of *"wholly and exclusively for the purpose of business or profession"* and hence eligible for deduction as a business expense under sec. 37(1). The same donation may also qualify for deduction under sec. 80G. In such a case, the option remains with the assessee to claim the expenditure either as a business expense under sec. 37(1) or as deduction for donation under Sec. 80G but not under both. An assessee may exercise the option most beneficial to him but cannot claim the benefit of the same donation under more than one provisions of the Act [*Jaswant Trading Co.* v. *CIT* [1995] 212 ITR 24/[1996] 85 Taxman 639 (Raj.)].

(*iv*) **Source of income no ground to deny deduction -** Taxability of the source of the donation is not relevant. Deduction cannot be denied merely on the ground that the donation is made out of an income which is exempt from tax.

(*v*) **Violation of conditions of approval by the Donee Fund or institution does not affect the Donor's right to claim deduction -** The right of the donor to claim deduction for donation to an approved fund and compliance of conditions of approval by the donee fund or institution are two independent concepts. Deduction to the donor cannot be denied on the grounds that the donee institution did not comply with the conditions of the approval. Tax benefit to the donor gets neutralised by tax from the trust as its income becomes liable to be taxed due to the such violation. [*N. N. Desai Charitable Trust* v. *CIT* (2000) 246 ITR 452/123 Taxman 866 (Guj.)].

(*vi*) **Deduction cannot be allowed where gross total income is negative -** The opening words in Sec. 80G are *"in computing the total income of an assessee"*. In a case where there is no income earned by the assessee and, therefore, the question of computing total income does not arise, there appears to be no reason for giving the benefit of the deduction available under Sec. 80G. [*CIT* v. *S. Zoraster and Co. (S.)* (1988) 39 Taxman 261/(1989) 179 ITR 416 (Raj.)].

(*vii*) **No Deduction if a sum exceeding ₹ 2000 paid in cash [Section 80G(5D)] -** With effect from 1st June 2018 no deduction is allowed under this section when donation is made in cash exceeding ₹ 2000. Prior to its amendment by Finance Act, 2017 such disallowance was made when cash payment exceeded ₹ 10,000.

Classification of donations for the purposes of deduction:

Donations have been classified in two categories, keeping in view the rate of deduction :

Donations not subject to any ceiling or qualifying amount - Where Rate of Deduction is 100% of Donations Paid

Donation paid to the following funds or intuitions is fully deductible in computing the total income, irrespective of the amount paid:

1. National Defence Fund; or
2. Prime Minister's Armenia Earthquake Relief Fund; or
3. The Africa (Public Contributions—India) Fund; or
4. The Prime Minister's National Relief Fund; or the Prime Minister's Citizen Assistance and Relief in Emergency Situations Fund (PM CARES FUND) with retrospective effect from 1-4-2020;
5. National Foundation for Communal Harmony; or
6. The Maharashtra Chief Minister's Relief Fund; or
7. A University or any educational institution of national eminence as may be approved by the Director-General (Income-tax Exemption); or

8. Any Zila Saksharta Samiti, constituted in any district under the chairmanship of the Collector of that district for the improvement of primary education in villages and towns in such district and for literacy and post-literacy activities (w.e.f. 1-4-1996). "Town" means a town which has a population of not exceeding one lakh as per latest census published before the first day of the previous year; or
9. The National Blood Transfusion Council or State Blood Transfusion Council which has its sole object as to the control, supervision, regulation or encouragement in India of the services related to operation and requirements of blood banks; or
10. Any fund set up by a State Government to provide a medical relief to the poor; or
11. The Army Central Welfare Fund or the Indian Naval Benevolent Fund or the Air Force Central Welfare Fund established by the armed forces of the Union for the welfare of past or present members of such forces or their dependents; or
12. The Andhra Pradesh Chief Minister's Cyclone Relief Fund, 1996; or
13. The National Illness Assistance Fund; or
14. The Chief Minister's Relief Fund or the Lieutenant Governor's Relief Fund in respect of any State or Union Territory. The deduction is allowed subject to the following conditions:
    (*i*) such fund is the only fund of its kind established in the State or the Union Territory;
    (*ii*) such fund is under the overall control of the Chief Secretary or the Department of Finance of the State or the Union Territory, as the case may be; and
    (*iii*) such fund is administered in such manner as may be specified by the State Government or the Lieutenant Governor, as the case may be; or
15. National Cultural Fund, set up by the Central Government; or
16. National Sports Fund, set up by the Central Government; or
17. Fund for Technology Development and Application; or
18. National Trust for Welfare of Persons with Autism, Cerebral Palsy, Mental Retardation and Multiple Disabilities (constituted under sec. 3(1) of the National Trust for Welfare of Persons with Autism, Cerebral Palsy, Mental Retardation and Multiple Disabilities Act, 1999); or
19. Any fund, set up by the State Government of Gujarat for providing relief exclusively to the victims of earthquake in Gujarat w.e.f. 3-2-2001; or
20. Any trust, institution or fund for providing relief to the victims of earthquake in Gujarat; or
21. The National Children Fund; or

22. National Sports Fund; or
23. National Cultural Fund; or
24. Fund for Technology Development and Application; or
25. Swachh Bharat Kosh w.e.f. A.Y. 2015-16; or
26. Clean Ganga Fund w.e.f. A.Y. 2015-16; or
27. National fund for Control of Drug Abuse w.e.f. A.Y. 2016-17.

Donations Subject to Qualifying Amount

In certain cases, deduction for donation is allowed not for actual donations paid but for the qualifying amount of donation. Such cases are given as below:

1. Donation paid by any assessee to the government or any local authority, to be utilised for any charitable purpose other than the purpose of promoting family planning; or
2. Donation paid by any assessee to an authority constituted in India under any law enacted either for the purpose of dealing with and satisfying the needs for housing accommodation or for the purpose of planning, development or improvement of cities, towns and villages, or for both; or
3. Donation given by any person for the renovation or repair of any such temple, mosque, gurudwara, church or other place as is notified by the Central Government to be of historic, archaeological or artistic importance or to be a place of public worship of renown throughout any State or States; or
4. Donation given by any person for any corporation established by the Central Government or any State Government for promoting the interests of the members of a minority community (w.e.f. 1-4-1995); or
5. Donation paid by any assessee to any other fund or institution which is approved by the Commissioner under Rule 11AA [Sec. 80G(5)(*vi*)]; or
6. Donation given by any person to government or any such local authority, institutions, or association as may be approved in this behalf by the Central Government to be utilised for the purpose of promoting family planning.

Qualifying Amount

(*i*) Aggregate of donations paid to institutions/funds as aforesaid; or

(*ii*) 10% of Modified Gross Total Income

whichever is less is the Qualifying Amount.

Modified gross total income	₹	₹
Gross total income		xxxx
Less: Aggregate of:		

	Modified gross total income	₹	₹
(*i*)	**Share of profit in AOP entitled to rebate u/s 86.	xxxx	
(*ii*)	Any amount qualifying for deduction from GTI under Sections 80C to 80U except for deduction for donation u/s 80G itself.	xxxx	
(*iii*)	Any long-term capital gain [Sec. 112(2)]	xxxx	
(*iv*)	Any short-term capital gain arising from the transfer of an equity share or a unit of equity-oriented fund [Sec. 111A(2)].	xxxx	
(*v*)	Any income to a NRI by way of dividend or interest from investment of convertible foreign exchange referred to u/ss 115A, 115AB, 115AC, 115ACA and 115AD.	xxxx	
		xxxx	xxxx
	Modified gross total income		*xxxx*

Explanation - Where no member of AOP has taxable income exceeding ₹ 2,50,000 in his individual capacity and the company is not a partner in AOP, the share of profit from such AOP is included in the total income of the member only for rate purposes. The member is entitled to claim rebate on such profit under Sec. 86 at the average rate of tax applicable to total income. Where any member of AOP has got income exceeding taxable limit or company is a partner in AOP, share of profit of the member from such AOP is exempt from tax [Sec. 86 *r.w.* Sec. 167B].

The following amendments have been inserted by virtue of the Finance Act, 2020. These provisions are effective from 1-4-2021.

Statement of receipt of donations [Sec. 80G(5)(*viii*)] - Institutions or Funds under this section are required to prepare a statement of receipts of donations and file the same before the Income tax authority in the prescribed time. Any correction in the statement by rectification of any mistake or to addition, deletion or update the information furnished in the statement can also be made.

Certificate to donors [Sec. 80G(5)(*ix*)] - Institution or funds under this section are required to furnish to the donors, a certificate specifying the amount of donation in such manner, containing such particular within such time from the date of receipt of donation as may be prescribed.

Deduction for donor only on basis of information of done [Sec. 80G(*2A*)] - A donor claiming deduction in its returns in respect of the donation made to an institution or funds, shall be allowed on the basis of information relating to said donation furnished by the institution or fund to the prescribed income tax authority or the person authorized by such authority, subject to verification in accordance with the risk management strategy formulated by the board from time to time.

New Regime of Registration - The Finance Act, 2020 introduced a new regime for registration of trusts or institutions shall file an application before the Commissioner or Principle Commissioner within the prescribed time limits to sought registration under section 80G. Procedure and time limit to file an application for registration under section 80G is same as the procedure for registration under Sec. 12AB.

(15) Deduction in respect of Donations for Scientific Research or Rural Development [Sec. 80GGA]

Every assessee is entitled to claim deduction in respect of donation made to specified institutions for scientific research or rural development. However, an assessee engaged in business or profession cannot claim this deduction. [Sec. 80GGA(3)]. This restriction is to avoid double deduction because the items of specified contributions are already deductible in computing business income under sec. 35, sec. 35AC, sec. 35CCA and sec. 35CCB. Further, no deduction is allowed in respect of any sum paid in cash exceeding ₹ 10,000.

Double deduction not allowed [Sec. 80GGA(4)]

Where a donation is also eligible for deduction under any other provision of the Act, the assessee has a choice either to claim it under sec. 80GGA or under the other provision but not under both. Once a deduction is claimed and allowed under sec. 80GGA, it does not qualify for deduction under any other provision of the Act either for the same assessment year or any other assessment year.

Donations qualifying for deduction

Donations made to the following institutions qualify for deduction:

(*a*) Any sum paid to a research association, approved under sec. 35(1)(*ii*), which has the object to undertake a research, is allowed to be deducted. The research may be in social science or statistical research or for any other purpose.

(*b*) Any sum paid to a university, college, or other institution, approved under sec. 35(1)(*ii*), to be used for scientific research. The research may be in social science or statistical research or for any other purpose.

(*c*) Any sum paid to an approved association or institution, which has as its object the undertaking of any programme of rural development, to be used for the purposes of carrying out any approved programme of rural development (under sec. 35CCA).

(*d*) Any sum paid to an approved association or institution, which has as its object the training of persons for implementing programmes of rural development is fully deductible.

(*e*) Any sum paid for approved welfare project to a public sector company or a local authority or an association or institution approved under sec. 35AC, is allowed to be deducted.

(*f*) Any sum paid to a rural fund set up and notified by the Central Government under sec. 35CCA is deductible.

(*g*) Any sum paid to a National Urban Poverty Eradication Fund set up and notified by the Central Government u/s 35CCA, is allowed to be deducted.

Withdrawal of approval/notification, subsequent to the payment of donation, not to affect the deduction allowed [*Explanation* to Sec. 80GGA(2)]

Where the deduction has been allowed to an assessee in respect of any sum paid to (*i*) a scientific research association, university or college etc. for scientific/statistical research; or (*ii*) an association/institution for carrying out the programme of rural development or training persons for implementing such programme; or (*iii*) a public sector company/local authority/an association or institution for carrying out eligible project, and subsequent to such payment by an assessee, the approval/notification in respect of such association/institution or programme has been withdrawn, the earlier deduction allowed to the assessee for such payment cannot be withdrawn.

Deduction allowed on the basis of information provided by the payee [*Explanation* to sec. 80GGA] - The Finance Act, 2020 has inserted an explantion w.e.f. 1-6-2020 which provides that the claim of the assessee for a deduction claimed in the return of income for any assessment year filed by him will be allowed on the basis of information relating to such sum furnished by the payee to the prescribed income-tax authority or the person authorised by such authority, subject to verification in accordance with the risk management strategy formulated by the Board from time to time.

The above information has to be furnished by the payee in terms of sec. 35(1A).

(16) Deduction in respect of contributions given by companies to Political Parties [Sec. 80GGB]

Where an Indian company contributes during the previous year any sum to (*i*) any political party registered under Representation of People Act, or (*ii*) an electoral trust, such sum is fully allowed as a deduction in computing the total income of the company. There is no limit on the amount of contribution. A foreign company is not eligible to claim deduction in respect of contribution to political parties.

However, no deduction is allowed for any sum which is contributed by way of cash.

(17) Deduction in respect of any sum given by any person to Political Parties [Sec. 80GGC]

Where any person (*except a local authority and artificial juridical person wholly or partly funded by the government*) contributes during the previous year any sum to any political party registered under Representation of People Act or an electoral trust, such sum is fully allowed as a deduction in computing the total income of the person. There is no limit on the amount of contribution. However, no deduction is allowed for any such sum which is contributed by way of cash.

DEDUCTIONS OFFERING PROFIT-LINKED INCENTIVES

(1) Deduction in respect of Profits and Gains from Industrial Undertaking or Enterprise Engaged in Infrastructural Development [Sec. 80-IA]

Deduction under this section is available to an assessee who derives any profits and gains from an undertaking or an enterprise carrying on any of the following business:

(*i*) Infrastructure facility;

(*ii*) Telecommunication services;

(*iii*) Industrial parks;

(*iv*) Power generation, its transmission/distribution/renovation and modernisation of distribution lines;

(*v*) Reconstruction of a power unit [Sec. 80-IA(4)].

Since the operational period of 'Telecommunication Services' (w.e.f. 1 April, 1995 to 31 March, 2005) and 'Industrial Parks' (w.e.f. 1 April, 1995 to 31 March, 2006) is already over, the two schemes have not been discussed.

The relevant provisions in this connection are explained as below :

(*i*) Infrastructure facility [Sec. 80-IA(1), (2), (3) & (4)(*i*)]:

An Indian company or a consortium of Indian companies or an authority established under any Central/State Act can claim this deduction subject to the following conditions:

(*a*) It should provide infrastructure facility and thereby derive profits from an undertaking or enterprise carrying on the business of (*i*) developing or (*ii*) operating and maintaining or (*iii*) developing, operating and maintaining any infrastructure facility

(*b*) There should be an agreement with the Central Government

(*c*) The operations should start on or after 1st April 1995. However no deduction will be available where any enterprise that starts the development or operation and maintenance of the infrastructure facility on or after the 1st day of April, 2017.

(*d*) No deduction is allowed if the return of income is not furnished on or before the due date, specified under sec. 139(1). **[Sec. 80AC]**

Quantum of Deduction - 100% deduction of its profits derived from such business for 10 consecutive years out of 15 years, beginning from the year in which the undertaking begins to operate such facility. Where 'infrastructure facility' is a road, highway project or water supply project, the deduction is allowed for 10 years out of 20 years at the option of the assessee [Proviso to Sec. 80-IA(2)].

Infrastructure facility means - [*Explanation* to sec. 80-IA(4)]

- A road including toll road, a bridge or a rail system;
- A highway project including housing or other activities being an integral part of the highway project;
- A water supply project, water treatment system, irrigation project, sanitation and sewerage system, or solid waste management system.
- A port, airport, inland waterway or inland port.

Circular:

(*i*) Structures at the ports for storage, loading and unloading, etc. can be included in the definition of 'port', provided the concerned port authority has issued a certificate to that effect [Circular No. 10/2005, dated 16-12-2005].

(*ii*) Effluent treatment and conveyance system is treated as infrastructure facility [Circular No. 1/2006, dated 12-1-2006].

(*iii*) Navigational channel in the sea is also be treated an infrastructure facility. It is operative from the assessment year 2008-09 and onward.

It must be noted that the Finance Act, 2016 changed the incentives in respect of the infrastructure facility from profit based deduction to the asset based deduction as provided in sec. 35AD. Under sec. 35AD an asset based deduction can be availed by the specified business, *i.e.*, developing or operating and maintaining or developing, operating and maintaining, a new infrastructure facility, which commences its operation on or after 1-4-2017. Thus, it could be said that in relation to infrastructure facility business (as specified), if the relevant operation starts on or before 31-3-2017, it would be eligible for the profit based incentive deduction under section 80-IA; and if the relevant operation starts on or after 1-4-2017, it would be eligible for the asset based incentive deduction under section 35AD.

(*ii*) Undertaking set up for power generation or laying new transmission lines/renovation of existing network of transmission [Sec. 80-IA(4)(*iv*)] :

An undertaking, set up for the prescribed object during the specified period, is entitled to claim the deduction subject to the following conditions:

(*i*) It is set up in any part of India for the generation of power and begins to generate power at any time during the period w.e.f. 1 April, 1993 to 31 March, 2017; or

(*ii*) It stars transmission or distribution by laying a network of new transmission or distribution lines at any time during the period w.e.f. 1 April 1999 to 31 March, 2017. However, deduction is allowed for profits, derived from laying network of new lines for transmission or distribution; or

(*iii*) It undertakes substantial renovation and modernisation of the existing lines at any time during the period beginning on 1 April, 2004 to 31 March, 2017. "Substantial renovation and modernisation" means an increase in plant and machinery in the network of transmission or distribution lines by at least 50% of the book value of such plant and machinery as on 1st April, 2004.

(*iii*) Undertaking, set up for reconstructions of a power generating plant by an Indian Company :

Where an Indian company has set up a power generating plant, it is entitled to claim the deduction in computing its total income provided the following conditions are complied with :

(*i*) it is set up before 30 November, 2005 with majority equity participation by public sector company to enforce the security interest of the leader of company, owning the power generation plant;

(*ii*) it is notified before 31 December, 2005 by the Central Government; and

(*iii*) it begins to generate or transmit or distribute power before 31st March, 2011.

Computation of profits [Sec. 80-IA(5)] - Profits and gains of eligible business are computed as if it is the only source of income of the assessee during the previous year, relevant to the initial assessment year and to every subsequent year for which the determination is made.

Audit Report to be filed along with the 'Return' [Sec. 80-IA(7)] - No deduction is allowed unless the accounts are audited by a chartered accountant before the specified date referred to in sec. 44B and the assessee furnishes by that date and the report of such audit is furnished along with the return of income in the prescribed Form No. 10CCB (Rule 18BBB), duly signed and verified by such accountant [Sec. 80-IAC(7)].

Inter-transfer of goods/services [Sec. 80-IA(8)] - Inter-transfer of goods or services between the 'eligible business' (under Sec. 80-IA) to 'any other business' of the assessee or *vice versa* should be made at market value on the date of their transfer, failing which the Assessing Officer is empowered to recompute the profit of 'eligible source' as if the transfer had been made in either case at the market value.

More than ordinary profits arising from the specified source [Sec. 80-IAB(10)] - Where more than ordinary profits arise to the assessee from specified sources [under sec. 80-IAB] because of a close connection among the assessee and any other person, the Assessing Officer is empowered to recompute the profits of such business for the purposes of deduction. If the aforesaid arrangement involves a specified domestic transaction [under sec. 92BA], the amount of profits from such transaction is determined keeping in view the arm's length price [under sec. 92F]. It is operative from the assessment year 2013-14.

Suspension of the exemption-benefit [Sec. 80-IAB(11)] - The Central Government may notify that the exemption cannot apply to any class of industrial undertaking or enterprise w.e.f. specified date. It may hold any inquiry before taking any such decision.

Computation of profits [Sec. 80-IA(5)] - Profits and gains from industrial undertakings or enterprises, engaged in infrastructure development is computed as if the eligible business is the only source of income of the assessee during the tax holiday period.

Profit from housing or other activities, being an integral part of highway project [Sec. 80-IA(6)] - Profits from housing or other activities which are an integral part of highway project, are not liable to be taxed, provided the following conditions are satisfied:

(*i*) *Profits to be computed in accordance with Rule 18BBE* - Where the assessee follows regular method of accounting, the profits should be computed under that method in accordance with the provisions of this Act. Where profits cannot be computed in respect of such activities under regular method of accounting, the profits may be computed according to percentage of completion of such activities during the relevant previous year.

(*ii*) *Profit to be transferred to special reserve* - The profit, from the housing and other activities, computed as above, should be transferred to a special reserve account.

(*iii*) *Utilisation of reserve* - The amount of reserve should be utilised for highway project, excluding housing and other activities, before the expiry of three years following the year in which such reserve was created. The unutilised amount of reserve is chargeable to tax as the income of the year in which such transfer took place.

Amalgamation or Demerger [Sec. 80-IA(12)] - Where any undertaking of an Indian company is transferred to another Indian company in a scheme of amalgamation or demerger before the expiry of the period of deduction it is the amalgamated company or resulting company which is entitled to claim the deduction for the unexpired period.

However, where transfer of company or undertaking by way of amalgamation or demerger takes place on or after 1 April 2007, no deduction is allowed under Sec. 80-IA to the amalgamated or resulting company for the unexpired period. [Sec. 80-IA(12A)].

Double deduction not permissible [Sec. 80-IA(9)] - Where the amount of profits and gains of eligible business (to which this Section applies) is claimed and allowed as deduction under this Section, deduction to the extent of such profits and gain will not be allowed under any other provisions of this chapter under the heading 'C- Deductions in respect of certain income' and the aggregate amount of deduction should not exceed the amount of profits derived under sec. 80-IA. (There exists an issue whether deduction under sec.80-IA or 80-IB could be allowed if sec. 80HHC is already availed. Since the court was divided in its opinion the matter was referred to a larger bench and decision is pending. [*Asstt. CIT* v. *Micro Labs Ltd.* (2015) 64 taxmann.com 199/(2016) 237 Taxman 74/380 ITR 1 (SC)].

No deduction if works contracts awarded nothing contained in this section shall apply in relation to a business referred to in sub-section (4) which is in the nature of a works contract awarded by any person (including the Central or State Government) and executed by the undertaking or enterprise. [*Explanation* to Sec.80-IA]

Case Law : ***CIT* v. *Chetak Enterprises (P.) Ltd.* [2020] 115 taxmann.com 108/272 Taxman 509 (SC)**

Facts: 'C 's claim to deduction under sec. 80-IA was denied on the grounds that it was a successor company to an erstwhile partnership firm and it was the firm which had entered into an agreement with Rajasthan Government for construction of road and collection of toll tax. Since original bid for said work was made by a firm and work order was issued to said firm; the mandatory requirement of section 80-IA(4)(*i*)(*a*) being company owning infrastructure facility was not compiled with and no agreement in terms of section 80-IA(4)(*i*)(*b*) was made by assessee-company with State Government for collection of toll tax.

Held: Although the agreement was initially executed between erstwhile partnership firm and State Government, it was with clear understanding that as and when partnership firm was converted into a company, name of company in agreement so executed be recorded recognizing change. Since original agreement entered into with firm automatically stood converted in favour of 'C' the condition for claiming deduction Section 80-IA was fulfilled and deduction allowed.

Case Law : ***CIT* v. *Container Corporation of India* [2018] 93 taxmann.com 31/255 Taxman 334/404 ITR 397 (SC)**

Facts: 'C' being a government Company, was engaged in the business of handling and transportation of containerized cargo and operating activities were mainly carried out at its Inland Container Depots (ICDs), Container Freight Stations (CFSs) and Port Side Container Terminals (PSCTs) spread all over the country. The assessee filed its returns for relevant years and claimed deduction under various heads including deduction under section 80-IA which was rejected.

Held: While the term Inland Port has not been defined, the term port, in commercial terms, is a place where vessels are in a habit of loading and unloading goods. The ICDs function for the benefit of exporters and importers located in industrial centers which are situated at distance from seaports. The purpose of introducing them was to promote the export and import in the country as these depots acts as a facilitator. The Notification issued by the Central Board of Excise & Customs (CBEC) dated 24-4-2007 holds that considering the nature of work carried out at these ICDs they can be termed as Inland Ports. ICDs are Inland Ports and subject to the provisions of the section and deduction can be claimed for the income earned.

(2) Deduction in respect of Profits and Gains of an Undertaking or Enterprise Engaged in the Development of Special Economic Zone [Sec. 80-IAB]

Where the assessee is a 'developer' earning profits from the business of developing a 'Special Economic Zone,' it is allowed a 100% deduction for the profits derived from such business for 10 consecutive years out of 15 years beginning from the year in which a Special Economic Zone has been notified by the Central Government. However, the Special Economic Zone should be notified on or after April 1 2005 and the development of special economic zone should begin on or before 1st April 2017. Where a developer transfers the operation and maintenance to another developer, the transferee developer is allowed deduction for the unexpired period in the 10 consecutive assessment years.

For the purposes of this section, "Developer" is either (*i*) a person or (*ii*) a State Government, granted a letter of approval [under Sec. 3(10) of Special Economic Zones Act, 2005] by the Central Government and includes a 'co-developer' [Sec. 2(*g*) of Special Economic Zones Act, 2005].

Computation of Profits [Sec. 80-IAB(3)] - The profit is computed presuming that the eligible business is the only source of income during the previous year:

- Unabsorbed losses and allowances or carry forward losses and allowances of any other business of the assessee cannot be set-off against the profits of the eligible business for the purpose of the deduction u/s 80-IA.
- Unabsorbed losses and allowances or carry forward losses and allowances of the eligible business will, for the purpose of this deduction, may be set-off against the profits of the eligible business even if they were set-off against the profits of other business of the assessee in computing its total income.

Return of income [Sec. 80AC] - Deduction is allowed, provided return of income is furnished on or before the due date specified under Sec. 139(1).

Audit of accounts [Sec. 80-IA(7) r.w. Sec. 80-IAB(3)] - The accounts of the assessee should be audited. The assessee should furmish the return income along with the report of such audit in the prescribed form duly signed and verfied by the chartered accountant.

Double deduction not allowed [Sec. 80-IA(9) r.w. Sec. 80-IAB(3)] - Where any amount of profit is deducted under this Section, no deduction is allowed for such profits under any other provisions of this chapter.

Transfer of Goods between various other businesses of the assessee to be considered at their Market Value [Sec. 80-IA(8) r.w. Sec. 80-IAB(3)] - Any transfer of goods from the undertaking to another business of the assessee or *vice versa* must be at the market value of such goods on the date of transfer. "Market value" for this purpose means price that such goods may fetch in the open market. However, where determining such market value present exceptional difficulties, the Assessing Officer may compute 'transfer value' on such reasonable basis as he may deem fit.

Adjustment of more than ordinary profits arising due to transaction between assessee and closely connected person [Sec. 80-IA(10) r.w. Sec. 80-IAB(3)] - Where more than ordinary profits arise from the eligible business because of the close connection between the assessee carrying on the eligible business and any other person, the Assessing Officer may allow the deduction on the basis of such profits as may be reasonably expected to arise from eligible business.

Amalgamation or Demerger [Sec. 80-IA(12) r.w. Sec. 80-IAB(3)] - Where any undertaking of an Indian company is transferred to another Indian company in a scheme of amalgamation or demerger before the expiry of the period of deduction, it is the amalgamated company or resulting company which is entitled to claim the deduction under this section for the unexpired period.

(3) Deduction in respect of specified business [Sec. 80-IAC]

The Finance Act, 2016 provided for deduction in respect of profits and gains derived by a start-up under this section w.e.f. assessment year 2017-18. Accordingly, an assessee, being an eligible start-up, shall be allowed a deduction of an amount equal to 100% of the profits and gains derived from such business. Such deduction is available for 3 consecutive assessment years out of 10 assessment years beginning from year in which the eligible start-up is incorporated subject to fulfilment of the following conditions:

(*i*) The assessee is an eligible startup *i.e.* a company or a limited liability partnership incorporated on or after 1st day of April, 2016 but before the 1st day of April, 2024 with a total turnover not exceeding ₹ 100 crore (w.e.f. 1-4-2021) (previously ₹ 25 crore) and holds a certificate of eligible business from the Inter-Ministerial Board of Certification as notified in the Official Gazette by the Central Government; [Sec. 80-IAC(1) r/w *Explanation*].

(*ii*) Such assessee is carrying on eligible business *i.e.* a business carried out by an eligible start-up engaged in innovation, development or improvement of products or processes or services or a scalable business model with a high potential of employment generation or wealth creation. [Sec. 80-IAC(1) r/w *Explanation*].

(*iii*) The profits and gains are derived from eligible business and are included in the gross total income of the assessee. [Sec. 80-IAC(1)]

(*iv*) The startup is not formed by splitting up, or the reconstruction, of a business already in existence. However, an exception is made when such start-up which is formed as a result of the re-establishment, reconstruction or revival by the assessee of the business of any such undertaking as referred to in sec. 33B, in the circumstances and within the period specified in that section. [Sec. 80-IAC(3)(*i*)]

(*v*) The startup is not formed by the transfer of machinery or plant previously used for any purpose to new business [Sec. 80-IAC(3)(*ii*)].

Computation of profits [Sec. 80-IAC(4) r.w. Sec. 80-IA(5)] - Profits and gains from industrial undertakings or enterprises, engaged in infrastructure development is computed as if the eligible business is the only source of income of the assessee during the tax holiday period.

Audit of accounts [Sec. 80-IAC(4) r.w. Sec. 80IA(7)] - The accounts of the assessee should be audited. The assessee should furnish the return income along with the report of such audit in the prescribed form duly signed and verified by the chartered accountant.

Inter-transfer of goods/services [Sec. 80-IAC(4) r.w. Sec. 80-IA(8)] - Inter-transfer of goods or services between the 'eligible business' (under Sec. 80-IA) to 'any other business' of the assessee or *vice versa* should be made at market value on the date of their transfer, failing which the Assessing Officer is empowered to re-compute the profit of 'eligible source' as if the transfer had been made in either case at the market value.

Double Deduction not Permissible [Sec. 80-IAC(4) r.w. Sec. 80-IA(9)] **-** Where the amount of profits and gains of eligible business (to which this Section applies) is claimed and allowed as deduction under this Section, deduction to the extent of such profits and gain will not be allowed under any other provisions of this chapter under the heading 'C- Deductions in respect of certain income' and the aggregate amount of deduction should not exceed the amount of profits derived under Sec. 80-IAC.

More than ordinary profits arising from the specified source [Sec. 80-IAC(4) r.w. Sec. 80-IAB(10)] **-** Where more than ordinary profits arise to the assessee from specified sources [under sec. 80-IAB] because of a close connection among the assessee and any other person, the Assessing Officer is empowered to recompute the profits of such business for the purposes of deduction. If the aforesaid arrangement involves a specified domestic transaction [under sec. 92BA], the amount of profits from such transaction is determined keeping in view the arm's length price [under sec. 92F]. It is operative from the assessment year 2013-14.

Suspension of the exemption-benefit [Sec. 80-IAB(11)] **-** The Central Government may notify that the exemption cannot apply to any class of industrial undertaking or enterprise w.e.f. specified date. It may hold any inquiry before taking any such decision.

(4) Deduction in respect of profits and gains from housing projects [Sec. 80-IBA]

The Finance Act, 2016 introduced this section w.e.f. 1-4-2017 to provide for a deduction of an amount equal to 100% of the profits and gains from housing projects subject to the following conditions:

(*i*) The project should be approved by the competent authority after the 1st day of June, 2016, but on or before the 31st day of March 2022;

(*ii*) The project should be completed within a period of 5 years from the date of approval by the competent authority. Where approval is obtained more than once, the project shall be deemed to have been approved on the date on which the building plan of such housing project was first approved by the competent authority; and the project shall be deemed to have been completed when a certificate of completion of project as a whole is obtained in writing from the competent authority;

(*iii*) The carpet area of the shops and commercial establishment included in the housing project should not exceed 3% of the aggregate carpet area;

(*iv*) Minimum Measurement of Plot:

- Prior to 1-4-2018, when the project was located within the cities of Chennai, Delhi, Kolkata or Mumbai or within the distance, measured aerially, of 25Kms from the municipal limits of these cities, the built up area should not have been less than 1000 square metres. This provision is now omitted and hence the limit of 2000 square meter would apply.
- For cities other than in Chennai, Delhi, Kolkata or Mumbai the land should measure not less than 2000 sq. mt.

(*v*) The project is the only housing project on the plot of land as specified above.

(*vi*) Minimum Carpet area:

- Where the project is located within the cities of Chennai, Delhi, Kolkata or Mumbai the carpet area of the residential unit comprised in the housing project should not exceed 30 square metres.
- Where the project is located in any other place the carpet area should not exceed 60 Square meters.

(*vii*) Where a residential unit in the housing project is allotted to an individual, no other residential unit in the housing project shall be allotted to the individual or the spouse or the minor children of such individual.

(*viii*) Minimum Built-up area:

- Prior to 1-4-2018 where the project is located within the cities of Chennai, Delhi, Kolkata or Mumbai or within the distance, measured aerially, of 25Kms from the municipal limits of these cities, the project should utilise not less than 90% of the floor area ratio permissible in respect of the plot of land under the rules to be made by the Central Government or the State Government or the local authority, as the case may be. This provision has been omitted by the Finance Act, 2017 and therefore the limit of 80% as provided for other cities applies.
- For cities other than Chennai, Delhi, Kolkata or Mumbai should utilise not less than 80% of the permissible floor area ratio.

(*ix*) The assessee should maintains separate books of account in respect of housing project:

(*i*) For the purposes of this clause rental housing project" means a project which is notified by the Central Government in the Official Gazette under this clause on or before the 31st day of March, 2022 and fulfils such conditions as may be specified in the said notification.

W.e.f 1-4-2022, a new sub-section (1A) has been inserted whereby the gross total income of an assessee includes any profits and gains derived from the business of developing and building rental housing project, there shall be allowed a deduction of an amount equal to 100% of the profits and gains derived from such business.

When the projects are approved on or after the 1st day of September, 2019 the following conditions will be applicable

(*i*) Minimum Measurement of Plot

- where such project is located within the metropolitan cities of Bengaluru, Chennai, Delhi National Capital Region (limited to Delhi, Noida, Greater Noida, Ghaziabad, Gurugram, Faridabad), Hyderabad, Kolkata and Mumbai (whole of Mumbai Metropolitan Region), the project should be on a plot of land measuring not less than 1000 sq.mt.
- For other cities it should not be less than 2000 sq.mt.

(*ii*) Minimum Carpet area

- where such project is located within the metropolitan cities of Bengaluru, Chennai, Delhi National Capital Region (limited to Delhi, Noida, Greater Noida, Ghaziabad, Gurugram, Faridabad), Hyderabad, Kolkata and Mumbai (whole of Mumbai Metropolitan Region) the carpet area of the residential unit comprised in the housing project should not exceed 60 sq. mt.
- For any other city it is 90 sq.mt.

(*iii*) Minimum Floor area

- where such project is located within the metropolitan cities of Bengaluru, Chennai, Delhi National Capital Region (limited to Delhi, Noida, Greater Noida, Ghaziabad, Gurugram, Faridabad), Hyderabad, Kolkata and Mumbai (whole of Mumbai Metropolitan Region), the project utilises not less than ninety per cent of the floor area ratio permissible in respect of the plot of land under the rules to be made by the Central Government or the State Government or the local authority, as the case may be.
- for cities other than the one mentioned above the project should utilize not less than 80% of the permissible floor area ratio.

(*iv*) The project is the only housing project on the plot of land as specified.

(*v*) The stamp duty value of a residential unit in the housing project does not exceed ₹ 45,00,000.

Double Deduction Not Permissible [Sec. 80-IBA(5)] - Where the amount of profits and gains of eligible business (to which this Section applies) is claimed and allowed as deduction under this Section, no deduction is allowed from the gross total income under any other Section of the Act.

(5) Deduction in Respect of Certain Undertaking in Northern-Eastern States [Sec. 80-IE]

An assessee deriving profits from a certain undertakings in Northern Eastern States of Arunachal Pradesh, Assam, Manipur, Meghalaya, Mizoram, Nagaland, Sikkim and Tripura is allowed a 100% deduction for 10 consecutive assessment years commencing with the initial assessment year relevant to the previous year in which the undertaking begins to manufacture or produce articles or things or completes substantial expansion; subject to the following conditions [Sec. 80-IE(3)]:

(*a*) The undertaking has been set up in the Northern-Eastern States during the period commencing from 1 April 2007 to 31 March 2017 to undertake the following objects :

(*i*) to manufacture or produce any eligible article or thing;

(*ii*) to undertake substantial expansion to manufacture or produce any eligible article or thing;

(*iii*) to carry on any eligible business.

(*b*) Undertaking should be new and not formed by splitting up or reconstruction of an existing business: The object of these incentives is to promote new investment and not just relocation of existing ones. Therefore, it has been provided that the eligible undertaking should be new and not formed by splitting up reconstruction of an existing business. However, this condition does not apply where the undertaking is discontinued due to extensive damage or destruction of its building, machinery or plant and furniture on account of natural disasters, civil disturbance, accidental fire or explosion, enemy action, etc., and such undertaking re-established within three years from the end of such previous year.

(*c*) *New plant and machinery to be used by the undertaking:* Use of old plant and machinery is prohibited except under the following cases:

Exceptions:

(*i*) This condition also does not apply to any transfer, either in whole or in part, of machinery or plant previously used by State Electricity Board. The transfer may or may not be in pursuance of the splitting up or reconstruction of the Board under Part VIII of Electricity Act, 2003.

(*ii*) Second-hand plant or machinery imported and put to use for the first time in India is not to be regarded as machinery or plant previously used, provided the following conditions are satisfied:

- It was used outside India by a person other than the assessee.
- Such plant and machinery is used in India for the first time.
- No depreciation in respect of such plant and machinery has been allowed or is allowable under the Act for a period prior to its installation by the assessee.

(*iii*) Where the value of plant or machinery previously used by the assessee is transferred to the new undertaking, such value should not exceed 20% of the total value of plant or machinery used in the new undertaking.

Term explained: [Sec. 80-IE(7)] :

Eligible article or thing: It means article or thing other than the following:

(*i*) Tobacco and manufactured tobacco substitutes as covered by goods falling under Chapter 24 of the First Schedule to the Central Excise Tariff Act, 1985; or

(*ii*) Pan masala as covered under Chapter 21 of the First Schedule to the Central Excise Tariff Act, 1985; or

(*iii*) Plastic carry bags of less than 20 microns as specified by the Ministry of Environment and Forests *vide* Notification Nos. S.O. 705(E), dated 2 September 1999 and S.O. 698(E), dated 17 June 2003; and

(*iv*) Goods falling under Chapter 27 of the First Schedule to the Excise Tariff Act, 1985, provided by petroleum oil or gas refineries.

Substantial expansion: Substantial expansion means increase in the investment in the plant and machinery by at least 25% of the book value of plant and machinery (before taking depreciation in any year) as on the 1st day of the previous year in which substantial expansion was undertaken.

Eligible business: Eligible business means the business of:

(*i*) hotel (not below two star category);

(*ii*) adventure and leisure sports including ropeways;

(*iii*) providing medical and health services in the nature of nursing home with a minimum capacity of 25 beds;

(*iv*) running an old age home;

(*v*) operating vocational training institute for hotel management, catering and food craft, entrepreneurship, development nursing and para-medical, civil aviation related training, fashion designing and industrial training;

(*vi*) running information technology related training centre;

(*vii*) manufacturing of information technology hardware; and

(*viii*) bio-technology.

Return of income to be furnished: Return of income should be furnished on a before the due date fixed for furnishing the return of income.

Accounts to be audited [Sec. 80-IA(7) r.w. Sec. 80-IE(5)] : The accounts of the undertaking should be audited by a chartered accountant for the relevant year for which deduction is claimed. The report of such audit should be furnished along with the return of income in the prescribed form duly signed and verified by the chartered accountant.

Computation of profits [Sec. 80-IE(5) r.w. Sec. 80-IA(5) and Sec. 80-IA(7) to (12)] - Subject to the following, the profits are computed in accordance with the provisions of the Act under the head "Profits and Gains from Business or Profession".

Eligible business to be considered as the only source of income during the previous year - The profits is computed presuming that the eligible business is the only source of income during the previous year:

- Unabsorbed losses and allowances or carry forward losses and allowances of any other business of the assessee cannot be set-off against the profits of the eligible business for the purpose of the deduction u/s 80-IE.
- Unabsorbed losses and allowances or carry forward losses and allowances of the eligible business are, be set-off against the profits of the eligible business for the purpose of this deduction, even if they were set-off against the profits of other business of the assessee in computing its total income.

Transfer of Goods between various other businesses of the assessee to be considered at their market value - Any transfer of goods from the undertaking to another business of the assessee or *vice versa* must be at the market value of such goods on the date of transfer. Market value for this purpose means price that such goods may fetch in the open market. However, where determining such market value may present exceptional difficulties, the Assessing Officer may compute their transfer value on such reasonable basis as he may deem fit.

Adjustment of more than ordinary profits arising due to transaction between assessee and closely connected Person [Sec. 80-IA(10) r.w. Sec. 80-IAB(3)] - Where more than ordinary profits may be expected to arise from the eligible business owing to the close connection between the assessee carrying on the eligible business and any other person, the Assessing Officer may allow the deduction on the basis of such profits as may be reasonably expected to arise from eligible business.

Amalgamation or Demerger [Sec. 80-IA(12) r.w. Sec. 80-IE(5)] - Where any undertaking of an Indian company is transferred to another Indian company in a scheme of amalgamation or demerger before the expiry of the period of deduction:

(*a*) No deduction is allowed under this section to the amalgamating company or the demerged company for the previous year in which the amalgamation or demerger takes place.

(*b*) The amalgamated company or resulting company is entitled to claim the deduction in a manner as if no amalgamation or demerger had taken place and it is entitled to claim the deduction for the unexpired period.

Double deduction not allowed [Sec. 80-IE(4)] - Where a deduction has been allowed under this Section, no deduction is allowed in respect of such profits under (*i*) Sec. 10A or (*ii*) Sec. 10AA or (*iii*) Sec. 10B or Sec. 10BA now not in operation or under any provision of this chapter.

(6) Profits and Gains from Business of Collecting and Processing of Bio-degradable Waste [Sec. 80JJA]

An assessee deriving profits from the following specified business, is allowed to claim 100% deduction in respect of such profits for a period of 5 consecutive assessment years, relevant to the previous year in which such business in commenced:

(*i*) Business of collecting and processing or treating of bio-degradable waste for generating power, or

(*ii*) Producing bio-fertilizers, bio-pesticides, or

(*iii*) Other biological agents, or

(*iv*) For producing bio-gas, or

(*v*) Making pellets or briquettes for fuel or organic manure.

(7) Deduction in respect of Employment of New Employees [Sec. 80JJAA]

An assessee carrying on any business which is subject to audit requirement under sec. 44AB derives profit from such business, 30% of additional employee cost is allowed to be deducted for 3 assessment years including the assessment year relevant to the previous year in which such employment is provided subject to the following conditions:

(*i*) The business should not be set up by way of splitting up or reconstruction of an existing business. Provided that if business is formed as a result of re-establishment, reconstruction or revival by the assessee of the business in the circumstances and within the period specified in sec. 33B then the deduction shall be allowed.

(*ii*) The business should not be acquired by the assessee by way of transfer from any other person or as a result of any business reorganization.

(*iii*) It has furnished along with the return of income the report of the accountant in the prescribed form. The requirement has been substituted by Finance Act, 2020 w.e.f. 1-4-2021 which provides the assessee to furnish the report of the accountant in prescribed Form 10DA (Rule 19AB) before the specified date referred to in Section 44AB.

Additional Employee Cost - Means the total emoluments paid or payable to additional employees employed during the previous year. However, in the case of existing business, "additional employee cost" is taken as nil if there is no increase in the number of employees from the total number of employees employed as on the last day of the preceding year or if emoluments are paid otherwise than by an account payee cheque or account payee bank draft or by use of electronic clearing system through a bank account. Finance Act, 2019 has included that if payment of emolument is made through such other electronic mode as may be prescribed under Rule 6ABBA then it may not constitute additional employee cost and the cost would be nil.

However, in the first year of a new business, emoluments paid or payable to employees employed during that previous year shall be deemed to be the additional employee cost.

Additional Employee - Means an employee who has been employed during the previous year and whose employment has the effect of increasing the total number of employees employed by the employer as on the last day of the preceding year. However, such employee will not be considered as additional employee if:

(*a*) total emoluments payable is more than ₹ 25,000 per month; or

(*b*) the entire contribution is paid by the Government under the notified Employees' Pension Scheme; or

(*c*) he is employed for less than 240 days during the previous year (150 days in the business of manufacturing of apparel or footwear or leather products); or

(*d*) he does not participate in the recognised provident fund.

Where a new employee is employed during the previous year for less than minimum period (240/150 days) but he is employed for more than such minimum period in immediately succeeding year, then he will be treated as new employee in the succeeding year and deduction under the section will be allowed in respect of his emolument.

(8) Deduction in respect of Certain Incomes of Offshore Banking Units and International Financial Services Centre [Sec. 80LA]

Deduction under this section is available on eligible income to an assessee being :

(*i*) A scheduled bank and having an Offshore Banking Unit in a Special Economic Zone; or

(*ii*) A foreign bank outside India and having an offshore banking unit in a Special Economic Zone; or

(*iii*) A unit of an International Financial Services Centre.

"International Financial Service Centre" means an International Financial Service Centre which has been approved by the Central Government.

"Unit" means a unit set up by an entrepreneur in a Special Economic Zone and includes an existing unit, an offshore banking unit and a unit in an International Financial Services Centre, whether established before or after the commencement of this Act [Sec. 2(*3C*) of Special Economic Zones Act, 2005].

Incomes Eligible for Deduction [Sec. 80LA(2)]

The following incomes are eligible for deduction:

(*i*) Income from an offshore banking unit in Special Economic Zone.

(*ii*) Income from business referred to u/s 6(1) of Banking Regulation Act, 1949 with an undertaking located in a Special Economic Zone or with any other undertaking which develops, develops and operates and maintains a Special Economic Zone.

(*iii*) Income from any unit of the International Financial Services Centre from its business for which it has been approved for setting up in such a Centre in a Special Economic Zone.

(*iv*) arising from the transfer of an asset, being an aircraft or a ship, which was leased by a unit referred to in clause (*c*) to a person, subject to the condition that the unit has commenced operation on or before the 31st day of March, 2024 (w.e.f. 1-4-2022).

No deduction is allowed unless the return of income is furnished along with the following documents:

- Report of a chartered accountant certifying that the amount of deduction has been correctly claimed.
- A copy of the permission obtained under sec. 23(1)(*a*) of the Banking Regulation Act, 1949 or copy of permission or registration obtained under the International Financial Services Centres Authority Act, 2019 [Sec. 80LA(3)].

Quantum of Deduction:

- 100% of the eligible income is deductible for 5 consecutive assessment years beginning with the assessment year relevant to previous year in which the permission is obtained under sec. 23(1)(*a*) of the Banking Regulation Act, 1949 or permission or registration under the Securities and Exchange Board of India Act, 1992 or any other relevant law was obtained and 100% deduction for the next 5 consecutive years thereafter [Sec. 80LA(1)].
- In case of an assessee being a Unit of an International Financial Services Centre 100% of the eligible income is deductible for any 10 consecutive assessment years out 15 assessment years beginning with the assessment year relevant to previous year in which the permission is obtained under sec. 23(1)(*a*) of the Banking Regulation Act, 1949 or permission or registration under the Securities and Exchange Board of India Act, 1992 or (w.e.f. 1-4-2022) registration under the International Financial Services Centre Authority Act, 2019 was obtained.

(9) Deduction in respect of certain inter-corporate dividends [Sec. 80M]

When a company receives dividend by virtue of its shareholding in another company, such dividends are known as inter-corporate dividends. Accordingly, where a domestic company receives dividend from another domestic company or foreign company or business trust ("specified entities"), deduction under this section is available to the recipient company which is the amount of dividend so received. For the purpose, the recipient domestic company needs to distribute the dividend one month prior to the due date of filing of return of income; the deduction would be restricted to the extent of dividend "distributed"; and once the deduction is allowed, it would not be allowed in any other previous year. [Sec. 80M(2)]

(10) Deduction in respect of certain Producer Companies [Sec. 80PA]

An assessee being a producer company with a turnover of less than ₹ 100 crore carrying on eligible business is allowed 100% deduction on profits derived from such eligible business. The deduction in this section is allowed for the previous year relevant to an assessment year commencing on or after the 1st day of April, 2019, but before the 1st day of April, 2025. The Assessee must file its returns of income within specified time. [Sec. 80AC]. This section is operational w.e.f. 1-4-2019.

Eligible Business means:

(*a*) the marketing of agricultural produce grown by the members; or

(*b*) the purchase of agricultural implements, seeds, livestock or other articles intended for agriculture for the purpose of supplying them to the members; or

(*c*) the processing of the agricultural produce of the members.

However, in a case where the assessee is entitled also to deduction under any other provision of this Chapter, the deduction under this section shall be allowed with reference to the income, if any, as referred to in this section included in the gross total income as reduced by the deductions under such other provision of this Chapter. [Sec. 80PA(2)]

CHAPTER 14

Agricultural Income and Tax Liability

INTRODUCTION

Agriculture as a subject falls within State List and Entry 46 therein expressly covers taxes on agricultural income. Therefore, only State Governments are empowered to tax this income by virtue of Art. 246(3) of the Constitution read with Entry 46 in List II of the Seventh Schedule. Consequently, agricultural income is exempt under sec. 10(*1*) for the purposes of the Income-tax Act, which is an enactment of the Central Government.

However, even though the power to tax agricultural income vests with the State Governments, power to define what is agricultural income remains with the Central Government. This is because Art. 366(*1*) of the Constitution defines 'agricultural income' to mean 'agricultural income as defined for the purposes of the enactments relating to Indian Income-tax.' Accordingly, the Income-tax Act, 1961 defines agricultural income in sec. 2(*1A*) which will then be exempt.

Now even as the Income-tax Act defines agricultural income, the very term 'agriculture' remains undefined in the Act. The meaning of the term agriculture therefore is derived from the judicial interpretation. It is for the assessee to prove that the income sought to be taxed is agricultural income exempt from taxation. If he fails to prove that it is agricultural income, he is chargeable to tax on such income [*CIT* v. *Ramakrishna Deo* (1959) 35 ITR 312 (SC)].

MEANING OF AGRICULTURE

The meaning of agriculture is "field cultivation" ('agar' = field + 'cultura' = cultivation). In cultivation, two agricultural operations are involved-basic and subsequent.

Basic Operations - Agriculture in its primary sense denotes the cultivation of the field and is restricted to cultivation of the land in the strict sense of the term, meaning thereby tilling of the land, sowing of seeds, planting and similar operations on the land. These are basic operations and they require the expenditure of human skill and labour upon the land itself. The kind of basic operation required depends upon the nature of the crop intended to be raised [*CIT* v. *Raja Benoy Kumar Sahas Roy* (1957) 32 ITR 466 (SC)].

Subsequent Operations - Such operations are absolutely necessary for the purpose of effectively raising the produce and are to be performed after the produce sprouts from the land, *e.g.* weeding, digging the soil around the growth, removal of undesirable undergrowth, and all operations which foster the growth and preservation of the produce not only from insects and pests but also from depradation from outside, tending, pruning, cutting, harvesting and rendering the produce fit for the market, would all be agricultural operations when taken in conjunction with the basic operations. The human labour and skill spent in the performance of these subsequent operations cannot be said to have been spent on the land itself [*CIT* v. *Raja Benoy Kumar Sahas Roy* (1957) 32 ITR 466 (SC)].

Subsequent operations without basic operation do not constitute agriculture : The mere performance of subsequent operations on the products of the land, where such products have not been raised on the land by the performance of the basic operations, would not be enough to characterise them as agricultural operations. In order to invest them with the character of agricultural operations, these subsequent operations must necessarily be in conjunction with, and in continuation to the basic operations, which are the effective cause of the products being raised from the land. The subsequent operations divorced from the basic operations cannot constitute by themselves agricultural operations [*CIT* v. *Raja Benoy Kumar Sahas Roy* (1957) 32 ITR 466 (SC)].

Agriculture includes commercial crops also : Agriculture connotes not only the production of food grains and other primary produce for human consumption and animals, but also raising of commercial crops, that is, cotton, rubber, jute, tea, coffee, sugarcane, etc., things of artistic and decorative value, such as flowers, and creepers, materials of housing value, such as bamboo and timber, herbs of medicinal or health value and commodities of fuel value.

Growing potted plants in nursery may constitute agriculture only if basic operations are performed on land : Nursery means a piece of ground in which young plants or trees are reared until fit for transplantation. The keeping and running of a nursery does not generally involve the ordinary processes of cultivation in fields at all. Usually, nurseries are maintained and run as business quite independently of agriculture and there may be no process carried on upon the land at all in running a nursery. Even if the keeping of a nursery necessarily means the use of some land and earth for the purposes of rearing plants, that would not by itself amount to carrying on a primary agricultural operation in the sense of cultivating fields. Moreover, plants or seeds are not considered produce ready for the market in the ordinary sense [*H.H. Maharaja Vibhuti Narain Singh (H.H.)* v. *State of Uttar Pradesh* (1967) 65 ITR 364 (All.)].

However, if the plants reared in a nursery are the result of basic operations on the land expending human skill and labour thereon, and if after performance of the basic operations on land the resultant product grown on such part thereof is suitable for being nurtured in a pot with water or by placing them in the green house or in shade or after performing several operations such as weeding, watering, manuring, etc., and are made ready for sale, all these operations are agricultural operations and the plants are thus products of agriculture. So far as the seeds are concerned, it is not possible for the seeds to exist without the mother plants, and if the mother plant is grown on land, the seeds will be clearly a product of agriculture [*CIT* v. *Soundarya Nursery* (2000) 241 ITR 530/ (2002) 123 Taxman 372 (Mad.)].

Income from sapling or seedling

In order to avoid any further confusion relating to plants grown in a nursery, the Finance Act, 2008 inserted *Explanation 3* to sec. 2(*1A*) which clarifies that any income derived from saplings or seedlings grown in a nursery is deemed to be agricultural income. Accordingly, irrespective of whether the basic operations have been carried out on land, such income is treated agricultural income, qualifying for exemption.

Crop or trees of spontaneous growth: In regard to forest trees of spontaneous growth which grow on soil unaided by any human skill and labour and where no basic operations in agriculture are performed upon the soil itself by the assessee, there is no cultivation of the soil at all. Even though operations in the nature of forestry performed by the assessee may have the effect of nursing and fostering the growth of such forest trees, they have nothing in common with the basic operations in agriculture and cannot constitute agricultural operations unless they form part and parcel of and integrate themselves with such basic operations. However, where fresh trees are planted in place of the ones denuded and such new plantation and income thereof could be considered as agricultural income. In such situation, the Revenue authorities would be required to ascertain income attributable to spontaneous growth which will be non-agricultural income and income from replantation which will be agricultural income. [*Maharajadhiraj Sri Kameshwar Singh* v. *CIT* (1957) 32 ITR 587 (SC)].

The term "agriculture" does not extend to those activities which have some remote relation to the land, or are in some remote way connected with land : "Agriculture" in its primary sense denotes the cultivation of the field and is restricted to cultivation of the land in the strict sense of the term. There is no warrant at all for extending the term "agriculture" to all activities which have some relation to the land or are in any way connected with the land, for the term agriculture cannot be dissociated from its primary significance, which is that of cultivation of the land. The extension of the term "agriculture" to denote such activities as breeding and rearing livestock, dairy farming, butter and cheese-making, and poultry farming, fisheries, use of land for potteries or brick-kiln, stone quarries or for storing agriculture produce is not agricultural income, is an unwarranted distortion of the term [*CIT* v. *Raja Benoy Kumar Sahas Roy* (1957) 32 ITR 466 (SC)].

Case Law : ***Sri Ranganatha Enterprises* v. *CIT* [1998] 100 Taxman 552/232 ITR 568 (Kar.)**

Facts: The assessee was a licensee for tapping and vending of toddy and claimed income therefrom to be exempt from income tax being agricultural income.

Held: The activity of extracting toddy and vending of toddy is not an agricultural process and income derived therefrom is not an agricultural income. The burden of proof that the underlying income is agricultural income lies on the assessee.

DEFINITION OF AGRICULTURAL INCOME [SEC. 2(*1A*)]

'Agricultural income' means:

(*a*) Any rent or revenue derived from land which is situated in India and is used for agricultural purposes [Sec. 2(*1A*)(*a*)].

(*b*) Any income derived from agriculture from land which is situated in India and is used for agricultural purposes [Sec. 2(*1A*)(*b*)(*i*)].

(*c*) Any income derived from marketing process performed by cultivator or receiver of rent in kind [Sec. 2(*1A*)(*b*)(*ii*)].

(*d*) Any income derived from the sale of produce [Sec. 2(*1A*)(*b*)(*iii*)].

(*e*) Income from farm building [Sec. 2(*1A*)(*c*)].

(*a*) Any Rent or Revenue derived from land situated in India and is used for agricultural purpose [Sec. 2(*1A*)(*a*)] - Any income which is rent or revenue derived from land, situated in India and used for agricultural purposes is agricultural income. Thus, the following three conditions must be satisfied to qualify under this provision:

(*i*) Rent or revenue should be derived from land

(*ii*) Such land should be situated in India

(*iii*) Such land should be used for agricultural purposes.

(*i*) Any Rent or revenue should be derived from land

Rent is a payment by one person to another for the grant of right to use land. The landlord may not cultivate the land himself but may lease it on rent. Rent may be received in cash or in kind, that is, in the form of a share of crops. Both constitute agricultural income if the requisite conditions regarding location and use of land are fulfilled. It is noteworthy that the recipient of rent or revenue may or may not be the owner of agricultural land. The expression "any rent" includes rent received by superior tenant from sub-tenant under sub-lease or rent received by a mortgagee in possession of agricultural land.

The expression "revenue" is used in the broad sense of return, yield or income and not in the sense of land revenue. It covers income other than rent. For example, mutation fee which is paid to the landlord for recognising the transfer of holding by one tenant to another, is revenue from land.

Where *salami* is in the form of a lump sum non-recurring payment made by a prospective tenant to the landlord as a consideration for the settlement of agricultural land and parting with certain rights of the landlord in the land in favour of the prospective tenant, and is paid anterior to the constitution of relationship of landlord and tenant, it is not "rent" within the meaning of the word used in the definition of agricultural income. [Member for the Board of *Agricultural Income tax* v. *Sindhurani Chaudhurani* (1957) 32 ITR 169 (SC)]. However, *salami* can be a revenue. Where *salami* occurred as a normal and regular, though variable, feature of the Zamindar's receipts from his agricultural estates in a way that the interest in land is parted for a very short duration of time they were held revenue from agricultural land [*Jyotirindra Narayan Singh Chowdhury,* In re (1945) 13 ITR 263 (Cal.)].

Rent of revenue must have a direct nexus with agricultural operations: If income is received in lieu of rent or revenue of agricultural land or is inseparably connected with them it would still enjoy exemption as agricultural income. Revenue can be said to be derived from land only if the land is an immediate and effective source of the revenue and not a secondary and indirect source [*CIT* v. *Raja Bahadur Kamakhaya Narayan Singh* (1948) 16 ITR 325 (PC)]. Thus, revenue or income derived indirectly from land cannot be agricultural income. The following examples make the point clear:

(*a*) Dividend paid by a company out of its agricultural income to the shareholder is not revenue or income derived from land, because the immediate and effective source of the dividend is the shareholding and not the land [*Mrs. Bacha F. Guzdar* v. *CIT* (1955) 27 ITR 1 (SC)].

(*b*) Interest on arrears of rent payable in respect of land used for agricultural purposes, is not agricultural income, for it is neither "rent" nor "revenue" derived from land [*CIT* v. *Raja Bahadur Kamakhaya Narayan Singh* (1948) 16 ITR 325 (PC)].

(*c*) An allowance called *malikana* paid by the government under a statutory obligation to a proprietor, dispossessed of his land, is not revenue derived from land. The immediate and effective source of the income is the government's statutory obligation to pay and not land [*Raja Mustafa Ali Khan* v. *CIT* (1948) 16 ITR 330 (PC). Also see, *Rani Ratnesh Kumari* v. *CIT* (1966) 62 ITR 830 (All.)].

(*d*) Income from supply of water from a well situated on agricultural land cannot be termed as agricultural income [*Sri Ranga Vilas Ginning and Oil Mills* v. *CIT* (1982) 9 Taxman 238/133 ITR 85 (Mad.)].

The assessee must have interest in the agricultural land: Agricultural income cannot be said to accrue to every person into whose hands the produce of the land passes. It is only the owner, landlord or *ryot*, or persons having a derivative interest in the land from these persons that can be said to "derive" income from the land by the performance of agricultural operations in it. Rent, revenue or income has to be derived by a person having some interest in land, and by virtue of the fact that he is the owner of that interest. For example, the profit accruing from the purchase of a standing crop and resale of it after harvest by a merchant having no interest in the land except a mere licence to enter upon the land and gather the produce as incidental to the transaction of purchase of standing crop differs radically in its character from income derived by way of rent or revenue or by the performance of agricultural operations by a person having an interest therein as owner, tenant or mortgagee with possession, etc. The profit in such a case is derived by entering into a contract of purchase of a commodity and by resale of that commodity at a higher price and it is not agricultural income. The land is not the direct or immediate or effective source of his income. The immediate and effective source is the trading operation of purchase of the standing crop and its resale in the market after harvesting the produce at an advantageous price [*CIT* v. *Maddi Venkatasubbayya* (1951) 20 ITR 151 (Mad.)].

(*ii*) Land must be used for Agricultural Purposes

The land must be used for agricultural purposes. Land is used for agricultural purposes by performing basic operations involving expenditure of human skills and labour prior to germination and subsequent operations after the produce sprouts. Subsequent operations without basic operation do not constitute agriculture [*CIT* v. *Raja Benoy Kumar Sahas Roy* (1957) 32 ITR 466 (SC)]. (See the above discussion).

(*iii*) Land must be Situated in India

Income should be derived from land which must be situated in India. If the land is situated outside India, income derived from such land even if used for agricultural purposes cannot be termed as agricultural income. Such income is outside the purview of the definition of the term agricultural income and therefore is not exempt under sec. 10(*1*).

Case Law : ***Vibha Agrotech Ltd.* v. *ITO* (2009) 120 ITD 182 (Hyd. - Trib.)**

Facts: 'V', being a company engaged in research, production and marketing of hybrid seeds, claimed part of its income as exempt as agricultural income. Assessing Officer rejected this claim holding that the main activity of assessee was development of high yielding crop hybrids for commercial purposes and production of basic seeds, which was then multiplied to hybrid seeds was subservient and an incidental activity.

Held: Since basic seeds sold by 'V' were result of primary as well as subsequent operations involving huge skills and efforts as defined under section 2(*1A*), same was an agricultural income entitled to exemption.

Case Law : ***CIT* v. *R.M. Chidambaram Pillai* (1977) 106 ITR 292 (SC)**

Facts: 'C' being a partner of firm owning tea estate and deriving income therefrom, received salary for services to the firm in addition to a share in profits of the firm. Issue arose if the salary received was wholly liable to tax or 60% of it ought to be exempt being agricultural income.

Held: A firm is not a legal person even though it has some attributes of personality. In Income-tax Act, a firm is a unit of assessment by special provisions but is not a full person. Since a contract of employment requires two distinct persons, *viz.*, the employer and the employee, there cannot be a contract of service, in strict law, between a firm and one of its partners. Payment of salary to a partner represents a special share of the profits. Salary paid to a partner retains the same character of the income of the firm and if such income is agricultural income, the salary of the partner will also be agricultural income. Since the firm is engaged in the business of growing and manufacturing tea, 60% of salary/interest paid by the firm to a partner will be treated as agricultural income in the hands of the partner.

(*b*) Any Income derived from Agriculture [Sec. 2(*1A*)(*b*)(*i*)]

Any income from agriculture derived from land, situated in India and used for agricultural purposes, is agricultural income. Any income upon sale of standing crop or raw produce after harvest (without performing marketing process) by the cultivator, it is income from agriculture. Besides, if the crop is used by the cultivator or receiver of rent-in-kind for his consumption or is used as raw material in his business, the market value of such produce is agricultural income.

However, the income accruing to the assessee because it had purchased the ready harvested crops will not qualify for exemption. Similarly, profit earned by a trader by purchasing and selling a standing crop is not agricultural income to him, because he did not perform the basic operations on the land.

Subsidies and compensation for agricultural produce: The word "derived" is inextricably connected either with the land or with the building occupied by the cultivator or receiver of the rent-in-kind of any land with respect to which or the produce of which any operation mentioned in the definition of agriculture is carried on. Subsidies cannot be construed as "income derived from land" and hence are not agricultural income. [*Velimalai Rubber Company Ltd.* v. *State of Tamil Nadu* (1999) 240 ITR 232 (Mad.)]. On the other hand, compensation received from an insurance company for damages caused by hailstorm to the green leaf forming part of the assessee's tea garden represents income from agriculture [*CIT* v. *B. Gupta (Tea) (P) Ltd*. (1969) 74 ITR 337 (Cal.)] [*Camellia Tea Group Pvt. Ltd.* v. *CIT* (1993) 70 Taxman 350/203 ITR 80 (Cal.)].

Income from forests: In order to decide whether the income derived by the assessee from the sale of forest trees is agricultural income or not the crucial question to be answered is were those trees planted by the assessee or did they grow spontaneously? If those trees had grown spontaneously, then the income derived from the sale of those trees is not agricultural income. In such a case, it is wholly immaterial that the assessee has maintained a large establishment for the maintenance and preservation of the forests and assisting in the growth of the trees and has performed operations of a substantial character for the maintenance and improvement of the forests, because, *ex hypothesi,* he has performed no basic operations for bringing the forests into being [*CIT* v. *Ramakrishna Deo* (1959) 35 ITR 312 (SC)].

Miscellaneous income like grazing of cattle, compounding fee, sale of firewood, etc., will also constitute agricultural income if it is directly linked to agriculture: Miscellaneous income from agriculture should also be agricultural income except in respect of sale of trees of spontaneous growth. Income from grazing permits in respect of land which had been tilled and fenced as a result of human efforts is agricultural income but income from permitting grazing of cattle in grassland of spontaneous growth cannot be considered to be agricultural income. The compounding for unauthorised removal of produce belonging to the assessee and the income from sale of firewood will constiture agricultural income if such income can be directly linked to agricultural activity. However, mere registration fee or sale of tender forms could not be treated as agricultural income as they are not directly linked to agriculture [*CIT* v. *Tamil Nadu Forest Plantation Corporation* (2001) 248 ITR 331 (Mad.)].

Case Law : *Commissioner of Agricultural Income-Tax* v. *New Ambadi Estates Ltd.* (1967) 63 ITR 325 (SC)

Facts: 'N' had purchased an estate along with crops which had already been harvested and had paid separately for the crop. Receipts from the crop were claimed as agricultural income.

Held: Income in respect of crops already harvested was not derived by 'N' by carrying on any agricultural operations, or by performance of any process ordinarily employed by a cultivator to render the produce raised or received by it fit to be taken to the market. The crops which had already been harvested, were raised and removed from the land by the previous owner from whom 'N' purchased these crops. 'N' cannot be entitled to exemption.

(*c*) Any Income derived from marketing process performed by cultivator or receiver of rent-in-kind [Sec. 2(*1A*)(*b*)(*ii*)]

It may be possible that the cultivator or receiver of rent-in-kind may not find a market for the crop harvested. In order to make the produce a saleable commodity, it may be necessary to perform some kind of process on the produce. This may increase the value of the produce. Any income by performing such process to make raw produce fit for marketing is also agricultural income, provided the land is situated in India and used for agricultural purposes.

In order that an income might fall within the definition of agricultural income following points are considered:

(*i*) *The process to which the agricultural produce is subjected, whether manual or mechanical, should be one which is ordinarily employed by a cultivator:* The ordinary process employed to make the produce fit for marketing includes threshing, winnowing, cleaning, drying, crushing, boiling, decanting, etc. The nature of the process depends on the prevailing practice in the particular locality where the crop is grown and the assessee resides. The process adopted in one locality may not necessarily be adopted in other locality. It may differ from time to time and place to place.

(*ii*) *The said process should be employed in order to render the produce fit to be taken to market and not for any other purpose :* The produce must retain its original character in spite of the process, unless there is no market for selling it in that condition. If there is no market to sell the produce, then any process which is ordinarily employed to render it fit to reach the market where it can be sold would be covered by the definition [*CIT* v. *Woodland Estates Ltd.* (1965) 58 ITR 612 (Ker.)]. For example, tobacco leaves are ordinarily dried to make them suitable for sale. Hence, income from the sale of dried tobacco leaves is agricultural income. Similarly, there is no ready market for raw coffee. It has to be dried and cured before it can be sold. Hence, this process has to be performed to make the produce fit for marketing and any income from this process is agricultural income. Likewise, cereal plants are threshed out and winnowed in order to produce the grain. The process of threshing and winnowing is one ordinarily employed by the cultivator or receiver of rent-in-kind to render the produce fit to be taken to the market. Any income from this process is agricultural income, that is, income from the sale of straw.

(*iii*) *The produce must retain its original character in spite of the process unless there is not ready market in its raw form and the process is necessary to make it marketable:* The assessee must establish that the agricultural produce itself has got no market and only by converting the same into some other product, there can be a market.

Income derived by performing any marketing process on an agricultural produce that has a ready market in raw form is partly agricultural income and partly business income: If a product can be sold in its raw form (without any process), the income derived from the sale of such produce is agricultural income. However, if the same product goes through any kind of marketing process, the income derived from the sale of such product is partly agricultural and partly business. For example, unginned cotton has a ready market and the profit attributable to ginning operations is not agricultural income. Similarly, the green tea leaf is a marketable commodity, and the process of manufacturing it into tea fit for human consumption cannot be said to yield agricultural income. The manufacturing process cannot properly be said to be employed to render the tea leaves fit to be taken to the market. Likewise, if sugar cane is ordinarily marketed in a given area where sugar manufacturing factories are operating their purchasing centres, the process of converting sugar cane into jaggery (*gur*) or *rab* or refined sugar is not a process which can be said to be employed to render the produce fit to be taken to the market. Hence, the profits attributable to the process of converting sugar cane into jaggery (*gur*) or *rab* or refined sugar is not agricultural income in such cases.

Where mulberry leaves are fed to the silk worms and cocoons obtained from silk worms are sold in the market, the income is partly from agriculture and partly from business. Income derived by the assessee from sale of cocoons raised by it by growing and feeding mulberry leaves to silk worms is not agriculture income [*K. Lakshmanan & Co.* v. *CIT* (2000) 108 Taxman 167 (SC)]. Treatment of agriculture income can be extended only to the sale of mulberry leaves.

Case Law : ***CIT* v. *Stanes Amalgamated Estates Ltd.* (1998) 232 ITR 443 (Mad.)**

Facts: 'S' extracted eucalyptus oil from leaves of eucalyptus trees grown by it and claimed that income arising from sale proceeds of oil represented its agricultural income.

Held: Even under processing, the produce should not lose its identity and 'S' must establish that the agricultural produce itself has no market and only by converting the same into some other product there can be a market. Oil extracted from the eucalyptus leaves lose its original identity and 'S' could not prove that the eucalyptus leaves themselves had no market, the oil extracted from eucalyptus leaves could not be considered to be an agricultural produce within the meaning of Section 2(*1A*)(*b*)(*ii*).

(*d*) Any Income derived from the Sale of Produce [Sec. 2(*1A*)(*b*)(*iii*)]

Any income from the sale of produce of any land, situated in India and used for agricultural purposes, by the cultivator or receiver of rent-in-kind is agricultural income, provided the produce is not subjected to any process except marketing process ordinarily employed to render the produce fit for sale. Where the produce is subjected to any other process profit on such sale is partly from business and partly from agriculture. Such profits must be apportioned according to the prescribed rules, between business income and agricultural income. Only the agricultural income is exempt. Business profits are liable to tax.

(*e*) Income from Farm Building [Sec. 2(*1A*)(*c*)]

Income from farm building is to be computed as if it were income chargeable under the head "house property". Net income so computed is treated as agricultural income, provided the following conditions are satisfied:

(*i*) *Occupancy and ownership of the farm building [Sec. 2(*1A*)(*c*)]:* The farm building may be occupied either by the receiver of rent or revenue, or the receiver of rent-in-kind of any land situated in India and used for agricultural purposes. Where the farm building is occupied by the receiver of rent or revenue (in cash), the building must be owned by him. If it is not owned but occupied by him (as tenant), the rent received by the owner of this building is chargeable to tax as income from house property. If he owns the farm building but does not occupy it, the income from the building (computed on the basis of annual value) is not agricultural income. It is income from house property and chargeable to tax. Therefore, in the case of receiver of rent or revenue (in cash) the income from farm building is agricultural income, provided it is owned and occupied by him.

Where the farm building is occupied by the cultivator or the receiver of rent-in-kind of any land, the income from this building is agricultural income, provided the produce of this land is not subjected to manufacturing process (excepting ordinary marketing process to make the raw produce a saleable commodity) by the cultivator or the receiver of rent-in-kind. Here, the farm building may not be owned by the cultivator or the receiver of rent-in-kind. If it is occupied by him (as tenant), the rent paid is agricultural income to the owner of this building. If the farm building is owned and occupied by him, the income from such building (computed on the basis of annual value) is agricultural income to him. If it is owned but not occupied by him, the income from this building is not agricultural income. It is income from house property which is liable to tax. Thus, the farm building may not be owned by the cultivator or the receiver of rent-in-kind but it must be occupied by him and he should not subject the produce to any manufacturing process. If any of these conditions is not satisfied, the income from farm building is not agricultural income.

(*ii*) *Location of farm building [Sec. 2(*1A*)(*c*)(*i*)]:* The farm building should be on or in the immediate vicinity of the land. The land must be situated in India and used for agricultural purposes.

(*iii*) *Use of the farm building [Sec. 2(1A)(c)(i)]:* The farm building may be used as a dwelling-house, or as a store-house, or as an out-building (out-house). It must be used for the aforesaid purposes by the receiver of the rent or revenue (in cash) or the cultivator or the receiver of rent-in-kind because of his connection with the land. It is not enough to use the building for the aforesaid purpose. There should also be justification in every case that the building is required for the aforesaid purposes. Thus, if the building is required as a dwelling-house by the cultivator, it has to be shown that a dwelling-house is necessary on the land or in its immediate vicinity for the efficient supervision and proper growth of the crop. If the dwelling-house is required by the receiver of the rent (in cash), he has to justify that a dwelling-house is necessary in the immediate vicinity of the land for the collection of the rent. That is to say, the tenants must be so numerous and large that a dwelling-house is necessary. If the building is required for a store-house, the produce of the land must be of sufficient quantity to justify the need of a store-house. Once requirement of the building is established for the aforesaid purpose, it is not open to the tax authorities to inquire how much of the dwelling-house, or store-house or out-building is necessary for such purposes and to charge the excess accommodation to tax. There must be a *bona fide* use of the farm building either as a dwelling-house, or as a store-house or as an out-building. The burden of proof lies on the assessee that the building was used for the aforesaid purposes.

Where farm building is used for non-agriculture purposes, any income accruing/arising from non-agricultural use will not be treated as agricultural income. Thus, where farm houses are let out for residential purposes, marriage functions or other business purposes, income from such letting cannot be treated as agriculture income [*Explanation 2* to Sec. 2(*1A*)].

(*iv*) (*a*) *Land assessed to land revenue or assessed to a local rate [Sec. 2(1A)(c)(ii)]:* Income from farm building is considered as agricultural income if the land is assessed to land revenue in India or is subject to a local rate, assessed and collected by the officers of the government, Union or State. Local rates are levied for the benefit of local bodies. Examples of such rates are road cess, irrigation cess, education cess, library cess, etc. Local rates must be assessed and collected by the officers of the government and not by the officers of local bodies.

It should be noted that the land should be assessed to land revenue or should be subject to a local rate in the present and not that it was assessed to land revenue or it was subject to a local rate in the past.

(*b*) *Location of land:* Where the land is not so assessed to land revenue or subject to a local rate, it should not be situated :

- within the area of a municipality/cantonment board with a population of 10,000 or more, or
- within such distance which is notified as below :

It should not be situated within the jurisdiction of the municipality or cantonment board, having a population of 10,000 or more;

Distance of land from the local limits of municipality/cantonment board	Population of the municipality or cantonment board, figures of which have been published before first day of the previous year
(*i*) Up to 2 Kilometers from the local limits of the municipality/cantonment board Population of the municipality/cantonment board	Population of the municipality/cantonment board exceeds 10,000 but does not exceed 1,00,000
(*ii*) Up to 6 kilometers from the local limits of the municipality/cantonment board Population of the municipality/cantonment board	Population of the municipality/cantonment board exceeds 1,00,000 but does not exceed 10,00,000
(*iii*) Up to 8 kilometers from the local limits of the municipality/cantonment board	Population of the municipality/cantonment board exceeds 10,00,000

Population Ceiling applies to Municipality as a Whole - It is the population of the municipality or cantonment board that has to be taken into account as a whole and not the population of the street, ward, village where the agricultural land is situated. "Municipality" may be called by any name such as municipal corporation, town area committee, notified area committee, etc. The population statistics is to be taken according to the preceding census, the figures of which have been published before the first day of the previous year.

AGRICULTURAL SALARY

Agricultural income does not lose its exemption merely because it is earned from employment. If the employee is vested with the possession of the agricultural land in such a manner that he collects the income in his own right as a beneficiary, the remuneration from such employment is agricultural income. For example, where a trust estate, comprising of agricultural lands, decides to remunerate its manager by giving him possession of a certain portion of its "agricultural estate" with intention that the manager should appropriate towards his remuneration the rents or profits earned from the portion of agricultural land allotted to him, such rents and profits will be earned under employment but exempt from income tax as constituting agricultural income. The manager or employee under such an arrangement has a right either to cultivate the land himself or lease the same to a tenant of his choice. Any income derived by him under such an arrangement is agricultural income as the direct source of income is the land and not the contract of employment.

If the employee is not vested with the right to possess any portion of the agricultural land for his beneficial employment, but he is required to manage the agricultural land on behalf of his employer, the remuneration payable to the employee cannot be agricultural income as the direct source of income is not the land but contract of employment. The mere fact that the remuneration is paid out of the agricultural income of the employer is wholly irrelevant consideration.

INCOME PARTLY AGRICULTURAL AND PARTLY BUSINESS

Where agricultural produce is subjected to any manufacturing process, the profit from the sale of finished product is partly from business and partly from agriculture. Profit attributable to agriculture is exempt while business profit is liable to tax. A similar situation may arise when the agricultural produce is utilised as a raw material in business. Profits from such business are partly from agriculture and partly from business. Therefore, it is necessary to apportion profits in such cases between business profits and agricultural profits. Rules 7 and 8 of Income-tax Rules, 1962, contain necessary provision in this respect.

Computation of Profits from Business and Agriculture where Produce is utilised in Business [Rule 7]

Where the cultivator or the receiver of rent-in-kind utilises agricultural produce in his business as raw material or its sale proceeds are credited by him in the accounts of his business, the market value of such produce is deducted in computing taxable profits of such business. No further deduction is to be allowed in respect of any expenditure incurred by the cultivator or the receiver of rent-in-kind. Thus, the market value of the produce represents agricultural income which is exempt from tax. Hence, it is deductible from business profits. Examples of such cases can be traced in sugar mills, flour mills, cloth mills, etc. For example, if a sugar mill crushes the sugar cane grown by it on its farms, the market value of such sugar cane is to be deducted in computing taxable profits from the sale of sugar. If sugar mill has debited only the cost of such sugar cane, the difference of market value of such sugar cane and its cost price is further to be deducted in computing taxable profits [Rule 7].

Under Rule 7(2) Market value shall be deemed to be as follows:

Where the agricultural produce is ordinarily sold in the market in its raw state or after application to it of any marketing process ordinarily employed by the cultivator or the receiver of rent-in-kind to render it fit to be taken to market. [Rule 7(2)(*a*)].	Market value is determined according to the average price at which the produce is sold during the relevant previous year.
Where the produce has no market in its raw form or after application [Rule 7(2)(*b*)].	Market value is the aggregate of: (*i*) the expenses of cultivation; (*ii*) the land revenue or rent paid for the area in which it was grown; and (*iii*) such amount of profits as the Assessing Officer may find reasonable, having regard to circumstances in each case.

Meaning of Market- "Market" in the context of Rule 7 does not mean an open market where buyers and sellers get together for the purpose of purchase and sale of goods. No special significance can be read into the phrase "ordinarily sold". The principle that the value of a property is the price which it may fetch if sold in the open market, is a well-known method of valuation. It is well-settled that existence of an open market is not a pre-condition for application of this principle. There may or may not be an actual market where buyers and sellers congregate to purchase and sell goods. Where there is no such open market, an estimate of the market price may be arrived on hypothetical basis. [*Thiru Arooran Sugars Ltd.* v. *CIT* (1997) 93 Taxman 579/227 ITR 432 (SC)].

For example, a manufacturer of sugar may purchase sugar cane from the market, and also may have their own cane fields where sugar cane is cultivated, which is then entirely consumed by their factory. Since the profits made by the assessee from the sale of sugar may arise from agricultural activities as well as manufacturing activities, the income earned needs to be divided into two, agricultural income and non-agricultural income. No tax is leviable on agricultural income but the profit generated by the non-agricultural activities is liable to be taxed under the Act. If the assessee also bought sugar cane from other farmers year after year in the ordinary course of business, the price at which he bought sugar cane must be taken to be the market price of the sugar cane grown and used for internal consumption for the purpose of determining the value of agricultural income. On the other hand, if the price of sugar cane is controlled by the government, the controlled price would be taken as the market price because it is this price that a willing buyer and a willing seller were expected to transact business. [*Thiru Arooran Sugars Ltd.* v. *CIT* (1997) 93 Taxman 579/227 ITR 432 (SC)].

Apportionment of Profits into Agricultural Profits and Business Profits, Arising from the Manufacture of Rubber [Rule 7A]

Income derived from the sale of centrifuged latex or cenex or latex-based crepes (such as pale latex crepe) or brown crepes (such as estate brown crepe, re-milled crepe, smoked blankit crepe or flat bark crepe) or technically specified block rubbers manufactured or processed from field latex or coagulum obtained from rubber plants grown by the seller in India is computed as if it were income derived from business. 35% of such income is deemed to be income, liable to be taxed and the balance 65% of such income is deemed to be agricultural income.

In computing such income, the assessee is entitled to claim deduction in respect of the cost of planting rubber plants in replacement of plants that have died or became permanently useless in an area already planted, provided such area has not been previously abandoned. In determining such cost, no deduction is allowed in respect of the amount of any subsidy which is not includible in the total income under sec. 10(*31*).

Apportionment of Profits into Agricultural Profits and Business Profits arising from the Manufacture of Coffee [Rule 7B]

Income derived from the sale of coffee grown and cured by the seller in India is computed as if it were derived from business and 25% of such income is deemed to be income liable to tax [Rule 7B(1)].

Income derived from the sale of coffee grown, cured, roasted and grounded by the seller in India, with or without mixing of chicory or other flavouring ingredients, is computed as if it were income derived from business. 40% per cent of such income is deemed to be income liable to be taxed and the balance 60% of such income is deemed to be agricultural income [Rule 7B(1A)].

In computing such income, the assessee is entitled to claim the deduction in respect of the cost of planting coffee plants in replacement of the plants that have died or become permanently useless in an area already planted, provided such area has not been previously abandoned. In determining such cost, no deduction will be allowed in respect of the amount of any subsidy which is not inclusible in the total income under sec. 10(*31*).

Apportionment of Profits into Agricultural Profits and Business Profits, arising from the Manufacture and Sale of Tea [Rule 8]

60% of the profits derived from sale of tea, grown and manufactured by the seller in India, is deemed to be agricultural profits. Hence, it is exempt from tax. The remaining 40% of such profits is deemed to be business profits which is liable to tax.

Allowance is made for the cost of replacement of tea bushes that have died or become permanently useless in an area already planted, if such an area has not been previously abandoned. For the purpose of determining such cost, no deduction is allowed in respect of the amount of any subsidy, which is exempt from tax under sec. 10(*30*).

INCLUSION OF AGRICULTURAL INCOME FOR COMPUTATION OF TAX [SEC. 2(*2*) OF ANNUAL FINANCE ACT]

Agricultural income is exempt from tax under sec. 10(*1*) but is included in the total income for rate purpose. The object of aggregating the net agricultural income with non-agricultural income is to tax the non-agricultural income at higher rates (Table 14.1).

TABLE 14.1: AGGREGATION OF NET AGRICULTURAL INCOME

Assessee	Conditions for aggregation
Individual, Hindu Undivided Family, an Association of Persons or Body of Individuals, and Artificial Juridical Person	When (*i*) agricultural income exceeds ₹ 5,000; and (*ii*) the total income (non-agricultural) exceeds the exemption limit the whole of such income is to be taken into account for computation of income tax. Where net agricultural income does not exceed ₹ 5,000, the provisions of aggregation do not apply.
	Step 1 Income tax is calculated on the aggregate of non-agricultural total income + net agricultural income, as if such income is the total income.
	Step 2 Income tax is calculated on the net agricultural income + exemption limit as if such income is the total income.
	Step 3 The amount of income tax as calculated under Step 1 is to be reduced by the amount of income tax as calculated under Step 2.
	Step 4 Tax payable is increased by surcharge @ 10%, if total non-agricultural income exceeds ₹ 1 crore.
	Step 5 Cess on income-tax and surcharge.
Company, firm assessed as such, cooperative society and local authority	Agricultural income is not aggregated.

Computation of Net Agricultural Income

As stated earlier, though agricultural income is exempt from income tax, it is included in the total income of an Individual, Hindu Undivided Family, an Association of Persons or Body of Individuals, and Artificial Juridical Person where the agricultural income exceeds Rs. 5,000 and the non-agricultural income exceeds the exemption limit. The net agricultural income needs to be computed for the purpose of aggregation in accordance with the rules as shown in Table 14.2.

TABLE 14.2: RULES FOR COMPUTATION OF NET AGRICULTURAL INCOME

Any rent or revenue derived from land which is situated in India and is used for agricultural purposes. [Sec. 2(*1A*)(*a*)]	This is computed under the head "Income from Other Sources" [Rule 1]
Any income derived from agriculture from land which is situated in India and is used for agricultural purposes. [Sec. 2(*1A*)(*b*)(*i*)]	This is computed under the head "Profits and Gains from Business or Profession" [Rule 2]
Any income derived from marketing process performed by cultivator or receiver of rent in kind [Sec. 2(*1A*)(*b*)(*ii*)]	

Any income derived from the sale of produce [Sec. 2(*1A*)(*b*)(*iii*)]	
Income from farm building [Sec. 2(*1A*)(*c*)]	This is computed under the head "Income from House Property" [Rule 3]
Income derived from the sale of centrifuged latex or cenex or latex based crepes (such as pale latex crepe) or brown crepes (such as estate brown crepe, re-milled crepe, smoked blanket crepe or flat bark crepe) or technically specified block rubbers manufactured or processed from field latex or coagulum obtained from rubber plants grown by the seller in India [Rule 7A]	(*i*) This is computed as if it were income derived from business. (*ii*) 35% of such income is liable to tax as business income and 65% of such income is agricultural income [Rule 4]. (*iii*) Allowance is made for the cost of replacement of rubber plants that have died or become permanently useless in an area already planted, if such an area has not been previously abandoned but no deduction is made in respect of the amount of any subsidy, which is exempt from tax under sec. 10(31)
Income derived from the sale of coffee grown and cured by the seller in India [Rule 7B(1)] Income derived from the sale of coffee grown, cured, roasted and grounded by the seller in India, with or without mixing chicory or other flavouring ingredients [Rule 7B(1A)]	(*i*) This is computed as if it were income derived from business. (*ii*) 75% of such income is agricultural income and balance 25% is liable to tax as business income [Rule 4 r.w. rule 7B(1)]. (*iii*) Income is computed as if it is from business. 60% of such income is agricultural and 40% is treated as business income [Rule 7B(1A)]. (*iv*) Allowance is made for the cost of replacement of rubber plants that have died or become permanently useless in an area already planted, if such an area has not been previously abandoned but no deduction is made in respect of the amount of any subsidy, which is exempt from tax under sec. 10(*31*)
Income from sale of tea grown and manufactured by the seller [Income-tax Rule 8]	This is computed as if it were income derived from business. (*i*) 60% of such income is agricultural income and balance 40% is liable to tax as business income [Rule 4]. (*ii*) Allowance is made for the cost of replacement of tea bushes that have died or become permanently useless

	in an area already planted, if such an area has not been previously abandoned but no deduction is made in respect of the amount of any subsidy, which is exempt from tax under sec. 10(*30*)
Where an assessee is a member of an AOP or BOI (other than an HUF, company or firm) which in the previous year has either no income chargeable to tax; or has non-agricultural income not exceeding the taxable amount but has any agricultural income	The agricultural income or loss is computed in accordance with these rules and the share of the assessee in the agricultural income or loss so computed is regarded as his agricultural income or loss [Rule 5]
Set-off of agricultural loss	(*i*) Any loss incurred in agriculture is allowed to be set-off against any other income from agriculture during the same year (*ii*) A member of AOP or BOI cannot set-off his share of agricultural loss from AOP or BOI against his agriculture income [Rule 6]
Deduction for State taxes on agricultural income	Any tax levied by a State government on agricultural income is allowed as a deduction in computing net agricultural income [Rule 7]
Set-off of unabsorbed agricultural loss	Any unabsorbed agricultural loss can be carried forward and set-off only against agricultural income within the prescribed time-limit of 8 years. For example, any unabsorbed agricultural loss for the previous year relevant to the assessment year 2007-08 can be carried forward and set-off in the assessment year 2015-16 but agricultural loss relating to assessment year 2006-07 cannot be carried forward and set-off in the assessment year 2015-16 [Rule 8].
Agricultural loss not to be aggregated	Where the net result of computation of agricultural income is a loss, it is to be disregarded and agricultural income is taken as *Nil* [Rule 9]. An agricultural income is aggregated for rate purposes only if it is in excess of ₹ 5,000, net agricultural loss is ignored for the purpose of aggregation for rate purpose.
Rounding off	Net agricultural income is rounded off to the nearest multiple of ₹ 10 [Rule 10]

CHAPTER 15

Charitable Trusts and Religious Institutions

INTRODUCTION

Charitable and Religious Trusts/Institutions

Charitable or religious trusts/institutions stand to promote the welfare of the public and hence the income-tax law provide exemption to such entities. Sec. 11 is a general provision that allows exemption to all institutions that are charitable and sec. 10(*23C*) is a specific provision allowing exemption to educational institutions and hospitals. (Refer to Chapter 4).These exemptions can be availed as long as the income of such trust is not misused or diverted to non-charitable objects. The taxation of charitable and religious trusts is governed by Chapter III of the Income-tax Act which contains secs. 11, 12, 12A, 12AA, 12AB and 13. While secs. 11 and 12 contains the provisions that exempts certain incomes of charitable and religious trusts, sec.13 provide for incomes that are not so eligible for exemption. Secs. 12A and 12AA are concerned with the Registration and the Registration Procedure. Sec.12AB have introduced a new regime of registration w.e.f. 1-4-2021.

Sec.11 Exempts incomes of charitable or religious trusts. While the term 'Charitable purpose' has been defined *vide* sec. 2(15), there exists no statutory definition of the term 'religious purpose'. There could however be instances when given the nature of activity such as supply of fodder and taking care of cattle and animals,it could be both for a charitable as well as religious purpose Vallabhdas *Karsondas Natha* v. *CIT* [1947] 15 ITR 32 (Bom.).

Religious Purpose

According to Black's Law Dictionary "religion" means :- man's relation to Divinity, to reverence, worship, obedience, and submission to mandates and precepts of supernatural or superior beings. In its broadest sense, it includes all forms of belief in the existence of superior beings exercising power over human beings by volition, imposing rules of conduct, with future rewards and punishments. Bond uniting man to God, and a virtue whose purpose is to render God worship due him as source of all being and principle of all Government of things. For the purposes of income tax provision, religious purpose includes the advancement and propagation of a religion and its tenets. The distinction between a charitable trust and a religious trust is that a charitable trust is always public but a religious trust may be public or private [*CIT* v. *Jamal Mohammad Sahib* (1941) 9 ITR 375 (Mad.)].

Case Law : ***Bai Hirbai Rahim Aloo Paroo & Kesarbai Dharamsey Kakoo Charitable & Religious Trust* v. *CIT* [1968] 68 ITR 821 (Bom.)**

Facts: Two sisters 'H' and 'K' of Khoja community created trusts with the dominant intention of trust to hold an annual majlis or a meeting in remembrance of anniversary of Imam Hussein Saheb, who is subject of highest veneration by Khojas to which sect 'H' and 'K' belonged. Exemption was not granted on ground that trust was not created wholly for religions or charitable purposes.

Held: While 'Majlis' may impliy any educational or cultural purposes, it is essentially a religious meeting in the context in which it is used here, namely, "remembrance of the anniversary of the Imam Hussain Saheb". Where the main purpose of the endowment was such remembrance and holding an annual majlis on that occasion to celebrate it, there must necessarily be prayers offered and the reading of the Holy Koran and whether the reading was in public or private, it would still be a valid purpose of a public religious endownment. The income of trusts was exempt.

Case Law : ***CIT* v. *Ahmedabad Rana Caste Association* (1983) 140 ITR 1 (SC)**

Facts: 'A' an association of persons held diverse properties under legal obligation for the purposes of spread education in the Rana community, ender medical assistance to the community, promote unity and brotherhood amongst the members of the community and so on.

Held: Arranging Bhandara on the occasion of Havan or Shravan procession *i.e.* dinner of Brahmins was for religions purpose, if not charitable purpose. Exemption could be availed.

Charitable Purpose [Sec. 2(15)]

Charitable purpose includes relief of the poor, education, yoga, medical relief, preservation of environment (including water sheds, forests and wild life) and preservation of monuments or places or objects of artistic or historic interest; and advancement of any other object of general utility.

However, advancement of any other object of general public utility is not a charitable purpose, if it involves the carrying on of any activity in the nature of trade, commerce or business or any activity of rendering any service in relation to any trade, commerce or business for a cess or fee or any other consideration, irrespective of the nature of use or application or retention of income from such activity unless—

(*i*) such activity is undertaken in the course of actual carrying out of such advancement of any other object of general public utility; and

(*ii*) the aggregate receipts from such activity or activities during the previous year do not exceed 20% of the total receipts of the trust or institution, undertaking such activity or activities of that previous year. [Proviso to sec. 2(15)].

The Figure below clearly explicates the definition.

FIGURE 15.1: CHARITABLE PURPOSE

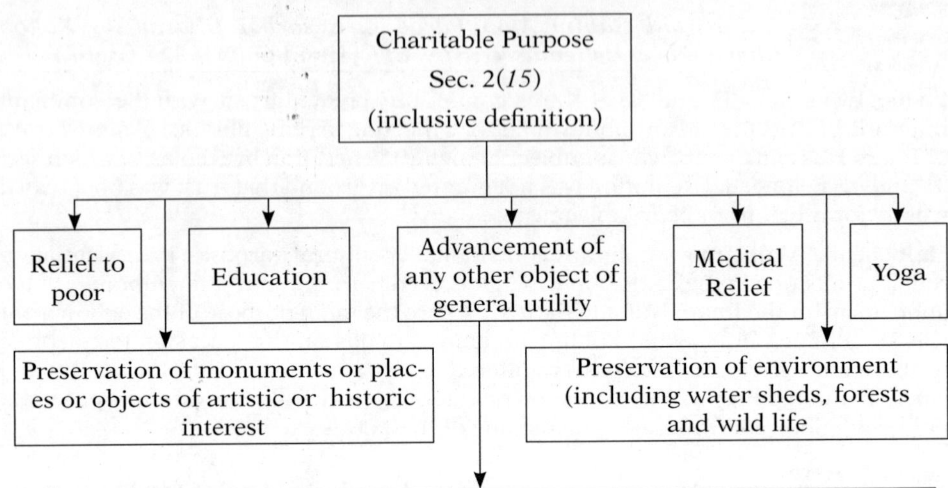

Relief to the poor - The relief to poor people may be a relief to the poor public at large or relief to a particular section of the poor public, for example, relief to poor coffee or tea planters, brick-kiln workers, and so on. The relief to poor does not necessarily mean giving them free doles or alms; it may take some other shape like seeking better reward for labour.

An object beneficial to a section of the public is an object of general public utility - To serve a charitable purpose it is not necessary that the object should be to benefit the whole of mankind or all persons in a country or state. The word *Public* need not be understood as the general public and it is sufficient if a section of the public (as distinguished from a specified individual) is benefited [*CIT* v. *Riding Club* (1987) 32 Taxman 295/168 ITR 393 (AP)]. However, the section of the community sought to be benefited must be sufficiently definite and identifiable by some common quality of a public or impersonal nature. [*Ahmedabad Rana Caste Association* v. *CIT* (1971) 82 ITR 704 (SC)]. Acts which would be useful to a particular community to promote unity and brotherhood among its members and bring about complete development of all aspects of the life of members of the community are charitable purposes. [*CIT* v. *Ahmedabad Rana Caste Association* (1983) 140 ITR 1 (SC)].

"Advancement of any other activity of general public utility" are words of wide import. Raising of moral, intellectual, economic, social and political conditions of people in general is an object of general public utility.

Case Law : ***CIT* v. *United Way of Baroda*[2020] 121 taxmann.com 5/275 Taxman 328 (Guj.)**

Facts: 'U' a charitable institution registered under section 12A, was engaged into health and human services for purpose of improving quality of life in society. Main objective of 'U' included mobilizing resources from local communities and applying them for strengthening services in education, health and human care and other social sectors of under privileged. 'U' filed its return of income declaring nil income after claiming exemption under section 11. Assessing Officer noted that 'U' received income from organizing event of garba during navratri festival by way of selling tickets and giving food stalls on rent etc. which constituted huge part of its income and concluded that activities of 'U' could not be held to be for advancement of any other object of general public utility as per sec. 2(*15*).

Held: Since profit making was not the driving force or objective of 'U', any income generated by assessee from events like garba was to be utilized fully for purposes of objects of the advancement of any other object of general public utility and 'U' would not be hit by proviso to section 2(*15*). It was eligible for exemption under sec. 11.

GENERAL PRINCIPLES OF APPLICATION OF PROVISO TO SEC. 2(*15*)

The proviso to sec. 2(*15*) is applicable to the entities whose purpose is 'advancement of any other object of general public utility (GPU). Hence, such entities will not be eligible for exemption under sec. 11 or sec. 10(*23C*), if they carry on commercial activity. In a significant ruling, the Supreme Court *ACIT* v. *Ahmedabad Urban Development Authority* [2022] 143 taxmann.com 278 (SC) has clarified the application of the proviso to sec. 2(*15*). Accordingly,

- Generally no commercial or business or trading activity ought to be engaged by an assessee advancing GPU.
- However, in the course of achieving the object of GPU, the concerned trust, society, or other such organization, can carry on trade, commerce or business or provide services in relation thereto for consideration, provided that (*i*) the activities of trade, commerce or business are connected ("actual carrying out..." inserted w.e.f. 1-4-2016) to the achievement of its objects of GPU; and (*ii*) the receipt from such business or commercial activity or service, does not exceed the quantified limit, as amended over the years (₹ 10 lakhs w.e.f. 1-4-2009; then ₹ 25 lakhs w.e.f. 1-4-2012; and now 20% of total receipts of the previous year, w.e.f. 1-4-2016).
- Thus, the Act does not envision pure charity in the sense that the performance of an activity without any consideration. Therefore, for achieving a general public utility object, if the concerned trust, society etc. involves itself in activities that entail charging amounts only at cost or marginal mark up over cost, and also derive some profit, the prohibition.

- Generally, the charging of any amount towards consideration for such an activity (advancing general public utility), which is on cost-basis or nominally above cost, cannot be considered to be "trade, commerce, or business". It is only when the charges are significantly above the cost incurred by the assessee in question, that they would fall within the mischief of "cess, or fee, or any other consideration" towards "trade, commerce or business".
- For example, Gandhi Peace Foundation disseminating Mahatma Gandhi's philosophy through museums and exhibitions and publishing his works, for nominal cost is not business.
- The requirement in sec. 11(4A) of maintaining separate books of account is to be read harmoniously with sec. 2(*15*) which facilitates ensuring that the quantitative limit prescribed in the proviso to section 2(*15*), has not been breached.
- This ruling would be applicable to all Statutory Regulators, Trade Promotion Bodies, Non-Statutory Bodies, Sports Association, Private Trust. In case of statutory corporation, board or any other body set up by the state government or central governments, for achieving 'public functions/services' such as housing, industrial development, supply of water, sewage management, supply of food grain, development and town planning, etc. may resemble trade, commercial, or business activities. However, since their objects are essential for advancement of public purposes/functions, any receipts by them are *prima facie* eligible for exemption from tax.

In view of the 2008 Amendment to sec. 2(*15*) the 'predominant test' propounded by the Supreme Court ruling in *ACIT* v. *Surat Art Silk Cloth Manufacturers, Association* (1980) 2 SCC 31 has been overruled by the Ahmedabad Urban Development Authority case. The 'predominant test' that now stands redundant had provided that if the primary or dominant purpose of a trust or institution is charitable, another object which may be non-charitable which is merely ancillary or incidental to the primary or dominant purpose, would not prevent the trust from being valid charity. Further, when proceeds from such non-charitable activities were ploughed back to GPU, the same continued to be exempt from tax. The ruling in Ahmedabad Urban Development Authority emphasised that post 2008, the very engagement in trade, commerce or business was prohibited and therefore the question of ploughing it back had been retendered redundant and as also the 'predominant test'.

Conditions to be fulfilled for being Eligible for Exemption [Sec. 12A]

In order to avail exemption to the income of any trust or institution under secs. 11 and 12, the following two conditions must be complied with:

(*a*) the trust should be registered

(*b*) accounts of such trust should be audited.

Under the newly substituted sub-sec. (*b*) to sec. 12A(1) where the total income of the trust/institution exceeds the basic exemption limit, it is required to get its books of account audited. Under the existing scheme of things, there are no specific books of account that the trust is required to maintain. The Finance Act, 2022 by virtue of sec.12A(1)(*b*) mandates maintaining books of account that may be prescribed. Exemption shall be allowed only if the return of income is furnished under sec. 139(1) (w.e.f. 1.4.2023).

New Registration Regime [sec. 12AB]

Every charitable or religious trust or institution that sought to avail exemption for its income under secs. 11 and 12, were required to comply with the following two conditions:

(*a*) the trust should be registered [Sec. 12A and sec.12AA].

(*b*) accounts of such trust should be audited [Sec.12A].

Further registrations are also obtained under sec. 80G so that donors to such entities can claim a deduction from their total income.

Since the process of registration was completely manual and scattered all over the country, in order to simplify the compliance for the new and existing charity institutions, a new registration regime has been put in place by the Finance Act 2020. The process of registration under the new regime will be completely electronic and a unique registration number (URN) shall be issued to all new and existing charity institutions. Such centralised registration will enable to create a national register of such trusts or institutions and weed out those which have remained defunct.

Following points must be noted :

(*a*) **Existing Exempt Entities Need to Apply Afresh** - All charitable or religious entities, educational institutions or hospitals etc. that is already registered and granted approval under secs. 12A, 12AA, 10(23C) and 80G have to apply for fresh registration under sec. 12AB within three months from 1.10.2020 *viz.* on or before 31.12.2020 failing which the registration granted earlier would cease to operate.

(*b*) **No Perpetual Registration** - The registrations will come with an approval valid for 5 years beginning from the AY 2021-22, after which a renewal have to be sought again. Under the erstwhile regime registrations granted under sec.12AA or sec.12A were perpetual in nature unless cancelled by the concerned Income-tax authority. The new regime scrapped this concept of perpetual registration and certification.

(*c*) **Provisional Registration newly introduced** - The charitable or religious trusts etc. newly coming into existence will be granted a provisional registration for 3 years. Such provisional registration may be applied for only before commencement of activities. If the trust/institution has already commenced activities, it is required to apply for regular registration.

(*d*) **Conditions to be satisfied for grant of Registration -** Under the old regime, while granting registration revenue authorities were required to check the twin conditions of the 'objects being charitable in nature' and 'the activities being genuine'. The Finance Act, 2019 added a third aspect which is 'compliance of such requirements of any other law for the time being in force by the trust or institution as are material for the purpose of achieving its objects'. (w.e.f. 1.9.2019). These remain the same under the new regime as well.

TABLE 15.1: NEW REGISTRATION REGIME [SEC. 12AB]

Section	Particulars	By when should application to be made	Period of Validity of Registration and Approval	Renewal Application
12AB(1) (a) r.w.s. 12A(1)(*ac*) (*i*)	Existing Trusts exempt under old provisions (secs. 12A, 12AA, 10(23C), 80G) applying under new provisions (sec.12AB)	Between 1.1.2020 to 31.12.2020 (CBDT Press release dt. 08.05.2020)	Order granting automatic approval for a period of 5 years (beginning from AY 2021-22)	Accept within 3 months from the end of the month in which application was received
12AB(1) (b) r.w.s. 12A(1)(*ac*) (*ii*)	Trusts granted registration under sec.12AB applying for renewal after expiry of 5 year	At least 6 months prior to date of expiry	Call for documents and conducting inquiries and after the authority is satisfyied about (*i*) object of trust (*ii*) genuineness of activities and (*iii*) compliance with requirement of any other law Either grant the registration for period for 5 years or reject the application after giving an opportunity of being heard	Within 6 months from the end of the month in which application was received
12AB(1) (b) r.w.s. 12A(1)(*ac*) (*iii*)	Trusts coming into existence for the first time applying for provisional registration for 3 years under sec. 12AB	(*a*) apply for provisional registration only before activities commence (*b*) apply for regular registration if activities have commenced.		
12AB(1) (b) r.w.s. 12A(1)(*ac*) (*iv*)	Trust/Board etc. formed under Central/State/Provincial statute exempt under sec.10(23C), (46) has become inoperative due to sec. 11(7)	6 months prior to commencement of the AY from which said registration is sought to be made operative.		
12AB(1) (b) r.w.s. 12A(1)(*ac*) (*v*)	Trust modifying the objects applies	Within 30 days of date of modification		

Section	Particulars	By when should application to be made	Period of Validity of Registration and Approval	Renewal Application
12AB(1) (*c*) r.w.s. 12A(1)(*ac*) (*vi*)	In any other case not covered above (Pending application under the old regime)	At least 1 month before the commencement of relevant previous year,	Order granting provisional approval for a period of 3 years with copy to such trust	Within 1 month from the end of the month in which application was received

Cancellation of Registration - Where registration of a trust or an institution has been granted and subsequently, the Principal Commissioner or Commissioner, is satisfied that the activities of such trust or institution are not genuine or are not being carried out in accordance with the objects of the trust or institution, as the case may be, he shall pass an order in writing cancelling the registration of such trust or institution after affording a reasonable opportunity of being heard [Sec. 12AB(4), (5)].

The Finance Act, 2022 substitutes the existing provisions of sec.12AB(4) and (5) with new sub-sections to stipulate that having granted registration of a trust or an institution, where the Principal Commissioner or Commissioner

(*a*) has noticed occurrence of one or more specified violations during any previous year; or

(*b*) has received a reference from the Assessing Officer under sec. 143(3) or

(*c*) such case has been selected in accordance with the risk management strategy, formulated by the Board from time to time,

the such Principal Commissioner or Commissioner shall pass an order in writing cancelling the registration of such trust or institution after calling for such documents and information or making such inquiry and affording a reasonable opportunity of being heard. [Sec. 12AB(4)].

Specified Violation in this regard comprise in:

(*i*) application of income of trust for objects other than for the objects of the trust or institution

(*ii*) application of income of trust for private religious purposes, which does not enure for the benefit of the public

(*iii*) having a business which is not incidental to the attainment of its objectives

(*iv*) failure to maintain separate books of account in respect of the business which is incidental to the attainment of its objectives

(*v*) the trust or institution established for charitable purpose created or established after the commencement of this Act, has applied any part of its income for the benefit of any particular religious community or caste

(*vi*) any activity being carried out by the trust or institution : is not genuine; or is not being carried out in accordance with all or any of the conditions subject to which it was registered. [*Explanation* to sec.12AB(4)].

(*vii*) where application furnished for registration on there e-portal is incomplete or the information is false or incorrect (inserted by the Finance Act, 2023)

EXEMPTION OF INCOME [SEC. 11]

Subject to the clubbing provisions (under sec. 60 to sec. 63), the following figure captures an overview of the income that is exempt under sec. 11 and further explained in details.

FIGURE 15.2: INCOME FROM CHARITABLE TRUSTS AND RELIGIOUS INSTITUTIONS

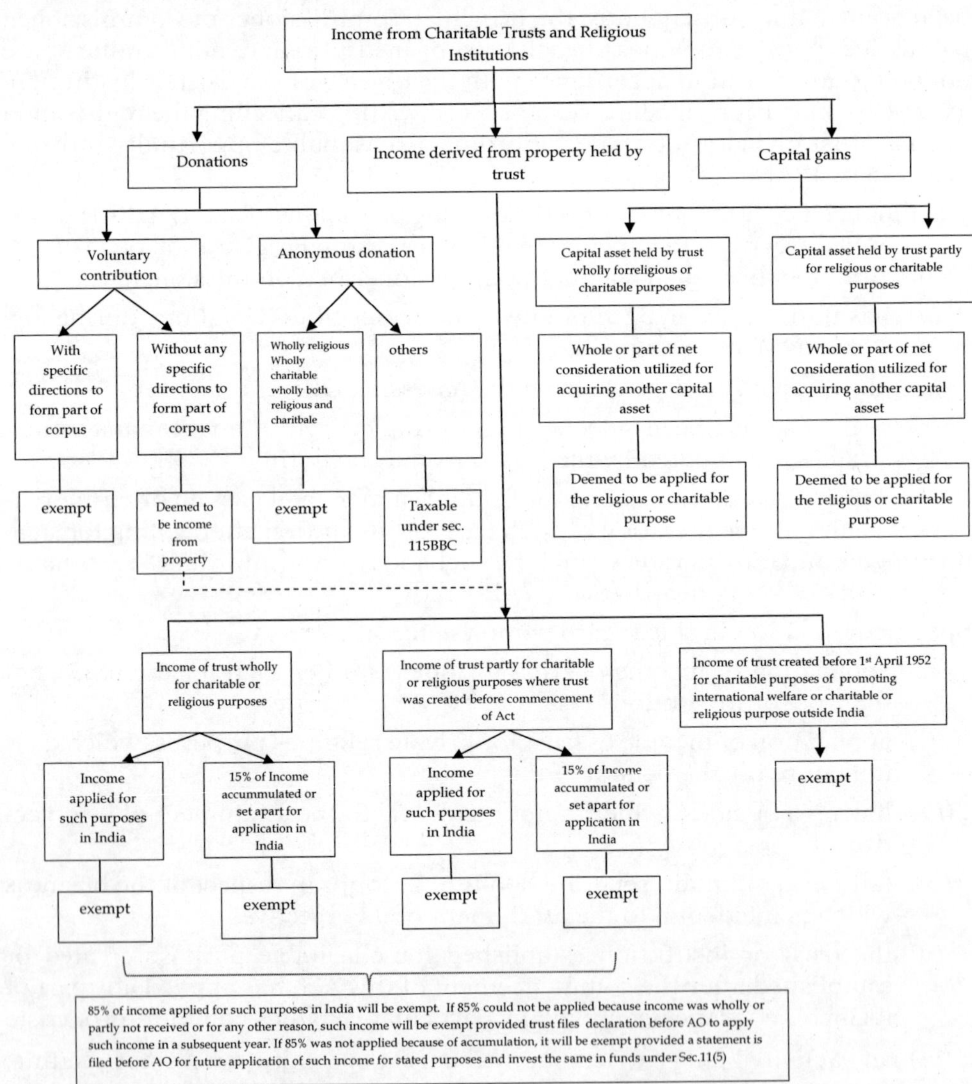

A. Voluntary Donations

Voluntary contribution forming part of corpus [Sec. 11(1)(d)] - Where income is received in the form of the voluntary contributions with a specific direction that it should form part of the corpus of the trust or institution, it is not included in the total income of such trust or institution. Where the donors contribute a certain amount towards the corpus of the assessee, with a direction that the interest earned from the amount also be applied towards the corpus, such interest is also exempted under sec. 11(1)(*d*) [*CIT* v. *Mata Amrithanandamayi Math Amritapuri* (2018) 94 taxmann.com 82/256 Taxman 62 (SC)]. The Finance Act, 2021 has further added a qualification subject which such voluntary contribution will be excluded from the total income of the trust or institution. Accordingly, voluntary contributions must be invested or deposited in one or more of the forms or modes specified in sec. 11(5) so as to be excluded from total income of the trust or the institution. This condition shall be operational w.e.f. 1.4. 2022. *Explanation 4(i)* to sec. 11(1) further clarifies that application for charitable or religious purposes from such corpus as shall not be treated as application of income for charitable or religious purposes unless to the extent of the amount of such corpus deposited or invested in any of the modes specified in Sec. 11(5).

Voluntary donations received for renovation or repair of temple, mosque etc. - By virtue of newly inserted *Explanation 3A* to sec.11(1)(*a*) through the Finance Act, 2022 provides option to the trust to treat voluntary contribution received for renovation or repair of temple, mosque etc. as a part of corpus. Accordingly, where the property held under a trust or institution includes any temple, mosque, gurdwara, church or other place notified under sec.80G(2)(*b*), any sum received by such trust or institution as voluntary contribution for the purpose of renovation or repair of such temple, mosque, gurdwara, church or other place, may, at its option, be treated by such trust or institution as forming part of the corpus of the trust or the institution, subject to the condition that the trust or the institution,—

(*a*) applies such corpus only for the purpose for which the voluntary contribution was made;

(*b*) does not apply such corpus for making contribution or donation to any person;

(*c*) maintains such corpus as separately identifiable; and

(*d*) invests or deposits such corpus in the forms and modes specified under sec. 11(5)

Where any of these conditions are breached, such voluntary contribution shall be treated as income of the trust/institution in that year. [*Explanation 3B* to sec. 11(1)(*a*)] (newly inserted by the Finance Act, 2022).

Donations and Grants-in-Aid are also income derived from Trust and eligible for exemption under Sec. 11(1)(a) - Donations received by a charitable trust would also constitute its income [*CIT* v. *Programme for Community Organisation*

(2001) 116 Taxman 608/248 ITR 1 (SC)]. Similarly, grants-in-aid are eligible for exemption under secs. 11(1)(*a*) and 12 and are in the nature of voluntary contributions. Grants-in-aid are made by government to provide certain institutions with sufficient funds to carry on their charitable activities and are in nature of voluntary contributions. Any conditions imposed by the government to the grants are merely intended to see that the amounts are properly utilised and does not detract from the voluntary nature of the grant. There was no element of any consideration in such grants-in-aid and the institutions or associations to which the grant is made have no right to ask for the grant. It is solely within the discretion of the government to make grants to institutions for a charitable cause. The government does not expect any return for the grants given by it to such institutions. There is nothing which is required to be done by the institutions for the government, which can be considered as a consideration for the grant [*CIT* v. *Gem and Jewellery Export Promotion Council* (1983) 13 Taxman 13/143 ITR 579 (Bom.)].

Income from trusts and institutions from Contributions [Sec.12]

Voluntary contributions other than the one forming a corpus [Sec.12(1)] - Any voluntary contributions (not being the corpus) received by a trust or an institution created wholly for charitable or religious purposes will be deemed to be income derived from property and the provisions applicable to that income will apply. *i.e* such income will qualify for exemption to the extent such income is utilised for the purposes of the trust or set apart for future application as referred to in sec. 11.

Value of any medical or educational services provided to interested persons by a Charitable Trust or Institution running a Hospital or Medical or Educational Institution are chargeable to tax [Sec. 12(2)] - Where a charitable or religious trust is running a hospital or a medical institution, or an educational institution and it provides medical or educational services to interested persons (that is, the author of the trust, trustee, substantial contributor contributing more than ₹ 50,000 during the year, or any relative of such persons) the value of medical/educational services is deemed to be the income of the trust or institution and such is chargeable to tax during the previous year in which such services are rendered. The term 'value' here refers to the value of any benefit or facility provided to such interested person for free or at a concessional rate. The exemption of Sec. 11 does not apply to the value of such services [Sec. 12(2)].

Donations received for Gujarat Earthquake victims chargeable to tax if conditions not fulfilled [Sec.12(3)] - Where a charitable trust or institution receives donations during the period from 26 January 2001 to 30 September 2001 for providing relief to the earthquake victims of Gujarat, it should be utilised for the said purpose. The trust is required to render the accounts in respect of such donations received and expenditure incurred to the prescribed authority on or before 30 June 2004. Any amount remaining unutilised till 31 March 2004, should be transferred to Prime Minister's National Relief Fund on or before 31 March 2004, failing which it is chargeable as the income of that previous year [Sec. 12(3)]. If such donations are utilised for any other purpose, it is deemed to be the income of the trust for that previous year and charged to tax accordingly. Similarly, if accounts of such income and expenditure are not rendered to the prescribed authority by 30 June 2004, it is deemed to be the income of the trust.

B. Anonymous Donations

In order to prevent channelisation of unaccounted money to charitable or religious trusts or institutions by way of anonymous donations, the Finance Act, 2006 introduced sec. 115BBC w.e.f. 1-4-2007.

Anonymous Donations Defined [Sec. 115BBC(3)] - Anonymous donations means any voluntary contribution [referred to under Sec. 2(24)(*iia*)] where person receiving such contribution does not maintain a record of the identity of the donor indicating his name, and address and such other particulars as may be prescribed. Such anonymous donations are not eligible for exemption.

Applicability [Sec. 115BBC(1)] - Following entities are chargeable in respect of anonymous donations:

(*i*) A trust or institution referred to in Sec. 11;

(*ii*) University or other educational institutions where annual receipts do not exceed ₹ 5 crore [Sec. 10(*23C*)(*iiiad*)] or any other university or educational institution approved by the [Commissioner of Income-tax [Exemptions] w.e.f. 15-11-2014] [Sec. 10(*23C*)(*vi*)] but not being a university/educational institution, financed wholly or substantially by the government;

(*iii*) Any hospital or other medical institution whose annual receipts do not exceed ₹ 5 crore [Sec. 10(*23C*)(*iiiae*)], or any other hospital or institution approved by the prescribed authority [Sec. 10(*23C*)(*via*)] but excluding such hospital or institutions as are financed, wholly or substitantially by the government;

(*iv*) Any fund or institution, established for charitable purposes and notified by the Central Government, having regard to the objects of the fund or institution and its importance throughout India or throughout any State or States [Sec. 10(*23C*)(*iv*)];

(*v*) Any trust (including any other obligation) or institution wholly for public religious purposes or wholly for public religious and charitable purposes and notified by the Central Government with a view to ensure that the income accruing thereto is properly applied for the objects thereof [Sec. 10(*23C*)(*v*)].

Rate of Tax [Sec. 115BBC] - Income tax payable on the anonymous donations received by a trust or institution is the aggregate of:

i. The amount of income-tax calculated at the rate of thirty per cent on the aggregate of anonymous donations received in excess of the higher of the following, namely:

a. five per cent of the total donations received by the assessee; or

b. ₹ 1,00,000

ii. The amount of income tax with which the assessee would have been chargeable had his total income been reduced by the aggregate of anonymous donations received in excess of the amount referred to in sub-clause (*a*) or sub-clause (*b*) of clause (*i*), as the case may be

Exemption to Anonymous donations [Sec.115BBC(2)]

As such exemption provisions of Secs. 11 and 12 do not apply to anonymous donations [Sec. 13(7)]. Therefore when trusts or institutions receive anonymous donation these are not exempt income. However, anonymous donation made to the trust or institution created or established (*a*) wholly for religious purposes or (*b*) for both *i.e.* for wholly charitable and religious are exempt. Anonymous donation shall be taxable for these trusts or institutions only if it is for any university or other educational institution or any hospital or other medical institution run by them.

For availing exemption under section 11 etc., an assessee needs to separately pass the test under section 115BBC subject to the exceptions. If a particular receipt turns out to be anonymous donation and same gets caught within mischief of sec. 115BBC; exemption of income to that extent cannot be availed under sec.11 even if the assessee applied 85 per cent of such anonymous donations for objects of trust. Sec. 13(7) clearly provides that nothing contained in sec. 11 or sec. 12 shall operate so as to exclude any anonymous donation (referred to in section 115BBC on which tax is payable under sec.115BBC) from the total income of the recipient. [*Shriram Bahuuddeshiya Sevabhavi Sanstha* v. *ITO* [(2020) 119 taxmann.com 203/185 ITD 614 (Pune-Trib.)].

Capital gains utilized for acquiring another capital asset [Sec. 11(1A)] :

Where a capital asset, being property held under trust, wholly for charitable or religious purposes, is transfered and whole or part of the net consideration is utilised for acquiring another capital asset to be so held, the capital gain arising from the transfer is deemed to have been applied for charitable or religious purposes to the following extent :

(*a*) (*i*) If the whole net consideration is utilised in acquiring the new capital asset, the whole amount of capital gain is deemed to have been applied for charitable or religious purposes.

(*ii*) If only a part of the net consideration is utilised for acquiring the new capital asset, an amount by which the cost of acquisition of the new asset exceeds the aggregate of the cost of acquisition of the capital asset transferred plus cost of improvement, if any, is treated to have been applied for such purposes.

(*b*) If a property, held under trust in part only for charitable or religious purposes, is transferred, proportionate amount of capital gain is treated to have been applied for charitable or religious purposes.

Case Law : ***CIT* v. *Ambalal Sarabhai Trust No. 3* (1988) 40 Taxman 369/173 ITR 683 (Guj.)**

Facts: 'A', a charitable trust sold certain shares that it held as capital assets of the trust to a purchaser. Under the sale agreement, 90% of the consideration remained with the purchaser in the form of an interest bearing fixed deposit and the remaining 10% received in cash were invested in a bank. 'A' claimed that the entire capital gains from the transaction were exempted under sec. 11(1A) as they were invested in a fixed deposit and a bank deposit. The revenue department rejected this contention, claiming that the deposits were merely unpaid purchase price which would be paid in instalments.

Held: Under *Explanation (iii)* to sec. 11(1A), the net consideration refers to the full value of the consideration for the transfer which is either received or accrues to 'A'. In this case, the entire net consideration was used by 'A' to acquire another capital asset – the fixed deposit and the bank deposit – and therefore, sec. 11(1A) would apply to exempt such amount.

3. Income from property held under the Trust

Property is a term of the widest import - It signifies every possible interest which a person can acquire, hold and enjoy. It includes both tangible as well as intangible property. Property in sec. 11 is used in the popular sense and includes securities or business or share in a business.

For the purpose of exemption, "income derived from property held under trust" should be understood in real and commercial sense. Provisions of Sec. 14 for determining "total income" under various heads of income are not relevant for this purpose [*CIT* v. *Rao Bahadur Calavala Cunnan Chetty Charities* (1982) 135 ITR 485 (Mad.)]; [*CIT* v. *Estate of V.L. Ethiraj* (1982) 136 ITR 12 (Mad.)]. The net income under the mercantile system of accounting (or total income under provisions of the Act) may include credits which are not capable of being applied. Therefore, for the purpose of exemption under sec. 11(1), the income derived from trust property and applied for charitable or religious purposes must be determined on commercial principles and in doing so, all outgoings including outgoings by way of income tax paid by the assessee-trust, must be deducted and it is only from the surplus income in the hands of the trustees that the question of application or accumulation or setting apart of income can arise.

"Property held under Trust" includes a business undertaking provided it is incidental to attainment of the main objective of the Trust and separate Books of Account are maintained for such business [Sec. 11(4), (4A)] - Where exemption is claimed in respect of income of business undertaking, such income is to be computed in accordance with the provisions of this Act, relating to assessment, and where the income is found in excess of the income as shown in the accounts of the undertaking, such excess is deemed to be applied to non-charitable or non-religious purposes and hence, liable to be taxed in the normal manner [Sec. 11(4)]. The exemption for business income applies if the business is incidental to the attainment of the objectives of the trust or institution and separate books of account are maintained for such business [Sec. 11(4A)]. A business whose income is utilized by the trust or the institution for the purpose of achieving the objectives of the trust or the institution is, surely, a business which is incidental to the attainment of the objectives of the trust [*Asstt. CIT* v. *Thanthi Trust* (2001) 115 Taxman 126/247 ITR 785 (SC)].

Apportionment of Agricultural and Non-agricultural Income of the Trust - Where agricultural and non-agricultural properties are held under trust for charitable purposes and no separate accounts are maintained, the Income-tax Officer has no option but to allocate the amount spent on charitable/religious purposes between agricultural and non-agricultural income in an appropriate ratio. For this purpose, it is not necessary that there should be a provision in the Income-tax Act and Rules. The Income-tax Officer has to take a reasonable and realistic view of what has happened which means that the amount applied towards specified purposes, namely, charitable/religious purposes, has necessarily got to be allocated in an appropriate proportion between agricultural and non-agricultural income and then the rule contained in section 11(1)(*a*) applied. [*CIT* v. *Panchayati Akhara Nirmal* (1991) 56 Taxman 61/190 ITR 121 (All.)].

Only real income to be considered - The exemption from tax granted by Sec. 11 must be confined to the real income of the trust. For example, the amount of income which is taken away by deduction at source under Sec. 194 is not available to the trust for application to charitable purposes and cannot be considered as income of the trust. Though sec. 198 provides that the amounts deducted by way of income tax is deemed to be "income received", what is deemed to be income can neither be spent nor accumulated for charitable purposes. The immunity from taxation that has been granted to the income of a charitable trust cannot be denied on the ground that the deemed income under Sec. 198 has not been actually spent for the purpose of charity [*CIT* v. *Jayashree Charity Trust* (1986) 159 ITR 280 (Cal.)].

Case Law : ***CIT* v. *Ganga Charity Trust Fund* (1986) 29 Taxman 413/162 ITR 612 (Gujarat)**

Facts: 'G' was following the mercantile system of accounting, and had paid certain amounts as income tax, which is claimed should be deducted when determining the net income from the property under sec. 11(1)(*a*).

Held: When the assessee is following an accrual based system, incomes on accrual basis may be reflected in the account books, but such notional income cannot be applied or set aside until it is actually received. If the assessee were made to pay income tax on such income, it would render the intended benefits under sec. 11 nugatory. Instead, the income from trust property must be determined on the basis of commercial principles, and in doing so all outgoings including payment of income tax must be deducted when determining the surplus amount based on which the percentages for application and setting aside may be calculated.

Income of the Trust should be applied for charitable or religious purposes [Sec.11(1)]:

Income applied for charitable or religious purposes in India [Sec.11(1)(*a*)] - Exemption under sec. 11(1) is available only for income that is applied for charitable or religious purposes in India. However, upto 15% such income can also be accumulated or set aside for charitable or religious purposes subject to certain conditions. Where such income is deemed to be applied or accumulated/set aside, the trust or institution is required to file Form 9A or Form 10 respectively. Such Forms must be filed at least two months prior to the filing of income tax returns under sec. 139(1) (w.e.f. 1.4.2023).

Donation to other trusts

Trusts or institutions are allowed to either apply mandatory 85% of their income either themselves or by making donations to the trusts with similar objectives. If donated to other trusts or institutions, the donation should not be towards corpus to ensure that the donations are applied by the donee trust or institutions. However, instances have come to the notice that certain trusts or institutions are trying to defeat the intention of the legislature by forming multiple trusts and accumulating 15% at each layer. By forming multiple trusts and accumulating 15% at each stage, the effective application towards the charitable or religious activities is reduced significantly to a lesser percentage compared to the mandatory requirement of 85%.

To curb such practices, the Finance Act, 2023 restricts the amount of donation made by a trust to another trust to 85% of the eligible donations. Thus, only 85% of the eligible donations made by a trust or an institution to another trust or institution shall be treated as application of income only to the extent of 85% of such donation.

Income applied for promoting international welfare [Sec. 11(1)(*c*)(*i*)] - Where income of the trust is applied to promote international welfare in which India is interested, such income is exempt to the extent it is applied for such purposes outside India provided such trust was created on or after 1 April, 1952

Income from property applied for charitable or religious purposes outside India [Sec. 11(1)(*c*)(*ii*)] - Where income is applied for charitable or religious purposes outside India, it is exempt from tax provided such trust was created before 1st April 1952 and the Board has directed to exclude it from the total income of the trust either by a general order or special order.

***It is immaterial whether the application of income is revenue or capital in nature* -** The word "applied" is wider in import than the word "expenditure". The money or amount may not go irretrievably when it is "applied" to a purpose. The application of the income can be for revenue or capital purposes. So long as the expenditure is incurred out of the income of the trust, even if such expenditure is for capital purposes on the objects of the trust, income would be exempt. Therefore, even capital expenditure incurred for charitable or religious purposes is considered as application of income and qualify for exemption under Sec. 11 [*CIT* v. *St. George Forane Church* (1988) 36 Taxman 42/170 ITR 62 (Ker.)].

Application to be considered on payment basis - Since existing provision was silent on whether the application of income could be allowed to such trusts on accrual basis following the mercantile system of accounting or on payment basis following the cash system, the Finance Act, 2022 offers some clarity. According to the newly inserted *Explanation* 7 to sec.11(7) application of income by any trust or institution will be on 'payment basis'. In other words, irrespective of the accounting method employed by the trust, any sum payable by any trust or institution shall be considered as application of income only when such sum is actually paid by it.

Payment of Taxes amounts to Applications - The expenditure incurred by way of payment of tax out of the current year's income has to be considered as an application for charitable purposes because the payment is made to preserve the corpus, the existence of which is absolutely necessary for the trust [*CIT* v. *Janaki Animal Ayya Nadar Trust* (1985) 23 Taxman 416/153 ITR 159 (Mad.)].

Repayment of Loans, taken for the Purpose of the Trust, amounts to Applications [Circular No. 100, dated 24.1.1973] - The repayment of loan, originally taken to fulfil one of the objects of the trust will amount to an application of the income for charitable and religions purposes.

If the object of the trust is advancement of education, granting of educational loans, even if interest bearing, will amount to applications of the income for charitable purposes. As and when the loans are returned to the trust, it is treated as income of the trust for that year.

The Finance Act, 2021 inserted *Explanation 4(ii)* to sec.11(1) w.e.f. 1.4.2022 clarifying this point. Accordingly, as a rule of thumb application for charitable or religious purposes, from any loan or borrowing, shall not be treated as application of income for charitable or religious purposes. However, repayment of loan or borrowing which was originally taken for the purposes of application for charitable or religious purposes will be treated as application to the extent the amount so repaid from the income of the trust or the institution.

Charitable Trusts and Religious Institutions Time limit of 5 years for refurbishing of corpus

The Finance Act, 2023 further imposes a cap of 5 years for refurbishing of corpus and repayment of loan. Thus, in order to claim the repayment of loan as application of income, the loan would have to be repaid within a period of five years. Further, conditions that are required to be satisfied in the case of application for charitable or religious purposes must also be satisfied while making the application from the corpus or loan or borrowing. These conditions are as follows:

(*i*) Such application should not be in the form of corpus donation to another trust.

(*ii*) TDS, if applicable, should be deducted on such application.

(*iii*) Application whereby payment or aggregate of payments made to a person in a day exceeds ₹ 10,000 in other than specified modes (such as cash) is not allowed.

(*iv*) Carry forward and set off of excess application is not allowed.

(*v*) Application is allowed in the year in which it is actually paid.

(*vi*) Application should not directly or indirectly benefit any specified related party.

These amendments will take effect from 1st April, 2023 and will accordingly apply to the assessment year 2023-24 and subsequent assessment years.

No deduction for depreciation - After 1 April 2015, no deduction or allowance is permitted when arriving at the income under Sec. 11, in respect of any asset which has been acquired as an application of income under the Section in the same or previous year [Sec. 11(6)].

Disallowances of expenditure In arriving at the income under sec.11, expenditures disallowed under sec. 40A(*a*)(*ia*) (failure to deduct tax at source) and under sec. 40A (3), (3A) payment in cash in excess of ₹ 10,000) will be disallowed. This disallowance is operational from 1.4.2019.

Case Law : ***CIT* v. *Janmabhumi Press Trust* (2000) 242 ITR 457 (Karnataka)**

Facts: 'J' had used the rental income earned during the assessment year towards the repayment of a loan which had previously been taken for the construction of a building to augment its income. The issue was whether this amounted to 'application' of the income for the purposes of exemption under sec. 11.

Held: When determining whether the assessee trust would be entitled to the benefit of sec. 11, the only question that need be considered is whether the income is applied for charitable purposes. In the present case, where the income was repay the loan taken to construct a building which would augment 'J's income, it should be treated as an 'application' of the income for charitable purposes.

Case Law : ***CIT* v. *Krishi Upaj Mandi Samiti, Raisinghnagar* [2016] 69 taxmann. com 425/240 Taxman 527/(2017) 390 ITR 59 (Rajasthan)**

Facts: 'K' had incurred an excess of expenditure for charitable purposes over the income earned in that previous year, which it sought to set off against the income earned in the assessment year. The Assessing Officer rejected this claim on the grounds that the excess in expenditure had been incurred out of the accumulated fund from previous years.

Held: Where the expenditure incurred in excess of the income in a previous year is sought to be set off against the income of a subsequent year, the assessee cannot be denied the benefits of exemption under sec. 11 merely because the expenses were incurred out of the accumulated fund.

Option to accumulate income and apply the same in subsequent year [Sec.11(2)] - It is not necessary that the income should have been applied for charitable or religious purposes only in the year in which the income had arisen. A trust is free to accumulate upto 15% of its income for future application (not exceeding 5 years). Where any such income is accumulated or set apart for application for such purposes in India, it is not included in total income.

However, 85% of its income should be applied for charitable purposes during the previous year. In computing the aforesaid percentage, the amount of donation or voluntary contributions, received for charitable or religious purposes, not forming part of the corpus of the trust, are also taken into account [Sec. 12(1)]. Where 85% of the income (referred to in sec. 11(1)) could not be applied for charitable or religious purposes in India either because such income could not be received, wholly or partly, during that year or for any other reason, the exemption may still apply under sec. 11(2), provided the following conditions are complied with:

(*a*) Assessing Officer should be informed about the purpose of accumulation

(*b*) Accumulated income should be invested according to sec.11(5)

(*a*) Information to Assessing Officer - The Assessing Officer is informed about the purpose of the accumulation and the period for which the income is being accumulated. The period of accumulation cannot exceed 5 years. The information is to be furnished in writing in the prescribed manner before the expiry of the time fixed for furnishing the return of income under Sec. 139(1) (Form No.10 as per Rule 17). In computing the period of 5 years, the period during which the income could not be applied for the purposes for which it is so accumulated or set apart due to an order or injunction of any court is excluded.

Notice of accumulation must be given to assessing authority before assessment is concluded - It is mandatory for the person claiming the benefit of Sec. 11(2) to intimate to the assessing authority the particulars required. If during the assessment proceedings, the Assessing Officer does not have the necessary information, the question of excluding such income from assessment does not arise at all. Therefore, it is necessary that the assessing authority must have this information at the time he completes the assessment. Further, any claim for giving the benefit of Sec. 11 on the basis of information supplied subsequent to the completion of assessment would mean that the assessment order will have to be reopened. The Act does not contemplate such reopening of the assessment [*CIT* v. *Nagpur Hotel Owners' Association* (2001) 114 Taxman 255/247 ITR 201 (SC)].

Time-limit within which notice is to be issued under sec. 11(2)*(a) *for accumulation of income - The statement under sec. 11(2)(*a*) must be furnished on or before the due date as specified under sub-section (1) of Section 139 for furnishing the return of income for the previous year [Sec. 11(2)(*c*)].

Where accumulation is for the purpose of the objects for which the trust is created, the assessee need not specify any specific purpose - It is true that specification of a certain purpose or purposes was needed for accumulation of the trust's income under sec. 11(2) of the Act. At the same time, the purpose or purposes to be specified cannot be beyond the objects of the trust. Plurality of the purposes of accumulation is not precluded but it depends on the precise purpose for which the accumulation is intended. Therefore, it is sufficient if the income is accumulated for the purpose of the trust. [*CIT* v. *Hotel & Restaurant Association* (2003) 132 Taxman 76/261 ITR 190 (Del.)].

Case Law : ***CIT* v. *Bochasanwasi Shri Akshar Purshottam Public Charitable Trust* [2018] 409 ITR 591/[2019] 102 taxmann.com 122/261 Taxman 229 (Gujarat)**

Facts: 'B' being a charitable trust claimed an exemption for certain portion of its income under Sec. 11(2) which was rejected on the grounds that 'B' had failed to specify the purpose for which the income was being set apart in the requisite Form of declaration. In its reply 'B' stated that it was undertaking two new hospital projects with modern amenities and that the board of trustees also passed a resolution in favour of setting aside such amount for the projects.

Held: Though a statement of the purpose for which the amount is being set aside would be required to avail exemption under sec. 11(2), however assessee's failure to include the same within the Form 10 declaration would not necessarily be fatal to its claim. The prime requirement is to state the purpose for which the income is being accumulated or set apart. Since 'B' had provided such a statement during the assessment proceedings, which was held to be sufficient for meeting the requirements of the provision.

(*b*) Statutory Form of Investment - The money so accumulated should be invested/deposited in statutory form of investment as laid down under sec. 11(5).

Accumulation in excess of 15% of income derived from property held under trust will enjoy exemption if such income is invested or deposited in statutory form of investment under sec. 11(5).

Only the accumulated amount in excess of 15% of the trust income needs to be invested in specified government securites and not the whole of the accumulated trust income. It is not required that for obtaining the benefit of the relaxation provided in sec. 11(2), the assessee has to invest the entire accumulated income in specified investment. [*CIT* v. *H.H. Marthanda Varma Elayaraja of Travancore Trust* (1981) 5 Taxman 278/129 ITR 191 (Ker.)].

Exception in cases where income invested or deposited cannot be applied for the purposes it was accumulated or set apart due to circumstances beyond the control of the assessee but is instead applied for other charitable or religious objects of the trust with the approval of the Assessing Officer [Sec. 11(3A)] - Where it is beyond the control of the assessee trust or institution to spend the income for which it was accumulated or set apart, the Assessing Officer may allow the assessee to apply the income so accumulated or set apart for any other religious or charitable purposes provided such other purposes are in conformity with the objects of the trust. In such cases, the exemption, granted to the assessee, cannot be forfeited and the provisions of Sec. 11(2) will continue to apply.

The Assessing Officer is not empowered to allow the application of income by way of a credit or payment to any trust or institution registered under section 12AA or to any other fund, institution, trust, hospital, university or other educational institution, or hospital or any other medical institution referred under clauses (*iv*), (*v*), (*vi*) and (*via*) of sec. 10(*23C*) except in the year in which the assessee trust or institution is dissolved [Proviso to sec. 11(3A)].

Case Law : ***CIT* v. *H.H. Marthanda Varma Elayaraja of Travancore Trust* (1981) 5 Taxman 278/129 ITR 191 (Kerala)**

Facts: The assessee claimed exemption under Sec. 11 for the unspent income that it had accumulated for future use. It invested the portion of the income which was over the 25% limit under sec. 11(1)(*a*), in the appropriate government securities, and sought an exemption for the entire income. The Commissioner rejected the assessee's claim on the grounds that the entire accumulated income was not invested in the approved government securities.

Held: The Court observed that the words *"money so accumulated"* in sec. 11(2)(*b*) in relation to the requirement of investing the amount, must be understood to mean the among which is being claimed for relaxation under sec. 11(2). This means that it would only apply to that income which is in excess of the limits specified in sec. 11(1)(*a*). Therefore, it is only the amount above the 25% threshold that would have needed to be invested as under the modes specified in sec. 11(5).

Year of Chargeability when acccumulated income under sec. 11(2) remains unapplied or applied in breach of certain conditions [Sec. 11(3)] - The benefit of exemption allowed to an assessee–trust for accumulation of its income in excess of 15% is subject to certain conditions and such benefit will be rolled back upon failure to comply. In such instances the amount of exemption allowed will be deemed to be the income of the assessee–trust. Accordingly, where any trust income accumulated in excess of 15% and in respect of which exemption is granted under sec. 11(2), upon happening of the following events, such income will be deemed to be the income of the specified previous year:

it is applied to purposes other than religious or charitable	deemed to be the income of the previous year in which it is so applied in
it ceases to be accumulated or set apart for application to religious or charitable purposes	deemed to be the income of the previous year in which ceases to be so accumulated or set apart
it ceases to remain invested in statutory form of investment specified under sec. 11(5)	deemed to be the income of the previous year in which ceases to remain so invested or deposited
it is not utilised for the purpose for which it is so accumulated or set apart within the allowed period of 5 years or in the year immediately following the expiry thereof	deemed to be the income of the previous year immediately following the expiry of the period aforesaid (*i.e.* sixth year)
it is credited or paid to any other trust or institution registered under sec. 12AA or sec.12AB	deemed to be the income of the previous year in which credited or paid
it is credited or paid to any other fund, institution, trust, hospital, university or other educational institution, or hospital or any other medical institution referred under clauses (*iv*), (*v*), (*vi*) and (*via*) of sec. 10(*23C*)	deemed to be the income of the previous year in which credited or paid

The Finance Act, 2022 makes a departure from the existing position where un-applied accumulated income was taxable in the sixth year. W.e.f. 1st April 2023, such accumulated funds that remains unutilised for the purpose for which it was accumulated or set apart will taxable the last previous year of the period for which the income was so accumulated or set apart.

Case Law : ***Maharaja Ranjit Singh War Museum Society, Ludhiana* v. *CIT* (2020) 121 taxmann.com 90/275 Taxman 640 (Punj. & Har.)**

Facts: 'M' was a charitable trust which was running a museum and was registered under Section 12AA. During the relevant year, 'M' made a donation the Punjab State War Heroes Memorial & Museum Society, which was not a society registered under Section 12AA, but was subsequently registered under the same.

Held: The amount of donation to another society was in violation of the conditions laid down in sec. 11(3)(d), and therefore, the amount which was donated would have to be treated as the income of the assessee.

DENIAL OF EXEMPTION IN CERTAIN CASES [SEC. 13]

The exemption is denied in the following cases:

1. Private Religious Trust not enuring for the benefit of the public not eligible for exemption [Sec. 13(1)(*a*)]

Any part of income from property held under trust for private religious purposes which does not enure to the benefit of the public is not exempt. However, if it is applied to charitable purpose or religious (public) purposes, the exemption applies to such income.

2. Charitable Trust for the benefit of a particular religious community or caste [Sec. 13(1)(*b*)]

If a charitable trust or institution is created or established after the commencement of this Act (that is, 31 March 1962), for the benefit of any particular religious community or caste, no part of the income applied to such purposes is exempt from income tax. But a trust or institution created or established for the benefit of the scheduled castes, tribes, backward classes or women and children is not deemed to be a trust or institution created or established for the benefit of a religious community or caste [*Explanation 2* of sec. 13]. A charitable trust or institution created or established before 1 April 1962, is entitled to exemption even if it is for the benefit of any particular religious community or caste.

3. Income of the Trust/Institution used for the benefit of interested persons [Sec. 13(1)(*c*)]

No exemption is available in respect of any income of a charitable/religious trust or institution if any part of the income of the trust or institution or any property of the trust or institution is used or applied for the benefit of interested persons. This is explained with the help of the table below:

TABLE 15.2: INCOME USED FOR THE BENEFIT OF INTERESTED PERSONS

Trust created or established on or after 1 April 1962 [Sec. 13(1)(c)(i)]	
Exemption is denied to any income if under terms of the trust or rules governing the institution, any part of such income enures directly or indirectly for the benefit of any person referred under Sec. 13(3)	
Trust whenever created [Sec. 13(1)(c)(ii)]	
Exemption is denied to any income if any part of such income or any property of the trust or institution is used or applied during the previous year directly or indirectly for the benefit of any person referred under sec. 13(3)	*Exceptions:* (*a*) Where the trust or institution is created before 1 April 1962 and application for the benefit of person referred under sec. 13(3) is by way of compliance with mandatory terms of the trust or mandatory rules governing the institution [First Proviso to sec. 13(1)(*c*)]. (*b*) Insofar as the application relates to a period before 1 June 1970 [Second Proviso to sec. 13(1)(*c*)].

Interested Person [Sec. 13(3)] - The 'interested person' are the following :

(*i*) the author of the trust or founder of the institution;

(*ii*) any person who has made a substantial contribution to the trust or institution, that is, any person whose total contribution up to the end of the relevant previous year exceeds ₹ 50,000;

(*iii*) where such author, founder or person is a Hindu Undivided Family, a member of the family;

(*iv*) any trustee of the trust or manager (by whatever name called) of the institution;

(*v*) any relative of any such author, founder, person, or member, trustee or manager as aforesaid. (It is not understood why the relative of a substantial contributor has been left out); and

(*vi*) any concern in which any of the persons referred to in clauses (*i*) to (*v*) has a substantial interest.

Where aggregate of the funds of the trust invested in a concern in which any interested person has a substantial interest does not exceed 5% of the capital of that concern, income other than the income earned from such investment is eligible for exemption and cannot be denied merely by reason that the funds of the trust or institution is invested in a concern in which the persons interested in the trust have a substantial interest. [Sec. 13(4)]

Relative [*Explanation 1* to sec. 13] - Relative in relation to an individual means: (*i*) spouse of the individual; (*ii*) brother or sister of the individual; (*iii*) brother or sister of the spouse of the individual; (*iv*) any lineal ascendant or descendant of the individual and of the spouse of the individual; (*v*) spouses of brother or sister of the individual; (*vi*) spouses of brother or sister of the spouse of the individual; (*vii*) spouses of any lineal ascendant or descendant of the individual; (*viii*) spouses of any lineal ascendant or descendant of the spouse of the individual; (*ix*) any lineal descendant of a brother or sister of either the individual or of the spouse of the individual [*Explanation 1* to sec. 13].

Case Law : ***CIT* v. *Bholaram Educational Society* (2019) 101 taxmann.com 193/260 Taxman 368 (SC)**

Facts: 'B' was a charitable trust running a school and paid rent to an HUF, whose karta was its trustee. The Assessing Officer took the view that this payment breached sec. 13(1)(*c*), and therefore, the assessee was not entitled to the exemption under sec. 11.

Held: Since rent charged by HUF was at the prevailing market rates and not excessive, the interested person did not derive any benefit, and 'B' could continue to derive the benefit of exemption under sec. 11.

Income deemed to be applied for the benefit of the interested persons [Sec. 13(2)] - The income or property of the trust or institution or any part of such income or property is deemed to have been used or applied for the benefit of interested persons in the following cases:

(*a*) If any part of the income or property of the trust or institution is, or continues to be lent to any interested person for any period during the previous year without either adequate security or adequate interest or both;

(*b*) If any land, building or other property of the trust or institution is, or continues to be, made available for the use of any interested person for any period during the previous year without charging adequate rent or other compensation;

(*c*) If any amount is paid by way of salary, allowance or otherwise during the previous year to any interested person out of the resources of the trust or institution for services rendered by that person to such trust or institution and the amount so paid is in excess of what may be reasonably paid for such services;

(*d*) If the services of the trust or institution are made available to any person during the previous year without adequate remuneration or other compensation;

(*e*) If any share, security or other property is purchased by or on behalf of the trust or institution from any interested person during the previous year for consideration which is more than adequate;

(*f*) If any share, security or other property is sold by or on behalf of the trust or institution to any interested person during the previous year for consideration which is less than adequate;

(*g*) If any income or property of the trust or institution is derived during the previous year in favour of any interested person. However, this clause does not apply where the income, or the value of the property or, as the case may be, the aggregate of the income and the value of the property, so diverted does not exceed one thousand rupees;

(*h*) If any funds of the trust or institution are, or continue to remain, invested for any period during the previous year (not being a period before the 1 January 1971), in any concern in which any interested person has substantial interest.

New Penalty provision under sec. 271AAE for passing on unreasonable benefits to trustee or specified persons (w.e.f. AY 2023-24)

The Finance Act, 2022 newly inserted a penalty provision by virtue of sec. 271AAE for passing on unreasonable benefits to trustee or specified persons. Accordingly, upon first instance of such violation, a sum equal to amount of income applied by such trust or institution for the benefit of specified person will be imposed as penalty. The penalty will be twice this amount upon any subsequent violation. The penalty under this section will be applicable to any other penalty that may apply.

4. Investment of the Funds is not in manner Specified by the Act [Sec. 13(1)(*d*)]

A charitable or religious trust or institution is denied the benefit of exemption under secs. 11 and 12 in the following cases:

(*a*) If any funds of the trust or institution are invested or deposited otherwise than in accordance with sec. 11(5);

 (*i*) after 28 February 1983 [Sec. 13(1)(*d*)(*i*)]; or

 (*ii*) before 1 March 1983 and continued to remain so invested or deposited after 30 November 1983 [Sec. 13(1)(*d*)(*ii*)]; or

(*b*) If any shares in a company, other than–

 (*i*) shares in a public sector company;

 (*ii*) shares prescribed as a form or mode of investment under sec. 11(5)(*xii*) are held by the trust or institution after 30 November 1983 [Sec. 13(1)(*d*)(*iii*)].

Meaning of Funds - In this context, "funds" normally and ordinarily mean cash on hand or cash at bank capable of being drawn upon and dealt with in a manner as desired by the person entitled or authorised to do so. It does not include actionable claims like promissory notes [*Auditor Dasaradha Rami Reddy Charities* v. *CIT* (1989) 44 Taxman 453/177 ITR 249 (Mad.)].

Exception - However, such exemption is not withdrawn in the following cases:

(*a*) Any assets held by the trust or institution where such assets form part of the corpus of the trust/institution as on 1 June 1973 [Proviso (*i*) to sec. 13(1)(*d*)].

(*b*) Any bonus shares allotted in relation to shares forming part of the corpus as on 1 June 1973 [Proviso (*ii*) to sec. 13(1)(*d*)].

(*c*) Any debentures issued by or on behalf of any company or corporation acquired by the trust or institution before 1 March 1983. However, where debentures issued by or on behalf of any company or corporation are acquired after 28 February 1983 but before 25 July 1991, exemption is denied only in respect of interest on such debentures and not the entire income of the trust/institution, provided that these are disinvested on or before 31 March 1992 [Sec. 13(5)].

(*d*) Any asset not mentioned in section 11(5), and which is not held by the trust or the institution, after the expiry of one year from the previous year in which such asset is acquired or 31 March 1993, whichever is later.

(*e*) Any funds representing the profits and gains of business of any previous year relevant to the assessment year from 1 April 1984 or any subsequent assessment year. However, this does not apply if the trust or institution has any income other than the profits and gains from business, unless it has maintained separate books of account with respect to such business.

Disallowance of proportionate income applied for specified persons/ interested persons/related persons [Sec.13(1)]

If trust/institution diverts income/provides excessive benefits to trustees/other specified persons or deploys its funds in prohibited investments only that part of income that is diverted/regarded as excessive benefit/deployed in prohibited investments would be taxable. This position has been upheld in certain rulings even before the amendment. As discussed above, such incomes will be taxable at a flat rate of 30 per cent without any deductions

Tax consequences for non-exempt incomes [Sec.164(2)]

When :

(*i*) income derived from property held under trust wholly for charitable or religious purpose,

(*ii*) income from voluntary contributions referred to in sec. 2(*24*)(*iia*) of the Act,

(*iii*) income from business being carried on incidentally to the main objective referred to in sec. 11(4A),

is not exempt under sec. 11 or sec. 12 of the Act, such income shall be charged to tax as if the relevant income, not so exempt was an income of an "Association of persons". Only that part of the relevant income which is not exempt under section 11 or section 12 is brought to tax, as the income of an AOP and the balance of income of the charitable trust / institution, will remain exempt.

Where tax exemption of such trust is forfeited because of the contravention of the provisions contained in sec. 13(1)(*c*) and/or section 13(1)(*d*), tax shall be charged on such income or part thereof at the maximum marginal rate of income-tax (including surcharge) applicable to the highest slab of income in the case of an Association of persons. [Proviso to sec. 164(2)]. In simple words,

MMR will apply only on that portion of income which is non-exempt owing to contravention of sec.13(1)(*c*) or (*d*) and not on the total income of the trust.

Computation of income of a trust in case of certain non-compliances [Sec. 13(10)] (newly inserted by the Finance Act, 2022)

Under the existing scheme, there is no explicit provision that determines computation of taxable income due to non-compliances. The Finance Act, 2022 newly inserted sub-sec. (10) to sec. 13 provides for computation such income after allowing deductions for revenue expenditure in India to the following conditions:

- Expenditure should not be a donation or contribution to any person.
- Expenditure incurred without with holding appropriate tax or expenditure incurred in cash beyond the prescribed threshold shall not be allowed.
- Expenditure incurred from the corpus or any loan or borrowing shall not be allowed.
- Depreciation on an asset, the cost of which is claimed as application of income in any year, shall not be allowed.

Further no deduction in respect of any expenditure or allowance or set off of any loss shall be allowed to the assessee under any other provision of this Act [Sec.13(11)].

Tax rates applicable on specified incomes [Sec. 115BBI] (newly inserted by the Finance Act, 2022)

Specified Incomes of trust or institutions, that is, income accumulated or set apart in excess of 15 percent would be taxable at a flat rate of 30 per cent without reduction of any expenditure or allowances or set off of losses. Other incomes (if any) of the trust/institution will be taxable per the currently applicable provisions.

Exit Tax on Charitable trust when it cease to exist or converts into a non-charitable entity (Secs. 115TD to 115TF) (inserted w.e.f. 1-6-2016)

A charitable trust may voluntarily wind up its activities and dissolve or may also merge with any other non-charitable institution, or to may convert into a non-charitable organisation. Moreover, it is always possible for charitable institutions to transfer assets to a non-charitable institution. In such cases, the existing law does not provide for a clarity as to how the assets of such a charitable institution shall be charged to tax.

Under provisions of sec. 11 certain amount of income of prior period can be brought to tax on failure of certain conditions. However, there is no provision in the Act which ensure that the corpus and asset base of the trust accreted over period of time, which was created with promise of it being used for charitable purpose, continues to be utilised for charitable purposes even after the trust has ceased to operate. Therefore, to ensure that the benefit conferred over the years by way of exemption is not misused and to plug the gap in law that allows the charitable trusts having built up corpus/wealth through exemptions being converted into non-charitable organisation with no tax consequences, Chapter XII-EB - Special Provision Relating to Tax on Accreted Income of Certain Trusts and Institutions is inserted with effect from June 1, 2016.

The Finance Act, 2022 extended the provisions of Chapter XII-EB and sections 115TD, 115TE and 115TF to the educational institutions, hospitals etc. covered under sec. 10(*23C*) as well.

Circumstances when exit tax levied [Sec. 115TD]

A tax which is in addition to income-tax chargeable in hands of entity and leviable at the maximum marginal rate on the accreted income in case of :

(*i*) conversion into, or

(*ii*) merger with, any non-charitable form, or

(*iii*) on transfer of assets of a charitable organisation on its dissolution to a non-charitable institution.

Levy of exit tax on non-filling of application

Instances have come to the notice where certain trusts and institutions have not applied for the regular registration after taking the provisional registration or have not applied for the re-registration/approval. In such instances, the trusts or institutions were escaping exit tax. The Finance Act, 2023 makes sec. 115TD applicable on failing to apply for registration/approval, provisional registration/approval or re-registration/approval, as the case maybe. The date of conversion of the trust or institution shall be considered to be the last date for making an application for registration.

Deemed Conversion [Sec. 115TD(3)] - A trust or institution shall be deemed to have been converted into any from (not eligible for registration under sec. 12AA) in a previous year, if:

(*a*) The registration granted to it under section 12AA has been cancelled ; or

(*b*) It has modified its objects and not applied for fresh registration (or fresh registration application has been rejected)

(*c*) It has failed to make an application for re-registration or renewal

Meaning of accreted income [Sec. 115TD(2)] - Accreted income shall be amount of aggregate of fair market value of total assets as reduced by the liability as on the specified date (*i.e.*, the date of conversion, merger or dissolution) in accordance with the method of valuation as may be prescribed under Rule 17CB.

The following shall be ignored for the purpose of computation of accreted income –

1. Any asset which is established to have been directly acquired be the trust or institution out of agricultural income as is referred to in section 10 (1).

2. Any asset acquired by the trust/institution during the period beginning from the date of its creation and ending on the date from which the registration under section 12AA became effective or deemed effective (however, this rule is valid only if the trust/institution has not been allowed any benefit of sections 11 and 12 during the said period). "Deemed" effective covers a case where due to first proviso to section 12A(2) the benefit of sections 11 and 12 have been allowed to the trust/institution in respect of any previous year prior to the year of registration.

Interest payable for non-payment of tax by trust or institution [Sec. 115TE]
Where the principal officer or the trustee of the trust or the institution and the trust or the institution fails to pay the whole or any part of the tax on the accreted income within the prescribed time, a simple interest @ 1 per cent per month or part of it shall be applicable for the period of non-payment.

Assessee-in-default if failure to pay tax on accreted income [Sec. 115TF]
If any principal officer or the trustee of the trust or the institution and the trust or the institution does not pay tax on accreted income in accordance with the provisions of sec. 115TD, then, he or it shall be deemed to be an assessee in default in respect of the amount of tax payable by him or it and all the provisions of this Act for the collection and recovery of income-tax shall apply.

CHAPTER 16 Dividend

MEANING OF DIVIDEND [SEC. 2(22)]

Dividend is paid by a company out of its profits. Thus, a share of profit received by a shareholder out of the profits of the company, proportionate to his shareholding, is termed as "dividends". But the legislature in defining dividend has added certain other receipts which otherwise may not have been called dividends. Dividend is an inclusive definition under sec. 2(*22*) as follows:

- **Distribution of Accumulated Profits, Entailing the Release of Company's Assets [Sec. 2(*22*)(*a*)]** - Any distribution of accumulated profits, whether capitalised or not, by a company to its shareholders is deemed to be dividend if it entails the release of all or any part of its assets. Distribution of accumulated profits may be in cash or in kind.

  If accumulated profits are distributed in cash, it is dividend within the meaning of the Act as it had reduced the assets of the company.

  Where accumulated profits are distributed in kind, market value of asset, to the extent of accumulated profits, is deemed to be dividend, [*CIT* v. *Central India Industries Ltd.* (1971) 82 ITR 555 (SC)]. For example, the company distributes its investment to its shareholders. The market value of investment on the date of such distribution, to the extent of accumulated profits, is liable to be taxed as dividend in the hands of a shareholder.

  Renunciation of Right Shares, covered by Accumulated Profits - Where a company becomes entitled to "right shares" of a company in which it is itself a shareholder and instead of taking up these "right shares" it renounces its rights in favour of its shareholders in proportion to their shareholding, such distribution of the right amounts to dividend [*Kantilal Manilal* v. *CIT* (1961) 41 ITR 275 (SC)]. If a company applies its accumulated profits for buying the share of another company and then distributes those shares among its own shareholders, there would be distribution of accumulated profits entailing release of the company's assets. In such a case, the shareholders are deemed to have received dividends in money's worth.

  Shares Distributed as Dividend must be valued at Market Value - When shares are distributed as dividend, amount of dividend should be taken to be the market value of those shares as on date on which person concerned becomes entitled to those shares; the fact that shareholder retains them and does not sell them is irrelevant. It would be wrong to say that when shares are distributed as dividend, the person who receives them gets only their face value in terms of money. What he really receives is the market value of those shares as on the date he became entitled to those shares [*CIT* v. *Central India Industries Ltd*. [1971] 82 ITR 555 (SC)].

Capitalisation of Profit in case of Equity Shareholders not treated as Deemed Dividend - Capitalisation of accumulated profits does not entail the release of the company's assets. A company may capitalise its accumulated profits by issuing bonus shares to its equity shareholders. These bonus shares may either be ordinary or preference shares on one hand, or redeemable preference shares on the other. Capitalisation of the accumulated profits keeps the assets of the company intact. Assets which were represented by the accumulated profits continue to remain as part of a company's assets, the only difference being that instead of the assets being profits, they are capitalised and become part of the capital of the company. There is thus no deemed dividend to be included in the total income of a shareholder.

But whenever such bonus shares are paid off, the distribution to the holders of bonus shares is deemed to be dividend as it entails the release of the company's assets. Thus, if a shareholder who was issued bonus shares, transfers such shares, and later on the company redeems such shares, the amount received on redemption, including premium, if any, is taxable as dividend in the hands of the purchaser. It is to be noted that the purchaser cannot deduct the cost of purchasing such shares as no capital expenditure is allowed in computing the taxable income from dividends.

- **Distribution of Bonus Shares to Preference Shareholders [Sec. 2(*22*)(*b*)]** - Where a company capitalises its accumulated profits and issues bonus shares to preference shareholders, the market value of such shares is assessable as dividend. Preference shareholders are entitled to the refund of their capital and nothing more. Issue of bonus shares would entitle them to claim more amount than what they invested. Thus, issue of bonus shares to preference shareholder is deemed to be dividend even though it does not entail a release of company's assets. Therefore, the market value of such bonus shares is taxable as dividend in the hands of a preference shareholder.

- **Distribution of Debentures or Debenture Stock or Debenture Certificate by a Company to its Shareholders to the extent of Accumulated Profits [Sec. 2(*22*)(*b*)]** - If a company distributes debentures or debenture stock or debenture certificate in any form, *i.e.* in the form of a promissory note or a post-dated cheque to its shareholders; whether with or without interest, such distribution to the extent it possesses accumulated profits, is deemed to be dividend though there is no release of company's asset in this case.

The certificates are valued at the market rate and if there is no market rate, they should be valued according to well-known principles of valuation, e.g. the solvency of the debtor company, the rate of interest as compared to market rate and the period of redemption. Such income would be the income of the year in which such certificates are issued.

- **Distribution in Liquidation [Sec. 2(*22*)(*c*)]** - Any distribution made to the shareholders of a company on its liquidation, to the extent to which the distribution is attributable to the accumulated profits of the company immediately before its liquidation, whether capitalised or not, is deemed to be dividend income. Thus, any distribution made out of the profits of the company after the date of liquidation cannot be deemed to be dividends. It is a repayment towards capital.

  Distribution can be Less than Capital Invested - There is no warrant for the proposition that the distribution in a winding up does not attract tax even if it is out of accumulated profits unless the capital has been repaid in full. The shareholder may have made a loss by subscribing to the capital of the company and may have, in the distribution, received much less than the capital subscribed. Yet, such receipt is taxable [*Vidyutrai Y. Desai* v. *CIT* [1958] 33 ITR 510 (Bom.)].

  Exceptions - Any distribution attributable to accumulated profits as on the date of liquidation is deemed to be dividend. However, there are two exceptions to this:

  (*i*) *Distribution to preference shareholders in respect of shares issued for full cash consideration* - Any distribution on the date of liquidation to the extent of accumulated profits is not deemed to be a dividend if the distribution is made in respect of shares issued for full cash consideration and the holder is not entitled to participate in the surplus assets in the event of liquidation.

  Preference shareholders are not entitled to participate in the surplus assets in the event of liquidation. They are only entitled to a return of their share money which they had paid either in full or in part, as the case may be, but to no more. Therefore, the return to such a shareholder either in liquidation proceeding or on reduction of capital of the company would really be in the nature of a return of capital.

  The exception applies in respect of preference shares which have been issued for full cash consideration. Where, on the other hand, the shares in question have been only partially paid up and the shareholder gets from the liquidator the full nominal value of the share, then the difference between the amount partly paid up and full face value is regarded as dividend within the meaning of this definition.

  (*ii*) *Distribution to equity shareholders who have been issued bonus shares after 31 March 1964 but before 1 April 1965* - Where distribution is made to equity shareholders in respect of bonus shares which were issued by capitalisation of the profits after 31 March 1964 and before 1 April 1965, it is not deemed to be dividend. The exception has been granted because during this period there was a tax on notional capital gains arising on allotment of bonus shares. Hence the exemption has been provided.

From 1 April 1965 and onwards, there is no tax on notional gains on the allotment of bonus shares. Hence, the exemption does not apply from 1 April 1965.

- **Distribution on Reduction of Share Capital [Sec. 2(*22*)(*d*)]** - A company may utilise its accumulated profits for reducing the share capital. Therefore, any distribution to its shareholders by a company on the reduction of its capital to the extent to which the company possesses accumulated profits is deemed to be dividend. For example, after obtaining the court's approval, the company reduces ₹ 5,00,000 share capital, ₹ 5 per share. The accumulated profits on the date of resolution amount to ₹ 4,00,000. Any distribution to this extent is deemed to be dividend. Mr. *X* holds 1,000 shares of this company. He gets ₹ 5,000. Out of this, ₹ 4,000 is taxable as dividend.

  Amount should be Bifurcated into Dividend and Capital Gains - The amount distributed by a company on reduction of its share capital has two components: distribution, attributable to accumulated profits and distribution, attributable to capital (except capitalised profits). To the extent of the accumulated profits, whether such accumulated profits are capitalised or not, the return to the shareholder on the reduction of his share capital is a return of such accumulated profits. This part would be taxable as dividend. The balance may be subject to tax as capital gains, if they accrue [*CIT* v. *G. Narasimhan* [1999] 102 Taxman 66/236 ITR 327 (SC)].

- **Loan by a Closely Held Company to a Specified Shareholder [Sec. 2(*22*)(*e*)]** - Any payment by way of loan or advance, made by a closely held company, after 31 May 1987,

  - to a shareholder who is the beneficial owner of 10% or more equity capital of the company, or
  - to any concern in which such shareholder is a member or a partner and in which he has a substantial interest (hereafter in this clause referred to as the said concern), or
  - any payment by any such company on behalf, or for the individual benefit, of any such shareholder, is deemed to be dividend to the extent it is covered by the accumulated profits, excluding capitalised profits. If the loan is not covered by the accumulated profits, it is not deemed to be dividends.

Loan or Advances to be given to a person who is Registered Shareholder **-** Deeming provision is attracted where loan or advances, covered by accumulated profits, are given by a closely held company to a shareholder, beneficially holding 10% or more equity share capital of the company. Thus, first a person should be a shareholder, that is, the shares should stand registered in his name in the register of shareholders of the company. Even though a person has purchased shares and he is in physical possession of those shares, he cannot be regarded as a shareholder till the shares are registered in his name [*H.K. Mittal* v. *Asstt. CIT* (1994) 49 ITD 653 (Delhi - Trib.)]. Thus, where an HUF is the beneficial owner of shares which stand registered in the name of its *Karta*, any loan advanced by the company to the HUF cannot be treated as 'deemed dividend' as HUF is not the registered shareholder [*Rameshwarlal Sanwarmal* v. *CIT* (1980) 3 Taxman 1/122 ITR 162 (SC)].

Shareholder includes a Corporate Entity **-** Section 2(*31*) defines a "person" which takes within its ambit not only individual but also a corporate entity. Thus, where subsidiary company grants loan to its holding company, sec. 2(*22*(*e*) could apply if other conditions are satisfied [*Sadhana Textiles Mills (P.) Ltd.* v. *CIT* (1991) 188 ITR 318 (Bom.)].

Should it be a Registered Shareholder as well Beneficial Shareholder?

From 1-4-1988, the definition of deemed dividend under sec. 2(*22*)(*e*) was amended to include advancing of such loans to a shareholder who was a beneficial shareholder holding not less than 10% of the voting power. Issue arose whether for applicability of sec. 2(*22*)(*e*) the shareholder in question should be both, registered as well as beneficial shareholder holding not less than 10% of the voting power. The Delhi High Court in *CIT* v. *Ankitech (P.) Ltd.* [2011] 11 taxmann.com 100/199 Taxman 341/[2012] 340 ITR 14 (Delhi) both conditions have to be satisfied *i.e.* shareholder has to be a registered shareholder as well as beneficial shareholder. The Supreme Court in *National Travel Services* v. *CIT* [2018] 89 taxmann.com 332/253 Taxman 243/401 ITR 154 (SC) doubted this ruling of Ankitech to observe that the whole object of the amended provision would be stultified if this was accepted. The matter has been placed before the Chief Justice of India in order to constitute an appropriate Bench of three Judges in order to have a relook at the entire question.

Payment may be towards Personal Liabilities of Shareholder **-** Section covers not only advances and loans to shareholder but any other payments by the company on behalf of or for the individual benefit of shareholder, such as payments of shareholder's personal expenses, income-tax dues, insurance premia, etc., to the extent of the accumulated profits of the company [*CIT* v. *K. Srinivasan* [1963] 50 ITR 788 (Mad.)].

Fact of Repayment of Loan is not relevant **-** The Legislature has deliberately not made the subsistence of the loan or advance, or its being outstanding on the last date of the previous year relevant to the assessment year, a pre-requisite for raising the statutory fiction. In other words, even if the loan or advance ceased to be outstanding at the end of the previous year, it can still be deemed as a "dividend" if the other four conditions factually exist to the extent of the accumulated profits, possessed by the company [*Smt. Tarulata Shyam* v. *CIT* [1977] 108 ITR 345 (SC)] [*See* also *Miss P. Sarada* v. *CIT* [1998] 96 Taxman 11 (SC)].

Duration of Loan not relevant - A temporary advance for a very short period of 23 days out of the accumulated profits to a shareholder was held to be deemed dividend. Even if the loan is not granted to such a shareholder directly, but it is given to a third person who is acting on behalf of, or for the individual benefit of such shareholder, the loan amount, covered by accumulated profits, is treated as dividends.

Every Debit to the Account, not a Loan - Loan refers to a lending of money and acceptance by the other party to repay that sum of money. A transaction of sale of goods on credit does not amount to loan although a debt is created [*Lakmichand Muchhal* v. *CIT* (1961) 43 ITR 315 (MP)].

Date of Accumulated Profits - Accumulated profits have to be taken on the date on which loan is advanced by the company to its substantially interested shareholder. Thus, where a company reduced its share capital and thereafter grants loan to a shareholder, accumulated profits first should be reduced by the amount of reduction of share capital. The balance amount of accumulated profits be considered under sec. 2(*22*)(*e*) for the purposes of loan.

Apportionment of Loan according to Percentage of Shareholding not Permissible - The amount of loan, covered by accumulated profits, cannot be treated dividend only in proportion of the percentage of shareholding. The whole amount of loan, covered by accumulated profits, is deemed to be dividend. Thus, where a shareholder, holding 20% shares, borrows ₹ 1,00,000, covered by accumulated profits, the entire amount of loan is to be treated dividend and not the proportionate amount of 20% of ₹ 1,00,000, that is, ₹ 20,000 [*CIT* v. *Arati Debi* (1978) 111 ITR 277 (Cal.)].

Exceptions - There are two exceptions to the deeming fiction under sec. 2(*22*)(*e*):

(*i*) *Lending of money is a substantial part of the business of the company* - If the loan is granted in the ordinary course of its business and lending of money is a substantial part of the company's business, the loan or advance to a shareholder is not deemed to be a dividend.

The phrase "in the ordinary course of business" implies that even in the case of money-lending company, if the circumstances show that the loan is arranged so as to defeat tax liability, there could arise a dividend.

(*ii*) *Distribution of dividend subsequent to a loan* - Where loan had been treated as dividend, and subsequently the company declares and distributes the dividend to all its shareholders, including the borrowing shareholder, and the dividend so paid is set off by the company against the borrowing, the dividend so declared on the second occasion is not to be treated as a dividend.

Loan by a Closely Held Company to a Specified Concern [Sec. 2(*22*)(*e*)] - Where a member of a concern, holding 20% share of its income is also a shareholder of a closely held company, holding 10% of its equity capital, any payment by way of loan or advance after 31 May 1987, by such company to such concern is deemed to be dividends to the extent the company possesses accumulated profits. Accordingly, such concern is assessible for deemed dividend. It is operative from the assessment year 1988-1989 and onward.

Case Law : ***L. Alagusundaram Chettiar* v. *CIT* [2001] 252 ITR 893/[2002] 121 Taxman 587 (SC)**

Facts: 'A' was the MD of a textile mill where one 'K' was employed at a very low salary. 'K' took loan in the name of his HUF which was also running textile handicraft business. The Assessing Officer found that 'K' had advanced almost half amount of loan to 'A' and concluded that loan taken by 'K' was actually on behalf of and for the benefit of 'A' and assessed the same in 'A's hands.

Held: Since the payments were made for the benefit of 'A', the amount of loan was deemed to be the dividends in the hands of 'A' being the shareholder-managing director.

Case Law : ***Vikram Krishna* v. *Principal CIT* [2020] 114 taxmann.com 197/269 Taxman 477 (SC) (SLP against High Court order dismissed which in turn had dismissed appeal against Tribunal ruling)**

Facts: 'V' was director of company holding 50% shares of said company, was sought to be taxed for ₹ 1 crore as deemed dividend under sec. 2(*22*)(*e*). 'V' contended that this ₹ 1 crore was an advance received from the company for an agreement to sell the land but the deal did not materialize and therefore the amount was refunded. The total amount received was ₹ 1.8 crores and 'V' repaid only ₹ 78 lakhs after 8 months. The Company never claimed any interest on such delayed payment and 'V' being the director could not explain which banks or other institutions were approached by the company to ensure that the deal comes through.

Held : since 'V' failed to give adequate evidence and cogent and credible evidences about the transaction, an inference that is drawn is that the Agreement to Sell and cancellation of such deed is merely a cover up, a camouflage for giving loan to 'V' and liability under sec. 2(*22*)(*e*) arises.

Meaning of Accumulated Profits [*Explanation 1* and *Explanation 2* to Sec. 2(*22*)]

Accumulated profits include all profits of the company whether capitalised or not up to the date of such distribution or payment but any capital gain arising before 1 April 1946, and from 1 April 1948 to 31 March 1956 is excluded from accumulated profits [*Explanation 1* to Sec. 2(*22*)]. The reason for exclusion is that capital gain was exempt from tax during this period. Thus, accumulated profits include the balance standing to the credit of profit and loss account + current profits of the year in which the distribution or payment is made up to the date of such distribution or payment + general reserve + investment allowance/

development rebate reserve + capitalised profits, *i.e.* bonus shares issued out of profits + tax-free profits, *i.e.* agricultural income + capital gains chargeable to tax [*Tea Estate India (P.) Ltd.* v. *CIT* (1976) 103 ITR 785 (SC)]. Provision for depreciation, or taxation are not included in accumulated profits.

Profit to be understood in the Commercial Sense - The expression 'accumulated profits' means profit in the commercial sense and not assessable or taxable profits liable to tax as income [*P.K. Badiani* v. *CIT* (1976) 105 ITR 642 (SC)]. For example, expenses actually disbursed but disallowed in assessment, say, expenditure disallowed as excessive under Sec. 40A(2), cannot form part of accumulated profits because although disallowed for the purposes of assessment, the money (profit) has, commercially, gone out of the hands of the assessee. However, this does not apply to bogus or fraudulent expenses because these have not been incurred as such [*Rajpal Brothers (P.) Ltd.* v. *CIT* (1971) 80 ITR 463 (Bom.)]. Similarly, surplus on revaluation of assets, arising by mere book entries, cannot be considered as profits in the commercial sense. Therefore, the same cannot be treated as part of accumulated profits.

Deemed Profit not to be treated a part of Accumulated Profit - "Balancing charge" under sec. 41(2), being fictionally a withdrawal of excess depreciation allowed, does not represent accumulated profits. Similarly, deemed dividend cannot be included in accumulated profits. For example, B Ltd. holds shares in C Ltd. B Ltd. takes loan from C Ltd. The loan is assessed as deemed dividends in the hands of B Ltd. under Sec. 2(*22*)(*e*). Such deemed dividend, fictionally assessed, cannot be included in the accumulated profits within the meaning of that expression in Sec. 2(*22*) [*CIT* v. *Urmila Ramesh* [1998] 96 Taxman 533 (SC)].

Scope of Accumulated Profits in case of Compulsory Acquisition - Accumulated profits include all profits of the company up to the date of liquidation whether capitalised or not. But where liquidation is consequent on the compulsory acquisition of an undertaking by the government or any corporation owned or controlled by the government, the accumulated profits do not include any profits of the company prior to the three successive previous years immediately proceeding the previous year in which such acquisition took place [*Explanation 2* to Sec. 2(*22*)].

Meaning of Concern [*Explanation 3* to sec. 2(22)]

The term "concern" means a Hindu undivided family, or a firm, or an association of person, or a body of individuals or a company. Thus, where the *Karta* of an HUF has got 20% share out of the income of HUF and he holds at least 10% equity share of a closely held company, on behalf of the HUF, any loan or advance, covered by accumulated profits, by such company to such HUF is assessable as deemed dividend in the hands of HUF even though the HUF is not a registered shareholder.

EXCLUSION FROM THE SCHEME OF DIVIDEND

From the assessment year 2000-01 and subsequent years the following payment/distribution cannot be deemed to be dividend:

(*a*) *Payment on buy back of shares [Sec. 2(22)(*iv*)]* - Any payment made by a company on purchase of its own shares from a shareholder in accordance with the provisions of Sec. 77A of the Companies Act, 1956 is not deemed to be dividend.

Buy back of shares by a company amount to reduction of share capital. If the company utilises its reserve to buy back its shares, it would have been liable to dividend tax. However, now it cannot be deemed as dividend because of the specific exclusion under sec. 2(*22*)(*iv*).

On buy back of the shares, the shareholders are liable only to capital gain under sec. 46A.

(*b*) *Distribution of shares by resulting company to the shareholders of demerged company [Sec. 2(22)(*v*)]* - Any distribution of shares by the resulting company to the shareholders of demerged company on account of demerger is not deemed to be dividend. It is immaterial whether or not there is any reduction of share capital in the demerged company.

Basis of Charge of Dividend Income [Sec. 8]

(*a*) *Regular dividend* - Dividend which is declared by the company at its Annual General Meeting under the Companies Act is deemed to be the income of the previous year in which it is so declared. The date of receipt by the assessee is immaterial.

(*b*) *Notional dividend* - Notional dividend as contemplated under sec. 2(*22*) (*a*), (*b*), (*c*) and (*d*) is deemed to be the income of the previous year or accounting year in which it is distributed. Distribution connotes something actual and not notional. It can be a physical distribution or it could be a constructive distribution, *e.g.* crediting the amount due to the respective account of a shareholder.

Notional dividend under sec. 2(*22*)(*e*) is deemed to be the income of the accounting year in which it is paid.

(*c*) *Interim dividend* - Interim dividend is deemed to be the income of the previous year in which the amount of such dividend is unconditionally made available by the company to a shareholder. In other words, it is chargeable to tax on receipt basis.

Place of Accrual of Dividend [Sec. 9(1)(*iv*)]

The dividend payable by an Indian company outside India is deemed to accrue or arise in India. Thus, a non-resident is liable to tax in respect of the dividend distributed by an Indian company outside India.

But dividend paid by a foreign company outside India is not deemed to accrue or arise in India. It means a non-resident cannot pay tax on dividend received outside India from a foreign company. Dividend from foreign companies, even if operating in India, is taxable only when it is paid in India.

Shares sold-cum-Dividend

Dividend accrues not from day-to-day but only when it is declared. Thus, where an assessee buys shares-*cum*-dividend just before the declaration of dividend by the company, he is liable to be taxed on the whole amount of dividend declared by the company. He cannot be allowed any deduction of the amount paid to the seller in respect thereof. The additional sum so paid is regarded as part of the cost of the shares to the assessee buying them. Likewise, the seller is not assessable in respect of the sum received in lieu of dividends from the buyer. Such a sum is regarded as part of the consideration of the shares sold and thus does enter into computation of capital gain. Therefore, the nature of transaction-*cum*-dividend and ex-dividend is to be ignored.

DIVIDEND RECEIVED FROM DOMESTIC COMPANIES

Dividend Distribution Tax was introduced in the year 1997 through sec. 115-O thereby making the domestic companies liable to pay tax on distribution of dividend and exempting dividend incomes in the hands of shareholders under sec. 10(*34*). DDT was abolished in 2002 but re-introduced in 2003. It was however realized that high net worth individuals and non-natural persons such as companies received huge dividend incomes were unjustly benefiting since dividend incomes were exempt in the hands of the shareholder and two, dividends were subjected to a flat rate of tax of 15% under DDT.

In order to address this situation, the Finance Act, 2016 introduced sec. 115BBDA w.e.f. 1.4.2017 whereby shareholder receiving the dividend income of more that ₹ 10 lakhs; then such shareholder have also to pay tax under this section @10%.

The Finance Act, 2020 has abolished DDT and accordingly, secs. 115-O, 115BBDA and the exemption under sec.10(*34*) has been scrapped. Liability to pay tax on dividend income now has been placed on the door step of the shareholder and tax rate will apply in accordance with the tax slab of their total income. Thus progressive form of taxing dividend incomes has been introduced.

Insofar as corporate shareholders are concerned when resident companies receive dividend from other domestic companies, they shall be taxed as per the applicable corporate tax rates. In case of non-resident corporate shareholders, a withholding tax @20% is applicable sec. 195. This rate could be lower if the benefit under the tax treaty is available to such shareholder.

Dividends received from a foreign company

When Indian Holding companies received dividends from their foreign subsidiary in which the said Indian company holds 26% or more in nominal value of equity shares, the dividend is taxable @15% under sec. 115BBD without any allowance for deducting expenditures. Thus, there was a parity in tax rates whether dividend was received from a domestic company on which DDT was paid and when dividend was received from a foreign company. With the abolition of DDT by the Finance Act, 2020, this provision shall also no longer be applied. The Finance Act, 2022 has also done away with application of sec. 115BBD with effect from 1-4-2023.

Conversion of Dividend received in Foreign Currency into Indian Currency - Dividends paid by a foreign company can be converted into Indian currency at the telegraphic transfer buying rate of such currency on the specified date. "Specified date" is the last day of the month immediately preceding the month in which dividend is declared, distributed or paid by the company (Rule 115).

Deduction for Inter-Corporate Dividend [Sec. 80M]

Simply put, inter-corporate dividend is when one company, being a shareholder in another company, receives dividend from this another company. Under DDT, the burden to pay tax on dividend was on the company declaring and distributing such dividend and it was tax-free in the hands of the recipient company. Since DDT was abolished and tax was payable by the shareholders, there existed a possibility of double taxation of dividend income when these were received by company-shareholders. In other words, when dividends would be received by a company, being a shareholder in another company, the recipient company would be liable to pay tax on such dividend income. Subsequently, when the recipient company declared and distributed dividends (from its income that included dividend income on which tax is already paid) to its own shareholders, these shareholders were also required to pay tax on dividend income. This would result into dividend being taxed twice, one when it was received by the company, two, when it was received by shareholders of the recipient company.

In order to avoid this double taxation, a deduction under Sec. 80M can be availed by the domestic companies. Under this provision, domestic companies can claim a deduction to the least of the following:

(*a*) Amount of Dividend received from other Domestic Company/Foreign Company/Business Trust.

(*b*) Amount of Dividend distributed by the said Domestic Company, *i.e.*, Receiver, one month prior to the date for furnishing Return of Income under sec. 139(1).

Thus, by granting a deduction of either the dividend received or the dividend distributed from the gross total income, the cascading effect of tax and thereby double taxation of dividend income is averted.

Buy-back by Company

By virtue of sec. 2(*22*)(*iv*) payments made by companies for buy-back of shares were excluded from the definition of dividend. Since buy-back was not dividend at all, no dividend distribution tax was payable on such payment by the company (although shareholders were chargeable for capital gains tax but that was also only from 1-4-2000 and before that). Thus, companies were subjected to dividend distribution tax when they distributed profits to the shareholders in the form of dividends, but incurred no tax consequences at the time of buy-back. Taking advantage of this companies began to resort to buy-back of shares and made payments thereunder so as to avoid paying DDT.

Buy-back is essentially a scheme whereby a company repurchases a certain amount of its shares. Once taken back, these shares are extinguished by the company. Such reduction in the number of shares improves earnings per share of the existing shareholders. Buy-backs are also strategically resorted to by the promoters when they seek to increase their holdings in the company and avoid any takeover bids through open markets. However, since there was no tax imposed on such buy-back, it provided a safe haven to those who wished to circumvent DDT.

To curb such attempts, the Finance Act, 2013 introduced sec. 115QA whereby domestic companies engaging into buy-back are subjected to a buy-back tax at the rate 20%. While initially buy-back tax was imposed only on unlisted companies, the Finance Act, 2019 extended its application to the listed companies as well with retrospective effect from 5-7-2019. However, BBT will not be charged to listed companies that have made a public announcement of the buy-back of shares before 5-7-2019 but actual buy-back of shares happens on or after 05-07-2019 [Proviso to Sec. 115QA]. This tax is in addition to the income-tax that the company is liable to pay. Such buy-back tax paid cannot be claimed as a deduction either by the company or the shareholder from their incomes.

CHAPTER 17 Double Taxation Relief

This chapter provides tax relief to an assessee who has been taxed doubly on the same income under the Indian Income-tax Act as well as under the taxation laws of any other country. The main purpose of allowing benefit or relief under a Double Tax Avoidance Agreement (DTAA) was to ensure that assessees do not suffer tax twice. However, over the years there have been instances where the income in question having been left to be taxed by the other country was exempt in that other country, leading to double non-taxation. In such instances it was doubted if the assessee could be extended the benefit of DTAA at all. The Court rulings had held that insofar as the income was 'liable to tax' in the other country, the condition for applying DTAA was fulfilled and it was not necessary that the income should have been actually taxed in the other country. In the absence of any definition of 'liable to tax', there is was ambiguity in this regard.

The Finance Act, 2021 has inserted a definition of 'liable to tax' under sec. 2(*29A*) whereby 'liable to tax', in relation to a person and with reference to a country, means that there is an income-tax liability on such person under the law of that country for the time being in force and shall include a person who has subsequently been exempted from such liability under the law of that country.

BILATERAL RELIEF [SEC. 90]

The Central Government is empowered to make agreement in respect of tax administration and management with the government of foreign countries.

Agreement for Granting Relief [Sec. 90(1)(*a*)] - The Central Government may enter into agreement with the government of a foreign country to provide relief in respect of income on which tax has been paid in India as well as in that country. In order to promote mutual economic relations, trade and investment, the Central Government may also enter into agreement to grant relief in respect of income which is chargeable to tax in India as well as in that country.

Agreement to Avoid Double Taxation [Sec. 90(1)(*b*)] - The Central Government may enter into agreement with the government of a foreign country to avoid double taxation of income in India and in that country without creating opportunities for non-taxation or reduced taxation through tax evasion or avoidance (including through treaty-shopping arrangements aimed at obtaining reliefs provided in the said agreement for the indirect benefit to residents of any other country or territory).

Agreement for Exchange of Information [Sec. 90(1)(*c*)] - The Central Government may enter into agreement with the government of a foreign country for exchange of information to prevent evasion or avoidance of income tax in India and in that country or to investigate cases of such evasion or avoidance.

Agreement for Recovery of Tax [Sec. 90(1)(*d*)] - The Central Government may enter into agreement with the government of a foreign country for mutual recovery of income tax of one country in another country.

Beneficial Provisions of the Act to Supersede the Provisions of Double Taxation Avoidance Treaty [Sec. 90(2)] - Where the Central Government has entered into agreement with the government of a foreign country to provide relief against double taxation or to prevent avoidance of double taxation, the provisions of the Income-tax Act do not apply to an assessee who is covered by double taxation avoidance treaty. However, if the provisions of the Act are more beneficial to such assessee, such beneficial provisions supersede the provisions of the double taxation avoidance treaty.

Application of General Anti-Avoidance Rule [Sec. 90(2A) w.e.f. 1-4-2016] - From the assessment year 2016-17 and subsequent years, the provisions of General Anti-Avoidance Rules under Chapter X-A (secs. 95 to 102) supersede the provisions of 'Double Taxation Relief'.

Terms Not Defined to have the Same Meaning as Assigned to it in the Notification [Sec. 90(3)] - Where any term used in Income-tax Act or Double Taxation Avoidance Treaty has not been defined, such term has got the same meaning as has been assigned to it in the Notification issued by the Central Government, provided such meaning is not inconsistent with the provisions of the Act or agreement.

Certificate of residence [Sec. 90(4)(5)] - No relief is allowed [under sec. 90(1)(*a*)/(*b*)/(*c*)/(*d*)] to any assessee, not being a resident, unless (*i*) he has obtained a certificate of residence in any country outside India [Sec. 90(4)] and (*ii*) provides such documents or information as may be prescribed [under Rule 21AB(3) and (4) in Form Nos. 10FA and 10FB].

Adoption by Central Government of Agreements between Specified Associations for Double Taxation Relief [Sec. 90A] - Any specified association in India may enter into an agreement with any specified association in the specified territory outside India.

The Central Government may, by Notification in the Official Gazette [under sec. 90A(1)], make such provisions as may be necessary for adopting and implementing such agreement for:

- Grant of double taxation relief in respect of income on which tax has been paid under this Act and also in specified territory outside India; or
- Avoidance of double taxation of income under this Act and in specified territory outside India; or

- Exchange of information for the prevention of evasion or avoidance of income tax; or
- Recovery of income tax under this Act and specified territory outside India.

On notification of such agreement, the provisions of this Act remain applicable to such assessee to the extent they are more beneficial to him [Sec. 90A(2)].

From the assessment year 2016-17 and subsequent years, the provisions of General Anti-Avoidance Rules under Chapter X-A (Secs. 95 to 102) supersede the provisions of 'Double Taxation Relief'.

Any term used but not defined in the Income-tax Act or, in the said agreement has got the same meaning as assigned to it in the Notification by the Central Government, unless the context requires otherwise and it is not inconsistent with the provisions of the Income-tax Act or the said agreement.

Terms defined:

(i) **"Specified Association"** - Means any notified institution, association or body, whether incoporated or not, functioning under any law for the time being in force in India or the laws of the specified territory outside India.

(ii) **"Specified Territory"** - Means any area outside India notified by the Central Government.

Applicability: The aforesaid provisions are applicable w.e.f. 1 June 2006.

UNILATERAL RELIEF [SEC. 91]

Where there is no agreement either to avoid double taxation or provide relief against double taxation with a foreign country, Indian Government provides a unilateral relief on doubly taxed income against income tax payable in India, provided the following conditions for the unilateral relief are satisfied:

(i) **Assessee to be Resident** - The assessee is "resident" in India during the previous year. Thus, if the assessee is non-resident during the previous year, no relief can be granted to him.

(ii) **Accrual of Foreign Income outside India** - Foreign income, taxable in India, accrues or arises outside India. Thus, the place of accrual of income must fall outside India.

(iii) **Foreign Income not to be deemed to Accrue or Arise in India** - If foreign income is deemed to accrue or arise in India under Sec. 9, no relief is provided against such doubly taxed income. For example, Mr. J has earned business profits of ₹ 20,00,000 in Japan from a business, controlled and managed from there. It includes business profit of ₹ 5,00,000 which is from business connection in India. Such profit is deemed to accrue or arise in India. No relief is allowed on such doubly taxed income.

(*iv*) **Payment of Tax on Foreign Income -** The assessee has paid tax on such foreign income outside India either by way of deduction of tax at source or otherwise.

PROCEDURE OF RELIEF

The relief is allowed against Indian income tax under four steps:

(*i*) **To Ascertain the Amount of Doubly-taxed Income -** The assessee is required to ascertain the amount of income which has been simultaneously taxed in India as well as in foreign country.

(*ii*) **To Determine the Average Rate of Indian Income Tax -** Average rate of Indian income tax should be determined. Such average is determined as under:

$$\frac{\text{Tax Payable in India}}{\text{Total Income}} \times 100$$

Tax payable in India is taken after providing any relief due under the provisions of this Act, but before providing double taxation relief under this section.

(*iii*) **To Determine the Average Rate of Foreign Income tax -** Average rate of foreign income tax should be determined. Such average is determined as follows:

$$\frac{\text{Foreign Income Tax}}{\text{Total Income}} \times 100$$

"Foreign income tax" means income tax and super tax actually paid in foreign country in accordance with corresponding laws in force in the said country after deduction of all relief due but before deduction of any relief due in the said country in respect of double taxation.

(*iv*) **To Ascertain the Amount of Relief -** Relief is allowed on the amount of doubly taxed income either at the average rate of Indian tax or at the average rate of Foreign Income Tax, whichever is lower. Thus, if average rate of Indian income tax is 25.75% and the average rate of Foreign Income Tax is 22.25%, relief is allowed against Indian Income Tax on the doubly taxed income @ 22.25%.

CHAPTER 18 Assessment of Individual

An "individual" means a natural person, that is, a human being. "Individual" includes a male, female, minor child, and a person of unsound mind. In the case of a minor or a person of unsound mind, the assessment is made on the guardian or trustee of such individual in representative capacity [under Sec. 161(1)]. An individual is taxed not only on his total income but in certain cases, he is assessable on incomes of other persons (under Secs. 60 to 64). The relevant provisions, relating to an individual, are explained as below :

COMPUTATION OF TOTAL INCOME

In computing total income of an individual, the following points play an important role:

Income earned in individual capacity

Income, earned by an individual may relate to the different heads, e.g. income from salary; income from house property; income from business or profession; capital gain and other sources.

Income by virtue of membership of other entities

An individual may also earn his income by virtue of his membership in other institution, explained as below :

(*i*) **As a Member of Partnership Firm -** Share of profit from a partnership firm, assessed as such is exempt from tax in the individual assessment of the partner [Sec. 10(*2A*)].

However, any remuneration by way of salary, bonus, commission which has been deducted in computing taxable profits of the firm, is taxable as business income in the hands of a partner [Sec. 28(*iv*)].

(*ii*) **As a Member of an Association of Persons -** If an individual is a member of an association of persons or body of individuals share-income from such association or body is included in his total income only for rate purposes, provided the association or body is chargeable to income tax at the normal rates on such income.

If total income of AOP is not chargeable to tax, his share of income is taxable in his total income and no rebate of tax is allowed to him.

If the AOP is chargeable to tax at the maximum marginal rate or at a higher rate, the share of profit from AOP is fully exempt in the individual assessment of the member.

(*iii*) **As a Member of a Company** - Where an individual is a shareholder of the domestic company, any dividend paid, distributed or declared is taxable in the hands of the shareholder at tax rate in accordance with the tax slab of their total income. Dividends from foreign company are fully taxable in the hands of the shareholder.

(*iv*) **Income from Impartiable Estate of HUF** - Any income from impartiable estate of an HUF is taxable in the individual assessment of the *Karta*.

Income to be included under Clubbing Provisions

Certain incomes of other persons are included in the total income of some other individual under clubbing provisions. Such incomes include the following:

(*i*) Transfer of income without transfer of the assets [Sec. 60].

(*ii*) Income arising from revocable transfer of assets [Sec. 61].

(*iii*) Remuneration to the spouse from a concern where the other spouse has got substantial interest [Sec. 64(1)(*ii*), *Explanation 2*].

(*iv*) Income arising to the spouse from an asset, transferred by other spouse without adequate consideration [Sec. 64(1)(*iv*), *Explanation 1*].

(*v*) Income arising to the son's wife from the assets transferred without adequate consideration by the father/mother-in-law [Sec. 64(1)(*vi*)].

(*vi*) Income from the transfer of asset for the benefit of spouse [Sec. 64(1)(*vii*)].

(*vii*) Transfer of assets for the benefit of son's wife [Sec. 64(1)(*viii*)].

(*viii*) Income from cross-transfers.

(*ix*) Income of the minor child [Sec. 64(1A)] - Income of a minor child is clubbed with the income of that parent whose income, without such clubbing, is greater, provided the marriage of the parents subsists. If marriage of the parent does not subsist, the income of the minor is clubbed in the income of that parent who maintains the child. However, no clubbing is allowed in respect of such income which is earned by the minor by his manual skill or expertise. Similarly, income of minor child, suffering from permanent physical disability, has also been excluded from the ambit of clubbing provisions.

Where income of a minor is clubbed with the income of the parent, such parent is entitled to claim exemption in respect of such income up to ₹ 1,500 for each such child.

(*x*) Income from converted property [Sec. 64(2)] - Where a member of a Hindu Undivided Family converts his self-acquired property into HUF property after 31 December 1969, income from such property is included in the total income of converting member. Where such property is partitioned, the share income of the property, allotted to the spouse of converting member, is included in his income.

Income of Husband and Wife governed by Portuguese Civil Code 1860 [Sec. 5A]

Under the Portuguese Civil Code, 1860 which is in force in Goa, Daman and Diu and Dadra Nagar Haveli; the communion of husband and wife under marriage is considered as an association of persons. The Finance Act, 1994 introduced Sec. 5A to the Income-tax Act whereby it was stipulated for income tax purposes, income of spouses governed by the Portuguese Civil Code, except income from salary, would be equally apportioned between such spouses and will be taxed in their individual capacities and not as association of persons or body of individuals. The salary income earned by a spouse will be taxable in the hands of that spouse alone.

Income from GDR [Global Depository Receipts, Sec. 115ACA]

Where total income of a "resident individual", an employee of an Indian company or its subsidiary, engaged in specified knowledge-based industry or service, includes income by way of (*i*) dividends, from GDR, or (*ii*) long-term capital gains on the transfer of GDR. Such income is taxed at concessional rate of 10%, provided the following conditions are satisfied.

Conditions:

(*i*) the assessee is an individual;

(*ii*) he is an employee of an Indian company or its subsidiary engaged in specified knowledge-based industry or service;

(*iii*) GDR are purchased by him from overseas Depository Bank outside India in foreign currency;

(*iv*) GDR are issued to him under stock-option scheme as notified by the Central Government;

(*v*) he is non-resident at the time of purchase of GDR;

(*vi*) he is resident at the time of accrual of the income from GDR;

(*vii*) he is also an employee of Indian company or its subsidiary, engaged in specified knowledge-based industry or service at the time of the sale of GDR. It is not necessary that he should be employee of the same company whose GDR he is holding at the time of accrual of income;

(*viii*) capital gain is computed without applying First and Second Proviso to Sec. 48. Thus, scheme of computing capital gain in foreign currency or scheme of indexation does not apply;

(*ix*) dividends from GDR is taxed on gross basis; and

(*x*) if any deduction is computable with reference to gross total income, the two incomes from GDR (dividend and capital gain) are excluded.

"*Specified knowledge-based industry or service*" means:

(*i*) information technology software;

(*ii*) information technology service;

(*iii*) entertainment service;

(*iv*) pharmaceutical industry;

(*v*) bio-technology industry; and

(*vi*) any other industry or service, as may be specified by the Central Government, by Notification in the Official Gazette. "Subsidiary" has got the meaning assigned to it in sec. 4 of the Companies Act, 1956 [now Sec. 2(*87*) of the Companies Act, 2013] and includes subsidiary incorporated outside India.

STEPS IN THE COMPUTATION OF TOTAL INCOME

After determining the residential status of the individual (under sec. 6), the following steps needs to be undertaken:

Computation of Total Income at a Glance

	Particulars	₹
1.	Compute taxable income headwise:	
	(*i*) Income from salaries [Secs. 15 to 17]	xxx
	(*ii*) Income from house property [Secs. 22 to 27]	xxxx
	(*iii*) Profits and gains of business or profession [Secs. 28 to 44DB]	xxxx
	(*iv*) Capital gains [Secs. 45 to 55A]	xxxx
	(*v*) Income from other sources [Secs. 56 to 59]	xxxx
2.	Adjustment of losses of the current year and carried forward losses [Secs. 70 to 80]	
3.	Gross total income	xxxx
4.	*Less*: Deductions in computing total income [Secs. 80C to 80U]	(–) xxx
	Net Taxable Income	xxxx
	Total income is rounded off to the nearest multiple of ₹ 10 [Sec. 288]	

Computation of Tax Liability

Tax liability of an assessee-individual is computed in the following manner:

		₹
1.	Compute gross income tax on the Net Taxable Income at the prescribed rates:	
	(*a*) Tax on winnings from lotteries, crossword puzzle, races including horse races, card games and other games of any sort or gambling or betting (under Sec. 115BB);	xxx
	(*b*) Tax on winnings from online games [Sec. 115BBJ]	xxx
	(*c*) Tax on long-term capital gains [Sec. 112(1)];	xxx
	(*d*) Tax on short-term capital gain [Sec. 111A];	xxx
	(*e*) Tax on GDR [Sec. 115ACA];	xxx
	(*f*) Tax on the balance of total income at the prescribed rates, contained in the First Schedule of the relevant AY	xxx
	Total gross income tax	xxx
2.	*Add:* Surcharge on income tax, if any, at the prescribed rate	xxx
	Tax after surcharge	xxx
3.	*Add:* Health and Education Cess [@ 4% of income tax and surcharge]	
	Total tax	xxx
4.	*Less:* (*a*) Rebate on share of profit from AOP under sec. 86 where AOP	(–) xxx
	(*b*) Relief under sec. 89(1), if any,	(–) xxx
	(*c*) Double taxation relief under sec. 91, if any	(–) xxx
	Tax due from the assessee	xxx
	Less: Prepaid taxes:	
	(*a*) Tax deducted at source	(–) xxx
	(*b*) Advance payment of tax	(–) xxx
	(*c*) Tax paid on self-assessment (under sec. 140A)	(–) xxx
	Tax payable/refund due to the assessee	xxx
	Tax payable is rounded off to the nearest multiple of ₹ 10 [Sec. 288B]	xxx

Rebate of Income-tax [Sec. 87A]

Where an individual is resident in India and his total income does not exceed ₹ 5,00,000, he is allowed the following 'Rebate' from gross income-tax :	₹	₹
Gross income on total income		***
Less : Rebate of income-tax:		
(*i*) Gross income-tax or	***	
(*ii*) ₹ 12,500,	12,500	
whichever is less, is deducted		(–) ***
Tax payable, if any –		***

Rebate under this section is up to ₹ 25,000 for resident individuals having total income of up to ₹ 7 lacs, under the new regime.

Rates of Income Tax on specified income for the Assessment Year 2024-25

Income tax is computed on specified income at the rates, given as below:

	Particulars of total income Rates of income tax	Rates of income tax
(*i*)	Winnings from lotteries, crossword puzzle, or race including horse race, or card games and other games of any sort, or from gambling or betting of any form or nature, whatsoever [Sec. 115BB]	30%
(*ii*)	Winnings from online games [Sec. 115BBJ]	30%
(*iii*)	Long-term capital gains (Sec. 112) from any asset, computed under indexation scheme (as contained in Second Proviso to Sec. 48)	20%
(*iv*)	Short-term capital gain from the sale of equity shares of a company or units of an equity-oriented fund where such transaction is chargeable to securities transaction tax [Sec. 111A]	15%
(*v*)	Dividends in respect of Global Depository Receipt [Sec. 115ACA]	10%
(*vi*)	Balance of total income: Income tax is charged as per rates given in the following table:	

Income-tax on the balance of Total Income

Old Regime

An individual resident in India, aged 80 years or more		An individual resident in India, aged 60 years or more but less than 80 years		Any other individual	
Slab of total income	Rate of tax	Slab of total income	Rate of tax	Slab of total income	Rate of tax
1. Up to ₹ 5,00,000	Nil	1. Up to ₹ 3,00,000	Nil	1. Up to ₹ 2,50,000	Nil
2. Up to ₹ 5,00,001 to 10,00,000	20%	2. Up to ₹ 3,00,001 to 5,00,000	5%	2. Up to ₹ 2,50,001 to 5,00,000	5%
3. Above ₹ 10,00,001	30%	3. Up to ₹ 5,00,001 to 10,00,000	20%	3. Up to ₹ 5,00,001 to 10,00,000	20%
		4. Above 10,00,001	30%	4. Above 10,00,001	30%

- Surcharge on Income tax
  - 10% if total income exceeds ₹ 50 lacs but does not exceed ₹ 1 crore.
  - 15% if total income exceeds ₹ 1 crore but does not exceed ₹ 2 crore

- 25% if total income exceeds ₹ 2 crore but does not exceed ₹ 5 crore
- 37% if total income exceeds ₹ 5 crore

(In case of short term capital gains covered under sec. 111A long term capital gain covered under sec. 112/112A and dividend income, surcharge could be restricted to 15%.

◆ Health and Education Cess at 4% of income tax and surcharge.

New Regime

The Finance Act, 2020 introduced a new section 115BAC for individuals/HUFs according to which a new Income tax slab has been introduced with effect from AY 2021-22. The Finance Act, 2023 has amended the tax slab of new regime as follows:.

Income slab	**Rate**
Upto ₹ 3,00,000	Nil
From ₹ 3,00,000 to 6,00,000	5%
From ₹ 6,00,000 to 9,00,000	10%
From ₹ 9,00,000 to 12,00,000	15%
From ₹ 12,00,000 to 15,00,000	20%
Above ₹ 15,00,000	30%

In order to avail this new tax slab, the assessee will have to forgo the following exemptions and deductions

Exemption under Leave Travel Concession - Sec. 10(*5*)

Exemption under House Rent Allowance - Sec. 10(*13A*)

Some allowance as prescribed under section 10(*14*) for this purpose

Exemption in respect of allowances received by MPs and MLAs as specified in section 10(*17*)

Exemption in respect of clubbing of Income - Sec. 10(*32*)

Deduction under section 10AA

Deduction in respect of Interest on housing loan - Sec. 24(*b*)

Additional depreciation - Sec. 32(1)(*iia*)

Section 32AD or Section 33AB or Section 33ABA or Section 35(2AA) or Section 35(1)(*iii*) or Section 35(1)(*iia*) or Section 35AD or Section 35CCC

Deduction under chapter VIA

The Finance Act, 2023 allows availing standard deduction under sec. 16(*ia*), deduction for family pension under sec. 57(*iia*), deductions under sec. 80CCD(2) for NPS, sec. 80CCH for Agnipath Scheme and sec. 80JJA - employment of new wage workers.

While previously the assessees were required to opt for the New regime of tax slab, the Finance Act, 2023 makes the new regime applicable as a default mode unless the assessee opts for the old regime.

- Surcharge on Income Tax
- 10% if total income exceeds ₹ 50 lacs
- 15% if total income exceeds ₹ 1 crore but does not exceed ₹ 2 crore
- 25% if total income exceeds ₹ 2 crore

  (In case of short term capital gains covered under sec. 111A, long term capital gains covered under sec. 112/112A and dividend income, surcharge would be restricted to maximum 15%)
- Health & Education Cess 4%.

Alternate Minimum Tax payable by a non-company assessee [Sec. 115JC to Sec. 115JF]:

Where regular income-tax payable by a non-company assessee for a previous year is less than 18.5% of the adjusted total income, he is liable to pay alternate minimum tax on adjusted total income @ 18.5% [Sec. 115JC(1)].

Adjusted Total Income [Sec. 115JC(2)]

Adjusted Total Income is arrived at by adding the back the following deductions to the total income, where such deductions were claimed:

(*i*) Any deduction claimed from gross total income, in computing total income, except deduction in respect of income of co-operative society (under sec. 80P); or

(*ii*) Any deduction in respect of newly established units in 'Special Economic Zones' (under sec. 10AA); or

(*iii*) Any deduction in respect of expenditure on specified business (under sec. 35AD).

Tax credit for alternate minimum tax [Sec. 115JD]

The assessee is allowed credit for the excess of alternate minimum tax paid over the regular income-tax payable for that year [Sec. 115JD(2)]. No interest is payable on the amount of such tax credit [Sec. 115JD(3)].

Set off of the excess tax [Sec. 115JD(5), (6)]

Where regular income-tax exceeds the alternate minimum tax, the tax credit is allowed to be set off to the extent of the excess of regular income-tax over the alternate minimum tax. The balance of tax credit is allowed to be carried forward for further set off [Sec. 115JD(5)].

If the amount of regular income-tax or alternate minimum tax is reduced or increased as a result of any order passed under this Act, the amount of tax credit allowed is also varied accordingly [Sec. 115JD(6)].

Time-Limit for set off [Sec. 115JD(4)]

No carry forward of tax credit is allowed beyond the fifteenth assessment year immediately succeeding the assessment year for which tax credit becomes allowable.

Interest on tax credit [Sec. 115JD(3)]

No interest is payable on the amount of tax credit, allowed to be carried forward.

Report of the Chartered Accountant [Sec. 115JC(3)]

Where the aforesaid provisions apply to an assessee, he is required to obtain a report from the chartered accountant, certifying that the adjusted total income and alternate minimum tax have been computed in accordance with prescribed law. Such report should be furnished on or before the specified date referred to in Sec. 44AB that is the date one month prior to the due date of filing of the return under sec. 139(1).

Non-Applicability of AMT provisions

- The provisions of AMT does not apply if the adjusted total income of such assessee does not exceed ₹ 20 lakhs [Sec.115JEE(2)].
- The Finance Act, 2020 inserted sec. 115BAC and sec. 115BAD to provide for concessional tax rates for Individuals/HUFs and resident co-operative society, respectively. Therefore, where individuals have opted for concessional rates under sec.115BAC and Sec.115BAD, then AMT provisions will not apply to such individuals [Sec.115JD(7)].

CHAPTER 19 Liability in Special Cases

INTRODUCTION

As a general rule, income tax being personal in nature, it is only the assessee earning such income will be liable to tax personally and the tax liability cannot be passed on to anyone else. However, in certain special circumstances, a person other than the assessee will be assessable to tax with respect to the income of the assessee. These special cases are discussed in this chapter.

LEGAL REPRESENTATIVES [SEC. 159]

Where a person dies, his legal representative shall be liable to pay any sum which the deceased would have been liable to pay in the same manner and to the same extent as the deceased [Sec. 159(1)]. Sec. 159(1) extends fictionally the legal personality of a deceased person but only for the duration of the previous year in the course of which he died and the income received either by him before his death or by his heirs and representatives after his death in that previous year alone became assessable to tax in the relevant assessment year. Any income received on behalf of the deceased which falls in a previous year subsequent to the previous year of death of the deceased cannot be assessed under sec. 159(1) [*CIT* v. *Amarchand N. Shroff* [1963] 48 ITR 59 (SC)].

Legal Representative - "Legal representative" has the meaning assigned to it in Sec. 2(11) of the Code of Civil Procedure, 1908 [Sec. 2(29)]. Accordingly, "legal representative" means a person who in law represents the estate of a deceased person and includes an executor, administrator, heir and any person who intermeddles with the estate of the deceased. The legal representative of the deceased is, for the purposes of this Act, deemed to be an assessee [Sec. 159(3)].

Assessment on Legal Representative [Sec. 159(2)]

For the purpose of making assessment (including an assessment, re-assessment or re-computation (under sec.147) of the income of the deceased, any proceeding taken against the deceased before his death is deemed to have been taken against the legal representative and may be continued against the legal representative from the stage at which it stood on the date of the death of the deceased. Further, any proceeding which could have been taken against the deceased if he had survived, may be taken against the legal representative [Sec.

159(2)]. Proceedings can be continued against the legal representative only if it were initiated during the lifetime of the assessee.

A legal representative cannot be liable for any proceedings initiated after the death of the assessee [*CIT* v. *C. V. Raghava Reddy (C.V.)* [1983] 12 Taxman 81/ (1984) 148 ITR 385 (AP)]. For instance, a notice under Sec. 148 cannot be issued to the legal representative for reopening the assessment of the deceased assessee [*Rupa Shyamsundar Dhumatkar* v. *ACIT* [2020] 120 taxmann.com 323/275 Taxman 453 (Bombay)].

It is incumbent under Sec. 159(2) of the Act on the part of the Assessing Officer to issue notice to the legal representatives of the deceased assessee to bring them on record and proceeded from the stage from where it was left at the time of death of the deceased assessee [*CIT* v. *Prabhawati Gupta* (1998) 231 ITR 188 (MP)]. However, mere omission to serve or any defect in the service of notices provided by procedural provisions does not efface or erase the liability to pay tax where such liability is created by distinct substantive provisions (charging sections). Any such omission or defect may render the order irregular, depending upon the nature of the provision not complied with, but certainly not void or illegal. Therefore, where proper notice is not issued to all legal representatives, fresh assessment can be made after giving proper notices. [*CIT* v. *Jai Prakash Singh* (1996) 85 Taxman 407/219 ITR 737 (SC)].

The computation of the income of the deceased's estate is to be made in the status applicable to the deceased, granting all reliefs which the deceased may be entitled to in respect of that status.

The Assessment on legal representative is to be made in respect of the income of the deceased only up to the date of his death and not up to the end of the Accounting Year in which death occurs. The assessment in respect of income of the deceased's estate for the period from the date of death up to the end of accounting year in which the death occurs is to be made on the executors. Thus, in respect of the year of death two separate and distinct assessments are made—one on the legal representative (under Sec. 159) in respect of the income of the deceased from the first day of the accounting year up to the date of death and the other on the "executors" in respect of income of the estate for the rest of the year [Sec. 168(3)]. This may result in lowering the rate and incidence of tax for the year. This position is not affected by the fact that the legal representatives (assessable under Sec.159) may be the same individuals who are assessable as executors (under Sec. 168). Assessment for the years or part thereof subsequent to the year of death are made on the executors till the administration of the estate is completed [Sec. 168(3)]. Thus, assessment on legal representative is made only for one year, namely, the assessment year corresponding to the accounting year of death.

Income which does not accrue from day-to-day cannot be apportioned on time basis, that is, income accruing up to the date of death and thereafter. Thus, if dividends have been declared after the date of death of the deceased, the whole of the dividend is taxable in the hands of the representative assessee/executors. Legal representative cannot be assessed on time basis.

Rights and Liabilities of Legal Representative [Sec. 159(1), (4), (5) and (6)]

Where a person dies, his legal representative is liable to pay any sum which the deceased would have been liable to pay if he had not died. Any sum includes income tax, penalty, fine, interest, and so on. Thus, legal representative is liable to pay penalty for the defaults committed by the deceased. Further, the legal representative, being an assessee for the purposes of the Act, is liable to penalty for his own defaults, for instance, penalty for having himself submitted an incorrect return of the income of the deceased [Sec. 159(3)].

The liability of the legal representative is limited to the extent to which the estate is capable of meeting the liability [Sec. 159(6)]. However, the legal representative is personally liable to the extent of the value of any asset of the estate which he disposes of while the liability for tax remains undischarged. The personal liability applies only in respect of tax and not in respect of penalty, fine or interest [Sec. 159(4)]. However, any amount payable by an assessee as a legal representative cannot be set-off from any refund of tax due to him in his personal capacity. [*Hasmukhalal* v. *Income-tax Officer* (2001) 117 Taxman 231/251 ITR 511 (MP)].

Where a legal representative is liable in respect of certain income as a legal representative, he cannot be assessable in respect of that very income in any other capacity [Sec. 161(2)]. The legal representative is entitled to reimbursement of any sum paid by him on behalf of the deceased from his estate [Sec. 162(1)]. The legal representative is also entitled to claim any refund due to the deceased [Sec. 238(2)].

Case Law : ***Urmilaben Anirudhha Sinhji Jadeja* [2020] 117 taxmann.com 504/273 Taxman 481 (Gujarat)**

Facts: 'U' was issued a notice under Sec.148 for the re-opening of the assessment of her deceased husband on the count that certain payments made towards booking a plot have not been reflected in the return of income filed by the decease husband and therefore had escaped assessment. 'U' challenged the notice bad, illegal, barred by limitation and without jurisdiction.

Held: Reopening notice issued against a dead person would be a nullity and the proceedings pursuant to reopening notice under Sec. 148 issued to a dead person could not be continued against legal representatives.

REPRESENTATIVE ASSESSEE [SEC. 160]

A representative assessee is liable to be taxed in respect of income which he receives or he is entitled to receive for any other person. The following persons have been held to be representative assessees:

(*i*) **Agent of a Non-resident [Sec. 160(1)(*i*)]** - The agent of a non-resident principal is assessable in respect of income which is deemed to accrue or arise in India [under Sec. 9(1)] to the non-resident. Such agent may be an express agent appointed by the non-resident principal or one who is treated as an agent by the Assessing Officer for the purpose of levying the tax in respect of such income. "Agent" in relation to a non-resident includes [under Sec. 163(1)] any person in India:

(*a*) who is employed by or on behalf of the non-resident; or

(*b*) who has any business connection with the non-resident; or

(*c*) from or through whom the non-resident is in receipt of any income, whether directly or indirectly; or,

(*d*) who is a trustee of the non-resident.

(ii) **Guardian or Manager of Minor, person of unsound mind [Sec. 160(1)(*ii*)]** - The guardian or manager of a minor, person of unsound mind is chargeable to tax in respect of the income which he receives or is entitled to receive on behalf of the beneficiary. It is immaterial whether the guardian is a *de facto* guardian or a *de jure* guardian.

(iii) **Court of wards, Administrator-General, Official Trustee or Receiver or Manager [Sec. 160(1)(*iii*)]** - The court of wards, the Administrator-General, the Official Trustee or any receiver or manager appointed by or under any order of a court and who receives or is entitled to receive any income on behalf or for the benefit of any person is assessable in respect of such income as representative assessee.

(iv) **Trustee [Sec. 160(1)(*iv*)(*v*)]** - (*a*) A trustee appointed under a trust declared by a duly executed instrument in writing whether testamentary or otherwise is assessable as representative assessee in respect of income which he receives or is entitled to receive on behalf or for the benefit of any person [Sec. 160(1)(*iv*)] (*b*) Likewise, a trustee under an oral trust is assessable as representative assessee in respect of income which he receives or is entitled to receive on behalf or for benefit of any person [Sec. 160(1)(*v*)].

Every representative assessee is deemed to be an assessee for the purpose of this Act [Sec. 160(2)].

Liability of Representative Assessee [Sec. 161]

The representative assessee is to be assessed in his own name on such incomes in respect of which he is a representative assessee. He is subject to the same duties, responsibilities and liabilities as if the income were received or beneficially held by him. But any such assessment is deemed to be made upon him in his representative capacity only and it is different from his personal assessment. The tax is to be levied upon and recovered from him in the like manner and to the same extent as it was leviable upon and recoverable from the person represented by him. The liability of the representative assessee is a vicarious liability and it is co-extensive with the liability of the person represented by him. Therefore, he is to be assessed in the status of the beneficiary. He is entitled to all such exemptions, deductions and abatements, as the beneficiary would have been entitled to in case of direct assessment [*Annamalai N.* v. *CIT* (1969) 73 ITR 809 (Mad.)]. He is also entitled to claim a refund where the total income of the beneficiary justifies such a claim. Where the beneficiary is not liable to tax at all in respect of certain income, there is no liability to tax on the representative assessee in respect of that income. Where a person is assessable in respect of any income in the capacity of a representative assessee, he cannot be assessed in respect of that income under any other provision of this Act [Sec. 161(2)].

Where a trustee is assessable as a representative assessee [under Sec. 160(*iv*)] in respect of any income which consists of or includes profits and gains of business, the whole of such income will be taxed in his hands at the maximum marginal rate of income tax as applicable to an association of persons [Sec. 161(1A)]. However, the trustee may not be assessed on such income at the maximum marginal rate if the profits and gains of business are receivable under a trust declared by any person by will exclusively for the benefit of any relative dependent on him for support and maintenance and such trust is the only trust so declared by him. In such case, the normal rate of income tax will apply [Second Proviso to Sec. 164(3)].

Right of Representative Assessee to Recover Tax [Sec. 162]

Every representative assessee who pays any sum in his representative capacity is entitled to recover the sum so paid from the person on whose behalf it is paid. He may also retain out of any money that may be in his possession or may come to him in his representative capacity, an amount equal to the sum so paid.

Any representative assessee who apprehends that he may be assessed as a representative assessee, may retain out of any money payable to the principal, a sum equal to his estimated liability. In the event of any disagreement between the principal and representative assessee as to the amount to be so retained, such representative assessee may secure from the Assessing Officer a certificate stating the amount to be so retained pending final settlement of the liability. The certificate so obtained is his warrant for retaining that amount. The amount recoverable from such representative assessee at the time of final settlement cannot exceed the amount specified in such certificate except to the extent to which such representative assessee may at such time have in his hands additional assets of the principal.

If the representative assessee fails to recover the tax from the real beneficiary, he cannot claim it as bad debt against his profit from business.

Direct Assessment of or Recovery from the Beneficiary not Barred [Sec. 166] - The Assessing Officer has the option to make an assessment on the representative assessee or a direct assessment on the person beneficially entitled to the income. Once the Assessing Officer has exercised his option and assessed either the representative assessee or the beneficial recipient of the income, he cannot thereafter assess the same income in the hands of the other. Even in a case where the assessment is made in respect of representative assessee, the recovery of tax can be made from the beneficiary because the representative is only a notional assessee whereas the beneficiary is the real assessee [*Ganesh Chander Dhar* v. *CIT* (1959) 35 ITR 84 (Cal.)].

Remedies against Property in cases of Representative Assessee [Sec. 167]

The Assessing Officer is empowered to recover the tax assessed on the beneficiary from the property vested in or under the control or management of the representative assessee in his representative capacity. The Assessing Officer has the same remedies against all property of any kind vested in or under the control or management of any representative assessee as he would have against the property of any person liable to pay tax. Such remedies are available in full and ample manner, irrespective of whether the demand is raised against the representative assessee or against the beneficiary.

Executors [Sec. 168]

Executor includes an administrator or other person administering the estate of the deceased person (*Explanation* to Sec. 168). An executor is a person who is appointed by the testator to carry out and execute his wishes and for that purpose, to administer his estate after his death. An administrator is a person who is not appointed by the testator, but who is granted letters of administration by a court to administer the estate. An administrator is in the same position as an executor.

Assessment on Executor

The executor or administrator is to be assessed on the income accruing from the estate of the deceased for a period commencing from the date of the death of deceased to the date when the administration of each estate is complete [Sec. 168(3)]. Till the date of death, the income was the income of the deceased and was vested in him. It is, therefore, assessable in the hands of the legal representative (under Sec. 159).

From the date of death, the estate and income therefrom are vested in the executors till the date of complete distribution to the beneficiaries of the estate according to their respective legacies. Therefore, the assessment is to be made from year to year, separately for all assessment years, on the total income of each completed previous year or part thereof, on the executors till such complete distribution of the estate [Sec. 168(3)].

After the administration of the estate is over, the executors would hold the residue as trustees; hence any assessment is to be made on the trustees. The distinction between an executor and a trustee is that an executor is the representative of the testator for all purpose while a trustee is representative of the legatees or the beneficiaries (Sec. 211 of the Indian Succession Act).

Residential Status of Executor

The residential status of the executor or administrator is the same as that of the deceased in the previous year in which death took place and the computation of income is to be made according to such status [Sec. 168(1)].

Taxable Entity of Executor

If there is only one executor or one administrator, he is to be assessed in the status of an individual. If there are more than one executors or administrators, their status is to be that of an association of persons [Sec. 168(1)]. The assessment of an executor or administrator (under Sec. 168) is separate from any assessment that may be made on him in respect of his own income [Sec. 168(2)].

Computation of Total Income

In computing the total income of any previous year, if any income from the estate is distributed or applied to the benefit of any specific legatee of the estate during the previous year, such income is to be excluded from the chargeable income of the estate for that previous year. The income so excluded is inclusible in the total income of such specific legatee in the year of receipt [Sec. 168(4)]. In computing the income from the estate, the executor is not entitled to deduct expenses of obtaining probate of will and letters of administration or any other expenditure directed to be incurred under the will of the deceased, for example, *shradh* expenses of the deceased. In fact, such expenses are mere application of the income after the same is earned.

Right of the Executor to Recover the Tax Paid [Sec. 169]

The executor or the administrator has the right to recover the tax paid by him in such capacity from the estate of the deceased. His rights are the same in this respect as that of the representative assessee (under Sec. 162).

CHAPTER 20 Income-tax Authorities

INTRODUCTION

In order to ensure efficient administration and to discharge executive and other appellate functions, the Income-tax Act entrusts such powers, functions and jurisdictions to the Central Board of Direct Taxes and the income-tax authorities as specified under Sec. 116. Central Board of Direct Taxes is the apex body of the Income-tax Department and charged with the administration of taxes. The officials of the Board in their *ex officio* capacity also function as a Division of the Ministry dealing with matters relating to levy and collection of direct taxes. Together with several other income-tax authorities, the administration and execution of the Income-tax Act is carried out.

With an objective of enhancing the efficiency of the delivery system of the Income Tax Department, and building and developing mutual trust between taxpayers and administrators, the Finance Act, 2020 introduced Taxpayers' Charter. Accordingly, Sec. 119A requires the Board to adopt and issue a Taxpayers' Charter that enumerates the rights and obligations of taxpayers. The Taxpayers Charter recognizes every taxpayers' right to be provided with fair, courteous, and reasonable treatment by the department and that every taxpayer shall be deemed to be honest unless there is a reason to believe otherwise, provide a mechanism to lodge a complaint and provide timely decisions. The Charter also refers to obligations of a taxpayers and expects taxpayers to be honest and compliant, keep accurate records, respond to tax department on time and pay the tax dues in a timely manner.

CENTRAL BOARD OF DIRECT TAXES

The Central Board of Direct Taxes is a statutory authority functioning under the Central Board of Revenue Act, 1963 [Sec. 2(12)]. It is the apex body entrusted with several tasks including organization of the set-up and structure of Income-tax Department, administrative planning, transfers and postings of officers in the cadre of Chief Commissioner of Income-Tax and Commissioner of Income-tax and so on. The Board may not perform all its functions while sitting as a single body. It may assign its various duties and functions to individual members constituting it. The Board is empowered to control the income-tax authorities. It may notify that any income-tax authority is subordinate to such other income-tax authority or authorities as may be specified in the notification [Sec.118].

Powers of the Board

The Board is vested with the following powers in its functioning:

(*i*) **Power to make Rules [Sec. 295]** - It has the power to make rules (under Sec. 295) for carrying out the purposes of this Act. The Rules may be made for whole or any part of India.

It may give retrospective operation to a rule but the date of operation cannot be prior to the date of commencement of this Act.

Generally, no retrospective effect is given to any rule so as to prejudicially affect the interest of assessees.

(*ii*) **Orders and Instructions to Subordinate Authorities [Sec. 119(1)]** - The Board may, from time to time, issue such orders, instructions and directions to other income-tax authorities as it may deem fit for the proper administration of this Act.

Authorities to follow such Orders - Income-tax authorities and all other persons employed in the execution of this Act are required to observe and follow such orders, instructions and directions of the Board.

No Instructions in Individual Cases - The Board does not issue any advance rulings/directions/instructions in individual cases to any income-tax authority [Instruction No. 796, dated 2 November 1974 F. No. 225/121/74-IT(A-II)].

No Interference with Appellate Functions of CIT (Appeals) - The Board cannot interfere with the discretion of the Commissioner (Appeals) in the exercise of his appellate functions.

No Interference with Quasi-judicial Functions of an Income-tax Authority - The Board cannot issue any order, instruction or direction to any income-tax authority to make a particular assessment or to dispose of a particular case in a particular manner [*J.K. Synthetics Ltd.* v. *Central CBDT* (1972) 83 ITR 335 (SC)] but general directions could be issued by the board to control the quasi-judicial function of the judicial authority [*Nathuram Kapoor* v. *ITO* (1979) 120 ITR 257/1 Taxman 434 (MP)].

(*iii*) **To lay down Guidelines, Principles or Procedures relating to Assessment, Collection of Revenue or Imposition of Penalties [Sec. 119(2)(a)]** - The Board may issue general or special orders in respect of any class of incomes or class of cases for the proper management of the assessment and collection of revenue for the said purpose [*Union Home Products Ltd.* v. *UOI* [1995] 215 ITR 758/[1996] 84 Taxman 303 (Kar.); *Sant Lal* v. *Union of India* (1996) 222 ITR 375/89 Taxman 272 (Punj. & Har.)].

The Board may even relax the provisions relating to furnishing return of income (Sec. 139), or making assessment/rectification (under Sections 143, 144, 147, 148, 154, 155) or charging mandatory interest for defaults in TDS (Sec. 201) or advance tax (Sec. 211) or interest for late return

(Sec. 230A) or interest for deferment of advance tax or under payment of advance tax (Secs. 234C, 234B) or fee for default in furnishing of statement (Sec. 234E) or return (Sec. 234F) or penalty for concealment (Sec. 271) or failure to deduct tax at source (Sec. 271C) or collect tax at source (Sec. 271CA) or failure to estimate advance tax correctly (Sec. 273).

Power of Relaxation be exercised in Public Interest - The power to relax the provisions of specified sections may be exercised by the Board if it is of the opinion that it is necessary to do so in the public interest.

(*iv*) **To Authorise any Income-tax Authority to admit Belated Claims for Exemption, Deduction, Refund and so on [Sec. 119(2)(*b*)]** - If the Board considers it desirable to avoid genuine hardship in any case or class of cases, it may authorise, by general or special order, any income-tax authority to admit an application of claim for any exemption, deduction, refund or any other relief under this Act after the expiry of the prescribed period and deal with the case on merits in accordance with law.

No Order can be Issued to CIT (Appeals) - The Board cannot issue any such direction to the Commissioner of Income Tax (Appeals).

(*v*) **To Relax any Provision relating to Headwise Computation of Income or Deductions allowable in computing Total Income [Sec. 119(2)(*c*)]** - Where the Board considers it desirable to avoid genuine hardship in any case or class of cases where the assessee has failed to comply with any requirement specified in any provision relating to headwise computation of income or deductions allowable in computing total income, it may pass a general order or special order relaxing any requirement contained in the said provision.

(*vi*) **Power to decide Jurisdiction** - The Board is empowered to decide jurisdictional matters of any income-tax authority and assign to them such functions as are to be performed by them [Sec. 120].

(*vii*) **Power to disclose Information** - The Board may disclose information relating to any assessee to any officer, authority or body performing any functions under any law relating to the imposition of any tax, duty or cess or dealing in foreign exchange under Foreign Exchange Regulation Act, 1973, if it considers such disclosure in public interest. The Board may also authorize any other income-tax authority to disclose such information (Sec. 138). The provisions are intended to facilitate exchange of information about tax evaders.

Other Powers of the Board, specified in Other Sections of the Act:

1. To declare any institution, association or body, whether incorporated or not, whether Indian or non-Indian, to be a company [Sec. 2(*17*)(*iv*)].
2. To declare a company, having no share capital, to be a company in which public has substantial interest. [Sec. 2(*18*)].

3. To specify exemption to the income of charitable trust for application of its income outside India [Sec. 11(1)(*c*)].
4. To notify profession for compulsory maintenance of account [Sec. 44AA].
5. To exercise control over income-tax authorities [Sec. 118].
6. To decide jurisdiction of income-tax authorities [Sec. 120].
7. To empower authorities with the power of search [Sec. 132].
8. To lay down the procedure of search [Sec. 132(14)].
9. To allow disclosure of information in certain cases [Sec. 138].
10. To lay down educational qualification for an authorised representative [Sec. 288].

INCOME-TAX AUTHORITIES

The following is the hierarchy of income tax authorities

1. The Central Board of Direct Taxes.
2. Principal Directors General of Income-tax or Principal Chief Commissioners of Income-tax (w.e.f. 1-6-2013).
3. Directors-General of Income-tax or Chief Commissioners of Income Tax.
4. Principal Directors of Income-tax or Principal Commissioners of Income-tax.
5. Directors of Income Tax or Commissioners of Income Tax or Commissioners of Income Tax (Appeals).
6. Additional Directors of Income Tax or Additional Commissioners of Income Tax or Additional Commissioners of Income Tax (Appeals).
7. Joint Directors of Income Tax or Joint Commissioners of Income Tax.
8. Deputy Directors of Income Tax or Deputy Commissioners of Income Tax or Deputy Commissioners of Income Tax (Appeals).
9. Assistant Directors of Income Tax or Assistant Commissioners of Income Tax.
10. Income-tax Officers.
11. Tax Recovery Officers.
12. Inspectors of Income Tax.

1. Appointment of Income-tax Authorities [Sec. 117]

The following provisions have been enacted in this connection.

(*i*) **Appointment by the Central Government [Sec. 117(1)]** - The Central Government may appoint such persons as it thinks fit to be the income-tax authorities.

(*ii*) **Delegated Authorities to appoint Income-tax Authorities below the Rank of an Assistant Commissioner or Deputy Commissioner [Sec. 117(2)] -** The Central Government, subject to its rules and orders regulating the conditions in public services and posts, may authorise the Board or a Principal Director-General or Director-General, a Principal Chief Commissioner or Chief Commissioner or a Principal Director or Director or a Principal Commissioner or Commissioner to appoint Income-tax authorities below the rank of an Assistant Commissioner or Deputy Commissioner [Sec. 117(2)].

(*iii*) **Appointment of Executive or Ministerial Staff by an Income-tax Authority, Authorised by the Board [Sec. 117(3)] -** The Board, subject to the rules and orders of the Central Government regulating the conditions of service in public services and posts, may authorise an income-tax authority to appoint such executive or ministerial staff as may be necessary to assist it in the execution of its functions.

2. Jurisdictions of Income-tax Authorities [Sec. 120]

Provisions dealing with jurisdiction of income-tax authorities are explained as follows:

(*i*) **Board to decide jurisdiction of income-tax authorities [Sec. 120(1), (2), (3)] -** Income-tax authorities are required to exercise such powers and perform such functions as are assigned to them by the Board and in accordance with the directions as are issued to them by the Board [Sec. 120(1)] [*Mrs. Uma Loomba* v. *CIT* (2000) 241 ITR 152/108 Taxman 232 (Delhi)]. The Board may also direct an income-tax authority higher in rank to perform the functions of an income-tax authority lower in rank. [*Explanation* to Sec. 120(1)].

The Board may authorise any other income-tax authority to direct to issue orders in writing to exercise the powers and perform the functions by all or any of the income-tax authority, subordinate to it.

In issuing the directions or orders the board or other income tax authorities authorized by it may have regard to any one or more of the following criteria, namely;- (*a*) territorial area; (*b*) persons or classes of persons; (*c*) incomes or classes of incomes; and (*d*) cases or classes of cases.

(*ii*) **Delegation of the functions of other authorities to the top authorities [Sec. 120(4)] -** The Board may authorise any (*i*) Principal Director General, or (*ii*) Director General or (*iii*) Principal Director or (*iv*) Director to perform such functions of any other income-tax authority as assigned to him by it.

The Board may, by general or special order, empower (*i*) Principal Director General or (*ii*) Director General, (*iii*) Principal Chief Commissioner or (*iv*) Chief Commissioner or (*v*) Principal Commissioner, or (*vi*) Commissioner, to issue orders in writing to the effect that the power and functions, assigned to the Assessing Officer in respect of (*i*) specified area, (*ii*) persons, or (*iii*) classes of persons, or (*iv*) income or cases or classes of cases have to be exercised or performed by an (*i*) Additional Commissioner or (*ii*) An Additional Director or (*iii*) Joint Commissioner or (*iv*) Joint Director.

(*iii*) **Delegation of concurrent jurisdiction to Assessing Officer [Sec. 120(5)]** - The Board or any other income-tax authority authorised by it may confer concurrent jurisdiction on the Assessing Officers. For the proper management of work, two or more Assessing Officers (whether or not of the same class) may be required to exercise and perform, concurrently, the powers and functions in respect of any area or persons or classes of persons or incomes or classes of income or cases or classes of cases.

Where such powers and functions are exercised or performed concurrently by the Assessing Officers of different classes, any authority lower in rank amongst them is required to exercise the powers and perform the functions as any higher authority amongst them may direct [Sec. 120(5)].

(*iv*) **Jurisdiction for furnishing Return of Income and other Notified Functions [Sec. 120(6)]** - The Board is empowered to regulate jurisdictional matters for the purposes of furnishing of the return of income or the doing of any other act or thing under the Act [Sec. 120(6)].

Jurisdiction of the Assessing Officers [Sec. 124]

Provisions dealing with the jurisdiction of the Assessing Officer are explained as below:

(*i*) **Assessing Officer vested jurisdiction on a Specified Area** - Where the Assessing Officer has been vested with jurisdiction over a specified area, he exercises jurisdiction on any person who resides in that area or who carries on business profession in that area or if he carries on business or profession at more than one place but the principal place of business profession falls in that area.

Normally, the principal place of business is that place where control and management is situated.

(*ii*) **Jurisdictional Dispute not appealable but to be decided by the specified authorities [Sec. 124(2), (3)]** - Where the assessee disputes the jurisdiction of the Assessing Officer on any ground (say, place of business and place of residence fall under different jurisdictions), the Assessing Officer cannot decide such dispute.

If the Assessing Officer is not satisfied about the correctness of the assessee's claim, he may refer the matter to the concerned Principal Director-General of Income-tax or the Principal Chief Commissioner of Income-tax before the assessment is made [Sec. 124(4)] If more than one authority exercises jurisdiction over that area and such authorities are not in agreement, the dispute is decided by the Board. The order passed by the Commissioner cannot be made a subject matter of the appeal.

[*Rai Bahadur Seth Teomal* v. *CIT* [1959] 36 ITR 9 (SC); *Nirmal Singh* v. *ITO* (I.T.A. No. 588/Asr/2016 and S.A. No. 13/Asr/2016)]

Jurisdictional dispute to be raised within the permissible time - No person can dispute the jurisdiction after the expiry of prescribed time-limit which is related to the furnishing of the return of income.

(*i*) **Where a Return has been Furnished -** Jurisdiction can be disputed either within one month from the date on which notice was issued under sec. 142(1) or sec. 143(2)or before completion of the assessment, whichever period is earlier.

(*ii*) **Where Return has not been Furnished -** Jurisdictional dispute may be raised either before the expiry of the time allowed to make a return under sec. 142(1) or sec. 148, or before a show cause notice is issued to make best judgment assessment under First Proviso to sec. 144, whichever period expires earlier.

(*iii*) Where Action has been taken: No person shall be entitled to call in question the jurisdiction of an AO where an action has been taken under sec. 132 or sec. 132A, after the expiry of one month from the date on which he was served with a notice under sec. 153A(1) or sec. 153C(2) or after the completion of the assessment, whichever period expires earlier [Sec.124(3)(c)].

(*iii*) **Assessing Officers' power extend to income or accruing or arising or received in area Non-obstante clause [Sec. 124(5)] -** Every Assessing Officer shall have all the powers conferred by or under this Act on an Assessing Officer in respect of the income accruing or arising or received within the area, if any, over which he has been vested with jurisdiction by virtue of the directions or orders issued under Sec. 120(1),(2).

Case Law : ***Mrs. Uma Loomba* v. *CIT* (2000) 241 ITR 152/108 Taxman 232 (Delhi)**

Facts: 'U' and another were individuals deriving income from their profession and business at Amritsar and later shifted to Delhi and carried their profession and business there. They continued to file their returns with the ITO at Amritsar and when served with a notice on search and seizure operations and later on other notices by the Assessing Officer in Delhi, challenged the jurisdiction of the Assessing Officer, Delhi. The revenue department contended that since 'U' had shifted to Delhi the Assessing Officer at Delhi held the natural jurisdiction over them.

Held: Once the two petitioners had their business/profession situated at Delhi, the assessing authority in Delhi having natural jurisdiction over the area would have jurisdiction to assess them, and could issue notices though referable to the period when they were assessed or were assessable at Amritsar.

Case Law : ***B.R. Industries* v. *CIT* [2002] 123 Taxman 92/255 ITR 593 (Delhi)**

Facts: 'B' challenged the jurisdiction of the assessing authority citing a relevant notification of the CBDT contending that only Joint Commissioner could function as the Assessing Officer and the ITO had no jurisdiction to deal with its case and therefore the Commissioner's order assigning jurisdiction to the ITO could not supersede the statutory notification.

Held: The Legislature in its wisdom has clearly spelt out that ordinarily the assessments have to be done by the AO and in some exceptional or special cases looking to the gravity, intricacy and complexity of the case, jurisdiction can be given to the Joint Commissioner and he will become the Assessing Officer in that specified case. By giving those powers to the Joint Commissioners in special and exceptional cases, the Assessing Officers have not been divested of their powers to carry out the assessments according to Sec. 120(1) and (2). The assessee cannot be given the discretion to choose its officer. No mandamus can be issued from the Court that the assessment should be carried out by a Joint Director in view of section 120(4)(*b*).

Power to Transfer Cases [Sec. 127]

The provisions dealing with transfer of a case from one Assessing Officer to another Assessing Officer are explained as follows:

(*i*) **Principal Director General or Director General or Principal Chief Commissioner or Chief Commissioner or Principal Commissioner or Commissioner -** Any such authority may transfer any case from subordinate AO to another subordinate AO [*CIT* v. *Rameshwar Prasad & Co.* (1991) 55 Taxman 29/188 ITR 291 (All.)].

Where both Assessing Officers are not subordinate to the same Director-General or Chief Commissioner or Commissioner, the transfer can be made on the agreement of the respective Principal Director-General or Director General, as the case may be.

Where the Principal Director-General or Director General, as the case may be are not in agreement the order transferring the case may, similarly, be passed by the Board or any such Principal Director General or Director General or Principal Chief Commissioner or Chief Commissioner or Principal Commissioner or Commissioner as the Board may, by notification in the Official Gazette, authorise in this behalf.

(*ii*) **Transfer to be made at any stage, either *suo motu* or on the request of assessee -** It is not necessary that a case should be transferred at the initial stage. It may be transferred at any stage of the proceedings, and shall not render necessary the re-issue of any notice already issued by the Assessing Officer or Assessing Officers from whom the case is transferred.

The Department may transfer a case *suo motu*. Transfer of case may also be made on the request of the assessee.

(*iii*) **Public Interest be the sole consideration for transfer -** Although the grounds for transfer have not been enlisted in the Section, it is evident that the sole consideration for the transfer should be public interest [*Jharkhand Mukti Morcha* v. *CIT* (1997) 95 Taxman 132/225 ITR 284 (Patna)].

(*iv*) **Reason for Transfer to be Recorded -** Reasons for the transfer should be recorded [*Rajesh Mahajan* v. *CIT* [2003] 126 Taxman 87/[2002] 257 ITR 577 (Punj & Har.)]. The power should not be exercised for extraneous or irrelevant considerations [*Jharkhand Mukti Morcha* v. *CIT* (1997) 95

Taxman 132/225 ITR 284 (Patna); *G. Mohandas* v. *CIT* (2000) 110 Taxman 229/244 ITR 32 (Mad.)]

(*v*) **Whenever possible opportunity of being heard be allowed to Assessee except in a case where the transfer is made in the same city -** Before any transfer is made, an opportunity of being heard must be allowed to the assessee wherever it is possible to do so. However, no such opportunity is allowed where the offices of such officers are situated in the same city, locality or place.

(*vi*) **Order to be communicated to the Assessee -** Failure to communicate order and reason for the order of transfer of case to the assessee render the order, transferring the case, invalid [*Ajantha Industries* v. *CBDT* (1976) 102 ITR 281 (SC); *Vinay Kumar Jaiswal* v. *CIT* (1996) 221 ITR 568 (All.)].

The power of transfer under section 127(1) is a quasi-judicial one and such power has to be exercised in a fair and reasonable manner and not in an arbitrary or mechanical way and passing a reasoned order is one of the requirements of fairness in action [*Benz Corporation* v. *ITO* (1998) 232 ITR 807 (Kerala)].

Case Law : ***Jharkhand Mukti Morcha* v. *CIT* (1997) 95 Taxman 132/225 ITR 284 (Patna)**

Facts: Four office-bearers of 'J' being a registered political party having its head office at Ranchi were alleged to have taken bribe from another political party for supporting it during the no-confidence motion in the Parliament. The matter was being investigated by the CBI and huge deposits, immovable properties some of them purchased in Delhi, were found either in their names or in the names of their family members. The investigation of case by the CBI was being monitored by the Delhi High Court. All the papers including the papers seized from the office of the 'J were also taken possession of by the CBI, Delhi but 'J' was being assessed by the Dy. Commissioner, Ranchi. Since no progress was being made in the cases in Ranchi, it had become necessary on account of administrative convenience and better coordinated investigation for proper assessment, to transfer their cases from Ranchi to Delhi. 'J' objected to the transfer.

Held: An order passed by Commissioner, Ranchi, in exercise of his power under section 127(2)(*a*) and with agreement of Commissioner, Delhi, transferring case of petitioner, a political party, with head office at Ranchi, along with other cases of office-bearers and members, to Delhi, on grounds of coordinated investigation, public interest, facilitating assessment proceedings, launching of prosecution, collection of revenue, after giving opportunity of hearing to petitioner and recording relevant and valid reasons for transfer, was valid in law.

Case Law : ***Ajantha Industries* v. *CBDT* (1976) 102 ITR 281 (SC)**

Facts: The Central Board of Direct Taxes sent a notice to 'A' under Sec. 127 proposing to transfer its case files "for facility of investigation" from the ITO at Nellore to the ITO Hyderabad and invited objections, if any, in writing to the proposed transfer. CBDT passed the transfer order, the validity of which challenged on the ground of violation of the principles of natural justice as before passing the order, no reasons were given nor communicated to 'A' in the said order.

Held: The requirement of recording reasons under section 127(1) is a mandatory direction under the law and non-communication thereof would not be saved by showing that the reasons existed in the file although not communicated to the assessee.

Case Law : ***Vinay Kumar Jaiswal* v. *CIT* [1996] 221 ITR 568 (All.)**

Facts: The Commissioner had transferred under Sec. 127 certain cases of 'V' who challenged the transfer order on the grounds no opportunity of hearing was given as required under Sec. 127 and the transfer had not been communicated. The department submitted that the petitioners had themselves filed objection before the Commissioner objecting to the proposed transfer and, hence, merely because they had not been given notice by the Commissioner the impugned order of transfer would not be vitiated

Held: Mere filing of the objection does not comply with the requirement of section 127 because unless the assessees know the reasons for the proposed transfer, they will not be able to properly meet the basis for the proposed transfer. Mere filing of the objection does not comply with the requirement of Sec. 127 because unless the assessees know the reasons for the proposed transfer, they will not be able to properly meet the basis for the proposed transfer.

Change of Incumbent of an Office [Sec. 129]

Whenever, during the pendency of any proceeding, an income-tax authority is succeeded by another, the successor may continue the proceeding from the stage at which his predecessor left the proceeding. [*Pradip Lamps Works* v. *CIT* (2001) 119 Taxman 269/169 CTR 1 (SC)]

Opportunity of Re-hearing - The assessee has the right to demand a re-hearing before the proceeding is so continued or the previous proceeding or any part thereof is re-opened or before any order of assessment is passed against him.

Faceless Jursidiction of Income-Tax Authorities [Sec. 130]

With effect from 1-11-2020, the Amendment Act, 2020 has inserted a new sec. 130 to empower the Central government to make a scheme to exercise the following functions in a faceless manner:—

(*a*) Exercise of all or any of the powers and performance of all or any of the functions conferred on or assigner to the Incometax authorities under Sec. 120; or

(*b*) Vesting the jurisdiction with the AO under sec. 124; or

(*c*) Exercise of power to transfer cases under sec. 127; or

(*d*) Exercise of the jurisdiction in case of change of incumbency under sec. 129

Such faceless scheme serves the purpose of imparting greater efficiency, transparency and accountability by—

(*i*) eliminating the interface between the income-tax authority and the assessee or any other person, to the extent technologically feasible;

(*ii*) Optimising utilisation of the resources through economies of scale and functional specialisation; and

(*iii*) Introducing a team-based exercise of powers and performance of functions by two or more income-tax authorities concurrently in respect of any area or persons or classes of persons or incomes or classes of income or cases or classes of cases, with dynamic jurisdiction.

Accordingly, the Central Government *vide* Notification No. 15/2022, dated 28-3-2022 notified the Faceless Jurisdiction of Income-tax Authorities Scheme, 2022. The Scheme is applicable with effect from 28-3-2022. Under this scheme, the jurisdiction of the Assessing Officer shall be vested in a faceless manner through automated allocation. Such jurisdiction shall be in accordance with and to the extent provided in:

(1) Section 144B with reference to making the faceless assessment of total income or loss of assessee;

(2) The Faceless Appeal Scheme, 2021 with reference to the disposal of appeals;

(3) The Faceless Penalty Scheme, 2021 with reference to the imposition of penalty under Chapter XXI of the Act;

(4) The e-Verification Scheme, 2021 with reference to:

   a. Calling for information under section 133,

   b. Collecting certain information under section 133, or

   c. Calling for information by the prescribed authority under section 133C, or

   d. Exercise of power to inspect the register of companies under section 134, or

   e. Exercise of power of Assessing Officer under section 135.

(5) The e-Settlement Scheme, 2021 with reference to the settlement of pending applications by the interim Board; and

(6) The e-advance rulings Scheme, 2022 with reference to dispute resolution for persons or class of persons, as specified by the Board, who may opt for dispute resolution under Chapter XIX-AA with reference to the dispute arising from any variation in the specified order fulfilling the specified conditions.

Power Regarding Discovery, Production of Evidence and so on [Sec. 131]

For the purposes of any proceeding pending under this Act, certain powers of civil court have been vested with income-tax authorities. These provisions are explained as below:

(*i*) **Vesting the Powers of the Civil Court with Income-tax Authorities to deal with any Proceeding Pending under this Act [Sec. 131(1)]**

- Under Code of Civil Procedure 1908, a civil court, while trying a suit, has the following powers:

(*a*) Discovery and inspection;

(*b*) Enforcing attendance of any person including an officer of a bank and examining him on oath;

(*c*) Compelling the production of books of account and other documents; and

(*d*) Issuing commissions.

To deal with any proceeding pending under this Act, Sec. 131(1) vests the same powers with Assessing Officer, Deputy Commissioner (Appeals), Joint Commissioner, Commissioner (Appeals), Principal Chief Commissioner or Chief Commissioner or Principal Commissioner or Commissioner. The proceedings must be an independent proceeding before the issue of notice under this section. [*Smt Rina Sen* v. *CIT* [1998] 101 Taxman 151/ [1999] 235 ITR 219 (Patna)]

Summoning of Witness for collecting Material for the Purposes of making an Assessment - The Assessing Officer may summon and examine witness from third parties to procure information and evidence. When the evidence of a witness is being taken, the witness has no right to be represented by an authorised representative but the assessee has the right to be represented by a lawyer [*Sarju Prosad Sharma* v. *ITO* (1974) 93 ITR 36 (Calcutta)].

Seeking Information from a Bank - Banks cannot be compelled to produce evidence which is not available in the taxable territories [Circular No. 8D(LXXVI-22) *Sarju Prosad Sharma* v. *ITO* [1974] 93 ITR 36 (Cal.)].

Enforcing Attendance - It is the duty of the Assessing Officer to enforce attendance of the witness if his evidence is found to be material [*Munnalal Muralidhar* v. *CIT* (1971) 79 ITR 540 (All.)].

Issuing Commissions - The income-tax authorities may issue a commission for any purpose for which a civil court may issue a commission, that is, to make a local investigation.

(*ii*) **Powers of Civil Courts be Exercised by Certain Income-tax Authorities to Inquire into Suspected Concealment even though no Proceeding is Pending [Sec. 131(1A)] -** If the Principal Director General or Director General or Principal Director or Director or Joint Director or Assistant Director or Deputy Director or the authorised officer has reason to suspect that any income has been concealed or is likely to be concealed by any person or class of persons within his jurisdiction, he may exercise the powers of civil court to investigate the suspected concealment even though no proceeding may be pending against such person before him. [*Peerless General Finance & Investment Co. Ltd.* v *AO* (2001) 117 Taxman 253/248 ITR 113 (All.)]

(*iii*) **Power to Impound and Retain Books and Documents [Sec. 131(3)]** - Income-tax authorities have been empowered to impound and retain in their custody any books of account or other documents produced before them in any proceeding. The Assessing Officer or an Assistant Director or Deputy Director are required to record reasons for impounding the books of account and if any of them wants to retain them for more than 15 days (excluding holidays), he has to obtain the prior approval of the Principal Chief Commissioner or Chief Commissioner or Principal Director General or Director General or Principal Commissioner or Commissioner or Principal Director or Director, as the case may be. Any other income-tax authority can impound and retain the books of account or documents without any time-limit.

Case Law : ***Peerless General Finance & Investment Co. Ltd.* v. *AO* [2001] 117 Taxman 253/248 ITR 113 (All.)**

Facts: 'P'engaged in the business of investment and social welfare scheme had branches and units at various places including Kanpur. 'P' was a regular income taxpayer and was assessed at Calcutta. 'P' offices in Calcutta and Kanpur received a number of summons under Sec.131 and letters from AO, Kanpur directing their appearance and for production of various documents. 'P' objected against the actions taken by the AO of Kanpur contending that as no enquiry or proceeding before any TDS officer in respect of any financial year concerned was pending, the summons issued was without jurisdiction and without authority of law, and that the seizure of books of account and documents in the course of survey and their retention under section 131(3) was illegal and invalid.

Held: The expression 'Assessing Officer' in section 2(*7A*) is not confined to an Assessing Officer making regular assessment only and includes others also who may come within purview of said section. There is no express provision in Sec. 131 to the effect that some proceedings must be pending before same income-tax authority who exercises power under Sec. 131. Since assessment proceedings were pending at Calcutta, this was not a case where no proceedings were pending at all and, hence, the AO, Kanpur had jurisdiction to exercise power under Sec. 131.

Search and Seizure [Sec. 132]

Searches are important means to unearth black money and to detect concealed income. Sec. 132 does not confer any arbitrary authority upon the revenue officers. The Commissioner or the Director of Inspection must have, in consequence of information, reason to believe that the statutory conditions for the exercise of the power to order search exist. He must record reasons for the belief and he must issue an authorization in favour of a designated officer to search the premises and exercise the powers set out therein. The condition for entry into and making search of any building or place is the reason to believe that any books of account or other documents which will be useful for, or relevant to, any proceeding under the Act may be found. If the officer has reason to believe that any books of account or other documents would be useful for, or relevant to, any proceedings under the Act, he is authorised by law to seize those books of account or other documents, and to place marks of identification therein, to make extracts or copies there from and also to make a note or an other inventory of any articles or other things found in the course of the search. Since by the exercise of the power a serious invasion is made upon the rights, privacy and freedom of the taxpayer, the power must be exercised strictly in accordance with the law and only for the purposes for which the law authorizes it to be exercised [*ITO* v. *Seth Brothers* [1969] 74 ITR 836 (SC).

If the action of the officer issuing the authorization or of the designated officer is challenged, the officer concerned must satisfy the court about the regularity of his action. If the action is maliciously taken or power under the section is exercised for a collateral purpose, it is liable to be struck down by the court. If the conditions for exercise of the power are not satisfied, the proceeding is liable to be quashed.Even a non-resident is amenable to search and seizure [*Ram Kumar Dhamuka* v. *UOI* (2001) 252 ITR 205/118 Taxman 535 (Raj.)].

Authorities empowered to order Search and Seizure [Sec. 132(1)] - Principal Director-General or Director General or Principal Director or Director or Principal Chief Commissioner or Chief Commissioner or Principal Commissioner or Commissioner or Additional Director or Additional Commissioner or Joint Director or Joint Commissioner is empowered to order for search and seizure.

Conditions to be satisfied to order Search and Seizure [Sec. 132(1) (*a*), (*b*), (*c*)] - Designated authority, as above, may order for search and seizure in cases where, in consequence of information in his possession, he has reason to believe [*Smt. Kavita Agarwal* v. *DIT* (2003) 264 ITR 472/133 Taxman 848 (All.)] that any of the followings conditions is satisfied:

(*a*) **Failure to produce any books of account or other documents as were required to be produced under summons issued under Sec. 131 or Sec. 142(1)** - Where the designated authority, in consequence of information in his possession, has reason to believe that, summons were issued under sec. 131 to any person compelling him to produce books of account and other documents, or notice was issued under sec. 142(1) to any person to produce or cause to be produced the books of account or other documents but such person has failed or omitted to produce or cause to be produced such books of account or other documents as were required by such summons or notice, he may order for search and seizure.

(OR)

(*b*) **Suspected non-compliance with summons or notice issued to any person as aforesaid** - Where the designated authority, in consequence of information in his possession, has reason to believe that any person to whom a summons or notice as aforesaid has been or might be issued may not, or would not, produce or cause to be produced, any books of account or other documents which are useful or relevant to any proceedings under this Act, he may order for search and seizure.

(OR)

(*c*) **Non-disclosure of concealed income or property -** Where the designated authority, in consequence of information in his possession, has reason to believe that any person is in possession of any money, bullion, jewellery or other valuable article or thing, representing either wholly or partly income or property which has not been or may not be disclosed for the purposes of this Act, he may order for search and seizure of the undisclosed income and property.

Under Sec. 132, 'reason to believe' is a condition precedent for search and seizure which cannot be equated with 'reason to suspect'. The expression 'reason to believe' postulates belief and the existence of reasons for that belief. The expression 'reason to believe' does not mean purely subjective satisfaction on part of authority in making the seizure but the reasons for the belief must have a rational connection or a relevant bearing for the formation of the belief, not extraneous or irrelevant for the said purpose. When places of persons of diverse activities and unconnected with each other are searched and their bank accounts are freezed, to get or gather materials and information to form a belief that the assessee is avoiding tax, it is wholly outside the scope of the search and seizure under the Act. Under the Income-tax Act, 'reason to suspect' is also available but subject to 'reason to believe'. Therefore, 'reason to suspect' in sub-sections (1A) and (4A) is subject to satisfaction of the primary test of 'reason to believe' under section 132(1). In other words, unless one successfully crosses the hurdle of 'reason to believe' under section 132(1), there is no scope to get attracted by sub-sections (1A) and (4A). [*Mahesh Kumar Agarwal* v. *Dy. DDIT* [2003] 133 Taxman 520/260 ITR 67 (Cal.)].

Information not to be based on rumour or gossip or hunch - The expression "information in his possession" should be construed as some valid, definite information in possession and not any imaginary or invalid information. The information should be credible and if there is some such information, the Court cannot go into the sufficiency of the information [*Kusum Lata* v. *CIT* (1989) 180 ITR 365/[1990] 48 Taxman 401 (Raj.); *Dy. DDIT* v. *Mahesh Kumar Agarwal* (2003) 130 Taxman 674/262 ITR 338 (Cal.)].

The reason to believe as recorded by the Income tax authority shall not be disclosed to any person, authority or Appellate Tribunal. [*Explanation* after the Fourth Proviso to sec. 132(1) inserted by the Finance Act, 2017 w.e.f. 1-4-1962]

Similarly the reason to suspect as recorded by the Income tax authority shall not be disclosed to any person, authority or Appellate Tribunal. [*Explanation* to sec. 132(1A) of the Finance Act, 2017 w.e.f. 1-10-1975].

Functions connected with Search Proceedings [Sec. 132(1)] - The Authorised Officer is required to perform the following functions in search proceedings:

(*i*) enter and search any building, place, vessel, vehicles or aircraft where he has reason to suspect that (*a*) the books of account or documents which are requisitioned [under sec. 142(1)] or which may be useful for any proceeding under this Act are kept; or (*b*) money, bullion, jewellery or other valuable article representing undisclosed income wholly or partly are kept;

(*ii*) break/open the lock of any door, box, locker, safe, almirah or other receptacle if the keys thereof are not available;

(*iii*) search any person who has got out of, or is about to get out of or is in the building, place, vessel, vehicle or aircraft, if the Authorised Officer has reason to suspect that such person has secreted about his person any such books of account, other documents, money, bullion, jewellery or other valuable article or thing;

(*iv*) require any person who is found to be in possession or control of any books of account or other documents maintained in the form of electronic record, to afford the Authorised Officer the necessary facility to inspect such books of account or other documents (w.e.f. 1 June 2002);

(*v*) seize any such books of account, other documents, money, bullion, jewellery or other valuable article or thing found as a result of such search;

(*vi*) place marks of identification on any books of account or other documents or make or cause to be made extracts or copies therefrom;

(*vii*) make a note or an inventory of any such money, bullion, jewellery or other valuable article or thing.

Title Deeds are not valuable articles or things - The expression "valuable article or thing" implies that the asset is such as could be converted into cash so that the tax liability of the assessee from undisclosed income could be duly satisfied. Documents of title do not carry any saleable interest and are not 'valuable things' or articles as contemplated under the Section [*Bhagwandas Narayandas* v. *CIT* (1975) 98 ITR 194 (Guj.)].

No Seizure of Stock-in-trade - In search proceedings, the Authorised Officer can neither seize bullion, jewellery or other valuable article or thing, forming part of the stock-in-trade of the business nor he can direct its owner in the immediate possession or control, not to deal with it or part with it without his prior approval. He may make a note or inventory of such stock-in-trade of the business [Fourth Proviso to Sec. 132(1)].

Restraint order in respect of unseizable items - Where it is not possible or practicable to take physical possession of any valuable article or thing or to remove it to safe place due to its volume, weight or other physical characteristics or due to its being of dangerous nature, the Authorised Officer may serve an order on the owner or person who is in the immediate possession or control thereof that he cannot remove, part with or otherwise deal with it, except with his prior permission. [Third Proviso to Sec. 132(1)] Such action of the Authorised Officer is deemed to be seizure of such valuable article or thing.

Place of search not falling within the jurisdiction of competent authority - If the Authorised Officer comes to know that the authorisation of search has not been authorised by competent authority, having jurisdiction over the search proceedings, but getting approval of the jurisdictional authority is likely to delay the matter and it may be prejudicial to the interest of revenue, he is competent to continue search proceedings in the larger interest of revenue.

Authorisation of search by specified authorities to be approved by the Board - The Additional Director or Additional Commissioner or Joint Director or Joint Commissioner cannot authorise search proceedings on or after 1st October, 2009 unless he has been empowered by the Board to do so.

Seeking police assistance in search proceedings [Sec. 132(2)(4)] - The authorised officer is empowered to seek services of any police officer or any officer of the Central Government or of both or any person or entity approved by the principal commissioner or the chief commissioner or the principal Director General or the Director General to assist him in search proceedings [Sec. 132(2)] It is the duty of every such officer to comply with such request.

During search proceedings, the authorised officer may examine on oath any person who is found in possession or control of any books of account, documents, money, bullion, jewellery or other valuable article [Sec. 132(4)].

Authenticity of documents found in search proceedings [Sec. 132(4A)] - Where any books of account, other documents, money, bullion, jewellery or other valuable articles are found in possession or control of any person in course of search proceedings, it is presumed that these belong to such person and the contents of books of account and other documents are correct.

Case Law : ***ITO* v. *Seth Brothers* [1969] 74 ITR 836 (SC)**

Facts: Upon completion of assessment 'S' was issued a notice that there was reason to believe that their income chargeable to tax had escaped assessment and it was proposed to reassess this income. In the meantime an information was received by the ITO that assessee were maintaining "duplicate records" and were evading assessment of their true income and that it was necessary to seize the records which may be found at premises in which assessee carried on the business. Accordingly the premises were searched and account books and certain documents were seized. some of the documents seized by the ITO were irrelevant for the purpose of any proceeding under the Act; that besides the documents belonging to the assessee, the ITO seized documents relating to the transactions of the allied concerns. Issue arose there was abuse of power conferred on ITO by section 132, and therefore, the proceedings should be quashed.

Held: Section 132 does not require specific mention by description of each particular document which has to be discovered on search: it is for the officer who is conducting the search to decide whether a particular document found on search is relevant for the purpose or not. Merely because the ITO made a search for and seized the books of account and documents in relation to business carried on in the names of other firms and companies, it could not be said the search and seizure were illegal.

Restraint Order in respect of books of account, other documents, money, bullion or jewellery and so on [Sec. 132(3)] - Where the Authorised Officer does not find it practicable to seize any books of account, other documents, money, bullion, jewellery or other valuable article or thing due to any other reason, (other than as referred above) he may serve an order on owner or the person who is in the immediate possession or control thereof that he should not remove, part with or otherwise deal with it without his prior approval [Sec. 132(3)] [*CIT* v. *Sandhya P. Naik* [2002] 253 ITR 534/124 Taxman 384 (Bom.); *B.K. Nowlakha* v. *UOI* (1992) 101 CTR 73 (Delhi)].

The power of seizure cannot be exercised in respect of assets or documents which are in the custody of the court [*K. Choyi* v. *Syed Abdulla Bafakky Thangal* [1980] 123 ITR 435 (SC); *Haneefa* v. *State of Kerala* [2004] 139 Taxman 147/[2005] 272 ITR 230 (Ker.)]. The power of seizure cannot be exercised where the source of acquisition of the asset is explained to the department [*Lalajibhai K. Soni* v. *ACIT* (1995) 213 ITR 114 (Guj.); *Smt. Sharda Agrawal* v. *DIIT* (1994) 210 ITR 690 (All.)]. Gold ornaments which are below the weight specified by the Board in its instructions, cannot be seized [*Pati Devi* v. *ITO* (1999) 240 ITR 727 (Kar.)].

Service of such order is not deemed to be a seizure.

Restraint Order remains in force for 60 Days - Any restraint order passed in respect of books of account, money, bullion, jewellery, and so on under Sec. 132(8A) cannot remain in force for a period exceeding 60 days from the date of the order.

Warrant of Authorisation to be in the Prescribed Form - Warrant of authorisation should be in the prescribed form and cannot be issued without specifying the person in respect of whom it has been issued [*Southern Herbals Ltd.* v. *DIT* [1994] 207 ITR 55]. It should be in writing under the signature of issuing officer and bear his seal.

Warrant of authorisation issued by Director-General or Director, Chief Commissioner or Commissioner of Income-tax or Deputy Director, Deputy Commissioner of Income-tax should be in Form No. 45 under sec. 132(1). Where it is issued by the Chief Commissioner or Commissioner of Income-tax, under Provisio to sec. 132(1), it should be in Form No. 45A. Where it is issued under Sec. 132(1A), it should be issued in Form No 45B [Rule 112], signed by Chief Commissioner or Commissioner.

Case Law : *B.K. Nowlakha* v. *UOI* [1992] 101 CTR 73 (Delhi)

Facts: 'N' carried on the business of dealing in handicraft items and during course of search in 'N''s premises, some highly valuable antique pieces of handcraft were found which had not been disclosed either to the Income-tax Department or to the Department of Antiquities. No seizure was effected but the revenue authorities purported to pass an order under section 132(3) restraining 'N' as well as the partners of the firm and their family members from operating or removing or dealing with the stock or other valuable articles or things lying in the premises. The entire room in which the stocks were lying was sealed. This restraint order was refreshed from time to time.

Held: It is the duty of the authorized officers to effect seizure wherever any valuable article or thing is found during the course of the search. The words 'not practicable to seizure' used in Sec. 132(3) have to be understood as where there is a practicable difficulty in effecting seizure, then an order under section 132(3) can be passed. Not knowing the value of the articles or whether they are antique or not cannot be regarded as a practical difficulty on the part of the authorized officer in effecting seizure. Therefore, the orders issued under Sec. 132(3) were not validly issued. Whenever there is a seizure of articles under Sec. 132(1) including a deemed seizure, an order has to be passed within 120 days of the seizure. Where no such order is passed, the goods have to be released.

Case Law : *M.K. Gabriel Babu* v. *Asstt. DIT* [1990] 186 ITR 435 [1991] 55 Taxman 18 (Ker.) [Upheld by the Division Bench in *CIT* v. *M.K. Gabriel Babu* [1991] 57 Taxman 146/188 ITR 464 (Ker.)]

Facts: In exercise of their powers under Sec.132(1), the revenue authorities searched the residence and business premises of the assessee and seized, *inter alia*, the immovable properties of 'G' and further directed him that inasmuch as he could not properly explain the sources of acquisition of these properties, he shall not transfer or otherwise alienate them. 'G' challenged the order of seizure and contended that the immovable properties were incapable of being seized under Sec. 132.

Held: On reading the provisions of section 132(1) it is clear that where the authorized officer has reason to suspect that the person concerned has hidden any books of account, other documents, money, bullion, jewellery or other valuable article or thing in his place of business, in any building, place etc. he has the power to search such place and also to seize such books of account, other documents, money, bullion, jewellery or other valuable article or thing. It is well established canon of construction that words and phrases occurring in a statute are to be taken not in an isolated or detached manner dissociated from the context in which they are used. It is also fundamental that if a word occurs in association with other words, which are well defined and understood, then that word takes colour from the words with which that word is associated. Thus, the words 'other valuable article or thing' used in section 132(1)(*c*) used in association with the words 'money, bullion, jewellery' cannot be said to include in its ambit immovable properties. Accordingly, the order of seizure of immovable properties including the prohibitory order contained therein was, therefore, set aside.

Examination of any person, found in possession of books of account, money, jewellery, and so on oath [Sec. 132(4)] - During the search proceedings, the Authorised Officer may examine on oath any person who is found in possession or control of any books of account, documents, money, bullion, jewellery or other valuate article or thing.

Examination may be made in connection with any matter, connected with any proceeding under the Act - The examination of any such person may not be merely in respect of any books of account, other documents or assets found as a result of the search but it may also cover all matters relevant for the purposes of any investigation, connected with any proceeding under this Act.

Any statement made during examination is used in evidence - Any statement made by such person during such examination may, therefore, be used in evidence in any proceeding under this Act.

Person examined on oath is free to attend to his normal duties after his statement is recorded - The Act does not give any power to the income-tax department to arrest an individual. Thus, once a statement is recorded during search, the department has no power to restrain such person from attending to his professional work [*L.R. Gupta* v. *Union of India* (1991) 59 Taxman 305 (Del.)].

Presumption regarding books of account, other documents, money, bullion, jewellery and so on found during the search [Sec. 132(4A)] - The law makes the following presumption in respect of aforesaid assets, found in possession or control of any person in the course of search:

(*a*) **Presumption as to ownership** - It is presumed that the books of account, other documents, money, jewellery or other valuable article or thing belongs to such person.

(*b*) **Presumption as to truthfulness** - It is presumed that the contents of such books of account and other documents are true.

(*c*) **Presumption as to signature** - It is presumed that the signature and every part of such books of account and other documents which purport to be in the handwriting of any particular person or which may reasonably be assumed to have been signed by or to be in the handwriting of any particular person, are in that person's handwriting.

(*d*) **Presumption as to stamped and attested documents** - In case of a document stamped, executed or attested, it is presumed that it was duly stamped and executed or attested by the person by whom it purports to have been so executed or attested.

Presumption not to apply for Criminal Offences - The presumption does not establish the ingredients of the criminal offences relating to wilful attempt to evade tax under Sec. 276C and false statement in verification under Sec. 277 [*Prem Das* v. *ITO* [1999] 103 Taxman 65/236 ITR 683 (SC); *N. Srinivasan* v. *Tmt Uma Rani* (2004) 141 Taxman 564/270 ITR 77 (Madras)].

Retention period of books of account [Sec. 132(8)] - The books of account or other documents seized during the course of search cannot be retained by the Authorised Officer for more than 30 days from the date of the assessment order or reassessment or recomputation under sec. 143(3) or sec. 144 or sec. 147 or order passed in search cases under sec. 153A.

Books can be returned on giving undertaking by the assessee - The object of retention of books is not to penalise the assessee or to confiscate the books forever. Where an undertaking had been obtained from the assessee–petitioner to the effect that as and when the department required the records they would be made available to it, a Single Judge would be justified in ordering the return of the books to the petitioner [*Director of Inspection* v. *K.C. & Co.* (1990) 185 ITR 475 (J&K)].

Extension of the Prescribed Period of Retention - The Authorised Officer may retain the books of account or other documents for more than the prescribed period of 30 days if the following two conditions are satisfied:

(*a*) **Recording of Reasons -** The Authorised Officer should record the reasons in writing for retention of the books of account or other documents for more than the prescribed period; and

(*b*) **Approval of the Prescribed Income-tax Authority -** The Authorised Officer is required to obtain the approval of the Principal Chief Commissioner or Chief Commissioner, Principal Commissioner or Commissioner, Principal Director General or Director-General or Principal Director or Director before the expiry of the prescribed period. There cannot a gap of a single day because Sec. 132(8) allows extension of time and not a fresh retention [*Survir Enterprises* v. *CIT* [1985] 22 Taxman 516/(1986) 157 ITR 206 (Delhi); *Nutan Sahkari Awas Samiti Ltd*. v. *DIT (Investigation)* (1994) 75 Taxman 486 (All.)].

Maximum retention period not to exceed 30 days after all the proceedings are completed [Proviso to Sec. 132(8)] - The Principal Chief Commissioner or Chief Commissioner, Principal Commissioner or Commissioner, Principal Director General or Director General or Principal Director or Director cannot authorise the retention of the books of account or other documents for a period exceeding 30 days after all the proceedings under this Act in respect of the years for which the books of account and documents are relevant, are completed.

Appeal to the Board against Extension of the Prescribed Period [Sec. 132(10)] - If a person legally entitled to the books of account or other documents seized in course of search, objects to the extension of retention period by the Principal Chief Commissioner or Chief Commissioner, Principal Commissioner or Commissioner, Principal Director General or Director General or Principal Director or Director, he may make an application to the Board. He may state therein the reasons for such objection and request for the return of the books of account or other documents. After giving an opportunity of being heard to the applicant, the Board may pass such orders as it thinks fit.

Obtaining Copies of any books of account or Documents seized during search [Sec. 132(9)] - The person from whose custody any books of account or other documents are seized during the course of search, may make copies thereof or take extracts therefrom in the presence of the authorised officer at such place and time as the authorised officer may allow in this behalf.

Authorised Officer to hand over the seized assets within the prescribed period to the Assessing Officer having jurisdiction over the defaulting person [Sec. 132(9A)] - Where the Authorised Officer has no jurisdiction over the person who has either failed or suspected to be a failure in producing books of account or other documents required to be produced in response of a notice issued to him under Sec. 131 or Sec. 142(1), or who has concealed the income or property, the Authorised Officer is required to hand over the seized assets within 60 days from the date on which the last of the authorisation of search was executed to the Assessing Officer who has jurisdiction over such person.

Provisional attachment of any property belonging to an assessee [Sec. 132(9B)] - Inserted by the Finance Act, 2017 w.e.f. 1-4-2017, Sec.132(9B) provides that where, during the course of the search or seizure or within a period of 60 days from the date on which the last of the authorisations for search was executed, the authorised officer, for reasons to be recorded in writing, is satisfied that for the purpose of protecting the interest of revenue, it is necessary so to do, he may with the previous approval of the Principal Director General or Director General or the Principal Director or Director, by order in writing, attach provisionally any property belonging to the assessee, and for the said purposes, the provisions of the Second Schedule shall, *mutatis mutandis,* apply.

Provisional attachment shall cease to have effect after expiry of certain period [Sec. 132(9C)] - Inserted by the Finance Act, 2017 w.e.f. 1-4-2017, Sec. 132(9C) provides that the provisional attachment made above [Sec.132(9B] shall cease to have effect after the expiry of a period of six months from the date of the order referred to in that section.

The Authorised Officer to estimate fair market value of property, make a reference to Valuation Officer and other procedures in that respect [Sec. 132(9D)] - Inserted by the Finance Act, 2017 w.e.f. 1-4-2017 Sec.132(9D) provides that the authorised officer may, during the course of the search or seizure or within a period of sixty days from the date on which the last of the authorisations for search was executed, make a reference to a Valuation Officer referred to in Sec. 142A, who shall estimate the fair market value of the property in the manner provided under that section and submit a report of the estimate to the said officer within a period of sixty days from the date of receipt of such reference.

Code of Criminal Procedure applicable to Search and Seizure [Sec. 132(13)] - The provisions of the Code of Criminal Procedure, relating to search and seizure, are also applicable to any search and seizure made under Sec. 132(1) or Sec. 132(1A).

Board empowered to make rules in respect of search and Seizure [Sec. 132(14)] - The Board is empowered to make rules to prescribe the procedure to be followed in search and seizure. It may make provisions to get ingress into any building, place, vessel, vehicle or aircraft where free ingress thereto is not available. The Board may also make rules to ensure safe custody of any books of account or other documents or assets seized.

Powers to requisition books of account [Sec. 132A] - "Powers to requisition books of account" and "powers of search and seizure" are complementary to each other and go hand-in-hand. 'Powers to requisition books of account' are explained as below:

(*i*) **Authorities empowered to requisition books of account [Sec. 132A(1)]** - The powers to requisition books of account may be exercised by the Principal Director-General or Director General or Principal Director or Director or the Principal Chief Commissioner or Chief Commissioner or Principal Commissioner or Chief Commissioner or Principal Commissioner or Commissioner. The authority exercising such powers is referred to as 'Requisitioning Officer' (RO).

Conditions to be satisfied for exercising such power [Sec. 132A(1) (*a*), (*b*), (*c*)] - The Principal Director-General or Director or the Principal Chief Commissioner or Chief Commissioner or Principal Commissioner or Commissioner in consequence of information in his possession has reason to believe:

(*a*) **Takeover by any other authority of any books of account or other documents which could not be produced under summons issued under sec. 131 or Notice issued under sec. 142(1)** - Where the designated authority in consequence of information in his possession has reason to believe that summons was issued under sec. 131(1) or notice was issued under sec. 142(1) to any person to produce or cause to be produced the books of account or other documents but such person has omitted or failed to produce them or cause to produce them and such books of account or other documents have been taken into custody by any officer or authority under any other law for the time being in force (such as Collector of Customs, Sales Tax Commissioner and others), it may authorise the Requisitioning Officer to requisition them from such authority/officer.

OR

(*b*) **Suspected non-compliance with summons or notice, issued to any person by aforesaid officers** - Where the designated authority, in consequent of information in his possession, has reason to believe that any books of account or other documents, useful for any proceeding under this Act, in respect of which summons or notice as aforesaid has been issued or might be issued, would not be produced or caused to be produced by such person on their return by the concerned officer or authority by whom they were taken over, it may authorise the requisitioning officer to requisition such books of account or other documents from the concerned officer or authority.

OR

(*c*) **Non-disclosure of income or property -** Where the designated authority, in consequence of information in his possession, has reason to believe that any asset, representing either wholly or partly, income or property, has not been or would not have been disclosed for the purposes of this Act by any person from whose possession or control such assets have been taken into custody by any officer or authority under any law for the time being in force, it may authorise the requisitioning officer to requisition such assets from the concerned officer or authority.

The reason to believe as recorded by the Income tax authority shall not be disclosed to any person, authority or Appellate Tribunal [*Explanation* to Sec.132(1) has been inserted by Finance Act, 2017 w.e.f. 1-4-1975]

Case Law : ***Samta Construction Co.* v. *Pawan Kumar Sharma* [1999] 107 Taxman 198/(2000) 244 ITR 845 (MP)**

Facts: 'S' being a firm engaged in the business of executing various kinds of work, deposited certain amount as earnest money with a Madhya Pradesh Nigam in connection with a bid for fishing rights which was subsequently returned since the work was not awarded to 'S'. When the draft to the bank went for clearance, it was seized by the department on the grounds that the said amount related to unexplained source of income of 'S' and, accordingly, the warrant of authorisation was sent to requisition the draft in exercise of the power under Sec. 132A. 'S' contended that the action of the department was totally illegal and without jurisdiction.

Held: For issue of warrant of authorisation under Sec. 132A(1)(*c*), an important condition required is that assets must have been taken into custody by any officer or authority under any other law for time being in force from any person who is in possession or control of such assets. Under the Banking Regulation Act, the banker cannot take into custody a draft from the possession or control of a person. When it is in the custody of the banker, the banker retains it on behalf of the customer. The banker cannot utilize the draft for any purpose other than what has been desired by the customer. Therefore, the bank draft presented for clearing by customer to the bank cannot be said to have been taken into custody by the bank to attract the applicability of the provision enshrined under Sec. 132A. The warrant of authorisation requisitioning the same by the competent authority was without jurisdiction and the proceedings in consequence thereof was quashed by the court.

Other relevant provision of sec. 132 and sec. 132B to apply [Sec. 132A(3)] - After receipt of such books of account, other documents, bullion, jewellery, other valuable articles or assets, it is presumed as if they have been seized from the person concerned to whom summons or notice was issued under sec. 132(1) or sec. 142(1) or which was in their possession or control prior thereto.

Such books of account and other documents can be retained/released in accordance with the provisions as are contained in sec. 132(4A) to sec. 132(14).

Such assets can be applied towards setting off the outstanding tax demands against such person in accordance with Sec. 132B.

Application of seized or requisitioned assets [Sec. 132B] - Provisions dealing with application of seized assets under Sec. 132 or requisitioned assets under Sec. 132A, are explained as below:

(*i*) **Order of application of the seized assets/requisitioned assets [Sec. 132B(1)] -** The assets seized under Sec. 132 or requisitioned under Sec. 132A are applied to meet the amount of existing liability in the following order:

(*a*) the amount of any liability under the Income-tax Act, 1961, the Wealth-tax Act, 1958, the Gift-tax Act, 1995, the Interest Tax Act, 1974.

(*b*) the amount of liability determined on completion of assessment or reassessment or recomputation and assessment of the year relevant to the previous year in which search is initiated or requisition is made or the amount of liability determined on completion of assessment for the block period under Sec. 158BC (now deleted), including any penalty or interest payable in connection with such assessment and in respect of which such person is in default or is deemed to be in default or the amount of liability arising on an application made before the Settlement Commission [under sec. 245C(1) w.e.f. 1-6-2015].

(*c*) **existing liability be met against asset which is to be released as source of its acquisition is explained to the AO [First and second provision to sec. 132B(1)] -** Where the person concerned makes an application for the release of an asset within 30 days from the end of the month in which the asset was seized and its source of acquisition is explained to the satisfaction of the Assessing Officer, the amount of any existing liability may be recovered out of such asset and the remaining portion, if any, of the asset may be realised, with the prior approval of the Principal Chief Commissioner or Chief Commissioner or Principal Commissioner or Commissioner, to the person from whose custody the assets were seized. Such asset is required to be released within a period of 120 days from the date on which the last of the authorisation for search under Sec. 132 or for requisition under Sec. 132A, as the case may be, was executed.

(*ii*) **Application of assets, consisting solely of money or partly of money and partly of other assets [Sec. 132B(1)] -** The Assessing Officer is required to apply such money in the discharge of the liabilities referred to in clause (*i*) aforesaid. The assessee is discharged of such liability to the extent of the money so utilised.

Recovery by other modes not barred [Sec. 132B(2)] - In addition to the above mode of recovery, the amount of existing tax liabilities may also be recovered by any other mode laid down under this Act.

Surplus of assets to be paid to the persons from whose custody the assets were seized [Sec. 132B(3)] - Any assets or proceeds thereof which remain after the liabilities referred to in clause (i) above are discharged, is made over or paid to the persons from whose custody the assets were seized.

Interest payable by the government on the surplus amount @ 0.5% p.a. [Sec. 132B(4)] - The Central Government is liable to pay simple interest @ 0.5% for every month or part thereof on the surplus amount. It is operative from the assessment year 2008-09 and subsequent years.

The period for which interest is payable begins from the date immediately following the expiry of 120 days from the date on which the last of the authorisation for search under Sec. 132 or requisition under Sec. 132A was executed to the date of completion of reassessment or recomputation.

The period for which interest is payable is rounded off, taking part of the month as full month.

Execution of Authorisation for Search - Execution of authorisation for search under Sec. 132 means the date of conclusion of the search as is recorded in the last *panchnama* in the case of a person in whose case the search warrant has been executed.

In the case of requisition under Sec. 132A, the execution of authorisation means the date when the authorised officer receives books, documents or assets.

Power to Call for Information [Sec. 133]

For making the assessment, collection of information is an important function in tax administration. Hence, some provisions have been inacted to empower tax authorities to call for information. Such provisions are explained as below:

(*i*) **Authorities empowered to call for Information -** The Assessing Officer, the Deputy Commissioner (Appeals), the Joint Commissioner or the Commissioner (Appeals) may call for information in respect of any proceeding which is pending under this Act. The power cannot be exercised to seek 'fishing' information which is unrelated to any 'proceeding' [*DBS Financial Services (P.) Ltd.* v. *Smt. M. George Second ITO* [1994] 73 Taxman 640/207 ITR 1077 (Bom.); *Devansh Exports* v *DCIT* (2018) 196 TTJ 665 (Kol.)].

Power of Survey [Sec. 133A]

The object of survey is different from that of search and seizure [*N. K. Mohnot* v. *Dy. CIT* [1995] 83 Taxman 238/215 ITR 275 (Mad.) affirmed by SC *N.K. Mohnat* v. *Dy. CIT* [1999] 104 Taxman 64/240 ITR 562 (Mad.); *Sri Venkateshwara Tourist Home (P.) Ltd.* v. *Asstt. DIT* (1998) 101 Taxman 710/233 ITR 736 (Karnataka)].

However, survey proceeding may be converted into search proceeding under Sec. 132 if the conditions of that section are satisfied [*Vinod Goel* v. *UOI* [2001] 118 Taxman 690/252 ITR 29 (Punj. & Har.); *Rich Udyog Network Ltd.* v. *Chief CIT* [2015] 63 taxmann.com 88/235 Taxman 313/(2016) 386 ITR 136 (All.)].

Provisions dealing with survey are explained as below:

(*i*) **Authorities empowered to Survey [Sec. 133A(1)] r.w. *Explanation* to Sec. 133A]** - An income-tax authority is empowered to survey a specified place at which business or profession is carried on.

For this purpose, "income-tax authority" means a Principal Commissioner or Commissioner or a Joint Commissioner, a Principal Director, or Director, a Joint Director, an Assistant Director or a Deputy Director or an Assessing Officer or a Tax Recovery Officer.

However, for the purposes of inspecting books of account at the place of business or profession or for the purposes of placing identification marks on such books or for the purposes of detecting lavish spending on any function, ceremony or event, income-tax authority also includes an inspector of income tax.

(*ii*) **Survey of Business Place, falling within the Jurisdiction of Income-tax Authority [Sec. 133A(1)]** - An income-tax authority may survey any place at which business or profession is carried on, provided such place falls within the limits of the area assigned to him or such place is occupied by a person in respect of whom he exercises jurisdiction or he is authorised by any income-tax authority exercising jurisdiction on any of them.

Functions in Survey [Sec. 133A(1)(3)] - While surveying the place of business, an income-tax authority is required to do the following:

(*a*) To inspect such books of account as are available at such place;

(*b*) To verify the cash, stock or other valuable article or thing which may be found therein;

(*c*) To collect such information as may be useful or relevant to any proceeding under this Act;

(*d*) If deemed necessary, place marks of identification on the books of account or other documents inspected by him and make or cause to be made extracts or copies therefrom.

(*e*) Impound and retain in his custody any books of account or other documents, inspected by him for such period as he thinks fit, provided he has recorded the reasons for doing so and if he wants to retain them for more than 10 days (exclusive of holidays), he has obtained prior approval of the Chief Commissioner or Director-General, as the case may be,

(*f*) Make an inventory of any cash, stock or other valuable article or thing checked or verified by him;

(g) Record the statement of any person, which may be useful or relevant to any proceeding under this Act.

Inclusive definition of business place [*Explanation* to Sec. 133A(1)] - For this purpose, the business place also includes a place at which books of account or other documents or any part of cash or stock or other valuable article or thing relating to business are or is kept.

Entry time to business place [Sec. 133A(2)] - An income-tax authority may enter any place of business or profession during business hours but survey operations can continue after business hours.

The section provides that the authority may 'enter' only during business hours. After such entry, no further limitation is imposed by the section regarding the period for which he may remain in that premises.

Entry time to any other place [Sec. 133A(2)] - An income-tax authority may enter any other place only after sunrise and before sunset.

Prior Notice not Necessary - The Section does not require prior notice of the survey to the given to be affected person [*N.K. Mohnot* v. *Dy. CIT* (1995) 215 ITR 275/83 Taxman 238 (Mad.); *Sri Venkateshwara Tourist Home (P.) Ltd.* v. *Asstt. DIT* (1998) 101 Taxman 710/233 ITR 736 (Karnataka)].

Premises not to be Sealed - Sec. 133A or sec. 132 nowhere provides for sealing of the business premises before or subsequent to the survey or even if there is difficulty in making survey [*Shyam Jewellers* v. *Chief Commissioner* 1990 Tax LR 696 (All.)].

To enter any office or business place to verify the compliance of TDS provisions [Sec. 133A(2A)] - Income-tax authorities may enter after sunrise and before sunset any business place in their jurisdiction to verify the application of the provisions, relating to 'tax deducted at source' or 'tax collected at source'. It is operative w.e.f. 1-10-2014.

No removal of cash, stock or other valuable article from the business place [Sec. 133A(4)] - An income-tax authority has no power to remove or cause to be removed any cash, stock or other valuable article or thing from the place he has entered.

(iii) **Power to collect information about unaccounted spending on any function, ceremony or event [Sec. 133A(5)] -** Where an assessee incurs an ostentatious expenditure on any function or ceremony, the income-tax authority is empowered to collect information about such expenditure from the assessee or any other person who is likely to possess information in this connection and may record his statement which may be used thereafter as an evidence. This may be done at the time such function or ceremony is over.

(iv) **Consequences of non-co-operation with Income-tax Authority [Sec. 133A(6)] -** Where any person does not allow the facility to income-tax authority to inspect books of account or other documents or check or verify any cash, stock or other valuable article or does not furnish any information or refuses or evades recording of his statement, the income-tax authority is empowered to exercise powers of discovery and inspection, enforcing the attendance of any person, compelling the production of books of account and other documents and issuing commissions under Sec. 131(1).

However, such power cannot be exercised by an Assistant Director or a Deputy Director or an Assessing Officer or a Tax Recovery Officer or an Inspector of Income Tax without obtaining the prior approval of the Joint-Director or the Joint-Commissioner, as the case may be.

Case Law : ***Sri Venkateshwara Tourist Home (P.) Ltd.* v. *Asstt. DIT* (1998) 101 Taxman 710/233 ITR 736 (Karnataka)**

Facts: During the survey operations at the business premises of 'V' certain documents were sorted out by the officers of the department and a notice under Sec. 131 was served directing 'V' to appear before them the same evening with the books of account and other details. 'V' sought to quash the notice on the ground that the action of the authority in seizing the books of account in the garb of the power under Sec. 131(3) was misuse of the provisions of Sec. 133A.

Held: Power of survey is different than that of seizure under Sec. 132. Seizure is taking possession contrary to the wishes of the owner of the property, whereas in survey the possession remains with the owner and only right of inspection of those books of account or documents could be exercised by the authorities having the power. Power of search implies an exploratory examination or probing into or seeking out something which is hidden and suspected. The power of survey does not confer any power to impound, seize or even to remove the documents from the business premises. The power by of impounding under Sec. 133A cannot be exercised unless there is non-cooperation. In the present case there was no evidence of non-cooperation for the purpose of exercising the power of impounding or seizure of the books of account and the action of the authorities was not justified in accordance with the provisions of law.

Case Law : ***Rich Udyog Network Ltd.* v. *Chief CIT* [2015] 63 taxmann.com 88/235 Taxman 313/[2016] 386 ITR 136 (All.).**

Facts: During the course of survey under section 133A, which was conducted after due approval of the Competent Authority, huge amount of cash was found from the premises of 'R' along with the incriminating documents showing huge cash transactions. The statement of the Director of 'R' was recorded under Sec. 131(1A), who could not explain the source of cashand various dubious entries in seized documents.

Held: From the perusal of the record, the warrant of authorisation was issued after according approval from the competent authority further, from the facts and the circumstances of the case after valid survey was conducted incriminating that came forward during the course of survey, a satisfactory note was placed before the competent authority, who after considering the material recorded his satisfaction. Such satisfaction recorded was in accordance with the provision of section 132 therefore, the conversion of survey proceedings under search proceedings was valid.

Case Law : ***Shyam Jewellers v. Chief Commissioner (Administration)* [1992] 196 ITR 243 (All.)**

Facts: A survey was conducted at shops of 'S', a firm carrying on the business in gold and silver, and shops sealed. Later on order of Court, the shop was reopened by the income-tax authorities who carried out a search and seized the entire gold ornaments and jewellery. 'S' filed writ petition subsequent to which final order was passed under section 132(5). The department mainly contented that the final orders had been passed and since 'S' had an alternative remedy of filing an appeal under Sec. 132(11), the writ petition should not be maintained.

Held: There is no absolute bar to the entertainability of a writ petition in suitable cases even if an alternative remedy is available.There is no provision for sealing of the business premises either under section 133A or section 132 or any other section of the Act. There is no provision for sealing of the business premises either under section 133A or section 132 or any other section of the Act. The Act of sealing of a particular business premises purported to be in exercise of powers under section 132 a deliberate act in gross violation of the specific provisions of law which the ITO or a higher officer was supposed to know and the said action was not only an abuse of the power or misuse of the power but was a malicious act with a collateral object. The sealing of the business premises for which there was no provision in law was in violation of the fundamental rights guaranteed to a citizen under article 19(1)(*g*) of the Constitution of India.

Power to Collect Certain Information [Sec. 133B]

Power to collect information is an important function of an income-tax authority. An income-tax authority is empowered to collect information which may be useful or relevant for the purposes of this Act.

An income-tax authority means a Joint Commissioner, an Assistant Director, or Deputy Director or an Assessing Officer. It includes an Inspector of Income Tax who is authorised by the Assessing Officer to exercise such power in the area in respect of which the Assessing Officer exercises jurisdiction.

Entering any Building/Place at which business is carried on for collecting information useful or relevant to the purposes of this Act [Sec. 133B(1)] - An income-tax authority may enter any building or place at which business or profession is carried on provided such building or place falls within the limit of the area assigned to him or is occupied by a person in respect of whom he exercises jurisdiction.

The income-tax authority may require any proprietor, employee or any other person, attending in any manner such business or profession, to furnish such information as he may require. Such information should be furnished in Form No. 45D under Income-tax Rule 112E.

Entry time [Sec. 133B(2)] - An income-tax authority may enter any place of business or profession during business hours.

No removal of cash, stock or other valuable article or thing [Sec. 133B(3)] - An income-tax authority has no power to remove or cause to be removed any cash, stock or other valuable article or thing from the place he has entered.

Power to call for information by prescribed income-tax authority [Sec. 133C]

Principal Director General or Director General or Principal Director or Director may require any person to furnish information or documents, verified in the prescribed manner, which may be useful or relevant to any inquiry or proceedings under this Act for the purposes of verification of information in their possession [Sec. 133C(1)].

In order to expedite the verification and analysis of information and documents so received, Sec. 133C(2)where any information or document has been received in response to the aforesaid notice, the prescribed income-tax authority may process such information or document and utilise such information and document in accordance with the scheme notified under Sec.135A(3) and make available the outcome of such processing to the AO [Sec. 133C(2)].

Faceless Collection of Information [Sec. 135A]

Taxation and Other Laws (Relaxation and Amendment of Certain Provisions) Act, 2020 w.e.f. 1-11-2020 has inserted a new section 135A to empower the Central government to make a scheme for faceless:

(*a*) Collecting information under Sec. 133 or Sec. 133B or Sec. 133C; or

(*b*) Exercising power to inspect the register of companies under Sec. 134; or

(*c*) Exercising the power of Assessing Officer under Sec. 135

For the purpose of giving effect to the scheme the Central Government may by notification direct that any provision of this act shall not apply or shall apply with such exceptions, modifications and adaptations as may be specified in the notification. [Sec 135A(2)]. Every notification issued under this section as soon as may be after the notification is issued, be laid before each House of Parliament. [Sec. 135A(3)].

Consequently, Sec.133C(2), which provides for the processing of information or documents received and making available outcome to the Assessing Officer, has also been amended to provide that the prescribed Income-tax authority may process and utilise such information and documents in accordance with the scheme made under section 133C(3) (Centralised Verification Scheme, 2019) or the provisions of section 135A (Faceless Collection of Information).

The Board may make a scheme for centralised issuance of notice and for processing of information or documents and making available the outcome of the processing to the AO. In exercise of such power, the CBDT *vide* Notification No. 5/2019 dated 30-1-2019, notified the Centralised Verification Scheme, 2019 [Sec.133C(3)]. Since, the Central Government has been empowered to form a new Faceless Scheme for the collection of information under Sec. 135A, the Centralised Verification Scheme, 2019 shall cease to exist the day when the Faceless Scheme comes into effect. [Sec. 133C(4)].

Power to Inspect Register of Companies [Sec. 134]

The Assessing Officer or the Deputy Commissioner (Appeals) or the Joint Commissioner, or the Commissioner (Appeals) or any subordinate authority, authorised by any of them in writing, may inspect any register of the members, debenture holders or mortgages of any company and may take their copies or copy of any entry therein.

Power of Principal Director-General or Director General, or Principal Director or Director, Principal Chief Commissioner or Commissioner or Principal Commissioner or Commissioner and Joint Commissioner to make any inquiry [Sec. 135]

Any such authority is competent to make any enquiry under this Act for this purpose. Such authority has got all the powers which are vested in an Assessing Officer under this Act in relation to the making of enquiries.

e-Verification Scheme, 2021

In exercise of the powers conferred by section 135A(1), (2), the Central Government *vide* Notification No. 137 /2021, dated 13-12-2021 has notified e-Verification Scheme, 2021. The same is effective from 13-12-2021. The Scheme applies with respect to collecting information under sections 133, 133B, 133C, the exercise of power to inspect registers of companies under section 134, and exercise of the power of AO under section 135. The Scheme shall be applicable to verify the mismatch of the information uploaded to the assessee's registered account. Where the mismatch between the amount accepted by the assessee and the amount reported by the reporting entity persists, the information after initial e-verification shall be run through a risk management strategy laid down by the Board. The information found to be no/low risk on such risk criteria or where no further action is required shall be processed for closure.

Proceeding before an Income-tax Authority to be Judicial Proceedings [Sec. 136]

Any proceeding under this Act before an income-tax authority is deemed to be a judicial proceeding within the meaning of Secs. 193, 228 and for the purposes of Sec. 196 of the Indian Penal Code and every income-tax authority is deemed to be a Civil Court for the purposes of Sec. 195 of the Code of Criminal Procedure but not for the purpose of Chapter XXVI of the Code of Criminal Procedure, 1973 (that is, provisions as to offences affecting the administration of justice).

Thus, if any false statement is made in proceeding before the Assessing Officer, a criminal court may take cognisance of the offence on a written complaint made by the Assessing Officer and such person may be punishable with imprisonment as per law [*Lalji Haridas* v. *State of Maharashtra* (1964) 52 ITR 423 (SC)].

Intentional insult to a public servant sitting in judicial proceeding is punishable under Sec. 228 of the Indian Penal Code with simple imprisonment for a term which may extend to six months or with fine which may extend to ₹ 1,000, or with both.

Intentional false evidence under Sec. 193 of Indian Penal Code is punishable with imprisonment which may extend to seven years. Similarly, anyone who represents knowingly a false evidence as true, is punishable under Sec. 196 of the Indian Penal Code in the same manner as if he has made a fabricated false evidence under Sec. 193 of the IPC.

Proceedings under FERA cannot be the Basis of Prosecution under Income-tax Act

Income-tax authorities cannot launch a prosecution for perjury on the basis of a statement recorded by the enforcement officer under the Foreign Exchange Regulation Act, 1973.

Income-tax proceedings are entirely different from and dissimilar to proceedings under FERA. Therefore, the ITO in exercise of his power under Sec. 136 cannot make use of statements recorded by the Enforcement Directorate for prosecuting deponents of those statements in a separate and independent proceeding under the Income-tax Act, on the ground that the deponents had retracted their statements given before the Enforcement Directorate [*K.T.M.S. Mohammed* v. *Union of India* (1992) 65 Taxman 130/197 ITR 196 (SC)].

CHAPTER 21

Procedure for Assessment

INTRODUCTION

Having earned income in a previous year, the assessee is required to pay tax on such income in the immediately following assessment year. For this purposes it is essential that every assessee makes an 'assessment' of its tax liability. In simple words, assessment means an estimation of the total income earned by an assessee and computation of tax payable on such income. The details of such incomes and taxes that may have already been paid by virtue of advance tax or TDS on income etc. is furnished by the assessee by filing a return of income. The correctness or otherwise of such returns filed by the assessee is then verified by the Income-tax.

After the expiry of the previous year in the prescribed form by the due date specified in this behalf [Sec. 139(1)]. Where a person fails to furnish voluntary return, the Assessing Officer may issue a notice to him to furnish such return [Sec. 142(1)(*ii*)].

Thereafter, the Assessing Officer is required to assess the income or loss, earned or suffered by the assessee. For this purpose, the Assessing Officer may require an assessee to produce books of account and such other information as he may require [Sec. 142].

Depending on facts of a case, the Assessing Officer may make a summary assessment [Sec. 143(1)] or scrutiny assessment [Sec. 143(3)]. Where the assessee does not comply with statutory obligations, the Assessing Officer may proceed to assess him to the best of his judgment [Sec. 144.].

He is empowered to assess an income escaping assessment (under sec. 147) and to assess an income in search proceedings (under Sec. 153A). He is required to complete all types of assessment within the prescribed time-limit (under sec. 153) and to rectify any mistake, if any, therein (under sec. 154 and sec. 155).

Finally, the Assessing Officer determines the tax liability of the assessee on the total income assessed by him. Due credit is given for pre-paid taxes by way of advance tax [Sec. 210] or tax deducted/collected at source [Sections 192 to 206C] or self-assessment tax, paid on furnishing the return of income [Sec. 140A] or double taxation relief due to the assessee (under sec. 90A).

If any tax is found due from the assessee, a 'Demand Notice' is issued to him for collecting such tax [Sec. 156].

The Figure below explains the same.

FIGURE 21.1: PROCEDURE FOR ASSESSMENT

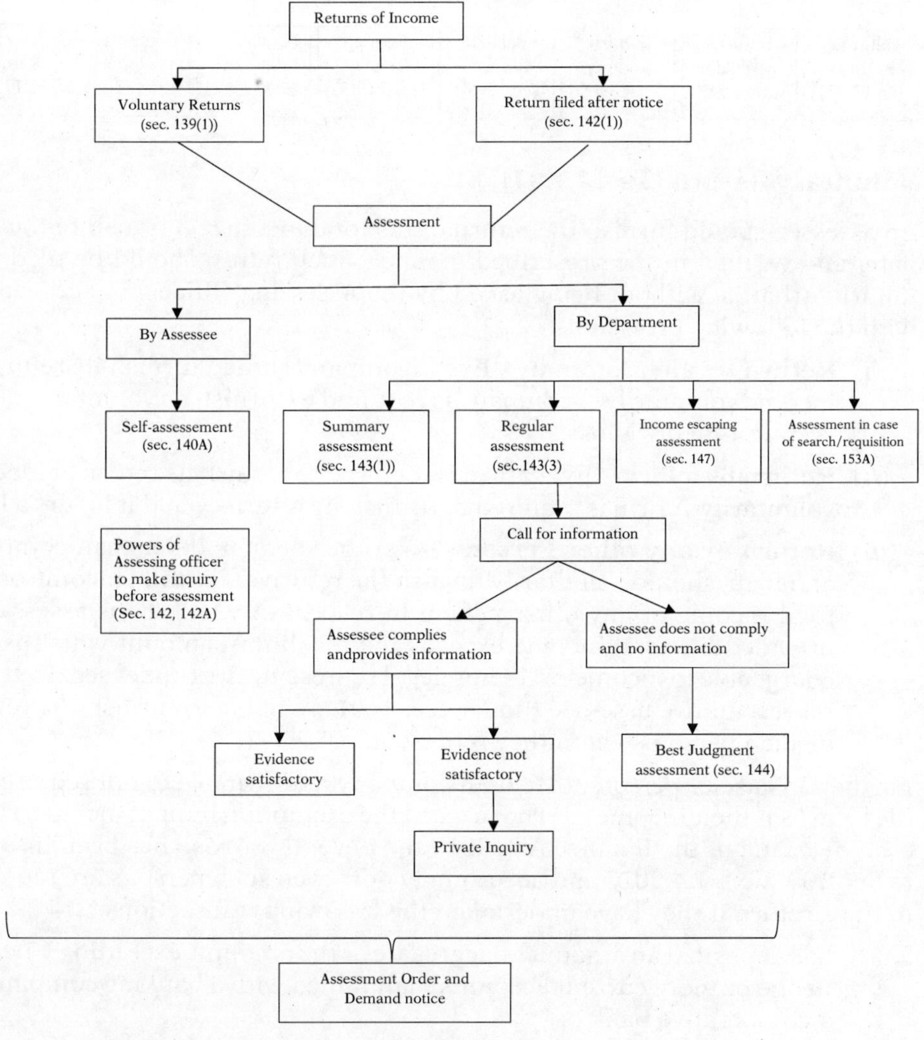

FILING THE RETURN OF INCOME [SEC. 139]

The following are the various returns that are filed:

FIGURE 21.2: OVERVIEW OF VARIOUS RETURNS

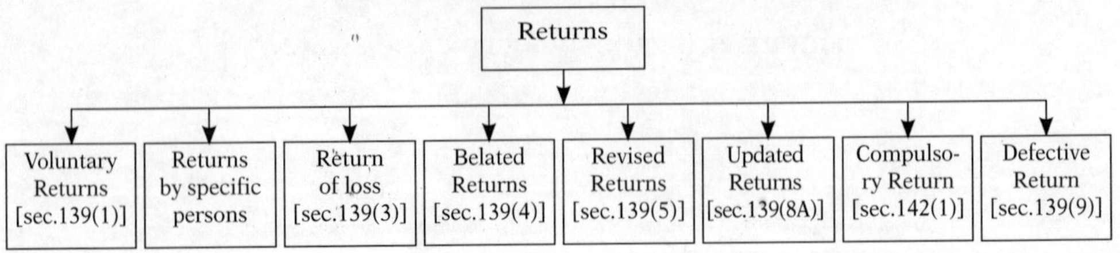

Voluntary Return [Sec. 139(1)]

An assessee should furnish the return of his total income on or before the due date, and verified in the prescribed manner. Such return should be filed voluntarily (that is, without being asked by the Assessing Officer) in accordance with the following provisions:

(*i*) **Return by any Company** - Every company should furnish its return of income voluntarily. A company is required to furnish its voluntary return even if it incurs a loss.

(*ii*) **Return by a Firm** - Every firm is required to furnish its return of income voluntarily. A firm is required to furnish its return even if it incurs a loss.

(*iii*) **Return by any other Person** - Any other person, other than company and firm, should voluntarily furnish the return of his total income or the total income of any other person in respect of which he is assessable, provided his total income exceeds the maximum amount which is not chargeable to income-tax. Thus, legal representative (under sec. 159) and representative assessee (under sec. 160) are liable to furnish the return of such persons whom they represent.

Further, in case of person other than company and firm, were not required to file returns if their incomes did not exceed the exemption limit of income. However, by virtue of the Finance Act, 2019 the Seventh Proviso has been inserted to Sec.139 w.e.f. 1.4.2020 and accordingly now even such persons are required to file a return if they have undertaken the following transactions:

(*a*) has deposited an amount or aggregate of the amounts exceeding ₹ 1 crore in one or more current accounts maintained with a banking company or a co-operative bank or

(*b*) has incurred expenditure of an amount or aggregate of the amounts exceeding ₹ 2 lakh for himself or any other person for travel to a foreign country or

(*c*) has incurred expenditure of an amount or aggregate of the amounts exceeding ₹ 1 lakh towards consumption of electricity or

(*d*) fulfils such other conditions as may be prescribed. [Fourth Proviso to Sec. 139(1)].

Further (*i*) the assessee is 'resident' other than 'not ordinarily resident' in India during the previous year; and

(*ii*) he holds, as a beneficial owner or otherwise, any asset (including financial interest in any entity) located outside India or has signing authority in any account located outside India.

or

he is a beneficiary of any asset (including any financial interest in any entity) located outside India. It is operative w.e.f. 1-4-2016.

'Beneficial owner' in respect of an asset means an individual who has provided, directly or indirectly, consideration for the asset for the immediate or future benefit, direct or indirect, of himself or any other person [*Explanation 4* to Sec. 139(1)].

'Beneficiary' in respect of an asset means an individual who derives benefit from the asset during the previous year and the consideration for the asset has been provided by any person other than the beneficiary [*Explanation 5* to Sec. 139(1)].

A co-operative society or a local authority is always required to furnish the return of its total income because the minimum exemption limit, not chargeable to tax, applies only to an individual, an HUF, an association of persons or body of individuals and artificial juridical person.

Non-residents not to file voluntary return in certain cases where tax has been deducted at source:

1. An assessee, having taxable income, exceeding the exemption limit, is required to furnish the voluntary return under Sec. 139(1). However, no return is required to be furnished, by a non-resident in the following cases provided tax has been deducted at source:

   (*i*) **Investment Income and Long-term Capital Gain [Sec. 115G] -** Where the total income of a non-resident Indian consisted only of investment income or income by way of long-term capital gains or both, no return is required to be furnished, provided the tax deductible at source has been deducted.

   "Investment income" means any income derived from a foreign exchange asset [Sec. 115C(*c*)].

   (*ii*) **Dividends and Interest [Sec. 115A(5)] -** Where the total income of a non-resident or a foreign company consists of only

   (*a*) by way of dividends, other than dividends referred to under Sec. 115-O, or

   (*b*) interest from government or Indian concern on moneys borrowed or debt incurred in foreign currency, or

   (*c*) interest received from an infrastructure debt fund referred to in Sec. 10(*47*);

   (*d*) Income by way of interest from an Indian Company;

(*e*) Income by way of interest on certain bonds and Government securities;

(*f*) Income by way of interest from a business trust to its unit holder;

(*g*) income from units of UTI or mutual fund [Specified under Sec. 10(*23D*)], purchased in foreign currency and the tax, deductible at source, has been deducted, no return is required to be furnished; or

(*h*) royalty or fees for technical services received from the government or an Indian concern, pursuant to an agreement approved by the Central Government or where it relates to a matter of industrial policy [Sec. 115A(5)].

(*iii*) **Dividends and Interest on Bonds/Shares, sold by Government [Sec. 115AC(4)] -** Where the total income of a non-resident assessee consists of only (*a*) by way of dividends other than dividends referred to under Sec. 115-O on certain Global Depository Receipts, or (*b*) interest on bonds of an Indian company or a public sector company sold by government, subscribed in convertible foreign exchange and the tax deductible at source has been deducted, no return is required to be furnished.

(*iv*) **Income from Participation of Games and other activities in India [Sec. 115BBA(2)] -** Where a non-resident foreign national receives any income by way of participation (*a*) in any game, (other than the winnings under Sec. 115BB) or (*b*) sports or (*c*) advertisement or (*d*) contribution of articles on sports events in India in newspapers/journals/magazines, and (*e*) tax deductible at source on such income has been deducted, it is not necessary for him to furnish the return of income.

(*v*) **Any amount relating to any Game played in India [Sec. 115BBA(2)] -** Where any sports association or institution receives any amount guaranteed to be paid or payable, in relation to (*a*) any game (other than winnings under Sec. 115BB) or (*b*) sport played in India, and (*c*) tax deductible at source has been deducted, it is not necessary for it to furnish the return of such income.

(*vi*) **Performance by an Entertainer [Sec. 115BBA(2)] -** Where any entertainer who is not a citizen of India and is a non-resident has earned the income through their performance in India, and tax deductible at source has been deducted, it is not necessary for them to furnish the return of such income.

TIME-LIMIT FOR FURNISHING VOLUNTARY RETURN [EXPLANATION 2 TO SEC. 139(1)]

From the assessment year 2001-02 and subsequent years, the return should be furnished on or before the due date which has been prescribed as follows:

TABLE 21.1: DUE DATES FOR FILING RETURN

Status of the assessee	Due date for furnishing return of income
1. Where the assessee is a company	by 31st October of the AY
2. Where the assessee is a person other than company:	
(*i*) Where accounts of the assessee are required to be audited under this Act or under any other law for the time being in force.	by 31st October of the AY
(*ii*) Where the assessee is a working partner of a firm whose accounts are required to be audited under this Act or under any other law for the time in force.	by 30th November of the AY
3. Where the assessee has entered into an international transaction or specified domestic transaction.	by 30th November
4. Where the return is furnished by any other assessee	by 31st July of the AY

When the last date of return is a holiday, return is to be filed on the next day - Where the last day for filing return of income/loss is a day on which the office is closed, the assessee may file the return on the next day afterwards on which the office is open. In such cases, the return is considered to have been filed within the specified time-limit [Circular No. 639 dated 13 November 1992].

Salaried person may furnish voluntary return through his employer [Sec. 139(1A)] - From the assessment year 2002-03 and onward, a salaried employee has the option to furnish his return of income through his employer who is liable to furnish 'Bulk Return' to the designated Assessing Officer on or before the due date of furnishing return.

The CBDT has notified two schemes for this purpose. The essential features of the two schemes are explained as below:

Electronic furnishing of returns of income [Sec. 139(1B) r.w. sec. 139D] - From the assessment year 2003-04, any assessee has the option to furnish a return of income for any previous year in accordance with a specified scheme in such form (including on a floppy diskette, magnetic cartridge tape, CD-ROM or any other computer readable media) as may be prescribed. The Board under Sec. 139D may make rules providing for—

(*i*) the class or classes of persons who are required to furnish the return in electronic form;

(*ii*) the form and manner in which the return in electronic form may be furnished;

(*iii*) the documents, statements, receipts, certificates or audited reports which may not be furnished along with the return in electronic form but have to be produced on demand before the assessing officer;

(*iv*) the computer resource or the electronic record to which the return in electronic form may be transmitted.

Exemption from filing return of income [Sec. 139(1C)] - The Central Government may exempt any class or classes of persons from the requirement of furnishing the return of income, subject to such conditions as may be specified.

Compulsory return under the order of the Assessing Officer [Sec. 142(1)(i)] - Where a person has not made a return of income before the end of the time allowed under Sec. 139(1) or before the end the relevant assessment year, the Assessing Officer may serve a notice on him after the end of the relevant assessment year, requiring him to furnish the return.

Such person has to furnish the return even if his taxable income is below the taxable limit or he is not otherwise assessable under any other provisions of the Act. Return should be furnished in the prescribed form, verified in the prescribed manner and setting forth such particulars as may be prescribed.

Compulsory return of loss, intended to be carried forward for future Set-off [Sec. 139(3)] - Where in any previous year, any person has sustained business loss or speculation loss under the head 'Profits and Gains from Business or Profession' or loss computed in respect of any specified business referred to in Sec. 35AD or long-term/short-term capital loss under the head 'Capital Gains' or loss from the activity of owning and maintaining race horses under the head 'income from other sources' and he intends to carry forward the loss for being set-off in future in accordance with law, he should furnish the return of loss, within the prescribed time-limit under Sec. 139(1), in the prescribed form, and containing such other particulars as may be prescribed [under Income-tax Rules 12 and 12A].

A company assessee is statutorily bound to furnish a loss return within the prescribed time-limit under Sec. 139(1). Intention to carry forward the loss is not relevant here.

Belated return be furnished within one year 'from the end of the assessment year' but before the assessment is completed [Sec. 139(4)] - Where any person has not filed a voluntary return within the time-limit allowed to him under Sec. 139(1), he may furnish such return for any previous year at any time before the expiry of one year from the end of the relevant assessment year or before completion of the assessment, whichever is earlier. Thus, the last date to file the revised or belated return is 31st March of the relevant Assessment Year.

According to the amended sec. 139(4) under the Finance Act, 2021 for the assessment year 2021-22 and subsequent assessment years, belated return can be filed at any time within three months prior to the end of the relevant assessment year or before completion of the assessment, whichever is earlier *i.e.* 31st December of the relevant Assessment Year.

Liability of Interest - The assessee remains liable for interest under Sec. 234A for late furnishing of return.

Trustees Required to Furnish Return of Charitable or Religious Trust [Sec. 139(4A)] - Every person in receipt of income derived from (*i*) voluntary contribution or (*ii*) property held under trust or other legal obligation wholly, or in part, for charitable or religious purposes, has to furnish return if the total income (computed without giving effect to the provisions of Sections 11 and 12) exceeds the exemption limit.

The return should be furnished by trustees in accordance with the provisions of Sec. 139(1) as aforesaid.

Return of Income of Political Party [Sec. 139(4B)] - If the total income of a political party (computed without giving effect to the provisions of Sec. 13A) exceeds the exemption limit, the chief executive officer of such a party (whether known as Secretary or by any other designation) is required to furnish the return of income in accordance with the provisions of Sec. 139(1).

Filing Return of Income by certain Associations, Institutions, Trust and Funds [Sec. 139(4C)] - Ignoring the exemption provisions of Sec. 10, if the total income of certain prescribed institution, fund, trust, association and such other institution exceeds the maximum limit which is not chargeable to tax, it is required to furnish the return of its income in the prescribed form, verified in the prescribed manner, setting forth such other particulars as may be prescribed. Such return should be furnished as if it were a return required to be furnished under Sec. 139(1).

Prescribed institution/association/fund/trust others are given below:

(*i*) Research association [Sec. 10(*21*)].

(*ii*) News agency [Sec. 10(*23B*)].

(*iii*) Professional association [Sec. 10(*23A*)].

(*iv*) Trust or institution promoting Khadi and village industries [Sec. 10(*23B*)].

(*v*) Any university or other educational institution whose receipts do not exceed ₹ 5 crore [Sec. 10(*23C*)(*iiiad*) or (*iiiab*)].

(*vi*) Any hospital or medical institution whose receipts do not exceed ₹ 5 crore [Sec. 10(*23C*)(*iiiae*) or (*iiiac*)].

(*vii*) Notified fund or institution [Sec. 10(*23C*)(*iv*)].

(*viii*) Notified trust or institution for public religious purposes [Sec.10(*23C*)(*v*)].

(*ix*) Any university or educational institution or a hospital or medical institution provided it is not wholly or mainly financed by government and its annual receipts do not exceed ₹ 5 crore [Sec. 10(*23C*)(*vi*)(*via*)].

(*x*) Registered trade union [Sec. 10(*24*)].

(*xi*) Any body or authority or Board or Trust, constituted by the Central Government or State Government for regulating any activity for the benefit of general public.

(*xii*) Infrastructure debt fund, set up in accordance with the guidelines notified by the Central Government.

Return by scientific research association or a University, or College or other Institution [Sec. 139(4D)] - Where any of the aforesaid entity gets any donation to be used for scientific research [Sec. 35(1)(*ii*)] or research in social science or statistical research [Sec. 35(1)(*iii*)], it has to furnish the return of its total income in accordance with the provisions of Sec. 139(1).

Return to be furnished by business trust [Sec. 139(4E)] - Every business trust, which is not required to furnish the return of income or loss under any other provision of this section, is liable to furnish the return of its income or loss in every previous year as if it is a return furnished under sec. 139(1).

Return to be furnished by investment fund [Sec. 139(4F)] - Every 'investment fund' (under Sec. 115UB), which is not required to furnish the return of income or loss under any other provision of this section, is liable to furnish the return of income in respect of its income or loss in every previous year as if it is a return, furnished under Sec. 139(1).

Revised Return furnished to rectify any mistake or omission [Sec. 139(5)] - If any person has furnished a voluntary return [Sec. 139(1)] or a belated return [Sec. 139(4)] and if he discovers any omission or wrong statement, not made knowingly or deliberately, he may furnish a revised return at any time before the expiry of one year from the end of the relevant assessment year or before completion of the assessment, whichever is earlier.

According to the amended Sec. 139(4) under the Finance Act, 2021 for the assessment year 2021-22 and subsequent assessment years, revised return can be filed at any time within three months prior to the end of the relevant assessment year or before completion of the assessment, whichever is earlier *i.e.* 31st December of the relevant assessment year.

Revised Return Restores Rectification of Accidental Mistakes - The right to file a revised return can be exercised to restore an omission or correct a wrong statement when it was inadvertent or accidental and not deliberate.

A second revised return may also be furnished correcting omission or wrong statement made in the first revised return [*Niranjan Lal Ram Chandra* v. *CIT* [1982] 134 ITR 352 (All.)]. It is the right of the assessee to furnish a revised return and no application for permission from the Assessing Officer is necessary [*Waman Padmanabh Dande* v. *CIT* [1952] 22 ITR 339 (Nag.)].

Right to file revised return cannot be exercised to change the method of Accounting - The right to furnish a revised return cannot be exercised to rewrite the books by changing the method of accounting [*Deepnarayan Nagu & Co.* v. *CIT* [1985] 21 Taxman 222/[1986] 157 ITR 37 (MP)].

Revised Return cannot be a Device to Condone the Consequence of False Return - Deliberate omissions, false and fraudulent statements fall outside the purview of revised return [*K.M. Bhatia* v. *CIT* [1992] 62 Taxman 430/193 ITR 379 (Guj.)].

The benefit of filing a revised return cannot be claimed by a person who has initially filed a return, knowing it to be false [*Addl. CIT* v. *Radhey Shyam* [1979] 1 Taxman 29/[1980] 123 ITR 125 (All.)]

Revised return does not condone penalty and prosecution for a deliberate false return, contained under Sec. 271 and Sec. 277.

Revision by Firm makes the Partners liable to Revise their Returns - If firm files a revised return, it is necessary that its partners should also file their revised returns [*N. Seenappa* v. *ITO* [1974] 97 ITR 528 (Mysore)].

Revised Return Dates Back to the Date of Original Return - When a revised return is furnished, the original return is deemed to have been withdrawn and substituted by a fresh return. A revised return merely makes good the shortcomings in the original return from which it suffered. Therefore, a revised return must be considered as filed when the original return was filed for the purpose of calculation of interest under Sec. 234A [*Dhampur Sugar Mills Ltd.* v. *CIT* [1973] 90 ITR 236 (All.)].

Case Law : ***Pr.CIT* v. *Babubhai Ramanbhai Patel* [(2017) 84 taxman.com 32/249 Taxman 470 (Guj.)]**

Facts: 'B' filed their return of income under Sec. 139(1) on 30 October 2005, where only taxable income was declared, and there was no mention of any speculation loss being suffered. However, when subsequently 'B' revised the return under Sec. 139(5), they included certain amount as speculation loss which was sought to be carried forward. The Assessing Officer rejected this claim on the grounds that it was not raised in the original return.

Held: When the return is duly revised within the prescribed time limits set by Sec. 139(5), the original return would no longer survive. Assessee's claim for carry forward of speculation loss was allowed.

DEFECTIVE RETURN [SEC. 139(9) R.W. EXPLANATION]

Provisions regarding defective returns are summarised below:

Return suffering from a Specified Defect is treated as Defective Return - While furnishing the return of income, an assessee is required to comply with certain conditions, laid down in *Explanation* to Sec. 139(9). If any such condition is not complied with, the return is treated as suffering from a defect and is called a defective return.

Conditions Only Illustrative and Not Exhaustive - The conditions laid down in the *Explanation* to Sec. 139(9) are only illustrative and not exhaustive [*CIT* v. *Rai Bahadur Bissesswarlal Motilal Malwasie Trust* [1992] 65 Taxman 273/195 ITR 825 (Cal.)]. Thus, on facts of a case, the Assessing Officer may treat a return as suffering from a defect, even though such defect is not covered by the said explanation.

Cases of Defective Return

The return is treated defective in the following cases:

(i) **Information about Income Computation not Furnished** - Where the annexures, statements and columns in the return relating to computation of income under each head, gross total income or total income have not been duly filled; or

(ii) **Tax Computation Statement Not Attached with the Return** - Where the return is not accompanied by the statement showing computation of tax payable; or

(iii) **Claiming Tax Credit without Attaching Proof of Payment** - Where the assessee claims tax credit in respect of advance tax or tax paid on self-assessment but fails to furnish the proof of payment along with the return.

Similarly, where the assessee claims tax credit for tax deducted at source but fails to attach a certificate of tax deducted at source or collected at source, the return is treated as defective.

However, the return of income is not treated defective if the certificate under Sec. 203 or Sec. 206 is not furnished by the deductor to the deductee and such certificate is produced within 2 years specified under Sec. 155(14).

(iv) **Assessee maintaining books of account but Accounting Statements not attached with return** - Where regular books of account are maintained but the copies of manufacturing account, trading account, profit and loss account or income and expenditure account or any other similar statements and balance sheet are not furnished along with the return; or

(v) **Information relevant to income computation not disclosed in a case where books of account not maintained** - Where regular books of account have not been maintained but the return is not accompanied by a statement indicating *(a)* the amount of turnover/gross receipt/gross profit, *(b)* expenses, *(c)* net profit and basis of computation, *(d)* total debtors and creditors, *(e)* closing stock, and *(f)* cash balance at the end of the accounting years; or

(vi) **Return Not Accompanied with Audited Accounts** - Where accounts have been audited but the copies of audited profit and loss account, balance sheet and auditor's report including cost audit report [where cost audit was conducted under Sec. 233B] have not been furnished along with the return; or

Where the accounts of a government company could not be audited because of the delay in the appointment of the auditors by the government and therefore, the return is furnished along with the provisional accounts to meet the requirements of due date under Sec. 139(1), it is to be treated as invalid return and the Assessing Officer may make best judgment assessment [*U.P. Rajya Vidyut Utpadan Nigam Ltd*. v. *Dy. CIT* [1993] 202 ITR 93 (All.)]; or

(*vii*) **Report of compulsory audit not attached with the return of income -** Where compulsory audit is required under Sec. 44AB but the report of such audit has not been furnished along with the return, or where the report of such audit has been furnished prior to the filing of the return but a copy of audit report under Sec. 44AB along with the proof of furnishing the report has not been filed along with the return; or

(*viii*) **Sole proprietor return not accompanied with a copy of his personal account -** In the case of sole proprietory business or profession, where the return is not accompanied by the copy of personal account of the proprietor; or

(*ix*) (*a*) **Return of firm/AOP/BOI not accompanied with a copy of the personal account of its partners/members -** Where a firm or AOP or BOI submits its return but individual personal account of the partner or member is not attached with that return, it is treated a defective return; or

(*b*) **Return of a partner of firm or a member of AOP/BOI not Accompanied with a Copy of his account in the Firm/AOP/BOI -** Where a partner of a firm or member of an Association of Persons or Body of Individuals submits his return of income without a copy of his account with said firm/AOP/BOI, such return is treated as defective.

Case Law : ***Dy. CIT* v. *Kunal Structure (India) Pvt. Ltd*. [2021] 123 taxmann. com 392/277 Taxman 401(SC)**

Facts: 'K' being a company filed its return on income on 10 September 2016. It then received a notice on 17 June 2017, intimating that the return was defective, and which granted time until 20 July 2017 to rectify the same. 'K' rectified the return and submitted it on 7 July 2017. The return was subsequently processed, and on 9 August 2018, 'K' received another notice that its return on income was selected for scrutiny. The assessee challenged this notice as being time barred, on the grounds that under Sec. 143(2), such notice must be sent before six months from the end of the financial year in which the return is furnished. The issue was whether the limitation period commences from the date of the original return which is 10 September 2016 or the date when rectified return of was filed that is 7 July 2017.

Held: For the purpose of computing the time period for limitation under Sec. 143(2), it is the date of filing of the original return which would be taken into account, and not the date on which the defects actually came to be removed. Therefore, the impugned notice being substantially after the period of limitation on its issuance, it was barred by such limitation and was not sustainable.

15 days' time to be allowed to the assessee to rectify the defects - The Assessing Officer is required to intimate such defect to the assessee and to allow him 15 days from the date of intimation to rectify such defect.

Extension of Time-limit - The Assessing Officer is empowered to extend the time-limit if the assessee makes an application seeking extension of time. The Assessing Officer may also allow further extension on the merits of the case.

Rectification of defect after the expiry of the Time-limit but before completion of the assessment - Where the assessee fails to rectify the defect within the time allowed or within extended time-limit, but rectifies before the assessment is made, the Assessing Officer may condone the defect and return may not be treated as invalid.

Defective return to be treated as invalid return when defect not rectified - Where the assessee does not rectify the defect, the Assessing Officer treats the return as invalid and other provisions of the Act will as if the assessee has failed to file the return.

The Assessing Officer may proceed according to the best of his judgment under Sec. 144.

Distinction between a defective return and invalid return - A defective return is not treated *ipso facto* as invalid return. It is only when the return contains any of the specified defects, the Assessing Officer communicates it to assessee but he fails to rectify the same within the specified time, the Assessing Officer may treat such return as invalid [*Kerala State Bamboo Corporation Ltd.* v. *CIT* (1998) 101 Taxman 296/(1999) 236 ITR 288 (Ker.)].

Provisions of defective return overrides the provisions of sec. 292B - Sec. 292B provides that return furnished cannot be deemed to be invalid merely by reason of any defect or omission in such return of income if such return of income is in conformity with the intent and purpose of this Act. However, the provisions of Sec. 139(9) would override other provisions of the Act including Sec. 292B [*National Insurance Co. Ltd.* v. *CIT* (1994) 72 Taxman 161/(1995) 213 ITR 862 (Cal.)].

Updated Return [Sec. 139(8A)] (newly inserted by the Finance Act, 2022) - In a move towards encouraging voluntary tax compliance and reducing tax litigation, a new provision has been inserted by the Finance Act, 2022. Sec. 139(8A) allows filing an updated return of income by any person, whether he has filed a return previously for the relevant assessment year, or not. Accordingly, any person may furnish an updated return for the relevant previous year within two years from the end of the relevant assessment year. Thus, Sec. 139(8A) provides a period of upto 2 years for filing such updated returns which is longer than the existing provisions say under sec. 139(4) (belated returns) or sec. 139(5) (revised return) which offer approximately 5 months to individual assessee, 2 months to company assessee and 1 month to an assessee entering into international transaction. However, such updated return will be accompanied with a payment of an amount equal to 25% as additional tax on tax and interest due where the updated return was filed after the time lines of belated returns and revised returns but before two years. Such additional tax will be 50% of the tax and interest due where updated return is filed after one year but before two years. [Sec. 140B which is newly inserted by the Finance Act, 2022 provide for this tax on updated return]. It is expected that such extended time of 2 years will nudge assessees for compliance and result in additional revenues for the government in a litigation free environment.

However, an updated return cannot be filed if the same is a return of loss or results in a refund or increases the refund due or decreases the total tax liability determined in earlier return. Further an updated return of an already updated return is not allowed.

Updated return cannot be filed in the following situations :

(*a*) where certain search proceedings has been initiated under section 132 or books of account or other documents or any assets are requisitioned under section 132A or

(*b*) where a survey has been conducted under section 133A or

(*c*) where a notice has been issued to the effect that any money, bullion, jewellery or valuable article or thing, seized or requisitioned under section 132 or section 132A in the case of any other person belongs to such person

(*d*) where a notice has been issued to the effect that any books of account or documents, seized or requisitioned under section 132 or section 132A in the case of any other person

(e) any proceeding for assessment or reassessment or recomputation or revision of income under this Act is pending or has been completed

(*f*) against whom criminal prosecution under Chapter XXII have been initiated for the relevant assessment year or

(*g*) any information has been received under specified under the Smugglers and Foreign Exchange Manipulators (Forfeiture of Property) Act, 1976 or the Prohibition of Benami Property Transactions Act, 1988 or the Prevention of Money-laundering Act, 2002 or the Black Money (Undisclosed Foreign Income and Assets) and Imposition of Tax Act, 2015 and the same has been communicated to him or under information exchange agreements with foreign countries.

The Central Board of Direct Taxes (CBDT) is also empowered to notify any person or class of person, who will not be eligible to file an Updated Return.

Difference between updated return and revised return - Updated return offers an opportunity to file update return even if the assessee may not have filed for the relevant assessment year. Revised Return can only be filed if the assessee have filed a return in the relevant assessment year. Updated return can be filed only if there is increase in tax liability. Revised return can be filed irrespective of the increase or decrease in tax liability.

Power of the Board to dispense with furnishing documents, etc., with the Return [Sec. 139C] - The Board may make rules providing for a class or classes of persons who may not be required to furnish documents, statements, receipts, certificates, audited reports, or any other documents, which are otherwise under any other provisions of this Act, except Sec. 139D, required to be furnished, along with the return but to be produced on demand before the Assessing Officer. The Board may also make rules to dispense with any condition treating a return as defective under clauses (*a*) to (*f*) under Sec. 139(9).

The Board may also include any of the conditions under clauses (*a*) to (*f*) under Sec. 139(9) in the Form of the return prescribed under Sec. 139(1) or Sec. 139(6).

Return by whom to be verified [Sec. 140] - Return of income should be signed and verified by the assessee. If a return is not signed and verified, it is not merely an inaccurate or incomplete return but it is not a return at all.

Unsigned return to be treated as invalid - If a return is filed without signature and verification, it is treated as invalid return [*Khialdas & Sons* v. *CIT* [1997] 94 Taxman 394/225 ITR 960 (MP)].

Unsigned return cannot be validated by issue of a notice - Signing and verification of a return is a mandatory requirement without which the return is treated as invalid. A notice issued under Sec. 143(2) in response to an unsigned and unverified return does not validate such invalid return [*Electrical Instrument Co.* v. *CIT* [2001] 116 Taxman 807/250 ITR 734 (Delhi)].

PERMANENT ACCOUNT NUMBER (PAN) [SEC. 139A]

Provisions relating to Permanent Account Number (PAN) are explained as below:

PAN Defined [Explanations (b), (c) to Sec. 139A] - The Permanent Account Number (PAN) is a ten-digit alphanumeric number, issued for the purpose of identification in the form of a laminated card. PAN is allotted on basis of applications without actual *de facto* clarification of identity or ascertainment of active nature of business activity, just as a facility to revenue to keep track of transactions. Therefore PAN could not be blindly and without consideration of surrounding circumstances treated as sufficiently disclosing identity of individual [*N. Tarika Property Invest. (P.) Ltd.* v. *CIT* [2014] 51 taxmann.com 387/227 Taxman 373 (SC)].

Persons Required to Obtain PAN [Sec. 139A(1), (1A)] - Sec.139A imposes a statutory obligation on the persons specified as below, to apply to the Assessing Officer for the allotment of Permanent Account Number (PAN):

(*i*) **Persons having Taxable Income -** Every person whose total income during any previous year exceeds the maximum amount which is not chargeable to income tax is required to apply for a PAN.

(*ii*) **Persons carrying on business or Profession -** Every person, who is carrying on any business or profession and whose total sales, turnover or gross receipts are or is likely to exceed a prescribed limit of ₹ 5,00,000 is required to apply for PAN. In their case, the question whether they have any taxable income under the Act or not is not at all relevant.

(*iii*) **Persons, being resident, entering into financial transactions exceeding specified limits -** Any resident person, other than an individual, which enters into a financial transaction of an amount aggregating to ₹ 2,50,000 in a financial year is required to apply for a PAN.

(*iv*) **Persons entering into Transactions Prescribed by the Board -** Any persons who intend to enter into such transaction as may be prescribed by the Board in the interest of the revenue

(*v*) **Persons liable to be assessed as representative assessee -** Every person in receipt of income derived from property held under trust or other legal obligation wholly or in part for charitable or religious purposes, and who is liable to be assessed as representative assessee in respect of such income, is also required to apply for PAN.

(*vi*) **Persons notified by the Central Government -** With effect from 1 June 2000, the Central Government may, by Notification, specify any class or classes of persons by whom tax is payable under the Income-tax Act or any tax or duty is payable under any other law [including importers and exporters, whether any tax is payable by them or not] and such persons are required, within the time mentioned in the notification, to apply to the Assessing Officer for allotment of PAN.

(*vii*) **Person notifed by Central Government for collecting certain Information -** For the purpose of collecting certain information which may be useful for or relevant to the purposes of this Act, the Central Government may specify any class of or classes of persons to apply to the Assessing Officer for the allotment of PAN within such time as may be specified. Such person, even if not liable to pay any tax under this Act, or whose turnover does not exceed the specified limit, is required to apply for the allotment of PAN. [Sec. 139A(1B)]. It is operative from 1 June 2006.

(*viii*) **Any other person -** Any person, not covered under the above categories, may apply to the Assessing Officer for the allotment of PAN under Sec. 139(3). In such case, the Assessing Officer is required to allot a PAN to such person 'forthwith'.

Necessity to have PAN [Sec. 139A(5), (5A), (5B), (5C), (6) r. w. Rules 114B, 114C and 114D]

It is statutory obligation to obtain PAN because it is required to be quoted in tax documents and certain financial transactions. Such cases are explained below:

(*i*) **Return, Challan or Correspondence with Income-tax Authority -** PAN is required to be quoted in all returns, correspondence with any income-tax authority, as well as on challan for payment of any sum due under this Act and quote such number in all documents, pertaining to such transactions as may be specified [Sec. 139A(5)].

(*ii*) **Receiving any Income subject to TDS -** Every person receiving any sum or income, from which tax is deducted at source, has to intimate his PAN to the person responsible for deducting such tax. However, such person may intimate General Index Register Number (GIRN) till such time the PAN is allotted [Sec. 139A(5A)].

(*iii*) **Person deducting tax at source to Quote PAN of the payee -** Where any person has paid any sum or income after deducting tax at source, he has to quote PAN of the payee to the tax authorities in any statement furnished under Sec. 192(2C), or in any certificate furnished under Sec. 203 or in all returns furnished in accordance with Sec. 206.

In addition, every person deducting tax is required to quote PAN of the deductee in all quarterly returns, prepared and delivered or cause to be delivered, in accordance with Sec. 200(3). It is operative from 1 June 2006 [Sec. 139A(5B)].

(*iv*) **Intimation of PAN by buyer or licensee or lessee of Alcoholic Liquor and Forest Produce -** Every buyer, licensee or lessee of alcoholic liquor, forest produce, or scrap etc., from a seller, has to intimate his PAN to the person responsible for collecting tax. It is operative from the assessment year 2007-08 and onward [Sec. 139A(5C)].

(*v*) **Every person collecting tax from the buyer of alcoholic liquor and forest produce to quote PAN of the buyer -** Every person collecting tax from the buyer of alcoholic liquor, forest produce, scrap and so on, has to quote PAN of the buyer or licensee or lessee to the tax authorities. [Sec. 139A(5D)].

From 1 June 2006, every person deducting tax is required to quote PAN of the deductee in all quarterly returns prepared and delivered or cause to be delivered in accordance with Sec. 206C(3).

(*vi*) **Quoting PAN in all documents pertaining to economic or Financial Transactions -** If certain economic or financial transactions are entered into on or after 1 November 1998, it is necessary to quote PAN.

***Suo Motu* Allotment of PAN [Sec. 139A(2)] -** The Assessing Officer may also allot PAN to any other person by whom tax is payable. From 1 June 2006, the Assessing Officer is now empowered to allot PAN to any person on the basis of prescribed transactions that come to his notice.

Only one PAN for a Person - A person can have only one PAN under the new series. Sec. 139A(7) of the Act specifically prohibits a person who has been allotted a PAN under the new series from applying, obtaining and possessing another PAN [*See* also, Proviso to Sec. 139A(4)].

Quoting of Aadhaar number [Sec.139AA]

Every person who is eligible to obtain Aadhaar number shall, on or after the 1st day of July, 2017, quote Aadhaar number:

(*i*) in the application form for allotment of permanent account number,

(*ii*) in the return of income.

Where the person does not possess the Aadhaar Number, the Enrolment ID of Aadhaar application form issued to him at the time of enrolment shall be quoted in the application for permanent account number or, as the case may be, in the return of income furnished by him.

Every person who has been allotted permanent account number as on the 1st day of July, 2017, and who is eligible to obtain Aadhaar number, shall intimate his Aadhaar number to such authority in such form and manner as may be prescribed, on or before 31st March, 2020 (Rule 114AAA). Provided that in case of failure to intimate the Aadhaar number, the permanent account number allotted to the person shall be made inoperative after the date so notified in such manner as may be prescribed.

The Finance Act, 2021 has inserted a new Sec. 234H to levy a fee for default in intimating the Aadhaar Number. Any person who is required to intimate his Aadhaar under Sec. 139AA(2) fails to do so shall be liable to pay a fee, as may be prescribed, not exceeding ₹ 1,000 at the time of making such intimation.

TYPES OF ASSESSMENT

Self-assessment [Sec. 140A]

Self-assessment is where an assessee himself assesses his tax liability on the income earned during the particular previous year and submits the returns to the revenue department. For the purposes of self-assessment an assessee is required to:

(*i*) Compute his total income under different heads taking into account the clubbing provisions (Secs. 60 to 64), provisions of carry forward and set-off of losses (Secs. 72 to 74A) and claim the deductions available to him under Secs. 80C to 80U.

(*ii*) Compute the tax payable on the total income in accordance with the rates applicable for that assessment year. Such tax payable is to be further adjusted as follows :

Particulars	₹	₹
Tax due on the total income, declared in the return :		xxx
Less: (*i*) Advance tax, if any, paid	xxx	
(*ii*) Any tax deducted or collected at source		
(*iii*) Any relief of tax claimed under Sec. 89 on account of salary paid in arrears or advance	xxx	

Particulars	₹	₹
(*iv*) Any relief of tax or deduction of tax claimed under Sec. 90 or 91 on account of tax paid in a country outside India	xxx	
(*v*) Any relief of tax claimed under Sec. 90A on account of tax paid in specified territory outside India	xxx	
(*vi*) Any tax credit claimed to be set-off under Sec. 115JAA	xxx	
(*vii*) Tax credit for alternate minimum tax under Sec. 115JD	xxx	
	xxx	(-)xxx
Amount of deficiency on which interest is to be charged	xxx	

The tax payable as computed aforesaid, must also include the interest payable for any delay in furnishing the return [Sec. 234A] or any default or delay in payment of advance tax [Secs. 234B and 234C] is paid before furnishing the return and the proof of payment of such tax is attached with the return.

Consequences of non-payment or under-payment - Assessee deemed to be in default [Sec. 140A(3)] - If any assessee fails to pay the whole or any part of such tax or interest or both, he is deemed to be an assessee in default in respect of such amount. Recovery proceedings may be started against him in respect of the unpaid amount. Penalty under Sec. 221 may also be imposed for the default.

Case Law : ***CIT* v. *Naresh Kumar Jaggi* [2015] 57 taxmann.com 442/370 ITR 401 (Delhi)**

Facts: 'N' admitted tax payable as per self-assessment under Sec. 140A and although he had paid certain amounts as advance tax, he had not paid the balance amount. Before a show cause notice could be issued under Sec. 140A(3), 'N' paid the balance amount. The Assessing Officer imposed a 100% penalty of the unpaid tax liability on the grounds that 'N' had failed to demonstrate a reasonable cause for the non-payment.

Held: Since there was no intention on the part of the assessee to deliberately delay or avoid payment of the tax and the eventual payment, albeit belated, was voluntarily made without the need for any coercive steps on the part of the revenue department, the penalty imposed was reduced to 25%.

POWER OF THE ASSESSING OFFICER TO MAKE INQUIRY BEFORE ASSESSMENT [SEC.142, SEC. 142A, SEC. 142B]

Under section 142(1) the Assessing Officer can undertake a preliminary investigation into an assessment. Thus, where any person who has made a return under Sec. 139 or in whose case the time allowed to furnish voluntary return [Sec. 139(1)] has expired, the Assessing Officer may serve a notice under sec. 142 to such a person requiring him to furnish the return of his income in the prescribed form and manner.

Production of Accounts or Documents - The Assessing Officer may ask to produce, or cause to be produced, such accounts or documents and to furnish in writing and verified in the prescribed manner information in such form and on such points or matters (including a statement of all assets and liabilities of the assessee, whether included in the accounts or not). However, when the assessee is required to furnish a statement of all assets and liabilities not included in the accounts, the previous approval of the Joint Commissioner must be obtained. Further, the Assessing Officer shall not require the production of any accounts relating to a period more than 3 years prior to the previous year [Proviso (*b*) to Sec. 142(1)]. This restriction applies only to accounts and does not apply to documents.

Direction for Special Audit [Sec. 142(2A)] - Having regard to the nature and complexity of the accounts, volume of the accounts, doubts about the correctness of the accounts, multiplicity of transactions in the accounts or specialized nature of the business of the assessee and the interest of the revenue, the Assessing Officer direct the assessee to get the accounts audited by an auditor or may require to get the inventory valued by a cost accountant.

Such auditor or cost accountant be nominated by the Principal Chief Commissioner or Chief Commissioner or Principal Commissioner or Commissioner in this behalf and required to furnish a report in the prescribed form duly signed and verified by such accountant and setting forth such particulars, as may be prescribed, and such other particulars as the Assessing Officer may require. However, the Assessing Officer shall not direct the assessee to get the accounts so audited or inventory so valued unless the assessee has been given a reasonable opportunity of being heard. (newly substituted sec. 142(2A) by the Finance Act, 2023)

Hearing opportunity to be given the assessee [Sec. 142(3)] The assessee should be given an opportunity of being heard in respect of material gathered on the basis of any inquiry (under Sec. 142(2) or any audit (under Sec. 142(2A)] and proposed to be utilised for the purposes of assessment.

Case Law : ***Pr. CIT* v. *Vilson Particle Board Industries Ltd.* (2020) 116 taxmann.com 12/271 Taxman 90/423 ITR 227 (Bom.)**

Facts: The Assessing Officer made a proposal for a special audit of the assessee without offering them an opportunity to be heard. However, the superior authority *i.e.* the Commissioner of Income Tax afforded the assessee an opportunity to be heard, before they (the Commissioner) gave their approval to the proposal of the Assessing Officer. The issue was whether this constituted sufficient compliance with the principle of natural justice – *audi alteram partem*.

Held: Assessing Officer is required to give pre-decisional hearing to assessee before making order proposing conduct of special audit under section 142(2A); in absence of pre-decisional hearing, decision to have special audit would be invalid, despite the Commissioner offering the assessee an opportunity to be heard before granting approval to the proposal for a special audit.

Estimation of value of assets by Valuation Officer [Sec. 142A] - For the purposes of making the assessment or re-assessment, the Assessing Officer may require a Valuation Officer to estimate the value of any asset, property or investment and submit a copy of report to him [Sec. 142A(1)].

He may also seek his opinion whether or not he is satisfied about the correctness or completeness of the accounts of the assessee [Sec. 142A(2)].

The valuation officer has to estimate the value of the asset, property or investment after taking into account such evidence as the assessee may produce and any other evidence in his possession, gathered during the course of hearing after having given the assessee an opportunity to be heard [Sec. 142A(4)].

Where the assessee does not co-operate, or comply with his directions the Valuation Officer may estimate the value of the asset, property or investment to the best of his judgment [Sec. 142A(5)].

The Valuation Officer is required to send his report to the Assessing Officer and the assessee within 6 months from the end of the month in which the reference was made to him [Sec. 142A(6)].

Thereafter, the Assessing Officer may proceed to make an assessment or re-assessment after giving an opportunity of being heard to the assessee [Sec. 142A(7)].

Faceless Inquiry or Valuation [Sec.142B]

In order to impart greater efficiency, transparency and accountability by:

(*a*) eliminating the interface between the income-tax authority or Valuation Officer and the assessee or any person to the extent technologically feasible;

(*b*) optimising utilisation of the resources through economies of scale and functional specialisation;

(*c*) introducing a team-based issuance of notice or making of enquiries or issuance of directions or valuation with dynamic jurisdiction the Central Government may make a scheme for the purposes of issuing notice under Sec.142(1) or making inquiry before assessment under Sec.142(2), or directing the assessee to get his accounts audited under Sec.142(2A), or estimating the value of any asset, property or investment by a Valuation Officer under section 142A.

Faceless Inquiry or Valuation Scheme, 2022

In exercise of the powers conferred by section 142B(1), (2), the Central Government *vide* Notification No. 19/2022 dated 30-3-2022 notified Faceless Inquiry or Valuation Scheme, 2022. The Scheme applies for:

(*a*) issuing notice under of section 142(1),

(*b*) directing the assessee to get his accounts audited under section 142(2A),

(*c*) estimating the value of any asset, property or investment by a Valuation Officer under section 142A.

The aforementioned process shall be in a faceless manner, through automated allocation.

Summary Assessment [Sec. 143(1)]

Where the return is checked to ascertain arithmetical accuracy (and not detailed scrutiny), it is called as summary assessment. Summary assessment is contemplated only in cases where the assessee has filed the return of income either as voluntary return under Sec. 139(1), or a belated return under Sec. 139(4) or a revised return under Sec. 139(5) or a return filed under the order of the Assessing Officer under Sec. 142(1). Thus, where no return of income is furnished by the assessee, no summary assessment is either contemplated or feasible. The Assessing Officer is required to make best judgment assessment in such cases.

The Assessing Officer undertakes the following steps to make a summary assessment:

1. Compute total income or loss after making the following adjustments, namely—

(*i*) any arithmetical error in the return be rectified; or

(*ii*) an incorrect claim, apparent from any information in the return, be adjusted.

"An incorrect claim, apparent from any information in the return" is defined to mean a claim on the basis of an entry, in the return—

(*a*) of an item, which is inconsistent with another entry of the same or some other item in such return; or

(*b*) in respect of which, information required to be furnished under this Act; or

(*c*) in respect of a deduction, where such deduction exceeds specified statutory limit which may have been expressed as monetary amount or percentage or ratio, or fraction.

(*ii*) disallowance of loss claimed, if return of the previous year for which set off of loss is claimed was furnished beyond the due date specified under Sec. 139(1)

(*iv*) disallowance of expenditure indicated in the audit report but not taken into account in computing the total income in the return

(*v*) disallowance of deduction claimed under Sections 10AA, 80-IA, 80-IAB, 80-IB, 80-IC, 80-ID, 80-IE, if the return is furnished beyond the due date specified under Sec. 139(1)

(*vi*) addition of income appearing in Form 26AS or Form 16A or Form 16 which has not been included in computing the total income in the return.

2. Compute tax or interest due from the assessee or a refund is due to him. Such tax payable is to be further adjusted as follows:

Particulars	₹	₹
Tax due on the total income disclosed in the return		xxxx
Add: Interest found payable by the assessee:		
(*i*) for late furnishing of return [Sec. 234A]		
(*ii*) for deferment of advance tax [Sec. 234C]		xxxx
(*iii*) for failure to pay advance tax or under-payment of advance tax [Sec. 234B]		xxxx
		xxxx
Less:		
(*i*) Advance tax paid;	xxxx	
(*ii*) Tax deducted or collected at source;		
(*iii*) Any relief allowable under Sec. 89;	xxxx	
(*iv*) Any relief allowable under Sec. 90 or Sec. 90A;	xxxx	
(*v*) Any relief allowable under Sec. 91; or	xxxx	
(*vi*) Tax paid on self-assessment under Sec. 140A;	xxxx	
(*vii*) Any amount paid otherwise by way of tax or interest;	xxxx	
	xxxx	(–) xxxx
Tax due from the assessee or refund due to him		xxxx

3. Intimation to be sent to thew assessee in case of any demand or refund - If any tax or interest is found due from the assessee, the Assessing Officer is required to send an intimation to the assessee within one year from the end of the financial year in which the return is furnished [Sec. 143(1)].

The intimation sent to him is deemed to be a Notice of Demand [Proviso to Sec. 156]. The assessee is required to pay such tax within the prescribed period failing which he is treated as an assessee in default. Consequently, recovery proceedings can be started against him. Where any refund is found due to the assessee on the basis of the return, the Assessing Officer is required to grant the same to the assessee and send an intimation to him. However, such intimation is not to be considered as an assessment order.

The assessee is entitled to appeal against the intimation order to the Commissioner (Appeals) under Sec. 246A(1).

REGULAR ASSESSMENT [UNDER SEC. 143(3) OR 144]

Regular assessment is of two types:

(*i*) Scrutiny assessment [Sec. 143(3)]; and

(*ii*) Best judgment assessment [Sec. 144].

The law relating to them is described below:

Scrutiny Assessment [Sec. 143(2) and (3)]

Where a return has been furnished under Sec. 139 or in response to a notice under Sec. 142(1) but the Assessing Officer is not inclined to accept it and considers it necessary to scrutinise to check any under-statement of income therein or under-payment of tax by the assessee, he is empowered to do so. For making the scrutiny of the return, the Assessing Officer is required to serve a notice on the assessee requiring him either to attend to his office on a date specified therein, or to produce, or cause to be produced, any evidence in support of the return. However, no notice under shall be served on the assessee after the expiry of 6 months from the end of the financial year in which the return is furnished [Proviso to Sec. 143(2) w.e.f. AY 2008-2009].

Where the assessee complies with the notice under Sec.143(2) and produces evidence in support of the return, but the Assessing Officer is not fully satisfied, he may issue further notices requiring the assessee to produce evidence on specified points [Re Lachmandas 2 ITC 1].

- If the Assessing Officer is satisfied with the evidence and information produced by the assessee in support of the return, he may make the assessment on the basis of such evidence.
- If the Assessing Officer is not satisfied as to the correctness of the account or evidence produced by the assessee, or he believes them to be false or unreliable, he may reject such accounts or evidence. Assessment must then be made under Sec. 143(3) on the basis of material collected by him through private inquiries. The Assessing Officer is not bound to disclose those sources to the assessee. However, where he proposes to use the result of private inquiry against the assessee, he should communicate to the assessee the substance of his information and provide an opportunity to him to rebut it [*Dhakeswari Cotton Mills Ltd.* v. *CIT* [1954] 26 ITR 775 (SC)]. Thus, principles of natural justice must be followed in the assessment proceedings and the assessee should have knowledge of the material which is going to be used against him so that he may be able to meet it [*Gargi Din Jwala Prasad* v. *CIT* [1974] 96 ITR 97 (All.)].

While no hard and fast rule exists to define the type of material on which the Assessing Officer should estimate the income of the assessee, arbitrary additions and guesswork must be avoided. The following points must be noted in this regard:

Summons can be issued under Sec. 131 to gather information from private parties - For the purposes of gathering relevant material, the Assessing Officer may issue summons under Sec. 131 for the examination of witness and production of documents from third parties to ascertain the assessee's income. He can, for instance, secure information and guidance by examining rivals in the trade of the assessee, or experts or past employees under the assessee, or managers who are acquainted with the particular business of the assessee. He may examine his own inspectors or surveyors if they can aid him and give information.

Local reputation, lifestyle the assessee and other relevant information may be taken into account - The Assessing Officer may also take into account the local reputation and position which the assessee occupies in the market, the style of living of the assessee and any acquisition of property by him during recent years, the increase in his total resources, the quantity of stocks carried by the assessee from year to year and whether the same is increasing or decreasing, and lastly the rate of profit earned generally in the business by other businessmen in the line.

Past history alone is not a sufficient basis to make assessment - Past history might be legitimate material, but that is not sufficient by itself to justify an assessment prejudicial to the assessee. There must be some material related to the accounting year which, taken with the history, may justify such assessment.

Information be gathered from other relevant sources - The Assessing Officer may gather information from the returns of TDS submitted under Sec. 201 and Sec. 285B, may inspect the register of members of any company (Sec. 134) and may call information in exercise of his powers under Sec. 133. He may further seek an authority of search and seizure under Sec. 132 and requisition of books of account or documents under Sec. 132B. He may enter business premises for inspection of accounts and documents (Sec. 133A).

Circumstantial evidence may be material for assessment - The material need not be direct evidence; it may be circumstantial evidence [*Homi Jehangir Gheesta* v. *CIT* [1961]41 ITR 135 (SC)]. Thus, from one admitted incident of suppression, the department may be entitled to infer that there were other similar incidents [*Bhimraj Pannalal* v. *CIT* [1961] 41 ITR 221 (SC)]. Similarly, entries in the books of third parties or inference from queries from third persons or discrepancy in stock found during the course of search may be circumstantial evidence for estimating profits [*CIT* v. *Southern Shipping Co. (P.) Ltd.* (2000) 241 ITR 464/ (2002) 123 Taxman 922 (Mad.)] [*CIT* v. *Golcha Properties (P.) Ltd.* (1997) 92 Taxman 356/227 ITR 391 (Raj.)] [*CIT* v. *Kalikoth Kunchi Timbers* (2000) 111 Taxman 306/246 ITR 202 (Ker.)].

Protective Assessment - If there is a doubt as to which person amongst the two is liable to be assessed in respect of certain income, parallel proceedings may be taken against both of them and an alternative assessment may be made.

Where it appears to the income-tax authorities that certain income has been received during the relevant previous year but it is not clear who has received that income, and *prima facie* it appears that the income may have been received either by A or by B or by both together, it would be open to the relevant income-tax authorities to determine the said question by taking appropriate proceedings against both A and B [*Lalji Harida*s v. *ITO* [1961] 43 ITR 387 (SC)].

While a protective assessment is permissible, protective recovery is not allowed [*Jagannath Bawri* v. *CIT* (1998) 234 ITR 464 (Gau.)].

Thus, after considering the evidence and such other particulars as the assessee may produce on specified points and he should take into account all relevant material, which he has gathered, the Assessing Officer is required to make an assessment of the total income or loss. After completing the assessment, the Assessing Officer is required to pass an assessment order in writing. The assessment order must contain a clear indication of the material on which the income is computed and/or estimated. If the order suffers from failure to indicate on what material or basis the income is assessed and tax determined, the assessment is bad and liable to be set aside.

The assessee is given due credit for any tax or interest paid by him under summary assessment [Sec. 143(1)]. The balance, if any, is deemed to be tax due from him. If no refund is due on regular assessment, the amount refunded under summary assessment is deemed to be tax payable by him. If amount refunded on summary assessment exceeds the amount refundable in regular assessment, the excess amount so refunded is deemed to be tax due from him. [Sec. 143(4)]. Accordingly, the Assessing Officer is required to issue a Demand Notice (under Sec. 156) specifying the sum payable by the assessee.

AO to make best judgment assessment in cases where notice is not complied with - Where the assessee does not comply with the notice and makes a default in producing the evidence, accounts or other information on specified points, the Assessing Officer is left with no choice but to make the assessment according to the best of judgment [Sec. 144].

BEST JUDGMENT ASSESSMENT [SEC. 144]

Where an assessee does not co-operate in the assessment proceedings with the taxing authorities and fails to discharge his statutory duty in the matter, the assessing authority is left with no option but to assess him to the best of his judgment. The Assessing Officer, after taking into account all relevant material which he has gathered, and after giving the assessee an opportunity of being heard, makes the assessment of the total income or loss to the best of his judgment and determine the sum payable by the assessee.

Best judgment assessment is of two types:

(*i*) Compulsory best judgment assessment; and

(*ii*) Discretionary best judgment assessment.

Compulsory best judgment assessment - The Assessing Officer is bound to make an assessment to the best of his judgment in any of the following cases:

(*i*) when any person fails to make the return required under Sec. 139(1),

(*ii*) when any person has not made a belated return under Sec. 139(4) or a revised return under section 139(5), or updated return under Sec. 139(8A), or

(*iii*) when any person fails to comply with all the terms of a notice issued under Sec. 142(1), (*iv*) when any person fails to comply with the direction issued under Sec. 142(2A) for getting the accounts audited, or

(*v*) when any person having made a return, fails to comply with all the terms of a scrutiny notice issued under Sec. 143(2).

Discretionary best judgment assessment - Where the Assessing Officer is not satisfied about the correctness or the completeness of the accounts of the assessee or where no method of accounting or accounting standard has been regularly employed by the assessee, the Assessing Officer may make the assessment to the best of his judgment under Sec. 144.

Best judgment assessment v. Scrutiny Assessment - The difference between scrutiny assessment under Sec. 143(3) and best judgment assessment under Sec.144 is that under scrutiny assessment the Assessing Officer has to assess to the best of judgment on the basis of evidence before him whilst under best judgment assessment he has often to assess to the best of his judgment in the absence of such evidence [*CIT* v. *Messrs. EinShin* [1947] 15 ITR 290 (Rangoon)].

Under the former, the Assessing Officer goes into more details while in the latter he acts in a summary manner due to the deliberate default of the assessee [*Dhanalakshmi Pictures* v. *CIT* [1983] 144 ITR 452 (Mad.)].

Underlying Principles to make best judgment assessment - While there are no provisions in the statute book, which can serve as a guide for making best judgment assessment, the following norms have been settled by the judicial pronouncements that may be followed in making the best judgment assessment.

Local repute of the Assessee, knowledge of previous returns and comparable cases may be taken into account for estimating total income - In making a best judgment, the Assessing Officer need not conduct a local inquiry and record the details and result of that inquiry [*CIT* v. *Laxminarain Badridas* [1937] 5 ITR 170 (PC)].

He may gather material from the assessee's accounts books of the relevant year or preceding years [*Jot Ram Sher Singh* v. *CIT* [1934] 2 ITR 129 (All.)].

He may compute the income of the assessee on the basis of a flat rate of profit, arrived at from comparable cases [*CIT & Excess Profits tax* v. *S. Sen* [1949] 17 ITR 355 (Orissa)].

He is not bound to confine himself to any special kind of material, in making the assessment [*Ram Kissendas Bagri* v. *CIT* [1927] 2 ITC 324 (Cal.)]. He need not take any evidence [*Gopinath Naik* v. *CIT* [1936] 4 ITR 1 (All.)].

Estimation of income must be honest and fair - The authority making a best judgment assessment must make an honest and fair estimate of the income of the assessee and though arbitrariness cannot be avoided in such an estimate, the same must not be capricious but should have a reasonable nexus to the available material and the circumstances of the case [*Brij Bhushan Lal Parduman Kumar* v. *CIT* [1978] 115 ITR 524 (SC)].

Guesswork be connected to available material - Though there is an element of guesswork in a 'best judgment assessment', it should not be a wild one, but should have a reasonable nexus to the available material and the circumstances of each case. Though the Section provides for a summary method because of the default of the assessee, it does not enable the assessing authority to function capriciously without regard to the available material [*State of Kerala* v. *C. Velukutty* [1966] 60 ITR 239 (SC)].

Power is not Arbitrary - The mere fact that the material placed by the assessee before the Assessing Officer is unreliable does not empower the officer to make an arbitrary order. The power to make a best judgment assessment is not an arbitrary power [*State of Orissa* v. *Maharaja Shri B.P. Singh Deo* [1970] 76 ITR 690 (SC)].

Rules of Justice, Equity and Good Conscience be the Guiding Spirit - In making best judgment, the Assessing Officer should not act dishonestly, vindictively or capriciously. He must exercise judgment in the matter [*CIT* v. *Laxminarain Badridas* [1937] 5 ITR 170 (PC)].

In making the best judgment assessment, the Assessing Officer should not be influenced by a desire to punish the assessee for the default, however culpable such default might be. He must not act dishonestly or vindictively or capriciously because he must exercise judgment in the matter. He must make what he honestly believes to be a fair estimate of the proper figure of assessment.

In making a best judgment assessment the Assessing Officer does not possess absolutely arbitrary authority to assess at any figure he likes and, that although he is not bound by strict judicial principles, he should be guided by rules of justice, equity and good conscience.

Where the best judgment assessment power has been conferred, the limits of the power are implicit in the expression 'best of his judgment'. Judgment is a faculty to decide matters with wisdom, truly and legally. Judgment does not depend upon the arbitrary caprice of a judge, but on settled and invariable principles of justice. Though there is an element of guesswork in a best judgment, it should not be a wild one, but should have reasonable nexus to the available material and the circumstances of each case.

Consequences of compulsory best judgment assessment:

(*i*) **Penalty of ₹ 10,000 Imposable for each Default** - The assessee is liable to pay penalties under Sec. 271(1)(*b*) for non-compliance with the terms of notice issued under Sec. 142(1) or 142(2A) or 143(2). The penalty imposable for each default is ₹ 10,000.

(*ii*) **Prosecution for failure to furnish Return or Non-compliance with Notice** - The assessee is liable to prosecution for wilful failure to file return under Sec. 276CC. The defaulter may be prosecuted with rigorous imprisonment for a minimum term of six months which may extend to seven years, provided tax evaded exceeds ₹ 25 lacs.

In any other case, the minimum rigorous imprisonment is three months which may extend to two years.

For non-compliance with the terms of notice issued under Sec. 142(1) or 142(2A) he may be prosecuted under Sec. 276D with rigorous imprisonment which may extend to one year or with fine.

Appeal against Best Judgment Assessment - The assessee can appeal against best judgment assessment under Sec. 246A(*a*). He can object to the amount of income assessed, or the amount of tax determined, or the amount of loss computed or to the status under which he is assessed.

FACELESS ASSESSMENT [SEC. 143(3A), (3B), (3C)]

The genesis of the present day Faceless Assessment Scheme dates back to the year 2015 when E-assessment Scheme first introduced on a pilot basis in metro cities. Subsequently the year 2017 saw the development of an integrated platform for electronic conduct of the assessment proceedings. It was the Finance Act, 2018 that took the faceless scheme to the next level by inserting sub-sections (3A), (3B) and (3C) to sec.143 w.e.f. 1-4-2018 which enabled the Central Government to come up with a Scheme for Faceless-Electronical Assessment.

The Central Government had introduced Faceless Assessment Scheme *vide* Notification No. 61/2019 dated 12th September 2019. Subsequently the scheme was renamed as Faceless Assessment Scheme *vide* Gazette notification dated 13-8-2020 bearing F.No. S.O. 2745(E). The said scheme came into force w.e.f.13-8-2020. The Scheme operated as per the Income Tax Act and Income Tax Rules. The Central Board of Direct Taxes (CBDT) decided the scope of the faceless assessment such as territorial area, persons, class of persons, incomes, class of incomes, cases or class of cases to whom this faceless assessment is applicable. It was directed that all the assessment orders shall be passed by NeAC in a faceless manner with the exceptions of (*i*) cases assigned to central charges (i.e. search and seizure cases); and (*ii*) cases under International Taxation (*i.e.* those related to non-residents or for transfer pricing proceedings). The Faceless Assessment Scheme was to be carried out through the National e-Assessment Centre (NeAC) along with other centers and units such as Regional e-Assessment Centres (ReAC), Assessment units (AUs), Verification Units (VUs) Technical Units (TUs) and Review Units (RUs) for reviewing the draft assessment order to check whether the facts, relevant evidence and law and judicial decisions have been considered in the draft order.

However, the Faceless Scheme formulated by a delegated legislation in the form of CBDT notification would have been a matter of concern in terms of its sanctity and validity and therefore the Taxation and Other Laws (Relaxation and Amendment of Certain Provisions) Act, 2020 passed by the Parliament inserted a new sec. 144B w.e.f. 1-4-2021. Thus, sec. 144B legislates the procedure of the conducting the faceless proceedings. The National e-Assessment Centre (NeAC) under the 2019 Scheme has been renamed as National Faceless Assessment Centre (NFAC) under sec. 144B.

With sec.144B being applicable, the Faceless Assessment Scheme, 2019 ceased to operate from 1.4.2021.One year of operationalizing of the Faceless Scheme under sec.144B proved to be wrought with various challenges. A cursory look at the same will help appreciate the point.

Assessment orders passed without granting virtual hearing against Principles of Natural Justice

Sec.144B(7) introduced by the Finance Act, 2021 comprised of a provision where in case a variation was proposed in draft assessment order or revised assessment order, such assessee or his legal representative could request a personal hearing to the revenue authorities. However, the provision did not mandate the authorities to grant such hearing upon request and it was left to the discretion of such authority. This provision was challenged by various assessees before different High Courts on the grounds that it is against the Principles of Natural Justice to pass orders without giving another party a chance of hearing. Several High Court rulings including *Sanjay Aggarwal* v. *National Faceless Assessment Centre* [2021] 127 taxmann.com 637/281 Taxman 282/436 ITR 180 (Delhi), *Mantra Industries Ltd*. v. *National Faceless Assessment Centre* [2021] 131 taxmann.com 165/283 Taxman 459 (Bom.) set aside such assessment orders which were passed without providing personal hearing to the assessee despite its requests.

Assessment Orders passed without issuing a prior show cause notice

Under Sec. 144B(1)(*xvi*)(*b*) in case any variation prejudicial to the interest of assessee is proposed, it was mandatory to serve a show cause notice calling upon such assessee to show cause as to why the proposed variation should not be made. However, in several matters final assessment orders were passed without issuing such show cause notice. High Courts have been setting aside such assessment that were made without following the mandated procedure of the Faceless Scheme. [*see* for instance *Novelty Merchants (P.) Ltd*. v. *National Faceless Assessment Centre* [2021] 131 taxmann.com 289/283 Taxman 385 (Delhi), *Pardesi Developers (P.) Ltd.* v. *National Faceless Assessment Centre* [2021] 131 taxmann.com 246/[2022] 441 ITR 696 (Delhi)].

Assessment Orders passed without providing reasonable time to respond

There have been several occasions when the assessees were not provided with reasonable time to respond to the show cause notice issued. Such final assessment orders that were passed without providing reasonable time to respond and with dysfunction of newly launched income tax e-filing portal, were challenged by assessees and duly set aside by the High Court. [*See* for instance *Centum Finance Ltd*. v. *National Faceless Assessment Centre* [2021] 131 taxmann.com 39/283 Taxman 232 (Delhi)].

The aforementioned lapses in following the mandatory procedure stipulated in sec.144B when read with sec. 144B(9) proved to be highly problematic. Sec.

144B(9) stipulates that all the assessments made on or after 1 April 2021 shall be carried out as per the procedure laid down under section 144B and failure to comply with the same will make such assessments *non-est*. Thus, assessments made in contravention of the procedure contained in the provisions of Sec. 144B would be fatal to such assessment in the light of sec. 144B(9) even if the same may result owing to some technical issue.

In order to iron out the difficulties discussed above, the Finance Act, 2022 has substituted the old sub-sections (1) to (8) of sec. 144B with new sub-section that are effective from 1.4.2022. Thus, the assessment [under sec. 143(3)], reassessment (under sec. 144) or recomputation (under sec. 147) shall be made in a faceless manner. The substituted provisions makes it mandatory to provide a personal hearing to the assessee through video conferencing when so requested. Sec. 144B(9) has been omitted in the substituted provisions with retrospective effect. Sec.144B(9) contains a strict provision that the assessment proceedings shall be void if the procedure mentioned in the section was not followed. According to the explanation furnished by the Memorandum to the Finance Bill, 2022 "a large number of disputes have been raised under this sub-section involving technical issues arising due to use of information technology, leading to unnecessary litigation. It is, therefore, proposed to omit this sub-section *i.e.*, sub-section (9) of section 144B from its date of inception." Such retrospective repealing of Sec.144B(9) would therefore save the matters from being void due to non-compliance with the procedure. It must be observed that the disputes mostly arose due to non-observance of Principles of Natural Justice which were further fortified due to the categorical presence of sec. 144B(9). Therefore, sec. 144B(9) was a significant safeguard against any arbitrary action. However, with the other provisions being amendment in light of the essential principles of natural justice and learning from the difficulties already faced, the Faceless Scheme has been further streamlined through substituted provisions. Now let us understand the Faceless Assessment procedure.

The following units facilitate the operation of the faceless system [Sec. 144B(3)]:

National Faceless Assessment Centre (NaFAC) to facilitate the conduct of faceless assessment proceedings in a centralised manner.

Assessment Units (AU) to conduct the faceless assessment, to perform the function of making assessment, including identification of points or issues material for the determination of any liability (including refund) under this Act, seeking information or clarification on points or issues so identified, analysis of the material furnished by the assessee or any other person, and such other functions as may be required for the purposes of making faceless assessment. The term "assessment unit", wherever used in this section, shall refer to an Assessing Officer having powers so assigned by the Board.

Verification Units (VU) to facilitate the conduct of faceless assessment, to perform the function of verification, which includes enquiry, cross verification, examination of books of account, examination of witnesses and recording of statements, and such other functions as may be required for the purposes of verification. The term "verification unit", wherever used in this section, shall refer to an Assessing Officer having powers so assigned by the Board.

It must be noted that the function of VU under this section may also be performed by a VU located in any other faceless centre set up under the provisions of this Act or under any scheme notified under the provisions of this Act; and the request for verification may also be assigned through the National Faceless Assessment Centre to such verification unit.

Technical Units (TU) to facilitate the conduct of faceless assessment, to perform the function of providing technical assistance which includes any assistance or advice on legal, accounting, forensic, information technology, valuation, transfer pricing, data analytics, management or any other technical matter under this Act or an agreement entered into under section 90 or 90A, which may be required in a particular case or a class of cases, under this section. The term "technical unit", wherever used in this section, shall refer to an Assessing Officer having powers so assigned by the Board.

Review Units (RU) to facilitate the conduct of faceless assessment, to perform the function of review of the income determination proposal assigned, which includes checking whether the relevant and material evidence has been brought on record, relevant points of fact and law have been duly incorporated, the issues requiring addition or disallowance have been incorporated and such other functions as may be required for the purposes of review. The term "review unit", wherever used in this section, shall refer to an Assessing Officer having powers so assigned by the Board.

The assessment unit, verification unit, technical unit and the review unit shall have the following authorities, namely:—

(*i*) Additional Commissioner or Additional Director or Joint Commissioner or Joint Director, as the case may be;

(*ii*) Deputy Commissioner or Deputy Director or Assistant Commissioner or Assistant Director, or Income-tax Officer, as the case may be;

(*iii*) such other income-tax authority, ministerial staff, executive or consultant, as may be considered necessary by the Board [Sec.144B(4)].

FIGURE 21.3: FACELESS ASSESSMENT SCHEME UNDER SEC. 144B (SUBSTITUTED BY THE FINANCE ACT, 2022)

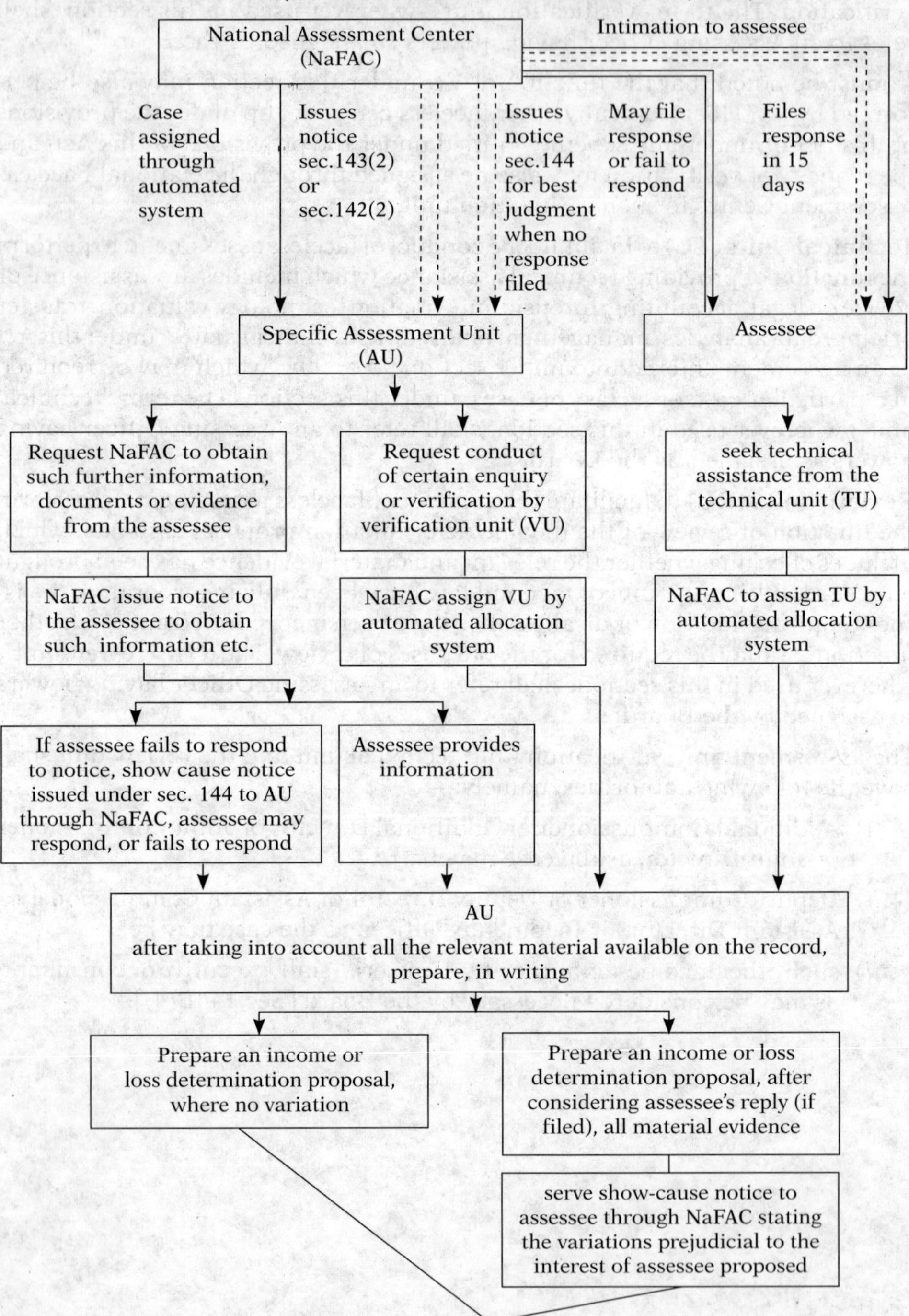

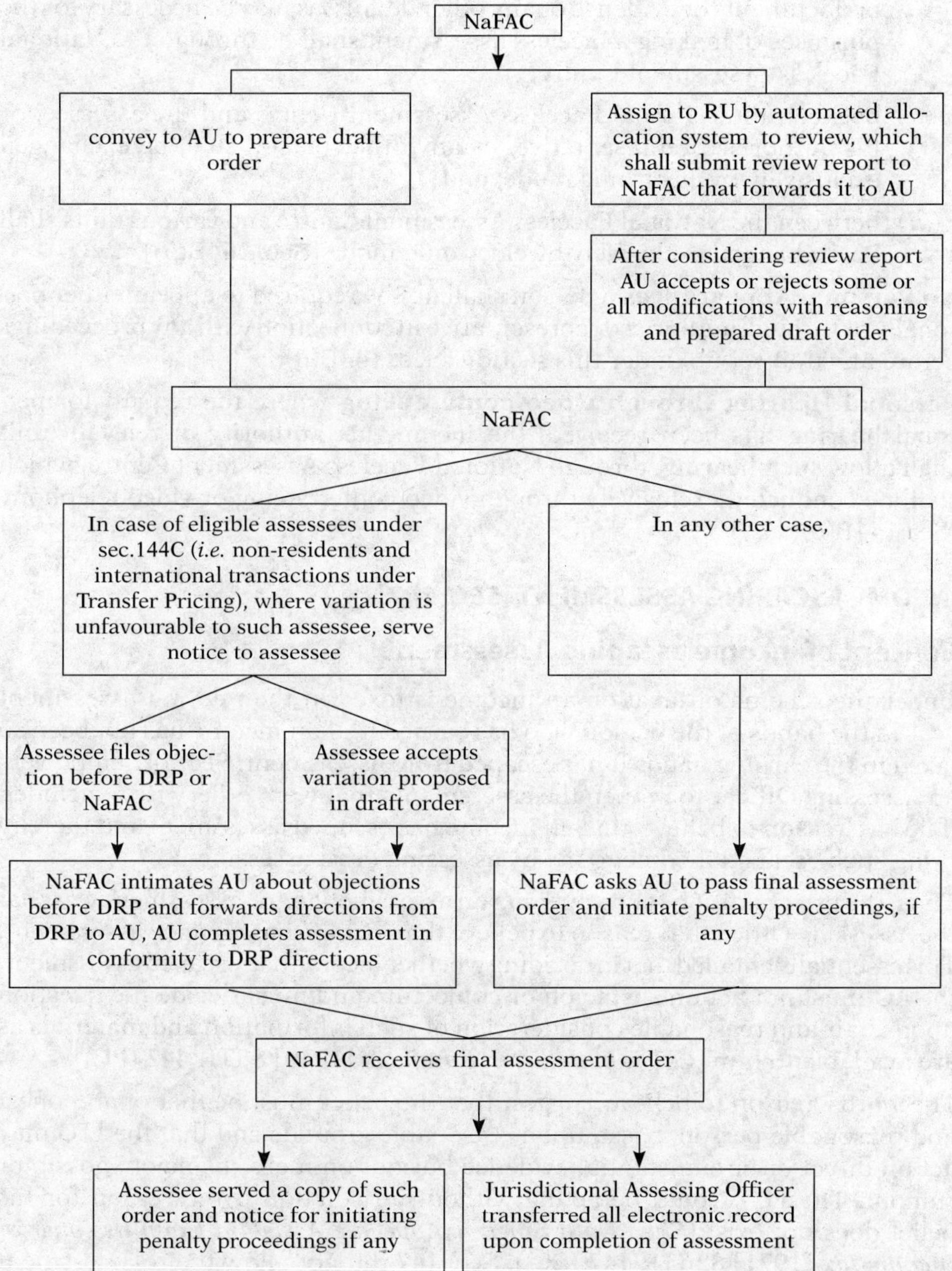

The following points must be noted about the faceless procedure:

Mode of Communication between Units All communications,—

(*i*) among the assessment unit, review unit, verification unit or technical unit or with the assessee or any other person with respect to the information or documents or evidence or any other details, as may be necessary for the purposes of making a faceless assessment shall be through the National Faceless Assessment Centre;

(*ii*) between the National Faceless Assessment Centre and the assessee, or his authorised representative, or any other person shall be exchanged exclusively by electronic mode; and

(*iii*) between the National Faceless Assessment Centre and various units shall be exchanged exclusively by electronic mode [Sec. 144B(5)].

No Personal Appearances a person shall not be required to appear either personally or through authorised representative in connection with any proceedings before any unit set up under this section [Sec. 144B(6)(*vi*)].

Personal Hearing through video conferencing where the request for personal hearing has been received, the income-tax authority of relevant unit shall allow such hearing, through National Faceless Assessment Centre, which shall be conducted exclusively through video conferencing or video telephony [Sec.144B(6)(*viii*)].

INCOME ESCAPING ASSESSMENT [SEC. 147]

Concept of Income escaping Assessment

Under the scheme of taxation an income is taxed in the relevant assessment year in the hands of the person who has earned it. If an income has not been so taxed in the earning hands it has escaped from assessment. Sec. 147 empowers an Assessing Officer to reopen the assessments that were otherwise concluded if he has 'reason to believe' that an income has escaped assessment and thereby bring such escaped income to tax by assessing or re-assessing it.

Thus, the pre-condition for re-opening an assessment or re-assessment was that the Assessing Officer has reason to believe that income has escaped assessment. This essentially entailed that in deciding whether income had escaped assessment, the AO must not act on suspicion or conjecture and must decide the question upon a fair and reasonable consideration of such information and materials as are available to him [*CIT* v. *Mahaliram Ramjidas* [1940] 8 ITR 442 (PC)].

The words 'reason to believe' suggest that the belief must be that of an honest and reasonable person, based upon reasonable grounds and that the ITO may act on direct or circumstantial evidence but not on mere suspicion, gossip or rumour. The ITO would be acting without jurisdiction if the reason for his belief does not exist [*Sheo Nath Singh* v. *Appellate Assistant Commissioner of Income-tax* [1971] 82 ITR 147 (SC)]. Sec. 147 did not allow the re-assessment of an income merely because of the fact that the Assessing Officer has a change of opinion with regard to the interpretation of law differently on the facts that were well within his knowledge even at the time of assessment [*ITO* v. *TechSpan India (P.) Ltd.* [2018] 92 taxmann.com 361/255 Taxman 152 (SC)].

Case Law : ***Pr.CIT* v. *Andaleeb Sehgal* [2021] 124 taxmann.com 247/277 Taxman 492 (SC)**

Facts: Assessing Officer sought to reopen assessment in case of assessee on ground that assessee had paid bribe to Iraqi officials and therefore same was required to be added to income of assessee. However, it was found that Assessing Officer had simply borrowed conclusions drawn by Enforcement Directorate without making any independent inquiry himself into matter.

Held: Reopening of assessment by the Assessing Officer on basis of borrowed investigation from the Enforcement Directorate without making any independent inquiry himself was not justified.

Case Law : ***Phool Chand Bajrang Lal* v. *CIT* [1993] 69 Taxman 627/203 ITR 456 (SC)**

Facts: 'P' being a company was allowed a deduction for interest on loans borrowed which subsequently turned out to be bogus loan and the lender had confessed that he was only a name-lender and had not advanced any loan to any party.

Held: Sec. 147 ensures that an assessee does not get away by wilfully making a false or untrue statement at the time of original assessment and when that falsity comes to notice, to turn around and say 'you accepted my lie, now your hands are tied and you can do nothing'. Thus, where subsequent to the conclusion of the original assessment, the ITO gets some fresh information which was not available at the time of the original assessment which enables him to form a reasonable belief that the income of the assessee has escaped assessment, he can reopen the assessment.

Case Law : ***ITO* v. *TechSpan India (P.) Ltd.* [2018] 92 taxmann.com 361/255 Taxman 152 (SC)**

Facts: 'T' engaged in the business of development and export of computer software and human resource claimed expenses commonly for both sources of income and also claimed deduction under Sec. 10A for the income from the software development. The return was selected for regular assessment and a show cause notice was issued under Sec. 134 to 'T' as to why the expenses claimed with regard to the allocation of common expenses between the two heads, *viz.,* software development and human resource development did not reveal any basis for such allocation. The issue was duly contested and the proceedings ended and the income was assessed as '*Nil*. Thereafter a notice was issued under Sec.148 on the ground that the deduction under section 10A had been allowed in excess.

Held: Section 147 does not allow the re-assessment of an income merely because of the fact that the Assessing Officer has a change of opinion with regard to the interpretation of law differently on the facts that were well within his knowledge even at the time of assessment. The notice which was issued in the original assessment proceedings under Sec. 143 makes it clear that the point on which the re-assessment proceedings were initiated included the question as to how and to what extent deduction should be allowed under Sec. 10A was well considered. Merely because of the fact that now the Assessing Officer is of the view that the deduction under Sec. 10A was allowed in excess, is nothing but a change of opinion on the same facts and circumstances which were already in his knowledge and re-opening cannot be allowed.

Problem with 'reason to believe' and an overhaul

The re-opening of assessment proceedings have been wrought with challenges and litigations pertaining to substantial and procedural issues. Take for instance the controversy discussed hereinabove whether the Assessing Officer indeed had 'reasons to believe' that the income had so escaped assessment or was it merely a change of opinion. Since the expression 'reason to believe' involved making subjective determination, the same was heavily litigated. Several other points of dispute emerged controverting whether before issuing notice the AO appropriately 'record his reasons', whether the assessee had disclosed 'fully and truly all material facts necessary for his assessment' and so on.

Substitution with the new provisions

In order to curtail unnecessary litigation and offering ease of doing business, the Finance Act, 2021 revamped the scheme of undertaking assessment escaping income. Accordingly, the existing Secs. 147, 148, 149 and 151 is substituted with the new sections. The new scheme of re-assessment comprise of the following provisions:

Sec. 147: Assessment of income escaping assessment;

Sec. 148: Issue of notice for re-assessment;

Sec. 148A: Procedure to be followed before issuing a notice for re-assessment;

Sec. 149: Time limit for issuing a notice for re-assessment;

Sec. 150: Assessment in pursuance of an order on appeal, etc. (no amendment has been proposed);

Sec. 151: Specified Authorities for authorising the issue of notice for re-assessment;

Sec. 151A: Faceless assessment of income escaping assessment; and

Sec. 153: Time limit for completion of assessment or re-assessment.

Newly substituted Sec. 147 makes a departure from the existing provision that required the AO to have a 'reason to believe' which was a major bone of contention. Whereas even under the new sec. 147, Assessing Officer is empowered to assess or reassess any income that has escaped assessment for any assessment year, however before making such re-assessment AO is required to conduct an inquiry under sec. 148A and then serve a notice to the assessee under sec. 148. Thus, under the new regime the Assessing Officer can initiate the proceedings only if he has information which suggests that some income has escaped the assessment.

However, if there is any income which is not related to the reason for which the assessment or reassessment proceedings are initiated comes in notice of the Assessing officer subsequently, then provisions of sec. 148A shall not apply to such subsequent issues and they can be very well adjudicated under the provisions of sec. 147 itself. [*Explanation 1* to sec. 147].

When income escaped assessment [*Explanations* to Sec. 148]

Unlike old regime when reassessment could be initiated on a 'reason to believe' that income escaped assessment, under the new regime Assessing Officer can initiate the proceedings only if he has the information which suggests that some income has escaped the assessment. *Explanation 1* to Sec. 148 provide the meaning of the 'information suggesting income escaping assessment' and *Explanation 2* to Sec. 148 stipulates when AO will be 'deemed to have information suggesting income escaping assessment'.

Information with Assessing Officer - The Assessing Officer must have information which suggests that the income chargeable to tax has escaped assessment in the case of the assessee for the relevant assessment year, that is

(*a*) any information in the case of the assessee for the relevant assessment year in accordance with the risk management strategy formulated by the Board from time to time

The Central Board of Direct Taxes (CBDT) formulates the Risk Management Strategy to identify the high-risk cases for the re-assessment. Such information would largely be done by the computer-based system on basis of pre-defined algorithms which may not be made public. The CBDT does the risk analysis based on the data gathered from various sources such as information about the specified financial transactions collected from the third parties under Section 285BA (Statement of Financial Transaction or Reportable Account) or the information received from other law enforcement agencies or the foreign countries

(*b*) any audit objection to the effect that the assessment in the case of the assessee for the relevant assessment year has not been made in accordance with the provisions of this Act; or

(*c*) any information received under an Information Exchange Agreement referred to in section 90 or section 90A of the Act; or

(*d*) any information made available to the Assessing Officer under the scheme notified under section 135A; or

(*e*) any information which requires action in consequence of the order of a Tribunal or a Court [*Explanation 1* to Sec. 148]

Deemed to have information - In case of the following proceedings, the Assessing Officer is deemed to have information suggesting escapement of income for three Assessment Years preceding the assessment year relevant to the year in which the proceedings are conducted:

(*a*) Search & Seizure (Sec. 132)

(*b*) Survey (Sec. 133A)

(*c*) Requisition of books of account, etc. relating to the assessee (Sec. 132A) or

(*d*) where money, bullion, jewellery or other valuables articles are seized in case of another person but belong to the assessee or books of account or documents seized or requisitioned in case of another person pertain to the assessee or contain information related to the assessee. [*Explanation 2* to Sec. 148]

Conducting inquiry, providing opportunity before issue of notice under sec. 148 [Sec. 148A]

When the AO has information as mentioned aforesaid, he must undertake the following procedure before issuing notice for reassessment:

(*a*) Conduct any enquiry, if required, with prior sanction of the specified authority, with respect to the information suggesting escapement of income;

(*b*) Provide the assessee an opportunity of being heard by serving a notice to show cause within such time as to why a notice under Sec. 148 should not be issued on the basis of information suggesting escapement of chargeable income and results of enquiry conducted, if any;

(*c*) Consider the reply of assessee, if any, furnished and basis the material including reply of the assessee, decide whether a notice is to be issued by passing an order, with the prior approval of specified authority, within 1 month from the end of the month in which the reply referred to in received/ time allowed to furnish a reply expires.

The aforesaid procedure is not required to be followed where the AO is deemed to have information suggesting escapement of assessment or where the Assessing Officer has received any information under the scheme notified under sec. 135A pertaining to income chargeable to tax escaping assessment for any assessment year in the case of the assessee.

Issue of Notice [Sec. 148]

Having thus conducted an inquiry, the Assessing Officer is obliged to serve a notice (along with a copy of the order passed) to the assessee before making any assessment, reassessment or recomputation. The assessee is required to furnish a return of income during the previous year relevant to the assessment year, in the prescribed form and verified in the prescribed manner within a period of three months from the end of the month in which such notice is issued or such further period as may be allowed by the Assessing Officer the basis of application made by assessee. However, any return furnished beyond the period allowed in shall not be deemed to be a return under sec. 139. A prior approval of the Principal Commissioner or Principal Director or Commissioner or Director must be obtained so as to issue such notice. However, no such approval shall be required where the Assessing Officer, with the prior approval of the specified authority, has passed an order under section 148A(*d*) to the effect that it is a fit case to issue a notice under this section. (Second proviso to Sec. 148(1) newly inserted by the Finance Act, 2022 so as to simplify the procedure).

Prior approval for assessment, reassessment or recomputation in certain cases [Sec. 148B] (newly inserted by the Finance Act, 2022 w.e.f. 1-4-2022)

No order of assessment or reassessment or recomputation under the Act shall be passed by an Assessing Officer below the rank of Joint Commissioner, except with the prior approval of the Additional Commissioner or Additional Director or Joint Commissioner or Joint Director, in respect of assessments consequent to search, survey and requisition to reduce avoidable inaccuracies.

Time limit for issuance of reassessment notice [Sec. 149]

The Finance Act, 2021 substituted the existing provision and reduced the time-limit for re-opening of assessment 3 years from the end of relevant assessment year.

In case where the AO has in his possession books of account or other documents or evidence which reveal that the income chargeable to tax, represented in the form of:

(*a*) Assets (including immovable property, being land or building or both, shares and securities, loans and advances, deposits in bank account),

(*b*) expenditure in respect of a transaction or in relation to an event or occasion, or

(*c*) an entry or entries in the books of account,

which has escaped assessment amounts to ₹ 50 lakhs or more, such assessment can be re-opened after 3 years but prior to 10 years (as amended by the Finance Act, 2022).

The aforesaid period of limitation shall exclude the period during which the proceeding under Sec. 148A is stayed by an order or injunction of any court. When income escaping assessment pertains to any expenditure in relation to an event or occasion and such expenditure was incurred over multiple previous year, a notice under Sec. 148 shall be issued for every such year [Sec. 149(1A) (newly inserted by the Finance Act, 2022)].

However, the new time limitation of 3 years shall not apply where search or requisition is initiated or made on or before 31st March 2021. In such cases, the assessment or reassessment or re-computation shall be continued as per the existing provision of Secs. 153A, 153B, 153C and 153D (First Proviso to Sec. 149). Further, no notice can be issued under the newly substituted Sec. 148 at any time in a case for the relevant assessment year beginning on or before 1st day of April 2021, if such notice could not have been issued at that time on account of being beyond the time limit of 6 years (Second Proviso to Sec. 149).

Since evidence of tax evasion may be reflected in the statements recorded or documents seized or impounded etc. during such action before 31st March, but issuance of notice related to such information or search may go beyond the time limitation provided due to the procedure involved. Therefore, important information related to revenue leakage cannot be proceeded on due to the paucity of time for searched conducted and information obtained as a consequence of these searches in the last few days of any financial year. Therefore, in cases where the information deemed to be with the Assessing Officer emanates from a statement recorded or documents impounded under summons or survey, as the case may be, on or before the 31st day of March of a financial year, in consequence of, a search initiated or last of the authorization executed under section 132 or a requisition made under section 132A, after the 15th day of March of such financial year, a period of fifteen days shall be excluded for the purpose of computing the period of limitation for issuance of notice under section 148 and the show cause notice issued under sec. 148A(*b*) in such case shall be deemed to have been issued on the 31st day of March of such financial year. It must be noted that an extension has been provided only for the time consumed in the procedure for issuance of notice under sec.148 or 148A, as the case may be. The impounding or the recording of the statement in consequence of the search or the search itself should be before the 31st March only. (Inserted by the Finance Act, 2023 to be effective from 1.4.2023)

The following table will provide a quick comparative between the old scheme of assessment of income escaping assessment and the newly substituting provisions:

TABLE 21.2: COMPARATIVE VIEW OF INCOME ESCAPING ASSESSMENT

Particulars	Old Scheme	New Scheme
Pre-requisite for initiating assessment, reassessment or recomputation (Sec. 147)	The Assessing Officer has reasons to believe that income has escaped assessment and also any other income chargeable to tax which has escaped assessment and which comes to his notice subsequently in the course of the proceedings	when such issue comes to his notice subsequently in the course of the proceedings under this section
Steps to be taken before issuing notice (Sec. 148)	Record reasons to believe that the income has escaped assessment	Follow the process laid down in Section 148A, namely: (*a*) Conduct an Inquiry; (*b*) Grant an opportunity of being heard to the assessee; (*c*) Consider reply of the assessee; (*d*) Pass an Order
Time-limit for issuance of Notice	4 to 6 Years	3 to 10 years

Old Provisions and New Controversy: Validity of Notices issued under old sec.148

As noted in the discussion so far, the Finance Act, 2021 overhauled the re-assessment proceedings and substituted the existing provisions contained in secs.

147, 148, 149 and 151 with effect from 1-4-2021. The old provisions ceased to be applicable w.e.f. 1-4-2021. However, by virtue of exercise of the power vested in it by sec. 3 of the Taxation and other Laws (Relaxation and Amendment of Certain Provisions) Act, 2020, the Central Government issued notifications, Notification No. 38/2021 dated 27 March 2021 and Notification No. 20/2021 dated March 31, 2021 whereby it extended the timelines for issue of notice under the old sec. 148 to 30-6-2021. Further, the said notification contained an *Explanation* that for the purposes of issuance of notice under sec. 148, the old provisions of secs. 148, 149 and 151 shall apply. In other words, with respect to these notices, the matter will continue to be governed by the old provisions.

Validity of such notices that were so issued under the old provision that were no longer applicable after 1-4-2021 were challenged by the different writ petitions before various High Courts. The issue was whether the Central Government under a delegated power is empowered to issue such notification extending time limit of issue notice even as the old provisions for reassessment has been substituted by Finance Act, 2021 and no longer applicable on or after 1-4-2021.

In writ petitions before them, the Allahabad High Court, Rajasthan High Court, Delhi High Court, Calcutta High Court, Madras High Court, Bombay High Court quashed the reassessment notices under sec.148 being bad in law.

However, the Supreme Court in *UOI* v. *Ashish Agarwal* [2022] 138 taxmann.com 64/286 Taxman 183 (SC) provided partial relief to the revenue department by upholding the notices issued as deemed to be issued under sec. 148A and ruling that the new provisions would govern such matters. The Supreme Court in its ruling balanced the interest of the assessees with that of the revenue department. It went to hold that the respective High Courts have rightly held that the benefit of new provisions shall be made available even in respect of the proceedings relating to past assessment years, provided sec. 148 notice has been issued on or after 1st April, 2021. The Supreme Court concede that after the amendment was enforced w.e.f. 1-4-2021 notices under the erstwhile sec. 148 ought not have been issued. However, the revenue department cannot be rendered remediless and the object and purpose of reassessment proceedings cannot be frustrated. Therefore, some leeway was shown. Instead of quashing and setting aside the reassessment notices issued under the erstwhile section 148, the Supreme Court deemed that these notices have been issued under sec. 148A as substituted by the Finance Act, 2021 and ordered that AO shall provide information and material to the assessee within 30 days so that assessee can reply within 2 weeks. Since under the new regime AO is required to conduct enquiry under sec. 148A before issue of notice under sec. 148 which will not be possible in these matters, the Supreme Court has provided one time relief and dispensed with conduct of enquiry in these matters. The Supreme Court's order is applicable all over India to reverse the orders passed by various High Courts and to the matters pending in over 9000 cases. Thus, the notices issued under old sec. 148 have as such not been upheld by the Supreme Court but deemed to have been issued under the new sec. 148. The assessee and revenue authorities will have to rely on the new provisions while proceeding with these matters (barring the requirement of conduct of enquiry under sec. 148 before issue of notice which has been dispensed with as a one-time measure).

Tax Rates on reassessment [Sec. 152(1)] - In an assessment or re-assessment or recomputation made under Sec. 147, the tax is charged at the rate in force in the relevant assessment year, that is, the year to which the assessment or re-assessment or recomputation relates, and not the year in which the assessment or re-assessment or recomputation is made.

Time limit for completion of assessments or reassessments [Sec. 153] - Provisions in respect of completing different types of assessments or re-assessment are explained as below:

Section	Particulars	Time-Period for completion of Assessment/Reassessment/Recomputation, as the case may be
Sec. 153(1)	Summary assessment (under Sec. 143)	Within 21 months the end of the assessment year in which the income was first assessable 18 months for AY 2018-19 12 months for AY 2019-20 18 months for AY 2020-21 9 months for AY 2021-22 and thereafter where an updated return under Sec. 139(8A) is furnished, an order of summary assessment may be made at any time before the expiry of 9 months from the end of the financial year in which such return was furnished (sec. 153(1A) newly inserted by the Finance Act, 2022)
Sec. 153(1)	Best Judgment assessment (under Sec. 144)	Within 21 months the end of the assessment year in which the income was first assessable 18 months for AY 2018-19 12 months for AY 2019-20 18 months for AY 2020-21 and 9 months for AY 2021-22 and thereafter where an updated return under Sec. 139(8A) is furnished,

Section	Particulars	Time-Period for completion of Assessment/Reassessment/Recomputation, as the case may be
		an order of best judgment assessment may be made at any time before the expiry of 9 months from the end of the financial year in which such return was furnished (sec. 153(1A) newly inserted by the Finance Act, 2022)
Sec. 153(2)	Income escaping assessment (under Sec. 147)	Within 9 months from the end of the financial year in which the notice of income escaping assessment is served on the assessee under Sec. 148. 12 months where notice is served on or after the 1st day of April, 2019
Sec. 153(3)	Fresh assessment or fresh order under sec. 92CA when order is set aside by the Appellate Tribunal (Sec. 254) or the Principal Commissioner or Commissioner (Sec. 263 or 264)	Within 9 months from the end of the financial year in which the set aside order is received by the Principal Chief Commissioner or Chief Commissioner or Principal Chief Commissioner or Commissioner 12 months where the order by Appellant Tribunal (Sec. 254) is received or order passed by the Principal Chief Commissioner or Chief Commissioner or Principal Commissioner or Commissioner (Sec. 263 or 264) on or after the 1st day of April, 2019.
Sec. 153(5)	Giving effect to any order passed by the Commissioner (Appeals) (under Sec. 250) or Appellate Tribunal (under Sec. 254), or High Court (under Sec. 260) or Supreme Court (under sec. 262), or Principal Commissioner or Commissioner (under Sec. 263), or under any other order (under	Within a period of three months from the end of the month is received by the Principal Chief Commissioner or Chief Commissioner or Principal Commissioner or Commissioner additional period of 6 months allowed if it is not possible for

Section	Particulars	Time-Period for completion of Assessment/Reassessment/Recomputation, as the case may be
	Sec. 264) or in an order of any court in a proceeding, otherwise than by way of appeal or reference or fresh order under sec. 92CA	the Assessing Officer or Transfer Pricing Officer to give effect to such order within the aforesaid period, for reasons beyond his control.
Sec.153(5A) (inserted by the Finance Act, 2022)	Transfer Pricing Officer giving effect to an order or direction under sec. 263 by an order under sec. 92CA forwards such order to the Assessing Officer	Within 2 months from the end of the month in which such order of the Transfer Pricing Officer is received by him
Sec. 153(6)	Subject to sec. 153(3), (5), (5A) where an assessment or re-assessment or recomputation is made on the assessee or any person to give effect to any finding or direction in any order passed by the Commissioner (Appeals) (under Sec. 250) or Appellate Tribunal (under Sec. 254), or High Court (under Sec. 260) or Supreme Court (under sec. 262), or Principal Commissioner or Commissioner (under Sec. 263), or under any other order (under Sec. 264) or in an order of any court in a proceeding, otherwise than by way of appeal or reference	Within 12 months from the end of the month in which such order is received or passed by the Principal Commissioner or Commissioner, as the case may be
Sec. 153(8)	Revival of Order [under Sec. 153A(2)]	(*i*) either within 1 year from the end of the month of such revival or (*ii*) within the period, specified in this section or Sec. 153B(1) whichever is later
Where any reference is made to Transfer Pricing Officer [under Sec. 92CA(1)], re-assessment may be completed within 2 years instead of 1 year.		

Finding or Direction-Implication thereof - The expression "finding" and "direction" are limited in their meanings.

The expression "finding" means a finding necessary for giving relief in respect of the assessment for the year in the question. Therefore, no decision can be said to be a finding unless it can be said of it that it was necessary for the disposal of the appeal [*CIT* v. *S. Raghubir Singh Trust* [1980] 3 Taxman 14/123 ITR 438 (SC)].

The expression "direction" must be an expressed direction, necessary for disposal of the case before the authority or the court. A direction by a statutory authority is in the nature of an order requiring its positive compliance [*Rajindar Nath* v. *CIT* [1979] 2 Taxman 204/120 ITR 14 (SC)].

Order to drop revision proceedings is not a "Finding" or "Direction" - Where the Commissioner dropped, by an order, the proceedings initiated under Sec. 263, it would be erroneous to say that the order contained any "finding" or "direction" so as to extend the period of limitation [*Raj Kishore Prasad* v. *ITO* (1990) 88 CTR (All.) 152].

Finding relating to the assessee [*Explanation* 2 to Sec. 153] - Where by an order passed in higher tax proceedings (under Sec. 250, 254, 260, 262, 263 or 264), any income is excluded from the total income of the assessee for any assessment year, then, an assessment of such income for another assessment year is deemed to be one made in consequence of or to give effect to any finding or direction contained in the said order.

Faceless Scheme for Income Escaping Assessment [Sec. 151A]

For the purposes of assessment, reassessment or re-computation under Sec. 147 or issuance of notice under Sec. 148 or sanction for issue of such notice under Sec. 151, so as to impart greater efficiency, transparency and accountability by—

(*a*) eliminating the interface between the income-tax authority and the assessee or any other person to the extent technologically feasible;

(*b*) optimising utilisation of the resources through economies of scale and functional specialisation;

(*c*) introducing a team-based assessment, reassessment, re-computation or issuance or sanction of notice with dynamic jurisdiction,

Central Government may make a scheme, by notification in the Official Gazette.

For the purpose of giving effect to the scheme, the Central Government may by notification in the Official Gazette, direct that any of the provisions of this Act shall not apply or shall apply with such exceptions, modifications and adaptations as may be specified in the notification [Sec. 151A(2)]. However no direction shall be issued after the 31st day of March, 2022. Every notification so issued shall, as soon as may be after the notification is issued, be laid before each House of Parliament [Sec. 151A(3)].

e-Assessment of Income Escaping Assessment Scheme, 2022

In exercise of the powers conferred by section 151A(1), (2), the Central Government *vide* Notification No. 18/2022 dated 29-3-2022 notified the e-Assessment of Income Escaping Assessment Scheme, 2022. The scheme is in effect from 29-3-2022. The Scheme provides that assessment, reassessment or recomputation under Section 147 and issuance of notice under Section 148 shall be done:

(*a*) Through automated allocation, in accordance with risk management strategy formulated by the Board as referred to in section 148 for issuance of notice, and

(*b*) In a faceless manner, to the extent provided in Section 144B with reference to making assessment or reassessment of total income or loss of assessee.

ASSESSMENT IN CASE OF SEARCH OR REQUISITION [SEC. 153A]

Searches conducted by the income-tax department are important means to unearth black money and to detect concealed income. When a search under sec. 132 is commenced or the books of account, other papers or the assets are requisitioned under sec. 132A after 31st May, 2003 but before 31st March, 2021; secs. 153A, 153B and 153C will govern the assessment Secs. 153A, 153B and 153C governs the assessment in case of search.

(*i*) **Issue of notice -** As a first step, the Assessing Officer issues a notice to the assessee where a search is initiated [under Sec. 132] or books of account, other documents or any assets are requisitioned [under Sec. 132A]. Under this notice, requiring such assessee to furnish return of income for 6 assessment years, immediately preceding the assessment year relevant to the previous year in which search is conducted or requisition is made. Thus, where search is initiated on 1 January 2016 the assessee is bound to furnish the return of income for the assessment years 2009–10 to 2014–15. However, the Central Government may make rules to specify the cases in which the Assessing Officer shall not be required to issue such notice.

No prior approval is required to be sought by the Assessing Officer to issue notice. [Sec. 153D]. It is not necessary that Assessing Officer should first detect undisclosed income before issuing such notice.

(*ii*) **Furnishing of returns by the assessee -** On receipt of the notice, the assessee is required to furnish the return of income in the prescribed form and verified in the prescribed manner, within such period as may be specified in the notice.

He has to furnish the return of income even if he has already furnished such returns for the period specified in the notice or even if the assessment of a particular year might have become time-barred under the normal provisions of Sec. 149.

While filing the return of income, the assessee is also required to pay any tax or interest, due from him under other provisions of the Act. The assessee is liable to pay interest under Sec. 234A for late furnishing or non-furnishing the return of income. He is also liable to pay interest under Sec. 234B for under-payment of advance tax. The assessee may be prosecuted (under Sec. 276CC) for failure to furnish the return of income.

(*iii*) **Estimation of total income -** The Assessing Officer is required to estimate the total income for each assessment year, covered under the notice, in accordance with the provisions of the Act described as below:

(*i*) Income is computed head-wise;

(*ii*) Clubbing provisions (Secs. 60 to 64) are also applicable;

(*iii*) Incomes computed head-wise are aggregated (Sec. 70 to Sec. 71);

(*iv*) Set-off and carry forward of losses is allowed (Secs. 72 to 80);

(*v*) Deductions admissible from gross total income (Sec. 80C to Sec. 80U) are allowed in determining total income.

The Assessing Officer is required to assess or re-assess the total income of each assessment year falling within such 6 assessment years in accordance with the following provisions:

(*i*) ***Abatement of Pending Assessment or Re-assessment* -** If any assessment or re-assessment for an assessment year, falling within the aforementioned 6 assessment years is pending on the date of initiation of the search [under Sec. 132] or making of requisition [under Sec. 132A], it stands abate.

Where the seized documents, books of account and other assets (money, bullion, jewellery, and others) belong to a person or persons, other than the person in relation to whom the search/requisitions proceedings were conducted and the Assessing Officer has no jurisdiction over such other person/persons, he is required to hand over the seized documents/assets to the Assessing Officer who has jurisdiction over such person/persons.

In case of such person/persons, if any assessment or re-assessment for an assessment year, falling within six assessment years preceding the assessment year relevant to the previous year in which search is conducted or requisition is made, is pending on the date of receiving the books of account or documents or assets seized or requisitioned by the Assessing Officer having jurisdiction on such person/persons, such assessment stand also abate.

(*ii*) ***Completed Assessment to be Re-opened* -** If an assessment for any assessment year, falling within the scheme of 6 assessment years, has already been completed before the date of such search/requisition, it is re-opened and its income is to be re-assessed under Sec. 153A.

(*iii*) ***Powers of Regular Assessment to be exercised in making Assessment or Re-assessment*** - While assessing or re-assessing the total income of any six assessment years, the Assessing Officer may exercise all such powers as are vested with him in making regular assessment.

Thus, the Assessing Officer may order for re-audit of the books of account under Sec.142(2A). He may hold inquiry and collect material from any source available to him. He may exercise the powers of discovery and information under Sec. 131. He may provide an opportunity of being heard to the assessee in the interest of natural justice.

(*iv*) **Determining tax liability** - The total income of an assessment year thus assessed is charged to tax at the rate or rates as are applicable for such assessment year under the Annual Finance Act of that year. In determining tax liability, credit is given for all taxes paid by the assessee in the form of advance tax, TDS, self-assessment tax, tax paid in pursuant to assessment, and so on.

Assessment of Income of any other person, other than searched person [Sec. 153C] - Sec. 153C governs a situation where search is conducted against a person and undisclosed assets/documents indicating undisclosed income are found as belonging to "other person" other than "searched person". Where the Assessing Officer is satisfied that any money, bullion, jewellery or other valuable article or thing or books of account or documents seized or requisitioned belongs or belong to a person other than the person referred to in the Sec. 153A, the books of account or documents or assets seized or requisitioned are handed over to the Assessing Officer having jurisdiction over such other person. Thereafter, that Assessing Officer is required to proceed against such person and issue notice to him and assess or re-assess him for such income in accordance with the provision of Sec. 153A.

Where books of account or documents or assets seized or requisitioned have been received by the Assessing Officer having jurisdiction over such other person after the due date for furnishing the return of income for the assessment year relevant to the previous year in which search is conducted under Sec. 132 or requisition is made under Sec. 132A, the following provisions govern such assessment:

(*a*) Where no return of income has been furnished in respect of such assessment year by such other person and no notice has been issued under Sec. 142(1) before the date of receiving the books of account or documents or assets seized or requisitioned by the Assessing Officer having jurisdiction over such person, such Assessing Officer is required to issue notice to such other person and assess or re-assess total income of such other person of such assessment year in the manner provided under Sec. 153A; or

(*b*) Where a return of income has been furnished in respect of such assessment year by such other person but no notice has been served to him under Sec. 143(2) and the limitation period of serving such notice has expired before the date of receiving the books of account or documents or assets seized or requisitioned by the Assessing Officer having jurisdiction over such other person, such Assessing Officer is required to issue notice and assess or re-assess total income of such other person in the manner provided in Sec. 153A; or

(*c*) Where assessment or re-assessment in respect of such assessment year has been made, before the date of receiving the books of account or documents or assets seized or requisitioned by the Assessing Officer having jurisdiction over such other person, such Assessing Officer is required to issue notice to such other person for such assessment year in the manner provided in Sec. 153A.

Nothing contained in this section shall apply in relation to a search initiated under section 132 or books of account, other documents or any assets requisitioned under section 132A on or after the 1st day of April, 2021 [Sec. 153(3)].

Time limit for the completion of assessment [Sec. 153B]

In case of person searched the assessment must be completed within 21 months from the end of the financial year in which last of the authorization for search under Sec. 132 or requisition under Sec. 132A was executed. Where the last of the authorisations for search was executed during the financial year commencing on the 1st day of April, 2018, the assessment must be completed within 18 months and where it was last executed during the financial year commencing on or after the 1st day of April, 2019, assessement must be completed within 12 months.

This time limit is increased by one year when it involves Transfer Pricing regulations.

However, in a case where the last of the authorisations for search under sec. 132 or requisition under sec. 132A was executed during the financial year commencing on the 1st day of April, 2020 or in case of other person referred to in sec. 153C, the books of account or document or assets seized or requisitioned were handed over under sec. 153C to the Assessing Officer having jurisdiction over such other person during the financial year commencing on the 1st day of April, 2020, the assessment in such cases for the assessment year commencing on the 1st day of April, 2021 shall be made on or before the 30th day of September, 2022 (sixth proviso to sec. 153B(1) inserted by the Finance Act, 2022).

Authorisation shall be deemed to have been executed.

In the case of search, on the conclusion of search as recorded in the last *panchnama* drawn in relation to any person in whose case the warrant of authorisation has been issued.

In the case of requisition under Sec. 132A, on the actual receipt of the books of account or other documents or assets by the Authorised Officer.

Time limit to complete assessment of such other person, other than the person searched - In case of any other person, time limit to complete the assessment is:

(*a*) 21 months (18 months or 12 months as referred above) from the end of the financial year in which last of the authorization for search under Sec. 132 or requisition under Sec. 132A was executed

or

(*b*) 9 months from the end of the financial year in which books of account or documents or assets seized/requisitioned are handed over to the AO having jurisdiction over such person;

whichever is later.

Exclusions

The aforesaid time period for completion of assessment excludes the following:

(*i*) the period during which the assessment proceeding is stayed by an order or injunction of any court;

(*ii*) the period commencing from the date on which the Assessing Officer makes a reference to the Valuation Officer under sec. 142A(1) and ending with the date on which the report of the Valuation Officer is received by the Assessing Officer; or

(*iii*) the time taken in re-opening the whole or any part of the proceeding or in giving an opportunity to the assessee of being re-heard under the provision to sec. 129; or

(*iv*) in a case where an application made before the Income-tax Settlement Commission is rejected by it or is not allowed to be proceeded with by it, the period commencing from the date on which an application is made before the Settlement Commission under sec. 245C and ending with the date on which the order under sec. 245D(1) is received by the Principal Commissioner or Commissioner under sub-section (2) of that section;

(*v*) the period commencing from the date on which an application is made before the Authority for Advance Rulings or before the Board for Advance Rulings;

(*vi*) the period commencing from the date on which a reference or first of the references for exchange of information is made by an authority competent under a Double Tax Avoidance Agreement;

(*vii*) the period commencing from the date on which a reference for declaration of an arrangement to be an impermissible avoidance arrangement is received by the Principal Commissioner or Commissioner; or

(*viii*) the period (not exceeding 180) commencing from the date on which a search is initiated under section 132 or a requisition is made under sec. 132A and ending on the date on which the books of account, or other documents or money or bullion or jewellery or other valuable article or thing seized under sec. 132 or requisitioned under sec. 132A, as the case may be, are handed over to the Assessing Officer having jurisdiction over such assessee.

Nothing contained in this section shall apply to any search initiated under section 132 or requisition made under section 132A on or after the 1st day of April, 2021 [Sec. 153B(4) (inserted by the Finance Act, 2022)].

RECTIFICATION OF MISTAKE [SEC. 154]

The power to rectify the mistake has been conferred on the tax authorities to ensure justice to both, the assessee the Revenue. It is not discretionary. It must be exercised if the requisite conditions are satisfied.

Mistake sought to be rectified, must be apparent from the record [Sec. 154(1)] - The mistake to be rectified must be one which is apparent from the record [*R.S. Lala Jessa Ram* v. *CIT* (1927) 2 ITC 342 (Lah)].

The plain meaning of the word "apparent" is that it must be something which appears to be so *ex facie* that it is incapable of argument or debate. Therefore, a mistake can be regarded as apparent only when it is glaring, obvious or self-evident mistake and not something which can be established by a long-drawn process of reasoning on points or in respect of which there may be two opinions [*CIT* v. *Lakshmi Prasad Lahkar* [1994] 74 Taxman 112 (Gau.)].

Glaring and Obvious Mistake of Law be Rectified - If mistake of fact, apparent from the record of the assessment order can be rectified, a mistake of law, which is glaring and obvious, can also be similarly rectified [*M.K. Venkatachalam* v. *Bombay Dyeing & Mfg. Co. Ltd.* [1958] 34 ITR 143 (SC)].

Mistake arising on a subsequent interpretation of law by Supreme Court or Jurisdictional High Court to be Rectified - A decision of the Supreme Court declaring a particular tax levy as invalid has the effect that such levy was at no time good. Consequently, where the ITO levied tax and subsequently the levy was rendered invalid by the Supreme Court there was a mistake apparent from the record which could be rectified by the ITO [*Walchand Nagar Industries Ltd.* v. *V.S. Gaitonde, ITO* [1962] 44 ITR 260 (Bom.)].

In the presence of a definite opinion of the jurisdictional High Court, the same and prevails is binding on the functionaries working within the territorial jurisdiction of that Court. The authorities by citing the opinion of another High Court, cannot say that the point is debatable and thus is not a mistake apparent on the face of the record. An order passed by the assessing authority by ignoring the opinion of the jurisdictional High Court is a mistake apparent on the face of the record and the authority would be justified in issuing a notice and passing an order of rectification [*CIT* v. *Ram Lal Babu Lal* [1998] 234 ITR 776/(2000) 109 Taxman 177(Punj. & Har.)].

"Record" includes entire Proceeding - The 'record' contemplated in these provisions does not mean only the order of assessment but it includes all proceedings and materials on which the assessment is based. Therefore, the Assessing Officer is entitled, to look into the whole evidence and the law applicable to ascertain whether there was an error.

"Record" under Sec. 154, means record of the case, comprising the entire proceedings including documents and material produced by the parties and taken on record by the authorities which were available at the time of passing of the order which is the subject-matter of the proceedings for rectification. They cannot go beyond the records and look into fresh evidence or material which were not on record at the time the order sought to be rectified was passed [*Gammon India Ltd.* v. *CIT* [1995] 80 Taxman 591/214 ITR 50 (Bom.)].

The Section can operate only on the facts which are already on record and cannot be resorted to for introducing new facts.

Disallowance of statutory duties be rectified on furnishing the proof of payment - Where statutory duties under Sec. 43B were disallowed because proof of payment was not attached with the return on income, mistake may be rectified on production of proof of payment, made on or before the due date of furnishing return of income [Circular No. 669 dated 25 October 1993].

Unclaimed relief be allowed on facts of a case - If it was apparent from the record that the assessee was entitled to a particular relief, that relief could be granted to him by an order under Sec. 154 by rectifying the assessment even though that relief had not been claimed by the assessee in the original assessment proceedings [*CIT* v. *K.N. Oil Industries* [1983] 12 Taxman 189/142 ITR 13 (MP)].

Intimation issued under Sec. 143(1) not to be rectified after issue of notice under Sec. 143(2) - If a notice has been issued under Sec. 143(2) after sending the intimation under Sec.143(1), proceedings under Sec.154(1)(*b*) cannot be initiated for rectifying that intimation [*Lakhanpal National Ltd.* v. *Dy. CIT* [1997] 90 Taxman 12 (Guj.)].

Notification issued after completion of an assessment, mistake arising there from be rectified - Where Notifications under Sec. 10(*23C*) or Sec. 35(1) are issued much after the completion of the assessments of the assessment years to which such notification apply, there is a mistake apparent from the record which can be rectified under Sec. 154. However, while disposing of the rectification applications, the Assessing Officer must ensure that the conditions prescribed in the notifications are satisfied [Circular No. 725, dated 16 October 1995].

Authorities empowered to Rectify Mistake [Sec. 154(1)] - For rectifying any mistake apparent from the record, an income-tax authority (referred to in Sec. 116) may amend any order passed by it. [Sec. 154(1)(*a*)]. It may rectify any mistake committed

(*i*) in the verification of the return [under Sec. 143(1)] or

(*ii*) processing of statements of tax deducted at source [under Sec. 200A(1)], or

(*iii*) processing of tax collected at source [under Sec. 206(CB) w.e.f. 1-6-2015]

Rectification on instruction from Superior Officers not Permissible - The Assessing Officer should apply his independent mind to the facts of the case and should not be influenced or guided in the matter by any instruction of the Commissioner or any other superior authority. A rectification based on a notice which indicated that the rectification was proposed as per Commissioner's instructions would be invalid [*Rajputana Mining Agencies* v. *ITO* (1979) 118 ITR 585/1 Taxman 99 (Raj.)]; [*ITO* v. *Eastern Scales (P.) Ltd*. [1978] 115 ITR 323 (Cal.)].

Power of Successor in Office to rectify mistake - Where an incumbent of the office has changed, the successor in office may pass rectification order [*Sushil* v. *ITO* 35 ITR 386].

When an Assessing Officer had exercised his jurisdiction under Sec. 154 and rectified the assessment order, his successor, ITO could not sit in appeal over that order and cancel the same by exercising powers again under Sec. 154 [*ACIT* v. *Chemical Limes* [1984] 149 ITR 325 (Raj.)].

Valid Rectification Application be allowed even when it is time-barred - In all the cases where a valid application under clause (*b*) of sub-section (2) of Sec. 154 had been filed by the assessee within the statutory time-limit but was not disposed of by the authority concerned within the time specified under sub-section (7) of Sec. 154, it may be disposed of by that authority even after the expiry of the statutory time-limit, on merits and in accordance with law [Circular: No.73 (F. No. 245/13/71-A & PAC) dated 7 January 1972].

Rectification of an Order, which had been subject-matter of Appeal [Sec. 154(1A)] - Where any matter has been considered and decided in any proceeding by way of appeal or revision, relating to an aforesaid order (under Sec. 154(1) as above), the authority passing such order may amend that order [under Sec. 154(1)] in relation to any matter, other than the matter which has been so considered and decided [Sec. 154(1A)].

An authority cannot rectify that part of his order, which had been the subject-matter of appeal and has, therefore, merged in the appellate order [*P. Das & Co.* v. *Dy. CIT* [1996] 87 Taxman 28/217 ITR 29 (Gau.)].

However, even after the appeal has been decided, a mistake in that part of the order which was not the subject-matter of appeal and which was left untouched by the appellate authority, can be rectified by the authority which passed the order [*Central Indian Insurance Co. Ltd.* v. *ITO* [1963] 47 ITR 895 (MP)].

Power exercisable *suo motu* or on application [Sec. 154(2)] - The power of rectification may be exercised by the authority concerned on his own initiative, that is, on discovery by him of any mistakes apparent from the record.

The power may also be exercised if the assessee concerned points out such mistake or it is brought to the notice by the deductor of tax (w.e.f. 1-7-2012) or collector of tax (w.e.f. 1-6-2015)

If the rectifying authority is Commissioner (Appeals) or Appellate Tribunal, the Assessing Officer may bring any such mistake to the notice of the concerned authority also.

Where any mistake in relation to an intimation for summary assessment under Sec. 143(1) is brought to the notice of the Assessing Officer by the assessee, the

Assessing Officer is required to rectify such mistake within a period of three months from the end of the month in which it is brought to his notice. If no such rectification is made, the assessee may file an appeal to the Commissioner (Appeals), as the case may be. From 1 June 1994, direct appeal has been provided against summary assessment.

Notice of Rectification [Sec. 154(3)] - Where a rectification of mistake has the effect of enhancing an assessment or reducing a refund or otherwise increasing the liability of the assessee, or the deductor (w.e.f. 1-7-2012) or collector (w.e.f. 1-6-2015) the concerned authority is required to issue a show-cause notice to the assessee or the deductor or the collector of its intention so to do and a reasonable opportunity to be heard should be given to him before the mistake is rectified. But such opportunity need not be given if the order of rectification reduces the assessment. The assessee is not entitled to a notice where the rectification gives effect to certain relief due to the assessee as well as enhances liability in another respect and the net result after final calculation is a reduction in the total figure of assessment. It was held that the Assessing Officer cannot change *suo motu* the status of the assessee without giving an opportunity to him in that regard.

Rectification order to be passed in writing [Sec. 154(4)] - An order of rectification is to be passed by the concerned authority in writing.

Refund to be allowed where rectification order reduces the assessment [Sec. 154(5)] - Where the rectification of mistake has the effect of reducing the assessment or reducing the liability of the assessee or the deductor or the collector, the Assessing Officer is required to make any refund due to the assessee or the deductor or the collector.

Demand notice to be issued where rectification order enhances the Assessment or reduces Refund [Sec. 154(6)] - Where the rectification proceedings have the effect of enhancing the assessment or reducing a refund already made or otherwise increasing the liability of the assessee or the deductor or the collector the Assessing Officer is required to serve on the assessee or the deductor or the collector, notice of demand in the prescribed form specifying the sum payable by the assessee or the deductor or the collector. Such a demand is deemed to be a notice of demand (under Sec. 156) and treated as a valid demand with all consequences attending on its non-compliance.

Period of limitation [Sec. 154(7), (8)] - An order of rectification may be passed by the authority concerned before the expiry of four years from the end of the financial year in which the order, sought to be amended was passed [Sec. 154(7)].

However, where an application for amendment is made by the assessee on or after 1 June 2001 to an income-tax authority (referred to under Sec. 116), the authority is now required to pass the order within six months from the end of the month in which the application is received by it, either making the amendment or refusing to allow the claim [Sec. 154(8)]. The amendment is operative from 1 June 2001.

Appeal against Rectification Order - The assessee has a right of appeal against an order of rectification or amendment passed by the Assessing Officer under Sec. 154 or 155 [Sec. 246A(*c*)]. An appeal against an order of rectification passed by the Commissioner (Appeals) or the Commissioner lies with the Tribunal [Sec. 253(1)].

Rectification of Mistake from the Order of the Appellate Tribunal [Sec. 254(2)] - The Appellate Tribunal may rectify a mistake, apparent from the record, within four years from the date of the order passed by it. It may do so if the mistake is brought to its notice either by the assessee or the Assessing Officer. Where the amendment has the effect of enhancing an assessment or reducing a refund, or otherwise increasing the liability of the assessee, the assessee should be given an opportunity of being heard.

OTHER AMENDMENTS [SEC. 155]

1. Rectification of the Assessment of a Partner of FAS on account of Disallowance of Partner's Remuneration in the Income Computation of FAS [Sec. 155(1A)] - Where a completed assessment of a firm is reviewed under re-assessment proceedings (Sec. 147) or rectification proceedings (under Sec. 154) or appeal proceedings (under Secs. 250, 254, 260 and 262), or reference proceedings (Sec. 263 or 264) or proceedings before the Settlement Commission [Sec. 245D(4)], and it is found that any remuneration to any partner is not deductible [under Sec. 40(*b*)], the Assessing Officer is required to reduce the total income of the partner to the extent of the amount not so deductible.

Such rectification can be passed at any time within four years from the end of the financial year in which the final order was passed in respect of the firm.

The rectification can be made within four years from the end of the financial year in which the final order was passed in respect of AOP/Body.

2. Rectification of the Assessment of a Member of AOP or BOI on account of Re-assessment of the Total Income of AOP or BOI [Sec. 155(2)] - Where any loss or depreciations is re-computed under re-assessment proceedings (under Sec. 147) and accordingly, it becomes necessary to re-compute the total income of the assessee for the succeeding year or years, to which the loss or depreciation has been carried forward [under Sec. 72(1) or 73(2) or Sec. 74(1) or Sec. 74A(3)], the Assessing Officer is required to re-compute the total income in respect of such year or years.

The rectification may be made within four years from the end of the financial year in which the re-assessment order was passed (under Sec. 147).

3. Rectification of Total Income on Re-computation of Loss or Depreciation in Re-assessment Proceedings [Sec. 155(4)] - Where any loss or depreciation is re-computed under re-assessment proceedings (under Sec. 147) and accordingly, it becomes necessary to recompute the total income of the assessee for the succeeding year or years, to which the loss or depreciation has been carried forward [under Sec. 72(1) or 73(2) or Sec. 74(1) or Sec. 74A(3)], the Assessing Officer is required to re-compute the total income in respect of such year or years.

The rectification may be made within four years from the end of the financial year in which the re-assessment order was passed (under Sec. 147).

4. Rectification of Total Income on Chargeability of Capital Gain [Sec. 155(7B)] - Where a capital asset is transferred by a parent company to its wholly-owned subsidiary or *vice versa* it is not treated as transfer [Sec. 47(*iv*) (*v*)], provided the transferee company in either case is an Indian company. The exclusion ceases to apply and capital gain becomes chargeable to tax if the transferee company converts the capital asset into stock-in-trade or the parent company ceases to hold 100% shareholding of the subsidiary within the next eight years from the date of such transfer. In such a case, the Assessing Officer is required to rectify the assessment of the transferer company of the previous year in which transfer took place.

The rectification may be made within four years from the end of the previous year in which the capital asset was converted into stock-in-trade or the parent company ceases to hold 100% shareholding.

5. Rectification of Assessment to allow Deduction under Sec. 10A/10B/10BA [Sec. 155(11A)] - Where no deduction has been allowed in any assessment year under Sec. 10A/10B/10BA on the ground that such income has not been received in convertible foreign exchange in India or having been received or converted in convertible foreign exchange outside India, has not been brought to India with the approval of the Reserve Bank of India or such other authority as is authorised for regulating payments/dealings in foreign exchange and subsequently such income or part thereof has been received/brought into India in the manner aforesaid, the Assessing Officer is required to amend the order of assessment to allow deduction under Sec. 10A/10B/10BA in respect of such income or part thereof as is so received or brought into India. The assessment may be rectified within 4 years, reckoned from the end of the previous year in which such income or part thereof has been received in or brought into India.

Note : Sec. 10B and Sec. 10BA have ceased to operate w.e.f. 1st April, 2012 and w.e.f. 1st April, 2010 respectively.

6. Rectification of Total Income on account of Delayed Receipt of Convertible Foreign Exchange [Sec. 155(13)] - Where no deduction has been allowed in any assessment year under Sec. 80HHC, or Sec. 80HHD or Sec. 80HHE or Sec. 80-O or Sec. 80R, or Sec. 80RR or Sec. 80RRA, on the ground that such income has not been received in convertible foreign exchange in India and subsequently such income is brought to India in convertible foreign exchange with the approval of Reserve Bank of India or such authority as is authorised under any law for regulating payments and dealings in foreign exchange, the Assessing Officer is required to allow the deduction and amend the assessment order.

The rectification may be made within four years from the end of the previous year in which such income is received in or brought into India.

7. Rectification on Account of TDS Certificate [Sec. 155(14)] - Where no tax-credit was allowed for any tax deducted at source in regular assessment or summary assessment on the ground that the certificate of tax deducted at source was not filed along with the return, the Assessing Officer is required to rectify such assessment order if such certificate is produced before him within two years from the end of the assessment year in which such income is assessable. However, such rectification is allowed if the income from which tax has been deducted at source has been disclosed in the return.

The rectification order may be passed within four years from the end of the financial year in which the order sought to be amended was passed.

From the AY 2007–08 and subsequent years, the Assessing Officer is also authorised to rectify the order of assessment or summary assessment under the aforesaid conditions where credit from tax collected is not given on the ground that the certificate furnished under Sec. 206C was not filed with the returns and the said certificate is produced within 2 years from the end of the assessment year in which such income in assessable.

8. Rectification on account of full value of consideration [Sec. 155(15)] - Where land, building or both are transferred for a consideration which is less than the value adopted for the purposes of payment of stamp duty on their transfer, the Assessing Officer is required to compute capital gain under Sec. 50C on the basis of such value, treating it as the full value of consideration. However, if such value is revised/reduced under a reference made by the assessee under Sec. 50C(2), the Assessing Officer is required to re-compute the capital gain and rectify the original assessment. Such rectification can be made within four years from the end of the financial year in which the revisionary order was passed by the Valuation Officer under Sec. 50C(2).

9. Rectification of capital gain on account of compulsory acquisition of a capital asset in a case where compensation is reduced [Sec. 155(16)] - Where a capital asset is compulsorily acquired under any law and its consideration was fixed or enhanced with the approval of the Central Government or the Reserve Bank but subsequently it is reduced by any court, tribunal or other authority, the Assessing Officer is required to rectify such assessment within four years from the end of the previous year in which the order reducing the compensation was passed by any court, tribunal or other authority.

10. Rectification of royalty on account of revocation of patent or on account removal of the name of patentee from the patent register [Sec. 155(17)] - Where deduction has been allowed in respect of royalty in computing total income of an individual under Sec. 80RRB but subsequently the patent was revoked under the order of the Controller or the High Court under the Patent Act, 1970 or his name was removed from the patents register as patentee, the Assessing Officer is required to rectify the assessment of the relevant previous year within four years from the end of previous year in which the order of the Controller or High Court was passed.

11. Rectification of deduction for cess availed under Sec.40 [Sec.155(18)] (inserted by the Finance Act, 2022) - It may be recollected that the Finance Act, 2022 inserted a clarificatory explanation to Sec. 40(*a*)(*ii*) whereby disallowance for any taxes paid by an assessee while computing its profits under the head profits and gains form business or profession included disallowance for cess or surcharge paid. This was particularly to settle the controversy whether education and health cess paid could be claimed as allowable deduction. Now, this rectification provision has been correspondingly been included which stipulates that any deduction in respect of any surcharge or cess which was claimed and allowed in any previous year shall be deemed to be under-reported income of the assessee for the purposes of sec. 270A(3) and the Assessing Officer shall recompute the total income of the assessee for such previous year and make necessary amendment. The provisions of section 154 shall, so far as may be, apply thereto, the period of four years specified in sub-section (7) of section 154 being reckoned from the end of the previous year commencing on the1st day of April, 2021. However, where the assessee makes an application to the Assessing Officer in the prescribed form and within the prescribed time, requesting for recomputation of the total income of the previous year without allowing the claim for deduction of surcharge or cess and pays the amount due thereon within the specified time, such claim shall not be deemed to be under-reported income for the purposes of sec. 270A(3).

NOTICE OF DEMAND (SEC. 156)

When any tax, interest, penalty, fine or any other sum is payable in consequence of any order passed under this Act, the Assessing Officer is required to serve upon the assessee notice of demand in the prescribed form specifying the sum so payable. It is only when notice of demand is served on the assessee that the tax or any other sum of money covered by the notice becomes amount due to the government.

Demand Notice be Issued in the Prescribed Form - Notice of demand must in a form prescribed by the rules [*ITO* v. *Seghu Bucharah Setty* [1964] 52 ITR 538 (SC)]. Notice of demand for tax liability on assessment should be issued in Form No. 7 (Rule 15) and demand notice for advance tax liability should be issued in Form No. 28 (Rule 38). If a notice of demand is not in the proper form, the assessee cannot be regarded as a defaulter and no question of recovery under Sec. 220 arises.

Order to Charge Interest must be Specific - Sec. 156 makes it clear that notice of demand claiming interest can be issued only when there is a clause in the assessment order levying interest. To use the expression "charge interest, if any" or "charge interest as per rules" cannot be read to mean that the Assessing Officer has passed orders to "charge interest under all the aforesaid sections". The order to charge interest has to be specific and clear. The assessee must be made to know that the Assessing Officer, after applying his mind has ordered the charging of interest and under which of the sections of the Act.

When the assessment order is silent as to whether any interest is leviable, the notice of demand cannot go beyond the assessment order and the assessee cannot be served with any such notice demanding interest. Such a notice is to be quashed [*Uday Mishtan Bhandar and Complex* v. *CIT* (1996) 222 ITR 44/(1997) 90 Taxman 500 (Pat.)] [Affirmed by the Supreme Court in *CIT* v. *Ranchi Club Ltd*. [2001] 114 Taxman 414/247 ITR 209 (SC)].

Demand notice constitutes grounds for recovery proceedings - The service of the notice of demand constitutes the grounds for launching recovery proceedings and unless the notice of demand is served, neither proceedings can be instituted against a person for recovery of the amount of tax or other sum nor can the person concerned be treated as a defaulter.

If, however, the assessee is aware of the tax-liability on him and has factually moved the authorities for extension of time for payment, he may, on default, be treated as 'defaulter' and proceedings for recovery may be launched against him.

Incorrect notice be replaced by a new one - If the earlier notice is wrong, a correct notice of demand in conformity with the assessment can always be issued to the assessee without a formal rectification order [*CIT* v. *Karnani Industrial Bank Ltd*. [1978] 113 ITR 380 (Cal.)].

Demand notice issued prior to the death of the assessee remains valid even after death - If, after the service of notice of the demand, an assessee dies, it is not necessary that a fresh demand should be served on his heirs.

Demand Notice v. Death of the assessee - If, after the service of notice of demand, an assessee dies, it is not necessary that a fresh demand should be served on his heirs. But if the assessee dies before service of the demand notice, it is essential that each of the heirs who is sought to be made liable for recovery is served with a notice of demand.

***Variation in Tax Liability* v. *Notice of Demand* -** If there is an enhancement of tax over the amount mentioned in the original notice of demand in an appeal, the Assessing Officer is required to serve a fresh notice of demand only for the excess amount over what was specified and demanded in the original notice and recovery proceedings remains in operation. If there is reduction in the tax demand, no fresh notice need be served but the fact of reduction should be intimated to the assessee and Tax Recovery Officer [Sec. 3 of Taxation Laws (Continuation and Validation of Recovery Proceedings) Act,1964].

Time-limit to issue Demand Notice - A notice of demand must be served within a reasonable time. No time-limit has been laid down in the Act. A notice of demand issued fourteen months after the expiry of the assessment year was held to have been issued within reasonable time.

Intimation of Loss [Sec. 157] - When in the course of the assessment of the total income of any assessee, it is established that a loss has occurred which the assessee is entitled to have carried forward and set-off, the Assessing Officer is required to notify to the assessee by an order in writing the amount of such loss computed by him. Where an Assessing Officer does not notify to the assessee by an order in writing the amount of loss for any year as computed by him, the assessee is entitled to have the loss re-determined in a subsequent year [*CIT* v. *Khushal Chand Daga* (1961) 42 ITR 177 (SC)].

Faceless rectification, amendments and issuance of notice or intimation [Sec. 157A]

The Taxation and Other Laws (Relaxation and Amendment of Certain Provisions) Act, 2020, w.e.f. 1-11-2020 introduced Sec. 157A that provides for faceless rectification. For the purposes of rectification of any mistake apparent from record under Sec. 154 or other amendments under Sec. 155 or issue of notice of demand under Sec. 156, or intimation of loss under Sec. 157, so as to impart greater efficiency, transparency and accountability by the Central Government may make a scheme.

CHAPTER 22 Interest, Penalties, Offences and Prosecutions

INTRODUCTION

In order to ensure that assessees duly comply with the income tax laws, the Income-tax Act comprises of a range of provisions that impose interest and penalties and prosecute defaulters. While interests are compensatory in nature and penalties impose monetary punishment for non-compliers, prosecution initiates criminal proceedings against tax evaders, defaulters and non-compliers. Chapter XXI recognises defaults which are imposable with penalties, Chapter XXII deal with offences and prosecutions declare certain omissions and/or commissions as punishable offences.

The chapter is divided in three major heads: Interest, Penalties, Prosecution.

INTEREST

Interest is a compensatory levy payable by a defaulter. Thus, if the assessee delays the process of assessment or fails to discharge his tax obligation on due dates, he remains liable to pay interest. Similarly, if the government withholds the money due to the assessee, it remains liable to pay interest to the assessee for the delay in the payment. The following table provides a cursory glance at interest liability. Interest payment for delay in Advance tax is explained in detail separately.

TABLE 22.1: INTEREST AT A GLANCE

Section	Type of Default	Period of interest	Rate of Interest
234A(1)	**Interest for Default in furnishing the Return of Income** (*a*) Delay in furnishing or non-furnishing of (*i*) voluntary return of income [Sec. 139(1)] or (*ii*) the belated return of income [Sec. 139(4)] or (*i*) the return of income under the order of the Assessing Officer [Sec. 142(1)(*i*)]	Delayed Return: commencing on the date immediately following the due date for filing of return of income under Sec. 139(1) and ending on the date on which the return of income is furnished No Return: commencing on the date, immediately following the	

Section	Type of Default	Period of interest	Rate of Interest
		due date of furnishing the return of income and ending on the date on which best judgment assessment is completed	
	(*b*) Delay in furnishing or non-furnishing return beyond the time allowed in notice issued by Assessing Officer to furnish return of income (*i*) for income escaping assessment (Sec. 148); or (*ii*) for assessment in search cases (Sec. 153A) after completion of summary assessment [Sec. 143(1)] or (*iii*) regular assessment [made under Sec. 143(3) or Sec. 144 or Sec. 147]	Delayed return: Date immediately following the expiry of the time-limit allowed in the notice, issued under Sec. 148 or Sec. 153A, and ends on the date on which return is furnished No return: Commences from the date immediately after the expiry of the time-limit allowed in the notice and ends on the date on which reassessment or assessment in search cases is completed	1% on the amount of deficiency
234B(2)	Interest where tax is paid on self-assessment	Date of regular assessment up to the date on which tax is so paid	@ 1% on the amount of short fall
234B(2A) r.w. Sec. 245C w.e.f. 1-6-2015	Interest payable in settlement of cases (*a*) When application is made making full disclosure of the income	Commencing on 1 April of such assessment year and ending on the date on which such application is made	1% on the additional amount of income-tax
	(*b*) During the proceedings	Commencing on 1st April of such assessment year and ending on the date of such order	1% on the additional amount of income-tax
	(*c*) Where the Settlement Commission has increased or reduced the amount of total income to rectify any mistake	Commencing on 1st April of such assessment year and ending on the date of such order	1% on the additional amount of income-tax interest shall be increased or reduced accordingly
234B(3)	Interest payable on account of Reassessment or Recomputation due to short-fall in the payment of advance tax which is increased in respect of	Commencing from 1st April, next following such financial year and ending on the date of reassessment or recomputation	1% of difference amount between tax determined upon reassessment/recomputation and tax under regular assessment

Section	Type of Default	Period of interest	Rate of Interest
	(*i*) income escaping assessment (under Sec. 147) or (*ii*) assessment in case of search or requisition (under Sec. 153A)		
234C	Interest payable by the Assessee for Deferment of Advance Tax No interest if non-company assessee's tax deficiency is on non-recurring income subject to other conditions		1% of the amount of deficiency
234D	Interest payable by the Assessee on Excess Refund	From the date of grant of refund to the date on which such regular assessment is completed	@ 0.5% on such amount of refund which was not actually due to him
244A	Interest on Refunds payable by Government		
	(*a*) Refund of tax is due out of any tax collected or deducted at source or paid by way of advance tax	From 1 April of the assessment year to the date on which refund is granted	0.5% on such excess amount
	(*b*) Amount of refund is less that 10% of the amount of tax, found due to the assessee on summary assessment [Sec. 143(1)] or regular assessment [Sec. 143 or Sec. 144]		No interest
	(*c*) Refund of tax is due to the assessee on account of any other reason, say, excess payment of penalty or excess payment of self-assessment tax	from the date on which such tax or penalty was paid in excess, to the date on which the refund is granted	0.5% of the amount of refund
Sec. 244A not to apply to Cases of Search or Requisitions No Interest is payable for the Period of Delay attributable to the Assessee			

PENALTIES

Penalties Imposable

Penalty is a monetary punishment, imposed for the default, committed by an assessee. Income-tax law has enacted different penalties for different defaults, some of which are as follows:

TABLE 22.2: PENALTIES AT A GLANCE

Section	Type of Default	Quantum of Penalty	Authority
140A(3)	Failure to pay wholly or partly— (*a*) self-assessment tax/ fringe benefit tax, or	Such amount as may impose but not exceeding tax in arrears	Assessing Officer

Section	Type of Default	Quantum of Penalty	Authority
	(*b*) interest, and fee, or (*c*) both under Sec. 140A(1)		
158BFA(2)	Determination of undisclosed income of block period	Penalty cannot be less than 100 % of tax leviable in respect of undisclosed income but cannot exceed um : 300 % of such tax leviable	Assessing Officer or the Commissioner (Appeals)
221(1)	Default in making payment of tax	Such amount as may impose but not exceeding amount of tax in arrears	Assessing Officer
234E	Failure to file statement within time prescribed in Sec. 200(3) or in proviso to Sec. 206C(3)	₹ 200 for every day during which failure continues but not exceeding tax deductible/collectible	-
234F (w.e.f. 2018)	Default in furnishing return of income within time as prescribed under Sec. 139(1)	₹ 5000 ₹ 1000 if total income of the person does not exceeds ₹ 5 lakh	-
234G (w.e.f. 1-6-2020	Fee for default in submission of statement/certificate prescribed under Sec. 35/Sec. 80G	₹ 200 per day	-
234H (inserted by the Finance Act, 2021)	Fee for default relating to intimation of Aadhaar Number	Upto ₹ 1000	
270A(1) (Operative from 1-4-2017)	Under-reporting and misreporting of income	If under-reported income: a sum equal to 50% of the amount of tax payable If under-reported income is in consequence of any misreporting- 200% of the amount of tax payable on under-reported income	Assessing Officer, Commissioner (Appeals), Principal Commissioner or Commissioner
271A	Failure to keep, maintain, or retain books of account, documents, etc., as required under Sec. 44AA	₹ 25,000	The Assessing Officer or the Commissioner (Appeals)
271AAB(1A)	Where search has been initiated on or after 15-12-2016 and undisclosed income found	(*a*) 30% of undisclosed income of the specified previous year if assessee admits the undisclosed income; substantiates the manner in which it was derived; and on or before the specified date pays the tax, together with interest thereon and furnishes the	The Assessing Officer or the Commissioner (Appeals)

Section	Type of Default	Quantum of Penalty	Authority
		return of income for the specified previous year declaring such undisclosed income (*b*) 60% of undisclosed income of the specified previous year in any other case.	
271AAC	Income determined by way of Cash Credits (Sec. 68) or Unexplained investments (Sec. 69) or Unexplained money etc (Sec. 69A) or Amount of investment etc. not fully disclosed in books of account. (Sec. 69B) or Unexplained expenditure etc. (Sec. 69C) or Amount borrowed / repaid on hundi (Sec. 69D.)	10% of tax payable under section 115BBE. (No penalty if such income is reflected in the income tax return filed under section 139, and tax on the same paid under section 115BBE(1)(*i*). Further no penalty for under reporting and misreporting of income (sec. 270A) shall be imposed on the assessee in respect to income referred to herein)	Assessing Officer or Commissioner (Appeals)
271AAD	Penalty, if during any proceedings under the Act, it is found that in the books of accounts-maintained by assessee, there is: (*a*) A false entry; or (*b*) Any entry relevant for computation of total income of such person has been omitted to evade tax liability.	100% of such false entries or omitted entry	Assessing Officer or Commissioner (Appeals)
271AAE (w.e.f. 1-4-2023)	Penalty for passing on unreasonable benefits to trustee or specified persons by trusts or institutions covered under sec.10(23C)(*iv*)/(*v*)/(*vi*)/(*via*)	On first breach, 100% of amount applied for the benefit of such person Any subsequent breach, 200% of amount applied for the benefit of such person	Assessing Officer
271B	Failure to get accounts audited or furnish a report of audit as required under Sec. 44AB	One-half per cent of total sales, turnover or gross receipts, etc., or ₹ 1,50,000, whichever is less	Assessing Officer
271C	Failure to deduct tax at source, wholly or partly, under Secs. 192 to 196D (Chapter XVII-B) or failure to pay wholly or partly tax under Sec. 115-O(2) or proviso to section 194B	Amount equal to tax not deducted or paid	Joint Commissioner
271CA	Failure to collect tax at source as required under Chapter XVII-BB	Amount equal to tax not collected	Joint Commissioner

Section	Type of Default	Quantum of Penalty	Authority
271F	Failure to furnish return as required by section 139(1) or by its provisos before the end of the relevant assessment year	₹ 5,000 Note: Applicable upto the Assessment Year 2017-18	Assessing Officer
271FA	Failure to furnish an annual information return as required under section 285BA(1)(2)	₹ 500 for every day during which the failure continues	Prescribed Income-tax Authority
271FAA	Furnishing of inaccurate information in statement of financial transaction or reportable account	₹ 50,000	Prescribed income-tax authority
	Failure to furnish annual information return within the period specified in notice u/s 285BA(5)	₹ 1,000 per day of default	
271FAB	Section 9A provides that fund management activity carried out by an eligible offshore investment fund through an eligible fund manager acting on behalf of such fund shall not constitute business connection in India (subject to certain conditions). The provision requires that eligible investment fund shall furnish within 90 days from the end of the financial year a statement, in respect of its activities in a financial year, in the prescribed form containing information relating to fulfilment of specified conditions and such other information or documents as may be prescribed. Penalty to be levied if investment fund failed to comply with the requirement.	₹ 5,00,000	Prescribed income-tax authority
271GA	Section 285A provides for reporting by an Indian concern if following two conditions are satisfied: (*a*) Shares or interest in a foreign company or entity derive substantial value, directly or indirectly, from assets located in India; and (*b*) Such foreign company or entity holds such assets in India through or in such Indian concern.	Penalty shall be: (*a*) A sum equal to 2% of value of transaction in respect of which such failure has taken place, if such transaction had effect of, directly or indirectly, transferring right of management or control in relation to the Indian concern; (*b*) A sum of ₹ 5,000 in any other case.	Prescribed income-tax authority

Section	Type of Default	Quantum of Penalty	Authority
	In this case, the Indian entity shall furnish the prescribed information for the purpose of determination of any income accruing or arising in India under Section 9(1)(*i*). In case of any failure, the Indian concern shall be liable to pay penalty.		
271GB(1)	Failure to furnish report under section 286(2)	₹ 5,000 per day upto 30 days and ₹ 15,000 per day beyond 30 days	Prescribed Authority
271GB(2)	Failure to produce the information and documents within the period allowed under section 271GB(6)	₹ 5,000 for every day during which the failure continues.	Prescribed Authority
271GB(3)	Failure to furnish report or failure to produce information/documents under section 286 even after serving order under section 271GB(1) or 271GB(2)	₹ 50,000 for every day for which such failure continues beginning from the date of serving such order.	Prescribed Authority
271GB(4)	Failure to inform about inaccuracy in report furnish under section 286(2). Or furnishing of inaccurate information or document in response to notice issued under section 286(6).	₹ 5,00,000	Prescribed Authority
271H	Failure to deliver/cause to be delivered a statement within the time prescribed in section 200(3) or the proviso to section 206C(3), or furnishes incorrect information in the statement	Minimum penalty ₹ 10,000 but may extend to ₹ 1,00,000 (no penalty the prescribed statement has been furnished before the expiry of one year since the prescribed date after payment of the tax along with interest and fees)	Assessing Officer
271-I	As per section 195(6) of the Act, any person responsible for paying to a non-resident or to a foreign company, any sum (whether or not chargeable to tax), shall furnish the information relating to such payment in Forms 15CA and 15CB. Penalty shall be levied in case of any failure.	₹ 1,00,000	Assessing Officer
271J	Furnishing of incorrect information in any report or certificate by an accountant or	₹ 10,000 for each incorrect report or certificate	Assessing Officer or the Commissioner (Appeals)

Section	Type of Default	Quantum of Penalty	Authority
	a merchant banker or a registered valuer		
271K	Penalty of default in submission of statement/certificate prescribed under section 35/ Section 80G	₹ 10,000 to ₹ 1 lakh	Assessing Officer
272A(1)	Refusal or failure to : (*a*) Answer questions (*b*) Sign statement (*c*) Attend to give evidence or produce books of account, etc., in compliance with summons under section 131(1) (*d*) Comply with notices u/s 142(1)/143(2) or failure to comply with direction issued u/s 142(2A).	₹ 10,000 for each failure/ default	When default occurs in any proceeding before an income-tax authority not lower in rank than a Joint Director or a Joint Commissioner, such authority In case of default under (*d*) penalty is imposed by the income-tax authority who had issued the notice/ direction
272A(2)	Failure to : (*a*) Furnish requisite information in respect of securities as required under section 94(6); (*b*) Give notice of discontinuance of business or profession as required under section 176(3); (*c*) Furnish in due time returns, statements or certificates, deliver declaration, allow inspection, etc., under sections 133, 134, 139(4A), 139(4C), 192(2C), 197A, 203, 206, 206C, 206C(1A) and 285B; (*d*) Deduct and pay tax under section 226(2) (*e*) File a copy of the prescribed statement within the time specified in section 200(3) or the proviso to section 206C(3) (up to 1-7-2012)	₹ 500 for every day during which failure continues. (In respect of penalty for failure, in relation to a declaration mentioned in section 197A, a certificate as required by section 203 and returns u/ss 206 and 206C and statements under Section 200(2A) or section 200(3) or proviso to section 206C(3) or section 206C(3A), penalty shall not exceed amount of tax deductible or collectible)	In case of default under (*f*), Principal Chief Commissioner or Chief Commissioner or Principal Commissioner or Commissioner In any other case, Joint Commissioner or Joint Director (No order shall be passed without an opportunity of being heard in the matter)

Section	Type of Default	Quantum of Penalty	Authority
	(*f*) file the prescribed statement within the time specified in section 206A(1) (*g*) Failure to deliver or cause to be delivered a statement under Section 200(2A) or Section 206C(3A) within prescribed time. With effect from June 1, 2015, it is mandatory for an office of the Government, paying TDS or TCS, as the case may be, without production of a challan, to deliver a statement in the prescribed form and manner to the prescribed authority.		
272AA(1)	Failure to comply with section 133B	Not exceeding ₹ 1,000	Joint Commissioner or the Assistant Director or the Deputy Director or the Assessing Officer (No order shall be passed without an opportunity of being heard in the matter)
272B	Failure to comply with provisions relating to PAN or Aadhaar as referred to in section 139A/139A(5)(c)/(5A)/(5C)	₹ 10,000 for each default	Assessing Officer (No order shall be passed without an opportunity of being heard in the matter)
272BB(1)	Failure to comply with section 203A	₹ 10,000 for each failure/ default	Assessing Officer (No order shall be passed without an opportunity of being heard in the matter)
272BB(1A)	Quoting false tax deduction account number/tax collection account number/tax deduction and collection account number in challans/certificates/statements/documents referred to in section 203A(2)	₹ 10,000	Assessing Officer (No order shall be passed without an opportunity of being heard in the matter)

Section	Type of Default	Quantum of Penalty	Authority
272BBB	Failure to Comply with the Provisions of Tax Collection Number	₹ 10,000	Assessing Officer (No order shall be passed without an opportunity of being heard in the matter)

Post-2017 Penalty for under-reporting and misreporting of income [sec. 270A]

Since the penalty imposed under sec. 271(1)(*c*) was highly litigious, in order to rationalize and bring objectivity, certainty and clarity to the penalty provisions, the Finance Act, 2016 introduced a new sec. 270A. Sec. 270A replaced the concept of 'concealment of income' and 'filing inaccurate particulars of income' with the new concept of 'under reporting of income' and 'misreporting of income'. Accordingly, sec. 271 shall not apply to and in relation to any assessment for the assessment year commencing on or after the 1st day of April, 2017 and subsequent assessment years.

Under reporting of income: Sec. 270A(2) enlists instances where a person shall be considered to have under-reported his income as follows:

Particulars	Income assessed under regular provisions	Income assessed under MAT (sec. 115JB) or AMT (sec. 115JC) provisions
When Return is filed	Assessed Income is greater than Processed Income	Deemed total income assessed or reassessed is greater than Processed Deemed income
When Return is not filed	Assessed Income is greater than maximum amount not chargeable to tax	Deemed total income assessed is greater than maximum amount not chargeable to tax
When Reassessment	Reassessed Income is greater than income assessed or reassessed immediately before such reassessment	Deemed total income re-assessed is greater than deemed total income assessed or reassessed immediately before such reassessment
Income assessed or reassessed has the effect of reducing the loss or converting such loss into income		

Penalty for Intangible additions, which becomes tangible in subsequent assessment years [sec. 270A(4)]: Sec. 270A(4) includes yet one more instance to the list of unreported income, that is, intangible additions. Thus, any additions to income in earlier years or income deducted while computing loss in earlier years, which have not been penalised then and is now used to explain source of any receipt/ deposit/investment etc. in any subsequent year [*Anantharam Veerasinghaiah and Co.* v. *CIT* (1980) 123 ITR 457 (SC)].

Misreporting of income - Section 270A(9) lists out cases where underreporting shall be considered to be misreporting of income, which are:

(*a*) misrepresentation or suppression of facts;

(*b*) failure to record investments in the books of account;

(*c*) claim of expenditure not substantiated by any evidence;

(*d*) recording of any false entry in the books of account;

(*e*) failure to record any receipt in books of account having a bearing on total income; and

(*f*) failure to report any international transaction or any transaction deemed to be an international transaction or any specified domestic transaction, to which the provisions of Chapter X apply.

Exclusions from Under-reported income [Sec. 270A(6)]

Sec. 270A(6) certain genuine transactions are excluded from being under-reported income. These are as follows:

(*a*) the amount of income in respect of which the assessee offers *bona fide* explanation and the assessee has disclosed all the material facts to substantiate the explanation offered;

(*b*) the amount of under-reported income determined on the basis of an estimate;

(*c*) the amount of under-reported income determined on the basis of an estimate, if the assessee has, on his own, estimated a lower amount of addition or disallowance on the same issue, has included such amount in the computation of his income and has disclosed all the facts material to the addition or disallowance;

(*d*) the amount of under-reported income represented by Transfer Pricing addition, where the assessee had maintained information and documents as prescribed under section 92D, declared the international transaction under Chapter X, and, disclosed all the material facts relating to the transaction; and

(*e*) the amount of undisclosed income (during search cases) referred to in section 271AAB.

Authority imposing Penalty - Assessing Officer, Commissioner (Appeals), Principal Commissioner or Commissioner is empowered to levy the penalty under section 270A.

Quantum of Penalty

In case of underreporting of Income - 50% of the amount of tax payable on under-reported income

In case of underreporting of Income in consequence of any misreporting thereof - 200% of the amount of tax payable on under-reported income

Special Provisions for immunity from Imposition of Penalty and Initiation of Prosecutions [Sec. 270AA]

In order to reduce the litigation and to get the speedy recovery of the tax along with interest, sec. 270AA has also been introduced by the Finance Act, 2016 wherein immunity for imposition penalty and initiation of prosecution can be sought subject to fulfilment of certain conditions. Such immunity cannot be sought for cases of misreporting of income. Accordingly, the assessee can make an application to the Assessing Officer to grant immunity from the levy of penalty etc. within one month from the end of the month in which assessment order has been received, provided that

(*i*) the tax and interest payable as per the order of assessment or reassessment has been paid within the period specified in such notice of demand; and

(*ii*) no appeal has been filed

Penalty for false entry, etc., in books of account [Sec. 271AAD] - With the launch of Goods & Services Tax (GST), several cases of fraudulent claims of input tax credit (ITC) had been caught by the GST authorities. As a modus operendi of claiming ITC, fake invoices were obtained by the suppliers so to reduce their GST liability. Such fake invoices are only paper work without any actual supply of goods or services or any real business being carried on. Therefore, in order to deal strictly with such fraudulent arrangements, sec. 271AAD was introduced.

The Finance Act, 2020 introduced penalty for false entry in books of account under sec. 271AAD w.e.f. 1-4-2020. Accordingly, penalty is imposed for a false entry or any entry relevant to the computation of total income of such person has been omitted with the intention to evade any tax liability in the books of account maintained by him.

Such penalty under sec. 271AAD can also be levied on any other person who is in any manner involved in making such false entries *i.e.* the person who issues a false invoice or causes to make the wrongful entry is also liable to penalty.

Meaning of False Entry

For the purposes of this section, "false entry" includes use or intention to use—

(*a*) forged or falsified documents such as a false invoice or, in general, a false piece of documentary evidence; or

(*b*) invoice in respect of supply or receipt of goods or services or both issued by the person or any other person without actual supply or receipt of such goods or services or both; or

(*c*) invoice in respect of supply or receipt of goods or services or both to or from a person who does not exist. [*Explanation* to sec. 271AAD]

Quantum of Penalty - Penalty imposed shall be equal to the aggregate amount of false entries or omitted entries.

PROCEDURE TO IMPOSE PENALTY [SEC. 274]

The following general provisions apply for the imposition of penalties under this Act:

- **Assessee to be given a reasonable opportunity of being heard [Sec. 274(1)] -** No penalty can be imposed unless the assessee has been heard or has been given a reasonable opportunity of being heard [Sec. 274(1)]. If an opportunity to show cause is not given to the assessee, the imposition of a penalty is invalid [*Banarsi Das* v. *CIT* [1936] 4 ITR 217 (Lahore)]; [*Rajeev Kumar Gupta* v. *CIT* [1980] 4 Taxman 345/123 ITR 907 (All.)]. mere notice sent in a printed form without mentioning grounds would not satisfy requirement of law *Muninaga Reddy* v. *Asstt. CIT* [2018] 96 taxmann.com 230/[2019] 417 ITR 699 (Kar.)].

  Where an Assessing Officer is succeeded by another, the succeeding officer has also to give such opportunity if the case was not fully heard by his predecessor or if the assessee demands such opportunity of hearing (Sec. 129) [*Satprakash Ram Naranjan* v. *CIT* [1969] 71 ITR 646 (Punj. & Har.).

- **Power to impose penalty [Sec. 274(2)] -** The Income-tax Officer cannot impose a penalty exceeding ₹ 10,000 without the prior approval of the Joint Commissioner. Similarly, the Assistant Commissioner or Deputy Commissioner cannot impose penalty exceeding ₹ 20,000 without the prior approval of the Joint Commissioner.

  After imposing the penalty, an income-tax authority is required to send its copy to the Assessing Officer unless he is himself the Assessing Officer [Sec. 274(3)].

- **Proceedings can be Initiated at any time -** The Act does not contemplate initiation of penalty proceedings only on the completion of assessment proceedings. The words 'in the course of any proceedings' as occurring in Sec. 271(1) only indicate that such initiation of penalty proceedings can be made during the pendency of any proceedings under the Act [*Jyoti Prakash Mitter* v. *Union of India* [1978] 112 ITR 378 (Cal.)].

- **Quantum of Penalty to be determined according to the Law Prevailing on the date of default -** The quantum of penalty is determined in accordance with the law as it stands at the date when the default, which attracts penalty, is committed. The law as it stands in the assessment year, when the penalty is imposed, is of no relevance unless the concerned law has retrospective effect. The question whether an act or an omission is an offence must be determined by reference to the law as it stands at the time when the act is done or omission is made [*CIT* v. *Onkar Saran & Sons* (1992) 62 Taxman 440/195 ITR 1(SC)].

- **Communication of penalty order to AO [Sec. 274(3)] -** An income-tax authority who imposes the penalty is required to send a copy of such order forthwith to the Assessing Officer. Where the income-tax authority imposing the penalty is himself the Assessing Officer, this provision has no application.

- **Direction to initiate penalty proceedings, deemed to be satis-fa-ction of the Assessing Officer to initiate penalty proceedings [Sec. 271(1B)] -** Where any amount is added or disallowed in computing total income or loss of an assessee in any order of assessment or reassessment and the said order contains a direction for the initiation of penalty proceedings, such an order of assessment or reassessment is deemed to constitute satisfaction of the Assessing Officer for initiation of penalty proceedings.

- **Finding of assessment proceeding not automatically applicable to penalty proceedings -** Since the burden of proof in a penalty proceeding varies from that involved in an assessment proceeding, a finding in an assessment proceeding that a particular receipt is income cannot automatically be adopted as a finding to that effect in the penalty proceeding. In the penalty proceeding the taxing authority is bound to consider the matter afresh on the material before it and, in the light of the burden to prove resting on the revenue, to ascertain whether a particular amount is a revenue receipt. The fact that the assessment order contains a finding that the disputed amount represents income constitutes good evidence in the penalty proceeding but the finding in the assessment proceeding cannot be regarded as conclusive for the purposes of the penalty proceeding *Anantharam Veerasinghaiah& Co.* v. *CIT* [1980] 123 ITR 457 (SC)].

- **Penalty is not an Additional Tax -** The penalty is in addition to the income tax determined as payable by the assessee but penalty is not additional tax [*CIT* v. *Express Newspapers (P.) Ltd.* (1978)111 ITR 347 (Mad.)].

- ***Discretion to Levy or not to Levy Penalty* v. *Minimum Penalty* -** The fact that minimum penalty is prescribed does not mean that penalty must necessarily be imposed in every case. Even if a minimum penalty is prescribed, the competent authority to impose penalty is justified in refusing to impose penalty when there is a technical or venial breach of the provisions of the Act or where the breach flows from a *bona fide* belief that the offender is not liable to act in the manner prescribed by the statute [*Hindustan Steel Ltd.* v. *State of Orissa* [1972] 83 ITR 26 (SC)].

- **Power to Reduce or Waive Penalty [Sec. 273A]**

1. Reduction or Waiver of Concealment Penalty [Sec. 273A(1)/(2)/(3)] - The Principal Commissioner or Commissioner, whether on his motion or otherwise, is empowered to reduce or waive the penalty of concealment of income if the following conditions are satisfied by the assessee:

(*i*) He has made full disclosure of his income prior to any detection of concealment by the Assessing Officer;

(*ii*) He has co-operated in any enquiry relating to his assessment; and (*iii*) He has paid or made satisfactory arrangement for the payment of tax or interest payable for the relevant assessment year.

Waiver benefit available only once [Sec. 273A(3)] - The benefit of reduction/ waiver is available to the assessee only once. If the penalty has been reduced or waived once, the assessee is not entitled to seek any reduction/waiver for any other year in future.

Where the assessee has made an application under Sec. 273A for the waiver of penalty in respect of four assessment years, the Commissioner is not justified in waiving the penalty only for the first year and dismissing the application for other years on the ground that power under Sec. 273A is available only for one year [*Ram Sarandas Har Swaroop Mal* v. *CIT* (1990) 53 Taxman 42/186 ITR 503 (All.)].

The assessee is debarred from applying for obtaining relief more than once, but in one application he can collectively apply for relief in respect of different defaults committed for different assessment years at different times.

The prohibition operates only where an order has been passed 'in favour' of the assessee. If his application for waiver or reduction of penalty has been rejected for a particular year, he may apply for waiver for another year [*Shree Singhvi Bros.* v. *UOI* [1990] 53 Taxman 555/[1991] 187 ITR 219 (Raj.)].

2. Reduction or waiver of any other penalty [Sec. 273A(4)] - The Principal Commissioner or Commissioner is empowered to reduce or waive any other penalty payable by the assessee under this Act or stay or compound any proceeding for the recovery of any such amount.

Conditions for reduction of penalty or stay of recovery of penalty - The power of reducing any penalty or granting stay of penalty can be exercised if the following conditions are satisfied:

(*i*) The Principal Commissioner or Commissioner is satisfied that to do otherwise would cause genuine hardship to the assessee, having regard to the circumstances of the case; and

(*ii*) The assessee has co-operated in any inquiry relating to the assessment or any proceedings for the recovery of any amount due from him.

Recording of Reasons - Where an assessee makes an application to the Principal Commissioner or Commissioner for reduction or waiver of any penalty, after recording his reasons for doing so, the Principal Commissioner or Commissioner may reduce or waive the penalty:

- **Power of the Principal Commissioner or Commissioner to Grant Immunity from Penalty [Sec. 273AA] -** From April 2008 and onward, a person may make an application to the Principal Commissioner or Commissioner for granting immunity from penalty, subject to the following conditions:

  (*i*) he has made an application for settlement of his case under Sec. 245C and the proceedings for settlement have abated; and

  (*ii*) the penalty proceedings have been initiated under this Act.

No application can be made if penalty has been imposed after abatement of settlement proceedings.

The Principal Commissioner or Commissioner may grant immunity from imposition of penalty if he is satisfied that after abatement the person has co-operated with the income-tax authority in the proceedings before him and has made full and true disclosure of his income and the manner in which such income has been derived.

Withdrawal of Immunity - The immunity granted to a person can be withdrawn if such person fails to comply with any condition subject to which the immunity was granted. Thereafter, the provisions of this Act become applicable as if no such immunity was granted.

The Principal Commissioner or Commissioner may also withdraw the immunity if he is satisfied that such person had, in the course of proceedings, after abatement, concealed any particulars material to the assessment from income-tax authority or had given false evidence. Thereupon, such person becomes liable to the imposition of any penalty under this Act to which such person would have been liable, if no such immunity had been granted.

Scheme for E-Penalty [Sec. 274(2A)]

In order to ensure greater efficiency, transparency and develop a faceless interaction, the E-assessment Scheme 2019 was launched. To compliment this scheme, e-penalty provisions has been inserted to the Penalty Provisions under sec. 274(2A) w.e.f. 1-4-2020.

Accordingly, the Faceless Penalty Scheme, 2021 has been launched by the Central Government by virtue of notification No. 02/2021 dated 12-1-2021 and the directions for the implementation of the same *vide* notification No. 03/2021 dated 12-2-2021. Under this scheme 'faceless penalty' means the penalty proceedings conducted electronically in 'e-proceeding' facility through assessee's registered account in designated portal. For the purpose of conducting of the penalty proceedings in a faceless manner, the CBDT has set up the following Centres:

(*i*) **National Faceless Penalty Centre -** To facilitate the conduct of faceless penalty proceedings in a centralised manner and vest it with the jurisdiction to impose penalty in accordance with the provisions of this Scheme;

(*ii*) **Regional Faceless Penalty Centres** - As it may deem necessary, to facilitate the conduct of faceless penalty proceedings, which shall be vested with the jurisdiction to impose penalty in accordance with the provisions of this Scheme;

(*iii*) **Penalty Units** - As it may deem necessary, to facilitate the conduct of faceless penalty proceedings, to perform the function of drafting penalty orders, which includes identification of points or issues for imposition of penalty under the Act, seeking information or clarification on points or issues so identified, providing opportunity of being heard to the assessee or any other person, analysis of the material furnished by the assessee or any other person, and such other functions as may be required for the purposes of imposing penalty;

(*iv*) **Penalty Review Units -** As it may deem necessary, to facilitate the conduct of faceless penalty proceedings, to perform the functions of review of draft penalty order, which includes checking whether the relevant material evidence has been brought on record, whether the relevant points of fact and law have been duly incorporated in the draft order, whether the issues on which penalty is to be imposed have been discussed in the draft order, whether the applicable judicial decisions have been considered and dealt with in the draft order, checking arithmetical correctness of computation of penalty, if any, and such other functions as may be required for the purposes of review, and specify their respective jurisdiction. The Faceless Penalty Scheme was made applicable w.e.f. 12-1-2021.

It must be noted that by virtue of Order F. No. 187/4/2021-ITA-1 dated 20-1-2021 Central Board of Direct Taxes directed that National Faceless Assessment Centre /Regional Faceless Assessment Centres/ Assessment Units/ Review Units under the Faceless Assessment Scheme, 2019 will also act as the National Faceless Penalty Centre /Regional Faceless Penalty Centre/ Penalty Unit/Penalty Review Unit respectively.

Scope of penalties under the Faceless Penalty Scheme

Notification No. 03/2021 dated 12-1-2021 specifies that the provisions of Sec. 2, Sec. 120, Sec. 127, Sec. 129, Sec. 131, Sec. 133, Sec. 133C, Sec. 136 and Chapter XXI of the Income-tax Act shall apply to the procedure for imposing penalty in accordance with the Faceless Scheme of Penalty subject to the states exceptions, modifications and adaptations. Further by virtue of CBDT *vide* Order F. No. 187/4/2021-ITA-1 dated 26-2-2021 and 20-1-2021 notified that this scheme would not be applicable to the following cases:

(*a*) Penalty proceedings arising/pending in the Investigation Wing, the Directorate of I&CI, erstwhile DG (Risk-Assessment) or by any prescribed authority;

(*b*) Penalty proceedings arising out of any statute other than the Income-tax Act, 1961;

(*c*) All the penalties imposable by the officers of the level of Commissioner/ Director/Commissioner (Appeals/Appeal Unit);

(*d*) Penalty proceedings in cases assigned to Central Charges;

(*e*) Penalty proceedings in cases assigned to International Tax Charges; and

(*f*) Penalty proceedings arising in TDS charges.

The board has notified another class of penalties that shall not be covered by the Faceless Penalty Scheme, 2021.

It has been specified that penalty proceedings in cases where pendency could not be created on ITBA because of technical reasons or cases not having a PAN shall be out of the purview of the Faceless Penalty Scheme, 2021.

The procedure commences when any income tax authority or the National Faceless Assessment Centre refers a matter to the National Faceless Penalty Centre when such authority or NFAC has (*a*) initiated penalty proceedings and issued a show-cause notice for imposition of such penalty; or (*b*) recommended initiation of penalty proceedings.

The figure below demonstrates the procedure for the levy of e-penalty:

FIGURE 22.1: PROCEDURE FOR E-PENALTY

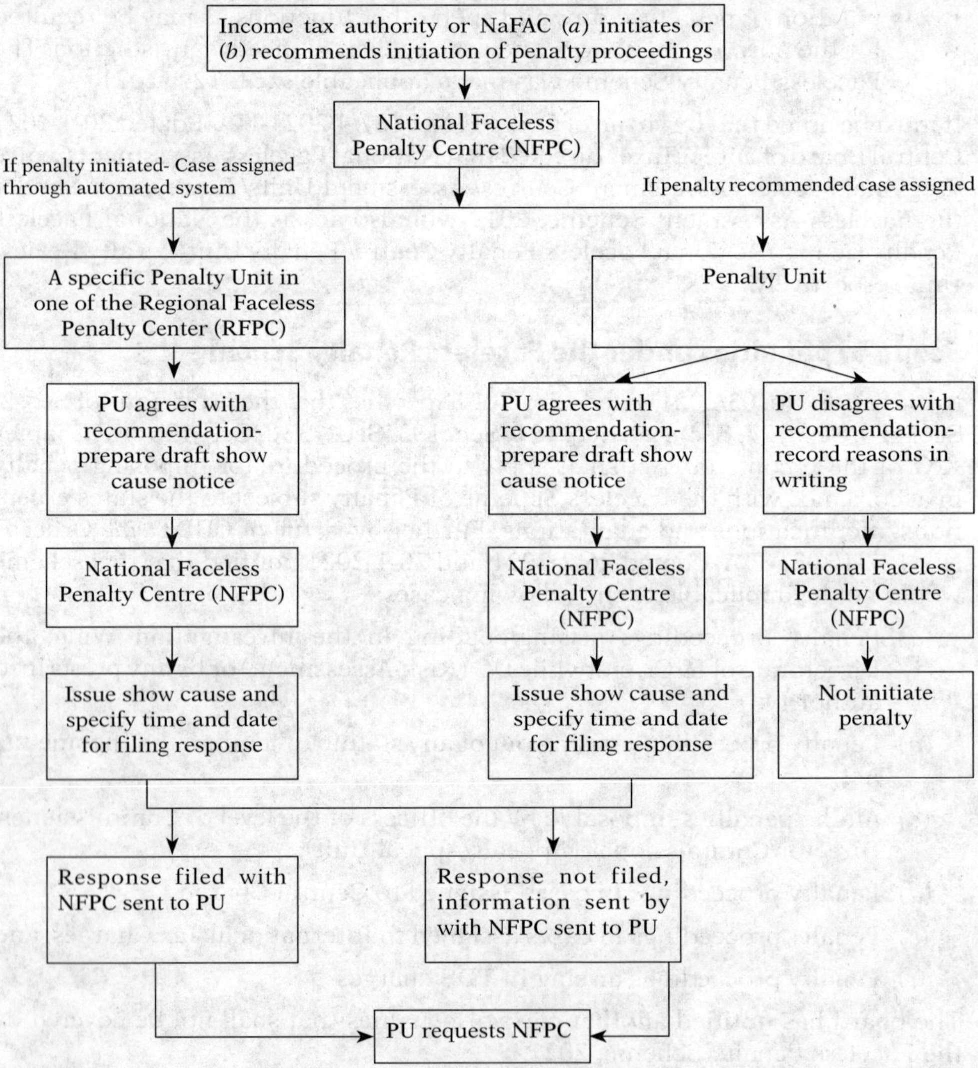

Income tax authority or NaFAC (*a*) initiates or (*b*) recommends initiation of penalty proceedings

National Faceless Penalty Centre (NFPC)

If penalty initiated- Case assigned through automated system

If penalty recommended case assigned

A specific Penalty Unit in one of the Regional Faceless Penalty Center (RFPC)

Penalty Unit

PU agrees with recommendation-prepare draft show cause notice

PU agrees with recommendation-prepare draft show cause notice

PU disagrees with recommendation-record reasons in writing

National Faceless Penalty Centre (NFPC)

National Faceless Penalty Centre (NFPC)

National Faceless Penalty Centre (NFPC)

Issue show cause and specify time and date for filing response

Issue show cause and specify time and date for filing response

Not initiate penalty

Response filed with NFPC sent to PU

Response not filed, information sent by with NFPC sent to PU

PU requests NFPC

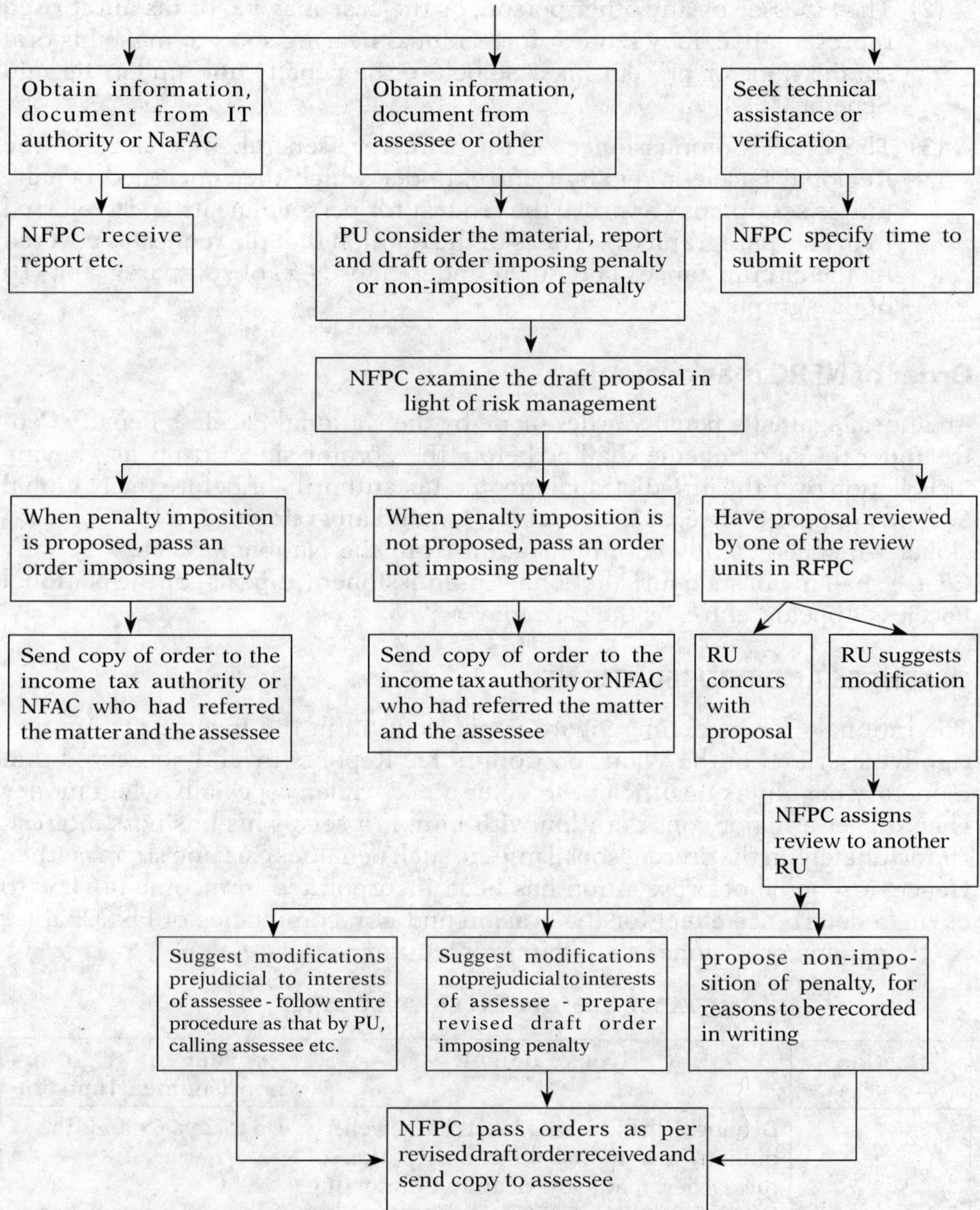

It must be noted that:

(1) A person shall not be required to appear either personally or through authorised representative in connection with any proceedings under the said Scheme before the income-tax authority at the National Faceless Penalty Centre or Regional Faceless Penalty Centre or penalty unit or penalty review unit set up under the said Scheme.

(2) The assessee or any other person, as the case may be, or his authorised representative, may request for personal hearing so as to make his oral submissions or present his case before the penalty unit under the said Scheme.

(3) The Chief Commissioner or the Director General, in charge of the Regional Faceless Penalty Centre, under which the concerned penalty unit is set up, may approve the request for personal hearing, as referred to in sub-paragraph (2), if he is of the opinion that the request is covered by the circumstances laid down under clause (*ix*) of sub-paragraph (B) of paragraph 4:

Order of NFPC is appealable

An appeal against a penalty order made by the National Faceless Penalty Centre under the said Scheme shall lie before the Commissioner (Appeals) having jurisdiction over the jurisdictional income-tax authority or before the National Faceless Appeal Centre, as the case may be; and any reference to the Commissioner (Appeals) in any communication from the National Faceless Penalty Centre shall mean such jurisdictional Commissioner (Appeals) or the National Faceless Appeal Centre, as the case may be.

OFFENCES AND PROSECUTIONS

The rationale for launching vigorous prosecution in the Income-tax Act was rightly described in the Wanchoo Committee Report. It rightly observed that monetary penalty is insufficient to deter a tax evader, especially when money is no longer a major consideration with him, if it serves his business interest. Unfortunately, in the present social milieu, such penalties carry no stigma either. Hence, a scheme of prosecution has been incorporated in income-tax law to create a deterrence effect for the evasion and non-compliance of tax. Chapter XXII contains provisions relating to prosecution.

TABLE 22.3: OFFENCES AT A GLANCE

Section	Type of default	Punishment (rigorous imprisonment) and fine
275A	Dealing with the Seized Assets like jewellery, bullion, any money in contravention of the Order made by Search Conducting Officer under sec. 132(1) (Second Proviso) or 132(3) in case of search and seizure	Up to 2 years and fine
275B	Failure to afford necessary facility to authorised officer to inspect books of account or other documents as required under section 132(1)(*iib*)	Up to 2 years and fine
276	Removal, concealment, transfer or delivery of property to thwart tax recovery	Up to 2 years and fine

Section	Type of default	Punishment (rigorous imprisonment) and fine
276A	Failure to comply with provisions of section 178(1) and (3)	6 months to 2 years and fine (not punishable if a reasonable cause for such failure is proved).
276B non-cognizable offence under section 279A	Failure to Pay tax deducted to the credit of Central Government (*i*) tax deducted at source under Chapter XVII-B (non-cognizable offence under sec. 279A), or (*ii*) tax payable u/s 115-O(2) or proviso to sec. 194B or 194R(1) first proviso or proviso to sec. 194S(1)	3 months to 7 years and fine
276BB	Failure to pay the tax collected by the seller of alcoholic liquor, tendu leaves, forest product etc. from the buyer under the provisions of sec. 206C	3 months to 7 years and fine
276C(1) non-cognizable offence under section 279A	Wilful attempt to evade tax, penalty or interest or under-reporting of Income (non-cognizable offence under section 279A)— (*a*) where tax sought to be evaded exceeds ₹ 25 lakh (w.e.f. 1-7-2012) (earlier ₹ 1 lakh) (*b*) in other cases	 6 months to 7 years and fine 3 months to 3 years (2 years w.e.f. 1-7-2012) and fine
276C(2) non-cognizable offence under section 279A	Wilful attempt to evade payment of any tax, penalty or interest (non-cognizable offence under section 279A)	3 months to 3 years (2 years w.e.f. 1-7-2012) and fine
276CC non-cognizable offence under section 279A	Wilful failure to furnish returns of fringe benefits under section 115WD/115WH or return of income under section 139(1) or in response to notice under section 142(1)(*i*) or section 148 or section 153A (non-cognizable offence under section 279A)— (*a*) where tax sought to be evaded exceeds ₹ 25 lakh (w.e.f. 1-7-2012) (earlier ₹ 1 Lakh) (*b*) in other cases (No prosecution if return furnished before expiry of assessment year or the tax payable (not being a company) as reduced by the advance tax self-assessment tax paid before	 6 months to 7 years and fine 3 months to 3 years and fine

Section	Type of default	Punishment (rigorous imprisonment) and fine
	expiry of the assessment year or a return is furnished by him under section 139(8A) within the time provided therein, TDS and TCS, does not exceed ₹ 10,000.	
276CCC	Wilful failure to furnish in due time return of total income required to be furnished by notice u/s 158BC(*a*)	3 months to 3 years and fine
276D	Wilful failure to produce accounts and documents under section 142(1) or to comply with a notice under section 142(2A)	Up to 1 year and fine
277 non-cognizable offence under section 279A	False statement in verification or delivery of false account, etc. (non-cognizable offence under section 279A)	
	(*a*) where tax sought to be evaded exceeds ₹ 25 lakh (w.e.f. 1.7.2012) (earlier ₹ 1 lakh)	6 months to 7 years and fine
	(*b*) in other cases	3 months to 3 years and fine
277A	Falsification of books of account or document, etc., to enable any other person to evade any tax, penalty or interest chargeable/leviable under the Act	3 months to 3 years and fine
278 non-cognizable offence under section 279A	Abetment of false return, account, statement or declaration relating to any income or fringe benefits chargeable to tax (non-cognizable offence under section 279A)	
	(*a*) where tax, penalty or interest sought to be evaded exceeds ₹ 25 lakh (w.e.f. 1-7-2012) (earlier ₹ 1 lakh)	6 months to 7 years and fine
	(*b*) in other cases	3 months to 3 years and fine
278A	Second and subsequent offences (*i*) for failure to deduct or pay tax (under Sec. 276B or sec. 276BB); or (*ii*) for wilful attempt to evade tax [under Sec. 276C(1)]; or (*iii*) for failure to furnish return of income (under Sec. 277CC); or (*iv*) for false statement in verification, and so on (under Sec. 277); or (*v*) for abetment of false return, and so on (under Sec. 278)	6 months to 7 years and fine

Section	Type of default	Punishment (rigorous imprisonment) and fine
280(1)	Disclosure of particulars by public servants in contravention of section 138(2) [Prosecution to be instituted with previous sanction of Central Government under section 280(2)]	Up to 6 months (simple/ rigorous) and fine

Punishment not to be imposed in certain cases [Sec. 278AA] - Notwithstanding anything contained in the provisions of section 276A, section 276AB, 50 [or section 276B, section 276BB no person shall be punishable for any failure referred to in the said provisions if he proves that there was reasonable cause for such failure.

When offences are committed by Companies [Sec. 278B] - When an offence under this Act has been committed by a company, such company and every person who was in charge of and was responsible to the company for the conduct of its business at the time when such offence was committed, both are deemed to be guilty of the offence. Therefore, both are liable to be proceeded against and punished accordingly. However, if such a person proves that the offence was committed without his knowledge or that he had exercised all due diligence to prevent the commission of such offence, he is not liable to any punishment [Sec. 278B(1)].

Where an offence under this Act has been committed by a company and it is proved that the offence has been committed with the consent or connivance of, or is attributable to any neglect on the part of, any director, manager, secretary or other officer of the company, such director, manager, secretary or other officer is deemed to be guilty of that offence and is liable to be proceeded against and punished accordingly [Sec. 278B(2)].

The aforesaid provisions are also applicable to a firm, an association of persons or a body of individuals, whether incorporated or not. It is so because the term "company" for purposes of these provisions has been defined (under *Explanation* to Sec. 278B) to include a firm, an association of persons or a body of individuals, whether incorporated or not; the term "director" in relation to a firm means a partner thereof and in relation to an association of persons or a body of individuals means any member controlling the affairs thereof.

Where an offence has been committed by a company and the punishment for such offence is imprisonment and fine, such company is punishable with fine and any person who was in charge of the company for the conduct of its business at the time the offence was committed and also director, manager, secretary or other officers of the company are liable to be proceeded against and punished in accordance with the provisions of this Act. It is operative from 1 October 2004.

When offences are committed by Hindu Undivided Families [Sec. 278C] - When an offence under this Act has been committed by a Hindu Undivided Family, the Karta is deemed to be guilty of the offence and is liable to be proceeded against and punished accordingly. However, the Karta is not liable to any punishment if he proves that the offence was committed without his knowledge or that he had exercised all due diligence to prevent the commission of such offence [Sec. 278C(1)].

Where an offence under this Act has been committed by a Hindu Undivided Family and it is proved that the offence has been committed with the consent or connivance of, or is attributable to any neglect on the part of any member of the Hindu Undivided Family, such member is deemed to be guilty of that offence and is liable to be proceeded against and punished accordingly [Sec. 278C(2)].

◆ Procedure governing prosecution proceedings

While the Criminal Procedure Code, 1973 govern the procedure with respect to the prosecution under the Income-tax Act and the evidence and burden of proof is to be discharged by the prosecution as per the Indian Evidence Act, 1872, some departures are also made in the Income-tax Act. In certain instances, specific provisions of the Income-tax Act shall prevail. Take for instance, presumption of *mens rea* [sec. 278E] in the Income-tax Act. Unlike criminal law jurisprudence which presumes an accused to be innocent until proven guilty and the burden is on the prosecution to prove beyond reasonable doubt that the accused committed the offense with a culpable state of mind; sec. 278E Income-tax Act presumes culpable mental state of the accused and the burden to prove otherwise is on the accused. Similarly, under sec. 360 of the Criminal Procedure Code, when the offence is punishable only with fine or imprisonment of less than seven years and the convict is more than twenty one years of age, such convict not having any earlier conviction can be granted a release on probation of good conduct or after admonition. However, sec. 292A of the Income-tax Act specifically states that nothing contained in sec. 360 of Cr.P.C. shall apply to a convict under the Income-tax Act unless such person is less than eighteen years of age. Similarly, sec. 278D presumes that documents, accounts, assets etc, found in possession of the assessee during the search and seizure in accordance with sec. 132(4A) shall be presumed to be belonging to such assessee and can be tendered by the prosecution in evidence against such person.

Further, certain acts of omission and/or commissions are punishable both under the Income-tax Act and the Indian Penal Code and yet some others when prosecuting under IPC is more appropriate for instance when a person makes a false statement on oath or is absconding service of summons. While there is no bar on the Income-tax Authorities to prosecute an offender under both Income-tax Act and IPC, such offender cannot be punished twice for the same offence, once under Income-tax Act and then under the IPC. Thus, Income-tax Act has to be read in conjunction with Cr.P.C., IPC and the Indian Evidence Act.

Procedure within the Administration

The Central Board of Direct Taxes has been issuing guidelines from time to time in the form of Prosecution Manual to provide the departmental procedure that leads to prosecution proceedings.

1. The Assessing Officer/ADIT/TRO identifies the cases for launching prosecution. Once the case is identified on the basis of the records of the assessee, such officer sends the proposal containing brief facts and details of the offence committed to the respective Commissioner.
2. The Commissioner examines the proposal and if finds it prima facie fit to be proceeded with, issue a show cause notice to the assessee. Such assessee is required to file a reply.
3. If Commissioner is satisfied with the reply of the assessee he may not grant sanction to the Assessing Officer to file complaint before the Court. If no reply is received or after considering the reply is found fit to be proceeded with, CIT may seek opinion of the Prosecution Counsel and thereafter accord his sanction to launch prosecution. The Assessing Officer with the help of the Prosecution Counsel file the complaint in appropriate jurisdictional Court.

Procedure before Court

1. On the basis of complaint filed, the court issues summons to the accused along with the copy of complaint and provide a date to attend the Court. If having received the summons, the accused does not appear before the Court, a warrant can be issued to ensure that the accused presents before the Court.
2. If on hearing the accused and considering other evidences, the court opines that there is no apparent case against the said accused, the complaint will be dismissed. If after hearing the accused, the Court opines that there is substance in the complaint, the Court will frame a charge of the offences purportedly committed by the accused on the basis of the complaint and considering primary evidence. The proceedings shall continue as per the Criminal Procedure Code and trial will begin.
3. The trial may result in an acquittal or conviction. If the trial results in a conviction, then an appeal to the Court of Session will lie under S. 374(3) of the Criminal Procedure Code. Further appeals from the order of the Sessions Court will lie before High Court and thereafter Supreme Court.

◆ **Power of the Commissioner to Grant Immunity from Prosecution [Sec. 278AB]**

From 1 April 2008 and onward, a person may make an application to the Principal Commissioner or Commissioner for granting immunity from prosecution if he has made an application for settlement under Sec. 245C and the proceedings for settlement have abated under Sec. 245HA. However, no such application can be made to the Principal Commissioner or Commissioner after institution of the prosecution proceedings after abatement.

The Principal Commissioner or Commissioner Principal may, subject to such conditions as he thinks fit to impose, grant immunity from prosecution for any offence under this Act, if he is satisfied that the person, after the abatement, co-operated with the income-tax authority in the proceedings before him and he his made a full and true disclosure of his income and the manner in which such income has been derived.

Withdrawal of the Immunity - The immunity granted to a person stands withdrawn if such person fails to comply with any condition subject to which the immunity was granted. Thereupon, the provisions of this Act become applicable as if no such immunity had been granted.

The immunity granted may also be withdrawn by the Principal Commissioner or Commissioner if he is satisfied that such person had, in the course of any proceedings after abatement, concealed any particulars material to the assessment from the income-tax authority or had given false evidence. Therefore, such person may be tried for the offence with respect to which the immunity was granted or for any offence of which he appears to have been guilty in connection with the proceedings.

- **Presumption as to assets, books of account, etc. in certain cases [Sec. 278D] -** Where during the course of any search [under Sec. 132] any money, bullion, jewellery or other valuable article or any books of account or other documents have been found in the possession or control of any person and such assets or books of account, and such assets or books of account or other documents are tendered by the prosecution in evidence against such person or against any other person who induces in any manner another person to make a statement (relating to taxable income) which he knows to be false or does not believe to be true and thus induces him to commit an offence or evade tax, income-tax law makes the following presumptions in respect of such assets and books of account/documents:

  (*i*) such books of account/documents or assets belong to such person;

  (*ii*) contents of such books of account and documents are true;

  (*iii*) the signature and such books of account/documents which purport to be in the handwriting of any particular person, are in the handwriting of that person; and

  (*iv*) documents stamped, executed or attested are deemed to have been stamped, executed and attested by that person by whom it purports to have been so executed or attested [Sec. 278D(1)].

  Similar presumptions have been made in respect of any assets or books of account or documents, which have been taken into custody from the possession or control of any person by the officer or authority under any law, [under Sec. 132A(1)], are delivered to the requisitioning officer [under Sec. 132A(2)] and such assets, books of account/documents are tendered by the prosecution in evidence against such person [Sec. 278D(2)].

- **Presumption as to Culpable Mental State [Sec. 278E] -** In any prosecution for any offence under this Act, which requires a culpable mental state on the part of the accused, the existence of such mental state is to be presumed by the Court. However, the accused has a defence to prove the fact that he had no such mental state with respect to the act charged as offence in that prosecution.

"Culpable mental state" includes intention, motive or knowledge of a fact or belief or reason to believe, a fact.

For the purpose of this Section, a fact is to be proved only when the court believes it to exist beyond reasonable doubt and not merely when its existence is established by a preponderance of probability.

- **Prosecution to be at the instance of Principal Chief Commissioner or Chief Commissioner or Principal Commissioner or Commissioner [Sec. 279] -** A person cannot be proceeded against an offence [under Section 275A, or 275B or 276 or 276A or 276B or 276BB or 276C or 276CC or 276D or 277 or 277A or 278] with previous sanction of the Principal Commissioner or Commissioner or Commissioner (Appeals) or appropriate authority.

  Appropriate authority consits of three persons two of whom are the members the Indian Income-tax Service, Group A, holding the post of Commissioner of Income-tax or any equivalent or higher post and one in a member of the Central Engineering Service, Group A, holding the post of chief Engineer or any equivalent or higher post.

  A person cannot be proceeded against an offence (under Sec. 276C or Sec. 277) if the penalty imposed [under Sec. 271(1)] has been reduced or waived (under Sec. 273A).

  Any office may be compounded by the Principal Chief Commissioner or Chief Commissioner or Principal Director General or Director General.

  The concerned authority must properly apply his mind before sanctioning prosecution. His mere signature on the instrument to prosecute does not meet the requirement of the section [*ITO* v. *Abdul Razack* [1989] 47 Taxman 141/[1990] 181 ITR 414 (AP)].

  The principle of natural justice may, in certain cases, require that an opportunity of being heard be given to the assessee before launching the prosecution [*Shree Singhvi Bros.* v. *UoI* [1990] 53 Taxman 555/[1991] 187 ITR 219 (Raj.)].

  Prosecution of a public servant is invalid without the sanction for prosecution under Sec. 197 of the Criminal Procedure Code being obtained [*Ram Kirt Singh* v. *CIT* [1997] 95 Taxman 207/[1998] 230 ITR 804 (Patna)].

- **Prohibition Against Prosecution [Sec. 279(1A)] -** A person cannot be proceeded against for an offence of wilful attempt to evade tax (Sec. 276C) or 'false statement in verification' [Sec. 277] in relation to the assessment for an assessment year in respect of which the penalty imposed for concealment [Sec. 271(1)(*iii*)] has been reduced or waived by an order under Sec. 273A.

◆ **Power to Compound Offence [Sec. 279(2)] -** The Principal Chief Commissioner or Chief Commissioner or Principal Director General or Director-General may compound any offence. The compounding may be before or after the institution of proceedings. The Board is empowered to issue instructions or directions to other income-tax authorities for the proper composition of the offences. It may also issue instructions to obtain its prior approval before compounding the prosecution proceedings.

Where prosecution proceedings have been initiated, any statement made or account/document produced before an income-tax authority cannot be inadmissible as evidence for such proceedings merely on the ground that such statement, account or document was produced in the belief that the penalty imposed may be reduced or waived [under Sec. 273A] or that the offence in respect of which such proceeding was taken, may be compounded.

Immunity - The Central Government has the power to render immunity from prosecution for any offence under this Act (Sec. 291). A similar power rests with the Settlement Commission [Sec. 245H].

◆ **Proof of Entries in Records or Documents [Sec. 279B] -** Entries in records of an income-tax authority is admissible in evidence in any proceedings for the prosecution of any person for an offence. Such entries may be proved either by producing the records containing such entries or producing their certified copies, duly attested by an income-tax authority, stating that it is the true copy of the original entries contained in the records.

CHAPTER 23 Appeals and Revisions

INTRODUCTION

The right to appeal is a statutory right, that is, such right must be provided for by the Statute otherwise no appeal can lie. Under the Income-tax Act, where an assessee has been aggrieved with the orders passed by the income tax authority, such assessee can take a recourse to filing an appeal. There are several stages of appeals. Where at any stage, the revenue authority is dissatisfied with the order, the revenue department can also file an appeal.

Where an assessee is not satisfied with the orders of the Assessing Officer, the first appeal lies before Commissioner (Appeal) by virtue of Sec. 246A. Alternatively, the assessee may also apply to the Commissioner of Income-tax under Sec. 264 for revision of the orders of the Assessing Officer. It must be noted that such revisionary powers can be exercised by the Commissioner of Income-tax even suomoto when the orders of the Assessing Officer is erroneous and prejudicial to the interest of revenue [Sec. 263].

The following figure provides an overview of the various stages of appeals of tax dispute:

FIGURE 23.1 : STAGES OF APPEALS

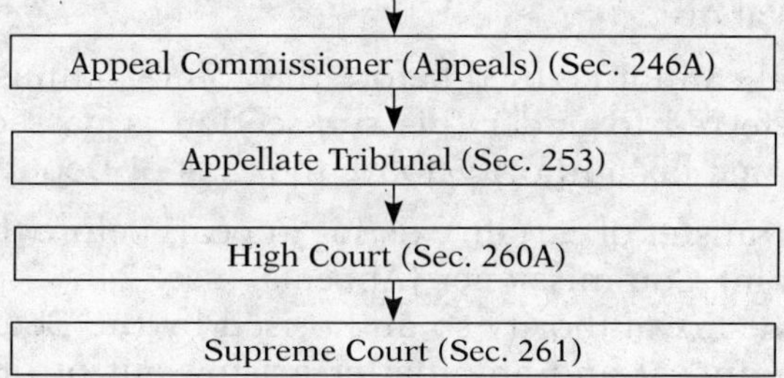

APPEAL BEFORE THE COMMISSIONER (APPEALS)

Appeals and Revisions (Finance Act, 2023)

As per the current scheme for appeals under the Act, the first appellate authority for an assessee aggrieved by any order issued under the Act is the Commissioner

(Appeals). Such Commissioner (Appeals) has the powers to confirm, reduce, enhance or annul/cancel an order of assessment or an order of penalty, after providing an opportunity of being heard to the assessee and the AO. The order passed by the Commissioner (Appeals) are appealable before the Appellate Tribunal.

However, owing to huge number of appeals and pendency thereof, the Commissioner (Appeals) are currently overburdened. In order to clear this bottleneck, the Finance Act, 2023 has introduced new authority for appeals at Joint Commissioner/Additional Commissioner level by virtue of sec. 246 to handle certain class of cases involving small amount of disputed demand. Such authority has all powers, responsibilities and accountability similar to that of Commissioner (Appeals) with respect to the procedure for disposal of appeals.

Thus, w.e.f. 1.4.2023, under sec. 246 the following appeals may be filed before Joint Commissioner (Appeals) by any assessee aggrieved by any of the following orders of an Assessing Officer (below the rank of Joint Commissioner) —

(*i*) an order being an intimation under sec. 143(1), where the assessee objects to the making of adjustments, or any order of assessment under sub-section (3) of section 143 or section 144, where the assessee objects to the amount of income assessed, or to the amount of tax determined, or to the amount of loss computed, or to the status under which he is assessed;

(*ii*) an order of assessment, reassessment or recomputation under sec. 147;

(*iii*) an order being an intimation under sec. 200A(1);

(*iv*) an order under sec. 201;

(*v*) an order being an intimation under sec. 206C(6A);

(*vi*) an order under sec. 206CB(1);

(*vii*) an order imposing a penalty under Chapter XXI; and

(*viii*) an order under sec.154 or sec.155 amending any of the orders mentioned in (*i*) to (*vii*) above.

However, an appeal cannot be filed before the Joint Commissioner (Appeals) where an order referred to under this sub-section is passed by or with the approval of an income-tax authority above the rank of Deputy Commissioner.

In order to enable transfer of certain existing appeals before the Commissioner (Appeals) to the Joint Commissioner (Appeals), sec. 246(2) provides that the Board or an income-tax authority so authorised by the Board in this regard may transfer such appeal and any matter arising out of or connected with such appeal and which is so pending, to the Joint Commissioner (Appeals) who may proceed with such appeal or matter, from the stage at which it was before it was so transferred. Such transfer by the Board also extends to matters being transferred from the Joint Commissioner (Appeals) to the Commissioner (Appeals) [sec. 246(3)]. However, where an appeal is transferred the assessee must be given an opportunity of hearing.

For the purposes of disposal of appeal by the Joint Commissioner (Appeals), the Central Government may make a Scheme, by notification in the Official Gazette, so as to dispose appeals in an expedient manner with transparency and accountability by eliminating the interface between the Joint

Commissioner (Appeals) and the appellant in the course of appellate proceedings to the extent technologically feasible and direct that any of the provisions of this Act relating to jurisdiction and procedure for disposal of appeals by Joint Commissioner (Appeals) shall not apply or shall apply with such exceptions, modifications and adaptations as may be specified in the notification (sec. 246(5)).

Procedure for filing appeal [Sec. 249(1)]

Every appeal shall be filed in Form No. 35 and verified in the prescribed manner. It shall be accompanied by a fees as follows, irrespective of the date of initiation of the assessment proceedings:

₹ 250 if the amount of total income computed by AO is ₹ 1 lakh

₹ 500, if computed income is ₹ 1 lakh to ₹ 2 lakh

₹ 1000, if computed income is more than ₹ 2 lakh

₹ 250 If computed income is less than ₹ 1 lakh or nil

Time limit for preferring an appeal [Sec. 249(2)]

In general the appeal must be filed within 30 days of the date on which intimation of the order sought to be appealed against is served on the appellant [*Section 249(2)(c)]*. However, in the following two instances, this limitation period of 30 days will operate thus:

1. Where the appeal relates to any tax deducted at source from payment made to a non-resident, (other than a company) or to a foreign company, any interest, other than interest on securities or any other sum chargeable under the provisions of the Income Tax Act (not being salaries) under Sec. 148, appeal must be filed within 30 days from the date of payment of tax deducted at source to the credit of the Central Government [Sec. 249(2)(*a*)].
2. Where the appeal relates to any assessment or penalty order, the appeals have to be presented within 30 days of the date of service of the notice of demand relating to that assessment or penalty order [Sec. 249(2)(*b*)].

Procedure for Appeal [Sec. 250]

With the launch of the Faceless Appeal Scheme, 2020 in 25th September, 2020 (now replaced with the Faceless Appeal Scheme, 2021 in 28th December, 2021) an electronic mode of procedure has been introduced which eliminates human interface. The CBDT issued directions dated 7th April, 2021 that the provisions of Faceless Appeal are applicable to appeals related to Income-tax Act, 1961 only and other Acts like, Wealth Tax Act, Securities Transaction Tax, Commodities Transaction Tax, and Equalization levy are not included in its scope.

However, within Income-tax Act as well, appeals relating to serious frauds, major tax evasion, sensitive and search matters, international tax and Black Money (Undisclosed Foreign Income and Assets) and Imposition of Tax Act, 2015 matters have not been currently covered under the Faceless Scheme and therefore the following procedure continues for the same:

Joint Commissioner (Appeals) or Commissioner (Appeals) shall fix a day and place for the hearing of the appeal and shall give notice of the same to the appellant and to the Assessing Officer against whose order the appeal is preferred.

The following shall have the right to be heard at the hearing of the appeal:

(*a*) The appellant, either in person or by an authorised representative.

(*b*) The Assessing Officer, either in person or by a representative.

The Joint Commissioner (Appeals) or Commissioner (Appeals) shall have the power to adjourn the hearing of the appeals from time to time. Before disposing any appeal,

(*a*) the Joint Commissioner (Appeals) or Commissioner (Appeal) may make such further enquiry as he deems fit, or

(*b*) may direct the Assessing Officer to make further enquiry and report as he deems fit, or

(*c*) may direct the Assessing Officer to make further enquiry and report the result of the same to the Joint Commissioner (Appeals) or Commissioner (Appeals).

The Joint Commissioner (Appeals) or Commissioner (Appeals) may, at the hearing of an appeal, allow the appellant to invoke additional grounds appeal if he is satisfied that the omission of that ground from the form of appeal was not wilful or unreasonable.

The order disposing the appeal shall be in writing and shall state the points for determination, the decision thereon and the reasons for the decision.

In every appeal, the Joint Commissioner (Appeals) or Commissioner (Appeal), where it is possible, may hear and decide such appeal within a period of one year from the end of the financial year in which such appeal is filed before him Joint Commissioner (Appeals) or Commissioner (Appeal) under Section 246A(1). On the disposal of the appeal, the Joint Commissioner (Appeals) or Commissioner (Appeals) shall communicate the order passed by him to the assessee and to the Chief Commissioner or Commissioner.

Powers of the Commissioner (Appeals) [Sec. 251]

In disposing of an appeal, the Commissioner (Appeals) shall have the following powers:

(*a*) In an appeal against an order of assessment, he may confirm, reduce, enhance or annul the assessment.

(*b*) In an appeal against an order imposing a penalty, he may confirm or cancel such order or vary it so as to either enhance or reduce the penalty.

(*c*) In any other case, he may pass such orders in the appeal as he deems fit.

The Commissioner (Appeals) shall not enhance an assessment or a penalty or reduce the amount of refund unless the appellant has had a reasonable opportunity of showing cause against such enhancement or reduction. While disposing an appeal, the Commissioner (Appeals) may consider and decide the facts arising out of the proceedings which in respect of order appealed against were carried notwithstanding that such matter was not raised before the Commissioner (Appeals) by the appellant.

Faceless Appeal before the Commissioner (Appeal) [Sec. 250(6B)]

In order to have greater efficiency, transparency and accountability and to optimise use of resources and technology, the Central Government has adopted a conscious policy of reducing human interface from the system. By virtue of the said policy, several processes under the Act has been made fully faceless. Faceless Scheme of Appeals was launched initially on a pilot basis and later as pan India at the stage of Commissioner (Appeals) in the year 2020. The Finance Act, 2021 extended such faceless scheme at the level of the Tribunal and the scheme is yet to be notified.

Accordingly, sec. 250(6B) provides for the introduction of an appellate system with dynamic jurisdiction by virtue of a Faceless scheme notified by the Central Government in this regard. The CBDT is empowered to specify the jurisdiction, or persons or class of persons, or incomes or class of incomes, or cases or class of cases to be covered by the Scheme. The allocation of cases is ensured through Data Analytics and Artifical Intelligence under the dynamic jurisdiction with central issuance of notices which would be having Document Identification Number (DIN). Thus, in Faceless Appeal Scheme, person shall not be required to appear either personally or through authorised representative in connection with any proceedings before the income-tax authority.

Accordingly, Faceless Appeal Scheme, 2020 was launched by the Central Government by virtue Notification No. 76/2020 dated 25 September 2020 and was effective from 25 September 2020. For the purposes of implementation of the Faceless Scheme, the Central Board of Direct Taxes set-up the following centres and units:

(*a*) **National Faceless Appeal Centre (NFAC) -** Will facilitate the conduct of e-appeal proceedings in a centralised manner. It is located at Delhi comprising of Principal Chief Commissioner of Income-tax, Commissioner of Income-tax, Additional/Joint CIT, Deputy/Assistant CIT. The Principal Chief Commissioner shall, with prior approval of CBDT, lay down the standards, procedures and processes for the effective functioning of the NFAC, RFACs and AUs;

(*b*) **Regional Faceless Appeal Centres (RFAC) -** Will facilitate the conduct of e-appeal proceedings. RFACs to be located in Delhi, Mumbai, Kolkata and Chennai; and (*c*) **Appeal Units (AU) -** Perform the function of disposing appeal, which includes admitting additional grounds of appeal, directing the National e-Assessment Centre or the Assessing Officer for making further inquiry, seeking information or clarification on admitted grounds of appeal, providing opportunity of being heard to the appellant, analysis of the material furnished by the appellant, review of draft order etc.

Under the Faceless Scheme of Appeal 2020 there was no compulsion on the part of the NFAC to grant personal hearing to the appellant. That is whilst appellant could request a personal hearing, granting of such personal hearing was at the discretion of the Chief Commissioner or Director General in charge of RFAC. Therefore, validity of the Faceless Scheme, 2020 had been subjected to litigation through several petitions filed before various High Courts including the one before Delhi High Court in *Lakshya Budhiraja* v. *UOI* [2020] 120 taxmann.com 385 (Delhi). The petitioner has sought that the scheme be declared as discriminatory, arbitrary and illegal to extent it provided a virtual hearing subject to the approval of the authorities concerned. It was alleged that in terms of the new Faceless Appeal Scheme, 2020, the right of being heard, even through the video conferencing mode shall be subject to the approval of the Chief Commissioner or the Director General and therefore the same is discretionary since the officer "may" or "may not" provide a right of personal hearing in the matter. Accordingly, it was contended that such mechanism is against settled principles of law and in violation of Article 14 of Constitution of India as well as against the principle of *audi alteram partem i.e.* no person should be judged without a fair hearing in which each party was to be given an opportunity to respond to evidence against them. A transfer petition was filed at the Supreme Court to seek transfer of all such matters challenging the Faceless Scheme before High Courts to Supreme Court [*Central Board of Direct Taxes* v. *Lakshya Budhiraja* [2021] 131 taxmann.com 51 (SC)]. It was in this matter that the Additional Solicitor General submitted before the Supreme Court on 1st October, 2021 that the department was already revisiting the Faceless Scheme of Appeals and sought a period of three months as it required a change of law. The matter was listed for 10th January, 2022.

This scheme has now been superseded and replaced with the Faceless Appeal Scheme 2021 by virtue of Notification No. 139/2020 dated 28th December, 2021. The scheme is effective from 28th December, 2021. The 2021 Scheme has revamped the scheme with notable changes that include mandatory granting of personal hearing through video conferencing upon request by appellant, removal of RFAC and elimination of Automated Examination Tool from the appeals procedure. In the Faceless Scheme, 2020, appeals were assigned to a specific appeal unit, and the Commissioner (Appeals) appointed under such appeal unit performed the e-proceeding functions. Now, the National Faceless Appeal Centre (NFAC) shall assign the appeal directly to a Commissioner (Appeals) of the appeal unit.

FIGURE 23.2: FACELESS APPEAL SCHEME, 2021

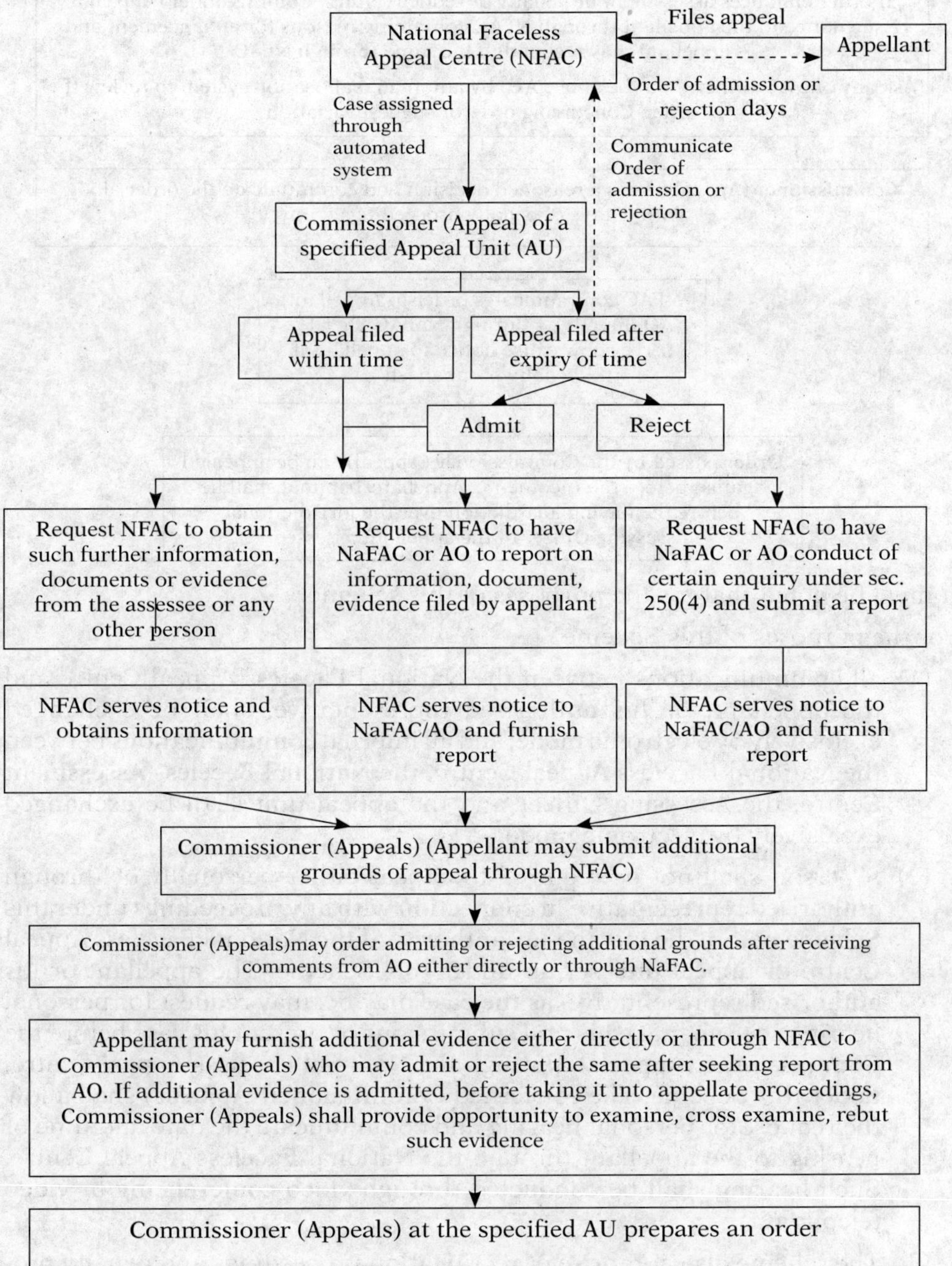

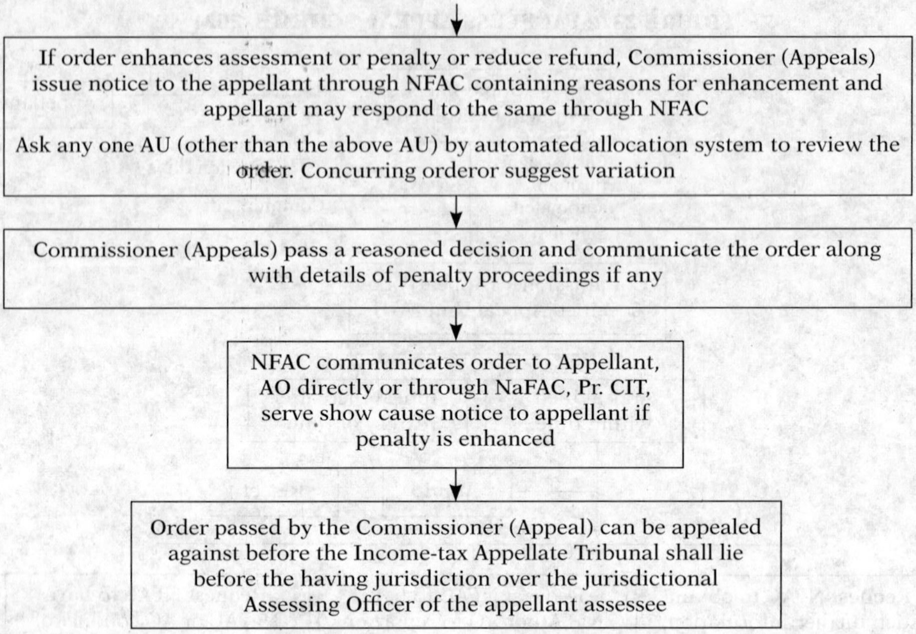

↓

If order enhances assessment or penalty or reduce refund, Commissioner (Appeals) issue notice to the appellant through NFAC containing reasons for enhancement and appellant may respond to the same through NFAC

Ask any one AU (other than the above AU) by automated allocation system to review the order. Concurring orderor suggest variation

↓

Commissioner (Appeals) pass a reasoned decision and communicate the order along with details of penalty proceedings if any

↓

NFAC communicates order to Appellant, AO directly or through NaFAC, Pr. CIT, serve show cause notice to appellant if penalty is enhanced

↓

Order passed by the Commissioner (Appeal) can be appealed against before the Income-tax Appellate Tribunal shall lie before the having jurisdiction over the jurisdictional Assessing Officer of the appellant assessee

It must be noted that for the purposes of this scheme:

For the purposes of this Scheme,

(1) all communications between the National Faceless Appeal Centre and the appellant, or his authorised representative, shall be exchanged exclusively by electronic mode; and all internal communications between the National Faceless Appeal Centre, the National Faceless Assessment Centre, the Assessing Officer and the appeal unit shall be exchanged exclusively by electronic mode.

(2) A person shall not be required to appear either personally or through authorised representative in connection with any proceedings under this Scheme before the income-tax authority at the National Faceless Appeal Centre or appeal unit set up under this Scheme. The appellant or his authorised representative, as the case may be, may request for personal hearing so as to make his oral submissions or present his case before the Commissioner (Appeals), through the National Faceless Appeal Centre, under this Scheme. The concerned Commissioner (Appeals) shall allow the request for personal hearing and communicate the date and time of hearing to the appellant through the National Faceless Appeal Centre. Such hearing shall be conducted through video conferencing or video telephony.

(3) The scheme also comprise of rectification proceedings and penalty proceedings in the course of appeal proceedings, for non-compliance of any notice, direction or order issued under this Scheme.

REVISION BY THE COMMISSIONER OF INCOME TAX

(*a*) Revision of orders prejudicial to the interest of the Revenue [Sec. 263]

Since the right to appeal against the orders of the Assessing Officer is available only to the assessee and not to the Revenue Department, the Commissioner of Income-tax is vested with the right to revision of such orders passed by the Assessing Officer. Thus, under Sec. 263 if the Principal Commissioner or Commissioner considers that any order passed by the Assessing Officer is erroneous insofar as it is prejudicial to the interests of the revenue, he may revise such an order.

The revision order is to be completed in the following stages (1) The Principle Commissioner or Commissioner may call for and examine the record of any proceeding under this Act and form a *prima facie* opinion that the order passed by the Assessing Officer or Transfer Pricing Officer, as the case may be, is erroneous insofar as it is prejudicial to the interests of the revenue. (2) Thereafter an opportunity of being heard must be given to the assessee. (3) After making such inquiry as he deems necessary, the Principle Commissioner or Commissioner shall pass such order thereon as the circumstances of the case justify, including —

(*i*) an order enhancing or modifying the assessment, or cancelling the assessment and directing a fresh assessment; or

(*ii*) an order modifying the order under section 92CA; or

(*iii*) an order cancelling the order under section 92CA and directing a fresh order under the said section.

Since the expression 'erroneous' and 'prejudicial to the interests of revenue' was not defined in the Act, it remained a highly contentious issue. In order to provide clarity on this issue, the Finance Act, 2015 inserted *Explanation 2* to Sec. 263. Accordingly, an order passed by the Assessing Officer shall be deemed to be erroneous in so far as it is prejudicial to the interests of the revenue, if, in the opinion of the Principal Chief Commissioner or Chief Commissioner or Principal Commissioner or Commissioner,—

(*a*) the order is passed without making inquiries or verification which should have been made;

(*b*) the order is passed allowing any relief without inquiring into the claim;

(*c*) the order has not been made in accordance with any order, direction or instruction issued by the Board under Sec. 119; or

(*d*) the order has not been passed in accordance with any decision which is prejudicial to the assessee, rendered by the jurisdictional High Court or Supreme Court in the case of the assessee or any other person.

This *Explanation* applies prospectively from 1-4-2015.

Limitation period for revision

Revision order cannot be made after the expiry of 2 years from the end of the financial year in which the order sought to be revised was passed [Sec. 263(2)]. In computing the period of limitation, the time taken in giving an opportunity to the assessee to be reheard under the proviso to Sec. 129 and any period during which any proceeding under this section is stayed by an order or injunction of any court shall be excluded [*Explanation* to Sec. 263(2)].

However, this limitation period of 2 years will not apply in the case of an order which has been passed in consequence of, or to give effect to, any finding or direction contained in an order of the Appellate Tribunal, National Tax Tribunal, the High Court or the Supreme Court [Sec. 263(3)].

Case Law : ***Pr.CIT* v. *Shree Gayatri Associates* [2019] 106 taxmann.com 31/263 Taxman 672 (SC)**

Facts: 'S' being a developer of real estate, was subjected to search operations, during which certain unaccounted income was disclosed. The Assessing Officer passed an order of assessment which was sought to be revised by the Commissioner who was of the opinion that such order of assessment was erroneous and prejudicial to the interest of Revenue.

Held: It could be concluded that the Assessing Officer had carried out detailed inquiries regarding the money transactions by 'S' and this was supported with a detailed correspondence between Assessing Officer and the assessee during the course of assessment proceedings. Since the Assessing Officer had made detailed inquires, the revision orders of the Commissioner was set aside.

(*b*) Revision of other orders

The Principal Chief Commissioner or Chief Commissioner or Principal Commissioner or the Commissioner of Income Tax may revise any order of an authority subordinate to him either suo motu or on an application by the assessee for such revision [Sec. 264(1)]. He may make such enquiry and may pass such order as he thinks fit but such order cannot be prejudicial to the assessee [Sec. 264(1)].

- In case of a *suo motu* action, the Principal Chief Commissioner or Chief Commissioner or Principal Commissioner or the Commissioner cannot revise an order made by the subordinate authority if the order had been made more than 1 year back [Sec. 264(2)].
- In the case of an application for revision by the assessee, the application must be made within one year from the date on which the order in question was communicated to him or the date on which he otherwise came to know of it, whichever is earlier [Sec. 264(3)]. The Principal Chief Commissioner or Chief Commissioner or Principal Commissioner or the Commissioner of Income Tax may

condone the delay and admit an application made after the expiry of that period, if he is satisfied that the assessee was prevented by sufficient cause from making the application within that period.

The application for revision by the assessee is to be accompanied by a fee of ₹ 500 [Sec. 264(5)]. Every such application for revision by an assessee shall be disposed by passing an order within one year from the end of the financial year in which such application is made by the assessee for revision [Sec. 264(6)]. In computing this time period of 1 year, the time taken in giving an opportunity to the assessee to be re-heard under the proviso to Sec. 129 and any period during which any proceeding under this section is stayed by an order or injunction of any court shall be excluded. This time limit of 1 year will not apply when a revisional order is passed in consequence of or to give effect to any finding or direction contained in an order of the Appellate Tribunal, the High Court or the Supreme Court [Sec. 264(7)].

The revisional order cannot be passed in the following cases:

(*i*) When the order is appealable to the Commissioner (Appeals), such order cannot be revised until the time within which such appeal may be made expires. If an appeal has been made to the Commissioner (Appeals), the revisional power cannot be exercised while the appeal is pending but it may be exercised after the appeal has been disposed of.

(*ii*) If the order is appealable to the Commissioner (Appeals) or the Appellate Tribunal, revisional power cannot be exercised until the time within which such appeal may be made expires unless the assessee has waived his right of appeal. If an appeal has been made, the revisional powers cannot be exercised while the appeal is pending but it may be exercised after the appeal has been disposed of. If the Commissioner (Appeals) or the Appellate Tribunal refuses to entertain an appeal on the ground that it is time barred, or grants permission to the appellant to withdraw the appeal, the order cannot be said to be the "subject of an appeal" and the assessee would be entitled to apply to the Commissioner for revision.

Faceless Revision orders [Sec. 264A]

The Taxation and Other Laws (Relaxation and Amendment of Certain Provisions) Act, 2020, w.e.f. 1-11-2020 introduced Sec. 264A that provides for faceless revision orders. For the purposes of revision of orders under Sec. 263 or Sec. 264, so as to impart greater efficiency, transparency and accountability by—

(*a*) eliminating the interface between the income-tax authority and the assessee or any other person to the extent technologically feasible;

(*b*) optimizing utilisation of the resources through economies of scale and functional specialisation;

(*c*) introducing a team-based revision of orders, with dynamic jurisdiction, the Central Government may make a scheme, by notification in the Official Gazette [Sec. 264A(1)].

For the purpose of giving effect to the scheme the Central Government many by notification in the Official Gazette, direct that any of the provisions of this Act shall not apply or shall apply with such exceptions, modifications and adaptations as may be specified in the notification [Sec. 264A(2)]. However, no direction shall be issued after the 31st day of March, 2022. Every notification so issued shall, as soon as may be after the notification is issued, be laid before each House of Parliament [Sec. 264A(3)].

APPEAL BEFORE APPELLATE TRIBUNAL

In general a 'Tribunal' can be understood as a body tasked with discharging quasi-judicial functions with the primary objective of providing a special forum for specific type of disputes and for faster and more efficacious adjudication of issues.

The Income-tax Appellate Tribunal (ITAT) is a quasi-judicial body and is the responsibility of the Ministry of Law and Justice of the Government of India. However, this does not mean that the ITAT is controlled by the Ministry. ITAT functions as an independent authority without any interference by any Ministry or Department of the Government of India in the discharge of the functions entrusted to it by law. ITAT is a final fact finding authority and therefore when ITAT has arrived at its own conclusions or facts after the consideration of the evidence before it, the Court will not interfere.

Constitution of the Tribunal [Sec. 252]

The Tribunal constitutes of a President, Vice-President and judicial and accountant members. A bench of Tribunal is comprised of a judicial member and an accountant member. The qualifications, appointment, term of office, salaries and allowances, resignation, removal and the other terms and conditions of service of the President, Vice-President and other Members of the Appellate Tribunal appointed after the commencement of Part XIV of Chapter VI of the Finance Act, 2017, shall be governed by the provisions of Sec. 184 of that Act. Pursuant to its rule making power under Sec. 184, the Central Government had enacted the Appellate Tribunal and Other Authorities (Qualifications, Experience and Other Conditions of Service of Members) Rules, 2017. The constitutional validity of Part XIV of Finance Act, 2017 was challenged before the Supreme Court in *Rojer Mathew* v. *South Indian Bank Ltd.* [2019] 111 taxmann.com 208 (SC). It was contended that Part XIV which was passed as a Money Bill, amongst other things had also sought to amend the existing legislations providing for the various tribunals in the country and to introduce a whole new regime to govern them including providing for the amendments to the payment of salaries, emoluments, compensations etc. In the process, this matter also raised larger questions with respect to the independence and jurisdiction of the tribunals.

While the question in respect of vires of Part XIV of the Finance Act, 2017 being in the nature of Money Bill was placed before a larger bench, insofar as the Sec. 184 was concerned, the same was struck down in its entirety since Sec.

184 was found being contrary to parent enactment and principles envisaged in Constitution.

Subsequently, the Central Government in its notification dated 21st February, 2020 released a new set of rules under the Tribunal, Appellate Tribunal and other Authorities (Qualifications, Experience and other Conditions of Service of Members) Rules, 2020. These rules provide for the qualifications of the President, Vice-President and the judicial and accountant members of the ITAT as follows:

(1) A person shall not be qualified for appointment as President unless he is a sitting or retired Judge of a High Court and who has completed not less than seven years of service as a Judge in a High Court or a Vice-President of the Income-tax Appellate Tribunal

(2) The Central Government may appoint one or more members of the Income-tax Appellate Tribunal to be the Vice-President or, as the case may be, Vice-Presidents thereof.

(3) A person shall not be qualified for appointment as a Judicial Member, unless, —

  (*i*) he has, for a combined period of ten years, been a District Judge and Additional District Judge; or

  (*ii*) he has been a member of the Indian Legal Service and has held a post of Additional Secretary or any equivalent or higher post for two years; or

  (*iii*) he has been an advocate for twenty-five years.

(4) A person shall not be qualified for appointment as an Accountant Member, unless, —

  (*i*) he has for twenty-five years been in the practice of accountancy, - (*a*) as a chartered accountant under the Chartered Accountants Act, 1949 (38 of 1949); or (*b*) as a registered accountant under any law formerly in force; or partly as such registered accountant and partly as a Chartered Accountant; or

  (*ii*) he has been a member of the Indian Revenue Service (Income-tax Service Group 'A') and has held the post of Principal Commissioner of Income-tax or any equivalent or higher post for two years and has performed judicial, quasi-judicial or adjudicating function for three years.

Appealable orders in case of appeal by the taxpayer [Sec. 253(1)]

Appealable orders before ITAT

(*a*) An assessee can prefer an appeal before the ITAT in respect of following orders:

- ◆ Rectification order passed by the Commissioner of Income-tax (Appeals) under Sec. 154; or

- Order passed by the Commissioner of Income-Tax (Appeals) under Sec. 250, Sec. 270A, Sec. 271, Secs. 271A, 271AAB, 271AAC, 271AAD, 271J or Sec. 272A; or
- An order passed by a Joint Commissioner (Appeals) under section 154, section 250, section 270A, section 271, section 271A, section 271AAC, section 271AAD or section 271J
- an order passed by,—

  A Principal Commissioner or Commissioner under section 12AA or section 12AB or under 80G(5)(*vi*) or under section 263 or under section 270A or under section 271 or under section 272A or an order passed by him under section 154 amending any such order; or a Principal Chief Commissioner or Chief Commissioner or a Principal Director General or Director General or a Principal Director or Director under section 263 or under section 272A or an order passed by him under section 154 amending any such order.
- An order of penalty passed by a Principal Chief Commissioner or Chief Commissioner or a Principal Director General a Director General or a Principal Director or Director under Sec. 272A.
- An order passed by the Assessing Officer under Sec.115VZC(1) rejecting the assessee from tonnage tax scheme.
- An order passed by the Assessing Officer under scrutiny assessment [Sec. 143(3)] or under income escaping assessment (Sec. 147) or under assessment in cases of search or requisition (Sec. 153A) or under assessment of income of any other person, other than the person searched (Sec. 153C) with the approval of the Principal Commissioner of Income-tax or Commissioner of Income-tax as referred to in Sec. 144BA(12) being assessment after invocation of General Anti-avoidance Rules or an order passed under Sec. 154 or under Sec. 155 in respect of such order (applicable from 1-4-2016).

(*b*) **The Income- tax Department may also prefer an appeal before ITAT (Departmental appeal) [Sec. 253(2)]**

If the Principal Commissioner of Income-tax or Commissioner of Income-tax objects to the order passed by the Joint Commissioner (Appeals) or Commissioner of Income-tax (Appeals) under Sec. 154 or Sec. 250, then he may direct the Assessing Officer to make an appeal to the ITAT against the orders of the Joint Commissioner (Appeals) or Commissioner of Income-tax (Appeals).

Faceless Scheme [Sec. 253(8)] - In order to impart greater efficiency, transparency and accountability by—

(*a*) optimizing utilisation of the resources through economies of scale and functional specialisation;

(*b*) introducing a team-based mechanism for appeal to the Appellate Tribunal, with dynamic jurisdiction, the Central Government may make a scheme for the purposes of departmental appeal under Sec. 253(2) to the Appellate Tribunal. For the purpose of giving effect to such scheme, the Central Government may direct that any of the provisions of this Act shall not apply or shall apply with such exceptions, modifications and adaptations as may be specified in the notification [Sec. 253(9)]. However no direction shall be issued after the 31st day of March, 2024. (The Finance Act, 2022 has extended this current date to 31st march 2024 from originally 31st March 2023. The Tribunal is deemed to be a civil court for all purposes of Sec. 195 and Chapter XXXV of the Code of Criminal Procedure, 1898. Therefore a scheme governing the procedures to be followed by such a body needs to be formulated after due consultation with the Ministry of Law and Justice. Hence an extension of the date. Further every such notification issued, as soon as may be after the notification is issued, be laid before each House of Parliament [Sec. 253(10)].

Time-limit for presenting appeal [Sec. 253(3)]

An appeal to ITAT must be filed within a period of 60 days from the date on which order sought to be appealed against is communicated. The ITAT condone the delay and may admit an appeal even after the period of 60 days if it is satisfied that there was sufficient cause for not presenting the appeal within the prescribed time.

Procedure for filing appeal [Sec. 253(6)]

Every appeal shall be filed in Form No. 36 and verified in the prescribed manner. It shall be accompanied by a fees as follows, irrespective of the date of initiation of the assessment proceedings:

₹ 500/- if the amount of total income computed by AO is ₹ 1 lakh

₹ 1,500/-, if computed income is ₹ 1 lakh to ₹ 2 lakh

1% of the assessed income (subject to maximum of ₹ 10,000), if computed income is more than ₹ 2 lakh

₹ 500 for any other case not following above.

Cross-objections to be filed by the other party [Sec. 253(4)]

The Assessing Officer or the assessee, as the case may be, on receipt of notice that an appeal against an order has been preferred by the other party may file a memorandum of cross-objections, within 30 days of the receipt of notice, whether or not he may not have appealed against such order or any part thereof. Such memorandum must be verified in the prescribed manner and such memorandum shall be disposed of by the Appellate Tribunal as if it were an appeal presented within the specified period.

The Appellate Tribunal may condone the delay and admit an appeal or permit the filing of a memorandum of cross-objections after the expiry of the relevant period if it is satisfied that there was sufficient cause for not presenting it within that period.

An application for stay of demand shall be accompanied by a fee of five hundred rupees [Sec. 253(7)].

Order of Appeal [Sec. 254]

The Appellate Tribunal may, after giving both the parties to the appeal an opportunity of being heard, pass such orders thereon as it thinks fit. In every appeal, the Appellate Tribunal, where it is possible may hear and decide such appeal within a period of 4 years from the end of the financial year in which such appeal is filed under Sec. 253(1) [Sec. 254(2A)]. The Appellate Tribunal have the discretion to award any cost of any appeal [Sec. 254(2B)].

The Appellate Tribunal may, after considering the merits of the application made by the assessee, pass an order of stay in any proceedings relating to an appeal filed under Sec. 253(1). However, such a stay order can be for maximum 182 days from the date of the stay order subject to the condition that the assessee deposits at least 20% of the amount of tax, interest, fee, penalty, or any other sum payable under the provisions of this Act, or furnishes security of equal amount in respect thereof. The Appellate Tribunal shall dispose of the appeal within the period of stay specified in the order [First Proviso to Sec. 254(2A)] .

Where appeal is not disposed of within the said period of stay, an extension of stay can be granted by the Appellate Tribunal provided the assessee has made an application seeking such extension and complied with the condition of deposit of tax in the first proviso and the Tribunal is satisfied that the delay in disposing of the appeal is not attributable to the assessee. However, the total period of stay taking the original stay period and the extended stay period cannot exceed 365 days [Second Proviso to Sec. 254(2A)] .

If such appeal is not so disposed of within the period allowed, the order of stay shall stand vacated after the expiry of such period or periods, even if the delay in disposing of the appeal is not attributable to the assessee [Third Proviso to Sec. 254(2A)].In its recent ruling the Supreme Court in *Dy. CIT* v. *Pepsi Foods Ltd*. [2021] 126 taxmann.com 69/282 Taxman 10 (SC) that such automatic vacation of a stay upon expiry of 365 days even if the delay in disposing of appeal is not attributable to assessee, would be both arbitrary and discriminatory and, therefore, liable to be struck down as offending Article 14 of Constitution of India. The Third Proviso to Sec. 254(2A) has been read down. Consequently, it will now be read without the word "even" and the words "is not" after the words "delay in disposing of the appeal". In other words, any order of stay shall stand vacated after the expiry of the period or periods mentioned in the Section only if the delay in disposing of the appeal is attributable to the assessee.

The Appellate Tribunal may, at any time within 6 months from the date of the order, with a view to rectifying any mistake apparent from the record, amend any order passed by it and shall make such amendment if the mistake is brought to its notice by the assessee or the Assessing Officer. But, any amendment which has the effect of enhancing an assessment or reducing a refund or otherwise increasing the liability of the assessee shall not be made unless the Appellate Tribunal has given notice to the assessee of its intention to do so and has allowed the assessee a reasonable opportunity of being heard.

The Appellate Tribunal shall send a copy of any orders passed by it to the assessee and to the Principal Commissioner or Commissioner. Such order of the Tribunal shall be final unless the same have been further appealed against before the High Court.

Procedure for Appellate Tribunal [Sec. 255]

The powers and functions of the Appellate Tribunal may be exercised and discharged by benches constituted by the President of the Appellate Tribunal from amongst the members thereof. Ordinarily, the bench shall consist of one judicial member and one accountant member. However, the President or any other member of the Appellate Tribunal, authorised in this behalf by the Central Government, may, sitting singly, dispose of any case which has been allotted to the Bench of which he is a member and which pertains to an assessee whose, total income as computed by the Assessing Officer in the case does not exceed ₹5,00,000 [Sec. 255(3)].

The President may, for the disposal of any particular case, constitute a Special Bench consisting of three or more members, one of whom shall necessarily be a judicial member and one an accountant member.

If the members of a Bench differ in opinion on any point, the point shall be decided according to the opinion of the majority if there is a majority. But if the members are equally divided, they shall state the point or points on which they differ and the case shall be referred by the President of the Appellate Tribunal for hearing on such point or points by one or more of the other members of the Appellate Tribunal. Such point or points shall be decided according to the opinion of the majority of the members of the Appellate Tribunal who have heard the case including those who first heard it [Sec. 255(4)].

The Appellate Tribunal shall have the power to regulate its own procedure and the procedure of Benches thereof in all matters arising out of the exercise of its powers or of the discharge of its functions including the places at which the Benches shall hold their sittings [Sec. 255(5)].

The Appellate Tribunal shall have, for the purpose of discharging its functions, all the powers which are vested in the Income-tax authorities under Sec. 131 and any proceeding before the Appellate Tribunal shall be deemed to be a judicial proceeding and for the purpose of Section 196 of the Indian Penal Code, the Appellate Tribunal shall be deemed to be a Civil Court for all purposes of Section 195 and Chapter XXXV of the Code of Criminal Procedure [Sec. 255(6)].

Faceless Appeals to the Appellate Tribunal

Having already initiated reforms in the Finance Act, 2020 to reduce human interface and to ensure efficiency and transparency; the Finance Act, 2021 takes these reforms to the next level. Thus a faceless scheme is to be launched for ITAT proceedings. It may be noted that a faceless assessment scheme, faceless appeal scheme and faceless penalty scheme is already rolled out and on similar lines Tribunal proceedings will also be designed.

The Finance Act, 2021 introduced sub-sec. (7) to Sec. 255 with respect to appeals to the Appellate Tribunal. Accordingly, in order to impart greater efficiency, transparency and accountability by—

(*a*) eliminating the interface between the Appellate Tribunal and parties to the appeal in the course of appellate proceedings to the extent technologically feasible

(*b*) optimizing utilisation of the resources through economies of scale and functional specialisation;

(*c*) introducing an appellate system with dynamic jurisdiction,

the Central Government may make a scheme for the purposes of disposal of appeals by the Appellate Tribunal.

For the purposes of giving effect to the scheme the Central Government may direct that any of the provisions of this Act shall not apply to such scheme or shall apply with such exceptions, modifications and adaptations as may be specified in the notification to the Scheme [Sec. 255(8)]. However, no such direction shall be issued after the 31st day of March, 2024. (The Finance Act, 2022 has extended this current date to 31st march 2024 from originally 31st March 2023. The Tribunal is deemed to be a civil court for all purposes of Sec. 195 and Chapter XXXV of the Code of Criminal Procedure, 1898. Therefore a scheme governing the procedures to be followed by such a body needs to be formulated after due consultation with the Ministry of Law and Justice. Hence an extension of the date. Further every such notification issued, as soon as may be after the notification is issued, be laid before each House of Parliament [Sec. 255(9)].

APPEAL BEFORE HIGH COURT

Sec. 260A provides that an appeal shall lie to the High Court from every order passed in appeal by the Appellate Tribunal if the High Court is satisfied that the case involves a substantial question of law.

The Principal Chief Commissioner or the Chief Commissioner or the Principal Commissioner or the Commissioner or an assessee being aggrieved by the order passed by the Appellate Tribunal may file an appeal to the High Court within 120 days of the date on which the order appealed against is received by the such party. The memorandum of appeal must precisely state the substantial question of law involved. The High Court may condone the delay in filing an appeal when it is satisfied that there was sufficient cause for not filing the same within that period.

If the High Court is satisfied that a substantial question of law is involved in any case, it shall formulate that question. The appeal shall be heard only on the question so formulated, and the respondents shall at the hearing of the appeal, be allowed to argue that the case does not involve such question. However, the High Court may for reasons to be recorded, hear the appeal on any other substantial question of law not formulated by it, if it is satisfied that the case involves such question.

The High Court shall decide the question of law so formulated and deliver such judgment thereon containing the grounds on which such decision is founded and may award such cost as it deems fit. The High Court may determine any issue which has not been determined by the Appellate Tribunal or has been wrongly determined by the Appellate Tribunal on such substantial question of law.

An appeal filed before the High Court shall be heard by a bench of not less than two judges of the High Court and shall be decided in accordance with the opinion such Judges or the majority, if any [Sec. 260B(1)]. Where, however, there is no such majority, the part of law upon which they differ shall be referred to one or more of the Judges of the High Court and shall be decided according to the opinion of the majority of the Judges who have heard the case including those who first heard it [Sec. 260B(2)].

The High Court also has power to stay a proceeding for recovery of demand arising out of the assessment order pending disposal of appeal. Where the High Court delivers a judgment in an appeal filed before it under Section 260A, effect shall be given to the order passed on the appeal by the Assessing Officer on the basis of a certified copy of judgement [Sec. 260(1A)].

Unless otherwise provided in any section of the Income-tax Act, the provisions of the Code of Civil Procedure, 1908 relating to appeals to the High Court shall, as far as may be, apply in the case of appeals under this section [Sec. 260A(7)].

APPEAL BEFORE SUPREME COURT

An appeal shall lie to the Supreme Court :

(*a*) from any judgment of the High Court delivered before the Supreme Court lies against the judgment delivered by the High Court on the reference application made to it by the Tribunal (under Sec. 256) against an order made under Sec. 254 before the 1st day of October, 1998, or

(*b*) an appeal made to High Court in respect of an order passed under Section 254 on or after that date provided the High Court certifies the case to be fit for appeal to the Supreme Court.

The High Court provides a certificate of fitness when the issue involved raises a substantial question of law or if the question requires to be resolved given that it has been interpreted differently by different courts or it is a question of otherwise great public or private importance. An application of fitness for appeal to the Supreme Court has to be made within 60 days from the date of the High Court's judgment (under Article 132 of the Schedule to the Limitation Act, 1963). The time required for taking a certified copy of the High Court's judgment is to be excluded in computing such a period of limitation.

When the High Court refuses to certify a case to be fit for appeal to the Supreme Court, an application for special leave to appeal can be made to the Supreme Court under the writ jurisdiction of Article 136 of the Constitution.

The Code of Civil Procedure, 1908 relating to the appeal to the Supreme Court are applicable in the case of appeals under Section 261 in the same manner as they are applicable in the case of appeals from decrees of a High Court [Section 262(1)].

Where the judgment of the High Court is changed or reversed in the appeal, effect is given to the order of the Supreme Court [Sec. 262(3)]. To award the cost of an appeal is at the discretion the Supreme Court [Sec. 262(2)]. When such cost is awarded by the Supreme Court which has not been complied with, a petition may be made to the appropriate High Court for execution of the order of the Supreme Court [Sec. 266]. The High Court may transmit the order for execution to any court subordinate to it [Sec. 266].

Faceless Effect of orders [Sec. 264B]

For the purposes of giving effect to an order under Sec. 250, 254, 260, 262, 263 or 264, so as to impart greater efficiency, transparency and accountability by—

(*a*) eliminating the interface between the income-tax authority and the assessee or any other person to the extent technologically feasible;

(*b*) optimizing utilisation of the resources through economies of scale and functional specialisation;

(*c*) introducing a team-based giving of effect to orders, with dynamic jurisdiction, the Central Government, may make such scheme by notification in the Official Gazette [Sec. 264B(1)].

For the purpose of giving effect to the scheme the Central Government may by notification in the Official Gazette, direct that any of the provisions of this Act shall not apply or shall apply with such exceptions, modifications and adaptations as may be specified in the notification [Sec. 264(2)]. However, no direction shall be issued after the 31st day of March, 2022. Every notification so issued shall, as soon as may be after the notification is issued, be laid before each House of Parliament [Sec. 264B(3)].

SPECIAL PROVISION FOR AVOIDING REPETITIVE APPEALS

It is a given that litigation in India is a time intensive and resource intensive endeavour. Given the pendency of cases in the courts, final disposal of matters takes several months and often years. Therefore, in order to avoid repetitive appeals, especially when an identical question of law is already pending before a forum, Chapter XIV-A of the Income tax Act, 1961 comprise of special provisions. The chapter has been in the statute book since 1-10-1984.

Litigation management when in an appeal by revenue an identical question of law is pending before jurisdictional High Court or Supreme Court

Sec.158AA provides that where the Commissioner or Principal Commissioner is of the opinion that any question of law arising in the case of an assessee (relevant case) is identical with a question of law arising in his case for another assessment year (other case) which is pending in appeal before the Supreme

Court against an order of High Court which was in favour of assessee, he may direct the Assessing Officer to make an application to the Appellate Tribunal stating that an appeal on the question of law in the relevant case may be filed when the decision on the question of law becomes final in the other case, subject to the acceptance of the same by the assessee.

Procedure when assessee claims identical question of law is pending before High Court or Supreme Court [Sec. 158A]

Where an assessee claims that any question of law arising in his case for an assessment year which is pending before the Assessing Officer or any appellate authority is identical with a question of law arising in his case for another assessment year which is pending before the High Court or Supreme Court, on reference or appeal, as the case may be, he may furnish to the Assessing Officer or the appellate authority, a declaration in Form 8 (Rule 16), that if the Assessing Officer or the appellate authority, agrees to apply in the relevant case the final decision on the question of law in the other case, he shall not raise such question of law in the relevant case in appeal before any appellate authority or any High Court or Supreme Court.

Where such declaration is furnished to any appellate authority, the appellate authority shall call for a report from the Assessing Officer on the correctness of the claim made by the assessee and, where the Assessing Officer makes a request to the appellate authority to give him an opportunity of being heard in the matter, the appellate authority shall allow him such opportunity.

The Assessing Officer or the appellate authority, as the case may be, may, by order in writing,

(*a*) admit the claim of the assessee if he or it is satisfied that the question of law arising in the relevant case is identical with the question of law in the other case; or

(*b*) reject the claim if he or it is not so satisfied.

Where a claim is admitted,

(*a*) the Assessing Officer or the appellate authority may make an order disposing of the relevant case without awaiting the final decision on the question of law in the other case; and

(*b*) the assessee shall not be entitled to raise, in relation to the relevant case, such question of law in appeal before any appellate authority or Court.

When the decision on the question of law in the other case becomes final, it shall be applied to the relevant case and the Assessing Officer or the appellate authority, shall, if necessary, amend the order in conformity to such decision.

Such an order shall be final and shall not be called in question in any proceeding by way of appeal, reference or revision under this Act.

Procedure when in an appeal by revenue an identical question of law is pending before Supreme Court [Sec. 158AA] (not effective from 1-4-2022)

The Finance Act, 2015 inserted sec. 158AA this time offering litigation management, this time when an appeal by revenue on an identical question of law was pending before Supreme Court.

Accordingly, where the Commissioner or Principal Commissioner is of the opinion that any question of law arising in the case of an assessee for any assessment year is identical to a question of law arising in his case for another assessment year which is pending before the Supreme Court, in an appeal or a special leave petition, against the order of the High Court in favour of the assessee, he may, instead of directing the Assessing Officer to appeal to the Appellate Tribunal, direct the Assessing Officer to make an application to the Appellate Tribunal in the prescribed form within 60 days from the date of receipt of the order of the Commissioner (Appeals) stating that an appeal on the question of law arising in the relevant case may be filed when the decision on the question of law becomes final in the other case.

Such application can be directed to be made by the Commissioner or Principal Commissioner only if an acceptance is received from the assessee to that effect. In case no such acceptance is received, the Commissioner or Principal Commissioner shall proceed in accordance with Sec. 253(2)/(2A).

Where the order of the Commissioner (Appeals) is not in conformity with the final decision on the question of law in the other case, the Commissioner or Principal Commissioner may direct the Assessing Officer to appeal to the Appellate Tribunal against such order and save as otherwise provided in this section all other provisions of Part B of Chapter XX shall apply accordingly.

Every appeal such shall be filed within 60 days from the date on which the order of the Supreme Court in the other case is communicated to the Commissioner or Principal Commissioner.

The Finance Act, 2022 has grandfathered Sec. 158AA and by virtue of a proviso inserted to the section, no such direction shall be given on or after the 1st day of April, 2022. Instead, provisions similar to sec. 158AA has now been extended to the matters pending before the High Court as well and for the same purpose, a new sec. 158AB has been inserted.

Procedure where an identical question of law is pending before High Courts or Supreme Court [Sec. 158AB] (newly inserted by the Finance Act, 2022 w.e.f. 1-4-2022)

Notwithstanding anything contained in this Act, where the collegiumis of the opinion that—

(*a*) any question of law arising in the case of an assessee for any assessment year (such case being herein referred to as the relevant case) is identical with a question of law arising,—

(*i*) in his case for any other assessment year; or

(*ii*) in the case of any other assessee for any assessment year; and (*b*) such question is pending before the jurisdictional High Court under sec. 260A or the Supreme Court in an appeal under sec. 261 or in a special leave petition under article 136 of the Constitution, against the order of the Appellate Tribunal or the jurisdictional High Court, as the case may be, which is in favour of such assessee (such case being herein referred to as the other case),the collegium may, decide and inform the Principal Commissioner or Commissioner not to file any appeal, at this stage, to the Appellate Tribunal under sub-section (2) of section 253 or to the jurisdictional High Court under sub-section (2) of section 260A in the relevant case against the order of the Joint Commissioner (Appeals) or the Commissioner (Appeals) or the Appellate Tribunal, as the case may be.

The Principal Commissioner or the Commissioner shall, on receipt of a communication from the collegium, notwithstanding anything contained in sub-section (3) of section 253 or clause (*a*) of sub-section (2) of section 260A, direct the Assessing Officer to make an application to the Appellate Tribunal or the jurisdictional High Court, as the case may be, in such form as may be prescribed within a period of 120 days from the date of receipt of the order of the Joint Commissioner (Appeals) or the Commissioner (Appeals) or of the Appellate Tribunal, as the case may be, stating that an appeal on the question of law arising in the relevant case may be filed when the decision on such question of law becomes final in the other case.

The Principal Commissioner or Commissioner shall direct the Assessing Officer to make such an application only if an acceptance is received from the assessee to that effect. In case no such acceptance is received, the Principal Commissioner or Commissioner shall, notwithstanding anything contained in sub-section (3) of section 253 or clause (*a*) of sub-section (2) of section 260A, proceed in accordance with the provisions contained in sub-section (2) of section 253 or in clause (*c*) of sub-section (2) of section 260A.

Where the order of the Joint Commissioner (Appeals) or the Commissioner (Appeals) or the order of the Appellate Tribunal, as the case may be, is not in conformity with the final decision on the question of law in the other case, as and when such order is received, the Principal Commissioner or Commissioner may direct the Assessing Officer to appeal to the Appellate Tribunal or the jurisdictional High Court, as the case may be, against such order and save as otherwise provided in this section all other provisions of Part B and Part CC of Chapter XX shall apply accordingly.

Every appeal shall be filed within a period of 60 days to the Appellate Tribunal or 120 days to the High Court, as the case may be, from the date on which the order of the jurisdictional High Court or the Supreme Court in the other case is communicated to the Principal Commissioner or the Commissioner (having jurisdiction over the relevant case), in accordance with the procedure specified by the Board in this behalf.

Explanation.—For the purposes of this section, "collegium" means a collegiums comprising of two or more Chief Commissioners or Principal Commissioners or Commissioners, as may be specified by the Board in this behalf.

SETTLEMENT OF CASES

Abolition of Settlement Commission

It was in consequence to the recommendations made by the Direct Taxes Enquiry Committee (Popularly known as Wanchoo Committee) that provision for a Settlement Commission was made under Chapter XIX-A w.e.f. 1-4-1976 as a scheme that provided an extra-legal remedy to an assessee who dodged taxes but wanted to remain law-abiding thereafter. Thus, Settlement Commission being a quasi-judicial body left the door open for a compromise with an errant assessee and at the same time ensuring that the government received taxes due which would otherwise require lengthy administrative procedures and years of litigation.

However, the Finance Act, 2021 has discontinued the Settlement Commission with immediate effect on 1st February, 2021. Therefore, no fresh applications can be made under this Chapter. Insofar as pending applications are concerned which have not been declared invalid (under Sec. 245D(2C) or no orders have been passed under Sec. 245D(4), an Interim Board for Settlement has been constituted under Sec. 245AA.

Constitution of Interim Board for Settlement [Sec. 245AA]

Under Sec. 245AA one or more Interim Board for Settlement may be constituted. Such Interim Board shall consist of three members, each being an officer of the rank of Chief Commissioner, as may be nominated by the Board [Sec. 245AA(2)]. If the Members of the Interim Board differ in opinion on any point, the point shall be decided according to the opinion of the majority. On and from the 1st day of February, 2021, all the provisions such as exercise of powers provisional attachment, exclusive jurisdiction over the case, inspection of reports and power to grant immunity and so on that were available to the Income-tax Settlement Commission shall be available to the Interim Board for the purposes of disposal of pending applications. Accordingly, by virtue of Sec. 245DD(3) Power of Settlement Commission to order provisional attachment to protect revenue, Section 245F(3) Powers and procedure of Settlement Commission, 245G(3) to inspect, or obtain copies of, any reports made by any income-tax authority to the Settlement Commission, 245H(3) Power of Settlement Commission to grant immunity from prosecution and penalty shall be exercised by the Interim Board for Settlement and the provisions of such sections shall *mutatis mutandis* apply to the Interim Board as they apply to the Settlement.

The assessee is given an option to the pending application within a period of three months from the date of commencement of the Finance Act, 2021 and intimate the Assessing Officer about the same in the prescribed manner [Sec. 245M(1)]. Where the assessee so exercises his option and withdraws the application, the proceedings with respect to the application shall abate on the date on which such application is withdrawn and the Assessing Officer, or, as the case may be, any other income-tax authority before whom the proceeding at the time of making the application was pending, shall dispose of the case in accordance with the provisions of this Act as if no application had been made [Sec. 245M(5)]. However, the income-tax authority shall not be entitled to use the material and other information produced by the assessee before the Settlement Commission or the results of the inquiry held or evidence recorded by the Settlement Commission in the course of proceedings before it [Second Proviso to Sec. 245M(5)]

Where the assessee does not exercise the option to withdraw the application within the specified time, the pending application shall be deemed to have been received by the Interim Board for further process and decision [Sec. 245M(2)].

e-Settlement Scheme, 2021

In order to :

(*a*) eliminate the interface between the Interim Board and the assessee in the course of proceedings,

(*b*) optimize utilisation of the resources through economies of scale and functional specialization,

(*c*) introduce a mechanism with dynamic jurisdiction under Sec. 245D(11) the Central Government may frame a Faceless scheme for the purposes of settlement in respect of pending applications by the Interim Board. It may direct that any of the provisions of this Act shall not apply or shall apply with such exceptions, modifications and adaptations as may be specified in the notification. However, no such direction shall be issued after the 31st March, 2023.

Accordingly, by virtue of Notification No. 129/2021 dated 1-11-2021, the Central Government has notified e-Settlement Scheme, 2021. This Scheme shall be applicable with effect from 1-11-2021 to pending applications in respect of which the applicant has not exercised the option under sec. 245M(1) and which has been allotted or transferred by Central Board of Direct Taxes to an Interim Board. The detail proceedings of the e-settlement scheme is as follows:

FIGURE 23.3 : E-SETTLEMENT SCHEME, 2021

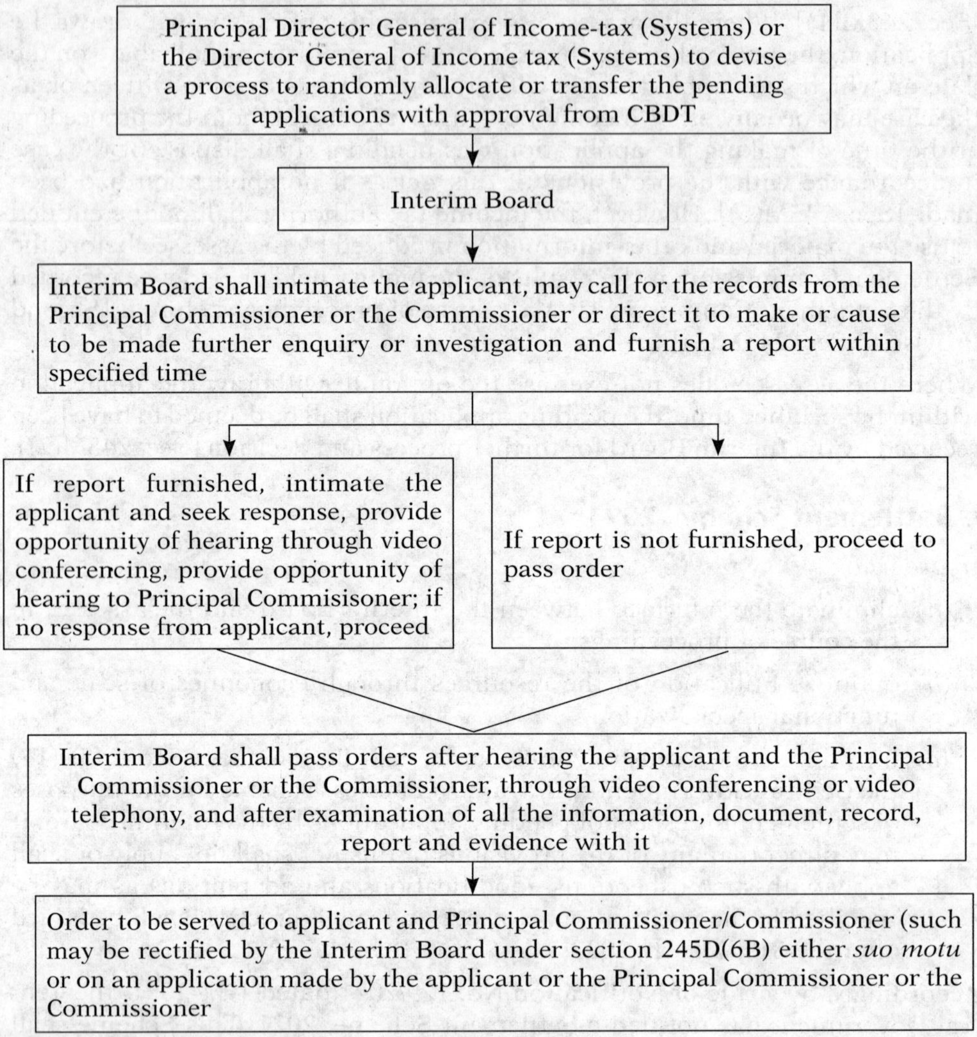

Principal Director General of Income-tax (Systems) or the Director General of Income tax (Systems) to devise a process to randomly allocate or transfer the pending applications with approval from CBDT

↓

Interim Board

↓

Interim Board shall intimate the applicant, may call for the records from the Principal Commissioner or the Commissioner or direct it to make or cause to be made further enquiry or investigation and furnish a report within specified time

↓

If report furnished, intimate the applicant and seek response, provide opportunity of hearing through video conferencing, provide opportunity of hearing to Principal Commisisoner; if no response from applicant, proceed

If report is not furnished, proceed to pass order

↓

Interim Board shall pass orders after hearing the applicant and the Principal Commissioner or the Commissioner, through video conferencing or video telephony, and after examination of all the information, document, record, report and evidence with it

↓

Order to be served to applicant and Principal Commissioner/Commissioner (such may be rectified by the Interim Board under section 245D(6B) either *suo motu* or on an application made by the applicant or the Principal Commissioner or the Commissioner

It must be noted that:

(1) The proceedings before the Interim Board shall not be open to the public and no person (other than the applicant, his employee, the concerned officers of the Interim Board or the Income-tax authority or the authorised representatives) shall, without the permission of the Interim Board, remain present during such proceedings, even on video conferencing or video telephony.

(2) All communications between the Interim Board and the applicant, or his authorised representative, and between the Interim Board and the Principal Commissioner or the Commissioner shall be exchanged by electronic mode.

(3) No personal appearance before the Interim Board. The applicant shall not be required to appear either personally or through authorised representative in connection with any proceedings under this Scheme before the Interim Board or before any Income-tax Authority or ministerial staff posted with the Interim Board.

(4) The Interim Board, at its discretion, direct the publication of orders or portions containing the rulings of the Interim Board with such modifications as to names and other particulars therein, as it may deem fit.

Dispute Resolution Committees

With the discontinuance of the Settlement Commission from 1st February, 2021, a new forum is proposed by the Finance Act, 2021 in the form of Dispute Resolution Committees. Thus, Chapter XIX-AA is inserted with effect from the 1st day of April, 2021.

Under Sec. 245MA(2), the Dispute Resolution Committee is empowered to reduce or waive any penalty imposable under this Act or grant immunity from prosecution for any offence punishable under this Act in case of a person whose dispute is resolved under this Chapter.

Thus, the benefit of dispute resolution by formation of the Dispute Resolution Committee can be opted by such persons or class of persons specified by the Central Board of Direct taxes in respect of dispute arising from any variation in the specified order and who fulfil the specified conditions [Sec. 245MA(1)].

Accordingly, the following specified conditions must be fulfilled by a person [*Explanation* (*a*) to Sec. 245MA] :

(1) no order of detention should have been made under the provisions of the Conservation of Foreign Exchange and Prevention of Smuggling Activities Act, 1974;

(2) no prosecution has been instituted for any offence punishable under the provisions of the Indian Penal Code, the Unlawful Activities (Prevention) Act, 1967, the Narcotic Drugs and Psychotropic Substances Act, 1985, the Prohibition of *Benami* Transactions Act, 1988, the Prevention of Corruption Act, 1988 or the Prevention of Money-laundering Act, 2002 and the person has been not been convicted of any offence punishable under any of these Acts;

(3) no prosecution has been initiated by an income-tax authority for any offence punishable under the provisions of this Act or the Indian Penal Code or for the purpose of enforcement of any civil liability under any law for the time being in force, or such person has been convicted of any such offence consequent upon the prosecution initiated by an Income-tax authority;

(4) such person should not be notified under Sec. 3 of the Special Court (Trial of Offences Relating to Transactions in Securities)Act, 1992;

(5) such other conditions, as may be prescribed.

Dispute Resolution option can be availed in respect of the specified order. *Explanation (b)* to Sec. 245MA defines specified order as such order, including draft order, as may be specified by the Board, and

(*a*) aggregate sum of variations proposed or made in such order does not exceed ₹ 10 lakh

(*b*) such order is not based on search initiated under section 132 or requisition under section 132A in the case of assessee or any other person or survey under section 133A or information received under an agreement referred to in section 90 or section 90A

(*c*) where return has been filed by the assessee for the assessment year relevant to such order, total income as per such return does not exceed ₹ 50 lakh.

The Assessing Officer shall pass an order giving effect to the resolution of dispute by the Dispute Resolution Committee within a period of one month from the end of the month in which such order is received. [Sec. 245MA(2A) inserted by the Finance Act, 2022 w.e.f. 1-4-2022].

By virtue of Notification No. 26/2022, dated 5-4-2022 the Central Government has notified Income-tax (Seventh Amendment) Rules, 2022 for constitution of DRC.

DRC shall be constituted for every region of the Principal Chief Commissioner of Income-tax for dispute resolution. The dispute resolution committee, which shall consist of three members, including two retired officers from the Indian Revenue Service who have held the post of commissioner of income tax or higher post for five years and one serving officer not below the rank of principal commissioner of income-tax. Members will have a tenure of three years [Rule 44DAA]. An application to the DRC shall be made in Form No. 34BC by the person, who opts for dispute resolution under section 245MA. Such application shall be accompanied by a fee of ₹ 1,000 [Rule 44DAB]. DRC, subject to prescribed conditions, shall grant waiver of penalty imposable or immunity from prosecution or both, in respect of the order which is the subject matter of resolution, if it is satisfied that such person has:

(*i*) paid the tax due on the returned income in full if available; and

(*ii*) Co-operated with the Dispute Resolution Committee in the proceedings before it [Rule 44DAC].

E-Dispute Resolution Scheme, 2022

In order to impart greater efficiency, transparency and accountability by—

(*a*) eliminating the interface between the Dispute Resolution Committee and the assessee in the course of dispute resolution proceedings to the extent technologically feasible;

(*b*) optimizing utilisation of the resources through economies of scale and functional specialisation;

(*c*) introducing a dispute resolution system with dynamic jurisdiction the Central Government may make a scheme, by notification in the Official Gazette, for the purposes of dispute resolution under this Chapter [Sec. 245MA(3)]. For the purposes of giving effect to such scheme, the Central Government may direct that any of the provisions of this Act shall not apply or shall apply with such exceptions, modifications and adaptations as may be specified in the said notification [Sec. 245MA(4)]. However no such direction shall be issued after the 31st day of March, 2023. However, the Central Government may amend any direction issued on or before 31st March, 2023 by notification in the official gazette. Every notification issued with respect such scheme, as soon as may be after the notification is issued, be laid before each House of Parliament [Sec. 245MA(5)].

By virtue of Notification No. 27/2022, dated 5-4-2022 the Central Government notified e-Dispute Resolution Scheme, 2022 to dispose of application facelessly. The detailed scheme of faceless dispute resolution is as follows:

FIGURE 23.4 : E-DISPUTE RESOLUTION SCHEME, 2022

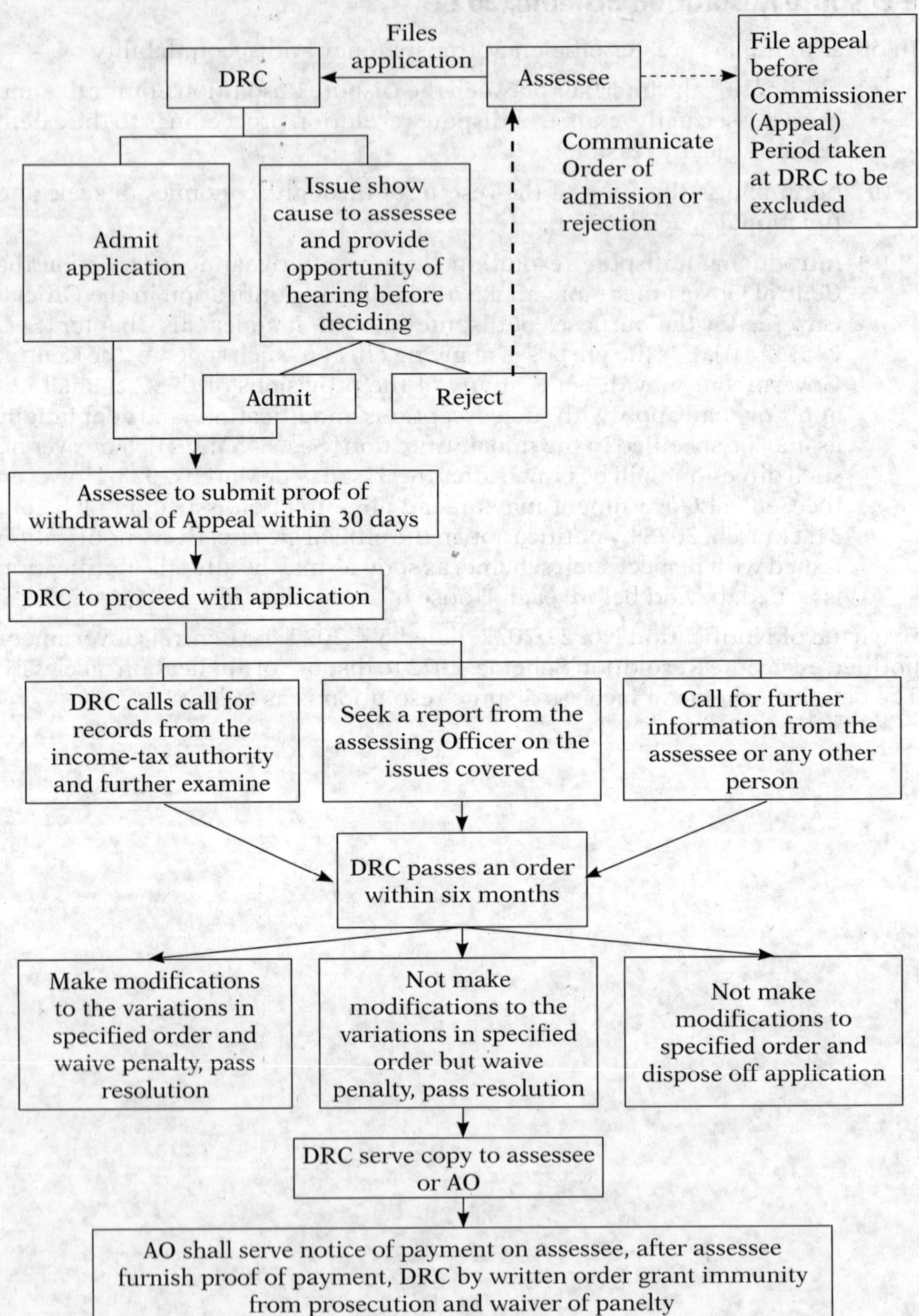

No appeal or revision shall lie against the modified order.

The Dispute Resolution Committee may at any stage of the dispute resolution proceedings, if considered necessary, for reasons to be recorded in writing and after giving an opportunity of being heard to the assessee, decide to terminate the dispute resolution proceedings if,—

(*i*) the assessee fails to cooperate during the course of dispute resolution proceedings; or

(*ii*) the assessee fails to respond to, or submit any information in response to, a notice issued to him; or

(*iii*) the Committee is satisfied that the assessee has concealed any particular material to the proceedings or had given false evidence;

(*iv*) the assessee fails to pay the demand as required in clause (*xviii*) of sub-paragraph (1) of paragraph 4.

It must be noted that :

(1) The proceedings before the Dispute Resolution Committee shall not be open to the public and no person (other than the assessee, his employee, the concerned officers of the Dispute Resolution Committee or the income-tax authority or the authorised representatives) shall, without the permission of the Dispute Resolution Committee, remain present during such proceedings, even on video conferencing or video telephony.

(2) All communications between the Dispute Resolution Committee and the assessee or the authorised representative of the assessee or any other person, as the case may be, shall be exchanged exclusively by electronic mode, to the extent technologically feasible; and all internal communications between the Dispute Resolution Committee, or any income-tax authority shall be exchanged exclusively by electronic mode.

(3) No personal appearance before the Dispute Resolution Committee. A person shall not be required to appear either personally or through authorised representative in connection with any proceedings under this Scheme before the Dispute Resolution Committee or income-tax authority. However, the assessee or any other person, as the case may be, or his authorised representative, may request for personal hearing so as to make his oral submissions or present his case before the Dispute Resolution Committee. The Dispute Resolution Committee may approve the request for personal hearing. Where the request for personal hearing has been approved by the Dispute Resolution Committee, such hearing shall be conducted through video conferencing, including use of any telecommunication application software which supports video telephony.

Monetary limits for filing of appeals by Income Tax Department

In recognition of the substantial pendency of appeals of the Income Tax Department before various appellate forums, the CBDT has been continuously working towards litigation management. To effectively reduce taxpayer grievances/

litigation and help the Department focus on litigation involving complex legal issues and high tax effect, Department have been prescribing monetary limits for filing appeals by them. Such monetary limits have been revised from time to time. These were last revised on 11th July, 2018 *vide* CBDT Circular No. 3 of 2018. In Press Release dated 8th August, 2019 the same has been enhanced as follows:

Appellate Forum	Existing Monetary Limit (₹)	Revised Monetary Limit (₹)
Before Income Tax Appellate Tribunal	20,00,000	50,00,000
Before High Court	50,00,000	1,00,00,000
Before Supreme Court	1,00,00,000	2,00,00,000

CHAPTER 24 Advance Ruling

INTRODUCTION

Given the number of litigations emerging out of tax disputes and their pendency in the Courts of Law, the system of Advance Ruling was introduced by the Finance Act, 1993. Advance ruling facilitates assessees in obtaining clarity about the tax implications of the transactions they are undertaking and their tax liability in advance. It thereby facilitated in avoiding expensive and time consuming litigation which also lead to uncertainties and unpredictability for the assessee, especially foreign investors.

Chapter XIX-B provides the full scheme of advance ruling whereby, applicants can obtain a ruling from the Authority for Advance Ruling (AAR) on issues that may arise at the time of determination of tax liability. By virtue of the Finance Act, 2021 the existing Authority for Advance Ruling shall cease to operate on and from such date as the Central Government may notify. Instead, Boards for Advance Rulings shall be constituted for giving advance rulings under this Chapter on or after such date as the Central Government may notify. Accordingly, CBDT by virtue of Notification No. 96/2021 and Notification No. 97/2021, dated 1-9-2021 has notified that AAR shall cease to operate with effect from September 1, 2021. Further, the Boards for Advance Rulings has been constituted having its headquarters at Delhi and Mumbai, to give advance rulings under Chapter XIX-B of the Act on or after 1-9-2021.

Authority for Advance Ruling replaced with Boards for Advance Rulings

Under Sec. 245-OB one or more Boards for Advance Ruling may be constituted and the same will replace the existing AAR. All the pending applications with the AAR in respect of which an order has not been passed before the notified date shall be transferred to the Board.

The Board will be providing advance ruling the meaning of which continues to remain in its existing form. Thus advance ruling under Sec. 245N means:

(*i*) a determination by the Authority in relation to a transaction which has been undertaken or is proposed to be undertaken by a non-resident applicant; or (*ii*) a determination by the Authority in relation to the tax liability of a non-resident arising out of a transaction which has been undertaken or is proposed to be undertaken by a resident applicant with such non resident and such determination shall include the determination of any question of fact specified in the application;

(*iii*) a determination or decision by the Authority in respect of an issue relating to computation of total income which is pending before any income-tax authority or the Appellate Tribunal;

(*iv*) a determination or decision by the Authority whether an arrangement, which is proposed to be undertaken by any person being a resident or a non-resident, is an impermissible avoidance agreement as referred to in Chapter X-A General Anti-Avoidance Rules.

Thus, the Board, like its predecessor AAR, may determine not only a transaction but also the tax liability arising out of a transaction and such determination may include a determination of issue of fact or issue of law.

Applicants : The aforesaid advance ruling can be sought be the following applicants as per Sec. 245N(*b*) :

(*a*) A non-resident;

(*b*) A resident who has undertaken or proposes to undertake one or more transactions of value of ₹ 100 crore or more in total [Notification No. 73, dated 28-11-2014];

(*c*) A public sector company as defined in Sec. 2(*36A*) [Notification No. 11456 dated 3.8.2000];

(*d*) Any person (resident or non-resident) making an application for determining whether an arrangement, is an impermissible avoidance agreement as referred to in Chapter X-A dealing with GAAR.

The Finance Act, 2017 merged the AAR with respect to Income-tax, Customs, Excise and Service Tax into one and therefore the applicants also includes those under Sec. 28E(*c*) of the Customs Act, 1962; Sec. 23A(*c*) of the Central Excise Act, 1944; Sec. 96A(*b*) of the Finance Act, 1994. And therefore applicants under these Acts were also recognized as applicants under Sec. 245N(*b*). The same shall be omitted with effect from such date as the Central Government may notify.

Constituting Members of Board for Advance Rulings

Unlike AAR that consisted of a Chairman and various Vice-Chairman, revenue members and law members the Board for Advance Rulings shall consist of two members, each being an officer not below the rank of Chief Commissioner, as may be nominated by the Board [Sec. 245-OB]. This is a significant departure from the erstwhile composition of AAR where persons having knowledge of law and judicial interpretation were in majority. Thus, the Chairperson of AAR were retired judges of the Supreme Court or retired Chief Justice of High Court or retired Judge of a High Court who had served in that capacity for a minimum period of seven years and the Vice-Chairperson was also a retired Judge of a High Court. However, an absence of judicial members on the newly constituted Boards for Advance Rulings with only departmental officers as members may be seen as compromising neutrality and likely to be subjected to challenge in the Courts of law.

Powers of the Authority [Sec. 245U]

All the powers of the AAR under Sec. 245R as well as the procedure for application under Sec. 245U shall *mutatis mutandis* apply to the Board for Advance Rulings as they apply to the AAR:

(1) The Authority shall have all the powers of a civil court under the Code of Civil Procedure, 1908 as are referred to in Sec. 131 of this Act.

(2) The Authority shall be deemed to be a civil court for the purposes of Sec. 195, but not for the purposes of Chapter XXVI, of the Code of Criminal Procedure, 1973 and every proceeding before the Authority shall be deemed to be a judicial proceeding within the meaning of Secs. 193 and 228 and for the purpose of section 196 of the Indian Penal Code.

Procedure on receipt of application [Sec. 245R]

All the powers of the AAR under Sec. 245R *mutatis mutandis* apply to the Board for Advance Rulings as they apply to the AAR:

(1) An applicant desirous of obtaining an advance ruling may make an application in such form and in such manner as may be prescribed, stating the question on which the advance ruling is sought. The application shall be made in quadruplicate and be accompanied by a fee of ₹ 10,000 or such fee as may be prescribed in this behalf, whichever is higher. An applicant may withdraw an application within thirty days from the date of the application [Sec. 245Q].

(2) On receipt of an application, the Authority shall forward a copy of the application to the Principal Commissioner or Commissioner and, if necessary, call upon him to furnish the relevant records. The Authority may, after examining the application and the records called for, by order, either allow or reject the application. However the following applications cannot be entertained by AAR:

   (*a*) when the question raised is already pending before any income-tax authority or appellate tribunal or any Court.

(*b*) when the question involves determination of fair market value of any property.

(*c*) when the question relates to a transaction which is designed *prima facie* for the avoidance of income-tax; (except when an application is made by a public sector company or to determine whether an arrangement proposed to be undertaken is an impermissible avoidance arrangement under Chapter X-A dealing with General Anti-Avoidance Rules).

(3) Where an application is allowed, the AAR shall, after examining such further material as may be placed before it by the applicant or obtained by the AAR, pronounce its advance ruling on the question specified in the application. No application shall be rejected unless an opportunity has been given to the applicant of being heard, either in person or through a duly authorized representative (The term "Authorised representative" shall have the meaning assigned to it in section 288(2)). Where the application is rejected, reasons for such rejection shall be given in the order. The Authority shall pronounce its advance ruling in writing within six months of the receipt of application.

(4) A copy of the advance ruling pronounced by the Authority, duly signed by the Members and certified in the prescribed manner shall be sent to the applicant and to the Principal Commissioner or Commissioner, as soon as may be, after such pronouncement.

Binding value of the ruling [Sec. 245S]

The advance ruling pronounced by the Authority shall be binding only—

(*a*) on the applicant who had sought it;

(*b*) in respect of the transaction in relation to which the ruling had been sought; and

(*c*) on the Principal Commissioner or Commissioner, and the income-tax authorities subordinate to him, in respect of the applicant and the said transaction.

The ruling shall remain binding as aforesaid unless there is a change in law or facts on the basis of which the advance ruling has been pronounced.

Advance ruling to be void in certain circumstances [Sec. 245T]

Where the Authority finds, on a representation made to it by the Principal Commissioner or Commissioner or otherwise, that an advance ruling pronounced by it has been obtained by the applicant by fraud or misrepresentation of facts, it may, by order, declare such ruling to be *void ab initio*. Upon such declaration all the provisions of this Act shall apply to the applicant as if such advance ruling had never been made.

Binding value of the ruling [Sec. 245S]

Unlike the ruling of AAR that was binding on the applicant in respect of the transaction in relation to which the ruling had been sought and the on the income-tax authorities in respect of the applicant and the said transaction, the ruling of the Board does not create such a binding.

Faceless Scheme for Advance Ruling

Further, in order to impart greater efficiency, transparency and accountability by—

(*a*) eliminating the interface between the Board for Advance Rulings and the applicant in the course of proceedings to the extent technologically feasible;

(*b*) optimising utilisation of the resources through economies of scale and functional specialisation;

(*c*) introducing a dispute resolution system with dynamic jurisdiction.

the Central Government may make a scheme, by notification in the Official Gazette, for the purposes of giving advance rulings under this Chapter by the Board for Advance Rulings [Sec. 245R(9)].

For the purposes of giving effect to such scheme, the Central Government may direct that any of the provisions of this Act shall not apply or shall apply with such exceptions, modifications and adaptations as may be specified in the said notification [Sec. 245R(10)]. However no such direction shall be issued after the 31st day of March, 2023. Every notification issued with respect such scheme, as soon as may be after the notification is issued, be laid before each House of Parliament [Sec. 245R(11)].

Right to Appeal

While there was no right to appeal available to the parties with respect the rulings of AAR, the same could be challenged under the writ jurisdiction of under article 226/227 of the Constitution before the High Court or under Article 136 of the Constitution before the Supreme Court.

However, the Finance Act, 2021 by virtue of newly inserted Sec. 245W provides a right to appeal against the ruling of the Board for Advance Ruling. Accordingly, if the parties are aggrieved by any ruling pronounced or order passed by the Board for Advance, they may appeal to the High Court against such ruling or order of the Board of Advance Rulings within 60 days from the date of the communication of that ruling or order, in such form and manner, as may be prescribed. The High Court may condone the delay in filing the appeal and grant further period of 30 days for filing such appeal.

Faceless Scheme of Appeal

In order to impart greater efficiency, transparency and accountability by—

(*a*) optimising utilisation of the resources through economies of scale and functional specialisation;

(*b*) introducing a team-based mechanism with dynamic jurisdiction, the Central Government may make a scheme for the purposes of filing appeal to the High Court by the Assessing Officer [Sec. 245W(2)].

For the purposes of giving effect to such scheme the Central Government may direct that any of the provisions of this Act shall not apply or shall apply with such exceptions, modifications and adaptations as may be specified in the notification [Sec. 245W(3)]. However no such direction shall be issued after the 31st day of March, 2023.

Every notification so issued shall, as soon as may be after the notification is issued, be laid before each House of Parliament [Sec. 245W(4)].

e-Advance Ruling Scheme, 2022

Pursuant to the powers conferred under sec. 245R(9), (10) and sec. 245W(2), (3); the Central Government has notified the 'e Advance Ruling Scheme, 2022' which is applicable w.e.f. 18-1-2022. Accordingly, Notification 7/2022 dated 18-1-2022 by CBDT prescribes the procedure for submission, handling and disposal of the applications for advance rulings, before the Board for Advance Rulings. This Scheme shall be applicable with effect from 18-1-2022 to applications of advance rulings made under section 245Q(1) or transferred under section 245Q(4). The following are details of the scheme:

FIGURE 24.1 : E-ADVANCE RULING SCHEME, 2022

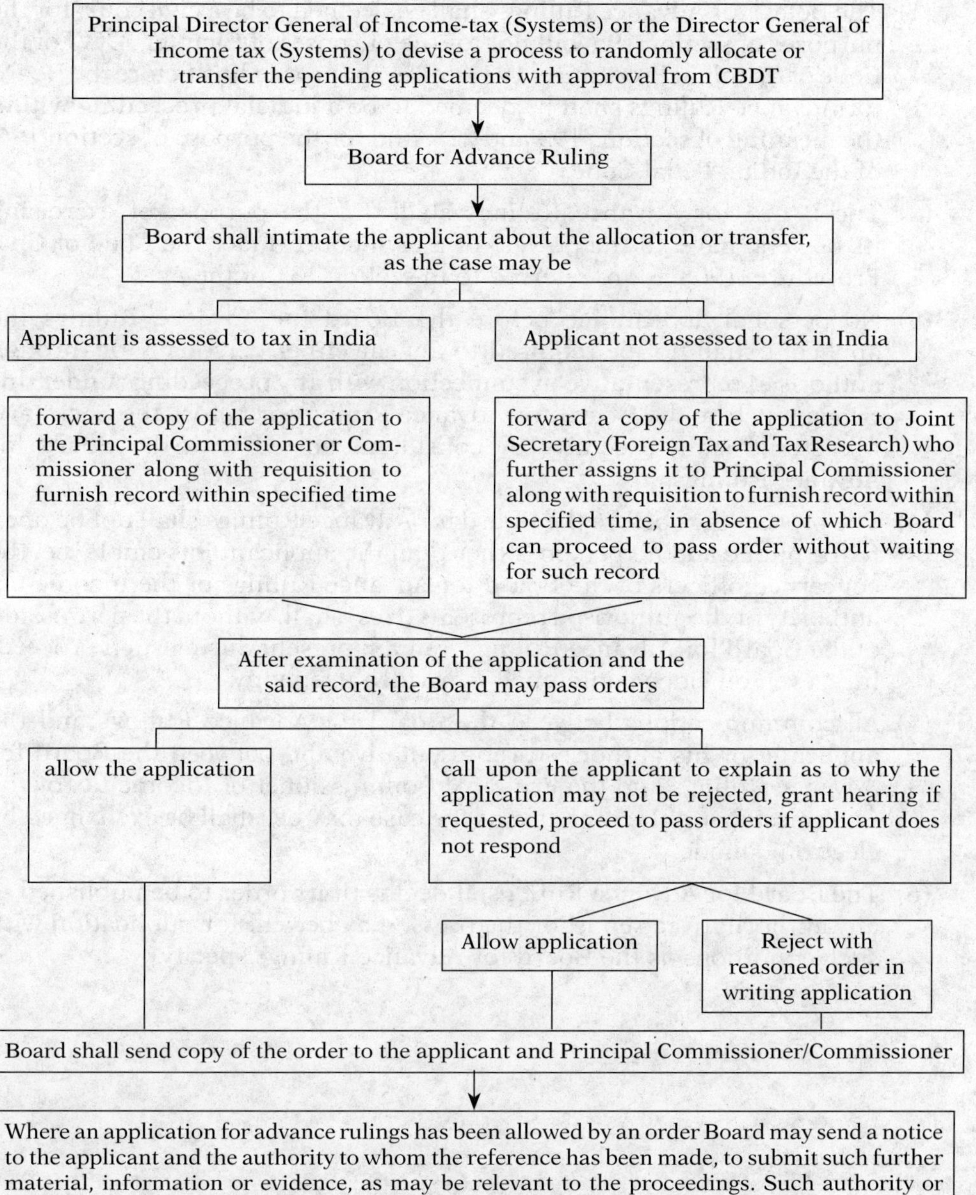

It must be noted that:

(1) The Board for Advance Rulings shall be deemed to be a civil court for the purposes of section 195, but not for the purposes of Chapter XXVI of the Code of Criminal Procedure, 1973 and every proceeding before the Board for Advance Rulings shall be deemed to be a judicial proceeding within the meaning of sections 193 and 228, and for the purpose of section 196, of the Indian Penal Code.

(2) The Board for Advance Rulings shall, for the purpose of exercising its powers, have all the powers of a civil court under the Code of Civil Procedure, 1908 as are referred to in section 131 of the Act.

(3) No personal appearance before the Board for Advance Rulings the applicant shall not be required to appear either personally or through authorised representative in connection with any proceedings under this Scheme before the Board for Advance Rulings or before the Secretary, ministerial staff, executive or consultant posted with the Board for Advance Rulings.

(4) The proceedings before the Board for Advance Rulings shall not be open to the public and no person (other than the applicant, his employee, the concerned officers of the Board for Advance Rulings or the Income-tax authority or the authorised representatives) shall, without the permission of the Board for Advance Rulings, remain present during such proceedings, even on video conferencing or video telephony.

(5) All communications between the Board for Advance Rulings and the applicant, or his authorised representative and between the Board for Advance Rulings and the Principal Commissioner of Income-tax or the Commissioner of Income-tax, as the case may be, shall be exchanged by electronic mode.

(6) The Board for Advance Rulings, if deems fit its order to be published in any authoritativea report or the press, may be sent for publication with such conditions as the Board for Advance Rulings specify.

CHAPTER 25 Deduction of Tax at Source

INTRODUCTION

The canon of convenience and the canon of economy discussed in Chapter 1 guided creation of a tax system where taxes are collected at a time that is most convenient for the assessee and at a minimal cost of collection for the administrators. In keeping with these principles of taxation, collection of income tax is not deferred till the completion of assessment of income and the principle of 'pay as you earn' is embodied in the Income-tax Act through various provisions. So that even when in principle income-tax is payable on any income in the subsequent assessment year, tax on such income is payable almost instantaneously in part by way of (*i*) deduction of tax at source (TDS) or (*ii*) collection of tax at source (TCS) or (*iii*) advance payment of tax [under Sec. 192(1A) r.w. Sec. 190(1)].

Under TDS provisions, the payer of income is required to deduct tax from certain payments at the prescribed rates and pay such tax to the credit of the Central Government within the prescribed time, failing which he is deemed to be an assessee in default and becomes liable to penalties. It must be noted that primary liability to pay the tax remains with that of the recipient of such income being an assessee. Therefore, where neither there is a provision to deduct tax at source nor income-tax has been deducted in accordance with the prescribed provisions, income-tax is payable by the assessee direct by way of advance tax. [Sec.191]. Apart from economic principles, TDS provisions also aid in ensuring that tax collections are made at the time of the release of payments from the very source of such payments *i.e.* the payer so that any possibilities of the revenue loss owing to the recipient being not traceable or chances of tax evasions are negated.

TDS PROVISIONS

The scheme of deduction of tax at source applies to a range of incomes discussed below at the rates specified. If the PAN of the deductee is not intimated to the deductor, tax will be deducted at the source by virtue of section 206AA either at the rate given in the table or at the rate of 20 per cent, whichever is higher. Further, under section 94A(5), if payment or credit is made or given to a deductee who is located in a notified jurisdictional area, tax is deductible at the rate given in the table or at the rate of 30 per cent, whichever is higher.

The amount of tax, is deducted at source, is rounded off to the nearest multiple of ₹ 10. For this purpose, any part of a rupee, consisting of paise is ignored. Thereafter, if such amount is not a multiple of ₹ 10, and the last figure in that amount is five or more, it is increased to next higher amount which is a multiple of ₹ 10 and if last figure is less than five, the amount is reduced to the next lower amount which is a multiple of ten [Sec. 288B].

Grossing up of Tax Free Income [Sec. 195A] - Where under any agreement or arrangement (other than the arrangement to pay tax free non-monetary perquisite referred to in sec. 192(1A)), the payer of any income is liable to bear the tax on it, such income should be grossed up because the income tax so paid is treated income of the payee.

For this purpose, such income should be increased to such amount as would be equal to the net amount payable after deduction of tax at source thereon.

1. Deduction of Tax at source from Salary [Sec. 192]

Payment covered	Salaries
Deductor- Payer	Employer
Deductee- Recipient	Employee
Time of Deduction	At the time of making payment
Rate of Tax	Rate of tax applicable to an individual according to the tax rate slab. (Including surcharge, health and education cess)

TDS where employee works with more than one employer [Sec. 192(2)]

Where an employee is employed simultaneously under more than one employer, tax will be deducted by each employer separately. However, the employee must furnish the details of the income under the head "Salaries", due or received from other employer or employers, the tax deducted there from and such other particulars as may be prescribed to any one employer of his choice so that the tax may be deducted on the total income of the employee at one end.

Right of adjustment [Sec. 192(3)]

The person responsible for making the payment as aforesaid [under Sec. 192(1) or Sec. 192(1A) or Sec. 192(2) or Sec. 192(2A)] is empowered to increase or reduce the amount to adjust any excess or deficiency arising out of the prior deduction or failure to deduct during the financial year.

Particulars of any other income also to be furnishes [Sec. 192(2B)]

Where a salaried assessee has also got income from sources, other than salary for the same financial year, he is bound to disclose such income to the person deducting tax at source from salary income (Rule 26B).

If he has also suffered any loss under any head of income, it cannot be taken into account for deducting tax at source except a loss on 'income from house property'.

Evidence or proof to be furnished by the assessee [Sec. 192(2D)]

For the purpose of estimating the income of the assessee or for computing tax deductible at source [under sec. 192(1)], the person responsible for making the payment to the employee has to obtain evidence or proof or particulars of the prescribed claims, including claim of set off of loss, in such form and such manner as may be prescribed.

It is operative w.e.f. 1-6-2015.

Statement of perquisites or profits in lieu of salary [Sec. 192(2C)]

A person responsible for paying any income, chargeable under the head 'Salaries' has to furnish to the person to whom the payment is made a statement, giving correct and complete particulars of perquisited or profits in lieu of salary provided to him and the value thereof in Form Nos. 12BA and 16 under Rule 26A.

TDS on non-monetary perquisites [Sec. 192(1A), (1B)]

An employer has the option to pay tax on non-monetary perquisities provided by him to an employee. Such tax is determined at the average rate of income-tax, computed at the rates in force for the financial year on the income, chargeable under the head "Salaries" including income by way of non-monetary perquisites.

Relief when salary is paid in arrears or in advance [Sec. 192(2A) r.w. Sec. 89(1)]

Where an assessee is an employee of the (*i*) Government or (*ii*) company or (*iii*) co-operative society or (*iv*) local authority or (*v*) university or (*vi*) institution or (*vii*) association or (*viii*) body and he is paid salary (*i*) in advance or (*ii*) in arrears or (*iii*) of more than 12 months, or (*iv*) by way of profits in lieu of salary, he may furnish such details to the person deducting tax at source.

Thereupon, such person has to compute the relief on the basis of such particulars and take it into account for deducting tax at source.

2. Deduction of Tax from Dividends [Sec. 194]

Payment covered	Dividend and Notional Dividend under sec. 22
Deductor- Payer	Principal Officer of an Indian company or a company which has made the prescribed arrangements for the declaration and payment of any dividend (including dividends on preference shares)
Deductee- Recipient	Resident Shareholder (non-resident shareholder under sec. 195)
Time of Deduction	At the time making payment in any mode In case of notional dividend under sec. 22, at the time of distribution of payment
Rate of Tax	10% (7.5% w.e.f. 14-5-2020 to 31-3-2021) (no surcharge, education cess)

Exemption from TDS [First and Second Provisons to Sec. 194]

No tax is deducted at source from dividends paid or distributed in the following cases:

(*i*) Dividends are paid to an individual shareholder where dividend is paid upto ₹ 5,000 in a mode other than cash.

(*ii*) Dividends paid or credited to Life Insurance Corporation of India in respect of any shares owned by it or in which it has full beneficial interest;

(*iii*) Dividends paid or credited to General Insurance Corporation of India in respect of shares owned by it or in which it has full beneficial interest;

(*iv*) Dividends paid to any other insurer in respect of any shares owned by it or in which it has full beneficial interest.

3. Winnings of Lottery or Crossword Puzzle [Sec. 194B]

Payment covered	Winnings from Lottery or crossword puzzle
Deductor- Payer	Any person so responsible for the payment
Deductee- Recipient	Any person
Time of Deduction	At the time of payment
Rate of Tax	30% (no surcharge or health and education cess)

TDS is deductible where the amount or aggregate of amounts exceeds ₹ 10,000.

TDS when winnings are partly paid in cash and partly in kind - Where the winnings are wholly in kind, the person responsible for releasing it is required not to release it unless tax has been paid in respect of such winnings. Similarly, where the winnings are partly in cash and partly in kind, but the cash part of the winnings is not sufficient to meet the liability of deduction of tax in respect of whole of the winnings, the person responsible for paying/releasing such winnings is required not to pay/release such winnings unless tax has been paid in respect of such winnings [Second Proviso to Sec. 194B]. This section shall not apply to deduction on winnings from any online game on or after 1.4.2023.

It must be noted that:

- The lottery agents are generally grouped into various categories according to the number of tickets purchased by them for the purpose of 'Lucky Dip Draws'. For each category, the prizes are awarded through draws of the lucky tickets. These prizes are lotteries and hence tax has to be deducted at source.

- Winnings from Chit Fund Scheme is also winnings from lotteries and hence tax is deductible at source [*CIT* v. *Sanjiv Kumar* (1980) 4 Taxman 97 (Punj. & Har.)]. In these schemes, chits are taken at regular intervals and any person whose name comes first, is entitled to get full amount without further contributions. The prize money comes from the interest earned from the subscriber contributions. As the subscribers have a chance to win the prizes, the amount received without further contributions is winning from lottery and hence tax is deductible.

- **Winnings on Unclaimed/Unsold Lottery Tickets does not Attract Deduction:** Where the winnings on unsold and unclaimed prizes on lottery tickets are credited to the account of the agent under the terms of agreement, no tax can be deducted at source, since Sec. 194B contemplates such deduction only in the case of actual payment of prize moneys. In case of unclaimed and/or undisbursed prize money, winning is not from lottery and, as such, the provisions of Sec. 194B for deduction of income tax at source are not applicable in respect thereof [*Director of State Lotteries* v. *Asstt. CIT* [1999] 238 ITR 1/[2000] 108 Taxman 88 (Gau.)].

4. Winnings from online games [Sec. 194BA inserted by the Finance Act, 2023]

Any person responsible for paying to any person any income by way of winnings from any online game during the financial year shall deduct income-tax on the net winnings in his user account, computed in the manner as may be prescribed, at the end of the financial year at the rates in force. Where there is a withdrawal from user account during the financial year, the income-tax shall be deducted at the time of such withdrawal on the net winnings comprised in such withdrawal, as well as on the remaining amount of net winnings in the user account, computed in the manner as may be prescribed, at the end of the financial year.

In a case where the net winnings are wholly in kind or partly in cash, and partly in kind but the part in cash is not sufficient to meet the liability of deduction of tax in respect of whole of the net winnings, the person responsible for paying shall, before releasing the winnings, ensure that tax has been paid in respect of the net winnings.

For the purposes of this section—

(*a*) "computer resource", "internet" and "online game" shall have the meanings respectively assigned to them in section 115BBJ;

(*b*) "online gaming intermediary" means an intermediary that offers one or more online games;

(*c*) "user" means any person who accesses or avails any computer resource of an online gaming intermediary;

(*d*) "user account" means account of a user registered with an online gaming intermediary.

5. Winning from Horse Race [Sec. 194BB]

Payment covered	Winnings from Horse Race
Deductor- Payer	Any person being a book maker or a person holding licence for horse racing so responsible for the payment
Deductee- Recipient	Any person
Time of Deduction	At the time of payment
Rate of Tax	30% (no surcharge or health and education cess)

TDS is deductible where the amount or the aggregate of amounts exceeds ₹ 10,000.

The obligation to deduct tax at source applies only where horse race winnings are paid by a book-maker or a person to whom a licence has been granted by the government for horse racing in any race course or for arranging for wagering or betting in any race course. A "book-maker" is a person who carries on the business of receiving or negotiating bets. He may carry on business on his own account or as a servant or agent of any other person. He may carry on the business occasionally or regularly.

6. Rent [Sec. 194-I]

Payment covered	Rent of land, building, plant, machinery and furniture
Deductor- Payer	(*i*) Any person not being an individual or HUF paying such rent (*ii*) An individual or a HUF carrying on any business or profession and the total sales, gross receipts or turnover from the business or profession carried on by him exceed ₹ 1 crore in case of business or ₹ 50 lakh in case of profession
Deductee- Recipient	Any resident person
Time of Deduction	(*i*) At the time crediting the amount (*ii*) At the time of payment Whichever is earlier
Rate of Tax	2% on rent for plant, machinery, equipment 10% on rent for land, building (including factory building) or land appurtenant thereto or furniture or fittings

Exemption from TDS

- No tax is required to be deducted at source if amount paid or credited to the account of service provider does not exceed ₹ 1,80,000 during the previous year [First proviso to Sec. 194-I]
- Where income is credited or paid to a 'business trust', [refered under Sec. 10(*23FCA*)], no tax can be deducted at source.

The following clarifications are issued Circular No. 715 dated 8 August 1995 and Circular No. 718 dated 22 August 1995:

- **Sub-letting for Putting up a Hoarding -** If a person has taken a particular space on rent and thereafter sub-lets the same fully or in part for putting up a hoarding, he is liable to TDS under Sec. 194-I and not under Sec. 194C.
- **Non-refundable Deposit liable to TDS -** In cases where the tenant makes a non-refundable deposit, tax has to be deducted at source as such deposit represents the consideration for the use of the land or the building, and, therefore partakes the nature of rent [as defined in Sec. 194-I]. If however, the deposit is refundable, no tax is deductible at source. If the

deposit carries interest, tax to be deducted on the amount of interest as well.

- **Warehousing Charges liable to TDS -** Warehousing charges are subject to deduction of tax [under Sec. 194-I].
- **Service Tax not liable to TDS -** If the municipal taxes, ground rent, and so on are borne by the tenant, no tax is deducted on such sum.
- **Joint payees having Definite Share in Property -** If there are a number of payees, each having definite and ascertainable share in the property, the limit of ₹ 1,80,000 applies to each of the payee/co-owner separately.
- **Income Content of the Payment to be Ignored -** The tax is to be deducted from the actual payment and there is no need of computing notional income in respect of a deposit, given to the landlord. If the deposit is adjustable against future rent, the deposit is in the nature of advance rent, subjected to TDS.
- **Format of Agreement not relevant -** In cases where the agreement is styled as a business centre agreement, the incidence of deduction of tax at source is not be affected, since it does not depend upon the nomenclature but on the content of the agreement as mentioned in clause (i) of *Explanation* to Sec. 194-I.
- In cases of composite arrangement for user of premises and provision of manpower for which consideration is paid as a specific percentage of turnover, if the composite agreement is in essence an agreement for taking the premises on rent, tax is deducted under Sec. 194-I from payments thereof.
- **Letting of a Part of Building -** The definition of the term "any land" or "any building" includes a part or a portion of such land or building and hence Sec. 194-I applies to rent paid for the use of only a part or a portion of any land or building [Circular No. 718 dated 22 August 1995.]
- **Payment for Regular Hotel Accommodation, liable to TDS -** Payments made for *hotel accommodation taken on regular basis is in the nature of rent subject to TDS under Sec. 194-I.* Where earmarked rooms are let out for a specified rate and specified period, it is construed to be an accommodation on 'regular basis'. Similar is the case, where a room or set of rooms are not earmarked, but the hotel has a legal obligation to provide such types of rooms during the currency of the agreement. However, where a rate contract is made with a hotel to ensure lower room rent over a specified period and there is no obligation on the part of the hotel to let out earmarked rooms at a specified rate for a specified period, such case falls to outside the scope of TDS provisions and it cannot be said that the accommodation has been hired on regular basis [Circular No. 5 dated 3 July 2002].

7. Payment on transfer of any immovable property other than agricultural land in rural area in India [Sec. 194-IA]

Payment covered	Consideration on transfer of any immovable property other than agricultural land in rural area in India
Deductor- Payer	Any person being a transferee responsible for paying (other than the person referred to in sec. 194LA)
Deductee- Recipient	Resident transferor
Time of Deduction	(*i*) At the time crediting the amount (*vi*) At the time of payment Whichever is earlier
Rate of Tax	1% or the stamp duty value of such property, whichever is higher

Exemption from TDS

No such deduction can be made where the consideration for the transfer of an immovable property and the stamp duty value of such property, are both less than ₹ 50 lakh [Sec. 194-IA(2)].

For deducting tax at source, it does not matter whether such person has been allotted 'Tax deduction account number' or 'Tax collection account number' [under sec. 203A r.w. Sec. 194-IA(3)].

8. Payment of Rent by Certain Individuals/HUFs [Sec. 194-IB]

Meaning of Rent [*Explanation* to Sec. 194-IB]

"Rent" means any payment, by whatever name called, under any lease, sub-lease, tenancy or any other agreement or arrangement for the use of any land or building or both.

Payment covered	Rent towards land or building (rent means any payment, by whatever name called, under any lease, sub-lease, tenancy or any other agreement or arrangement for the use of any land or building or both Explanation to Sec.194-IB).
Deductor- Payer	(*i*) Any person responsible for paying such sum (other than the ones referred to in Sec. 194-I) (*ii*) An individual or a HUF carrying on any business or profession and the total sales, gross receipts or turn-over from the business or profession carried on by him exceed ₹ 1 crore in case of business or ₹ 50 lakh in case of profession
Deductee- Recipient	Any Resident
Time of Deduction	(*i*) At the time crediting the amount for the last month of the previous year or the last month of tenancy, if the property is vacated during the year, as the case may be (*ii*) At the time of payment Whichever is earlier
Rate of Tax	5%

Exemption from TDS

No such deduction can be made if the rent payment does not exceed ₹ 50,000/- per month.

For deducting tax at source, it does not matter whether such person has been allotted 'Tax deduction account number' or 'Tax collection account number' [under sec. 203A r.w. Sec. 194-IA(3)].

9. Payment under Joint Development Agreement [Sec. 194-IC]

Payment covered	Consideration for Joint Development Agreement (excluding consideration in kind).
Deductor- Payer	(*i*) Any person not being an individual or HUF responsible for paying such sum (not being consideration in kind) (*ii*) An individual or a HUF carrying on any business or profession and the total sales, gross receipts or turnover from the business or profession carried on by him exceed ₹ 1 crore in case of business or ₹ 50 lakh in case of profession
Deductee- Recipient	Any Resident person
Time of Deduction	(*i*) At the time crediting the amount (*ii*) At the time of payment Whichever is earlier
Rate of Tax	10%

10. Fees for Professional/Technical Services [Sec. 194J]

Payment covered	Fees for professional/technical services/royalty/ remuneration or fees or commission to the director of a company/non-compete fee under sec. 28(*va*)
Deductor- Payer	(*i*) Any person not being an individual or HUF responsible for paying such sum (*ii*) An individual or a HUF carrying on any business or profession and the total sales, gross receipts or turnover from the business or profession carried on by him exceed ₹ 1 crore in case of business or ₹ 50 lakh in case of profession
Deductee- Recipient	Resident transferor
Time of Deduction	(*i*) At the time crediting the amount (*ii*) At the time of payment Whichever is earlier
Rate of Tax	2% in case of fees for technical services (not being a professional services) or royalty where such royalty is in the nature of consideration for sale, distribution or exhibition of cinematographic films 2% in case of business of call centre 10% in any other case

Terms Explained:

Professional services - Means services rendered by a person in the course of carrying on legal, medical, engineering, or architectural profession or accountancy or technical consultancy or interior decoration or advertising or such other profession as may be notified by the CBDT.

Fees for technical services - Means any consideration (including any lump sum consideration) for rendering of any managerial, technical or consultancy services, but does not include any consideration (for such service) which is taxable under the head "Salaries". Where technical services are provided under maintenance contracts. TDS provisions remain in operation.

Exemption from TDS

No deduction is required to be made if :

- any sums paid or credited to the account of the payee on or after 1 July 1995.
- any sums paid or credited to the account of the payee does not exceed ₹ 30,000.
- any sums paid or credited to the account of the payee exclusively for personal purposes of such individual or any member of Hindu undivided family.

11. Payment of Compensation on Acquisition of certain Immovable Property [Sec. 194LA]

Payment covered	Consideration received for compulsory acquisition under any law any immovable property (other than agricultural land or any building or part thereof)
Deductor- Payer	Any person responsible for payment
Deductee- Recipient	Resident person
Time of Deduction	(*iii*) At the time crediting the amount (*iv*) At the time of payment Whichever is earlier
Rate of Tax	10%

Exemption Limit :

Where the amount of such payment or the aggregate amount of such payments to a resident during the financial year does not exceeds ₹ 2,00,000, no tax is deducted at source.

12. Income by way of interest from Indian company [Sec. 194LC]

Payment covered	Interest on monies borrowed in foreign currency from a source outside India
Deductor- Payer	An Indian company or a business trust

Deductee- Recipient	A non-resident, not being a company or to a foreign company
Time of Deduction	(*i*) At the time crediting the amount (*ii*) At the time of payment Whichever is earlier
Rate of Tax	5% (4% if income is as per clause (*c*) below) (9% as per clause (*d*) below)

Interest incomes under this section pertain to the borrowings as follows and rate of interest should be approved by the Central Government:

(*a*) Interest in respect of monies borrowed in foreign currency outside India:

- under a loan agreement at anytime on or after 1st day of July, 2012 but before 1st day of July, 2023, or
- by way of issue of long term infrastructure bonds at any time on or after 1st day of July, 2012 but before 1st day of October, 2014; or
- by way of issue of any long-term bond including long-term infrastructure bond at any time during the 1st day of October, 2014 but before the 1st day of July, 2023.

Such loans should be approved by the Central Government, or

(*b*) Interest in respect of monies borrowed from a source outside India by way of issue of rupee denominated bond before the 1st day of July, 2023, or

(*c*) Interest in respect of monies borrowed from a source outside India by way of issue of any long-term bond or rupee denominated bond on or after the 1st day of April, 2020 but before the 1st day of July, 2023, which is listed only on a recognised stock exchange located in any International Financial Services Centre.

(*d*) Interest in respect of money borrowed from a source outside India by way of issuance of any long-term bond or rupee denominated bond on or after 1st July, 2023, which is listed only on a recognised stock exchange located in International Financial Services Centre.

13. Payment of certain amounts in cash [Sec. 194N]

Payment covered	Cash exceeding ₹ 1 crore (₹ 20 Lakhs if returns not filed by the recipient)
Deductor- Payer	Banks, Co-operative Society engaged in carrying on the business of banking, Post Office
Deductee- Recipient	Any recipient (in case of co-operative society payment unit is ₹ 3 crore)
Time of Deduction	(*i*) At the time crediting the amount (*ii*) At the time of payment Whichever is earlier

Rate of Tax	2% (when amount exceeds ₹ 1 crore) 2% (when amount exceeds ₹ 20 lakhs but not ₹ 1 crore if the recipient has not filed returns under sec. 139 for three years) 5% (when amount exceeds ₹ 1 crore if the recipient has not filed returns under sec. 139(1) for three years)

Exemption

No TDS deduction is required when any payment is made to—

(*i*) the Government;

(*ii*) any banking company or co-operative society engaged in carrying on the business of banking or a post office;

(*iii*) any business correspondent of a banking company or co-operative society engaged in carrying on the business of banking, in accordance with the guidelines issued in this regard by the Reserve Bank of India under the Reserve Bank of India Act, 1934;

(*iv*) any white label automated teller machine operator of a banking company or co-operative society engaged in carrying on the business of banking, in accordance with the authorisation issued by the Reserve Bank of India under the Payment and Settlement Systems Act, 2007;

(*v*) Any other recipient that may be specified by the Central Government in consultation with Reserve Bank of India.

14. Payment of certain sums by e-commerce operator to e-commerce participant [Sec. 194-O] [Inserted by the Finance Act, 2020 w.e.f. 1.10.2020]

Payment covered	Gross amount of such sales or services or both of an e-commerce participant facilitated by an e-commerce operator through its digital or electronic facility or platform (by whatever name called)
Deductor- Payer	e-commerce operator
Deductee- Recipient	e-commerce participant
Time of Deduction	(*i*) At the time crediting the amount (*ii*) At the time of payment Whichever is earlier
Rate of Tax	1%

Terms explained [*Explanation* to Sec.194-O]

(*i*) electronic commerce means the supply of goods or services or both, including digital products, over digital or electronic network.

(*ii*) e-commerce operator means a person who owns, operates or manages digital or electronic facility or platform for electronic commerce.

(*iii*) e-commerce participant means a person resident in India selling goods or providing services or both, including digital products, through digital or electronic facility or platform for electronic commerce.

(*iv*) services includes "fees for technical services" and fees for "professional services", as defined in the *Explanation* to Sec. 194.

Exemption from TDS [Sec.194-O(2)]

No deduction for TDS is required when the gross amount of sale or services or both of an e-commerce participant, being an individual or Hindu undivided family through e-commerce operator does not exceed ₹ 5 lakh and such e-commerce participant has furnished his Permanent Account Number or Aadhaar number to the e-commerce operator.

It must be noted that

- Where any payment made by a purchaser of goods or recipient of services directly to an e-commerce participant for the sale of such goods or provision of such services or both but facilitated by an e-commerce operator, it shall be deemed to be the amount credited or paid by the e-commerce operator to the e-commerce participant and shall be included in the gross amount of such sale or services for the purpose of TDS this section [Sec.194-O(1) *Explanation*].
- The Central Board of Direct Taxes may, issue guidelines for the purpose of removing the difficulty with the approval of the Central Government and such guidelines shall be laid before each House of Parliament, and shall be binding on the income-tax authorities and on the e-commerce operator [Sec.194-O(4), (5)].

15. Deduction of tax in case of specified senior citizen [Sec. 194P]

Payment covered	Gross total income comprising of no income other than pension and interest received from the same specified bank where pension is received (after allowing general deductions under Chapter VIA (Secs. 80C to 80U) and rebate under sec. 87A)
Deductor- Payer	Banking company as may be specified by the Central Government by a notification in Official Gazette
Deductee- Recipient	Resident individual being 75 year or more of age and having income in the form of pension and no other income other than interest received from the same specified bank where pension is received and who has furnished such a declaration verified by the bank
Time of Deduction	-
Rate of Tax	Existing tax rate slab

16. Deduction of tax on benefit or perquisite in respect of business or profession [Sec. 194R (inserted by the Finance Act, 2022)]

Payment covered	Any benefit or perquisite, whether convertible into money or not, arising from business or the exercise of a profession
Deductor- Payer	Any person responsible for providing such benefit or perquisite (in case of an individual or a HUF carrying on any business or profession only when the total sales, gross receipts or turnover from the business or profession carried on by him exceed ₹ 1 crore in case of business or ₹ 50 lakh in case of profession)
Deductee- Recipient	Resident engaged in business or profession
Time of Deduction	before providing such benefit or perquisite
Rate of Tax	10%

This provision shall apply to any benefit or perquisite, whether in cash or kind or partly in cash and partly in kind.

Exemption from TDS

No deduction for TDS is required when the value or aggregate of value of the benefit or perquisite provided or likely to be provided to such resident during the financial year does not exceed ₹ 20,000.

17. Payment on transfer of virtual digital asset [Sec. 194S (inserted by the Finance Act, 2022)]

Payment covered	Any sum by way of consideration for transfer of a virtual digital asset
Deductor- Payer	Any person responsible for paying (in case of an individual or a HUF carrying on any business or profession only when the total sales, gross receipts or turnover from the business or profession carried on by him exceed ₹ 1 crore in case of business or ₹ 50 lakh in case of profession; or being an individual or HUF not having income from the head 'Profits and Gains from Business or Profession)
Deductee- Recipient	Any resident
Time of Deduction	(*i*) At the time of credit of such sum to the account of the resident or (*ii*) At the time of payment of such sum by any mode, Whichever is earlier (Where consideration is wholly in kind or in exchange of virtual asset or is partly in cash and partly kind, the payer must ensure to deduct tax before releasing such consideration)
Rate of Tax	1%

Exemption from TDS

No deduction for TDS is required when consideration is payable by :

(*a*) An individual or a HUF carrying on any business or profession only when the total sales, gross receipts or turnover from the business or profession carried on by him exceed ₹ 1 crore in case of business or ₹ 50 lakh in case of profession; or being an individual or HUF not having income from the head 'Profits and Gains from Business or Profession and the value or aggregate value of such consideration does not exceed ₹ 50,000.

(*b*) Any other person and the value or aggregate value of such consideration does not exceed ₹ 10,000.

Other sums paid or payable to non-resident [Sec. 195]

Where any other sum is payable to a non-resident, tax is deducted at source in accordance with the following provisions :

Deduction of tax in respect of interest [Sec. 195(1)]

Where any person is responsible to pay either to non-resident, not being a company or to a foreign company any interest (*i*) from infrastructure debt fund (under Sec. 194LB), or (*ii*) interest from Indian company (under Sec. 194LC), or (*iii*) interest on certain bonds and Government securities (under Sec. 194LD) or any other sum, other than 'Salaries', he is required to deduct tax either at the time of payment thereof in cash or by issue of cheque or draft or by any other mode, whichever is earlier.

Where interest is payable by the Government or public sector bank or public financial institution, tax is deducted at the payment thereof either in cash or by issue of cheque or draft or any other mode.

Deduction of tax is made at the rate of income-tax in force.

No tax is deducted at source in respect of any dividend out of distributed profits of domestic companies under Sec. 115-O].

Determination of appropriate proportion, chargeable to tax [Sec. 195(2)] - Where the payer of income to the non-resident is of the opinion that whole of the income, other than salary, may not be chargeable to tax, he may request the Assessing Officer to determine the appropriate proportion, chargeable to tax.

On determination of such sum, tax is deducted on that proportion of the sum which is so chargeable.

Exemption certificate [Sec. 195(3), (4), (5)] - The receiver of interest may apply to the Assessing Officer to grant him a certificate to receive such interest without deduction of tax at source.

Where any such certificate is granted, every person responsible to pay such interest or other sum to the person to whom such certificate has been granted has to pay such interest or other sum without deducting tax at source so long the certificate remains in force [Sec. 195(3)].

Such certificate remains in force till the expiry of the period, specified therein or, if it is cancelled by the Assessing Officer before the expiry of such period, till such cancellation [Sec. 195(4)].

The Board is empower tó make rules to admit such application and grant such certificate subject to the rules connected therewith [Sec. 195(5)].

The person responsible for paying any sum to a non-resident (not being a company) or to a foreign company is required to furnish such information, relating to payment of such sum in Form Nos. 15CA & 15CB (under Rule 37BB), irrespective of its chargeability [Sec. 196(6) w.e.f. 1-6-2015].

Assessing Officer to determine the chargeable proportion of the sum [Sec. 195(7)] - The Board may specify a class of persons or cases where the payer of income may apply to the Assessing Officer to determine the appropriate proportion of sum chargeable, and upon such determination tax has to be deducted on that proportion of the sum which is so chargeable.

Interest or dividend or other sums payable to Government, Reserve Bank or certain corporations [Sec. 196]

No tax can be deducted by any person from any sum payable to—

(*i*) the Government, or

(*ii*) the Reserve Bank of India, or

(*iii*) a corporation established under Central Act which is exempt from income-tax on its income, or

(*iv*) a Mutual Fund, registered under securities and Exchange Board of India Act, 1992 or set up by a public sector bank or public financial institution or authorised by Reserve Bank of India, where such sum is payable to it by way of interest or dividend in respect of any securities or shares, owned by it or in which it has full beneficial interest or any other income, accruing or arising to it.

Exemption Certificate or deduction of Tax at Lower Rates [Sec. 197] - Where the total income of an assessee justifies no deduction of tax or justifies deduction of tax at lower rates, he may apply to the Assessing Officer (having jurisdiction over him) requesting him to issue a certificate to the effect that either no tax may be deducted at source or be deducted at lower rates.

Copy of the declaration by the assessee to be delivered to the Department [Sec. 197A(2)] - Where any income is paid without deduction of tax [under Sec. 197A(1) or (1A) or (1C)], the payer of such income is required to file a copy of the declaration of the assessee to the Principal Chief Commissioner or Chief Commissioner or Principal Commissioner or Commissioner on or Before the seventh day of the month next following the month in which the declaration is furnished to him.

Certificate of lower rate not to issued without PAN [Sec. 206AA(4)] - If the applicant has not furnished the PAN, he cannot be issued a certificate for deduction of tax at lower rates.

Nil tax declaration not acceptable in absence of PAN [Sec. 206AA] - Where tax deductee insists not to deduct tax at source because his total income in the specified is nil, tax has to be deducted at source if he has failed to furnish his 'Permanent Account Number.'

Similarly, tax has to be deducted at source from any income of a senior citizen of the age of 60 years or more from 'specified sources' even though he claims his total income to be nil but failed to furnish his 'Permanent Account Number.'

Consequences of declaration becoming invalid [Sec. 206AA(3)] - If the declaration becomes invalid, the deductor is required to deduct tax at source.

Special provision for deduction of tax at source for non-filers of income-tax return [Sec. 206AB] [w.e.f. 1-7-2021]

The Finance Act, 2021 has introduced Sec. 206AB that subjects habitual non-filers of income tax to a higher TDS rate. Accordingly, a person who has :

(*a*) not filed the returns of income for both of the two assessment years immediately prior to the previous year in which tax is required to be deducted; and

(*b*) where time limit of filing return of income u/s 139(1) has expired; and

(*c*) where aggregate of tax deducted and collected at source is more than ₹ 50,000 in each of these two previous years

will be subjected to higher rates of TDS under this section. In order to ensure that all the persons in whose case significant amount of tax has been deducted do furnish their return of income, the Finance Act, 2022 by virtue of an amendment to Sec. 206CCA has reduced the non-filing from two years requirement to one year. Thus a person who has not filed the returns of income for the assessment year immediately prior to the previous year in which tax is required to be deducted will be subjected to the provisions of this section.

Thus, where tax is required to be deducted at source under the provisions of Chapter XVIIB (other than the exceptions cited below) any sum or income or amount paid, or payable or credited, by the deductee to such specified person referred to above, the tax shall be deducted at :

(*i*) twice the rate specified in the relevant provision of the Act; or

(*ii*) twice the rate or rates in force; or

(*iii*) rate of 5%

whichever is higher.

Exceptions

(1) The higher TDS provision under this section will not apply, where TDS was required to be deducted under the following: Sec. 192 TDS on Salary, Sec. 192A TDS on payment of accumulated balance due to an employee, Sec.194B - TDS on winnings from lottery or crossword puzzle, Sec. 194BA - TDS on winning of online games, Sec. 194BB TDS on winnings from horse race, Sec. 194-IA TDS on payment on transfer of any immovable

property other than agricultural land in rural area in India Sec. 194-IB TDS on Payment of Rent by Certain Individuals/HUFs, Sec. 194LBC TDS on income in respect of investment in securitization trust, Sec. 194M TDS on works contract, commission etc. by individual or HUFs, Sec.194N TDS on payment of certain amounts in cash.

(2) This section shall not apply to a non-resident who does not have a permanent establishment in India or any person not required to furnish return of income notified by the Central Government [Proviso to Sec. 206AB(3)].

Special provision for collection of tax at source for non-filers of income-tax return [Sec. 206CCA]

The Finance Act, 2021 has introduced Sec. 206CCA that subjects habitual non-filers of income tax to a higher TDS rate. Accordingly, a person who has:

(*a*) not filed the returns of income for both of the two assessment years immediately prior to the previous year in which tax is required to be deducted, and

(*b*) where time limit of filing return of income u/s 139(1) has expired; and

(*c*) where aggregate of tax deducted and collected at source is more than ₹ 50,000 in each of these two previous years will be subjected to higher rates of TDS under this section. In order to ensure that all the persons in whose case significant amount of tax has been deducted do furnish their return of income, the Finance Act, 2022 by virtue of an amendment to Sec. 206CCA has reduced the non-filing from two years requirement to one year. Thus a person who has not filed the returns of income for the assessment year immediately prior to the previous year in which tax is required to be deducted will be subjected to the provisions of this section.

Thus, where tax is required to be collected at source under the provisions of Chapter XVII-BB, on any sum or amount received by a person from such person specified as above, the tax shall be collected at :

(*i*) at twice the rate specified in the relevant provision of the Act; or

(*ii*) at the rate of 5%

Whichever is higher.

However, this section shall not apply to a non-resident who does not have a permanent establishment in India for the purposes of this sub-section, the expression or a person who is not required to furnish the return of income and is notified by the Central Government [Proviso to Sec. 206CCA(3)]. The term Permanent establishment includes a fixed place of business through which the business of the enterprise is wholly or partly carried on [*Explanation* to Sec. 206CCA].

GENERAL PROVISIONS WITH RESPECT TO TDS

Tax Deducted at Source is Income deemed to be received [Sec. 198] - The tax which has been deducted at source is a part of the income of the assessee. It is deemed to have been received by him. Therefore, while computing the taxable income of an assessee, the amount actually received plus tax deducted at source, that is, the gross amount due to him is taken into consideration.

Tax paid by the employer on the value of non-monetary perquisite provided to the employee is not be deemed to be income of the employee. However, amount of tax deducted in the foreign country is not treated the income of the assessee [*CIT* v. *Ambalal Kilachand* [1994] 210 ITR 844/[1995] 81 Taxman 435 (Bom.)].

Credit to the Deductee for tax deducted at source [Sec. 199] - Any tax deducted at source and paid to the Central Government is treated as payment of tax on behalf of the person from :

(*i*) whose income the deduction was made, or

(*ii*) of the owner of security, or

(*iii*) of the depositor, or

(*iv*) of the owner of property, or

(*v*) of the unit holder, or

(*vi*) of the shareholder, as the case may be [Sec. 199(1)].

Where the employer has paid tax on the value of non-monetary perquisites under Sec. 17(2)] provided to the employee, the amount of tax paid by the employer is treated as the tax paid on behalf of the person in respect of whose income such payment has been made [Sec. 199(2)].

The Board is empowered to make rules (under Rule 37BA) to give credit in respect of tax deducted at source or tax paid on behalf a person [Sec. 193(3)].

Bar against Direct Demand on Assessee [Sec. 205] - Where tax is deductible at source, the assessee cannot be required to pay tax to the extent to which the tax has been deducted.

Statement of Tax Deducted at Source to be given to the Assessee [Sec. 203AA] - Director General of Income-tax (Systems/NSDL or any person authorised by it, is required to prepare and deliver to every person from whose income the tax has been deducted or in respect of whose income the tax has been paid a statement in Form No. 26AS by 31 July, following the financial year which taxes were deducted or collected or paid, specifying the amount of tax deducted or paid and such other particulars as may be prescribed.

Payee Required to furnish Permanent Account Number [Sec. 206AA] - Where any person is entitled to receive any sum or income or amount on which tax is deductible at source, he has to furnish his Permanent Account Number to the 'tax-deductor'.

If he fails to provide his 'Permanent Account Number', tax is to be deducted at the higher of the following rates:

(*i*) at the rate specified in the relevant provision, applicable to him, or

(*ii*) at the rate or rate in force, or

(*iv*) at the rate of 20% (where the tax is required to be deducted under Sec. 194Q rate of 5% applies w.e.f. 1st July, 2021).

Permanent Account Number, quoted by two parties to be same [Sec. 206AA(5)] - The deductee should furnish his Permanent Account Number to the deducter.

The 'PAN', quoted by both of them indicate the same, in all correspondence, bills, vouchers and other documents, sent to each other.

Consequences of providing invalid PAN [Sec. 206AA(6)] - Where the 'Permanent Account Number', provided by the deductor is invalid or does not belong to the deductee, it is deemed as if the deductee has not furnished his 'Permanent Account Number' to the deductor. Accordingly, the tax has to be deducted at a rate which is maximum out of the three rates as specified under Sec. 206AA(1) aforesaid.

Duty of Person deducting Tax

Obtain a Tax Deduction and Collection Account Number [Sec. 203A] - Every person, who is required to deduct or collect tax at source, but who has not been allotted a tax deduction or tax collection account number, should apply for the allotment of such number within the prescribed time to the Assessing Officer.

Issue a Certificate for tax deducted [Sec. 203 r.w. Rule 31] - Tax deductor is required to issue a certificate to the tax-deductee specifying the amount so deducted, the rate at which the tax has been deducted and such other particulars as may be prescribed.

Where an employer has paid tax on the perquisites provided to an employee [under Sec. 192(1A)], he has to issue a Certificate, specifying the amount so paid, the rate at which the tax has been paid and such other particulars as may be specified.

The certificate is furnished quarterly within the time-limit, specified below :

Quarter ending	Due date
(*i*) 30th June	31st July of the financial year
(*ii*) 30th September	31st October of the financial year
(*iii*) 31st December	31st January of the financial year
(*iv*) 31st March	31st May of the financial year immediately following the financial year in which deduction is made

Deposit the tax deducted with the Central Government [Sec. 200] - Any person deducting tax at source is liable to pay the sum so deducted to the credit of the Central Government within the prescribed time [Sec. 200(1)].

Consequences of Failure to Deduct or Pay [Sec. 201]

Payer assessee-in default - If any person, including principal officer of a company, liable to deduct tax at source either:

(*i*) does not deduct the whole or any part of the tax, or

(*ii*) after deduction fails to pay the tax as required under the Act,

such person is deemed to be an assessee-in-default in respect of such tax.

Similarly, where an employer opts to pay tax on the value of non-monetary perquisite provided by him to his employee but fails to pay such tax in accordance with the provisions of this Act, he is also deemed to be an assessee-in-default.

However, the Assessing Officer is required not to impose penalty on such person under Sec. 221 unless he is satisfied that such person failed to deduct and pay the tax without good and sufficient reasons [Sec. 201(1)].

Payer not an assessee-in-default if payee paid tax - The payer mentioned above is not deemed to be an assessee-in-default if the payee has :

(*i*) has furnished the return of income (under Sec. 139);

(*ii*) has taken such sum in the return of his income;

(*iii*) has paid tax on the income disclosed in the return; and

(*iv*) has furnished a certificate from chartered accountant to this effect in Form No. 26A under Income-tax Rule 31AB.

Interest liability on default - If any such person, principal officer or company does not deduct the whole or any part of the tax, or after deducting fails to pay it as required by or under this Act, the defaulter is liable to pay simple interest as below:

(*i*) at 1% for every month or part thereof on the amount of such tax from the date on which such tax was dedutible to the date on which such tax is deducted; and

(*ii*) at 1.5% for every month or part thereof on the amount of such tax from the date on which the tax was deducted to the date on which such tax is actually paid.

Such interest has to be paid before furnishing the statement [under Sec. 200(3)].

There was a confusion whether interest is payable when default in collection of tax or payment of tax continues. The Finance Act, 2022 clarifies that such interest will be payable when the default in collection of tax is a continuing one and interest shall be paid by the person in accordance with the order made by the Assessing Officer in this regard. [Proviso to Sec. 201(1A)].

Failure to pay tax after its deduction [Sec. 201(2)] - Where the tax has been deducted as aforesaid but it has not been paid, the amount of tax together with the amount of simple interest thereon as aforesaid, is a charge upon all the assets of the defaulter.

Time-barred [Sec. 201(3)] - No person can be deemed to be an assessee-in-default for failure to deduct the whole or any part of the tax from a person resident in India at any time after the expiry of 7 years from the end of the financial year in which the payment is made or credit is given.

TAX COLLECTION AT SOURCE (TCS)

1. TCS on certain lease/licence/contract [Sec. 206C(1C)]

Payment covered	Lease, License Agreement/Contract/Transfer of any right, interests for use of parking lot, toll plaza or mining and quarrying excluding mineral oil *i.e.* petroleum and natural gas
Person who collects the tax	Licensor/Leassor/Grantor of rights, interests
Person from whom tax should be collected	Licensee/Lessee/Grantee of rights, interests (other than a public sector company)
Time of Deduction	(*i*) At the time debiting the amount (*ii*) At the time of receipt Whichever is earlier
Rate of Tax	2%

2. TCS on sale of Motor Vehicle [Sec. 206C(1F)]

Payment covered	Consideration for sale of a motor vehicle of the value exceeding ₹ 10 lakh
Person who collects the tax	Seller
Person from whom tax should be collected	Buyer
Time of Deduction	At the time of receipt
Rate of Tax	1% (0.75% during the period from 14-5-2020 and 31-3-2021)

3. TCS on sales of any goods [Sec. 206C(IH) (w.e.f. 1-10-2020)]

Payment covered	Consideration for sale of any goods of the value or aggregate of such value exceeding ₹ 50 lakh [other than the goods being exported out of India or goods covered in sec. 206C(1),(1F), (1G)]
Person who collects the tax	Seller
Person from whom tax should be collected	Buyer
Time of Deduction	At the time of receipt
Rate of Tax	0.1% (three-fourth of the rate during the period from 14-5-2020 and 31-3-2021) 5% in absence of PAN/Aadhaar

Terms Explained

"buyer" means a person who purchases any goods, but does not include,—

(A) the Central Government, a State Government, an embassy, a High Commission, legation, commission, consulate and the trade representation of a foreign State; or

(B) a local authority as defined in the *Explanation* to Sec.10(*20*); or

(C) a person importing goods into India or any other person as the Central Government may, by notification in the Official Gazette, specify for this purpose, subject to such conditions as may be specified therein;

"seller" means a person whose total sales, gross receipts or turnover from the business carried on by him exceed ₹ 10 crore during the financial year immediately preceding the financial year in which the sale of goods is carried out, not being a person as the Central Government may, by notification in the Official Gazette, specify for this purpose, subject to such conditions as may be specified therein.

Exemption from TCS

No TCS is required to be collected by the seller if the buyer is liable to deduct tax at source under any other provision of this Act on the goods purchased by him from the seller.

If any difficulty arises in giving effect to the provisions of this section, the Central Board of Direct Taxes may issue, guidelines for the purpose of removing the difficulty with the approval of the Central Government and such guidelines shall be laid before each House of Parliament, and shall be binding on the income-tax authorities and on the person liable to collect the sum [Sec. 206C(1-I), (1J)].

GENERAL PROVISIONS OF TCS

Tax collection at Lower Rate [Sec. 206C(9), (10), (11)] - Where the Assessing Officer is satisfied that the total income of the buyer or the lessee or the licencee justifies the collection of the tax at any lower rate than the rate specified, the Assessing Officer is required, on an application made by the buyer/lessee/licensee in Form No. 13 in this behalf, to give to him a certificate for collection of tax at such lower rate.

Where such certificate is given, the person responsible for collecting the tax is, until such certificate is cancelled by the Assessing Officer, to collect the tax at the rates specified in such certificate. The certificate remains valid for the assessment year specified in that certificate unless it is cancelled by the Assessing Officer at any time before the expiry of the specified period.

An application for a fresh certificate may be made, if required, after the expiry of the period of validity of the earlier certificate. The certificate is valid only for the person named therein. The certificate is issued direct to the person responsible for collecting the tax under advice to the buyer or lessee or licencee who made an application for issue of such certificate.

Credit to the Payee for Tax collected at Source [Sec. 206C(4)]

Any amount of tax collected and paid to the credit of the Central Government is deemed to have been paid on behalf of the person from whom the amount has been collected. Such person is given tax credit for the assessment year for which income is assessable to tax.

Other modes of Recovery not affected [Sec. 206C(2)] - Power to recover tax by collection is without prejudice to any other mode of recovery.

Certificate of Tax collected at Source [Sec. 206C(5)]

The prescribed income-tax authority [The Director-General of Income Tax (System)] or the person so authorised by it, is required to issue a statement to the buyer or to the licensee or lessee, specifying the amount of tax collected and such other particulars as may be prescribed after the end of each financial year in the prescribed (Form No. 26AS) to the buyer or lessee specifying the amount of tax collected. Such statement is to be given by 31 July after the end of such financial year (Rule 31AB – Form No. 26AS).

Penalty for Failure to deliver the Return/Certificate [Sec. 272A(2)]

Where any person collecting tax at source fails to furnish the return of tax collection or fails to issue the certificate to the buyer or lessee for the tax collected within the prescribed time, he is liable for penalty which is ₹ 100 per day for every day during which the failure continues.

Consequences for Non-collection or Non-payment of Tax collected [Sec. 206C(6), (6A), (7)]

Where any person, responsible to collect tax, fails in such duty, he incurs many tax obligations, explained as below:

Liability to pay tax [Sec. 206C(6)] : If any person is responsible to collect tax but he fails to collect the tax in accordance with the prescribed provisions, he is liable to pay the tax to the credit of the Central Government [Sec. 206C(6) r.w. Sec. 206C(3)].

Defaulter deemed to be an assessee-in-default [Sec. 206C(6A)] : Where any person is responsible for collecting tax but (*i*) he does not collect the whole or any part of the tax or (*ii*) after collecting, fails to pay the tax as required under this Act, he is deemed to be an assessee-in-default in respect of such tax, without prejudice to any other consequences which he may incur.

Exception for treating an assessee-in-default

Where any tax collector, other than the jeweller, fails to collect the whole or any part of the tax on the amount received from a buyer or licensee or lessee or on the amount debited to the account of the buyer or licensee or lessee cannot be deemed to be an assessee-in-default in respect of such tax provided such buyer or licensee or lessee—

(*i*) has furnished his return of income (under Sec. 139);

(*ii*) has taken into account such amount for computing;

(*iii*) has paid the tax due on the income declared by him in such return of income; and

(*iv*) furnishes a certificate to this effect in Form No. 27BA (under Rule 37J).

Liability to pay interest [Sec. 206C(7)] - If any person, responsible for collecting tax, does not collect it or after collection fails to pay it, he is liable to pay simple interest @ 1% per month or part thereof on the amount of such tax from the date on which such tax was collectible to the date on which such tax was actually paid. There was confusion whether interest is payable when default in the collection of tax or payment of tax continues. The Finance Act, 2022 clarifies that such interest will be payable when the default in collection of tax is a continuing one and interest shall be paid by the person in accordance with the order made by the Assessing Officer in this regard. [Proviso to Sec. 206C(7)].

Such interest is paid before furnishing the quarterly statement for each quarter.

Where the buyer or licensee or lessee is not deemed to be in default under the first proviso to Sec. 206C(6A)], the interest is payable from the date on which such tax was collectible to the date of furnishing of return of income by such buyer or licensee or lessee.

CHAPTER 26 Advance Payment of Tax

INTRODUCTION

Advance tax is basically a device to ensure a steady flow of tax revenue to government exchequer without having to wait for the actual crystallisation of the tax liability on completion of the previous year. Since income tax is a charge on the total income of the previous year as assessed to tax in the assessment year, the actual tax liability on total income of the previous year crystallises only in the relevant assessment year. However, the scheme of advance tax requires every assessee to estimate his current income and if the tax liability on the estimated current income exceeds the specified tax-ceiling, the assessee is required to pay the estimated tax in installments during the financial year itself. Thus, an assessee is required to pay tax as he earns and therefore the scheme of advance tax is also known *'Pay as you Earn Scheme'*.

Liability to pay advance tax [Sec. 207(1)]

Tax is payable in advance during the financial year in respect of the 'current income' which is chargeable to tax in the assessment year, immediately following the financial year. Each and every income is subject to advance tax even if such income is subject to deduction of tax at source or any income is subject to a special rate of tax. Every assessee is liable to pay advance tax irrespective of his residential status that is, whether 'resident' or 'non-resident'.

Agent liable to pay advance tax on behalf of non-resident - The liability of the agent to pay advance tax on behalf of the non-resident principal may arise if the Assessing Officer serves him with a notice under Sec. 163 and after hearing him decides to treat him an agent for the non-resident principal. Once a person is held to be an agent for the non-resident principal for a particular assessment year, he may be required to pay advance tax for that year [*Premier Auto* v. *ITO* [1970] 76 ITR 1 (SC)]. This procedure is required to be followed for each relevant assessment year. An agent cannot be held liable to pay advance tax simply on the ground that he was assessed as an agent in the past year [*ITO* v. *Tata Engineering & Locomotive Co. Ltd*. [1969] 71 ITR 457 (SC)].

Exemption from advance tax [Sec. 207(2)] - No advance tax is payable by an individual, resident in India, if such individual :

(*i*) does not have any income chargeable under the head profits and gains from business or profession", and

(*ii*) is of the age of 60 years or more at any time during the previous year.

Conditions of liability to pay advance tax [Sec. 208] - Advance tax is payable during the financial year in every case provided the advance tax payable is ₹ 10,000 or more.

Completion of regular assessment for any past assessment year is not a bar for payment of Advance Tax by an Assessee [Sec. 210(1)] - Where the advance tax liability of an assessee for any financial year is ₹ 10,000 or more, he is liable to pay advance tax according to his own estimate for such year even if he has not been assessed so far by way of regular assessment (under Sec. 143(3) or Sec. 144).

Installment of advance tax and due dates of payment [Sec. 211]

An assessee is liable to pay advance tax in instalments at the prescribed rates on due dates, failing which he is liable to pay interest for under payment of advance tax [under Sec. 234C].

1. Any advance tax paid on or before 31 March, is also treated as tax paid during the financial year.
2. If a notice of demand is served on the assessee by the Assesssing Officer for the payment of advance tax after the expiry of any of the due dates as aforesaid, the assessee should pay the appropriate amount of advance tax on or before such due dates which remain unexpired after the service of such notice [Sec. 211(2)].

TABLE 26.1: INSTALMENTS AND DUE DATES OF PAYMENT OF ADVANCE TAX

Instalment	**assessee**	
	Due date of instalment	**Particulars**
1st	On or before 15th June	Up to 15% of advance tax
2nd	On or before 15th September	Up to 44% of advance tax
3rd	On or before 15th December	Up to 75% of advance tax
4th	On or before 15th March	Up to 100% of advance tax

An assessee who declares his business or professional income in accordance with the presumptive basis of taxation under Sec. 44AD(1) or Sec. 44ADA(1) is required to pay upto 100% of advance tax.

Date of delivery of cheque is the date of payment of advance tax.

When advance tax is paid by cheque, the date of payment of advance tax is the date on which the assessee delivers the cheque to the ITO. [*J &J Dechane* v. *CIT* [1990] 182 ITR 345 (AP)].

Computation of Advance [Sec. 209]

Advance tax payable for any financial year should be computed on or before the due date fixed for the payment of advance tax, keeping in view the residential status of an assessee in accordance with the relevant provisions in the manner as tabulated below:

TABLE 26.2: COMPUTATION TABLE OF ADVANCE TAX

	Particulars	Amt.(₹)
Step 1	**Compute Gross Total Income** head-wise [secs. 15-59], taking into account the clubbing provisions, if applicable [Secs. 60-64], provisions of set-off and carry forward of losses [Secs. 70 to 74A]	
	Income from Salary	
	Income from House Property	
	Profits and Gains from Business or Profession	
	Capital Gains	
	Income from Other Sources	
	Gross Total Income	
Step 2	**Compute Net Taxable Income** after allowing General Deductions [Secs. 80C to 80U]	
	Net Taxable Income	
Step 3	**Compute tax payable** on the Net Taxable income at the rates in-force during the financial year, relevant to the assessment year, as applicable (In computing tax payable by an individual and an HUF, the provisions of aggregating net agricultural income should also be taken into account in accordance with law for determining the rate of tax applicable to non-agricultural income)	
	Tax Payable on Net Taxable Income	
	Add: Surcharge	
	Health and Education Cess	
	Less: Rebate, if any	
	Relief, if any	
	Total Tax Liability	

	Particulars	Amt.(₹)
Step 4	**Adjust tax Prepaid taxes** Total Tax Liability Less: Any TDS/TCS Any relief of tax allowed under double taxation [Secs. 90, 90A, 91] Any MAT/AMT credit **Advance tax due from an assessee**	
Step 5	Apply the relevant percentage on the amount of advance tax payable to determine the amount payable in the relevant instalment of advance tax. **Amount payable by way of instalment of advance tax**	

It must be noted that:

1. Where any income, subject to TDS, is included in total income for computing advance tax, tax deductible at source on such income is computed on the gross amount of such income (*i.e.* without allowing expenses incurred in earning such income) at the prescribed rate for the relevant financial year.
2. Tax payable is rounded off to the nearest multiple of ₹ 10. For this purpose, any part of the rupee, consisting of paisa, is ignored. Thereafter, where such amount is not a multiple of ten, and the last figure in that amount is five or more, such amount is increased to the next higher amount which is a multiple of ten. If the last figure of such amount is less than five, the amount is reduced to the next lower amount which is a multiple of ten.
3. An assessee is free to revise the estimate of his/its total income on or before any instalment payable and determine the amount of instalment in the manner as explained in the computation table.

Payment of advance tax by the assessee on his own accord or in pursuance of order of Assessing Officer [Sec. 210(1)]

It is obligatory for every person to pay advance tax according to his/its estimate without any notice from the Assessing Officer.

After making the payment of first or second instalment of advance tax, an assessee can revise the remaining instalments of advance tax in accordance with his revised estimate of current income and pay tax accordingly. [Sec. 210(2)]

Computation of tax will be on current income estimated by the assessee at the rates in force during the financial year.

From the tax so computed, tax already deducted or collected at source will be further reduced.

Payment of advance tax in pursuance of order of Assessing Officer [Sec. 210(3)]

However, the Assessing Officer is also empowered to issue a notice to any person liable to pay advance tax under Sec. 210, directing him to pay advance tax. Where any person has been assessed for any previous year by way of regular assessment and in the opinion of the Assessing Officer, such person is liable to pay advance tax, he may serve a Notice of Demand in Form No. 28 (under Rule 38) on such person. Demand Notice for advance tax may be issued at any time during the financial year but not later than the last day of February of the relevant financial year, specifying the amount of advance tax and the number of instalment or instalments in which such tax is to be paid.

The Assessing Officer may also amend the Notice of Demand (*i*) if the assessment of a subsequent previous year, is completed by way of regular assessment; or (*ii*) if the assessee discloses higher income in the return furnished before 1st March in response to a notice issued under Sec. 142(1).

Basis of Computation of Advance Tax - The Assessing Officer is required to compute advance tax liability in such a case on the basis of higher of the two incomes:

(*a*) total income of the latest assessed previous year by way of regular assessment;

(*b*) total income disclosed in the return for any subsequent previous year.

Adjustment for Tax deductible at Source - The Assessing Officer is also required to give due adjustment for the amount of tax deductible at source on the income included in the current income on which advance tax is payable.

- **Payment of Advance Tax to be made by the assessee either as per notice of demand or as per his own estimate** - On receipt of the Notice of Demand, the assessee is liable to pay advance tax accordingly. However, if such assessee considers that the advance tax payable on current income of the relevant financial year (for which notice has been issued) may be less, he may send an intimation to the Assessing Officer in the Form No. 28A and pay advance tax accordingly [Sec. 210(5)]. Conversely, if the advance tax payable on current income of the relevant financial year is higher than the amount specified in the Demand Notice, he should pay advance tax according to his estimate [Sec. 210(6)]. The assessee is not required to send the estimate to the Assessing Officer.

- **Consequences for Non-payment of Advance Tax -** Where an assessee who is served with a Notice of Demand by the Assessing Officer (under Sec. 210) to pay advance tax, neither pays such tax as directed by the notice on or before the date on which any such instalment (as is not paid) becomes due nor pays advance tax according to his estimate of current income, he is deemed to be an assessee-in-default [Sec. 218].

Credit of Advance Tax [Sec. 219]

When any sum is paid by or recovered from an assessee as advance tax (other than a penalty or interest) shall be treated as a payment of tax in respect of the income of the period which would be the previous year for an assessment for the assessment year next following the financial year in which it was payable, and credit therefor shall be given to the assessee in the regular assessment.

Interest for defaults in payment of the Advance Tax [Sec. 234B]

Where an assessee is liable to pay advance tax (under Sec. 208) but has failed to pay such tax or where advance tax paid during the previous year is less than 90% of the assessed tax, the assessee is liable to pay interest on such deficiency. Interest is charged @ 1% p.m. on the amount of deficiency for the period of default.

Interest for deferment of the Advance Tax [Sec. 234C]

Interest is charged on the amount of deficiency @ 1% per month for the period of default.

CHAPTER 27

Collection and Recovery of Tax

INTRODUCTION

Before the completion of regular assessment, tax is collected by way of 'advance payment of tax' and 'deduction of tax at source'. After completion of the regular assessment, if any tax, interest, penalty, fine or such dues is found payable by the assessee, the Assessing Officer is required to serve Notice of Demand upon the assessee under Sec. 156 in the prescribed form, specifying the sum so payable. The assessee has to pay the amount as per Notice of Demand during the prescribed time-limit to escape penalties, prosecution and recovery proceedings.

COLLECTION OF TAX

Time and place to deposit the tax [Sec. 220(1)]

Any amount, not being advance tax, as specified in the Notice of Demand (issued under Sec. 156) should be paid within 30 days of the service of the notice at the place, to the person mentioned in the notice. But if the Assessing Officer has reason to believe that it is detrimental to Revenue to allow the full period of 30 days for depositing the tax, he may, with the previous approval of the Joint Commissioner, reduce the period of 30 days and may direct the assessee to pay the specified amount within such time as specified by him in the Notice of Demand.

Appeal against notice of demand [Sec. 220(1A)]

Where an appeal is filed against 'Demand Notice', it remains valid till the disposal of appeal by the last appellate authority. Such 'Notice of Demand' remains effective under Sec. 3 of the Taxation Laws (Continuation and Validation of Recovery Proceedings) Act, 1964.

Extension of time for payment of tax [Sec. 220(3)]

If the assessee is not in a position to pay within the specified time he must seek extension of time by making an application to the Assessing Officer before the expiry of due date in order to escape penalty [under Sec. 221]. If the application is made after the expiry of the date fixed for payment, the Assessing Officer is not empowered to entertain it. So it is liable to be rejected.

On receipt of an application before the expiry of due date, the Assessing Officer is empowered to extend the date of payment or may allow payment by instalments. While granting the extension he may impose such conditions as he may think fit according to the merits of each case.

The Assessing Officer has no power to reduce or waive the interest which becomes payable after the expiry of the period specified in the Notice of Demand.

Consequences of failure to pay the tax [Sec. 220]

The assessee to be deemed in default [Sec. 220(4)] - If the amount as specified in the Notice of Demand is not paid within such time, or extended time, as allowed by the Assessing Officer, at the place and to the person mentioned in the said notice, the assessee is deemed to be in default [Sec. 220(4)]. Where the assessee was allowed to pay the amount by instalments, if any installment is not paid within the time fixed by the Assessing Officer, the whole amount remaining outstanding under unexpired instalments is deemed to have fallen due at the same time when any due instalment is not paid and the assessee is deemed to be in default [Sec. 220(5)].

Exceptions: There are two exceptions to the above rule:

(*a*) *Assessee may not be treated in default during pendency of appeal* [*Sec. 220*(*6*)]: Where the assessee has filed an appeal against the order of an Assessing Officer to the Commissioner (Appeals) (Sec. 246A), the Assessing Officer may, at his discretion, not treat the assessee in default in respect of the amount which is in dispute during the pendency of the appeal.

(*b*) *Tax on non-repatriable foreign income* [*Sec. 220*(7)] : Where an assessee has been assessed in respect of foreign income, arising in a country the laws of which prohibit or restrict the remittance of money into India, the Assessing Officer is required not to treat the assessee being in default in respect of proportionate amount of tax on such foreign income as cannot be brought into India. The Assessing Officer cannot treat the assessee in default so long the prohibition or restriction on the remittance of such foreign income into India continues. In order to avail the benefit of exception the assessee must establish that he has made full, complete and *bona fide* attempts for repatriation of the money into India.

It should be noted that if such foreign income has been utilised or could have been utilised for the purpose of any expenditure actually incurred by the assessee outside India or if the income, whether capitalised or not, has been brought into India in any form, such foreign income is deemed to have been brought into India (*Explanation* to Sec. 220).

(*i*) Payment of Interest [Sec. 220(2)]

If the assessee fails to pay the amount specified in the Notice of Demand within the period as may be prescribed by the Assessing Officer, he is liable to pay simple interest @ 1% p.m. or part thereof. Interest is charged on such amount after the expiry of the prescribed period to the date when the amount specified in the Notice of Demand is actually paid. It should be noted that interest has to be paid by the assessee even if extension of time was granted by the Assessing Officer. The liability for payment of interest is absolute and unconditional. If the amount on which any interest was payable is reduced as a result of any order passed in rectification, appeal or revision, the amount of interest is also to be reduced accordingly. The amount of excess interest already paid is refunded to the assessee. For charging interest, the amount on which interest is payable is rounded off to the nearest multiple of ₹ 100. Any fraction of ₹ 100 is ignored. Any fraction of a month is deemed to be a full month (Rule 119A).

if tax is refunded pursuant to first appeal, but later restored and paid in second appeal, interest cannot be levied on refund made - Where the assessee initially paid the tax as per demand notice under Sec. 156, but later got the tax refunded pursuant to appellate order, and later on, the tax became due from the assessee pursuant to the decision of the High Court setting aside the appellate order, the Revenue is not entitled to demand interest in regard to the amount which was refunded to the assessee on the basis of appellate order, especially when the assessee had promptly satisfied the demand made by the Revenue in regard to the tax originally assessed [*Vikrant Tyres Ltd.* v. *First ITO* [2001] 115 Taxman 202/247 ITR 821 (SC)].

Interest cannot be charged in the rectification order itself - Sec. 220(2) gives power to the Assessing Officer to levy interest only if the amount specified in any particular demand has not been paid in accordance with Sec. 220(1).Where an order of rectification is made under Sec. 154 and a notice of additional demand is issued thereafter for the amount determined by that order, interest under Sec. 220(2) can be levied on the amount of demand only if there is no payment of the amount covered by the rectification order in accordance with the Notice of Demand. The rectification order itself cannot include interest under Sec. 220(2) [*Bharat Commerce and Industries Ltd.* v. *CIT* [1994] 76 Taxman 132/210 ITR 13 (Delhi)].

Company court can disallow Interest in appropriate cases - The court's powers under Sec. 446(2)(*b*) of the Companies Act are overriding of any other law and the company court may disallow department's claim for interest under Sec. 220(2) in appropriate cases [*ITO* v. *Official Liquidator* [1982] 138 ITR 136/[1983] 14 Taxman 496 (Ker.)].

Appellate Commissioner can Grant Stay - The Commissioner (Appeals) is also vested with the powers of granting stay order, which is not only necessary but expedient for effective adjudication of appeal [*Prem Prakash Tripathi* v. *CIT* [1994] 75 Taxman 107/208 ITR 461 (All.)].

Reduction or Waiver of Interest [Sec. 220(2A)] - The Principal Chief Commissioner or Principal Commissioner or Commissioner may reduce or waive the amount of interest payable by an assessee if he is satisfied that:

(*i*) Payment of such amount would cause genuine hardship to the assessee.

(*ii*) The default in the payment of the amount on which interest was payable was due to circumstances beyond the control of the assessee.

(*iii*) The assessee has co-operated in any enquiry relating to the assessment or any proceeding for the recovery of any amount due from him.

Speaking order is necessary on application [Sec. 220(2A)] - When an application is filed under Sec. 220(2A) the authority concerned is called upon to take a quasi-judicial decision. If it is satisfied that the reasons contained in the application may bring the case under clauses (*i*), (*ii*) and (*iii*) of Sec. 220(2A), it has the power either to reduce or waive the amount of interest. Even though in the said sub-section, it is not stated that any reasons are to be recorded in the order deciding such an application, it is implicit in the said provision that whenever such an application if filed, the same should be decided by a speaking order. Principles of natural justice in this regard is clearly applicable. A decision which is taken by the authority under Sec. 220(2A) can be subjected to judicial review, as was sought to be done in the instant case by filing a petition under Article 226; this being so and where the decision of the application may have repercussions with regard to the amount of interest which an assessee is required to pay, it is imperative that some reasons are given by the authority while disposing of the application [*Kishan Lal* v. *Union of India* [1998] 230 ITR 85 (SC)].

Double charge of interest to be prohibited [Sec. 220(2B)/(2C)] - Where interest is charged under Sec. 201(1A) on the amount of tax specified in the intimation under Sec. 200A(1) for any period, no interest can be charged on the same amount for the same period under Sec. 220(2) [Sec. 220(2B)].

Similarly, where interest is charged under Sec. 206C(7) on the amount of tax specified in the intimation issued under Sec. 206CB(1) for any period, no interest is charged on the same amount for the same period.

(*ii*) Penalty for Non-payment of Tax [Sec. 221]

The assessee is liable to penalty for non-payment of tax within the prescribed time. The Assessing Officer may impose such amount by way of penalty as he thinks fit and in case of continued default he may increase the amount of penalty from time to time but the total amount of penalty will not exceed the amount of tax remaining outstanding.

When an order of assessment itself is set aside on appeal, any order imposing penalty for non-payment of the tax demanded falls to the ground.

Thus, where the amount of tax is wholly reduced on appeal, the amount of penalty imposed earlier is to be cancelled and the amount of penalty, if paid, is to be refunded [Sec. 221(2)].

Levy of Penalty is Discretionary - Imposition of penalty is not automatic but discretionary. The exercise of discretion cannot be arbitrary but depends on the facts and circumstances of the case [*CIT* v. *Dadu Ulala* [1987] 34 Taxman 322/[1988] 170 ITR 491 (Raj.)].

Whether penalty should be levied or not, and if so, what should be the quantum of penalty, it depends upon the particular facts and circumstances of each case, which should primarily concern whether the default was wilful or merely accidental.

Penalty cannot be levied for Non-payment of Interest - Since 'tax' and 'interest' are different in character and the definition of 'tax' in Sec. 2(*43*) does not cover interest, penalty under Sec. 221(1) cannot be imposed for non-payment of interest [*Shreeniwas & Sons* v. *ITO* [1974] 96 ITR 562 (Cal.)].

Penalty cannot be levied for Non-payment of Penalty - No penalty can be imposed for non-payment of penalty since the definition of 'tax' does not include 'penalty' [*Chhotey Lal* v. *ITO* [1968] 69 ITR 709 (All.)]; [*Kunhalauamma* v. *ITO* [1968] 68 ITR 840 (Ker.)].

RECOVERY OF TAX

There are different modes of recovery of tax under the Income-tax Act. Tax Recovery Officer and the Assessing Officer have been empowered to recover the outstanding amount of tax from the defaulting assessee in accordance with law."Tax Recovery Officer" means Income-tax officer who is authorised by the Principal Commissioner or Commissioner, by general or special order in writing, to exercise the powers of a Tax Recovery Officer. He may also exercise or perform such powers and functions as are conferred on, or assigned to, an Assessing Officer under this Act and which may be prescribed [Sec. 2(*44*)] .

Following procedure under Secs. 222 to 225 is adopted for the recovery of tax and any other sum:

Certificate to Tax Recovery Officer [Sec. 222(1)] - Where an assessee is in default or is deemed to be in default on account of non-payment of tax, the Assessing Officer may forward to the Tax Recovery Officer a certificate under his signature specifying the amount of arrears due from the assessee.

On receipt of the certificate, the Tax Recovery Officer may proceed to recover from the defaulting assessee the amount specified in the certificate.

Service of Notice - The TRO is first required to serve a notice on the assessee to pay the arrears of tax, interest, or penalty as specified in the certificate within 15 days from the date of service of such notice, failing which recovery proceedings can be started. The TRO is required to draw a Certificate of Recovery under Rule 117B in Form No. 57.

Different Modes of Recovery - For this purpose the Tax Recovery Officer may adopt any one or more methods provided in the Second Schedule and Income tax (Certificate Proceedings) Rules, 1962. These methods are given below:

(*a*) Attachment and sale of the assessee's movable property (Rule 20 or 47, Schedule II).

(*b*) Attachment and sale of the assessee's immovable property (Rules 48 to 68, Schedule II).

(*c*) Appointment of a Receiver for the management of the movable and immovable properties of the assessee (Rules 69 to 72, Schedule II).

(*d*) Arrest of the assessee and his detention in prison (Rules 73 to 81, Schedule II).

Movable or immovable property includes any property transferred by the assessee on or after 1 June 1973 directly or indirectly without adequate consideration to his spouse or minor child or son's wife or son's minor child. Where property stands in the name of assessee's minor child or son's minor child, recovery proceedings can be taken against such property even after attaining of majority by such child [*Explanation* to Sec. 222].

Tax Recovery Officer by whom recovery is to be effected [Sec. 223(1)] – The TRO competent to take action under Sec. 222 must be—

(*a*) within whose jurisdiction the assessee carries on his business or profession or within whose jurisdiction the principal place of his business or profession is situated or

(*b*) within whose jurisdiction the assessee resides or any movable or immovable property of the assessee is situated.

For the purpose of recovery proceedings, jurisdiction to the TRO is assigned under the orders or directions issued by the Board, or by the CCIT/CIT who is authorised in this behalf by the Board under Sec. 120.

Where an assessee has property within the jurisdiction of more than one Tax Recovery Officer and the Tax Recovery Officer to whom the certificate was issued by the Assessing Officer.

(*a*) is not able to recover the entire amount by the sale of a property within his jurisdiction or

(*b*) he is of the opinion that for the purpose of speedy recovery of tax it is necessary to transfer the certificate to any other Tax Recovery Officer, he may transfer the certificate to another Tax Recovery Officer within whose jurisdiction the assessee resides or has the property. If only partial amount is to be recovered by such other Tax Recovery Officer, he may send only a certified copy of the certificate specifying the amount to be recovered by such other Tax Recovery Officer. The Tax Recovery Officer has to proceed to recover tax as if the certificate has been sent to him by the Assessing Officer [Sec.223(2)].

Validity of the certificate, amendments or cancellation thereof [Sec.224] - When the certificate is sent by the Assessing Officer to the Tax Recovery Officer, the assessee is not entitled to dispute the correctness of the assessment or the validity of the certificate drawn up by the TRO on any ground, whatsoever. The Tax Recovery Officer cannot entertain any objection raised by the assessee [*Union of India* v. *Bikash Chandra Ghosh* [1970] 78 ITR 524 (Cal.)].

Tax Recovery Officer is empowered to correct any clerical or arithmetical mistake brought to his notice.

However, if any TRO is assigned the powers/functions of the Assessing Officer, by the Principal Chief Commissioner or Commissioner he may rectify the apparent mistake from the record [Rule 117C].

Stay of proceedings in pursuance to certificate [Sec. 225] - Tax Recovery Officer is empowered to allow time to the defaulting assessee to pay the arrears of tax and thus he may stay the recovery proceedings until the expiry of the time granted.

Where the liability of an assessee has been finally reduced on an appeal or under other proceedings under the Act after the initiation of recovery proceedings, the Tax Recovery Officer is empowered to withdraw or cancel the recovery certificate accordingly.

Similarly, if the demand is reduced but the order of reduction is subject to further proceeding under the Act, the TRO may stay the recovery of such amount pertaining to the said reduction for the period for which the appeal or other proceeding remains pending.

Attachment or Sale of Property - The TRO may attach the movable or immovable property of the assessee for the recovery of tax assessed. However, such property as is exempt from attachment under Code of Civil Procedure, 1908, cannot be attached. Any objection against attachment of the property may be investigated by the TRO and can be set aside if the objection is found *bona fide*. The fixed deposit receipt is not a negotiable instrument, but could be assigned with the concurrence of the bank in favour of other persons. Amount in the fixed deposit could be attached by the income-tax authorities under the Proviso to Sec. 226(3) of the Act [*Vysya Bank Ltd.* v. *Jt. CIT* [2000] 109 Taxman 106/241 ITR 178 (Kar.)].

The TRO may sell the attached property. No sale is made on Sunday or any other general holiday recognised by the State Government or a local holiday in the area in which the sale is to take place.

No immovable property can be sold after the expiry of 3 years from the end of the financial year in which the demand notice for the recovery of dues for which the immovable property has been attached, has become conclusive.

Adjustment of Sale Proceeds - The sale proceeds are first adjusted against the amount due under the certificate. If there is any balance after such adjustment, it is utilised to set-off against any other amount recoverable from the assessee under this Act on the date on which the assets are realised.

The balance, if any, after such adjustment, is refunded to the defaulting assessee.

Where the property of the defaulter consists of a business, the TRO may attach the business and appoint a person as receiver to manage the business. The profits and gains of the business after defraying the expenses of the business, are to be adjusted towards the discharge of the assessed dues and balance, if any, is paid to the defaulter.

Defaulter to be committed to Civil Prison - Where the defaulter obstructs the recovery proceedings, the TRO may issue a notice to commit him to civil prison. If the defaulter commits a default in appearance or is to likely to abscond or leave the local limits of the jurisdiction of the TRO, he may issue a warrant for the arrest of the defaulter. However, the TRO cannot arrest and detain in civil prison a woman or a minor or a person of unsound mind.

Other Modes of Recovery [Sec. 226]

Where no certificate has been drawn up under sec. 222 as discussed above, the Assessing Officer may recover the tax by any one or more of the modes provided in this section [Sec. 226(1)]. Where a certificate has been drawn up under sec. 222, the Tax Recovery Officer may recover the tax by any one or more of the modes provided in this section [226(1A)].

(*i*) Recovery by Deduction from Salary [Sec. 226(2)]

If the assessee has the income chargeable under the head 'salaries', the Assessing Officer or Tax Recovery Officer may require any person, responsible for making the payment by way of salary to the assessee, to deduct the arrears of tax due from the assessee and pay it to the credit of the Central Government or such other person as the Board may direct.

Any amount of salary which is exempt from attachment under Sec. 60 of the Code of Civil Procedure, 1908 cannot be applied for the purpose of deduction of arrears of tax. As per provisions of the said Section, first ₹ 200 of salary and balance 50% of the salary cannot be attached.

For the purpose of attachment of salary, it is not necessary that the arrears of tax should also be of income chargeable under the head "salaries". The arrears of tax may be of any head of income.

***Salary of Third-party Debtor cannot be Attached* -** There is no provision that the salary of a third party, who is a debtor of the assessee, can be attached and recovered 'as an arrear of tax' [*Smt. Tejal R. Amin* v. *Asstt. CIT* [1994] 75 Taxman 543/208 ITR 103 (Guj.)].

(*ii*) Recovery from Debtors or would-be Debtors [Sec. 226(3)]

The Assessing Officer or Tax Recovery Officer may issue notice at any time to any debtor or would-be debtor of the assessee to pay the specified sum in the notice to the credit of the Central Government either forthwith or within such time as specified by the Assessing Officer or in case of would-be debtor when it becomes due. A copy of the notice is also to be forwarded to the assessee at his last known address by the Assessing Officer or Tax Recovery Officer. The liability of the debtor or would-be debtor cannot exceed the sum due from them to the assessee.

Similarly, the Assessing Officer or Tax Recovery Officer may also issue notice to any person who holds or may subsequently hold any money on behalf of the assessee.

Any person to whom such notice has been issued by the Assessing Officer or Tax Recovery Officer is duty-bound to pay the sum to the extent the money is due from him to the assessee or the sum specified in the notice, whichever is less, to the credit of the Central Government. The Assessing Officer or Tax Recovery Officer is required to grant receipt for the amount so paid in compliance with the notice. The person so paying is fully discharged from his liability to the assessee to the extent of the amount so paid.

Where a person to whom the notice has been issued fails to make the payment, he is deemed to be an assessee in default in respect of the sum specified in the notice and recovery proceedings can be started against him under Sec. 222 to 225 by issuing a certificate to Tax Recovery Officer as if the tax was due from him personally. If such person is an employee also, his employer cannot be required to deduct such amount from his salary income under Sec. 226(2) [*Smt Tejal R. Amin* v. *Asstt. CIT* [1994] 75 Taxman 543/208 ITR 103 Guj.].

Proceedings can continue only if Debtor-Creditor Relationship Subsists - Where the dual relationship of debtor and creditor does not exist, the mode of recovery under Sec. 226(3) cannot be resorted to, since they are in the nature of garnishee proceedings. Where the claim has got time-barred, the debtor could not be proceeded against for recovery of amount due from the creditor under Sec. 226(3) [*T.R. Rajakumari* v. *Tax Recovery Commissioner* [1979] 116 ITR 306 (Mad.)].

Tax must have been Assessed and Remained Unpaid - A garnishee order could be passed only if income tax had been assessed and had remained unpaid *[All India Reporter Ltd.* v. *Ramchandra D. Datar* [1961] 41 ITR 446 (SC)].

Notice cannot be Issued to Winner of Lottery when Payer has Deducted Tax at Source - Where, in respect of winnings from lotteries, obtained by the assessee, the person responsible for payment, deducted tax at source but failed to deposit the amount to the credit of government, the department can recover the tax only from the said person by treating him as an assessee-in-default, instead of proceeding to recover the amount from the assessee. The assessee cannot be doubly saddled with the tax liability [*Asstt. CIT* v. *Om Prakash Gattani* [2000] 242 ITR 638/[2001] 117 Taxman 549 (Gau.)].

(*iii*) Recovery from money under court custody [Sec. 226(4)]

If any money belonging to the defaulting assessee is under the custody of any court, the Assessing Officer or Tax Recovery Officer may apply to such court for payment to him either of the entire money under its custody or a sum equal to the arrears, whichever is less.

Money lying in execution Court - Money lying in execution court continues to belong to judgment debtor till it is disbursed among creditors and payment of money to credit or after application under Sec. 226(4) does not render such application infructuous. [*Lakshman Swarup Om Prakash* v. *Union of India* [1998] 97 Taxman 354/229 ITR 662 (SC)].

(*iv*) Recovery by distraint and sale of movable property [Sec. 226(5)]

The Assessing Officer or Tax Recovery Officer, with the previous approval of the Principal Chief Commissioner or Chief Commissioner, may recover any arrears of tax due from the assessee by distraint and sale of his movable property in the manner laid down in the Third Schedule.

(*v*) Recovery through State Government [Sec. 227]

If the recovery of tax in any area has been entrusted to a State Government under Article 258(1) of the Constitution, the State Government may direct the local authorities of the area that the arrears of tax due from the defaulting assessee may be recovered in the same manner as prescribed for the recovery of municipal and local taxes.

(*vi*) Recovery of Tax in Pursuance of Agreement with Foreign Countries [Sec. 228A]

The provision has been inserted by the Finance Act of 1972 with effect from 1 April 1972. It enables the Central Government to enter into agreement with foreign governments for the recovery of taxes. The Board may forward a certificate received from a foreign government with which a bilateral agreement exists, to the Tax Recovery Officer within whose jurisdiction such property is situated. The Tax Recovery Officer is required to recover the tax in the same manner as he would have recovered if the certificate has been received from an Indian Assessing Officer. Similarly, if the Assessing Officer finds that the assessee has property in a country outside India, with which a bilateral agreement exists, he may issue a certificate specifying the amount of tax arrears and forward it to the Board. The Board may take such action as it may deem appropriate having regard to the terms of the agreement with such country.

(*vii*) Recovery of Penalties, Fine, Interest and other Sums [Sec. 229]

Any sum, imposed by way of interest, fine, penalty or any other sum, payable under the provisions of this Act, is recoverable in the manner provided in this Chapter for the recovery of arrears of tax.

(*viii*) Recovery through Tax Clearance Certificate [Sec. 230]

Any person:

(*i*) who is not domiciled in India; or

(*ii*) who is domiciled in India; but

(*a*) who intends to leave India as an emigrant; or

(*b*) who intends to proceed to another country on a work permit to take up an employment or other occupation in that country,

cannot be allowed to leave India unless he has obtained a tax clearance certificate from the competent authority.

It is the duty of the owner or charter of the ship or aircraft to satisfy himself that the person travelling by his ship or aircraft has obtained the necessary certificate. If he fails to do so he is personally liable to pay the amount of such tax found due from such person. If he fails to pay he is treated as an assessee-in-default and the tax can be recovered by any of the methods discussed above.

Notice to Assessee is Necessary - A notice to the defaulter is necessary as insistence of a clearance certificate affects, though remotely, the right of the holder of a passport to go abroad. An opportunity of being heard after the issue of notice under Sec. 230(2) to the owner of the aircraft satisfy the mandate of natural justice [*Dr. Jayanti Dharma Teja* v. *ITO* [1984] 16 Taxman 165/148 ITR 316 (AP)]

Satisfaction of the Income-tax Authority must be Objective – It is no doubt, true that the words 'in the opinion of an income-tax authority in Sec. 230(1)' means the subjective satisfaction of the authority, but that subjective satisfaction must be arrived at in an objective way, that is, there must be some material on the basis of which such opinion could be reasonably formed as it affects the right to go abroad, which is part of the right of liberty [*Dr. Jayanti Dharma Teja* v. *ITO* [1984] 16 Taxman 165/148 ITR 316 (AP)].

(*ix*) Recovery by Suit [Sec. 232]

The various modes of recovery are not exhaustive. The Central Government has the right to enforce payment by other methods open to it under any other law relating to the recovery of debts due to the government. The right may be exercised even when the recovery of tax is being effected from the assessee by any mode under this Act. Thus, the government may institute a suit for the recovery of the arrears due from the assessee under any other law even when the recovery proceedings are going on under this Act.

Faceless Collection and Recovery of Tax [Sec. 231]

In order to ensure faster clearance, a reduced interface between taxpayers and officers, and enhanced transparency and optimum utilization of resources, the Central government launched the scheme of e-assessment in 2019 on pilot basis which is now being extended to all India basis and to various processes involved including collection and recovery of taxes in a faceless manner.

Accordingly, under sec.231(1) the Central Government may make a scheme, for faceless recovery.

VIVAD SE VISHWAS ACT, 2020

The extant tax disputes and prolonged litigation in involved in tax demands, the recovery of taxes due to the revenue department proves to be a long drawn process. In order to encourage erring assessees to comply with tax laws and simultaneously ensure timely recovery of taxes, the government has been coming up with Voluntary Disclosure of Income schemes from time to time. More recently the Vivad se Vishwas Act, 2020 was enacted to wrap up such pending litigations and timely collect tax arrears. The Vivad se Vishwas Act, 2020 has its genesis in the Vivad se Vishwas Scheme which in turn was launched in line with a scheme called Kar Vivad Samadhan Scheme, 1998. The 1998 Scheme extended to both direct and indirect taxes and aimed to settle tax arrears and end pending litigations claims for such arrears. Despite the 1998 scheme providing for immunity from prosecution and penalty under Income Tax Act and other fiscal statutes in India if the concerned assessee declares its tax arrears and paid the same, it failed to meet the expected targets in terms of revenue collections through such voluntary disclosure.

The Direct Tax Dispute Resolution Scheme, 2016 was introduced to wrap up matters pending before the first appellate authority, *i.e.* the Commissioner of Income Tax (Appeals). The Vivad se Vishwas Scheme was announced during the 2020 Budget with an aim to reduce the pending income tax litigations at various appellate forums and timely collection of the revenue. Subsequently, the Vivad se Vishwas Act was enacted in March 2020.

The Scheme requires an appellant being a person in whose case an appeal or a writ petition or special leave petition has been filed either by him or by the income-tax authority or by both, before an appellate forum and such appeal or petition is pending as on 31 January 2020 to make a declaration with respect to tax arrears and pay the same. It is applicable to all appeals/petitions either with the Commissioner of Income-tax (Appeals), Income-tax Appellate Tribunal, High Court, or the Supreme Court which is pending on 31st January 2020. Such declaration was to be filed on or before 31st December 2020. However, this date was further extended to 28th February 2021.Under Sec. 6 of the Vivad Se Vishwas Act, a declarant is granted immunity from initiation of proceedings in respect of offence and imposition of penalty or charge any interest under the Income-tax Act in respect of tax arrear if such declarant complies with all the requirements of this Act [Sec. 6].

Tax arrears is defined in Sec. 2(1)(*o*) as :

(*i*) the aggregate amount of disputed tax, interest chargeable or charged on such disputed tax, and penalty leviable or levied on such disputed tax; or

(*ii*) disputed interest; or

(*iii*) disputed penalty; or

(*iv*) disputed fee,

as determined under the provisions of the Income-tax Act.

Procedure to be followed – The procedure to be followed is as under:

(1) The declarant shall file a declaration with respect to tax arrears before the designated authority in such form and verified in such manner as may be prescribed [Sec.4]. The declarant is also required to give an undertaking in respect of the tax arrear, whereby he waives all rights under any law or in equity or agreement entered into by India with any country or territory outside India of any nature [Sec. 4(5)].

(2) Upon receipt of such declaration, the designated authority shall grant a certificate to the declarant within 15 days containing particulars of the tax arrear and the amount payable after such determination [Sec. 5(1)].

(3) The declarant shall pay the amount determined within 15 days of the date of receipt of the certificate and intimate the details of such payment to the designated authority in the prescribed form and thereupon the designated authority shall pass an order stating that the declarant has paid the amount [Sec. 5(2)].

(4) Consequent to such declaration,

- the appeal before the Income-tax Appellate Tribunal or Commissioner (Appeals) shall be deemed to be withdrawn.
- If the appeal or writ petition is pending before the High Court or the Supreme Court, such appeal or writ shall be withdrawn with the leave of the Court.
- Where the declarant has initiated any proceeding for arbitration, conciliation or mediation, or has given any notice thereof under any law for the time being in force or under Double Tax Avoidance Agreement or under Bilateral Investment Protection Treaty such claims in such proceedings shall be withdrawn [Sec. 4].

It must be noted that such declaration shall be presumed never to have been made if,—

(*a*) any material particular furnished in the declaration is found to be false at any stage;

(*b*) the declarant violates any of the conditions referred to in this Act;

(*c*) the declarant acts in any manner which is not in accordance with the undertaking given by him.

in such cases, all the proceedings and claims which were withdrawn under Sec. 4 and all the consequences under the Income-tax Act against the declarant shall be deemed to have been revived.

Amounts Payable under the Act

The assessee will be required to pay the following amounts under this scheme:

Nature of tax arrear	Amount payable under this Act on or before the 31st day of December, 2020 or such later date as may be notified	Amount payable under this Act on or after the 1st day of January, 2021 or such later date as may be notified but on or before the last date
Tax arrear is aggregate of disputed tax, interest chargeable or charged on such arrears and penalty leviable or levied on such tax	100% of the disputed tax, *i.e.*, without taking into consideration interest and penalty	110% of the disputed tax
Tax arrear relates to disputed interest or disputed penalty or disputed fee	25% of the disputed interest or disputed penalty or disputed fee	30% of the disputed liability

Inapplicability of the Act in certain instances :

Under Sec. 9 provisions of the Act shall not apply to:

(*i*) Tax arrear arising in respect of assessment in respect of search or requisition cases under Sec. 153A and Sec. 153C of the Income-tax Act.

(*ii*) Cases in which prosecution has been instituted on or before the date of declaration.

(*iii*) tax arrear in respect of cases relating to undisclosed income arising from a source or undisclosed asset located outside India.

(*iv*) Assessments made on the basis of any information received under an agreement referred to in section 90 or 90A.

(*v*) any person in respect of whom an order of detention has been made under the provisions of the Conservation of Foreign Exchange and Prevention of Smuggling Activities Act, 1974 on or before the filing of declaration, subject to certain conditions provided in the scheme.

(*vi*) any person in respect of whom prosecution has been instituted for any offence punishable under the provisions of the Unlawful Activities (Prevention) Act, 1967, the Narcotic Drugs and Psychotropic Substances Act, 1985, the Prevention of Corruption Act, 1988, the Prevention of Money Laundering Act, 2002, the Prohibition of Benami Property Transactions Act, 1988 has been instituted on or before the filing of the declaration or such person has been convicted of any such offence punishable under any of those Acts.

(*vii*) in respect of whom prosecution has been initiated by an Income-tax authority for any offence punishable under the provisions of the Indian Penal Code or for the purpose of enforcement of any civil liability under any law for the time being in force, on or before the filing of the declaration or such person has been convicted of any such offence consequent to the prosecution initiated by an Income-tax authority.

(*viii*) to any person notified under section 3 of the Special Court (Trial of Offences Relating to Transactions in Securities) Act, 1992 on or before the filing of declaration.

CHAPTER 28 Refunds

Basis of Refund: Excess Payment of Tax [Sec. 237]

If any person satisfies the Assessing Officer that the amount of tax paid by him or on his behalf or treated as paid by him or on his behalf for any assessment year exceeds the amount with which he is properly chargeable under this Act for that year, he is entitled to a refund of the excess.

The provision comes into operation when tax has been actually paid and not before such payment [*Amritsar Produce Exchange,* In re [1937] 5 ITR 307 (Lahore)]. Refunds cannot be denied to an assessee on the ground of some technical glitch by the computer system and auto-generation or any other difficulty [*Vodafone Idea Ltd.* v. *CIT* [2019] 111 taxmann.com 147/267 Taxman 408 (Bom.)].

Claim of refund in respect of income included in the total income of another person [Sec. 238]

Ordinarily, a refund is to be claimed by the person who has made excess payment of tax. However, where the income of one person is included in the total income of another person, the latter alone is entitled to a refund in respect of such income [Sec. 238(1)]. Thus, a minor child, whose income is clubbed with that of the father, is not entitled to any refund in respect of that income. If a refund is due in such a case, it should be claimed by the father. Similarly, where due to death, incapacity, liquidation or other cause, a person is unable to claim any refund due to him, the legal representative, or the trustee or guardian or receiver, as the case may be, is entitled to claim or receive such refund for the benefit of such person or his estate [Sec. 238(2)].

CASES OF REFUND

1. **Cases where Refund is granted by the Assessing Officer *suo motu***

   In the following two cases, refund is granted by the Assessing Officer *suo motu*:

   (*i*) Refund where pre-paid taxes exceed the tax determined on assessment - Where an assessee furnishes the return of his income, the Assessing Officer is required to determine his total income and tax liability on assessment. If the amount of taxes pre-paid by the assessee by way of advance tax or tax deducted at source or tax paid on self-assessment or otherwise, exceeds the amount of tax determined on assessment, the Assessing Officer is required to refund such excess *suo motu* and an intimation is sent to the assessee [Sec. 143(1)(*ii*)]

(*ii*) **Refund on Appeal [Sec. 240] -** Where an assessment is reduced in appeal or other proceedings under this Act, like, *e.g.* reference to Court [Sec. 260A, Sec. 262], rectification (Sec. 154) or revision (Sec. 263 or Sec. 264), and as a result any amount becomes refundable, the Assessing Officer is bound to refund the amount to the assessee without any claim being made by the assessee [*Sohan Pathak and Sons* v. *CIT* [1962] 46 ITR 523 (All.)].

However, the amount of such refund may be set-off against any other sum remaining payable by such person under this Act (Sec. 245).

Refund vs. Fresh Assessment [Proviso to Sec. 240] - Where by the order passed in appeal or other proceedings under this Act, the assessment is set aside or cancelled and the Assessing Officer has been directed to make a fresh assessment, the refund, if any, becomes due only after making the fresh assessment [*CIT* v. *Chittor Electric Supply Corporation* [1995] 78 Taxman 269/212 ITR 404 (SC)].

Refund vs. Annulment of Assessment [Proviso to Sec. 240] - Where an assessment is annulled by the order passed in appeal or other proceedings under this Act, the refund, if any, becomes due only of such amount as is paid in excess of the amount chargeable on the total income returned by the assessee.

2. Cases where refund is granted on claim made by the assessee [Sec. 239]

Every claim for refund under this shall be made by furnishing a return in accordance with the provisions of sec. 139. Say for example where any tax has been deducted at source or has been paid in advance but at the year-end the assessee discovers that his income is not taxable, such assessee can make a claim for refund. Such claim for refund shall be accompanied by a return in the form prescribed under sec. 139 unless the claimant has already made such a return to the Assessing Officer. (under Rule 41):

(*i*) **Refund Claim is to be furnished in Form No. 30 -** The assessee should furnish the claim of refund in Form No. 30 to the Assessing Officer exercising jurisdiction over him. However, the question of making the claim for refund in the prescribed form is judicially controversial.

Letter for refund not treated a proper application - Where the assessee simply wrote a letter, claiming the refund, it was not treated as a proper application for a refund since it was not in the prescribed Form [*Sardar Bahadur Sardar Indra Singh Trust* v. *CIT* [1954] 26 ITR 670 (Cal.)].

Claim in proper form not a bar to seek refund - The prescribed Form could not be used to bar the claim of the assessee to a refund of tax on the super technical ground that his application was not in the prescribed Form. By prescribing a given Form, the framers of the rule intended to facilitate the refund and not to bar or hinder the claim of the assessee for getting his money back [*Deep Chand Jain* v. *ITO* [1983] 15 Taxman 522/[1984] 145 ITR 676 (Punj. & Har.)].

Non-resident claiming refund on account of TDS - Where refund claim is made by a non-resident whose total income is made up only of income taxed at source, the claim for refund should be made to the Assessing Officer, Non-resident Refund Circle, Mumbai.

(*ii*) **Refund claim to be accompanied by a certificate of TDS -** Where any part of total income consists of dividends or any other income from which tax has been deducted at source under Secs. 192 to 194 and Sec. 194A and Sec. 195, the claim should be accompanied by the certificates prescribed under Sec. 203.

(*iv*) **Mode of presenting the Claim -** The claim may be presented by the claimant in person or through a duly authorised agent or may be sent by post.

(*v*) **Time-limit for presenting the claim [Sec. 239(2)] -** The claim for refund should be made within one year from the last day of the relevant assessment year.

Belated claims for refund - By virtue of the power conferred on the Central Board of Direct Taxes under Sec. 119(2), it is fully competent to admit an application for a refund even after the expiry of the period prescribed under sec. 239, for avoiding genuine hardship in any case or class of cases - *Jaswant Singh Bambha* v. *CBDT* [2005] 142 Taxman 528 (Punj. & Har.) (FB). However, there should be sufficient reasons for condonation of delay in filing returns of income, assessee's claim for refund, in the absence of which such claim cannot be allowed [*T.V. Hameed* v. *UOI* [2012] 17 taxmann.com 163/205 Taxman 83 (Ker.)]. It is desired that only genuine cases should be considered for the purposes of condoning the delay and the application should not be disposed of in a routine manner. When claim for refund was delayed due to inadvertence and oversight of the auditor of the assessee, delay was condoned. [*G.V. Infosutions (P.) Ltd*. v. *Dy. CIT* [2019] 102 taxmann.com 397/261 Taxman 482 (Delhi)].

3. Cases when refund is claimed when no tax was deductible [Sec. 239A (newly inserted by the Finance Act, 2022 w.e.f. 1.4.2022)]

Under Sec. 248 where a person who has deducted tax on any income paid to a non-resident may appeal to the Commissioner (Appeals) for a declaration that no tax was required to be deducted on such income. However, such an appeal could be filed only after making the payment of tax so deducted. Therefore, under the existing provisions, such person was compelled to enter an appellate process before the Commissioner (Appeals) and had no recourse to approach the Assessing Officer to request for refund of the tax that was as such not deductible. The newly inserted Sec. 239A offers this recourse to such a person to file an application for refund of such tax deducted before the Assessing Officer. If such a person is not satisfied with the order of the Assessing Officer, he may appeal against such order before the Commissioner (Appeals) under Sec. 246A. Accordingly, the provisions of Sec. 248 will not apply in cases where the date of tax payment to the credit of the Central Government is on or after 01.04.2022.

Correctness of assessment not to be questioned [Sec. 242]

While making a claim for refund, the assessee is not entitled to question the correctness of the assessment or any other matter, which has become final and conclusive.

The assessee cannot ask for a revision, review or modification of the assessment under the cloak of applying for a refund or otherwise to go behind the finality of the assessment [*Ramkrishna Ashanna Bukekar* v. *CIT* [1956] 30 ITR 833 (Nagpur)]. If an assessment is unjustified in law and the tax has been paid on the basis of such assessment, the assessee should go in appeal against such assessment and not apply for a refund [*CIT* v. *The Tribune* Trust [1948] 16 ITR 214 (PC)].

Withholding of refund in certain cases [Sec. 241A]

For every assessment year commencing on or after the 1st day of April, 2017, where refund of any amount becomes due to the assessee under the provisions of sec.143(1) and the Assessing Officer may withhold the refund up to the date on which assesement is made if having regard to the fact that a notice has been issued in respect of such return he is of the opinion that the grant of the refund is likely to adversely affect the revenue. The reasons for such opinion must be recorded in writing and withholding of refund is with the previous approval of the Principal Commissioner or Commissioner.

Set-off of refund against tax remaining payable [Sec. 245]

Where any refund is found due to the assessee, the Assessing Officer or the Commissioner (Appeals) or the Principal Chief Commissioner or the Chief

Commissioner, as the case may be, may set-off the amount of refund due to the assessee against the sum remaining payable under this Act from him [Sec. 245].

The assessee has no right against this. No opportunity of being heard can be given to the assessee. An order, passed in writing, informing the assessee about such set-off, is sufficient. The set-off can be applied even against such sum remaining payable from the assessee, the recovery of which has become time-barred. Sum remaining payable from the assessee also includes a tax on foreign income, the remittance of which is prohibited by the laws of that foreign country.

Prior Intimation Mandatory before Adjustment : It must be noted that the task of adjusting the refund towards the arrears of tax payable by the assessee is not a quasi-judicial proceeding. Therefore, Sec. 245 does not require any show-cause notice being given, calling upon the assessee to explain as to why the adjustment should not be made, nor does it contemplate any hearing. All that sec. 245 requires the authorities to do is to make a readjustment after giving an intimation in writing to such person of the action proposed to be taken under this section. The authorities are not required to go beyond what the section itself requires them to do. Therefore, before any set-off refund due against sums payable is made, a prior intimation to the assessee is mandatory [*Vijay Kumar Bhati* v. *CIT* [1993] 71 Taxman 629/[1994] 205 ITR 110 (Delhi)]. Adjustment made without such intimation will be ineffective and bad in law [*J.K. Industries Ltd.* v. *CIT* [1999] 238 ITR 820 (Cal.)].

Set-off allowed only against the Demand payable by the same person to whom Refund is Due Adjustment of refund can be made against the demand of the person to whom the refund is due [*Archana Shukla* v. *JCIT* (2000) 112 Taxman 573/244 ITR 829 (Delhi)]. Thus, the refund due to an individual cannot be adjusted against the demand arrears of the deceased father [*Hasmukh Lal* v. *ITO* (2001) 117 Taxman 231/251 ITR 511 (MP)]. But the amount of refund due to the firm cannot be set-off against the sum remaining payable from the partners. It is to be refunded to the firm so that all debts of the firm are discharged and the accounts taken.

Set-off permissible against Demand under this Act Refund is to be set-off only against the demand found payable under this Act and not under any other Act. Thus, the refund amount cannot be adjusted against demand under Interest Act or Sales Tax Act and so on [*State Bank of Patiala* v. *CIT* (1999) 105 Taxman 326/239 ITR 421 (Punj. & Har.)].

Set-off permissible against a Time-barred Tax Demand

The set-off can be applied even against such sum remaining payable from the assessee, the recovery of which has become time-barred under Secs. 222 to 228A.

INTEREST ON REFUNDS

1. **Interest payable by the Assessee on Excess Refund [Sec. 234D]**

   Where any refund is granted to an assessee on summary assessment [Sec. 143(1)] but it is found on completion of regular assessment that no refund is due to the assessee or the amount refunded exceeds the amount refundable on regular assessment, the assessee remains liable to pay interest on such amount of refund which was not actually due to him.

Interest is payable @ 0.5% per month or part thereof for the period from the date of grant of refund to the date on which such regular assessment is completed. Where an income escaping assessment [Sec. 147] or an assessment in search cases [Sec. 153A] is made for the first time, it is also treated as a regular assessment for this purpose [*Explanation* to Sec. 234D].

2. **Interest on Refunds payable by Government [Sec. 244A]**

Where any refund becomes due to the assessee out of any tax collected or deducted at source or paid by way of advance tax, such amount is required to be refunded to him without any delay, failing which the government is liable to pay interest on delayed refund. Such interest is payable on such excess amount @ 0.5% p.m. or part thereof from 1 April of the assessment year to the date on which refund is granted (that is, the date of issue of refund voucher). [Sec.244A(1)]

However, no interest is payable if the amount of refund is less than 10% of the amount of tax, found due to the assessee on summary assessment [Sec. 143(1)] or regular assessment [Sec. 143 or Sec 144]. **[Proviso to Sec. 244A(1)].**

Where refund of tax is due to the assessee on account of any other reason, say, excess payment of penalty or excess payment of self-assessment tax and so on, interest is payable on the amount of refund @ 0.5% p.m. or part thereof from the date on which such tax or penalty was paid in excess, to the date on which the refund is granted.

Additional interest on the amount of refund - In a case where a refund arises as a result of giving effect to an order under CIT (Appeals) (sec. 250), or Tribunal (sec. 254) or High Court (sec. 260) or Supreme Court (sec. 262) or Revision of orders prejudicial to revenue by CIT (sec. 263) or Revision of other orders by CIT (sec. 264) wholly or partly, the assessee shall be entitled to receive, in addition to the interest payable as mentioned above, additional interest on such amount of refund if there is a delay in giving effect order calculated **at the rate of 3 per cent per annum**, for the period beginning from the date following the date of expiry of the time allowed under sec.153(5) to the date on which the refund is granted. This does not cover an order of making a fresh assessment or reassessment. [sec. 244A(1A)]

However, where proceedings for assessment or reassessment are pending in respect of an assessee, in computing the period for determining the additional interest payable to such assessee under this sub-section, the period beginning from the date on which such refund is withheld by the Assessing Officer in accordance with and subject to provisions of sec.

245(2) and ending with the date on which such assessment or reassessment is made, shall be excluded.

Interest on refund of TDS: Where a refund of any amount becomes due to the deduct or in respect of any amount paid to the credit of the Central Government under Chapter XVII-B, such deduct or shall be entitled to receive, in addition to the said amount, simple interest thereon calculated at the rate of 0.5% per cent for every month or part of a month comprised in the period, from the date on which—

(*a*) claim for refund is made in the prescribed form, or

(*b*) tax is paid, where refund arises on account of giving effect to an order under section 250 or section 254 or section 260 or section 262,

to the date on which the refund is granted [sec. 244A(1B)]. However, where proceedings for assessment or reassessment are pending in respect of an assessee, in computing the period for determining the additional interest payable to such assessee under this sub-section, the period beginning from the date on which such refund is withheld by the Assessing Officer in accordance with and subject to provisions of sec. 254(2) and ending with the date on which such assessment or reassessment is made, shall be excluded.

No Interest is payable for the period of delay attributable to the assessee [Sec. 244A(2)] - Where the proceedings, resulting in the refund, are delayed for reasons attributable to the assessee, whether wholly or in part, such period is excluded from the period for which interest is payable. Where any question arises relating to the period to be excluded, it is decided by the Principal Chief Commissioner or Chief Commissioner or Principal Commissioner or Commissioner whose decision is final.

Sec. 244A not to apply to cases of search or requisitions - The said provisions do not apply to search cases - Sec. 132 is a self-contained code and it also provides for payment of interest. By virtue of Sec. 132(6), the assets seized in search operations have to be dealt with in accordance with Sec. 132B and Sec. 132B(4) provides for, in clear terms, payment of simple interest at the rate of .5% on the amount retained. Therefore, Sec. 244A has no application while dealing with the cases of seized assets under Sec. 132 [*Manohar Lal* v. *CIT* [2001] 118 Taxman 104(MP)].

Right to receive Refund, not dependant on Application for Refund – A reading of the plain language of Sec. 244A(1) and its two clauses make it clear that the right to receive interest on the amount of refund does not depend on the submission of an application by the assessee. Rather, it follows as a natural corollary to the assessee's right to receive a refund. Therefore, the mere fact that the application filed by the assessee was decided expeditiously, cannot be made a ground for declining its prayer for an award of interest [*National Horticultural Board* v. *Union of India* [2002] 125 Taxman 922/253 ITR 12 (Punj. & Har.)].

CHAPTER 29

Tax Implications on Business Re-organisation

INTRODUCTION

The globalisation and liberalisation of economies received further boost with the advancement of technology and the proliferation of the Internet resulted into increase in the cross border trade and stiff market competition. Company form of doing business unleashed vast potentials to capture newer markets, offer fresh line of products and services, improvise upon existing techniques and explore possibilities of collaborations and creating expertise. Various forms of business reorganisation facilitate stimulating growth, consolidating expertise and gaining a competitive advantage in doing business. The diagram below demonstrates various modes in which business reorganisation can be carried out.

FIGURE 29.1: FORMS OF BUSINESS RE-ORGANISATION

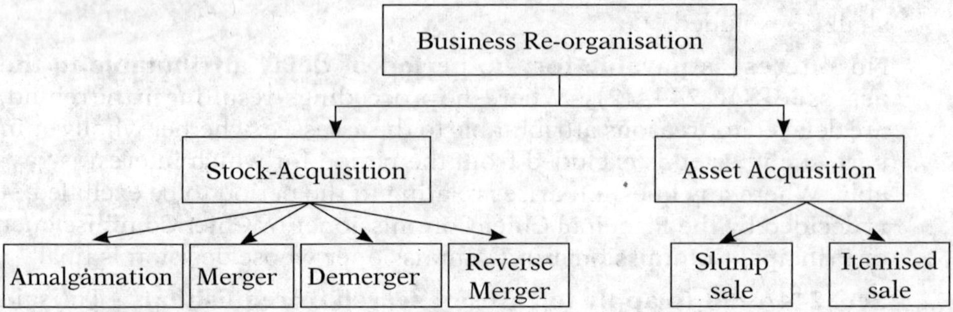

Since business reorgansiation impacts not only the immediate parties involved that is the companies in question but also stakeholders such as shareholders, consumers, competition in the markets, stock exchange, taxation; schemes of business-reorganisation are required to comply with several laws and regulations. This chapter will focus on the tax implications of business reorganisation strategies on the companies and its shareholders.

AMALGAMATION

In general business parlance, amalgamation is understood as the combining of two or more companies resulting in a new company by putting all the assets and liabilities of both the entities into one. Merger on the other hand is happens when two companies merge into each other and the survivor company continues to keep its name and accepts all the assets and liabilities of the other company which shuts down and no longer remains into existence. In that sense, amalgamation is different from mergers since unlike mergers none of the companies in a scheme of amalgamation continue to exist and a wholly new legal entity comes into being.

Amalgamation and mergers typically happen between the companies engaged in the same line of business or those that share some similarity in operations. It thus helps the companies involved to either gain a larger market share or acquire expertise in a particular production or servicing. Sometimes companies as a matter of expansion and diversification plans also prefer to go for amalgmations and mergers. However, the Income-tax Act does not distinguish between amalgamation and merger.

Definition of amalgamation - For the purposes of the Income-tax Act, Sec. 2(1B) defines amalgamation as the merger of one or more companies with another company or the merger of two or more companies to form one company. The company (or companies) which so merge is referred to as the **amalgamating company**. The company with which it merges or which is formed as a result of the merger is referred to as the **amalgamated company**.

Such amalgamation must fulfil the following conditions:

(*i*) all the property of the amalgamating company becomes the property of the amalgamated company;

(*ii*) all the liabilities of the amalgamating company become the liabilities of the amalgamated company by;

(*iii*) shareholders holding a minimum 75% of the shares in the amalgamating company (other than shares already held therein immediately before the amalgamation by, or by a nominee for, the amalgamated company or its subsidiary) become shareholders of the amalgamated company;

(*iv*) such merging is not the result of the acquisition of the property of one company by another company pursuant to the purchase of such property by the other company or as a result of the distribution of such property to the other company after the winding up of the first-mentioned company.

(1) Consequences for the shareholders of amalgamating company:

Exemption from capital gains for the shareholders of the amalgamating companies [Sec. 47(*ii*)] - When a shareholder transfers shares held by him in the amalgamated company pursuant to the scheme of amalgamation, such transfer of shares is not considered as a transfer at all and therefore no capital gains tax is payable. However, this exemption is subject to the fulfilment of the following conditions:

(*i*) consideration received for such transfer of shares is in the form of allotment of any share or shares in the amalgamated company except where the shareholder itself is the amalgamated company, and

(*ii*) the amalgamated company is an Indian company.

Cost of acquisition when shares received in amalgamation are subsequently transferred [Sec. 49(2)] - Where subsequently the shares allotted in the amalgamated company are transferred by such shareholder, it will attract capital gains tax. For the purposes of computation of capital gains tax therefore, the cost of acquisition will be taken as the cost of acquisition of the shares in the amalgamating company.

For example, say X Co. merges with Y Co. in a scheme of amalgamation. Thus X Co. is the amalgamating company and Y Co. is the amalgamated company. When 'A' being a shareholder of X Co. transfer his 100 shares (which he had purchased at ₹ 100 each) to Y Co. under this scheme of amalgamation and receive 150 shares of Y Co. this was not a transfer under sec. 47(*ii*) and no capital gains are chargeable in the hands of 'A'. However, subsequently, when 'A' transfers these 150 shares of Y Co. it will attract capital gains tax and the cost of acquisition for the purposes of computation will be taken as the cost of acquisition for shares of X Co. *i.e.* ₹ 100 for each share.

(2) Consequences for amalgamating company:

Exemption from capital gains in the hands of the amalgamating companies [Sec. 47(*vi*)] - When an amalgamating company transfers shares held by it to the amalgamated company pursuant to the scheme of amalgamation, such transfer of shares is not considered as a transfer at all and therefore no capital gains tax is payable. However, the amalgamated company must be an Indian company.

Exemption from capital gains in case of international restructuring with respect to Indian company [Sec. 47*via*)] - When both the parties in the scheme of amalgamation are foreign companies and there is a transfer of shares held in an Indian company, such transfer is not considered as a transfer at all, and therefore no capital gains tax is payable. However, such exemption is subject to fulfilment of the following conditions:

(*a*) Minimum 25% of the shareholders of the amalgamating foreign company must continue to remain shareholders of the amalgamated foreign company, and

(*b*) such transfer does not attract tax on capital gains in the country, in which the amalgamating company is incorporated.

Exemption from capital gains in case of international restructuring with respect to foreign company having underlying assets in Indian company [Sec. 47(*viab*)] - When both the parties in the scheme of amalgamation are foreign companies and there is a transfer of shares held in a foreign company which is directly or indirectly deriving its value substantially from the shares of an Indian company, such transfer is not considered as a transfer at all and therefore no capital gains tax is payable. However, such exemption is subject to fulfilment of the following conditions:

(*a*) Minimum 25% of the shareholders of the amalgamating foreign company must continue to remain shareholders of the amalgamated foreign company, and (*b*) such transfer does not attract tax on capital gains in the country, in which the amalgamating company is incorporated.

Meaning of deriving its value substantially from the assets located in India [*Explanation 6 to Sec. 9(1)(*i*)*]

(*i*) Such assets located in India may be tangible or intangible in nature;

(*ii*) The value of such assets exceeds ₹ 10 crore;

(*iii*) The value represents at least 50% of the value of all the assets owned by the company or entity.

Exemption from capital gains in case of a scheme of amalgamation of a banking company with a banking institution sanctioned and brought into force by the Central Government [Sec. 47(*viaa*)] - When banking company transfers a capital asset to the banking institution under a scheme of amalgamation which is sanctioned and brought into force by the Central Government under Sec. 45(7) of the Banking Regulation Act, 1949; it is not considered as a transfer and therefore no capital gains tax is payable.

Banking company shall have the meaning assigned to it in Sec. 5(*c*) of the Banking Regulation Act, 1949.

Banking institution shall have the same meaning assigned to it in Sec. 45(15) of the Banking Regulation Act, 1949.

(3) Consequences for amalgamated company:

- **Expenditures and Deductions -** Upon amalgamation, the following expenditures and deductions that would have been claimed by the amalgamating company shall be available to the amalgamated company instead:

  (*i*) Expenditure on scientific research [Sec. 35(5)] - Where any capital asset on scientific research is transferred in a scheme of amalgamation, the deduction for expenditure on such capital asset will be allowed to the amalgamated company (being an Indian company) and not to the amalgamating company. Therefore, the provisions for claiming deductions from profits on scientific research expenditure shall apply to the amalgamated company as they would have applied to the amalgamating company if the latter had not so sold or otherwise transferred the asset.

  (*ii*) Expenditure on know-how [Sec. 35AB(3)] - Where there is a transfer of an undertaking under a scheme of amalgamation and the amalgamating company was entitled to a deduction for expenditure on know-how, then it is the amalgamated company that is entitled to claim the deduction in respect of such undertaking to the same extent and in respect of the residual period as it would have been allowable to the amalgamating company.

(*iii*) **Expenditure for obtaining licence to operate telecommunication services [Sec. 35ABB] -** Where, in a scheme of amalgamation, the amalgamating company sells or otherwise transfers the licence to the amalgamated company (being an Indian company); deduction for expenditure incurred for obtaining the licence shall be available to the amalgamated company and not to the amalgamating company. Therefore, the provisions for claiming deductions from profits on this expenditure shall apply to the amalgamated company as they would have applied to the amalgamating company if the latter had not so sold or otherwise transferred the licence.

(*iv*) **Amortisation of certain preliminary expenses [Sec. 35D(5)] -** Where the undertaking of an Indian company which is entitled to the deduction with respect to amortization of certain preliminary expenses is transferred before the expiry of the period of 10 years to another Indian company in a scheme of amalgamation, such deduction shall be available to the amalgamated company and not to the amalgamating company. Provisions under this section shall apply to the amalgamated company as they would have applied to the amalgamating company as if the amalgamation had not taken place.

(*v*) **Amortisation of expenditure incurred under voluntary retirement scheme [Sec. 35DDA(5)] -** Where the assessee, being an Indian company, is entitled to the deduction under Sec.35DDA for amortization of expenditure incurred under a voluntary retirement scheme, and such undertaking is transferred before the expiry of the period of 10 years to another Indian company in a scheme of amalgamation, such deduction shall be available to the amalgamated company and not to the amalgamating company. Provisions under this section shall apply to the amalgamated company as they would have applied to the amalgamating company as if the amalgamation had not taken place.

(*vi*) **Deduction for expenditure on prospecting, etc., for certain minerals [Sec. 35E(7)] -** Where the undertaking of an Indian company which is entitled to the deduction under Sec.35E for expenditure on prospecting etc., for certain minerals is transferred before the expiry of the period of 10 years to another Indian company in a scheme of amalgamation, such deduction shall be available to the amalgamated company and not to the amalgamating company. Provisions under this section shall apply to the amalgamated company as they would have applied to the amalgamating company as if the amalgamation had not taken place.

(*vii*) **Deductions in respect of profits and gains from industrial undertakings or enterprises engaged in infrastructure development, etc. [Sec. 80-IA(12)] -** Where any undertaking of an Indian company which is entitled to the deduction under Sec.

80-IA is transferred before the expiry of the period specified to another Indian company in a scheme of amalgamation, such deduction shall be available to the amalgamated company and not to the amalgamating company. Provisions under this section shall apply to the amalgamated company as they would have applied to the amalgamating company as if the amalgamation had not taken place.

(*viii*) **Deduction in respect of profits and gains from certain industrial undertakings other than infrastructure development undertakings [Sec. 80-IB(12)]** - Where any undertaking of an Indian company which is entitled to the deduction under Sec.80-IB is transferred before the expiry of the period specified to another Indian company in a scheme of amalgamation, such deduction shall be available to the amalgamated company and not to the amalgamating company. Provisions under this section shall apply to the amalgamated company as they would have applied to the amalgamating company as if the amalgamation had not taken place.

◆ **Deemed Profits of amalgamating company chargeable for the amalgamated company [Sec. 41(1)]** - Where the amalgamating company had availed an allowance or deduction in respect of loss, expenditure or trading liability incurred by it and subsequently the amalgamated company obtains any by way of remission or cessation of such loss or expenditure, such amount will be deemed to be profits of the amalgamated company.

◆ **Transfer of capital assets**

(*i*) **When capital asset (other than block of asset is transferred) [*Explanation* 7 to Sec. 43(1)]** - Where any capital asset is transferred by the amalgamating company to the amalgamated company, in a scheme of amalgamation and the amalgamated company is an Indian company, the actual cost of the transferred capital asset to the amalgamated company shall be taken to be the same as it would have been if the amalgamating company had continued to hold the capital asset for the purposes of its own business.

(*ii*) **When block of asset is transferred [*Explanation* 2 to Sec. 43(6)]** - Where any block of assets is transferred by the amalgamating company to the amalgamated company in a scheme of amalgamation, and the amalgamated company is an Indian company, then the actual cost of the block of assets for the amalgamated company shall be the written down value of the block of assets for the amalgamating company would be the actual cost of the assets to the assessee less depreciation actually allowed to the company. The words 'actually allowed' mean as 'limited to depreciation actually taken into account or granted and given effect to, *i.e.,* debited by the Assessing Officer against the incomings of the business in computing the taxable income of the assessee *Madeva Upendra Sinai* v. *Union of India* [1975] 98 ITR 209 (SC) followed in *CIT* v. *Doom Dooma India Ltd*. [2009] 178 Taxman 261/310 ITR 392 (SC). Therefore, any unabsorbed depreciation of the amalgamating company should not be deducted in computing the written down value of the assets in the hands of the amalgamated company *CIT* v. *Silical Metallurgic Ltd* [2010] 324 ITR 29 (Mad).

(*iii*) **When capital assets are transferred as stock-in-trade [Sec. 43C(1)] -** Where an asset not being an asset referred to in the provisions of the Income-tax Act 1961 which becomes the property of an amalgamated company under a scheme of amalgamation, is sold after the 29th day of February, 1988, by the amalgamated company as stock-in-trade of the business carried on by it, the cost of acquisition of the said asset to the amalgamated company in computing the profits and gains from the sale of such asset shall be the cost of acquisition of the said asset to the amalgamating company, as increased by the cost, if any, of any improvement made thereto, and the expenditure, if any, incurred, wholly and exclusively in connection with such transfer by the amalgamating company.

◆ **Carry forward and set off of accumulated loss and unabsorbed depreciation allowance in amalgamation [Sec. 72A]**

This Section creates a legal fiction whereby the accumulated loss and the unabsorbed depreciation of the amalgamating company is deemed to be the loss, or as the case may be, allowance for unabsorbed depreciation of the amalgamated Company for the previous year in which the amalgamation was affected. The benefit under this section cannot be denied ostensibly merely because the revenue department would suffer loss as a result of amalgamation of two loss-making companies [*CIT* v. *Sadashiva Sugars Ltd*. [2017] 80 taxmann.com 352 (Karnataka)]. Accordingly, in respect of the following amalgamations, the accumulated loss and the unabsorbed depreciation of the amalgamating company can be availed by the amalgamated company:

(*a*) a company owning an industrial undertaking or a ship or a hotel with another company; or

(*b*) a banking company referred to in the Banking Regulation Act, 1949 with a specified bank; or

(*c*) one or more public sector company or companies engaged in the business of operation of aircraft with one or more public sector company or companies engaged in similar business,

(*d*) an erstwhile public sector company with one or more company or companies, if the share purchase agreement entered into under strategic disinvestment restricted immediate amalgamation of the said public sector company and the amalgamation is carried out within five year from the end of the previous year in which the restriction on amalgamation in the share purchase agreement ends:

Provided that the accumulated loss and the unabsorbed depreciation of the amalgamating company, in case of an amalgamation referred to in (*d*) above, which is deemed to be the loss or, as the case may be, the allowance for unabsorbed depreciation of the amalgamated company, shall not be more than the accumulated loss and unabsorbed depreciation of the public sector company as on the date on which the public sector company ceases to be a public sector company as a result of strategic disinvestment. According to *Explanation (*iii*)* to clause (*d*) strategic disinvestment means the sale of share holding by the Central Government or any State Government or a Public sector company in a public sector company which results in the reduction of its share holding to below 51% along with transfer of control to the buyer. This condition of below 51% will apply only where the holding was above 51% before sale.

***Conditions to be fufilled* -** Such a set off or carry forward shall be allowed to the amalgamated company only when:

(*a*) the amalgamating company:

(*i*) has been engaged in the business, in which the accumulated loss occurred or depreciation remains unabsorbed, for three or more years;

(*ii*) has held continuously as on the date of the amalgamation at least three–fourths of the book value of fixed assets held by it two years prior to the date of amalgamation;

(*b*) the amalgamated company:

(*i*) holds continuously for a minimum period of five years from the date of amalgamation at least three–fourths of the book value of fixed assets of the amalgamating company acquired in a scheme of amalgamation;

(*ii*) continues the business of the amalgamating company for a minimum period of five years from the date of amalgamation;

(*iii*) fulfils such other conditions as may be prescribed to ensure the revival of the business of the amalgamating company or to ensure that the amalgamation is for genuine business purposes.

The underlying objective of allowing carry forward and set off to the amalgamated company is to ensure that an industry which has otherwise become unviable in the hands of the amalgamating company is not closed down and is somehow revived by framing a scheme of amalgamation. The idea is that the amalgamated company will continue the business in the public interest and in the interests of employment of the workers involved. It is in aid of or in furtherance of the achievement of that object that a fiction is created whereby the amalgamated company which in fact had not made the losses is allowed to carry forward the loss incurred by the amalgamating company. This concession is not available when the amalgamation is followed by a closing down of the business, sending out most of the workmen and the amalgamated company or as in this case, a subsidiary of the amalgamated company starts a new business or industry of its own altogether with practically a new workforce. *Indian Metals & Ferro Alloys Ltd.* v. *Union of India* [2003] 133 Taxman 817/262 ITR 553 (Ori).

In a case where any of the conditions laid down above are not complied with, the set off of loss or allowance of depreciation made in any previous year in the hands of the amalgamated company shall be deemed to be the income of the amalgamated company chargeable to tax for the year in which such conditions are not complied with [Sec.72A(3)].

Meaning of certain terms

(*a*) *accumulated loss*, means so much of the loss of the amalgamating company under the head, 'Profits and gains of business or profession' (not being a loss sustained in a speculation business) which such amalgamating company, would have been entitled to carry forward and set off under the provisions dealing with the carry forward and set off of business losses under the Income-tax Act, 1961 if the amalgamation had not taken place.

(*b*) *industrial undertaking*, means any undertaking which is engaged in:

- (*i*) the manufacture or processing of goods; or
- (*ii*) the manufacture of computer software; or
- (*iii*) the business of generation or distribution of electricity or any other form of power; or
- (*iv*) the business of providing telecommunication services, whether basic or cellular, including radio paging, domestic satellite service, network of trunking, broadband network and internet services; or
- (*v*) mining; or
- (*vi*) the construction of ships, aircrafts or rail systems.

(*c*) *unabsorbed depreciation*, means so much of the allowance for depreciation of the amalgamating company which remains to be allowed and which would have been allowed to the amalgamating company under the provisions of the Income–tax Act, 1961, if the amalgamation had not taken place.

- **Carry forward and set-off of accumulated loss and unabsorbed depreciation allowance in scheme of amalgamation of banking company in certain cases [Sec. 72AA]** - Where there has been an amalgamation of a banking company with any other banking institution under a scheme sanctioned and brought into force by the Central Government under the Banking Regulation Act, 1949, the accumulated loss and the unabsorbed depreciation of such banking company shall be deemed to be the loss or, as the case may be, allowance for depreciation of such banking institution and other provisions of the Income-tax Act, 1961 relating to set-off and carry forward of loss and allowance for depreciation shall apply accordingly.

DEMERGERS

A demerger is generally defined as the transfer of a company's business undertakings to another company, which can either be a newly incorporated company which may be the subsidiary company of the transferor company or an external party altogether. The company whose undertakings are being so transferred is called the demerged company and the other company is known as the resulting company. There are different types of demergers. A demerger when a particular division or a line of business of a company is divested to become a separate company is called a spin-off. Both the companies exist as separate legal entities and the demerged company. Another form of demerger called a split is when a company decides to split its businesses into separate companies and thereby creates new companies and the demerged company is dissolved. In certain other instances, the company may sell off its business line to an external party which is called equity carved out. It must be noted that spin-off and split do not involve a sale to an external party.

For the purposes of Income-tax Act, demerger provisions are as discussed below.

Definition of Demerger Under Sec.2(*19AA*) demerger, in relation to companies, means the transfer of one or more undertakings of a demerged company to any resulting company pursuant to a scheme of arrangement under Secs. 391 to 394 of the Companies Act, 1956 (now Secs. 230 to 232 of the Companies Act, 2013). **Demerged company** means the company whose undertaking is transferred, pursuant to a demerger, to a resulting company [Sec. 2(*19AAA*)]. **Resulting company** means one or more companies (including a wholly owned subsidiary thereof) to which the undertaking of the demerged company is transferred in a demerger and, the resulting company in consideration of such transfer of undertaking, issues shares to the shareholders of the demerged company and includes any authority or body or local authority or public sector company or a company established, constituted or formed as a result of demerger [Sec. 2(*41A*)].

Such demerger must fulfil the following conditions:

(*i*) all the property of the undertaking being transferred by the demerged company becomes the property of the resulting company;

(*ii*) all the liabilities relatable to the undertaking being transferred by the demerged company becomes liabilities of the resulting company;

(*iii*) the property and the liabilities of the undertaking or undertakings being transferred by the demerged company are transferred at values appearing in its books of account immediately before the demerger;

(*iv*) in consideration of the demerger, the resulting company issues its shares to the shareholders of the demerged company on a proportionate basis except where the resulting company itself is a shareholder of the demerged company;

(*v*) shareholders holding minimum 75% of the shares in the demerged company (other than shares already held therein immediately before the amalgamation by, or by a nominee for, the resulting company or its subsidiary) become shareholders of the resulting company;

(*vi*) such demerging is not the result of the acquisition of the property or assets of the demerged company or any undertaking thereof by the resulting company;

(*vii*) the transfer of the undertaking is on a going concern basis;

(*viii*) the demerger is in accordance with the conditions, if any, notified under Sec.72A(5) by the Central Government in this behalf.

The definition of 'demerger' would be satisfied if the undertaking demerged is hived off as a going concern, that means, if it constitutes a business activity capable of being run independently for a foreseeable future. To ensure that it is a going concern, while sanctioning a Scheme, it can certainly be examined whether essential and integral assets like plant, machinery manpower without which it would not be able to run as an independent unit have been transferred to the demerged company. However, there is no requirement under the provisions of the Income-tax Act, 1961 or the Companies Act, 2013, for the transfer of all common assets and/or liabilities relatable to the Undertaking being demerged. Therefore, while framing a scheme of demerger, the existing and the resulting companies after ensuring that both of them are a going concern, are free to negotiate which common asset/liability would be transferred to which undertaking *Indo Rama Textile Ltd.*, In re [2012] 23 taxmann.com 390/[2013] 212 Taxman 462 (Del.).

Meaning of certain expressions

Undertaking shall include any part of an undertaking, or a unit or division of an undertaking or a business activity taken as a whole, but does not include individual assets or liabilities or any combination thereof not constituting a business activity [*Explanation 1* to Sec. 2(*19AA*)].

Liabilities shall include:

(*a*) the liabilities which arise out of the activities or operations of the undertaking;

(*b*) the specific loans or borrowings (including debentures) raised, incurred and utilised solely for the activities or operations of the undertaking; and

(*c*) so much of the amounts of general or multipurpose borrowings, if any, of the demerged company as stand in the same proportion which the value of the assets transferred in a demerger bears to the total value of the assets of such demerged company immediately before the demerger [*Explanation 2* to Sec.2(*19AA*)

In order to avail the tax neutrality and carry forward benefits upon demerger, the scheme of demerger requires to meet the stringent conditions mentioned aforesaid. In order to facilitate disinvestment of public sector companies, the

Finance Act, 2021 has inserted *Explanation 6* to Sec. 2(*19AA*) defining a demerger. Accordingly, the reconstruction or splitting up of a public sector company into separate companies shall be deemed to be a demerger, if:

(*a*) such reconstruction or splitting up has been made to transfer any asset of the demerged company to the resulting company and the resulting company;

(*b*) is a public sector company on the appointed day indicated in such scheme, as may be approved by the Central Government or any other body authorised under the provisions of the Companies Act, 2013 or any other law for the time being in force governing such public sector companies in this behalf;

(*c*) fulfils such other conditions as may be notified by the Central Government in the Official Gazette in this behalf;

Deemed demergers

The splitting up or the reconstruction of any authority or a body constituted or established under a Central, State or Provincial Act, or a local authority or a public sector company, into separate authorities or bodies or local authorities or companies, as the case may be, shall be deemed to be a demerger if such split up or reconstruction fulfils such conditions as may be notified in the Official Gazette, by the Central Government [*Explanation 4* to Sec. 2(*19AA*)].

Further, the reconstruction or splitting up of a company, which ceased to be a public sector company as a result of the transfer of its shares by the Central Government, into separate companies, shall be deemed to be a demerger, if such reconstruction or splitting up has been made to give effect to any condition attached to the said transfer of shares and also fulfils such other conditions as may be notified by the Central Government in the Official Gazette [*Explanation 5* to Sec. 2(*19AA*)].

(1) Consequences for the shareholders of demerged company

When shareholders of a demerged company are issued shares of the resulting company owing to the demerger, there are no tax consequences on the receipt of such shares of the resulting company. However, when such shares are subsequently sold by the shareholder, capital gains tax will be attracted. For the computation of capital gains, the cost of acquisition of the shares in the resulting company shall be the amount which bears to the cost of acquisition of shares held by the assessee in the demerged company the same proportion as the net book value of the assets transferred in a demerger bears to the net worth of the demerged company immediately before such demerger [Sec. 49(2C)].

For the purposes of this provision, "net worth" shall mean the aggregate of the paid up share capital and general reserves as appearing in the books of account of the demerged company immediately before the demerger [*Explanation* to Sec. 49(2C)]. The cost of acquisition of the original shares held by the shareholder in the demerged company shall be deemed to have been reduced by the amount as so arrived at under the Income-tax Act, 1961.

(2) Consequences for the demerged company

Exemption from capital gains in the hands of demerged company [Sec. 47(*vib*)] - When a demerged company transfers a capital asset to the resulting company in a scheme of demerger, it is not considered a transfer at all and therefore no capital gains tax gets attracted in the hands of the demerged company.

Exemption from capital gains in case of international restructuring with respect to shares in Indian company [Sec. 47(*vic*)] - When both parties in a demerger are foreign companies and there is a transfer of shares held in an Indian company by the demerged foreign company to the resulting foreign company, such transfer is not considered as a transfer at all and therefore no capital gains tax is payable. However, such exemption is subject to the fulfilment of the following conditions :

(*a*) Minimum 25% of the shareholders of the demerged foreign company continue to remain shareholders of the resulting foreign company; and

(*b*) such transfer does not attract tax on capital gains in the country, in which the demerged foreign company is incorporated

However, the provisions of Sec. 391 to 394 of the Companies Act, 1956 (now Secs. 230 to 232 of the Companies Act, 2013) shall not apply in case of demergers referred to in this Section [Proviso to Sec. 47(*vic*)].

Exemption from capital gains in case of international restructuring with respect to foreign company with underlying assets in Indian company [Sec. 47(*vicc*)] - When both the parties in a demerger are foreign companies and there is a transfer of shares held in a foreign company which is directly or indirectly deriving its value substantially from the shares of an Indian company, such transfer is not considered as a transfer at all and therefore no capital gains tax is payable. However, such exemption is subject to fulfilment of the following conditions:

(*a*) Minimum 25% of the shareholders of the demerged foreign company must continue to remain shareholders of the resulting foreign company; and

(*b*) such transfer does not attract tax on capital gains in the country, in which the demerged company is incorporated.

However, the provisions of Secs. 391 to 394 of the Companies Act, 1956 (now Sec. 230 to Sec. 232 of the Companies Act, 2013) shall not apply in case of demergers referred to in this section [Proviso to Sec. 47(*vicc*)].

(3) Consequences for the resulting company

Exemption from capital gains in the hands of shareholders of demerged company [Sec. 47(*vid*)] - Any transfer or issue of shares by the resulting company to the shareholders of the demerged company in a scheme of demerger where the transfer or issue is made in consideration of demerger of the undertaking, is not considered as transfer and therefore no capital gains tax is attracted.

- **Expenditures and Deductions -** Upon demerger, the following expenditures and deductions that would have been claimed by the demerged company shall be available to the resulting company instead.

  (*i*) Expenditure on know-how [Sec. 35AB(3)] - Where there is a transfer of an undertaking under a demerger and the demerged company was entitled to a deduction for expenditure on know-how, then it is the resulting company which is entitled to claim deduction in respect of such undertaking to the same extent and in respect of the residual period as it would have been allowable to the demerged company.

  (*ii*) Expenditure for obtaining licence to operate telecommunication services [Sec. 35ABB] - Where, in a demerger, the demerged company sells or otherwise transfers the licence to the resulting company (being an Indian company); deduction for expenditure incurred for obtaining the licence shall be available to the resulting company and not to the demerged company. Therefore, the provisions for claiming deductions from profits on this expenditure shall apply to the resulting company as they would have applied to the demerged company if the latter had not so sold or otherwise transferred the licence.

  (*iii*) Amortisation of certain preliminary expenses [Sec. 35D(5)] - Where the undertaking of an Indian company which is entitled to the deduction with respect to amortization of certain preliminary expenses is transferred before the expiry of the period of 10 years to another Indian company in a demerger, such deduction shall be available to the resulting company and not to the demerged company. Provisions under this section shall apply to the resulting company as they would have applied to the demerged company as if the demerger had not taken place.

  (*iv*) Amortisation of expenditure incurred under voluntary retirement scheme [Sec. 35DDA(5)] - Where the assessee, being an Indian company, is entitled to the deduction under Sec.35DDA for amortization of expenditure incurred under voluntary retirement scheme and such undertaking is transferred before the expiry of the period of 10 years to another Indian company in a demerger, such deduction shall be available to the resulting company and not to the demerged company. Provisions under this section shall apply to the resulting company as they would have applied to the demerged company as if the demerger had not taken place.

  (*v*) Deduction for expenditure on prospecting, etc., for certain minerals [Sec. 35E(7)] - Where the undertaking of an Indian company which is entitled to the deduction under Sec.35E for expenditure on prospecting etc., for certain minerals is transferred before the expiry of the period of 10 years to another Indian company in a demerger, such deduction shall be available to the resulting company and not to the demerged company. Provisions under this section shall apply to the resulting company as they would have applied to the demerged company as if the demerger had not taken place.

(*vi*) **Deductions in respect of profits and gains from industrial undertakings or enterprises engaged in infrastructure development, etc. [Sec. 80-IA(12)] -** Where any undertaking of an Indian company which is entitled to the deduction under Sec. 80-IA is transferred before the expiry of the period specified to another Indian company in a demerger, such deduction shall be available to the resulting company and not to the demerged company. Provisions under this section shall apply to the resulting company as they would have applied to the demerged company as if the demerger had not taken place.

(*vii*) **Deduction in respect of profits and gains from certain industrial undertakings other than infrastructure development undertakings [Sec. 80-IB(12)] -** Where any undertaking of an Indian company which is entitled to the deduction under Sec.80-IB is transferred before the expiry of the period specified to another Indian company in a demerger, such deduction shall be available to the resulting company and not to the demerged company. Provisions under this section shall apply to the resulting company as they would have applied to the demerged company as if the demerger had not taken place.

- **Deemed Profits of demerged company chargeable for the resulting company [Sec. 41(1)] -** Where the demerged company had availed an allowance or deduction in respect of loss, expenditure or trading liability incurred by it and subsequently the resulting company obtains any by way of remission or cessation of such loss or expenditure, such amount will be deemed to be profits of the resulting company.

- **Transfer of capital assets**

(*i*) **When capital asset (other than block of asset is transferred) [*Explanation* 7A to Sec. 43(1)] -** Where any capital asset is transferred by the demerged company to the resulting company, in a demerger and the resulting company is an Indian company, the actual cost of the transferred capital asset to the resulting company shall be taken to be the same as it would have been if the demerged company had continued to hold the capital asset for the purposes of its own business.

(*ii*) **When block of asset is transferred [*Explanations 2A* and *2B* to Sec. 43(6)]** - Where any block of assets is transferred by the demerged company to the resulting company in a demerger, and the resulting company is an Indian company,

the written down value of the block of assets of the demerged company shall be reduced by the written down value of the assets transferred to the resulting company pursuant to the demerger.

the written down value of the block of assets in the case of the resulting company shall be the written down value of the transferred assets of the demerged company immediately before the demerger.

Carry forward and set off of accumulated loss and unabsorbed depreciation allowance in demerger [Sec. 72A] - In the case of a demerger, the accumulated loss and the allowance for unabsorbed depreciation of the demerged company shall be allowed to be carried forward and set off in the hands of the resulting company where such loss or unabsorbed depreciation is directly relatable to the undertakings transferred to the resulting company [Sec. 72A(4)].

Where such loss or unabsorbed depreciation is not directly relatable to the undertakings transferred to the resulting company, be apportioned between the demerged company and the resulting company in the same proportion in which the assets of the undertakings have been retained by the demerged company and transferred to the resulting company, and be allowed to be carried forward and set off in the hands of the demerged company or the resulting company, as the case may be [Sec. 72A(5)].

The Central Government may, for the purposes of this section, by notification in the official gazette, specify such conditions as it considers necessary to ensure that the demerger is for genuine business purposes.

Meaning of certain terms

(*a*) *accumulated loss*, means so much of the loss of the demerged company under the head, 'Profits and gains of business or profession' (not being a loss sustained in a speculation business) which such demerged company, would have been entitled to carry forward and set off under the provisions dealing with the carry forward and set off of business losses under the Income-tax Act, 1961 if the demerger had not taken place.

(*b*) *industrial undertaking*, means any undertaking which is engaged in:

- (*i*) the manufacture or processing of goods; or
- (*ii*) the manufacture of computer software; or
- (*iii*) the business of generation or distribution of electricity or any other form of power; or
- (*iv*) the business of providing telecommunication services, whether basic or cellular, including radio paging, domestic satellite service, network of trunking, broadband network and internet services; or

(*v*) mining; or

(*vi*) the construction of ships, aircrafts or rail systems.

(*d*) *unabsorbed depreciation*, means so much of the allowance for depreciation of the demerged company which remains to be allowed and which would have been allowed to the demerged company under the provisions of the Income–tax Act, 1961, if the demerger had not taken place.

SLUMP SALE

Sec. 2(*42C*) of the Income-tax Act defines slump sale as the transfer of one or more undertakings as a result of the sale for a lump sum consideration without values being assigned to the individual assets and liabilities in such transfer.

Since 'slump sales' involved a transfer of an undertaking, it was not possible to compute cost of acquisition of such an undertaking and consequently, slump sales were not taxable under the capital gains head. In order to plug this gap and tax slump sales Sec. 50B was inserted in the Income-tax Act, 1961 *vide* the Finance Act, 1999 with effect from 1-4-2000.Whenever there were any profits made on account of a slum sale by an assessee, it was subjected to Sec. 50B is a special provision for the computation of capital gains in case of slump sale. Depending upon the period of holding it could be a long-term or a short-term capital gain. Where slump sale involves the transfer of a capital asset being one or more undertakings owned and held by an assessee for less than 36 months immediately preceding the date of its transfer, it is considered as short-term capital gain.

For the purposes of the computation of the capital gains, the net worth of the undertaking or the division transferred is deemed to be the cost of acquisition and the cost of improvement [Sec.50B(2)].

Capital Gains = Sale Consideration- Net Worth

Net worth = Value of total assets of the undertaking or division - Value of liabilities of such undertaking or division as appearing in its books of account [*Explanation 1* to Sec. 50B]

Whether slump exchange amounts to Slump sale

Since the statute uses the term slump 'sale' there existed a controversy whether it should be strictly construed so as to cover only those transactions that meet the classical requirement of sale, that is when transfer is accompanied by monetary, and only monetary consideration; or could slump sale provision also apply when consideration was received in the form of shares and thereby being an exchange. The courts were divided in their opinion on this issue. The Bombay High Court in *CIT* v. *Bharat Bijlee Ltd*. [2014] 46 taxmann.com 257/224 Taxman282/365 ITR 258 (Bom.) restricted the meaning of slump sale as only transfers that were purely sale in return of monetary consideration, so that when preference shares or bonds were received as consideration, it was an exchange and hence no longer a sale. The Delhi High Court in *SREI Infrastructure Finance Ltd*. v. *Income-tax Settlement Commission* [2012] 20 taxmann.com

476/207 Taxman 74/251 CTR 129 (Del.) took a view that the expression 'sale' in the term 'slump sale' should not be given a restrictive meaning so as to apply it only to 'sales' in a narrow sense and not to 'transfers' under section 2(*47*) that included exchange.

The Finance Bill, 2021 has put this controversy to rest. Slump sale has been defined as the transfer of one or more undertakings by any means for a lump sum consideration without values being assigned to the individual assets and liabilities in such sales [Sec. 2(*42C*)]. Thus, the broad view taken by the Delhi High Court has been endorsed by the legislature.

Taxation in case of succession to business in the event of business reorganization or restructuring [Sec.170]

Chapter XV of the Income-tax Act provides liability for tax in certain special cases, one of which is the case of business reorganization or restructuring. The following portions details out tax liability in such instances.

Predecessor and Successor to be assessed on Pre-succession and Post-succession Profits respectively [Sec. 170(1)]

Where a person carrying on any business or profession has been succeeded therein by any other person in any year, there are two assessments for that year; one on the predecessor in respect of the income of the previous year from the commencement of the year up to the date of succession and a second on the successor in respect of the income of the previous year from the date of succession to the end of the previous year. Thus, the predecessor is to be assessed on pre-succession profits and the successor is to be assessed on the post-succession profits. The incomes of the predecessor and the successor must be computed separately, and each must be granted the deductions and allowances appropriate to his case. The assessment of each must be separate and distinct.

Succession implies that there is an end of an entity carrying on the business and its place has been taken by an entirely new entity to run, in continuity and as a going concern, the same business. The tests of change of ownership, integrity, identity and continuity of a business have to be satisfied before it can be said that a person "succeeded to the business of another". Succession implies the devolution of the business as a whole. But, it is not essential in every case that the successor firm should have mathematically the same extent of the business as the predecessor firm nor does it mean that the successor firm should have taken over all the assets and liabilities of the predecessor firm. It is sufficient if there is substantial identity and similarity in the nature and extent of the activities carried on between the two firms and the major portion of the liabilities and assets of old partnership have been taken over by the new firm [*Kansiram Ganpatrai* v. *CIT* (1953) 23 ITR 314 (Pat.)].

Assessment to be made on the Successor where Predecessor cannot be found [Sec. 170(2)]

If the predecessor cannot be found, the assessment is to be made on the successor in respect of the income of the year in which succession took place up to the date of succession and of the year preceding that year. For this purpose "income" includes any capital gain accruing from the transfer of the business or profession as a result of the succession [*Explanation* to Sec. 170]. Thus, the successor is assessable only in respect of the income of the predecessor from the business in which succession has taken place and any gain accruing from the transfer of the business.

An assessment of the successor in respect of the income of the predecessor can be made only when the predecessor "cannot be found". An assessment cannot be made on the successor when the predecessor is alive and his whereabouts are known or can be ascertained [*Pt. Deo Sharma* v. *ITO* (1972) 84 ITR 633 All.]. It would be incorrect to say that a firm which has been dissolved "cannot be found" when its partners are alive and their whereabouts are known. But a company has ceased to exist and is struck off the register of companies is one which "cannot be found". [*CIT* v. *Express Newspapers Ltd*. (1960) 40 ITR 38 (Mad.), affirmed *CIT* v. *Express Newspapers Ltd.* (1964) 53 ITR 250 (SC)].

An assessment of the successor is to be made in like manner and to the same extent as it would have been made on the predecessor. The phrase "in like manner and to the same extent" connotes that the deductions and allowances in computing the business income are to be allowed with reference to the predecessor's status, and likewise, the tax is to be calculated according to the status of the predecessor.

Recovery of Tax, assessed on the Predecessor, from the Successor where Predecessor cannot be found [Sec. 170(3)]

If the tax assessed on the predecessor in respect of the income of the previous year in which succession took place up to the date of succession or of the year preceding that year cannot be recovered from him, recovery of such tax can be made from the successor. Before the recovery of such tax from the successor, the Assessing Officer has to record a finding that the tax assessed on the predecessor cannot be recovered from him. The successor is entitled to recover the tax, assessed on the predecessor, paid by him, from the predecessor. Tax for this purpose includes any penalty, fine or interest payable by the predecessor.

Modification of returns by the successor [Sec. 170A] (inserted by the Finance Act, 2022 w.e.f. 1.4.2022)

It was experienced that the process of business reorganisation or restructuring proved to be a long-drawn process. So that there was an indefinite timeline between the entity initiating the process of reorgansiation by filling an application with the adjudicating authority or any High Court and the issue of the orders by such authority concluding the same and the order taking effect.

During the pendency of the court proceedings the income tax proceedings and assessments are carried on and often completed on the predecessor entities only the difficulty arose when Courts have held such proceedings and consequent assessments illegal as the predecessor assessee ceases to exist in the midst of a perfectly valid and legal proceeding. The Supreme Court in *Pr. CIT* v. *Maruti*

Suzuki India Ltd. [2019] 107 taxmann.com 375/265 Taxman 515/416 ITR 613 (SC) held when assessee company was amalgamated with another company and had therefore lost its existence, the assessment order subsequently passed in the name of said non-existing entity would be a nullity.

Hence, till the decision of the court on the amalgamation scheme is received, the proceedings of the Income-tax Act were to be continued in the case of the predecessor only and such proceedings once completed, cannot become illegal as a result of subsequent orders of any court. Further, post such reorganization, the affairs of the successor entity go through a complete change with effect from the date from which such reorganization takes place. This also affects the final accounts of such entities as they are unable to modify their already filed returns in accordance with the reorganization.

In order to remove this anomaly, the Finance Act, 2022 has inserted a new section 170A to enable entities going through such business reorganization to file modified returns for the period between the date of effectivity of the order and the date of issuance of the final order of the competent authority.

However, certain issues have come to the fore since the insertion of section 170A in the Act last year. These pertain to the entities who have previously furnished the return for the relevant assessment year, the obligation on the Assessing Officer (AO) for passing or modifying assessment or reassessment orders, the requirement of furnishing modified return etc. In order to avoid any unintended litigation, the Finance Act, 2023 has amended sec. 170A w.e.f. 1.4.2023.

The newly substituted sec. 170A provides that notwithstanding anything contained in section 139, in a case of business reorganisation, where prior to the date of order of the tribunal or the High Court or Adjudicating Authority as defined in section 5(1) of the Insolvency and Bankruptcy Code, 2016, any return of income has been furnished for any assessment year relevant to a previous year, by an entity to which such order applies, the successor shall furnish, within a period of six months from the end of the month in which the said order was issued, a modified return in the form and manner, as may be prescribed, in accordance with and limited to the said order. This would also enable modification of the returns filed by the predecessor wherever required.

Since there was no provision of the procedure to be followed by the Assessing Officer after the modified return is furnished by the successor entity, sec.170A(2) provides the same. Accordingly, if proceedings of assessment or reassessment for the relevant assessment year have been completed on the date of furnishing of modified return as above, the Assessing Officer shall pass an order modifying the total income of the relevant assessment year in accordance with the order of the business reorganisation and taking into account the modified return so furnished. Where proceedings of assessment or reassessment for the relevant assessment year are pending on the date of furnishing of modified return as above, the Assessing Officer shall pass an order assessing or reassessing the total income of the relevant assessment year in accordance with the order of the business reorganisation and taking into account the modified return so furnished.

For the purposes of such assessment or reassessment, unless provided otherwise, all other provisions of the Act shall apply and the tax shall be chargeable at the rate applicable to such assessment year. For the purposes of this section business reorganisation is means the reorganisation of business involving the amalgamation or demerger or merger of business of one or more persons and "successor" means all resulting companies in a business reorganisation, whether or not the company was in existence prior to such business reorganisation.

CHAPTER 30 Tax Planning, Tax Evasion, Tax Avoidance

TAX PLANNING

Tax planning is an arrangement made by an assessee to reduce its tax liability by resorting to the means lawfully available to it. For instance, when an individual designs his investment in such savings instruments like National Savings Certificate or say borrows a housing loan and avails deductions for interest paid and principal amount repaid and thereby minimize tax liability, it is perfectly legal for him to do so. Similarly companies, firms etc. can avail the deductions, exemptions, allowances offered under the statutory provisions and thereby reduce their taxes through effective tax planning. Tax Planning thereby has the sanctity of law and the words of Lord Tomlin that "Every man is entitled, if he can, to order his affairs so that the tax attaching under the appropriate Acts is less than it otherwise would be" [*IRC* v. *Duke of Westminster* (1936) 19 TC 490] has found resonance is several jurisdictions including India. The Supreme Court of India in *McDowell & Co.* v. *CTO* (1985) 22 Taxman 11/154 ITR 148 (SC) observed that "tax planning may be legitimate provided it is within the framework of the law".

TAX EVASION

Tax evasion results when the assessee flagrantly violates the provisions of the law and evades payment of tax. For instance, under-reporting profits by manipulating the sales records. Tax evasion also results in reduced taxes or no taxes at all by resorting to illegal means and by flouting the statutory provisions.

TAX AVOIDANCE

Tax avoidance marks a grey area between tax planning and tax evasion. It is not perfectly legal as tax planning but is not outrightly illegal as tax evasion. Tax avoidance is loosely understood as such an arrangement by an assessee that results in minimizing the tax by exploiting the loopholes in the statute and deriving the benefit which truly speaking the legislation did not intend to offer. Tax Avoidance involves planning by resorting to colourable devices with the intent to defraud the revenue and although all transactions and schemes therein are on the face of it legally correct in their form; these militate against the spirit of the law in substance and therefore unacceptable.

FIGURE 30.1: TAX PLANNING, TAX AVOIDANCE AND TAX EVASION

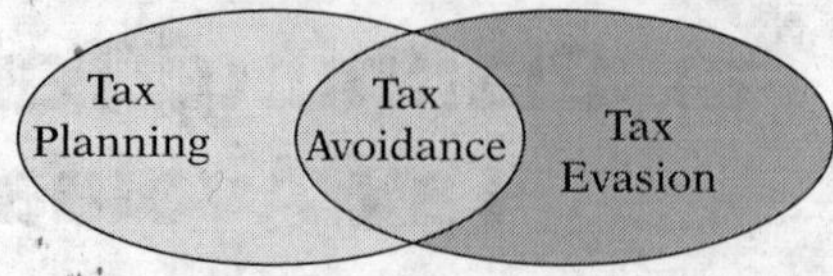

Being on the borderlines of tax planning and tax evasion, tax avoidance mechanisms are peculiarly difficult to detect and adjudicate. The judicial interpretation of the 'substance over form' doctrine has only been getting more complex over time with sophisticated measures of tax avoidance by the assessees. The recently inserted General Anti-Avoidance rules (discussed later in this chapter) to the Income-tax Act only marks the codification of the experience and instances of tax avoidance over all these years.

JUDICIAL INTERPRETATION OF TAX AVOIDANCE

Indian jurisprudence on tax avoidance has been heavily influenced by the English jurisprudence on tax avoidance and therefore it is worthwhile to trace the development in the Courts in England to then appreciate the Indian approach. The prevalent theory considered it perfectly open for persons to evade Income-tax if they could do so legally. 'No man in this country is under the smallest obligation, moral or other, so to arrange his legal relations to his business or to his property as to enable the Inland Revenue to put the largest possible shovel into his stores' [*Lord Clyde Ayrshire Pullman Motor Services & Ritchie* v *CIR* (1929) 14 TC 754]. The initial arrangements however remained more or less simple and a literal approach progressively underwent a shift towards a more purposive interpretation with the sophistication of tax avoidance devices as discussed below:

Single-step transactions and Literal Interpretation - The case of *IRC* v. *Duke of Westminster* (1936) 19 TC 490 involved a single-step transaction whereby the Duke who could not have otherwise claimed any deductions for the wages paid to certain domestic employees on his estate, sought the same by paying the employees an annuity instead. The revenue authorities in England rejected the form of this transaction and hence the deduction but the House of Lords held in favour of the Duke. What emerged from this case is the famous dicta of Lord Atkin, the cardinal principle that '*given that a document or transaction is genuine, the court cannot go behind it to some supposed underlying substance.*' Several jurisdictions around the world including India have endorsed this principle of the Duke of Westminster.

Circular transactions and Purposive Interpretation - This literal and formal approach to accepting the form of the transaction underwent a changed with the ruling in *W T Ramsay Ltd.* v *IRC* [1981] STC 174 which had adopted a circuitous mechanism to obtain the desired tax benefit. The case involved an attempt to shelter capital gains tax on the sale of a farm by creating capital loss and thereby off-setting the same in a self-cancelling manner. Whilst the House of Lords accepted that none of the steps involved individually were a sham, the scheme when looked at as a whole should be treated as a nullity for tax purposes.

Lord Wilberforce went to hold that '*while obliging the court to accept documents or transactions, found to be genuine, as such, it does not compel the court to look at a document or a transaction in blinkers, isolated from any context to which it properly belongs. If it can be seen that a document or transaction was intended to have effect as part of a nexus or series of transactions, or as an ingredient of a wider transaction intended as a whole, there is nothing in the doctrine to prevent it being so regarded; to do so in not to prefer form to substance, or substance to form.*'

Thus, even as the Court in *Ramsay* conceded the dicta of the Duke of Westminster that if documents are genuine and the form of it should be accepted by the Court; it added a caveat by stating that such documents or transactions though genuine should not be looked in blinkers or in isolation to one another. If upon such a wholesome approach the transaction appears to attain a tax consequence that was not intended by the legislation, the Westminster's doctrine does not prevent the Court from preferring the substance over the form or *vice versa*. It must be noted that Ramsay only added a qualifier to the Westminster's principle and had not overruled the same.

Commercial Substance Doctrine and Fiscal Nullity Doctrine - Yet another significant layer to the evolving jurisprudence on tax avoidance was added by *Furniss* v. *Dawson* (1984) 55 TC 324. The case involved a linear scheme with an inserted step in between to avoid payment of tax. The case arose out of the intention of the shareholders in a family company to sell their shares to an independent purchaser. Had the shares been sold directly for cash to the independent purchaser, capital gains tax would be attracted immediately. Instead, they were advised to set up an offshore subsidiary company, exchange their shares for the shares in the subsidiary company (a transaction exempt from capital gains tax is a group company transfer) and later the subsidiary sold the shares to the identified independent purchaser and thereby defer payment of capital gains tax till the time shares in the subsidiary company were realized.

The House of Lords held that steps inserted in a pre-ordained series of transactions with no commercial purpose other than tax avoidance should be disregarded for tax purposes, notwithstanding that the inserted step (*i.e.* the introduction of the subsidiary company Green Jacket) had a business effect. Thus, when the inserted step, although having a business effect, had no business purpose apart from the deferment of tax the same is liable to be disregarded and the tax benefit sought denied.

The emergence of New Realism and the difficulties it created - The combined effect of *Ramsay* and *Furniss* resulted in preordained series of transactions being looked at as a whole rather than in blinkers and as a consequence steps devoid of any commercial purpose except deferment or avoidance of tax were disregarded. In what is popularly dubbed in England as the emergence of new realism, several arrangements and schemes entered into by the assessee and producing tax benefits were scrutinized by revenue authorities under the lens of *Ramsay* and *Furniss,* and the arrangement was disregarded. One thereby reached from one end of the spectrum to the other end where any scheme of tax reduction was looked at with suspicion. The balance was restored with the decisions in that *Craven* v. *White* [1989] App. Cas. 398 and *Fitzwilliam* v. *IRC* (1993) STC 502 that held that Revenue cannot start with the question as to whether the transaction was a tax deferment/saving device but apply the look-at test to ascertain its true legal nature. It reminded that genuine strategic planning had not been abandoned.

The above discussion with respect to tax avoidance jurisprudence in the UK is not an exhaustive one but a selective one, only to gain insights into the phases that were encountered in the UK and a recount of a more or less similar experience in India.

The Indian Experience with Tax Avoidance

It can be safely said that the Indian jurisprudence tax avoidance was highly influenced with the three cases - *McDowell and Co. Ltd.* v. *CTO* AIR 1986 SC 649, *Union Of India* v. *Azadi Bachao Andolan* (2003) 132 Taxman 373/263 ITR 706 (SC) and more recently the largest corporate tax case of *Vodafone International BV* v. *Union of India* However before launching the discussion on these cases maps the long drawn connects with English jurisprudence.

Resonating with the Westminster's principle it was a well-settled legal position in India that while determining tax liability the taxing authorities are not entitled to ignore the legal character of the transaction which is the source of the receipt and to proceed on what they regard as "the substance of the matter. The Judicial Committee of the Privy Council in The *Bank of Chettinad Ltd. Colombo* v. *CIT* (1940) 8 ITR 522 (PC) fully approved the Westminster's principle. This position was further consolidated in *CIT* v. *B M Kharwar* (1969) 72 ITR 603 (SC) where the Supreme Court held that taxing authority is entitled and is indeed bound to determine the true legal relation resulting from a transaction. If the parties have chosen to conceal by a device the legal relation, it is open to the taxing authorities to unravel the device and to determine the true character of the relationship. But the legal effect of the transaction cannot be displaced by probing into the 'substance of the transaction'. This principle applies alike to cases in which the legal relation is recorded in a formal document and to cases where it has to be gathered from evidence-oral and documentary and conduct of the parties to the transaction. Again in *CIT* v. *A. Raman & Co*. (1968) 67 ITR 11(SC) took a line that avoidance of tax liability by so arranging commercial affairs that distributes charges of tax is not prohibited. A taxpayer may resort to a device to divert the income before it accrues or arises to him. The effectiveness of the device depends not upon considerations of morality, but on the operation of the Act. The legislative injunction in taxing statutes may not, except on peril of penalty, be violated, but it may lawfully be circumvented.

McDowell and Co. Ltd. v. *CTO* AIR 1986 SC 649: In *McDowells's* decision Justice Ranganath Misra proposed that tax planning may be legitimate provided it is within the framework of the law. Colourable devices cannot be part of tax planning and it is wrong to encourage or entertain the belief that it is honourable to avoid the payment of tax by resorting to dubious methods. It is the obligation of every citizen to pay the taxes honestly without resorting to subterfuges. Justice Chinappa Reddy in his part of judgment went on to hold *'that in the very country of its birth, the principle of Westminster has been given a decent burial. The Courts are now concerning themselves not merely with the genuineness of a transaction, but with the intended effect of it for fiscal purposes. No one can now get away with a tax avoidance project with the mere statement that there is nothing illegal about it. We think that time has come for us to depart from the Westminster principle as emphatically as the British Courts have done. It is neither fair not desirable to expect the legislature to intervene and take care of every device and scheme to avoid taxation. It is up to the Court to take stock to determine the nature of the new and sophisticated legal devices to avoid tax and consider whether the situation created by the devices could be related to the existing legislation with the aid of 'emerging' techniques of interpretation'*

McDowell's decision was seen as having altered the tax avoidance jurisprudence of India and the Westminster's principle was no longer applicable in India. However a balanced approach to distinguishing tax planning from tax avoidance continued to prevail that the decision in McDowell cannot be read as laying down that every attempt at tax planning is illegitimate and must be ignored, or that every transaction or arrangement which is perfectly permissible under law, which has the effect of reducing the tax burden of the assessee, must be looked upon with disfavour [*M.V. Valliappan* v. *ITO* (1988) 37 Taxman 46/170 ITR 238 (Madras)].

Union of India v. *Azadi Bachao Andolan* (2003) 132 Taxman 373/263 ITR 706 (SC): It was fervently urged to the Court in *Azadi Bachao Andolan* McDowell has changed the concept of fiscal jurisprudence in this country and any tax planning which is intended to and results in avoidance of tax must be struck down by the Court. The case was surrounding a circular issued by the Central Board of Direct Taxes whereby Assessing Officers in India were required to consider the tax residency certificate issued by Mauritius authorities to non-residents as a sufficient proof of their residence in Mauritius making them eligible under the Indo-Mauritius Double Tax Avoidance Agreement and the consequent exemption from capital gains tax in India. It was contended that owing to such blanket acceptance, shell companies having only post-box addresses in Mauritius that had routed their investment in Indian companies through Mauritius and no substantial business other than such investment in Indian companies were avoiding payment of capital gains tax in India and no tax was imposed on them in Mauritius as well resulting into double non-taxation. The Court however did not agree with the view of Justice Chinappa Reddy in *McDowells* that the *Duke of Westminster* is dead, or that its ghost has been exorcised in England. went on to reiterate that the tax planning was never abandoned The Supreme Court in Azadi Bachao Andolan went on to remind the judgment of the Privy Council in *the Bank of Chettinad* that had wholeheartedly approved the dicta of *Westminster* which was the law in this country when the Constitution came into force. This position continues to hold good by reason of Article 372 unless abrogated by an Act of Parliament, or by a clear pronouncement of this Court. Since *Mc Dowells* ruling nowhere overruled or dissented from this position, it could not be said that it changed the fiscal jurisprudence of this country.

Vodafone International Holdings BV v. *Union of India* (2012) 17 taxmann.com 202/204 Taxman 408/341 ITR 1 (SC): The Vodafone case is the biggest corporate tax case in India. The issue simply put was about the capital gains tax claims of Indian revenue authorities over a share purchase agreement entered into between two non-resident companies outside India with respect to shares of the third non-resident company, serving as Special Purpose Vehicle, having a substantial share in an Indian joint venture in telecom market through a network of downstream companies. The following flow chart demonstrates the facts:

FIGURE 30.2: VODAFONE FACTS

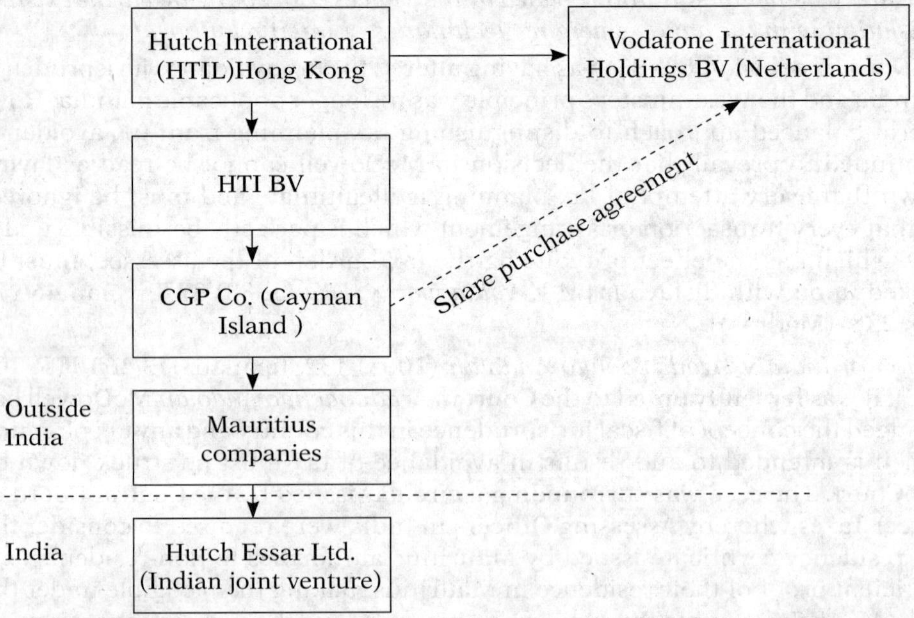

Hutch International (HTIL)Hong Kong
Vodafone International Holdings BV (Netherlands)
HTI BV
CGP Co. (Cayman Island)
Share purchase agreement
Outside India
Mauritius companies
India
Hutch Essar Ltd. (Indian joint venture)

Apart from the dispute about whether capital gains tax was chargeable in India since the company whose shares were being purchased held substantial controlling interest in Indian joint ventures, the contention was that this whole arrangement to purchase shares of an offshore company and hence indirectly gaining control over the Indian joint venture was a colourable device and a mechanism to avoid payment of tax. The Supreme Court was called upon to decide whether there was inherently a conflict between its ruling in *McDowells* which departed from Westminster principle and required to the Courts to consider the substance over form and *Azadi Bachao Andolan* that disagreed with such departure from Westminster. Reconciling the two decisions, the Supreme Court in the Vodafone case ruled that there was no conflict between *McDowells* and *Azadi Bachao Andolan* rulings since even under McDowells the majority judgment held tax planning is legitimate provided it is within the framework of law and it is only colourable devices that cannot be a part of tax planning. Justice Chinappa Reddy's who also concurred with the view of the majority made the proposition about departing from the Westminster principle only in the context of artificial and colourable devices of tax avoidance and not otherwise from tax planning altogether.

Having thus clarified the ground position, the Supreme Court in Vodafone ruling reiterated the "look at" principle enunciated in *Ramsay* wherein it was held that while ascertaining the legal nature of the transaction, the Revenue or the Court must look at a document or a transaction as a whole and not to adopt a dissecting approach. The Revenue cannot start with the question as to whether the impugned transaction is a tax deferment/saving device but that it should apply the "look at" test to ascertain its true legal nature and that genuine strategic tax planning has not been abandoned by any decision of the English Courts till date.

Holding structures and Special Purpose Vehicles are strategic devices cushions an investor by absorbing economic and financial shocks if any from the investment destination and at times serve as exit routes. Several factors such as the participation in investment, the duration of time during which the Holding Structure exists, the period of business operations in India, generation of taxable revenues in India; the timing of the exit, and the continuity of business on such exit are to be considered before concluding if the scheme or arrangement was for tax avoidance. In the light of these factors, there was no tax avoidance indulged by the companies in question.

Having learned from the experience of the past, it was a felt need to introduce General Anti-Avoidance Rules (GAAR) so as to offer a statutory response to address tax avoidance practices.

GENERAL ANTI-AVOIDANCE RULES (GAAR)

GAAR provisions in the Income-tax Act codify the 'substance over form' rule of the judicial interpretation of when an assessee is understood as having indulged in tax avoidance and sought a tax benefit that was not intended by the legislation to be offered. Chapter X of the Income-tax Act comprising of Secs. 95 to 102 is applicable from the AY 2018-19 onwards. The provisions of this Chapter apply in addition to, or in lieu of, any other basis for the determination of tax liability, in accordance with such guidelines and subject to conditions as may be prescribed . According to a clarification made in Circular No. 7 of 2017 issued by CBDT wherever the Specific Anti-Avoidance Rules ("SAAR") are not sufficient to curb tax avoidance practices, GAAR would become applicable as per the facts and circumstances of the case. Thus, it is made clear by the said Circular that provisions of GAAR and SAAR can coexist.

Accordingly, notwithstanding anything contained in the Income-tax Act, an arrangement entered into by an assessee may be declared to be an impermissible avoidance arrangement having a main purpose of tax benefit then consequences shall follow.

FIGURE 30.3: STEPS IN GAAR APPLICATION

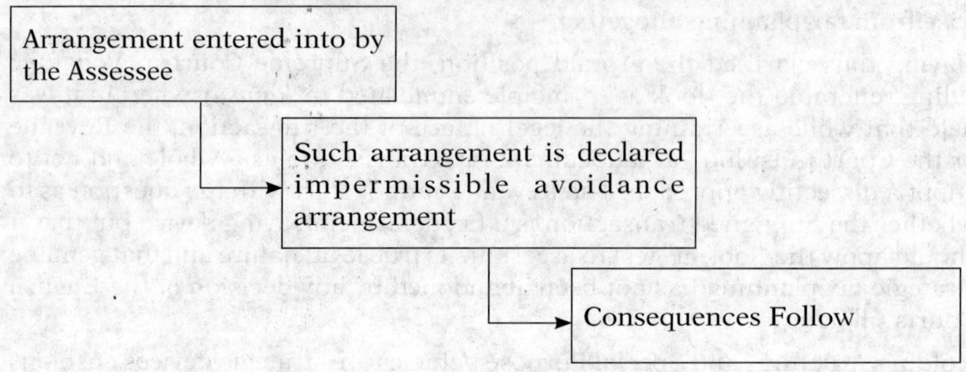

Step 1: Arrangement [Sec. 102(1)] - For this purpose the term Arrangement according to Sec.102(1) means any step in, or a part or whole of, any transaction, operation, scheme, agreement or understanding, whether enforceable or not, and includes the alienation of any property in such transaction, operation, scheme, agreement or understanding. Thus, the term arrangement has been defined very broadly to include different modes or designs, be it written or unwritten and GAAR provisions are not necessarily confined to the whole arrangement and may apply even to a step or a part of the arrangement.

Step 2: Impermissible Avoidance Arrangement [Sec. 96] - When such arrangement is declared an impressible avoidance arrangement under Sec.96, consequences shall follow. Impermissible avoidance arrangement means an arrangement, the main purpose of which is to obtain a tax benefit, and it—

(*a*) creates rights, or obligations, which are not ordinarily created between persons dealing at arm's length;

(*b*) results, directly or indirectly, in the misuse, or abuse, of the provisions of this Act;

(*c*) lacks commercial substance or is deemed to lack commercial substance under Section 97, in whole or in part; or

(*d*) is entered into, or carried out, by means, or in a manner, which are not ordinarily employed for *bona fide* purposes .

Meaning of Tax Benefit [Sec.102(10)]: Tax benefit includes a reduction in total income or an increase in loss or a reduction or avoidance or deferral or increase in a refund of tax or other amount payable by application of Income-tax Act or payable under the Income-tax Act as a result of a tax treaty.

An arrangement shall be deemed to lack commercial substance when:

(*i*) The substance/effect of the agreement on the whole is inconsistent with or differs significantly from the form of its individuals steps or part; or

(*ii*) Involves/includes - round trip financing (including the kind of agreement detailed in Sec. 97(2), an accommodating party, elements that have the effect of offsetting or cancelling each other; or a transaction which is conducted through one or more persons and disguises the value, location, source, ownership or control of funds which is the subject matter of such transaction;

(*iii*) Involves location of an asset/transaction/place of residence of any party which is without any substantial commercial purpose other than obtaining tax benefit for a party; or

(*iv*) It does not have a significant effect upon the business risks or net cash flows of any party to the arrangement apart from any effect attributable to the tax benefit that would be obtained. [Sec.97]

The burden of proof on the assessee - An arrangement shall be presumed, unless proved to the contrary by the assessee, to have been entered into for the main purpose of obtaining a tax benefit, if the main purpose of a step/part is to obtain a tax benefit. This is the case, notwithstanding the fact that the main purpose of the whole arrangement is not to obtain a tax benefit.

Further, it has been clarified that the following may be relevant but not sufficient for determining if an arrangement lacks commercial substance or not-the period/time for which the arrangement (including operations therein) exists; the fact of payment of taxes, directly or indirectly, under the arrangement; the fact that an exit route (including transfer of any activity or business or operations) is provided by the arrangement.

A party to an arrangement shall be an 'accommodating party' (whether or not the party is a connected person in relation to any party to the arrangement), if the main purpose of the direct/indirect participation of that party in the arrangement, in whole or in part, is to obtain a tax benefit for the assessee directly or indirectly.

Step 3: Consequences of impermissible avoidance arrangement [Sec. 98] -

When an arrangement is declared thus to be impermissible, the consequences that follows is a denial of a tax benefit or benefit under a tax treaty and such consequence that is deemed appropriate, in the circumstances of the case. For application of this provision, any equity may be treated as debt or *vice versa*, any accrual/receipt of a capital nature may be treated as of revenue nature or *vice versa*, any expenditure, deduction, relief or rebate may be recharacterized The appropriate manner includes but is not limited to the following—

(*a*) disregarding, combining or recharacterising any step/part or whole of, the impermissible avoidance arrangement;

(*b*) treating the impermissible avoidance arrangement as if it had not been entered into or carried out;

(*c*) disregarding any accommodating party or treating any accommodating party and any other party as one and the same person;

(*d*) deeming persons who are connected persons in relation to each other to be one and the same person for the purposes of determining tax treatment of any amount;

(*e*) reallocating amongst the parties to the arrangement—

(*i*) any accrual, or receipt, of a capital nature or revenue nature; or

(*ii*) any expenditure, deduction, relief or rebate;

(*f*) treating—

(*i*) the place of residence of any party to the arrangement; or

(*ii*) the situs of an asset or of a transaction,

at a place other than the place of residence, location of the asset or location of the transaction as provided under the arrangement; or

(*g*) considering or looking through any arrangement by disregarding any corporate structure .

Inapplicability of GAAR provisions

Under the Income-tax Rules, 1962. Rule 10U GAAR provisions shall not apply to the following :

(*a*) Where the tax benefit does not exceed ₹ 3 crores;

(*b*) a Foreign Institutional Investor, being an assessee under the Act has not taken the benefit of a DTAA agreement referred to in section 90 or section 90A as the case may be and who has invested in listed securities, or unlisted securities, with the prior permission of the competent authority, in accordance with SEBI regulations;

(*c*) non-residents in relation to investment made by them in off shore derivative instruments;

(*d*) income arising on transfer of investments made before the 1st day of April, 2017.

REFERENCE TO PRINCIPAL COMMISSIONER OR COMMISSIONER IN CERTAIN CASES [SEC. 144BA]

The initiation of GAAR proceedings commences with a reference made by the Assessing Officer to the Principal Commissioner. When the Assessing Officer, at any stage of the assessment or reassessment proceedings before him having regard to the material and evidence available, considers that it is necessary to declare an arrangement as an impermissible avoidance arrangement and to determine the consequence of such an arrangement within the meaning of Chapter X-A, then, he may make a reference to the Principal Commissioner or Commissioner in this regard. The figure below explains the entire procedure under Sec. 144BA:

FIGURE 30.4: PROCEDURE FOR DECLARING AN ARRANGEMENT AS BEING AN IMPERMISSIBLE AVOIDANCE AGREEMENT

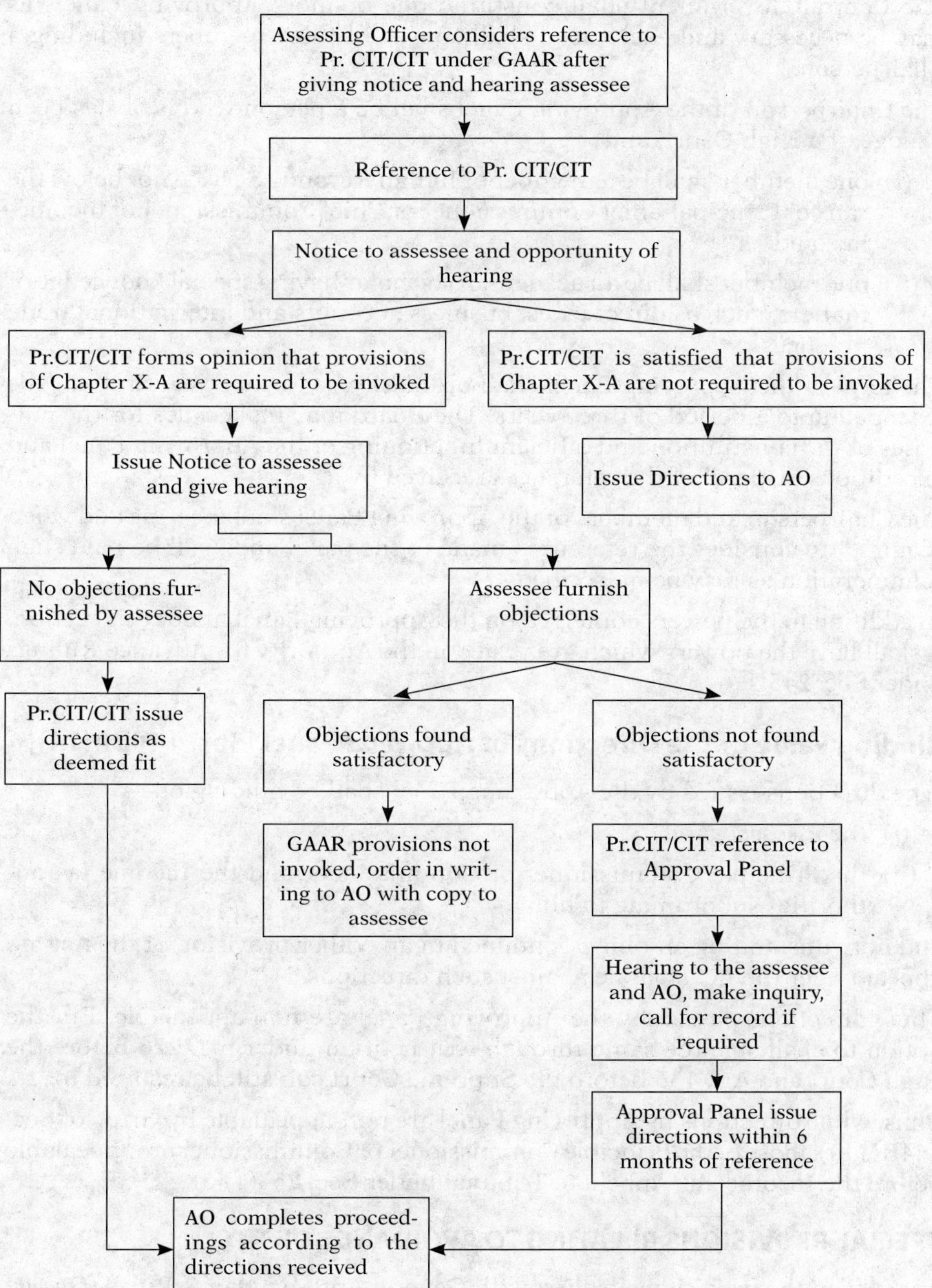

Constitution of Approving Panel [Sec. 144BA(15) to (21)]

The Central Government shall constitute one or more Approving Panels as may be necessary and each panel shall consist of three members including a Chairperson.

The Chairperson of the Approving Panel shall be a person who is or has been a judge of a High Court, and

(*i*) one member shall be a member of Indian Revenue Service not below the rank of Principal Chief Commissioner or Chief Commissioner of Income-tax; and

(*ii*) one member shall be an academic or scholar having special knowledge of matters, such as direct taxes, business accounts and international trade practices.

The term of the Approving Panel shall ordinarily be for one year and may be extended upto a period of three years. The Board may make rules for the purposes of the constitution and efficient functioning of the Approving Panel and expeditious disposal of the references received by it.

The Chairperson and members of the Approving Panel shall meet, as and when required, to consider the references made to the panel and shall be paid such remuneration as may be prescribed.

In addition to the powers conferred on the Approving Panel under this section, it shall have the powers which are vested in the Authority for Advance Rulings under Sec. 245U.

Binding value of the Directions of Approval Panel [Sec. 144BA(14)]

The directions issued by the Approving Panel shall be binding on—

(*i*) the assessee; and

(*ii*) the Principal Commissioner or Commissioner and the Income-tax authorities subordinate to him,

and notwithstanding anything contained in any other provision of the Act, no appeal under the Act shall lie against such directions.

Thus, directions passed by the Approving Panel are non-appealable. But the option to challenge the same through writ petition under Art. 226 before the High Court and Art. 136 before the Supreme Court can still be resorted to.

Thus, while directions by Approving Panel are non-appealable by virtue of Sec. 144BA(14), those of the Principle Commissioner or Commissioner are appealable before the Income Tax Appellate Tribunal under Sec. 253(1)(*e*).

SPECIAL PROVISIONS RELATING TO AVOIDANCE OF TAX

Apart from the provisions dealing with General Anti-Avoidance Rules (GAAR) as discussed above, there are also Special Anti-Avoidance Rules (SAAR) in the Income-tax Act in the form of transfer pricing regulations. Transfer pricing is a process whereby the prices of inter-transfer of goods or services between the associate enterprise are manipulated to distort their profits. As different countries have different tax rate structure, transfer pricing is employed by associate enterprises to minimise the tax liability of the group as a whole by inflating/increasing profit margin of an associate enterprise operating in low tax jurisdiction. It was the rampant misuse of transfer pricing by multinationals, operating in international field, which had forced the Government to regulate transfer price mechanism.

Chapter X of the Income-tax Act comprises of Special Provisions Relating to Avoidance of Tax from Secs. 92 to 94B and are operational from the AY 2002-03. The rationale of the transfer pricing regulations is to ensure that the true income of an assessee is brought to tax and there is no avoidance of tax by transfer of income from India to any other tax jurisdiction by virtue of the influence exercised by the associated enterprises. The provisions of Chapter X of the Act compute income in relation to a controlled transaction between an assessee and its associated enterprise having regard to the arms length price and thereby nullify the effect of transfer of income to a jurisdiction outside India.

However, even as the transfer pricing regulations are applicable to a controlled transaction which is then computed at an arms length price, income that is brought to tax is tax any notional income but real income. It must be noted that Chapter X does not artificially broaden, expand or deviate from the concept of "real income". Real income means profits arrived at on commercial principles. Profits and gains should be true and correct profits and gains, neither under nor over-stated. Arm's length price seeks to correct distortion and shifting of profits to tax the actual income earned by a resident/domestic AE. The profit which would have accrued had arm's length conditions prevailed is brought to tax. Misreporting, if any, on account of non-arm's length conditions resulting in lower profits, is corrected *Sony Ericsson Mobile Communications India (P.) Ltd.* v. *CIT* (2015) 55 taxmann.com 240/231 Taxman 113/374 ITR 118 (Delhi).

While originally transfer pricing regulations were applicable only on international transactions beyond a specified limit, these are now extended even to the specified domestic transactions. Accordingly, transactions that are suspected of having indulged in transfer pricing are re-computed at an arms length price as per one of the recognized methods in the statute for the purposes of arriving at the value to be taxed. The following are the essential elements for the application of transfer pricing regulations:

(*a*) It is an international transaction or specified domestic transaction;

(*b*) Such transactions are undertaken with associated enterprise, either or both of whom are non-residents;

(*c*) These are not carried out at arms length.

1. International Transaction [Sec. 92B]

"International transaction" means a transaction that is between two or more associated enterprises, either or both of whom are non-residents. It may be in the nature of purchase, sale or lease of tangible or intangible property, or provision of services or lending or borrowing money or any other transaction having a bearing on profits, income, losses or assets of such enterprises. It includes a mutual agreement or arrangement between two or more associated enterprises for the allocation or apportionment of, or any contribution to, any cost or expenses incurred or to be incurred in connection with a benefit, service or facility provided or to be provided to anyone or more of such enterprises.

A 'transaction' includes an arrangement, understanding or action in concert;

(*a*) whether or not such arrangement, understanding or action is format or in writing; or

(*b*) whether or not such arrangement, understanding or action is intended to be enforceable by legal proceedings.

Thus, all types of arrangements, understanding or actions in concert, whether oral or written, whether formal or informal, whether intended to be enforceable by legal proceedings or not are covered [Sec. 92F(*v*)].

The following 5 categories of transactions have been included in the definition of international transaction :

(*a*) the purchase, sale, transfer, lease or use of tangible property;

(*b*) the purchase, sale, transfer, lease or use of intangible property;

(*c*) capital financing, including guarantee, purchase or sale of marketable securities etc.;

(*d*) provision of services including provision of market research, administration, technical service, repairs, design, consultation, etc.;

(*e*) a transaction of business restructuring or reorganisation, entered into by an enterprise with an associated enterprise, irrespective of the fact that it has bearing on the profit, income, losses or assets of such enterprises at the time of the transaction or at any future date.

Case Law : ***Bharti Airtel Ltd.* v. *Addl. CIT* (2014) 43 taxmann.com 150/63 SOT 113 (Delhi-Trib.)**

Facts: 'B' issued corporate guarantee on behalf of its associated enterprise for which no consideration was charged. The TPO held the transaction to be international transaction and proceeded to compute ALP. 'B' contended that it had not incurred any cost therefore no transfer pricing adjustment should be made.

Held: Although the explanation to the definition of the term 'international transaction included providing a "Guarantee", the items in the exhaustive list of explanation has to be read in conjunction with the main provision that required the transaction to have a bearing on profits, incomes, losses, or assets of such enterprises. Therefore, the onus is on the revenue authorities to demonstrate that the transaction is of such a nature as to have "bearing on profits, income, losses or assets" of the enterprise. Since in the present case the transaction of corporate guarantee did not have any real impact on the "profits, income, losses or assets" of the enterprise no transfer pricing adjustment could be made.

Deemed International Transaction [Sec. 92B(2)]

A transaction between an enterprise and another person is also deemed to be an international transaction entered into between two associated enterprises if any of the following situations exists:

(*i*) there is a prior agreement in relation to the relevant transaction between such other person and the associated enterprise; or

(*ii*) The terms of the relevant transaction are determined in substance between such other person and the associated enterprise. Where the enterprise or associated enterprise or both of them are non-residents, irrespective of whether such other person is a non-resident or not.

2. Domestic Transaction [Sec. 92BA]

The fountainhead of the extension of transfer pricing regulation to domestic transactions was the recommendation of the Supreme Court in *CIT* v. *Glaxo SmithKline Asia (P.) Ltd.* (2010) 195 Taxman 35. The Court was dealing with an issue under Sec. 40A(2) as to whether the assessee-company and its service provider were related companies and whether the allocation of cross-charges by the assessee was the correct test applied. While dismissing the revenue's appeal the Court commented that the larger issue which needed to be addressed was, whether Transfer Pricing Regulations should be limited to cross-border transactions or could be extended to domestic transactions. Although domestic transactions involving in the under-invoicing of sales and over-invoicing of expenses ordinarily would be revenue neutral in nature, in the following two circumstances tax arbitrage would be possible—

(*i*) If one of the related companies is a loss-making company and the other is a profit-making company and profit is shifted to the loss-making concern; and

(*ii*) If there are different rates for two related units [on account of different status, area-based incentives, nature of the activity, etc.] and if profit is diverted towards the unit on the lower side of the tax arbitrage. For example, the sale of goods or services from non-SEZ area, [taxable division] to SEZ unit [non-taxable unit] at a price below the market price so that taxable division will have less taxable profit and non-taxable division will have a higher profit exemption.

All these complications arise in cases where fair market value is required to be assigned to the transactions between related parties in terms of section 40A(2). To get over this situation, the matter needs to be examined by the CBDT. The matter has been examined by the CBDT and it is of the view that amendments would be required to be made to the provisions of the Act, if such Transfer Pricing Regulations are required to be applied to domestic transactions between related parties under section 40A(2).

The Supreme Court went on to recommend that the Finance Ministry and the CBDT should examine whether Transfer Pricing Regulations can be applied to domestic transactions between related parties under Sec. 40A(2) by making amendments to the Act.

Accordingly, the Finance Act, 2012 extended the transfer pricing regulations to specified domestic transactions w.e.f. 1-4-2013 where the aggregate of the transactions entered into by the assessee in the previous year exceeds ₹ 20 crores (previously it was ₹ 5 crore). Under Sec. 92(2A) any allowance for an expenditure or interest or allocation of any cost or expenses or any income in relation to the Specified Domestic Transaction shall be computed having regard to the Arm's Length Price.

Sec. 92BA defines specified domestic transactions to mean any of the following transactions, not being an international transaction:

a. **All transactions under Sec. 80A -** Under Sec. 80A(6) when transaction value of the internal transfer of goods or services between various units / undertakings of the assessee does not correspond to the market value of such goods or services, then for the purposes of any deduction, the profits and gains of such undertaking or unit or enterprise or eligible business shall be computed as if the transfer had been made at the market value of such goods or services.

b. **Transactions of Undertaking availing tax holiday for infrastructure development, hospitals etc. under Sec. 80-IA -** It was often experienced that assessees operating in sectors that were offered tax holidays could attempt to avoid payment of tax by parking their extra profits in such units/businesses. In order to curb such attempts, the following have been included in the definition of specified domestic transaction.

c. **Internal transfer of goods or services referred to in section 80-IA(8) -** If the internal transfer of goods or services is not at market value, then profits or gains of transacting units shall be computed, as if, transfer, in either case, had been made at market value of such goods or services. The onus is on the taxpayer to prove that the internal transfer is at ALP.

d. **More than ordinary profits from any business transacted between the assessee and other person as referred to in Sec. 80-IA(10) -** Where it appears to the Assessing Officer that, owing to the close connection between the assessee carrying on the eligible business to which deduction under sec.80-IA applies and any other person, or for any other reason, the course of business between them is so arranged that the business transacted between them produces to the assessee more than the ordinary profits which might be expected to arise in such eligible business, the Assessing Officer shall take the profits as may be reasonably be deemed to have been derived for the purposes of the deduction under this section.

e. **Any transaction referred to in any other section under Chapter VI-A or section 10AA, to which provisions of Sec. 80-IA(8), (10) -** Transactions to which profit-linked deductions under Chapter VI-A applies or to which Sec.10AA exempting profits of units located in Special Economic Zone applies, and where the internal transfer of goods or services are not at market value or where such units enjoying exemptions/deductions derive more than ordinary profits due to close connection (similar to the ones in Sec. 80-IA(8), (10) will be computed at arms length.

f. **More than ordinary profits on any business transacted between the persons referred to in Sec. 115BAB(6) -** Where an assessee avails concessional rate of tax under Sec. 115BAB being a new domestic company into manufacturing, and it appears to the Assessing Officer that owing to the close connection, the course of business transacted between such person and another is so arranged so as to result into more than the ordinary profits to such person the Assessing Officer shall take the amount of profits as may be reasonably deemed to have been derived therefrom.

g. Any business transacted between the assessee are other person referred to in sec. 115BAE(4).

h. Any other transaction as may be prescribed.

3. Associated Enterprises [Sec. 92A]

An enterprise would be regarded as "associated enterprise" of another enterprise if:

(*a*) it participates, directly or indirectly, through one or more enterprises, in the management or control or capital of the other enterprise; or

(*b*) the person participating directly or indirectly, or through one or more intermediaries, in the management or control or capital of the other enterprise.

Deemed Associated Enterprises [Sec. 92A(2)] - Two or more enterprises will be deemed to be associated enterprises, if, at any time during the previous year:

(*i*) one enterprise holds, directly or indirectly, shares carrying not less than 26% of the voting power in the other enterprises; or

(*ii*) any person or enterprise holds, directly or indirectly, shares carrying not less than 26% of the voting power in both these enterprises; or

(*iii*) a loan advanced by one enterprise to the other enterprise constitutes not less than 51% of the book value of the total assets of the other enterprise; or

(*iv*) one enterprise guarantees not less than 10% of the total borrowings of the other enterprise; or

(*v*) more than 50% of the board of directors or members of the governing board, or one or more executive directors or executive members of the governing board of one enterprise, are appointed by the other enterprise; or

(*vi*) more than 50% of the board of directors or members of the governing board, or one or more executive directors or members of the governing board of both the enterprises are appointed by the same person or persons; or (*vii*) the manufacture or processing of goods or articles or business carried out by one enterprise is wholly dependent on the use of know-how, patents, copyrights, trademarks, licences, franchises or any other business or commercial rights of similar nature, or any data, documentation, drawing or specification relating to any patent, invention, model, design, secret formula or process of which the other enterprise is the owner or in respect of which the other enterprise has exclusive rights; or

(*viii*) one enterprise or its nominee, supplies and influences the prices and other conditions relating 90% or more of raw material and consumables required for the manufacture or processing of goods or articles carried out by the other enterprise; or

(*ix*) the goods or articles manufactured or processed by one enterprise, are sold to the other enterprise or its nominees and the prices and other conditions relating thereto are influenced by such enterprise; or

(*x*) where one enterprise is controlled by one individual, the other enterprise is also controlled by such individual or his relative or jointly by such individual and relative of such individual; or

(*xi*) where one enterprise is controlled by an HUF, the other enterprise is controlled by a member of such HUF, or by a relative of a member of such HUF or jointly by such member and his relative; or

(*xii*) where one enterprise is a firm, or association of persons, or body of individuals, the other enterprise holds at least 10% interest in such firm, association of persons or body of individuals; or

(*xiii*) any relationship of mutual interest, as may be prescribed, exists between the two enterprises.

4. Computation of Income from International Transaction having regard to Arm's Length Price [Sec. 92]

Any income arising from an international transaction is computed having regard to the arm's length price [Sec. 92(1)]. In computing such income, the allowance for any expense or interest arising from an international transaction is also be determined having regard to the arm's length price [*Explanation* to Sec. 92(1)].

Where in an international transaction or specified domestic transaction, two or more associated enterprises enter into a mutual agreement or arrangement for the allocation or apportionment of, or any contribution to, any cost or expense incurred or to be incurred in connection with a benefit, service or facility provided or to be provided to any one or more enterprises, the cost or expense allocated or apportioned or as the case may be, contributed by any such enterprise is determined having regard to the arm's length price of such benefit, service or facility, as the case may be [Sec. 92(2)].

5. Determination of Arm's Length Price

The exercise of determining the ALP in respect of international transactions between the related enterprises is aimed to determine the price, which would have been charged for products and services, as nearly as possible, in case such international transactions were not controlled by virtue of them being executed between related parties. The object of the exercise is, thus, to remove the effect of any influence on the prices or costs that may have been exerted on account of the international transactions being entered into between related parties. It is, at once, clear that for the exercise of determining ALP to be reliable, it is necessary that the controlled transactions be compared with uncontrolled transactions which are similar in all material aspects.

"Arm's length price" means a price which is applied or proposed to be applied in a transaction between persons other than associated enterprises, in uncontrolled conditions [Sec. 92F(*ii*)]. Thus, a price at which independent enterprises deal with each other should be reckoned as the arm's length price where market forces are at play. The arm's length price in relation to an international transaction is determined by the most appropriate method having regard to the nature of transaction or class of transaction or class of associated persons or functions performed by such persons or such other relevant factors as the board may prescribe.

Methods of Determining Arm's Length Price

The following methods are in operation for determining arm's length price:

(a) **Comparable Uncontrolled Price (CUP) method [Rule 10B]:** CUP method compares the price of goods sold or services rendered in a controlled transaction with the price of similar products or services charged by independent uncontrolled enterprises.

CUP method is useful in the sale–purchase of standardised products.

(b) **Re-sale price method (RPM) [Rule 10B*(b)*] -** Where associate enterprise performs only marketing functions and does not make any value addition, RPM may be used to determine arm's length price. RPM reduces the margin from the retail price to work out arm's length.

(c) **Cost Plus Method (CPM) [Rule 10B*(c)*] -** Under CPM, first the cost incurred by the enterprise in a controlled transaction is worked out and then a "cost plus mark-up" is added to it to work out arm's length price. "Cost plus mark-up" is worked out on the basis of a comparable transaction, carried out by an independent enterprise.

(d) **Profit Split Method (PSM) [Rule 10B*(d)*] -** Under PSM, first the overall profit from the controlled transaction is worked out. Thereafter, this profit is split between the controlled enterprises on the basis of functions performed by them, assets used by them and the risk borne by them.

(e) **Transactional Net Margin Method (TNMM) [Rule 10B*(e)*] -** TNMM examines the net profit margin, realised by the assessee from a controlled transaction, to an appropriate base (that is, cost, sales or assets, etc.). Thus, it uses the ratio of net profit to assets or net profit to sales realised

by a taxpayer from a controlled transaction. If a comparable controlled transaction entered into by the same enterprise is available, it may provide most suitable margin to be applied.

(*f*) **Any other method [Sec. 92C(1)(*f*)]** - Any other method, as may be specified by the Board, may also be taken into consideration to determine the arm's length price.

6. Determination of Arm's Length Price by the Assessing Officer [Sec. 92C(3), (4)]

While the prime responsibility of determining and applying arm's length price is on the assessee, Sec. 92C(3) also authorises the Assessing Officer to determine the arm's length price in the following cases:

(*a*) where the price charged or paid in an international transaction has not been determined in accordance with the method as referred to above [under Sec. 92C(1)/(2)]; or

(*b*) where any information and document relating to an international transaction have not been maintained by the assessee in the prescribed manner [under Sec. 92D(1) and rules made thereunder]; or

(*c*) where the information and data used in the computation of arm's length price is not reliable or correct; or

(*d*) the assessee has failed to furnish, within the specified time, any information or document which he was required to furnish by the Assessing Officer or CIT (Appeals) by a notice under Sec. 92D(3).

In such cases, the Assessing Officer may determine the arm's length price in an international transaction or specified domestic transaction in accordance with above methods [under Sec. 92C(1)/(2)] on the basis of material, or information or document in his possession. The Assessing Officer is required to give a show-cause notice to the assessee for fixing such price [Proviso to Sec. 92C(3)].

Where an arm's length price is determined by the Assessing Officer, he may compute the total income of the assessee having regard to the arm's length price so determined [Sec. 92C(4)]. Where total income of the assessee is enhanced under such computation, the Assessing Officer is required not to allow any deduction under Sec. 10A, or Sec.10B, or Sec.10AA in respect of the amount by which the total income of the assessee is so enhanced after such computation.

Where total income of an associated enterprise is computed [under Sec. 92C(4)] on determination of the arm's length price, paid to another associated enterprise from which tax has been deducted or deductible at source [under Chapter XVIIB], the income of other associated enterprise cannot be recomputed by reason of such determination of arm's length price in the case of first-mentioned person [Second Proviso to Sec. 92C(4)].

7. Reference to Transfer Pricing Officer [Sec. 92CA w.e.f. 1-6-2002]

When any assessee has entered into an international transaction or specified domestic transaction and the Assessing Officer considers it necessary or expedient so to do, he may, with the previous approval of the Commissioner, refer the computation of the arm's length price in relation to the said international transaction or specified domestic transaction to the Transfer Pricing Officer [Sec. 92CA(1)].

"Transfer Pricing Officer" means a Joint Commissioner or Deputy Commissioner or Assistant Commissioner, authorised by the Board to perform all or any of the functions of an Assessing Officer specified in Secs. 92C and 92D in respect of any person or class of persons [*Explanation* to Sec. 92CA].

Faceless determination of arms length price

The Central Government may make a scheme for the purposes of determination of the arm's length price so as to impart greater efficiency, transparency and accountability by—

(*a*) eliminating the interface between the Transfer Pricing Officer and the assessee or any other person to the extent technologically feasible;

(*b*) optimising utilisation of the resources through economies of scale and functional specialisation;

(*c*) introducing a team-based determination of arm's length price with dynamic jurisdiction. [Sec. 92CA(8)]

In order to give effect to such scheme, the Central Government may direct that any of the provisions of this Act shall not apply or shall apply with such exceptions, modifications and adaptations as may be specified in the notification provided that no direction shall be issued after 31st March, 2024 [Sec. 92CA(9)]. (The Finance Act, 2022 has extended this date to 31st March, 2024 from the original date of 31st March, 2022). Every notification so issued shall, as soon as may be after the notification is issued, be laid before each House of Parliament [Sec. 92CA(10)].

8. Safe Harbour Rule [Section 92CB r/w Rules 10TA to 10TG]

As the name itself suggests, Safe Harbour Rule means circumstances in which the revenue shall accept the Transfer Price declared by the assessee. It comprise of such margin/range within which the transfer price declared by the assessee will not attract any further scrutiny. The determination of ALP under Sec. 92C or 92CA as well as incomes deemed to accrue or arise under Sec. 9(1)(*i*) shall now be subjected to SHR.

Under this section the Central Board for Direct Taxes is empowered to make Safe Harbour Rules (SHR). Rule 10TA to Rule 10TG of the IT Rules covers provision relating to SHR in respect of International Transaction. Rule 10TD covers the safe harbour limit for different categories of transaction. Further, the SHR has now been extended to Specified Domestic Transaction and Rule 10TH to 10HD covers the same.

9. Advance Pricing Agreement [Section 92CC]

Transfer Pricing provisions and determination of arms length price remained highly contested and wrought with litigations. Therefore in order to provide certainty in terms of applying transfer pricing methods and also to avoid litigation, the provisions for Advance Pricing Agreements were introduced by the Finance Act, 2012 w.e.f 1-7-2012.

Accordingly, Sec. 92CC empowers the Central Board of Direct Taxes to enter into APA with any person for determining the ALP or the manner in which ALP is to be determined in relation to an international transaction with approval from the Central Government. Finance Act, 2020 expanded the scope of APA with the non-resident in respect to determining the income deemed to accrue or arise in India under Sec. 9(1)(*i*) or specifying the manner in which the said income is to be determined.

Such agreement will be binding between the tax authorities and the person on whose behalf it has been agreed upon and will be valid for a period of 5 consecutive assessment years. However, in case of a change in law or facts having bearing on the agreement the same shall not be binding. Rule 10Q of the IT Rules, 1962 provides for revision of the agreement on account of a change in law or change in critical assumption or failure to meet a condition subject to which the agreement has been entered into happens. In the case of multilateral or bilateral agreement revision can also happen if a request is made by the competent authority. This revision can be done either suo motu by the board or upon the request made by the assessee. The board has been provided with the power to cancel the agreement under Rule 10R subject to fulfilment of the condition mentioned in the rule.

The agreement could also be declared *void ab initio* by the Board, with approval from the Central Government if it is found that the agreement has been obtained by way of defraud or misrepresentation.

Effect to Advance Pricing Agreement [Sec. 92CD]

Where an assessee enters into the APA which applies to previous year but the return of which has already been filed by the assessee under Sec. 139, such person shall file a modified return within a period of three months from the end of the month in which the said agreement was entered into, in accordance with and limited to the agreement.

Subject Index*

* Number(s) after each entry denotes page No.(s).

Profits and gains of business or profession